11th International Conference on Recent Advances in Natural Language Processing (RANLP 2017)

Varna, Bulgaria

2 – 8 September 2017

ISBN: 978-1-5108-5522-9

TABLE OF CONTENTS

Parameter Transfer across Domains for Word Sense Disambiguation

Sallam Abualhaija
L3S Research Center
Leibniz University
abualhaija@l3s.de

Nina Tahmasebi
Department of Swedish
University of Gothenburg
nina.tahmasebi@svenska.gu.se

Diane Forin
Department of Applied
Mathematics & Modelling
Polytech Lyon
diane.forin@etu.univ-lyon1.fr

Karl-Heinz Zimmermann
Institute of Embedded Systems
Hamburg University of Technology
k.zimmermann@tu-harburg.de

Abstract

Word sense disambiguation is defined as finding the corresponding sense for a target word in a given context, which comprises a major step in text applications. Recently, it has been addressed as an optimization problem. The idea behind is to find a sequence of senses that corresponds to the words in a given context with a maximum semantic similarity. Metaheuristics like simulated annealing and D-Bees provide approximate good-enough solutions, but are usually influenced by the starting parameters. In this paper, we study the parameter tuning for both algorithms within the word sense disambiguation problem. The experiments are conducted on different datasets to cover different disambiguation scenarios. We show that D-Bees is robust and less sensitive towards the initial parameters compared to simulated annealing, hence, it is sufficient to tune the parameters once and reuse them for different datasets, domains or languages.

1 Introduction

Word sense disambiguation (WSD) is a well known problem in natural language processing (Agirre and Edmonds, 2007; Yarowsky, 1992). It is defined as the task of identifying the most likely meaning of a target word given the surrounding context. For example, in the sentence "The *mouse* of my computer is broken", the word *mouse* means "a computer device". WSD is an essential step in many applications like machine translation (Vickrey et al., 2005), lexical simplification (Specia et al., 2012) and many others (Ide and Véronis, 1998) and of particularly importance for creat-

ing accurate text understanding systems using the massive amounts of widely available text.

There are different methods to solve the WSD problem; supervised and knowledge-based methods rely on predefined sense inventories (Agirre and Edmonds, 2007; Martínez et al., 2007; Pedersen et al., 2005), and unsupervised methods that include sense induction and discrimination (Navigli, 2012; Brody et al., 2006; Schütze, 1998). Supervised methods generally achieve the best results (Navigli et al., 2007), however, they require strenuous effort to prepare annotated corpora or hand-crafted sense inventories. In addition, it is a process that has to be repeated for every language and domain especially since words change their senses over time (Tahmasebi et al., 2011; Kulkarni et al., 2015). In this paper, we rely on knowledge-based methods for WSD that make use of an existing knowledge-base like WordNet (Miller et al., 1990) and do not require annotated corpora. Our method can however work with any sense inventory, be a collaboratively created resource like Wiktionary [1] or an induced set of senses.

We will address WSD as an optimization problem (Schwab et al., 2012; Pedersen et al., 2005); Given a sequence of words as an input, a corresponding sequence of senses with the maximum semantic similarity should be returned as the output. The straight forward method considers all possible sense combinations in the context window to find the exact optimal solution. However, this method suffers from the combinatorial explosion problem, where the time complexity grows exponentially with the input size. So, WSD as an optimization problem is considered NP-hard (Dorigo and Stützle, 2004).

Approximate algorithms (metaheuristics) are

---

[1] https://www.wiktionary.org/

used to overcome the complexity problems and find near-optimal solutions while exploring as little of the search space as possible. Different metaheuristics have been applied to WSD, including but not limited to, the ant colony algorithm (ACA) (Schwab and Guillaume, 2011), simulated annealing (SA) (Cowie et al., 1992), genetic algorithm (GA) (Zhang et al., 2008) and D-Bees (Abualhaija and Zimmermann, 2016). The results have been good (Schwab et al., 2012), but the major concern is that they are sensitive towards their initial parameters due to their stochastic behavior. Therefore, to guarantee a good performance, parameters should be estimated for every language and domain beforehand.

In this paper, we study the parameter estimation of two metaheuristics for WSD, namely D-Bees (Abualhaija and Zimmermann, 2016) and SA (Cowie et al., 1992). We hypothesize that if metaheuristics are stable with respect to the initial parameters, the parameters can be tuned once on some dataset and then used on other datasets regardless of the domain or language. We test our hypothesis by studying how the best parameter settings for D-Bees and SA perform when tested on another domain.

Next, we explain the background. In Sec. 3, we glue the different pieces of this work together in one pipeline. Experiments and results are presented in 4. In Sec. 5 the results are further analyzed and compared. Finally, we conclude and give an outlook on future work in Sec. 6.

2 Background

2.1 WSD as an Optimization Problem

The WSD problem can be formulated as follows (Pedersen et al., 2005; Abualhaija and Zimmermann, 2016). Given a sequence of n words $W = (w_1, w_2, \ldots, w_n)$, a sequence of senses $\sigma = (s_1, s_2, \ldots, s_n)$, with a corresponding sense s_i for each word w_i, $1 \leq i \leq n$. Let $\mathcal{S} = \{\sigma_1, \ldots, \sigma m\}$ be the set of all sequences of senses corresponding to all sense combinations of the words in the context window (the search space). The objective function is then $\mathrm{argmax}_{\sigma \in \mathcal{S}} \ell(\sigma)$, where ℓ is the score assigned to a sequence of senses. In our experiments, the score is calculated using a variant of the Lesk algorithm (eLesk) (Banerjee and Pedersen, 2002). This optimization approach has the advantage that all the words in the context window are disambiguated simultaneously.

2.2 Metaheuristics for WSD

We choose D-Bees and simulated annealing algorithms because the first has a comparable performance on both English and German (Abualhaija et al., 2017), while the latter is considered a baseline for many metaheuristics since it has a solid formulation, performed well on the SemEval 2007 dataset, and has few parameters to tune (Schwab et al., 2012; Tchechmedjiev et al., 2012).

The D-Bees Algorithm

D-Bees is inspired by the bee colony optimization approach (Teodorović, 2009). Given a sequence of n words, one word is chosen to represent a (virtual) hive, i.e., the word from which the search starts. Only the hive produces bee agents, and sends them to explore the search space, each holding one of its senses and looking for similar senses from the context words.

The D-Bees algorithm comprises of several forward and backward passes. In a forward pass, the bee agents construct a partial solution incrementally by appending a sense from the next word based on the sense frequency and then updating the quality according to the similarity value between the senses until a predefined number of moves is reached. After that, the bee agents return to the hive to exchange information initiating the backward pass.

In the hive, each bee agent performs two probabilistic decisions based on the qualities of their partial solutions. Loyalty decides whether the bee agent exploits its partial solution further or abandons it. In case of abandoning it, another partial solution should be followed (recruitment). The bee agents with good partial solutions act as recruiters and be followed. Following means that the two bee agents fly together in the next forward pass until the point where they stopped last time, from there on they can act independently.

These two passes are alternated until no more target words are to be disambiguated. The bee agent with the best found solution is stored. After a given number of iterations the best solution is returned as the output. More details can be found in (Abualhaija and Zimmermann, 2016).

Simulated Annealing

Simulated Annealing (SA) was first applied to the WSD problem by Cowie et al. (1992) and reimplemented by Schwab et al. (2012). Given a sequence of n words, SA starts with an initial sequence (σ)

by assigning a sense to each word in the sentence; either randomly or based on some heuristic; e.g., using the most frequent sense.

All the definitions of the senses and the related senses are retrieved, preprocessed and stored in a list of lemmas. For this list, the redundancy (R) is calculated as $\sum (f - 1)$, such that f represents the frequency of a lemma occurs in the list. Each solution has an associated energy function (E) to be minimized, and is defined as $E = \frac{1}{1+R}$, where R is the redundancy.

At each iteration, the solution is modified by changing a sense of a randomly chosen word and creating a new solution, which is accepted by a probability $p = \exp^{-\Delta(E)/T}$, where $\Delta(E)$ is the difference between the energy values of the new and old solutions, and T is the temperature. The temperature is decreased by a cooling factor λ after each iteration. This process is repeated until a stopping criterion and the best found solution is returned.

2.3 Parameter Tuning

Parameter tuning is defined as a meta-optimization problem (Talbi, 2009). Given a base algorithm (e.g. D-Bees), and evaluation metric, the parameter estimation algorithm is used to find the parameter configuration of the base algorithm which performs the best for a specific dataset and domain.

In this work we use the Focused Iterated Local Search (ILS) (Hutter et al., 2007; Montero et al., 2014), which is a stochastic local search-based method suitable to tune stochastic metaheuristics. The intuition behind is to test all the possible parameter configurations by changing one parameter value at a time (one-exchange concept), and report the parameter configuration that results in the best performance.

Focused ILS starts with an initial parameter configuration and modifies it randomly. It uses a fixed number of random moves for perturbation, and always accepts the better or equally good parameter configurations. However, it reinitializes the search at random with some probability.

The parameter estimation is performed on a sample of the dataset (training set). The resulting best found parameter configuration is then evaluated on an independently sample of the dataset, the test set. The parameter estimation problem for WSD is defined formally by Tchechmedjiev et al. (2012).

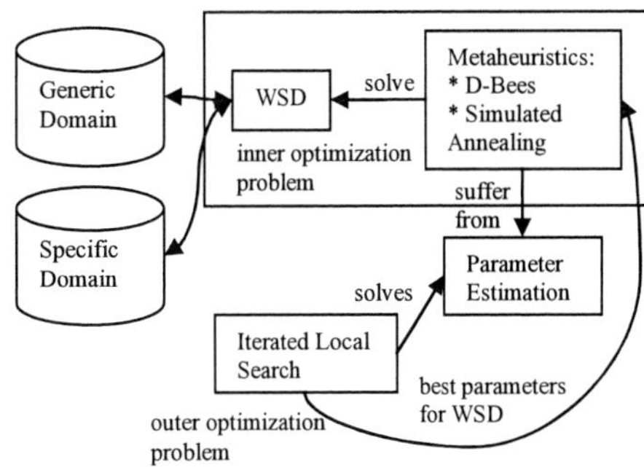

Figure 1: Parameter estimation meta-optimization diagram for WSD problem.

3 Optimizing the Optimizers

Fig. 1 shows the recursive view of the problem. That is, metaheuristics like D-Bees and SA are used to solve WSD as an optimization problem. However, to get the best performance of these algorithms, the initial parameters should be tuned beforehand. The senses in a generic domain dataset usually follow a different distribution than the ones in a specific domain where rare senses (or rather jargons) tend to be more prominent. Therefore, we designed the experiments to test parameters (i) within one dataset and (ii) across domains.

Parameters of the Metaheuristics

D-Bees has three main parameters that influence its performance. First, the hive-mode for choosing the hive and has two possible values: {"mini", "random"}. "mini" considers a word that has a minimal number of senses to limit the search and speed up the convergence whereas "random" refers to choosing uniformly at random. Second, the number of moves in a forward pass (c) : $c \in \{n/3, n/2\}$ where n is the number of words. This parameter controls the exploration process. So, using $n/2$ as an upper-bound ensures focusing on the good solutions early on and avoids prolonging the convergence. Finally, the number of recruiting bee agents (r) : $r \in \{b/3, b/2, 3 \cdot b/4, b - 1\}$, b is the number of bee agents. The upper-bound $b - 1$ reflects responding to better solutions quickly, as honeybees in nature.

SA has two parameters for which the values are chosen inspired by Cowie et al. (1992); Schwab et al. (2012). The temperature $T \in \{70, 200, 400, 600, 700, 800, 900, 1000, 1100, 1200\}$ and the cooling factor $\lambda \in \{0.1, \ldots, 0.9\}$.

4 Experiments and Results

The task is to estimate good parameters for each algorithm on the WSD problem by maximizing the F-measure. The best parameters are then tested on a test set and the results are compared to the most frequent sense baseline (MFS). In order to arrive to a valid conclusion, we use the Wilcoxon non-parametric statistical test.

4.1 Datasets

Tuning experiments are conducted using two datasets from the SemEval campaign. SemEval 2007 task 7 (Navigli et al., 2007) considers a coarse-grained disambiguation and is composed of five different texts (d001 – d005). Apart from d004, the corpus is general domain, and the precision of the MFS baseline is 78.89%. Second is SemEval 2010 task 17 (Agirre et al., 2009) which contains three texts (en1 – en3) on a specific domain (environment). The F-measure of the MFS baseline is 50.50%.

In our experiments we split each dataset into a training and a test set. For SemEval 2007 we used d001 or d004 as a training set and the rest for testing, while for SemEval 2010 we used en1 for training and the rest for testing.

4.2 Training Parameters (intra-Domain)

We start by comparing the parameters when trained and tested on the same corpus. The D-Bees results are compared against the MFS baseline because both introduce a bias on sense frequency when selecting the sense of the next word, also there is no previous literature on D-Bees. The baseline for SA is reported in (Schwab et al., 2012), this way we can test the parameter estimation algorithm compared to what was reported in the literature.

Fig. 2 shows the results of the top-10 parameters using d001, and tested on the rest of the texts of SemEval 2007. It can be proved that the top 10 parameters perform significantly better on the test set of the same corpus than the baseline with a confidence interval of 90% in both cases. Similarly, Fig. 3 and Fig. 4 summarizes the D-Bees and SA parameters behavior on SemEval 2007 dataset excluding d004 and SemEval 2010 excluding en1, respectively(d004 and en1 are used as training sets). For D-Bees, the baseline is the de-

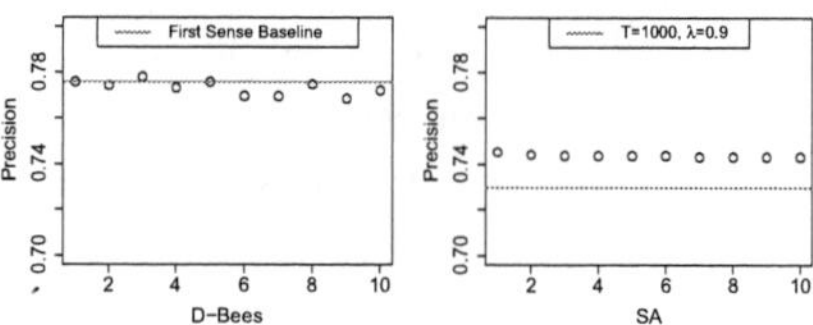

Figure 2: Top-10 parameters on SemEval 2007 excluding d001.

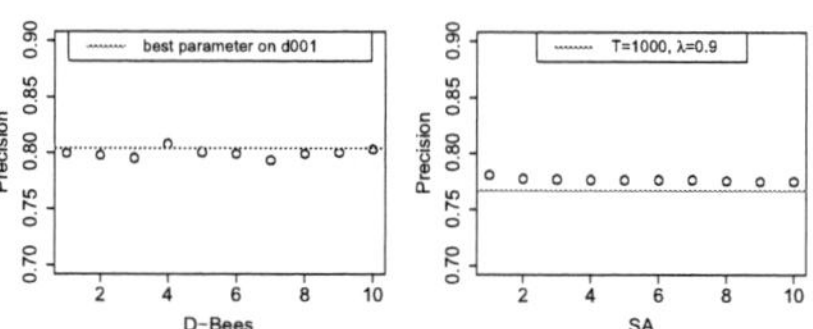

Figure 3: Top-10 parameters on SemEval 2007 excluding d004.

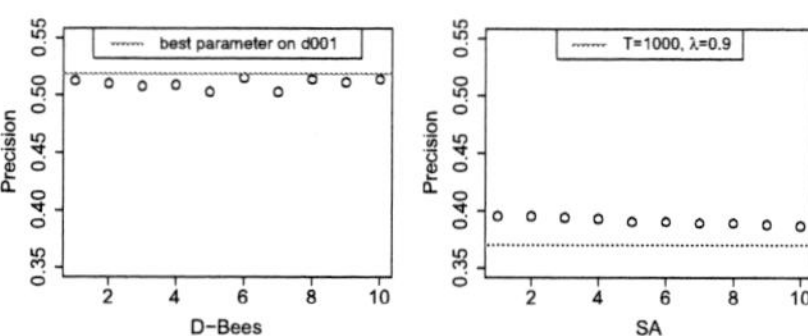

Figure 4: Top-10 parameters on SemEval 2010 excluding en1.

fault parameter found on d001 in order to get an impression about how parameters trained on general domain perform on a specific one.

It can be observed that the behavior of the best parameters found on the two datasets do not vary for both algorithms.

4.3 Transferring Parameters (inter-Domain)

Next we test how parameters perform when transferred across domains and datasets. If the parameters that are trained on corpus (or domain) A perform better than a certain baseline for corpus (or domain) B, then these parameters are suitable for use. It follows that the algorithm is less sensitive towards the dataset, or the domain of dataset. Therefore, the parameters do not necessarily have to be re-estimated. Otherwise the baseline is sufficient.

Fig. 5 shows the top-10 parameters found by training on d001 of SemEval 2007 and testing on SemEval 2010 dataset. The baseline for D-Bees corresponds to the best parameter trained on en1

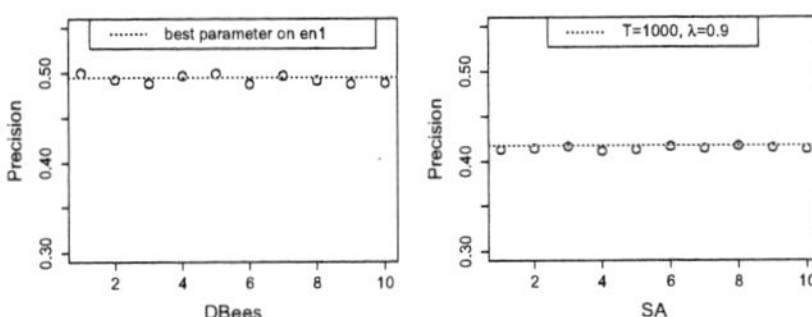

Figure 5: Top-10 parameters on d001 tested on SemEval 2010.

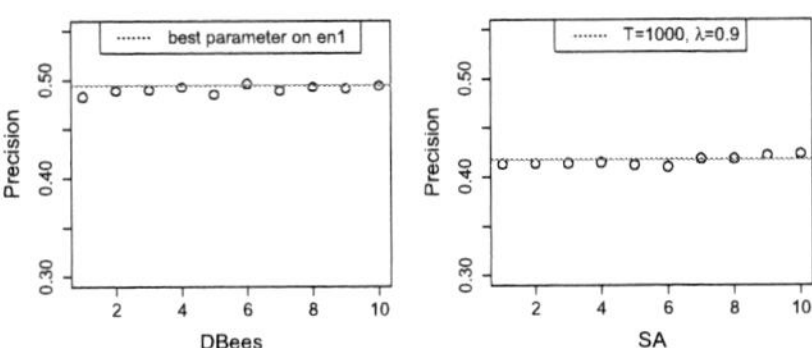

Figure 6: Top-10 parameters on d004 tested on SemEval 2010.

and tested on the rest of SemEval 2010 dataset. For SA, the baseline is the same as in the previous experiments which corresponds eventually to training the parameters on d001 from SemEval 2007 corpus. This makes the baselines for both algorithms equivalent.

It can be observed that some of the parameters of D-Bees significantly outperform the baseline, while for SA, the baseline performs best. Training the parameters of D-Bees on a generic domain then using them on another specific one is performing well. On the contrary, SA appears to be more sensitive towards the dataset.

In Fig. 6, the parameters are trained on d004 of SemEval 2007, considering d004 text as a specific domain on "computer science" and tested on the SemEval 2010. As expected, using the Wilcoxon test the performance of the parameters found on en1 are on par with those found on d004. It follows that training parameters on a specific domain dataset and then testing on a different specific domain one might work, but with a low certainty.

The last case is testing how well the parameters perform on a generic domain dataset (SemEval 2007) when trained on a specific domain from another dataset (SemEval 2010). Fig. 7 shows the results of this case, where the baseline outperforms all the parameters significantly for both algorithms. This supports our earlier argument that senses might have different distributions in specific domains.

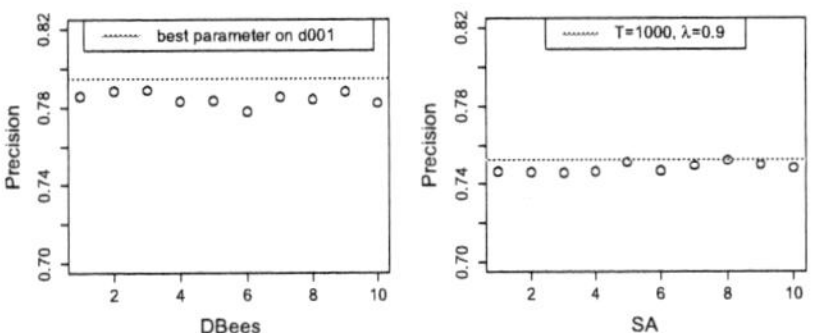

Figure 7: Testing the top-10 en1 parameters on SemEval 2007 dataset.

5 Analysis and Discussion

In this section, we discuss the results of solving the recursive problem, that is solving WSD using metaheuristics. In the first part we show the performance of using the best found parameters on the corresponding SemEval task. Then, we discuss the results of these parameters with the insight of their performance on the dedicated task.

5.1 Influence on WSD Results

Going back to the original problem (WSD), we compare the performance of D-Bees with the other participating systems reported in both SemEval 2007 and 2010 tasks. We focus on D-Bees and not SA because the former performs better in both parts of the recursive problem, WSD as well as parameter estimation. Also we apply D-Bees on the whole dataset to obtain a fair comparison with the other reported systems in the task.

Tab. 1 shows the performance of D-Bees on SemEval 2007 (Navigli et al., 2007). It can be observed that the results of D-Bees are outperformed mainly by supervised systems and are comparable to the first sense baseline (MFS). In general texts MFS disambiguates the target words to a large extent. Therefore, the chance to hit the correct meaning is high. Unlike MFS, D-Bees considers other frequent senses as well, which might match more precise meanings of the words provided that the definitions of the senses are close to each other because WordNet is fine-grained. This makes the D-Bees algorithm promising.

Tab. 2 shows the performance of D-Bees on SemEval 2010 using both best found parameters on the generic and specific domain. We report the precision and recall similar to the task (Agirre et al., 2009). The two D-Bees versions perform somewhat close although none beats the MFS baseline. The D-Bees (specific) is the next best system. This supports the conclusion that parameters trained on a general domain can be applied

Table 1: Comparison of D-Bees with 100% coverage evaluated on Semeval 2007 Task 7 († ≡ Supervised Method).

System	F-Measure (%)
UoR-SSI†	83.21
Nus-PT†	82.5
Nus-ML†	81.58
LCC-WSD†	81.45
GPLSI†	79.55
D-Bees	79.46
MFS Baseline	78.89
UPV-WSD†	78.63
Degree (Babelnet)	77.01
PageRank (Babelnet)	72.60
TKB-UO	70.21
RACAI-SYNWSD	65.71

Table 2: A comparison of D-Bees with the knowledge-based systems on SemEval 2010 Task 17.

System	Precision (%)	Recall (%)
MFS Baseline	50.5	50.5
D-Bees (specific)	50.0	50.0
CFILT-3	51.2	49.5
Treematch	50.6	49.3
D-Bees (generic)	48.9	48.9
kyoto-2	48.1	48.1
RACAI-MFS	46.1	46.0
UCF-WS	44.7	44.1
HIT-CIR-DMFS-1.ans	43.6	43.5
IIITH2-d.r.l.baseline.05	49.6	43.3

on a specific one with a decent performance. The other way around however, does not work.

5.2 Parameter Tuning

Our experiments show that D-Bees achieves F-score of 79.46% and 48.9% on SemEval 2007 and 2010 respectively using parameters trained on a generic domain. Adjusting the parameter to the specific domain increases the performance to 50.0% on SemEval 2010, the best of all evaluated systems. While SA achieves 24.0% and 40.0% using the best parameters trained on SemEval 2007 and SemEval 2010 respectively. We find that D-Bees performs comparable to the state-of-the-art (Abualhaija and Zimmermann, 2016; Schwab et al., 2012). The results of SA indicate that it is sensitive towards its parameters, thus have to be tuned beforehand for every domain and language.

Lemmas and part of speech tags of the words are not offered in SemEval 2010, so the performance of the WSD system depends partially on the lemmatizer and POS-tagger. Also, errors in pre-processing lead to an unstable behavior of D-Bees. Nevertheless, D-Bees shows a robust behavior by achieving scores on par with the MFS and the best systems. For the specific domain, the parameters of D-Bees perform better when the number of recruiters is greater than at least half of the bee agents, unlike on a generic domain where a third is sufficient.

The sensitivity of both algorithms is further analyzed on the lexical substitution task for English and German (Abualhaija et al., 2017). For D-Bees we used the parameters found on SemEval 2007 dataset (d001) and the default parameters as given by Cowie et al. (1992) for SA. D-Bees achieves competitive results for both languages, while the performance of SA could be improved by tuning the parameters on the testing language. This supports the conclusion that D-Bees algorithm is less sensitive towards its initial parameters.

6 Conclusion and Outlook

In this paper, we tested the hypothesis that metaheuristics are good approximation algorithms to solve the WSD optimization problem. We compared D-Bees to SA and found that D-Bees performs better for WSD. We studied the parameter tuning problem since metaheuristics could be sensitive towards their initial parameters. We found that transferring the parameters across domains (i.e., training on one domain and testing on another) works well for D-Bees, which reduces the need to tune the parameters on each new WSD scenario and dataset.

In some sense, we could find robustness in the parameters across datasets (D-Bees best performance compared to SA) but more limited transferability across domains. We believe that this difficulty can be avoided by including knowledge about the corpus domain from the lexical resource. D-Bees beats most unsupervised methods in both SemEval 2007 and 2010 contests. This makes it suitable for solving the WSD problem. Our experiments deduced clues on how to choose parameters for specific domain.

Acknowledgement

This work was partially funded by the German Federal Ministry of Education and Research (BMBF) under the project K3 (13N13548).

References

Sallam Abualhaija, Tristan Miller, Judith Eckle-Kohler, Iryna Gurevych, and Karl-Heinz Zimmermann. 2017. Metaheuristic approaches to lexical substitution and simplification. In *Proceedings of the 15th Conference of the European Chapter of the Association for Computational Linguistics (EACL 2017)*. Association for Computational Linguistics.

Sallam Abualhaija and Karl-Heinz Zimmermann. 2016. D-bees: A novel method inspired by bee colony optimization for solving word sense disambiguation. *Swarm and Evolutionary Computation* 27:188 – 195.

Eneko Agirre, Oier López De Lacalle, Christiane Fellbaum, Andrea Marchetti, Antonio Toral, and Piek Vossen. 2009. Semeval-2010 task 17: All-words word sense disambiguation on a specific domain. In *Proceedings of the Workshop on Semantic Evaluations: Recent Achievements and Future Directions*. Association for Computational Linguistics, pages 123–128.

Eneko Agirre and Philip Glenny Edmonds. 2007. *Word sense disambiguation: Algorithms and applications*, volume 33. Springer Science & Business Media.

Satanjeev Banerjee and Ted Pedersen. 2002. An adapted lesk algorithm for word sense disambiguation using wordnet. In *Computational linguistics and intelligent text processing*, Springer, pages 136–145.

Samuel Brody, Roberto Navigli, and Mirella Lapata. 2006. Ensemble methods for unsupervised wsd. In *Proceedings of the 21st International Conference on Computational Linguistics and the 44th annual meeting of the Association for Computational Linguistics*. Association for Computational Linguistics, pages 97–104.

Jim Cowie, Joe Guthrie, and Louise Guthrie. 1992. Lexical disambiguation using simulated annealing. In *Proceedings of the 14th conference on Computational linguistics-Volume 1*. Association for Computational Linguistics, pages 359–365.

Marco Dorigo and Thomas Stützle. 2004. *Ant Colony Optimization*. Bradford Company, Scituate, MA, USA.

Frank Hutter, Holger H Hoos, and Thomas Stützle. 2007. Automatic algorithm configuration based on local search. In *AAAI*. volume 7, pages 1152–1157.

Nancy Ide and Jean Véronis. 1998. Introduction to the special issue on word sense disambiguation: the state of the art. *Computational linguistics* 24:2–40.

Vivek Kulkarni, Rami Al-Rfou, Bryan Perozzi, and Steven Skiena. 2015. Statistically significant detection of linguistic change. In *Proceedings of the 24th International Conference on World Wide Web*. ACM, pages 625–635.

David Martínez et al. 2007. Supervised corpus-based methods for wsd. In *Word Sense Disambiguation*, Springer, pages 167–216.

George A Miller, Richard Beckwith, Christiane Fellbaum, Derek Gross, and Katherine J Miller. 1990. Introduction to wordnet: An on-line lexical database*. *International journal of lexicography* 3:235–244.

Elizabeth Montero, María-Cristina Riff, and Bertrand Neveu. 2014. A beginner's guide to tuning methods. *Applied Soft Computing* 17:39–51.

Roberto Navigli. 2012. A quick tour of word sense disambiguation, induction and related approaches. In *International Conference on Current Trends in Theory and Practice of Computer Science*. Springer, pages 115–129.

Roberto Navigli, Kenneth C Litkowski, and Orin Hargraves. 2007. Semeval-2007 task 07: Coarsegrained english all-words task. In *Proceedings of the 4th International Workshop on Semantic Evaluations*. Association for Computational Linguistics, pages 30–35.

Ted Pedersen, Satanjeev Banerjee, and Siddharth Patwardhan. 2005. Maximizing semantic relatedness to perform word sense disambiguation. *University of Minnesota supercomputing institute research report UMSI* 25:2005.

Hinrich Schütze. 1998. Automatic word sense discrimination. *Computational linguistics* 24:97–123.

Didier Schwab, Jérôme Goulian, Andon Tchechmedjiev, and Hervé Blanchon. 2012. Ant colony algorithm for the unsupervised word sense disambiguation of texts: Comparison and evaluation. In *COLING*. pages 2389–2404.

Didier Schwab and Nathan Guillaume. 2011. A global ant colony algorithm for word sense disambiguation based on semantic relatedness. In *Highlights in Practical Applications of Agents and Multiagent Systems*, Springer, pages 257–264.

Lucia Specia, Sujay Kumar Jauhar, and Rada Mihalcea. 2012. Semeval-2012 task 1: English lexical simplification. In *Proceedings of the First Joint Conference on Lexical and Computational Semantics-Volume 1: Proceedings of the main conference and the shared task, and Volume 2: Proceedings of the Sixth International Workshop on Semantic Evaluation*. Association for Computational Linguistics, pages 347–355.

Nina Tahmasebi, Thomas Risse, and Stefan Dietze. 2011. Towards automatic language evolution tracking, a study on word sense tracking. In *Joint Workshop on Knowledge Evolution and Ontology Dynamics*.

El-Ghazali Talbi. 2009. *Metaheuristics: From Design to Implementation*. Wiley Publishing.

Andon Tchechmedjiev, Jérôme Goulian, Didier Schwab, and Gilles Sérasset. 2012. Parameter estimation under uncertainty with simulated annealing applied to an ant colony based probabilistic wsd algorithm. In *Proceedings of the First International Workshop on Optimization Techniques for Human Language Technology*. pages 109–124.

Dušan Teodorović. 2009. Bee colony optimization (bco). In *Innovations in swarm intelligence*, Springer, pages 39–60.

David Vickrey, Luke Biewald, Marc Teyssier, and Daphne Koller. 2005. Word-sense disambiguation for machine translation. In *Proceedings of the conference on Human Language Technology and Empirical Methods in Natural Language Processing*. Association for Computational Linguistics, pages 771–778.

David Yarowsky. 1992. Word-sense disambiguation using statistical models of roget's categories trained on large corpora. In *Proceedings of the 14th Conference on Computational Linguistics - Volume 2*. Association for Computational Linguistics, Stroudsburg, PA, USA, COLING '92, pages 454–460.

Chunhui Zhang, Yiming Zhou, and Trevor Martin. 2008. Genetic word sense disambiguation algorithm. In *Intelligent Information Technology Application, 2008. IITA'08. Second International Symposium on*. IEEE, volume 1, pages 123–127.

What Sentence are you Referring to and Why? Identifying Cited Sentences in Scientific Literature

Ahmed Abura'ed
Universitat Pompeu Fabra
Large Scale Text Understanding
Systems Lab
TALN / DTIC
Barcelona, Spain
ahmed.aburaed@upf.edu

Luis Chiruzzo
Universidad de la República
Facultad de Ingeniería
Instituto de Computación
Montevideo, Uruguay
luischir@fing.edu.uy

Horacio Saggion
Universitat Pompeu Fabra
Large Scale Text Understanding
Systems Lab
TALN / DTIC
Barcelona, Spain
horacio.saggion@upf.edu

Abstract

In the current context of scientific information overload, text mining tools are of paramount importance for researchers who have to read scientific papers and assess their value. Current citation networks, which link papers by citation relationships (reference and citing paper), are useful to quantitatively understand the value of a piece of scientific work, however they are limited in that they do not provide information about what specific part of the reference paper the citing paper is referring to. This qualitative information is very important, for example, in the context of current community-based scientific summarization activities. In this paper, and relying on an annotated dataset of co-citation sentences, we carry out a number of experiments aimed at, given a citation sentence, automatically identify a part of a reference paper being cited. Additionally our algorithm predicts the specific reason why such reference sentence has been cited out of five possible reasons.

1 Introduction

Scientific publications such as scientific papers are some of the most valuable sources of human knowledge, containing information as relevant as how to cure diseases, create medicaments or construct useful life-saving machines; they are permanent records of what has been discovered so far (Kuhn, 1970). The amount of scientific publications is growing at unprecedented rates (Bornmann and Mutz, 2015; Saggion and Ronzano, 2016) with recent estimates indicating that a new research paper is published every 13 seconds. Scientific research needs awareness of what has been discovered or published before us to progress: as Newton has put it, "If I have seen further it is by standing on the shoulders of Giants."

The value of a scientific article is sometimes assessed by the number of publications citing the article, although this way of measuring research is well established, it is only quantitative, leaving qualitative considerations out of the picture. Although over the years several works have been interested in qualitative aspects related to paper citations (Moravcsik and Murugesan, 1975; Spiegel-Rosing, 1977; Teufel et al., 2006; Abu-Jbara et al., 2013; Athar, 2011; Shotton, 2010; Fisas et al., 2016; Valenzuela et al., 2015), recently, in the context of the Computational Linguistics Scientific Summarization Challenge (Jaidka et al., 2016) (CL-SciSumm hereafter), one task was identified as relevant to citation analysis: given a scientific paper – the reference, and another paper citing it, the task is to determine what part of the reference the citing paper is referring to, and also what particular aspect is being cited (e.g. the aim of the paper? the method?). In this paper we investigate how to address the above task and present a system which uses unsupervised sentence similarity metrics and supervised machine learning to address the challenge.

The contributions of this paper are as follows:

- A thorough comparison of several sentence matching algorithms relying on discrete and continuous word representations;

- An state-of-the-art method for matching citing sentences to cited sentences in scientific literature; and

- A trainable method for identifying citing facets which, in terms of precision, achieves competitive performance.

Proceedings of Recent Advances in Natural Language Processing, pages 9–17,
Varna, Bulgaria, Sep 4–6 2017.

2 Related Work

Recent studies proposed to take advantage of the scientific papers citation network mainly to approach scientific literature summarization. This section discusses some of the most related studies that tried to identify which reference paper sentences have been cited and also tried to identify the discourse facet of the reference sentence. Nomoto et al. (2016) aimed to detect a part of the reference paper that is most related to a given citation made by a citation paper through producing a hybrid model consisting of TFIDF and Neural Network (NN), he used the Neural Network to adapt the embedding model used in the question answering domain to provide a scoring function and built the TFIDF part based on the test data of the CL-SciSumm 2016 corpus. The training data, comprising of triples of citance, the true reference and the set of false references for the citance, was used to perform a Stochastic gradient descent search while sentence selection was based on a dissimilarity score (i.e. MMR). Li et al. (2016) used a Support Vector Machines (SVM) classifier to identify the spans of text in the reference paper matching each citance. They also used a combination of methods such as: idf similarity, Jaccard similarity and context similarity leading into the following methods: Sentence fusion, Jaccard Cascade method, Jaccard Focused method, SVM method, etc. Cao et al. (2016) considered the problem of identifying the reference text sentences that most precisely reflect the citance as a ranking problem which they modeled using SVM Rank, they also used a decision tree classifier to identify the facet that a citance belongs to. Moraes et al. (2016) used cosine similarity based on TFIDF weights for sentences with multiple incremental modifications and SVMs with a tree kernel. Moreover, the best results were obtained by cosine similarity. Di Iorio et al. (2013) presented a tool named CiTalO to automatically deduce the nature of citations by combining techniques of ontology learning from natural language, sentiment-analysis, word-sense disambiguation, and ontology mapping. CiTalO extracts information about the nature, the motivations and the goals of each citation. Many configurations were applied with CiTalO including: filtered citations, in which all synsets of which WordNet's gloss is not aligned with the natural language description of the property in consideration were filtered out; sentiment, including sentiment polarity emerging from the text in which the citation is included. CiTalO was tested by comparing its results with a human classification of the citations. Finally, Saggion et al. (2016) presented two supervised approaches for identifying RP's text spans and facet classification. They trained the sentence matching approach using only reference sentences in the gold standard which proved to be uneffective in testing data.

3 CL-SciSumm Challenge and Corpus

In the CL-SciSumm 2016 evaluation (Jaidka et al., 2016) participants were given a set of clusters, each one composed of n documents where one is a reference paper (RP) and the n-1 remaining documents are referred to as citing papers (CPs) since they cite the reference paper. Given this set-up, researchers were asked to address the following two tasks:

- **Task A**: For each citance in the CP (i.e., a reference to the RP), identify the spans of text (cited text spans) in the RP that most accurately reflect the citance.

- **Task B**: For each cited text span, identify what **facet** of the paper it belongs to, from a predefined set of facets, namely: *Aim, Hypothesis, Implication, Results* or *Method*.

There was an additional summarization task which we do not address here due to space constraints.

3.1 Dataset

In the experiments to be presented in this paper, we have relied on the CL-SciSumm 2016 corpus which provides training, development and testing data arranged in clusters of reference paper and the papers citing it. The corpus also contains text files that represent the gold manual annotations indicating the facet and the text span(s) in the reference paper that best represent each citance. Figure 1 shows an example of one line of the gold manual annotations provided by the CL-SciSumm organizers.

4 Text Processing

Each document in the clusters was annotated using processing resources from the following freely available tools: GATE system (Maynard et al., 2002), the SUMMA library (Saggion, 2008) and

```
Citance Number: 60 | Reference Article:  J96-3004.xml | Citing Article: W12-1011.xml |
Citation Marker Offset:  ['41'] | Citation Marker:  Sproat et al., 1996 | Citation Offset:
['41'] | Citation Text:  <S sid ="41" ssid = "5">Indeed, even native speakers can agree on
word boundaries in modern Chinese only about 76% of the time (Sproat et al., 1996).</S> |
Reference Offset:  ['325'] | Reference Text:  <S sid ="325" ssid = "34">The average agreement
among the human judges is .76, and the average agreement between ST and the humans is .75, or
about 99% of the interhuman agreement</S> | Discourse Facet:  Results_Citation | Annotator:
Ankita Patel |
```

Figure 1: One line example of the gold manual annotation provided by the CL-SciSumm 2016 corpus.

the Dr Inventor library (Ronzano and Saggion, 2015).

The GATE system was used to tokenize, sentence split, part of speech tag, manage gazetteers and lemmatize each document. Teufel's (Teufel et al., 2000) action and concept Lexicons were used to create gazetteers lists to identify in text scientific concepts (e.g. *research*: analyze, check and gather; *problem*: violate, spoil and mistake, and *solution*: fix, cure and accomplish). The Dr Inventor's library for analysing scientific documents was additionally applied to each document to generate rich semantic information such as citation marker, BabelNet concepts (Navigli and Ponzetto, 2012), causality markers, co-reference chains, and rhetorical sentence classification. The library classifies each sentence of a paper based on a rhetorical category of scientific discourse among: Approach, Background, Challenge, Outcome and FutureWork. In other words, it predicts the probability of the sentence of belonging to one of the five discourses provided. See (Fisas et al., 2016) for more details about the corpus used for training the classifier. Finally, the SUMMA library was used to produce term vectors, normalized term vectors, BabelNet synset ID vectors, normalized babelnet synset ID vectors, terms n-grams (up to two) and part of speech n-grams (up to two) for each document.

5 Matching Citations to Reference Papers

In this section, we present methods to, given a citation sentence, identify the sentence or sentences in the reference paper being referred to. First, we present a method based on current continuous word representations. This method did not provide the expected performance. Then, we present a method based on more traditional bag-of-words representations which performed reasonably well when compared to results from the CL-SciSumm Challenge.

5.1 Sentence Embeddings

Word embeddings are continuous vector representations for words. This technique tries to map a set of words into a set of n-dimensional continuous vectors, where the dimension n is much lower than the number of words in the vocabulary. There are a number of ways for training such word representations, for example the word2vec algorithms Continuous Bag of Words and Skipgram (Mikolov et al., 2013) are amongst the most popular ones. In our experiments we used a pretrained word embeddings collection trained over 100 billion words from the Google News dataset[1]. It comprises 3 million words and phrases embedded in a 300 dimensional space. We also used two word embedding models (dimensions 100 and 300) trained with scientific papers text[2](Liu, 2017) from the ACL Anthology Reference Corpus (Bird, 2008). We performed experiments using only Google News vectors (GN), only ACL vectors of size 100 (ACL100) or 300 (ACL300), and also using the concatenation of GN and ACL100 or ACL300 vectors.

Having the embeddings for the words it is possible to generate embeddings for larger units like phrases or sentences. There are several ways of creating sentence embeddings, in our experiments we averaged the word embeddings for each word in the sentence. This is a very simple approach that has nonetheless given good results to problems such as extractive summarization (Kågebäck et al., 2014) and semantic classification (White et al., 2015).

Using these sentence embeddings, we tried to identify the sentences in the reference paper (RP) that more accurately reflect the citance by calculating the sentence embedding for each citance sentence (sentences from the citing paper) and the sentence embedding for each RP sentence. Then

---

[1]https://code.google.com/archive/p/word2vec/
[2]https://github.com/liuhaixiachina/Sentiment-Analysis-of-Citations-Using-Word2vec/tree/master/trainedmodels

return the most similar sentences from the RP to any of the citance sentences according to cosine similarity.

We used the `gensim` library (Řehůřek and Sojka, 2010) for working with word embeddings. Table 1 summarizes the performance of these experiments. The number following the experiment name indicates the number of retrieved sentences we considered for each experiment, we tried retrieving different number of sentences (2, 5, 8 and 10) and optimized against the development corpus for the best F1 score. The best result has 0.101 of F1 score averaged over the test corpus documents, and was attained considering the top 2 sentences from the RP according to cosine similarity.

5.2 Words, BabelNet Concepts and Sentence Similarity Measures

We relied on two different sentence representations produced by the SUMMA library and two different text similarity measures. Sentences were represented either as word-vectors (W) or BabelNet-vectors (B) where each vector component (a word or a BabelNet synset) was weighted using a tf*idf weighting schema. For calculating the BabelNet vectors, we used the BabelNet service to get the list of synsets used in each sentence, and we calculated tf*idf over that. Where the similarity measures are concerned we used cosine similarity (C) or the Jaccard coefficient (J). Given a citation sentence in the CP, and a sentence in the RP, we computed four similarity values: the cosine similarity using word vectors (WC), the cosine similarity using BabelNet vectors (BC), the jaccard similarity using word vectors (WJ), and the jaccard similarity using BabelNet Vectors (BJ). We then performed another experiment using a modified version of the jaccard similarity (MJ) that takes into consideration the inverted frequency of words as well. For this experiment we calculated the tf*idf weighting schema over both training and development sets of documents, performing stemming of words and using only the first characters of every word so that words like "structure" and "structural" are considered the same token. The modified jaccard similarity between two sentences s_1 and s_2 is defined in equation 1, and it gives more weight to matching words that are infrequent in the corpus.

$$MJ(s_1, s_2) = \frac{\sum_{t \in s_1 \cap s_2} 2^{idf(t)}}{|s_1 \cup s_2|} \quad (1)$$

We optimize F-score on the training data searching for the best similarity threshold and the top number of sentences to retrieve for each citing sentence. Results for the test data are presented in Table 2. The table shows each configuration with the threshold used to retrieve sentences (i.e. similarity > thr) and the number of top RP sentences retrieved for each CP citance. As it can be observed the best performance is achieved using the modified jaccard similarity. Our results improve the state of the art performance obtained in the CL-SciSumm 2016 evaluation for this task.

To better comprehend the results of our approach we did a comparison with the top four results obtained by participants at the CL-SciSumm 2016 challenge. See Table 3.

6 Identifying Citation Facets

In this section, we present experiments aiming at identifying the facet the cited text span belongs to. We modeled pairs of reference and citance sentences as a feature vector. Then, we used such pair representation to enable the training of classification algorithms tailored to determine whether a cited text span belongs to one out of five predefined facets: *Aim*, *Hypothesis*, *Implication*, *Results* or *Method*. We rely on the WEKA machine learning framework (Witten et al., 2016) as a tool to conduct our experiments. We first describe the set of features used to generate the feature vectors for instance representation to then describe the machine learning algorithms used.

6.1 Features

Sentence position: we use three features that are based on the location of the sentence in the document:

- Sentence position: the position of the sentence in the reference paper.

- Section Sentence position: the position of the sentence in the section of the paper.

- Facet position: five binary features indicating whether the sentence is in a section indicating one of the target facets. We designed a set of keywords to determine if a section title belongs to a given facets (e.g. the word "method" indicates a section dealing with the facet *Method*). In case any of the title's words belong to a given facet, the value of that facet feature will be 1 otherwise it will be 0.

Table 1: Performance of the sentence embedding experiments.

Method	Top	Avg. Precision	Avg. Recall	Avg. F-Measure
GN	2	0.079	0.13	0.096
ACL100	2	0.055	0.084	0.066
ACL300	2	0.074	0.117	0.089
GN+ACL100	2	**0.082**	**0.132**	**0.101**
GN+ACL300	2	0.081	0.129	0.099

Table 2: Performance of the word vectors and similarity metrics experiments on test data.

Method	Thr	Top	Avg. Precision	Avg. Recall	Avg. F-Measure
WC	0.0	8	0.025	0.179	0.044
BC	0.0	8	0.023	0.124	0.039
WJ	0.1	2	0.084	0.138	0.105
BJ	0.1	2	0.079	0.111	0.092
MJ	0.1	2	**0.123**	**0.201**	**0.151**

Text similarity: We rely on the cosine similarity between the pair of citing and reference sentence using word and BabelNet synsets vectors (see Section 5.2).

Rhetorical Category Probability Features: We mentioned in Section 4 that the Dr Inventor library predicts the probability of a sentence being in one of five possible categories (different from the CL-SciSumm task): Approach, Background, Challenge, Outcome and FutureWork. Even though Dr Inventor library has different mapping from our targeted discourse facets, we believe this information could be useful for classification. Therefore, We use such probabilities as features for citing and reference sentences. **Dr Inventor Sentence related features**: We utilize an additional set of features produced by Dr Inventor:

- Citation marker: three features to represent the number of citation markers in the reference sentence, citing sentence and the pair of sentences together.

- Cause and effect: two features to represent if the reference or citing sentence participates to the formulation of one or more causal relations by specifying the cause or the effect.

- Co-reference Chains: three features to represent the number of nominals and pronominals chained in the reference sentence, citing sentence and the pair of sentences together.

Scientific Gazetteer Features: As mentioned in Section 4 the documents were enriched with Teufel's action and concept Lexicon gazetteers lists producing the total of 58 lists. Each list is used to produce a feature which is the ratio of words in the sentence matching the list to the number of words in the sentence. The features are computed for the reference sentence, the citing sentence, and their combination, giving rise to 174 features.

Bag-of-word Features: eight string features are produced to represent the *bigram lemmas*, *POS-tags bigram*, *lemmas* and *POS-tags* for both the reference and the citing sentences.

7 Facets Experiments

After having the complete set of features based on the pair of sentences, we trained algorithms over the training dataset based on 432 training instances distributed as follows: Aim (72), Implication (26), Result (76), Hypothesis (1), Method (257). We evaluated the performance of several classification algorithms including: Support Vector Machines(SMO), Naive Bayes, IBK, Random Committee, Logistic and Random Forest. Then, we performed 10-fold cross validation experiments with the training data in order to decide which algorithm to use during testing. To achieve the best approach, we investigated feature selection on training data. We split the set of features by the top ten, twenty and thirty percent of features then we evaluated the classification algorithms on each set of features in addition to the whole training feature set. We choose the best three performing algorithms for each set of features to create our models. See Table 4 for a list of feature sets and the best three algorithm (10-fold cross validation).

8 Facets Classification Results

We performed nine system runs to identify the facets for each matched pair of reference and

13

Table 3: A comparison with the top four results by participants at CL-SciSumm 2016

Team	best Approach	Avg. Precision	Avg. Recall	Avg. F
Nomoto et al. (2016)	TFIDF + neural network,	0.091	0.111	0.100
Li et al. (2016)	Sentence Fusion + Jaccard Focused	0.082	**0.262**	0.125
Cao et al. (2016)	SVM Rank	0.088	0.131	0.103
Moraes et al. (2016)	TF-IDF+ST+SL	0.096	0.224	0.133
Our approach	MJ	**0.123**	0.201	**0.151**

Table 4: A list of the best three algorithm for each feature set based on 10-fold cross validation. Precision, Recall and F-measure results for each configuration are shown.

Features	Algorithm	Avg. Precision	Avg. Recall	Avg. F-Measure
top 10%	SMO	0.920	0.921	0.920
	Logistic	0.924	0.926	0.924
	Random Committee	0.882	0.880	0.874
top 20%	SMO	**0.936**	**0.938**	**0.936**
	Logistic	0.918	0.919	0.917
	Naive Bayes	0.876	0.877	0.875
top 30%	SMO	0.934	0.935	0.934
	Logistic	0.929	0.926	0.926
	IBK	0.891	0.889	0.889
all features	SMO	0.929	0.931	0.928
	Logistic	0.914	0.910	0.910
	IBK	0.908	0.907	0.907

citing sentences in the testing dataset; we used the gold annotations to identify the matched sentences, after identifying the facet, we produced the output annotations in a format consistent with the CL-SciSumm 2016 corpus. We evaluated each system by comparing its output with the gold annotations provided in the corpus. Table 5 presents the evaluation results of the nine system runs based on models generated from different features sets. What can be noticed from the evaluation result is that the best performing system is the one using the Support Vector Machines (SMO) using the whole feature set.

However, this evaluation considers an *ideal scenario* in which the facet classifier is invoked for gold standard matches. Therefore, we also evaluated the Support Vector Machines (SMO) classifier used to identify the facets over each pair of matched sentences according to the best matching system described in Section 5.

Finally, to improve our facet system, we retrained its model after adding information from the development dataset making the total of 897 training instances distributed as follows: Aim (145), Implication (71), Result (168), Hypothesis (19), Method (494) and combining each pair of reference and citing sentences together before producing the Bag-of-word Features making the total number of string features to four instead of eight. The merging between the reference and citing sentences is motivated by representing each pair of reference and citing sentences as one entity instead of having two separate entities on each part of the pair. The evaluation can be seen in Table 6.

In comparison with CL-SciSumm 2016 challenge teams our approach scores directly after the best team's results. Please see Table 7 for such comparison.

What can be noticed at Table 7 is that our approach achieves higher precision than Li et al. approach but their approach has higher recall outperforming our system as a result. However, we believe that there are two reasons for such contrast: First, Li et al. used Jaccard Focused method for their matches system and then applied a Voting method which combines the results from three methods (Subtitle Rule, High Frequency Word and SVM classifier) to achieve the best results with the most votes for Facet Identification. On the other hand, our system did not use a voting mechanism instead we used a set of features including features which are equivalent to their methods (except their High Frequency Word feature). Second, our approach performed poorly over some of the testing clusters due to some noise in the gold annotations, such as a higher number of references to the title than expected (cluster P98-1046: 9 out of 31 annotations). We also show a set of results that exclude some of the most problematic clusters.

Table 5: Evaluation results of the nine system runs over the gold standard matched pair of sentences based on models generated from different features sets

Features	Algorithm	Avg. Precision	Avg. Recall	Avg. F-Measure
top 10%	SMO	0.7081	0.6243	0.6618
	Logistic	0.5263	0.4638	0.4916
	Random Committee	0.7294	0.6463	0.6835
top 20%	SMO	0.7458	0.6603	0.6985
	Logistic	0.5520	0.4889	0.5171
	Naïve Bayes	0.5422	0.4766	0.5057
top 30%	SMO	0.7494	0.6634	0.7019
	Logistic	0.5263	0.4689	0.4946
	IBK	0.5131	0.4493	0.4777
all	**SMO**	**0.7519**	**0.6657**	**0.7043**
	Logistic	0.3223	0.2797	0.2986
	IBK	0.5889	0.5162	0.5486

Table 6: Evaluation results of the improved best SMO system over the matched pair of sentences based on the best performing match system

Features	Algorithm	Avg. Precision	Avg. Recall	Avg. F-Measure
all	SMO	0.635	0.155	**0.242**

Table 7: A comparison with the top team (best results) at the CL-SciSumm 2016 applied on the testing dataset

System	Testing Clusters	Algorithm	Avg.Precision	Avg.Recall	Avg.F-Measure
Li et al.	all	Jaccard Focused	0.581	0.230	0.314
Our approach	all	SMO	0.635	0.155	0.242
Our approach	excluding worst cluster	SMO	0.683	0.168	0.263
Our approach	ex. worst two clusters	SMO	0.738	0.185	0.288
Our approach	ex. worst three cluters	SMO	0.748	0.200	0.308

9 Conclusion

In this paper, we have presented several unsupervised sentence similarity metrics used to identify the sentences in a reference paper that most accurately reflect a citing sentence in a citing paper, and a supervised machine learning system to identify the facet that sentence belongs to, from a predefined set of facets. We used the CL-SciSumm 2016 corpus in which we utilized text processing and summarization tools to enrich the corpus with annotations which were used to compute the features for the supervised machine learning system as well as the vectors used by the unsupervised sentence similarity metrics. Our systems performed well when compared to participants of the CL-SciSumm 2016 challenge; for matches identification we obtained 0.151 F-score, an improvement over the best system so far which achieved 0.134 F-score. For facet identification we obtained 0.704 F-score in cross-validation experiments and 0.242 F-score when the facet identification system is combined with the sentence matching algorithm. Although our F-score result was lower than the best system which got 0.314, our system achieved better Precision than the best system. Our facet approach performed poorly over some of the testing clusters due to errors in the gold annotations. These errors could be attributed to noisy OCR output from processing the original PDF files or to the fact that a single annotator was responsible for each document cluster. We plan to extend this work by addressing the summarization task and also comparing how our models work on better curated datasets.

Acknowledgments

This work is (partly) supported by the Spanish Ministry of Economy and Competitiveness under the Maria de Maeztu Units of Excellence Programme (MDM-2015-0502) and by the TUNER project (TIN2015-65308-C5-5-R, MINECO/FEDER, UE).

References

Amjad Abu-Jbara, Jefferson Ezra, and Dragomir R Radev. 2013. Purpose and polarity of citation: Towards NLP-based bibliometrics. In *HLT-NAACL*. pages 596–606.

Awais Athar. 2011. Sentiment analysis of citations using sentence structure-based features. In *Proceedings of the ACL 2011 Student Session*. Association for Computational Linguistics, Stroudsburg, PA, USA, pages 81–87.

Steven Bird. 2008. The ACL anthology reference corpus: A reference dataset for bibliographic research in computational linguistics .

Lutz Bornmann and Rüdiger Mutz. 2015. Growth rates of modern science: A bibliometric analysis based on the number of publications and cited references. *JASIST* 66(11):2215–2222.

Ziqiang Cao, Wenjie Li, and Dapeng Wu. 2016. PolyU at CL-SciSumm 2016. In *BIRNDL@ JCDL*. pages 132–138.

Angelo Di Iorio, Andrea Giovanni Nuzzolese, and Silvio Peroni. 2013. Towards the automatic identification of the nature of citations. In *SePublica*. pages 63–74.

Beatríz Fisas, Francesco Ronzano, and Horacio Saggion. 2016. A multi-layered annotated corpus of scientific papers. In *Proceedings of the Tenth International Conference on Language Resources and Evaluation LREC 2016, Portorož, Slovenia, May 23-28, 2016.*.

Kokil Jaidka, Muthu Kumar Chandrasekaran, Sajal Rustagi, and Min-Yen Kan. 2016. Overview of the CL-SciSumm 2016 shared task. In *Proceedings of the Joint Workshop on Bibliometric-enhanced Information Retrieval and Natural Language Processing for Digital Libraries (BIRNDL) co-located with the Joint Conference on Digital Libraries 2016 (JCDL 2016), Newark, NJ, USA, June 23, 2016.*. pages 93–102.

Mikael Kågebäck, Olof Mogren, Nina Tahmasebi, and Devdatt Dubhashi. 2014. Extractive summarization using continuous vector space models. In *Proceedings of the 2nd Workshop on Continuous Vector Space Models and their Compositionality (CVSC)@ EACL*. Citeseer, pages 31–39.

Thomas S. Kuhn. 1970. *The structure of scientific revolutions*. University of Chicago Press, Chicago.

Lei Li, Liyuan Mao, Yazhao Zhang, Junqi Chi, Taiwen Huang, Xiaoyue Cong, and Heng Peng. 2016. CIST system for CL-SciSumm 2016 shared task. In *BIRNDL@ JCDL*. pages 156–167.

Haixia Liu. 2017. Sentiment analysis of citations using word2vec. *arXiv preprint arXiv:1704.00177* .

Diana Maynard, Valentin Tablan, Hamish Cunningham, Cristian Ursu, Horacio Saggion, Kalina Bontcheva, and Yorick Wilks. 2002. Architectural elements of language engineering robustness. *Natural Language Engineering* 8(2-3):257–274.

Tomas Mikolov, Kai Chen, Greg Corrado, and Jeffrey Dean. 2013. Efficient estimation of word representations in vector space. *ICLR Workshop* .

Luis Moraes, Shahryar Baki, Rakesh Verma, and Daniel Lee. 2016. University of Houston at CL-SciSumm 2016: SVMs with tree kernels and sentence similarity. In *BIRNDL@ JCDL*. pages 113–121.

Michael J Moravcsik and Poovanalingam Murugesan. 1975. Some results on the function and quality of citations. *Social studies of science* 5(1):86–92.

Roberto Navigli and Simone Paolo Ponzetto. 2012. BabelNet: The automatic construction, evaluation and application of a wide-coverage multilingual semantic network. *Artif. Intell.* 193:217–250.

Tadashi Nomoto. 2016. Neal: A neurally enhanced approach to linking citation and reference. In *BIRNDL@ JCDL*. pages 168–174.

Radim Řehůřek and Petr Sojka. 2010. Software Framework for Topic Modelling with Large Corpora. In *Proceedings of the LREC 2010 Workshop on New Challenges for NLP Frameworks*. ELRA, Valletta, Malta, pages 45–50. `http://is.muni.cz/publication/884893/en`.

Francesco Ronzano and Horacio Saggion. 2015. Dr. Inventor Framework: Extracting structured information from scientific publications. In *International Conference on Discovery Science*. Springer, pages 209–220.

Horacio Saggion. 2008. SUMMA: A robust and adaptable summarization tool. *Traitement Automatique des Langues* 49(2):103–125.

Horacio Saggion, Ahmed AbuRa'ed, and Francesco Ronzano. 2016. Trainable citation-enhanced summarization of scientific articles. In *Proceedings of the Joint Workshop on Bibliometric-enhanced Information Retrieval and Natural Language Processing for Digital Libraries (BIRNDL) co-located with the Joint Conference on Digital Libraries 2016 (JCDL 2016), Newark, NJ, USA, June 23, 2016.*. pages 175–186.

Horacio Saggion and Francesco Ronzano. 2016. Natural language processing for intelligent access to scientific information. In *COLING 2016, 26th International Conference on Computational Linguistics, Tutorial Abstracts, December 11-16, 2016, Osaka, Japan*. pages 9–13.

D. Shotton. 2010. CiTO, the citation typing ontology. *Journal of Biomedical Semantics* 1.

Ina Spiegel-Rosing. 1977. Science studies: Bibliometric and content analysis. *Social Studies of Science* 7(1):97–113.

Simone Teufel, Advaith Siddharthan, and Dan Tidhar. 2006. An annotation scheme for citation function. In *Proceedings of the 7th SIGdial Workshop on Discourse and Dialogue*. Association for Computational Linguistics, Stroudsburg, PA, USA, SigDIAL '06, pages 80–87.

Simone Teufel et al. 2000. *Argumentative zoning: Information extraction from scientific text*. Ph.D. thesis, Citeseer.

Marco Valenzuela, Vu Ha, and Oren Etzioni. 2015. Identifying meaningful citations. In *AAAI Workshop: Scholarly Big Data*.

Lyndon White, Roberto Togneri, Wei Liu, and Mohammed Bennamoun. 2015. How well sentence embeddings capture meaning. In *Proceedings of the 20th Australasian Document Computing Symposium*. ACM, page 9.

Ian H Witten, Eibe Frank, Mark A Hall, and Christopher J Pal. 2016. *Data Mining: Practical machine learning tools and techniques*. Morgan Kaufmann.

A Comparison of Feature-Based and Neural Scansion of Poetry

Manex Agirrezabal[1] and **Iñaki Alegria**[1] and **Mans Hulden**[2]
IXA NLP Group[1]   Department of Linguistics[2]
Department of Computer Science   University of Colorado
Univ. of the Basque Country (UPV/EHU) `mans.hulden@colorado.edu`
`manex.aguirrezabal@ehu.eus`
`i.alegria@ehu.eus`

Abstract

Automatic analysis of poetic rhythm is a challenging task that involves linguistics, literature, and computer science. When the language to be analyzed is known, rule-based systems or data-driven methods can be used. In this paper, we analyze poetic rhythm in English and Spanish. We show that the representations of data learned from character-based neural models are more informative than the ones from hand-crafted features, and that a Bi-LSTM+CRF-model produces state-of-the art accuracy on scansion of poetry in two languages. Results also show that the information about whole word structure, and not just independent syllables, is highly informative for performing scansion.

1 Introduction

I don't like to brag and I don't like to boast[1]
Questi non ciberà terra né peltro,[2]
Мой дядя самых честных правил,[3]

The above are examples of metered poetry in English, Italian and Russian. If the English example is read out loud, it is probably rendered in a continuous deh-deh-**dum** pattern. In the second example, the line consists of eleven beats where some syllables (in fixed positions) are more prominent than others.[4] The Russian example is part of a poem written completely in iambic meter (using a recurring deh-**dum** sound pattern).[5] A person able to read texts in Russian would most likely produce this recurring pattern when reciting the poem. A far more interesting question is whether

this rhythmic structure of the poem can be discovered without possessing complete understanding of the language. Or, whether we could even analyze it without any knowledge of the language in question. These are a difficult challenge for NLP that involve knowledge about linguistics, literature and computer science.

To understand the underlying prosodic structure of a poem independently of the language, a necessary core piece of knowledge concerns the typological relationship between different poetic traditions. This work represents the first steps towards an understanding of how to incorporate such knowledge into practical systems. To this end, we scan[6] the rhythm of poems using data-driven techniques with two languages.[7] In our previous work we tested basic techniques on English poetry (Agirrezabal et al., 2016a); in this research we improve the results using deep learning and extend the experiments to include Spanish poetry. The analysis of the results and adopting our models to perform fully unsupervised and language independent poetry analysis is our current challenge.

2 Scansion

Performing scansion of a line of poetry involves marking the rhythmic structure of that line, along with feet (groups of syllables) and rhyme patterns across lines (Corn, 1997; Fabb, 1997; Steele, 1999). In this work, however, we address only the task of inferring the stress sequence for each verse (a sequence of words or syllables).

2.1 English

Poems in English contain repeating patterns of syllable stress groupings, better known as feet, and

---

[1]Dr. Seuss' *Scrambled Eggs Super!*

[2]Dante Alighieri's *The Divine Comedy*(Canto I, Inferno).

[3]Alexander Pushkin's *Eugene Onegin*.

[4]As a rule of thumb, the 10th beat is always stressed.

[5]A complete reading of each poem should convince the reader that this pattern is present throughout.

[6]The common term for annotating poetry with stress levels.

[7]The repository with the data and techniques: `https://github.com/manexagirrezabal/herascansion/`

Proceedings of Recent Advances in Natural Language Processing, pages 18–23,
Varna, Bulgaria, Sep 4–6 2017.

according to the type of foot used, i.e. the number of syllables in each, several meters can be employed. The most common ones are iambic feet (bal-**loon**), trochaic (**jun**-gle), dactylic (**ac**-cident) or anapestic (com-pre-**hend**).

The length of a metrical line is expressed by the number of feet found in regular lines. Thus a dimeter has two feet, a trimeter three, a tetrameter four, and so on (pentameter, hexameter, heptameter,...). The most common meter in English is iambic pentameter, e.g.

O change | *thy thought,* | *that I*
may change | *my mind,*

Although poems show an overall regularity throughout lines, poets tend to vary some parts of verse slightly, with various artistic motives for doing so, as in

Grant, if thou wilt, thou art beloved of many

This differs from the previous example by its prominent **dum**-deh-deh-**dum** pattern early on—**grant**, if thou **wilt**—known in the literature as a 'trochaic variation'. Another variation is that, while the poem is iambic overall, the final syllable in the line should be stressed, but it instead ends with an unstressed **ny**-syllable. Appending an unstressed syllable at the end of an iambic line is a common departure of a set form in English poetry called *feminine ending*. An automated scansion system must be aware of, or learn, such common variants and be able to apply them consistently.

2.2 Spanish

In the Spanish poetic tradition, several metrical structures have been popular over time (Quilis, 1984; Tomás, 1995; Caparrós, 1999). In this work, because of corpus availability, we have only focused on a specific time period, the Golden Age. In this period the main meter of poetry was the hendecasyllable, in which each line of verse consists of eleven syllables. The stress sequence is quite regular and usually the 10th syllable is stressed. Other syllable positions are also stressed and the specifics of the pattern leads to a rich categorization of hendecasyllabic lines, which is outside our current scope of work.

One of the challenges in analyzing Spanish poetry is the use of syllable contractions, also known as synaloephas, to force verses with more than eleven syllables into hendecasyllabic structures. Because of this, when scansion is performed, not all the syllables receive a stress value. As one of our intentions was to reproduce the experiments and methods of previous work, we have created a heuristic to assign a stress value to each syllable (by adding unstressed syllables and maintaining lexical stresses when possible).

2.3 Automated scansion

Automated scansion is a vibrant topic of research. Recent work often casts this as a prediction problem, where receiving a sequence of words in a poem as input we must predict the stress patterns for each of them. This prediction is often approached in one of two different ways; either following expert-designed **rules** that guide the marking, or learning from patterns in labeled data. Rule-based work include Logan (1988); Hartman (2005); Plamondon (2006); McAleese (2007); Gervas (2000); Navarro-Colorado (2015); Agirrezabal et al. (2016b). Currently, data-driven techniques are becoming more popular due to the availability of tagged data. Some works that employ data and get information from it are Hayward (1996); Greene et al. (2010); Hayes et al. (2012); Agirrezabal et al. (2016a); Estes and Hench (2016).

3 Corpora

As the gold standard material for training the English metrical tagger, we used a corpus of scanned poetry, For Better For Verse (4B4V), from the University of Virginia (Tucker, 2011).[8] The entire collection consists of 78 poems, approximately 1,100 lines in total. Sometimes several analyses are given as correct, as there is some natural ambiguity when performing scansion—about 10% of the lines are ambiguous with two or more plausible analyses given.

For the Spanish language portion we make use of a corpus of Spanish Golden-Age Sonnets (Navarro-Colorado et al., 2016) available on GitHub.[9] This is a collection of poems from the 16th and 17th centuries, which has been manually checked, contains approximately 135 sonnets and almost 2,000 lines. These poems were written by seven different well-known authors.

---

[8] http://prosody.lib.virginia.edu/
[9] https://github.com/bncolorado/
CorpusSonetosSigloDeOro

English
*The **jaws** that bite, the **claws** that catch!*   Eight segments, four strong beats
Spanish
*su **fábrica** en tus **ruinas** adelanta,*   Eleven segments, three strong beats

4 Methods

We follow the intuitions outlined in Agirrezabal et al. (2016a) and we use the same set of linguistically motivated features. The feature templates include current and surrounding words, syllables, POS-tags and lexical stresses, among other simpler ones. This paper extends the work as more current methods—neural network models in particular—and a new language is explored.

The earlier feature-based systems require manual extraction of features where for each syllable in the dataset we extract a set of 10 basic feature templates extended by another set of 54 feature templates. Neural network based methods do not need this feature extraction phase.

We have extended the methods and frameworks presented in Agirrezabal et al. (2016a) to analyze verses in the two datasets. The algorithms include the Averaged Perceptron,[10] (Rosenblatt, 1958; Freund and Schapire, 1999), Hidden Markov Models (Rabiner, 1989; Halácsy et al., 2007), and Conditional Random Fields (CRFs)[11] (Lafferty et al., 2001; Okazaki, 2007). Beyond this, we also performed further experiments by employing Bidirectional LSTMs with a CRF layer (Lample et al., 2016).[12]

Initially, we performed preliminary experiments using an Encoder-Decoder model[13] (Bahdanau et al., 2014; Kann and Schütze, 2016) and also Recurrent Neural Network Language Models[14] (Mikolov et al., 2010), but these performed less well in our experiments.

The specific Bi-LSTM+CRF model from Lample et al. (2016) is an architecture that is suitable for our problem.[15] Words are modeled with a character-based RNN with LSTM, which produces two vectors. The forward vector will have a representation of the character sequence from the left to the right. The backward one will have the same in the reversed order. Our insight is that this character-based LSTM captures the phonological structure of the word from its graphemes/characters. These two vectors are concatenated together with the whole word's embedding (the embeddings could be pre-trained from larger corpora or trained jointly for the task). The vector of these three elements will represent each word in the sequence. Then, for each word, there will be a word-level LSTM, which will produce an output for each word, with its right and left context information. Finally, this output will go through a CRF layer to get the optimal output. For details, we refer the reader to Lample et al. (2016).

We performed several experiments. In some cases, the models were designed to learn a direct mapping from syllables to stresses (**S2S**[16]). In other cases, for each syllable we extracted its respective feature templates (10 or 64) and learned from that data (S2S with more features). With the neural model, the dataset consisted of sequences of words or syllables and the framework had to infer the output (the stress). If the input was a sequence of words, as some words can have more than one syllable, the output had to be a stress pattern, and not only a single stress value (**W2SP**[17]). We decided to use this learning mode to check if the inclusion of independently pre-trained word embeddings would improve our results.[18] When the input was a sequence of syllables separated by spaces, word structure information could be lost. In order to handle this, we included word boundary markers (**WB**) in some experiments.

5 Evaluation and Results

We performed a 10-fold cross-validation to evaluate our models, due to the small size of the tagged datasets.

In assessing each of the annotated lines, we evaluate our system by checking the error-rate obtained by using Levenshtein distance comparing each line from the automatically analyzed poem against a hand-made scansion from the Gold Stan-

---

[10] `https://bitbucket.org/mhulden/pyperceptron`

[11] `https://github.com/jakevdp/pyCRFsuite`

[12] `https://github.com/glample/tagger`

[13] See the `machine_translation` example at `https://github.com/mila-udem/blocks-examples`

[14] `https://github.com/karpathy/char-rnn/`

[15] In this description, the elements in a sequence can be either words or syllables, separated by spaces.

[16] Syllable to Stress.

[17] Word to Stress Pattern.

[18] We saw slight improvements in the results by including pre-trained word embeddings in the English dataset, but improvements were not significant.

	English		Spanish	
	Per Syllable (%)	Per Line (%)	Per Syllable (%)	Per Line (%)
ZeuScansion (Agirrezabal et al., 2016b)	86.78	26.21	-	-
Scandroid (Hartman, 2005)	89.78	42.95	-	-
Gervas (2000)*	-	-	-	**88.73**
Perceptron$_{10}$ (S2S)	84.86	29.32	74.54	0.31
Perceptron$_{64}$ (S2S)	89.34	43.36	92.25	40.78
HMM (S2S)	90.43	49.88	92.57	45.40
CRF$_{10}$ (S2S)	89.66	50.16	85.30	19.20
CRF$_{64}$ (S2S)	91.41	55.30	93.37	57.00
Bi-LSTM+CRF (S2S)	91.26	55.28	95.13	63.68
Bi-LSTM+CRF+WB (S2S)	**92.96**	**61.39**	98.74	88.82
Bi-LSTM+CRF (W2SP)	89.39	44.29	**98.95**	**90.84**

Table 1: Results of the classifiers in the English and Spanish datasets. The first lines show three rule-based scansion systems, ordered according to their overall performance. The next group displays the results presented in Agirrezabal et al. (2016a) (gray cells) together with the results on the Spanish dataset under the same conditions. The last three lines show the accuracies of the neural network architecture.

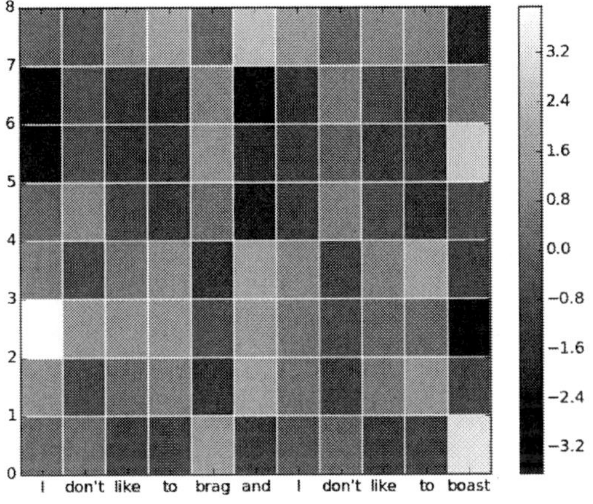

Figure 1: Output layer activations of the Bidirectional LSTM (8 different outputs), which will be the input of the CRF layer. The input sentence is *"I don't like to brag and I don't like to boast"*.

dard (Graves, 2012, p. 13). We do this in order to avoid overly penalizing a single missing or superfluous syllable, something which would shift an entire pattern to the left or right and potentially produce a count where all syllables would be counted as incorrect even though only one syllable was missing or added.

Table 1 shows the results obtained compared with the ones presented in Agirrezabal et al. (2016a), by applying the same methods with the same parameters. Results from that work are shown with a gray colored background.

In figure 1 the output of the Bidirectional LSTMs can be seen, showing the first line of *"Scrambled Eggs Super!"*. The columns that represent the stressed syllables (2nd, 5th, 8th and 11th syllables) stand out clearly. This representation is used as input for the CRF layer, which finds the optimal resulting sequence.

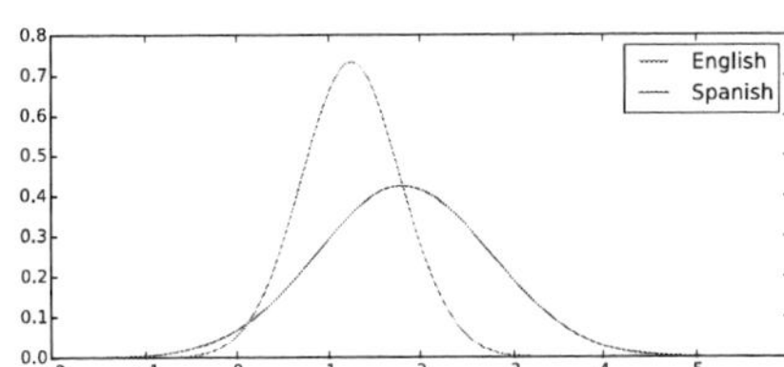

Figure 2: Syllable length in Spanish and English.

6 Discussion and Future Work

Inspecting the results in table 1, we conclude that the Spanish dataset is more regular, as results generally are better. In the work by Agirrezabal et al. (2016a) 10 potentially language-agnostic features were used, and the extrapolation to Spanish seems to show that these features are not well-suited as language-agnostic features because of their small impact on the results. This claim should be better demonstrated by performing further experiments in more languages.

Also, it can be inferred that word structure in Spanish plays a key role, mainly because the inclusion of word boundaries (or just word information) improves results significantly compared with systems that do not. In table 1, the Perceptron-based results are significantly improved upon by using 64 feature templates (according to a Welch's two-sample t-test ($p < 0.05$)).[19] The same can be seen in the case of CRFs and also when word boundary information is provided to the Bidirectional LSTM. The importance of knowing word boundaries in Spanish can be attributed to the fact that while English words tend to be monosyllabic, not all Spanish words will contain a syllable boundary marker, making it an informative characteristic. Figure 2 shows the differences of English and Spanish words' average syllable length. The results of the Bidirectional LSTM show that if tagged data is available, very good results can be obtained with neural network based structured predictors, without the use of additional linguistic information (such as, lexical stress, POS-tags, etc.). Tentatively, it could be said that the models infer the phonological information inherent to the words, although showing this conclusively requires further experiments.

The results serve to prompt several new strands of research in the domain. Our main goal is to be able to analyze poems with minimal supervision, including knowledge of the language in question, with unsupervised learning of rhythmic patterns being our long-term goal, possibly extending the unsupervised work done in Greene et al. (2010). We also intend to use the neural network based metrical analyzer as a meter checker in an automatic poetry generation system, such as Manurung (2003); Toivanen et al. (2013); Gervás (2014); Oliveira et al. (2014).

Acknowledgments

The first author's work has been partially funded by the University of the Basque Country (UPV/EHU) in collaboration with the Association of the Friends of Bertsolaritza under the Zabalduz program. We also want to acknowledge the anonymous reviewers, as their feedback improved both the current paper and contained suggestions for future research.

References

Manex Agirrezabal, Iñaki Alegria, and Mans Hulden. 2016a. Machine Learning for Metrical Analysis of English Poetry. In *Proceedings of COLING 2016, the 26th International Conference on Computational Linguistics, Osaka, Japan*. pages 772–781.

Manex Agirrezabal, Aitzol Astigarraga, Bertol Arrieta, and Mans Hulden. 2016b. ZeuScansion: a Tool for Scansion of English Poetry. *Journal of Language Modelling* 4(1):3–28.

Dzmitry Bahdanau, Kyunghyun Cho, and Yoshua Bengio. 2014. Neural Machine Translation by Jointly Learning to Align and Translate. *arXiv preprint arXiv:1409.0473* .

José Domínguez Caparrós. 1999. *Diccionario de Métrica Española*. Alianza Editorial.

Alfred Corn. 1997. *The Poem's Heartbeat: A Manual of Prosody.*. Copper Canyon Press.

Alex Estes and Christopher Hench. 2016. Supervised [Machine Learning for Hybrid Meter. *on Computational Linguistics for Literature* page 1.

Nigel Fabb. 1997. *Linguistics and Literature : Language in the Verbal Arts of the World*. Blackwell. 2nd ISBN: 9780631192435. http://strathprints.strath.ac.uk/28825/.

Yoav Freund and Robert E. Schapire. 1999. Large Margin Classification Using the Perceptron Algorithm. *Machine learning* 37(3):277–296.

Pablo Gervas. 2000. A Logic Programming Application for the Analysis of Spanish Verse. In *Computational Logic—CL 2000*, Springer, pages 1330–1344.

Pablo Gervás. 2014. Composing Narrative Discourse for Stories of many Characters: A Case Study over a Chess Game. *Literary and Linguistic Computing* page fqu040.

Alex Graves. 2012. *Supervised Sequence Labelling with Recurrent Neural Networks*. Springer.

Erica Greene, Tugba Bodrumlu, and Kevin Knight. 2010. Automatic Analysis of Rhythmic Poetry with Applications to Generation and Translation. In *Proceedings of the 2010 Conference on Empirical Methods in Natural Language Processing*. Association for Computational Linguistics, pages 524–533.

Péter Halácsy, András Kornai, and Csaba Oravecz. 2007. HunPos: an open source trigram tagger. In *Proceedings of the 45th Annual Meeting of the ACL on Interactive Poster and Demonstration Sessions*. Association for Computational Linguistics, pages 209–212.

Charles O. Hartman. 2005. The Scandroid 1.1. http://oak.conncoll.edu/cohar/Programs.htm.

Bruce Hayes, Colin Wilson, and Anne Shisko. 2012. Maxent Grammars for the Metrics of Shakespeare and Milton. *Language* 88(4):691–731.

---

[19]The current word is one of the feature templates.

Malcolm Hayward. 1996. Analysis of a Corpus of Poetry by a Connectionist Model of Poetic Meter. *Poetics* 24(1):1–11.

Katharina Kann and Hinrich Schütze. 2016. MED: The LMU system for the SIGMORPHON 2016 Shared Task on Morphological Reinflection. *ACL 2016* page 62.

John Lafferty, Andrew McCallum, and Fernando C. N.H Pereira. 2001. Conditional Random Fields: Probabilistic Models for Segmenting and Labeling Sequence Data .

Guillaume Lample, Miguel Ballesteros, Sandeep Subramanian, Kazuya Kawakami, and Chris Dyer. 2016. Neural Architectures for Named Entity Recognition. In *Proceedings of NAACL-2016, San Diego, California, USA*. Association for Computational Linguistics.

Harry M Logan. 1988. Computer Analysis of Sound and Meter in Poetry. *College Literature* pages 19–24.

Ruli Manurung. 2003. *An evolutionary algorithm approach to poetry generation*. Ph.D. thesis, School of informatics, University of Edinburgh.

G McAleese. 2007. *Improving Scansion with Syntax: an Investigation into the Effectiveness of a Syntactic Analysis of Poetry by Computer using Phonological Scansion Theory*. Ph.D. thesis, Open University.

Tomas Mikolov, Martin Karafiát, Lukas Burget, Jan Cernockỳ, and Sanjeev Khudanpur. 2010. Recurrent Neural Network based Language Model. In *Interspeech*. volume 2, page 3.

Borja Navarro-Colorado. 2015. A Computational Linguistic Approach to Spanish Golden Age Sonnets: Metrical and Semantic Aspects. *Computational Linguistics for Literature* page 105.

Borja Navarro-Colorado, Maria Ribes Lafoz, and Noelia Sánchez. 2016. Metrical Annotation of a Large Corpus of Spanish Sonnets: Representation, Scansion and Evaluation. In *Proceedings of the Language Resources and Evaluation Conference*.

Naoaki Okazaki. 2007. CRFsuite: a fast implementation of Conditional Random Fields (CRFs). http://www.chokkan.org/software/crfsuite/.

Hugo Gonçalo Oliveira, Raquel Hervás, Alberto Díaz, and Pablo Gervás. 2014. Adapting a Generic Platform for Poetry Generation to Produce Spanish Poems. *International Conference on Computational Creativity* .

Marc R Plamondon. 2006. Virtual Verse Analysis: Analysing Patterns in Poetry. *Literary and Linguistic Computing* 21(suppl 1):127–141.

Antonio Quilis. 1984. *Métrica Española*. Ariel Barcelona.

Lawrence R. Rabiner. 1989. A Tutorial on Hidden Markov Models and selected Applications in Speech Recognition. *Proceedings of the IEEE* 77(2):257–286.

Frank Rosenblatt. 1958. The Perceptron: a Probabilistic Model for Information Storage and Organization in the Brain. *Psychological review* 65(6):386.

Timothy Steele. 1999. *All the Fun's in how you Say a Thing: an Explanation of Meter and Versification*. Ohio University Press Athens.

Jukka Toivanen, Matti Järvisalo, and Hannu Toivonen. 2013. Harnessing Constraint Programming for Poetry. *International Conference on Computational Creativity* .

Navarro Tomás Tomás. 1995. *Métrica Española*. Ed. Labor.

Herbert F Tucker. 2011. Poetic Data and the News from Poems: A for Better for Verse Memoir. *Victorian Poetry* 49(2):267–281.

Persian–Spanish Low-Resource Statistical Machine Translation Through English as Pivot Language

Benyamin Ahmadnia[1], Javier Serrano[1], Gholamreza Haffari[2]
[1]Autonomous University of Barcelona, Cerdanyola del Valles, Spain
[2]Monash University, Clayton, VIC, Australia
{benyamin.ahmadnia, javier.serrano}@uab.cat
gholamreza.haffari@monash.edu

Abstract

This paper is an attempt to exclusively focus on investigating the pivot language technique in which a bridging language is utilized to increase the quality of the *Persian–Spanish* low-resource Statistical Machine Translation (SMT). In this case, *English* is used as the bridging language, and the *Persian–English* SMT is combined with the *English–Spanish* one, where the relatively large corpora of each may be used in support of the *Persian–Spanish* pairing. Our results indicate that the pivot language technique outperforms the direct SMT processes currently in use between *Persian* and *Spanish*. Furthermore, we investigate the sentence translation pivot strategy and the phrase translation in turn, and demonstrate that, in the context of the *Persian–Spanish* SMT system, the phrase-level pivoting outperforms the sentence-level pivoting. Finally we suggest a method called combination model in which the standard direct model and the best triangulation pivoting model are blended in order to reach a high-quality translation.

1 Introduction

The goal of Statistical Machine Translation (SMT) is to translate a source language sequences into a target language by assessing the plausibility of the source and the target sequences in relation to existing bodies of translation between the two languages. The presence of sizable bodies of aligned parallel corpora affects the SMT systems function and performance. On the other hand, gathering parallel data in practice becomes an issue due to the high costs and the limitation in scope which as a result may constrain the related research and its applications. Therefore, the scarcity of parallel data for many language pairs is amongst the main issues in SMT. (Babych et al., 2007).

Corpora of this type are usually rare, especially for under-resource pairs such as *Persian* and *Spanish*. Even for well-resource languages, such as those included in *Europarl* (Koehn, 2005), which covers the language of debates in the *European Parliament*, SMT performance degrades significantly while being applied to a slightly different domain. Therefore, with a change in the domain, the performance loses its efficiency. A common solution to the lack of parallel data is using pivot language technique (El-Kholy and Habash, 2013). This technique is used to generate a systematic SMT when a proper bilingual corpus is lacking or the existing ones are weak. This issue becomes significant when there are languages with inefficient NLP (Natural Language Processing) resources to be able to provide an SMT system. However, there are sufficient resources between them and some other languages. Though it is claimed that, the intermediary languages do not lead to an improvement in general case, this idea can be employed as a simple method to enrich the translation performance even for existing systems (Matusov et al., 2008).

In this paper we display how this idea acts effectively concerning the low-resource *Persian-Spanish* language pair. Besides, we examine a selective combination approach to efficiently blend a pivot and a direct model developed by a given parallel corpora to achieve better coverage and overall translation quality. We increase the obtained in-

Proceedings of Recent Advances in Natural Language Processing, pages 24–30,
Varna, Bulgaria, Sep 4–6 2017.

formation through picking the relevant portions of the pivot model that do not interfere with the more trusted direct model.

2 Language Issues

SMT has proven to be successful for a number of language pairs. However, as soon as the *Persian* language is involved with any sort of machine translation, a number of difficulties are encountered. Of other common languages, *English* seems to be the best language to pair with *Persian*, since it is best supported by resources such as large corpora, language processing tools, and syntactic tree banks. *Persian* is the complete opposite, with a significant shortage of digitally available text, both parallel and monolingual. Other language pairs make use of parallel corpora of many millions of sentences, giving any applied system a huge database to work from, and thus output much more accurate results. *Persian* is morphologically rich, with many characteristics not shared by other languages. It makes no use of articles ("a", "an", "the"), there is no distinction between capital and lower-case letters, and symbols and abbreviations are rarely used. Sentence structure is also different, *Persian* placing parts of speech such as nouns, subjects, adverbs and verbs in different locations in the sentence, and sometime even omitting them altogether. Some *Persian* words have many different versions of spelling, and it is not uncommon for translators to invent new words. This can result in an Out-Of-Vocabulary (OOV) output.

The *Spanish* language utilizes the Latin alphabet, with a few special letters; Vowels with an acute accent (á, ú, é, í, ó), (u) with an umlaut (ü), and an (n) with a tilde (ñ). The *Spanish* language spelling system, due to a substantial number of reforms, is almost perfectly phonemic and, therefore, easier to learn than the majority of languages. The *Spanish* language is pronounced phonetically. However, beware of the trilled (r) which is somewhat complex to reproduce. The letters (b) and (v) are almost indistinguishable. The letter (h) is silent. *Spanish* language punctuation is very close to, but not the same as *English*. There are a few significant differences. For example, in *Spanish*, exclamation and interrogative sentences are preceded by inverted question and exclamation marks. Also, in a *Spanish* conversation, a change in speakers is indicated by a dash, while in *English*, each speaker's remark is placed in separate

paragraphs. Formal and informal translations address several different characteristics. Inflection, declination and grammatical gender are important features of the *Spanish* language.

In both *Persian* and *Spanish* languages, the word-order is different from *English* in two ways; First, the modifier comes before the word it modifies. Second, the sentences follow a "Subject", "Object", "Verb" (SOV) order.

3 Baseline Translation System

The SMT paradigm has, as its most important elements, the idea; That probabilities of source and target sentences can find the best translations. Frequently used paradigms of SMT on the log-linear model are the *phrase-based SMT*, the *hierarchical phrase-based SMT*, and the *ngram-based SMT*. In our experiments we use the phrase-based SMT system with the maximum entropy framework (Berger et al., 1996).

$$\hat{y}_1^I = \arg\max_{y_1^I} P(x|y) \qquad (1)$$

The phrase-based SMT model is an example of the *noisy-channel* approach, where we can present the translation hypothesis t as the target sentence (given s as a source sentence), maximizing a log-linear combination of feature functions:

$$\hat{y}_1^I = \arg\max_{y_1^I} \left\{ \sum_{m=1}^{M} \lambda_m \, h_m(x_1^J, y_1^J) \right\} \qquad (2)$$

This equation called the *log-linear* model, where λ_m corresponds to the weighting coefficients of the log-linear combination, and the feature functions $h_m(x,y)$ to a logarithmic scaling of the probabilities of each model. The translation process involves segmenting the source sentence into source phrases s, translating each source phrase into a target phrase t, and reordering these target phrases to yield the target sentence $\hat{t}$.

4 Pivoting Strategy for SMT

High-quality data set is not always available for training the SMT systems. One of the possible ways to solve this impasse is to using a third language as a bridge one for which there exist high-quality source–pivot and pivot–target bilingual resources. Pivot-based strategies which are employed for SMT systems can be classified into three categories (Wu and Wang, 2007);

Transfer method: This method, which is also recognized as *cascade* or *sentence translation pivot strategy*, translates the text in the source language to the pivot through employing a source–pivot translation model, and subsequently translate it to a target language utilizing a pivot–target translation model.

Triangulation method: This method is known as *phrase-table multiplication* or *phrase translation pivot strategy*, which combines the corresponding translation probabilities of the translation models for the source–pivot and the pivot–target languages, thus generating a novel model for the source–target translation.

Synthetic corpus method: This method attempts to develop a synthetic source–target corpus by translating the pivot part in the source–pivot corpus, into the target language by means of a pivot–target model, and translating the pivot part in the target–pivot corpus into the source language with a pivot–source model. Eventually, it combines the source sentences with the translated target sentences or combines the target sentences with the translated source sentences. However, it is complicated to create a high-quality translation system with a corpus compiled merely by an MT system.

In the present paper, we will rely on the first and the second methods for doing our SMT pivoting experiments.

4.1 Transfer Pivoting Method

In the sentence translation pivot strategy, first the *Persian* sentences are translated into the *English* ones, followed by translation of these *English* sentences into the *Spanish* ones separately. We choose the highest scoring sentence amongst the *Spanish* sentences.

In this methodology for assigning the best *Spanish* candidate sentence s to the input *Persian* sentence p, we maximize the probability $P(s|p)$ by defining hidden variable e, which stands for the pivot language sentences, we gain:

$$\arg \max_{p} P(s|p)$$

$$= \arg \max_{p} \sum_{e} P(s, e|p)$$

$$= \arg \max_{p} \sum_{e} P(s|e, p) \, P(e|p) \quad (3)$$

Assuming that, p and s are independent given e:

$$\approx \arg \max_{p} \sum_{e} P(s|e) \, P(e|p) \quad (4)$$

In Equation (4) summation on all e sentences is difficult, so we replace it by maximization, and Equation (5) is an estimate of Equation (4):

$$\approx \arg \max_{p} \max_{e} P(s|e) \, P(e|p) \quad (5)$$

Instead of searching all the space of e sentences, we can just search a subspace of it. For simplicity we limit the search space in Equation (6). A good choice is e subspace produced by the *k-best* list output of the first SMT system (source-pivot):

$$\approx \arg \max_{p} \max_{e \in k-best(s)} P(s|e) \, P(e|p) \quad (6)$$

In fact each sentence p of the *Persian* test set is mapped to a subspace of total e space and search is done in this subspace for the best candidate sentence s of the second SMT system (pivot–target).

4.2 Triangulation Pivoting Method

Concerning the phrase translation pivot strategy, we directly create a *Persian–Spanish* phrase translation table from a *Persian–English* and an *English–Spanish* phrase-table.

In this technique, phrase p in the source–pivot phrase-table is connected to e, and this phrase e is associated with phrase s in the pivot–target phrase-table. We link the phrases p and s in the new phrase-table for the source–target. For scoring the pair phrases of the new phrase-table, assuming $P(e|p)$ as the score of the *Persian–English* phrases and $P(s|e)$ as the score of the *English–Spanish* phrases, then the score of the new pair phrases p and s, $P(s|p)$, in *Persian– Spanish* phrase-table is counted:

$$P(s|p) = \sum_{e} P(s, e|p) \quad (7)$$

e is a hidden variable and actually stands for the phrases of pivot language:

$$P(s|p) = \sum_{e} P(s|e, p) \, P(e|p) \quad (8)$$

Assume that, p and s are independent, given e:

$$P(s|p) \approx \sum_{e} P(s|e) \, P(e|p) \quad (9)$$

For simplicity the summation on all the *e* phrases is replaced by maximization, then Equation (9) is approximated by:

$$P(s|p) \approx \max_{e} P(s|e)\, P(e|p) \qquad (10)$$

Applying a translation model on a small bilingual corpus alone will result in a poor translation system performance. Therefore, the cause of such a poor performance is sparse data. Aiming at improving this performance, we can utilize additional source–pivot and pivot–target parallel corpora. Furthermore, more than one pivot languages can be utilized in order to enrich the quality of the translation performance. Different pivot language may catch different language phenomenon and can improve translation quality by adding quality source–target phrase pairs.

If we include *k* pivot languages, *k* pivot models can be estimated. *Linear interpolation* is employed for combining all these generated models with the standard model trained with the source-target corpus. Equations (11) and (12) demonstrate the estimation of the phrase translation probability and the lexical weight respectively.

$$P(s|t) = \sum_{i=1}^{k} \alpha_i\, P_i(s|t) \qquad (11)$$

$$P(s|t,\alpha) = \sum_{i=1}^{k} \beta_i\, P_i(s|t,\alpha) \qquad (12)$$

Where $P(s|t)$ and $P(s|t,\alpha)$ denote the phrase translation probability and the lexical weight trained with the source–target corpus estimated by using pivot languages. Both α_i and β_i are interpolation coefficients. Meanwhile $\sum_{i=1}^{k} \alpha_i = 1$, and $\sum_{i=1}^{k} \beta_i = 1$.

5 Experimental Framework

The data is gathered from in-domain *Tanzil* parallel corpus[1] (Tiedemann, 2012). In this corpus, the *Persian–Spanish* part encompasses more than *(68K)* parallel sentences, nearly *(2.06M)* words in the *Persian* side, and more than *(1.45M)* words in the *Spanish* side. Besides, the *Persian–English* part includes more than *(1M)* parallel sentences, around *(30.88M) Persian* words, and more than *(26.14M) English* words. The *English–Spanish* part contains more than *(138K)* parallel sentences,

approximately *(2.37M)* words in the *English* side, and over *(1.94M)* words in the *Spanish* side. Table below presents the corpus statistics, which have been used in our experiments, including the source and the target languages information in each direction.

Direction	Pe-En	En-Es	Pe-Es
Sentences	1,028,996	138,822	68,601
Src. Words	30,872,937	376,933	2,058,231
Trg. Words	26,143,026	1,932,696	1,454,778

Table 1: Corpus statistics

To examine the size factor on our SMT systems, data were compiled into two sets including System(1) and System(2). The *tokenize.perl* script has been employed for tokenizing all datasets. System(1) training part consists of *(10K)* sentences and it spreads almost *(50K)* sentences to System(2) with nearly *(60K)* sentences. In order to conduct the tuning and the testing steps, we gathered parallel texts from *Tanzil* corpus. *(3K)* sentences for the tuning, and *(5K)* sentences for the testing step were extracted.

MOSES package[2] (Koehn et al., 2007), is employed for training our SMT systems. Through employing *MOSES* decoder, *fast-align* approach (Dyer et al., 2013), is applied for word alignment. We employ *3-grams* language model for all SMT systems and they are developed by means of the *KenLM* toolkit (Heafield et al., 2013). In addition, for evaluating the systems performance, we use the *BLEU* metric. We set the beam-size to *(100)*, and the distortion limit to *(6)*. We restrain the maximum target phrases to *(6)* that are loaded for each source phrase, and we draw on the same other default features of *MOSES* toolkit.

For the translation systems we conduct two sets of experiments with different data sizes. The training data is collected from the beginning of the same parallel corpus, so the larger training set includes the smaller one. For instance, in the experiments with small dataset sizes, the two phrase-tables employed to shape a new table in the phrase pivoting method are extracted in turn from the *Persian–English* and the *English–Spanish* translation systems.

For conducting the first phase of our experiments, *English* was utilised by the transfer pivoting system as an interface between two separate phrase-based SMT systems, specifically a

---

[1] http://opus.lingfil.uu.se/Tanzil.php

[2] http://www.statmt.org/moses

Persian–English direct system and an *English–Spanish* direct system. Besides, while translating *Persian* to *Spanish*, the *English* top-1 output of the *Persian–English* system was forwarded as input to the *English–Spanish* system. The *English* language model which was used to train the *Persian–English* system is developed from the counterpart of the *Spanish* data used to build the *Spanish* language model in our considered parallel corpus.

For applying the triangulation method during the second portion of our experiments, we required to create a phrase-table to train the phrase-based SMT system. Therefore, a *Persian–English* phrase-table and an *English–Spanish* phrase-table were needed. Based on these tables, we formed a *Persian–Spanish* phrase-table. Furthermore, a matching algorithm that identifies parallel sentences pairs among the tables were utilized. After identifying candidate sentence pairs, we finally used a classifier to determine if the sentences in each pair are a good translation for each other and update our *Persian–Spanish* phrase-table with the selected pairs. Table below illustrates the results of both *Persian–Spanish* standard direct, and pivot-based translation systems through *English* as the intermediary language.

BLEU	System(1)	System(2)
Direct	19.07	19.39
Transfer	20.33	20.78
Triangulation	21.02	21.55

Table 2: The BLEU scores comparing the performance of direct with pivoting Persian–Spanish SMT systems, through two training data sizes

As expected, by an increase in the dataset size, the *BLEU* score rises. For the large size of training data set, the best result of the direct translation system is *(19.39)* point in term of the *BLEU*. Also the system achieved a *BLEU* score of *(21.55)* for the phrase-level pivoting, while for the sentence-level pivoting the system achieved *(20.78) BLEU* point.

The results indicate that, the pivot-based translation method is suitable for the scenario that there exist large amounts of source–pivot and pivot–target bilingual corpora and only a little source–target bilingual data. Thus we selected *(10K)*, and *(60K)* sentence pairs from the source–target bilingual corpora to simulate the lack of source–target bilingual data. As seen in Table 2, in phrase pivoting portion, the *Persian–English–Spanish* relative increase from System(1) to System(2) is approximately *(10.25%)*, and in sentence pivoting portion, the *Persian–English–Spanish* relative increase from System(1) to System(2) is *(10.22%)*. This suggests that, we are making better use of the available resources. The differences between pivot language method and direct translation approach are statistically significant confidence level.

6 Direct and Pivot Combination

We examine a combination approach so as to achieve a higher coverage and a better translation quality, aiming at efficiently merging both a phrase-based pivot and a direct translation models developed from a given parallel corpora.

In particular, this approach is an attempt to combine the direct and triangulation models in order to rise the amount of the gained information. We use *MOSES* toolkit as it lets employing the multiple translation tables for doing the combination experiments. In order to achieve this aim, several combination models are approachable and practical. In the current paper, we employ a combination model where the translation options are gathered from one table, and additional options are collected from other tables. Reaching similar translation options in multiple tables, we form separate translation options for each occurrence with different scores. Table 3 reveals the comparison between the findings of the basic combination technique with those of the best multiplication pivot translation and the direct translation models.

BLEU	Direct + Triangulation
System(1)	21.88
System(2)	22.02

Table 3: The BLEU scores of the combination experiments between the best triangulated and the direct SMT models for Persian–Spanish languages

The findings indicate that, merging and combining these two models, results in an improvement in the performance.

7 Previous Work

The pivot language approach has been previously applied for diverse purposes. For instance developing a technique for mining the web to collect parallel corpora for low-density language pairs (Resnik and Smith, 2003), and running new SMT system for languages *Catalan–English* with no parallel corpus (Gispert and Mariño, 2006).

In a research conducted by Utiyama and Isahara (2007), the use of pivot language through phrase translation and sentence translation are investigated. Moreover, Wu and Wang (2007) discuss three methods for pivot strategies in their findings including phrase translation method (i.e. triangulation), transfer method, and synthetic method.

Some researchers investigated the SMT system with pivot language technique. For example Babych et al. (2008) used *Russian* language as a pivot for translating from *Ukrainian* to *English*. Their comparison revealed that it is possible to achieve better translation quality with pivot language approach.

Habash and Hu (2009) compared two approaches for *Arabic–Chinese* MT system with direct MT system through *English* as a pivot language. The findings of their study indicated that using *English* as a pivot language in either approach outperforms direct translation from *Arabic* to *Chinese*.

In another study, Bakhshaei et al. (2010) used *English* as a bridging language while translating from *Persian* to *German* and concluded that using the pivot technique in phrase-level combination outperforms direct translation system. Furthermore, Al-Hunaity et al. (2010) presented a comparison between two common pivot strategies; phrase translation and sentence translation in order to enhance *Danish–Arabic* SMT system. According to their findings, it is illustrated that sentence pivoting overtakes phrase pivoting when common parallel corpora are not available.

Nakov and Ng (2012) try to exploit the similarity between resource-poor languages and resource-rich languages for the translation task.

Paul et al. (2013) debates over criteria to be considered for selection of good pivot language. Use of source-side segmentation as pre-processing technique is demonstrated by Kunchukuttan et al. (2014).

Dabre et al. (2015) used multiple decoding paths (MDP) to overcome the limitation of small sized corpora.

8   Conclusion

In this paper, we compared two common pivot language translation methods comprising *phrase-level pivoting* and *sentence-level pivoting* for low-resource *Persian–Spanish* SMT by employing *English* as an intermediary language.

Through conducting controlled experiments using the *Tanzil* corpus, we assessed the performances of these two methods against the performance of directly trained SMT system. The findings of our experiments revealed that utilising *English* as a bridging language in either approaches outperforms direct translation method from *Persian* to *Spanish*. Our best result is the phrase translation pivoting system scores higher than the best result of the sentence translation pivoting system by *(0.77) BLEU* points, and also higher than the best result of the *Persian–Spanish* direct translation system by *(2.16) BLEU* points.

Furthermore, the performance of a combination model between two different translation approaches on the translation quality is investigated in this paper. In order to apply this combination model, we employed the best pivoting translation model (phrase-level) along with the best standard direct translation model for attaining a high-quality translation. The results reveal that combining these two models cause an improvement in the performance quality. The *BLEU* score for this new combined translation system enhanced by *(+0.33)* point in comparison with the best triangulated system, and *(+2.49)* point in comparison with the best standard direct translation system for *Persian–Spanish* language pair.

Acknowledgments

The authors would like to express their sincere gratitude to Vahede Nosrati (PhD candidate at Monash University, Australia), for all her support. The authors have benefited from her erudition and thoughtful comments which truly enriched the present work.

References

Mossab Al-Hunaity, Bente Maegaard, and Dorte Hansen. 2010. Using english as a pivot language to enhance danish-arabic statistical machine translation.

Bogdan Babych, Anthony Hartley, and Serge Sharoff. 2008. Translating from under-resourced languages: Comparing direct transfer against pivot translation. In *Proceedings of MT Summit XI*.

Bogdan Babych, Anthony Hartley, Serge Sharoff, and Olga Mudraya. 2007. Assisting translators in indirect lexical transfer. In *Proceedings of ACL 2007: the 45th Annual Meeting of the Association of Computational Linguistics*.

Somaye Bakhshaei, Shahram Khadivi, and Noushin Riahi. 2010. Farsi-german statistical machine translation through bridge language. In *Proceedings of IST, 5th International Symposium on Telecommunications*.

Adam L. Berger, Stephen Della Pietra, and Vincent J. Della Pietra. 1996. A maximum entropy approach to natural language processing. *Computational Linguistics* 22(1):39–71.

Raj Dabre, Fabien Comieres, Sadao Kurohashi, and Pushpak Bhattacharyya. 2015. Leveraging small multilingual corpora for smt using many pivot languages. In *Proceedings of HLT-NAACL 2015, the Human Language Technology Conference of the North American Chapters of the Association of Computational Linguistics*. pages 1192–1202.

Chris Dyer, Victor Chahuneau, and Noah A. Smith. 2013. A simple, fast, and effective reparameterization of ibm model 2.

Ahmed El-Kholy and Nizar Habash. 2013. Language independent connectivity strength features for phrase pivot statistical machine translation.

Adria De Gispert and Jose B. Mariño. 2006. Catalan-english statistical machine translation without parallel corpus: bridging through spanish.

Nizar Habash and Jun Hu. 2009. Improving arabic-chinese statistical machine translation using english as pivot language.

Kenneth Heafield, Ivan pouzyrevsky, Jonathan H. Clark, and Philipp Koehn. 2013. Scalable modified kneser-ney language model estimation. In *Proceedings of ACL 2013, the 51st Annual Meeting of the Association of Computational Linguistics*. pages 690–696.

Philipp Koehn. 2005. Europarl: A parallel corpus for statistical machine translation. In *Proceedings of AAMT: the 10th Machine Translation Summit*. Phuket, Thailand, pages 79–86.

Philipp Koehn, Hieu Hoang, Alexandra Birch, Chris Callison-Burch, Marcello Federico, Nicola Bertoldi, Brooke Cowan, Wade Shen, Christine Moran, Richard Zens, Chris Dyer, Ondrej Bojar, Alexandra Constantin, and Evan Herbst. 2007. Moses: Open source toolkit for statistical machine translation. In *Proceedings of ACL: the 45th Annual Meeting of the Association of Computational Linguistics*.

Anoop Kunchukuttan, Ratish Pudupully, Rajen Chatterjee, Abhijit Mishra, and Pushpak B. Tacharyya. 2014. The iit bombay smt system for icon 2014 tools contest. In *Proceedings of ICON 2014, the Natural Language Processing Tools Contest*.

Evgeny Matusov, Student Member, Gregor Leusch, Rafael E. Banchs, Nicola Bertoldi, Daniel Dchelotte, Marcello Federico, Muntsin Kolss, Young suk Lee, Jose B. Mariño, Matthias Paulik, Salim Roukos, Holger Schwenk, and Hermann Ney. 2008. System combination for machine translation of spoken and written language. In *Proceedings of IEEE: Transactions on Audio, Speech and Language Processing*. pages 1222–1237.

Preslav Nakov and Hwee T. Ng. 2012. Improving statistical machine translation for a resource-poor language using related resource-rich languages. *JAIR: Journal of Artificial Intelligence Research* pages 179–222.

Michael Paul, Andrew Finch, and Eiichrio Sumita. 2013. How to choose the best pivot language for automatic translation of low-resource languages? In *Proceedings of TALIP 2013, the ACM Transactions on Asian Language Information*.

Philip Resnik and Noah A. Smith. 2003. The web as a parallel corpus. *CL: Journal of Computational Linguistics* 29(3):349–380.

Jorg Tiedemann. 2012. Parallel data, tools and interfaces in opus. In *Proceedings of ELRA: European Language Resources Association*. pages 2214–2218.

Masao Utiyama and Hitoshi Isahara. 2007. A comparison of pivot methods for phrase-based statistical machine translation. In *Proceedings of HLT-NAACL 2007, the Human Language Technology Conference of the North American Chapters of the Association of Computational Linguistics*. pages 484–491.

Hua Wu and Haifeng Wang. 2007. Pivot language approach for phrase-based statistical machine translation. In *Proceedings of ACL: the 45th Annual Meeting of the Association of Computational Linguistics*. pages 856–863.

Simple Open Stance Classification for Rumour Analysis

Ahmet Aker[a,b] and **Leon Derczynski**[a] and **Kalina Bontcheva**[a]

Department of Computer Science, University of Sheffield[a]
Department of Information Engineering, University of Duisburg-Essen[b]
a.aker@is.inf.uni-due.de, leon.derczynski@sheffield.ac.uk
K.Bontcheva@sheffield.ac.uk

Abstract

Stance classification determines the attitude, or stance, in a (typically short) text. The task has powerful applications, such as the detection of fake news or the automatic extraction of attitudes toward entities or events in the media. This paper describes a surprisingly simple and efficient classification approach to open stance classification in Twitter, for rumour and veracity classification. The approach profits from a novel set of automatically identifiable problem-specific features, which significantly boost classifier accuracy and achieve above state-of-the-art results on recent benchmark datasets. This calls into question the value of using complex sophisticated models for stance classification without first doing informed feature extraction.

1 Introduction

Stance detection is the problem of classifying the attitude taken by an author in a short piece of text. Typical stances include showing support, denying, commenting on or querying an existing claim or fact. Knowing the stance that authors hold in response to claims, e.g. in online commentary, gives useful insights. It can reveal rumours and fake news claims as the discourse around them is monitored (Procter et al., 2013). Stance reflects how certain authors are of a claim's veracity (Biber, 2006), which enables the effective detection of potential false rumours (Lukasik et al., 2015). Stance also reveals how online populations react to business and political news.

This paper addresses the general-purpose, or *open* stance classification task. This is distinct from *target-specific* stance classification, as in Au-

genstein et al. (2016) and Mohammad et al. (2016), which focus on stances towards known, pre-determined targets. In the latter task, the target has already been extracted, from e.g. conversational cues. Target-specific stance classification is suited to situations where the target is already known, such as analyses of a specific product or political actor. In contrast, the open stance classification task is appropriate in emerging news or novel contexts, such as working with online media or streaming news analysis.

Open stance classification is often applied in rumour resolution. Since attitudes in discourse around a claim are indicative not only of the controversiality of the claim, but also can act as a proxy for its veracity, it is reasonable to consider the application of open stance detection for rumour analysis. Indeed, many approaches to rumour and fake news analysis rely on this signal (Derczynski et al., 2017)[1]. In veracity analysis, the claim is already known, and the goal is to gather observations and analyse crowd reaction in order to resolve the claim. Instead of being concerned with specific targets, we apply non-targeted – *open* – stance analysis to messages replying to a claim, where the target may vary but the high-level rumour topic rumour remains the same.

Our simple approach to open stance classification implements common features used in stance classification reported by related work (e.g. bag-of-words, named entities, user activity information, URL presence). We extend this with problem-specific features (which we refer to as the AF features) designed to capture how users react to tweets and express confidence in them. Our results show adding these features gives significantly higher performance on benchmark datasets, compared to recent state-of-the-art systems.

---

[1] http://approximatelycorrect.com/2017/01/23/is-fake-news-a-machine-learning-problem/

Proceedings of Recent Advances in Natural Language Processing, pages 31–39,
Varna, Bulgaria, Sep 4–6 2017.

The outline of the paper is as follows. First we describe related work (Section 2) and then introduce our method along with the classification techniques used and features extracted (Section 3). Next, Section 4 describes our experimental setups, followed by results in Section 5. We report on feature analysis in Section 6, prior to concluding the paper (Section 7).

2 Related Work

The first study that tackles automatic stance classification is that of Qazvinian et al. (2011). With a dataset containing 10K tweets and using a Bayesian classifier and three types of features categorised as "content", "network" and "Twitter specific memes", the authors achieved an accuracy of 93.5%. Similar to them, Hamidian and Diab (2015) perform rumour stance classification by applying supervised machine learning using the dataset created by Qazvinian et al. (2011). However, instead of Bayesian classifiers, the authors use J48 decision tree implemented within the Weka platform (Hall et al., 2009). The features from Qazvinian et al. (2011) are adopted and extended with time-related information and the hastags themselves, instead of the content of the hashtag as used by Qazvinian et al. (2011). In addition to the feature categories introduced above, Hamidian and Diab (2015) introduce another feature category, namely "pragramatic". The pragmatic features include named entity, event, sentiment and emoticons. The evaluation of the performance is casted as either 1-step problem containing a 6 class classification task (not rumour, 4 classes of stance and not determined by the annotator) or 2-step problem containing first a 3 class classification task (non-rumour, rumour, and not determined), followed by a 4 class classification task (stance classification). The two step approach achieves better performance with 82.9% F-1 measure, compared to 74% with the 1-step approach. The authors also report that the best performing features were the content based features and the worst performing ones – the network and Twitter specific features. In their most recent paper, Hamidian and Diab (2016) introduce the Tweet Latent Vector (TLV) approach that is obtained by applying the Semantic Textual Similarity model proposed by Guo and Diab (2012). The authors compare the TLV approach to their own earlier system, as well as to the original features of Qazvinian et al. (2011) and show that the TLV approach outperforms both baselines.

Liu et al. (2015) use a rule-based method and show that it outperforms the approach reported by Qazvinian et al. (2011). Zeng et al. (2016) enrich the feature sets investigated by earlier studies by features derived from the Linguistic Inquiry and Word Count (LIWC) dictionaries (Tausczik and Pennebaker, 2010). Lukasik et al. (2016) investigate Gaussian Processes as rumour stance classifier. For the first time the authors also use Brown Clusters to extract the features for each tweet. Unlike researchers above, Lukasik et al. evalute on the rumour data released by Zubiaga et al. (2016b), where they report an accuracy of 67.7%. This result is achieved when the classifier is trained on $n - 1$ rumours and tested on the nth rumour. However, the authors achieve substantially better results when a small proportion of the in-domain data (data from the nth rumour) is also included in the training (68.6% accuracy). Performance scores differ substantially from those in the studies described above, given that Lukasik et al. (2016) tackled classification of stance in new rumours that differ from those in the training set.

Subsequent work has also tackled stance classification for new, unseen rumours. Zubiaga et al. (Zubiaga et al., 2016a) moved away from the classification of tweets in isolation, focusing instead on Twitter 'conversations' (Tolmie et al., 2015) initiated by rumours, as part of the PHEME project (Derczynski and Bontcheva, 2014). They looked at tree-structured conversations initiated by a rumour and followed by tweets responding to it by supporting, denying, querying or commenting on the rumour.

Rumour stance classification for tree structured conversations has also been studied in the RumourEval shared task at SemEval 2017 (Derczynski et al., 2017). Subtask A there consisted of stance classification of individual tweets discussing a rumour within a conversational thread as one of *support*, *deny*, *query*, or *comment*. Eight participanting teams submitted results to this task. Most of the systems viewed this task as a 4-way single tweet classification task, with the exception of the best performing system by Kochkina et al. (2017), as well as the systems by Wang et al. (2017) and Singh et al. (2017). The winning system addressed the task as a sequential classification problem, where the stance of each tweet takes into consideration the features and labels of the preceding tweets. The system by Singh et al. (2017) takes as input pairs of source and reply tweets, whereas Wang et al. (2017) addressed class imbalance by decomposing the problem into a two step classification task – first distinguishing between comments and non-comments and then classifying non-comment tweets as one of support, deny or query. Half of the systems employed ensemble classifiers, where classification was obtained through majority voting (Wang et al., 2017; García Lozano et al., 2017; Bahuleyan and Vechtomova, 2017; Srivastava et al., 2017). In some cases the ensembles were hybrid, consisting both of machine learning classifiers and manually created rules, with differential weighting of classifiers for different class labels (Wang et al., 2017; García Lozano et al., 2017; Srivastava et al., 2017). Three systems used deep learning, with Kochkina et al. (2017) employing LSTMs for sequential classification, Chen et al. (2017) using convolutional neural networks (CNN) for obtaining the representation of each tweet, assigned a probability for a class by a softmax classifier and García Lozano et al. (2017) using CNN as one of the classifiers in their hybrid conglomeration. The remaining two systems by Enayet and El-Beltagy (2017) and Singh et al. (2017) used support vector machines with a linear and polynomial kernel respectively.

3 Method

3.1 Data

In our experiments we used two different data sets: RumourEval dataset (Derczynski et al., 2017) and the PHEME dataset (Zubiaga et al., 2016b). In the PHEME dataset the authors identify rumours associated with events, collect conversations sparked by those rumours in the form of replies and annotate each of the tweets in the conversations for stance. These data consist of tweets from 5 different events: Ottawa shooting, Ferguson riots, Germanwings crash, Charlie Hebdo and Sydney siege. Each dataset has a different number of rumours where each rumour contains tweets marked with stance annotations: "supporting", "questioning", "denying" or "commenting". A summary of the data is given in Table 1.

The RumourEval dataset is derived from the PHEME dataset, however, for the purpose of the RumourEval shared Task A the data has a given

Dataset	Rumours	S	D	Q	C
Ottawa shooting	58	161	76	64	481
Ferguson riots	46	192	83	94	685
Charlie Hebdo	74	236	56	51	710
Sydney siege	71	89	4	99	713

Table 1: PHEME Data: Counts of tweets with supporting (S), denying (D), questioning (Q) and commenting (C) labels in each event collection.

split into training and testing. This provides an established basis for evaluation. The training data draws from stories in 2014–2016, from the earlier PHEME dataset. The evaluation split covers two new stories, both from 2016: first, the disappearance of Marina Joyce, a British Youtube personality, who was rumoured to have been abducted in July 2016. There was significant speculation in social media, and the case was brought to a concrete resolution as the police investigated and posted an open public response. The second story was that Hillary Clinton had pneumonia during mid-September 2016. The prevalence and spread of this story could be tracked easily, and it emerged in a short space of time, though among background noise of speculative, unsubstantiated claims about her and her opponent's health. More details about this dataset can be obtained from the SemEval website[2].

In keeping with prior work (Zeng et al., 2016; Lukasik et al., 2016; Zubiaga et al., 2016a), our experiments assume that incoming tweets already belong to a particular rumour, e.g. a user is tracking tweets related to a certain rumour. For each new tweet, features are extracted into a feature vector, which is then used to assign each tweet its stance towards the rumour.

3.2 Classifiers

We experiment with three different, well known machine learning classifiers: (1) a decision tree, J48; (2) Random Forests (Breiman, 2001); and (3) an Instance Based classifier (K-NN). For the Random Forest we use 50 trees (*-I 50*). Pruning is enabled for J48. Finally we run the Instance Based classifier with *-I -K 10* settings.

3.3 Features

Prior work on stance classification investigated various features which can be categorized into linguistic, message-based, and topic-based cate-

---

[2]http://alt.qcri.org/semeval2017/task8/

gories (Mendoza et al., 2010; Qazvinian et al., 2011; Hamidian and Diab, 2015; Liu et al., 2015; Zeng et al., 2016; Lukasik et al., 2016; Zubiaga et al., 2016a). The following list summarizes the features adopted in this work.

- **BOW (Bag of words)**: For this feature we first create a dictionary from all the tweets in the out-of-domain dataset. Next each tweet is assigned the words in the dictionary as features. For words occurring in the tweet the feature values are set to the number of times they occur in the tweet. For all other words "0" is used.

- **Brown Cluster:** Brown clustering is a hard hierarchical clustering method and we use it to cluster words in hierarchies. It clusters words based on maximising the probability of the words under the bigram language model, where words are generated based on their clusters (Liang, 2005). In previous work, it has been shown that Brown clusters yield better performance than directly using the BOW features (Lukasik et al., 2015). Brown clusters are obtained from a bigger tweet corpus that entails assignments of words to brown cluster ids. We used 1000 clusters, i.e. there are 1000 cluster ids. All 1000 ids are used as features however only, ids that cover words in the tweet are assigned a feature value "1". All other cluster id feature values are set to "0".

- **POS tag:** The BOW feature captures the actual words and is domain dependent. To create a feature that is not domain dependent, we added Part of Speech (POS) tags as additional feature. Similar to the BOW feature we created a dictionary of POS tags from the entire corpus (excluding the health data) and used this dictionary to label each tweet with it – binary, i.e. whether a POS tag is present.[3] However, instead of using just single POS tags, we created sequences containing bi-gram, tri-gram and 4-gram POS tags. Feature values are the frequencies of POS tag sequences occurring in the tweet.

- **Sentiment:** This is another domain-independent feature. Sentiment analysis reveals the sentimental polarity of the tweet such as whether it is positive or negative. We used the Stanford sentiment(Socher et al., 2013) tool to create this feature. The tool returns a range from 0 to 4 with 0 indicating "very negative" and 4 "very positive". First, we used this as a categorical feature but turning it to a numeric feature gave us better performance. Thus each tweet is assigned a sentiment feature whose value varies from 0 to 4.

- **NE:** Named entity (NE) is also domain independent. We check for each tweet whether it contains *Person, Organization, Date, Location* and *Money* tags and for each tag present, "1" is added, or a "0" otherwise.

- **Reply:** This is a binary feature, which is assigned "1" if the tweet is a reply to a previous one, or a "0" otherwise. Tweet reply information is extracted from the tweet metadata. Again this feature is domain independent.

- **Emoticon:** We created a dictionary of emoticons using Wikipedia[4]. In Wikipedia those emoticons are grouped by categories, which we use as a feature. If any emoticon from a category occurs in the tweet, we assign for that category feature the value "1" – otherwise "0". Again similar to the previous features this feature is domain independent.

- **URL:** This is again domain independent. We assign the tweet "1" if it contains any URL, or "0" otherwise.

- **Mood:** Mood detection analyses textual content using different view points or angles. Mood detection is performed using the tool from (Celli et al., 2016), which analyses tweets from five different angles: amused, disappointed, indignant, satisfied and worried. For each of this angles it returns a value from -1 to +1. We use the different angles as the mood features and the returned values as the feature value.

- **Originality score**: This is the count of tweets the user has produced, i.e. "statuses count" in the Twitter API.

- **isUserVerified(0-1)**: Whether the user is verified or not.

- **NumberOfFollowers**: Number of followers the user has.

---

[3]We also experimented with frequencies of POS tags, i.e. counting how many times a particular POS tag occurs in the tweet. The counts then have been normalized using mean and standard deviation. However, the frequency based POS feature negatively affected classification accuracy, so it has been omitted from the feature set.

[4]https://en.wikipedia.org/wiki/List_of_emoticons

34

- **Role score**: This is the ratio between the number of followers and followees (i.e. NumberOfFollowers/NumberOfFollowees).
- **Engagement score**: the number of tweets divided by the number of days the user has been active (number of days since the user account creation till today).
- **Favourites score**: The "favourites count" divided by the number of days the user has been active.
- **HasGeoEnabled(0-1)**: User has enabled geo-location or not.
- **HasDescription(0-1)**: User has description or not.
- **LenghtOfDescription in words**: The number of words in the user description.
- **averageNegation**: We determine using the Stanford parser (Chen and Manning, 2014) the dependency parse tree of the tweet, count the number of negation relation ("neg") that appears between two terms and divide this by the number of total relations.
- **hasNegation(0-1)**: Tweet has negation relationship or not.
- **hasSlangOrCurseWord(0-1)**: A dictionary of key words[5] is used to determine the presence of slang or curse words in the tweet.
- **hasGoogleBadWord(0-1)**: Same as above but the dictionary of slang words is obtained from Google.[6]
- **hasAcronyms(0-1)**: The tweet is checked for presence of acronyms using a acronym dictionary.[7]
- **averageWordLength**: Average length of words (sum of word character counts divided by number of words in each tweet).
- **hasQuestionMark(0-1)**: The tweet has "?" or not.
- **hasExclamationMark(0-1)**: The tweet has "!" or not.
- **hasDotDotDot(0-1)**: Whether the tweet has "..." or not.
- **numberOfQuestionMark**: Count of "?" in the tweet.
- **NumberOfExclamationMark**: Count of "!" in the tweet.
- **numberOfDotDotDot**: Count of "..." in the tweet.

- **Binary regular expressions applied on each tweet**: .*(rumor?—debunk?).*, .*is (that—this—it) true.*, etc. In total there are 10 features covering regular expressions.

This work extends the features above, with new additional problem-specific features (**AF features**). AF features score the level of confidence in a tweet. We compute scores for surprise (*surpriseScore (SS)*), doubt (*doubtScore (DS)*), certainty (*noDoubtScore (NDS)*) and support (*supportScore (SPS)*) towards rumourous tweets. For each of these features a list of typical words is collected. We use this list to compute a cumulative vector using word2Vec (Mikolov et al., 2013). For each word in the list, we obtain its word2Vec representation, add them together and finally divide the resulting vector by the number of words to obtain the cumulative vector. Similarly a cumulative vector is computed for the words in the tweet excluding acronyms, named entities and URLs. We use cosine to compute the angle between those two cumulative vectors to determine each of the scores. Our word embeddings comprise the vectors published by Baroni et al. (2014). The full list of tweet confidence AF features is as follows:

- **surpriseScore (SS)**: cosine between embedding of tweet content and the list of surprise words, e.g. "surprise", "wonder", etc.
- **doubtScore (DS)**: cosine between embedding of tweet content and the list of doubt words, e.g. "doubt", "uncertain", etc.
- **noDoubtScore (NDS)**: cosine between embedding of tweet content and the list of certainty words, e.g."surely", "sure", etc.
- **supportScore (SPS)**: cosine between embedding tweet content and the list of support words, e.g. "support", "confirm", etc.
  Furthermore, the following two AF features are included:
- **initialTweetSim (ITS)** captures tweets that tend to support rumours. Every rumour is initiated by a tweet. We compute the cosine similarity based on word2Vec of the tweet being classified to the first tweet in the rumour thread. If the tweet is just a simple re-retweet of the initial tweet, this is taken as an evidence that the tweet is supportive of that tweet.
- **isQuestion (IQ)** indicates whether a tweet starts with an interrogative. The feature is binary and aims to capture questioning tweets.

---

[5] www.noswearing.com/dictionary
[6] http://fffff.at/googles-official-list-of-bad-words
[7] www.netlingo.com/category/acronyms.php

Classifier	All features	w.o. AF
Decision tree	74.16	72.25
Random Forest	**79.02**	76.54
IBk	75.59	73.02
Baseline-Turing	78.4	–

Table 2: Accuracy scores of different stance classifiers for the RumourEval dataset. The baseline is the best performing system in the SemEval evaluation **Turing**.

4 Experimental Setup

4.1 Baselines

On the RumourEval dataset we run different classifiers (see Section 3.2). We compare the performance of these classifiers against the best-performing system from the RumourEval challenge, namely **Turing** (Kochkina et al., 2017).

We also run all the classifiers from the RumourEval dataset on the PHEME dataset. The results are compared against the following baseline systems reported on the PHEME dataset:

- **Gaussian Processes (GP)** reported by Lukasik et al. (2015).
- **Hawkes Processes (HP)** reported by Lukasik et al. (2016). HPs make use of both temporal and textual information of tweets.

4.2 Training-Testing Settings

We have two different settings. In the first setting we use the SemEval training data to train the models and apply on the testing data. In the second setting we perform training and testing on the PHEME dataset. For the PHEME dataset, we follow the leave one out (LOO) strategy taken by Lukasik et al. (2016) to construct the training and testing data. In LOO n-1 rumours (all tweets within these rumours) are used for training and the resulting model is tested on the nth rumour. Finally, results are macro-averaged.

5 Results

As shown in Table 2 (column two of the table) the best performing learner on the RumourEval dataset is the Random Forest classifier. It achieves the accuracy of *79.02*, higher than any participating system in the RumourEval Task A.[8]

The results on the PHEME dataset are shown in Table 3. Overall the best performing classifier is the J48 decision tree learner. The difference

in accuracy scores between the classfiers is tested for significance using paired t-test (p<0.001). J48 is only significantly better than IBk and J48 for the *Ottawa shooting* event type. In the remaining event types, J48 performs better, but not significantly better than IBk and Random Forest.

All classifiers J48, IBk and Random Forest, however, outperform the **GP** and **HP** baselines on all event types [9].

What these results demonstrate is that simpler classifiers, such as J48 and Random Forest can outperform significantly more sophisticated machine learning methods (GPs and HPs in this case, and LSTMs in the RumourEval case), thanks to the additional knowledge captured in the rich feature set. In contrast, for example, the GP and HP models relied primarily on BOW and Brown clustering features.

6 Feature Analysis

The results described in Section 5 are based on features reported by related work, enhanced by us with AF features (Section 3.3). We repeat the experiments with AF features removed from the feature set, in order to quantify the extent of their contribution.

For the RumourEval dataset the results are shown in column 3 of Table 2. The omission of the AF features leads to a performance decrease for all classifiers. The accuracy scores also fall below that of the SemEval winner **Turing** – the state-of-the-art system on the RumourEval dataset.

The results on the PHEME dataset are shown in Table 4. The exclusion of the AF features leads to an overall drop in performance when compared to the same classifiers in Table 3. However, these differences are not significant and the classifiers with AF features removed still perform at least as well as the GP and HP baselines (for the event type *Ferguson riots*), or outperform the baselines (for all other event types).

Table 5 shows the accuracy scores of the Random Forest stance classifier, the best performing system on the RumourEval dataset when each AF feature is removed in turn. The results indicate that each AF feature contributes to the accuracy boost in stance classification. The highest accu-

---

[8]The results are reported in http://alt.qcri.org/semeval2017/task8/index.php?id=results

[9]Although the significance test could not be run for the baselines, as the single data point values are not available, the proportion of difference in accuracy and the fact that it is the same data sets let us assume that the classifiers significantly outperform the baselines.

classifier	Ottawa shooting	Ferguson riots	Charlie Hebdo	Sydney siege	macro mean
IBk	70.31*	72.35	**78.33** (ref)	75.44	74.10
Decision tree	**76.28** (ref)	**75.20** (ref)	78.21	**80.01** (ref)	**77.42**
Random Forest	69.39*	69.16	74.57	74.49	71.90
Baseline - GP	62.28	64.31	70.66	65.04	65.57
Baseline - HP	67.77	68.44	72.93	68.59	69.43

Table 3: Accuracy scores for different stance classifiers on the PHEME dataset. * indicates a significant difference to ("ref") scores for each column of the table respectively as indicated by the paired t-test with $p < 0.001$.

classifier	Ottawa shooting	Ferguson riots	Charlie Hebdo	Sydney siege	macro mean
IBk / AF	69.26	69.54	77.09	73.28	72.29
J48 / AF	75.62	74.85	77.05	79.21	76.68
Random Forest / AF	67.87	68.31	75.40	72.57	71.03

Table 4: Accuracy scores of different stance classifiers on the PHEME dataset with AF features removed.

Features	Accuracy
All features	**79.02**
All without AF	76.54
All without ITS	78.55
All without SS	77.59
All without SPS	78.16
All without DS	78.36
All without NDS	77.59
All without IQ	78.64

Table 5: Contribution of each AF feature. Accuracy scores are for the Random Forest classifier on RumourEval data set with each feature removed in turn.

racy loss results from removing the surprise (SS) and certainty (NDS) scores and the least – when the *isQuestion* (IQ) feature is removed. None of the AF feature removals cause a significant drop in accuracy. However, the loss is significant ($p < 0.0001$) when all AF features are removed.

Both RumourEval and PHEME dataset evaluations show that the AF features play an important role in terms of achieving higher accuracy for tweet-based stance classification. They also show the importance of task or problem-specific feature engineering and point out that it is possible with some feature engineering effort to outperform state-of-the-art techniques that are typically considered more powerful and sophisticated than traditional learning methods.

7 Conclusion

This paper tackled the problem of stance classification of tweets towards rumours. In our approach we use a simple classification approach, combining common features reported by related studies with our novel AF features, to boost overall ac-curacy. Our results show that this approach leads to significantly better results on both RumourEval and PHEME datasets compared to current state-of-the-art systems. Furthermore, our results show that the omission of the AF features proposed in this work leads to significantly lower performance. Adding AF to the feature set causes our approach to outperform the best performing system on the RumourEval dataset. These results show the importance of task- or problem-oriented feature engineering.

The proposed features are content based and work on text level. In our future work we plan to investigate features that are able to capture communication behaviours between users. We also plan to apply stance information as a feature in rumour veracity classification.

Acknowledgments

This work was partially supported by the European Union funded COMRADES (grant agreement No. 687847) and PHEME projects (grant agreement No. 611223), as well as an EPSRC career acceleration fellowship (EP/I004327/1).

References

Isabelle Augenstein, Tim Rocktäschel, Andreas Vlachos, and Kalina Bontcheva. 2016. Stance detection with bidirectional conditional encoding. In *Proceedings of the 2016 Conference on Empirical Methods in Natural Language Processing*. Association for Computational Linguistics, Austin, Texas, pages 876–885. https://aclweb.org/anthology/D16-1084.

Hareesh Bahuleyan and Olga Vechtomova. 2017. UWaterloo at SemEval-2017 Task 8: Detecting

Stance towards Rumours with Topic Independent Features. In *Proceedings of SemEval*. ACL.

Marco Baroni, Georgiana Dinu, and Germán Kruszewski. 2014. Don't count, predict! a systematic comparison of context-counting vs. context-predicting semantic vectors. In *Proceedings of ACL*. pages 238–247.

Douglas Biber. 2006. Stance in spoken and written university registers. *Journal of English for Academic Purposes* 5(2):97–116.

Leo Breiman. 2001. Random forests. *Machine learning* 45(1):5–32.

Fabio Celli, Arindam Ghosh, Firoj Alam, and Giuseppe Riccardi. 2016. In the mood for sharing contents: Emotions, personality and interaction styles in the diffusion of news. *Information Processing & Management* 52(1):93–98.

Danqi Chen and Christopher D Manning. 2014. A fast and accurate dependency parser using neural networks. In *Proceedings of EMNLP*. pages 740–750.

Yi-Chin Chen, Zhao-Yand Liu, and Hung-Yu Kao. 2017. IKM at SemEval-2017 Task 8: Convolutional Neural Networks for Stance Detection and Rumor Verification. In *Proceedings of SemEval*. ACL.

Leon Derczynski and Kalina Bontcheva. 2014. PHEME: Veracity in Digital Social Networks. In *Proceedings of the UMAP Workshops*.

Leon Derczynski, Kalina Bontcheva, Maria Liakata, Rob Procter, Geraldine Wong Sak Hoi, and Arkaitz Zubiaga. 2017. SemEval-2017 Task 8: RumourEval: Determining rumour veracity and support for rumours. In *Proceedings of SemEval*. ACL.

Omar Enayet and Samhaa R. El-Beltagy. 2017. NileTMRG at SemEval-2017 Task 8: Determining Rumour and Veracity Support for Rumours on Twitter. In *Proceedings of SemEval*. ACL.

Marianela García Lozano, Hanna Lilja, Edward Tjörnhammar, and Maja Maja Karasalo. 2017. Mama Edha at SemEval-2017 Task 8: Stance Classification with CNN and Rules. In *Proceedings of SemEval*. ACL.

Weiwei Guo and Mona Diab. 2012. Modeling sentences in the latent space. In *Proceedings of ACL*. Association for Computational Linguistics, pages 864–872.

Mark Hall, Eibe Frank, Geoffrey Holmes, Bernhard Pfahringer, Peter Reutemann, and Ian H Witten. 2009. The weka data mining software: an update. *ACM SIGKDD explorations newsletter* 11(1):10–18.

Sardar Hamidian and Mona T Diab. 2015. Rumor Detection and Classification for Twitter Data. In *Proceedings of SOTICS*.

Sardar Hamidian and Mona T Diab. 2016. Rumor identification and belief investigation on twitter. In *Proceedings of NAACL-HLT*. pages 3–8.

Elena Kochkina, Maria Liakata, and Isabelle Augenstein. 2017. Turing at SemEval-2017 Task 8: Sequential Approach to Rumour Stance Classification with Branch-LSTM. In *Proceedings of SemEval*.

Percy Liang. 2005. *Semi-supervised learning for natural language*. Ph.D. thesis, Massachusetts Institute of Technology.

Xiaomo Liu, Armineh Nourbakhsh, Quanzhi Li, Rui Fang, and Sameena Shah. 2015. Real-time rumor debunking on twitter. In *Proceedings of CIKM*. ACM, pages 1867–1870.

Michal Lukasik, Trevor Cohn, and Kalina Bontcheva. 2015. Classifying tweet level judgements of rumours in social media. *arXiv preprint arXiv:1506.00468* .

Michal Lukasik, P. K. Srijith, Duy Vu, Kalina Bontcheva, Arkaitz Zubiaga, and Trevor Cohn. 2016. Hawkes processes for continuous time sequence classification: an application to rumour stance classification in twitter. In *Proceedings of the 54th Meeting of the Association for Computational Linguistics*. Association for Computer Linguistics, pages 393–398.

Marcelo Mendoza, Barbara Poblete, and Carlos Castillo. 2010. Twitter under crisis: can we trust what we rt? In *Proceedings of the workshop on social media analytics*. ACM, pages 71–79.

Tomas Mikolov, Ilya Sutskever, Kai Chen, Greg S Corrado, and Jeff Dean. 2013. Distributed representations of words and phrases and their compositionality. In *Advances in neural information processing systems*. pages 3111–3119.

Saif M Mohammad, Svetlana Kiritchenko, Parinaz Sobhani, Xiaodan Zhu, and Colin Cherry. 2016. Semeval-2016 task 6: Detecting stance in tweets. *Proceedings of SemEval* 16.

Rob Procter, Jeremy Crump, Susanne Karstedt, Alex Voss, and Marta Cantijoch. 2013. Reading the riots: What were the police doing on twitter? *Policing and society* 23(4):413–436.

Vahed Qazvinian, Emily Rosengren, Dragomir R Radev, and Qiaozhu Mei. 2011. Rumor has it: Identifying misinformation in microblogs. In *Proceedings of EMNLP*. pages 1589–1599.

Vikram Singh, Sunny Narayan, Md Shad Akhtar, Asif Ekbal, and Pushpak Bhattacharya. 2017. IITP at SemEval-2017 Task 8: A Supervised Approach for Rumour Evaluation. In *Proceedings of SemEval*.

Richard Socher, Alex Perelygin, Jean Y Wu, Jason Chuang, Christopher D Manning, Andrew Y Ng, and Christopher Potts. 2013. Recursive deep models for semantic compositionality over a sentiment treebank. In *Proceedings of EMNLP*. volume 1631, page 1642.

Ankit Srivastava, Rehm Rehm, and Julian Moreno Schneider. 2017. DFKI-DKT at SemEval-2017 Task 8: Rumour Detection and Classification using Cascading Heuristics. In *Proceedings of SemEval*. ACL.

Yla R Tausczik and James W Pennebaker. 2010. The psychological meaning of words: Liwc and computerized text analysis methods. *Journal of language and social psychology* 29(1):24–54.

Peter Tolmie, Rob Procter, Mark Rouncefield, Maria Liakata, and Arkaitz Zubiaga. 2015. Microblog analysis as a programme of work. *arXiv preprint arXiv:1511.03193* .

Feixiang Wang, Man Lan, and Yuanbin Wu. 2017. ECNU at SemEval-2017 Task 8: Rumour Evaluation Using Effective Features and Supervised Ensemble Models. In *Proceedings of SemEval*. ACL.

Li Zeng, Kate Starbird, and Emma S Spiro. 2016. #unconfirmed: Classifying rumor stance in crisis-related social media messages. In *Proceedings of ICWSM*.

Arkaitz Zubiaga, Elena Kochkina, Maria Liakata, Rob Procter, and Michal Lukasik. 2016a. Stance classification in rumours as a sequential task exploiting the tree structure of social media conversations. In *Proceedings of COLING*.

Arkaitz Zubiaga, Maria Liakata, Rob Procter, Geraldine Wong Sak Hoi, and Peter Tolmie. 2016b. Analysing how people orient to and spread rumours in social media by looking at conversational threads. *PLoS ONE* 11(3):1–29. https://doi.org/10.1371/journal.pone.0150989.

An Extensible Multilingual Open Source Lemmatizer

Ahmet Aker[a,b] and **Johann Petrak**[a] and **Firas Sabbah**[b]
Department of Computer Science, University of Sheffield[a]
Department of Information Engineering, University of Duisburg-Essen[b]
a.aker@is.inf.uni-due.de, johann.petrak@sheffield.ac.uk
firas.sabbah@stud.uni-due.de

Abstract

We present GATE DictLemmatizer, a multilingual open source lemmatizer for the GATE NLP framework that currently supports English, German, Italian, French, Dutch, and Spanish, and is easily extensible to other languages. The software is freely available under the LGPL license. The lemmatization is based on the Helsinki Finite-State Transducer Technology (HFST) and lemma dictionaries automatically created from Wiktionary. We evaluate the performance of the lemmatizers against TreeTagger, which is only freely available for research purposes. Our evaluation shows that DictLemmatizer achieves similar or even better results than TreeTagger for languages where there is support from HFST. The performance drops when there is no support from HFST and the entire lemmatization process is based on lemma dictionaries. However, the results are still satisfactory given the fact that DictLemmatizer is open-source and can be easily extended to other languages. The software for extending the lemmatizer by creating word lists from Wiktionary dictionaries is also freely available as open-source software.

1 Introduction

The process of lemmatization is an important part of many computational linguistics applications such as Information Retrieval (IR) and Natural Language Processing (NLP). In lemmatization, inflected forms of a lexeme are mapped to a canonical form that is referred to as the lemma. The task of finding the correct lemma for a word in context is often complicated by the fact that a word can be the inflected form of more than one lexeme each of which may have different lemmas. Lemmas can be used in various ways for NLP, for instance, to improve the performance of text similarity metrics. For this application, all words are mapped to their lemma before a similarity is calculated. Lemmas are also often used in information retrieval and information extraction to better identify and group terms which occur in their inflected forms.

The task of finding lemmas is different and harder than finding stems. Stemming is often used as a much cruder heuristic approach to map inflectional forms of words to some canonical form, but unlike lemmatization does not differentiate between different lexemes which could have the same inflectional form and it is possible for the stem of a word to not be a valid lexeme of the language.

The TreeTagger (Schmid, 2013) software provides lemmatization for 20 languages including English, German, Italian, French, Dutch and Spanish. However, it is not open source and it is not straightforward to use it for non-research or commercial applications. There exist a few other lemmatizers which are open for non-research purposes (Lezius et al., 1998; Perera and Witte, 2005; Bär et al., 2013; Cappelli and Moretti, 1983)[1]. However, these lemmatizers are mostly concerned with only one language and do not provide a broad coverage like the TreeTagger.

In this paper, we describe GATE DictLemmatizer, a plugin for the GATE NLP framework[2] (Cunningham et al., 2011) that performs lemmatization for English, German, Italian, French, Dutch, and Spanish and is freely available under the LGPL license. The GATE NLP framework is one of the most widely used frameworks for

---

[1] https://github.com/giodegas/morphit-lemmatizer
[2] https://gate.ac.uk

Proceedings of Recent Advances in Natural Language Processing, pages 40–45,
Varna, Bulgaria, Sep 4–6 2017.

applied natural language processing. It is implemented in Java, freely available under the permissive LGPL license and can be extended through plugins.

Our method combines the Helsinki Finite-State Transducer Technology (HFST)[3] (Lindén et al., 2011) and word-lemma dictionaries obtained from Wiktionary. Since we use separate dictionaries depending on the word category, the method also depends on a POS tagger for the language. The word dictionaries are obtained automatically from Wiktionary[4] data dumps. The code for creating the dictionaries automatically is available as free and open-source software.[5] This software can be used to easily add dictionaries for new languages to the DictLemmatizer. The plugin also contains the HFST models for the 4 languages for which models are available: English, German, French and Italian.[6]

The rest of the paper is structured as follows. First we describe our method of performing lemmatization (Section 2). Our lemmatizer uses automatically generated lemma dictionaries. The process of obtaining such dictionaries from Wiktionary is outlined in Section 3. In Section 4 we detail the release information. Next, in Section 5 we evaluate the performance of our lemmatizer. We use the TreeTagger for comparison. We conclude in Section 6.

2 Method

To obtain lemmas we combine two strategies: the Helsinki Finite-State Transducer Technology (HFST)[7] and word-lemma dictionaries obtained from Wiktionary[8]. For both strategies, it is necessary to know the coarse-grained word categories such as "noun", "verb", "adposition" for each word.

For this purpose, the lemmatizer requires the Universal POS tags[9] from the Universal Dependencies project. In GATE (Cunningham et al.,

2011), POS tags can be created using different methods or plugins, however for the evaluation in this paper we use the ANNIE POS-tagger (Cunningham et al., 2002) for English and the Stanford CoreNLP POS tagger (Toutanova et al., 2003) for all other languages. These language-specific POS tags are then converted to Universal Dependencies tags using mappings adapted from

```
https://github.com/slavpetrov/
universal-pos-tags
```
(Petrov et al., 2011).

The lemmatizer first tries to look up each word form in the dictionary that matches the language and word category of the word. Currently there are lists for the following categories: adjective, adposition, adverb, conjunction, determiner, noun, particle, pronoun, verb. If the word form is found in the dictionary, the corresponding lemma is used. Pre-generated dictionaries for the six supported languages are included with the plugin.

If the word could not be found in the dictionary, an attempt is made to find the lemma by using the HFST model for the language, if it is available. The HFST model returns for each word all possible morphological variants. This makes it difficult to directly find the lemma for the word. We therefore implemented rules that use the Universal POS tag information and extract the correct lemma. E.g. for the word "computers" the HFST returns the following options:

```
compute[V]+ER[V/N]+N+PL
computer[N]+N+PL
```

Since we know from the POS tagger that "computers" is a noun we can use that information and extract from the HFST list the entry that refers to a noun ([N]) - "computer".

The HFST models are freely available only for a few languages. For any language where there is no HFST model, our lemmatizer will rely only on the Wiktionary-based dictionaries.[10]

3 Parsing dictionaries

We implemented a Java based tool that allows users to extract lemma information from the Wiktionary API. With this tool it is easy to create dictionaries for additional languages not included in the lemmatizer distribution. We refer to this tool as Wiktionary-Lemma Extractor. It fetches for a

---

[3] http://www.ling.helsinki.fi/
kieliteknologia/tutkimus/hfst/
[4] https://www.wiktionary.org/
[5] https://github.com/ahmetaker/
Wiktionary-Lemma-Extractor
[6] https://sourceforge.net/
projects/hfst/files/resources/
morphological-transducers/
[7] http://www.ling.helsinki.fi/
kieliteknologia/tutkimus/hfst/
[8] https://www.wiktionary.org/
[9] http://universaldependencies.org/u/
pos/all.html

[10] In this case, it is also possible to make DictLemmatizer work without any POS tags at all by merging the original dictionaries per word type into one dictionary for unknown/unidentified POS type.

given word form its lemma from the Wiktionary page. In addition the tool expects the language information, such as English, German, etc. Once these pieces of information are provided the tool fetches through the Wiktionary API the English version of the Wiktionary page for the queried word. The English Wiktionary page is divided into different areas where each area conveys a particular information such as lemma, synonym, translation, etc. Our tool isolates the lemma area and finds the non-inflected form for the queried word. The queried word and the non-inflected form are saved into a database to be used as dictionary lookup.

4 Software Availability

4.1 GATE DictLemmatizer Plugin

Most of the tools and resources for the GATE NLP framework are created as separate plugins which can be used as needed for a processing pipeline. The approach for finding lemmas described earlier has been implemented as a GATE plugin and is freely available from `https://github.com/GateNLP/ gateplugin-dict-lemmatizer`. This plugin only implements the lemmatization part since there are already several plugins for tokenisation, sentence splitting, and POS-tagging included or separately available for GATE.

4.2 Wiktionary-Lemma Extractor

Similar to the GATE Plugin for lemmatization we make our Wiktionary-Lemma Extractor publicly available through github[11]. Along with the code we also provide a client that ease the creation of new dictionaries. The client just expects the input of the target language such as English, German, Turkish, Urdu, etc. The client first collects all possible words for that particular language from Wiktionary titles, determines for each title word its lemma and finally extract the lemma dictionaries. These lemma dictionaries can then be directly injected into the GATE Plugin.

5 Evaluation

We evaluated DictLemmatizer and compared it to TreeTagger on the following corpora:

- English British National Corpus (EN-BNC) (Consortium, 2007; Clear, 1993)

- German Tiger Corpus (DE-Tiger) (Brants et al., 2004)

- Universal Dependencies English tree bank (EN-UD) (Bies et al., 2012)

- Universal Dependencies French tree bank (FR-UD)

- Universal Dependencies German tree bank (DE-UD)

- Universal Dependencies Spanish tree bank (ES-UD)

- Universal Dependencies Spanish Ancora corpus (ES-Ancora)

For more information on the Universal Dependencies tree banks see McDonald et al. (2013).

All corpora were converted to GATE documents using format specific open-source software[12][13][14]. The software and setup for carrying out all evaluation is also available online.[15]

Note that for this comparison, the GATE Generic Tagger Framework plugin[16] was used to wrap the original TreeTagger software. This plugin does not use the full processing pipeline of the original TreeTagger software[17] but instead just uses the `tree-tagger` binary to retrieve per-token information.

All corpora were converted so that the token boundaries from the corpus were preserved for the conversion to GATE format. However, for the evaluation, the tokens produced by the annotation pipeline are based on the GATE tokenizer and can therefore differ from the correct tokens as present in the tree bank. We list the performance of the tokeniser used together with the performance of the lemmatizer on the tokens which match exactly. Some corpora use corpus-specific ways to represent multi-token words or multi-word tokens which cannot be represented in an identical way as GATE annotations and so these cases get excluded

---

[11]`https://github.com/ahmetaker/ Wiktionary-Lemma-Extractor`

[12]`https://github.com/GateNLP/ corpusconversion-bnc`

[13]`https://github.com/GateNLP/ corpusconversion-tiger`

[14]`https://github.com/GateNLP/ corpusconversion-universal-dependencies`

[15]`https://github.com/johann-petrak/ evaluation-lemmatizer`

[16]`https://gate.ac.uk/userguide/sec: parsers:taggerframework`

[17]

from the evaluation. Results of the evaluation reported in accuracy are shown in Table 1.

From the results in Table 1 we can see that for English and German, DictLemmatizer outperforms TreeTagger. For French, TreeTagger achieves better performance in the test corpora; however, for the training corpora DictLemmatizer achieves better results. For Spanish, the TreeTagger results are much better. The reason for this is that apart from TreeTagger's outstanding performance on the Spanish corpora, the HFST inducer is not used in our Lemmatizer for Spanish because there is no HFST model available, so the lemmatization is performed only using the lemma dictionaries obtained from Wiktionary.[18] Although there is a big performance difference for the Spanish language, we consider that this result is satisfactory given the restrictions.

To get a better indication of the performance of each of the two strategies for the other languages, we also performed evaluations using the DictLemmatizer where we used only the dictionary-based or only the HFST-based approach. Table 2 shows the results for all corpora except Spanish (where only the dictionary is used by default). We can see that for English and German the performance of using just HFST and using just lemma dictionaries achieve comparable results, though using only lemma dictionaries is always slightly better. This pictures looks different when we look at the French language. There using only HFST clearly wins against using only the lemma dictionaries and achieves around 10% better accuracy. Nevertheless both resources are complementary and when combined boost the results as seen in Table 1.

In addition to the Wiktionary source, the word lists can be extended by an annotated training corpus. We tested this by finding the 500 most frequent incorrect assignments on each of the Universal Dependencies training corpora grouped by target POS tag and adding those to the dictionaries for each language. The evaluations using those extended word lists are shown in 1 with the indication "DL-TR". This improves the accuracy on all Universal Dependencies training and test sets and on the BNC corpus, but slightly decreases ac-

curacy on the Tiger corpus.

Along with the accuracy figures, we also recorded the time needed to process each corpus (see Table 1). The timing information only gives a rough indication because we show the results of a single run only, and because the machine was under different load for different runs. Also note that the times for the TreeTagger include the overhead of wrapping the original TreeTagger binary for use in a Java plugin. The implementation of the Generic Tagger Framework plugin executes the binary for every document, so the timing information includes the overhead for this and thus also depends on the average document size for a corpus, while the timing for the DictLemmatizer does not. However, from these rough results we can still see that DictLemmatizer is always significantly faster than the TreeTagger for the concrete GATE-plugin implementations that were compared.

6   Conclusion

In this paper we presented a lemmatizer for six languages: English, German, Italian, French, Dutch and Spanish that is easily extensible to other languages. We compared the performance of our lemmatizer to the one of TreeTagger. Our results show that our lemmatizer achieves similar or better results when there is support from HFST. In case there is no HFST support we still achieve satisfactory results.

Both the DictLemmatizer and the lemma dictionary collector software are available freely for commercial use under the LGPL license. The dictionary collector can be used to easily extend the lemmatizer to new languages that are currently not included in DictLemmatizer.

Acknowledgments

This work was partially supported by the European Union under grant agreement No. 687847 COMRADES and PHEME project under the grant agreement No. 611223.

References

Daniel Bär, Torsten Zesch, and Iryna Gurevych. 2013. Dkpro similarity: An open source framework for text similarity. In *ACL (Conference System Demonstrations)*. pages 121–126.

Ann Bies, Justin Mott, Colin Warner, and Seth Kulick. 2012. English web treebank LDC2012T13. Web

---

[18]In our evaluation we focused on languages which are rich in resources and high performing lemmatizers such as English, German and French and also supported by HFST and languages that are less rich in terms of resources and also has no support by the HFST tool such as Spanish.

Corpus	TT	DL	DL-TR	Time DL	Time TT
EN-BNC	0.927	0.938	**0.958**	1:47:23	3:11:29
EN-UD-Test	0.922	0.945	**0.972**	0:00:14	0:11:08
EN-UD-Train	0.920	0.941	**0.972**	0:01:18	1:14:54
DE-Tiger	0.804	**0.940**	0.925	0:12:12	0:53:07
DE-UD-Test	0.841	0.915	**0.946**	0:00:44	0:13:34
DE-UD-Train	0.783	0.910	**0.944**	0:05:08	3:02:56
FR-UD-Test	0.902	0.881	**0.961**	0:00:12	0:03:00
FR-UD-Train	0.882	0.896	**0.973**	0:04:10	1:31:28
ES-Test	0.904	0.779	**0.936**	0:00:18	0:01:47
ES-Train	0.884	0.797	**0.954**	0:02:41	0:45:50
ES-Ancora-Test	**0.993**	0.806	0.950	0:00:26	0:05:30
ES-Ancora-Train	**0.993**	0.807	0.953	0:07:21	0:58:06

Table 1: Performance of TreeTagger (TT) and our Dictionary Lemmatizer (DL) and Dictionary Lemmatizer trained on the UD training set (DL-TR) on different corpora. Figures are accuracy of lemma (ignoring case) for tokens matching the corpus token boundaries, times are in HH:MM:SS.

Corpora	HFST	Lemma Dicts
BNC-EN	0.89	0.924
UD-Test-EN	0.905	0.933
UD-Train-EN	0.90	0.928
Tiger-DE	0.812	0.853
UD-Test-DE	0.827	0.827
UD-Train-DE	0.817	0.827
UD-Test-FR	0.878	0.799
UD-Train-FR	0.894	0.819

Table 2: Performance of DictLemmatizer (HFST only and Wiktionary lemma dictionary only) on different corpora.

Download. Philadelphia: Linguistic Data Consortium.

Sabine Brants, Stefanie Dipper, Peter Eisenberg, Silvia Hansen-Schirra, Esther König, Wolfgang Lezius, Christian Rohrer, George Smith, and Hans Uszkoreit. 2004. Tiger: Linguistic interpretation of a german corpus. *Research on Language and Computation* 2(4):597–620. https://doi.org/10.1007/s11168-004-7431-3.

Amedeo Cappelli and Lorenzo Moretti. 1983. *Aspetti della rappresentazione della conoscenza in linguistica computazionale*, volume 5. Pacini.

Jeremy H. Clear. 1993. The digital word. MIT Press, Cambridge, MA, USA, chapter The British National Corpus, pages 163–187. http://dl.acm.org/citation.cfm?id=166403.166418.

BNC Consortium. 2007. The british national corpus, version 3 (bnc xml edition). Distributed by Oxford University Computing Services on behalf of the BNC Consortium. http://www.natcorp.ox.ac.uk/. http://www.natcorp.ox.ac.uk/.

Hamish Cunningham, Diana Maynard, Kalina Bontcheva, and Valentin Tablan. 2002. GATE: A Framework and Graphical Development Environment for Robust NLP Tools and Applications. In *Proceedings of the 40th Anniversary Meeting of the Association for Computational Linguistics (ACL'02)*.

Hamish Cunningham, Diana Maynard, Kalina Bontcheva, Valentin Tablan, Niraj Aswani, Ian Roberts, Genevieve Gorrell, Adam Funk, Angus Roberts, Danica Damljanovic, Thomas Heitz, Mark A. Greenwood, Horacio Saggion, Johann Petrak, Yaoyong Li, and Wim Peters. 2011. *Text Processing with GATE (Version 6)*.

Wolfgang Lezius, Reinhard Rapp, and Manfred Wettler. 1998. A freely available morphological analyzer, disambiguator and context sensitive lemmatizer for german. In *Proceedings of the 17th international conference on Computational linguistics*. Association for Computational Linguistics, pages 743–748.

Krister Lindén, Erik Axelson, Sam Hardwick, Miikka Silfverberg, and Tommi Pirinen. 2011. HFST—framework for compiling and applying morphologies pages 67–85.

Ryan McDonald, Joakim Nivre, Yvonne Quirmbach-Brundage, Yoav Goldberg, Dipanjan Das, Kuzman Ganchev, Keith Hall, Slav Petrov, Hao Zhang, Oscar Tackstrom, Claudia Bedini, Nuria Bertomeu Castello, and Jungmee. 2013. Universal dependency annotation for multilingual parsing. In *Lee Proceedings of ACL 2013*.

Praharshana Perera and René Witte. 2005. A self-learning context-aware lemmatizer for german. In

Proceedings of the conference on Human Language Technology and Empirical Methods in Natural Language Processing. Association for Computational Linguistics, pages 636–643.

Slav Petrov, Dipanjan Das, and Ryan T. McDonald. 2011. A universal part-of-speech tagset. *CoRR* abs/1104.2086. http://arxiv.org/abs/1104.2086.

Helmut Schmid. 2013. Probabilistic part-ofispeech tagging using decision trees. In *New methods in language processing*. Routledge, page 154.

Kristina Toutanova, Dan Klein, Christopher D. Manning, and Yoram Singer. 2003. Feature-rich part-of-speech tagging with a cyclic dependency network. In *Proceedings of the 2003 Conference of the North American Chapter of the Association for Computational Linguistics on Human Language Technology*. Association for Computational Linguistics, Stroudsburg, PA, USA, NAACL '03, pages 173–180.

Universal Dependencies for Arabic Tweets

Fahad Albogamy
School of Computer Science,
University of Manchester,
Manchester, M13 9PL, UK
albogamf@cs.man.ac.uk

Allan Ramsay
School of Computer Science,
University of Manchester,
Manchester, M13 9PL, UK
allan.ramsay@cs.man.ac.uk

Abstract

To facilitate cross-lingual studies, there is
an increasing interest in identifying linguistic universals. Recently, a new universal scheme was designed as a part of
universal dependency project. In this paper, we map the Arabic tweets dependency
treebank (ATDT) to the Universal Dependency (UD) scheme to compare it to other
language resources and for the purpose of
cross-lingual studies.

1 Introduction

Universal Dependency (UD) is a common scheme
proposed by (Agic et al. 2015) to support cross-
lingual studies and to compare the scheme in
question to other language resources. Dependency treebanks have been developed for many
languages such as Arabic, Czech and Turkish.
However, each treebank has different labelling annotation and was built according to a specific linguistic theory. Due to these variations, a treebank
for one language cannot be easily compared to a
treebank for another language, so using a universal
framework is an appealing method of overcoming
these variations. From a parsing point of view, it is
difficult to compare parser output in one language
to that in another if their training data is based
on different labelling schemes, because parsing results can be influenced by the number of annotation labels and different linguistic analyses across
languages, as demonstrated by (McDonald et al.
2011) through a cross-lingual parsing study.

To facilitate cross-lingual studies, there is an
increasing interest in identifying linguistic universals. In POS tagging, the Google universal
POS tagset was developed by (Petrov et al. 2011),
which contains 12 main POS tags aiming to cover
the common categories that exist in any language.

In parsing, a set of 41 dependency labels and
a universal annotation scheme was developed by
(McDonald et al. 2013) and used to convert ten
language treebanks for the purpose of multilingual parsing. Recently, a new universal scheme
was designed as a part of universal dependency
project (Agic et al. 2015; Nivre et al. 2016). This
scheme is based on the universal Stanford dependency (De Marneffe et al. 2006) and the Google
universal POS tagset. We have mapped mapped
the Arabic tweets dependency treebank (ATDT)
(Albogamy et al. 2017) to the Universal Dependency (UD) scheme to compare it to other language resources and for the purpose of cross-
lingual studies. The ATDT is a corpus of Arabic
tweets that have been annotated with information
on deep syntactic structure. This paper summaries
the conversation and mapping of the ATDT to the
UD scheme and outlines some structural changes
and specific dependency labels introduced during
the mapping process.

2 Mapping the Arabic tweets POS tagset to the universal POS tagset

To facilitate cross-lingual POS tagging and parsing studies, the (Google) universal POS tagset was
designed by (Petrov et al. 2011). Its aim is to
simplify POS tagsets and unify them across languages. The ATDT used a tagset obtained by unifying the tagsets from AMIRA, MADA and Stanford. The resulting tagset consists of the main
POS tags both coarse- and fine-grained in addition
to Twitter-specifics tags (Albogamy and Ramsay
2016). Table 1 shows the mapping of Arabic
tweets POS tagset to the universal POS tagset.
Most of the POS mappings made from the Arabic Tweets POS tagset to the universal POS tagset
are intuitive. There are two types of mapping:
one-to-one (e.g. JJ $\rightarrow$ ADJ), many-to-one; fine-

Proceedings of Recent Advances in Natural Language Processing, pages 46–51,
Varna, Bulgaria, Sep 4–6 2017.

<table>
<tr><th colspan="3" align="center">Universal POS Mappings</th></tr>
<tr><th>UD Tagset</th><th>Arabic Tweets Tagset</th><th>Gloss</th></tr>
<tr><td>ADJ</td><td>JJ</td><td>Adjective</td></tr>
<tr><td>ADP</td><td>IN</td><td>Preposition</td></tr>
<tr><td rowspan="2">ADV</td><td>RB</td><td>Adverb</td></tr>
<tr><td>WRB</td><td>Wh-adverb</td></tr>
<tr><td>AUX</td><td>AUX</td><td>auxiliary</td></tr>
<tr><td>CCONJ</td><td>CC</td><td>Coordinating conjunction</td></tr>
<tr><td>DET</td><td>DET</td><td>Definite,article</td></tr>
<tr><td>INTJ</td><td>UH</td><td>Interjection</td></tr>
<tr><td>NOUN</td><td>NN</td><td>Common noun</td></tr>
<tr><td>NUM</td><td>CD</td><td>Cardinal number</td></tr>
<tr><td>PART</td><td>RP</td><td>Particle</td></tr>
<tr><td rowspan="4">PRON</td><td>DT</td><td>Demonstrative pronoun</td></tr>
<tr><td>PRP</td><td>Subject pronoun</td></tr>
<tr><td>SPRP</td><td>Clitic personal pronoun</td></tr>
<tr><td>WP</td><td>Relative pronoun</td></tr>
<tr><td>PROPN</td><td>NNP</td><td>Proper noun</td></tr>
<tr><td>PUNCT</td><td>PUNC</td><td>Punctuation</td></tr>
<tr><td>SCONJ</td><td>CO</td><td>Subordinating conjunction</td></tr>
<tr><td>SYM</td><td>-</td><td>symbol</td></tr>
<tr><td>VERB</td><td>VB</td><td>Verb</td></tr>
<tr><td>X</td><td>-</td><td>other</td></tr>
<tr><td>-</td><td>AC</td><td>Accusative mark</td></tr>
<tr><td>-</td><td>AGR</td><td>Nouns agreement</td></tr>
<tr><td>-</td><td>FUT</td><td>Future mark</td></tr>
<tr><td>-</td><td>PERS</td><td>Person mark for verbs</td></tr>
<tr><td>-</td><td>TNS</td><td>Verb tense</td></tr>
<tr><td>-</td><td>EMOJ</td><td>Emoji</td></tr>
<tr><td>-</td><td>EMOT</td><td>Emoticons</td></tr>
<tr><td>-</td><td>LINK</td><td>Url or link</td></tr>
<tr><td>-</td><td>MEN</td><td>MEN</td></tr>
<tr><td>-</td><td>REP</td><td>Reply</td></tr>
<tr><td>-</td><td>RET</td><td>Retweet</td></tr>
<tr><td>-</td><td>USERN</td><td>Username</td></tr>
</table>

Table 1: Mapping of Arabic tweets POS to Universal POS tagset. '-' marks unused POS tags.

grained tags mapped to a coarse-grained tag (e.g. DT, PRP, SPRP and WP → PRON). However, there are Arabic tweets POS tags that cannot be mapped to the universal POS tagset. Some of them are related to Twitter phenomena (i.e. REP, MEN, LINK, USERN, RET, EMOT and EMOJ), whereas the others resulting from splitting clitics (i.e. AC, AGR, FUT, PERS and TNS). Therefore, they should be taken into consideration when mapping to the universal tagset. It should be noted that information is lost when fine-grained tags are mapped to coarse-grained tags. Consequently, the relationship and meaning between words and structure is often lost. For example, if we map PRP and WP to PRON then the parser cannot distinguish between ordinary pronouns and relative pronouns. As a result, we will not see that relative clauses have different structures from other clauses. '@' token which is attached with username in tweets has multiple tags. So, assigning tags to tweet items is not an entirely trivial activity. The tagger has also to learn when '@' is a reply and when it is a retweet or a mention (Albogamy and Ramsay 2016).

It is worth mentioning that taggers are generally more accurate on coarse-grained tagsets than fine-grained ones. (Marton et al. 2013) showed that using a fine-grained tagset by a tagger (e.g. MADA) can decrease the accuracy of the parser. This is because the tagger is likely to make more mistakes when using a fine-grained tagset, and these mistakes can have substantial knock-on effects on the performance of the parser. Therefore, we use the coarse-grained tagset in our tagger.

3 Mapping the Arabic tweets dependency scheme to the Universal Dependency scheme

The Universal Dependency scheme (UD15) consists of 41 dependency labels. Table 2 shows the mapping of the Arabic tweets dependency treebank (ATDT) scheme to the UD15 scheme. Some labels in the UD15 annotation scheme do not apply to the Arabic tweets language, marked '-' in Table 2. The mapping process involves some structural changes and it introduces more specific dependency labels as described below.

3.1 Structural changes

coordination The Arabic tweets treebank treats a coordinating conjunction (e.g. و 'and') as the head and the coordinates as its daughter. On the other hand, the universal dependency annotation scheme treats the first coordinate as the head of the coordination, and the rest of the phrase as its daughter to the right.

cop In Arabic language, a copula is used in past tense forms and negated sentences. The copula is treated as a verb in the Arabic tweets treebank. So, it can function as the root of a dependency tree. However, the UD15 scheme treats the predicate as the head of the sentence, and the copula as its daughter.

case vs prepcomp The UD15 scheme attaches the head of a preposition phrase to the verb, and makes the preposition a daughter of the object, saying that it is a case-marker on the noun. On the other hand, the Arabic tweets treebank makes the preposition the head of a prepositional phrase, with the noun labelled as prepcomp (i.e. as the complement of the preposition)

aux vs auxcomp In the Arabic tweets treebank, the non-main (auxiliary) verb in a sentence functions as the head, and this relation is labelled as auxcomp. In the UD15, the auxiliary is usually taken to be a daughter of a verb.

zero-copula Arabic has zero-copula feature. A zero-copula sentence consists of an NP and predications (another NP, an adjective, a PP). In the Arabic tweets treebank, the subject is taken to be the head of a zero-copula sentence whereas the UD15 assumes that the predication is the head of the sentence.

The choice of whether to make a preposition the head or a daughter of the following noun phrase (NP), and of whether to make an auxiliary the head or a daughter of the following verb, depends on the underlying linguistic theory. We are using a version of the grammar of Arabic described by (Alabbas and Ramsay 2012) in which a preposition is taken to be the head of a preposition phrase (PP) and an auxiliary is taken to be the head of a sentence. They undertook experiments that showed that Arabic dependency parsing is more accurate when using the above structures.

3.2 Twitter-specific relations

To use a parser to extract Arabic tweets syntactic structure, we should be familiar with the grammatical structure of Arabic tweets and train the parser on it. Tweets have many phenomena such as mentions, replies, retweets, hashtags, links

and etc. (Albogamy and Ramsay 2015). These elements become parts of tweets text and they will play grammatical roles in this context. In this section, we will discuss the grammatical structure of Arabic tweets.

UD Dependency Label Mappings		
Universal Label	**Arabic Tweets label**	**Gloss**
root	root	root
acl	Whmod	clausal modifier of noun (adjectival clause)
advcl	advcl	adverbial clause modifier
advmod	Advmod	adverbial modifier
amod	-	adjectival modifier
appos	-	appositional modifier
aux	auxcomp	auxiliary
case	predcomp	case marking
cc	cc	coordinating conjunction
ccomp	xcomp	clausal complement
clf	-	classifier
compound	-	compound
cop	-	copula
csubj	Subj	clausal subject
dep	-	unspecified dependency
det	det	determiner
discourse	-	discourse element
dislocated	-	dislocated elements
expl	-	expletive
fixed	-	fixed multiword expression
flat	-	flat multiword expression
goeswith	-	goes with
iobj	-	indirect object
list	-	list
mark	-	marker
nmod	nmod	nominal modifier
nsubj	subj	nominal subject
nummod	-	numeric modifier
obj	obj	object
obl	-	oblique nominal
orphan	-	orphan
parataxis	-	parataxis
punct	-	punctuation
reparandum	-	overridden disfluency
vocative	vocative	vocative
xcomp	xcomp	open clausal complement
-	Link	verbal argument or modifier
-	Men	verbal argument
-	Reply	usually the root
-	Retweet	usually the root
-	Usern	daughter of retweet, or mention or reply
-	Emot	modifier
-	Emoj	modifier

Table 2: Mapping of Arabic tweets treebank scheme to UD15 scheme. '-' marks unused dependency labels.

Arabic tweets have new elements which are not part of the normal Arabic language. These elements have syntactic function in tweets. For example, both the hashtags and the mention in (1) are parts of the tweet syntactic structure.

عندك سؤال عن القبول في #الجامعة ؟   (1)
#محادثة _الجامعةاسال عن طريق برنامج
@UniAdmissionمن لتحصل على اجابة

These new elements cannot be assigned the traditional POS tags. This means that they cannot easily be dealt with using traditional grammar, and hence it is important to discover their grammatical roles. As seen above, these elements are part of tweets so they must have grammatical relations with the rest of tweets, but because they are new parts and do not exist in the MSA grammar we need to know what kinds of relations they have. There are some efforts in the literature aiming at parsing English tweets. In (Kong et al. 2014) they developed a dependency parser for English tweets, but they omitted most of the tweets elements from the material to be parsed which leads to losing parts of the content of the tweet. In contrast, in this research we will try to discover the structures of Arabic tweets by taking into account all tweet constructions and we argue that all the new tweet elements play grammatical roles. One way to discover their grammatical roles is to rewrite tweets in ordinary more formal Arabic and try to preserve the meaning as far as possible, which will help us to understand the relationships between these elements and to analyse tweets structures. We will show a few examples of grammatical functions which can be played by these elements and present their dependency trees.

1. The link in tweet (2) is a Twitter-specific element and functions as the subject of a zero-copula senetence:
   (2) Original tweet صورة لاحد عشاق جيرارد http://t.co/vY0feFK3F2
   Transliteration Gerrard's fans one-of picture http://t.co/vY0feFK3F2
   Paraphrase to MSA http://t.co/vY0feFK3F2 هذه صورة لاحد عشاق جيرارد
   Paraphrase to English http://t.co/vY0feFK3F2 (is) a picture of one of Gerrard's fans

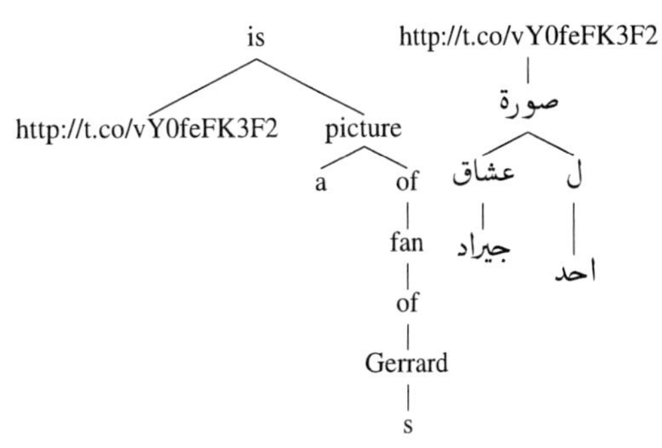

Figure 1: Dependency tree for tweet (2). Left: (English) Right: (Arabic).

2. The link in tweet (3) is a Twitter-specific element and works as a modifier:
   (3)   Original   tweet انها تمطر:http://t.co/mT2feDS5n5
   Transliteration http://t.co/mT2feDS5n5 : raining it's
   Paraphrase   to   MSA http://t.co/mT2feDS5n5 انها تمطر:انظر الصورة
   Paraphrase to English It is raining : see the picture http://t.co/mT2feDS5n5

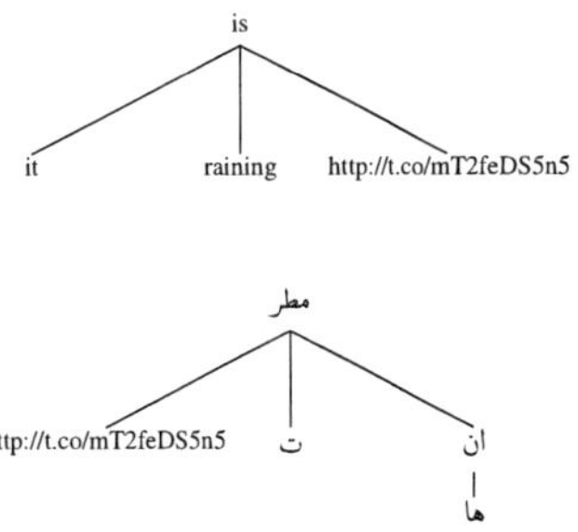

Figure 2: Dependency tree for tweet (3). Top: (English) Bottom: (Arabic).

3. The reply mark is a Twitter-specific element and it is equivalent to "reply to someone" phrase. It works as a verb in tweet (4):
   (4)   Original   tweet انا سويت هذا @AhamedMoh
   Transliteration this did I @AhamedMoh
   Paraphrase to MSA @Ahamed- رد على Moh: انا سويت هذا
   Paraphrase to English Reply to @AhamedMoh: I did this

49

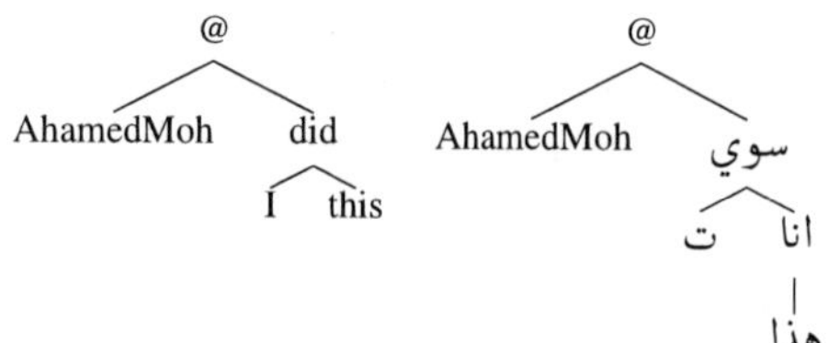

Figure 3: Dependency tree for tweet (4). Left: (English) Right: (Arabic).

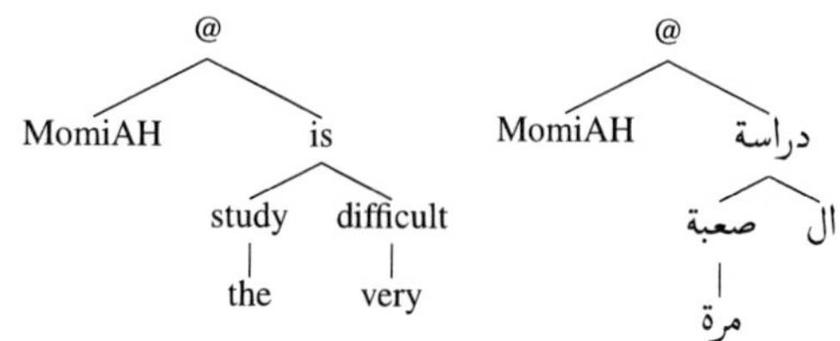

Figure 5: Dependency tree for tweet (6). Left: (English) Right: (Arabic).

4 Conclusion

In this paper, we have explained the importance of a universal annotation scheme in cross-lingual studies (e.g. cross-evaluate parsers). We have described the mapping of the Arabic POS tagset to the universal POS tagset and Arabic tweets dependency treebank to the Universal Dependency scheme. We have explained the mapping and conversion process in detail including structural changes. We have also discussed linguistic analyses of Arabic tweets and motivation for introducing specific dependency labels during the mapping process.

Acknowledgments

The authors would like to thank the anonymous reviewers for their encouraging feedback and insights. Fahad would also like to thank King Saud University for their financial support. Allan Ramsay's contribution to this work was partially supported by Qatar National Research Foundation (grant NPRP-7-1334-6 -039).

4. The mention mark is a Twitter-specific element and works as an object in tweet (5):

(5) Original tweet @FahadTiger انا قابلت اليوم

Transliteration @FahadTiger today met I

Paraphrase to MSA @FahadTiger انا قابلت اليوم

Paraphrase to English I met @FahadTiger today

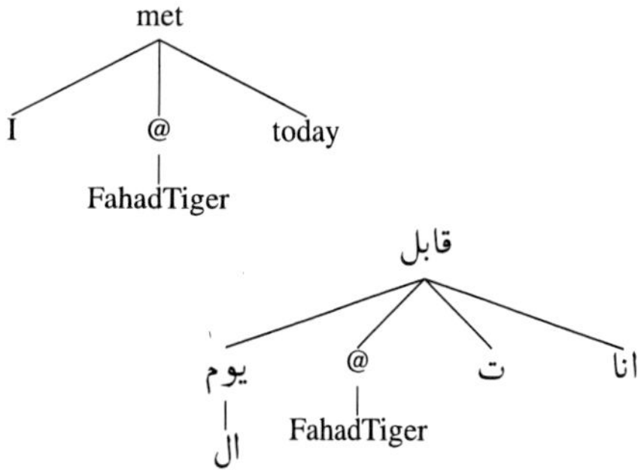

Figure 4: Dependency tree for tweet (5). Left: (English) Right: (Arabic).

5. The re-tweet is a discourse marker and it is equivalent to "someone says" phrase. It works as a verb in tweet (6) :

(6)Original tweet الدراسة صعبة مررررة @MomiAH:

Transliteration very difficult study @MomiAH:

Paraphrase to MSA @MomiAH يقول أن الدراسة صعبة جدا

Paraphrase to English @MomiAH says that the study is very difficult

References

Agic, Ž., M. J. Aranzabe, A. Atutxa, C. Bosco, J. Choi, M.-C. de Marneffe, T. Dozat, R. Farkas, J. Foster, F. Ginter, et al. (2015). Universal dependencies 1.1. *LINDAT/CLARIN digital library at Institute of Formal and Applied Linguistics, Charles University in Prague 3*.

Alabbas, M. and A. Ramsay (2012). Arabic treebank: from phrase-structure trees to dependency trees. In *Proceedings of the META-RESEARCH Workshop on Advanced Treebanking at the 8th International Conference on Language Resources and Evaluation (LREC)*, pp. 61–68.

Albogamy, F. and A. Ramsay (2015). POS tagging for Arabic tweets. In *Proceedings of the Conference on Recent Advances in Natural Language Processing (RANLP)*, pp. 1. Citeseer.

Albogamy, F. and A. Ramsay (2016). Fast and robust POS tagger for Arabic tweets using agreement-based bootstrapping. In *Proceedings of the Tenth International Conference on Language Resources and Evaluation (LREC)*.

Albogamy, F., A. Ramsay, and H. Ahmed (2017). Arabic tweets treebanking and parsing: A bootstrapping approach. In *Proceedings of the Third Arabic Natural Language Processing Workshop (WANLP)-EACL*, pp. 94.

De Marneffe, M.-C., B. MacCartney, Manning, and C. D (2006). Generating typed dependency parses from phrase structure parses. In *Proceedings of the International Conference on Language Resources and Evaluation (LREC)*, Volume 6, pp. 449–454. Genoa.

Kong, L., N. Schneider, S. Swayamdipta, A. Bhatia, C. Dyer, and N. Smith (2014). A dependency parser for tweets. In *Proceedings of the Conference on Empirical Methods in Natural Language Processing, Doha, Qatar*.

Marton, Y., N. Habash, and O. Rambow (2013). Dependency parsing of modern standard Arabic with lexical and inflectional features. *Computational Linguistics 39*(1), 161–194.

McDonald, R., S. Petrov, and K. Hall (2011). Multi-source transfer of delexicalized dependency parsers. In *Proceedings of the Conference on Empirical Methods in Natural Language Processing*, pp. 62–72. Association for Computational Linguistics.

McDonald, R. T., J. Nivre, Y. Quirmbach-Brundage, Y. Goldberg, D. Das, K. Ganchev, K. B. Hall, S. Petrov, H. Zhang, O. Täckström, et al. (2013). Universal dependency annotation for multilingual parsing. In *Proceedings of the Association for Computational Linguistics (ACL)(2)*, pp. 92–97.

Nivre, J., M.-C. de Marneffe, F. Ginter, Y. Goldberg, J. Hajic, C. D. Manning, R. McDonald, S. Petrov, S. Pyysalo, N. Silveira, et al. (2016). Universal dependencies v1: A multilingual treebank collection. In *Proceedings of the 10th International Conference on Language Resources and Evaluation (LREC 2016)*, pp. 1659–1666.

Petrov, S., D. Das, and R. McDonald (2011). A universal part-of-speech tagset. *arXiv preprint arXiv:1104.2086*.

Translating Dialectal Arabic as Low Resource Language using Word Embedding

Ebtesam H Almansor [1,2]**, Ahmed Al-Ani** [1]

[1]Faculty of Engineering and Information Technology, University of Technology Sydney, Sydeny, Australia
[2]Community College, Najran University, Najran, Saudi Arabia
EbtesamHussain.Almansor@student.uts.edu.au
Ahmed.Al-Ani@uts.edu.au

Abstract

A number of machine translation methods have been proposed in recent years to deal with the increasingly important problem of automatic translation between texts of different languages or languages and their dialects. These methods have produced promising results when applied to some of the widely studied languages. Existing translation methods are mainly implemented using rule-based and static machine translation approaches. Rule based approaches utilize language translation rules that can either be constructed by an expert, which is quite difficult when dealing with dialects, or rely on rule construction algorithms, which require very large parallel datasets. Statistical approaches also require large parallel datasets to build the translation models. However, large parallel datasets do not exist for languages with low resources, such as the Arabic language and its dialects. In this paper we propose an algorithm that attempts to overcome this limitation, and apply it to translate the Egyptian dialect (EGY) to Modern Standard Arabic (MSA). Monolingual corpus was collected for both MSA and EGY and a relatively small parallel language pair set was built to train the models. The proposed method utilizes Word embeddings as it requires monolingual data rather than parallel corpus. Both Continuous Bag of Words and Skip-gram were used to build word vectors. The proposed method was validated on four different datasets using a four-fold cross validation approach.

1 Introduction

Globally, social media networking platforms have witnessed a rapid increase in the last few years (Albogamy and Ramsay, 2015). Social media messages usually contain large amounts of noisy text. Thus, issues of the noisy text generation are increasing. A noisy text is an informal text that contains spelling error, slang, dialects and abbreviation (Li and Liu, 2012). Volumes of informal texts require efficient processing and analysis techniques such as sentiment analysis and summarization (Han and Baldwin, 2011). Also, these noisy texts need to be translated to their standard form to be more understandable. Therefore, various studies in Natural Language Processing (NLP) were focused on translating these texts (Han and Baldwin, 2011). This work explores dialectal Arabic translation.

Dialect Arabic words can be treated as non-standard words that are used in Arabic and thus, need to be translated to their standard forms (Sawaf, 2010; El-taher et al., 2016; Shaalan et al., 2007). Dialects are different from the Modern Standard Arabic (MSA), which is the official language in the Arab world. Studies that investigate dialectal Arabic mainly concentrate on rules and statistic level approaches (Sawaf, 2010; El-taher et al., 2016; Shaalan et al., 2007). While, these approaches need more effort to build the rules, however, the rules can not cover all the words. On the other hand, the static approach produced promising results when applied to some other languages, however, it needs large parallel datasets, dictionary and phrase tables (Mikolov et al., 2013).

Parallel corpus is one of the main components in many machine translation approaches (Xiang et al., 2013). However, this represents a big barrier for low resource languages, such as Arabic and its dialects. There are only few small dialectal datasets, such as the one which was constructed

Proceedings of Recent Advances in Natural Language Processing, pages 52–57,
Varna, Bulgaria, Sep 4–6 2017.

by Bouamor et al., (2014). Therefore, in this paper we proposed an effective approach that avoids using large parallel corpus and is based on word embedding.

Word embedding is also known also as distributed word representation (Mikolov et al., 2013). It can be implemented using neural networks with the aim of representing words as vectors based on semantic features. Word embedding was used in numerous NLP tasks, such as classification (Rahmawati and Khodra, 2016), language model (Bengio et al., 2003) and sentiment analysis (Altowayan and Tao, 2016). There are many types of word representation methods including Latent Semantic Analysis (LSA), Latent Dirichlet Allocation (LDA), Word2vec and Glove.

In this work, we employed Word2vec to translate the Egyptian dialect text to the Modern Standard Arabic. Monolingual data sets were collected from publicly available sources and a relatively small language pair set was built to train the model.

2   Related work

Unlike English and other international languages, the number of dialectal Arabic NLP studies that involve translation is relatively low. This could be related to a number of reasons that include the existence of various dialects. Arabic and dialectal Arabic could be considered as closely related languages and hence can be translated at the level of word level or character and rules (Sajjad et al., 2013; Durrani et al., 2010; Salloum and Habash, 2011). Previous research on machine translation of dialectal Arabic has focused on normalizing the dialectal word to MSA. Sajjad et al. (2013) have built character level model that attempts to map between dialect and Modern Standard Arabic (MSA) and train on small parallel corpus (Sajjad et al., 2013). The authors used this model to make the translation between Arabic dialect and English more effective (Sajjad et al., 2013). Another proposed approach that can translate dialect to MSA was developed using character level rule and morphological analysis (Sawaf, 2010). Salloum and Habash (2011) proposed a rule based approach that generate the Modern Standard Arabic paraphrases of the low frequency and out-of-vocabulary (OOV) dialect words (Salloum and Habash, 2011). A hybrid system that maps between the Egyptian Arabic and

MSA using Egyptian-MSA lexicon and morphological analysis was suggested by Abo Bakr et al. (2008). Zbib et al. (2012) built a language model to translate between dialect and English and trained it on a parallel corpus (Zbib et al., 2012). Furthermore, the Tunisian dialect (TUN) was translated to MSA with deep morphological process based on root and pattern (Hamdi et al., 2013). El-taher et al. (2016) built a model that contains rules, dictionary and language model to understand the context of the Egyptian dialect and translate it to MSA (El-taher et al., 2016). Another method was proposed to translate the Egyptian dialect using rules that are built on top of the Buckwalter Arabic Morphological Analyser (Shaalan et al., 2007).

The above approaches are mostly based on rules that can not cover every word. Also the lack of sufficient parallel data set is still a challenge to translate from any dialect to MSA. To overcome these limitations, we proposed a method that uses word embedding to capture semantic and syntactic features of the word without any rules. The proposed approach emanated from a monolingual data sets rather than parallel corpus. In this study, Word2vec is implemented using Skip-gram and Continuous Bag of Words (CBOW) translation models.

3   Proposed approach

3.1   Word2vec Translation Model

Word2vec was introduced by Mikolov et al. (2013) and it aims to present the words as vectors in low domination space. This model has been successfully applied to a number of NLP tasks such as sentiment analysis, translation and classification (Mikolov et al., 2013). It uses simple neural network (NN) for training and it is considered as prediction based model that can capture linguistic features such as semantic feature (Mikolov et al., 2013; Altowayan and Tao, 2016). There are different parameters that were used for learning NN including the window of the context, the size of the features and negative sample. These parameters help the network to learn representations of the word through training the corpus. Also, it attempts to capture words that are semantically similar between the source and target spaces. Word2vec is based on Skip-gram and Continuous Bag-of-Words (CBOW). The architecture of Skip-gram and CBOW are shown in Figure 1.

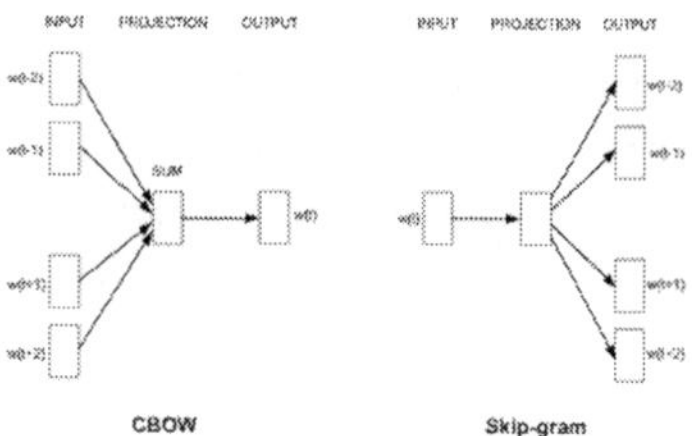

Figure 1: Continuous Bag-of-Word (CBOW) and Skip-gram models (Mikolov et al., 2013)

The model aimed to learn word representation and can be trained on large datasets. The CBOW attempts to predict the target word by combining the distributed representation of its surrounding words whereas, Skip-gram predicts the context by using the distributed representation of the input word (Mikolov et al., 2013). Also, there are two basic training objectives; hierarchical softmax and negative sampling. The Skip gram and CBOW use neural network (NN) to predict the neighbouring words by learning the word representation (Rong, 2014; Enríquez et al., 2016). Moreover, CBOW is fast and appropriate for large corpus while Skip-gram can be trained on small monolingual data sets.

$$skip - gram(D) = \frac{1}{T} \sum_{t=1}^{T} [\sum_{j=-k}^{k} \log p(w_{t+j}|w_t)] \tag{1}$$

$$CBOW(D) = \frac{1}{T} \sum_{t=1}^{T} [\sum_{j=k}^{t-k} \log p(w_j|w_{j+t})] \tag{2}$$

Suppose $D= w_1,..,w_t$ where k is the size of training context, equation (1) aims to maximize the average of log probability to predict the context words w_{t+j} based on the current word w_t (Mikolov et al., 2013). Whereas equation (2) computes the log probability of the target word w_i based on the surrounding words in the context (Chen et al., 2015).

Linear mapping can capture similar vectors from the source and target languages. Therefore, this mapping can learn the word translation matrix between different languages.

Translation matrix is based on a set of word pairs and their vectors. Consider $\{x_i, z_i\}_{i=1}^{n}$, where x_i and z_i are word vectors. These vectors have different dimensions (d_1, d_2), $x_i \in R_{d_1}$ is the representation of word i in source language and $z_i \in R_{d_2}$ is the vector of the translation (Mikolov et al., 2013). The translation matrix can be learned by equation (3)(Mikolov et al., 2013).

$$min \Sigma_{i=1}^{n} ||W_{x_i - z_i}||^2 \tag{3}$$

3.2   Language challenge

The Arabic language is considered as one of the six official languages of the United Nations (Aljlayl and Frieder, 2002; Ibrahim et al., 2015). It is spoken by 300 million people globally and considered to be a morphologically rich language (Cheriet, 2007; Aljlayl and Frieder, 2002). It has different structures from English and other languages. The Arabic language contains 28 letters and is written from right to left. There are two types of Arabic, Modern Standard Arabic (MSA) which is the formal Arabic language used in newspapers and books; and spoken varieties or Arabic dialect (DA), which is the language that is used in daily life and in social media (El-taher et al., 2016). There are different DAs such as Egyptian, Yemeni, Gulf, Iraqi and Levantine (Sajjad et al., 2013). However, these dialects are different from each other depending on the geographical distribution (Habash, 2010).

Arabic Natural Language Processing faces many challenges because Arabic is a morphologically rich language (Salloum and Habash, 2011). Arabic dialects are different from MSA and different from each other. Also, there are different features between dialects and Arabic as there is no rule for written set of grammar. For example, variation might be appeard orthographically, lexically and morphologically (Habash, 2010). In dialects there is no standard orthography which lead every dialects to spell same word in different ways, for instance (ميه ، مويه ، ماء) for water. Also, the ambiguity due to using diacritical marks which called Tashkiil in Arabic, this changes the meaning for the same word for example (شَعَرَ، شَعَر، شَعْر) for hair, feel and poetry respectively, where the diacritical marks make these words that are formed using the same letters having different meanings. Another feature is misspelling in dialect as they spell differently in MSA; for example, the word gold can be written as (ذهب) in MSA and as (دهب) in EGY. Although, these variations between Arabic and the various dialects, there is also similar semantic featuresas a result of similarity between them.

3.3 Pre-processing (Normalization)

Pre-processing is recognized as an essential step for a number of NLP tasks. Text normalization is one type of text pre-processing, which is defined as a process of transforming the non-standard words to their standard forms. For example, 2morrw should be transformed into tomorrow. Text normalization plays a major role in a number of Arabic Natural Language Processing tasks, such as information retrieval which included sentiment analysis, summarization, keywords, and topic detection. Arabic normalization may include deleting the diacritical marks to reduce the ambiguity. Consequently, we appliedd some normalization steps to clean our data sets and prepared them for the translation process. These steps included:

- Tokenization.

- Delete any diacritics from Arabic letter (Tshkula).

- Replace (إ، آ، أ) with (ا), replace (ة) with (ه) , replace (ؤ) with (و)and replace (ئ) with (ى).

- Remove non-Arabic words and punctuation marks (?, !).

4 Experiment and Result

4.1 Building monolingual Corpus

As a basic requirement for machine translation and other NLP tasks, data sets are needed to implement and validate proposed models. Both of parallel data and dictionaries are important for translation tasks. However, Arabic lacks sufficient parallel corpus. We could only find relatively small parallel corpus. Also, unlike some other languages there is no available parallel dictionary for Arabic dialects. Thus, we firstly built monolingual corpus for both the Egyptian and standard Arabic from Wikipedia and different resources that are publicly available. In this experiment we used four datasets for target language; MSA-EGY Wikipedia, bbc-arabic , osac-utf-8 corpus and lastly, cnn-arabic , Table 1 shows details for the data sets. Secondly, for the Egyptian dialect we had to construct a database with a reasonable size that incorporated the parallel data described in (Bouamor et al., 2014).

Table 1: Arabic and Egyptian data sets

Name	size
MSA-EGY Wikipedia	862MB
cnn-arabic	24MB
bbc-arabic	21MB
osac-uft8	178MB
MSA*	89KB
Egyptian*	86KM
Egyptian(own data)	143KM
parallel dictionary	375KM

4.2 Experiment

The following word2vec processes are used to translate the Egyptian dialect to the Modern Standard Arabic. Firstly, we normalized both the Arabic and the Egyptian data sets by using the steps that were mentioned in the pre-processing section. Secondly, two separate word vector models for target and source languages were built using CBOW and Skip-gram models. These models were applied on the data sets that were described in the previous section. The model parameters were set as 100 for the size of features, 5 for window size and 2 for minimum count which mean deleting any word that appear less than two times. Then, translation matrix was trained on the Arabic-Egyptian language pairs. In order to find semantic words translation based on the context, the model was trained on the monolingual data sets. Finally, testing was done in four-fold-cross-validation, i.e., 75% for training and 25% for testing.

4.3 Results

Monolingual data sets were used to evaluate our proposed model using Top@1 and Top@5 accuracy scores and a four-fold-cross-validation approach. As the translation was based on context, the predicted words are expected to be semantically and syntactically related to target words. Figure 2 shows the average accuracy of CBOW for Top@5 and Top@1 when applied to the four data sets of osac-utf8, Wikipedia, bbc-arabic and cnn-arabic, while Figure 3 shows the accuracy of Skip-gram model. The two figures show that CBOW produces better and more consistent results than Skip-gram. More specifically, the CBOW accuracy for all four datasets ranged between 77% and 81% and between 63% and 73%, for the Top@5 and Top@1 scores respectively. On the other hand, apart from the bbc-arabic data set, the Skip-gram was not found to achieve good result for the remaining three data sets (see Table 2). These results pointed out that the CBOW monolingual model was able to capture better semantically related words than Skip-gram. Also, the training time of CBOW is found to be faster than that of Skip-gram. Below are some examples of words and their translation as derived from CBOW and Skip-gram.

- عندهم [لديهم، لديه، لدينا، لديه، ثمه]

- هيبقى [سيبقى، سيظهر، ياخذ، للتاكيد، لايزال]

- إتنازلت [تخلت، استقلت، تخلي، تتنازل، تنازلت]

- ويعيش [ويعيش، يعيش، يتربى، فيعيش، فعاش]

English translation :

- They have[they have, he has, we have, he has, there is]

- Will remain[will remain, will appear, takes, for confirmation, still]

- Waived[waived, abandoned, resigned, waive, give up]

- Live[live, live, grow up, lived, lived]

As presented in the list above the words translated without any rules and some words translated based on the context. Even though, in some cases some words were not correctly translated, they still produced semantically related words e.g. القلق [النوم، والتوتر، والترنح، الدوخه، الترهل] which means in English Anxiety [sleep, tension, grogginess, dizziness, sag] which are all semantically related to the word anxiety.

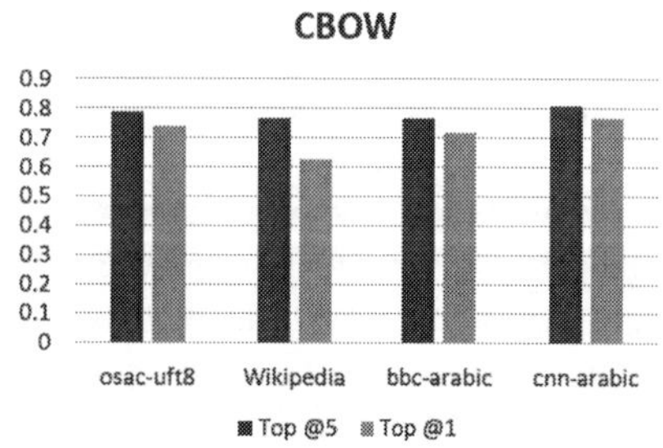

Figure 2: Top@5 and Top@1 for CBOW model.

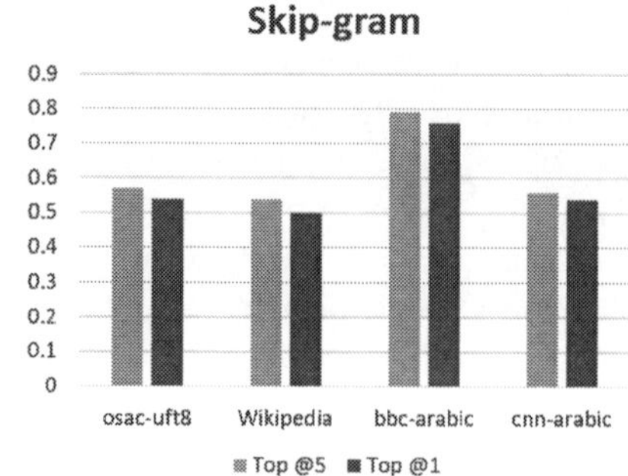

Figure 3: Top@5 and Top@1 for Skip-gram model

Table 2: The average of four-fold-cross-validation of all data sets

Model Name	Data set	Top@5	Top@1
CBOW	cnn-arabic	0.81	0.77
	bbc-arabic	0.77	0.72
	osac-utf8	0.79	0.74
	Wikipedia	0.77	0.63
Skip-gram	cnn-arabic	0.56	0.54
	bbc-arabic	0.79	0.76
	osac-utf8	0.57	0.54
	Wikipedia	0.54	0.50

5 Conclusion

Word embedding is a powerful approach in NLP. In this paper, word2vec was introduced to translate the Egyptian dialect to the Modern Standard Arabi. This approach solves the problem of parallel data as we can train the model on monolingual data. Word2vec has also shown that it can capture semantic features between MSA and EGY without any rules. Even though the model was only tested on small data set, it is expected to also perform well on large data sets. In future work, we plan to investigate the effect of other features at character level and other morphological features.

References

Fahad Albogamy and Allan Ramsay. 2015. POS Tagging for Arabic Tweets. In *RANLP*. pages 1–8.

Mohammed Aljlayl and Ophir Frieder. 2002. On Arabic search: improving the retrieval effectiveness via a light stemming approach. In *Proceedings of the eleventh international conference on Information and knowledge management*. ACM, pages 340–347.

A. A. Altowayan and L. Tao. 2016. Word embeddings for Arabic sentiment analysis. In *2016 IEEE International Conference on Big Data (Big Data)*. pages 3820–3825. https://doi.org/10.1109/BigData.2016.7841054.

Yoshua Bengio, Réjean Ducharme, Pascal Vincent, and Christian Jauvin. 2003. A neural probabilistic language model. *journal of machine learning research* 3(Feb):1137–1155.

Houda Bouamor, Nizar Habash, and Kemal Oflazer. 2014. A Multidialectal Parallel Corpus of Arabic. In *LREC*. pages 1240–1245.

Xinxiong Chen, Lei Xu, Zhiyuan Liu, Maosong Sun, and Huan-Bo Luan. 2015. Joint Learning of Character and Word Embeddings. In *IJCAI*. pages 1236–1242.

Mohamed Cheriet. 2007. Strategies for visual arabic handwriting recognition: issues and case study. In *Signal Processing and Its Applications, 2007. ISSPA 2007. 9th International Symposium on*. IEEE, pages 1–6.

Nadir Durrani, Hassan Sajjad, Alexander Fraser, and Helmut Schmid. 2010. Hindi-to-Urdu machine translation through transliteration. In *Proceedings of the 48th Annual meeting of the Association for Computational Linguistics*. Association for Computational Linguistics, pages 465–474.

Fatma El-zahraa El-taher, Alaa Aldin Hammouda, and Salah Abdel-Mageid. 2016. Automation of understanding textual contents in social networks. In *Selected Topics in Mobile & Wireless Networking (MoWNeT), 2016 International Conference on*. IEEE, pages 1–7.

Fernando Enríquez, José A Troyano, and Tomás López-Solaz. 2016. An approach to the use of word embeddings in an opinion classification task. *Expert Systems with Applications* 66:1–6.

Nizar Y Habash. 2010. Introduction to Arabic natural language processing. *Synthesis Lectures on Human Language Technologies* 3(1):1–187.

Ahmed Hamdi, Rahma Boujelbane, Nizar Habash, and Alexis Nasr. 2013. The effects of factorizing root and pattern mapping in bidirectional Tunisian-standard Arabic machine translation. In *MT Summit 2013*. pages pas–d.

Bo Han and Timothy Baldwin. 2011. Lexical normalisation of short text messages: Makn sens a# twitter. In *Proceedings of the 49th Annual Meeting of the Association for Computational Linguistics: Human Language Technologies-Volume 1*. Association for Computational Linguistics, pages 368–378.

Hossam S Ibrahim, Sherif M Abdou, and Mervat Gheith. 2015. MIKA: A tagged corpus for modern standard Arabic and colloquial sentiment analysis. In *Recent Trends in Information Systems (ReTIS), 2015 IEEE 2nd International Conference on*. IEEE, pages 353–358.

Chen Li and Yang Liu. 2012. Normalization of Text Messages Using Character-and Phone-based Machine Translation Approaches. In *INTERSPEECH*. pages 2330–2333.

Tomas Mikolov, Quoc V Le, and Ilya Sutskever. 2013. Exploiting similarities among languages for machine translation. *arXiv preprint arXiv:1309.4168* .

Dyah Rahmawati and Masayu Leylia Khodra. 2016. Word2vec semantic representation in multilabel classification for Indonesian news article. In *Advanced Informatics: Concepts, Theory And Application (ICAICTA), 2016 International Conference On*. IEEE, pages 1–6.

Xin Rong. 2014. word2vec parameter learning explained. *arXiv preprint arXiv:1411.2738* .

Hassan Sajjad, Kareem Darwish, and Yonatan Belinkov. 2013. Translating Dialectal Arabic to English. In *ACL (2)*. pages 1–6.

Wael Salloum and Nizar Habash. 2011. Dialectal to standard Arabic paraphrasing to improve Arabic-English statistical machine translation. In *Proceedings of the first workshop on algorithms and resources for modelling of dialects and language varieties*. Association for Computational Linguistics, pages 10–21.

Hassan Sawaf. 2010. Arabic dialect handling in hybrid machine translation. In *Proceedings of the conference of the association for machine translation in the americas (amta), denver, colorado*.

Khaled Shaalan, Hitham Bakr, and Ibrahim Ziedan. 2007. Transferring egyptian colloquial dialect into modern standard arabic. In *International Conference on Recent Advances in Natural Language Processing (RANLP–2007), Borovets, Bulgaria*. pages 525–529.

Lu Xiang, Yu Zhou, and Chengqing Zong. 2013. An Efficient Framework to Extract Parallel Units from Comparable Data. In *Natural Language Processing and Chinese Computing*, Springer, pages 151–163.

Rabih Zbib, Erika Malchiodi, Jacob Devlin, David Stallard, Spyros Matsoukas, Richard Schwartz, John Makhoul, Omar F Zaidan, and Chris Callison-Burch. 2012. Machine translation of Arabic dialects. In *Proceedings of the 2012 conference of the north american chapter of the association for computational linguistics: Human language technologies*. Association for Computational Linguistics, pages 49–59.

Using English Dictionaries to generate Commonsense Knowledge in Natural Language

Ali Almiman
University of Manchester
UK, Manchester
M13 9PL
a.almiman@mu.edu.sa

Prof. Allan Ramsay
University of Manchester
UK, Manchester
M13 9PL
allan.ramsay@cs.man.ac.uk

Abstract

This paper presents an approach to generating common sense knowledge written in raw English sentences. Instead of using public contributors to feed this source, this system chose to employ expert linguistics decisions by using definitions from English dictionaries. Because the definitions in English dictionaries are not prepared to be transformed into inference rules, some preprocessing steps were taken to turn each relation of word:definition in dictionaries into an inference rule in the form left-hand side $\Rightarrow$ right-hand side. In this paper, we applied this mechanism using two dictionaries: The MacMillan Dictionary and WordNet definitions. A random set of 200 inference rules were extracted equally from the two dictionaries, and then we used human judgment as to whether these rules are 'True' or not. For the MacMillan Dictionary the precision reaches 0.74 with 0.508 recall, and the WordNet definitions resulted in 0.73 precision with 0.09 recall.

1 Introduction

According to Lin and Pantel (2001), text is considered to be the most important source of human knowledge. Thus, various algorithms have been implemented in the field of text mining, e.g., document clustering Larsen and Aone (1999), identifying prototypical documents Rajman and Besançon (1998), or finding term associations Lin et al. (1998) hyponym relationships Hearst (1992), and discovering inference rules Lin and Pantel (2001). This paper presents another way of extracting inference rules using English dictionaries, for instance: *"X is very old $\Rightarrow$ X is aged", "X use a bicycle $\Rightarrow$ X cycle", "X provide Y $\Rightarrow$ X afford Y" and "X does Y in every occasion $\Rightarrow$ X always Y"*. In some of the natural language processing (NLP) applications, common sense knowledge is considered to be an important topic. One of the common sense resources is inference rules. For instance, consider the query to a textual entailment (TE) system: *T: "The vaccination also affords protection against polio." H: "The vaccination also provides protection against polio."* If the system cannot recognise the relationship between "X afford Y" and "X provide Y", it might not be able to find the entailment between these two sentences. We call them inference rules as they contain directional (asymmetric) relations.

A traditional way of generating inference rules is to write them manually. However, although hand-crafted rules might be very reliable and accurate, they are not the ideal procedure way to follow in order to generate thousands of rules. This is because it consumes a lot of time and effort, and it is not very likely that humans could make a complete set of rules. Some previous attempts have used public contributors to feed their set of common sense knowledge; for instance, Open Mind Common Sense (OMCS) Singh et al. (2002) and YAGO Suchanek et al. (2008) encourage people to participate in feeding their data by playing word games such as Verbosity. Although permitting the public to contribute to databases aids in enlarging these databases, it may also affect the projects credibility as there are no restrictions on the contributors' background and expertise. Another way of discovering inference rules was the work resulting from the Discovery of Inference Rules from Text algorithm (DIRT) by Lin and Pantel (2001). Lin and Pantel have applied a distributional hypothesis to paths in dependency trees in order to extract similar contexts, and then they generate in-

Proceedings of Recent Advances in Natural Language Processing, pages 58–63,
Varna, Bulgaria, Sep 4–6 2017.

ference rules.

In this paper, we want to make parsable rules that can be used in an inference engine that operates over parsed statements and questions. A suitable resource from which to extract inference rules are language dictionaries, as they show relationships between a word and its definition. However, dictionary definitions are not written as inference rules. Therefore, we need to preprocess the definitions into the required form. However, a lot of what can be found in dictionaries cannot be preprocessed into that form; therefore, we used a series of patterns to recognise sentences that will be transformable and subsequently we do the transformation.

The reminder of this paper is organized as follows. In the next section, we illustrate why we have chosen the MacMillan dictionary, followed by a discussion of some preprocessing steps. In section 3, we illustrate the mechanism of how we construct inference rules out of given definitions in The MacMillan dictionary. In section 3, we test the same mechanism on another dictionary (the WordNet definitions). In section 4, we evaluate our work by using human judgment to check the validity of the extracted inference rules. Finally, in section 5, there is a conclusion and future research.

2 The MacMillan Dictionary (TMDC)

A major advantage of language dictionaries is that they offer definitions for each word in a particular language. These definitions may be written differently from one dictionary to another in terms of length and complexity; however, we aim to use shorter definitions in order to make clear and concise inference rules. An appropriate choice for this task is *"The MacMillan Dictionary"* (TMDC), as it is usually utilizes short and patterned sentences in its definitions when compared to other well-known dictionaries, such as the Oxford and Cambridge dictionaries.

2.1 Word Collection

In addition to containing simple-form definitions, TMDC contains a set of 7,500 marked words that are believed to denote 93% of the everyday English words[1]; this set of words is used as the scope for this experiment during the current phase. This

No	Category	Count
1	abbreviation	1
2	adjective	1283
3	adverb	335
4	conjunction	16
5	determiner	10
6	interjection	12
7	modal verb	10
8	noun	3447
9	number	6
10	preposition	22
11	pronoun	33
12	verb	1431
	Total	6,606

Table 1: Collected domain

set of words is not provided in a separate list, and the only way to check whether a word is marked is to look up the targeted word in the dictionary. An automated solution was used to collect these words by employing Wiktionary's top 100,000[2] most frequently-used English words and looking up all of these words. If a word is in red font, it is an important word that needs to be added to our collection. The red words are added to our list of word collection if the source parge of the definition of the target word contains the class `<h1 class="redword">`. Each of these words has a part of speech tag (POS), and for common sense knowledge we are looking for the open class domain words, i.e., nouns, verbs, adjectives and adverbs. Additionally, some words are amongst the important words in one tag and are not in the other tags; e.g., *"knot"* is only added as a noun, not as a verb. After filtering the results, we have a collection of 6,606 words; Table [1] shows the categories of the extracted words and some statistics about them.

2.2 Definitions Extraction

In this step, the definitions for the extracted open-class words from the previous phase are investigated. For each word from the previous step, we have extracted its definitions and saved the word with its POS and definitions in a new dictionary. The target words represent the keys of that dictionary, and each word has an inner-dictionary with

---

[1]Source: http://www.macmillandictionaryblog.com/the-words-you-need-follow-the-red-words-and-stars

[2]If Wicktionary does not list all the tenses and forms for every word, then it is expected that the top 10,000 words is enough to do this step.

```
<span class="DEFINITION" resource="dict-
british"><span class="SEP
DEFINITION-before"> </span>a <a href=
"http://www.macmillandictionary.com/
dictionary/british/person" class="QUERY"
title="person">person</a></span> <div
class="EXAMPLES"...
```

Figure 1: A portion of a definition source page from MacMillan Dictionary

POS and definitions as values within it. To determine the POS, we have looked for the class `<span class="PART-OF-SPEECH">` in the source code, and have only added its definitions if it lies within one of the open-class word tags. Every definition has an example; therefore, it was easy to allocate the definitions on the source page between the definition class `<span class="DEFINITION">` and the examples class `<div class="EXAMPLES">`. Some words in the definitions have their own pages in the dictionary; these words are written in the definition class with a link to their pages. For example, the Figure [1] shows an example for the word (*"person"*) that is listed with the link to its own page in the dictionary.

2.3 Definiens Patterns

In order to generate inference rules out of these definitions, we need to turn each word:definition relationship into a parsable sentence. For instance, the sentence that we would like to receive from the definition *"human: a person"* is: *"X is a human if X is a person"*. Similarly, for all similar definitions, i.e., nouns with definitions constructed of a determiner and a noun should be produced in a similar way. To make rules for producing such sentences, we looked for the most frequently used patterns amongst each of the open-class word definitions. In order to find the most common patterns, we assigned another feature to the dictionary generated from the previous step called *"tagged-definition"*. Each definition has a tagged definition that is a copy of the definition that has been tokenized, and each of its words is assigned to its POS. For instance, the definition *"a person"* has the tagged definition [a!!DT person!!NN], where the two exclamation marks are used to split the word from its POS. To produce these tags, we employ a *"brill tagger"* with the *"Maximum like-*

lihood tagger" as an underlying tagger that are trained on the English treebank from the Universal Dependency Treebank (UDT). After applying this feature to all of the definitions in the dictionary, we have counted how many times each pattern occurrs. A definition pattern is the sequence of the part of speech tags that is written in the tagged definition. From the collected pattern counters, we see that some patterns are used very frequently. Among the noun class definitions, the pattern [DT NN] *"human: a person"* occurs more than 80 times, and the pattern [DT NN NN], e.g., *"advisory: an official warning"* occurs a similar number of times. Within the adjective definitions, the most commonpattern is [RB JJ], e.g., *"ancient: very old"*, used in nearly 90 definitions, and [RB] is repeated more than 40 times amongst the adverbs, e.g., *"absolutely: completely"*. Nearly all of the patterns for the verb definitions begin with TO, and the most frequent pattern is [TO VB DT NN], occurring more than 65 times, e.g., *"conquer: to win a victory."*

2.4 Re-writing Definitions

As mentioned in section [2.3], all of the words obtained and their definitions have to be transformed into complete sentences. To re-write these definitions, there are two main factors that specify the final output of the sentencethe word class, i.e., the noun, verb, adjective or adverb, and the definition pattern.

Nouns:

It is observed that the definition patterns for nouns very often begin with a determiner (DT. In addition to the [DT NN] and [DT NN NN] patterns mentioned earlier, there are other patterns, such as [DT NN IN NN], e.g., *"age: a period of history"* and [DT JJ NN], e.g., *"asset: a major benefit."* Other instances have a different type of determiner; such as cardinals (CD), as in the following definition: *"course: one of the parts of a meal."* By using the capturing groups feature in regular expressions, both DT and CD can be grouped under a determiner group, e.g., `(?P<det>\S*!!(DT|CD)?)`, which means that it announces a group called det that contains any word with one of the following tags (DT or CD), if they exist. For noun definitions, the rule can be straightforward, as most of the extracted patterns are similar; hence, the rule can be written as:

```
("noun", "ˆ(?P<det>\S*!!(DT|CD)?)\s*(?P<MOD>
(\S*!!(IN|JJ|NN|DT)\s*)*)$", "X is a %s
if X is \g<det> \g<MOD>")
```

This regular expression pattern has three parts: the word tag, the definition pattern and the output sentence format. In this example, the word tag is noun, and the second part is looking for definitions that begin with or without a determiner, followed by the rest of the definition. The third part is going to print the string, where %s refers to the word itself and \g<det> \g<MOD> refers to the values for these groups. This single rule may be sufficient to cover all the noun definitions that we obtained in this experiment.

Adjectives:

In general, the extracted examples and patterns for adjective definitions begin with an adverb (RB). For instance, the most common pattern is [RB JJ]; followed by [RB JJ CC JJ], e.g., *"appalling: very unpleasant and shocking"*; and [RB VB], e.g., *"awake: not sleeping."* These definitions can be re-written in a similar way to the nouns. In adjective definitions, it is not common to have articles in their heads (at the beginning of the pattern); therefore, the most common expression pattern for adjectives is

```
("adjective", "ˆ(?P<MOD>(\S*!!(IN|JJ|NN|DT)
\s*)*)$", "X is %s if X is \g<MOD>")
```

This regular expression used to rewrite the previous example as *"X is awake if X is not sleeping."*

Verbs:

Verbs are different than the previous couple of categories as there may be different types of verbs. A verb is called an *intransitive verb* if it does not take an object, e.g., *"He ran"*, or a *transitive verb* if the verb requires an object, e.g., *"He drives a bus for living"*, and a *ditransitive verbs*, when the verb requires two objects *"Maureen gave Dan the pencil"*. All of these types of verbs exist, but the dictionary did not provide enough information about transitivity. Looking at the examples of verb definitions we obtained that contain direct objects, we conclude that there are two distinct forms of objects. An object might occur as a particular word that delivers a special meaning to the definition, e.g., *"cycle: to use a bicycle"*, as there are not many objects that can replace the word "bicycle". Another form of direct object

occurs as generic objects that can take different values, as in *"afford: to provide something."* The general object word "something" can be substituted with any noun, e.g., *"afford a car"* means *"to provide a car"*. So, to make generic rules for verbs, we look for indefinite NPs with empty nouns such as *"something"*, *"someone"*, or *"somebody"*, which we replace with variables. We defined a variable called 'GENERIC' that contains all of the empty noun examples in order to re-write them as variables within the regular expression. In the output, we turn the existing 'GENERIC' into a variable (Y). Consider the following regular expression (regex) pattern:

```
("verb", "ˆ(?P<to>\S*!!TO?)\s*(?P<MV>verb)
(?P<REST1>word*?)(?P<OBJ>GENERIC) \s*
(?P<REST2>word*?)$", "X %s Y if X \g<MV>
\g<REST1> Y \g<REST2>").
```

Using this rule turn an examples such as *"assist: to help someone"* into *"X assist Y if X help Y"*. Similarly, for definitions that contain more than one generic object, we turn *"give: to pass something to someone"* into *"X give Y Z if X pass Y to Z"*.

Adverbs:

Generally, we find the extracted adverb definitions to be very short. There are many cases in which the definition contains only one word, e.g., *"commonly: usually"*. An example of a definition that contains more than one word can be seen in *"always: on every occasion."* An adverb is, generally, used to modify verbs, adjectives, or other adverbs; therefore, variables are introduced in all of their definitions. One word definitions can take the variable just after the definition, e.g., *"X commonly Y if X usually Y"*, according to this rule:

```
("adverb", "ˆ(?P<RB>\S*!!RB?)\s*$", "X %s
Y if X \g<RB> Y")
```

In the other case, in which the definition contains more than one word, the definition often begins with a preposition (IN), so we add an auxiliary verb (does) followed by the variable (Y) in front of the preposition, e.g., *"X always Y if X does Y on every occasion"*, according to the following rule:

```
("adverb", "ˆ(?P<IN>\S*!!IN?)\s*(?P<MOD>
(\S*!!(DT|JJ)\s*)*)(?P<HD>nn*)
(?P<POSTMOD>(\S*!!IN\s*nn\s*)*)$",
"X does Y %s if X does Y \g<IN> \g<MOD>
```

```
\g<HD> \g<POSTMOD>")
```

When we applied these regular expressions to the set of definitions we obtained, we were able to extract 4,613 sentences. Most of these sentences are "nouns", which is not surprising as most of the tokens for words are actually nouns. Nouns are 62.9% of the total generated sentences, followed by verbs which are 28.6%. In contrast, the adjective rules produced only 6.6% of the total sentences generated, and the lowest ranking is for adverbs, which are only 1.8% of the total output.

2.5 Transforming to Inference Rules

In this step, we are turning the sentences obtained from section [2.4] into inference rules of the form: `LHS ⇒ RHS`. All the sentences generated have a form where there is a main-clause followed by an if-clause, where each clause has a shared variable; e.g., X, Y, or both. The example *"X is awake if X is not sleeping"* shows that there is a shared variable (X). If a main-clause precedes an if-clause, a reader can understand it as whenever the if-clause is true, the main-clause is true too. This is a similar notion to the Horn clause inference rules, where for each rule `A ⇒ B`, whenever A is true, then so is B. Inspired by this notion, we converted all of these sentences into rules, in which each rule has an antecedent (left-hand side, LHS) and a consequence (right-hand side, RHS) in the form of `LHS ⇒ RHS`. The consequences of the main-clauses occupying the rules are in the obtained sentences, while if-clauses, excluding the conditional word "if" at the beginning, represent the antecedents of the rules.

To check the validity of our process of making inference rules, we tried the same procedure on another dictionary, which is the *"WordNet Definitions"*.

3 WordNet Definitions (WDFS)

In WordNet, there is a library incorporating the definitions of most of the words it contains, and nearly all of the words that we collected from TMDC exist in WordNet. The difference is that in WordNet, the dictionary deals with the words as synsets that contain all the similar words. For instance, `wordnet.synsets("back")` returns a list of similar items, as follows:

```
[Synset('back.n.01'),
Synset('rear.n.05'),
Synset('back.n.03'),
Synset('back.n.04'),
Synset('spinal_column.n.01'),
Synset('binding.n.05'),
Synset('back.n.07'),Synset('back.n.08'),
Synset('back.n.09'),
Synset('back.v.01'),
Synset('back.v.02'), ... etc].
```

Each of the 117,000 synsets in WordNet are linked together depending on their relational concept, and this explains why we can see synsets other than "back". As they fall in the same synset list, we extracted all the definitions for the synsets of the word "back". As the word class is essential in the rewriting process, we make our search for the synset more precise by looking for `wordnet.synsets("back", "n")` if we want nouns, "v" for verbs, and so on. We collected the words' definitions in a separate dictionary in the same way that we did for TMDC. Next, we applied the regular expressions in section [2.4] to the obtained definitions. We were able to rewrite 3,630 sentences in this collection. Amongst these sentences, nouns represent 56.6% of the domain size, while adjectives represent 31.2% and only 10.5% are adverbs. The most surprising result is that the minority were verbs, which are only 1.7% of the total domain size. The main reason for this is that our very selective regular expression rule was not suitable for the definitions in WordNet, as we expected verb definitions to begin with the word 'to' and contain generic objects.

4 Results

At this stage we have approximately 8,000 inference rules, and the accuracy of these rules must be assessed. To evaluate these rules, we took a random sample of 200 inference rules, 100 rules from each dictionary. We took into consideration the percentage that each word class represents in both dictionaries. The sample rules were uploaded to a web page and native English speakers were asked to see if these rules are correct in regards to both meaning and grammar. For each rule, there are three options: "yes" if a referee believes the rule is correct, "no" if the rule is wrong, and "skip" if the referee was not sure about the answer. As the number of rules is quite large for an online survey, we made the order of rules dynamic so that the rules with fewer answers appear first in the list. Additionally, to get precise percentages, we want to have the same number of answers on all of the questions, so we make the question disappear when there are a certain amount of answers. In this experiment, four answers for each question was our target, and whenever a rule received 75% "yes" answers the rule is considered to be true; otherwise it is false. Of the 200 inference rules, 148 rules were judged as 'true', and from these answers we calculated the precision for each word class; they are presented in Table [2]. To calculate the precision and the recall, we used the following equations [1] and [2],respectively:

$$precision = \frac{R}{100} \qquad (1)$$

$$recall = \frac{R}{100} \times \frac{M}{N} \qquad (2)$$

Where N represents the number of definitions that we were looking at, and M denotes the number of definitions that were picked out as being potential rules. the constant (100) denotes the sample domain size for each dictionary and R means inference rules that were judged 'True'. Applying equation [2] for TMDC, we got 0.68 recall, and 0.126 recall for WDFS.

	TMDC	WDFS	TMDC+WDFS
Nouns	69.3%	76.7%	72.8%
Verbs	78.5%	100%	80.0%
Adj	83.3%	67.7%	70.2%
Adv	100%	72.7%	80.0%
Total	74.0%	73.0%	74.0%

Table 2: TMDC & WDFS sample's precision

The rules obtained from TMDC are slightly more precise than the ones taken from the WDFS, as they were 'True' in 74% of the cases compared to 73% in WDFS, as shown in Table [2]. There are two samples that afforded 100% precision, verbs in WDFS and adverbs in TMDC; this is because we used tight patterns for them, meaning that while we only got a small number of examples, they were very precise.

5 Conclusion

In this paper we have presented an algorithm to extract common sense knowledge. This knowledge is essential for inference systems, as it provides tools that help prove systems can derive a match between two items if they have a relationship. In this experiment, The MacMillan Dictionary and WordNet definitions were used to extract

inference rules from definitions of a set of more than 5,000 important words. Even though the recall was quite low in the WDFS, it gives the impression that if this mechanism was applied to all the +155,000 WordNet definitions[3], it would generate a large number ($\approx$ 14,000) of inference rules. For future research, we are going to extract more inference rules from other dictionaries so that we can build a richer common sense knowledge base.

References

Marti A Hearst. 1992. Automatic acquisition of hyponyms from large text corpora. In *Proceedings of the 14th conference on Computational linguistics-Volume 2*. Association for Computational Linguistics, pages 539–545.

Bjornar Larsen and Chinatsu Aone. 1999. Fast and effective text mining using linear-time document clustering. In *Proceedings of the fifth ACM SIGKDD international conference on Knowledge discovery and data mining*. ACM, pages 16–22.

Dekang Lin and Patrick Pantel. 2001. Dirt - discovery of inference rules from text. In *Proceedings of the seventh ACM SIGKDD international conference on Knowledge discovery and data mining*. ACM, pages 323–328.

Shian-Hua Lin, Chi-Sheng Shih, Meng Chang Chen, Jan-Ming Ho, Ming-Tat Ko, and Yueh-Ming Huang. 1998. Extracting classification knowledge of internet documents with mining term associations: a semantic approach. In *Proceedings of the 21st annual international ACM SIGIR conference on Research and development in information retrieval*. ACM, pages 241–249.

Martin Rajman and Romaric Besançon. 1998. Text mining: natural language techniques and text mining applications. In *Data mining and reverse engineering*, Springer, pages 50–64.

Push Singh, Thomas Lin, Erik T Mueller, Grace Lim, Travell Perkins, and Wan Li Zhu. 2002. Open mind common sense: Knowledge acquisition from the general public. In *OTM Confederated International Conferences" On the Move to Meaningful Internet Systems"*. Springer, pages 1223–1237.

Fabian M Suchanek, Gjergji Kasneci, and Gerhard Weikum. 2008. Yago: A large ontology from wikipedia and wordnet. *Web Semantics: Science, Services and Agents on the World Wide Web* 6(3):203–217.

---

[3] source: http://wordnet.princeton.edu/wordnet/man/wnstats.7WN.html

A Hybrid System to apply Natural Language Inference over Dependency Trees

Ali Almiman
University of Manchester
UK, Manchester
M13 9PL
`a.almiman@mu.edu.sa`

Allan Ramsay
University of Manchester
UK, Manchester
M13 9PL
`allan.ramsay@cs.man.ac.uk`

1 Introduction

In the last decade, there has been a surge of interest in the problem of textual inference, which systems can use to automatically determine whether a hypothesis, H, can be inferred from a given text, T. A variety of approaches have been explored ranging from shallow-but-robust to deep-but-brittle. Systems that have tried to avoid semantic representations have applied shallow techniques on natural language snippets, such as measuring lexical overlaps (Jijkoun and Rijke 2005), extracting pattern-based relations (Romano et al. 2006), or applying approximate matching to predicate-argument structure (Hickl et al. 2006). Although these methods are robust and effective, they are not suitable for problems that require multi-steps of inference, such as in the FraCaS multi-premise problems that follow, because the task that they are designed to address simply does not involve applying sequences of rules:

P1: Both leading tenors are excellent.
P2: Leading tenors who are excellent are indispensable.

H: Both leading tenors are indispensable.

Multi-step inferences are more usually carried out by transforming the given sentences into formal representations and then applying a theorem prover to check inferential validity, as described by Akhmatova (2005). Although these approaches can solve multi-step inferences, they are limited by the difficulty of extracting formal paraphrases from freely occurring texts (MacCartney and Manning 2007). In particular, such systems generally require the input texts to be analysed in terms of a grammar with semantically annotated rules. The widespread occurrence of ambiguous and, worse, extra- and a-grammatical

sentences makes this extremely challenging.

In this work, we explore a different way to deal with this problem by developing a theorem prover that accepts natural language dependency trees instead of translating them into a logical format. All the sentences are parsed using a version of MALT-Parser[1] trained on the Penn TreeBank. This has the advantage that we do not need to annotate the rules of the grammar with semantic interpretations (indeed, there **is** no grammar to annotate) and that we can do at least something useful with ill-formed or otherwise anomalous texts.

2 The Hybrid System

2.1 Building a Theorem Prover

To make an inference engine that can benefit from background knowledge, we must utilize an idea that is similar to existing theorem provers. Since all of the inference rules that we use in this experiment are Horn clauses, we mimicked the strategy that works well for proving Horn clauses in existing theorem provers. Consider the standard rule of modus ponens for propositional logic:

$$B \to A, B \vdash A \qquad (1)$$

This suffices as the basis for a simple backward-chaining inference engine for Horn clauses, which can be used to capture a substantial portion of the kind of knowledge that underpins natural language.

We will rewrite this rule as (2) to enable generalisation to first-order logic and thence to our system. This version of the rule introduces a step which would lead to substantial inefficiency if it were implemented in a simple-minded way for propositional logic, but which leads very naturally

---

[1]The acronym stands for the Models and Algorithms for Language Technology Parser, and it is freely available at http://www.maltparser.org

Proceedings of Recent Advances in Natural Language Processing, pages 64–70,
Varna, Bulgaria, Sep 4–6 2017.

to the version used in standard first-order theorem provers.

$$B \rightarrow A', A = A', B \vdash A \qquad (2)$$

In first-order logic (FOL), a theorem prover can prove (A) if Rule [3] applies, where A is **unified** rather than identified with a term that leads to B.

$$B \rightarrow A', A \oplus A', B \vdash A \qquad (3)$$

From the rules [2 and 3], it can be seen that the main difference is the matching relationship between the items A and A'. We have as a general rule that you can infer A from B and $B \rightarrow A'$ if A and A' are equivalent: in propositional logic, two formule are equivalent if they are identical; and in first-order logic they are equivalent if they are unifiable. But this suggests that we could obtain other kinds of logic by exploring other notions of equivalence, e.g. the kind of matching algorithm used in textual entailment systems ($\approx$) as in Rule [4].

$$B \rightarrow A', A \approx A', B \vdash A \qquad (4)$$

Before it looks for inference rules, the inference engine checks whether there is any fact that approximately matches the goal using the rule [5]

$$A', A \approx A' \vdash A \qquad (5)$$

.

2.1.1 Approximate matching

It is possible to obtain a variety of logics by changing the matching algorithm: Pulman (1997), for instance, proposes a unification algorithm that allows predicates as well as terms to be treated as variable to allow for a range of higher-order phenomena. The approximate matching relation we propose is defined as follows.

Let T and T' be two dependency trees with heads H, H' and sets of daughters D, D', where D and D' may be empty. Then $T \approx T'$ if

(i) H is a hypernym of H', as proposed byBaroni et al. (2012). We use WordNet as a source for determining hypernym relations between open-class words. For instance, *"I found a cat"* $\approx$ *"I found an animal"*, because *"cat"* $\sqsubset$ *"animal"*. In addition to relationships between WordNet open-class words, we made some hierarchical relationships between generalized quantifiers according to

suggestions from the literature on natural logic (MacCartney and Manning 2008; Icard 2012; Vendler 1962; Kayne 2007; Poesio 1994; Barwise and Cooper 1981). The highest level of that hierarchy is shared between the following quantifers: *all = every = each = (the + plural)*. Some other relationships are: *most $\sqsubset$ many, many $\sqsubset$ some, a few $\sqsubset$ some* and *each $\sqsubset$ several*. If there are three quantifiers (α, β, σ), where $\alpha = \beta$ and $\alpha \sqsubset \sigma$, then we conclude that the relationship is $\beta \sqsubset \sigma$. Therefore, all of the root-level words have the same subsumption relationship with the other quantifiers. For example, from *"all"* = *"every"*, and *"all"* $\sqsubset$ *"some"*, we conclude that *"every"* $\sqsubset$ *"some"*, *each$\sqsubset$ "some"* and so on.

(ii) There is an order-preserving mapping m from D into D' such that

   (a) $D_i \approx m(D_i)$ for every D_i in D
   (b) if D'_j is not in the range of m then D'_j is headed by a modifier (i.e. an adjective or a preposition)

The first part of this allows us to match sentences where the premise contains a word that is a hypernym of some word in the hypothesis.

Consider the pair *T: "He saw a man"* and *H: "He saw a human"*, and assume that the parse trees for these two are `[saw: VB, [he: PN], [man: NN, [a: DT]]]` and `[saw: VB, [he: PN], [human: NN, [a: DT]]]`. These trees will match because as we recurse down through them we find that every subtree in the first is headed by a hypernym of the corresponding subtree in the second.

The second part allows us to skip modifiers; thus, if the subtree in T has an extra modifier, the approximate matching algorithm is allowed to skip that modifier and tries to match the rest. For example, *T: "He saw a fat man"* and *H: "He saw a human "*; when the system tries to find the match between `[man: NN, [fat: JJ]]` and `[human: NN]`, it unifies *"man"* with *"human"*, and skips the adjective.

Also, the system is allowed to skip prepositional modifiers, e.g., *T: "He saw a man in the gymnasium"* and *H: "He saw a human"*, because the subtree *'in the gymnasium'* is headed by a modifier. This makes it possible to cope with examples that could not be handled if we treated the texts as strings and used a string-edit algorithm.

(iii) Both the word-level and the phrase-level matching algorithms are asymmetric. For instance, in *I saw a man $\subseteq$ I saw a human*, if someone saw a man that means the person saw a human; however, *I did not see a man $\not\subseteq$ I did not see a human*. To handle this issue, we add polarity marking to lead the direction of matching. By default, every node of a parsed tree gets a positive mark (+), which means that the context is positive and the matching direction works from left to right. There is a list of words that swap the direction of matching if they exist; e.g., *"no, not, doubt"*, if any of these words is present, then the polarity marking is swapped for all its daughters. There is a list of words that change the direction of the matching if they occur; e.g., *"no, not, doubt"*. If any of these words occur, it changes the polarity marking for all the following nodes. For instance *"I doubt that he likes it"* is turned into `[(doubt,+), [(I,-)], [(likes,-), [(that,-)], [(he,-)], [(it,-)]]]`.

It is important to note that this matching algorithm is non-deterministic: a tree may contain several modifiers, and it may be that choosing to skip over one rather than another will have consequences at a later stage of analysis.

2.1.2 Backward chaining

As mentioned above, to do a proof this system requires set of facts and a set of inference rules in addition to the goal sentence and tries to deduce the proof using a backward-chaining algorithm. This means that it begins with the goal sentence and looks for a matching sentence in the set of facts. If there is no fact that matches this goal, the system looks through the rules to find an inference rule that leads to the given text, T. If that rule is found, the system tries to prove its antecedent. As proving the antecedent is not guaranteed, this algorithm is also a non-deterministic algorithm. We thus have a combination of non-deterministic algorithms: it is important to interweave these ap-

propriately – it may that the backward-chaining algorithm fails if we match the daughters of a pair of trees one way but will succeed if we match them differently (e.g. by skipping over different modifiers). Given that these are independent sets of choices, maintaining the two choice stacks is a challenge. We deal with this issue by using continuation programming (Landin 1998), using the standard call stack as the backtrack stack amd treating return from a function call as failure.

2.2 Inference rules

The backtracking algorithm outlined above requires us to have a collection inference rules. For instance, to find the relationship between *T:"He saw a man in the gymnasium"* and *H: "He saw a man in the large room with equipment for exercising the body"*, there is an inference rule that states: `'X is a large room with equipment for exercising the body ⇒ X is a gymnasium.'` This kind of rule is definitional, and there is no available source that we know of that uses such inference rules in natural language representation. In most cases, the existing inference rules either annotate their information with some special symbols, e.g., (...), or written as paraphrasing sentences; e.g., DIRT (the discovery of inference rules from text). The former status does not suit our needs as we are trying to avoid logical annotations, and the latter looks for symmetrical relations while we are looking for asymmetrical relations. From this point of view, we made our set of definitional inference rules in Section [2.2.1]. To solve multiple hypothesis tasks, we are looking for inference rules that contain more than one item on the left hand side (LHS) and one on the right hand side (RHS). Therefore, a set of syllogistic inference rules were extracted from the FraCaS multiple-premise examples, and they are presented in Section [2.2.2].

2.2.1 Definitional inference rules

One of the richest sources in which to find definitional information are language dictionaries. Therefore, we chose a selection of 5,000 words from The MacMillan Dictionary (TMDC) and converted the definitions from the form (word:definition) into an inference rule, such as `X is a defintion ⇒ X is a word`, where X is a variable. To make this transformation, we make the word:definition relationship into a sentence and parse it; for instance, we turn the definition *"aged: very old"* into *"X is aged if X is very old"*. The forms of these sentences vary depending on the category of the word. For nouns and adjectives, we turned all the definitions from word:definition into `"X is word if X is a definition"`. We have established two different types of definitions for verbs. A verb is called *"intransitive"* if it does not take an object, such as *"He ran"*; and a verb is called *"transitive"* if it requires an object, such as *"He drives a bus for living."* To make generic rules for verbs, we look for indefinite NPs with empty nouns such as *"something", "someone",* or *"somebody",* which we replace with variables. For instance, *"afford: to provide something"* has been turned into `"X afford Y if X provide Y"` and *"run: to move quickly to a place using legs and feet"* into *"X run if X move quickly to a place using legs and feet"*. It is very very common to have one-word definitions of adverbs, such as: *"commonly: usually"*, and as adverbs are used as modifiers in English sentences we turn them into `"X commonly Y if X usually Y"`. There are cases where an adverbs definition contains more than one word, such as, *"always: on every occasion"*. These words are turned into `"X always Y if X does Y on every occasion"`. At this stage, we have a main-clause followed by an if-clause, and each clause has a shared variable. To transform these sentences into inference rules, we replace the conditional word *"if"* with a right arrow ($\Rightarrow$) and bring the if-clause as an antecedent and the main-clause as a consequence of that rule; e.g., `"X is very old ⇒ X is aged"`.

2.2.2 Syllogistic inference rules

To handle multi-step inference tasks, inference rules with multiple antecedents were extracted from the FraCaS test suite. Multiple-premise FraCaS examples were used because they have words that are shared in both the hypothesis H and the premise $P's$; also, they are marked for their inferential validity. The task is to replace any open-class shared word into a variable. For instance, the example in Figure [1] is transformed into the inference rule in Figure [2].

P1: "Both leading tenors are excellent."
P2: "Leading tenors who are excellent are indispensable."

H: "Both leading tenors are indispensable."

Figure 1: A multi-premise FraCaS example

P1: "Both X are Y."
P2: "X who are Y are Z."

H: "Both X are Z."

Figure 2: A form of syllogistic inference rule

After parsing these sentences, the final form of the syllogistic inference rule will be:

```
[[are:  VX, [?Y: NN, [both:  DT],
[?X: JJ]], [?Z: JJ]], [?Y: NN,
[?X: JJ], [are:  VX, [who:  WP],
[?Z: JJ], [are:  VX, [?A: JJ]]]]
⇒ [are:  VX, [?Y: NN, [both:
DT], [?X: JJ]], [?A: JJ]]
```

These rules were extracted from all of the two-premise FraCaS problems that are judged to be entailed.

2.3 Proving process

When the theorem prover receives an input of both a premise and a goal, it starts from the goal and works toward the hypothesis. A proof can be found from the first step, such as when the inference engine successfully found a fact that approximately matches the given goal. If none of the facts match the goal, then the theorem prover looks at the inference rules; is there is any rule with a head that matches the goal? When no rule's head matches the goal, then there is no way to prove this goal. If there is only one rule with a matching head, then the inference engine sets the head as a new goal and tries to prove the premise using the same steps as the first goal. This step can be done repeatedly until the engine finds a way of getting to a block. If more than one rule is suitable the engine tries all of them in turn. If it fails with the first rule, then it tries the second, and so on, until it finds the proofif it exists. Every variable in the rules has a value, and the value for free variables is `'???'`. The theorem prover can bind any value to free variables, and when the proof is complete an unbind step is taken to free these variables.

Algorithm 1 Pseudo-code for the theorem prover

```
 1: prove ( goal, facts, rules, contn )
 2:    if goal = [] :
 3:       contn()
 4:    if isList(goal) :
 5:       prove(hd(goal), facts, rules,
          lambda: prove(tl(goal), facts,
          rules, contn))
 6:    else:
 7:       for f in facts:
 8:          match(goal, f, contn)
 9:          ⊙
10:       for LHS → RHS in rules:
11:          match(goal, RHS, lambda:
          prove(LHS, facts, rules, contn))

12:          ⊙
```

In Algorithm [1], there is an illustration of the steps that the theorem prover takes. We reach the points marked with ⊙ only if the previous step fails; i.e., if using the fact or rule did not lead to a proof. At that point, we automatically move to the next choice. Figure 3 shows the interactions between the search for a useful fact or rule and the approximate matching algorithm: note in particular that there are three places where something gets added to the backtrack stack – after a fact is found, after some way of matching a rule to the current goal is found, and after that rule has been chosen. When a branch of the search space fails, the algorithm will uniformly pick any one of these stored choices to explore.

3   Evaluation and Results

From Section [2.2], we were able to extract 4,613 definitional inference rules. Unsurprisingly, most of these rules were extracted from nouns as they represent 62.9% of the total words, followed by verbs, representing 28.6%. Adjectives comprise only 6.6% of the words, and the lowest number of words are adverbs, comprising only 1.8% of the total number of rules. To evaluate these rules, we have randomly extracted a sample of 100 rules, considering the percentage that each word category covers. Therefore, the greatest number of the sample rules were for nouns, followed by verbs, and so on. This sample was uploaded as an on-

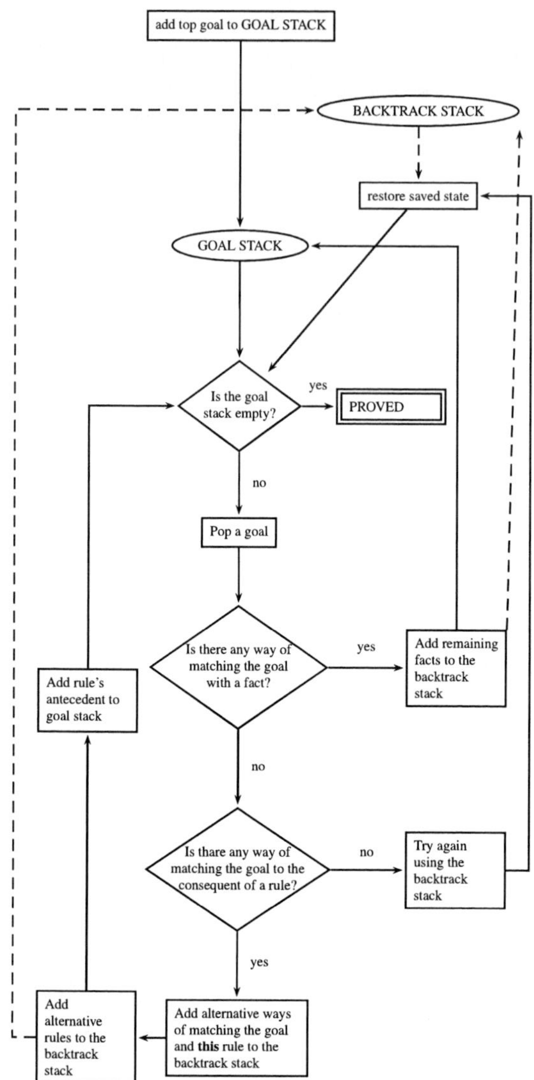

Figure 3: Overall architecture

line survey, and we asked native speakers to check whether these are true inference rules or not. For each rule, there are three options. *"Yes"*, if a referee believes the rule is correct; *"No"*, if the rule is wrong; and *"Skip"*, if a referee is not sure about the answer. Each question was limited to four answers, so whenever a question (rule) received four answers it disappeared from the survey to make sure that we have a similar quantity of opinions on all of our sample rules. After obtaining the survey results, we calculated the precision and the recall using the following equations, [6] and [7], respectively:

$$Precision = \frac{R}{100} \qquad (6)$$

$$Recall = \frac{R}{100} \times \frac{M}{N} \qquad (7)$$

Where N represents the number of definitions that we were looking at, and M denotes the number of definitions that were picked out as being potential rules. The constant (100) denotes the sample domain size, and R denotes the inference rules that were judged as True. From the previous equations, we got 74.0% precision with a recall of 0.68. Using the FraCaS examples, we have applied two different tests: (a) single premise problems test, and (b) a double premise problems test.

For single premise problems, we only employ our approximate matching features as the problems only contain a single premise with a single hypothesis. Amongst the 192 single premise problems that FraCaS test suite has, there are nine problems with an 'undefinite' answer, so they were excluded. MacCartney and Manning (2007) label some answers as 'undefinite' if they lack either hypothesis or well-defined answers. From the remaining 183 problems, we extracted the number of problems for which we could glean the right tree; the number of trees extracted totaled 70 sentences. These problems spread over nine different topics, and most of these topics require more robust parsers and matching techniques, such as anaphora and ellipsis. Therefore, we did the first test on two topics to which we can apply our approximate matching algorithms, which are generalized quantifiers and adjectives. By excluding the non-related topics, the number of problems was reduced to 28. When this system proves a problem, it is marked as a yes; otherwise both no and unknown answers are marked as no. Table [1] details the number of problems that our system observed, and shows how many times the system received a right answer. The four columns under the approximate matching table cell illustrate the status of each technique in each of the four tests. The first test is carried out by switching the word relations on (denoted in the table as: σ), and switching off the other techniques, i.e., detHyps (γ) and skipping modifiers (δ). The last line shows how many right answers can be received when all three techniques are switched on.

Topic	Q	Approximate matching techniques			
		$\sigma = 1$ $\gamma = 0$ $\delta = 0$	$\sigma = 0$ $\gamma = 1$ $\delta = 0$	$\sigma = 0$ $\gamma = 0$ $\delta = 1$	$\sigma = 1$ $\gamma = 1$ $\delta = 1$
Quant	20	12	12	19	19
Adj	8	5	5	6	7
Total	28	17	17	25	26

Table 1: First test on 28 single-premise FraCaS problems

For double-premise problems, we use our set of syllogistic rules that are actually generated from the same set of problems. Since our system is able to bind items to free variables, we were able to make all of the double-premise examples. However, we were looking for generic rules that can be used for more than one example, and consequently we reduced the number of rules used. From the 74 double-premise rules that we have extracted from the set, we were able to find only four generic rules that are able to solve more than one problem; these are shown in Table [2].

Generic rule	Problem No.
G.R(1)	`fracas-002`
	`fracas-003`
G.R(2)	`fracas-066`
	`fracas-067`
	`fracas-068`
G.R(3)	`fracas-134`
	`fracas-135`
G.R(4)	`fracas-157`
	`fracas-159`

Table 2: A list of the FraCaS examples covered by generic rules

The number of generic rules and the examples that they cover could be extended if we did not face the issue of getting different trees for quite similar sentences. This problem, however, is common with data-driven parsers and it has been mentioned by Kouylekov and Magnini (2005), who found more than 30% of similar trees in their test set parsed differently. In FraCaS problems, the shared words are always identical, therefore, there are no available examples to test the approximate matching techniques. Regarding to this problem, we have made up a test by replacing some identical terms to approximatly match terms and checked the sanity of our system on these problems.

4 Conclusion

In this paper, we have explored a new approach to solve natural language inference issues. To make shallow systems less shallow, we applied dependency trees to theorem provers in order to benefit from the advantages of avoiding the step of translating sentences to logic. What we have found is that it is important to have correct trees, and because no reliable, data-driven dependency parser exists, the problem is considered to be very difficult. One way to overcome this problem is by using a chunker instead of parsers, as this system is able to deal with any kind of tree. Another modification is that we add a full stop at the end of each sentence, and then we make that final full stop the root of the tree, and we chunk its daughters. This move makes it easier to control the shapes of trees, but similar to the issue for rule-based parsers that there is no complete set of rules can be written.

References

Elena Akhmatova. 2005. Textual entailment resolution via atomic propositions. In *Proceedings of the PASCAL Challenges Workshop on Recognising Textual Entailment*. Citeseer, volume 150. 1

Marco Baroni, Raffaella Bernardi, Ngoc-Quynh Do, and Chung-chieh Shan. 2012. Entailment above the word level in distributional semantics. In *Proceedings of the 13th Conference of the European Chapter of the Association for Computational Linguistics*. Association for Computational Linguistics, pages 23–32. 2

Jon Barwise and Robin Cooper. 1981. Generalized quantifiers and natural language. *Linguistics and philosophy* 4(2):159–219. 2

Andrew Hickl, John Williams, Jeremy Bensley, Kirk Roberts, Bryan Rink, and Ying Shi. 2006. Recognizing textual entailment with lccs groundhog system. In *Proceedings of the Second PASCAL Challenges Workshop*. volume 18. 1

Thomas F Icard. 2012. Inclusion and exclusion in natural language. *Studia Logica* pages 1–21. 2

Valentin Jijkoun and M Rijke. 2005. Recognizing textual entailment using lexical similarity. In *Proceedings Pascal 2005 Textual Entailment Challenge Workshop*. 1

Richard S Kayne. 2007. Several, few and many. *Lingua* 117(5):832–858. 2

Milen Kouylekov and Bernardo Magnini. 2005. Recognizing textual entailment with tree edit distance algorithms. In *Proceedings of the First Challenge Workshop Recognising Textual Entailment*. pages 17–20. 6

Peter J Landin. 1998. A generalization of jumps and labels. *Higher Order Symbolic Computation* 11(2):125–143. 3

Bill MacCartney and Christopher D Manning. 2007. Natural logic for textual inference. In *Proceedings of the ACL-PASCAL Workshop on Textual Entailment and Paraphrasing*. Association for Computational Linguistics, pages 193–200. 1, 6

Bill MacCartney and Christopher D Manning. 2008. Modeling semantic containment and exclusion in natural language inference. In *Proceedings of the 22nd International Conference on Computational Linguistics-Volume 1*. Association for Computational Linguistics, pages 521–528. 2

Massimo Poesio. 1994. Discourse interpretation and the scope of operators. Technical report, DTIC Document. 2

S G Pulman. 1997. Higher order unification and the interpretation of focus. *Linguistics & Philosophy* 20(1):73–115. 2

Lorenza Romano, Milen Kouylekov, Idan Szpektor, Ido Dagan, and Alberto Lavelli. 2006. Investigating a generic paraphrase-based approach for relation extraction. In *EACL*. 1

Zeno Vendler. 1962. Each and every, any and all. *Mind* 71(282):145–160. 2

Ensembles of Classifiers for Cleaning Web Parallel Corpora and Translation Memories

Eduard Barbu

Institute Of Computer Science / University of Tartu

eduard.barbu@ut.ee

Abstract

The last years witnessed an increasing interest in the automatic methods for spotting false translation units in translation memories. This problem presents a great interest to industry as there are many translation memories that contain errors. A closely related line of research deals with identifying sentences that do not align in the parallel corpora mined from the web. The task of spotting false translations is modeled as a binary classification problem. It is known that in certain conditions the ensembles of classifiers improve over the performance of the individual members. In this paper we benchmark the most popular ensemble of classifiers: Majority Voting, Bagging, Stacking and Ada Boost at the task of spotting false translation units for translation memories and parallel web corpora. We want to know if for this specific problem any ensemble technique improves the performance of the individual classifiers and if there is a difference between the data in translation memories and parallel web corpora with respect to this task.

1 Introduction

Translation memories are databases that store sentence segments in one language with their corresponding translation in another language. The origin of translation units in translation memories is diverse. Mostly, they come from professional translators, but some translation memory databases (e.g. MyMemory (Trombetti, 2009)) accept contributions from online contributors. Translation memories are integrated in computer-assisted translation tools and they are among the most used repositories of information by professional translators. For various reasons (e.g. the negligence of the translators, malicious users that spam through collaborative interfaces), a significant number of translation units in translation memories are false translations.

However, a similar resource can be obtained by mining the web (or large crawled documents repositories like Common Crawl) for parallel corpora. The pipeline for web mining starts with parallel sites discovery, parallel web documents identification and finishes with the alignment of parallel sentences in the documents. The resulting resource contains errors. This happens because either the automatic document pairing fails or because the sentence aligning fails.

Below there is an example of two translation units for the language pairs English-Italian and English-French that should be discarded.

1. An example for English-Italian language pair extracted from a translation memory.
   English segment. Weight loss category.
   Italian segment. Studi sulle linee di categoria.
   English translation of the Italian segment : "Studies concerning categories".

2. An example for English-French language pair produced by mining the web.
   English segment. The hotel has a minivan shuttle and took us on a complementary basis to several places which were a bit far to walk as one of us was injured skiing.
   French segment. Nous allons vivre un moment magique...aperitif dans la "bodega" , puis menu degustation dans une petite salle intimiste.
   English translation of the French segment: "We will live a magic moment ... aperitif in

Proceedings of Recent Advances in Natural Language Processing, pages 71–77,
Varna, Bulgaria, Sep 4–6 2017.

the "bodega", then menu tasting in a small intimate room."

The pace at which translation memories grow nowadays and the web parallel corpora are built makes it impossible to perform manual cleaning[1]. Given the size of modern translation memories and parallel corpora, automatic solutions have been proposed. They state the problem as a binary classification task. Given a translation unit, a classifier should return "yes" if the segments in the translation unit are true translation and "no" otherwise.

In this paper we explore various methods for building ensembles of classifiers to tackle the problem of spotting false translations in translation memories and web parallel corpora. It has been shown (Dietterich, 2000) that the ensembles of classifiers can work better than the individual classifiers in certain conditions. We want to know what the difference is between the data coming from web parallel corpora and the data coming from translation memories with respect to this task.

The rest of the paper has the following organization. The next section presents the related work. In section 3, the features used and the ensemble of classifiers are introduced. In section 4 we describe the data used for training and testing the classifiers and the results of the classifiers evaluation. The paper ends with the conclusions.

2 Related Work

Most people that mine large corpora from the web use Gale-Church score (Gale and Church, 1993) to filter the translation units. Please notice that Moses statistical machine translation engine includes a python script[2] for this purpose. However, this simple technique is clearly insufficient as none of the translation units in the examples above can be discarded with the Gale-Church score. According to our knowledge, the first study that uses a classifier to identify sentences that are translations in (comparable) corpora is Munteanu (2005). They use a maximum likelihood classifier trained on a set of features that are similar to the word alignment features we use (see section 3 for details) .

In Barbu (2015) we were the first to train a set of supervised classifiers to spot false translations in translation memories. An unsupervised approach for the same task was proposed in Jalili Sabet (2016). They use a set of features that capture the similarity between the segments in a translation unit, use them to induce training labels and train a set of base classifiers with Extremely Randomized Trees (Geurts et al., 2006). The most relevant attempts to spot false translation units in translation memories are surveyed in Barbu (2016). One of the most successful systems is trained not only on features related to translation quality, but also on features related to grammatical errors and features related to fluency and lexical choice (Wolff, 2016).

The previous supervised works focused on tuning and evaluation of the individual classifiers. The only research that uses ensemble of classifiers are Barbu (2015) which trained a Random Forest and Jalili Sabet (2016) which used Extremely Randomized trees. However, they did not attempt to combine individual classifiers in a systematic way and compare the performance of the individual classifiers with the performance of the ensembles of classifiers. Moreover, we are the first to test the classifiers on data coming from both parallel corpora and translation memories in a multilingual setting. This is important because there are data providers that want to clean the translation memories and the data collected from the web using a single trained model per language pair.

3 Classification

In this section we first present the individual classifiers and the motivation for choosing them, then the ensemble of classifiers and finally the features computed for the translation units to be classified.

3.1 Classifiers

The individual classifiers selected are among the widely used classifiers in the literature : *Decision Tree*, *Logistic Regression*, *Support Vector Machines* with the linear kernel, *Support Vector Machines* with the radial basis function kernel, *K-Nearst Neighbors*.

The ensembles of classifiers are meta-classifiers that combine the results of multiple classifiers. We presume that the ensemble of classifiers has a better generalization performance than the individual classifiers. We have explored the following popu-

---

[1] For example, MyMemory receives approximately 15 million contributions per month.

[2] The script is called gacha.py

lar ensemble techniques.

- *Majority Voting.* The meta-classifiers' predicted class is the class mostly voted by the individual classifiers. For example, if we have an ensemble composed of three classifiers and the vote assigned to a translation unit is (1,1,0), that is the first two classifiers predict that the result is positive and the third classifier that the result is negative, then the meta-classifier chooses the positive class. It can be proven that if the classifiers are independent and the error rated are not correlated, then the majority voting error rate is lower than the individual classifiers error rate (Dietterich, 2000).

- *Stacking.* As in majority voting case the individual classifier's predictions are combined. However, the final decision is taken by another classifier that is trained on the labels outputted by the classifiers in the ensemble.

- *Ada Boost.* Boosting is a machine learning technique that creates an accurate prediction combining many weak classifiers. A weak classifier is a classifier that performs slightly better than random guessing. Each weak classifier is trained on a random set of the training set. Ada Boost (Freund and Schapire, 1997) assigns weights to each training example. The assigned weight represents the probability that the training example appears in the training set. At each step the examples that were incorrectly predicted by a classifier have their weights increased and the examples that were correctly predicted have the weights decreased. Ada Boost assigns weights to each classifier based on the classifier accuracy. The classifiers that have better accuracy receive higher weight.

- *Bagging* Bagging (bootstrap aggregating) (Breiman, 1996) is an ensemble technique where the individual classifiers in the ensemble are trained on bootstrap samples (random samples taking from initial training set with replacement). The prediction for the test set is done as in the *Majority Voting* ensemble.

3.2 Features

The features used by the classifiers and computed for both training and test sets are either word alignment features, presence/absence features or miscellaneous features. The features are for the most part the features we have introduced before (Barbu, 2015). We have re-engineered some of them and replaced the similarity between the target segment and translation of the source segment with the word alignment features. In this way we no longer rely on an expensive machine translation system. Please notice that to compute some features, like word alignment features for example, you need a word aligner trained on a large parallel corpus.

1. Word Alignment Features. The idea behind word alignment features is that the word alignments provide an important clue for the hypothesis that source and target segments are translations. We compute the number of aligned words in source and target segments and the longest contiguous zone of aligned and unaligned words.

   - *Source (Target) Word Ratio.* The number of words in the source (target) segment that are aligned divided by the total number of words in the source (target) segment.
   - *Max Source (Target) Aligned Zone Ratio.* The number of words in the source (target) longest aligned continuous zone divided by the total number of words in the source (target) segment.
   - *Max Source (Target) Unaligned Zone Ratio.* The number of words in the source (target) longest unaligned continuous zone divided by the total number of words in the source (target) segment.

2. Presence/Absence Features. These features signal the presence/absence of an entity (URL, email address, named entity, etc.) in source and target segments. Furthermore, if the entities are present in both source and target segments, their ratio is computed. These features capture the intuition that if an entity is present in the source segment and if the target segment is a translation of the source segment it is very probable that the same entity is present in the target segment.

   - *Entity Features.* These features are *tag, URL, email, name entity, punctuation, number, capital letters, words in capital letters*. The value of these features is 1 if the source or target segments contain a tag, URL, email, name entity, punctuation, capital letters or words written in capital letters, otherwise is 0.

- *Entity Similarity Features*. If a feature explained under *Entity Features* except for *capital letters* and *words in capital letters* exists, the cosine similarity between the source and target segments entity vectors is computed. Therefore, we compute a feature for the tag similarity, punctuation similarity, URL similarity, etc.

- *Capital letters word difference*. The value of this feature is the ratio between the difference of the number of words containing at least a capital letter in the source segment and the target segment and the sum of the capital letter words in the translation unit. It is complementary to the feature *capital letters*.

- *Only capital letters difference*. The value of the feature is the ratio between the difference of the number of words containing only capital letters in the source segment and the target segments and the sum of only the capital letter words in the translation unit. It is complementary to the feature *words in capital letters*.

3. Miscellaneous Features. The rest of the features we compute fall under miscellaneous features category because they are not easily categorized.

  - *language difference*. If the language codes identified by a language detector for the source and target segments coincide with the language codes declared for the same source and target segments, then the feature is 1, otherwise is 0.

  - *Gale Church score*. This feature is the slightly Gale-Church score described in the equation 1 and introduced in Tiedemann (2011). This score reflects the idea that the length of the source (l_s) and target segments (l_d) that are true translations is correlated. We expect that the classifiers learn the threshold that separates the positive and negative ex-

amples. However, relying exclusively on the Gale-Church score is tricky because there are cases when a high Gale-Church score is perfectly legitimate. For example, when the acronyms in the source language are expanded in the target language.

$$CG = \frac{l_s - l_d}{\sqrt{3.4(l_s + l_d)}} \qquad (1)$$

4 Results and Discussion

4.1 Data

The setting we presuppose is that of a data provider that has a huge amount of translation memories and data crawled from the web and wants to train a unique model per language pair to clean both translation memories and data collected from the web. As we showed in (Barbu, 2015) a cross validation setting tends to overestimate the performance of the model. Therefore the training and test data for the English-Italian language pair is a random sample of multiple translation memories inside the MyMemory database. The test data is enriched with translation units from an aligned parallel English-Italian web site. The training and test data for English-French is a random sample from approximately 17 million translation units resulted from crawling and aligning at the sentence level a large number of parallel English-French sites. The crawling and alignment of the web sites have been performed with the ILSP crawler (Papavassiliou et al., 2013). The training and test sets have been annotated with positive and negative labels by an annotator and checked by a supervisor. The size of the training and test data and the distribution of positive and negative examples is given in table 1. The percentage of negative data in training and test set for English-French language pair is around 50%. This percentage is much higher than the percentage of negative data in English-Italian data sets. These figures are not a surprise because the data in translation memories has less noise than the data crawled and aligned from the web.

The features are computing using TM Cleaner, a publicly available software written by the author [3]. The individual classifiers and almost all ensembles of classifiers used in the experiments are im-

---

[3]https://github.com/SoimulPatriei/TMCleaner/tree/master/TMCleaner-MMT-API

Set	Training		Test	
Language Pair	en-it	en-fr	en-it	en-fr
Positive	2764	510	356	144
Negative	901	436	83	151
Total	3665	946	439	295

Table 1: The distribution of positive and negative translation units in training and test sets

Classifier	F1 Positive	F1 Negative	Balanced Accuracy
RBF	0.93	0.72	0.82
KN	0.93	0.65	0.77
DT	0.93	0.69	0.78
SK	0.93	0.69	0.8
BG	0.93	0.69	0.81
AB	0.93	0.73	0.84
MV	0.94	0.72	0.82
LR	0.94	0.73	0.82
LN	0.95	0.76	0.84

Table 2: Classification Results for English-Italian

Classifier	F1 Positive	F1 Negative	Balanced Accuracy
KN	0.81	0.77	0.8
DT	0.84	0.83	0.83
MV	0.86	0.86	0.86
LR	0.86	0.85	0.85
LN	0.86	0.86	0.86
RBF	0.86	0.86	0.86
AB	0.86	0.86	0.86
SK	0.87	0.86	0.86
BG	0.88	0.88	0.88

Table 3: Classification Results for English-French

plemented in the machine learning library scikit-learn (Pedregosa et al., 2011).

The word alignment features are computed using the fast align (Dyer et al., 2013) version modified in Modern Machine Translation project[4]. This version allows training a word alignment model on a parallel corpus and the use of the aligned model for obtaining the word alignments on a test set. The fast align in Modern Machine Translation is trained on English-Italian and English-French parallel corpora containing approximately 100 millions parallel words each.

The language codes assigned to English, Italian and French segments are computed with the language detector Cybozu[5].

The *Majority Voting* and the *Stacking* ensembles combine the results of all individual classifiers presented in section 3. The *Stacking* meta-classifier is logistic regression. *Ada Boost* uses 500 decision trees weak learners. The *Bagging* ensemble technique combines the results of 500 decision trees classifiers.

The results for English-Italian and English-French are presented in tables 2 and 3.

For each individual and ensemble of classifiers we compute the F1 score for positive and negative class and the balanced accuracy (BA). The first column lists a short name form for the classifiers. RBF stays for *Support Vector Machine* with RBF kernel, KN for *K-Nearst Neighbors*, DT for *Decision Tree*, SK for *Stacking*, BG for *Bagging*, AB for *Ada Boost*, MV for *Majority Voting*, LR for *Logistic Regression* and LN for *Support Vector Machines* with linear kernel. In both tables the classifiers are ordered by the F1 score for the positive class. The ensembles of classifiers are emphasized with bold font.

In figures 1 and 2 the F1 positive scores and F1 negative scores are plotted for English-Italian and English-French language pairs. With continuous line we connect the F1-scores for the positive class and with dashed line we connect the F1-scores for the negative class. As in the above tables the classifiers are ordered in ascending order according to F1 positive score.

For English-Italian language pair the best F1-scores for positive and negative classes are obtained by *Support Vector Machines* with linear kernel. For English-French language pair the clear winner is the Bagging ensemble. The difference between the performances of the classifiers for positive and negative classes is substantial for the English-Italian test set. The difference between the best performing classifiers for the positive class (*Support Vector Machines* with linear kernel) and negative class (*Support Vector Machines* with linear kernel) respectively is 19 percents. The difference between the worst performing classifier for the positive class, *Support Vector Machines* with RBF kernel and the worst performing classifier for the negative class *K-Nearst Neighbors* is 28 percents. Instead, for English-French test set, the

[4] http://www.modernmt.eu
[5] https://github.com/shuyo/language-detection

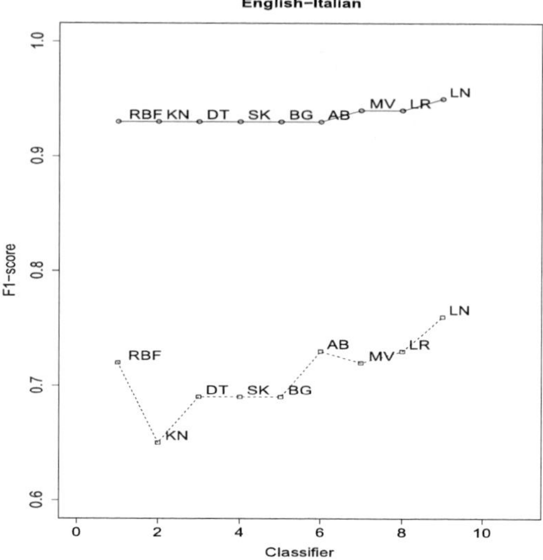
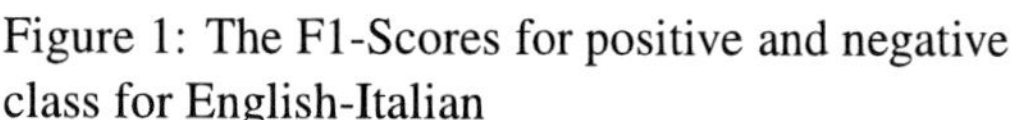
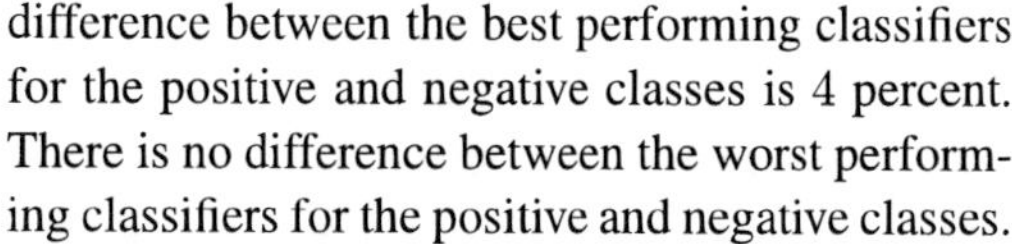

Figure 1: The F1-Scores for positive and negative class for English-Italian

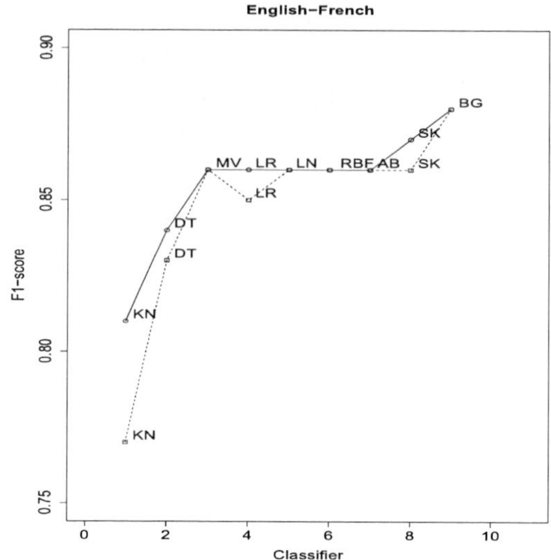

Figure 2: The F1-Scores for positive and negative class for English-French

difference between the best performing classifiers for the positive and negative classes is 4 percent. There is no difference between the worst performing classifiers for the positive and negative classes.

These results lead to the conclusion that it is much harder to distinguish between a positive and a negative translation unit in a translation memory than in parallel corpora crawled from the web. The translation units in parallel web corpora contain errors due to misalignment. They are easier to spot because it is less probable that the aligned segments have overlapping vocabulary.

According to balanced accuracy measure, the *Ada Boost* ensemble is as good as *Support Vector Machine* with the linear kernel for the mixed English-Italian test set. The *Bagging* Ensemble is the best classifier for English-French test set with the other ensembles and the *Support Vector Machine* with Linear kernel coming next.

5   Conclusions

In this paper we have tested well-known ensembles of classifiers (*Majority Voting, Stacking, AdaBoost* and *Bagging*) in the task of finding translation units that are not true translations in translation memories and parallel web corpora. Translation memories curators and researchers that build parallel corpora for machine translations can benefits from the results of this study.

To evaluate the performance of ensemble clas-

sifiers we have compared them against individual classifiers like *Support Vector Machines* and *K-Nearst Neighbors*. English-Italian translation units have better quality than the English-French translation units. For English-Italian language pair the ensemble classifiers are no better than the individual classifiers. If we order them according to the balanced accuracy measure, *Ada Boost* ensemble is as good as *Support Vector Machine* with the linear kernel. If we evaluate the classifiers according to F1-scores for positive and negative class then the *Support Vector Machine* with the linear kernel is the winner. For English-French language pair the *Bagging* Ensemble wins for both Balanced Accuracy and F1-scores.

The ensemble classifiers are more appropriate for data crawled and aligned from the web parallel sites. However, the quality of the content of the parallel sites together with the crawling and the alignment methodology play a big role in the decision to use or not an ensemble classifier. If the parallel sites are of good quality and the mapping methodology is very accurate, then it might well be the case that the resulting translation units have a quality close to translation memories. In this case using an ensemble classifier does not improve over a classifier like *Support Vector Machines*. If one is interested in mining a large amount of web sites with variable content quality, then using ensemble classifiers could the solution. The final destination of the translation units matters as well. If they are used to improve a translation memory, then the quality matters and even a 2-percent improvement in the classifier performance is a success. If the translation units are used to train a SMT system, then a slightly cleaner resource does not have an impact over the BLEU score or the translation quality.

6 Reproducibility

To reproduce the results in this paper please go to the link bellow. The folder the link is pointing to is inside TM Cleaner package. Inside the folder you will find a README file. Follow the instructions to run the individual classifiers, the ensembles of classifiers the evaluation scripts and the R scripts for reproducing the graphs in this paper:

```
https://github.com/SoimulPatriei/
TMCleaner/tree/master/
TMCleaner-MMT-API/Reproducibility
```

References

Eduard Barbu. 2015. Spotting false translation segments in translation memories. In *Proceedings of the Workshop Natural Language Processing for Translation Memories*. Association for Computational Linguistics, Hissar, Bulgaria, pages 9–16. http://www.aclweb.org/anthology/W15-5202.

Eduard Barbu, Carla Parra Escartín, Luisa Bentivogli, Matteo Negri, Marco Turchi, Constantin Orasan, and Marcello Federico. 2016. The first automatic translation memory cleaning shared task. *Machine Translation* 30(3):145–166. https://doi.org/10.1007/s10590-016-9183-x.

Leo Breiman. 1996. Bagging predictors. *Mach. Learn.* 24(2):123–140. https://doi.org/10.1023/A:1018054314350.

Thomas G. Dietterich. 2000. Ensemble methods in machine learning. In *Proceedings of the First International Workshop on Multiple Classifier Systems*. Springer-Verlag, London, UK, UK, MCS '00, pages 1–15. http://dl.acm.org/citation.cfm?id=648054.743935.

Chris Dyer, Victor Chahuneau, and Noah A. Smith. 2013. A simple, fast, and effective reparameterization of IBM model 2. In *HLT-NAACL*. The Association for Computational Linguistics, pages 644–648.

Yoav Freund and Robert E Schapire. 1997. A decision-theoretic generalization of on-line learning and an application to boosting. *J. Comput. Syst. Sci.* 55(1):119–139. https://doi.org/10.1006/jcss.1997.1504.

William A. Gale and Kenneth W. Church. 1993. A program for aligning sentences in bilingual corpora. *COMPUTATIONAL LINGUISTICS* .

Pierre Geurts, Damien Ernst, and Louis Wehenkel. 2006. Extremely randomized trees. *Mach. Learn.* 63(1):3–42. https://doi.org/10.1007/s10994-006-6226-1.

Masoud Jalili Sabet, Matteo Negri, Marco Turchi, and Eduard Barbu. 2016. An unsupervised method for automatic translation memory cleaning. In *Proceedings of the 54th Annual Meeting of the Association for Computational Linguistics (Volume 2: Short Papers)*. Association for Computational Linguistics, Berlin, Germany, pages 287–292. http://anthology.aclweb.org/P16-2047.

Dragos Stefan Munteanu and Daniel Marcu. 2005. Improving machine translation performance by exploiting non-parallel corpora. *Comput. Linguist.* 31(4):477–504. https://doi.org/10.1162/089120105775299168.

Vassilis Papavassiliou, Prokopis Prokopidis, and Gregor Thurmair. 2013. A modular open-source focused crawler for mining monolingual and bilingual corpora from the web. In *Proceedings of the Sixth Workshop on Building and Using Comparable Corpora*. Association for Computational Linguistics, Sofia, Bulgaria, pages 43–51. http://www.aclweb.org/anthology/W13-2506.pdf.

F. Pedregosa, G. Varoquaux, A. Gramfort, V. Michel, B. Thirion, O. Grisel, M. Blondel, P. Prettenhofer, R. Weiss, V. Dubourg, J. Vanderplas, A. Passos, D. Cournapeau, M. Brucher, M. Perrot, and E. Duchesnay. 2011. Scikit-learn: Machine learning in Python. *Journal of Machine Learning Research* 12:2825–2830.

Jörg Tiedemann. 2011. *Bitext Alignment*. Number 14 in Synthesis Lectures on Human Language Technologies. Morgan & Claypool, San Rafael, CA, USA. https://doi.org/10.2200/s00367ed1v01y201106hlt014.

Marco Trombetti. 2009. Creating the world's largest translation memory. http://www.mt-archive.info/MTS-2009-Trombetti-ppt.pdf.

Friedel Wolff. 2016. Combining off-the-shelf components to clean a translation memory. *Machine Translation* 30(3):167–181. https://doi.org/10.1007/s10590-016-9186-7.

Exploiting and Evaluating a Supervised, Multilanguage Keyphrase Extraction Pipeline for Under-Resourced Languages

Marco Basaldella[*] and **Muhammad Helmy**[†] and **Elisa Antolli**
Mihai Horia Popescu and **Giuseppe Serra**[*] and **Carlo Tasso**[*]

Artificial Intelligence Laboratory, University of Udine
Via Delle Scienze, 208, Udine, Italy
[*]`{name.surname}@uniud.it`, [†]`alameldien.muhammad@spes.uniud.it`,
`antolli.elisa@spes.uniud.it`, `popescu.mihaihoria@spes.uniud.it`

Abstract

This paper evaluates different techniques for building a supervised, multilanguage keyphrase extraction pipeline for languages which lack a gold standard. Starting from an unsupervised English keyphrase extraction pipeline, we implement pipelines for Arabic, Italian, Portuguese, and Romanian, and we build test collections for languages which lack one. Then, we add a Machine Learning module trained on a well-known English language corpus and we evaluate the performance not only over English but on the other languages as well. Finally, we repeat the same evaluation after training the pipeline over an Arabic language corpus to check whether using a language-specific corpus brings a further improvement in performance. On the five languages we analyzed, results show an improvement in performance when using a machine learning algorithm, even if such algorithm is not trained and tested on the same language.

1 Introduction

Automatic Keyphrase Extraction (herein AKE) is the task of extracting "a short list of phrases (typically from five to fifteen noun phrases) that captures the main topics discussed in a given document" (Turney, 2000). Recently, Automatic keyphrase extraction has received a lot of attention, because it has been successfully used in many natural language processing (hence NLP) and information retrieval tasks, such as text summarization (Zhang et al., 2004) or document clustering (Hammouda et al., 2005).

The AKE problem is tackled with different techniques. For example, researchers proposed

solutions using e.g. supervised Machine Learning algorithms (herein ML), graph-based ranking algorithms, or clustering techniques, the first being the most successful one (Hasan and Ng, 2014; Merrouni et al., 2016).

Resources to train and evaluate AKE algorithms are available for a variety of domains, like scientific papers, abstracts, newswire texts, emails, etc. (Hasan and Ng, 2014). However, AKE is typically performed on the English language, mainly due to the fact that datasets were not available in other languages. Recently, though, there has been a surge in interest in building AKE datasets in different languages, like French or Arabic (Bougouin et al., 2016; Helmy et al., 2016a).

Following this path, in this paper we propose a multilingual keyphrase extraction pipeline, which performs keyphrase extraction in English, Arabic, Italian, Portuguese and Romanian. However, while resources for English and Arabic are readily available, to our knowledge for the latter three languages there are no publicly available AKE datasets. Nevertheless, we show that it is actually possible to build an AKE pipeline for a language which lacks a gold standard. To prove our hypothesis, we first train a ML model that can extract keyphrases in English and Arabic. Then, we use that model to extract keyphrases in the other languages. Finally, we validate the proposed solution using expert knowledge.

2 Related Work

The problem of multilinguality in AKE is not new. It started in late 90's in order to provide approaches for IR users to handle multilingual documents: for example, Tseng (1998) built an unsupervised, language-independent AKE system and demonstrated its effectiveness on English and Chinese. Since then, many language-independent ap-

Proceedings of Recent Advances in Natural Language Processing, pages 78–85,
Varna, Bulgaria, Sep 4–6 2017.

proaches have been proposed, but most of them are still unsupervised or require the collection of ad-hoc corpora when evaluated on languages other than English.

For example, DegExt (Litvak et al., 2013) was introduced as an unsupervised language independent keyphrase extractor. DegExt uses a simple graph-based syntactic representation of text and web documents (Schenker et al., 2005). The evaluation was performed on an English corpus (DUC 2002) and one purpose-built corpus of 50 Hebrew documents.

Bougouin et al. (2013) proposed TopicRank as an unsupervised, language-independent AKE system. TopicRank creates a graph of the document where each node is a topic appearing in the document, then it uses graph ranking techniques to score the topics and select keyphrases belonging to the top ranked topics. The authors evaluate their approach on four datasets, two on the English language (the SEMEVAL 2010 corpus (Kim et al., 2010) and the Inspec dataset (Hulth, 2003)), and two on the French language, one freely available and one purpose-built by them.

DIKpE-G (Degl'Innocenti et al., 2014) was proposed as a novel multi-language, unsupervised, knowledge-based approach towards keyphrase generation. DIKpE-G integrates several kinds of knowledge for selecting and evaluating meaningful keyphrases, ranging from linguistic to statistical, meta/structural, social, and ontological knowledge, and it has been evaluated on the Italian language using a custom-built dataset of 50 scientific papers.

Finally, LIKE (Aquino et al., 2013) was presented as a supervised method that uses feedforward neural networks for automatically extracting keywords from a document regardless of the language used in it. While the authors claim that LIKE is a truly language-independent AKE system, it is trained and evaluated only on the English language.

3 Multilanguage Keyphrase Extraction

To build an AKE system for a specific language the first step is to understand which parts of the pipeline needs to be adapted. Therefore, we divide the AKE pipeline in modules and we identify the language-dependent ones:

1. Low-level NLP: sentence and word segmentation, part-of-speech tagging and stemming;

2. Candidate generation: selection of the possible keyphrases in the document. It is usually performed by detecting the phrases which match certain known part-of-speech tags patterns;

3. Feature extraction: candidates are assigned some features, like position in the text, frequency, etc.

4. Candidate scoring: the feature extracted in the previous step are used to assign a score to the candidates; then, the top ranked candidates are usually used to evaluate the pipeline.

In this work we focus on the first, second and fourth steps, which are the ones which rely mostly on language-specific knowledge, by implementing several AKE pipelines in the Distiller keyphrase extraction framework (Basaldella et al., 2015).

3.1 Low-level NLP

The first step of the AKE pipeline consists in preparing the document to identify the potential keyphrases, by splitting the text into sentences and the sentences into tokens and, finally, performing part-of-speech tagging, stemming and/or lemmatization.

We use off-the-shelf libraries to perform these tasks. For the English and Arabic languages, we used the Stanford CoreNLP library for all the tasks except stemming, since it offers state-of-the-art performance. Due to the limited availability of languages available for CoreNLP, for the Portuguese and Italian languages we used the the Apache OpenNLP[1] library with the default models for Portuguese and Ciapetti's models for the Italian language[2]. For the Romanian language, the models were not available, so we built them ourselves; we describe this process in Section 3.1.1.

To stem the tokens, we used the Tartarus stemmer (Porter, 1980) for all languages but Arabic, where lemmatization was used instead of stemming. Thus, the lemmatizer used for the Arabic language is the AraMorph lemmatizer (Buckwalter, 2002).

3.1.1 Romanian

We were not able to find any suitable CoreNLP or OpenNLP models for the Romanian language to

---

[1] https://opennlp.apache.org/
[2] https://github.com/aciapetti/opennlp-italian-models

perform sentence splitting, tokenization, and PoS tagging. Thus, we decided to build our own models for Apache OpenNLP using the ROMBAC[3] dataset (Ion et al., 2012).

The corpus contains about 41,000,000 words including punctuation and it is divided in five domains: journalism, pharmaceutics and medicine, law, biographies of Romanian literary personalities, and fiction. We tested different training/testing split to obtain the best possible performance. For the training of the sentence detector and tokenizer, we used the journalism domain, while to train the POS tagger we used the journalism, medicine, and fiction domains.

3.1.2 Arabic

Being very different from the Western languages we previously described (Farghaly and Shaalan, 2009; Habash, 2010), the Arabic language needed additional text preprocessing steps.

The text is cleaned by removing all unnecessary characters like the special Arabic punctuation marks, diacritics, and Kashida[4]. In addition, some Arabic characters have various forms which we normalize into a single one to decrease the processing complexity.

Another issue about Arabic is that punctuation is used differently than in English and other Western languages. In fact, Arabic has traditionally no punctuation, and it is still usual to find modern Arabic books written in this way (Dickins et al., 2016). In the other languages we analyze, we trivially assume that all the words of a keyphrase have to appear within the same sentence. Since it may be not possible to distinguish sentences in an Arabic input text, we follow the approach described in (Helmy et al., 2016b), assuming that the tokens of a keyphrase in the Arabic language should appear in the same syntactic noun phrase.

3.2 Candidate Generation

Candidate generation requires more domain knowledge than simply using an off-the-shelf library. To generate the candidate keyphrases, we scan the text for phrases that match certain part-of-speech tag sequences (we will call such sequences *PoS patterns* from now on). For example, for the present document, a valid keyphrase may be "mul-

tilingual keyphrase extraction", which PoS pattern is "(*adjective, noun, noun*)".

These patterns are typical of the AKE task and they require to be engineered by a domain expert, since they are significantly different from language to language. For example, the English phrase "*software engineering*" is translated in Italian as "*ingegneria del software*", where *del* is an *articulated preposition*, i.e. the union of an article with a preposition, a part of speech which does not exist in the English language. This example shows also that in some languages we will look for shorter n-grams, while other, more verbose languages may require a larger n. For example, in English we look typically up to 3-grams (Pudota et al., 2010; Kim et al., 2010), while in Italian our system will look for 1 to 5-grams.

For the English, Arabic, and Italian language, we used known PoS patterns from the literature (Basaldella et al., 2016; Helmy et al., 2016b; Basaldella et al., 2015). For the other languages, we were not aware of existing PoS patterns. For this purpose, we collected about 500 author assigned keyphrases both in Portuguese and Romanian from scientific repositories and we performed PoS tagging on them. Then, we picked the most frequent patterns, after manually removing or correcting the erroneous ones (e.g. pattern with only conjunctions, etc.).

3.3 Features Extraction

After the identification of the candidate keyphrases we assign to each of them seven features. Most of the features assigned to candidate keyphrases rely simply on statistical and structural information (like the position in the text, frequency, TF-IDF, and so on) (Hasan and Ng, 2014). While researchers have developed language-dependent features, based e.g. on part of speech tags (Hulth, 2003), on anaphora resolution (Basaldella et al., 2016) or based on external knowledge like Wikipedia (Medelyan et al., 2009), this kind of features requires long computational times and specialized tools which may not be available for all languages. Thus, we decided to leave them out of our pipeline.

In our system, we take four features from Pudota et al. (2010) and we use them for *unsupervised* keyphrase extraction only. These features are:

Normalized Frequency i.e. the number of times

---

[3]The Romanian Balanced Annotated Corpus

[4]Also called Tatweel, it is a form of Arabic text justification that, instead of adding whitespace, adds an horizontal, slightly curvilinear stroke between certain letters.

a candidate appears in the document normalized to the number of sentences;

Height i.e. the relative position of the first occurrence of the candidate in the document;

Depth i.e. the relative position of the last occurrence of the candidate in the document;

Lifespan i.e. the difference between the last and the first appearance of the candidate, i.e. given a candidate kp for a document d, $lifespan(kp, d) = depth(kp, d) - height(kp, d)$.

We add three other features to this set to perform supervised kephrase extraction, namely:

Frequency i.e. the number of times a keyphrase kp appears in a document d. While this feature may seem redundant with *normalized frequency*, our experiments showed that using both features leads to better results. To see why, just consider the word "candidate" in the present document: it has been repeated many times in the same sentence, e.g. in the definition of the *lifespan* feature;

TF-IDF i.e. one of the first features used for AKE along with *height* (Witten et al., 1999). A common statistic used in information retrieval to identify which candidates are peculiar of that particular document with respect to a corpus, is the product of the *term frequency tf* and the *inverse document frequency idf*;

DPM i.e. Document Phrase Maximality, is used to discriminate between overlapping keyphrases and it helped to reach new state-of-the-art performance in the AKE task (Haddoud and Abdeddaim, 2014). Given a document d and the candidate keyphrase kp, we define the set $sup(kp, d)$ of the *superterms* of kp candidate keyphrase, i.e. the set of the candidates that contain kp as a substring. For example, if we have a document d which talks about "*software engineering*", we have that "*software engineering*" $\in sup($"*software*"$, d)$.

3.4 Candidate Scoring

To score the candidates, the most trivial approach in this kind of AKE pipeline is to assign heuristically crafted weights to the features, like in Pudota

et al. (2010). Typically, however, one can train a machine learning algorithm over a dataset, like the SEMEVAL 2010 dataset (Kim et al., 2010), and use the generated model to identify keyphrases of new documents. Unfortunately, as pointed out in the introduction, datasets are available only for a minority of languages, so this is not always a viable option.

In our system we used three different scoring techniques. First, since we do not have training sets for all five languages, we assigned manual weights to four of our features, using values which have proven to work on the English language (Pudota et al., 2010). Then, we trained two models, one for English using the SEMEVAL 2010 dataset and one for Arabic using the AKEC dataset. Finally, we used the models trained on these languages to score keyphrases in Italian, Romanian and Portuguese as well.

3.4.1 Manual Weights

In this approach we follow a very simple technique. Given a candidate keyphrase kp, a feature f, and the set of the features F, we define $value(kp, f)$ as a function which returns the value of f for the candidate kp. For each feature, we also assign a weight w, whose value is defined below. Then, the score of a keyphrase kp is computed as follows:

$$score(kp) = \sum_{i=1}^{|F|} w_i \times value(kp, f_i)$$

As mentioned in Section 3.3, the features used in this step are *normalized frequency*, *height*, *depth*, and *lifespan*, and the values of their weights w_i are respectively 0.1, 0.32, 0.16 and 0.12, as presented in Pudota et al. (2010). We did not recompute the values of the weights by ourselves, because authors already proved its effectiveness, and since we just want to use them as a baseline.

3.4.2 Supervised Weights

The manual weights technique is trivially limited by the fact that these weights are used to compute a simple linear function. Many machine learning algorithms are instead able to learn nonlinear functions, and for this reason are commonly used for AKE in literature (Hasan and Ng, 2014).

Thus, in our final step we train a multilayer neural network to extract keyphrases in English and Arabic, using two different training sets.

For the English language, we use the dataset from the "SEMEVAL-2010 Task 5: Automatic Keyphrase Extraction from Scientific Articles" challenge (Kim et al., 2010) (herein, simply SEMEVAL 2010). For the Arabic language, the network has been trained on the recent AKEC corpus (Helmy et al., 2016a). The corpora have 244 and 160 documents respectively, of which 144 are used for training and 100 for testing in the SEMEVAL 2010 dataset, and 100 are used for training and 60 for testing in the AKEC dataset (see Table 1) .

The neural network has been trained using the `nnet` package in the R programming language using the *entropy* parameter. The network uses one neuron per input feature, a hidden layer with two times the input neurons, and one output neuron. The keyphrases are ranked according to the score assigned by the network, which is the value of the output neuron.

We use the models trained on these datasets to extract keyphrases in all our five languages. This is possible because the neural network ignored the text of the actual candidate keyphrase, since it does not receive any information about its words or about its meaning, but only statistical information about its appearance(s) in the input document.

4 Experimental Evaluation

While it is straightforward to analyze the performance of our model in English and Arabic since both the SEMEVAL 2010 and AKEC datasets provide test sets, for Italian, Portuguese and Romanian we are not aware of publicly available collections of keyphrase extraction datasets.

For this reason, we asked mother tongue speakers of these three languages to collect 20 documents per language and assign 15 keyphrases to each document, ranking them by importance. To have a further verification of our techniques, we did the same process for 20 documents in the English language as well. The collected datasets are described in Table 1. For English, Italian and Portuguese, we have collected similar datasets with a majority of scientific documents, which is reflected by mean of about 4000 words per document. For Romanian, we collected *mainly* newswire documents, so we have a mean of 800 words per document, close to the AKEC dataset. All the purpose-built datasets have a greater variability in the number of words with respect to the SEMEVAL 2010 and AKEC datasets, because

Dataset	Size	Mean length	σ length
Semeval 2010	244	8020	1946
AKEC	160	757	145
English	20	3717	1877
Italian	20	4699	3412
Portuguese	20	4335	2482
Romanian	20	802	730

Table 1: The datasets used to train and test the pipelines, with their number of documents, their mean length in words, and the standard deviation σ of the length in words.

while these datasets are composed by only one kind of documents with strict constraints on the length, our test datasets are mixed, containing scientific papers, newswire text, web pages, etc.

For all three approaches, we evaluate our algorithms using Precision computed on the top 5 extracted keyphrases (herein Precision@5 or P@5), and Precision and F1-score computed on the top 15 extracted keyphrases (herein P@15 and F1@15) and Mean Average Precision (MAP). Note that for our own datasets, since they have only 15 expert-assigned keyphrases, the Precision score and the F1 score on the top 15 candidates are equal[5], so for these datasets we show only the former.

5 Experimental Results

We present the results obtained in our experiments in Table 2. As expected, the manual weights method achieves the lowest performance. This is true in particular for the SEMEVAL 2010 dataset; on the other datasets, though, the performance is higher, with 40% and 46% P@5 score on the Portuguese language and Arabic language respectively. This scores seem to be particularly good, since the best performing system in the SEMEVAL 2010 challenge obtained 40% in P@5.

Using the English model we obtained better performance on the SEMEVAL 2010 dataset with 21% F-Score, which would be enough to be placed 9th over 19 systems in the challenge. Since we are not interested in getting the best score but we want to get an average AKE system, this result looks acceptable. Moreover, the score of our neural network greatly outperforms the manual baseline, so

---

[5]Because the size of the set of the retrieved documents is equal to the size of the set of the relevant documents, hence *Precision = Recall*.

Dataset	Pipeline	P@5	P@15	MAP	F1@15
English (SEMEVAL 2010)	Manual weights	0.13	0.1	0.076	0.10
	English model	**0.29**	**0.21**	**0.151**	**0.21**
	Arabic model	0.25	0.18	0.117	0.18
Arabic (AKEC)	Manual weights	0.46	0.37	0.158	0.145
	English model	**0.63**	0.47	0.185	0.18
	Arabic model	0.61	**0.48**	**0.190**	**0.19**
English	Manual weights	0.33	0.26	0.232	
	English model	**0.51**	**0.35**	**0.320**	
	Arabic model	0.47	0.32	0.280	
Italian	Manual weights	0.37	0.23	0.182	
	English model	**0.44**	**0.26**	**0.209**	
	Arabic model	0.41	0.23	0.185	
Portuguese	Manual weights	0.40	0.27	0.226	
	English model	0.42	0.24	0.221	
	Arabic model	**0.45**	**0.31**	**0.250**	
Romanian	Manual weights	0.34	0.26	0.229	
	English model	**0.47**	**0.3**	**0.266**	
	Arabic model	0.39	0.28	0.248	

Table 2: The results obtained with the different 15 experiment we executed.

were are satisfied and we decided to use it on the other languages.

The Arabic model obtains similarly satisfactory results on the AKEC dataset. We have no other systems to compare our model with, since the dataset has been recently released, but the 61% P@5 Score is hugely outperforming the best system in the SEMEVAL 2010 challenge and a 15% improvement over the manual weights, so we're satisfied with this result.

After we validated the machine learning models, we proceeded to use them for the other languages. Using the English and Arabic models to extract keyphrases in Italian, Portuguese, and Romanian offers *always* an improvement with respect to the manual weights, and the same holds for our English countercheck collection.

Analyzing the results for each language, we see that the English model outperforms the Arabic one on the English, Italian and Romanian language, while the Arabic model performs better on the Portuguese language only. Looking at the Precision@15 score, of particular interest is the English model on the English and Romanian collections, and the Arabic model again on the English collection and on the Portuguese one, all of which reach and/or surpass 30%, outperforming again the best performing systems on the SEMEVAL 2010 dataset.

Anyway, a direct comparison of our results with the one obtained in the SEMEVAL 2010 challenge is clearly not fair, since the documents in our collections are significantly shorter, so the problem we had to solve was easier (Hasan and Ng, 2014). This is the reason why our English model performs better on our collections than on the SEMEVAL 2010 dataset, the reason why the Arabic model performs better on the AKEC collection than on the other datasets, and a probable reason of the poor performance of the unsupervised weights, since Pudota et al. (2010) tailored them on documents with a different length.

6 Conclusions

Our approach showed that it is possible to build an effective supervised keyphrase extraction pipeline for an under-resourced language which lacks a keyphrase extraction gold standard by training it on another language. In fact, by training our AKE pipeline over English and Arabic, we were able to obtain good performance on Italian, Romanian and Portuguese as well.

As a future work, it should be considered to perform further experiments on documents in several languages coming from several domains and of different lengths, to further investigate if the performance of AKE depends more on the length or on the language of the document.

References

Germán Osvaldo Aquino, Waldo Hasperué, César Armando Estrebou, and Laura Cristina Lanzarini. 2013. A novel, language-independent keyword extraction method. In *XIX Congreso Argentino de Ciencias de la Computación*.

Marco Basaldella, Giorgia Chiaradia, and Carlo Tasso. 2016. Evaluating anaphora and coreference resolution to improve automatic keyphrase extraction. In *Proc. of International Conference on Computational Linguistics (COLING)*.

Marco Basaldella, Dario De Nart, and Carlo Tasso. 2015. Introducing distiller: a unifying framework for knowledge extraction. In *Proceedings of 1st AI*IA Workshop on Intelligent Techniques At Libraries and Archives co-located with XIV Conference of the Italian Association for Artificial Intelligence (AI*IA 2015)*. Associazione Italiana per l'Intelligenza Artificiale.

Adrien Bougouin, Sabine Barreaux, Laurent Romary, Florian Boudin, and Beatrice Daille. 2016. Termitheval: a french standard-based resource for keyphrase extraction evaluation. In *Proc. of International Conference on Language Resources and Evaluation (LREC)*.

Adrien Bougouin, Florian Boudin, and Béatrice Daille. 2013. Topicrank: Graph-based topic ranking for keyphrase extraction. In *Proceedings of the Sixth International Joint Conference on Natural Language Processing*. Asian Federation of Natural Language Processing, Nagoya, Japan, pages 543–551. http://www.aclweb.org/anthology/I13-1062.

Tim Buckwalter. 2002. Buckwalter {Arabic} morphological analyzer version 1.0 .

Dante Degl'Innocenti, Dario De Nart, and Carlo Tasso. 2014. A new multi-lingual knowledge-base approach to keyphrase extraction for the italian language. In *Proc. of 6th International Conference on Knowledge Discovery and Information Retrieval (KDIR)*. pages 78–85.

James Dickins, Sándor Hervey, and Ian Higgins. 2016. *Thinking Arabic translation: A course in translation method: Arabic to English*. Routledge.

Ali Farghaly and Khaled Shaalan. 2009. Arabic natural language processing: Challenges and solutions. *ACM Transactions on Asian Language Information Processing (TALIP)* 8(4):14.

Nizar Y Habash. 2010. Introduction to arabic natural language processing. *Synthesis Lectures on Human Language Technologies* 3(1):1–187.

Mounia Haddoud and Said Abdeddaim. 2014. Accurate keyphrase extraction by discriminating overlapping phrases. *Journal of Information Science* 40(4):488–500. https://doi.org/10.1177/0165551514530210.

Khaled M Hammouda, Diego N Matute, and Mohamed S Kamel. 2005. Corephrase: Keyphrase extraction for document clustering. In *International Workshop on Machine Learning and Data Mining in Pattern Recognition*. Springer, pages 265–274.

Kazi Saidul Hasan and Vincent Ng. 2014. Automatic keyphrase extraction: A survey of the state of the art. In *Proc. of the Annual Meeting of the Association for Computational Linguistics*.

Muhammad Helmy, Marco Basaldella, Eddy Maddalena, Stefano Mizzaro, and Gianluca Demartini. 2016a. Towards building a standard dataset for arabic keyphrase extraction evaluation. In *Proc. of 20th International Conference on Asian Language Processing (IALP)*. IEEE, pages 26–29.

Muhammad Helmy, Dario De Nart, Dante Degl'Innocenti, and Carlo Tasso. 2016b. Leveraging arabic morphology and syntax for achieving better keyphrase extraction. In *Proc. of 20th International Conference on Asian Language Processing (IALP)*. IEEE, pages 340–343.

Anette Hulth. 2003. Improved automatic keyword extraction given more linguistic knowledge. In *Proc. of the conference on Empirical methods in natural language processing*.

Radu Ion, Elena Irimia, Dan Stefanescu, and Dan Tufis. 2012. Rombac: The romanian balanced annotated corpus. In *Proceedings of the Eighth International Conference on Language Resources and Evaluation (LREC-2012)*. European Language Resources Association (ELRA), Istanbul, Turkey, pages 339–344.

Su Nam Kim, Olena Medelyan, Min-Yen Kan, and Timothy Baldwin. 2010. Semeval-2010 task 5: Automatic keyphrase extraction from scientific articles. In *Proc. of the International Workshop on Semantic Evaluation*.

Marina Litvak, Mark Last, and Abraham Kandel. 2013. Degext: a language-independent keyphrase extractor. *Journal of Ambient Intelligence and Humanized Computing* 4(3):377–387.

Olena Medelyan, Eibe Frank, and Ian H Witten. 2009. Human-competitive tagging using automatic keyphrase extraction. In *Proc of Conference on Empirical Methods in Natural Language Processing*.

Z. A. Merrouni, B. Frikh, and B. Ouhbi. 2016. Automatic keyphrase extraction: An overview of the state of the art. In *Proc. of IEEE International Colloquium on Information Science and Technology (CiSt)*.

Martin F Porter. 1980. An algorithm for suffix stripping. *Program* 14(3):130–137.

Nirmala Pudota, Antonina Dattolo, Andrea Baruzzo, Felice Ferrara, and Carlo Tasso. 2010. Automatic keyphrase extraction and ontology mining for content-based tag recommendation. *International Journal of Intelligent Systems* 25(12):1158–1186.

Adam Schenker, Abraham Kandel, Horst Bunke, and Mark Last. 2005. *Graph-theoretic techniques for web content mining*, volume 62. World Scientific.

Yuen-Hsien Tseng. 1998. Multilingual keyword extraction for term suggestion. In *Proceedings of the 21st annual international ACM SIGIR conference on Research and development in information retrieval*. ACM, pages 377–378.

Peter D. Turney. 2000. Learning algorithms for keyphrase extraction. *Information Retrieval* 2(4):303–336.

Ian H. Witten, Gordon W. Paynter, Eibe Frank, Carl Gutwin, and Craig G. Nevill-Manning. 1999. Kea: Practical automatic keyphrase extraction. In *Proceedings of the Fourth ACM Conference on Digital Libraries*. ACM, New York, NY, USA, DL '99, pages 254–255. https://doi.org/10.1145/313238.313437.

Yongzheng Zhang, Nur Zincir-Heywood, and Evangelos Milios. 2004. World wide web site summarization. *Web Intelli. and Agent Sys.* 2(1):39–53.

Multi-Lingual Phrase-Based Statistical Machine Translation for Arabic-English

Ahmed Bastawisy and **Mohamed Elmahdy**

Computer Science Department

German University in Cairo, Cairo, Egypt

`ahmed.bastawisy@student.guc.edu.eg, mohamed.elmahdy@guc.edu.eg`

Abstract

In this paper, we implement a multi-lingual Statistical Machine Translation (SMT) system for Arabic-English Translation. Arabic Text can be categorized into standard and dialectal Arabic. These two forms of Arabic differ significantly. Different mono-lingual and multi-lingual hybrid SMT approaches are compared. Mono-lingual systems do always result in better translation accuracy in one Arabic form and poor accuracy in the other. Multi-lingual SMT models that are trained with pooled parallel MSA/dialectal data result in better accuracy. However, since the available parallel MSA data are much larger compared to dialectal data, multi-lingual models are biased to MSA. We propose in the work, a multi-lingual combination of different mono-lingual systems using an Arabic form classifier. The outcome of the classier directs the system to use the appropriate mono-lingual models (standard, dialectal, or mixture). Testing the different SMT systems shows that the proposed classifier-based SMT system outperforms mono-lingual and data-pooled multi-lingual systems.

1 Introduction

The Arabic language is the largest still living Semitic language. Arabic is spoken by more than 350 million people around the world. It is also one of the five official languages of the United Nations, and the first official language of twenty-two countries known by the Arab world. Arabic is also used as a second language for more than 1.2 billion people.

Modern Standard Arabic (MSA) is currently considered the formal Arabic variety across all Arabic people. MSA is used in news broadcasts, newspapers, formal speech, books, movies subtiling, and whenever the target audience or readers come from different nationalities. However, MSA is not the natural language for everyday life communications and on social networks. In fact, dialectal Arabic is usually used in this case.

A major problem in all Arabic Natural Language Processing tasks, and in particular Statistical Machine Translation (SMT) is the existence of the Arabic dialects. There exist significant syntactic, morphological, and lexical differences between MSA and the different Arabic dialects. That is why they are sometimes considered as completely different languages (Soudi et al., 2012; Elmahdy et al., 2012)

There were big efforts exerted to improve Arabic-English SMT, most of these efforts were focused on MSA rather than dialectal Arabic. This is mainly due to the fact that the vast majority of available parallel Arabic data are for MSA, whilst relatively sparse and limited parallel data are available for dialectal Arabic (Alqudsi et al., 2014).

To tackle the problem of dialectal Arabic parallel data sparsity, in many previous, they have normalized dialectal words/phrases into corresponding MSA equivalents. This normalization, or pivoting, is basically a rule-based approach to paraphrase dialectal words into MSA. This normalization would allow the usage of existing MSA SMT systems (Salloum and Habash, 2013; Sawaf, 2010).

In (Zbib et al., 2012), instead of relying on normalization or pivoting, they have collected extra dialectal Arabic parallel in combination to existing MSA data. Results showed that the proposed pooling technique has improved translation accuracy for dialectal Arabic. However, MSA translation accuracy has slightly decreased.

Because of the complex morphological nature of Arabic, some prior work, as in (Lee, 2004), fo-

Proceedings of Recent Advances in Natural Language Processing, pages 86–89,
Varna, Bulgaria, Sep 4–6 2017.

cused on MSA morphological analysis to improve Arabic SMT.

The aim of this work is to build a Multilingual Arabic SMT system that supports MSA as well as dialectal Arabic. Another goal is that the addition of dialectal Arabic should not affect MSA translation accuracy. Moreover, since available MSA data are always larger than dialectal data, the system should not be biased to MSA.

In this paper, we propose training three different Arabic SMT models. One model for MSA, another system for Dialectal Arabic, and the last one is a hybrid model that is trained with a data pool of parallel Arabic-English for MSA and dialectal Arabic. A pre-classifier is built to choose the appropriate model to be used.

2 Translation Models

Throughout this work, all translation models were built using Giza Aligner and Moses SMT engine (Philipp et al., 2007). Three translation models have been created: MSA-English model, dialectal-English model, and hybrid-English model. To train the MSA-English translation model, a parallel dataset of 26M words was utilized from the ISI Arabic-English Automatically Extracted Parallel Text corpus (Dragos and Daniel, 2007). An independent MSA-English evaluation set of 300K words was used to tune the model. A MSA-English test set of 300K words is used to evaluate MSA-English translation accuracy.

To train the dialectal-English translation model, a parallel dataset of 2.7M words was utilized from the Arabic-Dialect/English Parallel Text corpus (Technologies et al., 2012) (notice the huge difference between the size of available MSA and dialectal data). An independent dialectal-English evaluation set of 300K words was used to tune the model. A dialectal-English test set of 300K words is used to evaluate MSA-English translation accuracy.

The hybrid translation model has been trained by pooling both training sets of MSA and dialectal parallel data that consists of 26M MSA words and 2.7M dialectal words. Model tuning was performed using the two evaluation sets of MSA and dialectal Arabic.

A statistical tri-gram language model is trained for English. Language model training set consists of 688M words from 2011 and 2012 articles (News Crawl) that is described in (Sofia, 2013).

The English language model is used to estimate the prior probability in all of the proposed SMT techniques.

The three translation models have been tested with the three testing sets (MSA, dialectal, MSA+dialectal). As shown in Table 1, the MSA model has resulted in BLEU score of 34.8, 2.6, and 18.7 on MSA, dialectal, and MSA+dialectal testing sets. It is clear that the MSA model performs poorly on dialectal Arabic data. Using dialectal Arabic model, the results were 4.1, 15.9, and 10.0 on MSA, dialectal, and MSA+dialectal respectively. It is clear that the dialectal model performs better on dialectal data, and performs poorly with MSA data. The hybrid model has resulted in a better acceptable accuracy across both MSA and dialectal Arabic. The hybrid model has resulted in 33.2, 12.3, and 22.8 BLEU for MSA, dialectal, and MSA+dialectal respectively. The hybrid model seemed to be a little bit biased towards MSA as the relative decrease in the accuracy was -4.6% relative the MSA baseline model, and -22.6% relative to the dialectal baseline model.

| Translation | Parallel data type | | |
model	MSA	Dialect.	MSA+Dialect.
MSA	34.8	2.6	18.7
Dialectal	4.1	15.9	10.0
Hybrid	33.2	12.3	22.8

Table 1: BLEU score for the different SMT systems on MSA, dialectal, and MSA+dialectal data.

3 Classification-Based Translation

Although before adding the classifier, MSA and Dialectal Arabic-English SMT systems accuracy were poor across the different variants, the hybrid system that was trained with both MSA and dialectal data has resulted in better accuracy. However, the aim of the Classification-Based Translation is to further improve the accuracy across both dialectal and MSA, and to overcome the bias problem of the hybrid model.

Two classification techniques have been used, the first technique is to classify input Arabic text into two classes Standard and Dialectal, and accordingly translate them with the appropriate system. The second technique is to classify input Arabic text into three classes Standard, Hybrid and Dialectal, and then use the appropriate system accordingly.

A tri-gram MSA language model is built for the sake of classification. More than 355M words from the Arabic Gigaword corpus (Parker et al., 2011) were used to train a MSA language model.

The MSA language model is used in text classification by scoring every input sentence by the language model. Sentences with high log likelihood are classified as MSA, whilst sentences with low log likelihood are classified as Dialectal.

3.1 First Classification Techniques

In the techniques, text segments are classified into two categories: MSA or dialectal. Two-passes optimization search was made to find the optimal language model scoring threshold between MSA and dialectal classes.

In the first pass, a coarse search was performed by varying classification threshold from 0.0 to -10.0 with a coarse step of 1.0. For each iteration, classification accuracy is evaluated. The initial optimal threshold was found to be -4.0 which has resulted in classification accuracy of 95.58% on the evaluation sets of MSA and dialectal Arabic.

In the second optimization pass, a fine step search was performed around the initial -4.0 threshold with a variable value of -3.0 to -5.0 with a step of 0.1. Figure 1 shows classifier's accuracy test with a fine step of 0.1 ($x = x-0.1$). As shown in the graph, the optimal threshold is -3.7 which has resulted in classification accuracy of 96.64%. Thus, threshold of -3.7 has been used.

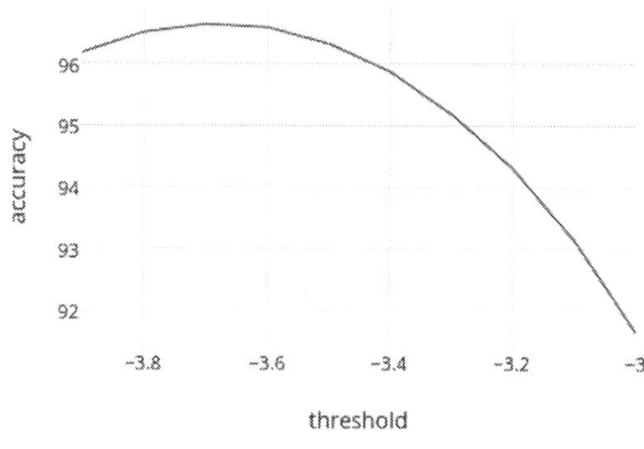

Figure 1: Fine tuning graph for MSA/dialectal classification threshold.

In this technique, the classifier works on classifying the test set and generating two file groups, the first group contains the MSA classified seg-

ments which have scored more than the threshold -3.7. The second group contains the dialectal Arabic classified segments which have scored below or equal the score threshold -3.7.

After that, each classified Arabic text file was translated with the corresponding SMT system, and then all translations were evaluated with the BLEU score test.

3.2 Second Classification Technique

In this technique, instead of having a sharp threshold between MSA and dialectal classes, we have created a window with the optimal threshold in the middle. Any sentence with a score that lies in this window is classified with a third class. That class is labeled the *mixture class*. It is assumed that any sentence in this class (very close to the threshold) might contain a mixture of dialectal and MSA words, which is a common case on social media for instance. The optimal window range has been found to be from -2.7 to -5.45. The three classes in this case are: Dialectal, MSA, and mixture.

The test set is classified into three file groups, the first group contains MSA sentences, which has scored more than the window upper bound -2.7, the second group has the Hybrid Arabic classified sentences, which has score within the window from -2.7 to -5.45, the third group has the Dialectal classified sentences, which has scored less than the window lower bound -5.45.

After that, each classified Arabic text file was translated with the corresponding SMT system, and then all translations were evaluated with the BLEU score test.

4 Experimental Results

The two classification-based translation techniques have been tested on a test set that combines both testing sets of MSA (300K words) and dialectal Arabic (300K words).

The first classification technique has resulted in a BLEU translation accuracy of 29.1 absolute outperforming the hybrid model with a relative increase in the accuracy of 27.6% as shown in Table 2.

The second classification technique has resulted in a BLEU translation accuracy of 29.0 absolute outperforming the hybrid model with a relative increase of 27.2%.

As shown in Table 2, both techniques have significantly improved translation accuracy in comparison to all of the three baseline systems. This means that introducing a pre-classification stage might be a helpful step in improving the performance of Arabic machine translation systems.

The BLEU score is slightly better in the first classification technique than the second one with an absolute difference of 0.1. This implies that it is enough to classify input Arabic text into just two categories instead of three.

Technique	BLEU	Relative
Hybrid Model	22.8	baseline
Classifier-based 1	29.1	+27.6%
Classifier-based 2	29.0	+27.2%

Table 2: Translation accuracy on MSA+dialectal parallel data for the hybrid model, classifier-based technique 1, and classifier-based technique 2.

5 Conclusions

This paper has focused mainly on enhancing the accuracy of SMT across MSA and dialectal Arabic. Three baseline Arabic-English SMT systems were built: MSA, dialectal, and Hybrid. MSA system resulted in significantly low accuracy on dialectal data, whilst dialectal system resulted in low accuracy on MSA data. The hybrid system performed with a better average accuracy across both MSA and dialectal data.

In order to classify input text into the correct variety of Arabic (dialectal or MSA), two classification techniques have been proposed. The first technique classifies the testing data into two categories, one to be translated with the MSA model, and the other to be translated with the dialectal model. The second technique classifies the testing data into three classes, one to be translated with the MSA model, one to be translated with the hybrid model, and the last one to be translated with the dialectal model.

Both techniques have significantly improved translation accuracy on a balanced testing set that contains equal amounts of MSA and dialectal data. The first technique resulted in a slightly better BLEU score than the second classification one.

References

Arwa Alqudsi, Nazlia Omar, and Khalid Shaker. 2014. Arabic machine translation: a survey. *Artificial Intelligence Review* 42(4):549–572.

Stefan Munteanu Dragos and Marcu Daniel. 2007. ISI Arabic-English Automatically Extracted Parallel Text LDC2007T08. Web Download. Philadelphia: Linguistic Data Consortium.

Mohamed Elmahdy, Rainer Gruhn, and Wolfgang Minker. 2012. *Novel Techniques for Dialectal Arabic Speech Recognition*. Springer-Verlag New York, 1 edition.

Young-Suk Lee. 2004. Morphological analysis for statistical machine translation. In *Proceedings of HLT-NAACL 2004: Short Papers*. Association for Computational Linguistics, pages 57–60.

Parker, Robert, et al. 2011. Arabic Gigaword Fifth Edition (LDC2011T11). Linguistic Data Consortium.

Koehn Philipp, Hoang Hieu, et al. 2007. Moses: Open Source Toolkit for Statistical Machine Translation. Annual Meeting of the Association for Computational Linguistics (ACL).

Wael Salloum and Nizar Habash. 2013. Dialectal Arabic to English machine translation: Pivoting through modern standard Arabic. In *HLT-NAACL*. pages 348–358.

Hassan Sawaf. 2010. Arabic dialect handling in hybrid machine translation. In *Proceedings of the conference of the association for machine translation in the americas (amta), denver, colorado.*

Sofia. 2013. News Crawl (articles from 2011 and 2012). web Download. Shared Task: Machine Translation.

Abdelhadi Soudi, Ali Farghaly, Gunter Neumann, and Rabih Zbib. 2012. *Challenges for Arabic Machine Translation*. Natural Language Processing 9. Benjamins, John.

Raytheon BBN Technologies, Linguistic Data Consortium, and Sakhr Software. 2012. Arabic-Dialect/English Parallel Text (LDC2012T09). Linguistic Data Consortium.

Rabih Zbib, Erika Malchiodi, Jacob Devlin, David Stallard, Spyros Matsoukas, Richard Schwartz, John Makhoul, Omar F Zaidan, and Chris Callison-Burch. 2012. Machine translation of arabic dialects. In *Proceedings of the 2012 conference of the north american chapter of the association for computational linguistics: Human language technologies*. Association for Computational Linguistics, pages 49–59.

Gap in pagination due to unavailable paper.

Pages 90-96

Inter-Annotator Agreement in Sentiment Analysis: Machine Learning Perspective

Victoria Bobicev

Department of Informatics and Systems Engineering
Technical University of Moldova
`victoria.bobicev@ia.utm.md`

Marina Sokolova

IBDA@Dalhousie University, Halifax, NS, Canada, and
University of Ottawa, Ottawa, ON, Canada
`sokolova@uottawa.ca`

Abstract

Manual text annotation is an essential part of Big Text analytics. Although annotators work with limited parts of data sets, their results are extrapolated by automated text classification and affect the final classification results. Reliability of annotations and adequacy of assigned labels are especially important in the case of sentiment annotations. In the current study we examine inter-annotator agreement in multi-class, multi-label sentiment annotation of messages. We used several annotation agreement measures, as well as statistical analysis and Machine Learning to assess the resulting annotations.

1 Introduction

Automated text analytics methods rely on manually annotated data while building their heuristics. Although manually annotated texts comprise a small part of a data set, learning algorithms extrapolate the results to the remaining part of the data set and beyond it. At the same time, development of annotation schemes and methods and their implementation attract considerably less research attention than building electronic resources or development of Machine Learning techniques. In this work, we study multi-class sentiment annotation of a *new* data set. The texts have been collected from an online health forum; three annotators annotated each text. Annotators could assign each text with one or more sentiment labels; 4 labels were predefined (*facts, gratitude, encouragement, confusion*) and could be supplemented by other sentiment labels, if annotators deemed the four given labels insufficient to cover sentiments found in the text. Our results show that metrics estimating inter-annotator agreement can be effectively used in deciding of sentiment categories and establishing annotation protocols. We apply Machine Learning (ML) techniques to compare human and automated recognition of sentiment labels.

2 Related Work

Inter-annotator agreement of multi-class sentiment annotations was analyzed in (Steinert, 2017). The author worked with 3255 German documents collected from social networks. Texts were 50 words in average, thus limiting topics and sentiments conveyed by individual messages. Six annotators annotated the documents with one of the following labels: Neg, Neut, Pos, No Sent, Undecided, and Irrelevant. Each document was annotated by three participants. Cohen kappa was used to estimate inter-annotator agreements between each pair of all the six annotators. The best kappa was 0.747 and the worst kappa was 0.480. The final message labels were selected by a majority voting algorithm.

Manual annotations and automated annotations were compared by Emi Ishita et al. (2010). The authors worked with 1,783 sentences collected from written statements of hearings held by a U.S. Senate Committee. Four annotators could annotate a sentence into 10 possible labels; each sentence obtained 3 labels on average; the obtained agreement was 0.30. Then a k-NN algorithm was applied to classify the sentences; it obtained F-score = 0.4. Then human annotations were evaluated in the same way as the automated classification, i.e. obtaining F measures against the final annotation called "ground truth". The best F-measure for human annotation was 0.70.

Proceedings of Recent Advances in Natural Language Processing, pages 97–102,
Varna, Bulgaria, Sep 4–6 2017.

600 sentences collected from English-language Spine-health forum were manually annotated by 60 Master's students, who were not health professionals (Melzi et al, 2014). Annotators used 6 basic emotions (Ekman, 1992): anger, disgust, fear, joy, sadness and surprise. Each sentence was annotated by two annotators. The inter-annotation coefficient Kappa was 0.26. 150 sentences from the same corpus were annotated by two health professionals. The agreement between health professional annotators and non-professionals was moderate, 0.46. The authors nevertheless proceeded with machine learning experiments; their best F-score was equal to 0.65.

150 topics from 115 documents (from the Blog Track at TREC 2008) were annotated in (Bermingham and Alan, 2009). An average of 3.6 annotators worked with each topic. Annotators' agreement was evaluated by Krippendorf alpha (Hayes and Krippendorf, 2007). Unlike Cohen and Fleiss kappa, the measure can assess agreement among a variable number of annotators and accepts non-annotated examples. The value of 0.4219 was obtained for sentence-level annotation for 5-class annotation; the authors considered such agreement as moderate. Bermingham and Alan emphasized necessity of further studies of different levels of annotations, i.e., sentence, paragraph and document levels.

3 The Data Set and Annotation

The data set. To build this data set, we collected messages posted on Introduction and IVF/FET/IUI Cycle Buddies sub-forums of InVitroFertilization.ca forum[1]. The structure of the posted discussions is similar to those posted on other online forums: a participant starts discussion by posting the first message; other participants join discussion by replying on the initial post or the following messages, thus creating coherent online conversations. The Introduction sub-forum contained 2,913 discussions, whereas the IVF/FET/IUI Cycle Buddies contained 3,771 discussions. The number of messages in a single discussion varied considerably: from hundreds to only a few messages.

Due to budgetary limitations, we restricted the number of annotated discussions. We selected 65 medium length discussions, with 10-20 posts in each discussion. Those discussions yielded in to-

tal 1000 posts. The messages were comparatively long, 126 words on average.

Annotation procedure. We adopted four labels from a label set proposed in (Sokolova and Bobicev, 2013); the label set was further analyzed in (Navindgi et al., 2016). We used three sentiment labels: *confusion, encouragement* and *gratitude* and the label *facts* for neutral factual information. We discarded the label *endorsement* that was created as combination of two labels *facts* and *encouragement* (Bobicev et al., 2015). Navindgi et al. (2016) demonstrated that this label confused machine learning algorithms and was not recognized properly.

As one message often conveyed > 1 sentiment, the resulting sentiment mosaic posed challenges to both one label and multi-labeled post annotation:

- one label annotation can be directly mapped into a multi-class classification problem; however, deciding on one sentiment label will artificially restrict annotators' choices, thus, leaving side important information about message sentiment and their annotation.
- multi-labeled annotation represents diversity of sentiments in individual posts; however, mapping multitudes of labels into multi-label machine learning is not a trivial task.

In this study, we have decided to combine the two approaches: first, allow multiple labels for one post; then generalize the received annotations into one label per post.

Preliminary text annotation. In the annotation guidelines we presented three sentiment labels and one for neural/factual information as default labels and then suggested that for each message annotators can indicate as many sentiments as they considered appropriate. Although the annotators were allowed to attach any number of any labels, in many cases they assigned only one predefined label per post: approx. 85% of the assigned labels were from the predefined set. New labels suggested by the annotators are reported in Table 1.

The final text annotation. To choose one label for each post based on all the labels assigned by annotators, we had to resolve the following situations: (1) All three annotators assigned the same label for a post; no other labels were assigned; that ideal case happened in 326 posts. (2) All three annotators assigned the same label for a post; however, other, non-matching labels were assigned too; in this case, the label indicated by all three annotators was selected as the final one: 297

---

posts. (3) All three annotators assigned same two labels for a post; no other labels were assigned; it happened for 26 posts; one annotator indicated the importance of the labels; we used this information and assigned the label she indicated first. (4) Of all labels attached to the post by all annotators only one label was used twice; this label was selected as the final one: 214 posts (5) Two or even three labels were used twice in annotation of the same post; in this case we kept the label marked as the most important; it happened for 95 posts; in four cases the most important label was not repeated by other annotators; we did not use these posts in the experiments. (6) All the annotators attached different labels to a post. This happened for 14 posts. Those posts remained ambiguous without the final label.

Table 1: New sentiments of 1st, 2nd and 3rd annotators.

Sentiment	1st	2nd	3rd
support		473	
cheering		158	
worry		124	
uncertainty		115	
compassion	53	96	17
hope	37	238	19
optimism		125	
dislike		92	
excitement	20		
concern		81	
sadness		38	
joy			5
happiness		36	3
disappointment	13		2
sadness	9		12
frustration	7		

Figure 1 reports labels assigned by annotators after we merged the additional labels. The first annotator tended to use more neutral labels whilst the second annotator attached more labels with sentiments. This problem was discussed in (Melzi et al., 2014) as health forums are about health problems, diagnosis, treatment, etc. Thus, some annotators, by empathy, associated negative emotion to factual information about diseases, symptoms and diagnoses.

In general, the first annotator attached fewer labels (average labels per post is 1.17; 83% of posts annotated with only one label); the second and the third annotators attached more labels (average labels per post is 1.35, 68% of posts annotated with only one label).

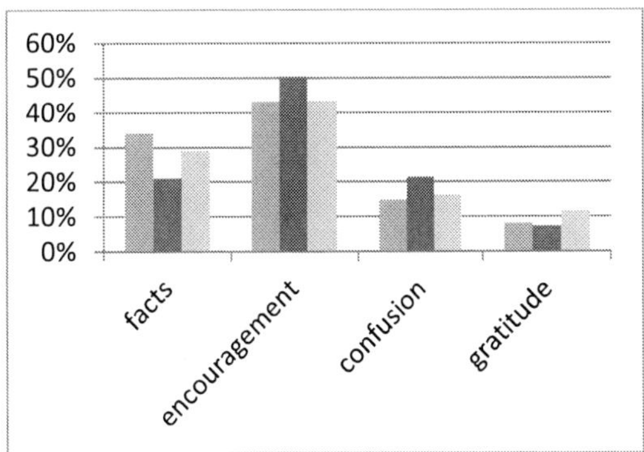

Figure 1: The ratio of labels used by all three annotators in the order: 1st, 2nd, 3rd.

4 Assessment of Inter-Annotator Agreement

Several inter-annotators metrics were proposed for inter-annotator agreement evaluation.

Per cent of agreement is the easiest and the most straightforward measure. The measure is often criticized (it does not differentiate between categories) but still it gives a basic approximation of annotators' agreement. As we have multiple labels per post, inter-annotator agreement was calculated for each label separately and the average for these four labels. The same situation is for three annotators. The pairwise agreement calculated for each pair of the annotators and the average are presented in Table 2.

Table 2: Per cent inter-annotator agreement for the four labels and three annotators. A1, A2, A3 are the annotators; the labels are: lab1 (encouragement), lab2 (facts), lab3 (confusion), lab4 (gratitude).

	lab1	lab2	lab3	lab4
A1vs A2	73%	72%	85%	88%
A2vs A3	73%	70%	83%	93%
A1vs A3	78%	74%	81%	87%
average	74.6%	71.8%	82.7%	89.1%

The average agreement is 79.6%; it shows a strong agreement. Agreement between pairs of the three annotators is almost uniform; we cannot say that some are better than others.

Comparing agreement per labels we see that lesser agreement was reached on *encouragement* and *facts*. This may be explained by the specific of the text: participants often asked to tell success stories to encourage them fighting with health issues. Thus, factual stories of illness and following recovery were frequently perceived as encouragement.

Inter-annotator agreement is often evaluated by Cohen's kappa (κ), Fleiss' kappa (K), Krippendorf's alpha (α) (Artstein, Poesio, 2008). Cohen's kappa and Fleiss kappa are Chance-Corrected Coefficients which means that they measure above chance agreement. The general formula for these coefficients is:

$$k = (Ao - Ae)/(1 - Ae) \qquad (1)$$

where Ao is observed agreement and Ae is expected agreement by chance if the annotators pick the labels randomly.

Cohen k. In case of Cohen k the expected agreement Ae is calculated basing on the assumption that random assignment of categories to the items is governed by prior distributions that are unique to each coder, and which are observed from their actual distribution. Cohen k is applied to two annotators only, thus we calculated it for each pair of our annotators (Table 3)

Table 3: Cohen's k for the annotation

	lab1	lab2	lab3	lab4
A1 vs A2	0.48	0.41	0.50	0.47
A1 vs A2	0.46	0.34	0.51	0.56
A1 vs A2	0.53	0.40	0.49	0.44
average	0.49	0.38	0.50	0.49

The average Cohen's k = 0.46 shows moderate agreement.

Fleiss k is generalization to more than two annotators; expected agreement is calculated on the basis on the assumption that random assignment of categories to items, by any annotator, is governed by the distribution of items among categories in the actual world (Table 4).

Table 4: Fleiss k for the annotation.

	lab1	lab2	lab3	lab4	average
Fleiss k	0.48	0.38	0.49	0.48	0.46
observed	0.75	0.72	0.83	0.89	0.80
expected	0.51	0.55	0.66	0.79	0.63

Krippendorf's alpha (α) is an agreement coefficient based on assumptions that expected agreement is calculated by looking at the overall distribution of judgments without regard to which coders produced these judgments. It applies to multiple coders, and it allows missing values. As in previous cases α is calculated for each label and then averaged in Table 5.

Table 5: Krippendorf's alpha (α)

	lab1	lab2	lab3	lab4	average
α	0.48	0.38	0.49	0.48	0.46

The average agreement is equal to 0.46 in all calculated metrics which is similar to 0.48 reported in (Bobicev, Sokolova, 2017) and is considered as moderate in (Artstein, Poesio, 2008).

In the current study, there was no considerable difference between the results of the inter-annotator metrics. Nevertheless, we conjecture that pairwise metrics can serve for the detection of the best annotator. For example, Nowak and Roger (2010) identified the best and the worst annotators (among 11 annotators) by calculating correlation between their labels and the final labeled set.

On the other hand, we can calculate annotator agreement per label and then use the result as an indicator of the label identification difficulty: labels with the best agreement are the easiest to detect and, vice versa, the worst agreement shows labels with the most problems for the annotators. Finally, annotator agreement can be used in analysis of the label sets and annotation instructions in order to improve annotation process and resolve annotation difficulties.

5 Experiments

We worked with the following sets of text:

(1) 970 posts, each post identified with one label;

(2) 326 posts with exact match of the labels assigned by the three annotators;

(3) 297 posts with a principal match: all 3 annotators agreed on 1 label but other labels were added;

(4) 214 posts with a partial agreement: two annotators selected one label which was considered the final one;

The complete set of 970 messages has the following distribution of labels: *confusion*: 146, *encouragement*: 494, *gratitude*: 69, *facts*: 261.

To estimate reliability of annotations (see Sec 4), we have run ML experiments on sets (1) – (3). We used several sets of features:

1. BOW – Bag of Words. All words from the whole corpus with the frequency at least 2; 3497 features.

2. SS – SentiStrength (Thelwall et al., 2012). All terms from SentiStrength lexicon which appear in our corpus.
3. SWN – SentiWordNet (Esuli, Sebastiani, 2006). All terms from SentiWordNet lexicon which appear in our corpus.
4. DM – DepecheMood (Staiano, Guerini, 2014). All terms from DepecheMood lexicon which appear in our corpus.
5. HA – HealthAffect (Sokolova, Bobicev, 2013). All terms from HealthAffect lexicon which appear in our corpus.

Table 6: Results of the 1st set of the experiments.

exper- iment	F	Fea- tures	algorithm
1	0.794	BOW	NB Multinomial
2	0.504	BOW	SVM
3	0.445	SWN	NB Multinomial
4	0.571	BOW	NB Multinomial

Note that SS, SWN, DM, HA showed reliable results in sentiment analysis studies (Bobicev et al., 2015). We applied Naive Bayes (NB), NB Text, NB multinomial, SVM machine learning algorithms in our experiments. To select the best results, we used 10-fold cross-validation and computed F-score (F). We used the majority class baseline. We run four experiments using the created sub-corpora (Table 6):
(1) 326 posts with exact match; baseline=0.536.
(2) 297 posts with agreement; baseline=0.362.
(3) 214 posts with partial agreement; baseline=0.283.
(4) All the 970 posts with one label; baseline=0.344.
The best result F=0.794 was obtained for the sub-corpus with exact match. For the whole corpus the best F-measure=0.571 was too obtained on the BOW feature set.

Table 7: Results of the 2nd set of the experiments on the selected set of features.

exper- iment	F	algorithm
1	0.797	NB Multinomial
2	0.628	NB Multinomial
3	0.527	NB Multinomial
4	0.646	NB Multinomial

Table 8: Classification per label

Class	F-Measure
confusion	0.562
facts	0.535
gratitude	0.441
encouragement	0.759

Feature selection Feature sets consisting of all words from the texts or from lexicons were comparatively large. We used Correlation-based Feature Subset Selection (Hall, 1999) which evaluates the worth of a subset of features by considering the individual predictive ability of each feature along with the degree of redundancy between them. We created a set of selected features from all 4 lexicons' merged features and have run the same 6 experiments on them. The results are presented in Table 7. Feature selection improved the learning results: F measure for the whole set is 0.652 which is much better than 0.571 on BOW features.

F-measures for the individual labels are presented in Table 8. We used the feature selection results obtained on all the 970 posts with 1 label, i.e. experiment # 4 in Table 7. *Encouragement* was classified significantly better than other categories: F-score = 0.759; the lowest F-score= 0.441 was obtained for classification of *gratitude*.

Those results may be explained by imbalanced distribution of categories: almost half of posts were labeled by *encouragement* (i.e., 494 posts out of 970 posts) while *gratitude* had been assigned to the smallest number of posts (i.e., 69 out of 970). Thus, the automate method had enough training data to recognize *encouragement*, but not enough training data for recognition of *gratitude*.

Table 9: Inter-annotator agreement calculated for automated classification and final labels.

label	Per cent Agreement	Cohen kappa
confusion	85.9	0.478
facts	76.7	0.380
gratitude	93.2	0.405
encouragement	74.5	0.489

To compare automated classification and human annotation we calculated agreement between the results of automated analysis and the final set of labels used in the experiments. Cohen kappa is the worst for *facts* (0.380) and the best for *encouragement* (0.489) (Table 9). Thus, humans and automated methods disagree more when they assign *facts* than when they assign **encouragement.**

6   Conclusions and Future Work

We have presented a study of multi-class sentiment annotation. We worked with a *new* data set of 970 texts collected from a health-related forum. To estimate the quality of annotations, we have applied several inter-annotation agreement metrics. We have shown how those metrics can be used in evaluation of sentiment categories and annotation schemes. Finally, we applied Machine Learning techniques to compare automated classification and human annotation of the same data.

Our future work will expand current studies to new data sets. We aim to investigate various protocols and procedures of generalization of sentiment annotations, and how those procedures affect Machine Learning sentiment classification.

References

Ron Artstein, Massimo Poesio. 2008 Inter-coder agreement for computational linguistics. Computational Linguistics Journal Volume 34 Issue 4, pages 555-596. doi: 10.1162/coli.07-034-R2

Adam Bermingham, Alan F. Smeaton. 2009 A study of inter-annotator agreement for opinion retrieval. In: SIGIR 2009 - The 32nd Annual ACM SIGIR Conference, pages 784-785.

Victoria Bobicev, Marina Sokolova and Michael Oakes. 2015. What Goes Around Comes Around: Learning Sentiments in Online Medical Forums. *Cognitive Computation*, 7(5): 609-621. http://dx.doi.org/10.1007/s12559-015-9327-y.

Victoria Bobicev, Marina Sokolova. 2017. Confused and Thankful: Multi-label Sentiment Classification of Health Forums. In: Mouhoub M., Langlais P. (eds) Advances in Artificial Intelligence. AI 2017. DOI: 10.1007/978-3-319-57351-9_33

Paul Ekman. 1992. An argument for basic emotions. Cognition and Emotion, vol. 6(3-4), pp. 169–200.

Andrea Esuli and Fabrizio Sebastiani. 2006. SENTI-WORDNET: A Publicly Available Lexical Resource for Opinion Mining, In Proceedings of the 5th Conference on Language Resources and Evaluation (LREC'06), pages 417-422.

Mark A. Hall. 1999. Correlation-based Feature Selection for Machine Learning, Ph.D. thesis, University of Waikato.

Andrew F. Hayes and Klaus Krippendorff. 2007. Answering the Call for a Standard Reliability Measure for Coding Data. Communication Methods and Measures Journal Volume 1, Issue 1, pp. 77-89.

Emi Ishita, Douglas W. Oard, Kenneth R. Fleischmann, An-Shou Cheng, Thomas Clay Templeton. 2010. Investigating multi-label classification for human values. Proceedings of the Association for Information Science and Technology. http://dx.doi.org/10.1002/meet.14504701116

Soumia Melzi, Amine Abdaoui, Jérôme Azé, Sandra Bringay, Pascal Poncelet, Florence Galtier. 2014. Patient's rationale: Patient Knowledge retrieval from health forums. eTELEMED 2014 : The Sixth International Conference on eHealth, Telemedicine, and Social Medicine.

Soumia Melzi, Amine Abdaoui, Jérôme Azé, Sandra Bringay, Pascal Poncelet, Florence Galtier. 2014. Patient's rationale: Patient Knowledge retrieval from health forums. eTELEMED 2014 : The Sixth International Conference on eHealth, Telemedicine, and Social Medicine.

Stefanie Nowak, Stefan Roger. 2010. How reliable are annotations via crowdsourcing? a study about inter-annotator agreement for multi-label image annotation. In: Proceedings of the international conference on Multimedia information retrieval - MIR'10, p. 557.

Marina Sokolova and Victoria Bobicev. 2013. What Sentiments Can Be Found in Medical Forums? In Galia Angelova, Kalina Bontcheva, Ruslan Mitkov: Recent Advances in Natural Language Processing, RANLP 2013, Bulgaria.

Jacopo Staiano, Marco Guerini. 2014. DepecheMood: a Lexicon for Emotion Analysis from Crowd-Annotated News. Proceedings of the 52nd Annual Meeting of the Association for Computational Linguistics, pages 427-433. http://www.anthology.aclweb.org/P/P14/

Kai Steinert. 2017 Collaborative Web-Based Short Text Annotation with Online Label Suggestion. MA Thesis, TU Darmstadt.

Mike Thelwall, Kevan Buckley, Georgios Paltoglou. 2012. Sentiment strength detection for the social Web, Journal of the American Society for Information Science and Technology, 63(1), 163-173. doi>10.1002/asi.21662.

Fast and Accurate Decision Trees for Natural Language Processing Tasks

Tiberiu Boros[*,**], Stefan Daniel Dumitrescu[**] and Sonia Pipa[**]

[*]Adobe Experience Manager, Machine Learning, Adobe Systems
[**]Research Institute for Artificial Intelligence, Romanian Academy
{boros}@adobe.com, {sdumitrescu,sonia}@racai.ro

Abstract

Decision trees have long been used in many machine-learning tasks; they have a clear structure that provides insight into the training data and are simple to conceptually understand and implement. We present an optimized tree-computation algorithm based on the original ID3 algorithm. We introduce a tree-pruning method that uses the development set to delete nodes from overfitted models, as well as a result-caching method for speed-up. Our algorithm is 1 to 3 orders of magnitude faster than a naive implementation and yields accurate results on our test datasets.

1 Introduction

Decision trees (DTs) are a well-established classification/prediction methodology in machine learning, in which the model is (as the name suggests) a tree where each node is a decision and each leaf represents an output class (label/distribution). A node can have any number of children, but commonly, most algorithms implement only binary trees with binary questions. Decision-tree classifiers are a very popular choice, mainly because they are easy to train and, by analyzing the tree structure one can easily validate certain assumptions or gain a better understanding of the corpora/task as opposed to, for example, neural networks in which the model is a matrix of numbers offering no insight.

DTs have been widely used in natural and spoken language-processing tasks such as tagging (Schmid, 2013), named entity recognition (NER) (Szarvas et al., 2006), letter-to-sound (LTS) conversion (Pagel et al., 1998), text categorization (Lewis and Ringuette, 1994), parameter estima-

tion for statistical parametric speech synthesis (Zen et al., 2007).

One of the drawbacks of decision trees is their relatively modest performance in classification tasks. Current state-of-the-art approaches in natural language processing and other research fields employ more powerful methodologies, such as Support Vector Machines (SVMs), Conditional Random Fields (CRFs), and complex neural network architectures.

In what follows, we propose an optimized decision tree computation algorithm which follows the guidelines of the Iterative Dichotomiser 3 (ID3) algorithm (Quinlan, 1986), but computes entropy and information gain using a single pass over the training data. We also address the issue of overfitting the training set by introducing a tree-pruning algorithm that tunes an already existing tree using a development set. For significant speed increase we implement a result-caching method. We show that tree-pruning achieves up-to-par accuracy on our datasets by comparing results obtained using (a) the unpruned version of the tree (b) the pruned version of the tree and (c) various state-of-the-art methods in identical training and testing conditions.

We argue that the training speed-boost obtained by using our computational enhancements, as well as the accuracy-boost obtained by tree-pruning make DTs a desirable choice for feature-engineering and for real-life applications, whenever speed of implementation/training with slightly lower results are acceptable.

2 Related Work

The simple and robust principle behind decision trees made them an ideal choice for both academic and industrial (applied) research. There are several papers that address construction and optimiza-

Proceedings of Recent Advances in Natural Language Processing, pages 103–110,
Varna, Bulgaria, Sep 4–6 2017.

tion principles applied, from which we selected those relevant to our approach. Su and Zhang (2006) use independent information gain (IIG) to speed-up the process of tree construction and reduce the complexity of the calculus, Dai and Ji (2014) introduce an algorithm designed for distributed computation of trees, based on mapreduce. Quinlan (1987) introduces one of the first tree-pruning strategies, while Mehta et al. (1995) and Rastogi and Shim (1998) use the a more principled approach, based on the Minimum Description Length (MDL). Though MDL strategies work very well and are currently the main ingredient of statistical parametric speech synthesis (Zen et al., 2009), for simple NLP tasks they add "overhead" and increase computational complexity at training time. Other approaches to decision tree optimization are aimed straight at tree-construction strategies and refer to randomization, bagging and boosting (Dietterich, 2000).

Our proposed optimization methods (a) are based on the original ID3 algorithm with the **"missing-attribute" extension** and (b) focus on discrete features (not continuous values).

3 Enhanced ID3 Computation

The Iterative Dichotomizer 3 (ID3) is an algorithm created by Ross Quinlan to generate a decision tree from a dataset. The computation starts with the entire dataset S at the root node. For each iteration, the feature having the largest information gain $IG(S)$ is located among the unused features. The set S is then split and the two children of the current node are created: one for the examples that contained the selected feature and second for those that did not. The algorithm continues recursively for each newly created node, until one of the stop conditions is encountered:

- A subset contains only examples belonging to the same class. In this case, the node is turned into leaf labeled with the name of the class.

- There is no unused feature to select, but the examples still do not belong to the same class. The node is also turned into a leaf, this time labeled with the most common class in the subset.

- We do not obtain any information gain when splitting by any unused feature. In this situa-

tion, the created leaf is also labeled with the most common class in current subset.

The output of this algorithm will be a decision tree, with each non-terminal node representing the selected feature on which the data was split, and the terminal nodes (leafs) representing the class label of the final subset of the branch.

3.1 Speed-Optimized Computation of Entropy and Information Gain

Before describing our proposed optimizations, we have to clarify our view of the algorithm's data representation style. The standard way to view a dataset is that of a examples (instances) having a number of attributes and an output class. Each attribute (e.g. Temperature) can have several values (multinomial attribute, e.g. Hot, Average, Cold), an instance being a collection of a particular value for each of the available attributes. The ID3 implementation we propose handles missing features and treats attributes as a bag-of-words, meaning that an instance might have a feature like Temperature_Hot, or Temperature_Cold. This allows greater flexibility, especially for NLP tasks, and is essentially similar to the classic data representation style.

Returning to the ID3 algorithm training procedure, the decision to select a feature over another is given by the information gain. Given a dataset S with M features and N classes, information gain $IG_i(S)$ is the measure of the difference in entropy in S after it was split on feature i, meaning we measure how much the uncertainty in S has decreased by choosing to split by i. This implies running over S for each of the M features to compute $IG_i(S)$ and selecting the maximum value. Choosing to split by feature i will yield, two complementary subsets of S, one having all examples (instances) that have feature i, named the Yes_i subset, the other having the remaining examples that do not have feature i (the No_i subset). Iteratively, for each subset we have to find the next feature to split on, again running over all the examples in the subsets. We propose a way around these multiple passes over the dataset that brings a significant speed increase.

Starting from the definition, information gain is the difference in entropy of the initial set S and after the set was split on feature i (in all T subsets).

$$IG_i(S) = H(S) - \sum_{t \in T} (P(t) \cdot H(t)) \quad (1)$$

where $H(S)$ is the entropy of the initial set S, $H(t)$ the entropy of subset t, and $P(t)$ is the fraction of elements in t over the entire $|S|$. We note $|S|$ as the number of instances in S.

$$H(S) = -\sum_{x=1}^{N} P_x \cdot \log_2 P_x \qquad (2)$$

where P_x is the number of instances of class x divided by $|S|$.

The optimization we propose in this paper is based on creating a contingency matrix. By having a matrix that stores partial results and additional information, we are able to reduce the number of operations that are repeatedly executed in the classical implementation of the ID3 algorithm.

The proposed matrix is presented in Table 1, where $O_{1,N}$ notation is used for the N output classes, and $F_{1,M}$ marks the M unique features. Cells at index $[i, j]$ (from position $[1, 1]$ to $[M, N]$) keep the number of instances in the dataset that contain feature F_i of class O_j. To compute $H(S)$ and $IG_i(S)$ for every feature i, an iteration through the dataset is required. To skip this step we add an extra row and column to the matrix: the $M+1^{th}$ row stores the total number of instances of class O_j and the $N+1^{th}$ column stores the number of instances that have label F_i.

Starting from the Entropy and Information Gain formulas, we developed the following set of equations to compute these measures using the partial results stored in matrix.

a	O_1	O_2	O_3	O_4	...	O_n	
F_1	2	0	5	0	...	0	X_1
F_2	0	0	1	0	...	0	X_2
F_3	1	3	1	7	...	0	X_3
F_4	20	0	1	0	...	1	X_4
...	...	...	...	...	...	...	...
F_m	1	0	4	1	...	10	X_m
	Y_1	Y_2	Y_3	Y_4	...	Y_n	

Table 1: Computation matrix

Now, the entropy $H(S)$ can be written as:

$$H(S) = -\sum_{i=1}^{N} \frac{a[M+1, i]}{|S|} \log_2 \frac{a[M+1, i]}{|S|} \qquad (3)$$

where a is our proposed contingency matrix and $a[M+1, i]$ refers to the last row that counts the number of instances having output class O_i.

To calculate $IG_i(S)$, considering i as the attribute to split on, we have to subtract from $H(S)$ the entropy of the subsets multiplied by the probability of splitting by feature i. The subsets, in our implementation, are always two: the Yes subset containing all instances that have feature i and the No subset, with instances not containing feature i:

$$IG_i(S) = H(S) - \\ [P_{feat_i} \cdot H(Yes) + \overline{P_{feat_i}} \cdot H(No)] \qquad (4)$$

Where P_{feat_i} is:

$$P_{feat_i} = \frac{a[i, N+1]}{|S|} \qquad (5)$$

with $a[i][N+1]$ being the number of instances that contain feature i, meaning the number of instances in the Yes subset. The $\overline{P_{feat_i}}$ is the complement of P_{feat_i}, meaning the number of instances in the No subset divided by the total number of instances in $|S|$.

Moving on, the entropies of $H(Yes)$ and $H(No)$ are:

$$H(Yes) = -\sum_{x \in Yes} P_{Yes_x} \cdot \log_2 P_{Yes_x} \qquad (6)$$

$$H(No) = -\sum_{x \in No} P_{No_x} \cdot \log_2 P_{No_x} \qquad (7)$$

so $IG_i(S)$ becomes:

$$IG_i(S) = H(S) \\ -\sum_{x \in X} (-P_{feat_i} \cdot P_{Yes_x} \log 2 P_{Yes_x} \\ - (\overline{P_{feat_i}} \cdot P_{No_x} \log 2 P_{No_x}) \qquad (8)$$

$$P_{Yes_x} = P_{Yes_{i,j}} = \frac{a[i, j]}{a[i, N+1]} \qquad (9)$$

$$P_{No_x} = P_{No_{i,j}} = \frac{a[M+1, j] - a[i, j]}{|S| - a[i, N+1]} \qquad (10)$$

where $a[i, j]$ means the number of instances having feature i and output class O_j; $a[i, N+1]$ is the number of instances that have feature i; $a[M+1, j] - a[i, j]$ is the number of instances of class O_j minus those in the Yes subset; $|S| - a[i, N+1]$ is the number of instances that do not have feature i (the number of instances in the No subset).

Finally,parametrized by i and j, $IG_i(S)$ becomes:

$$IG_i(S) = H(S)$$
$$- \sum_{j=1}^{N}(-P_{feat_i} \cdot P_{Yes_{i,j}} \log 2P_{Yes_{i,j}}$$
$$- (\overline{P_{feat_i}} \cdot P_{No_{i,j}} \log 2P_{No_{i,j}}) \quad (11)$$

It can be seen that the calculation is now performed in a single operation, using the extra row and column of the contingency matrix.

The purpose of creating this contingency matrix is to avoid iterating at each step through all of the training examples, an amount that can vary from hundreds to hundreds of millions of instances, each with any number of features. The size of the contingency matrix itself is small as it does not very by the number of instances but by the number of features and classes, usually orders of magnitude smaller than the training corpus itself.

3.2 Decision-Tree Pruning

As with machine learning algorithms, data sparseness combined with noise will likely yield overfitted models, which means that the constructed tree will model a features/label combination that will never exists in real data. There are, of course, several techniques that can be used to prevent this from happening such as increasing the train-set size, decreasing the number of features and performing frequency cut-off over features and labels, but these are general guidelines applicable to any classifier. In what follows we propose a simple method to prevent overfitting the training data by introducing the possibility to use a development set in the training process.

Though our proposed methodology is simple and intuitive and is inspired by the idea to reduce the tree-size be replacing a node with one of its subtrees presented in (Quinlan, 1993). However, in our approach we rely on the development set to perform this step. The idea is simple: use the standard ID3 to build a decision tree and then iteratively run a tree-pruning procedure until there are no more improvements on the development set. The algorithm can be outlined as:

1. Construct an initial tree using the available training data;

2. Take each node and measure the accuracy on the development set as if the node were a ter-

minal leaf with the most probable output label[1];

3. If there are no improvements on the development set, stop the algorithm and return the current tree structure; Otherwise update the tree structure by removing the node with the highest accuracy gain and return to step 2.

Though trivial, our experiments showed that this is an effective approach to prevent the tree from over-fitting the training data and it provides significantly better accuracy rates on the test set, actually bringing the results very close to those obtained using state-of-the-art classifiers (see subsection 4.3).

The naive way to implement this algorithm is to compute the best performing tree-structure at every iteration (t) by pruning part of the tree and measuring the accuracy on the development data. This means that, at every step i_t, for a tree structure with k_t nodes (k_t is used to denote the remaining number of nodes at step t) the algorithm has to go through the entire development set, compute the predicted label using the new tree structure and measure the new accuracy. While this approach works for small datasets and trees, larger number of nodes and development examples render this algorithm unusable. For instance, in our initial experiments we let this algorithm run for 24 hours on a part-of-speech tagging corpus for Romanian (see section 4.3 for details) and it only pruned 26 nodes, while the actual convergence number was 245 nodes.

The prerequisites for computing the accuracy gain by pruning a node are the following: (a) the algorithm has to know which is the most probable label that the unmodified tree structure would predict if the runtime prediction algorithm would pass through the current node; (b) the algorithm has to know what would be the overall accuracy of the unmodified tree structure; (c) the algorithm has to compute the new accuracy figures if the node would be transformed into a leaf assigned with the most probable label. Because we already know the ground-truth for all the examples (training and development) and we can easily compute the prediction values for both the training and the development set before each iteration, we can speed-up

---

[1] When we compute the most probable label we use the data in the training set, because we don't want to completely bias the tree towards the development data.

accuracy computation at the expense of memory by caching the results.

As such, for every node (n) inside the tree, we compute 3 vectors (g_n, s_n and f_n) which have a length equal to the number of unique labels (l).

- g_n is used to cache the counts of each unique label generated by **training examples** that pass through this node at runtime;

- s_n is used to cache the counts of **successful predictions** for each unique label, generated by **development set examples** that pass through this node at runtime;

- s_n is used to cache the counts of **unsuccessful predictions** for each unique label, generated by **development set examples** that pass through this node at runtime;

By pruning a node we actually wind up generating correct prediction for all example instances of the most probable label an incorrectly classify all other examples. As such, for each node (n) we can compute the most probable label (l) as

$$l = argmax(g_n) \qquad (12)$$

and the accuracy gain (A_n) as:

$$A_n = \frac{(s_{n,l} + f_{n,l}) - \sum s_n}{E} \qquad (13)$$

where E is the total number of examples in the development set.

As such, we compute g_n in the initialization step of our algorithm and we update s_n and f_n by performing a single pass on the development set before each tree-pruning iteration. This means that for a tree with 15K nodes (which is not rare), we only require a single pass over the development set, instead of 15K passes, which makes this approach practically 15K faster than the naive implementation.

4 Experimental Validation

To provide a thorough evaluation of our proposed methodologies, we are (a) providing a clear view over the computation-time enhancements by comparing a naive ID3 implementation with our own version of the algorithm (subsection 4.2) and (b) demonstrate how we mitigate model over-fitting issues using tree-pruning by comparing our results to state-of-the-art methods in identical testing conditions (subsection 4.3)

4.1 Corpora Description

For our algorithm validation process we have selected a number of training datasets which we can use in our evaluation. The choice of these datasets is driven by reproducibility, in the sense that we have access to both training and datasets on which state-of-the-art methods were tuned and tested. Before we proceed with the actual evaluation of our system we will shortly review these datasets to familiarize the reader with the tasks themselves. Arguably, there are many other resources that can be used in the validation process, but we feel that the selected datasets provide a fair coverage on most of the typical NLP tasks. The chosen datasets refer to: (a) letter-to-sound (LTS); (b) syllabification; (c) part-of-speech tagging; (d) text classification and (e) tokenization

- **The LTS lexicon** used in our validation process contains two sub-datasets: the CMU-Dictionary (Weide, 2005) and the Romanian Speech Synthesis Database (Stan et al., 2011);

- **The syllabification lexicon** is the automatically Onset-Nucleus-Coda (ONC) (Bartlett et al., 2008) labeled corpora also has two sub-corpora, for Romanian and English;

- **The part-of-speech lexicon** is based on the coarse part-of-speech datasets (Petrov et al., 2011) provided in the Universal Dependencies Database (Nivre et al., 2016);

- **Morphological attributes lexicon** is compiled from the Universal Dependencies Database based on the specifications of Zeman (2008);

- **The text classification datasets** contain the WebKB dataset (Craven et al., 1998), and 20 newsgroups (20ng);

- **The tokenization corpus** is automatically extracted from the multilingual training-files provided with Universal Dependencies.

Before we proceed with the actual validation we must clarify the testing conditions regarding morphological attribute resolution. As mentioned, the training data was compiled from the Universal Dependencies treebank. The morphological labels strictly refer to attributes such as gender, number, case etc. and not to the part-of-speech itself

Table 2: Training time on the selected corpora, reported using the naive and optimized implementations of the algorithm

Dataset	# examples	# features	# labels	Naive	Optimized
LTS EN (CMUDICT)	666771	295	159	212.7s	9.8s
LTS RO (RSS)	53491	206	48	14.6s	0.18s
SYL EN	1373012	240	22	720.2s	12.9s
SYL RO	4760735	291	25	885.4s	41.9s
TAG EN (UD)	204605	2133	17	5811.3s	19.8s
TAG RO (UD)	185113	2403	17	4956.1s	19.1s

(which is actually used as an input feature). The original files are in CONLL format[2] and the attributes are stored in a special column in the form of key/value pairs. In order to create our training data we used the following procedure:

1. We went through the entire training data and we grouped attributes by their key, thus obtaining attribute groups;

2. We created separate training, development and test files for each individual attribute group;

3. For every word/token, we used the following features, extracted from every word inside a 5-token window (centered on the current item): coarse part-of-speech, first 4 characters of the word (4 individual features), last 4 characters of the word (also 4 individual features), word style (lowercased, capitalized or uppercased)

4.2 Training Speed Optimization

To check our proposed optimization technique we will measure the training speed gain for each of the previously mentioned datasets. Table 2 shows the training time measured for both the naive and optimized implementations of the algorithm. To ensure comparable results, we verified that the naive and optimized tree structures are identical.

The table shows that our proposed implementation of the algorithm speeds up training time by a 1-3 orders of magnitude compared to the naive tree construction. This translates in the ability to perform a significantly larger number of tests during feature selection and tuning phases. To our knowledge, there is no other implementation of any tool or classifier that can build a **comparable model** in such a short period of time.

<hr>

[2]http://universaldependencies.org/format.html - accessed 2017-05-03

4.3 Accuracy-Boost Using Tree-Pruning

To prove that our tree pruning strategy is effective on real life data, in what follows we are going to compare the accuracy of the un-pruned trees to that of pruned trees. For reference, we are also going to report the highest accuracy of any other state-of-the-art method, provided that the testing conditions are identical. Table 3 summarizes the results and, as can be seen, the results obtained using the pruned tree are significantly better that the un-pruned version and are very close to state-of-the-art results reported by other authors. The notable difference on the tagging set between the ID3 classifier and the CRF is mostly influenced by the fact that the CRF implementation generates label bi-grams and uses a Viterbi decoder to select an optimal state sequence. A similar approach can also be obtained using the ID3 tree, but the tree-pruning part would require a different methodology for computation and optimization and it was currently out-of-scope. However, when it comes to morphology extracted from local word features, the ID3 implementation is closer to the CRF results, mainly because morphologic attribute resolution is not influenced by bi-grams (we are not saying that there are no context dependencies between the attributes of words - we imply that these dependencies are not easily handled by the simple use of label bi-grams).

*The results reported in Jiampojamarn et al. (2008) are probably obtained using a different split or corpora preparation (filtering) procedure. In practice when we tried to reproduce the results with an identical feature template, using the same classifier, we only achieved a 65.19% accuracy on our test-set.

For letter-to-sound and syllabification we report word-accuracy (not label accuracy which is significantly higher) and for document classification we report the number of correctly classified examples.

Table 3: Accuracy figures for the selected datasets, reported for the pruned, un-pruned and reference state-of-the-art methods and algorithms

Dataset	Un-pruned			Pruned			State-of-the-art			
	Train	Dev	Test	Train	Dev	Test	Name	Train	Dev	Test
LTS EN	72.67	56.93	56.47	67.58	64.11	63.18	MIRA	N/A	N/A	**71.99***
LTS RO	98.36	93.24	93.44	97.07	95.31	95.05	MIRA	N/A	N/A	**96.29**
Syl EN	94.77	82.63	83.21	89.31	87.89	85.58	CRF	N/A	N/A	**86.22**
Syl RO	99.27	98.89	98.97	99.21	99.07	**99.16**	CRF	N/A	N/A	99.10
Tag EN	97.28	94.03	93.98	96.05	95.13	95.04	CRF	N/A	N/A	**97.63**
Tag RO	98.78	93.12	93.02	96.42	95.68	95.48	CRF	N/A	N/A	**96.72**
Morph En	–.–	–.–	97.22	–.–	–.–	**98.46**	Custom	N/A	N/A	93.82
Morph RO	–.–	–.–	94.81	–.–	–.–	**95.76**	Custom	N/A	N/A	95.56
Tok EN	–.–	–.–	–.–	–.–	–.–	**99.05**	GRU	N/A	N/A	98.69
Tok RO	–.–	–.–	–.–	–.–	–.–	**99.80**	GRU	N/A	N/A	99.55
WebKB	99.76	75.35	74.11	86.10	81.78	**78.15**	LSI	N/A	N/A	75.56
20NG	99.96	51.72	52.16	81.85	72.32	**62.91**	LSI	N/A	N/A	62.78

Because the current version of the UD corpus was newly released, there are no official papers that evaluate any state-of-the art methods on the latest release of the corpora. However, in this case we compare the pruned tree results with the results reported on the official UD page (tokenization - using Gated Recurrent Units (GRUs) (Straka et al., 2016)). Also, we were unable to evaluate tokenization results in a "static manner", because token boundaries for a given character index depend on the previously generated breaks. Thus, we only provide the final evaluation results over the test set. Also, we must mention that in order to keep the testing conditions similar to previously reported results we did not alter the tests sets in any way and we used 10% of the original training data for building our development sets.

The state-of-the-art results obtained for WebKB and 20NG are based Latent Semantic Indexing (LSI) (Zelikovitz and Hirsh, 2001).

5   Conclusions and Future Work

We introduced our optimized version of the ID3 tree-computation algorithm, as well as a method to fine-tune an existing tree using a development set to selectively prune it. The later mentioned algorithm is also optimized for speed using a result-caching approach.

We showed that by fine-tuning a tree structure one can achieve results comparable to state-of-the art classifiers. We argue that decision trees can be easily used in the feature selection process of any machine learning algorithm. Combined with the enhanced computation time and tree-pruning methodology make this a useful contribution, especially in the field of natural language processing where working with discrete features in a bag-of-words fashion is common.

Additionally, the results reported in section 4.3 are obtained by simply extracting features inside the context-window and not by introducing any predefined feature-sets. This is not the case for the state-of-the art results to which we compared our system to, where the features are actually the result of complex careful crafting of feature templates. The robust principles behind decision trees do not require an extensive feature engineering process. Instead, the constructed tree can offer a good overview of the task and dataset itself and can actually guide the process of constructing feature templates for other classifiers. Finally, one very important note about this implementation is that it was used during the preparation of a shared task which involved more that 50 datasets on which various tasks had to be performed. The enhanced speed of this algorithm allowed us to make over 1000 training runs and explore a rich set of features, in the short available time, which, without the optimization would otherwise had been impossible.

Our implementation of the enhanced ID3 algorithm is written in C++ and we provide a JAVA library for the tree-pruning and prediction algorithms. The tool is freely available and can be downloaded[3].

---

[3]http://slp.racai.ro/

References

Susan Bartlett, Grzegorz Kondrak, and Colin Cherry. 2008. Automatic syllabification with structured svms for letter-to-phoneme conversion. In *ACL*. pages 568–576.

Mark Craven, Andrew McCallum, Dan PiPasquo, Tom Mitchell, and Dayne Freitag. 1998. Learning to extract symbolic knowledge from the world wide web. Technical report, DTIC Document.

Wei Dai and Wei Ji. 2014. A mapreduce implementation of c4. 5 decision tree algorithm. *International Journal of Database Theory and Application* 7(1):49–60.

Thomas G Dietterich. 2000. An experimental comparison of three methods for constructing ensembles of decision trees: Bagging, boosting, and randomization. *Machine learning* 40(2):139–157.

Sittichai Jiampojamarn, Colin Cherry, and Grzegorz Kondrak. 2008. Joint processing and discriminative training for letter-to-phoneme conversion. In *ACL*. pages 905–913.

David D Lewis and Marc Ringuette. 1994. A comparison of two learning algorithms for text categorization. In *Third annual symposium on document analysis and information retrieval*. volume 33, pages 81–93.

Manish Mehta, Jorma Rissanen, Rakesh Agrawal, et al. 1995. Mdl-based decision tree pruning. In *KDD*. volume 21, pages 216–221.

Joakim Nivre, Marie-Catherine de Marneffe, Filip Ginter, Yoav Goldberg, Jan Hajic, Christopher D Manning, Ryan McDonald, Slav Petrov, Sampo Pyysalo, Natalia Silveira, et al. 2016. Universal dependencies v1: A multilingual treebank collection. In *Proceedings of the 10th International Conference on Language Resources and Evaluation (LREC 2016)*. pages 1659–1666.

Vincent Pagel, Kevin Lenzo, and Alan Black. 1998. Letter to sound rules for accented lexicon compression. *arXiv preprint cmp-lg/9808010* .

Slav Petrov, Dipanjan Das, and Ryan McDonald. 2011. A universal part-of-speech tagset. *arXiv preprint arXiv:1104.2086* .

J. Ross Quinlan. 1986. Induction of decision trees. *Machine learning* 1(1):81–106.

J. Ross Quinlan. 1987. Simplifying decision trees. *International journal of man-machine studies* 27(3):221–234.

J Ross Quinlan. 1993. *C4.5: programs for machine learning*. Elsevier.

Rajeev Rastogi and Kyuseok Shim. 1998. Public: A decision tree classifier that integrates building and pruning. In *VLDB*. volume 98, pages 24–27.

Helmut Schmid. 2013. Probabilistic part-ofispeech tagging using decision trees. In *New methods in language processing*. Routledge, page 154.

Adriana Stan, Junichi Yamagishi, Simon King, and Matthew Aylett. 2011. The romanian speech synthesis (rss) corpus: Building a high quality hmm-based speech synthesis system using a high sampling rate. *Speech Communication* 53(3):442–450.

Milan Straka, Jan Hajic, and Jana Straková. 2016. Ud-pipe: Trainable pipeline for processing conll-u files performing tokenization, morphological analysis, pos tagging and parsing. In *Proceedings of the Tenth International Conference on Language Resources and Evaluation (LREC 2016)*.

Jiang Su and Harry Zhang. 2006. A fast decision tree learning algorithm. In *AAAI*. volume 6, pages 500–505.

György Szarvas, Richárd Farkas, and András Kocsor. 2006. A multilingual named entity recognition system using boosting and c4. 5 decision tree learning algorithms. In *International Conference on Discovery Science*. Springer, pages 267–278.

Robert Weide. 2005. The carnegie mellon pronouncing dictionary [cmudict. 0.6].

Sarah Zelikovitz and Haym Hirsh. 2001. Using lsi for text classification in the presence of background text. In *Proceedings of the tenth international conference on Information and knowledge management*. ACM, pages 113–118.

Daniel Zeman. 2008. Reusable tagset conversion using tagset drivers. In *LREC*.

Heiga Zen, Takashi Nose, Junichi Yamagishi, Shinji Sako, Takashi Masuko, Alan W Black, and Keiichi Tokuda. 2007. The hmm-based speech synthesis system (hts) version 2.0. In *SSW*. Citeseer, pages 294–299.

Heiga Zen, Keiichi Tokuda, and Alan W Black. 2009. Statistical parametric speech synthesis. *Speech Communication* 51(11):1039–1064.

An Evolutionary Algorithm for Automatic Summarization

Aurélien Bossard[*] and Christophe Rodrigues[**]

[*]LIASD - EA 4383, Université Paris 8, Saint-Denis, France
bossard@iut.univ-paris8.fr
[**]Léonard de Vinci Pôle Universitaire, Research Center, Paris La Défense, France
christophe.rodrigues.bento@gmail.com

Abstract

This paper proposes a novel method to select sentences for automatic summarization based on an evolutionary algorithm. The algorithm explores candidate summaries space following an objective function computed over ngrams probability distributions of the candidate summary and the source documents. This method does not consider a summary as a stack of independent sentences but as a whole text, and makes use of advances in unsupervised summarization evaluation. We compare this sentence extraction method to one of the best existing methods which is based on integer linear programming, and show its efficiency on three different acknowledged corpora.

1 Introduction

Automatic summarization systems are essential components of information systems. Indeed, increase of numerical information sources can have a negative effect on online content reading and assimilation. Summarizing such content can allow users to better apprehend it. Automatic summarization has therefore become one of the first research in natural language processing field (Luhn, 1958) and still remains a widely spread topic.

In order to validate the benefits obtained from new methods or parametrization, the automatic summarization field needs robust evaluation methods. Evaluating automatic summaries, just like evaluating automatic translation, is a complex task. Until early 2000s, only two types of approach existed: entirely manual evaluation with a reading grid and semi-automatic evaluations that compare automatic summaries with human written references. Since, entirely automatic approaches that allow for evaluating a summary without a human reference (writing it is the most time-consuming task in evaluation) emerged and have recently achieved good performances, using probabilistic models (Louis and Nenkova, 2009; Saggion et al., 2010).

Probabilistic models for automatic summarization evaluation are natural: a summary and its source have to share the same distribution of concepts. As they have proven performant for evaluation, using them to guide automatic summarization process seems obvious, although it has to our knowledge not been already tested. As opposed to the most part of automatic summarization methods that use encoded metrics, we here propose to consider automatic summarization as the maximization of a natural score: the divergence between the concepts distribution in the source and the concepts distribution of a candidate summary.

So we view automatic summarization as choosing the best summary among a very large set of candidate summaries upon a metric that is computed on the whole candidate summary. This leads us to the use of an evolutionary algorithm in order to naturally select the best summaries.

While other recent papers (Li et al., 2013; Nishikawa et al., 2014; Peyrard and Eckle-Kohler, 2016) integrate sophisticated and task-specific preprocessings and postprocessings, and handle semantics using complex representations, this paper proposes a new generic and directly usable sentence extraction method for automatic summarization. This method explores the candidate summaries space using an evolutionary algorithm. This algorithm aims at finding an approximate solution of the maximization of an objective function computed over a candidate summary. We first present iterative methods and exploratory analysis methods for automatic summarization. We then expose our sentence extraction method and

Proceedings of Recent Advances in Natural Language Processing, pages 111–120,
Varna, Bulgaria, Sep 4–6 2017.

the evaluation protocol: it is compared to one of the best methods in the automatic summarization field. Finally, we discuss our results.

2 Related Work

Iterative Selection Automatic summarization systems generally combine a centrality score for text portions and an extraction method for these portions. The first automatic summarization systems (Luhn, 1958; Edmundson, 1969) simply extracted most central portions. MMR method (Carbonell and Goldstein, 1998) allows for iterative text portions extraction given a centrality score and a redundancy score. CSIS-based method (Radev, 2000) removes from a list of text portions sorted by centrality every one that shares too much information with a higher ranked. These methods share a major drawback: generated summaries depend mostly on the first selected text portion. Therefore, they are exposed to omitting summaries made of average ranked sentences that reflect correctly the overall content of the source documents when combined together.

Optimization Other methods emerged recently to overcome this problem. They consist in exploring the space of all candidate summaries in order to find the one that maximizes an objective function. This problem is exponential in input sentences as there are C_m^n candidate summaries composed of n sentences for a corpus of m sentences. For example, choosing 10 sentences over 200 leads to 10^{25} possible solutions. Adding constraints on text portions selection and using ILP[1] help delimiting the problem and finding (not always) an exact solution (McDonald, 2007; Gillick and Favre, 2009b). The search space is limited by constraints on text portions length and by constraints that avoid including text portions that do not provide additional information. Whereas Gillick and Favre (2009b) select summaries based on the maximization of bigram occurrences, Li et al. (2013) try to maximize the similarity between summaries and sources bigram frequencies. These methods have proven to be very efficient. However, the use of an ILP solver enforces to modelize the problem as a linear functions, so does not allow for complex functions that could better take into account the structure of the automatic summarization problem.

---

[1]Integer Linear Programming

Liu et al. (2006); Nandhini and Balasundaram (2013); Shigematsu and Kobayashi (2014) propose to look for an approximate solution using a genetic algorithm. As opposed to ILP extraction methods, these methods are free of any constraints on the objective function. However, these methods keep on considering a summary as a set of independent portions of text, and do not take advantage of the new structure of the problem that we propose: a summary is not considered as a whole. Considering a summary as a whole allows for a better space exploration and more complex objective functions. Alfonseca and Rodríguez (2003) use a "standard GA" without describing it and several fitness scores, whose main metric is cosine-tfidf similarity between sources and candidate summaries. However, this similarity has obtained poor results when used as an automatic evaluation metric (Nenkova et al., 2007). So this metric should not be used as fitness score for automatic summarization. As opposed to Alfonseca and Rodríguez (2003), we define a new, non-standard, and fully replicable evolutionary algorithm combined with an extension of an agreed-upon automatic evaluation metric.

Supervised Learning (Litvak et al., 2010; Bossard and Rodrigues, 2011) use genetic algorithms for supervised learning of parameters in order to tune automatic summarization systems. Nishikawa et al. (2014); Takamura and Okumura (2010); Sipos et al. (2012) perform structured output learning to maximize ROUGE scores. These approaches suffer from the complexity of machine learning model. Moreover, it requires learning data and is very task-specific. Recently, Peyrard and Eckle-Kohler (2016) proposed to use an approximation of ROUGE-N score combined to an ILP solver. The approximation of ROUGE-N score is performed with supervised learning. The results obtained outperform state-of-the art methods on DUC 2002 and 2003 corpora.

In contrast to supervised learning, we propose to use a fully unsupervised method that allows for summarizing even when no manual reference is available. We here propose to use scoring functions based on probabilistic models of source documents and candidate summaries. The smoothing used for building probability distributions considers a candidate summary as a whole, not as a set of independent sentences. This complex objective function requires a constraint-free optimization algorithm. So evolutionary algorithms seem appropriate. In the meantime, the scoring functions we use allow to benefit more of evolutionary algorithms.

3 Our Method

Louis and Nenkova (2009) have proposed an entirely unsupervised function for automatic summary evaluation. The evaluation method has proved efficient as it strongly correlates to Pyramid score, a semi-automatic score used in TAC evaluation campaigns to assess automatic summaries informational quality (Nenkova et al., 2007). Saggion et al. (2010) confirmed the relevance of the approach. The method is entirely unsupervised, so it does not need any human reference. This makes it perfectly fit to be used as an objective function in a guided space exploring algorithm.

Our objective function computes the probability distribution of tokens in the source documents with the probability distribution of tokens in the summaries. Tokens can be words, ngrams or even semantic concepts. The objective function is based on (Louis and Nenkova, 2009) that handles automatic evaluation using Jensen-Shannon(JS) divergence.

The JS divergence can be considered as a symmetric version of Kullback-Leibler divergence (KL). KL divergence is defined as the average number of bits wasted by coding samples belonging to P using another distribution Q, an approximate of P (Louis and Nenkova, 2009). In our case, the two distributions are those for words (or concepts) in the input and the summary.

Given two distributions P and Q, here is the definition of JS divergence:

$$JS(P||Q) = \frac{1}{2}[KL(P||A) + KL(Q||A)]$$

with : $A = \frac{P+Q}{2}$ the mean distribution of P and Q; $KL(P||A)$ the Kullback-Leibler divergence:

$$KL(P||Q) = \sum_w p_P(w) log_2 \frac{p_P(w)}{p_Q(w)}$$

Louis and Nenkova (2009) use a simple weighted Laplace smoothing over probabilities.

$$p(w) = \frac{C(w)+\delta}{N+\delta \times 1.5 \times |V|}$$

with : $C(w)$ the number of occurrences of w; N the overall number of tokens; V the vocabulary, and $\delta = 0.0005$.

3.1 Unigram Distribution Objective Function

This objective function (Uniprob) fits the exact automatic evaluation function described above and in (Louis and Nenkova, 2009).

3.2 Bigram Simple Sum Objective Function

Bigram simple sum objective function (Bisimple) consists in summing all bigram weights in a candidate summary. Candidate summaries get a high score if they are composed of the most frequent bigrams in the source documents.

3.3 Bigram Cosine Objective Function

Bigram cosine objective function (Bicos) consists in a cosine similarity between source and candidate summaries bigram vector. This objective function is used in (Alfonseca and Rodríguez, 2003).

3.4 Bigram Distribution Objective Function

Lin (2004) has shown that ROUGE semi-automatic evaluation metrics are more correlated to manual evaluation when using bigrams rather than unigrams when it comes to compare summaries and references of a standard length: 50 words and more. Therefore, we make the assumption that a probabilistic model based on bigrams outcomes one based on unigrams for our objective function. Moreover, we smooth probabilities using Dirichlet smoothing (MacKay and Peto, 1994), that adds to every count of a token in a summary its probability in the source documents. Dirichlet smoothing is more faithful to the data (Zhai and Lafferty, 2004) than Laplacian smoothing while remaining simple to compute. With Dirichlet smoothing, the probability of a token t in a summary S is computed this way:

$$p_{dir}(t|S) = \frac{C_S(t)+\mu p_{ML}(t|D)}{N_S+\mu}$$

with: D the source documents; $C_S(t)$ the number of occurrences of t in S; $p_{ML}(t|D)$ the maximum likelihood of t in D; N_S the number of tokens in S; and μ a constant parameter called pseudo-frequency.

Candidate summaries are subsets of source documents, so smoothing is only applied to summaries.

However, this objective function (Biprob) may have a major drawback: it favors summaries whose probability distributions are close to source documents. If these source documents are highly redundant, the summaries that are rated high on this objective function would also be redundant.

3.5 Evolutionary Algorithm

We here describe the evolutionary algorithm we developed and use for maximization of our objective function. This evolutionary algorithm differs from traditional genetic algorithms as described below, to better handle automatic summarization problem. In fact, automatic summarization tasks often bound the summaries length in words, not in number of sentences. So the number of sentences extracted in a summary depends on both maximum summary length and each sentence length. That is why we cannot use a standard problem model in which every candidate summary would be an individual with n genes, n being the number of sentences to extract. Having a specific representation of the individuals leads to defining new operators on these individuals. So the mutation and hybridization mutators differ from what we are used to because of the structure of our problem.

Individuals Definition   Each individual (= a candidate summary) is defined by a set of chromosomes (= sentences). A chromosome codes for a sentence. The number of chromosomes in the set of an individual is variable, while there is an upper threshold for the sum over the length of all chromosomes in words. This requires some adaptations to the classic mutation and hybridization operators, that we define below.

Algorithm Sequence   At generation 0, a starting population is created randomly. It contains N individuals, where $N = N_p + N_m + N_h$, where N_p, N_m and N_h are the parameters of the evolutionary algorithm for the next generations. For each of the next generations:

- N_p is the number of parents;

- N_m is the number of mutated individuals;

- N_h is the number of hybridated individuals.

Then N_p parents are selected to generate by mutation and by hybridation N_m and N_h additional individuals. The parents and the individuals they generated constitute a new generation. N_g generations are iteratively created this way. At the end, the individual that maximizes the objective function is selected.

Starting Population Selection N individuals are randomly generated. A new sentence is randomly added to an individual until the length constraint is reached:

$$\exists s \in S \backslash I\, s.t. \sum_{s_i \in I} length(s_i) + length(s) < maxLength,$$

with I an individual and S the sentences in source documents.

Parents Selection   Parents selection can be performed through different methods. These methods favor space exploration or exploitation by selecting the best individuals. We chose a selection method that is a compromise between exploration and exploitation : tournament selection. N_p tournaments composed of $\frac{N}{N_p}$ individuals – with N the total population size – are randomly created. The best individual in each tournament is selected as a parent for the next generation.

Mutation Operator   We cannot use classic mutation operators: changing one gene for another. Selecting a too long sentence would violate the summary length constraint while selecting a too short sentence would let the new candidate summary to be evaluated against other summaries that are longer. Our mutation operator is defined as follows : a chromosome (sentence) is randomly deleted from an individual. The individual is then randomly filled with new chromosomes until the length constraint is no longer satisfiable.

Hybridization Operator   The chromosomes of two individuals (here, parents) are put together in a single set. A new individual is then created with chromosomes randomly selected from this set. Once no more chromosome matches the length constraint, the individual is randomly filled with chromosomes from the source documents. This operation does not guarantee that chromosomes from both individuals will be selected, so it is completely different from traditional hybridization operators. Proceeding this way is however mandatory in order to create individuals that will satisfy the summary length constraint.

4   Experiment

We compare our summarization method to three *baselines* on TAC 2008, TAC 2009 evaluation campaigns corpora[2]. We also use the French cor-

---

[2]The corpora are available on request at `http://www.nist.gov/tac/data/index.html`.

pus RPM2[3] evaluation that share a similar structure with the TAC 2008 and 2009 corpora.

4.1 Corpora

TAC 2008, 2009 and RPM2 are composed of two distinct parts: the first one is dedicated to standard multi-document summarization. The second is dedicated to update summarization: the goal is to summarize information in the update set, assuming that the user has already read the information in the standard set. The following TAC campaigns concern guided summarization: writing summaries for a given topic where the topic falls into a predefined category, including "Accidents and Natural Disasters", "Attacks", "Health and Safety", "Endangered Resources", and "Trials and Investigations". The goal is to encourage a deeper linguistic analysis, and summarization systems must take into account each task specificity in order to produce coherent summaries. So, post 2009 TAC campaigns are out of this article scope.

TAC 2009 standard summarization corpus is composed of 44 sets of 10 documents each: english-written news articles. The task consists in generating a 100 words summary for every document set. Average document length is 6330 words.

4.2 Our System

Document Preprocessing The documents are first cleaned: all tags and meta-information are removed.

Tokenization and Sentence Splitting We first use the default tokenizer of the POS-tagging tool tree-tagger[4] (Schmid, 1994). Tree-tagger is also used for POS-tagging (not used in the English system) and sentence splitting.

Stemming Words are stemmed via the Porter stemmer for TAC 2008 and 2009 corpora. For RPM2, we implemented the French snowball stemmer[5].

Bigrams Filtering Bigrams composed of two stopwords are pruned. A stoplist composed of the 200 more frequent English words is used for this

purpose. For the French corpus, a word is considered as a stopword if it is tagged as either a determiner or a preposition.

Sentence Selection Sentence selection is performed by the evolutionary algorithm described in Section 3.5 using the three objective functions described in Sections 3.4, 3.1 and 3.2.

Evolutionary Algorithm Parameters We empirically tuned the number of generations using TAC 2009 test dataset in order to increase the probability that the algorithm converges. TAC 2009 test dataset and evaluation datasets are strictly disjoint. Here are the parameters of the evolutionary algorithm: $N_p = N_h = N_m = 160$ and $N_g = 160$.

First Sentences Salience TAC 2009 corpus is a news corpus composed for the most part of news wires and articles. First sentences are often considered as more salient than the other ones. (Gillick et al., 2009a) upweight by a factor 2 the concepts that appear in the first sentence of a document and thus reach a 16% gain in automatic evaluation metrics on TAC 2009 corpus. Our systems also upweight by a factor 2 the bigrams in the first sentences. We test its effect in Section 5.

4.3 Baselines

We implemented two baselines:

- *lexmmr*: common scoring method LexRank (Erkan and Radev, 2004), followed by MMR (Carbonell and Goldstein, 1998) to perform redundancy removal;

- *ILP*: the sentence selection method of (Gillick et al., 2009a) described in Section 2.

These two systems have the same preprocessing, tokenizing, stemming, filtering, and first sentence bigrams weighting as ours, so they can be compared efficiently.

ILP1 baseline is based on ICSI summarization system (Gillick et al., 2009a) which is considered as state-of-the-art in a recent study (Hong et al., 2014). ICSI employ different heuristics/preprocessings, *eg* pronominal references removal, relative dates and "said" clauses removal. In order to efficiently compare sentence extraction methods, we here use a generic version of ICSI system: sentence extraction is processed using the

---

[3]The corpus is available on request at `http://lia.univ-avignon.fr/fileadmin/documents/rpm2/`

[4]Treetagger: `http://www.cis.uni-muenchen.de/~schmid/tools/TreeTagger/`

[5]Snowball: `http://snowball.tartarus.org/algorithms/french/stemmer.html`

		Baselines				Evolutionary algorithm based systems				
		lexmmr	hextac	ILP1	ILP2	uniprob	biprob	bisimple	bicos	Oracle
TAC2008	ROUGE-1	.3134	-	.3713	.3716	.3546	**.3804**	.3752	.3497	.4262
	ROUGE-2	.0647	-	.1075	.1027	.0816	**.1103**	.1065	.0930	.1718
TAC2009	ROUGE-1	.3361	.3794	.3729	.3837	.3509	**.3855**	.3846	.3586	.4348
	ROUGE-2	.0787	.1065	.1053	.1096	.0821	**.1173**	.1128	.0961	.1782
RPM2	ROUGE-1	.3203	-	.4126	.4126	.3843	**.4250**	.3801	.4071	.4407
	ROUGE-2	.0889	-	.1568	.1568	.1472	**.1683**	.1473	.1491	.2039
Overall	ROUGE-1	.3236	-	.3793	.3837	.3655	**.3904**	.3798	.3634	.4321
	ROUGE-2	.0745	-	.1154	.1151	.0961	**.1234**	.1163	.1042	.1800

Table 1: Average results of all systems on TAC 2008, 2009 and RPM2

same solver as ICSI system (glpk) but preprocessings are limited to the strict minimum: the same as our system, described in 4.2. This way it can be efficiently compared to our evolutionary based sentence extraction method. As in (Gillick et al., 2009a), sentences of less than 10 words and bigrams that do not appear more than twice are not taken into account; in ILP2, we add the last rule in ICSI summarization system: sentences that do not share at least one word in common with the query are pruned. This way, we can compare more efficiently ILP baselines to our system that does not take query into account. The only difference between ICSI summarization system and ILP2 lies in processings that are not related to the sentence selection module.

The last baseline (*hextac*) is TAC 2009 third *baseline* : human generated extractive summaries (Genest et al., 2009). This baseline stands for determining the best summary we can achieve using purely extractive methods. Therefore, comparing its results to a pure extractive summarizer is informative. However, as the goal of this system is to produce good summaries for a human judge, its automatic scores could be lower than manual ones. In fact, human extractors can emphasize linguistic quality and global coherence rather than pure information extraction.

4.4 Oracle Experiments

We want to estimate the upper bound that a system based on our evolutionary algorithm and a probabilistic model can achieve. For this purpose, we define a new objective function. The objective function described above compares distributions between candidate summaries and source documents. If we suppose that manual summaries are available (which is the case in ROUGE evaluation campaigns), then we can directly compute distributions between candidate summaries and manual ones. So doing, we obtain an evolutionary approach guided by an Oracle. Given the small size of manual summaries used as source documents,

we don't use any smoothing at all.

This oracle is a good way to fit to the manual summaries. However, it is not optimal in all cases. The manual summaries are indeed small and are not necessarily composed of bigrams also present in source documents. This can cause the distribution divergences to be less precise.

5 Results

We here use the same ROUGE parameters as for TAC evaluation campaings[6].

5.1 General Results

Table 1 presents the results obtained by all the systems and baselines described in Section 4.2 on three corpora : TAC 2008, TAC 2009 and RPM2. The best system, whatever the evaluation metric, is *biprob*, that uses our evolutionary algorithm and JS divergence between bigrams distributions on source documents and candidate summaries as objective function. It outperforms *ILP1* and *ILP2* baselines. *ILP1* and *ILP2* baselines have the same ROUGE scores on RPM2 corpus, as RPM2 is not query-oriented. One can notice that *biprob* and human baseline *hextac* are really close in terms of ROUGE scores.

Biprob system as well as *ILP* baselines outperform the human generated *hextac* baseline. It means that both systems succeed in extracting as many salient information as a human. However, *hextac* summaries outperform automatic summaries in terms of linguistic quality: coherence, ordering...

5.2 Impact of First Sentence Bigrams Upweight

All of the three corpora are only composed of newswire articles and share the same information structure. The central information is located in the first sentences. Figure 1 shows *biprob* and *ILP* baseline ROUGE-2 scores when the upweight

---

[6]ROUGE-1.5.5.pl -c 95 -r 1000 -n 2 -m -a -x -d file

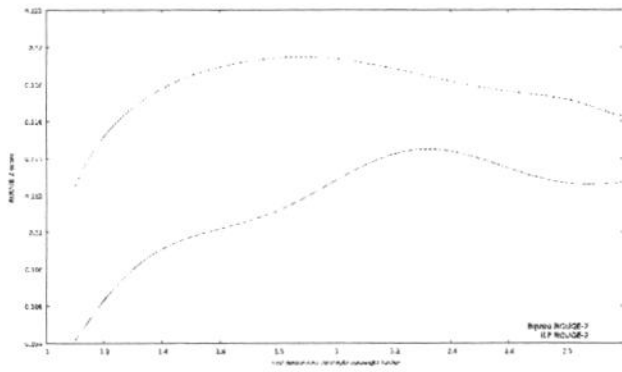

Figure 1: *Biprob* system and *ILP1* baseline results depending on first sentences concepts upweight value

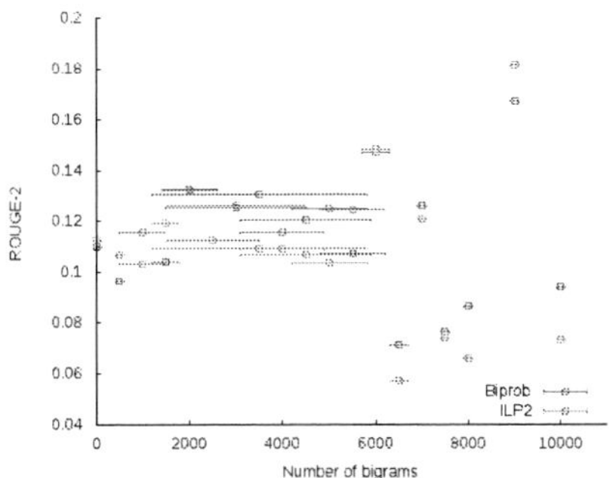

Figure 2: ROUGE-2 scores on all topics depending on topic size in bigrams

factor of first sentence bigrams varies on our three corpora. Increasing first sentences concepts weight improves ROUGE-2 scores of both ILP baseline and *biprob* on the overall score over the three corpora. The maximum is reached around the factor 2, as assumed by Gillick et al. (2009a). Our experiment confirms that weighting up first sentence concepts with a factor 2 is efficient on newswire articles corpora.

5.3 Impact of Input Size

Figure 2 presents ROUGE-2 scores of ILP1 baseline and Biprob depending on the number of bigrams in the source documents for all corpora. The x error bar shows the number of topics that are concerned by a point. One can see that the two systems are really close for small topics. However, for topics with a larger number of bigrams, Biprob tends to outperform ILP1 (except for number of bigrams intervals with a small number of examples).

5.4 Impact of Bigram Filtering

Taking into account only the bigrams that appear more than twice for ILP baselines increases results (as also noticed in (Gillick et al., 2009a)), so we tested a probability distribution that keeps

only these bigrams. The results are not as good as when computing probability distribution over all bigrams. This can be linked to the fact that our method performs better when the number of bigrams as input is high.

5.5 Convergence on TAC 2009 Data

Figure 3 shows the average fitness score (= bigram distribution objective function) of each generation for every topic of TAC 2008, TAC 2009 and RPM2 corpora for 12 different runs of the evolutionary algorithm. We can see that the scores seem to converge quite fast on average, before the 50th generation.

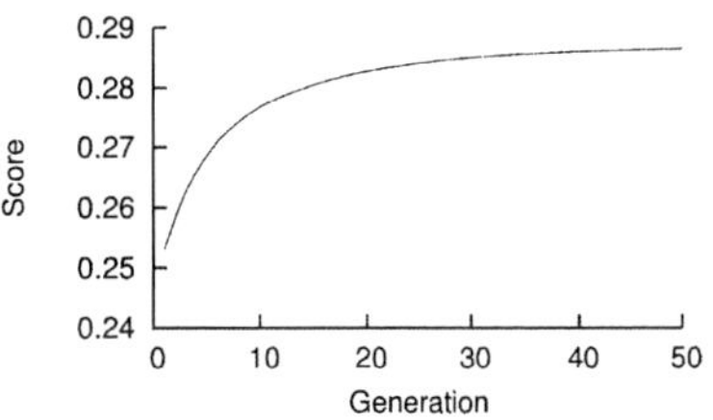

Figure 3: Average fitness scores of all topics in TAC 2008, 2009 and RPM2 corpora depending on the generation.

The Figure 3 presents the fitness average scores on all evaluation topics. Convergence speed depend on several factors: data dispersal, exploration space size... Figure 4 shows the convergence speed for the most populated topic of our three corpora: the D0918 topic from TAC 2009. It prints the average score, and the score standard deviation for D0918 topic on 12 different runs. This can give us an idea of the algorithm convergence in the worst case, speaking of exploration space size.

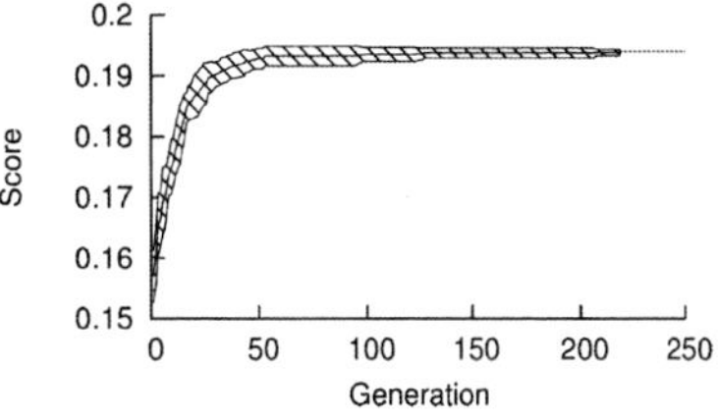

Figure 4: Average scores and standard deviation of scores for D0918 topic depending on the generation.

The algorithm converges near the 220th generation, and the topic is composed of 575 sentences. There are more than 5×10^{13} candidate summaries that match the 100 words length limit, and the evolutionary algorithm has always reached convergence after exploring 70400 different candidate summaries.

5.6 Oracle Results

One can see in table 1 that, as expected, our Oracle performs more than 50% better than every of our systems. This means that there are summaries composed of sentences in the source documents that are closer to the reference summaries than those chosen by our objective functions. The 50% difference in ROUGE-2 scores shows that there is room for improvement.

6 Discussion

In this article, we proposed a sentence extraction method for automatic summarization that allows for good summaries on our three evaluation corpora. Our method outperforms a state-of-the-art sentence extraction method based on an ILP model by more than 6.4% on the combined score of our three evaluation corpora.

We show that Jensen-Shannon divergence outperforms cosine similarity as objective function in our evolutionary algorithm. This confirms the conclusions of (Louis and Nenkova, 2009) on the evaluation of metrics for automatic summary evaluation.

Thanks to the use of an evolutionary algorithm rather than an ILP-based method, the score computation and constraints are totally free and not limited by ILP modelization constraints. However, the objective functions described here do not handle redundancy. A candidate summary will be well scored if its probability distribution sticks to the one of the source documents. So, if the source documents display high redundancy on a given information, our method could generate redundant summaries. However, other objective functions that handle redundancy can be implemented as well as constraints on candidate summaries generation. Our system does not try to improve linguistic quality: sentences articulation is not managed. Methods such as lexical chains (Barzilay and El-hadad, 1999) could be implemented to the objective function or used as post-treatment.

The method proposed in the article uses an evolutionary algorithm and objective functions that imply heavy computation. Several solutions can be brought to this problem: using GPU architecture for faster computation of distribution divergences as the evolutionary algorithm can be easily parallelized, or finding a linear approximation of the divergence distribution function so it can be used inside an ILP solver.

At last, an evolutionary algorithm needs a fine parameters tuning: population size, mutants and cross over percentage. Although we parameterized the algorithm so it finds a good solution for every topic of our three corpora, their influence on the algorithm convergence should be further studied using different data sets.

Extractive automatic summaries can outperform (in terms of ROUGE scores) human extractive summaries. It brings us to the upper limit that one can achieve with purely extractive methods, and to question the methods to consider from now on: sentence compression, generative paradigms for specialized summaries, or sentence rephrasing to achieve a better textual cohesion.

7 Conclusion

For automatic summarization, finding a summary (as good as possible) without an Oracle or any reference summary is an unsupervised task. In this paper, we show that automatic summarization can be achieved using recent advances in automatic summarization evaluation. In particular, we explore automatic summarization under the hypothesis that source documents and summaries have to share the same bigram distribution.

We present a sentence extraction evolutionary algorithm for automatic summarization capable of improving summary generation after generation based only on distribution computation. We show that this extraction algorithm achieves good results compared to state-of-the-art method on three corpora. However, the system can be improved in several ways: the objective function can be improved to better evaluate candidate summaries or be approximated to be used in a faster algorithm. If ROUGE-2 scores used in this paper are heavily correlated to human metrics, the evaluation needs to be pushed further using fully manual metrics such as Pyramid.

References

Enrique Alfonseca and Pilar Rodríguez. 2003. *Generating Extracts with Genetic Algorithms*, Springer Berlin Heidelberg, Berlin, Heidelberg, pages 511–519.

Regina Barzilay and Michael Elhadad. 1999. Using lexical chains for text summarization. *Advances in automatic text summarization* pages 111–121.

Aurélien Bossard and Christophe Rodrigues. 2011. Combining a multi-document update summarization system cbseas with a genetic algorithm. In Ioannis Hatzilygeroudis and Jim Prentzas, editors, *Combinations of Intelligent Methods and Applications*, Springer Berlin Heidelberg, volume 8 of *Smart Innovation, Systems and Technologies*, pages 71–87.

Jaime Carbonell and Jade Goldstein. 1998. The use of MMR, diversity-based reranking for reordering documents and producing summaries. In *SIGIR'98: Proceedings of the 21st ACM SIGIR Conference.* pages 335–336.

H. P. Edmundson. 1969. New methods in automatic extracting. *Journal of the ACM* 16(2):264–285.

Güneş Erkan and Dragomir R. Radev. 2004. Lexrank: Graph-based centrality as salience in text summarization. *Journal of Artificial Intelligence Research (JAIR)* .

Pierre-Etienne Genest, Guy Lapalme, and Mehdi Yousfi-Monod. 2009. Hextac: the creation of a manual extractive run. In *Proceedings of the Second Text Analysis Conference*. Gaithersburg, Maryland, USA.

Dan Gillick and Benoit Favre. 2009b. A scalable global model for summarization. In *Proceedings of the Workshop on Integer Linear Programming for Natural Language Processing*. Association for Computational Linguistics, pages 10–18.

Dan Gillick, Benoit Favre, Dilek Hakkani-tr, Berndt Bohnet, Yang Liu, and Shasha Xie. 2009a. The ICSI/UTD summarization system at TAC 2009. In *Proceedings of Workshop on Summarization task at TAC 2009 conference*.

Kai Hong, John Conroy, Benoit Favre, Alex Kulesza, Hui Lin, and Ani Nenkova. 2014. A repository of state of the art and competitive baseline summaries for generic news summarization. In *Proceedings of the Ninth International Conference on Language Resources and Evaluation (LREC'14)*. European Language Resources Association (ELRA), Reykjavik, Iceland.

Chen Li, Xian Qian, and Yang Liu. 2013. Using supervised bigram-based ilp for extractive summarization. In *ACL 2013*. The Association for Computer Linguistics, pages 1004–1013.

Chin-Yew Lin. 2004. Rouge: A package for automatic evaluation of summaries. In *Proc. ACL workshop on Text Summarization Branches Out*. page 10.

Marina Litvak, Mark Last, and Menahem Friedman. 2010. A new approach to improving multilingual summarization using a genetic algorithm. In *Proceedings of the 48th Annual Meeting of ACL*. ACL '10, pages 927–936.

Dexi Liu, Yanxiang He, Donghong Ji, and Hua Yang. 2006. Genetic algorithm based multi-document summarization. In Qiang Yang and Geoff Webb, editors, *PRICAI 2006: Trends in Artificial Intelligence*, Springer Berlin Heidelberg, volume 4099 of *Lecture Notes in Computer Science*, pages 1140–1144.

Annie Louis and Ani Nenkova. 2009. Automatically evaluating content selection in summarization without human models. In *Proc. of the 2009 EMNLP Conference : Volume 1*. ACL, pages 306–314.

H.P. Luhn. 1958. The automatic creation of literature abstracts. *IBM Journal* 2(2):159–165.

David J.C. MacKay and Linda C. Bauman Peto. 1994. A hierarchical dirichlet language model. *Natural Language Engineering* 1:1–19.

Ryan McDonald. 2007. *A study of global inference algorithms in multi-document summarization*. Springer.

Kumaresh Nandhini and Sadhu Ramakrishnan Balasundaram. 2013. Use of genetic algorithm for cohesive summary extraction to assist reading difficulties. *Applied Computational Intelligence and Soft Computing* 2013:8.

Ani Nenkova, Rebecca Passonneau, and Kathleen McKeown. 2007. The pyramid method: Incorporating human content selection variation in summarization evaluation. *ACM Trans. Speech Lang. Process.* 4(2).

Hitoshi Nishikawa, Kazuho Arita, Katsumi Tanaka, Tsutomu Hirao, Toshiro Makino, and Yoshihiro Matsuo. 2014. Learning to generate coherent summary with discriminative hidden semi-markov model. In *COLING 2014, 25th International Conference on Computational Linguistics, Proceedings of the Conference: Technical Papers, August 23-29, 2014, Dublin, Ireland*. pages 1648–1659. http://aclweb.org/anthology/C/C14/C14-1156.pdf.

Maxime Peyrard and Judith Eckle-Kohler. 2016. Optimizing an approximation of rouge - a problem-reduction approach to extractive multi-document summarization. In *Proceedings of the 54th Annual Meeting of the Association for Computational Linguistics (ACL 2016)*. Association for Computational Linguistics, volume Volume 1: Long Papers, pages 1825–1836.

Dragomir R. Radev. 2000. A common theory of information fusion from multiple text sources step one: cross-document structure. In *Proceedings of the 1st SIGdial workshop*. Association for Computational Linguistics, pages 74–83.

Horacio Saggion, Juan-Manuel Torres-Moreno, Iria da Cunha, and Eric SanJuan. 2010. Multilingual summarization evaluation without human models. In *Proceedings of the 23rd International Conference on Computational Linguistics: Posters*. Association for Computational Linguistics, Stroudsburg, PA, USA, COLING '10, pages 1059–1067.

Helmut Schmid. 1994. Probabilistic part-of-speech tagging using decision trees. In *Proceedings of the International Conference on New Methods in Language Processing*. Manchester, UK.

Haruka Shigematsu and Ichiro Kobayashi. 2014. Topic-based multi-document summarization using differential evolution for combinatorial optimization of sentences .

Ruben Sipos, Pannaga Shivaswamy, and Thorsten Joachims. 2012. Large-margin learning of submodular summarization models. In *Proceedings of the 13th Conference of the European Chapter of the Association for Computational Linguistics*. Association for Computational Linguistics, Stroudsburg, PA, USA, EACL '12, pages 224–233. http://dl.acm.org/citation.cfm?id=2380816.2380846.

Hiroya Takamura and Manabu Okumura. 2010. Learning to generate summary as structured output. In Jimmy Huang, Nick Koudas, Gareth J. F. Jones, Xindong Wu, Kevyn Collins-Thompson, and Aijun An, editors, *CIKM*. ACM, pages 1437–1440.

Chengxiang Zhai and John Lafferty. 2004. A study of smoothing methods for language models applied to information retrieval. *ACM Trans. Inf. Syst.* 22(2):179–214.

Building Chatbots from Forum Data:
Model Selection Using Question Answering Metrics

Martin Boyanov, Ivan Koychev
Faculty of Mathematics and Informatics
Sofia University "St. Kliment Ohridski"
Sofia, Bulgaria
mboyanov@gmail.com
koychev@fmi.uni-sofia.bg

Preslav Nakov, Alessandro Moschitti,
Giovanni Da San Martino
Qatar Computing Research Institute
HBKU, Doha, Qatar
{pnakov,amoschitti}@hbku.edu.qa
gmartino@hbku.edu.qa

Abstract

We propose to use question answering (QA) data from Web forums to train chatbots from scratch, i.e., without dialog training data. First, we extract pairs of question and answer sentences from the typically much longer texts of questions and answers in a forum. We then use these shorter texts to train seq2seq models in a more efficient way. We further improve the parameter optimization using a new model selection strategy based on QA measures. Finally, we propose to use extrinsic evaluation with respect to a QA task as an automatic evaluation method for chatbots. The evaluation shows that the model achieves a MAP of 63.5% on the extrinsic task. Moreover, it can answer correctly 49.5% of the questions when they are similar to questions asked in the forum, and 47.3% of the questions when they are more conversational in style.

1 Introduction

Recently, companies active in diversified business ecosystems have become more and more interested in intelligent methods for interacting with their customers, and even with their employees. Thus, we have seen the development of several general-purpose personal assistants such as Amazon's Alexa, Apple's Siri, Google's Assistant, and Microsoft's Cortana. However, being general-purpose, they are not a good fit for every specific need, e.g., an insurance company that wants to interact with its customers would need a new system trained on specific data; thus, there is a need for specialized assistants.

This aspect is a critical bottleneck as such systems must be engineered from scratch. Very recently, models based on neural networks have been developed, e.g., using seq2seq models (Vinyals and Le, 2015). Such models provide shallow solutions, but at the same time are easy to train, provided that a large amount of dialog data is available. Unfortunately, the latter is a critical bottleneck as (*i*) the specificity of the domain requires the creation of new data; and (*ii*) this process is rather costly in terms of human effort and time.

Many real-world businesses aiming at acquiring chatbot technology are associated with customer services, e.g., helpdesk or forums, where question answering (QA) sections are often provided, sometimes with user evaluation. Although this data does not follow a dialog format, it is still useful to extract pairs of questions and answers, which are essential to train seq2seq models. Typically, forum or customer care sections contain a lot of content, and thus the requirement about having large datasets is not an issue. The major problem comes from the quality of the text in the pairs that we can extract automatically. One solution is to select data using crowdsourcing, but the task will still be very costly given the required size (hundreds of thousands of pairs) and its complexity.

In this paper, we propose to use data extracted from a standard question answering forum for training chatbots from scratch. The main problem in using such data is that the questions and their associated forum answers are noisy, i.e., not all answers are good. Moreover, many questions and answers are very long, e.g., can span several paragraphs. This prevents training effective seq2seq models, which can only manage (i.e., achieve effective decoding for) short pieces of text.

Proceedings of Recent Advances in Natural Language Processing, pages 121–129,
Varna, Bulgaria, Sep 4–6 2017.

We tackle these problems by selecting a pair of sentences from each questions–answer pair, using dot product over averaged word embedding representations. The similarity works both (*i*) as a filter of noisy text as the probability that random noise occurs in the same manner in both the question and the answer is very low, and (*ii*) as a selector of the most salient part of the user communication through the QA interaction.

We further design several approaches to model selection and to the evaluation of the output of the seq2seq models. The main idea is, given a question, (*i*) to build a classical vector representation of the utterance answered by the model, and (*ii*) to evaluate it by ranking the answers to the question provided by the forum users. We rank them using several metrics, e.g., the dot product between the utterance and a target answer. This way, we can use the small training, development and test data from a SemEval task (Nakov et al., 2016b) to indirectly evaluate the quality of the utterance in terms of Mean Averaged Precision (MAP). Moreover, we use this evaluation in order to select the best model on the development set, while training seq2seq models.

We evaluate our approach using (*i*) our new MAP-based extrinsic automatic evaluation on the SemEval test data, and (*ii*) manual evaluation carried out by four different annotators on two sets of questions: from the forum and completely new ones, which are more conversational but still related to the topics discussed in the forum (life in Qatar). The results of our experiments demonstrate that our models can learn well from forum data, achieving MAP of 63.45% on the SemEval task, and accuracy of 49.50% on manual evaluation. Moreover, the accuracy on new, conversational questions drops very little, to 47.25%, according to our manual evaluation.

2 Related Work

Nowadays, there are two main types of dialog systems: sequence-to-sequence and retrieval-based. Here we focus on the former. Seq2seq is a kind of neural network architecture, initially proposed for machine translation (Sutskever et al., 2014; Cho et al., 2014). Since then, it has been applied to other tasks such as text summarization (See et al., 2017), image captioning (Vinyals et al., 2017), and, of course, dialog modeling (Shang et al., 2015; Li et al., 2016; Gu et al., 2016).

The initial seq2seq model assumed that the semantics of the input sequence can be encoded in a single vector, which is hard, especially for longer inputs. Thus, attention mechanisms have been introduced (Bahdanau et al., 2015). This is what we use here as well.

Training seq2seq models for dialog requires large conversational corpora such as Ubuntu (Lowe et al., 2015). Unstructured conversations, e.g., from Twitter, have been used as well (Sordoni et al., 2015). See (Serban et al., 2015) for a survey of corpora for dialog. Unlike typical dialog data, here we extract, filter, and use question-answer pairs from a Web forum.

An important issue with the general seq2seq model is that it tends to generate general answers like *I don't know*, which can be given to many questions. This has triggered researchers to explore diversity promotion objectives (Li et al., 2016). Here, we propose a different idea: select training data based on performance with respect to question answering, and also optimize with respect to a question answering task, where giving general answers would be penalized.

It is not clear how dialog systems should be evaluated automatically, but it is common practice to use BLEU (Papineni et al., 2002), and sometimes Meteor (Lavie and Agarwal, 2007): after all, seq2seq models have been proposed for machine translation (MT), so it is natural to try MT evaluation metrics for seq2seq-based dialog systems as well. However, it has been shown that BLEU, as well as some other popular ways to evaluate a dialog system, do not correlate well with human judgments (Liu et al., 2016). Therefore, here we propose to do model selection as well as evaluation extrinsically, with respect to a related task: Community Question Answering.

3 Data Creation

In order to train our chatbot system, we converted an entire Community Question Answering forum into a set of question–answer pairs, containing only one selected sentence for each question and for each answer.[1] We then used these selected pairs in order to train our seq2seq models. Below, we describe in detail our data selection method along with our approach to question-answer sentence pair selection.

---

[1] We released the data here: `http://goo.gl/e6UWV6`

3.1 Forum Data Description

We used data from a SemEval task on Community Question Answering (Nakov et al., 2015, 2016b, 2017). The data consists of questions from the Qatar Living forum[2] and a (potentially truncated) thread of answers for each question. Each answer is annotated as *Good, Potentially Useful* or *Bad*, depending on whether it answers the question well, does not answer well but gives some potentially useful information, or does not address the question at all (e.g., talks about something unrelated, asks a new question, is part of a conversation between the forum users, etc.). The goal of the task is to rank the answers so that *Good* answers are ranked higher than *Potentially Useful* and *Bad* ones. The participating systems are evaluated using Mean Average Precision (MAP) as the official evaluation metric.

The data for SemEval-2016 Task 3, subtask A comes split into training, development and test parts with 2,669/17,900, 500/2,440 and 700/3,270 questions/answers, respectively. In addition, the task organizers provided raw unannotated data, which contains 200K questions and 2M answers. Thus, our QA data consists of roughly 2M answers extracted from the forum. We paired each of these answers with the corresponding question in order to make training question–answer pairs for our seq2seq system. We made sure that the development and the testing datasets for SemEval-2016 Task 3 were excluded from this set of training question–answer pairs.

We used the annotated development and test sets both to carry out our new model selection, as explained in Section 4.2, and our new evaluation, as described in Section 5. Both model selection and our proposed evaluation are based on extrinsic evaluation with respect to the SemEval task.

3.2 Sentence Pair Selection

As the questions and the comments[3] in Qatar Living can be quite long, we reduced the question-answer pairs to single-sentence pairs. In particular, given a question-answer pair, we first split the question and the answer from the pair into individual sentences, and then we computed the similarity between each sentence from the question and each sentence from the answer. Ultimately, we kept the most similar pair.

We measured the similarity between two sentences based on the cosine between their embeddings. We computed the latter as the average of the embeddings of the words in a sentence. We used pre-trained word2vec embeddings (Mikolov et al., 2013a,b) fine-tuned[4] for Qatar Living (Mihaylov and Nakov, 2016), and proved useful in a number of experments with this dataset (Guzmán et al., 2016; Hoque et al., 2016; Mihaylov et al., 2017; Mihaylova et al., 2016; Nakov et al., 2016a).

More specifically, we generated the vector representation for each sentence by averaging 300-dimensional word2vec vector representations after stopword removal. We assigned a weight to the word2vec vectors with TF×IDF, where IDF is derived from the entire dataset. Note that averaging has the consequence of ignoring the word order in the sentence. We leave for future work the exploration of more sophisticated sentence representation models, e.g., based on long short-term memory (Hochreiter and Schmidhuber, 1997) and convolutional neural networks (Kim, 2014).

4 Model Selection and Evaluation

In this section, we describe our approach to automatic evaluation as well as model selection for seq2seq models.

4.1 Evaluation

Intrinsic evaluation. We evaluated our model *intrinsically* using BLEU as is traditionally done in dialog systems.

Extrinsic evaluation. We further performed *extrinsic* evaluation in terms of how much the answers we generate can help solve the SemEval CQA task. In particular, we input each of the test questions from SemEval to the trained seq2seq model, and we obtained the generated answer. Then, we calculated the similarity, e.g., TF×IDF-based cosine (see below for more detail), between that seq2seq-generated answer and each of the answers in the thread, and we ranked the answers in the thread based on this similarity. Finally, we calculated MAP for the resulting ranking, which evaluates how well we do at raning the *Good* answers higher than the not-Good ones (i.e., *Bad* or *Potentially Useful*). As a baseline, we used the MAP ranking produced by comparing the answers to the question (instead of the generated answer).

4.2 Model Selection

The training step produces a model that evolves over the training iterations. We evaluated that model after each 2,000 minibatch iterations. Then, among these evaluated models, we selected the best one, which we used for the test set. We used three model selection approaches, optimizing for MAP and for BLEU calculated on the development set of the SemEval-2016 Task 3, and for the seq2seq loss on the training dataset.

Seq2seq loss. We consider the loss that the seq2seq model optimizes during the training phase. Notice that in this case no development set is required for model selection.

Machine translation evaluation measure (BLEU). A standard model selection technique for seq2seq models is to optimize BLEU. Here, we calculated multi-reference BLEU between the generated response and the *Good* answers in the thread (on average, there are four *Good* answers out of ten in a thread). We then take the average score over all threads in the development set.

Extrinsic evaluation based on MAP. The main idea for this model selection method is the following: given a question, the seq2seq model produces an answer, which we compare to each of the answers in the thread, e.g., using cosine similarity (see below for detail), and we use the score as an estimation of the likelihood that an answer in the thread would be good. In this way, the list of candidate comments for each question can be ranked and evaluated using MAP. We used the gold relevancy labels available in the development dataset to compute MAP.

More formally, given an utterance u_q returned by the seq2seq model in response to a forum question, we rank the comments $c_1, \ldots, c_n$ from the thread according to the values $r(u_q, c_i)$. We considered the following options for $r(u_q, c_i)$:

- **cos**: this is the cosine between the embedding vectors of u_q and c_i, where the embeddings are calculated as the average of the embedding vectors of the words, using the fine-tuned embedding vectors from (Mihaylov and Nakov, 2016);

- **BLEU**: this is the sentence-level BLEU+1 score between u_q and c_i;

- **bm25**: this is the BM25 score (Robertson and Zaragoza, 2009) between u_q and c_i;

- **TF×IDF**: we build a TF×IDF vector, where the TF is based on the frequency of the words in u_q, and the IDF is calculated based on the full SemEval data (all 200K questions and all 2M answers), we then repeat the procedure to obtain a vector for c_i, and finally we compute the cosine between these two vectors;

We also define a variant of each of the $r(x, y)$ functions above, where the similarity score is further summed with the TF×IDF-cosine similarity between the question and the comment (**+qc-sim**). Finally, we define yet another metric, **Avg**, as the average of all $r()$ functions defined in this section.

5 Experiments

We compare the model selection approaches described in Section 4.2 above, with the goal to devise a seq2seq system that gives fluent, *good* and informative answers, i.e., avoids answers such as *"I don't know"*.

5.1 Setup

Our model is based on the seq2seq implementation in TensorFlow. However, we differ from the standard setup in terms of preprocessing, postprocessing, model selection, and evaluation.

First, we learned subword units using byte pair encoding (Sennrich et al., 2016) on the full data. Then, we encoded the source and the questions and the answers using these learned subword units. We reversed the source sequences before feeding them to the encoder in order to diminish the effect of vanishing gradients. We also applied padding and truncation to accommodate for bucketing. We then trained the seq2seq model using stochastic gradient descent.

Every 2,000 iterations, we evaluated the current model with the metrics from Section 4.2. These metrics are later used to select the model that is most suitable for our task, thus avoiding overfitting on the training data.

In our experiments, we used the following general parameter settings: (*i*) vocabulary size: 40,000 subword units; (*ii*) dimensionality of the embedding vectors: 512; (*iii*) RNN cell: 2-layered GRU cell with 512 units; (*iv*) minibatch size: 80; (*v*) learning rate: 0.5; (*vi*) buckets: [(5, 10), (10, 15), (20, 25), (40,45)].

	Optimizing for	MAP	BLEU	Iteration	Ans. Len.
1	MAP	63.45	9.18	192,000	10.56
2	BLEU	62.64	8.16	16,000	16.31
3	seq2seq loss	62.81	7.00	200,000	8.73
4	Baseline	52.80	-	-	-

Table 1: Evaluation results using the seq2seq model and optimizing during training for MAP (on DEV) vs. BLEU (on DEV) vs. the seq2seq loss (on TRAIN). The following columns show some results on TEST when selecting the best training model on DEV (for MAP and BLEU) and on TRAIN (for the seq2seq loss). We report BLEU and MAP, as well as the iteration at which the best value was achieved on DEV/TRAIN, and the average length of the generated answers on TEST.

	MAP	
Ranking Metric	Dev	Test
TF×IDF+qc-sim	63.56	63.45
TF×IDF	62.46	62.03
cos-embeddings+qc-sim	62.97	62.90
cos-embeddings	62.21	62.13
bm25+qc-sim	62.81	61.96
bm25	62.88	61.77
BLEU+qc-sim	62.67	62.73
BLEU	59.94	59.82
Avg	62.84	62.33

Table 2: MAP score for the ranking strategies defined in Section 4.2, evaluated on the development and on the test datasets.

5.2 Results and Discussion

In our first experiment, we explore the performance of seq2seq models produced by optimizing MAP using the different variants of the similarity function $r()$ from Section 4.2, with MAP for model selection. The results in Table 2 show that **TF×IDF+qc-sim** performs best. The results are consistent on the development (63.56) and on the test datasets (63.45). The absolute improvement with respect to **cos-embeddings+qc-sim** is +0.59 on the development and +0.55 on the test dataset, respectively.

In a second experiment, we compared model selection strategies when optimizing for MAP (**TF×IDF+qc-sim**) vs. BLEU vs. seq2seq loss. We further report the results for a baseline for the SemEval2016 Task 3, subtask A (Nakov et al., 2016b), which picks a random order for the answers in the target question-answer thread. The results are shown on Table 1. For each model selection criterion, we report its performance and statistics on the test dataset about the model that was best-performing on the development dataset.

We can see that doing model selection according to MAP yielded not only the highest ranking performance of 63.45 but also the best BLEU score. This is even more striking if we consider that BLEU tends to favor longer answers, but the average length of the seq2seq answers is 10.56 for MAP and 16.31 for BLEU score. Thus, we have shown that optimizing for an extrinsic evaluation measure that evaluates how good we are at telling *Good* from *Bad* answers works better than optimizing for BLEU.

6 Manual Evaluation and Error Analysis

We evaluated the three approaches in Table 1 on 100 relatively short questions.[5] First, we randomly selected 50 questions from the test set of SemEval-2016 Task 3. However, we did not use the original questions, as they can contain multiple sentences and thus can be too long; instead, we selected a single sentence that contains the core of the question (and in some cases, we simplified it a bit further). We further created 50 new questions, which are more personal and conversational in nature, but are still generally related to Qatar. The answers produced by the three systems for these 100 questions were evaluated independently by four annotators, who judged whether each of the answers is good.

6.1 Quantitive Analysis

Table 3 reports the number of good answers that each of the annotators has judged to be good when the model is selected based on BLEU, MAP, and seq2seq loss. The average of the four annotators suggests that optimizing for MAP yields the best overall results. Note that all systems perform slightly worse on the second set of questions.

---

[5]The questions and the outputs of the different models are available at `http://goo.gl/w9MZfv`

	Optimizing for	# *Good* answers according to				Avg.
		Ann. 1	Ann. 2	Ann. 3	Ann. 4	
questions 1-50						
1	MAP	23	29	21	26	24.75 (49.50%)
2	BLEU	8	15	11	8	10.50 (21.00%)
3	seq2seq loss	18	26	21	28	23.25 (46.50%)
questions 51-100						
4	MAP	28	20	13	29	22.50 (45.00%)
5	BLEU	9	5	2	6	5.50 (11.00%)
6	seq2seq loss	25	14	11	24	18.50 (37.00%)
questions 1-100						
7	MAP	51	49	34	55	47.25 (47.25%)
8	BLEU	17	20	13	14	16.00 (16.00%)
9	seq2seq loss	43	40	32	52	41.75 (41.75%)

Table 3: Number of good answers according to manual annotation of the answers to 50+50 questions by the three models from Table 1.

This should be expected as the latter are different from those used for training the models. Overall, the MAP-based system appears to be more robust, with only 2.25 points absolute decrease in performance (compared to 5 and 4.75 for the systems using BLEU and seq2seq loss, respectively).

6.2 Qualitative Analysis

We now analyze the quality of the generated answers from the manual evaluation. Instead of looking at overall numbers, here we look at some interesting cases, shown in Tables 4 and 5.

First, we can confirm that the answers generated by the model that was optimized for BLEU seem to be the worst. We attribute this to the relatively early iteration when the optimal BLEU occurs and also to the nature of the BLEU metric. BLEU tries to optimize for n-gram matching. Thus, the selected model ultimately prefers longer utterances, while the other two models focus on providing a short focused answer; this is especially true for the first part of the manual test set as shown in Table 4, where we can find "safe" answers with stopwords, which do not have much informative content, but are a good bet, e.g., "good luck", "I think that", "it is good to", etc.

In examples 1 and 6, we can see that only the MAP-based model addressed the question directly. The other models are a better fit to the language model, and thus failed to produce the target named entity. In example 1, they produced a generic answer, which can be given in response to many questions.

Example 5 shows how the models have trouble handling exclusion/negation. The model was able to copy the named entity, which is generally a good thing to do, but not here. If the question was simply "Where can I go running?", the answer would have been good.

Note that the responses to the questions from the second group are more personal, e.g., they start with "I think", "I will", etc. Finally, we can see the well-known problem with seq2seq models: repetition. This is evident in examples 3, 13, 14.

7 Conclusion

Building dialog systems, e.g., in the form of chatbots, has attracted a lot of attention recently and thus has become a crucial investment for many companies. Progress in neural networks, especially in seq2seq models, has made it possible to quickly and directly learn chatbots from data. However, the availability of domain-specific training data coming from real dialogs is a critical bottleneck for the development of dialog systems.

We addressed the problem by producing training data from Community Question Answering (CQA) forums. We further applied sentence selection based on word embeddings in order to retain only meaningful pairs of short texts, which can be more effectively used for training seq2seq models.

Moreover, we introduced the use of extrinsic evaluation based on a CQA task using MAP to select the most effective models among those generated during training, using a development set of good user answers available from the cQA data.

#	Model	Example
1		*How good are Karwa services?*
	BLEU	good luck
	seq2seq	good luck
	MAP	**karwa is good .**
2		*Which is the best spa in Doha?*
	BLEU	lulu
	seq2seq	**al sharq spa**
	MAP	**al sharq spa**
3		*Which is better: Qtel or Vodafone?*
	BLEU	go for the bank
	seq2seq	**vodafone**
	MAP	vodafone is better than vodafone .
4		*Can you recommend a good Vet in Doha?*
	BLEU	good luck
	seq2seq	**dr . choc**
	MAP	**dr . choc**
5		*Where can I go running; other than the Corniche?*
	BLEU	i think it is a good place to go to doha .
	seq2seq	corniche
	MAP	corniche
6		*Are there any cameras on the roundabouts in Qatar?*
	BLEU	i think it is a good offer for a few months .
	seq2seq	there are many cars in qatar .
	MAP	**there is no radar in qatar .**
7		*What is the best mall in Doha to buy good furniture?*
	BLEU	lulu is good
	seq2seq	carrefour
	MAP	**ikea**

Table 4: Output of our chatbot when using different model selection strategies for some simplified questions from Qatar Living, which we used for the first part of our manual evaluation. The good answers are shown in bold.

#	Model	Example
8		*Do you like fast food?*
	BLEU	**i like the one in doha**
	seq2seq	**i do n ' t eat food .**
	MAP	**i hate food .**
9		*What is your favorite beach in Qatar?*
	BLEU	i think it is a good place
	seq2seq	**sealine beach**
	MAP	**sealine beach**
10		*Tell me bot, what do you know about Qatar?*
	BLEU	i think it is a good offer to qatar .
	seq2seq	qatar living
	MAP	**qatar is a country .**
11		*What are the things about Qatar you like the most?*
	BLEU	i think it ' s a good one ...
	seq2seq	qatar is a country .
	MAP	**qatar is the best place to live .**
12		*Are you looking forward to the FIFA World Cup in 2022?*
	BLEU	i think it was a good one in doha
	seq2seq	i will win the world cup .
	MAP	i will win the world cup .
13		*Do you think the fast food in Qatar is of good quality?*
	BLEU	i think it is a good place to go to doha .
	seq2seq	**food is good .**
	MAP	food is good for food .
14		*What is the most useful thing that you can tell me about life in Qatar?*
	BLEU	i love my life ...
	seq2seq	life is life ... : - rrb -
	MAP	**life is beautiful ...**
15		*Do you need to Google to give me an answer?*
	BLEU	i think you can get a good one in your home
	seq2seq	i will give you the answer .
	MAP	**i would like to answer .**

Table 5: Output of our chatbot for some new, conversational questions related to Qatar, which we created and used for the second part of our manual evaluation. The good answers are shown in bold.

We also used MAP to perform automatic evaluation of system accuracy against the test set annotated for the CQA task. This was not explored before.

Finally, we carried out manual evaluation with four different annotators on two different sets of questions: the first set used simplified questions taken from the CQA data, whereas the second one was composed of new, conversational-style questions that we generated. Thus, the questions of the second set are rather different from those used to train the systems; yet, they are about topics that are generally discussed in the training data.

We have found that the seq2seq model can learn from CQA-derived data, producing accurate answers when answering forum questions according to automatic and manual evaluation, with MAP of 63.45, and accuracy of 49.50, respectively. Moreover, the accuracy on completely new questions drops by only few points, i.e., to 47.25, according to our manual evaluation.

Interestingly, our model selection is more accurate than using the loss of the seq2seq model, and performs much better than BLEU. Indeed, the latter seems not to be very appropriate for evaluating chatbots, as our manual analysis shows.

In future work, we would like to study new methods for selecting data, so that the overall system accuracy can improve further. We also plan to try sub-word embedding representations (Bojanowski et al., 2017) that could better capture typos, which are common in Web forums, and to experiment with other languages such as Arabic. Last but not least, we want to explore adversarial dialog training and evaluation (Bruni and Fernandez, 2017; Kannan and Vinyals, 2016; Li et al., 2017; Yu et al., 2017).

Acknowledgments

This research was performed by the Arabic Language Technologies group at Qatar Computing Research Institute, HBKU, within the Interactive sYstems for Answer Search project (IYAS).

References

Dzmitry Bahdanau, Kyunghyun Cho, and Yoshua Bengio. 2015. Neural machine translation by jointly learning to align and translate. In *Proceedings of 3rd International Conference on Learning Representations*. San Diego, California, USA, ICLR '15.

Piotr Bojanowski, Edouard Grave, Armand Joulin, and Tomas Mikolov. 2017. Enriching word vectors with subword information. *Transactions of the Association for Computational Linguistics* 5:135–146.

Elia Bruni and Raquel Fernandez. 2017. Adversarial evaluation for open-domain dialogue generation. In *Proceedings of the 18th Annual SIGdial Meeting on Discourse and Dialogue*. Saarbruecken, Germany, SIGDIAL '17, pages 284–288.

Kyunghyun Cho, Bart van Merrienboer, Caglar Gulcehre, Dzmitry Bahdanau, Fethi Bougares, Holger Schwenk, and Yoshua Bengio. 2014. Learning phrase representations using RNN encoder–decoder for statistical machine translation. In *Proceedings of the Conference on Empirical Methods in Natural Language Processing*. Doha, Qatar, EMNLP '14, pages 1724–1734.

Jiatao Gu, Zhengdong Lu, Hang Li, and Victor O.K. Li. 2016. Incorporating copying mechanism in sequence-to-sequence learning. In *Proceedings of the 54th Annual Meeting of the Association for Computational Linguistics*. Berlin, Germany, ACL '16, pages 1631–1640.

Francisco Guzmán, Lluís Màrquez, and Preslav Nakov. 2016. Machine translation evaluation meets community question answering. In *Proceedings of the 54th Annual Meeting of the Association for Computational Linguistic*. Berlin, Germany, ACL '16, pages 460–466.

Sepp Hochreiter and Jürgen Schmidhuber. 1997. Long short-term memory. *Neural Comput.* 9(8):1735–1780.

Enamul Hoque, Shafiq Joty, Lluís Màrquez, Alberto Barrón-Cedeño, Giovanni Da San Martino, Alessandro Moschitti, Preslav Nakov, Salvatore Romeo, and Giuseppe Carenini. 2016. An interactive system for exploring community question answering forums. In *Proceedings of the 26th International Conference on Computational Linguistics*. Osaka, Japan, COLING '16, pages 1–5.

Anjuli Kannan and Oriol Vinyals. 2016. SeqGAN: Sequence generative adversarial nets with policy gradient. In *Proceedings of the NIPS 2016 Workshop on Adversarial Training*. Barcelona, Spain.

Yoon Kim. 2014. Convolutional neural networks for sentence classification. In *Proceedings of the Conference on Empirical Methods in Natural Language Processing*. Doha, Qatar, EMNLP '14, pages 1746–1751.

Alon Lavie and Abhaya Agarwal. 2007. Meteor: An automatic metric for MT evaluation with high levels of correlation with human judgments. In *Proceedings of the Second Workshop on Statistical Machine Translation*. Prague, Czech Republic, WMT '07, pages 228–231.

Jiwei Li, Michel Galley, Chris Brockett, Jianfeng Gao, and Bill Dolan. 2016. A diversity-promoting objective function for neural conversation models. In *Proceedings of the North American Chapter of the Association for Computational Linguistics: Human Language Technologies*. San Diego, California, USA, NAACL-HLT '16, pages 110–119.

Jiwei Li, Will Monroe, Tianlin Shi, Sébastien Jean, Alan Ritter, and Dan Jurafsky. 2017. Adversarial learning for neural dialogue generation. In *Proceedings of the 2017 Conference on Empirical Methods in Natural Language Processing*. Copenhagen, Denmark, EMNLP '17, pages 2147–2159.

Chia-Wei Liu, Ryan Lowe, Iulian Serban, Mike Noseworthy, Laurent Charlin, and Joelle Pineau. 2016. How NOT to evaluate your dialogue system: An empirical study of unsupervised evaluation metrics for dialogue response generation. In *Proceedings of the Conference on Empirical Methods in Natural Language Processing*. Austin, Texas, USA, EMNLP '16, pages 2122–2132.

Ryan Lowe, Nissan Pow, Iulian Serban, and Joelle Pineau. 2015. The Ubuntu dialogue corpus: A large dataset for research in unstructured multi-turn dialogue systems. In *Proceedings of the 16th Annual Meeting of the Special Interest Group on Discourse and Dialogue*. Prague, Czech Republic, SIGDIAL '15, pages 285–294.

Todor Mihaylov, Daniel Balchev, Yasen Kiprov, Ivan Koychev, and Preslav Nakov. 2017. Large-scale goodness polarity lexicons for community question answering. In *Proceedings of the 40th International ACM SIGIR Conference on Research and Development in Information Retrieval*. Tokyo, Japan, SIGIR '17, pages 1185–1188.

Todor Mihaylov and Preslav Nakov. 2016. SemanticZ at SemEval-2016 task 3: Ranking relevant answers in community question answering using semantic similarity based on fine-tuned word embeddings. In *Proceedings of the 10th International Workshop on Semantic Evaluation*. San Diego, California, USA, SemEval '16, pages 804 – 811.

Tsvetomila Mihaylova, Pepa Gencheva, Martin Boyanov, Ivana Yovcheva, Todor Mihaylov, Momchil Hardalov, Yasen Kiprov, Daniel Balchev, Ivan Koychev, Preslav Nakov, Ivelina Nikolova, and Galia Angelova. 2016. SUper team at SemEval-2016 task 3: Building a feature-rich system for community question answering. In *Proceedings of the 10th International Workshop on Semantic Evaluation*. San Diego, California, USA, SemEval '16, pages 836–843.

Tomas Mikolov, Ilya Sutskever, Kai Chen, Greg Corrado, and Jeffrey Dean. 2013a. Distributed representations of words and phrases and their compositionality. In *Proceedings of the 26th International Conference on Neural Information Processing Systems*. Lake Tahoe, Nevada, USA, NIPS'13, pages 3111–3119.

Tomas Mikolov, Wen-tau Yih, and Geoffrey Zweig. 2013b. Linguistic regularities in continuous space word representations. In *Proceedings of the 2013 Conference of the North American Chapter of the Association for Computational Linguistics: Human Language Technologies*. Atlanta, Georgia, USA, NAACL-HLT '13, pages 746–751.

Preslav Nakov, Doris Hoogeveen, Lluís Màrquez, Alessandro Moschitti, Hamdy Mubarak, Timothy Baldwin, and Karin Verspoor. 2017. SemEval-2017 task 3: Community question answering. In *Proceedings of the 11th International Workshop on Semantic Evaluation*. Vancouver, British Columbia, Canada, SemEval '17, pages 27–48.

Preslav Nakov, Lluís Màrquez, and Francisco Guzmán. 2016a. It takes three to tango: Triangulation approach to answer ranking in community question answering. In *Proceedings of the Conference on Empirical Methods in Natural Language Processing*. Austin, Texas, USA, EMNLP '16, pages 1586–1597.

Preslav Nakov, Lluís Màrquez, Walid Magdy, Alessandro Moschitti, Jim Glass, and Bilal Randeree. 2015. SemEval-2015 task 3: Answer selection in community question answering. In *Proceedings of the 9th International Workshop on Semantic Evaluation*. Denver, Colorado, USA, SemEval '15, pages 269–281.

Preslav Nakov, Lluís Màrquez, Alessandro Moschitti, Walid Magdy, Hamdy Mubarak, abed Alhakim Freihat, Jim Glass, and Bilal Randeree. 2016b. SemEval-2016 task 3: Community question answering. In *Proceedings of the 10th International Workshop on Semantic Evaluation*. San Diego, California, USA, SemEval '16, pages 525–545.

Kishore Papineni, Salim Roukos, Todd Ward, and Wei-Jing Zhu. 2002. BLEU: A method for automatic evaluation of machine translation. In *Proceedings of the 40th Annual Meeting on Association for Computational Linguistics*. Philadelphia, Pennsylvania, USA, ACL '02, pages 311–318.

Stephen Robertson and Hugo Zaragoza. 2009. The probabilistic relevance framework: BM25 and beyond. *Found. Trends Inf. Retr.* 3(4):333–389.

Abigail See, Peter J. Liu, and Christopher D. Manning. 2017. Get to the point: Summarization with pointer-generator networks. In *Proceedings of the 55th Annual Meeting of the Association for Computational Linguistics*. Vancouver, British Columbia, Canada, ACL '17, pages 1073–1083.

Rico Sennrich, Barry Haddow, and Alexandra Birch. 2016. Neural machine translation of rare words with subword units. In *Proceedings of the 54th Annual Meeting of the Association for Computational Linguistics*. Berlin, Germany, ACL '16, pages 1715–1725.

Iulian Vlad Serban, Ryan Lowe, Peter Henderson, Laurent Charlin, and Joelle Pineau. 2015. A survey of available corpora for building data-driven dialogue systems. *CoRR* abs/1512.05742.

Lifeng Shang, Zhengdong Lu, and Hang Li. 2015. Neural responding machine for short-text conversation. In *Proceedings of the 53rd Annual Meeting of the Association for Computational Linguistics and the 7th International Joint Conference on Natural Language Processing*. Beijing, China, ACL-IJCNLP '15, pages 1577–1586.

Alessandro Sordoni, Michel Galley, Michael Auli, Chris Brockett, Yangfeng Ji, Margaret Mitchell, Jian-Yun Nie, Jianfeng Gao, and Bill Dolan. 2015. A neural network approach to context-sensitive generation of conversational responses. In *Proceedings of the Conference of the North American Chapter of the Association for Computational Linguistics: Human Language Technologies*. Denver, Colorado, USA, NAACL-HLT '15, pages 196–205.

Ilya Sutskever, Oriol Vinyals, and Quoc V. Le. 2014. Sequence to sequence learning with neural networks. In *Proceedings of the 27th International Conference on Neural Information Processing Systems*. Montréal, Québec, Canada, NIPS '14, pages 3104–3112.

Oriol Vinyals and Quoc V. Le. 2015. A neural conversational model. *CoRR* abs/1506.05869.

Oriol Vinyals, Alexander Toshev, Samy Bengio, and Dumitru Erhan. 2017. Show and tell: Lessons learned from the 2015 MSCOCO image captioning challenge. *IEEE Trans. Pattern Anal. Mach. Intell.* 39(4):652–663.

Lantao Yu, Weinan Zhang, Jun Wang, and Yong Yu. 2017. SeqGAN: Sequence generative adversarial nets with policy gradient. In *Proceedings of the 31st Conference on Artificial Intelligence*. San Francisco, California, USA, AAAI '17, pages 2852–2858.

Mining Association Rules from Clinical Narratives

Svetla Boytcheva　　　**Ivelina Nikolova**　　　**Galia Angelova**

Institute of Information and Communication Technologies

Bulgarian Academy of Sciences

25A Acad. G. Bonchev Str., 1113 Sofia, Bulgaria

svetla.boytcheva@gmail.com {iva,galia}@lml.bas.bg

Abstract

We propose a method that processes raw informal medical texts (from health forums) and formal texts (outpatient records) in Bulgarian language in order to extract typical word co-occurrences in the form of association rules. When mining these rules we use some context information and small terminological lexicons to generalize the extracted frequent patterns. This allows to study informal expressions of medical terminology and to identify automatically typical descriptions of types of patient statuses. The paper presents association rules generated from 300,000 outpatient records and 1,425 forum postings and discusses their evaluation and usefulness. Employing this unsupervised data mining approach we hope to overcome the lack of linguistic resources that can support successful NLP analysis of clinical narratives in Bulgarian.

1 Introduction

Clinical narratives written by medical experts are a growing source of patient-related information that can be used in medical research and healthcare management. In addition, informal medical texts and conversations in social networks and popular TV broadcasts increase significantly. Public forums for medical consultations exist as well where doctors provide opinions and answer questions. In this case medical experts abandon the professional style of clinical writings (brief reports in cryptic form with medical terminology and specific words, abbreviations, acronyms, and phrases of their professional jargon). They switch to informal, conversational style (avoiding terminology, using casual words for popular explanations,

with shorter and simpler sentences etc.). Differences between informal and formal communication are often addressed in translation where the objective is to reproduce language in all its variety. In (Lozano and Matamala, 2009) the authors analyse how the original English medical terminology, used to give a special atmosphere and to reproduce a real professional context in the television series E.R., was translated in colloquial language to reach a broad audience of Spanish native speakers in the Spanish dubbed version. The original English terms were manually categorized based on their degree of formality in order to differentiate between formal and informal medical language. Then rules for selecting translations in different settings were elaborated. This structuring enabled to approach systematically the evaluation of translation. Many mistakes have been found in the translation of medical terminology, hence lowering the realism of the dubbed version. The conclusion is that terminology misuse is rather often in informal communication.

Here we also consider formal and informal medical texts but as input data for mining Association Rules (AR) that explicate stable collocational patterns of terms and words. The overall objective is to find frequent patterns of lexical co-occurrences which, as we suppose, will help to structure patient descriptions. In general there are no standard templates how patients are to be examined, e.g. in diabetes there is no predefined structured questionnaire how to document the status of a diabetic patient in the form of indicators and their values. Earlier attempts to structure patient status descriptions took us months to study a large number of patient records and weeks of manual work to produce feature-value templates that were discussed with medical experts (Boytcheva et al., 2010). Now we believe that ARs will discover automatically attributes and their values as

Proceedings of Recent Advances in Natural Language Processing, pages 130–138,

Varna, Bulgaria, Sep 4–6 2017.

the latter are expressed by lexical units in the free text descriptions. Therefore it is important to consider patient-related texts in records produced by medical doctors as well as informal texts written by the patients themselves. In addition for low resource languages like Bulgarian, Data Mining provides better instruments to discover new knowledge than Text Mining via shallow analysis and information extraction techniques. We propose a method that processes raw formal clinical narratives (outpatient records, OR) and informal texts (postings in health forums) in Bulgarian language. Some context information is taken into consideration when mining the ARs, which is an original aspect of the proposal. Small terminological lexicons provide generalization of extracted frequent patterns. This approach allows to map informal expressions of medical terminology to the formal ones and to study in parallel both the professional and colloquial medical language.

The paper is structured as follows. Section 2 overviews related work. Section 3 presents the materials used and Section 4 - the methods. Section 5 details the experiments. Section 6 contains the conclusion and plans for future work.

2   Related Work

Almost no electronic resources with medical terminology exist for Bulgarian language (except for terms in standard medical nomenclatures) so we are interested in terminology extraction for low resource languages. For Polish, linguistic analysis and statistical methods identify automatically phrases that cover 84% of the occurring medical terms in over 1,200 discharge letters (Marciniak and Mykowiecka, 2014). At the top of the ranked list, only 4% out of 400 terms were incorrect. Another work deals with term extraction from sparse, ungrammatical and informally-written texts with domain-specific contents (Ittoo and Bouma, 2013). This paper focuses on rare (low frequency) terms, detects multi-word terms of arbitrarily lengths which are often disregarded by existing term extraction systems, and involves external resources (Wikipedia) to support domain-specific term extraction and assessment of accuracy. A rather high F1-measure is achieved (88% against a baseline of 77%) and successful extraction of terms regardless of their length.

Discovering frequent word sequences also provides useful hints about analysis of units in for-

mal and informal texts. A method for extraction of all maximal frequent word sequences, which allows for gaps, is presented in (Ahonen-Myka, 1999). The algorithms in (Ahonen-Myka, 2002) include pruning of all stop words, which might be problematic in case of terminological expressions. No stemming is applied since inflexion endings might be meaningful, moreover their removal will combine sequences and in this case some low-frequency variations can exceed together the selected frequency threshold. In (Ahonen-Myka and Doucet, 2005) the discovery of maximal frequent word sequences is re-considered in the light of collocation discovery, where "collocation" is a recurrent, stable multiword expression without gaps. The authors assume that most existing methods for collocation discovery cannot be straightforwardly extended to find sequences with length more than 5 words, when applied to large corpora.

Text mining extracts essential information from texts while data mining (in particular ARs) discovers novel knowledge about the subject. ARs that are found in texts are used in various kind of document-processing applications, for instance:

(i) Text classiffication based on ARs: sentences of documents are viewed as basic text units (Haralambous and Lenca, 2014). This approach is enriched by linguistic knowledge (delivered by the Stanford dependency parser). Words are replaced by their hyperonyms in WordNet, to optimize the itemsets. In the training phase ARs are mined from sentences. At the classification stage, for each sentence s in a document d the system finds the most confident AR that can be applied to it (i.e., such that the itemset of the rule is entirely contained in the itemset of the sentence). An aggregation procedure classifies the document by taking class by class the sum of rule confidence and selecting the class with the highest sum. The evaluation was done on 7,000 texts of Reuters corpus. The experiments show that using dependency property (*nsubj*) to select a word is a better choice than the one provided by the *tf-idf*-based method. However, no alternative classification techniques are applied in parallel to the same text collection so no real conclusion can be drawn about the effectiveness of the suggested approach.

(ii) Elucidating domain concepts based on ARs: the paper (Yolcular, 2011) presents 12 ARs that can point to significant medical concepts mined in 600 otorhinolaryngology discharge notes written

in Turkish language. The n-gram method was used for discovering terms co-occurrences. A dataset of concept candidates has been generated for the validation step and then the Predictive Apriori algorithm for AR mining was applied to validate the candidate concepts.

(iii) Explication of relations among text units: (Sizov and Öztürk, 2012) present the SmoothApriori algorithm that finds association relations between sentences which may reveal a cause-effect type of relation or have a more implicit nature. SmoothApriori uses similarity between items; compared to a previously proposed SoftApriori algorithm, which also makes use of similarity, it is able to utilize similarity values directly rather than reducing them to binary values similar/not-similar. The evaluation was done on "Findings as to Risk" section of 208 Air Investigation Reports, published by the Transportation Board of Canada. Many top confidence rules, automatically generated by SmoothApriori, are interesting and make sense. Some rules connect consecutive sentences in the same text but the implicit discourse relation of causality is explicated. This application illustrates the potential of using ARs in various areas.

The results presented here integrate text and data mining ideas, extending further our previous developments (Boytcheva et al., 2017).

3   Materials

We work with two data sources: ORs submitted to the Bulgarian National Health Insurance Fund (NHIF) and content from the online medical portal *puls.bg*[1]. The ORs concern 10,000 diabetic patients and were produced by Endocrinologists (ESs) (set **S00**) and General Practitioners (GPs) (set **S05**) in 2012–2013. In total these are 330,666 records, semi-structured files with predefined XML-format. We use only two free text fields of these ORs: "*Anamnesis*" and "*Patient Status*". The corpus of informal medical texts includes postigns at *puls.bg* forum (set **SF**). We process all questions and comments from three sub-forums[2] amounting to 1,425 records.

Fig. 1 presents the distribution of words (items) in the sets after stemming and stop words removal.

We analyzed how the sources vocabularies are distributed in different categories using available lexicons. Table 1 presents the distribution of cate-

---

[1]http://puls.bg
[2]Diabetes, Smoking cessation, Thyroid gland

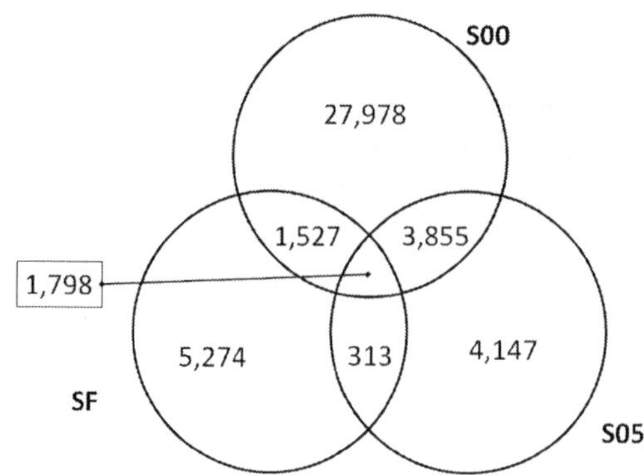

Figure 1: Corpus vocabulary

gories in subsets of 20% of the vocabulary in $S00$, 35% in $S05$ and 55% in SF.

Set	$S00$	$S05$	SF
common words	10.7%	15.1%	36.6%
medical terms	1.2%	1.6%	1.2%
names of diseases	5.8%	10.9%	12.0%
treatment	0.4%	0.8%	0.7%
symptoms	0.8%	1.9%	1.7%
abbreviations	0.6%	1.4%	0.6%
not classified	79.6%	66.8%	44.2%

Table 1: Vocabulary distribution in training sets

The items of SF are mainly general lexica (36.6%) and names of diseases (12.2%). The most frequent units are stop words (43%) followed by numerical values (5%), some common words like have/has, year, value, month, examination, problem, result etc. signaling for the duration of the symptoms and medical terms signaling for the location of the finding - endocrine, hormon, thyroid gland.

The items of $S00$ are mainly common words and names of diseases. The most frequent units are stop words (19.84%), numerical values (7.54%), names of anatomic organs and systems as well as their conditions: breath, abdomen, liver, rhytmic, soft, RR (Riva Roci), vesicular, pulmo, limbs.

Similarly to $S00$, the items of $S05$ are mainly common words and names of diseases. Some of the most frequent units are stop words (17.12%), numerical values (12.60%), and indicators related to diabetes concepts like: sugar, treatment, activity, diabetes, rythmic, type, breath, BSP (blood sugar profile).

The analysis of corpus items (Table 2) shows that in the intersection $S4$ of the three training corpora, some 34% are general words from the top

Set	S1	S2	S3	S4
common words	39.5%	22.1%	34.8%	34.0%
medical terms	1.8%	2.2%	1.7%	1.7%
names of diseases	25.4%	18.1%	30.4%	32.3%
treatment	1.4%	1.3%	1.6%	1.7%
symptoms	4.3%	3.4%	5.5%	6.1%
abbreviations	1.4%	2.2%	1.8%	1.8%
not classified	24.2%	48.6%	22.3%	20.6%

Table 2: Common vocabulary in the training sets, where $S1 = S00 \cap SF, S2 = S00 \cap S05, S3 = S05 \cap SF, S4 = S00 \cap S05 \cap S0F$

10,000 most frequent words in Bulgarian, names of diseases (32.2%), symptoms (6.1%), abbreviations (1.8%) and other medical terms (1.7%).

The common items for SF and $S05$ represent terminology related to diabetes. This is not surprising because the forum topic is about diabetes and $S00$ contains ORs written by Endocrinology specialists. Examples of such items are: enlarged, weight, hemoglobin, insulin, examination, pain, control, glycated, treatments, blood, sugar, consisting, profile, diabetes etc.

The common items for SF and $S00$ are mainly terms related to medical examinations. This is also easy to explain since SF consists of informal texts and $S00$ contains clinical notes of General Practitioners. Examples of items common for SF and $S00$ are: treatment, procedure, drugs, complains, pain, examination, condition, consultation, normal, increased, control, changed, etc.

The common items for $S05$ and $S00$ are mainly terms concerning patient status - names of anatomic organs and systems. Examples of such items are: succusio renalis, palpated, non-painful, enlarged, ripple, pink, terminal, height, weight, limbs, pulmonary, good, breathe, family, edema, vesicular, complained, RR, liver, neck, rhythmically, peripheral, diabetes, control, heart, etc.

4 Text Analysis Methods

Our approach has three main phases: *preprocessing* which converts the text documents into itemsets, *processing* based on frequent pattern mining (FPM) techniques and elicitation of ARs, and *postprocessing* that filters, maps and generalizes rules by using context information and small lexicons (Fig. 2). The system processes input texts in unicode format and is language independent in principle (stemming and stopword filtering can be replaced by modules for another language).

4.1 Preprocessing

We have three text collections: SF - questions and comments in forum postings, $S05$ and $S00$ - the free texts of "*Anamnesis*" and "*Patient Status*" sections of ORs written by ESs and GPs correspondingly. Each text in SF, $S05$, and $S00$ is turned to a sequence of word stems in their original order, using blank spaces and punctuation delimiters as tokenization separators. Stop words and numbers may be essential for some patterns so they are preserved and generalized - replaced by the constants STOP and NUM correspondingly. After this step the punctuation is eliminated because it is often erroneosly written or missing in both forums and in ORs.

Let S be one collection. The vocabulary used in all documents of S will be called *items* $W = \{w_1, w_2, ..., w_n\}$. For the collection S we extract the set of all different documents $P = \{p_1, p_2, ..., p_N\}$, where $p_i \subseteq W$. This set corresponds to transactions; the associated unique transaction identifiers (*tids*) shall be called **pids** (patient identifiers). Each patient interaction with a doctor (question or comment in SF or an anamnesis or patient status section of an OR in $S00$ and $S05$) is viewed as a single document in P.

4.2 Processing

Our documents are written in different styles: the forum texts have quite informal syntax structure while the ORs are written in telegraphic style with phrases rather than full sentences. Usually the ORs list attribute-value (*A-V*) pairs - anatomic organs/systems and their status/condition:

$$A_1V_1, ..., A_nV_n|V_1A_1, ..., V_nA_n .$$

> **E.g.:** Кор - ритмична нормофреквентна сърдечна дейност, Крайници- хипестезия от дистален тип, везикуларно дишане. (*Cardiovascular system - rhythmic norm frequent heartrate, limbs - hypoesthesia distal type, vesicular breath.*)

where A_1=*Cardiovascular system*, A_2=*limbs* and A_3=*breath* are attributes and their corresponding values are $V1$=*rhythmic norm frequent heartrate*, $V2$=*hypoesthesia distal type* following A_1 and A_2 and $V3$=*vesicular* preceeding A_3.

Attribute names contain phrases and abbreviations in Cyrillic and Latin. Values can be long descriptions in case of status complications.

The order of *A-V* pairs can vary and parts of the value descriptions can surround the attributes:

$$V_1...V_kAV_{k+1}...V_n.$$

133

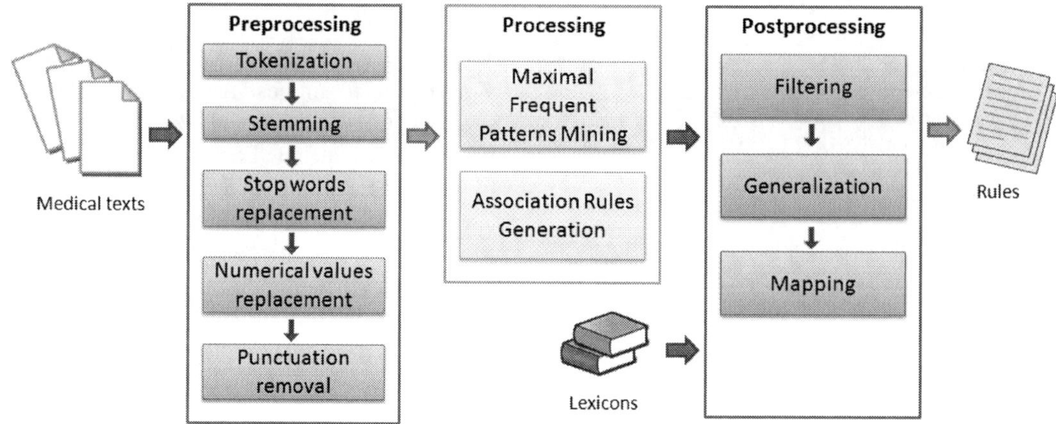

Figure 2: System Architecture

E.g.: Об.везикуларно дишане, средни и дребни хрипчета в белодробните основи... (*Ac.vesicular breathing, moderate and small wheezes in the lungs' bases...*)

where A=*breathing* and the surrounding words describe the status (attribute value).

It is also possible that some attributes share the same value:

$$A_1, A_2, ..., A_n V | V A_1, A_2, ..., A_n.$$

E.g.: хепар ет лиен неувеличени, Глава и шия - б.о., Кожа и видими лигавици бледорозови, ... (liver and spleen not enlarged, Head and neck - without peculiarities, Skin and visible mucous membranes pale pink, ...)

At the same time the informal texts in the health forum contain descriptions of patient status in a rather sparse form with much richer language and wider context around the triggering terms.

E.g.: Здравейте, моля ви кажете какво да правя, сърцето ми прескача от над 3 часа и то доста често... (*Hello, please tell me what to do, my heart skips over three hours and quite often...*)

Thus, when searching for frequent patterns, we consider a window of more than 10-12 words around each attribute. The rich terminology and flexible syntax structure hinder the application of traditional methods for extraction of collocations with gaps. These approaches would rather find the OR clishe phrases as collocations with highest frequency, moreover many *A-V* pairs would be erroneously considered as *n*-grams.

E.g.: Positive examples:
(forum) електронна цигара (*electronic cigar*)
(forum) щитовидна жлеза (*thyroid gland*)
(ORs) общо състояние (*general condition*)
(ORs) щитовидна жлеза (*thyroid gland*)
Negative examples:
(forum) имам Хашимото (*I have Hashimoto*)
(ORs) диабет тип (*diabetes type*)
(ORs) мек неболезнен (*soft non-painful*)

Therefore we treat documents as bag of words rather than sequences, they are transformed to itemsets with single word occurrences only.

Given a set of pids S, support of an itemset I is the number of pids in S that contain I. We denote it as $supp(I)$. We define a threshold called *minsup* (minimum support). A frequent itemset (FI) I is one with at least minimum support count, i.e. $supp(I) \geq minsup$. The task of FPM of S is to find all possible frequent itemsets in S.

Most FPM algorithms generate all possible frequent patterns (FPs). The search space grows exponentially with the size of W. Summarized information for data relations can be extracted as maximal frequent itemsets (MFI). The condensed information not only accelerates the process, reducing redundancy, but also decreases significantly the number of frequent patterns for post-analysis.

An implication in the form $I \Rightarrow J$ is called *association rule*, where $I \subset W, J \subset W, I \cap J = \emptyset$. I is called antecedent or ancestor and J is called consequent. Support of a rule is the number of pids in S that contain $I \cup J$, i.e.

$$sup(I \Rightarrow J) = sup(I \cup J) = P(I \cup J).$$

If $C\%$ of the documents in S that contain I, contain also J, then the association rule $I \Rightarrow J$ holds with *confidence C* in S, i.e. this is the condition probability

$$conf(I \Rightarrow J) = P(J|I) = \frac{sup(I \cup J)}{sup(I)}.$$

The task of ARs mining in collection S is to generate all ARs with confidence above the user defined confidence (*minconf*) and support above user defined support (*minsup*). Rules that satisfy both a minsup and minconf are called *strong*.

However, even for reasonable values of minconf and minsup, big datasets yield huge sets of strong ARs. Thus we can use an additional filter called *lift* that is defined as the ratio of the confidence of the rule and the confidence of its consequent.

$$lift(I \Rightarrow J) = \frac{P(I \cup J)}{P(I)P(J)}.$$

The lift represents the strenght of the relation between the consequent and its antecedent. A lift value < 1 indicates independence between them. If the lift value is > 1, this indicates that the antecedent and consequent appear together more often than expected, i.e. are correlated. Such rules are potentially usefull for predicting the consequent in new sets.

For ARs generation we use algorithms for mining all ARs with the lift measure in a transaction database (Agrawal and Srikant, 1994) with implementation at SPMF[3]. In the experiments we applied the FPmax algorithm (Grahne and Zhu, 2003) for MFI and All Association Rulse with FP-Growth with lift (Han et al., 2004).

4.3 Postprocessing

In order to find certain correlation among rare items, the minimal support needs to be set rather low. This causes generation of a huge amount of ARs and most of them are redundant. Adapting methods of Ashrafi et al. (2007), we apply some techniques for redundant ARs removal. In addition we select only those ARs that fulfill the requirements to have support, confidence and lift above predefined thresholds minsup and minconf. The lift value is very important because it gives additional information about the usefulness of the generated rules. Thus we filter only ARs with lift > 1. This is a necessary condition but not a sufficient one. For instance we obtain ARs like:

везикулар кожа => *STOP*

where STOP is a marker for a stop word, "везикулар" means "vesicular" (concerning breath) and "кожа" means "skin". This rule has high support (about 8%), confidence (0.999) and although its lift (1.429) is quite high, obviously it is useless. Thus we add some additional constraints, like removing all ARs with consequent that contains only the $STOP$ constant.

At the next step we perform AR generalization, based on small lexicons. We use some terms as seeds and rule based prediction about the features of other words that appear in similar rules at the same position. Initially generalization is applied for symptoms/conditions and complains:

- For association rules $R_1 : I \cup X \Rightarrow J$ and $R_2 : I \cup Y \Rightarrow J$ in case X and Y are symptoms/conditions for the same anatomic organ/systems C, we replace them by the marker "$STATUS(C)$" and define a more general rule $R_C : I \cup STATUS(C) \Rightarrow J$.

- For association rules $R_1 : I \Rightarrow J \cup X$ and $R_2 : I \Rightarrow J \cup Y$ in case X and Y are symptoms/conditions for the same anatomic organ/systems G, we replace them by the marker "$STATUS(G)$" and define a more general rule $R_G : I \Rightarrow J \cup STATUS(G)$.

> **E.g.:** R_1: лигавици => розови (*Oral mucosa => pink*)
> R_2: лигавици => бледи (*Oral mucosa => pale*)
> R_G: лигавици => STATUS(G)
>   (*Oral mucosa => STATUS(G)*)
> G=лигавици (*Oral mucosa*)

The variety of all status conditions is huge but some complications are rare and it is unlikely to have them all included in ARs. The main generalization advantage is that more general rules will help to predict/recognize some status conditions in the text that are not included in our original lexicon. The main disadvantage is that not all markers $STATUS(i)$ are equivalent, i.e. the status descriptions for different anatomic systems and organs can differ. Thus we can not apply further generalization of already generalized rules.

Finally the ARs generated for different collections are mapped to each other in order to study the specifics of the extracted collocations in formal and informal medical language. As result we are able to enrich the possible contexts of the medical terminology occurring in both types of text (Figure 3). Thus we can define word embeddings for some terms included in ARs for all three sets. For some item $w_i \in W$ and collection S we define its context for all ARs in S such that: $C_S(w_i) = \{I | I \Rightarrow J \cup w_i\}$. In particular when $I \Rightarrow J \cup w_i$ holds in S then it also holds that $I \Rightarrow w_i$. Thus $C(w_i) = \bigcup C_S(w_i)$ is the observed context of item w_i for all collections. The observation of the terminology context will help for further study of its nature.

5 Experiments and Findings

The experiments were performed on the collections SF, $S00$ and $S05$. SF consists of informal

---

[3]http://www.philippe-fournier-viger.com/spmf/index.php?link=algorithms.php

Set	$S05.1$	$S05.2$	$S05.3$	$S00.1$	$S00.2$	$S00.3$	$SF.1$	$SF.2$	$SF.3$
pids	48,129	48,129	48,129	215,326	215,326	215,326	1,141	1,141	1,141
FI	465,454	359,032	342,118	421,238	386,132	344,215	2,161	1,977	1,977
MFI	759	500	388	1,659	1,619	1,605	453	455	439
AR	4,985,268	3,084,677	3,482,135	1,596,953	1,455,634	1,345,088	202	147	176
minsup	0.05	0.05	0.05	0.04	0.04	0.04	0.02	0.02	0.02

Table 3: Generated association rules with minconf=1.0 and minlift=1.1 for 9 training sets

Set	$S05.1$	$S05.2$	$S05.3$	$S00.1$	$S00.2$	$S00.3$	$SF.1$	$SF.2$	$SF.3$
pids	12,032	12,032	12,032	53,831	53,831	53,831	284	285	285
all	99.98%	99.99%	99.98%	99.99%	99.99%	99.99%	95.43%	96.01%	97.34%
max 2,000	99.96%	100.00%	99.95%	100.00%	100.00%	99.99%	95.43%	96.01%	97.34%

Table 4: Evaluation of the generated association rules for 9 test sets

text and is rather small. $S00$ and $S05$ contain sections of ORs. $S00$ corresponds to ORs produced by GPs and is significantly larger than the other two collections. It presents more sparse information than $S05$ which contains more focused information about the specific domain of diabetes. For each of SF, $S00$ and $S05$ three experiments are provided by non-exhaustive cross-validation (3 iterations on sets in ratio 4:1 training to test). The sets are denoted by their original set name and the number of experiment, e.g. for the set $S05$ there are three training sets $S05.1$, $S05.2$, and $S05.3$.

Table 3 presents numbers of constructions found in the FPM experiments: pids, frequent itemsets, MFI and ARs. In ARs generation for all collections we used minconf=1.0 but different minsup depending on the sets' size. We considered only ARs with lift > 1.1.

Filter the rules with lift <1.1 and consequent STOP automatically reduced approx. 50% of the ARs for $S05$ and $S00$, where language is more formal with limited vocabulary and strong support. The same constraints lead to about 40% reduction of the ARs in SF which has rich vocabulary and small support. The distribution of the lift measure values in these two types of sets - formal vs informal was also quite different. Lift variation in $S05$ and $S00$ is much smaller than in SF.

Table 4 presents the evaluation of the generated ARs. Two types of tests are performed: with all generated ARs and for the top 2,000 ARs according to their antecedents' cardinality. High precision in consequent prediction is seen for all sets.

Some ARs bring new knowledge about patient status description:

> корем ==> мек неболезн
> (*abdomen => soft non-painful*)

This rule has not too high support (about 5%) but its lift is higher than 1.1. It is a reasonable rule which connects lexical units describing an anatomic organ and its typical status.

The following AR has also very high lift - 12.21 and represents a set of attributes and values describing the condition of a diabetic patient. All of them are terms or typical phrasal expressions in the domain of diabetes.

> тургор видим шия ссс запаз общо състояни ==>
> розов кожа
> (*turgour visible neck ccc preserved general condition =>*
> *pink skin*)

In the following OR excerpt, items from the AR antecedent are highlighted in blue and the predicted consequent items are highlighted in pink:

> Запазено общо състояние . Глава - склери чисти. Видими лигавици - розови. Кожа - розова , норм. тургор. Шия . -щит.жлеза- увеличена 1А. Не се палпират увеличени лимфни възли. Дихат. с-ма-чисто везикуларно дишане. ССС - ритмична нормофреквентна сърдечна дейност.
> (*Preserved general condition* . *Head - clear ciliary body.* *Visible* *tissue -* *pink. Skin - pink* , *normal* *turgor. Neck* *-thyroid gland- enlarged 1A. Lymph nodes do not palpate enlarged. Respiratory system-clear vesicular breathing.* *Circulatory system* *- normal heart rhythm.*)

The support sets of the ARs present patients with different profiles. In general several ARs can represent the conditions of different anatomic organs and systems of one patient and thus the initial profiling groups can be partitioned into profiling subgroups. Thus patients can be clustered in groups with similar health condition. A more detailed analysis of patients that belong to several profile groups is a task for further investigation.

Although generalization did not decrease significantly the total number of ARs, the new general rules help to process unseen status descriptions in other collections of medical documents.

ARs mapping. By collapsing equal ancestors of the ARs generated from the respective data sets we observe regularities which describe the medical language in the ORs on the one hand and the informal language from the medical forum on the other hand. Figure 3 presents ARs whose ancestor contain "thyroid gland". The larger ellipses denote the ancestors of the rules and the smaller ones linked through arrows are the consequents. $SFrule1$ and $SFrule2$ (in gray) are result of processing the SF dataset; $S05ruleset1$ and $S05ruleset2$ come from the dataset $S05$. Each of the rule sets represents several rules with equal ancestor.

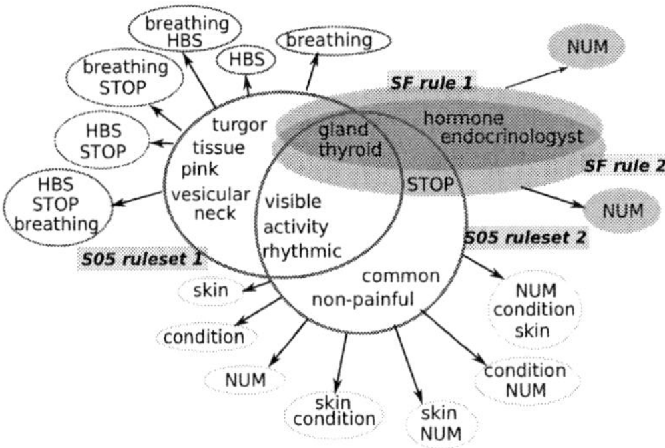

Figure 3: Mapping of ARs from forum data and ORs from Endocrinology professionals.

Among the extracted ARs from SF only 21 contain the terms "thyroid" and "gland" either in the ancestor or in the consequent whereas in the ARs resulting from $S05$ there are 3,985 ARs containing both terms. This shows that the informal language of non-specialists, although in medical topics, is rather difficult to formalize. The patterns in SF are short with up to 5 tokens in the ancestor vs. up to 14 tokens in the ARs coming from $S05$. Only 3 rules in SF have equal ancestors, in contrary the ancestors often can be collapsed in $S05$ and the same ancestor can have up to 62 different consequents. The ARs coming from $S05$ are also much longer, they describe related symptoms and/or diseases. As shown on Figure 3 the various consequents may be numerous but their vocabulary is not so rich. In $S05ruleset1$ there are only 3 tokens in the union of consequent vocabularies. Finally we note that the circles of mappings, as illustrated in Fig. 3, also suggest different profiles of patients experiencing eventual changes of thy-

roid.

6   Conclusion and Further Work

By fusing information from ORs written in a formal language with informal medical forum texts and applying frequent pattern matching techniques, we manage to extract and generalize ARs describing the context of medical terminology in the domain of diabetes. The obtained patterns have the means of stable term subsets which occur in the documents with a window longer than the usually utilized ones. In this sense our approach delivers higher benefits for generating resources that describe the terminology in the Diabetes domain in comparison to the word frequency based techniques such as *tf*, *tf-idf*. Moreover, the FP matching techniques have the advantage of being unsupervised thus they do not require any external knowledge or annotated data and can successfully deal with big data.

We generalize ARs for the common terms in three sets: terms related to diabetes generated by processing SF and $S05$ as well as terms related to medical examinations obtained by processing of SF and $S00$. We generalize also rules describing the context of terms describing the patient status, output from the processing of $S05$ and $S00$. These resources shall be further employed for automatic analysis of formal and informal medical records, symptoms and condition recognition.

Acknowledgments

The research presented here is partially supported by the grant SpecialIZed Data MIning MethoDs Based on Semantic Attributes (IZIDA), funded by the Bulgarian National Science Fund in 2017–2019, and the project DFNP-100/04.05.2016 "Automatic analysis of clinical text in Bulgarian for discovery of correlations in the Diabetic Registry" funded by the Bulgarian Academy of Sciences in 2016-2017. The team acknowledges also the support of Medical University – Sofia, the Bulgarian Ministry of Health and the Bulgarian National Health Insurance Fund.

References

Rakesh Agrawal and Ramakrishnan Srikant. 1994. Fast algorithms for mining association rules in large databases. In *Proceedings of the 20th International Conference on Very Large Data Bases.*

Morgan Kaufmann Publishers Inc., San Francisco, CA, USA, VLDB '94, pages 487–499. http://dl.acm.org/citation.cfm?id=645920.672836.

Helena Ahonen-Myka. 1999. Finding all maximal frequent sequences in text. In *Mladenic and Grobelnik (Eds.), Proc. 16th Int. Conf. on ML ICML-99, Workshop on ML in Text Data Analysis, J. Stefan Institute, Ljubljana.* pages 11–17.

Helena Ahonen-Myka. 2002. Discovery of frequent word sequences in text. In *Proceedings of the ESF Exploratory Workshop on Pattern Detection and Discovery.* Springer-Verlag, London, UK, UK, pages 180–189. http://dl.acm.org/citation.cfm?id=647915.738872.

Helena Ahonen-Myka and Antoine Doucet. 2005. Data Mining Meets Collocations Discovery. In *Inquiries into Words, Constraints and Contexts, Festschrift in the Honour of Kimmo Koskenniemi,* CSLI Publications, Center for the Study of Language and Information, University of Stanford, pages 194–203. https://hal.archives-ouvertes.fr/hal-00324775.

Mafruz Zaman Ashrafi, David Taniar, and Kate Smith. 2007. Redundant association rules reduction techniques. *Int. J. Bus. Intell. Data Min.* 2(1):29–63. https://doi.org/10.1504/IJBIDM.2007.012945.

Svetla Boytcheva, Galia Angelova, Zhivko Angelov, and Dimitar Tcharaktchiev. 2017. Mining comorbidity patterns using retrospective analysis of big collection of outpatient records. *Health Information Science and Systems* (to appear). Springer Int. Publishing. https://link.springer.com/journal/13755.

Svetla Boytcheva, Ivelina Nikolova, Elena Paskaleva, Galia Angelova, Dimitar Tcharaktchiev, and Nadia Dimitrova. 2010. Obtaining status descriptions via automatic analysis of hospital patient records. *Informatica* 34(3):269–278. http://www.informatica.si/index.php/informatica/article/view/301/300.

Gosta Grahne and Jianfei Zhu. 2003. High performance mining of maximal frequent itemsets. In *6th Int. Workshop on High Performance Data Mining.* pages 135–143.

Jiawei Han, Jian Pei, Yiwen Yin, and Runying Mao. 2004. Mining frequent patterns without candidate generation: A frequent-pattern tree approach. *Data mining and knowledge discovery* 8(1):53–87.

Yannis Haralambous and Philippe Lenca. 2014. Text classification using association rules, dependency pruning and hyperonymization. *Proc. of DMNLP, Workshop at ECML/PKDD, Nancy, France, CEUR Workshop Proceedings 1202, pp. 65-80 .*

Ashwin Ittoo and Gosse Bouma. 2013. Term extraction from sparse, ungrammatical domain-specific documents. *Expert Systems with Applications* 40(7):2530 – 2540. https://doi.org/https://doi.org/10.1016/j.eswa.2012.10.067.

Dolores Lozano and Anna Matamala. 2009. The translation of medical terminology in tv fiction series: the spanish dubbing of e.r. *Vigo International Journal of Applied Linguistics* 6:73–87.

Małgorzata Marciniak and Agnieszka Mykowiecka. 2014. Terminology extraction from medical texts in polish. *Journal of Biomedical Semantics* 5(1):24. https://doi.org/10.1186/2041-1480-5-24.

Gleb Sizov and Pinar Öztürk. 2012. Mining of association relations in text. *Proc. Norsk informatikkonferanse, 2012, pp. 37-48, http://www.nik.no/2012/1-4-sizov12MiningOfAssociationRelationsInText.pdf .*

Basak Oguz Yolcular. 2011. Concepts extraction from discharge notes using association rule mining. *World Academy of Science, Engineering and Technology* (59):1031.

Sentence-Level Multilingual Multi-modal Embedding for Natural Language Processing

Iacer Calixto
ADAPT Centre
Dublin City University
Glasnevin, Dublin 9
`iacer.calixto@adaptcentre.ie`

Qun Liu
ADAPT Centre
Dublin City University
Glasnevin, Dublin 9
`qun.liu@adaptcentre.ie`

Abstract

We propose a novel discriminative ranking model that learns embeddings from multilingual and multi-modal data, meaning that our model can take advantage of images and descriptions in multiple languages to improve embedding quality. To that end, we introduce an objective function that uses pairwise ranking adapted to the case of three or more input sources. We compare our model against different baselines, and evaluate the robustness of our embeddings on image–sentence ranking (ISR), semantic textual similarity (STS), and neural machine translation (NMT). We find that the additional multilingual signals lead to improvements on all three tasks, and we highlight that our model can be used to consistently improve the adequacy of translations generated with NMT models when re-ranking n-best lists.

1 Introduction

Distributional semantic models (DSMs) compute word vector representations from text based on word co-occurrence patterns. However, these models suffer from an obvious limitation since the meaning of a word is derived entirely from connections to other words, i.e. they do not take extra-linguistic modalities into account and thus lack *grounding* (Glenberg and Robertson, 2000). This is the case not only of widely adopted word-level DSMs, e.g. word2vec (Mikolov et al., 2013), but also of sentence-level DSMs, e.g. skip-thought vectors (Kiros et al., 2015).

In this work, we address this issue and expand on the idea of training sentence-level multi-modal embeddings (Kiros et al., 2014; Socher et al., 2014), introducing a model that can be trained not only on images and their monolingual descriptions but also on additional multilingual image descriptions when these are available. We believe that having multiple descriptions of one image, regardless of its language, is likely to increase the coverage and variability of ideas described in the image, which may lead to a better generalisation of the depicted scene semantics. Moreover, a similar description expressed in different languages may differ in subtle but meaningful ways.

To that end, we introduce an objective function that uses pairwise ranking (Cohen et al., 1999) adapted to the case of three or more input sources, i.e. an image and multilingual sentences (§3). Our objective function links images and multiple sentences in an arbitrary number of languages, and we validate our idea in experiments where we use the Multi30k data set (§4).

We evaluate our embeddings in three different tasks: an image–sentence ranking (ISR) task (§6), in both directions, where we find that multilingual signals improve ISR to a large extent, i.e. the median ranks for English are improved from 8 to 5 and for German from 11 to 6, although the impact on ranking sentences given images is less conclusive; two sentence textual similarity (STS) tasks (§7), finding consistent improvements over a comparable monolingual baseline and outperforming the best published SemEval results; a neural machine translation (NMT) task (§8), where we use our model to re-rank n-best lists generated by different NMT models and report consistent improvements. Our main contributions are:

- we introduce a novel ranking-based objective function to train a discriminative model that utilises not only *multi-modal* but also *multilingual* data;
- we compare our proposed multilingual multi-modal embedding (MLMME) to embeddings

Proceedings of Recent Advances in Natural Language Processing, pages 139–148,
Varna, Bulgaria, Sep 4–6 2017.

trained on only one language (Kiros et al., 2014) on three different tasks (ISR, STS and NMT), as well as the Skip-Thought vectors when applicable (Kiros et al., 2015), and find that our model consistently improves over comparable monolingual baselines in all tasks but ranking sentences given images, where results are mixed.

2 Background and Related work

Multi-modal distributional semantic models try to expand DSMs and include inputs from additional modalities other than text as a means to address the grounding problem (Glenberg and Robertson, 2000). At the word level, Bruni et al. (2014) propose deriving word and image vectors, where the word vector representations are based on co-occurrence counts in text corpora, and the images are represented using a bag-of-visual-words method with Scale-Invariant Feature Transform (SIFT) vectors (Lowe, 1999, 2004) extracted from a data set of tagged images. These two representations are concatenated and merged using Singular Value Decomposition. Silberer and Lapata (2014) use stacked auto-encoders to map words and images to one same shared multi-modal embedding space. Their image representation is obtained using attribute classifiers that predict visual attributes (e.g., has wings, made of wood) for given words, proposed in Farhadi et al. (2009). Lazaridou et al. (2015) expand the word2vec *skip-gram* (Mikolov et al., 2013) into a multi-modal *skip-gram* model by incorporating image features extracted from pre-trained Convolutional Neural Networks (CNNs). Visual features obtained with pre-trained CNNs are widely used in transfer learning scenarios, such as in visual question answering (Zhang et al., 2016), to train multi-modal word embeddings (Lazaridou et al., 2015) or in multi-modal neural machine translation (Calixto et al., 2017).

All these DSMs have in common that they learn models at the word-level. Nonetheless, there are many models that propose to learn sentence-level (Kiros et al., 2015; Arora et al., 2017) or even paragraph-level vector representations (Le and Mikolov, 2014). Similarly to their word-level counterparts, these models are trained based on text signals only.

At the sentence level, Kiros et al. (2014) propose a multi-modal embedding model trained to map sentences and images into one shared multi-modal embedding space, where the sentences are encoded using Recurrent Neural Networks (RNN). In a similar vein, Socher et al. (2014) utilised Recursive Neural Networks, i.e. RNNs that operate on parse trees, as their sentence encoder. They both utilised pre-trained CNNs to extract image features and a pairwise ranking function to train their multi-modal embeddings.

We build on previous work and extend the idea of training multi-modal sentence-level embeddings to the scenario where the training data is not only *multi-modal*, but also *multilingual*. We thus put forward a model that integrates images and an arbitrary number of descriptions in different languages.

3 Multilingual and multi-modal embeddings (MLMME)

Our model has two main components: one *textual* and one *visual*. In the textual component, we have K different languages L_k, $k \in [1, K]$, and for each language we use a recurrent neural network (RNN) with gated recurrent units (GRU) (Cho et al., 2014) as a sentence encoder. Let $S^k = \{w_1^k, \ldots, w_{N_k}^k\}$ denote sentences composed of word indices in a language L_k, and $X^k = (x_1^k, x_2^k, \cdots, x_{N_k}^k)$ the corresponding word embeddings for these sentences, where N_k is the sentence length. An RNN Φ_{enc}^k reads X^k word by word, from left to right, and generates a sequence of annotation vectors $(h_1^k, h_2^k, \cdots, h_{N_k}^k)$ for each embedding x_i^k, $i \in [1, N_k]$. For any given input sentence, we use the corresponding encoder RNN's last annotation vector $h_{N_k}^k$ for that language L_k as the sentence representation, henceforth v^k.

In our visual component we use publicly available pre-trained models for image feature extraction. Simonyan and Zisserman (2014) trained deep CNNs for classifying images into one out of 1000 ImageNet classes (Russakovsky et al., 2015). We use their 19-layer VGG network (VGG19) to extract feature vectors for all images in our dataset. More specifically, we use *global* features extracted from the penultimate fully-connected layer of the VGG19 network, which consists of a $4,096$D feature vector, henceforth FC7.

Each training example consists of a tuple *(i)* sentences S^k in L_k, $\forall k \in [1, K]$, and *(ii)* the associated image these sentences describe. Given a training instance, we retrieve the embeddings $X^k = \{x_1^k, \ldots, x_{N_k}^k\}$ for each sentence S^k using one separate word embedding matrix for each language k. A sentence embedding representation v^k is then obtained by applying the encoder Φ_{enc}^k onto each embedding $x_{1:N_k}^k$ and using the last annotation vector $h_{N_k}^k$ of each RNN, after it has consumed the last token in each sentence. An image feature vector $q \in \mathbb{R}^{4096}$ is extracted using the VGG19 CNN so that $d = W_I \cdot q$ is an image embedding and W_I is a model parameter. Also, image embeddings d and sentence embeddings v^k, $\forall k \in [1, K]$ are normalised to unit norm and have the same dimensionality. Finally, $s_i(d, v^k) = d^\top \cdot v^k, k \in [1, K]$ is a function that computes the similarity between images and sentences in any language, and $s_s(v^k, v^l) = (v^k)^\top \cdot v^l, \forall k, l \in [1, K], k \neq l$, computes the similarity between sentences in two different languages.[1]

We now describe two *pairwise ranking* functions used in our objective, one that scores sentences and images, and another one that scores sentences in two different languages. Our model takes into consideration not only the relation between sentences in a given language and images computed by the $s_i(\cdot, \cdot)$ function, but also sentences in different languages in relation to each other, computed by $s_s(\cdot, \cdot)$. Our sentence–image, *multi-modal* ranking function is given in (1):

$$R_{\text{MM}} = \sum_d \sum_r \max\{0, \alpha - s_i(d, v^k) + s_i(d, v_r^k)\} +$$
$$\sum_{v^k} \sum_r \max\{0, \alpha - s_i(v^k, d) + s_i(v^k, d_r)\},$$
$$k \in K, \qquad (1)$$

where v_r^k (subscript r for *random*) is a contrastive or non-descriptive sentence embedding in language L_k for image embedding d and vice-versa, and α is a model parameter, i.e. the *margin*. R_{MM} learns to rank a sentence embedding v^k in language L_k, $k \in K$, against an image embedding d, and vice-versa. Our sentence–sentence, *multilingual* ranking function is (2):

$$R_{\text{ML}} = \sum_{v^k} \sum_r \max\{0, \alpha - s_s(v^k, v^l) + s_s(v^k, v_r^l)\} +$$
$$\sum_{v^l} \sum_r \max\{0, \alpha - s_s(v^l, v^k) + s_s(v^l, v_r^k)\},$$
$$k \in K, l \in K, l \neq k, \qquad (2)$$

where v_r^k is a contrastive or non-descriptive sen-

tence embedding in language L_k for sentence v^l in language L_l, and vice-versa. In both R_{MM} and R_{ML}, contrastive terms are chosen randomly from the training set and resampled at every epoch.

Finally, our optimisation function in Equation (3) minimises the linearly weighted combination of R_{MM} and R_{ML}:

$$\min_{\theta_k, W_I} \beta R_{\text{MM}} + (1 - \beta) R_{\text{ML}}, \forall k \in K,$$
$$0 \geq \beta \geq 1, \qquad (3)$$

where θ_k includes all the encoder RNNs parameters for language L_k, and W_I is the image transformation matrix. β is a model hyperparameter that controls how much influence a particular similarity (*multi-modal* or *multilingual*) has in the overall cost. We illustrate the model in Figure 1.

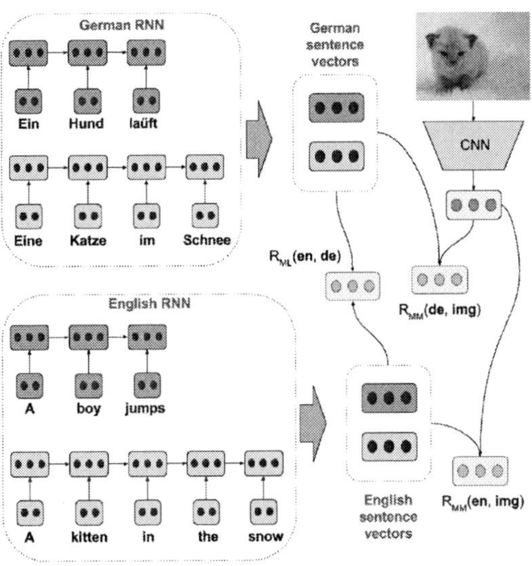

Figure 1: Multilingual multi-modal embedding trained with images and their English and German descriptions. The sentences in red denote contrastive examples, whereas the sentences in blue are descriptive of the image.

The two extreme scenarios are $\beta = 0$, in which case only the multilingual similarity is used, and $\beta = 1$, in which case only the multi-modal similarity is used. If the number of languages $K = 1$ and $\beta = 1$, our model computes the Visual Semantic Embedding (VSE) of Kiros et al. (2014).

4 Datasets

The original Flickr30k data set contains 30k images and 5 English sentence descriptions for each image (Young et al., 2014). We use the Multi30k

---

[1]In this work, both s_i and s_s are implemented as the dot product, but they could be any other suitable function.

		English						German				
	Skip-T.	VSE		Ours				VSE	Ours			
		paper	current	β=1	β=.75	$\beta = 0.5$	$\beta = 0.25$	current	β=1	β=.75	$\beta = 0.5$	$\beta = 0.25$
Sentence to image												
r@1	<u>18.2</u>	16.8	16.5	23.0 (+6.2)	**24.9** (+8.1)	22.3 (+5.5)	21.3 (+4.5)	<u>13.5</u>	**21.6** (+8.1)	20.3 (+6.8)	20.3 (+6.8)	19.5 (+6.0)
r@5	41.9	<u>42.0</u>	41.9	49.3 (+7.3)	**52.3** (+10.3)	48.3 (+6.3)	45.5 (+3.5)	<u>36.6</u>	**48.8** (+12.2)	45.0 (+8.4)	43.7 (+7.1)	43.0 (+6.4)
r@10	53.5	<u>56.5</u>	54.4	61.1 (+4.6)	**63.6** (+7.1)	58.4 (+1.9)	56.7 (+0.2)	<u>49.0</u>	**59.5** (+10.5)	56.6 (+7.6)	55.4 (+6.4)	54.4 (+5.4)
mrank	9	<u>8</u>	9	6	**5**	6	7	<u>11</u>	**6**	7	8	8
Image to sentence												
r@1	26.8	23.0	<u>30.7</u>	**33.1** (+2.4)	30.7 (+0.0)	27.4 (−3.3)	26.7 (−4.0)	<u>30.5</u>	**32.3** (+1.7)	24.9 (−5.6)	23.0 (−7.5)	21.8 (−8.7)
r@5	54.9	50.7	<u>**57.8**</u>	57.2 (−0.6)	55.4 (−2.4)	54.5 (−3.3)	51.4 (−6.4)	<u>56.0</u>	**58.6** (+2.6)	52.3 (−3.7)	48.4 (−7.6)	49.8 (−6.2)
r@10	67.5	62.9	<u>**70.6**</u>	68.7 (−1.9)	65.6 (−5.0)	64.0 (−6.6)	61.9 (−8.7)	<u>**68.9**</u>	68.1 (−0.8)	63.6 (−5.3)	62.8 (−6.1)	61.3 (−7.6)
mrank	5	5	<u>**4**</u>	4	4	4	5	<u>**4**</u>	4	5	6	6

Table 1: We show results for our MLMME model evaluated on the M30k$_C$ test set when trained using different values of β, and two monolingual baselines: the Skip-thought vectors (Skip-T.) of Kiros et al. (2015) and the VSE model of Kiros et al. (2014), where *paper* are the results reported in their paper and *current* were obtained when re-training their model. Best monolingual results are underlined and best overall results appear in bold. We show improvements over the best monolingual baseline in parenthesis.

data set (Elliott et al., 2016), which consists of two expansions of the Flickr30k.

To train NMT models (§8) we use the *translated Multi30k*, henceforth M30k$_T$, where for each of the 30k images in the original Flickr30k, one of its English descriptions is manually translated into German by a professional translator. Training, validation and test sets contain 29k, 1014 and 1k images respectively, each accompanied by one translated sentence pair in English and German. In all other experiments (§6 and §7), we use the *comparable Multi30k*, henceforth M30k$_C$, an expansion of the Flickr30k where 5 German descriptions were collected for each image in the original Flickr30k independently from the English descriptions. Training, validation and test sets contain 29k, 1014 and 1k images respectively, each accompanied by 5 English and 5 German sentences.

We split the M30k$_C$'s validation set in two and use the first 500 images and their corresponding bilingual sentences for model selection and the remaining 514 images and bilingual sentences for model evaluation. Source and target languages were estimated over the entire vocabulary, i.e. ∼22 English and ∼34 German tokens.

5 MLMME experimental setup

For each language we train a separate 1024D encoder RNN with GRU. Word embeddings are 620D and trained jointly with the model. All non-recurrent matrices are initialised by sampling from a Gaussian $\mathcal{N}(0, 0.01)$, recurrent matrices are random orthogonal and bias vectors are all initialised to zero. We apply dropout (Srivastava et al., 2014) with a probability of 0.5 in both text and image

representations, which are in turn mapped onto a 2048D multi-modal embedding space. We set the margin $\alpha = 0.2$. Our models are trained using stochastic gradient descent with Adam (Kingma and Ba, 2015) with minibatches of 128 instances.

As our main baseline, we retrain Kiros et al. (2014) monolingual models separately on the M30k$_C$'s English and German sentences (+images), whereas model MLMME is trained on the entire M30k$_C$.

When processing English sentences and images, we additionally use the pre-trained Skip-Thought vectors (Kiros et al., 2015), more specifically the 4800D *combine-skip* vectors as a second baseline. We follow the authors description[2] on how to do it: *(i)* we use their pre-trained encoders to compute the English sentence representations, i.e. a 4800D vector; *(ii)* we train their model on the M30k$_C$ training set using their image–sentence ranking model; *(iii)* we select the model with the best performance of the M30k$_C$ validation set and use it to compute results in the test set.

6 Image↔Sentence Ranking

In Table 1, we show results for the monolingual English Skip-thought vectors of Kiros et al. (2015), the monolingual VSE English and German models of Kiros et al. (2014) and our MLMME models on the M30k$_C$ data set and evaluated on images and bilingual sentences. Recall-at-k ($r@k$) measures the mean number of times the correct result appear in the top-k retrieved entries and *mrank* is the median rank.

---

[2] `https://github.com/ryankiros/`
`skip-thoughts#image-sentence-ranking`

First, we note that multilingual models show consistent improvements in ranking images given sentences. All our models, regardless of the value of the hyperparameter β ($= .25, .5, .75, 1$), show strong improvements in recall@k (up to $+12.2$) and median rank (in English, the mrank is reduced from 8 to 5 and in German from 11 to 6 in comparison to the best model by Kiros et al. (2014)). Nevertheless, when ranking sentences given images, results are less conclusive. The best results achieved by our multilingual models, for both languages, are observed when $\beta = 1$, with the recall@k slightly deteriorating as we include more multilingual similarity, i.e. $\beta = .75, .5, .25$, and the median rank also slightly increasing for English (from 4 to 5) and German (from 4 to 6). In short, model MLMME consistently improves over all baselines when ranking images given sentences, and applying model MLMME with $\beta{=}1$ to rank sentences given images performs comparably to the monolingual VSE baseline and clearly improves over using the Skip-Thought model on the same task.

6.1 Discussion

Using image features are crucial in *grounding* the sentence vector representations. We note that using $\beta{=}0$ in Equation 3 is equivalent to using only multilingual similarity scores (eq. 2), and no multi-modal similarities (eq. 1). However, in the training data there are multiple sentences describing one same image, and by not using the multi-modal similarity the model loses the ability to generalise and project semantically similar sentences, i.e. sentences that describe one same image, close together. In other words, the model has no way of mapping the comparable sentences that describe one same image together, since the link between these sentences are the image they describe.

In practice, we noted that using $\beta = 0$ leads to a model that cannot learn to rank sentences given images and vice-versa, i.e. the results for median ranks in Table 1 when $\beta = 0$ drop to chance levels. For that reason, we do not include $\beta = 0$ in our hyperparameter search for the experiments we report in Sections 7 and 8.

7 Semantic Textual Similarity

In the semantic textual similarity task, we use our model to compute the distance between a pair of sentences (distances are equivalent to cosine

Test set	VSE	Our model				SemEval best
		$\beta{=}1$	$\beta{=}.75$	$\beta{=}.5$	$\beta{=}.25$	
in-domain data						
IMG$_1$	.791	.797	.819	**.826**	.817	.821
IMG$_2$	.834	.880	.882	.885	**.886**	.864

Table 2: Pearson rank correlation scores for semantic textual similarities in two different SemEval test sets. IMG$_1$: image descriptions (2014), IMG$_2$: image descriptions (2015).

similarity and therefore lie in the $[0, 1]$ interval). Gold standard scores for all tasks are given in the $[0, 5]$ interval, where 0 means complete dissimilarity and 5 complete similarity. We simply use the cosine similarity distance and scale it by 5, directly comparing it to the gold standard scores. There is no SemEval data set including the German language, therefore we only use our English encoders to compute embedding vectors for both sentences in each entry in the test set. We report results for the two in-domain similarity tasks in SemEval, specifically the image description similarity tasks from years 2014 (Agirre et al., 2014) and 2015 (Agirre et al., 2015).

In Table 2, we note that our MLMME model consistently improves on the monolingual baseline of Kiros et al. (2014) in the two in-domain similarity tasks, and our best models also outperform the best published SemEval results.

We note that we only use the English side of our models (+images) in these two evaluations, but we do not directly use our German encoders since there are no German sentences in the SemEval STS task. Nonetheless, training on additional German sentences—incorporated in our model via the German encoder—clearly increases the quality of the English encoder, specially for lower values of β as can be seen in Table 2. These are interesting results, showing that the additional multilingual data brings holistic effects to the entire model and makes the overall model better.

8 Neural Machine Translation (NMT)

In this set of experiments, we use model MLMME to re-rank n-best lists generated with baseline text-only NMT models. Arguably, the main advantage of using such discriminative models to re-rank n-best lists instead of directly training a multi-modal NMT model is the shorter training time . Whereas training the discriminative MLMME model on the Multi30k data set takes $\sim$6 hours, training a multi-modal NMT model on the same data set usually takes many days.

In order to evaluate how VSE and MLMME models perform in n-best list re-ranking, we train NMT baselines based on the model of Bahdanau et al. (2015) using different hyper-parameter settings. All NMT models have an encoder bidirectional RNN with GRU (one 1024D single-layer forward RNN and one 1024D single-layer backward RNN). Source and target word embeddings are 620D each and both are trained jointly. All non-recurrent matrices are initialised by sampling from a Gaussian ($\mu = 0, \sigma = 0.01$), recurrent matrices are orthogonal and bias vectors are all initialised to zero. The decoder is an attention-based RNN with GRU and is a neural LM (Bengio et al., 2003).

NMT models are trained using stochastic gradient descent with Adadelta (Zeiler, 2012) and minibatches of size 40, where each training instance consists of one English sentence, one German sentence and one image. We apply early stopping for model selection based on BLEU scores. We evaluate our models' translation quality quantitatively in terms of BLEU4 (Papineni et al., 2002), METEOR (Denkowski and Lavie, 2014), and TER (Snover et al., 2006) and we compute statistical significance using approximate randomisation computed with the MultEval toolkit (Clark et al., 2011).

8.1 NMT baselines

We train one *weak* model, one *regular* model and one *optimised* NMT model on the translated Multi30k training data set (without images) to translate from English into German. In order to train these three different models, we search for the best dropout and L2 regularisation weight combination by observing model performance on the validation set. The search space for the dropout hyperparameter is the set $\{0.0, 0.1, 0.2, \ldots, 0.9, 1.0\}$, and for the L2 regularisation weight is the set $\{0.0, 1e{-}1, 1e{-}2, \ldots, 1e{-}9, 1e{-}10\}$.

Weak model   Our *weak* model is the text-only NMT baseline model trained with no regularisation, i.e. L2 regularisation weight is 0.0 and dropout probability is 0.0. It corresponds to the model with the worst performance on the translated Multi30k validation set.

Regular model   Our *regular* model is a text-only NMT baseline model with medium-performance regularisation. Specifically, from the hyperparameter search on the translated Multi30k validation set, we use a weight of $1e{-}8$ to scale the L2 regularisation term and a dropout of 0.5;

Optimised model   Our *optimised* model is the text-only NMT baseline model that has the best performance on the translated Multi30k validation set, according to our dropout and L2 regularisation hyper-parameters search. This corresponds to the model with no L2 regularisation, i.e. L2 weight is 0.0, and dropout with probability 0.2.

8.2 N-best re-ranker

We first use the three different NMT models we have just described to generate n-best lists ($n \in \{20, 50\}$) for each entry in the M30k$_T$ validation and test sets. Second, we use the monolingual VSE model (Kiros et al., 2014) trained on German sentences and images to compute the distance between translations into German and images, for all entries in the M30k$_T$ validation and test sets. We also use our MLMME models trained with $\beta \in \{.25, .5, .75, 1\}$ to compute the distance between German and English sentences with $s_s(\cdot, \cdot)$, and between a German sentence and an image using $s_i(\cdot, \cdot)$, for all entries in the M30k$_T$ validation and test sets.

We then train an n-best list re-ranker on the M30k$_T$ validation set's 20-best (50-best) lists with k-best MIRA (Crammer and Singer, 2003; Cherry and Foster, 2012), and use the new distances as additional features to the original MT log-likelihood $p(Y \mid X)$. We finally apply the optimised weights to re-rank the test set's 20-best (50-best) lists.

8.3 Results

In Tables 3 and 4, we show results obtained with the *weak*, the *regular*, and the *optimised* models when used to re-rank 20-best and 50-best lists, respectively. We compute 20- and 50-best lists to be able to observe whether the different models we use in re-ranking generate consistent results, regardless of the size of the n-best lists.

In order to measure of the quality of the n-best lists generated by the different models, we compute their oracle scores. The difference between the oracle scores for the n-best lists generated by the weak and the regular model is considerable: 8.8/10.4 BLEU, 7.9/8.0 METEOR, and

	BLEU		METEOR		TER	
Weak NMT model						
baseline	25.7		43.1		56.1	
+ VSE	25.8	(+0.1)	43.2	(+0.1)	56.1	(-0.0)
+ MLMME, $\beta = 1$	26.1	(+0.4)	**44.4**†‡	(+1.3)	55.5	(-0.6)
+ MLMME, $\beta = 0.75$	26.1	(+0.4)	44.3†‡	(+1.2)	55.9	(-0.2)
+ MLMME, $\beta = 0.5$	26.0	(+0.3)	43.9†‡	(+0.8)	55.9	(-0.2)
+ MLMME, $\beta = 0.25$	**26.3**†‡	(+0.6)	44.3†‡	(+1.2)	**55.2**†‡	(-0.9)
oracle	33.1		51.4		46.5	
Regular NMT model						
baseline	32.4		50.7		51.9	
+ VSE	32.2	(-0.2)	50.7	(+0.0)	52.6	(+0.7)
+ MLMME, $\beta = 1$	**33.8**†‡	(+1.4)	**51.4**†‡	(+0.7)	49.0‡	(-2.9)
+ MLMME, $\beta = 0.75$	33.5‡	(+1.1)	51.3†‡	(+0.6)	49.0‡	(-2.9)
+ MLMME, $\beta = 0.5$	**33.8**†‡	(+1.4)	**51.4**†‡	(+0.7)	**48.6**†‡	(-3.3)
! + MLMME, $\beta = 0.25$	33.7‡	(+1.3)	**51.4**†‡	(+0.7)	49.4‡	(-2.5)
oracle	41.9		59.3		41.2	
Optimised NMT model						
baseline	35.3		52.3		44.9	
+ VSE	32.3	(-3.0)	49.8	(-2.5)	46.5	(+1.6)
+ MLMME, $\beta = 1$	35.3‡	(+0.0)	**52.7**†‡	(+0.4)	**44.5**‡	(-0.4)
+ MLMME, $\beta = 0.75$	35.2‡	(-0.1)	52.6‡	(+0.3)	44.6‡	(-0.3)
+ MLMME, $\beta = 0.5$	35.1‡	(-0.2)	52.3‡	(+0.0)	44.9‡	(-0.0)
+ MLMME, $\beta = 0.25$	**35.7**‡	(+0.4)	**52.7**‡	(+0.4)	**44.5**‡	(-0.4)
oracle	43.2		59.7		37.8	

Table 3: MT evaluation metrics computed for 1-best translations generated with three NMT baselines, and for 20-best lists re-ranked using VSE and MLMME as discriminative features. Results improve significantly over the corresponding 1-best baseline (†) or over the translations obtained with the VSE re-ranker (‡) with $p = 0.05$.

	BLEU		METEOR		TER	
Weak NMT model						
baseline	25.7		43.1		56.1	
+ VSE	25.8	(+0.1)	43.5†	(+0.4)	56.1	(-0.0)
+ MLMME, $\beta = 1$	26.2	(+0.5)	**44.6**†‡	(+1.5)	55.4	(-0.7)
+ MLMME, $\beta = 0.75$	**26.4**†	(+0.7)	44.5†‡	(+1.4)	55.6	(-0.5)
+ MLMME, $\beta = 0.5$	25.9	(+0.2)	43.9†	(+0.8)	55.9	(-0.0)
+ MLMME, $\beta = 0.25$	**26.4**†‡	(+0.7)	44.5†‡	(+1.4)	**55.0**†‡	(-1.1)
oracle	36.2		53.8		43.4	
Regular NMT model						
baseline	32.4		50.7		51.9	
+ VSE	32.7	(-0.3)	50.8	(+0.1)	51.4	(-0.5)
+ MLMME, $\beta = 1$	**34.2**†‡	(+1.8)	**51.6**†‡	(+0.9)	48.3‡	(-3.6)
+ MLMME, $\beta = 0.75$	34.1†‡	(+1.7)	**51.6**†‡	(+0.9)	47.6†‡	(-4.3)
+ MLMME, $\beta = 0.5$	34.0†‡	(+1.6)	51.4†‡	(+0.7)	**47.3**†‡	(-4.6)
+ MLMME, $\beta = 0.25$	34.1†‡	(+1.7)	**51.6**†‡	(+0.9)	48.5‡	(-3.4)
oracle	46.6		61.8		34.1	
Optimised NMT model						
baseline	35.3		52.3		44.9	
+ VSE	30.7	(-4.6)	47.9	(-4.4)	48.6	(+3.7)
+ MLMME, $\beta = 1$	35.4‡	(+0.1)	**52.7**†‡	(+0.4)	**44.4**†‡	(-0.5)
+ MLMME, $\beta = 0.75$	35.2‡	(-0.1)	52.5‡	(+0.2)	44.7‡	(-0.2)
+ MLMME, $\beta = 0.5$	35.1‡	(-0.2)	52.3‡	(+0.0)	44.7‡	(-0.2)
+ MLMME, $\beta = 0.25$	**35.6**‡	(+0.3)	52.6‡	(+0.3)	**44.4**†‡	(-0.5)
oracle	46.3		61.9		34.9	

Table 4: MT evaluation metrics computed for 1-best translations generated with three NMT baselines, and for 50-best lists re-ranked using VSE and MLMME as discriminative features. Results improve significantly over the corresponding 1-best baseline (†) or over the translations obtained with the VSE re-ranker (‡) with $p = 0.05$.

5.3/9.3 TER, for the 20-best and 50-best lists respectively. Nevertheless, the difference between the oracle scores for the n-best lists generated by the regular and the optimised model is not nearly as high: 1.2/−0.3 BLEU, 0.0/0.1 METEOR, and 3.4/0.8 TER, again for the 20-best and 50-best lists respectively. However, when we analyse the metrics scores obtained by re-ranked models, we see a considerable difference between the improvements brought by VSE and MLMME features to the regular and optimised models.

Weak model First of all, using VSE features to re-rank n-best lists generated by the weak model practically does not change translations. MLMME features have a strong impact on METEOR scores, suggesting that they are making translations more adequate by improving their word-level recall. Using MLMME features to re-rank significantly improves METEOR in relation to the baseline and to the translations obtained with the VSE-features re-ranked model, for all values of β and for all n-best list sizes.

The model re-ranked with MLMME features with $\beta = 0.25$ performs best in this scenario. It is the only model that significantly improves on the three automatic metrics over both the 1-best baseline and the VSE-features re-ranked model, for all n-best lists sizes ($p = 0.05$).

Regular model Again, using VSE features to re-rank n-best lists generated by the regular model does not change translations in practice. Nevertheless, VSE re-ranked models are the only ones to show some small deterioration in relation to the baseline, even though these differences are not statistically significant. Models re-ranked with MLMME features are consistently better than the baseline, for all values of β and $n \in \{20, 50\}$. They also show strong improvements on ME-TEOR scores in relation to both the baseline and to the translations obtained with the VSE-features re-ranked model, suggesting that they are still making translations more adequate by improving their word-level recall.

When applied to re-rank 50-best lists, MLMME features also significantly improve BLEU scores in relation to the baseline and to the translations obtained with the VSE-features re-ranked model, in spite of the values of β.

Optimised model First of all, we see that improving on the baseline using VSE or MLMME features becomes harder when applied to n-best lists generated by the optimised model. From looking at the results, perhaps the most apparent outcome is the poor results obtained when using VSE features in this scenario. Using the additional VSE features to re-rank consistently and significantly deteriorate translations, for all n-best lists sizes ($n = \{20, 50\}$). The same does not happen when using MLMME features to re-rank n-best lists. MLMME features lead to translations that consistenly improve over those obtained with the VSE-features re-ranked model, for all different configurations of MLMME models ($\beta = \{0.25, 0.5, 0.75, 1.0\}$).

Model MLMME with $\beta = 0.25$ or $\beta = 1.0$ obtain the best results regardless of the n-best list sizes. These are the only two models that also significantly improve on the corresponding 1-best baseline according to at least one of the metrics.

8.4 Final Remarks

In this set of experiments we evaluated how well VSE (Kiros et al., 2014) and MLMME models perform when used to compute features to re-rank n-best lists. We found that VSE features do not affect translations when n-best lists are generated by less optimised NMT models, but they become less attractive as the baseline NMT models used to generate n-best lists gets better, getting to the point of significantly harming BLEU, METEOR and TER in the case of a highly optimised model.

In general, MLMME features outperformed VSE features across different scenarios, and seem to have a stronger impact on re-ranking n-best lists generated with the regular model compared to the weak and optimised models. Nonetheless, when applied to translations generated with the optimised model, MLMME models with $\beta = 0.25$ or $\beta = 1.0$ achieve the best results. They consistently and significantly increase METEOR scores, for all n-best lists sizes ($n \in \{20, 50\}$), which is an important finding since NMT models are known to suffer from adequacy issues (Tu et al., 2016).

Finally, MLMME models take considerably less time to train compared to a fully fledged multi-modal NMT model: training MLMME models take $\sim$3–6 hours, whereas training a text-only attention-based NMT model should take $\sim$3–4 days.[3] Likewise, using MLMME models to compute features at inference time is fast: it takes the time to encode the source and target sentences with the corresponding source- and target-language RNNs, the image with the pre-trained CNN, and then performing three dot products: source·target, target·image, and source·image.

Arguably, our results puts MLMME models as attractive candidates to be included in an NLP pipeline for processing image descriptions.

9 Conclusions

We propose a new discriminative ranking model that incorporates both multilingual and multi-modal similarities, and obtain promising results in three different NLP tasks. We train our models using an objective function based on pairwise ranking. When applied to the task of image–sentence ranking, our model consistently outperforms all baselines when ranking images given sentences; our model when $\beta=1$ performs comparably to the monolingual VSE baseline, and the more weight we add to the multilingual similarity in the training objective, the worse the model ranks sentences given images. However, when applied to the task of Semantic Textual Similarity, our model outperforms the best published SemEval models in two image description similarity tasks, and when applied to re-rank n-best lists generated with different NMT models, they consistently improve translations as measured by three different MT metrics. We note that it has a consistent impact on METEOR, which is a recall-oriented metric that emphasises the *adequacy* of translations, which is precisely a problem that NMT models are known to suffer from (Tu et al., 2016). In the future we will train our model on a many-languages setting, with images and descriptions in $\sim$10 languages.

Acknowledgments

This project has received funding from Science Foundation Ireland in the ADAPT Centre for Digital Content Technology (`www.adaptcentre.ie`) at Dublin City University funded under the SFI Research Centres Programme (Grant 13/RC/2106) co-funded under the European Regional Development Fund and the European Union Horizon 2020 research and innovation programme under grant agreement 645452 (QT21).

---

[3]This is the case of training an English–German translation model, evaluated in this work, on the Multi30k data set.

References

Eneko Agirre, Carmen Banea, Claire Cardie, Daniel Cer, Mona Diab, Aitor Gonzalez-Agirre, Weiwei Guo, Inigo Lopez-Gazpio, Montse Maritxalar, Rada Mihalcea, German Rigau, Larraitz Uria, and Janyce Wiebe. 2015. SemEval-2015 Task 2: Semantic Textual Similarity, English, Spanish and Pilot on Interpretability. In *Proceedings of the 9th International Workshop on Semantic Evaluation (SemEval 2015)*. Denver, Colorado, pages 252–263. http://www.aclweb.org/anthology/S15-2045.

Eneko Agirre, Carmen Banea, Claire Cardie, Daniel Cer, Mona Diab, Aitor Gonzalez-Agirre, Weiwei Guo, Rada Mihalcea, German Rigau, and Janyce Wiebe. 2014. Semeval-2014 task 10: Multilingual semantic textual similarity. In *Proceedings of the 8th International Workshop on Semantic Evaluation (SemEval 2014)*. Dublin, Ireland, pages 81–91. http://www.aclweb.org/anthology/S14-2010.

Sanjeev Arora, Yingyu Liang, and Tengyu Ma. 2017. A Simple but Tough-to-Beat Baseline for Sentence Embeddings. In *International Conference on Learning Representations, ICLR 2017*. Toulon, France. https://openreview.net/pdf?id=SyK00v5xx.

Dzmitry Bahdanau, Kyunghyun Cho, and Yoshua Bengio. 2015. Neural Machine Translation by Jointly Learning to Align and Translate. In *International Conference on Learning Representations, ICLR 2015*. San Diego, California. http://arxiv.org/abs/1409.0473.

Yoshua Bengio, Réjean Ducharme, Pascal Vincent, and Christian Janvin. 2003. A Neural Probabilistic Language Model. *J. Mach. Learn. Res.* 3:1137–1155. http://dl.acm.org/citation.cfm?id=944919.944966.

Elia Bruni, Nam Khanh Tran, and Marco Baroni. 2014. Multimodal distributional semantics. *J. Artif. Int. Res.* 49(1):1–47. http://dl.acm.org/citation.cfm?id=2655713.2655714.

Iacer Calixto, Daniel Stein, Evgeny Matusov, Pintu Lohar, Sheila Castilho, and Andy Way. 2017. Using images to improve machine-translating e-commerce product listings. In *Proceedings of the 15th Conference of the European Chapter of the Association for Computational Linguistics: Volume 2, Short Papers*. Valencia, Spain, pages 637–643. http://www.aclweb.org/anthology/E17-2101.

Colin Cherry and George Foster. 2012. Batch tuning strategies for statistical machine translation. In *Proceedings of the 2012 Conference of the North American Chapter of the Association for Computational Linguistics: Human Language Technologies*. Montrèal, Canada, pages 427–436. http://aclweb.org/anthology/N12-1047.

Kyunghyun Cho, Bart van Merrienboer, Caglar Gulcehre, Dzmitry Bahdanau, Fethi Bougares, Holger Schwenk, and Yoshua Bengio. 2014. Learning Phrase Representations using RNN Encoder–Decoder for Statistical Machine Translation. In *Proceedings of the 2014 Conference on Empirical Methods in Natural Language Processing (EMNLP)*. Doha, Qatar, pages 1724–1734. http://www.aclweb.org/anthology/D14-1179.

Jonathan H. Clark, Chris Dyer, Alon Lavie, and Noah A. Smith. 2011. Better hypothesis testing for statistical machine translation: Controlling for optimizer instability. In *Proceedings of the 49th Annual Meeting of the Association for Computational Linguistics: Human Language Technologies: Short Papers - Volume 2*. Association for Computational Linguistics, Stroudsburg, PA, USA, HLT '11, pages 176–181. http://dl.acm.org/citation.cfm?id=2002736.2002774.

W. W. Cohen, R. E. Schapire, and Y. Singer. 1999. Learning to order things. *Journal of Artificial Intelligence Research* 10:243–270.

Koby Crammer and Yoram Singer. 2003. Ultraconservative online algorithms for multiclass problems. *Journal of Machine Learning Research* 3:951–991. https://doi.org/10.1162/jmlr.2003.3.4-5.951.

Michael Denkowski and Alon Lavie. 2014. Meteor Universal: Language Specific Translation Evaluation for Any Target Language. In *Proceedings of the Ninth Workshop on Statistical Machine Translation*. Baltimore, Maryland, USA, pages 376–380. http://www.aclweb.org/anthology/W/W14/W14-3348.

Desmond Elliott, Stella Frank, Khalil Sima'an, and Lucia Specia. 2016. Multi30K: Multilingual English-German Image Descriptions. In *Proceedings of the 5th Workshop on Vision and Language, VL@ACL 2016*. Berlin, Germany. http://aclweb.org/anthology/W/W16/W16-3210.pdf.

Ali Farhadi, Ian Endres, Derek Hoiem, and David Forsyth. 2009. Describing objects by their attributes. In *Proceedings of the IEEE Computer Society Conference on Computer Vision and Pattern Recognition (CVPR*. Miami, Florida, USA, pages 1778–1785. https://doi.org/10.1109/CVPR.2009.5206772.

A. Glenberg and D. Robertson. 2000. Symbol grounding and meaning: A comparison of high-dimensional and embodied theories of meaning. *Journal of Memory and Language* http://psych.wisc.edu/glenberg/.

Diederik P. Kingma and Jimmy Ba. 2015. Adam: A method for stochastic optimization. In *International Conference on Learning Representations, ICLR 2015*. San Diego, California.

Ryan Kiros, Ruslan Salakhutdinov, and Richard S. Zemel. 2014. Unifying visual-semantic embeddings with multimodal neural language models. *CoRR* abs/1411.2539. http://arxiv.org/abs/1411.2539.

Ryan Kiros, Yukun Zhu, Ruslan Salakhutdinov, Richard S. Zemel, Antonio Torralba, Raquel Urtasun, and Sanja Fidler. 2015. Skip-thought Vectors. In *Proceedings of the 28th International Conference on Neural Information Processing Systems*. MIT Press, Cambridge, MA, USA, NIPS'15, pages 3294–3302. http://dl.acm.org/citation.cfm?id=2969442.2969607.

Angeliki Lazaridou, Nghia The Pham, and Marco Baroni. 2015. Combining language and vision with a multimodal skip-gram model. In *Proceedings of the 2015 Conference of the North American Chapter of the Association for Computational Linguistics: Human Language Technologies*. Denver, Colorado, pages 153–163. http://www.aclweb.org/anthology/N15-1016.

Quoc Le and Tomas Mikolov. 2014. Distributed representations of sentences and documents. In *Proceedings of the 31st International Conference on Machine Learning (ICML-14)*.

David G. Lowe. 1999. Object Recognition from Local Scale-Invariant Features. In *Proceedings of the International Conference on Computer Vision-Volume 2 - Volume 2*. IEEE Computer Society, Washington, DC, USA, ICCV '99, pages 1150–. http://dl.acm.org/citation.cfm?id=850924.851523.

David G. Lowe. 2004. Distinctive Image Features from Scale-Invariant Keypoints. *Int. J. Comput. Vision* 60(2):91–110. https://doi.org/10.1023/B:VISI.0000029664.99615.94.

Tomas Mikolov, Ilya Sutskever, Kai Chen, Greg Corrado, and Jeffrey Dean. 2013. Distributed Representations of Words and Phrases and their Compositionality. In *Proceedings of the 26th International Conference on Neural Information Processing Systems, NIPS*. Lake Tahoe, Nevada, NIPS'13, pages 3111–3119. http://dl.acm.org/citation.cfm?id=2999792.2999959.

Kishore Papineni, Salim Roukos, Todd Ward, and Wei-Jing Zhu. 2002. BLEU: a Method for Automatic Evaluation of Machine Translation. In *Proceedings of 40th Annual Meeting of the Association for Computational Linguistics*. Philadelphia, Pennsylvania, USA, pages 311–318. https://doi.org/10.3115/1073083.1073135.

Olga Russakovsky, Jia Deng, Hao Su, Jonathan Krause, Sanjeev Satheesh, Sean Ma, Zhiheng Huang, Andrej Karpathy, Aditya Khosla, Michael Bernstein, Alexander C. Berg, and Li Fei-Fei. 2015. ImageNet Large Scale Visual Recognition Challenge. *International Journal of Computer Vision (IJCV)* 115(3):211–252. https://doi.org/10.1007/s11263-015-0816-y.

Carina Silberer and Mirella Lapata. 2014. Learning Grounded Meaning Representations with Autoencoders. In *Proceedings of the 52nd Annual Meeting of the Association for Computational Linguistics (Volume 1: Long Papers)*. Baltimore, Maryland, pages 721–732. http://www.aclweb.org/anthology/P14-1068.

K. Simonyan and A. Zisserman. 2014. Very deep convolutional networks for large-scale image recognition. *arXiv preprint arXiv:1409.1556* .

Matthew Snover, Bonnie Dorr, Richard Schwartz, Linnea Micciulla, and John Makhoul. 2006. A study of translation edit rate with targeted human annotation. In *In Proceedings of Association for Machine Translation in the Americas*. Cambridge, MA, pages 223–231.

Richard Socher, Karpathy Andrej, Q Le, Chris Manning, and Andrew Ng. 2014. Grounded Compositional Semantics for Finding and Describing Images with Sentences. *Transactions of the Association for Computational Linguistics* 2:207–218.

Nitish Srivastava, Geoffrey Hinton, Alex Krizhevsky, Ilya Sutskever, and Ruslan Salakhutdinov. 2014. Dropout: A simple way to prevent neural networks from overfitting. *Journal of Machine Learning Research* 15:1929–1958. http://jmlr.org/papers/v15/srivastava14a.html.

Zhaopeng Tu, Zhengdong Lu, Yang Liu, Xiaohua Liu, and Hang Li. 2016. Modeling Coverage for Neural Machine Translation. In *Proceedings of the 54th Annual Meeting of the Association for Computational Linguistics (Volume 1: Long Papers)*. Berlin, Germany, pages 76–85. http://www.aclweb.org/anthology/P16-1008.

Peter Young, Alice Lai, Micah Hodosh, and Julia Hockenmaier. 2014. From image descriptions to visual denotations: New similarity metrics for semantic inference over event descriptions. *Transactions of the Association for Computational Linguistics* 2:67–78.

Matthew D. Zeiler. 2012. ADADELTA: an adaptive learning rate method. *CoRR* abs/1212.5701. http://arxiv.org/abs/1212.5701.

Peng Zhang, Yash Goyal, Douglas Summers-Stay, Dhruv Batra, and Devi Parikh. 2016. Yin and Yang: Balancing and answering binary visual questions. In *Conference on Computer Vision and Pattern Recognition (CVPR)*. Las Vegas, Nevada, USA.

Role-based model for Named Entity Recognition

Pablo Calleja, Raúl García-Castro, Guadalupe Aguado-de-Cea, Asunción Gómez-Pérez
Ontology Engineering Group
Universidad Politécnica de Madrid, Spain
`{pcalleja,rgarcia,lupe,asun}@fi.upm.es`

Abstract

Named Entity Recognition (NER) poses new challenges in real-world documents in which there are entities with different roles according to their purpose or meaning. Retrieving all the possible entities in scenarios in which only a subset of them based on their role is needed, produces noise on the overall precision. This work proposes a NER model that relies on role classification models that support recognizing entities with a specific role. The proposed model has been implemented in two use cases using Spanish drug Summary of Product Characteristics: identification of therapeutic indications and identification of adverse reactions. The results show how precision is increased using a NER model that is oriented towards a specific role and discards entities out of scope.

1 Introduction

Information extraction (IE) has become a popular research topic in the last three decades, specially in the biomedical field. Most of the works in this field are focused on corpora provided by conferences or challenges such as JNLPBA (Kim et al., 2004) and on the exploitation of paper abstracts (Hunter and Cohen, 2006). Other works, closer to health applications, exploit resources like Electronic Health Records (EHR) (Meystre et al., 2008) and drug Summary of Product Characteristics (SPC) (Boyce et al., 2012).

While EHRs are usually short simple phrases written by doctors, SPCs are official and detailed documents that collect the essential scientific information of a drug for healthcare professionals. In Spain, the authorization of SPCs depends on the *Agencia Española de Medicamentos y Pro-*

ductos Sanitarios (AEMPS) and on the European Medicine Agency (EMA).

Named Entity Recognition (NER) is one of the most important tasks inside IE processes that consists in finding and classifying real-world entities denoted by a referent term or proper name (named entity). However, the state of the art is oriented to retrieve all the possible entities regardless if they are relevant or not to a concrete use scenario. Beyond paper abstracts and conference corpora, natural language documents display mixed information in which there are entities that are not relevant to a use scenario and that produce noise on the overall result of the NER task.

This is the case of SPCs, which are natural language documents that contain a lot of mixed valuable information for concrete use scenarios. This paper proposes a new method to create a NER model focused only on specific entities by taking into account the presented role of such entities in the corpus. Such role determines the general meaning and function of the entity in the corpus. The method has been implemented for two IE use cases over specific sections of SPCs in Spanish in collaboration with the AEMPS.

The paper is structured as follows. Section 2 describes related work and section 3 describes in detail the problem of documents with different entity roles. Section 4 proposes the method to create a NER model focused on entities which a specific role. Section 5 shows the application of the method over two use cases and section 6 discusses the obtained results. Finally, section 7 presents some conclusions and highlights future work.

2 Related Work

Normally, the main named entity types proposed in the literature are "person", "organization", "location" "dates", "time expressions" and "mone-

Proceedings of Recent Advances in Natural Language Processing, pages 149–156,
Varna, Bulgaria, Sep 4–6 2017.

tary expressions" (Grishman and Sundheim, 1996; Ferro et al., 2005). The biomedical field defines its own named entity types such as such as "protein", "drug" and "disease" (Rindflesch et al., 2000; Zhou et al., 2005). In contrast, other researchers classify entities into taxonomic models where some types are considered subtypes (i.e., children) of a high level one (e.g., "geological region" or "address" are subtypes of "location") (Sekine et al., 2002).

Nowadays, the state of the art of NER models shows that the best results are provided by supervised machine learning techniques (Nadeau and Sekine, 2007; Campos et al., 2012). However, these techniques require big annotated corpora such as (Kim et al., 2003; Moreno et al., 2017) to be trained. Thus, the use of machine learning techniques is limited in some domains in which there are not such annotated training corpora or there are not in a specific language.

Roles are defined and attached to text segments or entities in an IE task called template filling (Schank and Abelson, 1975; Steimann, 2000). These roles are defined by its acts or meaning in a given context and normally are associated with lexical-syntactic patterns (Patwardhan and Riloff, 2007). Nevertheless, this task in the biomedical domain is focused on event relations like cause-effect or drug-drug interactions (Settles, 2004).

3 Problem Setting

In this context, the current classifications covered in NER systems just deal with taxonomic types and are not meant to represent the entities' role. Nevertheless, as the conceptual model proposed by Steimann shows (Steimann, 2000), entity roles can also be represented as a classification model. For example in the biomedical domain, the taxonomic hierarchy of diseases is normally represented by the affection type such as "mental disorder" and "gastric disease". But, "adverse reaction" or "contraindication" are roles that an entity may have in a given context, and which can also be represented in a taxonomic form. This work proposes to introduce roles into the NER task in order to identify entities according such specific roles.

The following use cases are driven by a NER need in the AEMPS. In them, the agency needs to identify entities in drug SPC documents. However, it usually happens in those documents that there are entities with the same type (disease) but

Durante el tratamiento con Pramipexol Normon, las reacciones adversas pueden ser: *amnesia*, *confusión*, *hipersexualidad*, *delirio* y *mareo*. En base al análisis agrupado de los ensayos controlados con placebo, que incluyen un total de 1.778 pacientes con *enfermedad de Parkinson* tratados con Pramipexol y 1.297 pacientes con placebo.	
Trastornos del sistema nervioso	
Muy frecuentes	*mareo*, *somnolencia*
Frecuentes	*hipercinesia*
Poco frecuentes	*amnesia*
Trastornos gastrointestinales	
Frecuentes	*estreñimiento*, *vómitos*

Figure 1: Excerpt of the adverse reactions section

with different role, and the agency is only interested in those entities with a specific role.

The **therapeutic indication section** provides information about the diseases to be treated with the drug. However, it is sometimes verbose and includes information from other sections such as contraindications, diseases for which the drug should not be prescribed (e.g., *should not be used as a treatment for*), or diseases that refer to the medical record of the patient (e.g., *who does not have a recent history of*).

The **adverse reactions section** provides information about unwanted effects caused by the administration of a drug (diseases or disorders) and their frequency. However, sometimes it also contains therapeutic indication information to specify the adverse reactions. Figure 1 shows an example of the adverse reaction section; all the disease entities are in italics, but only the entities surrounded with a continuous black box are adverse reactions. The entities surrounded with a segmented black box represent other roles.

4 NER model for specific entity roles

The proposed NER model for specific entity roles requires the classification of the reflected roles of the named entities in taxonomic models. These models have to be created through manual tasks using a representative gold standard corpus as reference. The annotated entities must be classified by its named entity type and their position in the text (initial and final offset) must be identified.

Besides, the next assumptions are declared. First, that the entities annotated in the gold standard corpus have the role that must be recognized by the NER model (target role). Second, that the annotated entities always belong to a general named entity type (e.g., person, disease, etc.).

In this work, we define the terms pattern, entity type, entity role and role classification model as: A) A *pattern* is a particular contextual sequence

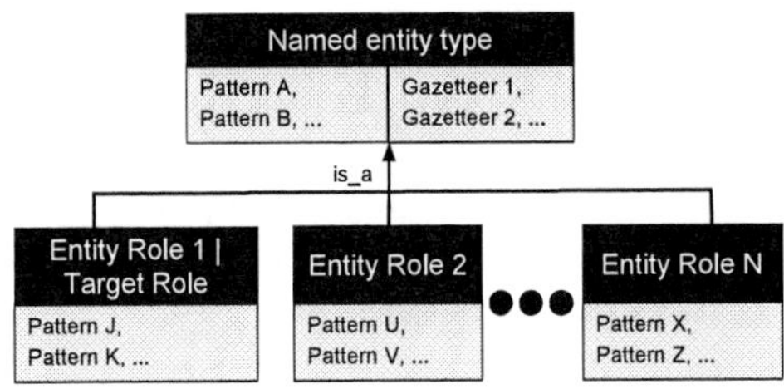

Figure 2: Role classification model representation

of hints that allows to identify an entity by its type or its role; patterns can be lexical, syntactic and layout-based. B) An *entity type* is defined as the classification group of an entity and it composed by sets patterns and gazetteers. C) An *entity role* is defined as a subtype of a named entity type that is characterized by a set of patterns in a specific corpus and describes an entity by its act or meaning in a given context. D) A *role classification model* describes the hierarchy of the different roles for a named entity type in a corpus; the role classification model is composed of a named entity type, one role defined as the target role and a set of zero or more non-target roles. The different roles are disjoint between them and inherit patterns and gazetteers from the entity type.

Figure 2 shows a representation of the role classification model. Once a role classification model is defined, the proposed NER algorithm uses it to identify named entities with a specific role.

4.1   Creation of the role classification model

The method to create a role classification model is composed of the following six tasks that are performed over a gold standard corpus:

1- Extraction of annotated entities. The first task is to collect all the annotated entities of one named entity type in the gold standard corpus.

2- Pattern detection of the annotated entities. The collected annotated entities are studied to detect lexical patterns (character combinations or affixes) that could represent the named entity type. Since lexical patterns do not represent role information, they are attached to the named entity type. Then, the context of the annotated entities is studied to find syntactic patterns (word combinations) and layout patterns (the format in which the information is presented); both types of patterns can represent the named entity type or the target role. Lexical and syntactical patterns are used to identify new possible entities in documents; however,

layout patterns are meant to attach roles or named entity types to entities previously identified.

Figure 1 shows an example in which the annotated entities are diseases inside a continuous black box. A lexical pattern is represented by the prefix "hiper_" that is commonly used in disease names. Also, a syntactic pattern represented by the word combination *reacciones adversas pueden ser:* (the adverse reactions could be:). This syntactic pattern is reflecting the target role of the gold standard corpus (adverse reactions) and all the entities under the scope of the pattern (until the full stop) have the target role. Finally, a layout pattern is also represented in the example. All the entities in the table that are not headers in bold are also diseases with the target role (adverse reactions).

3- Identification of gazetteers for the named entity type. Gazetteers are a common NER resource and there are many of them available for the most common named entity types. This task aims to identify gazetteers aligned with the annotated named entities to support the model on the identification of named entities with the same type.

4- Discovery of entities with different role. Using the selected gazetteers and the patterns identified in the previous tasks, a review of the corpus is made to detect named entities of the same type that have not been reflected in the gold standard corpus. Figure 1 shows three disease named entities inside a segmented black box that are not reflected in the gold standard corpus.

5- Pattern detection of the entities with different role. This task aims to detect syntactic and layout patterns of the entities that are not reflected in the gold standard corpus studying their context. These identified patterns represent other roles present in the corpus. The most common role interpretation is the complementary of the target role ($\neg$Target role). However, it is possible to define and classify different roles studying the gold standard corpus.

Figure 1 shows two examples with a syntactic pattern and a layout pattern. The first one is represented with the word combination *pacientes con* (patients with) that is reflecting diseases with the role for which the drug is prescribed. The second one is represented by rows in the table that are in bold font that is reflecting the classification role of the mentioned diseases.

6- Creation of the role classification model. This task aims to create the role classification model based on the named entity type. The named entity type is represented in the model as the upper class and it is composed by the set of patterns discovered in task 2 and the gazetteers identified in task 3; the patterns associated to the named entity type lack of role information. Then, the different roles are specified. First, the target role is represented by the set of patterns associated to the role discovered in task 2. Second, the rest of the roles are specified by the sets of patterns discovered in task 5. Finally, the role classification model of the named entity type could be represented as in Figure 2.

4.2 Role-based NER algorithm

The NER model executes the proposed Algorithm 1 for each role classification model to identify named entities with the target role, along with its span text and position.

The input of the algorithm is the document to be processed, the role classification model and whether a closed world assumption holds. The output is the set of identified named entities. In the algorithm, two sets of entities are defined: the set of entities without role (*entities*) and the set of entities with the target role (*targetEntities*). The algorithm is divided into five main steps. The first one (lines 5 to 11) is oriented to identify named entities by using the gazetteers of the named entity type. The second one (lines 13 to 16) uses the patterns of the entity type to identify named entities. Patterns are detected with the function *detectPattern*. These two tasks store their results in the *entities* set. The next task (lines 17 to 19) executes the patterns of the target role and stores the results in the *targetEntities* set. Then, the patterns of the non-target roles of the model are executed to identify and delete entities of the two sets (lines 20 to 27). Finally, if the NER model is oriented to a close world assumption (lines 28 to 32), the results are composed only by the entities of the *targetEntities* set. In other case, the results are the union between the *entities* set and *targetEntities* set.

5 Method Implementation

As mentioned in section 3, two projects in collaboration with the AEMPS have implemented the proposed NER model for specific roles. Both projects were oriented to the exploitation of different sections of the SPCs. The first aimed at automatically identifying therapeutic indications

---

Algorithm 1 Role-based NER algorithm

Input: Document d, RoleClassificationModel rcm, boolean cwa

Output: : Set of entities in document d

```
 1: target= rcm.TargetRole
 2: type= rcm.EntityType
 3: entities ← { }
 4: targetEntities ← { }
 5: for all gaz ∈ Gazetteers do
 6:     for all entry ∈ gaz do
 7:         if (termMatches(entry,d)) then
 8:             add(entities,entry)
 9:         end if
10:     end for
11: end for
12: aux ← { }
13: for all p ∈ type.Patterns do
14:     add(aux, detectPattern(p,d))
15: end for
16: entities ← entities ∪ aux
17: for all p ∈ target.Patterns do
18:     add(targetEntities, detectPattern(p,d))
19: end for
20: for all role ∈ rcm.NonTargetRoles do
21:     aux ← { }
22:     for all p ∈ role.Patterns do
23:         add(aux, detectPattern(p,d))
24:     end for
25:     entities ← entities - aux
26:     targetEntities ← targetEntities - aux
27: end for
28: if (cwa) then
29:     return targetEntities
30: else
31:     return entities ∪ targetEntities
32: end if
```

---

in the section with the same name. The second aimed at improving pharmacological surveillance processes through the identification of adverse reactions in the section with the same name.

The AEMPS provided one set of more than 1,000 SPCs in Spanish. From this set, 120 randomly selected SPCs were annotated by domain experts from the agency. The annotation process was made separately in two sections of the SPC: the therapeutic indication one and the adverse reaction one. In each section, the annotated diseases represent the target role of their section ("therapeutic indication" or "adverse reaction"). From these annotated SPCs, two gold standard corpora have been created with the two different sections.

In both projects, 80 SPCs of each gold standard corpus had been used to train their respective model and 40 to test them. The SPCs were selected randomly once for the two use cases. As the named entity type in both use cases is 'disease', the proposed gazetteers for task 3 of the role classification model method were extracted from the Spanish version of the medical dictionary MedDRA (Brown et al., 1999) and from the *Diccionario de siglas médicas* (Yetano Laguna, J., Alberola Cuñat, 2003).

5.1 Therapeutic indication section use case

The first use case aimed at automatically identifying those diseases that have the therapeutic indication role. The gold standard corpus used in this project was created from the therapeutic indication sections of 80 annotated SPCs.

The first two tasks of the method are to extract the annotated entities in the gold standard corpus and to identify patterns. Table 1 shows the patterns discovered through these tasks, which were reviewed by experts from the agency. Lexical patterns are represented by affixes in nouns that are commonly used in medicine like "_itis" (e.g., sinusitis). Lexical patterns are used to identify nominal phrases (NP) as a disease in which the noun contains at least one of the affixes. The nominal phrases include the adjectival phrases (AdjP) that are joined to the noun. The identified patterns had to be classified into patterns that belong to the named entity type and those that belong to the target role therapeutic indication. Lexical patterns are attached directly to the named entity type due to the lack of role information. Similarly, syntactic patterns 13 to 17 are language structures that represent only a disease. Syntactic patterns 18 to 22 represent the common structure to present therapeutic indications in SPCs, describing the target role of the entities.

This use case involved the identification of the named entity type disease, so the gazetteers proposed in the third task are MedDRA and *Diccionario de siglas médicas*. The next task involves the identification of disease entities that are not reflected in the gold standard by using the gazetteers and the patterns identified in the previous task. The context of the discovered entities was then studied to discover patterns of entities with different role. Table 2 shows the patterns identi-

Lexical Pattens			
1) _oma	2) _itis	3) _osis	4) _algia
5) _ema	6) _asis	7) _emia	8) _orrea
9) _penia	10) _plasia	11) hiper_	12) hipo_
Syntatic patterns			
13) {infección de + NP}		14) {enfermedad de + NP}	
15) {enfermedad + AdjP}		16) {afección de + NP}	
17) {virus de + NP}		18) tratamiento de + {NP}	
19) asociado a + {NP}		20) pacientes con + {NP}	
21) prevención de + {NP}		22) alivio de los síntomas de + {NP}	

Table 1: Patterns identified from the annotated entities in the therapeutic indication use case

Syntatic patterns	
23) sin + {NP}	24) que se hayan excluido + {NP}
25) excluyendo + {NP}	26) que no tiene + {NP}
27) siempre que no exista + {NP}	28) pero no + {NP}
29) no protege + {NP}	30) no se recomienda + {NP}
31) no debe ser utilizado + {NP}	32) no debe utilizarse + {NP}
33) no se ha demostrado/ documentado/ estudiado + {NP}	34) no se han realizado estudios + {NP}

Table 2: Patterns identified for entities with other role in the therapeutic indication use case

fied in the task. Experts from the AEMPS determined that patterns 23 to 27 attach the role "medical record" of the patient, while patterns 28 to 33 represent the role "contraindication", i.e., diseases for which the use of the drug is not recommended.

Finally, the role classification model was created representing the named entity type as the parent class with its patterns and gazetteers and the different discovered roles and their patterns as children classes.

5.2 Adverse reaction use case

The second use case aimed at identifying adverse reactions. As in the first project, the target entities for the NER model are diseases, but their role is "adverse reaction". The gold standard corpus used for this project was created from the adverse reaction section of the 80 annotated SPCs.

The first two tasks of the method are to extract the annotated entities and to identify patterns; table 3 shows the patterns identified for the entities. Lexical patterns are the same as presented in Table 1 (1 to 12). Also, other syntactic patterns were repeated (13 to 17). The new syntactic patterns (35 to 38) are diseases that are represented by fluctuation disorders of biological substances of the organism. The syntactic patterns in Table 3 are presented in sets having the same meaning with different words. For example, pattern 35 represents decrease of biological substances and there are four words to compose the pattern: *dismin-*

Lexical Pattens	
Patterns 1-12	
Syntatic patterns	
Patterns 13- 17	35) { (disminución | pérdida | reducción | descenso) de + NP}
36) { (prolongación | incremento | elevación | aumento) de + NP}	37) { (alteración | anormalidad | cambios | descompensación) de + NP}
38) { empeoramiento de + NP}	
Layout Patterns	
39) Entities inside tag <table>	40) Entities inside tag <p> below headers in tags <b>, <i> or <u>

Table 3: Patterns identified from the annotated entities in the adverse reaction use case

Syntatic patterns	
Patterns 18-21	41) potenciado por + {NP}
42) con el fin de evitar + {NP}	43) no se asocia + {NP}
44) no se observó + {NP}	45) sin indicios de + {NP}
46) en ensayos clínicos de + {NP}	47) en estudios clínicos de + {NP}
48) administración en combinación en + {NP}	
Layout Patterns	
49) Entities in tags <b>, <i> or <u>	

Table 4: Patterns identified for entities with other role in the adverse reaction use case

ución (decrease), *reducción* (reduction), *pérdida* (loss) and *descenso* (decline). None of these patterns contains information about the role. However, it has been observed that most of the adverse reactions presented in SPCs are represented in tables, indicating the affection classification type and their frequency. At the same time, documents that do not contain tables, also use the affection classification type as headers to enounce adverse reactions. Both layout patterns had been used to identify entities with the adverse reaction role. Pattern 39 associates entities that are inside the HTML table tag as an entity and pattern 40 identifies entities that are in the text under a header and associates them to the adverse reaction role.

As in the other use case, the next step was to identify other entities with the NE type disease that had not been reflected in the gold standard using the gazetteers and the identified patterns. The syntactic patterns found for these entities are presented in Table 4. In specific cases SPCs repeat the diseases with the "therapeutic indication" role (18, 21, 46-48). Other roles that have appeared are "medical interaction", "non adverse reaction" and "classification headers". "Medical interaction" (41-42) represents diseases that only appear in a specific case or diseases that could produce more adverse reactions. The "non adverse reaction" (43-45) role represents diseases that have not been discovered as adverse reactions during the drug clinical research. The last role is "classification headers" (49), general diseases that classify and enounce the adverse reactions. Finally, it was possible to represent the role classification model.

6 Evaluation

The model evaluation has been performed by measuring the results obtained over the 40 test documents of the gold standard corpus. Each use case has been evaluated separately with their own role classification model. The evaluation consisted of four experiments related with the main steps in which the role-based NER algorithm is divided. The first experiment only takes the results obtained by gazetteers. The second one adds the results obtained by the patterns of the named entity type disease. The third one uses the target role patterns to add or associate entities to the target role. Finally, the fourth one uses the patterns of the other roles to discard entities that are not associated to the target role. Both use cases work under the open world assumption; i.e., entities with no role are considered to be part of the target role.

The evaluation metrics used are precision (P), recall (R) and F-measure (F). The evaluation measures the detected entities under two matching criteria as proposed in other biomedical evaluations (Tsai et al., 2006). Normally, NER systems use the strict or exact matching criteria; the entity detected by the system and the entity annotated in the gold standard corpus must have the same span text and named entity type. However, the annotated entities of the provided gold standard corpus have problems in the consensus between annotators, i.e., the same entity with the same span text is annotated with different length (different offset in one side). Normally, the difference between annotations are adjectives that experts have taken or not into account in the annotation process, such as adjectives that describe a particular case of the patient's disease (e.g., *recurrente* (recurrent)) and adjectives that describes the intensity or degree (e.g., *grave* (severe)). Thus, the partial criteria allows that one of the span texts offsets can be different.

Table 5 presents the obtained results of the 4 experiments in use case 1. Firstly, experiment 1 denotes that gazetteers cover most of the entities in the corpus, but they are not representative enough to cover all of them. Experiment 2 shows how lexical and syntactic patterns detect more named entities thus improving the results of

	Strict			Partial		
	P	**R**	**F**	**P**	**R**	**F**
Exp. 1	0.8162	0.8531	0.8343	0.9243	0.9661	0.9448
Exp. 2	0.905	0.9153	0.9101	0.9665	0.9774	0.9719
Exp. 3	0.9176	0.9435	0.9304	0.9615	0.9887	0.9749
Exp. 4	0.9382	0.9435	**0.9408**	0.9831	0.9887	**0.9859**

Table 5: Therapeutic indication evaluation

	Strict			Partial		
	P	**R**	**F**	**P**	**R**	**F**
Exp. 1	0.8901	0.809	0.8476	0.9502	0.8636	0.9049
Exp. 2	0.8598	0.8274	0.8433	0.9429	0.9074	0.9248
Exp. 3	0.8598	0.8274	0.8433	0.9429	0.9074	0.9248
Exp. 4	0.872	0.8256	**0.8482**	0.9557	0.9048	**0.9296**

Table 6: Adverse reaction evaluation

the gazetteers. Experiment 3 shows how the patterns of the target role increase the recall. However, precision decreases because these syntactic patterns are overlapped with patterns with other role patterns. For example, sometimes pattern 18 *tratamiento de* (treatment of) overlaps with pattern 31 *no debe ser utilizado* (must not be used) in the sentence *no debe ser utilizado para el tratamiento de la rinitis* (must not be used in the treatment of the rhinitis). Experiment 4 demonstrates that applying the patterns of other roles to discard entities increases the final precision, with a minimal decrease in the recall.

The evaluation of the adverse reaction use case is presented in Table 6. Experiment 1 shows again that gazetteers cover most of the entities. The main problem that gazetteers have in this domain is the representation of disorders; MedDRA represents disorders with adjectives (e.g., *glucosa aumentada* (increased glucose)) and SPCs represent them in a nominal form (e.g., *aumento de glucosa* (increase of glucose)). This problem is solved in experiment 2 by using syntactic patterns that represent the nominal form of the disorders. Patterns of the named entity type increase recall significantly in the partial matching criteria. The results in the exact matching criteria reflect how the gold standard corpus is highly affected by the annotation problems. Experiment 3 shows no modification over the results. Layout patterns are associating discovered entities (in tables or under headers) to the target role and not discovering new ones. In spite of not improving the results, associating entities to the target role is critical if the experiment is not under the open world assumption. Experiment 4 finally shows that patterns from other roles are used to discard entities and the precision on the overall result increases.

7 Conclusions and Future Work

The evaluations of both use cases show how a NER model oriented by roles increases the precision of the obtained results in those natural language documents in which only some of the entities are required. Roles and their patterns allow to represent a classification model of the entities in a corpus and the NER algorithm uses the role classification model to identify named entities with a specific role. The proposed method to create a role classification model requires a gold standard corpus in which only the required entities are annotated, saving time in the annotation process.

Normally, the proposed role classification model could be represented with a target role and all the other roles joined as the complementary role ($\neg$Target role). However, these two specific use cases have also demonstrated that to precisely classify and define roles benefits the overall work because different sections have repeated roles and patterns. Thus, it is possible to create a complete role classification model for all the roles that could be reused and extended in different use cases for homogeneous domain-specific documents.

The main disadvantage of the method is that it requires very time-consuming tasks involving domain experts. Although the method is proposed for real use cases in which it is better to annotate only the required entities instead of annotating and classifying all of them, the patterns and the role that they represent have been discovered manually. This method performs the first approach to introduce entities roles inside the NER task in natural language documents in which the detection of specific entities according to a role is required.

As mentioned above, one of the most time-consuming tasks was the pattern detection. One of the first future lines of work regarding the proposed method is to explore automatic pattern detection using algorithms based on distributional semantics such as Latent Semantic Analysis (Konkol et al., 2015).

Acknowledgments

This work has been funded by the Agencia Española de Medicamentos y Productos Sanitarios and by project Datos 4.0 (TIN2016-78011-C4-4-R), of the Agencia Estatal de Investigación MINECO and Fondos FEDER.

References

R. Boyce, G. Gardner, and Henk H. 2012. Using natural language processing to identify pharmacokinetic drug-drug interactions described in drug package inserts. *Proceedings of the 2012 Workshop on Biomedical Natural Language Processing,* (BioNLP).

E. G. Brown, L. Wood, and S. Wood. 1999. The Medical Dictionary for Regulatory Activities (MedDRA).

D. Campos, S. Matos, and J. L. Oliveira. 2012. Biomedical named entity recognition: a survey of machine-learning tools. In *Theory and Applications for Advanced Text Mining.* InTech.

L. Ferro, L. Gerber, I. Mani, B. Sundheim, and G. Wilson. 2005. TIDES 2005 Standard for the Annotation of Temporal Expressions.

R. Grishman and B. Sundheim. 1996. Message Understanding Conference-6: A Brief History. *Proceedings of the 16th conference on Computational linguistics,* 1.

L. Hunter and K. B. Cohen. 2006. Biomedical language processing: What's beyond PubMed?

J. D. Kim, T. Ohta, Y. Tateisi, and J. Tsujii. 2003. GENIA corpus - A semantically annotated corpus for bio-textmining. In *Bioinformatics,* volume 19.

J. Kim, T. Ohta, Y. Tsuruoka, Y. Tateisi, and N. Collier. 2004. Introduction to the Bio-entity Recognition Task at JNLPBA. *Proceedings of the International Joint Workshop on Natural Language Processing in Biomedicine and Its Applications.*

M. Konkol, T. Brychcín, and M. Konopík. 2015. Latent semantics in named entity recognition. *Expert Systems with Applications,* 42(7).

S. M. Meystre, G. K. Savova, K. C. Kipper-Schuler, and J. F. Hurdle. 2008. Extracting information from textual documents in the electronic health record: a review of recent research. *IMIA Yearbook of Medical Informatics,* 2008(1).

Isabel Moreno, Ester Boldrini, Paloma Moreda, and M Teresa Romá-Ferri. 2017. Drugsemantics: a corpus for named entity recognition in spanish summaries of product characteristics. *Journal of Biomedical Informatics.*

D. Nadeau and S. Sekine. 2007. A survey of named entity recognition and classification. *Linguisticae Investigationes,* 30(30).

S. Patwardhan and E. Riloff. 2007. Effective Information Extraction with Semantic Affinity Patterns and Relevant Regions. *Proceedings of the 2007 Joint Conference on Empirical Methods in Natural Language Processing and Computational Natural Language Learning,* 7(June).

T. C. Rindflesch, L. Tanabe, J. N. Weinstein, and L. Hunter. 2000. EDGAR: extraction of drugs, genes and relations from the biomedical literature. *Pacific Symposium on Biocomputing. Pacific Symposium on Biocomputing.*

R. C. Schank and R. P. Abelson. 1975. Scripts, Plans, and Knowledge. *Proceedings of the 4th International Joint Conference on Artificial Intelligence.*

S. Sekine, K. Sudo, and C. Nobata. 2002. Extended named entity hierarchy. In *Third International Conference on Language Resources and Evaluation (LREC 2002).*

B. Settles. 2004. Biomedical Named Entity Recognition Using Conditional Random Fields and Rich Feature Sets.

F. Steimann. 2000. On the representation of roles in object-oriented and conceptual modelling. *Data and Knowledge Engineering,* 35(1).

R. T. Tsai, S. Wu, .i Chou, Y. Lin, D. He, J. Hsiang, T. Sung, and W. Hsu. 2006. Various criteria in the evaluation of biomedical named entity recognition. *BMC bioinformatics,* 7(1).

V. Yetano Laguna, J., Alberola Cuñat. 2003. *Diccionario de siglas médicas.* Ministerio de sanidad y consumo.

G. Zhou, D. Shen, J. Zhang, J. Su, and S. Tan. 2005. Recognition of protein/gene names from text using an ensemble of classifiers. *BMC bioinformatics,* 6 Suppl 1.

Gap in pagination due to unavailable paper.

Pages 157-163

Underspecification in Natural Language Understanding for Dialog Automation

John Chen
Interactions LLC
41 Spring Street, Suite 106
Murray Hill, NJ 07974 USA
jchen@interactions.com

Srinivas Bangalore
Interactions LLC
41 Spring Street, Suite 106
Murray Hill, NJ 07974 USA
sbangalore@interactions.com

Abstract

With the increasing number of communication platforms that offer variety of ways of connecting two interlocutors, there is a resurgence of chat-based dialog systems. These systems, typically known as *chatbots* have been successfully applied in a range of consumer and enterprise applications. A key technology in such chat-bots is robust natural language understanding (NLU) which can significantly influence and impact the efficacy of the conversation and ultimately the user-experience. While NLU is far from perfect, this paper illustrates the role of *underspecification* and its impact on successful dialog completion.

1 Introduction

With the coming of age of speech recognition technology, everyday spoken language expressions can be converted into text with a degree of accuracy that creates unprecedented opportunities for realizing natural and sophisticated human-machine conversations to accomplish routine tasks. In addition, there is a resurgence of text-based conversation systems, such as SMS and Chat, owing to the availability of communication platforms that make it convenient to configure human-machine *text* driven conversations. The potential opportunities of speech/text driven human-machine conversational system, collectively known as *virtual agents*, can only be realized if the user's request in spoken or typed form are *understood* by the virtual agent and acted on appropriately to fulfill users' requests.

It is often difficult to represent the precise meaning of a sentence given the inherent ambiguity in natural language. Furthermore, interpreting a user's sentence in the conversation context that is modulated by the user's perspective, further exacerbates the challenge of extracting the precise pragmatic import of a user's request. For practical applications, such as conversational agents and speech/text analytics systems, the meaning of a sentence may be approximated as one or more *actionable* labels associated with the input utterance. Such *actionable* labels are termed as *intents* and an *intent model* is used to uncover the intent from a user's utterance.

In practical applications, intent labels often conflate the linguistic meaning of a user sentence, the conversation context in which the utterance appears, and the rules of business that apply to that application. The intent model then directly disambiguates a user request and maps it to a representation that can be interpreted by the downstream system without the need for further inference mechanisms. Consequently, most of the intent labels in an application domain are specific to that particular domain and sometimes are even crafted specifically to the flow of a particular dialog system. While such a direct approach limits the reusability of the intent labels across application domains, the benefit of such an approach is it circumvents the intricacies of conventional knowledge acquisition and domain modeling that is necessary for inference on a domain-independent meaning representation.

The actionable meaning representation of a user input also identifies the target of the intent, typically called an *entity*. An entity is that part of the user request that identifies the object of the intent. Some examples of application-independent entities include a *person name, date, phone number, credit card, account number*. In addition to such generic entities, domain-specific entities such as names of services and names of products need to be identified. In order to provide an actionable representation, the orthographic differences in ref-

Proceedings of Recent Advances in Natural Language Processing, pages 164–170,
Varna, Bulgaria, Sep 4–6 2017.

erences to an entity need to be normalized and rendered in a canonical form (e.g. *Christmas, 12/25, December 25*).

In this paper, we discuss the NLU component of an enterprise-grade customer care chat system and highlight the benefits of under-specification of intents in automating chats. In Section 2, we discuss the details of the chat system and present the NLU model in Section 3. The impact of underspecification in NLU is discussed in Section 4 along with experiments and results.

2 Chat-based Customer Care

A chat-based customer care system we use in this study is shown in Figure 1. The user, or *Chat Client* interacts with the *Chat Platform* by typing in chat text in response to a system prompt that is displayed by the chat platform. The chat text is first routed to the *NLU* to determine the intent of the user's text. If the NLU determines the intents from the text with high confidence, the text is routed to the Dialog Manager through the Chat Platform. If the NLU is unable to determine the intent, the Chat Platform routes the text to a human (*Intent Analyst*) for intent determination. The intents identified from the user's text are used to update the dialog state in a *Dialog Manager*. Depending on the identity of the new dialog state, the Dialog Manager may prompt the user for more information, via the Chat Platform.

3 NLU in a Care Chatbot

A single chat utterance is tagged with three types of labels – *Intents*, *Entities*, and *Conversational handlers*. Intents are domain-specific labels such as *SALES*, *TECH_ASSISTANCE* and *BILLING* and generally expresses the action intended by the customer. There are 85 different types of intents in the customer care chat system under study. *Entity* labels represent the names of products or services mentioned in the user's text. These include, for example, entities such as *Headphones*, *Mobile Phone*, and *Insurance*. There are a total of 115 types of entities in the chat system. There is an ontology defined over intents and entities. For example, the general intent, *SALES*, is composed of more specific intents such as *PRICING, DISCOUNTS* or *LEASING*. An abridged version of the intent ontology is shown in Figure 2. Finally, conversational handlers are labels which are similar to speech acts, and guide the conversation, such as

LIVE AGENT or *CONFUSED*. There are 15 types of conversational handlers in the current system.

3.1 NLU Models

Three independent SVM classifiers are trained, one for each of intents, entities, and conversational handlers. Each of the classifier is modeled as a set of binary SVM classifiers, with each binary classifier predicting if the input is assigned or not assigned a particular label type. Consequently, for a given input chat utterance x, classification involves computing the following for each of intent (tn), entity (sv) and conversational labels (en).

$$y^* = \arg\max_{y \in tn, sv, en} F_y(x, y) \qquad (1)$$

Subsequently, the joint label is defined as $\langle tn^*, sv^*, en^* \rangle$.

The different classifiers use the same feature set $\mathcal{F}$, which is composed of three types of features – *application context, conversation context, utterance*. Features from the application context include the URL, the section and the subsection of the web page from which the chat session originated. Conversation context includes the dialog state identifier, and a bag of ngrams (unigrams and bigrams) extracted from all the utterances from the dialog until the current utterance. Utterance features are a bag of word ngrams that are extracted from the current user utterance.

3.2 Confidence Measures

In an attempt to boost the accuracy, we reject the decisions made by the classifier based on a measure of confidence computed using the score generated by the classifier. We experiment with the effect on accuracy that use of different confidence measures elicit.

We use the sigmoid to obtain probabilities from the scores assigned by the SVM classifiers.

$$P(tn^*) = \frac{1}{1 + exp(F_{tn}(x, tn^*))} \qquad (2)$$

This can be extended to a simple confidence measure on joint labels (*joint probability*) as in Equation 3.

$$jointprob = min(P(tn^*), P(sv^*), P(en^*)) \qquad (3)$$

We define another confidence measure (Equation 4) as the ratio of the probabilities of the first

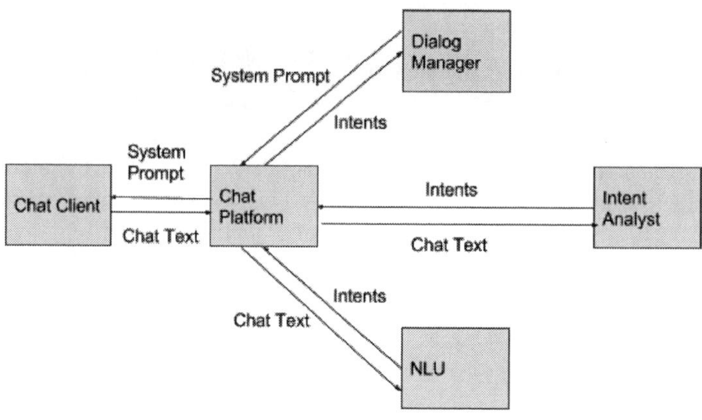

Figure 1: Architecture of the Chat Dialog system

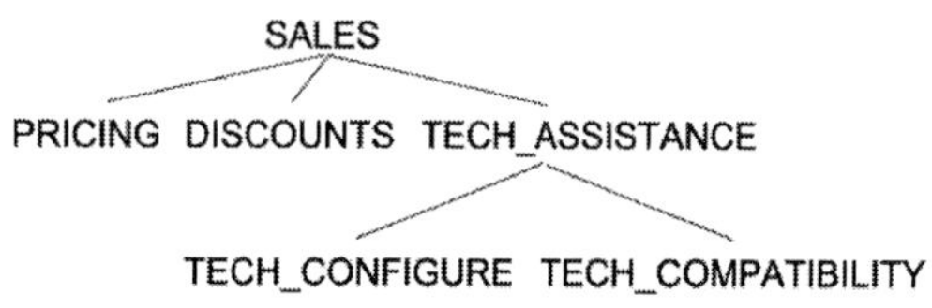

Figure 2: A sample view of the intent ontology.

(tn^*) and second best (tn^{*-1}) labels assigned by individual classifiers.

$$cf(tn^*) = \frac{P(tn^*)}{P(tn^{*-1})} \qquad (4)$$

In a similar manner as before, this can be extended to a confidence measure on joint labels (*joint ratio*) as in Equation 5.

$$cf_{jt} = min(cf(tn^*), cf(sv^*), cf(en^*)) \qquad (5)$$

4 Experiments and Results

The training corpus of 1.6 million examples of chat turns and test corpus of 57K chat turns are tagged with intents, entities and conversation handler labels.

Table 1 shows accuracies of the resulting classifiers. These are compared against baseline accuracies, which are obtained by tagging every test instance with the majority class type label. Conversational handlers are the easiest to predict, followed by Entities and Intents. Conversational handlers are easy because most turns are labeled as INFORM. Entities are moderately difficult. Its difficulty is similar to that of named entity recognition or entity linking. Complications include noisy text input or the need to find the main entity if multiple entities exist in the input. Unlike named entity recognition, there is no need to find the exact boundary of the entity mention in the input text. Intents are the most difficult.

Classification Task	Baseline	Accuracy
Intents	41.85	90.65
Entities	35.59	93.92
Conversational	90.81	99.01
Joint	7.41	84.86

Table 1: Accuracies of the different classifiers

Figure 3 shows accuraries of these classifiers as a function of training data size. As can be inferred by its relative ease of prediction, the classifier for conversational handlers has an accuracy with respect to training data size that plateaus early. Less than 200K samples can train a classifier with an acccuracy within 1.0% of one trained on 1.6 million samples. In contrast, accuracies of intent and entity classifiers increase more quickly as more samples are introduced into the training data.

The accuracies of the different classifiers as plotted against automation rate are shown in Figure 4. Here, a classifier returns a result if its confidence score is not less than a predefined threshold. The automation rate is the percent of input user utterances for which the classifier returns a result. The classifier accuracy is the percent of returned

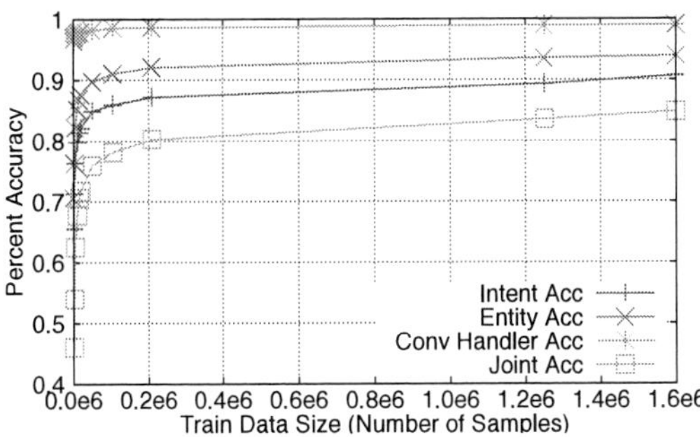

Figure 3: Classifiers' Accuracies as a Function of Training Data Size

results that are correct. Within such a framework, the accuracy of joint label prediction can be 90% or higher at an automation rate of 88% or lower.

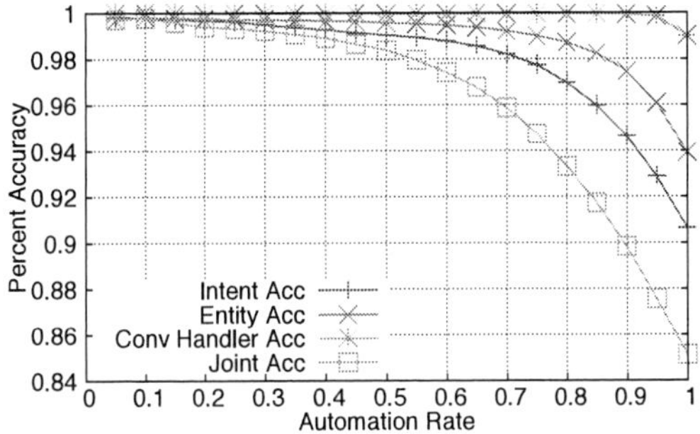

Figure 4: Accuracies of Different Classifiers versus Automation Rate

Instead of thresholding using joint probability, we may threshold the classifiers results using joint ratio. These two kinds of confidence scores are compared in an accuracy versus automation graph for joint labeling, as shown in Figure 5. Using joint ratio always gives better results. At 90% automation, joint ratio gives about 0.3% improvement in accuracy. The improvement in accuracy is only larger for automation rates between 30% and 90%.

The top 10 confusion pairs of the Task Names classifier are shown in Table 2. Most of them involve misclassification of SALES, either as a false positive or a false negative. This is probably because SALES is the most common class occurring in the data. SALES is an intent having the meaning of expressing interest in a product, before a purchase. Many of the intents that it is confused with, such as PRICING and SHIPPING_TIMES, have the same meaning, but they have additional, intent-specific meanings as well. For example, PRICING has the meaning of wanting to know the

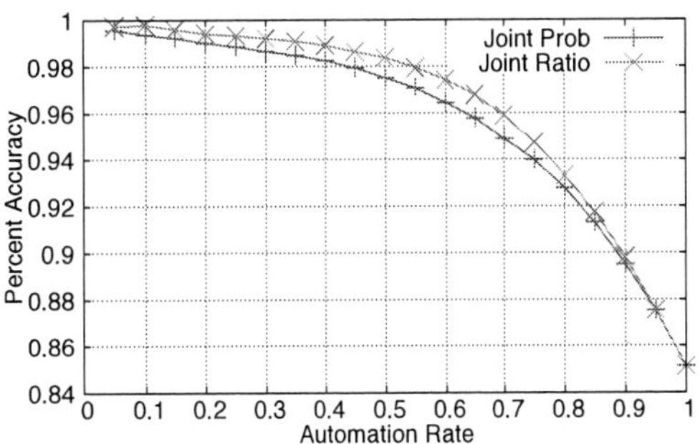

Figure 5: Accuracy vs. Automation for Different Confidence Metrics

price of a product while SHIPPING_TIMES has the meaning of wanting to know when a product can be delivered. Confusions arise for the classifier if one chat turn contains some phrases supporting the general SALES intent (want to buy) and other phrases supporting a more specific intent (how much for one?). The most prolific confusion pair, reference SALES and prediction NONE, happens often when the chat turn contains noise, such as misspellings like by instead of buy.

4.1 Underspecified Output and Its Impact on Automation

We are most interested in the models producing an accurate and unambiguous joint classification label. On the other hand, because the joint classification accuracy is only 84.86%, it is also interesting to explore if we can trade off some ambiguity for additional accuracy. In order to obtain n-best joint label results, we first define the probability of a joint label $P(tn, sv, en)$ as the product of probabilities of its constituent labels:

$$P(tn, sv, en) = P(tn)P(sv)P(en)$$

Then, the n-best joint labels are the n joint labels with the n highest probabilities, out of the n^3 possible combinations of each of the n-best labels from the three classifiers. The accuracy versus automation curves for n-best joint labels are shown in Figure 6. The biggest improvement in accuracy comes from moving from 1-best to 2-best results, with accuracy increasing from 84.8% to 92.7% at 100% automation. If we move to 4-best results, we get 95.9% accuracy at 100% automation.

We analyze the 2-best joint labeling results further by breaking down the joint labels into intents, entities, and conversation handlers. We can divide the test instances into different types (and their percentages) based on the kinds of differences be-

Correct Intent	Predicted Intent	% of All Errors
SALES	NONE	5.66
NONE	SALES	5.62
PRICING	SALES	4.31
SHIPPING_TIMES	SALES	3.79
DISCOUNTS_PURCHASE	SALES	3.48
SALES	FOREIGN_PURCHASE	3.29
TECH_ASSISTANCE	SALES	3.15
CHECKOUT_PROBLEM	SALES	3.08

Table 2: Top Confusion Pairs

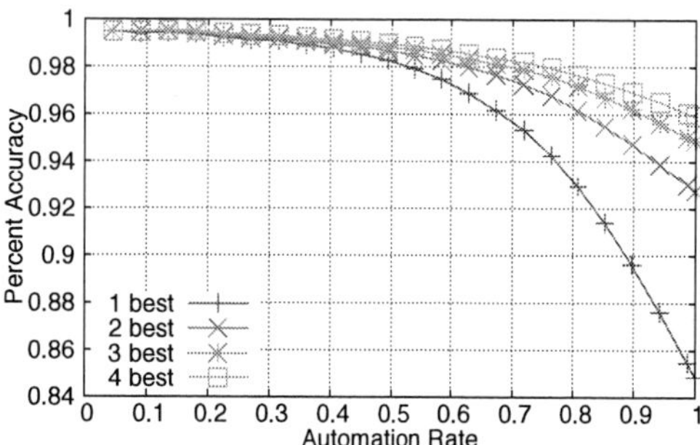

Figure 6: Accuracy vs. Automation for Different N-best Results

tween the 1-best and the 2-best results: (1) Only the intent labels are different (53.6%); (2) Only the entity labels are different (40.4%); (3) Only the conversational handler labels are different (6%) (4) More than two label types are different (1%).

Based on the encouraging analysis of the 2-best joint labeling results, we devise a *N-best Backoff (NBB)* system that uses the 2-best results that more accurately detects user intent. The major difference in NBB is that we allow the system to output *partial* answers if the 1-best answer is low confidence.

Given an input chat utterance, the 2-best joint labels are determined as previously outlined, along with a confidence score. If the score is above a predefined threshold, the system outputs the 1-best joint label. Otherwise, an algorithm *new_joint_label*, synthesizes a new joint label that takes into account the 2-best joint labels and the intent ontology.

The algorithm *new_joint_label* returns its input intent if the 1-best and 2-best intents are the same. The same is true for entities. If the 1-best and 2-best intents differ, then the algorithm checks if one is the parent of the other in the intent ontology. If so, it returns the more general, parent intent. If

the 1-best and 2-best entities differ, then no entity label is produced in our current chat system. However, if we had access to a entity ontology, a underspecification similar to the one for intents could be performed on entity labels as well. For conversational handlers, the algorithm simply returns the 1-best label. Therefore, currently, the algorithm focuses mainly on synthesizing a new intent, a focus that is justified by the fact that most of the time, it is the 1-best and 2-best intents that differ.

We evaluate NBB using two measures. The first measure is the *percent error* of the joint label returned by the system. If the system returns an entire label, i.e. none of intent, entity, or conversational handlers is $\langle empty \rangle$, then it is evaluated fully. If the system returns a partial label, then only the parts of the label that have been specified are evaluated. For example, if the system returns intent as *SALES* and entity as $\langle empty \rangle$, then only the intent is checked for correctness. The second measure is *partial miss percentage*. This is the percent of utterances for which the returned joint label is partially specified, i.e. the intent or entity of the joint label is $\langle empty \rangle$, or the intent of the joint label is a more general intent (e.g. *SALES*) than the reference intent (e.g. *TECH_ASSISTANCE*). This measure is meant to capture the percent of time that the user may experience a longer dialog because the system did not fully understand the users intent.

The evaluation results of NBB are shown in Figure 7. The percent on the Y axis is percent error or partial miss percentage, depending on the curve. The automation rate on the X axis is the percent of user utterances for which the classifier returns any result, even a partial result. A partial result is considered fully automated because the system does not rely on a human intent analyst to disambiguate the partial result. Instead, the system asks the user a clarification question.

These results are quite promising. It shows that at a 96% automation rate, the system can output intents with only 5% error. According to the nature of the algorithm, these intents may be partially specified. Still, the results show that at this automation rate, this will occur only 15% of the time, i.e. only 15% of the time will the system have to ask a clarification question in order to ask the user to repeat information that the system could not understand. The percent error can be driven below 5% as automation rate decreases, but in order to do so, the partial miss percentage increases approximately linearly.

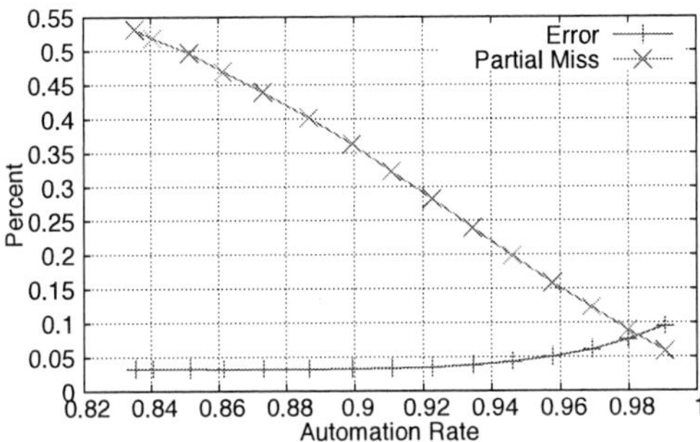

Figure 7: Percent Error/Partial Miss vs. Automation Rate

5   Related Work

Many dialog act ontologies are multidimensional and hierarchical, such that each utterance is tagged with one label from each dimension. DAMSL (Allen and Core, 1997) and its variants for different domains (Di Eugenio et al., 1998; Jurafsky et al., 1997; Dhillon et al., 2004) has four dimensions each of which has its own hierarchy. Utterances may receive more than one label, with each label DIAML (Bunt et al., 2010) has nine dimensions many of which are associated with their own hierarchies. Typically, these ontologies make a distinction between the discourse function of an utterance and its semantic content, the former being how the utterance guides the discourse and the latter concerning the topic under discussion. In our ontology, the former is represented as our conversational handlers. The latter is represented as our intents and entities. Conversational handlers are a flat set of classes rather than the rich hierarchies found in the literature. Conversely, intents and entities are relatively elaborate. These differ-

ences are rooted in the subtleties of our application which requires gathering quite specific information about the customer's requirements that can only be represented through a detailed ontology for semantic content.

Originally, work on dialog act classification largely involved processing of spoken input (Stolcke et al., 2000). Recently, it has expanded to processing of other modalities including email threads (Omuya et al., 2013), message board discussions (Kim et al., 2006), and tweets (Zhang et al., 2012). Still, most of these share in common prediction of dialog acts from a flat set of possibilities. One exception is the work of (Allen et al., 1996) where a symbolic parser predicts dialog acts from a hierarchical set. Unlike our work, Allen (1996) predicts a general rather than a specific dialog act only if the input is genuinely nonspecific. Another exception is the work of (Kang et al., 2013) where a SVM classifier predicts hierarchical dialog acts. It differs from our work because Kang (2013)'s system always predicts a general dialog act and a specific dialog act for the same input, the rationale being that specific dialog acts are more accurately predicted if the general dialog act is predicted first.

6   Conclusions

In this paper, we have discussed the NLU component of an enterprise-grade, chat-based routing application. We have analyzed the possible error reduction if the NLU were to output n-best labels. Based on the analysis, we have designed and implemented an underspecification algorithm and demonstrated the significant improvement in intent accuracy an automation of a system using underspecified intents derived from an intent ontology.

References

James Allen and Mark Core. 1997. Damsl: Dialogue act markup in several layers (draft 2.1). Technical report, Multiparty Discourse Group, Discourse Resource Initiative.

James F Allen, Bradford W Miller Bradford, Eric K Ringger, and Teresa Sikorski. 1996. A robust system for natural spoken dialogue. In *Proceedings of the 34th annual meeting on Association for Computational Linguistics*. Association for Computational Linguistics, pages 62–70.

Harry Bunt, Jan Alexandersson, Jean Carletta, Jae-Woong Choe, Alex Chengyu Fang, Koiti Hasida, Kiyong Lee, Volha Petukhova, Andrei Popescu-Belis, Laurent Romary, et al. 2010. Towards an iso standard for dialogue act annotation. In *Seventh conference on International Language Resources and Evaluation (LREC'10)*.

Rajdip Dhillon, Sonali Bhagat, Hannah Carvey, and Elizabeth Shriberg. 2004. Meeting recorder project: Dialog act labeling guide. Technical report, International Computer Science Institute, Berkeley.

Barbara Di Eugenio, Pamela W. Jordan, and Liina Pylkkänen. 1998. The coconut project: Dialogue annotation manual. Technical report, University of Pittsburgh.

Daniel Jurafsky, Elizabeth Shriberg, and Debra Biasca. 1997. Switchboard swbd-damsl shallow discourse function annotation (coders manual). Technical report, University of Colorado, Institute of Cognitive Science.

Sangwoo Kang, Youngjoong Ko, and Jungyun Seo. 2013. Hierarchical speech-act classification for discourse analysis. *Pattern Recognition Letters* 34(10):1119–1124.

Jihie Kim, Grace Chern, Donghui Feng, Erin Shaw, and Eduard Hovy. 2006. Mining and assessing discussions on the web through speech act analysis. In *Proceedings of the Workshop on Web Content Mining with Human Language Technologies at the 5th International Semantic Web Conference*.

Adinoyi Omuya, Vinodkumar Prabhakaran, and Owen Rambow. 2013. Improving the quality of minority class identification in dialog act tagging. In *Proceedings of NAACL-HLT 2013*. pages 802–807.

Andreas Stolcke, Klaus Ries, Noah Coccaro, Elizabeth Shriberg, Rebecca Bates, Daniel Jurafsky, Paul Taylor, Rachel Martin, Carol Van Ess-Dykema, and Marie Meteer. 2000. Dialogue act modeling for automatic tagging and recognition of conversational speech. *Computational linguistics* 26(3):339–373.

Renxian Zhang, Dehong Gao, and Wenjie Li. 2012. Towards scalable speech act recognition in twitter: Tackling insufficient training data. In *Proceedings of the Workshop on Semantic Analysis in Social Media*. Association for Computational Linguistics, pages 18–27.

Identification and Classification of the Most Important Moments in Students' Collaborative Chats

Costin-Gabriel Chiru and Remus Decea
University Politehnica from Bucharest
Splaiul Independenţei 313, Bucharest, Romania
costin.chiru@cs.pub.ro, remus.decea@gmail.com

Abstract

In this paper, we present an application for the automatic identification of the important moments that might occur during students' collaborative chats. The moments are detected based on the input received from the user, who may choose to perform an analysis on the topics that interest him/her. Moreover, the application offers various types of suggestive and intuitive graphics that aid the user in identification of such moments. There are two main aspects that are considered when identifying important moments: the concepts' frequency and distribution throughout the conversation and the chat tempo, which is analyzed for identifying intensively debated concepts. By the tempo of the chat we understand the rate at which the ideas are input by the chat participants, expressed by the utterances' timestamps.

1 Introduction

Nowadays, a chat system is an important element for any web-based business. On one hand, it allows the owners to find out about customers' opinion without increasing the expenses too much. On the other, it helps boosting the sales as the customers may find immediate help to surpass the problems they may stumble upon.

The importance of chat systems was also noticed by Zuckerberg, who said that messaging is "one of the few things people do more than social networking" (Hamburger, 2014).

Considering this increasing popularity of chat, many systems were developed to support it. However, simply helping the people talk about different facts is not always enough. Thus, there are situations when the information from such systems needs to be collected, analyzed and interpreted automatically. The computer supported collaborative learning (CSCL) systems are such examples.

CSCL is a pedagogical approach where learning takes place via interaction supported by several devices through Internet. Thus, technology becomes the main means of communication and resource sharing with the goal of obtaining new knowledge or distributing it. However, in this kind of systems, the tutor is not always available to answer the students' questions at the rate and moments when they are posed. Still, the information needs to be collected and analyzed and the results should be presented to the tutor for helping him/her in managing the class (either to answer or grade the students' comments). The most problematic situation is in the case of massive open online course (MOOC) systems, where there may be thousands of students enrolled for a class and, most of the time they may be geographically spread across the globe. This means that they may be online (and thus needing guidance) at different times during the day.

The collaboration theory (Stahl, 2002) states that technology should come with new media types that support "knowledge building". Moreover, these technologies should also help in the process of changing the role of the teacher (seen as a bottleneck element) in the learning act. In this context has arisen the need for chat analysis tools.

In this paper, we will present a chat analysis application that was meant to improve the work of Chiru and Trausan-Matu (2012) by creating a web-based application which also considers the timestamp of the students' utterances in the chat.

The paper continues with some theoretical background that the application is based on. Afterwards, we will present an overview of the existing application, along with the improvements that we added. After that, we will go through some implementation details, presenting the graphics and functionalities offered by the app. The paper will end with our conclusions and direction for furthering even more the work presented here.

Proceedings of Recent Advances in Natural Language Processing, pages 171–176,
Varna, Bulgaria, Sep 4–6 2017.

2 Theoretical Background

The starting point of the work presented in this paper is represented by the concept of voice introduced in the Polyphonic Theory (Trausan-Matu, 2009; Trausan-Matu and Rebedea, 2010). A voice can be perceived as a point of view shared by one or several participants in the chat. These voices interact throughout the conversation generating relationships that are similar to the sequential, transversal or counter-point ones from polyphonic music (Bakhtin and Emerson, 1993). According to Trausan-Matu's claim (2013), following Bakhtin's perspective, a voice may range from a word or an idea to a reply in a chat or even to an entire book. Words play an essential role: "the idea resembles the word, with which it forms a dialogical unity. Like the word, the idea wants to be heard, understood and 'answered' by other voices, from other positions" (Trausan-Matu, 2013).

Bakhtin extended this model from music to discourse, stating that the voice of others is an expression of what they affirm, write or think. Thus, the knowledge is gained through the interaction with the other existing voices: "rather than speaking about 'acquisition of knowledge,' many people prefer to view learning as becoming a participant in a certain discourse" (Sfard, 2000).

Starting from this concept, Chiru and Trausan-Matu (2012) came up with the idea that the most important moments in a discourse may be identified at the interaction of different voices from that discourse. Thus, considering the type of these interactions, they classified the important moments in 4 different categories: pivotal, convergent, singular and divergent. A pivotal moment appears when, in the same utterance, one voice "fades out" while another one appears for the first time. A convergent moment takes place when two or more voices appear for the last time in the same utterance. A singular moment may be found when several voices appear for the last time except for one, that continues through the discourse. A divergent moment is detected when two or more voices meet and afterwards they continue to appear in different areas of the conversation. Our work is based on the results obtained by Chiru and Trausan-Matu (2012) and is meant to improve them by also integrating the temporality in the analysis.

Thus, another direction that is relevant for our work was undertaken by Reimann (2009) and Chiu and Khoo (2005) who considered that temporality is a key component of learning concepts in the CSCL setting. Reimann introduced temporality analysis techniques based on sliders. Starting from their research, we investigated whether the time factor could play a role in identifying the important moments from conversations. Thus, using a slider, the developed application filters discourse as much as the user wants and points out the chat fragments that are "hotter" (where there are more utterances in a short time period).

3 Application Description

The developed application is a web app that offers visualization techniques for identifying the important moments from the students' collaborative learning chats. In this section, we will present a quick overview of the already existing application (as described in (Chiru and Trausan-Matu, 2012)) to understand its basic functionality. Afterwards, in section 4, we will detail the new features developed to extend this functionality so that to incorporate the utterances' temporality in the analysis.

3.1 Application Overview

The initial version of the application was built in Java and thus was only locally available. Its purpose was to semi-automatically identify the important moments that appeared in a collaborative learning chat, starting from the voices (important concepts) that were selected by the user. These moments were then shown to the end user in three different tabs that were related to the "voice visualization" process ("Word level", "Sentence level" and "Important moments") plus another one ("View File") where the chat was displayed along with the words selected by the user (or words belonging to the same lexical chain) which were highlighted for a better comprehension of their distribution. The "Word level" tab provides an analysis of the distribution of voices throughout the conversation, at the word level. In the "Sentence level" tab, the analysis is done at utterance level. Finally, the "Important moments" tab points out the important moments from a chat, classified as specified above. In these analyses, a dot represents either a word (as in "Word Level" tab) or an utterance (for the other two visualizations). The position of the dot is given by the relative position of that word/utterance in the whole text and the representation is similar to the position of a word in a written page (matrix representation, having a maximum number of dots per raw and continuing afterwards with the left side of the next raw).

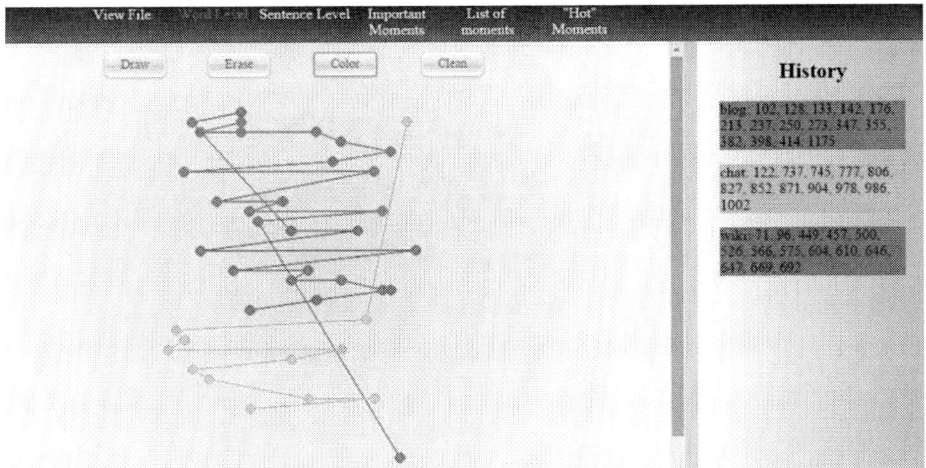

Figure 1: Word level graphic.

4 The Improved Application

The main problems that we identified at the existing application were related to its availability (only locally available), the user's intervention ((s)he had to choose the voices of interest) and the lack of use of temporal timestamps of the utterances. Thus, these are the main issues that we addressed and are presented in this paper. The new application's purpose is to automatically identify and suggest important moments that appear in a collaborative learning chat. These moments are then presented to the end user by 2 means: "voice visualization" graphics and "hot" moments identification. The additional information is presented on two new tabs: "List of moments", that presents all the important moments from a chat that were automatically identified; and "Hot moments", which adds-in the analysis relying on the time factor.

4.1 Application Overview

In this subsection, we will present the general graphics and functionalities of the web app, that were ported from the initial application. The first graphic shows the distribution of voices at a word level. Regardless of the conversation length, this graphic offers a suggestive illustration of the distribution of concepts by mapping them in a fixed-size window (see Fig. 1). As a new feature, by clicking a word from the graphic, the user is redirected in the "View File" tab to see the content of the chat, with the clicked word highlighted.

In Fig. 1 is depicted an example with the selection of 3 voices: one can easily see that the "blog" voice was present in the beginning of the conversation, while the "chat" topic was addressed in the later part of it. Also, in the "History" fragment of the screen, the arrays of positions of the respective concepts are shown. It should be noted that the "History" area is shared by other visualizations ("Sentence Level" and "Important Moments") and thus, by adding/removing/cleaning concepts to/ from any of these graphics will affect all of them.

To add a word to the graphic, the user would select that word from the vocabulary (not shown in Fig. 1) and press "Draw". To remove the last concept, the user should press "Erase", and to remove all the concepts, (s)he should press "Clean". The "Color" button changes the latest added concept's color, with a randomly generated one.

By clicking one of the dots, the screen will be re-directed to the "View Chat" tab, pointing to the position of that word's occurrence in the chat. This behavior is illustrated in Fig. 2, where the user pressed the third dot of the "blog" voice from Fig. 1. By adding this re-direction, the user may read in the context of the chat the utterance where the "blog" concept appeared (namely, at position 133, counting all the words from the chat).

The "Sentence Level" graphic is very similar with the previous one, the difference being that now the occurrences are not indexed by the position of the word itself, but by the position of the utterances they belong to.

The "Important Moments" view is a key part of the application, illustrating the most important moments from a chat. In the developed web app, the following shapes are used for illustrating them: pivotal moment – △; convergence moment - □; singular moment - ◊; divergent moment - ○. An example of such moments is provided in Fig. 3.

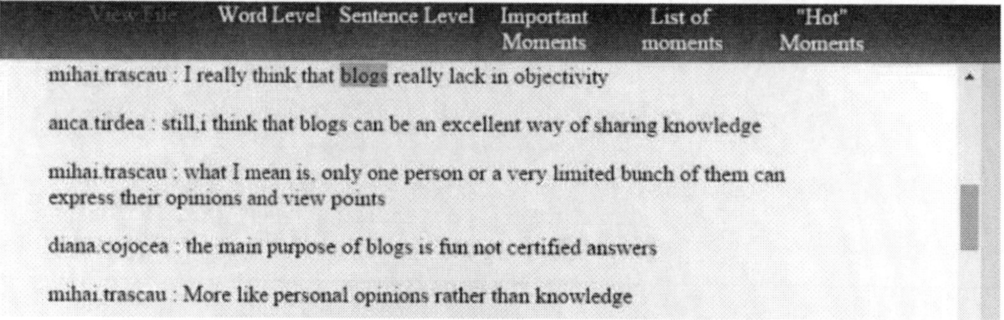

Figure 2: Highlight option for the "Word level" tab.

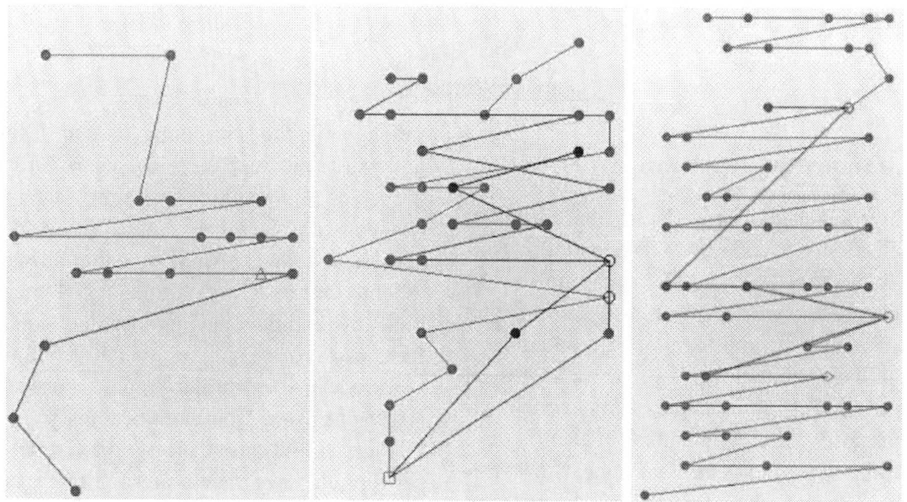

Figure 3: Examples of important moments.

4.2 List of Moments

In the initial version of the application, the user had to choose different voices to identify the important moments of the chat. This way, (s)he may oversee some of these moments, if wrong voices are chosen. Thus, we decided to add another view ("List of Moments") to provide an automatic analysis of the voices from the chat, that doesn't depend on the user's choice. Therefore, in this tab (see Fig. 4), the user has the option to select how many voices (s)he wants to see interacting and then the app detects all the important moments that can be identified using the chosen number of voices. That is, if the user chooses n voices, all the possible combinations of n concepts from the chat are considered, and then, all the moments that are identified are classified according to the criteria developed by Chiru and Trausan-Matu (2012). This way, the user's intervention is minimized, the only thing that (s)he has to input being the cardinality of the set of concepts to be analyzed.

4.3 Hot Moments

The last important element that we added to the existing application was the analysis of the utterances timestamps, which resulted in the "Hot Moments" view. The graphic from this tab is different from the others presented so far, as it doesn't consider the distribution of voices throughout the chat, but it relies on a different factor: time. Thus, it captures the moments when the participants are intensely disputing a subject. However, it should be noted that this functionality is available only for the chats that have the utterances' timestamps.

For this visualization, the user is allowed to adjust the maximum accepted delay between utterances, which is initially computed as the chat duration divided by the number of utterances that it contains. Thus, by adjusting the delay to a lower percentage of this value, some parts of the chat are cut off, the analysis consisting only in the parts of the chat that are "hotter". In Fig. 5 can be seen the

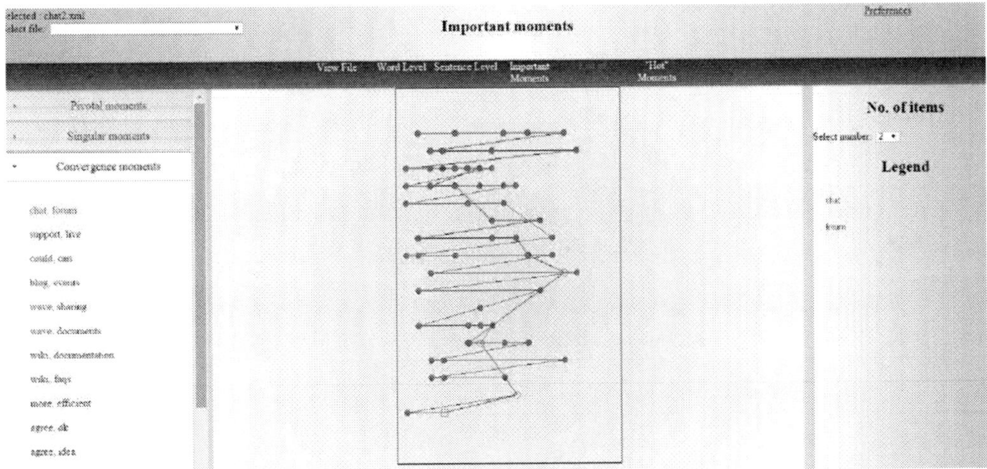

Figure 4: The List of Moments tab.

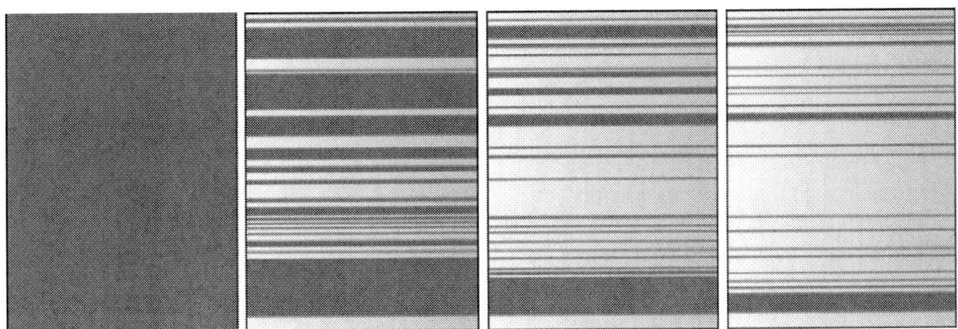

Figure 5: Hot moments sketch evolution (maximum delay is set in order from left to right to 100%, 75%,40% and 15%).

hot moments sketch's evolution when the maximum delay is set, in order, to: 100%, 75%, 40% and 15% of the original value. The green areas represent the chat fragments where the delay is less than the chosen percentage of the maximum delay, resulting in considering only highly debated fragments (from the temporality perspective).

The final aspect that we are going to mention here is the combination of "Hot Moments" and "Sentence Level" functionalities. Using this combination, the user can view if there is a strong connection between the appearances of certain concepts and the parts from the chat where an intense dispute is present. This way, the user can observe whether a concept was more intensely disputed compared to others.

For an easier readability, we also provide an overlap percentage between the sentences where the considered concepts were present and the ones that remained after filtering the chat according to the selected maximum delay. In Fig. 6, we provide an example of this functionality. Seeing this analysis, one can draw the conclusions that the "blog" (73%) and "wiki" (64%) concepts were more disputed than the "chat" (8%) one.

5 Conclusions and Future Developments

In this paper, we presented the improved version of an application for the identification and classification of important moments from the students' collaborative chats. Compared to the initial version, two factors were considered in the analysis: the concepts distribution throughout the chat and the intensity of dialogue in various fragments.

Using the visualization graphics, the user may see the main topics that were debated and may speculate whether the participants reached agreement or not. Moreover, the "Hot Moments" functionality offers the option to view the intensively disputed parts of a char. Furthermore, by combining the functionalities, it can be seen whether the "Hot Moments" overlap with the voices from the chat, leading to the discovery of inflammatory

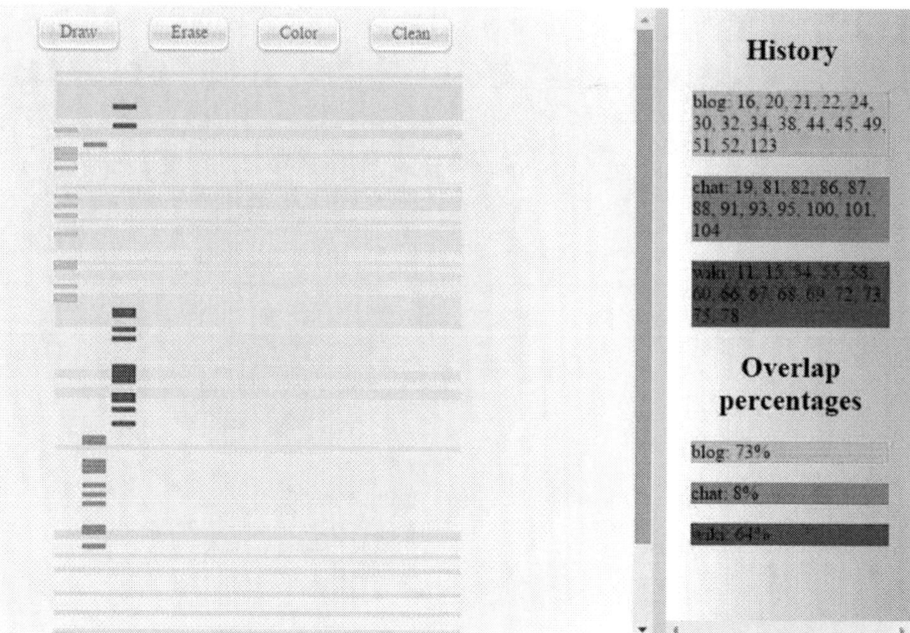

Figure 6: "Hot sentences": overlap of "Hot Moments" and "Sentence Level" graphics.

topics, along with the participants that let themselves carried in such intense (contradictory) talks.

The application allows the user to choose the concepts to be analyzed, but also shows the moments that were automatically identified for various sets of concepts. This way the influence of the user in the analysis is minimized, thus overcoming one of the issues of the initial application.

In terms of future work, an interesting improvement could be the possibility to offer collaborative analysis tools, so that multiple persons could participate in the analysis of the same chat.

Acknowledgments

This work has been partially funded by University Politehnica of Bucharest, through the "Excellence Research Grants" Program, UPB – GEX. Identifier: UPB–EXCELENȚĂ–2016, 09/26.09.2016.

References

M Mikhail Mikhailovich Bakhtin and Caryl Emerson. 1993. *Problems of Dostoevsky's poetics*. U of Minnesota Press.

Costin-Gabriel Chiru and Stefan Trausan-Matu. 2012. Identification and classification of the most important moments from students' collaborative discourses. In *Proc. of ITS*, pages 330–339.

Ming Ming Chiu and Lawrence Khoo. 2005. A new method for analyzing sequential processes dynamic multilevel analysis. *Small Group Research* 36(5): 600–631.

Ellis Hamburger. 2014. Mark Zuckerberg finally explains why he forced you to download the standalone messenger app. https://www.theverge.com/2014/11/6/7170791/mark-zuckerberg-finally-explains-why-he-forced-you-to-download-the.

Peter Reimann. 2009. Time is precious: Variable-and event-centred approaches to process analysis in cscl research. *Int. J. of CSCL* 4(3):239–257.

Anna Sfard. 2000. On reform movement and the limits of mathematical discourse. *Mathematical thinking and learning* 2(3):157–189.

Gerry Stahl. 2002. Contributions to a theoretical framework for cscl. In *Proc. of CSCL: Foundations for a CSCL Community*, pages 62–71.

Stefan Trausan-Matu. 2009. The polyphonic model of hybrid and collaborative learning. *Handbook of research on hybrid learning models: Advanced tools, technologies, and applications*, pages 466–486.

Stefan Trausan-Matu. 2013. A polyphonic model, analysis method and computer support tools for the analysis of socially-built discourse. *Romanian J. of Information Science and Tech.* 16(2-3):144–154.

Stefan Trausan-Matu and Traian Rebedea. 2010. A polyphonic model and system for inter-animation analysis in chat conversations with multiple participants. In *Int. Conf. on Intelligent Text Processing and Computational Linguistics*, pages 354–363.

Annotation of Entities and Relations in Spanish Radiology Reports

Viviana Cotik□**, Darío Filippo**△**, Roland Roller**⋆**, Hans Uszkoreit**⋆ **and Feiyu Xu**⋆

□Departamento de Computación, FCEyN, UBA, Argentina

vcotik@dc.uba.ar

△Hospital De Pediatría, Prof. Dr. Juan P. Garrahan, Argentina

dfilippo@garrahan.gov.ar

⋆Language Technology Lab, DFKI, Berlin, Germany

{firstname.surname}@dfki.de

Abstract

Radiology reports express the results of a radiology study and contain information about anatomical entities, findings, measures and impressions of the medical doctor. The use of information extraction techniques can help physicians to access this information in order to understand data and to infer further knowledge.

Supervised machine learning methods are very popular to address information extraction, but are usually domain and language dependent. To train new classification models, annotated data is required. Moreover, annotated data is also required as an evaluation resource of information extraction algorithms. However, one major drawback of processing clinical data is the low availability of annotated datasets. For this reason we performed a manual annotation of radiology reports written in Spanish. This paper presents the corpus, the annotation schema, the annotation guidelines and further insight of the data.

1 Introduction

Annotated data is required to evaluate information extraction algorithms and for training supervised machine learning methods. There is a scarcity of annotated corpora from the biomedical domain, in particular for non-English texts. There are two main reasons for that: first, the generation of new annotated data is expensive due to the need of expert knowledge, and, second, the ownership of the data is very discussed, specially when it refers to information that might identify the patient. Each country and institution has different regulations and some tasks -eg. anonymization-have to be performed before publishing the data.

So, although the availability of annotated data is a highly valuable asset for the research community, it is very difficult to access it. Furthermore, annotation guidelines have to be carefully designed and reviewed in an iterative process. They have to be clear enough so as to be followed by different annotators with a high annotation agreement. The important amount of information in short texts with complex terminology of the medical domain makes the guidelines definition difficult.

We are interested in supporting physicians with automatic text processing methods, such as named entity recognition (NER), relation extraction (RE) and negation and uncertainty detection in Spanish radiology reports. This could help to detect the main illnesses present among the patients, the patients evolution and to detect problems not expressed in an explicit way. See Sevenster et al. (2012) for an example of possible applications. To the best of our knowledge, there are no annotated datasets of Spanish medical reports which would be appropriate for our use case. For this reason, this work focuses on creating an annotated corpus of Spanish radiology reports.

The radiology reports used for this work are very short and are written by physicians after doing the examination of the patient. They show similarities to other clinical data in the fact that sentences are not always well formed and that many of them have a telegraphic style. There are also spelling mistakes and the use of non-standard abbreviations (that may include some named entities or negation markers, eg. *RD* for *riñon derecho - right kidney-*) is frequent. This, added to the use of specialized language of the medical domain, makes the annotation task difficult.

After describing briefly some previous guidelines definitions and annotated data (Section 2), this work describes the dataset used, the annotation schema and guidelines (Section 3). Then an

Proceedings of Recent Advances in Natural Language Processing, pages 177–184,
Varna, Bulgaria, Sep 4–6 2017."

analysis of the resulting annotated dataset is presented, that includes the number of entities and relations discovered by the annotators and the inter-annotator agreement among them (Section 4). Finally, Section 5 discusses the results of the dataset analysis and Section 6 presents conclusions.

2   Previous Works

The definition of guidelines is a time consuming and difficult task. There exist some previous definitions for more generic entity types (eg. persons, organizations and geographical locations). For example, MUC-7 and ACE competitions defined guidelines for the named entity recognition tasks organized by them in the past[1], [2]. The annotation criteria is not easy to establish. For example, both guidelines differ in the way that the name of a Saint has to be annotated.

ISO space[3] and ISO TimeML standards[4] establish guidelines of space-related features and of temporal relations.[5]

Wilbur et al. (2006) defined annotation guidelines to categorize segments of scientific sentences in research articles of the biomedical domain (see Shatkay et al. (2005)).

There is usually a scarcity of available data for the biomedical domain. The department of Radiology Informatics of Stanford University own a large dataset of radiology reports, that is not annotated, nor publicly available, as far as we know.[6] There are some annotated datasets available for languages different to Spanish in the clinical domain, eg. for English (Uzuner et al., 2011; Pradhan et al., 2013, 2014), for Swedish (Skeppstedt et al., 2014), for French (Névéol et al., 2015), for Polish (Mykowiecka et al., 2009) and for German (Roller et al., 2016). Oronoz et al. (2015) presented an annotated dataset in Spanish for adverse drug reactions analysis. Although the dataset is in

---

[1] http://itl.nist.gov/iaui/894.02/ related_projects/muc/proceedings/ne_ task.html

[2] https://www.ldc.upenn.edu/ sites/www.ldc.upenn.edu/files/ english-entities-guidelines-v5.6.6.pdf

[3] https://www.iso.org/standard/60779. html

[4] https://www.iso.org/standard/37331. html

[5] They have relation with our 'type of measure' entities (longitudinal, transversal, etc) and temporal relations (in the past, etc). See Subsection 3.2.

[6] http://langlotzlab.stanford.edu/ nlp-datasets/

Spanish and addresses the biomedical domain, it concerns a different use case and covers different information. Recently, Cruz et al. (2017) and Marimon et al. (2017) annotated negations in Spanish clinical reports.

3   Annotation Process

Our annotation guideline was improved within three iterations consisting of annotation and revision. In order to decrease the annotation time, entities, negation and uncertainty terms were pre-annotated automatically. Then, based on the annotation guideline, two native speakers of Spanish annotated the pre-annotated reports, making corrections and adding relations.

In this section we describe how we selected and anonymized the reports to be annotated, we present the annotation schema and guidelines, and the automatic and manual annotation process.

3.1   Data

A set of different kinds of ultrasound reports (e.g. kidney, abdominal, small parts, Doppler) provided by a hospital in Argentina were selected. They contain only one section, that includes findings, conclusions and suggestions.

3.1.1   Selection of the Dataset

Since we are interested in examining the existence of different health problems, we performed a selection of the reports to be annotated defining four sets. The first, called **hyperthrophic pyloric stenosis**, involves reports containing information about the pyloric muscle and pyloric canal, that might refer to pyloric stenosis (pyloric obstruction); the second, called **splenomegaly**, contains reports referring to the spleen, whether of normal size or enlarged; the third, called **appendicitis**, has reports that mention the appendix and that might or might not refer to appendicitis and the fourth, called **generic**, comprises a set of ultrasound reports corresponding to different body parts and possibly involving different findings or diseases not including the previous cases.

The first three sets are particularly interesting because the extraction of entities and relations among them could suggest possible medical problems, that might lead to surgical interventions. The first set is useful for studying entities and relation extraction in general terms.

For instance, taking into account the age of the patient and the size of the spleen it is possible to

determine whether the patient has splenomegaly (enlargement of the spleen) or not according to normal reference values. Furthermore, the visibility of the appendix, its maximal outer diameter not exceeding 6 mm and its non-compressibility are the most reliable criteria used in the diagnosis of acute appendicitis. The automatic detection of critical issues, such as appendicitis and pyloric stenosis, is of interest and is being studied (see e.g. Do et al. (2013) and Morioka et al. (2016)) and could allow their communication by pager or alternatives methods, as Lakhani and Langlotz (2009) describe.

Table 1 presents the number of files processed by each annotator for each report type. Overall 513 different files have been annotated.

report type	ann. 1	ann. 2	both	total
pyloric sten.	7	51	7	51
splenom.	123	31	13	141
append.	58	45	12	91
generic	176	83	29	230
Total	417	262	61	513

Table 1: Overview of annotated files.

3.1.2 Anonymization

Reports contain a report number, a patient identification number, the date of the study and the age of the patient. In some cases they also have information about the doctor or doctors who performed the ultrasonography and their medical license number. Names might be preceded with the title *Dr.* or *Dra.* (male or female doctor). In occasions, the medical license number is written after the doctor's name, sometimes it can appear without the doctors name. The license number can have been issued at a national (*MN*) or at a state level (*MP*).

Before performing the automatic and manual annotations reports had to be anonymized. Therefore, regular expressions were used considering the different ways of writing the title of the doctors (e.g. *DR, Dr., doctor, Dra.*), the doctor's names, the enrollment numbers and the order among them. Also names of the doctors appearing with titles or enrollments were searched to see if they appeared without titles and without enrollments and were removed. Patient and report identification were changed in a way that it is not possible to identify a patient. The date of the study was removed.

3.2 Annotation Schema

The following entities and characteristics were considered for the annotation:

findings (FI): entities corresponding to a pathological finding or diagnosis, eg. cyst, gallstone, abscess,

anatomical entities -or body parts- (AE): eg. breast, right thyroid lobe, liver,

location (LO): location in the body or in the body part, eg. medial, distal, peripheral, unilateral, apical, adjacent,

measure (ME): eg. 0.3 mm, 0.5 cc, 2 cm., 0.8 (cm.), large, small, scarce, minimum,

type of measure (TM): indication of the kind of measure that a number is referring to. eg. in *longitudinal 3 (cm) and transversal 1 (cm)*, *longitudinal* and *transversal* will be annotated as two type of measures and *3 (cm)* and *1 (cm)* as two measures, and

texture (TE): e.g. homogeneous or heterogeneous.

Other annotated concepts are the following ones:

negation (NT) and uncertainty terms (UT): We call them modifiers. e.g. were not detected and might correspond to,

abbreviations: e.g. *RI* for *riñon izquierdo* (*right kidney*), and

temporal terms (TT): terms that denote mentions to the past or that express conditionals. eg. previous, residual, old, preoperative, persistent and *had* and *if the patient has* for the phrases *the patient had fever (...)* and *if the patient has fever again (...)*.

The following binary relations were annotated:

occurs in: among findings and the part of the body where they occur (AE or LO). eg. in *vescícula biliar de paredes engrosadas, -thick(FI)-walled(LO) gallbladder(AE)-*, the finding (*engrosadas, -thick-*) occurs in the wall (LO),

located in: between location and an anatomical entity. The goal is to know where in an anatomical entity a finding is located. eg. in the example shown above, the walls (LO) are located in the gallbladder,

area of: associates an anatomical entity with a location. eg. in *kidneys without enlargement of the excretory pathway*, there is an *area of* relation among excretory pathway (LO) and kidney (AE),

has measure type: associates a type of measure with a measure (eg. in *longitudinal 3 (cm)*, *anteroposterior 0.54 (cm)*, the measure *3 (cm)* has measure type longitudinal),

measure of: associates a measure or a type of measure with an anatomical entity, a location or a finding. Also in *pyloric muscle thickness: 3.5 cm.*, there is a relation *measure of* from thickness (TM) to the pyloric muscle (AE) and a relation *has type* from thickness to 3.5 cm. (ME),

texture of: associates an entity of *texture* type to an anatomical entity, a finding or a location. eg. in *[kidneys](AE) of [conserved](TE) echotexture*, the conserved echotexture is related to AE kidneys,

negates: relates a negation term with a finding. eg. in *without enlargement*, the NT *without* is related with the FI *enlargement*,

speculates: relation among an uncertainty term and a finding. eg. in *compatible (UT) with [fatty liver] (FI)* the uncertainty term compatible is related with the fatty liver, and

not present: relates terms referring to the past or conditional terms and a finding. eg. in *gallblader(AE): history(TT) of cholecystectomy (FI)*, the cholecystectomy does not necessarily exist at the present moment and is related as not present with the temporal term.

Entities and relations to annotate were selected based on the named entities and relations that are interesting for physicians.

3.3 Annotation Guidelines

During the annotation process and discussion rounds with the annotators, the original annotation guideline was adjusted. The main annotation guidelines were following:

Largest possible term: as in MUC NER task definition[7] (see Appendix A.1.3), the largest possible term of a particular entity type (that contains as substring terms of the same entity type) has to be annotated (eg [[[retro[peritoneo]] vascular][8] should be annotated as retroperitoneo vascular - *vascular retroperitoneum-*).

Use of lexicons as resources: doubts about the category of an entity (sometimes it is not clear whether a term is, for example, an anatomical entity or its boundaries are not clear) should be

solved using RadLex[9] (it needs a translation into English) or UMLS,[10] (that exists for Spanish)[11]. **Existence of spelling errors:** terms with spelling errors should also be annotated.

Multi-name expressions/terms: unlike MUC-7 NER task definition, when there is elision of the head of one conjunct, the expression should be annotated as different terms (discontinuous expressions can be annotated by our annotation tool, eg. in the construction *intra and extrahepatic*, annotators were asked to annotate *intrahepatic* and *extrahepatic* as entities). The decision to annotate the different terms that form multi-word expressions was taken -after some discussion- because we want the gold standard to be correct and representative of the entities existing in the real world. However, to avoid too complex annotations, cases with more than three terms were annotated as a single *term*.

Relations across sentences: they have to be annotated (eg. in *orthotopic left kidney. Size diminished and (...)*, *size* refers to the *orthotopic left kidney* and a relation among them has to be annotated).

Abbreviations: the abbreviations of some entity types (eg. AE or FI) should not only be annotated as abbreviations, but also as entities (eg. in *RD -riñon derecho, right kidney-*, *RD* should be annotated as abbreviation and as anatomical entity as well).

Segmentation of annotations: if it is not clear if part of the term corresponds to a LO and part to an AE, if from the term it is clear where the AE is located, the whole term should be labeled as anatomical entity, else a segment might be labeled as LO and another as AE (eg. lymph node should be labeled as an AE, since it is possible to identify the location of lymph nodes in the body. The same occurs with *right iliac fossa*).[12] In *upper part of the head* it is not clear what exactly the upper part is. So *upper part* should be annotated as location and *head* as AE and *the tumor is located in the upper left part of the liver* should be annotated as follows: *the [tumor](FI) is located in*

---

[8]Words between brackets show valid anatomical entities.

[11]RadLex is more appropriate for the radiology domain, but has the disadvantage of not being translated into Spanish.

[12]RadLex should be used as a source to detect which is the largest possible concept corresponding to an AE (i.e. if right iliac fossa exists as AE in RadLex then it should be annotated as an AE)

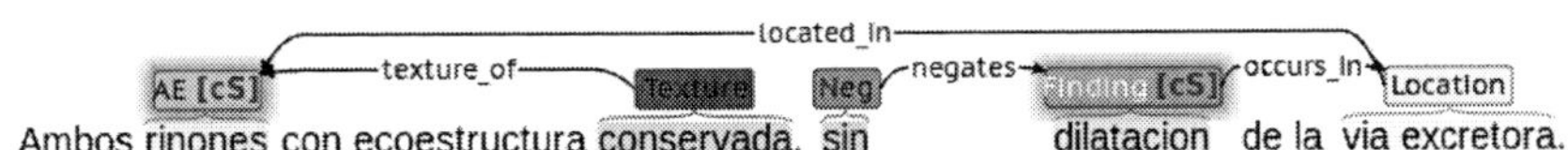

Figure 1: Both kidneys of conserved ecostructure, without enlargement of the excretory pathway.

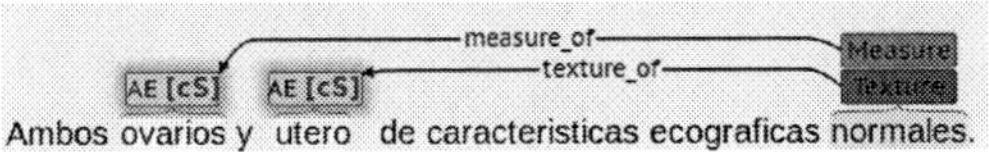

Figure 2: Both ovarys and uterus of normal eco-graphic signs.

the [upper](LO) [left part of the liver](AE).

Prioritize AE over LO: if there is a doubt as whether a term corresponds to an anatomical entity or to a location, it should be annotated as anatomical entity.

Prioritize findings over locations: if a concept refering to a finding includes a location, the largest possible concept that refers to a finding has to be annotated (eg. *pyloric stenosis* refers to a FI, that includes a location. Therefore, [pyloric stenosis](FI) should be chosen over [pyloric](AE) [stenosis](FI)).

Negation and uncertainty terms: negations and uncertainty terms should be annotated only if there is a relation among them and a finding.

Anatomical entities: anatomical entities have to be annotated although there is no relation among them and a finding (eg. in *right lobe of the liver has the usual size*, *right lobe of the liver* should be annotated, although it is not associated to any finding).

Some other decisions that had to be taken were how to annotate certain frequently occurring concepts in the best way. For example, we decided to always annotate *kidney implant* as an AE. Furthermore, *ovarian cyst* and *cyst in the ovary* should be annotated as [ovarian cyst](FI) instead of [ovarian](AE) [cyst](FI), and as cyst[FI] in the ovary[AE].

Figures 1 and 2 show examples of annotations of some sentences.

3.4 Automatic Pre-Annotation

In order to decrease the annotation time, entities were pre-annotated automatically. For this purpose, regular expressions, UMLS and a manually-created dictionary were used.

Regular expressions were used to detect the concept *measure*. *Anatomical entities* and *findings* were detected by the use of some semantic

types (STY) of UMLS (see mapping among our concepts and UMLS STYs in Table 2).

entity	UMLS STY
AE	Body Part, Organ, or Organ Component; Body Space or Junction; Body System; Tissue
FI	Anatomical Abnormality; Congenital Abnormality; Acquired Abnormality; Finding; Sign or Symptom; Pathologic Function; Disease or Syndrome; Mental or Behavioral Dysfunction; Neoplastic Process; Injury or Poisoning

Table 2: Mapping of UMLS Semantic Types to our annotation schema.

First, concepts of the Spanish UMLS were mapped to the radiology reports. If one of the corresponding semantic types corresponded to an anatomical entity or to a finding, then the concept was pre-annotated. Finally, a manually-created dictionary, that contains terms and their corresponding entity type -such as negation and uncertainty terms, locations or textures- was used. For example *no puede descartarse (cannot be discarded)* is mapped to *Uncertainty*. Many of the concepts in this dictionary have been included within an iterative process followed from the annotations performed by the annotators. A dictionary lookup algorithm was used to look for terms of UMLS and of the terms of the dictionary in the texts. Therefore, terms were stemmed using the Spanish Snowball implementation of NLTK.

After applying automatic pre-annotation, data was processed by human annotators. Annotations wrongly made by the tool were removed or corrected and missing concepts included.

3.5 Manual Annotation

The manual annotation was carried out by two Spanish native speakers: an advanced medicine student (6th year of the career) (Annotator 1) and a professional of a technical field (Annotator 2), that were not trained in medical document annotation. brat annotation tool (Stenetorp et al., 2012) was used for this purpose.

Many meetings were held with the annotators in order to solve doubts. After having annotated a first dataset (Annotation iteration 1 in Table 5) doubts and differences in criteria were reviewed and the annotation guidelines (described in Subsection 3.3) were written by the computational linguits with more detail. After two annotation-revision iterations, the final guidelines were defined and annotations were performed (in what we call iteration 3). Disagreements were solved by a computational linguist with expertise in the biomedical domain together with a physician.

4 Dataset Analysis

Once the annotation was performed, the annotated dataset was analyzed in order to know how many entities and relations of each type were found. The analysis of the annotations is calculated for the whole set of 513 annotated reports (not for each of the datasets described in section 3.1.1). For those reports annotated by both annotators the annotation done by the medical student was chosen.

type	total	different
anatomical	4398	405
finding	2637	745
location	722	201
measure	3210	975
texture	1890	74
type of measure	1127	72
negation	1489	51
uncertainty	109	26
abbreviations	880	105
temporal expressions	35	15
multi-name terms	788	210

Table 3: Type and amount of entities, modifiers and other characteristics.

Table 3 shows the number of entities, modifiers of entities and other characteristics (abbreviations, temporal expressions and multi-name terms). In all cases the total number of concepts and the number of different concepts is shown. It can be seen that there are a total of 880 abbreviations. 470 of them correspond to anatomical entities and 7 to findings. The rest correspond to type of measures (266), locations (20) and 117 have no associated entity type. Table 4 shows for each type of relation, the entities related by them, the total number of relations and the number of different relations appearing in the annotated texts.

There are 867 relations across sentences and a total of 10987 relations in the 513 reports. 7.89% of the relations are across sentence relations.

The most frequent multi-name terms are *via biliar extrahepática* (*extrahepatic bile duct*) (232) and *via biliar intra hepática* (*intrahepatic bile duct*) (219).

relation	entities	total	different
occurs in	FI-AE	2161	750
	FI-LO	233	218
located in	LO-AE	538	165
area of	AE-LO	65	53
measure of	TM-AE	1007	154
	TM-LO	46	36
	TM-FI	59	56
	ME-AE	1651	578
	ME-LO	74	48
	ME-FI	407	346
has meas. type	ME-TM	1123	831
texture	TE-AE	1495	192
	TE-LO	387	54
	TE-FI	90	37
negates	NG-FI	1478	164
speculates	UT-FI	96	86
not present	CT-FI	33	33

Table 4: Relations with more than five occurrences annotated among entities in iteration 3.

4.1 Inter-Annotator Agreement

To evaluate the consistency among the annotations performed by both annotators, the inter-annotator agreement (IAA) was calculated using the Cohen's Kappa coefficient (κ) (Cohen, 1960). κ was calculated with the scikit-learn toolkit on a token level.

Multiple annotations per token are possible (and are frequently used) due to various meanings and to the existence of nested or overlapping concepts, e.g. *normal* can be labeled as measure, as texture or as both of them (consider, for example, the phrase *normal size and echotexture*). For the calculation of the IAA we decided to consider that a token is labeled in the same way by both annotators if and only if both annotators assigned to it the exact same set of labels (or no label at all).

Table 5 shows the IAA for each of the annotation datasets. It can be appreciated that it improves in each annotation iteration step. Annotation dataset 3 was the final one, and was annotated once the annotation schema and criteria (see Subsections 3.2 and 3.3) were stabilized.

ann. iter.	# reports	# processed by both annotators	κ
1	16	16	0.5883
2	20	20	0.8577
3	513	61	0.8893

Table 5: IAA (κ) and number of annotated reports in different annotation iterations.

The subset of dataset 3 annotated by both annotators contains 427 tokens with more than one annotation of a total of 5894 tokens. That is 7.24% tokens belonged to more than one entity according to one of the annotators.

5 Discussion

As reported before, abbreviations are often used in our dataset. Considering that there are 7035 anatomical entities and findings (see Table 3), and that there are 477 abbreviations of anatomical entities and findings, we can think that about 6% of the anatomical entities and findings are written in an abbreviated way. Also, there is a total of 105 different abbreviations in 513 reports (see Table 3), which we consider a high number.

The other results of Table 3 are useful for the later use of this annotated dataset. Multi-name terms will probably not be easily recognized by standard entity recognition algorithms. The relation of findings with temporal expressions (see Table 4) should be taken into account to determine the factuality of a finding. The same occurs with terms that denote negation and uncertainty. Relations between sentences will be also difficult to discover.

As depicted in Table 5, the inter-annotator agreement improves in each annotation iteration step. This makes sense, since after each annotation iteration many meetings were held with both annotators to solve doubts and the annotation criteria was changed according to new questions the annotators asked until it stabilized. With this stabilized annotation guidelines, annotators performed the annotation of dataset 3, which had an inter-annotator agreement of 0.89.

We do not have an objective measure related to how the annotation easiness increased after the pre-annotation process. Eventhough, annotators reported that after some improvements of our manually built dictionary (occured after some 'annotation-automatic improvement of the dictionary' iterations) pre-annotations were much more accurate and that their annotation was much easier. We also noticed an increase of the reports annotated per hour.

Considering Tables 3 and 4, we can see that 56% of the findings are negated (1478 out of 2637). This might lead to future implementation of methods to detect negated findings in reports (see Chapman et al. (2001), and Cotik et al. (2015) for Spanish). Only 1.25% of the findings are reported as a past issue or as a conditional issue in the future (33 *not present* relations out of 2637 *findings*).

The development of the annotation criteria has not been an easy task. New entities (eg. location) had to be added to the initial annotation schema. The need to add these entities came from the actual annotation process and the questions that the annotators had. The initial set of relations grew also much more than expected due to the complexity of some of the sentences that revealed the existence of relations that were not considered initially.

In many cases it was not easy to determine if a concept belonged to an entity type or to another. In particular we found that a location can be referring to an anatomical entity and an anatomical entity to a location. Many doubts of this kind arose and helped us to define the definitive annotation guidelines (Section 3.3).

6 Conclusions

In this work we presented an annotation criteria developed for a set of radiology reports written in Spanish with the goal to be able to use the annotated corpus as an evaluation resource for name entity recognition and relation extraction and as input for the training of supervised learning methods to solve these tasks. We divided the total available set in four subsets in order to be able to extract in the future relations among the data that give further information (for instance, the existence of appendicitis), that might be useful for physicians and patients. We anonymized data and trained the annotators to do the annotation task.

The shortness of the texts, the abundance of acronyms and the specificity of the medical language made the annotation task difficult. Furthermore, it was not easy to keep up with the goal to achieve a simple annotation criteria.

The analysis of the annotated dataset shows some interesting characteristics, as the abundance of negated findings. That might lead to the development of negation detection algorithms. This annotated dataset is useful for its evaluation.

We noticed the importance of having annotators with expertise in the annotation task and in the medical domain and we consider that in this particular domain it is even more difficult than in others to obtain annotations from experts.

Acknowledgements

This research was supported by the German Federal Ministry of Economics and Energy (BMWi) through the project MACSS (01MD16011F).

References

Wendy Chapman, W. Bridewell, P. Hanbury, GF. Cooper, and BG. Buchanan. 2001. A simple algorithm for identifying negated findings and diseases in discharge summaries. *J Biomed Inform.* 34(5):301–310.

Jacob Cohen. 1960. A coefficient of agreement for nominal scales. *Educational and Psychological Measurement* 20(1):37–46.

Viviana Cotik, Vanesa Stricker, Jorge Vivaldi, and Horacio Rodriguez. 2015. Syntactic methods for negation detection in radiology reports in Spanish. In *ACL - Workshop on Replicability and Reproducibility in Natural Language Processing: adaptative methods, resources and software.* Buenos Aires, Argentina.

Noa Cruz, Roser Morante, Manuel J. Maña López, Jacinto Mata Vázquez, and Carlos L. Parra Calderón. 2017. Annotating negation in spanish clinical texts. In *Proceedings of the Workshop Computational Semantics Beyond Events and Roles.* Association for Computational Linguistics, Valencia, Spain, pages 53–58.

B. Do, A.S. Wu, J. Maley, S., and Biswal. 2013. Automatic retrieval of bone fracture knowledge using natural language processing. *J Digit Imaging* 26(4):709–13.

Paras Lakhani and Curtis P. Langlotz. 2009. Automated detection of radiology reports that document non-routine communication of critical or significant results. *J Digit Imaging* 23(6):647–57.

Montserrat Marimon, Jorge Vivaldi, and Núria Bel. 2017. Annotation of negation in the iula spanish clinical record corpus. In *Proceedings of the Workshop Computational Semantics Beyond Events and Roles.* Association for Computational Linguistics, Valencia, Spain, pages 43–52.

C. Morioka, F. Meng, R. Taira, J. Sayre, P. Zimmerman, D. Ishimitsu, J. Huang, L. Shen, and S. El-Saden. 2016. Automatic classification of ultrasound screening examinations of the abdominal aorta. *J Digit Imaging* 29(6):742–48.

Agnieszka Mykowiecka, Małgorzata Marciniak, and Anna Kupść. 2009. Rule-based information extraction from patients' clinical data. *Journal of Biomedical Informatics* 42(5):923 – 936. Biomedical Natural Language Processing.

Aurélie Névéol, Cyril Grouin, Xavier Tannier, Thierry Hamon, Liadh Kelly, Lorraine Goeuriot, and Pierre Zweigenbaum. 2015. CLEF ehealth evaluation lab 2015 task 1b: Clinical named entity recognition. In *Working Notes of CLEF 2015 - Conference and Labs of the Evaluation forum, Toulouse, France, September 8-11, 2015..*

Maite Oronoz, Koldo Gojenola, Alicia Pérez, Arantza Díaz de Ilarraza, and Arantza Casillas. 2015. On the creation of a clinical gold standard corpus in spanish: Mining adverse drug reactions. *Journal of Biomedical Informatics* 56:318 – 332.

Sameer Pradhan, Noémie Elhadad, Brett R South, David Martinez, Lee Christensen, Amy Vogel, Hanna Suominen, Wendy W Chapman, and Guergana Savova. 2014. Evaluating the state of the art in disorder recognition and normalization of the clinical narrative. *Journal of the American Medical Informatics Association* .

Sameer Pradhan, Noémie Elhadad, Brett R. South, David Martínez, Lee M. Christensen, Amy Vogel, Hanna Suominen, Wendy W. Chapman, and Guergana K. Savova. 2013. Task 1: ShARe/CLEF eHealth Evaluation Lab 2013. In *Working Notes for CLEF 2013 Conference , Valencia, Spain, September 23-26, 2013..*

Roland Roller, Feiyu Xu Hans Uszkoreit, Laura Seiffe, Michael Mikhailov, Oliver Staeck, Klemens Budde, Fabian Halleck, and Danilo Schmidt. 2016. A fine-grained corpus annotation schema of German nephrology records. *Proceedings of the Clinical Natural Language Processing Workshop* 28(1):69–77.

M. Sevenster, R. van Ommering, and Y. Qian. 2012. Automatically correlating clinical findings and body locations in radiology reports using MedLEE. *J Digit Imaging* 25(2):240–249.

Hagit Shatkay, W. John Wilbur, and Andrey Rzhetsky. 2005. Annotation guidelines [Online; accessed 28-04-2017].

Maria Skeppstedt, Maria Kvist, Gunnar H. Nilsson, and Hercules Dalianis. 2014. Automatic recognition of disorders, findings, pharmaceuticals and body structures from clinical text: An annotation and machine learning study. *Journal of Biomedical Informatics* 49:148 – 158.

Pontus Stenetorp, Sampo Pyysalo, Goran Topić, Tomoko Ohta, Sophia Ananiadou, and Jun'ichi Tsujii. 2012. brat: a web-based tool for NLP-assisted text annotation. In *Proceedings of the Demonstrations Session at EACL 2012.* Association for Computational Linguistics, Avignon, France.

Özlem Uzuner, Brett R South, Shuying Shen, and Scott L DuVall. 2011. 2010 i2b2/VA challenge on concepts, assertions, and relations in clinical text. *Journal of the American Medical Informatics Association* 18(5):552–556.

W John Wilbur, Andrey Rzhetsky, and Hagit Shatkay. 2006. New directions in biomedical text annotation: definitions, guidelines and corpus construction. *BMC Bioinformatics* 356(7).

Towards Replicability in Parsing

Daniel Dakota, Sandra Kübler
Indiana University
{ddakota, skuebler}@indiana.edu

Abstract

We investigate parsing replicability across 7 languages (and 8 treebanks), showing that choices concerning the use of grammatical functions in parsing or evaluation and the influence of the rare word threshold, as well as choices in test sentences and evaluation script options have considerable and often unexpected effects on parsing accuracies. All of those choices need to be carefully documented if we want to ensure replicability.

1   Introduction

Over the last 10 years, statistical constituent parsing has developed from a research area that mainly focused on parsing the Penn Treebank (Marcus et al., 1993) to covering more languages, including a wide range of morphologically rich languages, such as German or Arabic. While the extension across different languages resulted in many insights about parsing models for specific languages, the development also had a dramatic effect on replicability. For novices to become experts in parsing, they need not only understand the parsing algorithms and implementations, but must also become familiar with the intricacies of existing data sets and annotations across a range of languages. It should be a fairly well known fact that the Penn Treebank uses traces in form of numbers attached to constituent labels as well as empty categories. The failure to remove either traces or empty categories before training can lead to rather unexpected, low results, especially when the test data come from a different source and do not have empty categories in the sentences. After a careful study of the existing literature, we may also know that the German TiGer treebank (Brants et al., 2004) uses crossing branches, which

need to be resolved before parsing with a CFG parser, and that the method with which the crossing branches are resolved has an influence on parsing results (Boyd and Meurers, 2008). But it may not be generally known that the two major German treebanks, TiGer and TüBa-D/Z (Telljohann et al., 2015), do not attach punctuation signs into the tree structure, which can lead to unexpected results if not handled in preprocessing. Again, the method chosen to attach punctuation signs has an effect on parsing accuracy (p.c. W. Maier).

The problem becomes more serious if we conduct experiments across a wider range of languages, some of which we may not be familiar with, in order to demonstrate good parser performance across languages. It is exacerbated by often minimal descriptions of the methods used in preprocessing for published results. We argue that in order to enable replicability in parsing research, we need to be more explicit and detailed with regard to pre- and post-processing steps.

In the current paper, we show the effects of different decisions in two major design issues on parsing results: We investigate two issues during parsing and during evaluation. In parsing, we 1) have a closer look at the (non-)use of grammatical functions during training and testing, and 2) we investigate the effect of selecting the threshold for rare words. Grammatical functions (GFs) are part of most constituent annotation schemes (such as NP-SBJ for subjects or NP-TMP for temporal NPs in the Penn Treebank). Since parsers often delete these GFs by default in their output, it may not be immediately obvious that using them in training has an effect on the quality of the results. The threshold for rare words is often neglected in parsing experiments, but has a considerable influence on results. With regard to evaluation, we investigate decisions in the test set and in the evaluation parameters. More specifically, we investigate 1)

Proceedings of Recent Advances in Natural Language Processing, pages 185–194,
Varna, Bulgaria, Sep 4–6 2017.

the effects of test set size, which varies across languages. 2) We also show evaluation results using different settings of the evaluation script.

Since all of those decisions have an effect on parsing results, we argue that they need to be documented in parsing literature to ensure replicability of parsing results. Whereas in the past, concern about paper length forced authors to focus on important findings and conclusions, which resulted in the omission of many details, today this is not necessarily an issue as many conferences allow the inclusion of supplementary information for exactly such purposes as well as the ability to make publicly available any additional settings.

2 State of the Art

Replicability has started to appear as a topic in NLP and machine learning, for example as an IJCAI 2015 Workshop on Replicability and Reproducibility in Natural Language Processing[1], and it has been described as one of the potentially negative factors of shared tasks in NLP by Parra Escartín et al. (2017). However, there is little work on more specific areas such as parsing.

In many cases, decisions concerning preprocessing, parser settings, or evaluation settings are not described in parsing literature, thus requiring assumptions ranging from what function tags to be included in evaluation (Gabbard et al., 2006) to the exact specifications in accompanying evaluation parameter files (van Cranenburgh and Bod, 2013).

In the following, we look at a few highly cited papers to document common practices in the literature. It is not our aim to single out those authors, but we rather want to document that even high quality papers do not provide enough information for replicability, thus documenting the need for more rigorous guidelines.

2.1 Preprocessing

For German, Cheung and Penn (2009) report that they could not replicate experiments by Becker and Frank (2002): "While the test set used in the paper [by Becker and Frank] was manually corrected for evaluation, we did not correct our test set, because it would be difficult to ensure that we adhered to the same correction guidelines. No details of the correction process were provided in

the paper, ... Also, because we could not obtain the exact sets used for training, development, and testing, we had to recreate the sets by randomly splitting the corpus."

For English, Bod (2001) describes his preprocessing of the WSJ part of the Penn Treebank as follows: "All trees were stripped off their semantic tags, co-reference information and quotation marks." No further information is given. Charniak and Johnson (2005) describe their data split as "We used the division into preliminary training and preliminary development data sets described in (Collins, 2000)" but do not mention any preprocessing. Collins (2000) similarly defines his data split, but does not mention preprocessing. In their work on domain adaptation, McClosky et al. (2006) describe the splits they use for the Brown Corpus and the WSJ portion of the Penn Treebank, but they do not mention any preprocessing. Klein and Manning (2003) describe their use of the WSJ sections as: "For each model, input trees were annotated or transformed in some way, as in (Johnson, 1998)". The latter describes his tree transformations in detail, but only mentions the data splits without any details about preprocessing: "It is fairly straightforward to mechanically transform the Penn II tree representations in the WSJ corpus into something close to the alternative tree representations described above ...". In a multilingual setting, the only information Petrov and Klein (2007) provide concerns information about their treatment of the treebanks: "We trained models for English, Chinese and German using the standard corpora and splits as shown in Tab. 3. We applied our model directly to each of the treebanks, without any language dependent modifications." There is no information about preprocessing. And apart from the cross-references to previous papers shown in the quotes, there is no information about possible standards documented in earlier publications.

2.2 Evaluation

Johnson (1998) defines precision and recall, but does not provide information about implementation or parameters. Charniak and Johnson (2005) state that they "evaluated the performance of [their] reranking parser using the standard PARSEVAL metrics." (Bod, 2001) describes his evaluation as "We used 'evalb' to compute the standard PARSEVAL scores for our parse results. We

---

[1] https://sites.google.com/site/adaptivenlp2015/

	# train	# test	#POS	# GFs
Arabic (AR)	5k	1,958	35	20/52
Basque (EU)	5k	946	25	5
Chinese (ZH)	5k	1,905	33	26
English (EN)	5k	2,412	36	20
German (DE-TI)	5k	5,000	51	51
German (DE-Tü)	5k	5,000	54	51
Hebrew (HE)	5k	716	50	45
Swedish (SV)	5k	666	25	65

Table 1: Treebank Statistics.

focus on the Labeled Precision (LP) and Labeled Recall (LR) scores only in this paper, as these are commonly used to rank parsing systems." but does not provide information about parameter settings. McClosky et al. (2006) "We use evalb to calculate how similar the two sets of output are on a bracket level." Neither Collins (2000), Klein and Manning (2003) nor Petrov and Klein (2007) mention the evaluation script they use.

3 Experimental Setup

3.1 Treebanks

We focus on a range of languages, covering morphologically rich languages with different characteristics (Arabic, Basque, German, Hebrew, Swedish) and morphologically simpler languages (Chinese, English). For Arabic (Green and Manning, 2010), Basque (Aldezabal Roteta et al., 2008), Hebrew (Sima'an et al., 2001), the German TiGer treebank (Brants et al., 2004), and Swedish (Nivre and Megyesi, 2007), we use data from the 2013 and 2014 shared tasks on parsing MRLs (see (Seddah et al., 2013, 2014) for a description of treebank preparation). In addition, we utilize the Penn Chinese Treebank CTB5 (Xue et al., 2005), the Penn Treebank of English (Marcus et al., 1993), and the German TüBa-D/Z treebank (Telljohann et al., 2015).

Table 1 lists the sizes of the training and test sets in terms of number of sentences, and it lists the number of POS tags and function labels. For Arabic, we list the number of single function labels and the number of the combined ones. Since the treebanks vary considerably in size, we used the small SPMRL data sets of 5,000 sentences. Basque and Swedish are by far the smallest data sets, which also affects the size of the test set. However, these two languages also show extremes in terms of grammatical functions: With 5 GFs,

Basque has the lowest number, and Swedish the highest with 65.

It is common knowledge that the size of the tagset as well as the size of the GFs influences parsing results. However, it is difficult to separate effects of the POS tagset and the GFs from language characteristics. For this reason, the SPMRL shared tasks have concentrated on an evaluation that disregards the GFs for the inter-language comparison (Seddah et al., 2013, 2014).

3.2 Parser Setup

We use the Berkeley parser (Petrov and Klein, 2007), which has achieved state of the art results for a range of languages (Seddah et al., 2013, 2014). In order to ensure stable findings, we report results averaged over four train/test cycles using grammars trained with four different seeds. To ensure comparability, we use the same four seeds (1-4) for the grammar across all languages.

For all languages, we follow SPMRL and train on a subset of 5,000 sentences in order to eliminate effects of training set size. This size was chosen for ease of comparison to the SPMRL shared task and since it is the maximum training size available for the Swedish Treebank. We use gold POS tags for training and report results for both gold POS tags and parser internal tagging. Pre-processing for the English and Chinese treebanks involved removing traces and collapsing unary nodes into a single node using the Berkeley Parser Analyser (Kummerfeld et al., 2012, 2013).

3.3 Evaluation

We evaluate using the scorer for the SPMRL 2014 shared task[2], a reimplementation of EVALB[3] that allows for additional options such as scoring with grammatical functions and penalizing unparsed sentences. By default, EVALB only scores up to a *dash* that separates any complex label (e.g. SBJ-TMP) and inherently does not score GFs given this behavior. Furthermore, EVALB does not penalize unparsed sentences, and simply omits them from the final scores, reporting the number of unparsed sentences separately. This can be somewhat misleading, especially in cases of high numbers of unparsed sentences.

The average scores across the four grammars are reported with punctuation being scored, which

---

[2]http://spmrl.org/spmrl2014-sharedtask
[3]http://nlp.cs.nyu.edu/evalb/

is not standard practice for languages such as English, but whose inclusion influences parsing results (Kulick et al., 2006).

Results in section 4 and 5.1 are evaluated with a parameter file that deletes root nodes and accompanying brackets from gold and parsed files. Some treebanks contain additional root nodes that are not intrinsically part of the treebank, but are required for parsing (such as TiGer in which all punctuation is attached to a virtual root). However, the inclusion of these roots should not be included in evaluation as this can artifically increase scores. Additionally we enable settings that penalizes the parser for unparsed sentences and and score the POS tag but not the function labels (unless mentioned otherwise).

4 Parsing Decisions

In this section, we investigate decisions regarding grammatical functions (GFs) in parsing and/or evaluation as well as the influence of the rare word threshold on parsing results.

4.1 Grammatical Functions

We first investigate how decisions regarding the use of GFs influence parsing results. For each language, there are three settings: 1) NoGF: The complete experiment (training/parsing/evaluation) is carried out without grammatical functions. 2) Mixed: In this setting, we train and parse using GFs, but we ignore them in evaluation. I.e., the evaluation only considers the constituent structure, which is the standard setting for parsing English and has also been used for the SPMRL shared tasks even if parsers produced GFs. 3) AllGF: Here, the complete experiment, including evaluation, uses GFs. For the versions of trees without GFs, we remove GFs from the node to which they are attached. For example, NP-SBJ is shortened to NP.

The third setting may be a harsh evaluation for configurational languages, but for non-configurational languages, the GFs are the only indicators of subjects and direct objects and thus important information for many downstream applications.

The results of these experiments are shown in table 2.

POS tagging considerations The POS tagging results show several noteworthy trends. The first issue is that even in the setting where we provide gold POS tags, the POS tagging accuracy is generally lower than 100%. In these cases, the parser changes the POS tags because it cannot find a good analysis using the gold POS. I.e., the Berkeley parser trades POS tagging accuracy for parsability.

Swedish and the German TiGer treebank show the most untypical results: For gold POS, both reach (near-)perfect accuracy when no GFs are used, but when GFs are used in training/parsing or additionally for evaluation, the accuracy degrades to 92.58% and 89.66% for Swedish and to 90.16% and 86.25% for TiGer. The reason can be attributed to the fact that both the Swedish treebank and TiGer attach GFs to POS tags. A comparison of POS tagging accuracy between setting 1+2 (noGF/mixed) and 2+3 (mixed/allGF) for both treebanks shows that the former difference is twice as large as the latter. I.e., the parser more often changes from one POS tag to another rather than keeping the same POS tags and only changing the GF. When parsing with GFs, both parser internal and gold POS tags result in (near-)identical performance, suggesting that the parser is completely retagging all words to parse. A similar phenomenon has been observed by Maier et al. (2014) for German.

The most surprising results can be found in the comparison of not using GFs at all and using them for parsing but ignoring them in evaluation. For gold POS, we see almost identical results, but for automatically assigned POS tags, Arabic shows the smallest loss (0.52) and Swedish the highest (2.53), followed by German-TiGer (2.42). It is worth noting that the treebanks that attach GFs to POS tags, Swedish and TiGer, have the highest differences. These results show that using GFs internally has a noticeable negative effect on accuracy.

In conclusion, the decision whether to use GFs in parsing and evaluation has a considerable effect on POS tagging quality, which goes against our original expectations.

Parsing considerations When we look at the F-scores in table 2, we also see the expected decrease from parsing without GFs (noGF) to parsing and evaluation including GFs (allGF). There is a considerable decrease in the F-scores, ranging from 4.82 points (Basque) to >10 for Arabic, English, German, and Swedish, given gold POS tags. Thus, the divide does not correlate with morphological

Language	GFs	Gold POS				POS by parser			
		F-Score	Recall	Precision	POS	F-Score	Recall	Precision	POS
Arabic	noGF	76.82	75.98	77.66	99.98	73.88	72.73	75.06	94.24
	parse	74.19	73.94	74.44	99.93	71.63	70.95	72.32	93.72
	allGF	65.54	65.32	65.76	99.93	63.01	62.42	63.62	93.72
Basque	noGF	74.11	73.90	74.33	98.15	66.99	66.27	67.72	87.70
	mixed	72.57	72.12	73.04	98.14	65.35	64.22	66.51	87.10
	allGF	69.29	68.85	69.73	98.14	62.65	61.57	63.76	87.10
Chinese	noGF	83.52	83.18	83.87	99.94	72.43	71.08	73.82	88.37
	mixed	81.28	81.87	80.69	99.82	70.14	69.70	70.58	87.42
	eval	75.56	76.12	75.01	99.82	64.25	63.85	64.66	87.42
English	noGF	84.38	84.37	84.39	99.76	83.79	83.56	84.01	95.70
	mixed	82.30	82.69	81.90	99.72	81.86	81.91	81.80	95.12
	allGF	73.95	74.31	73.60	99.72	73.72	73.77	73.67	95.12
German-Ti	noGF	71.96	70.50	73.48	99.64	69.27	66.97	71.73	92.52
	mixed	65.72	64.34	67.18	90.16	65.73	64.34	67.17	90.10
	allGF	49.90	48.84	51.00	86.25	49.90	48.84	51.00	86.19
German-Tü	noGF	91.78	91.85	91.70	99.91	87.52	87.32	87.73	94.47
	mixed	90.70	91.01	90.41	99.82	85.88	85.92	85.85	93.53
	allGF	79.16	79.42	78.90	99.82	75.02	75.05	74.98	93.53
Hebrew	noGF	91.97	92.07	91.87	100.00	86.87	86.85	86.89	92.20
	mixed	89.92	90.14	89.70	100.00	84.58	84.70	84.45	91.30
	allGF	83.72	83.93	83.51	99.96	78.53	78.65	78.41	91.30
Swedish	noGF	82.88	82.66	83.10	100.00	79.06	78.73	79.39	95.11
	mixed	75.21	74.92	75.49	92.58	75.21	74.92	75.49	92.58
	allGF	63.22	62.97	63.46	89.66	63.22	62.97	63.46	89.66

Table 2: Results for training/parsing without GFs (noGF), training/parsing with GFs + evaluation w/o GFs (mixed), and training/parsing/evaluation with GFs (allGF).

richness, as we would have expected. The divide is unclear, but may partially depend on the annotation scheme or the number of GFs. However, further research is required to investigate this point. For Swedish and TiGer, the decrease is extreme, reaching almost 20 points for Swedish and >22 points for TiGer. This can be explained by the complete retagging (see above). I.e., the parser's performance is on a level of internally assigned POS tags. For automatic POS tags, the differences are similar or smaller.

However, there is a somewhat surprising decrease in F-scores between the setting in which we train/parse without GFs (noGF) and the setting where we use GFs in training/parsing but ignore them in evaluation (mixed). One would expect the presence of GFs to have only a minimal effect on phrase structure decisions. But results show decreases in the F-score, generally between 1.08 (German-TüBa-D/Z) and 2.63 (Arabic) for gold POS. Exceptions are Swedish with a drop of 7.67

points and German-Tiger with a decrease of 6.24 points. The drop is similar or less pronounced for parser internal POS tags.

In conclusion, we see several expected differences between the settings. But we also see unexpected differences, for example in the comparison of results between using or not using GFs in parsing if we do not consider them in the evaluation. Thus, if we do not delete GFs from the treebank data before we parse, we will obtain artificially low results, even when GFs are not part of the evaluation.

4.2 Handling Rare Words

The Berkeley parser's handling of rare words has been demonstrated to be biased towards an English lexicon (Hall et al., 2014). Rare words are mapped to classes based on automatically learned suffix and character information, as described by Petrov et al. (2006). During training, the parser performs smoothing over rare words, with a de-

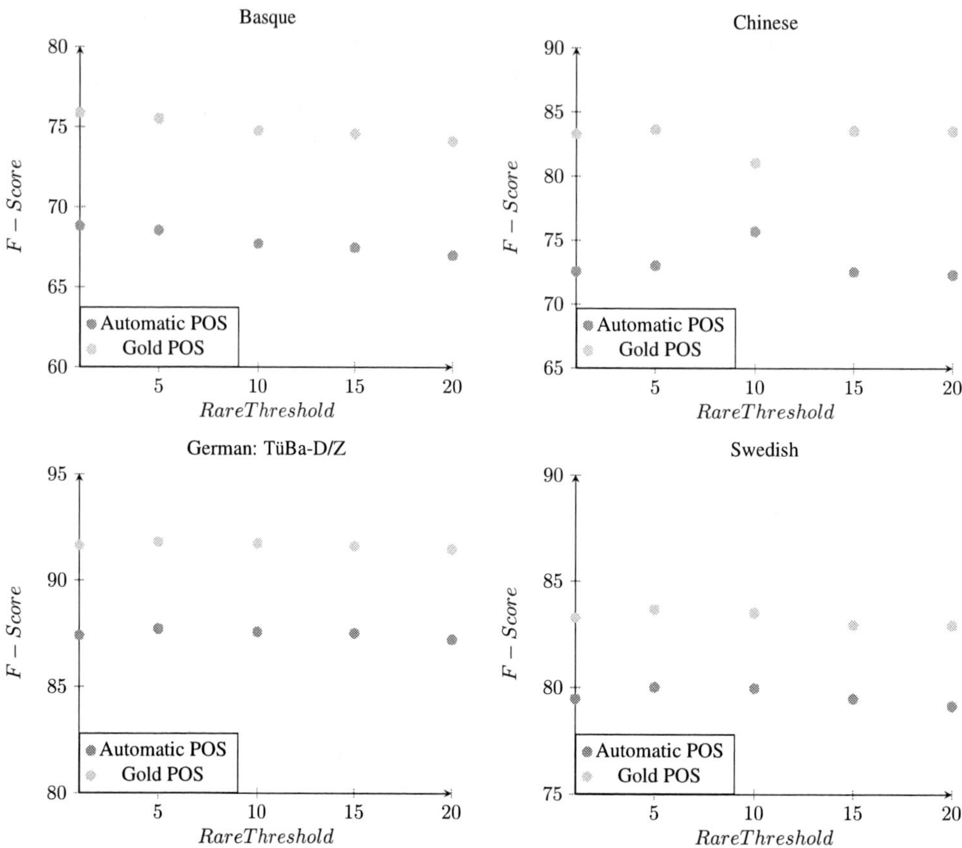

Figure 1: Experiments with different threshold for handling rare words.

fault threshold of 10. Some languages, such as Chinese, have additional lexicon information accessible to the parser (which we do not use here), but for most languages this is not the case. Yet when using the parser in a downstream application, the threshold for rare words at which the parser was trained has a direct impact on performance, particularly for languages with small training sets, but is often not adjusted.

The results of using different thresholds for rare words in the Berkeley parser are shown in figure 1. These experiments do not use grammatical functions. We show the results of four languages, Basque, Chinese, German using the TüBa-D/Z treebank, and Swedish.

The German results show only minimal differences in F-scores of around half a point. For Swedish, there is a difference of approximately 1 point. However, in both cases, the best setting is not the default setting of 10, but rather a lower threshold closer to 5. For Basque, the lowest setting of 1 provides the highest F-scores, and the dif-

ference to other settings reaches approximately 2 points. Given that differences in parsing results in the range of 0.5 points tend to be significant, this means that the differences are in the range of statistical significance.

The most interesting results, however, come from Chinese: In contrast to all other languages, in Chinese, we see a difference between the best threshold for the setting where we use gold POS tags as input for the parser, as opposed to having the parser assign POS tags internally. When using gold POS tags, a threshold of 10 gives us the lowest F-scores while for the automatic POS tags, it is the best setting. Additionally, the differences between settings are the most pronounced for Chinese, reaching more than 3 points (between 72.55 and 75.70 for automatic POS tags). The reasons for this behavior are unclear.

These results show very clearly that it is important to optimize the threshold for rare words, not only per language, but also per setting (gold POS tags versus automatic POS tags). And in order

Lang.	F_1	F_2	F_3	F_4	diff_{max}	# test_{orig}
Arabic	62.33	62.21	62.14	62.43	0.29	1,958
Basque	63.11	62.85	63.33	63.27	0.48	946
Chinese	64.86	63.29	63.97	64.42	1.57	1,905
English	73.36	72.70	73.88	73.68	1.18	2,412
German-TiGer	51.03	52.06	51.24	49.76	2.30	5,000
German-TüBa-D/Z	73.86	75.30	73.80	73.53	1.77	5,000
Hebrew	77.74	78.25	78.74	77.73	1.01	716
Swedish	63.47	63.54	62.48	63.01	1.06	666

Table 3: Parsing results based on sampled test sets of size 500.

to ensure replicability, it is important to document these parameter settings.

5 Evaluation Decisions

In this section, we have a closer look at decisions involving the evaluation step. We consider whether the size of the test set has an influence on parsing results. In other words, are some of the test sets too small to be representative? The other question concerns options that the evaluation scripts provide, such as deleting the virtual root that often serves as the unique root node that some parsers require.

5.1 Test Set Size

We investigate the effect of test set size by a controlled experiment in which we repeatedly randomly sample 500 sentences from the standard test set. The sampling is performed after parsing, which means that all the results we present are based on the same parses from section 4 (using automatic POS tags and GFs throughout). The number was chosen so that it is slightly below the size of the smallest test set (666 sentences for Swedish). We chose to repeat the sampling for each language four times. Rather than reporting the average and variance, we decided to show the actual results along with the difference between the highest and lowest result, to give the reader a better overview of the variation in results.

The results of evaluating the randomly sampled subsets are shown in table 3. They show that there are differences between 0.29 points (Arabic) and 2.30 (German-TiGer). Most of the differences are in the range between 1 and 1.8 points. Once again, we are in the range of statistical significance, and it is concerning to see that the selection of test sentences has such a large effect on parsing accuracy. It is also obvious that there is no correlation to the

original size of the test set given that the two German treebanks with the highest number of test sentences have the highest variance while the smallest variance is found in a mid-sized language, Arabic, and the smallest treebank, Swedish, is on the lower end.

5.2 Evaluation Script Settings

To demonstrate the impact of evaluation decisions on parsing results, we present three evaluation settings: 1) Standard: standard EVALB metrics where there is no penalty for unparsed sentences, no inclusion of a parameter file, and no evaluation of function labels; 2) +DEL: standard EVALB metrics with a parameter file that deletes root nodes from the gold and test data and accompanying brackets; 3) +PEN: EVALB metrics with a parameter file and penalties for unparsed sentences. We show results with these settings when integrating or ignoring GFs in the evaluation.

The results are shown in table 4. The good news is that for Arabic, Chinese, English, and Swedish, there is (virtually) no difference across the different setting. But for all other languages, there are differences, and some of them are considerable. If results change in a language, they decrease from the default setting to using the parameter file to penalizing the parser for unparsed sentences. For the German TiGer treebank, we see the highest decrease, the results degrade from 69.44 to 65.73 given GFs are not evaluated, and from 55.31 to 49.90 if GFs are evaluated. This means that leaving virtual roots or similar nodes in the parses or the grammar can have a significant effect on results. The results also show that the difference between deleting virtual roots (+DEL) and punishing the parser for unparsed sentences (+PEN) is generally minimal; the only exception is Basque when GFs are ignored in evaluation. This means

| | GFs in parse only | | | GFs in evaluation | | |
Lang.	standard	+DEL	+PEN	standard	+DEL	+PEN
Arabic	71.71	71.71	71.63	63.08	63.08	63.01
Basque	67.60	65.35	63.35	65.08	62.65	62.65
Chinese	72.45	72.45	72.43	53.47	53.47	53.45
English	81.89	81.89	81.86	73.75	73.75	73.72
German-TiGer	69.44	65.78	65.73	55.31	49.94	49.90
German-TüBa-D/Z	86.57	85.92	85.88	76.19	75.04	75.02
Hebrew	84.89	84.58	84.58	78.97	78.53	78.53
Swedish	75.36	75.36	75.21	63.34	63.34	63.22

Table 4: Parsing results based on different evaluation settings: +DEL = standard + parameter; +PEN = standard + parameter + parse penalty.

that the decision concerning the virtual roots often has more effect on results than the decision to punish the parser for unparsed sentences. Thus, their treatment needs to be reported to ensure replicability.

6 Conclusion and Future Work

In this paper, we have started looking into which factors can affect parsing results and replicability of results. We show that the choice of using grammatical functions in parsing and/or evaluation, the choice of the threshold for rare words, the choice of test sentences, and the choice of evaluation parameters all have considerable and potentially statistically significant effects on parsing results. Most of these details are not generally reported in research on parsing. However, only by reporting all choices meticulously, we can ensure replicability.

We have clearly just scratched the surface in this investigation. We will continue our investigation to better understand factors that influence parsing results, by having a closer look at how evaluation script settings influence parsing results, but also by investigating representational issues, such as double bracketing of sentences across different parser. We will also investigate more parsers. Preliminary results show that the LORG parser (Attia et al., 2010), a re-implementation of the Berkeley parser, shows systematic differences in how the choice of using grammatical functions and of the threshold for rare words influence parsing results.

References

Izaskun Aldezabal Roteta, Maria Jesús Aranzabe Urruzola, Arantza Diaz de Ilarraza Sánchez, and Enrique Fernández Terrones. 2008. From dependencies to constituents in the reference corpus for the processing of Basque. In *Procesamiento del Lenguaje Natural, n° 41 (2008)*. Anual de la Sociedad Española para el Procesamiento del Lenguaje Natural (SEPLN), pages 147–154.

Mohammed Attia, Jennifer Foster, Deirdre Hogan, Joseph Le Roux, Lamia Tounsi, and Josef van Genabith. 2010. Handling Unknown Words in Statistical Latent-Variable Parsing Models for Arabic, English and French. In *Proceedings of SPRML 2010*.

Markus Becker and Anette Frank. 2002. A Stochastic Topological Parser for German. In *Proceedings of the 19th International Conference on Computational Linguistics*. Taipei, Taiwan, COLING '02, pages 1–7.

Rens Bod. 2001. What is the minimal set of subtrees that achieves maximal parse accuracy. In *Proceedings of the 39th Annual Meeting of the Association for Computational Linguistics (ACL) and the 10th Conference of the European Chapter of the ACL (EACL)*. pages 66–73.

Adriane Boyd and Detmar Meurers. 2008. Revisiting the impact of different annotation schemes on PCFG parsing: A grammatical dependency evaluation. In *Proceedings of the ACL Workshop on Parsing German*. Columbus, OH.

Sabine Brants, Stefanie Dipper, Peter Eisenberg, Silvia Hansen, Esther König, Wolfgang Lezius, Christian Rohrer, George Smith, and Hans Uszkoreit. 2004. TIGER: Linguistic interpretation of a German corpus. *Research on Language and Computation, Special Issue* 2(4):597–620.

Eugene Charniak and Mark Johnson. 2005. Coarse-to-fine n-best parsing and MaxEnt discriminative reranking. In *Proceedings of the 43rd Annual Meeting of the Association for Computational Linguistics (ACL'05)*. Ann Arbor, MI, pages 173–180.

Jackie Chi Kit Cheung and Gerald Penn. 2009. Topological Field Parsing of German. In *Proceedings of the 47th Annual Meeting of the ACL and the 4th IJC-NLP of the AFNLP*. Suntec, Singapore, pages 64–72.

Michael Collins. 2000. Discriminative reranking for natural language parsing. In *Proceedings of the Seventeenth International Conference on Machine Learning (ICML)*. Stanford, CA.

Ryan Gabbard, Mitchell Marcus, and Seth Kulick. 2006. Fully parsing the Penn Treebank. In *Proceedings of the Human Language Technology Conference of the North American Chapter of the ACL*. New York, pages 184–191.

Spence Green and Christopher D. Manning. 2010. Better Arabic parsing: Baselines, evaluations, and analysis. In *Proceedings of the 23rd International Conference on Computational Linguistics*. Beijing, China, pages 394–402.

David Hall, Greg Durrett, and Dan Klein. 2014. Less grammar, more features. In *Proceedings of the 52nd Annual Meeting of the Association for Computational Linguistics*. Baltimore, Maryland, pages 228–237.

Mark Johnson. 1998. PCFG models of linguistic tree representations. *Computational Linguistics* 24(4):613–632.

Dan Klein and Christopher Manning. 2003. Accurate unlexicalized parsing. In *Proceedings of ACL-2003*. Sapporo, Japan, pages 423–430.

Seth Kulick, Ryan Gabbard, and Marcus Mitchell. 2006. Parsing the Arabic treebank: Analysis and improvements. In *Proceedings of the Treebanks and Linguistic Theories Conference*. Prague, Czech Republic, pages 31–42.

Jonathan K. Kummerfeld, David Hall, James R. Curran, and Dan Klein. 2012. Parser showdown at the Wall Street Corral: An empirical investigation of error types in parser output. In *Proceedings of the 2012 Joint Conference on Empirical Methods in Natural Language Processing and Computational Natural Language Learning*. Jeju Island, South Korea, pages 1048–1059.

Jonathan K. Kummerfeld, Daniel Tse, James R. Curran, and Dan Klein. 2013. An empirical examination of challenges in Chinese parsing. In *Proceedings of the 51st Annual Meeting of the Association for Computational Linguistics*. Sofia, Bulgaria, pages 98–103.

Wolfgang Maier, Sandra Kübler, Daniel Dakota, and Daniel Whyatt. 2014. Parsing German: How much morphology do we need? In *Proceedings of the First Joint Workshop on Statistical Parsing of Morphologically Rich Languages and Syntactic Analysis of Non-Canonical Languages (SPMRL-SANCL)*. Dublin, Ireland, pages 1–14.

Mitchell P. Marcus, Mary Ann Marcinkiewicz, and Beatrice Santorini. 1993. Building a large annotated corpus of English: The Penn Treebank. *Computational Linguistics* 19(2):313–330.

David McClosky, Eugene Charniak, and Mark Johnson. 2006. Reranking and self-training for parser adaptation. In *Proceedings of the 21st International Conference on Computational Linguistics and 44th Annual Meeting of the Association for Computational Linguistics (COLING-ACL)*. Sydney, Australia.

Joakim Nivre and Beáta Megyesi. 2007. Bootstrapping a Swedish treeebank using cross-corpus harmonization and annotation projection. In *Proceedings of the the 6th International Workshop on Treebanks and Linguistic Theories*. Bergen, Norway, pages 97–102.

Carla Parra Escartín, Wessel Reijers, Teresa Lynn, Joss Moorkens, Andy Way, and Chao-Hong Liu. 2017. Ethical considerations in nlp shared tasks. In *Proceedings of the First ACL Workshop on Ethics in Natural Language Processing*. Valencia, Spain, pages 66–73. http://aclweb.org/anthology/W17-1608.

Slav Petrov, Leon Barrett, Romain Thibaux, and Dan Klein. 2006. Learning Accurate, Compact, and Interpretable Tree Annotation. In *Proceedings of the 21st International Conference on Computational Linguistics and the 44th Annual Meeting of the Association for Computational Linguistics*. Sydney, Australia, pages 433–440.

Slav Petrov and Dan Klein. 2007. Improved Inference for Unlexicalized Parsing. In *Proceedings of Human Language Technologies 2007: The Conference of the North American Chapter of the Association for Computational Linguistics*. Rochester, NY, pages 404–411.

Djamé Seddah, Reut Tsarfaty, Sandra Kübler, Marie Candito, Jinho D. Choi, Richárd Farkas, Jennifer Foster, Iakes Goenaga, Koldo Gojenola Galletebeitia, Yoav Goldberg, Spence Green, Nizar Habash, Marco Kuhlmann, Wolfgang Maier, Joakim Nivre, Adam Przepiórkowski, Ryan Roth, Wolfgang Seeker, Yannick Versley, Veronika Vincze, Marcin Woliński, Alina Wróblewska, and Eric Villemonte de la Clergerie. 2013. Overview of the SPMRL 2013 shared task: A cross-framework evaluation of parsing morphologically rich languages. In *Proceedings of the Fourth Workshop on Statistical Parsing of Morphologically-Rich Languages*. Seattle, Washington, USA, pages 146–182.

Djamé Seddah, Reut Tsarfaty, Sandra Kübler, Marie Candito, Jinho D. Choi, Richárd Farkas, Jennifer Foster, Iakes Goenaga, Koldo Gojenola Galletebeitia, Yoav Goldberg, Spence Green, Nizar Habash, Marco Kuhlmann, Wolfgang Maier, Joakim Nivre, Adam Przepiórkowski, Ryan Roth, Wolfgang Seeker, Yannick Versley, Veronika Vincze, Marcin

Woliński, Alina Wróblewska, and Eric Villemonte de la Clergerie. 2014. Overview of the SPMRL 2014 shared task on parsing morphologically rich languages. In *Notes of the SPMRL 2014 Shared Task on Parsing Morphologically-Rich Languages*. Dublin, Ireland.

Khalil Sima'an, Alon Itai, Yoad Winter, Alon Altmann, and Noa Nativ. 2001. Building a tree-bank of Modern Hebrew text. *Traitement Automatique des Langues* 42:347–380.

Heike Telljohann, Erhard W. Hinrichs, Sandra Kübler, Heike Zinsmeister, and Kathrin Beck. 2015. Stylebook for the Tübingen Treebank of Written German (TüBa-D/Z). Seminar für Sprachwissenschaft, Universität Tübingen, Germany.

Andreas van Cranenburgh and Rens Bod. 2013. Discontinuous parsing with an efficient and accurate DOP model. In *Proceedings of the International Conference on Parsing Technologies (IWPT 2013)*. Nara, Japan.

Nianwen Xue, Fei Xia, Fu-Dong Chiou, and Martha Palmer. 2005. The Penn Chinese Treebank: Phrase structure annotation of a large corpus. *Natural Language Engineering* 11(2):207—238.

Gap in pagination due to unavailable paper.

Pages 195-200

On the Stylistic Evolution from Communism to Democracy: Solomon Marcus Study Case

Anca Dinu
Faculty of Foreign Languages
and Literatures
University of Bucharest
anca_d_dinu@yahoo.com

Liviu P. Dinu
Faculty of Mathematics
and Computer Science
University of Bucharest
ldinu@fmi.unibuc.ro

Bogdan C. Dumitru
Faculty of Mathematics
and Computer Science
University of Bucharest
bogdan27182@gmail.com

Abstract

In this article we propose a stylistic analysis of Solomon Marcus' publicistics, gathered in six volumes, aiming to uncover some of his quantitative and qualitative fingerprints. Moreover, we compare and cluster two distinct periods of time in his writing style: 22 years of communist regime (1967-1989) and 27 years of democracy (1990-2016). The distributional analysis of Marcus' text reveals that the passing from the communist regime period to democracy is sharply marked by two complementary changes in Marcus' writing: in the pre-democracy period, the communist norms of writing style demanded on the one hand long phrases, long words and clichés, and on the other hand, a short list of preferred "official" topics; in democracy, the tendency was towards shorter phrases and words, while approaching a broader area of topics.

1 Introduction

Authorship attribution became an important topic in the last decade, not only in computational linguistics, but also in applied areas such as forensics, journalism, education, etc. The most common scenario is the following: given some known sample documents from a small set of candidate authors, which of them wrote a certain document with unknown authorship ? (Koppel et al., 2009; Luyckx and Daelemans, 2008) A related question is author clustering, where, given a document collection, the task is to group documents written by the same author, so that each cluster corresponds to a different author.

Marcus (1989) identifies the following four situations in which text authorship is disputed:

- A text attributed to one author seems non-homogeneous, lacking unity, which raises the suspicion that there may be more than one author. If the text was originally attributed to one author, one must establish which fragments, if any, do not belong to him, and who are their real authors.

- A text is anonymous. If the author of a text is unknown, then based on the location, time frame and cultural context, we can conjecture who the author may be and test this hypothesis.

- If based on certain circumstances, arising from literature history, the paternity is disputed between two possibilities, A and B, we have to decide if A is preferred to B, or the other way around.

- Based on literary history information, a text seems to be the result of the collaboration of two authors; an ulterior analysis should establish, for each of the two authors, their corresponding text fragments.

Authorship analysis deals with the classification of texts into classes, based on the stylistic choices of their authors. The problem of authorship identification is based on the assumption that there are stylistic features that help distinguish the real author from any other possibility. This set of stylistic features was recently defined as linguistic fingerprint (or stylome), which can be measured, is largely unconscious and is constant (van Halteren et al., 2005).

Beyond the author identification and author verification tasks, recently other tasks occurred, like author profiling, author diarization, gender and age prediction, or author masking (given a document, paraphrase it so that the original style

Proceedings of Recent Advances in Natural Language Processing, pages 201–207,
Varna, Bulgaria, Sep 4–6 2017.

does not match that of its original author, any-more.) The main conference dedicated to authorship problems (PAN) organizes yearly competitions dedicated to these tasks (Trinidad et al., 2006; Rocha et al., 2017).

In this paper, we are interested in a related topic, strongly related with the stylistic fingerprint of an author, namely if an author preserves his stylome in two different political periods of his life. To be more precise, we want to see if we can discriminate between the essays written by an author in the communist period, and the essays written by the same author in the post-communism period. As a study case, we have chosen Solomon Marcus (1925-2016), one of the most prominent scientist and man of culture of modern Romania. As a scientist, he published in an impressive range of different fields, as mathematics, computer science, mathematical and computational linguistics, semiotics, etc. Marcus published about 50 books in Romanian, English, French, German, Italian, Spanish, Russian, Greek, Hungarian, Czech, Serbo-Croatian, and about 400 research articles in specialized journals in almost all European countries. He is one of the initiators of mathematical linguistics (Marcus 1970) and of mathematical poetics (cf. Encyclopaedia Universalis (French), vol. 9, 1971, p. 1057-1059, and vol. 13, 1989, p. 837), and has been a member of the editorial board of tens of international scientific journals covering all his domains of interest. One of his most famous books is probably *Mathematical Poetics* (Marcus 1973), which pioneered the interdisciplinary field of poetics and mathematical linguistics. As a man of culture, he has written an equally impressive amount of texts, having as main topics mathematical education, culture, science, children, etc. His wide interests and complex personality have left deep imprints in Romanian scientific and cultural world. In this article we propose a stylistic analysis of his publicistics texts gathered in six volumes (Marcus, 2012-2017), aiming to uncover some of his quantitative and qualitative fingerprints, and we test if we can distinguish between the essays written in two distinct periods of time in his writing style: 22 years of communist regime and 27 years of democracy.

2 The Corpus

The whole collection of Marcus' publications is available on print, in six volumes entitled *"Răni deschise"* (Opened wounds), consisting of almost 6000 pages and 1.056.400 words and spanning over a period of a half of century. The first volume comprises 1256 pages of texts, conferences and interviews, from 2002 to 2011 (and a few published before 1990). The second volume *"Cultură sub dictatură"* (Culture under dictatorship), of 1088 pages, and the third „Depun Mărturie" (I testify), of 668 pages, are collections of texts published between 1967 and 1989. The fourth volume *"Dezmeticindu-ne"* (Awaking), of 1030 pages, contains texts from the period immediately following the Romanian Revolution (December 1989) to the year 2011. The fifth volume of the collection, entitled *"Focul și Oglinda"* (The fire and the mirror), contains 709 pages and represents texts written by Marcus in 2012. Finally, the sixth and last volume, *"Eu doar întreb"* (I just ask) contains 592 pages and is written in 2013. From its foreword by Mihai Dinu, it is apparent that the publisher house (Spandugino) is preparing a final volume, with Marcus' texts from 2014 to 2016.

The input texts where provided in pdf format. Extracting texts required manual intervention in every volume to remove noise generating areas like images, text under images, etc. For conversion, we have used pdf to text converter. The resulted text where further processed to ensure proper diacritics. Python with NLTK library was used to extract tokens, phrases and other necessary information. TreeTagger was used for POS extraction. Hyphens where extracted using Pyhpen (python module), but further refinements where necessary to ensure a proper list of hyphens. One CVS file was created for every processed volume. It contains all the raw information necessary to perform future analysis on the texts. Extracting articles written until 1989 and after was performed in a semi-automatic approach. Regular expressions where used to detect article boundaries and human input was requested for validation.

3 Stylistic Analysis

One of the first attempts to uncover the stylistic fingerprint of an author was (Mendenhall, 1901), who tried to establish the authorship of texts from Shakespeare. Mendenhall argues in favor of the fact that words distribution, by their length, represents an essential feature of the style of an author. Such measurements abounded later on, quantifying almost anything, from the length of syllables, words and phrases, to the distribution of the part of speech. While this type of measurements has its merits, clues about the stylistic fingerprint of an author should be more about the unconscious text patterns of the author, which cannot be voluntarily controlled. From this category, stop words (or grammatical words, which do not have semantic content of their own, like pronouns, quantifiers or determiners, etc.) distribution is among the most popular features used to determine the stylome of an author (Mosteller and Wallace, 1964).

Rank	Freq.	Romanian Word	English Translation
1	2540	matematică	mathematics
2	1094	știință	science
3	941	problemă	problem
4	710	științific	scientific
5	695	teorie	theory
6	604	domeniu	field
7	594	fapt	fact
8	554	exemplu	example
9	538	cercetare	research
10	538	limbaj	language
11	534	activitate	activity
12	512	cultură	culture
13	512	matematician	mathematician
14	498	trebui	must
15	476	exista	exists
16	471	parte	part
17	450	vrea	want
18	433	privi	regards
19	392	rezultat	result
20	390	românesc	Romanian

Table 1: The most frequent 20 content words in communism

3.1 A Quantitative Analysis of Linguistic Objects

To analyze Marcus' style, we first gather quantitative evidence: the six volumes have all together 1.056.400 words, 50.596 sentences and 2.226.621 syllables. Thus, the texts yield an average of 20.8 words per sentence and of 2.1 syllables per word. Second, since the six volumes are chronologically ordered, we investigated the possibility that the texts differ in their style, before and after the fall of the communist regime. The two volumes written in the communist period (the second and the third volume) have a clear preference for longer

constructions: the average of number of words per sentence is 23.54 for the second volume and 24.95 for the third. Expectedly, the average for the rest of the volumes, written in democracy is sensibly lower, of around 20 words per sentence (even 18.2 for the fifth volume). Also, the same tendency occurs for the length of words: the communist period reveals a mean of 2.23 syllables per word for the second volume and of 2.24 syllables per word for the third, whilst the post-communist texts present a lower average of 2.01 syllables per word. Thirdly, we had a look at the way Marcus made use of the parts of speech in his texts from *"Răni Deschise"*. Thus, the distribution of the main parts of speech (verbs, nouns and adjectives) in Marcus' texts is as follows: 157.008 verbs, 309.613 nouns and 97.935 adjectives in all of the six volumes. It follows that Marcus used in average almost 3 verbs per sentence, 6.11 nouns per sentence and a much lower number of adjectives, which have a mean of fewer than 2 per sentence (1.93). Did Marcus make different use of the three categories of parts of speech in communism and democracy? The verbs distribution is rather the same over the two periods: about 3 verbs per sentence. However, the nouns and the adjectives present significant fluctuations. Thus, the average of adjectives per sentence from the second and third volumes, written in the communist period, is 2.64 and 2.82, respectively and the average of nouns per sentence is 7.75 and 7.68, respectively. As one can see, all of these values are homogenous and over the mean of the whole texts in the six volumes by almost one unit. On the contrary, the means of the adjective and nouns per sentence from the volumes written after 1989 are visibly lower than both the general mean and the mean from the communist period, as it follows: the average of adjectives (and nouns) per sentence, for the volumes one, four, five and six are, in this order: 1.64 (5.59), 1.85 (5.96), 1.41 (4.91) and 1.67 (5.51). Clearly, Marcus' appetite for nouns and adjectives diminished after the fall of the communism. It is already transparent that there is an obvious difference between the way Marcus wrote before and after the fall of communism.

3.2 Functional Words

But the preference for long words and phrases, and for more nouns and adjectives during the communist regime, might well have been voluntary, ac-

Rank	Freq.	Romanian Word	English Translation
1	3679	matematică	mathematics
2	2341	lucru	thing
3	1937	avea	have
4	1911	trebui	must
5	1686	spune	say
6	1592	știință	science
7	1504	vedea	see
8	1493	profesor	professor
9	1425	fapt	fact
10	1412	lume	world
11	1379	școală	school
12	1258	problemă	problem
13	1251	elev	student
14	1224	exista	exist
15	1218	cultură	culture
16	1188	viață	life
17	1156	vrea	want
18	1106	parte	part
19	1103	om	human
20	1098	educație	education

Table 2: The most frequent 20 content words in democracy

cording to the need to conform to the regime's norms, as well as the choice of the content words or topics.

What about the involuntary fingerprint of the two distinct periods? Was Marcus' style affected in depth? To answer this question, we resort to one of the most commonly accepted indicators of personal style of an author, namely the distribution of grammatical (functional) words, such as pronouns, determiners, prepositions, etc. Such lists of stop words were used for authorship attribution of texts with controversial paternity. We use here the list of 120 functional Romanian words (Dinu et al., 2012).

The first 15 functional words used by Marcus (and their raw frequencies) in all of the six volumes are the following: *în* (in 31.160) , *un* (a 29.411), *avea* (have 29.261), *fi* (be 28.223), *și* (and 27.486), *al* (of 17.851), *care* (which 17.229), *el* (he 16.906), *la* (at 16.088), *să* (to 14.591), *nu* (no 13.397), *ca* (that 11.202), *cu* (with 10.405), *mai* (more 9.503), *pe* (on 9.442).

For the communist period the first functional words are in volume 2: *un* (6206), *în* (6027), *și* (5408), *fi* (4519), *al* (4504), *avea* (4426), *care*

(2977), *el* (2906), *la* (2697), *cu* (2003), *mai* (1968), *nu* (1965), *să* (1834), *acest* (1553), *din* (from 1471); and in volume 3: *în* (3683), *un* (3610), *și* (3164), *fi* (2689), *al* (2542), *avea* (2304), *care* (1683), *el* (1578), *la* (1395), *mai* (1171), *cu* (1128), *nu* (1084), *să* (1024), *acest* (this 923), *că* (849).

One instantly notices that the second and the third volume, both written in the communist period, have almost identical stop word lists, with only two exceptions: in volume two the first two words are *un* (a) and *în* (in), while in volume three the order is reversed, but with a very small difference in frequency; also, the same thing happens with the words in positions 10 and 11, *cu* (with) and *mai* (more).

The post-communism volumes (1, 4, 5 and 6) are also very similar within the group with regard to the ranking of the stop words and they definitely differ in this respect from the other two volumes. We only give here the stop word lists for two of them, the rest being similar. The list of the first 15 stop words for the first volume is: *avea, fi, în, un, și, el, la, care, să, al, nu, că, pe, cu, mai;* and for the fifth is: *avea, în, fi, un, și, să, care, el, la, nu, al, că, pe, cu, acest.*

This natural grouping is confirmed by analyzing the similarity of the six rankings. The computation of the exact distance between any two of the stop words ranking revealed quite small values for the distance between the two volumes written before 1989, and a neat clustering in one group of the other volumes. To this end, it seems that even a scientist and a man of culture of Marcus' amplitude was subject to both voluntary and involuntary differences in writing style in communism versus democracy periods.

3.3 Clustering Experiments

We want to confirm the above global intuitions on randomly selected short texts. We have chosen 23 texts written before 1989 and an equal number of texts written between 2000 and 2013. We have extracted from each text a 120 functional words frequency list, ranked them by their frequency, and computed the distance between the obtained rankings. The distance we have chosen is rank distance (Dinu, 2003; Popescu and Dinu, 2008), an ordinal distance which was successfully used also in other problems of authorship (Dinu et al., 2008, 2012). One proper way to test the virtues of a dis-

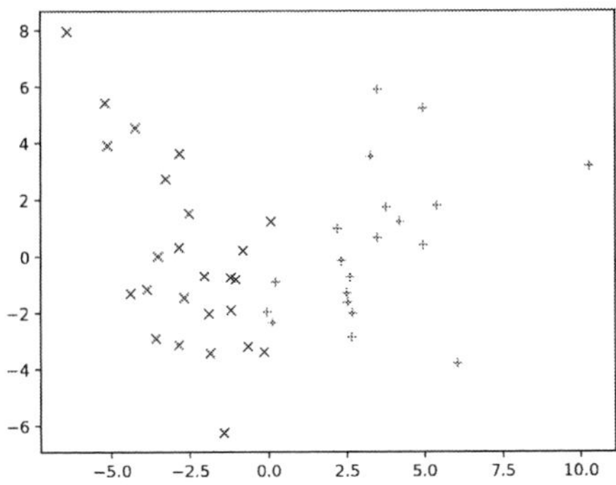

Figure 1: Clustering of random Marcus' texts from two distinct periods

tance measure is to use it as a base for a clustering algorithm (Duda et al., 2001). For our purposes, we applied a k-means clustering algorithm with k=2, corresponding to the two possible classes of texts: written before 1989 (in communism), and after 1989 (democracy). The results are plotted in figure 1, where by + we marked the texts written in communism period and by x the ones written in democracy.

One can clearly notice that out of the 46 texts, all 23 written after 1989 form a well separated group. For the other 23, 20 of them form a distinct cluster, while the remaining 3 marginally group with the texts written in democracy. Interestingly, those 3 texts were written immediately before the fall of the communism (one in 1988 and two in 1989). Could it be that professor Marcus understood it was the right time for the change?! This wouldn't be a surprise for those who knew him.

What is remarkable about this analysis is that the functional words were unconsciously used by the author in a different way in communism than in democracy period, and that we can distinguish the texts written in communism by an author on the base of such analysis.

4 Semantic Analysis

We also addressed some aspects of the distribution of the topics that Marcus tackled in his texts from *"Rani Deschise"*. To gain insight about the text content and his preferred topics, we employed the distribution of the content words. Since the texts are naturally divided in two periods (communism and democracy), an analysis of differences in se-

mantic content and topics between the two periods is compelling.

Rank	Keyness Value	Romanian Word	English translation
1	1949	matematică	mathematics
2	1264	problemă	problem
3	1101	ştiinţă	science
4	1010	teorie	theory
5	980	ştiinţific	scientific
6	839	privi	look
7	780	vrea	want
8	746	exista	exist
9	701	diferit	different
10	694	domeniu	domain
11	666	carte	book
12	630	asa-zis	so called
13	624	trebui	must
14	619	limbaj	language
15	611	românesc	Romanian
16	541	fapt	fact
17	531	numara	count
18	518	cercetare	research
19	508	matematician	mathematician
20	501	situatie	situation

Table 3: Keywords from *"Răni Deschise"* in communism

We have seen that, in what the length of the words and phrases and the distribution of parts of speech are concerned, the two periods clearly differ from one another, the traces of the omnipresent plethoric style of the communist period being present in detectable quantities in Marcus' text.

We performed a statistical analysis on Marcus' texts, using AntConc, a concordance tool made by Laurence Anthony, available as open source at www.laurenceanthony.net.

In a pre-processing step, we first obtained a word frequency list for each of the two periods. Because the words we are interested in are content words (words that have a semantic content of their own), the stop words were being excluded from the counting. Also, we lemmatized the corpus and we collapsed all words which have the same lemma into the same word.

Since Romanian is a highly inflectional language, this had the effect of dramatically reducing the word types. Thus, a word family such as *matematică, matematici, matematica, matemati-*

Rank	Keyness Value	Romanian Word	English translation
1	2215	lucru	thing
2	1887	trebui	must
3	1828	avea	have
4	1686	spune	say
5	1401	profesor	teacher
6	1349	scoală	school
7	1348	matematică	mathematics
8	1312	asa-zis	so called
9	1305	vrea	want
10	1297	vedea	see
11	1282	exista	exist
12	1280	elev	student
13	1257	educatie	education
14	1180	lume	world
15	1160	stii	know
16	1155	viată	life
17	1150	copil	child
18	1089	tv. romana	romanian tv
19	1022	afla	find out
20	996	intelege	understand

Table 4: Keywords from *"Răni Deschise"* in democracy

cile, matematicii, matematicilor, etc. (mathematics singular, mathematics plural, the mathematics singular, the mathematics plural, mathematics singular genitive, mathematics plural genitive, etc.) was conflated into a single word, *matematică*.

In table 1 and table 2 we give the first 20 most frequent words from both periods (the complete list of words is at http://nlp.unibuc.ro/resources/sm.pdf). One can see that Marcus' favorite topics in the texts from the communist period revolve around mathematics, research, science and culture, while the texts written in democracy target more areas of education (teacher, school, education, etc.).

Such frequency content word lists are quite transparent w.r.t Marcus's favorite topics (mathematics, language, teaching, education, etc.). A more in depth analysis is needed to detect differences between the topics addressed during the two periods. Thus, in a preliminarry analyses we give here a comparative report of the word usage in the texts from the two periods. We generated a keyword list, based on the keyness values for each word. A keyword list is a list of words which are unusually frequent in the texts, as compared with a reference corpus. We have generated a keyword list for both possible cases: one for the communist period, with the democracy texts as reference corpus and one for the democracy period, with the communist period texts as reference corpus. This time, we did not exclude the stop words, since the difference in use of both stop and content words from the two distinct writing periods might prove to be of interest. The key word generation method we have used is log likelihood. The keywords list was sorted by the keyness value, which is an indication of a preference for using a word in the corpus, as compared to the reference corpus. A statistically significant value of keyness, taken from a table of statistical values is 3.9 for a 5use of a word, as compared to the use of that word in a reference corpus. The bigger the value, the more significant the preference is. The keyness values of the keywords from the communist period texts, considering the democracy texts as reference corpus, start from a very high value of 1949 and for the democracy text, considering the communism texts as reference corpus, from 2215. This is a clear indication of an important semantic difference between the content of the texts from the two periods. In table 3 and 4, we give some of the most relevant words that have significant keyness values for both cases. Interestingly enough, he only speaks about the communism during the democracy period.

5 Conclusions

The distributional analysis of Marcus' text uncovers that the passing from the communist regime period to democracy is sharply marked by two complementary changes in Marcus' texts.

In the pre-democracy period, the communist norms of writing style demanded on the one hand long phrases, long words and clichés, and on the other hand a short list of preferred 'official' topics. On the contrary, in democracy, Marcus shortened the phrases and words (naturally becoming more concise) and approached a broader area of topics.

The clustering approach based on the preference of the author regarding the functional words shows that the functional words were unconsciously used by the author in a different way in communism than in democracy period, and they can be used to discriminate between the communist and post-communist texts of a given author.

In future works we plan to investigate more Romanian authors and to test the above hypothesis also for other languages.

6 Acknowledgements

Research supported by HerCoRe project, funded by Volkswagen Foundation (Project no. 91970).

References

Liviu P. Dinu. 2003. On the classification and aggregation of hierarchies with ifferent constitutive elements. *Fundamenta Informaticae 55.1* pages 39–50.

Liviu P. Dinu, Vlad Niculae, and Octavia-Maria Şulea. 2012. Pastiche detection based on stopword rankings: exposing impersonators of a romanian writer. *Proc. of the Workshop on Computational Approaches to Deception Detection. Association for Computational Linguistics* pages 72–77.

Liviu P Dinu, Marius Popescu, and Anca Dinu. 2008. Authorship identification of romanian texts with controversial paternity. *LREC 2008* pages 3392–3397.

R. O. Duda, P. E. Hart, and D. G. Stork. 2001. Wiley-Interscience Publication.

Moshe Koppel, Jonathan Schler, and Shlomo Argamon. 2009. Computational methods in authorship attribution. *Journal of the Association for Information Science and Technology* 60(1):9–26.

Kim Luyckx and Walter Daelemans. 2008. Authorship attribution and verification with many authors and limited data. In *Proceedings of the 22Nd International Conference on Computational Linguistics - Volume 1*. Association for Computational Linguistics, Stroudsburg, PA, USA, COLING '08, pages 513–520. http://dl.acm.org/citation.cfm?id=1599081.1599146.

Solomon Marcus. 1973. *Mathematische Poetik*. Ed. Academiei, Bucureşti-Athenaum Verlag, Frankfurt am Main.

Solomon Marcus. 1989. *Inventie si descoperire*. Ed. Cartea Romaneasca.

Solomon Marcus. 2012-2017. *Rani deschise (6 volumes)*. Ed. Spandugino.

Solomon Marcus, Ed. Nicolau, and S. Stati. 1970. *Introduzione alla linguistica matematica*. Casa editrice Riccardo Patron.

TC Mendenhall. 1901. *A mechanical solution of a literary problem*.

Frederick Mosteller and David Wallace. 1964. *Inference and disputed authorship: The Federalist*. Addison-Wesley, Massachusetts.

Marius Popescu and Liviu P. Dinu. 2008. Rank distance as a stylistic similarity. *COLING 2008* pages 91–94.

Anderson Rocha, Walter J. Scheirer, Christopher W. Forstall, Thiago Cavalcante, Antonio Theophilo, Bingyu Shen, Ariadne Carvalho, and Efstathios Stamatatos. 2017. Authorship attribution for social media forensics. *IEEE Trans. Information Forensics and Security* 12(1):5–33. https://doi.org/10.1109/TIFS.2016.2603960.

José Francisco Martínez Trinidad, Jesús Ariel Carrasco-Ochoa, and Josef Kittler, editors. 2006. *Progress in Pattern Recognition, Image Analysis and Applications, 11th Iberoamerican Congress in Pattern Recognition, CIARP 2006, Cancun, Mexico, November 14-17, 2006, Proceedings*, volume 4225 of *Lecture Notes in Computer Science*. Springer. https://doi.org/10.1007/11892755.

Hans van Halteren, R. Harald Baayen, Fiona J. Tweedie, Marco Haverkort, and Anneke Neijt. 2005. New machine learning methods demonstrate the existence of a human stylome. *Journal of Quantitative Linguistics* pages 65—77.

Building timelines of soccer matches from Twitter

Amosse Edouard
Université Côte d'Azur
Inria, CNRS, I3S, France
amosse.edouard@unice.fr

Elena Cabrio
Université Côte d'Azur
Inria, CNRS, I3S, France
elena.cabrio@unice.fr

Sara Tonelli
Fondazione Bruno Kessler
Trento, Italia
satonelli@fbk.eu

Nhan Le-Thanh
Université Côte d'Azur
Inria, CNRS, I3S, France
nhan.le-thanh@unice.fr

Abstract

This demo paper presents a system that builds a timeline with salient actions of a soccer game, based on the tweets posted by users. It combines information provided by external knowledge bases to enrich the content of tweets and applies graph theory to model relations between actions (e.g. goals, penalties) and participants of a game (e.g. players, teams). In the demo, a web application displays in nearly real-time the actions detected from tweets posted by users for a given match of Euro 2016. Our tools are freely available at https://bitbucket.org/eamosse/event_tracking.

1 Introduction

In the latest years, social media platforms have become a popular communication channel, thanks to their coverage and speed, which allow users to follow and comment events in real time. In particular, the need to monitor, categorize and organize information is very relevant during large sports events like the Olympic Games or FIFA World Cup, since several matches take place in a limited time span, sometimes in parallel. While summaries are usually made by journalists during the matches, user-generated content from microblogs can be used for the same purpose by building complete summaries of sports games from tweets. For example, Nichols et al. (2012) and Xu et al. (2013) present simple approaches based on the observation of peaks in the tweets' volume. Even though these works can effectively detect the most salient actions in games (e.g. goals), they fail to capture actions that do not generate high volumes of

tweets (e.g. shoots). To address this issue, we propose an algorithm to build a timeline with salient actions in sports games based on the tweets posted by users (Edouard et al., 2017). We combine information provided by external knowledge bases to enrich the content of the tweets and apply graph theory to model relations between actions (e.g. goal, penalties) and participants of a game (e.g. players, teams).

In this paper, we present the system built on top of such approach, resulting in a web-based application that displays a fine-grained, real-time summary of sub-events occurring in a soccer game based on the content of tweets, combined with information from external knowledge bases. In the remainder of the paper, we first describe the server component for real-time tweet processing (Section 2) and then the client component, displaying timelines to final users (Section 3).

2 The server component

The server component pipeline is displayed in Figure 1. It consists of the following components: tweet collection and preprocessing, Named Entity Recognition (NER) and timeline generation.

2.1 Tweet collection

The server component is configured to extract tweets either from the Twitter stream or from a local database. In both cases, it requires the names of the opposing teams to be provided (e.g. England VS Wales). To retrieve tweets from Twitter, we provide as query parameters to the Twitter streaming API a set of keywords, that are generated from the names of the teams. Soccer fans tend to use their teams standard abbreviation (e.g. ENG or WAL) more often than full names of the teams

Proceedings of Recent Advances in Natural Language Processing, pages 208–213,
Varna, Bulgaria, Sep 4–6 2017.

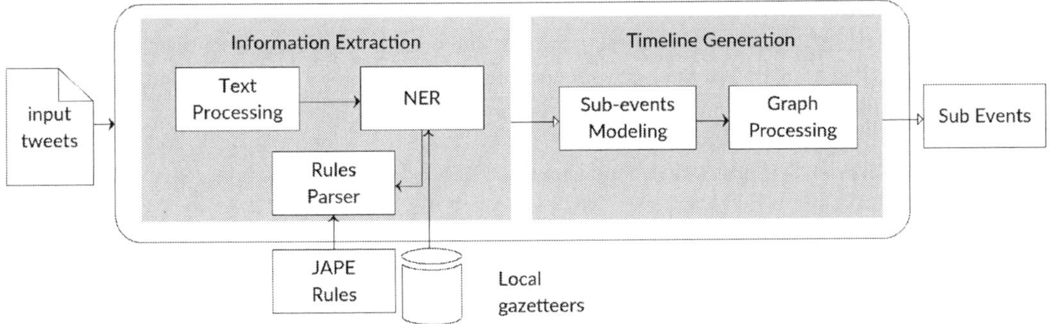

Figure 1: Server component pipeline in which data is flowing in the sense of the arrows. The input are tweets coming from Twitter stream or from a local database and the output is the sub-events detected from the input tweets.

(e.g. England, Wales). Based on this observation, we define heuristic rules to create keywords using different versions and combinations of the team names. For example eng, wal, engwal, waleng were used to query tweets related to the match between England and Wales. Furthermore, the keywords can be also enriched with other terms such as the competition (e.g. euro, euro2016) or soccer actions (e.g. goal).

2.2 Information Extraction Module

After retrieving the tweets, the pipeline extracts the participants and actions mentioned in the tweet, and sets relations between them. In the case of soccer, actions are defined by the Fédération Internationale de Football Association (FIFA). Table 1 shows the complete list of soccer actions detected in the current implementation of the system. Participants are players or teams who are involved in the actions. These information are extracted based on the following steps.

Tweet preprocessing. Input tweets are preprocessed in order to remove noise and redundant information similar to (Edouard et al., 2017). We clean the input tweets in order to remove repetitive characters (e.g. goooooaaaalll), emoticons or URL mentions. Manual inspection suggests that re-tweets are usually observed a few minutes after the original tweets have been sent. Thus, for the specific task of detecting real-time actions in soccer games, we make the assumption that re-tweets are not relevant to the actions reported in a current time window in our processing phase. Note that we do not perform stop words removal, since they are useful for determining relationships

between actions and participants (see Listing 1).

```
Rule: involved_in
Priority: 20
(
    {Lookup.minorType == "foot_action"}
    {Token.category == "IN"}*
    {Lookup.minorType == "football\_player"}

): participate
```

Listing 1: JAPE rule to detect relationship between actions and participants in tweets exploiting preposition and subordinating conjunctions.

NER module. For detecting mentions of actions and participants in tweets, we rely on GATE (Cunningham et al., 2002), because it includes a highly flexible NER tool that allows the integration of custom gazetteers. Indeed, in order to detect *actions*, we update its gazetteer based on the Sports Markup Language (Council, 2017), a controlled vocabulary used to describe sports events. SportsML core schema provides concepts allowing the description of events for 11 major sports including Soccer, American football, Basketball or Tennis. For soccer games, we extract actions such as goals, substitutions, yellow/red cards and penalties. Furthermore, we enrich the list of actions with synonyms extracted from Wordnet (Fellbaum, 1998).

For *participants*, we use football-data API[1] that, given a soccer game in input, returns the name of the teams and the players in each team. We employ a set of hand-crafted rules to define different mentions of players' and teams' names in tweets. For instance "giroud", "oliviergiroud" or "olivier_giroud" are considered as mentions

---

[1] http://api.football-data.org

Event	Description	Participants involved
D1P, D2P	Beginning of the first or second period	Both opponent teams
F1P, F2P	End of the first or second period	Both opponent teams
TIR	Shoot, goal attempt, blocked...	1 player
BUT	Goal, score	1 player
CGT	Substitution, replacement	2 players
CJA	Yellow card	1 player
CRO	Red card	1 player

Table 1: Set of actions detected by the system.

to "Oliver Giroud", a striker of the French national team. Finally, we update the GATE's local gazetteer with actions and participants according to the game.

We initialize GATE with the custom gazetteers and use its in-built NER to identify mentions of actions and participants in the tweets. Whenever actions and participants occur in the same tweet, we extract them and connect them through a link in a graph. Furthermore, we set additional links using JAPE (Java Annotation Pattern Engine) rules, a GATE-specific format to define regular expressions needed for pattern matching. As an example, we report in Listing 1 the JAPE rule matching all tokens whose type is "foot_action" and "football_player", separated by any preposition or subordinating conjunction, all matching patterns are labeled as a "participate".

2.3 Timeline generation

The output of the NER component is a list of quadruples $\langle a, p, t, \omega \rangle$, where a is a soccer action, p the participants, t the timestamp of the tweet and ω is the weight whose value is either $= 2$ if the relation is extracted from JAPE rules or $= 1$, otherwise. Next, the extracted entities are modeled in a temporal event graph. Specifically, we split the game in fixed time windows (e.g. 2 minutes), and create an event graph that models the relationships between actions and participants, represented by nodes, for each time window. The edges connecting two nodes correspond to the retrieved links, whose weight is increased every time a relation is found in a tweet.

At this stage, the weighted relations between actions and participants are considered as sub-event candidates. In a further step, we select the events (i.e. relations between actions and participants) that are to be included in a timeline by retaining those that are above an adaptive threshold. The thresholds are tuned by taking into account both the type of the action and the popularity of the teams involved in the game using Kreyszig standard score formula (Kreyszig, 2007). The detailed description of the algorithm, and its evaluation is presented in (Edouard et al., 2017). The output of the server component is thus a timeline where the extracted actions and participants are connected and temporally ordered.

2.4 Technical implementation

We implement the server component in the Java programming language. As local database, we use MongoDB[2] to store tweets and Twitter4J[3] to collect tweets from the Twitter streaming API.[4] We use the JGraph library (Naveh et al., 2008) to generate and process the event-graph. The server component also includes a socket listener allowing bidirectional communication between the server and the client component.

3 The client component: the web demo

The goal of the client component is two-fold. On the one hand, it displays the timelines containing the salient actions in the match and the statistics related to the selected soccer game (e.g. the current score, the ball possession). On the other hand, it allows users to modify the empirical threshold for the actions included in football games (see details below).

The client component is built as a web application with HTML5, CSS3 and Java Script libraries such as angularJS.[5] Data between the client and the server are exchanged using web socket. The web interface is inspired by the website of

---

[2]https://www.mongodb.com/
[3]http://twitter4j.org/en/index.html
[4]https://dev.twitter.com/streaming/overview
[5]Angular JS https://angularjs.org/

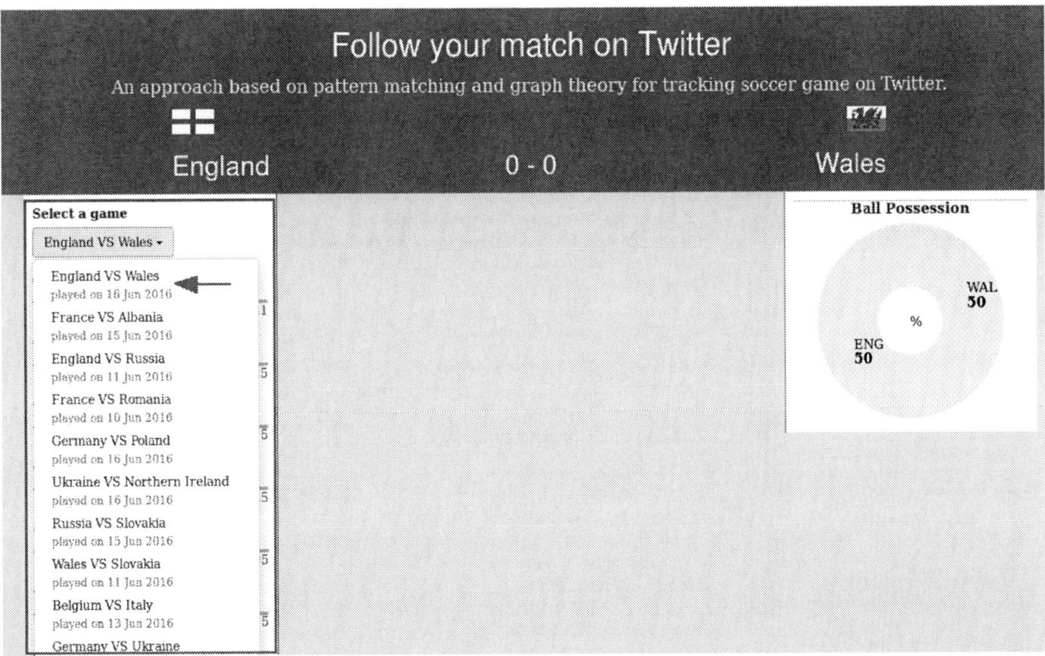

Figure 2: Screenshot of the web demo. To start, the user can select from a list the matches he wishes to track (for demo purposes, the list contains the matches from the first stage of the Euro 2016 championship.

The Guardian[6] describing soccer matches in real time. However, while the list of salient actions in The Guardian is manually compiled by journalists, our goal is to show that this can be automatized through our processing pipeline based solely on tweets.

End users can define different values from the client side: they can select a match and set the algorithm parameters, such as the frequency threshold, to retrieve the actions. Then, the server processes the tweets every two minutes (i.e the time-window) and notifies the clients when salient events are detected in the tweets.

In order to better describe the different demo components, we mark in the screenshot of the web platform (see Figure 3) its five main blocks: *i)* game selection, *ii)* threshold settings for actions selection, *iii)* ball possession, *iv)* salient actions, and *v)* updated score of the match.

Game Selection. For the purpose of the demo, the stream of tweets comes from a local database containing the tweets related to 24 games of the first stage of the Euro 2016 championship.[7] In the current implementation, the server can track

one game at a time, which can be selected from the list at the top of the left panel (see Figure 2 for the game selection list, and partition 1, Figure 3). Example matches are Switzerland-Albania or England-Wales.

Action thresholds. As introduced before, the action threshold is the minimal confidence value used by our algorithm to include or discard actions reported in tweets. The action threshold are automatically adapted according to the popularity of the game (i.e the more a game is discussed in tweets, the higher the thresholds and conversely). The lower the confidence, the smaller the number of tweets reporting a certain action on which the algorithm relies in order to add such action to the timeline (i.e. a lower threshold generates a higher number of actions in the timeline, detected with a lower confidence score). Conversely, the higher the threshold, the more confident the algorithm is (but less actions appear in the timeline). For each action, the user can easily modify the thresholds using the range sliders. Thus, the end user can adapt the different empirical values for the thresholds as needed.

---

[6]`https://goo.gl/MWc6dN`
[7]https://github.com/HackaTAL/2016/tree/master/Tweets

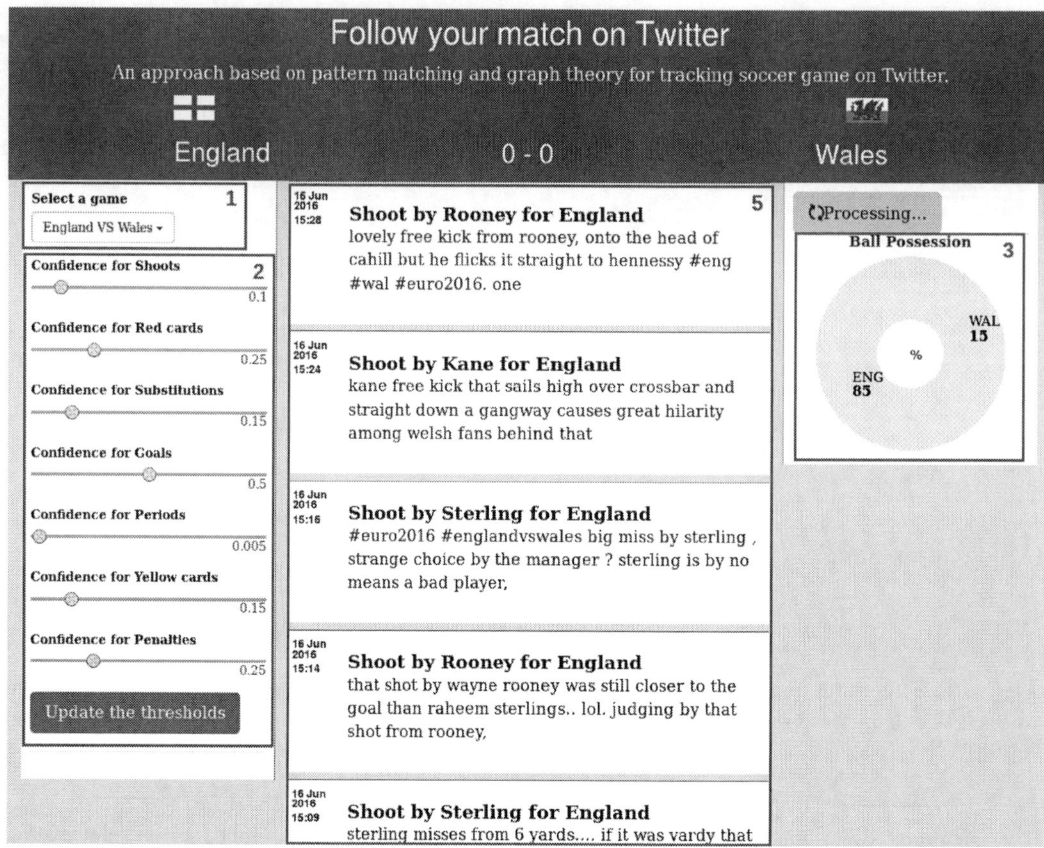

Figure 3: Screenshot of the timeline generated for the soccer game between England and Wales during the first stage of the Euro 2016 championship. The screenshot contains five main blocks : *i)* game selection, *ii)* threshold settings for actions selection, *iii)* ball possession, *iv)* salient actions, and *v)* updated score of the match

Ball possession. This functionality displays the ball possession for each team during a soccer game, i.e. the amount of time a team possesses the ball during a match, expressed as a percentage. To calculate that, we consider the amount of tweets describing actions of a certain team during a time window, i.e. the fact that a team or a player is mentioned in a tweet increases the ball possession score for that team. Ball possession is displayed as a pie chart at the bottom of the page and constantly updated (partition 3, Figure 3). The percentages of ball possession we obtain are very close to those reported by sports media. For instance, at the end of the England vs Wales match, The Guardian [8] reports 64/36 as the ratio of ball possession of the two teams, while we obtain a very similar ratio of 69/31.

Current score The panel at the top of the web page (partition 4, Figure 3) displays the current score of the match, as well as the scorers. When a player scores a goal, the match score is updated and the player name is displayed under the team he scored for, together with the time (see Figure 4). We retrieve the current score of the game from the tweets.

Salient actions. Actions detected in the tweets are displayed in a reversed chronological order to the end user (partition 5, Figure 3). For each action, its type (e.g. goal), the participants (e.g. Gareth Bale, Wales) and the time (e.g. 44 min) are provided. In addition, when an event is confirmed by our approach, we retrieve the content of the tweets that were used to detect this event and apply the approach proposed by (Mihalcea and Tarau, 2004) to produce a summary of the event. For instance, for the action "Shoot by Ram-

---

[8]E.g. `https://goo.gl/MWc6dN` Actions there are manually reported by sports journalists.

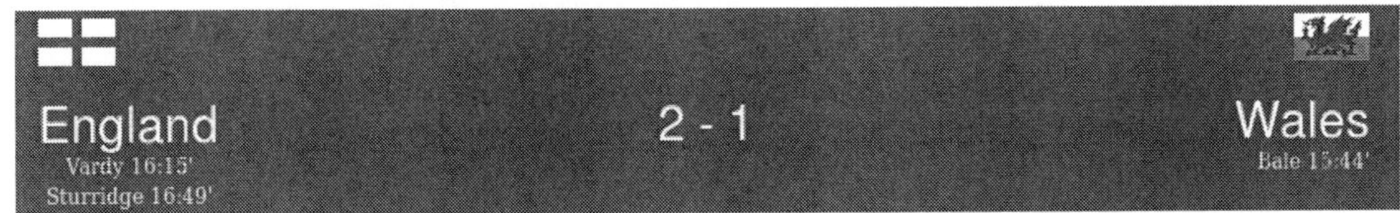

Figure 4: The score is constantly updated, and the players' name are added below the teams for which they score.

sey for Wales", we provide the following textual paragraph extracted from the tweets, also to show the supporters reaction to a certain action: *"aaron ramsey is by far a better player when he's playing for wales than arsenal #euro2016. aaronramsey ramsey shot from range"*. Or, for the action "Half time! England 2 - 1 Wales", we display *"i hope that's a blessing in disguise, now hodgson has to make a change at half time #engwal #euro2016 #optimistic"*.

3.1 Conference demo session

A video presenting the above described demo can be found at the following address: `https://goo.gl/EsI8Db`. During the demo session at the conference, participants are invited to test the different components of the web application live: they can select a game from the list of soccer games, click on "Start tracking the game", and experience with the creation of the timeline reporting the salient actions in the selected game. They are also invited to tune the threshold parameters, and compare the obtained results.

References

International Press Telecommunications Council. 2017. SportsML: A solution for sharing sports data. `https://iptc.org/standards/sportsml-g2/`. [Accessed 03-01-2017].

Hamish Cunningham, Diana Maynard, Kalina Bontcheva, and Valentin Tablan. 2002. GATE: A Framework and Graphical Development Environment for Robust NLP Tools and Applications. In *Proceedings of the 40th Anniversary Meeting of the Association for Computational Linguistics (ACL'02)*.

Amosse Edouard, Elena Cabrio, Sara Tonelli, and Le Thanh Nhan. 2017. You'll never tweet alone - building sports match timelines from microblog posts. In *Proceedings of RANLP 2017 - Recent Advances in Natural Language Processing conference*.

C. Fellbaum. 1998. *WordNet. An Electronic Lexical Database*. MIT Press.

Erwin Kreyszig. 2007. *Advanced engineering mathematics*. John Wiley & Sons.

Rada Mihalcea and Paul Tarau. 2004. Textrank: Bringing order into texts. Association for Computational Linguistics.

Barak Naveh et al. 2008. Jgrapht. *Internet: http://jgrapht.sourceforge.net* .

Jeffrey Nichols, Jalal Mahmud, and Clemens Drews. 2012. Summarizing sporting events using twitter. In *Proceedings of the 2012 ACM international conference on Intelligent User Interfaces*. ACM, pages 189–198.

Wei Xu, Ralph Grishman, Adam Meyers, and Alan Ritter. 2013. A preliminary study of tweet summarization using information extraction. *NAACL 2013* page 20.

You'll Never Tweet Alone
Building Sports Match Timelines from Microblog Posts

Amosse Edouard
Université Côte d'Azur,
Inria, CNRS, I3S, France
amosse.edouard@unice.fr

Elena Cabrio
Université Côte d'Azur,
Inria, CNRS, I3S, France
elena.cabrio@unice.fr

Sara Tonelli
Fondazione Bruno Kessler
Trento, Italy
satonelli@fbk.eu

Nhan Le-Thanh
Université Côte d'Azur,
Inria, CNRS, I3S, France
nhan.le-thanh@unice.fr

Abstract

In this paper, we propose an approach to build a timeline with actions in a sports game based on tweets. We combine information provided by external knowledge bases to enrich the content of the tweets, and apply graph theory to model relations between actions and participants in a game. We demonstrate the validity of our approach using tweets collected during the EURO 2016 Championship and evaluate the output against live summaries produced by sports channels.

1 Introduction

Historically, sports fans have watched matches either at the stadium or on TV, or have listened to them on the radio. In the latest years, however, social media platforms have become a new communication channel also to share information and comment on sports events, thus creating online communities of sports fans. Microblogs are particularly suitable, thanks to their coverage and speed, making them a successful channel to follow and comment on events in real time. Also sports teams and medias have benefited from these platforms to extend their contact networks, increase their popularity and exchange information with fans (Gibbs and Haynes, 2013; Özsoy, 2011). The need to monitor and organize such information is particularly relevant during big events like the Olympic Games or FIFA World Cup: several matches take place in a limited time span, sometimes in parallel, and summaries are manually made by journalists. A few approaches have recently tried to automa-

tize this task by recognizing actions in multimedia data (Hannon et al., 2011; Snoek et al., 2003; Snoek and Worring, 2005).

In this work, we investigate whether the same task can be performed relying only on user-generated content from microblogs. In fact, opinions shared by fans during sports matches are usually reactions to what is happening in the game, implicitly conveying information on the ongoing events. Existing works aimed at building complete summaries of sports games from tweets (Nichols et al., 2012; Xu et al., 2013) rely on the observation of peaks in the tweets' volume. Even though such approaches effectively detect the most salient actions in games (e.g. goals), they fail to capture actions that are not reported by many users (e.g. shoots). Moreover, they focus only on specific information: for example, Löchtefeld et al. (2015) and Alonso and Shiells (2013) are respectively interested in detecting in soccer games goals, yellow and red cards, and in detecting time and keywords, ignoring the players involved in the actions.

In this paper we perform a more complex task: we create a fine-grained, real-time summary of the sub-events occurring in sports games using tweets. We define a sub-event in a match as an action that involves one or many participants (e.g. a player, a team) at a given time, as proposed by Dou et al.. More specifically, we want to address the following research questions: *i) Is it possible to build detailed sports games summaries in a unsupervised fashion, relying only on a controlled vocabulary?*, and *ii) To what extent can Twitter be used to build a complete timeline of a game? Is information retrieved via Twitter reliable and sufficient?*

Proceedings of Recent Advances in Natural Language Processing, pages 214–221,
Varna, Bulgaria, Sep 4–6 2017.

2   Related Work

Most of the works that analyze the content of tweets for tracking sport events are based on spike detection on the stream of messages, to detect sub-events. To summarize event streams, Nichols et al. (2012) propose a method that identifies spikes in Twitter feed and selects tweets from a sub-event by scoring each of them based on phrase graph (Sharifi et al., 2010). This method may produce unexpected summary if most of the tweets published during the spike are not related to the sub-event. Kubo et al. (2013) generate live sports summary by prioritizing tweets published by good reporters. First, they identify spikes in the stream of an event as indicators of sub-events, and then the system tries to generate a summary by measuring the explanatory of the tweet by the presence of player's names, team names and terms related to the event. Similarly, when a spike is detected, Alonso and Shiells (2013) analyze the tweets published during the period to identify the most frequent terms which they use to describe spikes in a tweets' histograms (spikes are considered as sub-events). To summarize tweets on football, Jai-Andaloussi et al. (2015) create event clusters with similar documents, that are then automatically classified as relevant to football actions.

In the case of sports games, spikes do not necessarily characterize a sub-event. For example, when the crowd disagrees with the referees or a player, emotional tweets to express disagreement are published. On the other hand, actions with low importance (e.g. a shoot) or actions produced by non-popular teams or players (e.g. Albania) may not produce peaks in the volume of tweets. Thus, approaches solely based on spikes detection are unable to capture those actions. In our approach, we rely on Named Entities (NEs) to identify whether or not a tweet is related to a sports event. Besides, we rely on an adaptive threshold tuned according to the actions and the team (or player) of interest to evaluate whether or not the actions should be added to the timeline.

3   Proposed Approach

Although the approach we propose to detect sub-events in sports games and to build a timeline (Fig. 1) is general-purpose, we take as an example soccer games, so that we can use a consistent terminology. The pipeline can be applied to any sports as long as it is represented in the Sports Markup Language (Council, 2017).

First, a module for information extraction identifies actions (e.g. goals, penalties) and participants (e.g. player's names, teams) mentioned in tweets, setting relations between them (see examples in Table 1). Then, participants, actions and relations are modeled together in a temporal event-graph, taking into account also the time of the tweet. This leads to the creation of a timeline where actions and participants are connected and temporally ordered. The modules of this pipeline are described in detail in the following sections.

Tweets	Action	Particip.
kick off.... #engwal #euro2016 #teamengland	D1P	england wales
how has ramsey not got a yellow card yet every attempt to tackle has been a foul.	CJA	ramsey wales
goaaaaaaaaaaaal from bale woah #eng 0-1 #wal	BUT	bale wales

Table 1:   Detected actions and participants in tweets (England-Wales, June 16, 2016. D1P: First period begins, CJA: Yellow card, BUT: Goal).

3.1   Information Extraction

The first module retrieves participants and sub-events (or actions)[1] from tweets, and sets relations between them. In the case of soccer, actions are defined by FIFA, e.g. goals, penalties, yellow/red cards, etc. Participants are the actors who induce the actions. For soccer games, they are players and teams. To extract information we use GATE (Cunningham et al., 2002), because it includes a highly flexible NEs Recognition (NER) tool that allows the integration of custom gazetteers. To detect *actions*, we update its gazetteer based on the Sports Markup Language, a controlled vocabulary used to describe sports events. SportsML core schema provides concepts allowing the description of events for 11 major sports including Soccer, American football, Basketball and Tennis. For soccer games, we extract actions such as goals, substitutions, yellow/red cards and penalties. Furthermore, we enrich the list of actions with synonyms extracted from Wordnet (Fellbaum, 1998).

As for *participants*, we update the gazetteer using the football-data API[2] that, given a soccer game in input, returns the name of the teams and

---

[1]In this paper we use interchangeably the terms actions and sub-events to refer to actions in a sports game.

[2]http://api.football-data.org

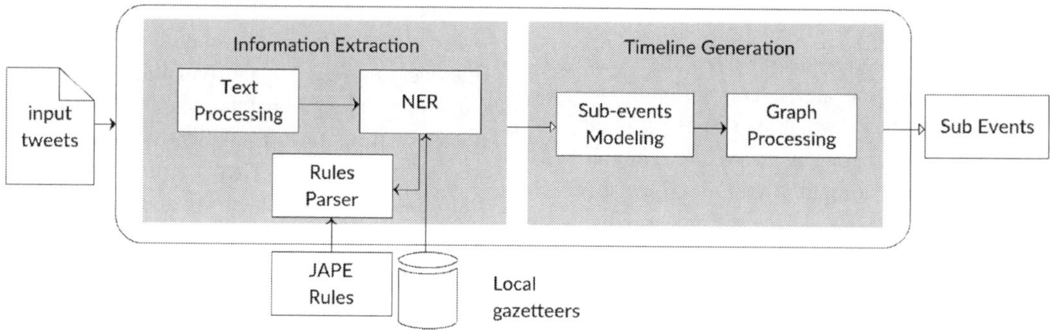

Figure 1: Sub-events extraction pipeline.

their players. We also apply some heuristics so as to associate different spelling variations to players' and teams' names. This is done by considering separately or by combining the different parts of the players' names (i.e. first name and last-name). For instance, *"giroud"*, *"oliviergiroud"* or *"olivier_giroud"* are all associated with *"Olivier Giroud"*, a player in the French national team.

We first pre-process the data using GATE in-built tweet normalizer, tokenizer and PoS-tagger. Then, we use the NER module integrating the two custom gazetteers we created. We also set links representing relations between actions and participants by means of JAPE (Java Annotation Pattern Engine) rules, a GATE-specific format to define regular expressions needed for pattern matching. Since relations detected through JAPE rules tend to be very accurate, we assign a weight $= 2$ to edges extracted from such rules. If an action and a participant appear in the same tweet but are not matched through a JAPE rule, we set a link with weight $= 1$, to account for a lower precision.

3.2 Timeline creation

Modeling sub-events. The output of the information extraction module (Fig. 1) is a list of tuples $\langle a, p, t, \omega \rangle$, where a is a sports action, t the timestamp of the tweet and p the participant involved and ω is the weight of the edge connecting a and p. These tuples are used to build a temporal event graph (see Figure 2). To retain temporal information on the sub-events, we split the game in fixed time windows, and create an event-graph that models the relationships between actions and participants for each time window. We refer to such graphs as *temporal graphs* (Verhagen et al., 2007) and we build them as follows:

- *Nodes*: Actions and participants are represented by nodes in the event-graph. First, we retrieve the nodes of the actions, and then we add the connected participants nodes;

- *Edges*: Nodes are connected by an edge if a relation can be set in the tweets published during the time-window. The occurrence of this relation is used to increase the weight of the edges. Relationships between participants are created for actions involving 2 or more participants (e.g. a substitution).

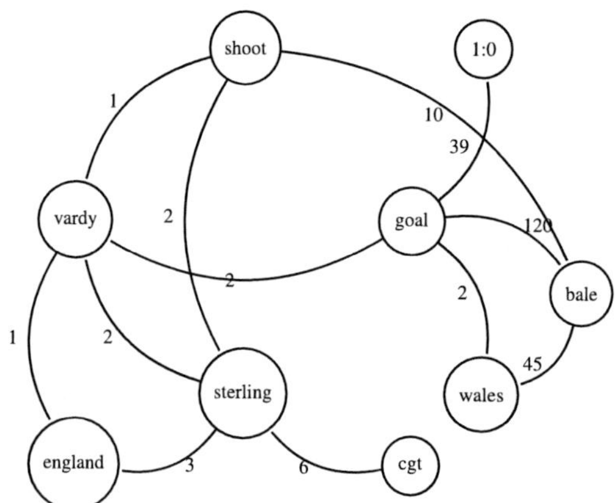

Figure 2: Event-graph for England-Wales.

Fig. 2 shows a temporal graph at time-window 22 of the game between England and Wales (Game #16 on June 16, 2016): we observe edges linking participants, e.g. connecting the node "Sterling" and "Vardy", retrieved from tweets requesting the substitution of "Sterling" by "Vardy". Both are linked also to the node "England', i.e. their team.

Processing the Event-Graphs. At this stage, the weighted relations between actions and partic-

216

ipants are considered as sub-event candidates. We cannot automatically include them in the timeline because they could represent opinions or wishes of the fans, as: *"how has ramsey not got a yellow card yet every attempt to tackle has been a foul"*. In general, we may assume that real sub-events in a game are reported by many users, while an action reported by a few users only is more likely to be a subjective post reflecting an opinion.

Most of the existing work set an empirical threshold to measure the importance of the actions (Alonso and Shiells, 2013; Marcus et al., 2011). However, we observe that the number of tweets generated for a given action is highly dependent on the game and the team or players involved. Thus, we find it useful to tune the thresholds by taking into account both the type of the action and the popularity of the teams involved in the game.

For each action belonging to a certain sport, we manually define an empirical threshold according to the importance of the action. For soccer, we can assume that a goal will trigger a higher number of tweets than a shoot. These empirical values can be defined by domain experts for each category of the sports we want to track. Based on the predefined thresholds, the interest of the games for people and the popularity of the opponent teams, we adjust the empirical thresholds using Kreyszig standard score formula (Kreyszig, 2007) as follows :

$$\varphi_{a,t} = \epsilon_a * \frac{\eta_{g,t} - \overline{\eta}_g}{\sigma_g} \qquad (1)$$

where $\varphi_{a,t}$ is the threshold for action a at time t of the game, ϵ_a the empirical threshold for a, $\eta_{g,t}$ the count of tweets related to the game at time t, $\overline{\eta}_g$ the mean count, σ_g the standard deviation of tweets related to the game in the past time windows.

Ranking Sports Actions. Let $A = \langle a, p, t, \omega \rangle$ be a quadruplet modeling an action a at time t, involving participants p and weighted by ω (i.e. the number of edges connecting a and p in the event graph). For each participant, we compute a standard score as follows:

$$z_{a,p,t} = \frac{\eta_{\omega_i} - \overline{\eta}_{\omega_i}}{\sigma_{\omega_i}} \qquad (2)$$

where η_ω is the weight of the edge in graph G that connects nodes a and p, $\overline{\eta}_\omega$ is the mean count of all the actions of type a induced by p, and σ_ω is the standard deviation of relationship between a and p over all past time windows. Thus, we evaluate

the action by taking the ratio between the standard score for each participant and the total standard scores for all the participants as follows :

$$z_{a,t} = \frac{z_{a,p_i,t}}{\sum\limits_{p_i \in P} z_{a,p_i,t}} \qquad (3)$$

At a given time t an action is added to the timeline iff there exists at least a participant p such that $z_{a,t} \geq \varphi_{a,t}$.

As shown in Algorithm 1, we first merge the current event graph and the graph from the previous time window (Line 1). Then, from the merged graph, we collect all vertices of type $foot\_action$ and for each we retrieve all connected nodes as participants of the action (Lines 4-6). We compute the adaptive threshold for each action and a standard score for each participant using equation 1 and 2, respectively (Lines 7-9). Finally, sub-event candidates are created with participants that have a score higher than the threshold of the action (Lines 10-16). For some actions, participants may not be required (e.g. beginning/end of periods in soccer), for such actions we consider both teams as participants in order to comply with equations (2 and 3). We remove from the event graph actions and participants involved in sub-events. Besides, nodes that were not related to sub-events are kept to be processed in the next time-window. However, if a node cannot be confirmed as related to sub-events in two consecutive time windows, we consider it as noise and simply discard it.

Before putting sub-events on a timeline, we perform a final check to see whether they have not been validated in the previous time window. If yes, it means that an action overlaps two time-windows, and the timestamp of the event must be updated, matching the time of the first occurrence. We consider two events identical if: *i)* they mention the same action and participants; *ii)* the number of tweets reporting the more recent action is lower than the number of tweets on the old one.

4 Experiments

4.1 Dataset

We experiment our framework on the Hackatal 2016 dataset[3], collected during the EURO 2016 Championship. A set of keywords were manually defined, including hashtags (#euro, #euro2016, #football) and the names of the teams involved in

---

[3] http://hackatal.github.io/2016/.

Algorithm 1 Algorithm to process a given event-graph to retrieve important sub-events.

```
 1: function GRAPH_PROCESSING(G_t, G_{t-1}, t)        ▷
       G_t - Event graph at time t, G_{t-1} - Event graph at t-1, t -
       current time
 2:     G = merge (G_t, G_{t-1})
 3:     E = ∅
 4:     for vertex ∈ G.vertices() do
 5:         if vertex is foot_action then
 6:             P = G.neighbors(node)
 7:             a = node.action
 8:             φ_{a,t} = compute (a, t)              ▷ equation 1
 9:             z_{a,t} = compute (a, P, t)           ▷ equation 3
10:             for z ∈ z_{a,t} do
11:                 if z ≥ φ_{a,t} then
12:                     event = (a, p, t)
13:                     E append (a, p, t)
14:                     G delete (a, p)
15:                 end if
16:             end for
17:         end if
18:     end for
19: end function
```

Time	Action	Participants
15:02	D1P	–
15:09	TIR	Sterling
...	...	...
15:44	BUT	Bale
15:48	F1P	–
16:04	CGT	Sterling; Vardy
16:18	BUT	Vardy

Table 2: A few examples of the sub-events that occurred in the game between England and Wales.

lection, and we consider one tweet per user in a time window. The input tweets are then analyzed with GATE. We use the JGraph library (Naveh et al., 2008) to create the event-graph. At each time-window, we create a new graph to model the relation between actions and participants detected in tweets. We process the event-graph with Algorithm 1 to detect real sub-events found in tweets.

4.3 Evaluation Strategies

We report on two different evaluation strategies. In the first one, we compare the output of our framework against the state of the art approach (Alonso and Shiells, 2013). There, sub-events are detected by identifying spikes in the Twitter stream. Since they do not detect participants, in this first comparison we also limit our evaluation to the action timeline, letting out additional information. We also compare the results with the gold standard timeline from manually created summaries by sports journalists. We show the results for three sample matches in Figures 4, 5 and 6.

In the second evaluation strategy, we evaluate our approach against the gold standard data described above. This time we include also the sub-event type, the time and participants information. Also, we consider three evaluation settings, namely *complete* matching, *partial* matching and *loose* matching. In the complete matching mode, we evaluate each sub-event detected by our system by taking into account the type of the sub-event, the participants and the time. A sub-event is considered correct if all three elements are correctly identified. In the partial mode, we consider the time and the type of the sub-events; and in the loose mode, we only consider the type. We set the error margin to 2 minutes while comparing the time, since this is the duration of the time-windows used to build the temporal graphs. Table 3 reports P/R/F1 for the same sample matches described above, as well as an average of the scores

the competition (e.g. France) as well as their short names (e.g. #FRA) and hashtags related to current games (e.g. #FRAROM for the game between France and Romania). For each game, tweets were collected for a two-hour time span, starting at the beginning of the game. For comparisons and to limit the complexity of the processing pipeline, we limit our analysis to tweets in English.

The dataset also contains the summary of the salient sub-events in each game, retrieved from journalistic reports (e.g. LeFigaro[4]). We consider these summaries as the ground truth while evaluating our approach. These summaries are defined as a set of triples ⟨time, action, participant⟩ where "time" is the time the sub-event occurs, the "action" is the type of the sub-event and "participants" are players or teams involved in the action. The sub-events include: the beginning of the periods (F1P, D1P), end of the periods (F1P, D2P), Shoot (TIR), Goal (BUT), Substitution (CGT), Red card (CRO) and Yellow card (CJA) (see Table 2).

4.2 Experimental Setting

We simulate the Twitter stream by grouping the tweets related to a game in intervals of two minutes, which we refer to as *time-windows*. Thus, we collect all the tweets published in a time-window in a single document which we give in input to our algorithm. In the preprocessing phase, we remove re-tweets if the original tweet is already in the col-

---

[4] http://sport24.lefigaro.fr

218

for 24 matches in the first stage of the competition.

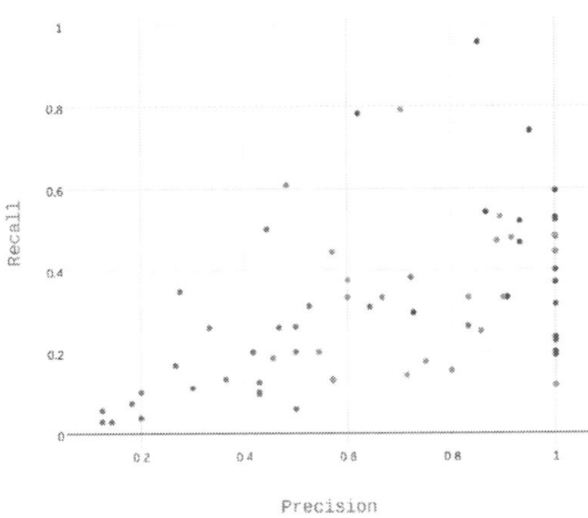

Figure 3: Precision Recall chart of the performances of our approach. X-axis is the average precision and Y-axis the average recall. Blue dots represent the loose matching, orange dots the partial matching and green dots the complete matching.

4.4 Results and discussion

The overall evaluation concerning the first 24 games in the EURO 2016 Championship (Table 3) shows that the approach is very accurate in some cases, while it suffers from low performance, especially recall, in other settings. If we compare the different actions (left-most columns in the table), we observe that the best performance is obtained when recognizing the start and the end of the match (last line in the table). For other actions, the performance varies across the three evaluation modes. For example, when considering participants to *shoot* actions, the approach fails to identify the correct player, probably because other players are likely to be mentioned in the same tweet. Fig. 3 provides an overview of the obtained performances with the different evaluation strategies.

We further focus on three sample matches: we plot in Fig. 4, 5 and 6 the sub-events detected by Alonso and Shiells, those detected by our approach, as well as the gold standard ones. We report in Tables 4, 5 and 6 P/R/F1 measures for the loose, partial and complete evaluation strategy.

The first game, England - Wales gained particular attention on Twitter. Fig. 4 shows the distribution of tweets during the game (in gray), distinguishing between tweets explicitly mentioning England (red line) and Wales (green). The

blue dots correspond to the sub-events identified by Alonso and Shiells's approach, while those detected by our approach and the ground truth are represented with yellow and green dots, respectively. The graphical representation shows that there is a significant correspondence between the sub-events detected by our approach and the gold standard ones. We can also observe that Alonso and Shiells fail to detect sub-events that do not produce spikes in the volume of tweets. Table 4 shows for the same match the average performance of our approach. In this case, our performance is affected by problems in detecting actions of type *substitution* and *shoots*.

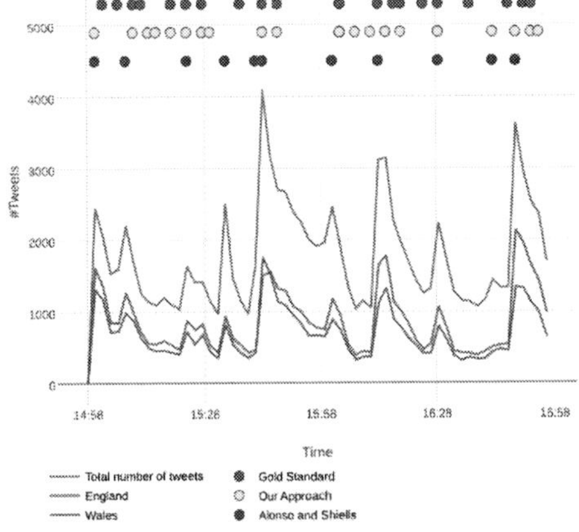

Figure 4: Sub-events in England-Wales.

A second example is the match France - Romania (see Fig. 5). Although the game was quite debated on Twitter, a few spikes were detected in the stream. In fact, during the first period the teams were barely mentioned, as indicated by the red and green curves on the graph. Instead, other teams were mentioned, which were not directly involved in the game. The second period seemed to be more interesting in terms of sub-events. Table 5 shows our performances. We obtain a 91.3% precision in the loose mode, since we detect 23 out of 34 sub-events in the game compared to 9 identified by Alonso and Shiells, and 21 of the detected sub-events were associated to the correct actions. However, the latency between the sub-events detected by our approach compared to the ground truth contributes in decreasing the performance of our approach in both intermediate and complete matching. For example, there is a huge peak at time 22:24 when *Stancu* equalizes for Romania, but we detect this action four minutes later since

	Loose			Partial			Complete		
actions	Prec	Rec	F1	Prec	Rec	F1	Prec	Rec	F1
goal	0.745	0.512	0.549	0.670	0.456	0.493	0.623	0.405	0.444
card	0.758	0.560	0.622	0.693	0.506	0.568	0.600	0.433	0.516
subt	0.859	0.629	0.693	0.627	0.460	0.510	0.501	0.374	0.438
shoot	0.643	0.203	0.292	0.571	0.185	0.264	0.548	0.167	0.243
period	0.814	0.656	0.706	0.655	0.517	0.562	0.585	0.462	0.523

Table 3: Experimental results of our approach for 24 games in the first stage of the Euro 2016 dataset

Methods	Prec	Rec	F-score
loose	0.852	0.958	0.902
partial	0.630	0.708	0.667
complete	0.444	0.500	0.470

Table 4: Performance on England- Wales.

most of the tweets in that time span discuss the penalty issue rather than the goal.

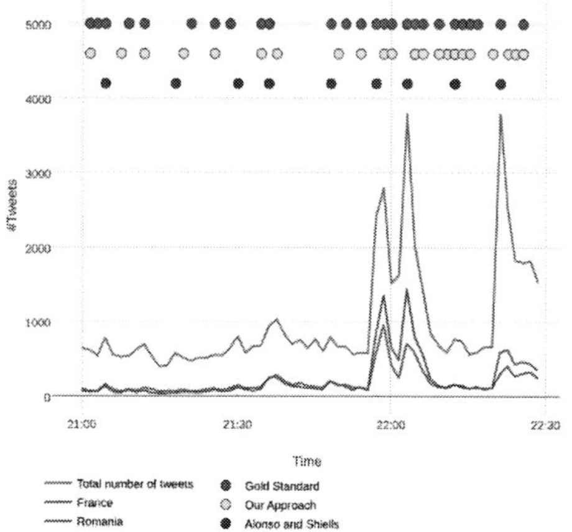

Figure 5: Sub-events in France-Romania.

Methods	Prec	Rec	F-score
loose	0.913	0.656	0.763
partial	0.696	0.500	0.582
complete	0.609	0.438	0.510

Table 5: Performance on France- Romania.

As a third example, we consider Belgium - Italy, that was less popular in terms of tweets than the previous ones. A few peaks are detected in the game (Fig. 6). This affects negatively the number of sub-events found by Alonso and Shiells, while our approach proves to have a better coverage, even if recall is on average lower than for the other matches. In most cases, we detect mentions of the actions, but we fail to detect the participants. Table 6 shows the overall performance of our approach. In the ground truth there were only a few tweets related to this game, and $\sim 50\%$ of them

were shoots. Our approach failed to identify them, impacting on the recall. On the other hand, all the events detected were correct.

Methods	Prec	Rec	F-score
loose	1.000	0.448	0.619
partial	0.923	0.414	0.572
complete	0.846	0.379	0.523

Table 6: Performance on Belgium- Italy.

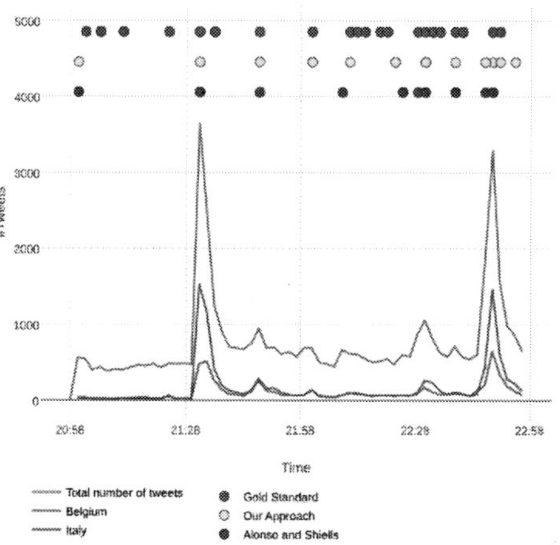

Figure 6: Sub-events in Belgium- Italy.

5 Conclusion and Future Work

In this paper, we have described a framework to generate timelines of salient sub-events in sports games exploiting information contained in tweets. Experiments on a set of tweets collected during EURO 2016 proved that our approach accurately detects sub-events in sports games when compared to news on the same events reported by sports media. While previous approaches focused only on detecting the type of the most important sub-events, we extract and model a richer set of information, including almost every type of sub-event and participants involved in the actions. As for future work, we plan to extend our approach to other sports (e.g. American football).

References

Omar Alonso and Kyle Shiells. 2013. Timelines as summaries of popular scheduled events. In *Proceedings of the 22nd International Conference on World Wide Web*. ACM, pages 1037–1044.

International Press Telecommunications Council. 2017. SportsML: A solution for sharing sports data. https://iptc.org/standards/sportsml-g2/. [Accessed 03-01-2017].

Hamish Cunningham, Diana Maynard, Kalina Bontcheva, and Valentin Tablan. 2002. GATE: A Framework and Graphical Development Environment for Robust NLP Tools and Applications. In *Proceedings of the 40th Anniversary Meeting of the Association for Computational Linguistics (ACL'02)*.

Wenwen Dou, K Wang, William Ribarsky, and Michelle Zhou. 2012. Event detection in social media data. In *IEEE VisWeek Workshop on Interactive Visual Text Analytics-Task Driven Analytics of Social Media Content*. pages 971–980.

C. Fellbaum. 1998. *WordNet. An Electronic Lexical Database*. MIT Press.

Chris Gibbs and Richard Haynes. 2013. A phenomenological investigation into how twitter has changed the nature of sport media relations. *International Journal of Sport Communication* 6(4):394–408.

John Hannon, Kevin McCarthy, James Lynch, and Barry Smyth. 2011. Personalized and automatic social summarization of events in video. In *Proceedings of the 16th international conference on Intelligent user interfaces*. ACM, pages 335–338.

Said Jai-Andaloussi, Imane El Mourabit, Nabil Madrane, Samia Benabdellah Chaouni, and Abderrahim Sekkaki. 2015. Soccer events summarization by using sentiment analysis. In *2015 International Conference on Computational Science and Computational Intelligence (CSCI)*. IEEE, pages 398–403.

Erwin Kreyszig. 2007. *Advanced engineering mathematics*. John Wiley & Sons.

Mitsumasa Kubo, Ryohei Sasano, Hiroya Takamura, and Manabu Okumura. 2013. Generating live sports updates from twitter by finding good reporters. In *Proceedings of the 2013 IEEE/WIC/ACM International Joint Conferences on Web Intelligence (WI) and Intelligent Agent Technologies (IAT)-Volume 01*. IEEE Computer Society, pages 527–534.

Markus Löchtefeld, Christian Jäckel, and Antonio Krüger. 2015. Twitsoccer: knowledge-based crowdsourcing of live soccer events. In *Proceedings of the 14th International Conference on Mobile and Ubiquitous Multimedia*. ACM, pages 148–151.

Adam Marcus, Michael S Bernstein, Osama Badar, David R Karger, Samuel Madden, and Robert C Miller. 2011. Twitinfo: aggregating and visualizing microblogs for event exploration. In *Proceedings of the SIGCHI conference on Human factors in computing systems*. ACM, pages 227–236.

Barak Naveh et al. 2008. Jgrapht. *Internet: http://jgrapht.sourceforge.net* .

Jeffrey Nichols, Jalal Mahmud, and Clemens Drews. 2012. Summarizing sporting events using twitter. In *Proceedings of the 2012 ACM international conference on Intelligent User Interfaces*. ACM, pages 189–198.

Selami Özsoy. 2011. Use of new media by turkish fans in sport communication: Facebook and twitter. *Journal of Human Kinetics* 28:165–176.

Beaux Sharifi, Mark-Anthony Hutton, and Jugal Kalita. 2010. Summarizing microblogs automatically. In *Human Language Technologies: The 2010 Annual Conference of the North American Chapter of the Association for Computational Linguistics*. Association for Computational Linguistics, pages 685–688.

Cees GM Snoek and Marcel Worring. 2005. Multimedia event-based video indexing using time intervals. *IEEE Transactions on Multimedia* 7(4):638–647.

Cees GM Snoek, Marcel Worring, et al. 2003. Time interval based modelling and classification of events in soccer video. In *Proceedings of the 9th annual conference of the advanced school for computing and imaging (ASCI), Heijen*. Citeseer.

Marc Verhagen, Robert Gaizauskas, Frank Schilder, Mark Hepple, Graham Katz, and James Pustejovsky. 2007. Semeval-2007 task 15: Tempeval temporal relation identification. In *Proceedings of the 4th International Workshop on Semantic Evaluations*. Association for Computational Linguistics, pages 75–80.

Wei Xu, Ralph Grishman, Adam Meyers, and Alan Ritter. 2013. A preliminary study of tweet summarization using information extraction. *NAACL 2013* page 20.

Graph-based Event Extraction from Twitter

Amosse Edouard
Université Côte d'Azur
Inria, CNRS, I3S, France
amosse.edouard@unice.fr

Elena Cabrio
Université Côte d'Azur
Inria, CNRS, I3S, France
elena.cabrio@unice.fr

Sara Tonelli
Fondazione Bruno Kessler
Trento, Italia
satonelli@fbk.eu

Nhan Le-Thanh
Université Côte d'Azur
Inria, CNRS, I3S, France
nhan.lethan@unice.fr

Abstract

Detecting which tweets describe a specific event and clustering them is one of the main challenging tasks related to Social Media currently addressed in the NLP community. Existing approaches have mainly focused on detecting spikes in clusters around specific keywords or Named Entities (NE). However, one of the main drawbacks of such approaches is the difficulty in understanding when the same keywords describe different events. In this paper, we propose a novel approach that exploits NE mentions in tweets and their entity context to create a temporal event graph. Then, using simple graph theory techniques and a PageRank-like algorithm, we process the event graphs to detect clusters of tweets describing the same events. Experiments on two gold standard datasets show that our approach achieves state-of-the-art results both in terms of evaluation performances and the quality of the detected events.

1 Introduction

Twitter has become a valuable source of timely information covering topics from every corner of the world. For this reason, NLP researchers have shown growing interest in mining knowledge from Twitter data. As a result, several approaches have been proposed to build applications over tweets, e.g. to extract structured representations/summary of newsworthy events (McMinn and Jose, 2015; Katragadda et al., 2017), or to carry out sentiment analysis to study users reactions (Agarwal et al., 2011; Kouloumpis et al., 2011). However, pro-

cessing tweets is challenging task, since information in Twitter stream is continuously changing in real-time, while at the same time there might be a high volume of redundant messages referring to the same issue or event.

In this work, we focus on event extraction from Twitter, consisting in the automated clustering of tweets related to the same event based on relevant information such as time and participants. Although there is no consensus in the NLP community on what an event is (Sprugnoli and Tonelli, 2017), our approach relies on the event definition by Dou et al. (2012), i.e. *"an occurrence causing change in the volume of text data that discusses the associated topic at a specific time. This occurrence is characterized by topic and time, and often associated with entities such as people and location"*.

Existing approaches to the task create clusters of tweets around event-related keywords (Parikh and Karlapalem, 2013), or NEs (McMinn and Jose, 2015). However, such approaches fail *i)* to capture events that do not generate spikes in the volume of tweets; and *ii)* to distinguish between events that involve the same NEs and keywords. Other approaches model the relationships between terms contained in the tweets relying on a graph representation (Katragadda et al., 2016), and retain the nodes with the highest number of edges as event candidates. However, the main drawbacks of these approaches are that *i)* they generate highly dense graphs, and *ii)* trending terms not related to events may be considered as event candidates.

To address such limitations, in this work we propose an unsupervised approach to detect open-domain events on Twitter, where the stream of tweets is represented through temporal event

Proceedings of Recent Advances in Natural Language Processing, pages 222–230,
Varna, Bulgaria, Sep 4–6 2017.

graphs, modeling the relations between NEs and the terms that surround their mentions in the tweets.

2 Related Work

Existing approaches to extract events from tweets can be divided into two main categories, namely closed-domain and open-domain event detection systems (Atefeh and Khreich, 2015). In the closed-domain, approaches are mainly focused on extracting a particular type of event, as for instance natural disasters (Panem et al., 2014). Works in the closed-domain scenario are usually cast as supervised classification tasks that rely on keywords to extract event-related messages from Twitter (Wang et al., 2012), to recognize event patterns (Popescu et al., 2011) or to define labels for training a classifier (Anantharam et al., 2015; Sakaki et al., 2010).

The open-domain scenario is more challenging, since it is not limited to a specific type of event and usually relies on unsupervised models. Among the works applying an unsupervised approach to event detection on Twitter, (McMinn and Jose, 2015) create event clusters from tweets using NE mentions as central terms driving the clusters. Thus, tweets mentioning the same entities are grouped together in a single cluster. Experiments on a public dataset of tweets show that this strategy outperforms other approaches such as Latent Sensitive Hashing (Petrović et al., 2010). Similarly, (Hasan et al., 2016) create clusters based on cosine similarity among tweets. Both works do not consider the temporal aspect of events and fail to capture terms or entities involved in different events at different time periods.

Very recently, Zhou et al. (2017) use a nonparametric Bayesian Mixture Model leveraged with word embeddings to create event clusters from tweets. In this approach, events are modeled as a 4-tuple $\langle y, l, k, d \rangle$ modeling non-location NEs, location NEs, event keywords and date. The work was focused on detecting events given a set of event-related tweets, which is however not applicable to a real scenario, where the stream of tweets can also contain messages that are not event-related. This scenario is simulated in the second experiment presented in this paper.

3 Approach description

In this section, we describe our approach for detecting open-domain events on tweets. The pipeline consists of the following components: Tweet pre-processing, Named Entity recognition and linking, graph creation, graph partitioning, event detection and event merging. Each step is described in the following subsections.

3.1 Tweet Preprocessing

The workflow starts by collecting tweets published during a fixed time window, which can be set as input parameter (e.g. 1 hour). Then, we apply common text preprocessing routines to clean the input tweets. We use TweetMotifs (O'Connor et al., 2010), a specific tokenizer for tweets, which treats hashtags, user mentions and emoticons as single tokens. Then, we remove the retweets, URLs, non ASCII characters and emoticons. It is worth mentioning that at this stage we do not perform stop word removal since stop words can be part of NEs (e.g. United States of America). As for hashtags, we define a set of hand-crafted rules to segment them into terms, is possible. We also try to correct misspelled terms using SymSpell[1], which matches misspelled tokens with Wordnet synsets (Fellbaum, 1998).

3.2 Named Entity Recognition and Linking

We use NERD-ML (Van Erp et al., 2013), a Twitter specific Named Entity Recognizer (NER) tool, to extract NE mentions in the tweets, since Derczynski et al. (2015) showed that it is one of the best performing tools for NER on Twitter data. Besides, NERD-ML not only recognizes the most common entity types (i.e. Person, Organization and Location), but tries also to link any term listed in external knowledge bases such as DBpedia[2] or Wikipedia. These are then associated with semantic classes in the NERD ontology.

3.3 Graph Generation

Previous works using graph-based methods to model relations between terms in text considered all terms in the input document as nodes and used their position in text to set edges (Andersen et al., 2006; Xu et al., 2013). Such approaches may generate a dense graph, which generally requires high computational costs to be processed.

---

[1] https://github.com/wolfgarbe/symspell
[2] http://dbpedia.com/

In this work, we assume that the terms surrounding the mention of a NE in a tweet define its context (Nugroho et al., 2015). Thus, we rely on the NE context to create event graphs, built as follows:

Nodes: We consider NE and k terms that precede and follow their mention in a tweet as nodes, where $k > 1$ is the number of terms surrounding a NE to consider while building the NE context.

Edges: Nodes in the graph are connected by an edge if they co-occur in the context of a NE.

Weight: The weight of the edges is the number of co-occurrences between terms in the NE context. In addition, each edge maintains as a property the list of tweets from which the relationship is observed

Formally, let $\mathcal{G}(\mathcal{V}, \mathcal{E})$ be a directed graph (or digraph) with a set of vertices $\mathcal{V}$ and edges $\mathcal{E}$, such that $\mathcal{E} \subset \mathcal{V} \times \mathcal{V}$. For any $\mathcal{V}_i \in \mathcal{V}$, let $In(\mathcal{V}_i)$ be the set of vertices that point to $\mathcal{V}_i$ (i.e. predecessors), and $Out(\mathcal{V}_i)$ be the set of vertices that $\mathcal{V}_i$ points to (i.e. successors).

Let $\mathcal{E}_i = (\mathcal{V}_j, \mathcal{V}_k)$ be an edge that connects node $\mathcal{V}_j$ to $\mathcal{V}_k$, we define ω_{ij} as the weight of $\mathcal{E}_i$, which is represented by the number of times relationships between $\mathcal{V}_j$ and $\mathcal{V}_k$ is observed in tweets published during a time window. An example of the graph created on 2011-07-07 with tweets related to the famine in Somalia and space shuttle to Mars is shown in Figure 1.

3.4 Graph Partitioning

At this stage, an event graph is generated to model relationships between terms in the NE contexts. We apply graph theory to partition the graph into sub-graphs, which will be considered as event candidates. Tweets related to the same events usually share a few common keywords (McMinn and Jose, 2015). In the event graphs, this phenomenon is expressed by stronger links between nodes related to the same event. In other words, the weight of edges that connect terms from tweets related to similar events are higher than edges between nodes that connect terms from tweets related to different events. The graph partitioning purpose is to identify such edges that, if removed, will split the large graph $\mathcal{G}$ into sub-graphs.

Let $\mathcal{E} = \{(\mathcal{V}_1, \mathcal{W}_1), (\mathcal{V}_2, \mathcal{W}_2), ..., (\mathcal{V}_n, \mathcal{W}_n)\}$ be a set of pair of vertices in a strongly connected graph $\mathcal{G}$. We define λ as the least number of edges whose deletion from $\mathcal{G}$ would split $\mathcal{G}$ into connected sub-graphs. Similarly, we define the edge-connectivity $\lambda(\mathcal{G})$ of $\mathcal{G}$ of an edge set $\mathcal{S} \subset \mathcal{E}$ as the least cardinality $|\mathcal{S}|$ such that $\mathcal{G} - \mathcal{S}$ is no longer strongly connected. For instance, given the graph in Figure 1 as input, the deletion of edges "mark/somalia" and "year/famine" will create two strongly connected sub-graphs, where the first one contains keywords related to "famine in Somalia" and other contains keywords related to "The space shuttle to Mars".

3.5 Event Detection

We assume that events from different sub-graphs are not related to each other. Thus, in the event detection sub-module, each sub-graph is processed separately. In a study on local partitioning, Andersen et al. (2006) show that a good partition of a graph can be obtained by separating high-ranked vertices from low-ranked ones, if the nodes in the graph have distinguishable values. We use a PageRank-like algorithm (Brin and Page, 1998) to rank vertices in the event-graph as follows :

$$S(V_i) = ((1 - d) + d \sum_{v_j \in In(V_i)} \frac{w_{ji}}{\sum_{v_k \in Out(V_k)} \omega_{jk}} S(V_j))\epsilon_i \tag{1}$$

where ω_{ij} is the weight of edge connecting V_i to V_j, d a dumping factor usually set to 0.85 (Brin and Page, 1998) and ϵ_i a penalization parameter for node i. In previous approaches (Mihalcea and Tarau, 2004), the penalization parameter is considered as a uniform distribution; instead, we define the penalization parameter of a node according to its tf-idf score. Due to redundant information in tweets, the score of the nodes can be biased by the trending terms in different time windows. Thus, we use the tf-idf score to reduce the impact of trending terms in the collection of tweets. Before computing the score with equation 1, we assign an initial value $\tau = 1/n$ to each vertex in the graph, where n is the total number of nodes in the graph. Then, for each node, the computation iterates until the desired degree of convergence is reached. The degree of convergence of a node can be obtained by computing the difference between the score at the current iteration and at the previous iteration, which we set to 0.0001 (Brin and Page, 1998).

As shown in Algorithm 1, we start by splitting the vertex set into high-ranked and low-ranked vertices based on a gauged parameter α (Line 3). Next, we process the vertices in the high-ranked subset starting from the highest ones, and for each

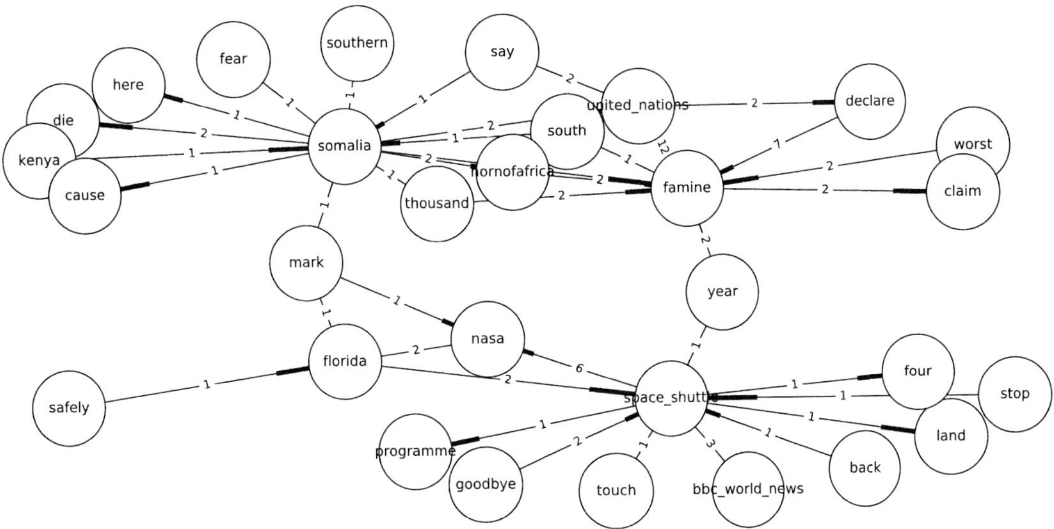

Figure 1: Graph generated on day "2011-07-07" from a sample of tweets related to the events about the famine in Somalia and the space shuttle to Mars.

candidate we select the highest weighted predecessors and successors as keywords for event candidates (Lines 4-9). After removing the edges between the keywords from the graph, if it becomes disconnected, we also consider the disconnected nodes as keywords for the event candidate (Lines 10-13). Based on the semantic class provided by the NER tool (see Section 3.2), we divide the keywords related to an event in the following subsets: *what* (i.e., the type of the event), *where* (i.e., the location in which the event happens), *who* (i.e., the person or organization involved). As for the date, we select the oldest tweets that report the event.

In the second stage of Algorithm 1, we further process the event candidates. First, we merge duplicate event candidates (Lines 22-35), i.e. those sharing common terms and having the same location or participants in the considered time window. A new event is thus built from the combination of terms and entities of the two event candidates. An event is considered as valid if at least a NE is involved, and if it occurs in a minimum number of tweets provided as input parameter.

3.6 Event Merging

We consider events in different time-windows as duplicate if they contain the same keywords, entities (e.g. person, organization, location) in an interval of k days, where k is an input parameter. When a new event is found as duplicate, we merge it with the previous detected event.

4 Experiments

Given a set of tweets, our goal is to cluster such tweets so that each cluster corresponds to a fine-grained event such as "Death of Amy Winehouse" or "Presidential debate between Obama and Romney during the US presidential election". We first describe the datasets, then we present the experimental setting. This section ends with a comparison of the obtained experimental results with state-of-the-art approaches.

4.1 Dataset

We test our approach on two gold standard corpora: the First Story Detection (FSD) corpus (Petrović et al., 2012) and the EVENT2012 corpus (McMinn et al., 2013).

FSD The corpus was collected from the Twitter streaming API[3] between 7th July and 12th September 2011. Human annotators annotated 3,035 tweets as related to 27 major events occurred in that period.After removing tweets that are no more available, we are left with 2,342 tweets related to one out of the 27 events. To reproduce the same dataset used by other state-of-the-art approaches, we consider only those events mentioned in more than 15 tweets. Thus, the final dataset contains 2,295 tweets describing 20 events.

EVENT2012 A corpus of 120 million tweets collected from October to November 2012 from

---

[3]dev.twitter.com/streaming/overview

225

Algorithm 1 Algorithm to process a given event-graph to retrieve important sub-events.

```
1: function GRAPH_PROCESSING(G, α)
2:     E = ∅
3:     H = {vᵢ ∈ vertex(G) if score(vᵢ) >= α}   ▷ Equation 1
4:     while H ≠ ∅ do
5:         G' = G.copy()
6:         vᵢ = H.pop()
7:         p = max(Wⱼ ∈ In(vᵢ))
8:         s = max(Wⱼ ∈ Out(vᵢ))
9:         keywords = set(p, vᵢ, s)
10:        G'.removeₑdges((p, vᵢ), (vᵢ, s))
11:        if not G'.connected() then
12:            append(keywords, disc_vertices(G'))
13:        end if
14:        who = person||organization ∈ keywords
15:        where = location ∈ keywords
16:        what = keywords − who − where
17:        tweets = tweet_from(keywords)
18:        when = oldest(tweets, date)
19:        event =< what, who, where, when >
20:        append(E, event)
21:    end while
22:    for e ∈ E do
23:        for e' in E do
24:            if what(e) ∩ what(e') then
25:                if who(e) ∩ who(e') then
26:                    merge(e, e')
27:                end if
28:                if where(e) ∩ where(e') then
29:                    merge(e, e')
30:                end if
31:            end if
32:        end for
33:        if not who(e) or not where(e) then
34:            discard(E, e)
35:        end if
36:    end for
       return E
37: end function
```

the Twitter streaming API, of which 159,952 tweets were labeled as event-related. 506 event types were gathered from the Wikipedia Current Event Portal, and Amazon Mechanical Turk was used to annotate each tweet with one of such event types. After removing tweets that are no longer available, our final dataset contains ∼43 million tweets from which 152,758 are related to events.

4.2 Experimental Setting

For each dataset, we compare our approach with state-of-the-art approaches. For the FSD dataset, we compare with LEM Bayesian model (Zhou et al., 2011) and DPEMM Bayesian model enriched with word embeddings (Zhou et al., 2017). For the EVENT2012 dataset, we compare our results with Named Entity-Based Event Detection approach (NEED) (McMinn and Jose, 2015) and Event Detection Onset (EDO) (Katragadda et al.,

2016).

In order to simulate a real scenario where tweets are continuously added to a stream, we simulate the Twitter stream with a client-server architecture which pushes tweets according to their creation date. We evaluate our approach in two different scenarios: in the first scenario, we consider tweets from the FSD dataset that are related to events and we classify them into fine-grained event clusters. In the second scenario, we adopt a more realistic approach in that we consider all the tweets from the EVENT2012 dataset (i.e event-related and not event-related ones), and we classify them into event clusters, discarding those that are not related to events.

Our approach requires a few parameters to be provided as input. In the experiments reported in this paper, we process the input stream with fixed time-window $w = 1$ hour. The minimum number of tweets for event candidates is set to $n = 5$. Finally, we empirically choose $t = 3$ days as the interval of validity for the detected events.

4.3 Results

Performance is evaluated both in terms of P/R/F1 and cluster purity.

Results on the FSD dataset: In this scenario, we consider an event as correctly classified if *all* the tweets in that cluster belong to the same event in the gold standard, otherwise the event is considered as misclassified. Due to the low number of tweets, we set the gauged parameter $\alpha = 0.5$ as the minimum score for nodes in the graph to be considered as useful for events. Table 1 shows the experimental results yielded by our approach in comparison to state-of-the-art approaches. Our approach outperforms the others, improving the F-score by 0.07 points w.r.t. DPEMM and by 0.13 w.r.t. LEM.

Approach	Precision	Recall	F-measure
LEM	0.792	0.850	0.820
DPEMM	0.862	0.900	0.880
Our Approach	0.950	0.950	0.950

Table 1: Evaluation results on the FSD dataset.

Furthermore, we evaluate the quality of the events, i.e. the clusters, in terms of purity, where the purity of an event is based on the number of tweets correctly classified in the cluster and the number of misclassified tweets. More specifically,

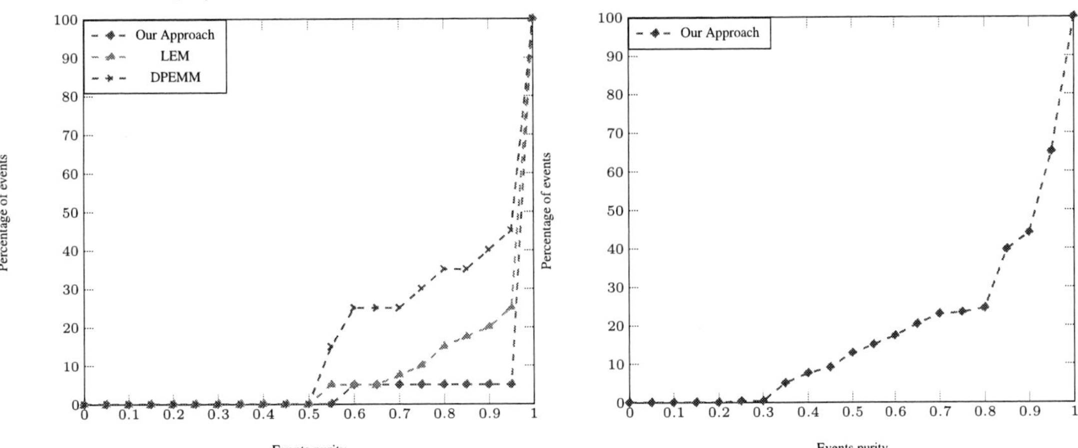

Figure 2: Purity of the events detected by our approach, LEM and DPEMM on the FSD dataset. The y-axis denotes the percentage of events and the x-axis the purity of the events.

Figure 3: Purity of the events detected by our approach on the event 2012 dataset. The y-axis denotes the percentage of events and the x-axis the purity of the events.

purity is computed as: $P_e = \frac{n_e}{n}$, where n_e is the number of tweets correctly classified and n the total number of tweets classified in that cluster. Figure 2 reports the purity of our approach compared to LEM and DPEMM, where each point (x, y) denotes the percentage of events having purity less than x. It can be observed that 5% of the events detected as well as DPEMM have purity less than 0.65 compared to 25% for LEM, while 95% of the events detected have purity higher than 0.95 compared to 75% for DPEMM and 55% for LEM.

Results on the EVENT2012 dataset: We also evaluate our approach on the EVENT2012 dataset using a more realistic scenario in which all the tweets (i.e. events related and non-event related tweets) are considered. Compared to the FSD dataset, the EVENT2012 dataset has more events and tweets and thus a larger vocabulary. We set the cutting parameter $\alpha = 0.75$ as the minimum score of nodes in the graph to be considered as important for events. We further detail the importance of the parameters α in Section 4.4. Also, since we include both event-related and not event-related tweets, we consider an event as correct if 80% of the tweets belong to the same event in the ground truth. Table 2 reports on the experimental results compared to the NEED and EDO approaches. In general, our approach improves the f-score by 0.07 points w.r.t. EDO and 0.23 points w.r.t. NEED. After a manual check of the output, we noticed

that some issues with precision may depend on the quality of the dataset, since some tweets related to events were not annotated as such in the gold standard. For example, we found that 9,010 tweets related to "BET hip hop award" were not annotated. The same was found for tweets concerning large events such as "the Presidential debate between Obama and Romney" or the "shooting of Malala Yousafzai, the 14-year old activist for human rights in Pakistan".

We also evaluate the purity of the events detected by our approach (Figure 3). We can observe that the quality of the detected events is lower than for the events detected on the FSD dataset. For instance, more than 20% of the detected events have purity *lower* than 0.7. As expected, event purity is mainly affected by the inclusion in the clusters of non event-related tweets.

Approach	Precision	Recall	F-measure
NEED	0.636	0.383	0.478
EDO	0.754	0.512	0.638
Our Approach	0,750	0.668	0.710

Table 2: Evaluation results on the EVENT2012 dataset.

4.4 Effect of the Cutting Parameter

We further experiment on the impact of the dangling parameter on the output of our model. The

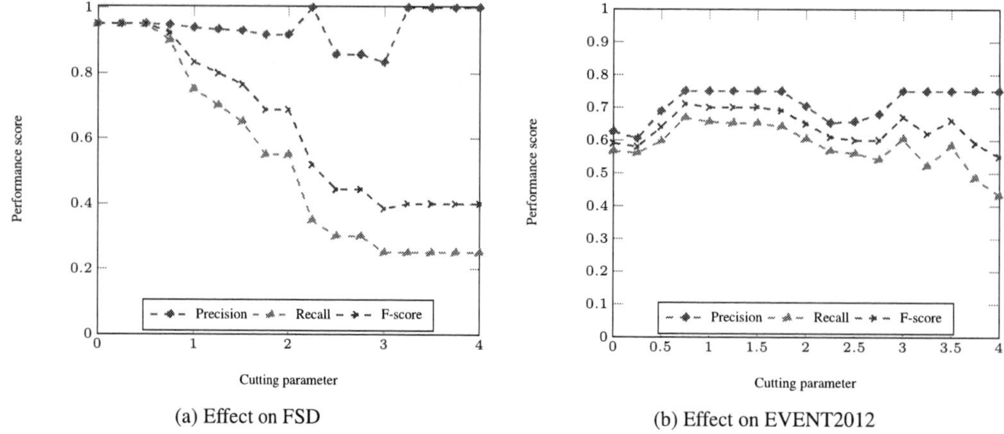

(a) Effect on FSD   (b) Effect on EVENT2012

Figure 4: Effect of the cutting parameter (α) on the performance of our approach.

dangling parameter α is used to separate the nodes of the event graph into high-ranked and low-ranked nodes, where the high-ranked nodes are used to extract keywords related to event candidates. We experiment different values for "α" and we evaluate their impact on the performance of our approach on both datasets.

In Figure 4a we show the performance of our model for $0 < \alpha \leq 4$ on the FSD dataset. We observe that higher value of α gives higher precision while lowering the recall. More specifically, for $\alpha \geq 3$ we obtain 100% precision and recall lower than 50%. On the other hand, the best performance is obtained for $\alpha \leq 0.5$. Since the FSD dataset contains $\sim 6,000$ unique words, at each time window the generated graph is strongly connected, thus the average minimum score of the nodes is higher than 0.5. For values higher than 0.5, important terms referring to events are ignored, mainly when they are related to events that do not generate a high volume of tweets. In our experiments, we also observe that higher values of α mostly affect the recognition of events with low number of tweets.

Figure 4b shows the performance of our model for different values of α on the EVENT2012 dataset. We observe that for different values of α, both precision and recall are affected. More specifically, the recall of the model tends to decrease for lower values of α. Without edge cutting (i.e. $\alpha = 0$), the recall of our model is similar to EDO. Overall, the impact of α is bigger on the EVENT2012 dataset than on FSD dataset. The variation of precision and recall curves is smaller for consecutive values of α w.r.t. to FSD. There

are two main reasons for that: *i)* the EVENT2012 dataset has a richer vocabulary, and *ii)* many events in the EVENT2012 dataset are similar to each other.

5 Conclusions and Future Works

In this paper, we described a model for detecting open-domain events from tweets by modeling relationships between NE mentions and terms in a directed graph. The proposed approach is unsupervised and can automatically detect fine-grained events without prior knowledge of the number or type of events. Our experiments on two gold-standard datasets show that the approach yields state-of-the-art results. In the future, we plan to investigate whether linking terms to ontologies (e.g. DBpedia, YAGO) can help in detecting different mentions of the same entity, for instance "German chancellor" and "Angela Merkel", as preliminarily shown in (Edouard et al., 2016). This can be used to reduce the density of the event graph. Another possible improvement would be to enrich the content of the tweets with information from external web pages resolving the URLs in the tweets.

References

Apoorv Agarwal, Boyi Xie, Ilia Vovsha, Owen Rambow, and Rebecca Passonneau. 2011. Sentiment analysis of twitter data. In *Proceedings of the workshop on languages in social media*. Association for Computational Linguistics, pages 30–38.

Pramod Anantharam, Payam Barnaghi, Krishnaprasad Thirunarayan, and Amit Sheth. 2015. Extracting city traffic events from social streams. *ACM*

Transactions on Intelligent Systems and Technology (TIST) 6(4):43.

Reid Andersen, Fan Chung, and Kevin Lang. 2006. Local graph partitioning using pagerank vectors. In *Foundations of Computer Science, 2006. FOCS'06. 47th Annual IEEE Symposium on*. IEEE, pages 475–486.

Farzindar Atefeh and Wael Khreich. 2015. A survey of techniques for event detection in twitter. *Computational Intelligence* 31(1):132–164.

Sergey Brin and Lawrence Page. 1998. The anatomy of a large-scale hypertextual web search engine. *Computer networks and ISDN systems* 30(1):107–117.

Leon Derczynski, Diana Maynard, Giuseppe Rizzo, Marieke van Erp, Genevieve Gorrell, Raphaël Troncy, Johann Petrak, and Kalina Bontcheva. 2015. Analysis of named entity recognition and linking for tweets. *Information Processing & Management* 51(2):32–49.

Wenwen Dou, K Wang, William Ribarsky, and Michelle Zhou. 2012. Event detection in social media data. In *IEEE VisWeek Workshop on Interactive Visual Text Analytics-Task Driven Analytics of Social Media Content*. pages 971–980.

Amosse Edouard, Elena Cabrio, Sara Tonelli, and Nhan Le Thanh. 2016. Semantic Linking for Event-Based Classification of Tweets. In *Proceedings of the Conference on Intelligent Text Processing and Computational Linguistics (CICLing)*.

C. Fellbaum. 1998. *WordNet. An Electronic Lexical Database*. MIT Press.

Mahmud Hasan, Mehmet A Orgun, and Rolf Schwitter. 2016. Twitternews: real time event detection from the twitter data stream. *PeerJ PrePrints* 4:e2297v1.

Satya Katragadda, Ryan Benton, and Vijay Raghavan. 2017. Framework for real-time event detection using multiple social media sources. In *Proceedings of the 50th Hawaii International Conference on System Sciences*.

Satya Katragadda, Shahid Virani, Ryan Benton, and Vijay Raghavan. 2016. Detection of event onset using twitter. In *Neural Networks (IJCNN), 2016 International Joint Conference on*. IEEE, pages 1539–1546.

Efthymios Kouloumpis, Theresa Wilson, and Johanna D Moore. 2011. Twitter sentiment analysis: The good the bad and the omg! *Icwsm* 11(538-541):164.

Andrew J McMinn and Joemon M Jose. 2015. Real-time entity-based event detection for twitter. In *International Conference of the Cross-Language Evaluation Forum for European Languages*. Springer, pages 65–77.

Andrew J. McMinn, Yashar Moshfeghi, and Joemon M Jose. 2013. Building a large-scale corpus for evaluating event detection on twitter. In *Proceedings of CIKM*. ACM, pages 409–418.

Rada Mihalcea and Paul Tarau. 2004. Textrank: Bringing order into texts. In Dekang Lin and Dekai Wu, editors, *Proceedings of EMNLP 2004*. Association for Computational Linguistics, Barcelona, Spain, pages 404–411.

Robertus Nugroho, Weiliang Zhao, Jian Yang, Cecile Paris, Surya Nepal, and Yan Mei. 2015. Time-sensitive topic derivation in twitter. In *International Conference on Web Information Systems Engineering*. Springer, pages 138–152.

Brendan O'Connor, Michel Krieger, and David Ahn. 2010. Tweetmotif: Exploratory search and topic summarization for twitter. In *ICWSM*. pages 384–385.

Sandeep Panem, Manish Gupta, and Vasudeva Varma. 2014. Structured information extraction from natural disaster events on twitter. In *Proceedings of the 5th International Workshop on Web-scale Knowledge Representation Retrieval & Reasoning*. ACM, pages 1–8.

Ruchi Parikh and Kamalakar Karlapalem. 2013. Et: events from tweets. In *Proceedings of the 22nd International Conference on World Wide Web*. ACM, pages 613–620.

Saša Petrović, Miles Osborne, and Victor Lavrenko. 2010. Streaming first story detection with application to twitter. In *Human Language Technologies: The 2010 Annual Conference of the North American Chapter of the Association for Computational Linguistics*. Association for Computational Linguistics, pages 181–189.

Saša Petrović, Miles Osborne, and Victor Lavrenko. 2012. Using paraphrases for improving first story detection in news and twitter. In *Proceedings of the 2012 Conference of the North American Chapter of the Association for Computational Linguistics: Human Language Technologies*. pages 338–346.

Ana-Maria Popescu, Marco Pennacchiotti, and Deepa Paranjpe. 2011. Extracting events and event descriptions from twitter. In *Proceedings of the 20th international conference companion on World wide web*. ACM, pages 105–106.

Takeshi Sakaki, Makoto Okazaki, and Yutaka Matsuo. 2010. Earthquake shakes twitter users: real-time event detection by social sensors. In *Proceedings of the 19th international conference on World wide web*. ACM, pages 851–860.

Rachele Sprugnoli and Sara Tonelli. 2017. One, no one and one hundred thousand events: Defining and processing events in an inter-disciplinary perspective. *Natural Language Engineering* 23(4):485–506.

Marieke Van Erp, Giuseppe Rizzo, and Raphaël Troncy. 2013. Learning with the web: Spotting named entities on the intersection of nerd and machine learning. In *# MSM*. Citeseer, pages 27–30.

Xiaofeng Wang, Matthew S Gerber, and Donald E Brown. 2012. Automatic crime prediction using events extracted from twitter posts. In *Social Computing, Behavioral-Cultural Modeling and Prediction*, Springer, pages 231–238.

Wei Xu, Ralph Grishman, Adam Meyers, and Alan Ritter. 2013. A preliminary study of tweet summarization using information extraction. *NAACL 2013* page 20.

Deyu Zhou, Liangyu Chen, and Yulan He. 2011. A simple bayesian modelling approach to event extraction from twitter. *Atlantis* page 0.

Deyu Zhou, Xuan Zhang, and Yulan He. 2017. Event extraction from Twitter using Non-Parametric Bayesian Mixture Model with Word Embeddings. In *Proceedings of the 15th Conference of the European Chapter of the Association for Computational Linguistics*. Valencia, Spain, pages 808–817.

Opinion Mining in Social Networks versus Electoral Polls

Javi Fernández, Fernando Llopis, Yoan Gutiérrez, Patricio Martínez-Barco, Álvaro Díez
Department of Software and Computing Systems, University of Alicante
{javifm,llopis,ygutierrez,patricio,adiez}@dlsi.ua.es

Abstract

The recent failures of traditional poll models, like the predictions in United Kingdom with the Brexit, or in United States presidential election with the victory of Donald Trump, have been noteworthy. With the decline of traditional poll models and the growth of the social networks, automatic tools are gaining popularity to make predictions in this context. In this paper we present our approximation and compare it with a real case: the 2017 French presidential election.

1   Introduction

Numbers leave no doubt: *social networks* are becoming more popular each day. According to the *Internet Live Stats* website[1], around 46% of the world population has an Internet connection today (July 2017), and around 55% of them are active users in a social network like *Facebook*[2] or *Twitter*[3]. This means around 2 billion people using social networks in the world. Beyond the sociological information they can bring, social networks have become a place where users not only can learn about what is happening around them, but also give opinions with respect to their environment. From a political point of view, they provide a lot of information on the possible degradations of the standard of living of a particular geographical area (Intagorn and Lerman, 2013). Others prefer to conduct studies of more reliable sources such as the news of the digital press (Leetaru et al., 2013).

Despite the slight decline in usage compared to previous years, *Twitter* still has an important use among Internet users, with more than 500 million tweets per day. But what allows Twitter to be one of the most popular data sources for social research is its open API[4] (Leetaru et al., 2013). It offers an *"unprecedented opportunity to study human communication and social networks"* (Miller, 2011). The access to the information turned over Twitter by millions of users can offer us a snapshot of the general state of each location. This information can help with the early detection of conflicts. In addition, if these studies are carried out in real-time, in the event of a catastrophe we can obtain critical information about in which areas it is a priority to act.

One of the possible uses of this information provided in real-time is the analysis of opinions of the citizens about the candidates to some electoral campaign, especially because the classic models of electoral polls are in crisis. The recent failures of these traditional models, like the predictions in United Kingdom with the Brexit, or in United States presidential election with the victory of Donald Trump, are very well-known. In a world in which information grows faster and faster, it is striking that models based on making hundreds of phone calls are still employed to predict results, like the surveys in the *Financial Times*[5] (see Figure 1). Traditional models obtain information that will be obsolete before it can be published or even processed. This obsolescence is not only due to the cost of information processing, but also due to people who are becoming more and more tired of talking to pollsters, and in many cases their intention to vote reflects a timely opinion, that may change during the electoral process.

Social networks allow to measure opinions and emotions of the citizens throughout the whole

---

[1] www.internetlivestats.com
[2] www.facebook.com
[3] twitter.com

[4] Application Programming Interface
[5] ig.ft.com/sites/france-election/polls

Proceedings of Recent Advances in Natural Language Processing, pages 231–237,
Varna, Bulgaria, Sep 4–6 2017.

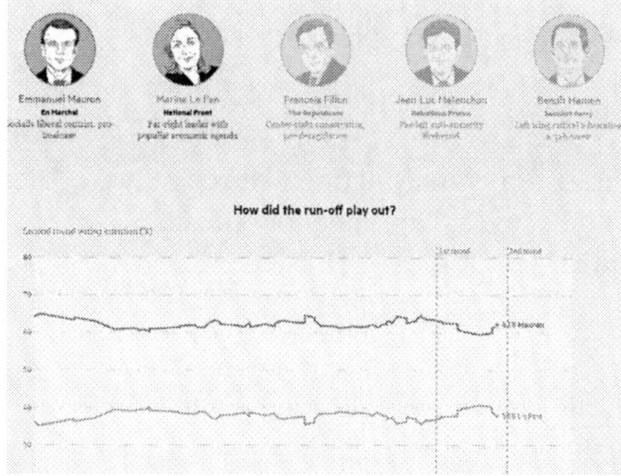

Figure 1: French election polls, Financial Times

electoral process. Users write their opinions about one candidate or another continuously. It is common to use the number of tweets or the *trending topics* as metrics to evaluate the reputation. But speaking a lot about someone does not imply the comments are necessarily positive. This is where the use of *Natural Language Processing* (NLP) and *Sentiment Analysis* (SA) techniques can be very useful, allowing to detect, with a reasonable degree of reliability, if the opinions about something are positive or negative.

In most of the cases, the users can provide information about their usual location or the place they write their messages. This allows to create studies with far more detail and information than traditional ones. However, location is not usually shared because of privacy or battery consumption. Some studies (Weidemann, 2014; Cebeillac and Rault, 2016) showed that the number of geolocated tweets is usually between 10% and 20%, but in our experience this number can be much lower, less than 5% in some contexts like politics. So, except some studies that use geolocation data to filter out unwanted messages (Poblete et al., 2011), most of them indicate that the users location is a field that determines with higher precision the geographical position of an user, and therefore their environment.

In this paper we present the *Social Analytics* system, developed by the *Natural Language Processing Group* (GPLSI) at the *University of Alicante*, a system that creates real-time reports summarising how different entities are being valued, based on the number of *positive*, *negative* or *neutral* opinions that users write about it, and the *audience* of those opinions (the number of followers of their authors). In addition, our system provides charts, aggregations, statistics, and advanced filters to show the information desired by the users. In previous works we studied the reputation in different contexts, but in this paper we present a study of the quality of the system to predict electoral results, and we compare it with a traditional model based on surveys. The context of experimentation chosen is the **2017 French presidential election**.

The article is structured as follows. In Section 2 we briefly describe the related work. Section 3 describes the architecture of our system. Section 4 will detail the formulas used to determine how the reputation of an entity is measured. Section 5 describes the evaluation, and Section 6 presents a series of conclusions and works that are currently being done to improve the system.

2 Related Work

Some other systems to visualize data from social networks exist, the majority of them focused only in statistics, but some others also adding semantic features as sentiment analysis (Marcus et al., 2011; Hao et al., 2011; Wang et al., 2012). There are also some public tools with this purpose, such as *SocialMention*[6]. In addition, there have been several studies in calculate the reputation of an entity, this is, how an entity is being valued in the Internet (Villena-Román et al., 2012; Amigó et al., 2014). Our proposal contains different statistical visualisations, reputation calculation, and advanced filtering by different dimensions, everything in real-time. The main goal of our system is to visualise the current state of an entity, what is being said about it, how it is being valued and, in some cases, make predictions about the future reputation of that entity.

It is essential to detect the polarity of the messages: if the data is expressing an opinion and, if it does, indicate if it is positive or negative. The field of *sentiment analysis* and *polarity classification* has been widely studied in the last years (Pang et al., 2008; Liu and Zhang, 2012; Mohammad, 2015; Ravi and Ravi, 2015). Two main approaches can be followed: *machine learning* and *lexicon-based*. *Machine learning* approaches perform very well in the domain they are trained on, but their performance drops when the same classifier is used in a different domain. In addition, if the number of features is big, the efficiency drops dra-

---

[6]www.socialmention.com

matically. *Lexicon-based approaches* make use of dictionaries of opinionated words and phrases to discern the polarity of a text. These approaches are usually faster than machine learning ones, as they employ predefined mathematical functions, but less effective in specific domains because they are (in general) more generic. The approximation we chose for our system is a hybrid approach, simple and fast enough to be used in real-time applications, but with a decent classification quality. This approach is described in Section 3.

Furthermore, in the case of Twitter, the usual location of the user is a free text field, so in some cases users can fill it with misspellings or an incorrect location. Obtain a real place from this field is a complex problem (Hecht et al., 2011; Peregrino et al., 2013). Our approximation to this problem is described in detail also in Section 3.

3   Architecture

In summary, our approximation downloads messages and comments from the social networks, extracts the useful information they contain (text, author, polarity, locations, etc.), and stores it in an efficient way to generate reports in real-time. We divided the system in three main modules: *listening*, *processing* and *presentation*, and uses three different databases (see Figure 2).

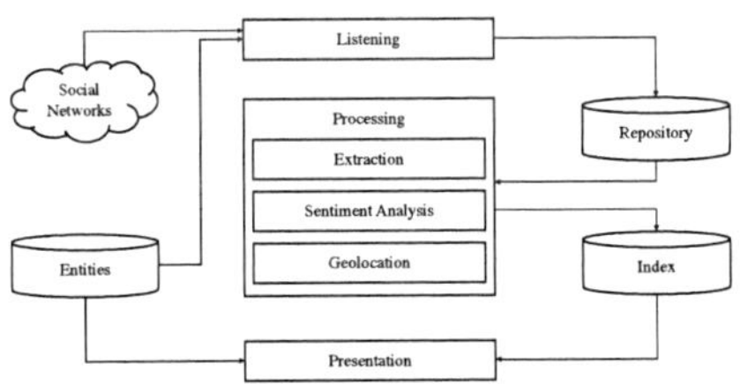

Figure 2: System architecture

3.1   Databases

First, we will describe the databases employed in our system. This will allow the reader to understand better how the concepts are represented and the information we want to fetch.

- **Entities**. In this database we store the entities of interest for the users. Users must manually assign terms (words, phrases, hashtags, or usernames) for each entity, that must

appear in a text to consider it is mentioning that entity. For example, in the context of the 2017 French presidential election, the entity *Emmanuel Macron* would contain terms like "emmanuel macron", "macron" or @emmanuelmacron.

- **Repository**. This is a temporary database in which we store the messages and comments found in social networks. Here, all the data is stored without any processing, and is deleted once processed.

- **Index**. This is also a messages and comments database. But here, the data is stored in a way that permits to perform analytics and statistics as efficiently as possible. We want to highlight that the data is only indexed and not stored, so it is not accessible anymore. We can only perform statistics, aggregations and filters.

3.2   Listening module

This module is responsible for downloading messages from the social networks. It does periodic search requests of the terms in the entities database, using the social network API (when available) to fetch the messages containing those terms. The frequency of the periodic searches depends on the API limits and the number of terms we have in the database. Some APIs allow to obtain these messages in streaming, that is, offering the messages as soon as they are published. In both cases, the fetched messages are stored in the *Repository* database.

3.3   Processing module

This module performs the data extraction, location detection and sentiment analysis of the fetched messages through the listening module. When available, we extract the text of the message, its publication date, its author, the users that are mentioned, the location where the message was written, and the usual location of the author.

In the case of Twitter, this last field is free text and users can write whatever they want. To obtain the most probable location we employ a very simple approximation. We indexed a places database (*Geonames*[7]), performing *exact* searches on it, and choosing the first result. We tried with more relaxed queries, but we preferred to obtain better precision and avoid false positives.

---

[7] http://www.geonames.org

From the text we also extract its polarity, that is, if the author is giving a positive, negative or neutral opinion about the entity. To detect this polarity we employ a hybrid supervised approach (Fernández et al., 2013, 2014a,b, 2015; Gutierrez et al., 2015). In summary, this approach builds a sentiment lexicon from a polarity dataset using statistical measures. It uses *skipgrams* as information units, to enrich the sentiment lexicon with combinations of words that do not appear explicitly in the text. The lexicon created is employed in conjunction with machine learning techniques to create the final classifier. This approach has been chosen mainly because of its balance between speed and accuracy.

3.4 Presentation module

This module refers to the user interface. Figure 3 shows the main view of the dashboard in our system. At a glance we can access all the data from different points of view:

- The number of mentions for each entity.

- The audience[10] (number of people) the messages of each entity can potentially reach.

- The entity reputation, a numeric value representing how users are valuing the entity (see Section 4).

- The more repeated words and hashtags.

- The most active users with the biggest number of publications, and the most mentioned users (usually the most replied users).

- The places the messages were written and the geographical origin of the authors of the messages.

- The polarity of the messages.

One of the important features of our system is that all the information shown can be filtered, in real-time, by date, polarity, author, location, etc.

4 Reputation

Using the number of positive, neutral and negative opinions detected, and the audience of those opinions, we can calculate a value of **reputation** for each entity in a specific time period. This metric is

a numeric value in the interval $[-1, +1]$, where -1 is the worst value of reputation and $+1$ is the best one. It is calculated using the formula in Equation 4, where e is the entity we are assessing; t is a time interval; $P_{e,t,+}$, $P_{e,t,0}$ and $P_{e,t,-}$ represent the set of publications containing a mention to the entity e in the time interval t with a positive, neutral and negative polarity respectively; a_p is the audience of the publication p; and d_t is the duration of the time interval t in milliseconds. Other statistics like the number of likes, retweets or clicks are not considered in this formula, mainly because they are not available at publication time (they are usually zero).

The inclusion of the time interval in the equation (d_t) is a way to give a higher reputation to those publications with a higher audience. For example, if an entity has negative mentions and reached 100 people in a minute, its reputation in that interval would be $-3 \cdot 100/(3 \cdot 100 + 60000) = -0.005$. However, if those publications reached 10,000 people, the reputation would be $-3 \cdot 10000/(3 \cdot 10000 + 60000) = -0.333$.

We want to highlight that in our system we consider neutral mentions ($p \in P_{e,t,0}$) as something positive, because being mentioned in social networks improves the reputation. In this way, if all the mentions are neutral, the reputation will be bigger than zero, while if there are no mentions, the reputation would be exactly zero.

$$pos = \sum_{p \in P_{e,t,+}} a_p \tag{1}$$

$$neg = \sum_{p \in P_{e,t,-}} a_p \tag{2}$$

$$neu = \sum_{p \in P_{e,t,0}} a_p \tag{3}$$

$$r_{e,t} = \frac{2 \cdot pos + neu - 2 \cdot neg}{2 \cdot (pos + neu + neg) + d_t} \tag{4}$$

In the context of the politics, this value of reputation between -1 and $+1$ may not be the most intuitive, because it is more common to use the *vote intention* measure. This is a percentage in the interval $[0\%, 100\%]$, where all the candidates sum 100% in every period of time. We made some additions in order to adapt our metrics to obtain a similar value. The formula for this new **collective reputation** is shown in Equation 5, where E is the set of all the entities to evaluate; and i is an entity inside the set E.

---

[10]This value is calculated by adding the number of followers of the authors of all the messages.

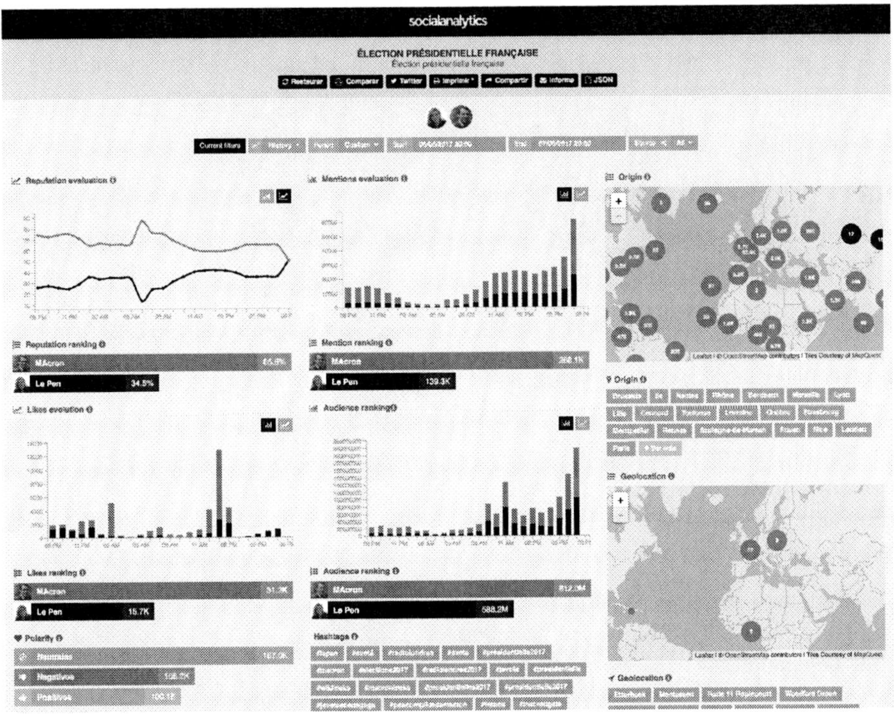

Figure 3: Main system dashboard, comparing the two main candidates in the French presidential election between May 4, 2017 and May 5, 2017 (Macron: orange, Le Pen: black)[9]

$$cr_{e,t} = \frac{r_{e,t} + 1}{\sum_{i \in E} (r_{i,t} + 1)} \cdot 100 \qquad (5)$$

This collective reputation is the metric we use in Figure 3 and the one we will use in the following Evaluation section.

5 Evaluation

The evaluation was performed in the context of the 2017 French presidential elections, specifically for the second round and the two most popular candidates: Emmanuel Macron and Marine Le Pen. In our opinion, this context was a suitable field of experimentation for the predictive use of our system, because:

- The circumscription was unique.

- There were only two candidates to evaluate.

- There was a lot of activity for both candidates, so there was a big number of messages to evaluate.

A week before the elections, we created an entity for each candidate. The terms chosen for Macron were "macron", "emmanuel macron", #macron, and @emmanuelmacron. For Le Pen, the terms were "le pen", "marine lepen", #lepen, and @lepen. Some days after, two predictions of election results were published on Twitter[11] (see Figure 5) (May 5, 2017 and May 6, 2017) the election day (May 7, 2017) using the proposed collective reputation. Some hours after the publication of our first prediction, a French television channel (BFMTV) published a poll that showed values[12] that were very similar to the ones given by our system (see Figure 4). However, our predictions were obtained in real-time, were easier to obtain, and were more economic.

During that weekend, the value of reputation for Macron was increased reaching the values of our second prediction[14] (see Figure 5). The final result was 66% for Macron and 33% for Le Pen. In our first consideration we concluded that the positive tendency of Twitter was not reflected in the final results. It is possible that if the election would be celebrated later, the result could not be

---

[11]twitter.com/fernandollopis/status/860463546597093376
[12]https://goo.gl/bzlwX1
[14]twitter.com/fernandollopis/status/860985783095885825

Figure 4: Vote intention published by BMFTV

the same. But what seems evident is that tendency of increase in Twitter.

There are other sociological aspects outside our study, but interesting to remark:

- We do not know the representation of the active French population with respect the total voting population.

- The influence of abstention in the final result.

- The information propagation speed and tendencies on the Internet respect the real vote propagation.

6 Conclusions

In this paper we presented the *Social Analytics* system. This system creates real-time reports summarising how different entities are being valued, providing a value of reputation for each entity. This reputation can be used to make comparisons with other entities and, in some cases, it can be useful to make predictions based on the current reputation of those entities.

The context of experimentation chosen was the second round of the 2017 French presidential election. In this simple case, with two candidates of electoral unique circumscription, the results prediction and tendencies in social networks have been very close to the final results, or at least as correct as the traditional polls. This opens a great amount of possibilities with respect the use of social networks, much more economic and updated, to measure the status of the candidates in electoral campaigns.

We open two research lines. The first is to continue experimenting with the reputation formula to obtain better and more accurate results. We will continue studying the concepts of number of mentions and audience, and how they affect each other.

The second goal is to improve the location detection of the authors, in order to be more accurate in geographic level results.

Acknowledgements

This research work has been partially funded by the University of Alicante, Generalitat Valenciana, Spanish Government, Ministerio de Educación, Cultura y Deporte and Ayudas Fundación BBVA a equipos de investigación científica 2016 through the projects TIN2015-65100-R, TIN2015-65136-C2-2-R, PROMETEOII/2014/001, "Plataforma inteligente para recuperación, análisis y representación de la información generada por usuarios en Internet" (GRE16-01) and "Análisis de Sentimientos Aplicado a la Prevención del Suicidio en las Redes Sociales" (ASAP).

References

Enrique Amigó, Jorge Carrillo-de Albornoz, Irina Chugur, Adolfo Corujo, Julio Gonzalo, Edgar Meij, Maarten de Rijke, and Damiano Spina. 2014. Overview of replab 2014: author profiling and reputation dimensions for online reputation management. In *International Conference of the Cross-Language Evaluation Forum for European Languages*. Springer, pages 307–322.

Alexandre Cebeillac and Yves-Marie Rault. 2016. Contribution of geotagged twitter data in the study of a social group's activity space. the case of the upper middle class in delhi, india. *Netcom. Réseaux, communication et territoires* (30-3/4):231–248.

Javi Fernández, José M Gómez, and Patricio Martínez-Barco. 2014a. A supervised approach for sentiment analysis using skipgrams. In *11th International Workshop on Natural Language Processing and Cognitive Science (NAACL)*.

Javi Fernández, Yoan Gutiérrez, José M Gómez, and Patricio Martınez-Barco. 2014b. Gplsi: Supervised sentiment analysis in twitter using skipgrams. In *Proceedings of the 8th International Workshop on Semantic Evaluation (SemEval 2014)*. pages 294–299.

Javi Fernández, Yoan Gutiérrez, José Manuel Gómez, Patricio Martínez-Barco, Andrés Montoyo, and Rafael Munoz. 2013. Sentiment analysis of spanish tweets using a ranking algorithm and skipgrams. In *XXIX Congreso de la Sociedad Espanola de Procesamiento de Lenguaje Natural (SEPLN 2013)*. pages 133–142.

Javi Fernández, Yoan Gutiérrez, David Tomás, José M Gómez, and Patricio Martínez-Barco. 2015. Evaluating a sentiment analysis approach from a business point of view .

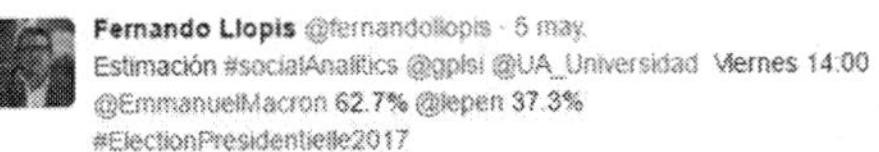

Figure 5: French presidential election prediction[13]

Yoan Gutierrez, David Tomas, and Javi Fernandez. 2015. Benefits of using ranking skip-gram techniques for opinion mining approaches. In *eChallenges e-2015 Conference, 2015*. IEEE, pages 1–10.

Ming Hao, Christian Rohrdantz, Halldór Janetzko, Umeshwar Dayal, Daniel A Keim, Lars-Erik Haug, and Mei-Chun Hsu. 2011. Visual sentiment analysis on twitter data streams. In *Visual Analytics Science and Technology (VAST), 2011 IEEE Conference on*. IEEE, pages 277–278.

Brent Hecht, Lichan Hong, Bongwon Suh, and Ed H Chi. 2011. Tweets from justin bieber's heart: the dynamics of the location field in user profiles. In *Proceedings of the SIGCHI Conference on Human Factors in Computing Systems*. ACM, pages 237–246.

Suradej Intagorn and Kristina Lerman. 2013. Mining geospatial knowledge on the social web. *Using Social and Information Technologies for Disaster and Crisis Management* pages 98–112.

Kalev Leetaru, Shaowen Wang, Guofeng Cao, Anand Padmanabhan, and Eric Shook. 2013. Mapping the global twitter heartbeat: The geography of twitter. *First Monday* 18(5).

Bing Liu and Lei Zhang. 2012. A survey of opinion mining and sentiment analysis. In *Mining text data*, Springer, pages 415–463.

Adam Marcus, Michael S Bernstein, Osama Badar, David R Karger, Samuel Madden, and Robert C Miller. 2011. Twitinfo: aggregating and visualizing microblogs for event exploration. In *Proceedings of the SIGCHI conference on Human factors in computing systems*. ACM, pages 227–236.

Greg Miller. 2011. Social scientists wade into the tweet stream. *Science* 333(6051):1814–1815.

Saif M Mohammad. 2015. Sentiment analysis: Detecting valence, emotions, and other affectual states from text. *Emotion measurement* pages 201–238.

Bo Pang, Lillian Lee, et al. 2008. Opinion mining and sentiment analysis. *Foundations and Trends® in Information Retrieval* 2(1–2):1–135.

Fernando S Peregrino, David Tomás, and Fernando Llopis. 2013. Every move you make i'll be watching you: geographical focus detection on twitter. In *Proceedings of the 7th Workshop on Geographic Information Retrieval*. ACM, pages 1–8.

Barbara Poblete, Ruth Garcia, Marcelo Mendoza, and Alejandro Jaimes. 2011. Do all birds tweet the same?: characterizing twitter around the world. In *Proceedings of the 20th ACM international conference on Information and knowledge management*. ACM, pages 1025–1030.

Kumar Ravi and Vadlamani Ravi. 2015. A survey on opinion mining and sentiment analysis: tasks, approaches and applications. *Knowledge-Based Systems* 89:14–46.

Julio Villena-Román, Sara Lana-Serrano, Cristina Moreno, Janine García-Morera, and José Carlos González Cristóbal. 2012. Daedalus at replab 2012: Polarity classification and filtering on twitter data. In *CLEF (Online Working Notes/Labs/Workshop)*. volume 60.

Hao Wang, Dogan Can, Abe Kazemzadeh, François Bar, and Shrikanth Narayanan. 2012. A system for real-time twitter sentiment analysis of 2012 us presidential election cycle. In *Proceedings of the ACL 2012 System Demonstrations*. Association for Computational Linguistics, pages 115–120.

Chris Donald Weidemann. 2014. *Geosocialfootprint (2013): Social media location privacy web map*. University of Southern California.

Corpus Creation and Initial SMT Experiments between Spanish and Shipibo-konibo

Ana-Paula Galarreta[1], **Andrés Melgar**[2] and **Arturo Oncevay-Marcos**[2]
[1]Departamento de Ciencias, [2]Departamento de Ingeniería
Grupo de Reconocimiento de Patrones e Inteligencia Artificial Aplicada
Pontificia Universidad Católica del Perú, Lima, Perú
{a.galarreta, amelgar, arturo.oncevay}@pucp.edu.pe

Abstract

In this paper, we present the first attempts to develop a machine translation (MT) system between Spanish and Shipibo-konibo (es-shp). There are very few digital texts written in Shipibo-konibo and even less bilingual texts that can be aligned, hence we had to create a parallel corpus using both bilingual and monolingual texts. We will describe how this corpus was made, as well as the process we followed to improve the quality of the sentences used to build a statistical MT model or SMT. The results obtained surpassed the baseline proposed (dictionary based) and made a promising result for further development considering the size of corpus used. Finally, it is expected that this MT system can be reinforced with the use of additional linguistic rules and automatic language processing functions that are being implemented.

1 Introduction

In Perú, there are around 47 indigenous or original languages according to the database of the Ministry of Culture (Ministerio de Cultura, Perú, 2016). Besides the official Spanish (Castillan) language, which is spoken by the majority of the population, there are other native languages that have remained throughout history in the different regions of the country. For instance, in the highlands, there are a lot of speakers from the Quechua family, followed by Aymara. Furthermost, in the Amazon region, there is a high density presence of many linguistic families between the different native communities, where Shipibo-konibo is one of the most studied languages by linguists at Perú (Valenzuela, 2003). Besides, nowadays there are a lot of efforts from the government in order to accelerate the integration of the communities that don't speak Spanish as the main language.

In this context, there is a need for computational resources to facilitate the accomplishment of tasks for the social inclusion of this native communities. As first steps, there are basic natural language processing (NLP) tools required for morphological or syntax analysis that are under development (Pereira et al., 2017). However one of the most important applications needed is a machine translation (MT) system, at least a prototype one.

MT systems may be rule (RBMT) or corpus driven (SMT). Also, there is an hybrid approach that integrates both of them (Costa-Jussa and Fonollosa, 2015). The RBMT system is based on the linguistic knowledge and could be very expensive to build in time and effort, while the SMT relies on the amount of parallel corpus available in order to obtain consistent results. Besides, there is a novel corpus-driven approach called Neural Machine Translation (NMT), but it could be less effective in low-resource scenarios unless there is another (rich-resourced) language involved as a pivot (Zoph et al., 2016).

In this context, it may seem that a SMT is not an appropriate approach for minority languages or with scarce digital resources. However, there have been different studies trying to take advantage of any small corpus they could. For instance, there were attempts for many pair of languages (involving a low resourced one) such as English-Lao, Myanmar and Thai (Pa et al., 2016); English-Estonian, Hungarian, Latvian, Lithuanian and Polish (Skadiņš et al., 2014) and also Persian-English (Salami et al., 2016).

While those studies use corpus with more than 50 000 sentences (for example, Skadiņš et al. (2014) obtained a BLEU score of 59.70 using a 0.5M en-hu corpus), our work will use at most the fifth part. Nevertheless, this does not stop

Proceedings of Recent Advances in Natural Language Processing, pages 238–244,
Varna, Bulgaria, Sep 4–6 2017.

this study and experiment, since the final goal is to be able to integrate the SMT system to a platform linked with more linguistic resources, taking advantage of rules, and other NLP functionalities such as POS-tagging or dependency parsing (Costa-Jussa and Fonollosa, 2015). In this sense, the individual results obtained were very promising considering the size of corpus used.

This study is organized as follows. Section 2 presents the Shipibo-konibo language. After that, Section 3 details the procedure followed to build our parallel corpus. Then, the experiment design is described in Section 4 and the obtained results are discussed in Section 5. Finally, we conclude the paper in Section 6, including future work proposals.

2 The Shipibo-Konibo Language

Shipibo-konibo (shp) is one of the most representative native languages in Perú, behind the Quechua language family, Aymara and Ashaninkas. It belongs to the Panoan family, which is an important subject of study of many linguist researchers in Perú (Adelaar et al., 2011; Zariquiey, 2006). This language is spoken by around 22k people in 150 communities, and is taught in almost 300 public schools (Ministerio de Educación, Perú, 2013b).

Shipibo-konibo is an agglomerative language, with a high use of common suffixes (130) plus some prefixes (13) for its words formation process. Thereby, this language has a very rich morphology, which increase the difficulty in an SMT task, because each variation of a word (flexed by an affix) would be taken into account as a completely new word. Also, the basic sentence order construction is SOV (subject-object-verb) unlike Spanish (SVO) (Valenzuela, 2003). An example of a translation (to English) could be seen in Figure 1.

3 Corpus Creation Procedure

The followed procedure consists mainly in the selection, preparation (that could includes digitalization, manual correction and translation) and alignment of a parallel corpus from different sources. We take into account two main domains for the corpus: religious and educational, and it is available in the project site[1]. The next subsections will

---

[1]`chana.inf.pucp.edu.pe/resources`

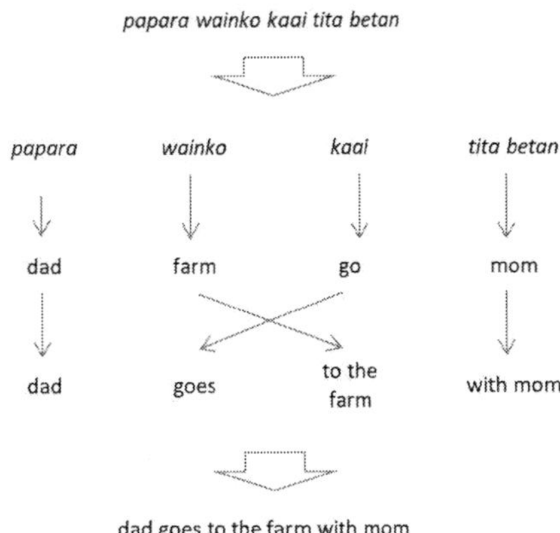

Figure 1: A translation sample between Shipibo-Konibo and English

detail the generation of the corpus and its later analysis at word level.

3.1 Generation of Parallel Corpus

In order to develop a SMT model, a large amount of parallel corpus is needed (Koehn, 2009). This kind of corpus is a very valuable resource for machine translation tasks but at the same time is a prohibitive element for low-resourced languages. In our case, Shipibo-konibo, as a minority language in Perú, has a very poor collection of digital text corpus, even monolingual ones. So it has been very difficult to identify texts translated between that language and Spanish.

Despite that, we decided to carry out an exhaustive search as a first step. In this context, we obtained a Shipibo-konibo to Spanish dictionary (which included translated sentences), laws, law proposals and the catholic Bible in both languages. However, the amount of parallel sentences obtained from the legal domain were too limited (1 142) and it was very difficult to increase the corpus size of that domain, due to the length of sentences and complexity of words used to write laws in Spanish.

The dictionary (James et al., 1993) included 5 143 translated sentences used to illustrate the meaning of the different terminology entries. Since each entry is different, we expected to have several out of vocabulary words (OOVW) when splitting the corpus into train-tune-test. For this reason, instead of using the dictionary examples to create a parallel corpus, we decided to elaborate rules from the entries in Shipibo-konibo and their

239

Table 1: Religious domain corpus: Token count per sentence

max number	shp		es	
of words	number of sentences	% of sentences	number of sentences	% of sentences
5	1 723	12.7	1 953	14.4
10	4 672	34.4	4 428	32.6
15	7 713	56.8	7 225	53.2
20	10 101	74.3	9 715	71.5
25	11 692	86.1	11 530	84.9
30	12 570	92.5	12 594	92.7
35	13 108	96.5	13 156	96.8

Table 2: Educational domain corpus (kindergarten book): Token count per sentence

max number	shp		es	
of words	number of sentences	% of sentences	number of sentences	% of sentences
5	983	49.9	523	14.4
10	1 595	84.3	1 224	64.7
15	1 742	92.1	1 565	82.8
20	1 798	95.1	1 691	89.4
25	1 828	96.7	1 754	92.8
30	1 848	97.7	1 793	94.8
35	1 862	98.5	1 826	96.6

correspondent translation. This procedure was tedious because only a scanned version of the dictionary was available.

In order to obtain the rules mentioned above, an OCR function was applied to the dictionary. However, the obtained text had several errors, which meant we had to correct it manually (with help of linguistic and engineering students). Finally, using information about the structure of the dictionary, we were able to obtain 13 783 rules to translate words directly from Shipibo-konibo to Spanish.

Regarding the religious domain, we were able to automatically obtain more than 10 000 phrases. Even though this corpus can not be enlarged or renewed we decided to run tests with it, since no one has analyzed the Bible in Shipibo-konibo before.

On the other side, because one of the main motivations to implement the translator is to use it in an educational context (to support the generation of bilingual education textbooks), we decided to translate educational text from Shipibo-konibo to Spanish and vice versa.

In the next subsections, we will detail the contents of each domain.

3.1.1 Religious Domain

The Bible is a common parallel corpus used in many experiments, regarding its limited size, due to the availability of many languages translations (Christodouloupoulos and Steedman, 2015). Using both Shipibo-konibo and Spanish Bibles, we semi-automatically aligned 9 804 versicles.

It is important to mention that not all of the Bible's books have been translated to Shipibo-konibo and that this translation may differ from the Spanish one. We identified several differences and had to make manual corrections in order to align the versicles. This is the case of chapter 3 of Joel's book (es), which was aligned with the last versicles of chapter 2 (shp).

Then, each versicle was split using specific punctuation signs (dots, colons, question and exclamation marks). For example, when Apocalypse 15:3 was split, 3 sentences were automatically obtained per language (Shipibo-konibo and Spanish):

shp: *[1] Jatianra ja Diossen yonoti Moiséssen bewá, itan *Corderon bewá bewai neskákana iki: [2] "Non Ibo Dios, jatíbi atipana koshi, itan ratéti jawékibo riki jatíbi min akábo; ponté, itan ikon riki min ikábo. [3] Mia riki jatíbiainoa joni-*

baon Apo

es: [1] Estos cantan el cántico de Moisés, servidor de Dios, y el cántico del Cordero: [2] Grandes y maravillosas son tus obras,Señor Dios, Todopoderoso. [3] Justicia y verdad guían tus pasos, oh Rey de las naciones.

en: [1] And they sing the song of Moses the servant of God, and the song of the Lamb, saying, [2] Great and marvellous are thy works, Lord God Almighty; [3] just and true are thy ways, thou King of saints.

Finally, we cleaned the text by removing all remaining punctuation signs (such as dashes and commas) and 13 587 sentences were obtained.

3.1.2 Educational Domain

An educational book used for kindergarten Shipibo-konibo students (Ministerio de Educación, Perú, 2013a) was translated by a human translator certified by the Ministry of Culture. As a result, 1 466 of the book's paragraphs were translated. Then, we split several paragraphs using punctuation signs. To split a paragraph, it had to fulfill both of the following conditions:

- The number of obtained phrases is the same for both languages.

- For all obtained phrases, the $ratio_{shp-es}$ of tokens was in a range value between 0.5 and 2 (see subsection 3.2.2).

After duplicated sentences were removed, we were left with 1 891 aligned sentences. For example, the following paragraph was split in 2 sentences:

shp: [1] ¿Jawe janerin min jeman jane?, [2] ¿Jawekeskamein min jema peokotai bena ika iki?

es: [1] ¿Cómo se llama tu comunidad?, [2] ¿Cómo se formó tu comunidad al principio?

en: [1] What is the name of your community?, [2] How was your community formed in the beginning?

3.2 Analysis of Parallel Corpora

Since manual validation of the human translations or the automatic alignments was not performed, we decided to obtain some descriptive information of the parallel corpus. Note that for the educational domain, only results from the kindergarten book are shown.

3.2.1 Token Count per Sentence

SMT systems are usually trained with short sentences (Dimeo, 2014), such as 10 tokens at most. In this case, in order to analyze the size of our corpus to know its usefulness, we decided to calculate the number of tokens for both Spanish and Shipibo-konibo sentences with a five-step variation. Results are shown on Table 1 and Table 2.

As we can observe, if we filter our corpus to limit sentence length to 10 tokens in Shipibo-konibo or Spanish, we would be left with less than 35% of total sentences. For this reason, we decided not to limit the sentence length to 10 or less tokens.

3.2.2 Ratio shp-es

We also calculated the Shipibo-konibo to Spanish ratio per sentence, using the following formula:

$$ratio_{shp-es} = \frac{tokens_{shipibo-konibo}}{tokens_{spanish}}$$

Since Shipibo-konibo is an agglutinate language, a sentence in Spanish usually presents fewer words in the Shipibo-konibo translated counterpart. Hence, we expected this ratio to be lower than 1 in most cases and this is true for the educational corpus. However, as seen in Figure 2, in the religious domain that statement does not follow the expected trend. We think this is due to the way the Bible was translated (from Spanish to Shipibo-konibo) and because of the nature of the texts: the missioners that translated it wanted to preserve the meaning of each sentence, so they probably used more words than usual.

3.2.3 Token Frequency

We determined the frequency of each token in both domains and observed that several tokens are *hapax legomenon* (HL) or words that appear only once within the corpus. We can see that information in Table 3.

Table 3: Token-level corpus stats: T = number of tokens; $|\mathcal{V}|$ = word vocabulary size or unique tokens; HLT = number of HL tokens (*hapax legomenon*).

	Religious		Educational	
	es	shp	es	shp
T	215 818	210 828	21 150	14 225
$|\mathcal{V}|$	14 386	20 500	2 629	2 793
HLT	6 706	11 898	1 324	1 642
%HLT	3.1	5.6	6.3	11.5

We also calculated the percentage of sentences that contain HL tokens, and those results are presented in Table 4. It was important to identify these HL tokens, since they would only appear in

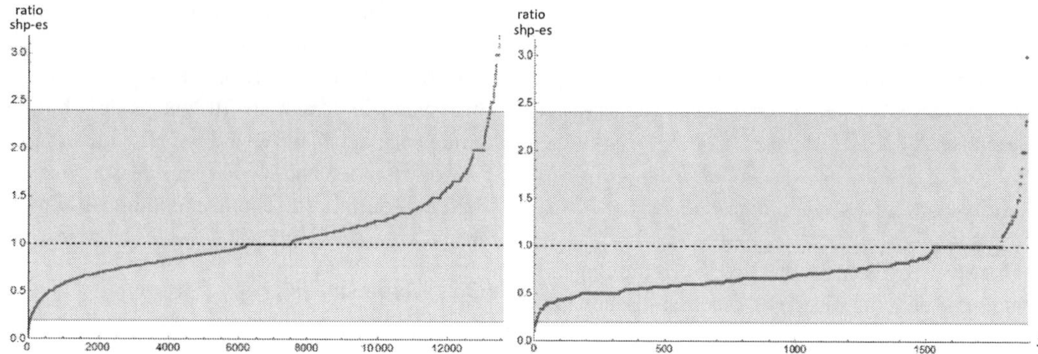

Figure 2: Sentence number (S) versus $ratio_{shp-es}$ for both the religious (left) and educational domain (right) corpus. The 96.6% of religious domain sentences have $ratio_{shp-es}$ values between 0.2 and 2.4, and 99.3% of educational domain sentences have $ratio_{shp-es}$ values between 0.4 and 2.4

one of the sub-datasets (train, validation or test). This means HL tokens present in the train subset would be the OOVW in the test subset, which can affect the overall result of the SMT system.

Table 4: Sentence-level corpus stats: S = total number of sentences or phrases; $SHLT$ = number of sentences or phrases that contains at least one HL token.

	Religious		Educational	
	es	shp	es	shp
S	13 587	13 587	1 891	1 891
$SHLT$	13 411	12 945	1 174	1 732
$\%SHLT$	98.7	95.3	62.1	91.6

4 Experiment

The corpus was split into train, tune/validation and test subsets, using a 80-10-10 proportion and an algorithm that avoids having too many unique tokens in a single subset. The number of sentences for each set is shown in Table 5. We decided not to remove sentences that contain this kind of tokens since, as seen in Table 4, we would be left with less than 10% of the original corpus.

Table 5: Number of sentences in train-tune-test subsets

	Train	Tune	Test	Total
Religious	10 021	1 263	1 263	12 547
Educational	1 429	184	184	1 797

Also, since we could not do a manual verification of all the aligned sentences (in both domains),

we decided to remove sentences that might not be correctly aligned, basing this decision in the token count and the $ratio_{shp-es}$.

A small sample of aligned sentences was taken and we observed that long sentences were usually misaligned. So, for both domains, we established a token count threshold of 35, considering that when this value is more strict, the corpus is smaller.

Using the same criteria, we analyzed the quality of the alignment using the $ratio_{shp-es}$. For the religious domain, we only selected sentences with $ratio_{shp-es}$ values between 0.2 and 2.4, and limited the token count to 35. For the educational domain the ratios were between 0.4 and 2.4, and the threshold was set to 35 also.

Then, we trained the SMT using the MOSES platform (Koehn et al., 2007). The texts were translated from Shipibo-konibo to Spanish and the language model was trained using 3-grams followed by some additional operations:

- **Test 1:** Initial experiment with 3-grams.

- **Test 2:** The unknown words (words that were not translated using MOSES) are directly translated (replaced) by the entry in the dictionary.

- **Test 3:** In the translation output, the consecutive duplicated words were removed.

- **Baseline:** Direct application of the dictionary rules in the Shipibo-konibo test file (replace of terms with their direct translation).

Table 6: BLEU scores obtained

Domain	min ratio	max ratio	max length	BLEU-1 score Baseline	BLEU score Test 1	BLEU score Test 2	BLEU score Test 3
Religious	0.2	2.4	35	4.90	4.31	4.32	**4.42**
Educational	0.4	2.4	35	6.99	13.86	13.90	**13.92**

Baseline: Original text translated using rules from dictionary.

BLEU score obtained in both domains is zero. We show BLEU-1 scores.

Test 1: Initial experiment

Test 2: OOVW were automatically translated using the dictionary

Test 3: Duplicated consecutive words were removed

5   Results and Discussion

As we can see in Table 6, the BLEU (Papineni et al., 2002) results obtained using the SMT system in the Educational domain greatly exceed the ones we got using only rules from the dictionary (baseline). A BLEU score of 4.31 was obtained for the religious domain. Besides, despite being trained with fewer sentences, the BLEU score for the educational domain was 13.86.

Also, replacing unknown tokens using dictionary rules (Test 2) and removing duplicated consecutive ones (Test 3) slightly improve the results.

The different scores between both domains may be explained by the sentence length of each corpus. As shown in Tables 1 and 2, 84.3% Shipibo-konibo sentences from the educational domain have 10 or less tokens and only 34.4% of Shipibo-konibo sentences from the religious domain have the same token count.

Another reason may be the simplicity of the educational corpus, since it was obtained from a kindergarten book. This means that all the sentences contains very simple words and belong to a very closed domain. On the other hand, the Bible contains several proper names and its different books were written by several authors in different periods of time, which adds the complexity level of the text.

6   Conclusions and Future Work

In this paper, we attempted the first steps of the implementation of a new language automatic translation pair between Spanish and Shipibo-konibo, a highly agglomerative native language from the peruvian Amazon. The main limitation in this study was the size of the parallel corpus available, and the great difference in the linguistic features between the language targets. Nevertheless, the results obtained surpassed the baseline proposed (dictionary based) for one of the domains analyzed (educational) and made a promising result for further development, since this corpus can be enlarged. We obtained a BLEU score of 4.42 for the religious domain corpus and 13.92 for the educational one.

As future work, this SMT implementation could be used as a part of an hybrid MT system guided mainly by rules, and also could incorporate other information related to the morphology (lemmas), POS-tags and syntax (dependency relations), since those language processing tools are currently under development. Regarding the morphological analysis, there could be test comparisons between the integration of a supervised (Pereira et al., 2017) or an unsupervised (Creutz and Lagus, 2005) word segmentation to the corpus in the Shipibo-konibo language, in order to identify which approach could improve further the results of the SMT system. In addition, NMT approaches may be tested if a third language could be added as a pivot for transfer learning (Zoph et al., 2016) or with the application of a data augmentation process for the parallel corpus (Fadaee et al., 2017). Finally, it is expected to achieve similar results with other close languages of the same family, in order to develop future pivots MT systems.

Acknowledgments

For this study, the authors acknowledge the support of the "Concejo Nacional de Ciencia, Tecnología e Innovación Tecnológica" (CONCYTEC Perú) under the contract 225-2015-FONDECYT, and the PAIP research program from the Vicerrectorado de Investigación, PUCP.

References

Willem Frederik Hendrik Adelaar, Pilar Valenzuela Bismarck, Roberto Zariquiey, and Rodolfo Marcial Cerrón-Palomino. 2011. *Estudios sobre lenguas andinas y amazónicas: homenaje a Rodolfo Cerrón-Palomino*. Pontificia Universidad Católica del Perú, Fondo Editorial.

Christos Christodouloupoulos and Mark Steedman. 2015. A massively parallel corpus: the bible in 100 languages. *Language resources and evaluation* 49(2):375–395.

Marta R Costa-Jussa and José AR Fonollosa. 2015. Latest trends in hybrid machine translation and its applications. *Computer Speech & Language* 32(1):3–10.

Mathias Creutz and Krista Lagus. 2005. *Unsupervised morpheme segmentation and morphology induction from text corpora using Morfessor 1.0*. Helsinki University of Technology.

Claire Dimeo. 2014. *Building an Automatic Translation System from English to Scots*. Master's thesis, University of Edinburgh.

Marzieh Fadaee, Arianna Bisazza, and Christof Monz. 2017. Data augmentation for low-resource neural machine translation. *arXiv preprint arXiv:1705.00440* .

Loriot James, Erwin Lauriault, and Dwight Day. 1993. *Diccionario Shipibo-Castellano*. Instituto Lingüístico de Verano.

Philipp Koehn. 2009. *Statistical machine translation*. Cambridge University Press.

Philipp Koehn, Hieu Hoang, Alexandra Birch, Chris Callison-Burch, Marcello Federico, Nicola Bertoldi, Brooke Cowan, Wade Shen, Christine Moran, Richard Zens, et al. 2007. Moses: Open source toolkit for statistical machine translation. In *Proceedings of the 45th annual meeting of the ACL on interactive poster and demonstration sessions*. Association for Computational Linguistics, pages 177–180.

Ministerio de Cultura, Perú. 2016. Base de datos de pueblos indígenas u originarios - Pueblos indígenas del Perú. Available in: http://bdpi.cultura.gob.pe.

Ministerio de Educación, Perú. 2013a. *Axeti kirika - Tsanas 4 Baritiayabaona. Cuaderno de Inicial Shipibo 4 años*. Ministerio de Educación.

Ministerio de Educación, Perú. 2013b. *Documento nacional de lenguas originarias del Perú*. Ministerio de Educación. URI: http://repositorio.minedu.gob.pe/handle/123456789/3549.

Win Pa Pa, Ye Kyaw Thu, Andrew Finch, and Eiichiro Sumita. 2016. A study of statistical machine translation methods for under resourced languages. *Procedia Computer Science* 81:250–257.

Kishore Papineni, Salim Roukos, Todd Ward, and Wei-Jing Zhu. 2002. Bleu: a method for automatic evaluation of machine translation. In *Proceedings of the 40th annual meeting on association for computational linguistics*. Association for Computational Linguistics, pages 311–318.

Jose Pereira, Rodolfo Mercado, Andres Melgar, Marco Sobrevilla-Cabezudo, and Arturo Oncevay-Marcos. 2017. Ship-lemmatagger: building an NLP toolkit for a peruvian native language. In *Text, Speech, and Dialogue: 20th International Conference, TSD 2017*. Springer. In-press.

Shahram Salami, Mehrnoush Shamsfard, and Shahram Khadivi. 2016. Phrase-boundary model for statistical machine translation. *Computer Speech & Language* 38:13–27.

Raivis Skadiņš, I Skadiņa, M Pinnis, A Vasiļjevs, and Tomas Hudik. 2014. Application of machine translation in localization into low-resourced languages. In *Proceedings of the Seventeenth Annual Conference of the European Association for Machine Translation (EAMT 2014)*. pages 209–216.

Pilar Valenzuela. 2003. *Transitivity in shipibo-konibo grammar*. Ph.D. thesis, University of Oregon.

Roberto Zariquiey. 2006. Reinterpretación fonológica de los préstamos léxicos de base hispana en la lengua shipibo-conibo. *Boletín de la Academia Peruana de la Lengua* 41.

Barret Zoph, Deniz Yuret, Jonathan May, and Kevin Knight. 2016. Transfer learning for low-resource neural machine translation. In *Proceedings of the 2016 Conference on Empirical Methods in Natural Language Processing*. Association for Computational Linguistics, pages 1568–1575.

Russian-Tatar Socio-Political Thesaurus: Methodology, Challenges, the Status of the Project

Alfiya Galieva, Tatarstan Academy of Sciences
amgalieva@gmail.com
Olga Nevzorova, Tatarstan Academy of Sciences & Kazan Federal University
onevzoro@gmail.com
Dilyara Yakubova, Tatarstan Academy of Sciences & Kazan Federal University
suleymanovad@gmail.com

Abstract

This paper discusses the general methodology and important practical aspects of implementing a new bilingual lexical resource – the Russian-Tatar Socio-Political Thesaurus that is being developed on the basis of the Russian RuThes thesaurus format as a hierarchy of concepts viewed as units of thought. Each concept is linked with a set of language expressions (words and collocations) referring to it in texts (text entries). Currently the Russian-Tatar Socio-Political Thesaurus includes 6,000 concepts, while new concepts and text entries are being constantly added to it.

The paper outlines main challenges of translating concept names and their text entries into Tatar, and describes ways of reflecting the specificity of the Tatar lexical-semantic system.

1 Introduction

At the present time, terminology resources for various domains and languages are being actively developed. For low-resource languages like Tatar, terminology compilation may be a challenge in many respects:
- because of the insufficient degree of terminology development that leads to absent relevant designations for special concepts in a language;
- because of lacking special sources for assembling terminology;
- because of lacking coherent terminology management at the terminology development stage as well as at the stage of usage, etc.

Automatic generation of domain-specific ontologies and thesauri may in many cases be a highly challenging task even for languages that possess special lexicographic resources. For the Tatar language, there is a relatively small amount of such resources, and most of available ones leave a lot to be desired.

The Russian-Tatar Socio-Political Thesaurus is structured in the same way as the RuThes thesaurus for Russian as a network of concepts and their lexical entries with basic semantic relations mapped between them (Loukachevitch and Dobrov, 2002a). The Tatar part of the Thesaurus is mainly being compiled by manually translating Russian terms represented in the Russian RuThes, into Tatar. Also, the Tatar language specific concepts and their lexical entries are added, so each part of the Thesaurus – the Russian and the Tatar one – represents a unique language-internal system of lexicalizations. At the same time, the languages are interconnected so that it is possible to go from the concepts and words in one language to corresponding items in the other.

The project of developing the Russian-Tatar Socio-Political Thesaurus is aimed at compiling the whole body of modern Tatar vocabulary related to the following basic domains: state government, economy, social life, justice, warfare, culture, religion; all of these items have Russian equivalents (correspondences) and are represented at the conceptual and lexical entries levels that are hierarchically arranged. This work is of great scientific and practical importance, since the Thesaurus is aimed at embracing all basic concepts and their lexical entries used in the modern Tatar-language socio-political domain. Socio-political vocabulary designates phenomena of social and political life and reflects basic topics raised in the society as well as its values. Being extremely sensitive to all kinds of innovations, socio-political vocabulary undergoes unceasing changes – new lexical items emerge

Proceedings of Recent Advances in Natural Language Processing, pages 245–252,
Varna, Bulgaria, Sep 4–6 2017.

while others become outdated relatively quickly. Thus, socio-political lexicons should be compiled on the data of constantly updated text collections.

The remainder of this paper is organized as follows. Section 2 outlines related works, and considerable attention is paid to the existing domain-specific thesauri. Section 3 gives a brief overview of the methodology used in the Thesaurus design and terminology collecting and translation. Section 4 presents main challenges encountered and ways to overcome these difficulties. Section 5 is devoted to one of the most interesting phenomena in Tatar socio-political discourse – a great number of domain-specific synonyms; the main causes of emerging synonymy are disclosed and structural types of synonyms are distinguished. Section 6 sketches out some technical aspects of implementing the new thesaurus and the current state of the project. Finally, Section 7 lists the conclusions and outlines the future work.

2   Related Works

The world of thesauri is not homogeneous. International organizations develop thesauri as means for document indexing and retrieval. Most of them (UNESCO thesaurus, Eurovoc) are multilingual and obey international standards, such as ISO 25964-1:2011. A different approach is implemented when a thesaurus is created as a lexical resource to be used in applications of computational linguistics and natural language processing. Such is Princeton WordNet Thesaurus, which gave start to many projects on creating national wordnets. Most important dictionary publishers create their own thesauri (Harper Collins, Oxford), both monolingual and multilingual, while some are being developed with the contribution of volunteers (Open Thesaurus) and therefore take much more time to complete. Some are developed manually and are more precise – although obviously more expensive than those developed automatically; some have open access, others not.

Another important distinction to be made is among general and domain-specific thesauri. As general thesauri give little coverage of the rich vocabulary of particular subject areas, domain-specific thesauri are required (Manning et al., 2008). They present an important instrument for extracting semantic information and term sense disambiguation (Maynard and Ananiadou, 1998).

Not all thesauri easily fall into one or the other group, like GEMET General Multilingual Environmental Thesaurus that was developed as an indexing, retrieval and control tool for the European Topic Centre on Catalogue of Data Sources and the European Environment Agency, although according to its creators it "was conceived as a "general" thesaurus, aimed to define a common general language, a core of general terminology for the environment" (About GEMET). Among domain-specific thesauri we can mention APA Thesaurus of Psychological Index Terms by the Association of Psychologists of America and AAT Art & Architecture Thesaurus by the Getty Research Institute. Both are aimed at making searching within their domain easier and more successful, but while the first one has no free online version, the second one is an open resource available as Linked Open Data. IATE Interactive Terminology for Europe Thesaurus has a different objective: it was created mainly for terminological and translation purposes.

As for the socio-political domain, several thesauri can be mentioned. One is the Gesis Thesaurus for the Social Sciences developed by Leibniz Institute for the Social Sciences for the content-oriented search by keywords. This multilingual resource (English, German, French and Russian) contains about 12,000 keywords and includes all the social science disciplines. The search may be carried out using alphabetic or systematic lists, and the user receives the following information on the term: descriptor, broader term, narrow term, combination and notation. Currently this Thesaurus is available in SKOS-format as Linked Open Data. Another example is the European Language Social Science Thesaurus, which is developed by UK Data Archive University of Essex and intended to be both an information retrieval and a terminological tool. It is currently available in nine languages and includes over 3,000 terms for most languages.

Important thesauri in the socio-political domain were created by RuThes developers. One is Thesaurus on Sociopolitical life that includes more than 62 thousand terms, words and proper names, more than 27 thousand concepts and 102 thousand conceptual relations (Loukachevitch and Dobrov, 2002). It presents "a hierarchical net of concepts constructed specially as a tool for different applications of automatic text processing. It contains a lot of terms from economic, financial, political, military, social, legislative, cultural and other spheres" (Loukachevitch and Dobrov, 2002). Another one is bilingual Russian-English Socio-Political Thesaurus that includes more than 32 thousand concepts, 78 thousand Russian terms and 85 thousand English terms (Ageev et al., 2006). For its creation, the developers combined methods of construction of information retrieval thesauri, the development of wordnets for various languages and ontology research.

3   Methodology of Designing the Thesaurus

Defining the principles for modeling a bilingual resource presupposes establishing the following: 1) the format of the vocabulary entry; 2) the volume and quality of the lexical material; 3) methods for identifying and resolving conflict situations arising in the process of translation (Galieva et al., 2017).

The Russian-Tatar Thesaurus is being developed in the format of the RuThes thesaurus. In the design of the Tatar part of the Thesaurus, the conceptual structure of RuThes is mainly preserved, i.e. the Tatar component is based on the list of concepts of RuThes. RuThes basic units are of conceptual nature rather than of linguistic one – they represent units of thinking that can be associated with several synonymous language expressions. Every concept should have distinctions from the related concepts; concepts are independent of contextual environment and should be expressed as specific sets of associated language expressions – text entries (Loukachevitch and Dobrov, 2002a).

The conceptual structure of RuThes determines the direction (sequence) of developing concepts in the Tatar part, and the basic structure of RuThes conceptual relations is preserved here as well. In cases when semantic relations between Tatar concepts do not correspond to those between the units of RuThes, these relations are established anew or revised.

The general methodology of creating the Tatar part of the Thesaurus includes the following steps.

1. Search for equivalents (corresponding terms) that are actually used in Tatar as translations of Russian terms.

2. Adding new concepts representing topics that are important for the socio-cultural life of the Tatar society but are not represented or represented insufficiently in the original RuThes (the list of required vocabulary is compiled, concept names and lexical entries are distinguished and arranged according to the RuThes structure).

3. Revising the relations between concepts considering the place of new concepts in the hierarchy of the existing ones, and if necessary, adding new concepts of intermediate level.

During the first stage, RuThes concept names and text entries are translated into Tatar. The sources of translation include bilingual general-purpose dictionaries, special socio-political dictionaries, Tatar texts on socio-political topics, and available Russian-Tatar parallel texts.

The main requirements to Tatar concept names are as follows:
- clarity of meaning;
- use of neutral and common lexical units for concept names;
- brevity of denomination;
- selecting the most precise, the most frequent and officially used denomination from several options if there are any.

The requirement of the concept name clarity supposes that a concept must be intuitively understood from its designation.

Due to the discrepancy between grammatical, semantic and lexical systems of the Russian and Tatar languages, the structure and length of concept names may significantly differ. In particular, because of lacking one-word terms in Tatar, in some cases we have to give their explanatory translations.

When designating concepts, ambiguous words may be used in individual sense, so we provide necessary comments in brackets to identify the meaning of the concept. Because of the differences between the word semantic structures of the languages, those comments and specifications often differ in the Russian and Tatar parts of the Thesaurus. Table 1 shows some peculiarities of use of Russian and Tatar polysemous words as concept names.

An important task is to represent the language specific features of Tatar in the Thesaurus both on contextual and lexical levels.

When compiling the list of Tatar terms, we use data of available corpora built for the Tatar language by now, each in open access:

Example of concept name in Russian	Example of concept name in Tatar
СУД (ГОСУДАРСТВЕННЫЙ ОРГАН) 'court of law (state institution)'	СУД 'court of law'
РУКОВОДСТВО (УЧЕБНОЕ ПОСОБИЕ) 'guidance, manual'	КУЛЛАНМАЛЫК 'guidance, manual'
СТАДО 'herd'	КӨТҮ (МАЛ КӨТҮЕ) 'herd (flock of cattle) '
СТОИМОСТЬ 'cost'	КЫЙММӘТ (ЧЫГЫМНАР КҮЛӘМЕ) 'cost (an amount of expenses)'

Table 1: Examples of ambiguous concept names: use of specifying comments.

1. The Corpus of Written Tatar (CWT) compiled by researchers of Kazan Federal University, Russia;

2. "Tugan Tel" Tatar National Corpus (TNC) developed at the Institute of Applied Semiotics of Tatarstan Academy of Sciences.

These Tatar corpora are constantly filled with new texts, and the bulk of socio-political texts in them is recent (unlike those in fiction texts), so we may argue that the corpora represent the actual usage of Tatar.

4   Challenges

The main challenges of the current project concern acquiring lexical data and representing all Tatar terms in actual use.

1. Search for equivalents (corresponding terms) that are actually used in Tatar as translations of Russian terms.

Search for translation equivalents and adequate correspondences practically used in texts in many cases becomes a laborious and time-consuming task because available bilingual Russian-Tatar dictionaries of the general lexicon (for example, Ganiev, 1997a) and special lexicons (Amirov, 1996; Ganiev, 1997b) are outdated, and new lexicons (for example, Tagirova and Timerkhanov, 2014) do not contain the required items.

The obsolescence of dictionaries becomes apparent in two main aspects:

1) the dictionaries are incomplete and do not contain entries reflecting present-day socio-political items widely used in Russia (such as *political correctness, lines of communication, framework agreement, taxable* and many others);

2) the dictionaries do not contain target language (Tatar) translation units in actual use, containing instead those that had been actively used in the Soviet era.

Consequently, available bilingual Tatar-Russian dictionaries, including special socio-political dictionaries, may be used in developing the Russian-Tatar Thesaurus with a certain proviso, because of the containing obsolete lexical data and lacking lexical items of current interest in many cases.

This circumstance significantly slows down the translation process and compels us to look through a huge amount of media texts and texts of official documents manually in search for appropriate Tatar terms.

2. Adding new concepts representing topics that are important for the socio-cultural life of the Tatar society but are not represented or represented insufficiently in the original RuThes.

We add single concepts and new branches of concepts related to issues of political, religious and cultural life of the Tatar society and reflecting peculiarities of the history of the Tatar people (for example, Islam-related concepts, concepts related to the socio-political structure of Oriental societies, Tatar ethnographic phenomena, etc.).

Table 2 represents this part of the work displaying the new EID AL-FITR concept designating an important religious holiday celebrated by Muslims worldwide; Eid Al-Fitr marks the end of Ramadan — the month of Islamic fasting.

Adding single new concepts often leads to revising relations between the existing ones and adding new intermediate concepts.

3. Revising relations between the concepts while considering the place of new concepts in the hierarchy of the existing ones.

This can be illustrated by an example. Inserting the new 'EID AL-FITR' concept required some changes in the RuThes concepts hierarchy; we entered the following concepts of the higher level:

- OFFICIAL HOLIDAY OF TATARSTAN REPUBLIC;
- MUSLIM HOLIDAY.

Besides, the existing CALENDAR DATE concept was supplemented by those of lower level:

- HIJRI CALENDAR DATE;
- GREGORIAN CALENDAR DATE.

Concept	Relationship with other concepts		Text entries of the concept
	Concepts above	**Associated concepts**	
УРАЗА ГАЕТЕ 'Eid Al-Fitr'	Above: ДИНИ БӘЙРӘМ 'religious holiday'	Association 1: УРАЗА 'Muslim fasting'	ураза гаете, ураза бәйрәме, рамазан гаете, рамазан бәйрәме
	Above: ТАТАРСТАН РЕСПУБ-ЛИКАСЫНЫҢ РӘСМИ БӘЙРӘМЕ 'official holiday of the Republic of Tatarstan'	Association 2: РАМАЗАН 'Ramadan'	
	Above: МӨСЕЛМАН ДИНЕ БӘЙРӘМЕ 'Muslim Holiday'	Association 3: УРАЗА ФИТЫРЫ 'Zakat al-Fitr'	
	Above: һИҖРИ КАЛЕНДАРЬ ДАТАСЫ 'Hijri calendar date'		
	Above: КАЛЕНДАРЬ ДАТАСЫ 'calendar date'		

Table 2: The new EID AL-FITR concept and its relationships with other concepts.

Adding the last two concepts seemed necessary due to principal dissimilarities between the European solar (Gregorian) calendar and the Islamic lunar calendar. Due to the fact that a year of the Islamic calendar is 10 or 11 days shorter than the solar year, dates of Muslim holidays shift forward every year as related to the European calendar. So, linking the concepts denoting Muslim holidays to the common CALENDAR DATE concept is insufficient, and therefore we are to mark-up the calendar type.

5 Synonymy in Tatar Socio-Political Vocabulary

Another challenge is related to the abundance of specific synonyms in the Tatar socio-political domain. This issue is quite interesting and deserves special attention.

Synonymy is one of fundamental concepts in linguistics that manifests itself at different language levels. A prevailing point of view in linguistics is that synonymy shows a high degree of language development, and that absolute (total) synonymy occurs infrequently because "yet even if near-synonyms do name one and the same thing, they name it in different ways: they present different perspectives on a situation (Divjak, 2010).

Available attitudes range from totally rejecting the idea of absolute (total) synonymy in language to claiming extreme rareness of them (Ulmann, 1967; Lyons, 1995). The situation with Tatar socio-political vocabulary in many respects refutes this thesis about rareness of absolute synonymy.

A great number of emerging total synonyms in Tatar occurred under the influence of a combination of intralinguistic and extralinguistic factors. The Tatar culture is located at the intersection of the Occidental and Oriental civilisations, which leads to active lexical borrowing both from the Arab-Muslim cultural area and the European cultural area; vocabulary borrowing from European languages is taking place through mediation of the Russian language, and, certainly, a huge amount of words and constructions are taken from Russian. Besides, a significant part of synonyms are built on the basis of Turkic and Tatar lexical material.

Therefore, words of different origin (Turkic and Tatar, Arabic and Persian, Greek, Latin, English and Russian) related to the same referent coexist in Tatar, which engenders a great number of synonyms at the single word level.

Table 3 illustrates redistribution of absolute synonyms of European and Arabic origin in corpus collections (for nouns the number of Nominative case forms, and not the number of lemmas, is given).

It is noteworthy that all words of Arabic origin presented in Table 3 entered Tatar active lexicon

Lexeme	English translation, PoS	Origin of the word	Number in the CWT	Number in the TNC
экономик	Economic (adj.)	Greek	621	676
икътисади		Arabic	27,351	22,274
политик	Political (adj.)	Greek	1,005	1,536
сәяси		Arabic	25,011	24,489
республика	Republic (noun)	Latin	316,667	258,433
җөмһүрият		Arabic	2,479	1,631
информацион	Informational (adj.)	Latin	858	807
мәгълүмати		Arabic	7,076	689
суд	Court of law (noun)	Russian	15,725	14,243
мәхкәмә		Arabic	8,718	8,101

Table 3: Distribution of synonyms coming from different languages (according to corpus data)

relatively recently, in the late 80's; nevertheless, they succeeded to push out the words of European origin with the same meaning that had been actively used in the language of the Soviet era.

Often words of Tatar (Turkic) origin formed of different stems by means of Tatar derivational affixes may compete among themselves. Table 4 represents quantitative distribution of synonymous words referred to the BUSINESSMAN concept, in corpus collections, and the number of their most frequent derivatives.

Lexeme	English translation	Number in the CWT	Number in the TNC
эшкуар	business-man	8,606	11,280
эшмәкәр		22,671	13,876
кәсәбәче		122	101
эшкуарлык	entrepreneurship (business activity)	2,641	3,852
эшмәкәрлек		6,454	4,207
кәсәбәчелек		67	54

Table 4: Tatar origin synonyms meaning 'businessman' and 'entrepreneurship (business activity)'

Currently most Tatar socio-political terms are formed by calquing (component-by-component translating) corresponding Russian terms. Diverse groups of specialists with dissimilar world-views and ideological guidelines develop Tatar terminology; in designing terminology they may principally be oriented at different cultural spaces dominated by different languages:
- Tatar and Turkic vocabulary;
- Arabic and Persian vocabulary;
- international Greek, Latin or English vocabulary;
- Russian vocabulary, etc.

Dissimilar preferences of terminology creators lead to the use of different designations for the same entity.

Some peculiarities of lexical, derivational and grammatical systems of the Tatar language also lead to originating of a great number of synonyms. On the level of multiword terms and phrases, lexical synonymy is complicated by the factor of differing grammatical structures in use.

For example, in Turkic languages the following grammatical patterns of noun phrases are regularly corresponding (abbreviations: N – noun, ADJ – adjective, PL – plural affix, POSS_3 – possessive affix, 3d person, NMZL – nominalizer):
ADJ +N and *N + N, POSS_3:*
икътисадый кризис (ADJ +N), *икътисад кризисы* (N + N, POSS_3)
'economic crisis'.

Such regular correspondences multiply the number of grammatical variants of multiword terms.

For example, we found in the media and official texts 9 noun phrases to designate the term *joint-stock company*; these are formed by 3 core nouns meaning '*company*' and are based on different grammatical patterns, see Table 5. All such synonyms are regarded as text entries of the same concept.

Since the linguistic situation in the Republic of Tatarstan is unstable, parallel denominations can be used for a wide range of phenomena, including some official names of departments and state structures. So, a separate task is to compile the most complete list of synonymous denominations related to the same concept in order to fix them as lexical entries for the Thesaurus, because lists of synonyms in available dictionaries are incomplete and in many cases limited to one word.

Grammatical model of the term	Term variants	Frequency of use in CWT
N,NMZL + N.POSS_3	акционерлык җәмгыяте,	4,320
	акционерлык ширкәте,	13
	акционерлык оешмасы	13
N, PL + N.POSS_3	акционерлар җәмгыяте,	274
	акционерлар ширкәте,	2
	акционерлар оешмасы	1
ADJ + N	акционер җәмгыять,	97
	акционер ширкәт,	4
	акционер оешма	14

Table 5: Texts entries of the concept JOINT-STOCK COMPANY

6 Status of the Project

Currently the Russian-Tatar Socio-Political Thesaurus contains 6,000 concepts and constantly grows. For the Thesaurus, special software and web interface have been designed.

The Thesaurus system is implemented in the format of a web application as a special site http://tattez.antat.ru/ and contains open and closed parts. The closed part is available to authorized users who have the authority to edit the Thesaurus; basic functions of adding new concepts and lexical entries, mapping relations between concepts, and referring to the data of Russian-Tatar dictionary are provided. An authorized user can also compare the conceptual structures of the Russian and Tatar parts of the Thesaurus, using a special markup reflecting the statuses of completeness and problems in description, and can also use convenient visualization tools with filtering by various parameters.

The main user functions in the open part of the system provide viewing the data, search and navigation through the concepts and text entries of the Thesaurus.

7 Conclusion

The Russian-Tatar Socio-Political Thesaurus is built as a hierarchical network of concepts and lexical entries from the most general to the most specific conceptual categories.

On the grounds of our research of Tatar socio-political terminology within the Thesaurus building project we can conclude that a certain Tatar terminology management is required. It may be descriptive (describing how terms are used in documents and media texts) and prescriptive (or even normative) to document compilers (prescribing what terms must be used in standard work and official documentation and how they must be used). Therefore, developing the bilingual Russian-Tatar Thesaurus that would cover all existing variants of terms might be an important step to achieving this, on condition of providing users with an effective access to information.

Coexistence of different centres of building Tatar terms and lack of coordination between them leads to instability and imbalance of terminology when diverse synonymous terms and terminological variants of different origin and structure may be in actual use. Therefore, an important task is to search for all synonymous denominations and variants to fix them all as text entries of corresponding concepts. Further extension of the Thesaurus requires development of methods of extracting domain-specific terms from texts and corpus data.

Acknowledgements

The reported study was funded by Russian Science Foundation, research project № 16-18-02074.

References

AAT Art & Architecture Thesaurus. http://www.getty.edu/research/tools/vocabularies/aat/

About GEMET - GEneral Multilingual Environmental Thesaurus. https://www.eionet.europa.eu/gemet/about?langcode=en

Alfiya M. Galieva, Alik V. Kirillovich, Natalia V. Loukachevitch, Olga A. Nevzorova, O.A., and Dzhavdet Sh. Suleymanov. 2017. *Sozdanie russko-tatarskogo tezaurusa po obshchestvenno-politicheskoj tematike: obshchie principy i aspekty realizacii* "Development of Russian-Tatar Socio-Political Thesaurus: General Principles and Aspects of implementation". In Nauchno-tekhnicheskaya informaciya. Seriya 2: Informacionnye processy i sistemy, 2:20-28.

APA Thesaurus of Psychological Index Terms. http://www.apa.org/pubs/databases/training/thesaurus.aspx

Christopher D. Manning, Prabhakar Raghavan, and Hinrich Schütze. 2008. *Introduction to information retrieval.* Cambridge University Press

Collins English Thesaurus. https://www.collinsdictionary.com/dictionary/english-thesaurus

Corpus of Written Tatar. http://search.corpus.tatar/en

Dagmar Divjak. 2010. *Structuring the lexicon: A clustered model for near-synonymy.* Vol. 43. Walter de Gruyter.

Diana Maynard and Sophia Ananiadou. 1998. *Term Sense Disambiguation Using a Domain-Specific Thesaurus.* In Proceedings of 1st International Conference on Language Resources and Evaluation (LREC), Granada, Spain.

ELSST European Language Social Science Thesaurus. https://elsst.ukdataservice.ac.uk/

Eurovoc. The EU's Multilingual Thesaurus. http://eurovoc.europa.eu/

F.I. Tagirova, A.A. Timerkhanov (ed.). 2014. *Russko-tatarskiy slovar aktualnoy leksiki* "Russian-Tatar dictionary of actual vocabulary". Kazan.

Fuat A. Ganiev. (ed.). 1997a. *Russko-tatarskiy slovar* "Russian-Tatar Dictionary. Moscow", Insan.

Fuat A. Ganiev. (ed.). 1997b. *Russko-tatarskiy obshchestvenno-politicheskiy slovar* "Russian-Tatar Socio-Political Dictionary". Kazan.

Fuat A. Ganiev. (ed.). 2005. *Tatarskiy tolkoviy slovar* "Tatar Explanatory Dictionary". Kazan.

GEMET Thesaurus. https://www.eionet.europa.eu/gemet

Gesis Thesaurus for the Social Sciences. http://www.gesis.org/en/services/research/tools/social-science-thesaurus/

IATE Interactive Terminology for Europe Thesaurus. http://iate.europa.eu/SearchByQueryLoad.do;jsessionid=VFzZw0dUdNLutE-TAg3EV5RA7t1P7QpalbDS1MJzgdU3hyk-bPp9P7!559570392?method=load

International Organization for Standardization. Thesauri and interoperability with other vocabularies. Part 1: Thesauri for information retrieval. https://www.iso.org/standard/53657.html

John Lyons. 1995. *Linguistic Semantics.* Cambridge University Press.

Kafil F. Amirov. (ed.). 1996. *Russko-tatarskiy yuridicheskiy slovar* "Russian-Tatar legal dictionary". Kazan.

M. Lynne Murphy. 2003. *Semantic Relations and the Lexicon.* Cambridge University Press.

Mikhail Ageev, Boris Dobrov, and Natalia Loukachevitch. 2006. *Socio-Political Thesaurus in Concept-Based Information Retrieval.* In: Peters C. et al. (eds) Accessing Multilingual Information Repositories. CLEF 2005. Lecture Notes in Computer Science, vol. 4022. Springer, Berlin, Heidelberg.

Natalia Loukachevitch and Boris Dobrov, 2002a. *Development and Use of Thesaurus of Russian Language RuThes.* In Proceedings of workshop on WordNet Structures and Standartisation, and How These Affect WordNet Applications and Evaluation. (LREC 2002) / Dimitris N. Christodoulakis, Gran Canaria, Spain: 65-70.

Natalia Loukachevitch and Boris Dobrov, 2002b. *Evaluation of Thesaurus on Sociopolitical Life as Information-Retrieval Tool.* In M.Gonzalez Rodriguez, C. Paz Suarez Araujo (Eds.) The Third International conference on Linguistic Resources and Evaluation (LREC-2002). – Vol.1 – 2002, Gran Canaria, Spain.

Open Thesaurus. http://openoffice-es.sourceforge.net/thesaurus/

Oxford Thesaurus. https://en.oxforddictionaries.com/

Roy Harris. 1973. *Synonymy and Linguistic Analysis.* Basil Blackwell.

RuThes Linguistic Ontology. http://www.labinform.ru/pub/ruthes/index_eng.htm

Stephen Ullmann. 1967: *Semantics, An Introduction to the Science of Meaning.* Basil Blackwell. Oxford Thesaurus for the Social Sciences. http://www.gesis.org/en/services/research/tools/social-science-thesaurus/

"Tugan Tel" Tatar National Corpus. http://corpus.antat.ru/

UNESCO Thesaurus. http://vocabularies.unesco.org/browser/thesaurus/en/

Wordnet. A lexical database for English. https://wordnet.princeton.edu/

On a Chat Bot Finding Answers with Optimal Rhetoric Representation

Boris Galitsky[1] and Dmitry Ilvovsky[2]
[1]Oracle Inc. Redwood Shores CA USA,
[2]National Research University Higher School of Economics
{boris.galitsky@oracle.com, dilvovsky@hse.ru}

Abstract

We demo a chat bot with the focus on complex, multi-sentence questions that enforce what we call *rhetoric agreement* of answers with questions. Chat bot finds answers which are not only relevant by topic but also match the question by style, argumentation patterns, communication means, experience level and other attributes. The system achieves rhetoric agreement by learning pairs of discourse trees (DTs) for question (Q) and answer (A). We build a library of *best* answer DTs for most types of complex questions. To better recognize a valid rhetoric agreement between Q and A, DTs are extended with the labels for communicative actions. An algorithm for finding the best DT for an A, given a Q, is evaluated.

1. Introduction

Over last few years, chat bots for efficient information access has become fairly popular. However, their relevance is still not as high as desired, which makes conversation longer, less efficient and less informative. For chat bots performing customer support capabilities, low relevance of answers and a lack in overall cohesiveness in support sessions may lead to customer frustration and as a result to a low customer retention.

Modern search engines are good at topical relevance; however, for a chat bot answers should not only be relevant but also need to follow certain style and specific session coherence. A sequence of clarification requests and intermediate answers need to form a logical sequence, not just be constrained by a certain topic or entity. Although an entity-based and topic-based relevance has been extensively explored, coherent flow of utterances in a dialogue in general and a rhetoric correlation between questions is a research area in its infancy.

In this demo paper we improve the cohesiveness of a chat bot session flow by learning correct and incorrect sequences of utterances. When an answer or a clarification expression is weakly rhetorically correlated with a question or a request, a user can identify a dialogue flow broken even when all utterances are about the same entity and therefore topical relevance is high.

The dialogue flow corruption due to a weak rhetoric correlation occurs mostly for complex (Chali et al., 2009; Galitsky, 2017), non-factoid dialogue sessions, involving clarification, explanation, comparison and other means to provide a chat bot user with a complete coverage on a topic or entity. Unsuitability of a request-response sequence usually becomes transparent via the ways an answer is communicated, explained or backed up. Examples of uncorrelated request-response pairs include:

- A chat bot user is a beginner and looks for a general recommendation but an answer is intended for professional, too specific, contains unnecessary arguments and details;

- A user formulated his ambiguous, controversial question relying on a contra-position, but a response just includes a set of plain facts, which are not opinionated;

- A user makes a claim, backs it up and asks for a confirmation. However, an answer just negates it without providing any support.

In the proposed system, rhetoric correlation is achieved via supervised learning of the sequences of utterances. We accumulate a set of correct utterance sequences, including question/answer pairs as our positive dataset, and a set of incorrect sequences and pairs – as the negative one.

Proceedings of Recent Advances in Natural Language Processing, pages 253–259,
Varna, Bulgaria, Sep 4–6 2017.

The proposed chat bot relies on a computational measure for how logical rhetoric structure of a question is correlated with that of an answer. The system forms a discourse tree (DT) representation for a question/answer pair based on Rhetoric Structure Theory (RST, Mann and Thompson, 1988, Figs 1 and 2), learns them and solves a Q/A pair classification problem of relating them into a class of valid (correct, appropriate answer) or invalid pairs.

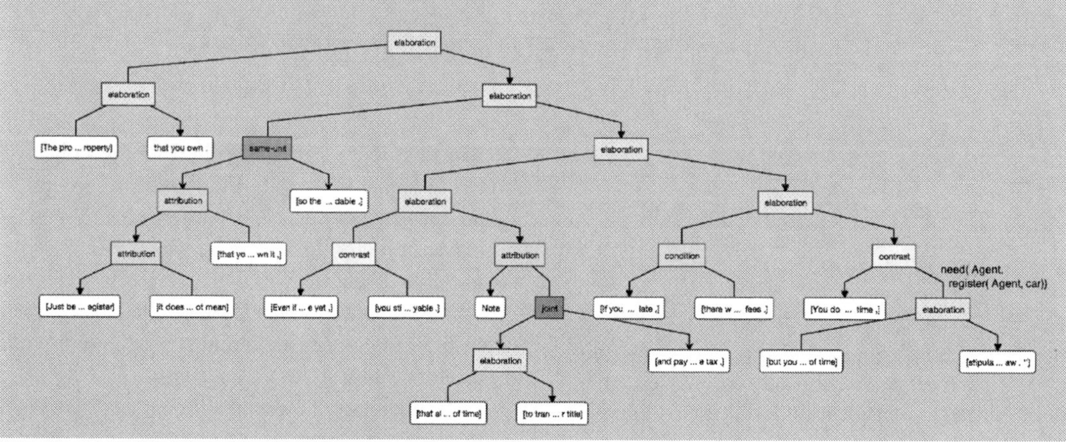

Fig. 1: Full discourse tree for the question

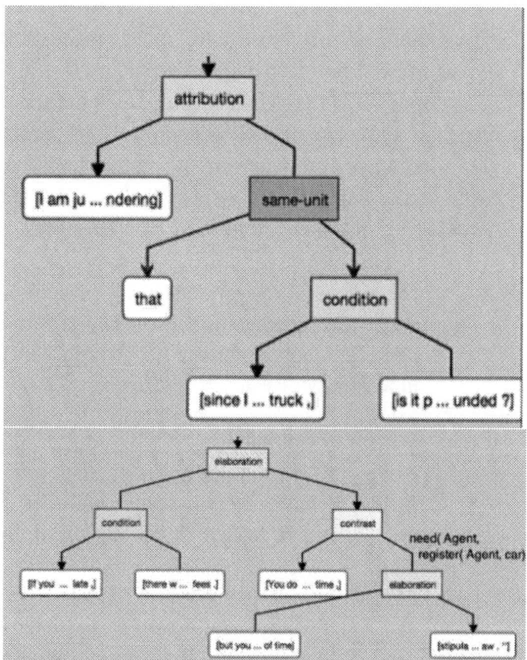

Figure 2: A fragment of a discourse tree for a question (on the top). A fragment of the discourse tree for the A that should be in agreement with this question (on the bottom)

Although the parsers producing discourse trees are constantly improving (Joty et al., 2013; Feng and Hirst, 2014), they identify too few rhetoric relations other than elaboration and joint. The scope of industrial applications of rhetoric-level analysis and rhetoric parsers is fairly restricted to content generation and summarization.

In our previous studies DTs have been found to assist in answer indexing to make search more relevant: query keyword should occur in nucleus rather than a satellite of a rhetoric relation (Galitsky et al., 2015). Hence we developed a chat bot that leverages rhetoric parsing.

A sample chat bot session is available at github.com/bgalitsky/relevance-based-on-parse-trees/blob/master/examples/botSessionExample.txt.

2. Adjusting Rhetoric Representation of Answer to that of a Question

In Fig. 3 we introduce an example of an initial question, a disambiguation request formed by the chat bot, the option selected by a user and the final response. We show that there is a certain correlation between their rhetoric representations, discourse trees for the initial question and the final answers. If a question has a set of certain rhetoric relations, its answer is expected to reflect them in some form. Rhetoric correlation is expected to facilitate a direct, exact and detailed answer. Moreover, rhetoric correlation reduces a number of intermediate disambiguation requests, the length of information access sessions and how many times a user reads irrelevant answers, on the pathway to a satisfactory answer.

The question is about property tax and insurance on a car. This Q is controversial: on one hand, all *owned properties are taxable*, and on the other hand, *the ownership is somewhat incomplete*. This controversy is expected to be addressed by a good answer, relevant not only in terms of topic but also in terms of rhetoric correlation. To provide such A, a responder makes a statement concerning the necessity to pay tax on whatever is owned irrespectively of the registration status.

My husbands' grandmother gave him his grandfathers truck. She signed the title over but due to my husband having unpaid fines on his license, he was not able to get the truck put in his name. I wanted to put in my name and paid the property tax and got insurance for the truck. By the time it came to sending off the title and getting the tag, I didn't have the money to do so. Now, due to circumstances, I am not going to be able to afford the truck. I went to the insurance place and was refused a refund. Since I am not going to have a tag on this truck, can I get the property tax refunded?

Are u talking about property tax refund, registration or insurance?

Insurance

The property tax is assessed on property that you own. Just because you chose to not register it does not mean that you don't own it, so the tax is not refundable. Even if you have not titled the vehicle yet, you still own it within the boundaries of the tax district, so the tax is payable. Note that all states give you a limited amount of time to transfer title and pay the use tax. If you apply late, there will be penalties on top of the normal taxes and fees. You don't need to register it at the same time, but you absolutely need to title it within the period of time stipulated in state law.

Figure 3: Chat bot log with a complex question, its clarification and answer (a demo screen-shot)

The reader can observe that since the question includes rhetoric relation of *Contrast*, the answer has to match it with a similar relation to be convincing. An adequate answer should clarify the difference between the presence and absence of the *contrast* clauses in the question. Otherwise, this answer would look incomplete. Characteristic sub-trees here are *Contrast-[Elaboration, ..., Elaboration]-Contrast*, which is present in question and therefore should also occur in the answer to match the argumentation style of the question.

A fragment of a DT with a special argumentation pattern used in a question is shown in Fig. 1. When a question is formulated with a chain *Attribution (to an authority) - Condition (if my case is covered by certain regulation issued by this authority)*, the answer is expected to confirm or reject this *Condition*. Indeed, there is a matching *Condition* relation in the answer, associated with *Elaboration* (Fig. 2, on the left).

To represent the rhetoric agreement better, we augment DT with the information how each discourse unit is communicated. Some edges of communicative DTs are labelled with the expressions for communicative actions (CAs) in the VerbNet (Kipper et. al., 2008) form (shown on the right of Fig. 2). Such DTs are called Communicative Discourse Trees (CDTs).

A high-level view of the full DTs for these Q and A is shown in Fig. 4. Both trees are merged into a single one for the purpose of automated learning of rhetoric agreement: a given pair can be (structurally) similar to Q/A pair of either positive or negative training set. Mapping of two occurrences of *Contrast* relations in Q into that of in A is shown by bolded arcs.

3. Maintaining a Sequence of Discourse trees

What does Clinton foundation do?

Most of the Clinton Foundation spending goes directly to programs that improve people's lives around the world

And what does Clinton foundation really do?

Becoming a Secretary of State, Hillary Clinton promised to distance herself from the Clinton Foundation. However, Clinton continued to have a cozy relationship with the foundation, having the US foreign policy for sale there. According to some sources, Clinton was granting access and favors to major Clinton Foundation donors

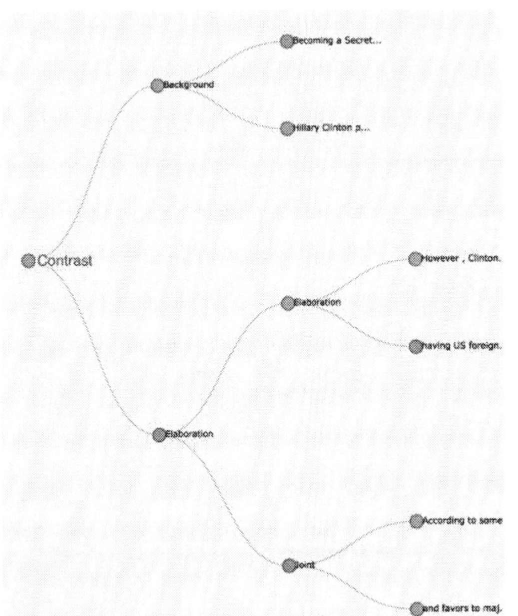

Figure 4: A dialogue and a discourse tree for the final answer.

In many cases, a current utterance needs to match the rhetorics of just a previous utterance. Howewer, in many cases not just a previous question but the whole chain needs to be taken into account (Fig.4).

The first utterance is perceived as a factoid (general) question and a common answer is given. However, this answer is followed by a sarcastic form of dissatisfaction, so the same question is repeated with *really* note. Now, instead of providing a general, common answer of the fits-for-all kind, the chat bot finds a controversial opinion about an entity in question. The controversy is expressed via the Contrast relation between the parts of this utterance: On one hand, a person's role is a Secretary of State, but on the other hand this person gives special favors to certain people.

A scenario template that is expected to be earned in this case is as follows:

1) A factoid question
2) A general factoid, definitional answer
3) Dissatisfaction with (2), expressed via sarcastic *really*. Repeated question.
4) Opinionated answer to the same question (2).

4. Identifying Rhetoric Correlation

A search engine dealing with complex questions such as Yahoo! Answers needs a systematic approach to assess the rhetoric agreement and select the most suitable answers among the relevant ones. DTs' features could be represented in a numerical space where a classification into valid or invalid Q/A pairs would be conducted, however structural information on DTs would not be leveraged. Conversely, rhetoric agreement could be measured in terms of maximal common sub-DTs, but it is computationally intensive and too sensitive to errors in DT construction. Therefore a DT-kernel learning approach is selected which applies SVM learning to a set of all sub-DTs of the DT for Q/A pair.

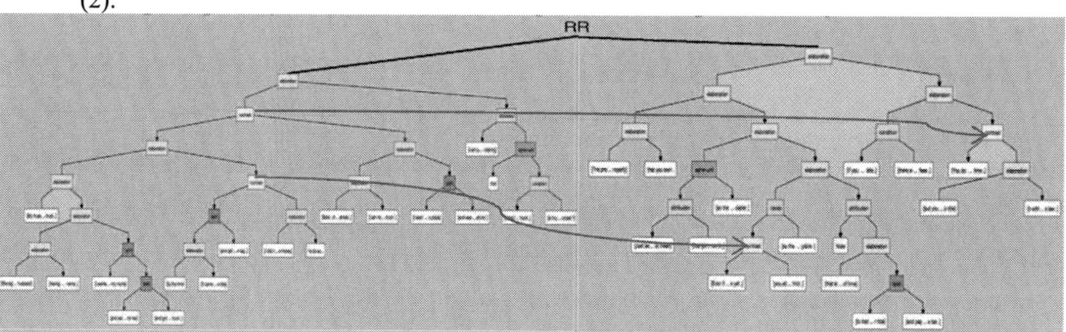

Figure 5: A high level view of the DT-Q – DT-A pair (full discourse trees for the example in Figure 3).

Tree kernel family of approaches is not very sensitive to errors in parsing (syntactic and rhetoric) because erroneous sub-trees are mostly random and will unlikely be common among different elements of a training set.

Given a positive dataset of valid Q/A pairs and a negative dataset of relevant Q/A pairs which are in a poor agreement, we attempt to recognize if a given Q/A pair is valid. Notice that a DT for Q and a DT for A can be arbitrary, but only DTs for a pair can be *valid* or *invalid*. Then this algorithm is applied to perform passage re-ranking of answers to achieve the highest possible rhetoric agreement maintaining relevance.

Tree Kernel (TK) learning for strings, parse trees and parse thickets is a well-established research area nowadays. The parse tree kernel counts the number of common sub-trees as the discourse similarity measure between two DTs. TK relies on the operation of generalization '^' which is applied at the level of parse and discourse trees, phrases, and words. A version of TK has been defined for DT by (Joty and Moschitti, 2014). In (Wang et al., 2013) special form of TK was used for discourse relation recognition. In this study we extend the TK definition for the CDT, augmenting DT kernel by the information on CAs. In Fig. 4 we have DT-A and DT-Q joined at the root, so that counting common sub-trees with nodes from DT-Q and nodes from DT-A provides a quantitative insight on how these DTs are coordinated.

A CDT can be represented by a vector V of integer counts of each sub-tree type (without taking into account its ancestors).

Only RST arcs of the same type of relation (*presentation* relation, such as *Antithesis, subject matter* relation, such as *Condition, and multinuclear* relation, such as *List*) can be matched when computing common sub-trees. We use N for a nucleus or situations presented by this nucleus, and S for satellite or situations presented by this satellite. *Situations* are propositions, completed actions or actions in progress, and communicative actions and states (including *beliefs, desires, approve, explain, reconcile* and others). Hence we have the following expression for RST-based generalization '$\wedge$' for two texts $text_1$ and $text_2$:

$$text_1 \ \wedge \ text_2 \ = \ \cup_{i,j} \ (rstRelation_{1i,} \ (...,...) \ \wedge \ rstRelation_{2j} \ (...,...))$$

where $I \in$ (RST relations in $text_1$), $j \in$ (*RST relations in* $text_2$). Further, for a pair of RST relations their generalization looks as follows: $rstRelation_1(N_1, \ S_1) \ \wedge \ rstRelation_2 \ (N_2, \ S_2) \ = \ (rstRelation_1 \wedge \ rstRelation_2)(N_1 \wedge N_2, \ S_1 \wedge S_2)$.

The texts in $N_1, \ S_1$ are subject to generalization as phrases. The rules for $rst_1 \wedge rst_2$ are as follows. If $relation\_type(rst_1) \ ! = relation\_type(rst_2)$ then similarity is empty. Otherwise, we generalize the signatures of rhetoric relations as sentences: $sentence(N_1, \ S_1) \wedge sentence \ (N_2, \ S_2)$ (Iruskieta et al., 2015).

We define CA as a predicate of the form *verb(agent, subject, cause),* where *verb* characterizes some type of interaction between involved *agents* (e.g., *explain, confirm, remind, disagree, deny*, etc.), *subject* refers to the information transmitted or object described, and *cause* refers to the motivation or explanation for the subject. To handle meaning of words expressing the subjects of CAs, we apply *word2vec* models (Mikolov et al., 2015). When verbs are identified in Qs and As, CAs are formed from the VerbNet patterns (example is shown on the right of Fig.2).

To compute similarity between the subjects of CAs, we use the following rule: If $subject1=subject2$, then $subject1\wedge subject2 = <subject1, POS(subject1), 1>$.

Otherwise, if they have the same part-of-speech, $subject1\wedge subject2 = <*, POS(subject1), word2vecDist(subject1\wedge subject2)>$. '*' is a placeholder for word lemma. If part-of-speech is different, generalization is an empty tuple. It cannot be further generalized.

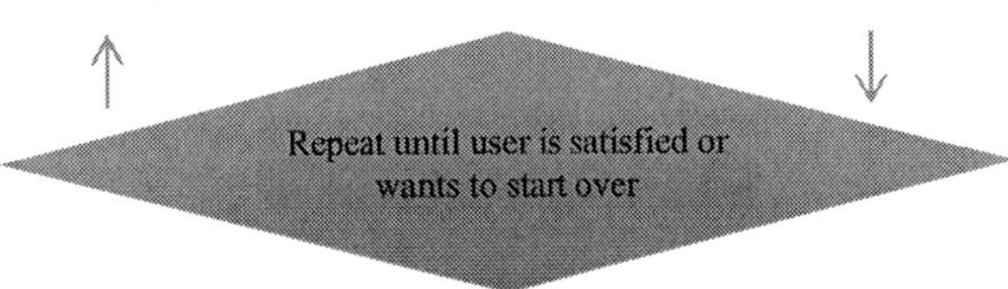

Figure 6: System architecture for a chat bot

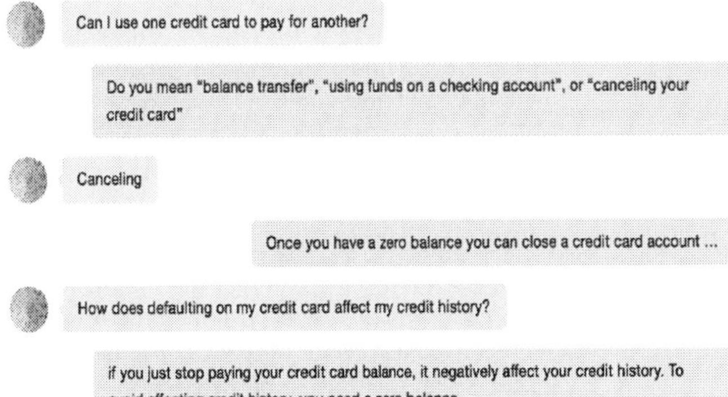

Figure 7: Sample dialogue. User questions and responses are aligned on the left and system responses - on the right

5. Chat Bot Implementation

The system architecture for a chat bot which relies on correlation of rhetoric structures of requests and response is shown in Figure 6.

Rhetoric agreement component combines Stanford NLP parsing, coreferences, entity extraction, DT construction (Surdeanu et al., 2013; Joty et al., 2016), VerbNet (Kipper et al., 2008) and Tree Kernel builder (Severyn et al., 2012) are integrated into one system stored at https://github.com/bgalitsky/relevance-based-on-parse-trees. This GitHub page contains the latest links, instructions on how to install resources and run the app.

The chat bot is optimized to minimize the amount of text the user needs to read in the course of getting to the answer. Instead of reading search results snippets and selecting the ones believed to be relevant, the system suggests the topics related to user question and options to drill into them or choose another one. This approach is better suited to personalization then conventional search engines, since user choice such as "financial product for a retired government employee" or "item for a toddler girl" is easier to formalize. A chat bot user is expected to read less and interact & clarify more to have a more efficient information access, which is also appropriate for mobile devices where text tends to be shorter and user interaction faster (Fig. 7).

6. Related Systems and Conclusions

Conventional search engines, from vertical to horizontal, do not use discourse level analysis, as far as the authors know. This is due to its computational load and hard compatibility with big data technologies. Most search engineers consider discourse analysis too abstract and too distant from applications.

Since rhetoric parsers for English has become more available and accurate, their application in search engine indexing is becoming more feasible. As precision and recall of search systems ignoring discourse level information deteriorates, users do not find products, services and information they need, leveraging of linguistic technologies including discourse become realistic for industrial systems.

Most chat bot vendors these days such as Microsoft's QnA Maker, IBM's Watson QnA Pair Ranker, botframework.com and Google's Api.ai provide an NLP chat bot platform. This platform is designed in a way so that the developers from the companies that acquired this platform can feed them with a random set of Q/A pairs and expect a reasonable relevance. Evaluation results for instances of these chat bot platforms are unavailable to the authors, but there is some evidence that the performance of above chat bots is limited when a user deviates from pre-set Q/A pairs.

Another family of chat bots is focused on simulation of intelligent human dialogues on an arbitrary topic instead of sharing searched information or performing a transaction. A number of chat bots are based on deep learning (Cho et al., 2014) of an extended training set of human dialogs. Deep learning-based chat bots are sometimes good at supporting a conversation on an arbitrary topic and building plausible utterances. However, these chat bots are not very suitable for domains such as product selling, financial transaction and customer support due to their non-deterministic nature.

We conclude that selection of answers without taking discourse correlation into account leads to a limited satisfaction with chat bots and search engines. Frequently, answers to user questions obtained from noisy user-generated content are of lower quality. This is true even for a popular content, since search engine optimization algorithms select from an available corpus and optimize the selection for efficient advertisement.

Although most search engines are good at answering popular, a few keyword-size queries, they are not good at answering complex, detailed, multi-sentence questions. The system employs the constructed library of rhetoric structures for answers that match most popular types of long questions. Using this library, a generic chat bot would be capable of providing not only topically relevant but exact, direct, properly backed up, rhetorically appropriate answers.

A web version of the chat bot is available at http://ec2-35-160-183-122.us-west-2.compute.amazonaws.com:8080/Chat bot/indexnew.html.

The bot is implemented in Oracle Mobile Cloud environment https://cloud.oracle.com/mobile.

Acknowledgements

The work of D. Ilvovsky was supported by the Russian Science Foundation under grant 17-11-01294 and performed at National Research University Higher School of Economics, Russia.

References

Chali, Y., Shafiq R. Joty, and Sadid A. Hasan. 2009. *Complex question answering: unsupervised learn-*

ing approaches and experiments. J. Artif. Int. Res. 35, 1 (May 2009), 1-47.

Vanessa Wei Feng and Graeme Hirst. 2014. A linear-time bottom-up discourse parser with constraints and post-editing. In *Proceedings of The 52nd ACL, Baltimore, USA, June*.

Galitsky, B. 2017. Matching parse thickets for open domain question answering, *Data & Knowledge Engineering*, V. 107, pp 24-50.

Galitsky, B. 2013. Machine learning of syntactic parse trees for search and classification of text. *Engineering Application of AI*, 26(3) 1072-91.

Galitsky, B, Ilvovsky, D. and Kuznetsov SO. 2015. *Rhetoric Map of an Answer to Compound Queries*. ACL-2, 681.

Shafiq R. Joty, Giuseppe Carenini, Raymond T Ng, and Yashar Mehdad. 2013. *Combining intra-and multi- sentential rhetorical parsing for document-level discourse analysis*. In *ACL (1)*, pages 486–496.

Shafiq R. Joty and A. Moschitti. 2014. *Discriminative Reranking of Discourse Parses Using Tree Kernels*. Proceedings of the 2014 Conference on Empirical Methods in Natural Language Processing (EMNLP), page

P. Jansen, M. Surdeanu and P. Clark. 2014. *Discourse Complements Lexical Semantics for Nonfactoid Answer Reranking*. ACL.

Mikel Iruskieta, Iria da Cunha and Maite Taboada. 2015. *A qualitative comparison method for rhetorical structures: identifying different discourse structures in multilingual corpora*. Language Resources and Evaluation, V. 49, I 2, pp 263–309.

William Mann and Sandra Thompson. 1988. Rhetorical structure theory: Towards a functional theory of text organization. Text-Interdisciplinary Journal for the Study of Discourse, 8(3):243–281.

Mikolov, Tomas, Chen, Kai, Corrado, G.S., Dean, Jeffrey. 2015. *Computing numeric representations of words in a high-dimensional space*. US Patent 9,037,464, Google, Inc.

Kipper, K. Korhonen, A., Ryant, N. and Palmer, M. 2008. *A large-scale classification of English verbs*. Language Resources and Evaluation Journal, 42, pp. 21-40.

Mihai Surdeanu, Thomas Hicks and Marco A. Valenzuela-Escarcega. 2015. *Two Practical Rhetorical Structure Theory Parsers*. Proceedings of the Conference of the North American Chapter of the Association for Computational Linguistics - Human Language Technologies: Software Demonstrations (NAACL HLT).

Webscope 2017. Yahoo! Answers Dataset. webscope.sandbox.yahoo.com/catalog.php?datatype=1.

Wang, W., Su, J., Tan, C.L. 2010. *Kernel Based Discourse Relation Recognition with Temporal Ordering Information*. ACL.

K. Cho, B. van Merrienboer, C. Gulcehre, F. Bougares, H. Schwenk, Y. Bengio. 2014. *Learning Phrase Representations using RNN Encoder-Decoder for Statistical Machine Translation*. EMNLP 2014.

A. Severyn, A. Moschitti. 2012. Fast Support Vector Machines for Convolution Tree Kernels. Data Mining Knowledge Discovery 25: 325-357.

Detecting Online Hate Speech Using Context Aware Models

Lei Gao
Texas A&M University
sjtuprog@tamu.edu

Ruihong Huang
Texas A&M University
huangrh@cse.tamu.edu

Abstract

In the wake of a polarizing election, the cyber world is laden with hate speech. Context accompanying a hate speech text is useful for identifying hate speech, which however has been largely overlooked in existing datasets and hate speech detection models. In this paper, we provide an annotated corpus of hate speech with context information well kept. Then we propose two types of hate speech detection models that incorporate context information, a logistic regression model with context features and a neural network model with learning components for context. Our evaluation shows that both models outperform a strong baseline by around 3% to 4% in F1 score and combining these two models further improve the performance by another 7% in F1 score.

1 Introduction

Following a turbulent election season, 2016's cyber world is awash with hate speech. Automatic detection of hate speech has become an urgent need since human supervision is unable to deal with large quantities of emerging texts.

Context information, by our definition, is the text, symbols or any other kind of information related to the original text. While intuitively, context accompanying hate speech is useful for detecting hate speech, context information of hate speech has been overlooked in existing datasets and automatic detection models.

Online hate speech tends to be subtle and creative, which makes context especially important for automatic hate speech detection. For instance,

(1) *barryswallows: Merkel would never say NO*

This comment is posted for the news titled by "German lawmakers approve 'no means no' rape law after Cologne assaults". With context, it becomes clear that this comment is a vicious insult towards female politician. However, almost all the publicly available hate speech annotated datasets do not contain context information.Waseem and Hovy (2016); Waseem (2016); Wulczyn et al. (2016); Ross et al. (2017).

We have created a new dataset consisting of 1528 Fox News user comments, which were taken from 10 complete discussion threads for 10 widely read Fox News articles. It is different from previous datasets from the following two perspectives. First, it preserves rich context information for each comment, including its user screen name, all comments in the same thread and the news article the comment is written for. Second, there is no biased data selection and all comments in each news comment thread were annotated.

In this paper, we explored two types of models, feature based logistic regression models and neural network models, in order to incorporate context information in automatic hate speech detection. First, logistic regression models have been used in several prior hate speech detection studies Chen et al. (2012); Burnap and Williams (2014); Van Hee et al. (2015); Hosseinmardi et al. (2015); Burnap and Williams (2015); Waseem and Hovy (2016); Wulczyn et al. (2016); Nobata et al. (2016) and various features have been tried including character-level and word-level n-gram features, syntactic features, linguistic features, and comment embedding features. However, all the features were derived from the to-be-classified text itself. In contrast, we experiment with logistic regression models using features extracted from context text as well. Second, neural network models Zhang et al. (2015); Tang et al. (2015); Yang et al. (2016) have the potential to capture compo-

Proceedings of Recent Advances in Natural Language Processing, pages 260–266,
Varna, Bulgaria, Sep 4–6 2017.

sitional meanings of text, but they have not been well explored for online hate speech detection until recently Pavlopoulos et al. (2017). We experiment with neural net models containing separate learning components that model compositional meanings of context information. Furthermore, recognizing unique strengths of each type of models, we build ensemble models of the two types of models. Evaluation shows that context-aware logistic regression models and neural net models outperform their counterparts that are blind with context information. Especially, the final ensemble models outperform a strong baseline system by around 10% in F1-score.

2 Related Works

Recently, a few datasets with human labeled hate speech have been created, however, most of existing datasets do not contain context information. Due to the sparsity of hate speech in everyday posts, researchers tend to sample candidates from bootstrapping instead of random sampling, in order to increase the chance of seeing hate speech. Therefore, the collected data instances are likely to be from distinct contexts.

For instance, in the Primary Data Set described in Djuric et al. (2015) and later used by Nobata et al. (2016), 10% of the dataset is randomly selected while the remaining consists of comments tagged by users and editors. Kwok and Wang (2013) built a balanced data set of 24.5k tweets by selecting from Twitter accounts that claimed to be racist or were deemed racist using their followed news sources. Burnap and Williams (2014) collected hateful tweets related to the murder of Drummer Lee Rigby in 2013. Waseem and Hovy (2016) provided a corpus of 16k annotated tweets in which 3.3k are labeled as sexist and 1.9k are labeled as racist. They created this corpus by bootstrapping from certain key words ,specific hashtags and certain prolific users. Warner and Hirschberg (2012) created a dataset of 9000 human labeled paragraphs that were collected using regular expression matching in order to find hate speech targeting Judaism and Israel. Hosseinmardi et al. (2015) extracted data instances from instagram that were associated with certain user accounts. Wulczyn et al. (2016) presented a very large corpus containing over 115k wikipedia comments that include around 37k randomly sampled comments and the remaining 78k comments were selected from wikipedia blocked comments.

Most of existing hate speech detection models are feature based and use features derived from the target text itself. Burnap and Williams (2014) experimented with different classification methods including Bayesian Logistic Regression, Random Forest Decision Trees and SVMs, using features such as n-grams, reduced n-grams, dependency paths, and hateful terms. Waseem and Hovy (2016) proposed a logistic regression model using character n-gram features. Djuric et al. (2015) used the paragraph2vec for joint modeling of comments and words, then the generated embeddings were used as feature in a logistic regression model. Nobata et al. (2016) experimented with various syntactic, linguistic and distributional semantic features including word length, sentence length, part of speech tags, and embedding features, in order to improve performance of logistic regression classifiers. Recently, Schmidt and Wiegand (2017) surveyed current approaches for hate speech detection, which interestingly also called to attention on modeling context information for resolving difficult hate speech instances.

3 The Fox News User Comments corpus

3.1 Corpus Overview

The Fox News User Comments corpus consists of 1528 annotated comments (435 labeled as hateful) that were posted by 678 different users in 10 complete news discussion threads in the Fox News website. The 10 threads were manually selected and represent popular discussion threads during August 2016. All of the comments included in these 10 threads were annotated. The number of comments in each of the 10 threads is roughly equal. Rich context information was kept for each comment, including its user screen name, the comments and their nested structure and the original news article. The data corpus along with annotation guidelines is posted on github[1].

3.2 Annotation Guidelines

Our annotation guidelines are similar to the guidelines used by Nobata et al. (2016). We define hateful speech to be the language which explicitly or implicitly threatens or demeans a person or a group based upon a facet of their identity such as gender, ethnicity, or sexual orientation. The la-

---

[1] https://github.com/sjtuprog/fox-news-comments

beling of hateful speech in our corpus is binary. A comment will be labeled as hateful or non-hateful.

3.3 Annotation Procedure

We identified two native English speakers for annotating online user comments. The two annotators first discussed and practices before they started annotation. They achieved a surprisingly high Kappa score Cohen (1960) of 0.98 on 648 comments from 4 threads. We think that thorough discussions in the training stage is the key for achieving this high inter-agreement. For those comments which annotators disagreed on, we label them as hateful as long as one annotator labeled them as hateful. Then one annotator continued to annotate the remaining 880 comments from the remaining six discussion threads.

3.4 Characteristics in Fox News User Comments corpus

Hateful comments in the Fox News User Comments Corpus is often subtle, creative and implicit. Therefore, context information is necessary in order to accurately identify such hate speech.

3.4.1 Context Dependent Comments

The hatefulness of many comments depended on understanding their contexts. For instance,

(3) *mastersundholm: Just remember no trabjo no cervesa*

This comment is posted for the news "States moving to restore work requirements for food stamp recipients". This comment implies that Latino immigrants abuse the usage of food stamp policy, which is clearly a stereotyping.

3.4.2 Implicit and creative language

Many hateful comments use implicit and subtle language, which contain no clear hate indicating word or phrase. In order to recognize such hard cases, we hypothesize that neural net models are more suitable by capturing overall composite meanings of a comment. For instance, the following comment is a typical implicit stereotyping against women.

(4) *MarineAssassin: Hey Brianne - get in the kitchen and make me a samich. Chop Chop*

3.4.3 Long Comments with Regional Focus of hatefulness

11% of our annotated comments have more than 50 words each. In such long comments, the hate-

ful indicators usually appear in a small region of a comment while the majority of the comment is neutral. For example,

(5) *TMmckay: I thought ...115 words...* ***Too many blacks winning, must be racist and needs affirmative action to make whites equally win!***

3.4.4 Disrespectful screen names

Certain user screen names indicate hatefulness, which imply that comments posted by these users are likely to contain hate speech. In the following example, commie is a slur for communists.

(6)*nocommie11: Blah blah blah. Israel is the only civilized nation in the region to keep the unwashed masses at bay.*

4 Context-aware Online Hate Speech Detection Models

4.1 Logistic Regression Models

In logistic regression models, we extract four types of features, word-level and character-level n-gram features as well as two types of lexicon derived features. We extract these four types of features from the target comment first. Then we extract these features from two sources of context texts, specifically the title of the news article that the comment was posted for and the screen name of the user who posted the comment.

For logistic regression model implementation, we use l2 loss. We adopt the balanced class weight as described in Scikit learn[2]. Logistic regression model with character-level n-gram features is presented as a strong baseline for comparison since it was shown very effective. (Waseem and Hovy, 2016; Nobata et al., 2016)

4.1.1 Word-level and Character-level N-gram Features

For character level n-grams, we extract character level bigrams, tri-grams and four-grams. For word level n-grams, we extract unigrams and bigrams.

4.1.2 LIWC Feature

Linguistic Inquiry and Word Count, also called LIWC, has been proven useful for text analysis and classification Pennebaker et al. (2001). In the LIWC dictionary, each word is labeled with several semantic labels. In our experiment, we use

---

[2]http://scikit-learn.org/stable/modules/generated/
sklearn.linear_model.LogisticRegression.html

the LIWC 2015 dictionary which contain 125 semantic categories. Each word is converted into a 125 dimension LIWC vector, one dimension per semantic category. The LIWC feature vector for a comment or its context is a 125 dimension vector as well, which is the sum of all its words' LIWC vectors.

4.1.3 NRC Emotion Lexicon Feature

NRC emotion lexicon contains a list of English words that were labeled with eight basic emotions (anger, fear, anticipation, trust, surprise, sadness, joy, and disgust) and sentiment polarities (negative and positive)(Mohammad and Turney, 2013). We use NRC emotion lexicon to capture emotion clues in text. Each word is converted into a 10 dimension emotion vector, corresponding to eight emotion types and two polarity labels. The emotion vector for a comment or its context is a 10 dimension vector as well, which is the sum of all its words' emotion vectors.

4.2 Neural Network Models

Our neural network model mainly consists of three parallel LSTM Hochreiter and Schmidhuber (1997) layers. It has three different inputs, including the target comment, its news title and its username. Comment and news title are encoded into a sequence of word embeddings. We use pre-trained word embeddings in word2vec[3]. Username is encoded into a sequence of characters. We use one-hot encoding of characters.

Comment is sent into a bi-directional LSTM with attention mechanism. (Bahdanau et al., 2014). News title and username are sent into a bi-directional LSTM. Note that we did not apply attention mechanism to the neural network models for username and news title because both types of context are relatively short and attention mechanism tends to be useful when text input is long. The three LSTM output layers are concatenated, then connected to a sigmoid layer, which outputs predictions.

The number of hidden units in each LSTM used in our model is set to be 100. The recurrent dropout rate of LSTMs is set to 0.2. In addition, we use binary cross entropy as the loss function and a batch size of 128. The neural network models are trained for 30 epochs.

____
[3]https://code.google.com/archive/p/word2vec/

4.3 Ensemble Models

To study the difference of logistic regression model and neural network model and potentially get performance improvement, we will build and evaluate ensemble models.

5 Evaluation

We evaluate our model by 10 fold cross validation using our newly created Fox News User Comments Corpus. Both types of models use the exact same 10 folds of training data and test data. We report experimental results using multiple metrics, including accuracy, precision/recall/F1-score, and accuracy area under curve (AUC).

5.1 Experimental Results

5.1.1 Logistic Regression Models

Table 1 shows the performance of logistic regression models. The first section of table 1 shows the performance of logistic regression models using features extracted from a target comment only. The result shows that the logistic regression model was improved in every metric after adding both word-level n-gram features and lexicon derived features. However, the improvements are moderate.

The second section shows the performance of logistic regression models using the four types of features extracted from both a target comment and its contextsThe result shows that the logistic regression model using features extracted from a comment and both types of context achieved the best performance and obtained improvements of 2.8% and 2.5% in AUC score and F1-score respectively.

5.1.2 Neural Network Models

Table 2 shows the performance of neural network models. The first section of table 2 shows the performance of several neural network models that use comments as the only input. The model names are self-explanatory. We can see that the attention mechanism coupled with the bi-directional LSTM neural net greatly improved the online hate speech detection, by 5.7% in AUC score.

The second section of table 2 shows performance of the best neural net model (bi-directional LSTM with attention) after adding additional learning components that take context as input. The results show that adding username and news title can both improve model performance. Using

Features	Input Contents	Accuracy	Precision	Recall	F1	AUC
char (baseline)	comment	0.738	0.549	0.469	0.504	0.733
+word	comment	0.735	0.548	0.443	0.488	0.736
+LIWC+NRC	comment	0.732	0.533	0.465	0.495	0.740
+word+LIWC+NRC	comment	**0.747**	**0.568**	**0.476**	**0.517**	**0.750**
	+ username	0.747	**0.576**	0.474	0.518	0.765
	+ title	0.745	0.558	0.496	0.523	0.761
	+ title+ username (**Best**)	**0.750**	0.572	**0.516**	**0.542**	**0.778**

Table 1: Performance of Logistic Regression Models

Model	Input Contents	Accuracy	Precision	Recall	F1	AUC
LSTM	comment	0.726	0.524	0.398	0.450	0.678
bi-LSTM	comment	0.720	0.513	**0.440**	0.473	0.682
bi-LSTM with attention	comment	**0.750**	**0.591**	0.437	**0.499**	**0.735**
	+ username	0.742	0.566	0.437	0.489	0.748
	+ title (**best**)	**0.766**	**0.614**	**0.499**	**0.548**	0.760
	+ title + username	0.755	0.589	0.496	0.532	**0.766**

Table 2: Performance of Neural Network Models

news title gives the best F1 score while using both news title and username gives the best AUC score.

5.1.3 Ensemble Models

Table 3 shows performance of ensemble models by combining prediction results of the best context-aware logistic regression model and the best context-aware neural network model. We used two strategies in combining prediction results of two types of models. Specifically, the Max Score Ensemble model made the final decisions based on the maximum of two scores assigned by the two separate models; instead, the Average Score Ensemble model used the average score to make final decisions.

We can see that both ensemble models further improved hate speech detection performance compared with using one model only and achieved the best classification performance. Compared with the logistic regression baseline, the Max Score Ensemble model improved the recall by more than 20% with a comparable precision and improved the F1 score by around 10%, in addition, the Average Score Ensemble model improved the AUC score by around 7%.

6 Analysis

6.1 Logistic Regression Models

As shown in table 1, given comment as the only input content, the combination of character n-grams, word n-grams, LIWC feature and NRC feature achieves the best performance. It shows that in addition to character level features, adding more features can improve hate speech detection performance. However, the improvement is limited. Compared with baseline model, the F1 score only improves 1.3%.

In contrast, when context information was taken into account, the performance greatly improved. Specifically, after incorporating features extracted from the news title and username, the model performance was improved by around 4% in both F1 score and AUC score. This shows that using additional context based features in logistic regression models is useful for hate speech detection.

6.2 Neural Network Models

As shown in table 2, given comment as the only input content, the bi-directional LSTM model with attention mechanism achieves the best performance. Note that the attention mechanism significantly improves the hate speech detection performance of the bi-directional LSTM model. We hypothesize that this is because hate indicator phrases are often concentrated in a small region of a comment, which is especially the case for long comments.

6.3 Ensemble Models

As shown in table 3, both ensemble models significantly improved hate speech detection performance. Figure 1 shows the system prediction results of comments that were labeled as hateful in the dataset. It can be seen that the two models per-

Model	Accuracy	Precision	Recall	F1	AUC
Char (Baseline)	0.738	0.549	0.469	0.504	0.733
Best Neural Network Model	0.766	0.614	0.499	0.548	0.760
Best Logistic Regression Model	0.750	0.572	0.516	0.542	0.778
Max Score Ensemble	0.740	0.539	**0.678**	**0.600**	0.794
Average Score Ensemble	**0.779**	**0.650**	0.496	0.560	**0.804**

Table 3: Performance of Ensemble Models

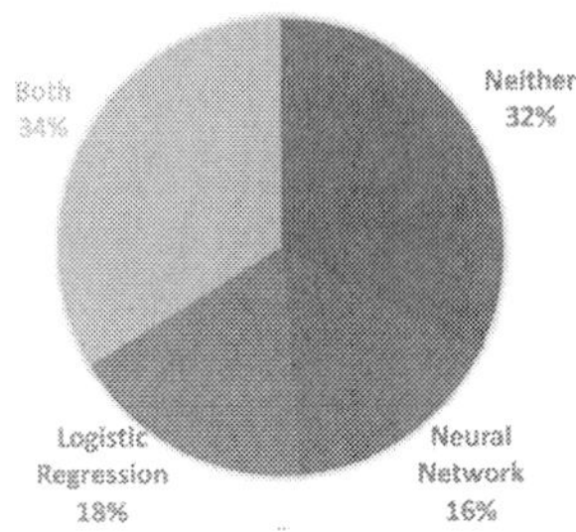

Figure 1: System Prediction Results of Comments that were Annotated as Hateful

form differently. We further examined predicted comments and find that both types of models have unique strengths in identifying certain types of hateful comments.

6.3.1 Strengths of Logistic Regression Models

The feature based logistic regression models are capable of making good use of character-level n-gram features, which are powerful in identifying hateful comments that contains OOV words, capitalized words or misspelled words. We provide two examples from the hateful comments that were only labeled by the logistic regression model:

(7)*kmawhmf:FBLM.*

Here FBLM means fuck Black Lives Matter. This hateful comment contains only character information which can exactly be made use of by our logistic regression model.

(8)*SFgunrmn: what a efen loon, but most femanazis are.*

This comment deliberately misspelled feminazi for femanazis, which is a derogatory term for feminists. It shows that logistic regression model is capable in dealing with misspelling.

6.3.2 Strengths of Neural Network Models

The LSTM with attention mechanism are suitable for identifying specific small regions indicating hatefulness in long comments. In addition, the neural net models are powerful in capturing implicit hateful language as well. The following are two hateful comment examples that were only identified by the neural net model:

(9)*freedomscout: @LarJass **Many religions are poisonous to logic and truth, that much is true**...and human beings still remain fallen human beings even they are Redeemed by the Sacrifice of Jesus Christ. So there's that. But the fallacies of thinking cannot be limited or attributed to religion but to error inherent in human motivation, the motivation to utter self-centeredness as fallen sinful human beings. **Nearly all of the world's many religions are expressions of that utter sinful nature**...Christianity and Judaism being the sole exceptions.*

This comment is expressing the stereotyping against religions which are not Christian or Judaism. The hatefulness is concentrated within the two bolded segments.

(10)*mamahattheridge: blacks Love being victims.*

In this comment, the four words themselves are not hateful at all. But when combined together, it is clearly hateful against black people.

7 Conclusion

We demonstrated the importance of utilizing context information for online hate speech detection. We first presented a corpus of hateful speech consisting of full threads of online discussion posts. In addition, we presented two types of models, feature based logistic regression models and neural network models, in order to incorporate context information for improving hate speech detection performance. Furthermore, we show that ensemble models leveraging strengths of both types of models achieve the best performance for automatic online hate speech detection.

References

Dzmitry Bahdanau, Kyunghyun Cho, and Yoshua Bengio. 2014. Neural machine translation by jointly learning to align and translate. *arXiv preprint arXiv:1409.0473*.

Pete Burnap and Matthew L Williams. 2015. Cyber hate speech on twitter: An application of machine classification and statistical modeling for policy and decision making. *Policy & Internet* 7(2):223–242.

Peter Burnap and Matthew Leighton Williams. 2014. Hate speech, machine classification and statistical modelling of information flows on twitter: Interpretation and communication for policy decision making. In *Proceedings of the Internet, Politics, and Policy conference*.

Ying Chen, Yilu Zhou, Sencun Zhu, and Heng Xu. 2012. Detecting offensive language in social media to protect adolescent online safety. In *Privacy, Security, Risk and Trust (PASSAT), 2012 International Conference on and 2012 International Confernece on Social Computing (SocialCom)*. IEEE, pages 71–80.

Jacob Cohen. 1960. A coefficient of agreement for nominal scales. *Educational and psychological measurement* 20(1):37–46.

Nemanja Djuric, Jing Zhou, Robin Morris, Mihajlo Grbovic, Vladan Radosavljevic, and Narayan Bhamidipati. 2015. Hate speech detection with comment embeddings. In *Proceedings of the 24th International Conference on World Wide Web*. ACM, pages 29–30.

Sepp Hochreiter and Jürgen Schmidhuber. 1997. Long short-term memory. *Neural computation* 9(8):1735–1780.

Homa Hosseinmardi, Sabrina Arredondo Mattson, Rahat Ibn Rafiq, Richard Han, Qin Lv, and Shivakant Mishra. 2015. Detection of cyberbullying incidents on the instagram social network. *arXiv preprint arXiv:1503.03909*.

Irene Kwok and Yuzhou Wang. 2013. Locate the hate: Detecting tweets against blacks. In *AAAI*.

Saif M Mohammad and Peter D Turney. 2013. Nrc emotion lexicon. Technical report, NRC Technical Report.

Chikashi Nobata, Joel Tetreault, Achint Thomas, Yashar Mehdad, and Yi Chang. 2016. Abusive language detection in online user content. In *Proceedings of the 25th International Conference on World Wide Web*. International World Wide Web Conferences Steering Committee, pages 145–153.

John Pavlopoulos, Prodromos Malakasiotis, and Ion Androutsopoulos. 2017. Deep learning for user comment moderation. *arXiv preprint arXiv:1705.09993*.

James W Pennebaker, Martha E Francis, and Roger J Booth. 2001. Linguistic inquiry and word count: Liwc 2001. *Mahway: Lawrence Erlbaum Associates* 71(2001):2001.

Björn Ross, Michael Rist, Guillermo Carbonell, Benjamin Cabrera, Nils Kurowsky, and Michael Wojatzki. 2017. Measuring the reliability of hate speech annotations: The case of the european refugee crisis. *arXiv preprint arXiv:1701.08118*.

Anna Schmidt and Michael Wiegand. 2017. A survey on hate speech detection using natural language processing. *SocialNLP 2017* page 1.

Duyu Tang, Bing Qin, and Ting Liu. 2015. Document modeling with gated recurrent neural network for sentiment classification. In *EMNLP*. pages 1422–1432.

Cynthia Van Hee, Els Lefever, Ben Verhoeven, Julie Mennes, Bart Desmet, Guy De Pauw, Walter Daelemans, and Véronique Hoste. 2015. Detection and fine-grained classification of cyberbullying events. In *International Conference Recent Advances in Natural Language Processing (RANLP)*. pages 672–680.

William Warner and Julia Hirschberg. 2012. Detecting hate speech on the world wide web. In *Proceedings of the Second Workshop on Language in Social Media*. Association for Computational Linguistics, pages 19–26.

Zeerak Waseem. 2016. Are you a racist or am i seeing things? annotator influence on hate speech detection on twitter. In *Proceedings of the 1st Workshop on Natural Language Processing and Computational Social Science*. pages 138–142.

Zeerak Waseem and Dirk Hovy. 2016. Hateful symbols or hateful people? predictive features for hate speech detection on twitter. In *Proceedings of NAACL-HLT*. pages 88–93.

Ellery Wulczyn, Nithum Thain, and Lucas Dixon. 2016. Ex machina: Personal attacks seen at scale. *arXiv preprint arXiv:1610.08914*.

Zichao Yang, Diyi Yang, Chris Dyer, Xiaodong He, Alex Smola, and Eduard Hovy. 2016. Hierarchical attention networks for document classification. In *Proceedings of NAACL-HLT*. pages 1480–1489.

Xiang Zhang, Junbo Zhao, and Yann LeCun. 2015. Character-level convolutional networks for text classification. In *Advances in neural information processing systems*. pages 649–657.

A Context-Aware Approach for Detecting Worth-Checking Claims in Political Debates

Pepa Gencheva[1], Preslav Nakov[2], Lluís Màrquez[2], Alberto Barrón-Cedeño[2], and Ivan Koychev[1]

[1]Sofia University "St. Kliment Ohridski", Bulgaria
[2]Qatar Computing Research Institute, HBKU, Qatar
pepa.k.gencheva@gmail.com, {pnakov, lmarquez, albarron}@hbku.edu.qa
koychev@fmi.uni-sofia.bg

Abstract

In the context of investigative journalism, we address the problem of automatically identifying which claims in a given document are most worthy and should be prioritized for fact-checking. Despite its importance, this is a relatively understudied problem. Thus, we create a new corpus of political debates, containing statements that have been fact-checked by nine reputable sources, and we train machine learning models to predict which claims should be prioritized for fact-checking, i.e., we model the problem as a ranking task. Unlike previous work, which has looked primarily at sentences in isolation, in this paper we focus on a rich input representation modeling the context: relationship between the target statement and the larger context of the debate, interaction between the opponents, and reaction by the moderator and by the public. Our experiments show state-of-the-art results, outperforming a strong rivaling system by a margin, while also confirming the importance of the contextual information.

1 Introduction

The current coverage of the political landscape in the press and in social media has led to an unprecedented situation. Like never before, a statement in an interview, a press release, a blog note, or a tweet can spread almost instantaneously and reach the public in no time. This proliferation speed has left little time for double-checking claims against the facts, which has proven critical in politics, e.g., during the 2016 presidential campaign in the USA, which was arguably impacted by fake news in social media and by false claims.

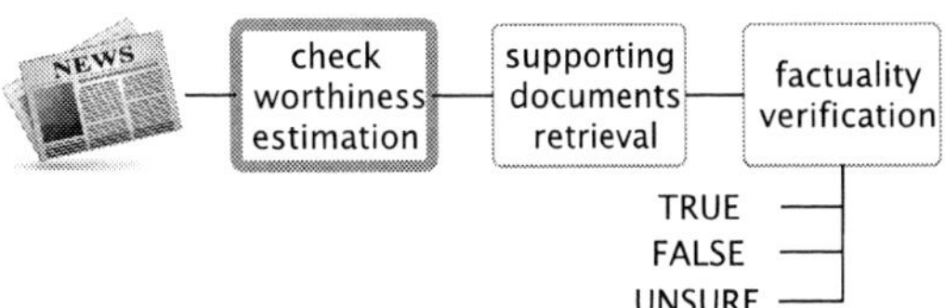

Figure 1: Information verification pipeline.

Investigative journalists and volunteers have been working hard trying to get to the root of a claim and to present solid evidence in favor or against it. Manual fact-checking has proven very time-consuming, and thus automatic methods have been proposed as a way to speed-up the process. For instance, there has been work on checking the factuality/credibility of a claim, of a news article, or of an information source (Castillo et al., 2011; Ba et al., 2016; Zubiaga et al., 2016; Ma et al., 2016; Hardalov et al., 2016; Karadzhov et al., 2017a,b; Nakov et al., 2017). However, less attention has been paid to other steps of the fact-checking pipeline, which is shown in Figure 1.

The process starts when a document is made public. First, an intrinsic analysis is carried out in which check-worthy text fragments are identified. Then, other documents that might support or rebut a claim in the document are retrieved from various sources. Finally, by comparing a claim against the retrieved evidence, a system can determine whether the claim is likely true or likely false. For instance, Ciampaglia et al. (2015) do this on the basis of a knowledge graph derived from Wikipedia. The outcome could then be presented to a human expert for final judgment.[1]

---

[1] As of present, fully automatic methods for fact checking still lag behind in terms of quality, and thus also of credibility in the eyes of the users, compared to what high-quality manual checking by reputable sources can achieve, which means that a final double-checking by a human expert is needed.

Proceedings of Recent Advances in Natural Language Processing, pages 267–276,
Varna, Bulgaria, Sep 4–6 2017.

In this paper, we focus on the first step: predicting check-worthiness of claims. Our contributions can be summarized as follows:

1. *New dataset:* We build a new dataset of manually-annotated claims, extracted from the 2016 US presidential and vice-presidential debates, which we gathered from nine reputable sources such as CNN, NPR, and PolitiFact, and which we release to the research community.

2. *Modeling the context:* We develop a novel approach for automatically predicting which claims should be prioritized for fact-checking, based on a rich input representation. In particular, we model not only the textual content, but also the context: how the target claim relates to the current segment, to neighboring segments and sentences, and to the debate as a whole, and also how the opponents and the public react to it.

3. State-of-the-art results: We achieve state-of-the-art results, outperforming a strong rivaling system by a margin, while also demonstrating that this improvement is due primarily to our modeling of the context.

We model the problem as a ranking task, and we train both Support Vector Machines (SVM) and Feed-forward Neural Networks (FNN) obtaining state-of-the-art results. We also analyze the relevance of the specific feature groups and we show that modeling the context yields a significant boost in performance. Finally, we also analyze whether we can learn to predict which facts are worth-checking with respect to each of the individual media sources, thus capturing their biases. It is worth noting that while trained on political debates, many features of our model can be potentially applied to other kinds of information sources, e.g., interviews and news.

The rest of the paper is organized as follows: Section 2 overviews related work. Section 3 describes the process of gathering and annotating the debates dataset. Section 4 describes our supervised approach to predicting fact-checking worthiness, including the explanation of the model and the information sources we use. Section 5 includes the evaluation and discusses the results. Section 6 provides further analysis. Finally, Section 7 presents the conclusions and outlines some lines for future research.

2 Related Work

The previous work that is most relevant to our work here is that of (Hassan et al., 2015), who developed the *ClaimBuster* system, which assigns each sentence in a document a score, i.e., a number between 0 and 1 showing how worthy it is for fact-checking. The system is trained on their own dataset of about 8 thousand debate sentences (1,673 of them worth-checking), annotated by students, university professors, and journalists. Unfortunately, this dataset is not publicly available, and contains sentences without context as about 60% of the original sentences had to be thrown away due to lack of agreement.

In contrast, we develop a new publicly-available dataset,[2] based on manual annotations of political debates by nine highly-reputed fact-checking sources, where sentences are annotated in the context of the entire debate. This allows us to explore a novel approach, which focuses on the context.

Note also that the *ClaimBuster* dataset is annotated following guidelines from (Hassan et al., 2015) rather than a real fact-checking website; yet, it was evaluated against CNN and PolitiFact (Hassan et al., 2016). In contrast, we train and evaluate directly on annotations from fact-checking websites, and thus we learn to fit them better.

Beyond the document context, it has been proposed to mine check-worthy claims on the Web. For example, Ennals et al. (2010a) searched for linguistic cues of disagreement between the author of a statement and what is believed, e.g., "falsely claimed that X". The claims matching the patterns go through a statistical classifier, which marks the text of the claim. This procedure can be used to acquire a corpus of disputed claims from the Web.

Given a set of disputed claims, (Ennals et al., 2010b) approached the task as locating new claims on the Web that entail the ones that have already been collected. Thus, the task can be conformed as recognizing textual entailment, which is analyzed in detail in (Dagan et al., 2009).

Finally, Le et al. (2016) argued that the top terms in claim vs. non-claim sentences are highly overlapping, which is a problem for bag-of-words approaches. Thus, they used a Convolutional Neural Network, where each word is represented by its embedding and each named entity is replaced by its tag, e.g., *person, organization, location.*

---

[2]The dataset and the source code are available in GitHub: `https://github.com/pgencheva/claim-rank`

Medium	1st	2nd	VP	3rd	Total
ABC News	35	50	29	28	142
Chicago Tribune	30	29	31	38	128
CNN	46	30	37	60	173
FactCheck.org	15	45	47	60	167
NPR	99	92	91	89	371
PolitiFact	74	62	60	57	253
The Guardian	27	39	54	72	192
The New York Times	26	25	46	52	149
The Washington Post	26	19	33	17	95
Total annotations	378	391	428	473	1,670
Annotated sentences	218	235	183	244	880

Table 1: Number of annotations in each medium for the 1st, 2nd and 3rd presidential and the vice-presidential debates.

Agreement Level	Number of Sentences	Cumulative Sum
9	1	1
8	6	7
7	5	12
6	19	31
5	26	57
4	40	97
3	100	197
2	191	388
1	492	880
Total number of sentences: 5,415		

Table 2: Agreement between the media represented as the number of sentences that n out of nine providers identified as worth-checking.

3 The CW-USPD-2016 Corpus on US Presidential Debates

We created a new dataset called CW-USPD-2016 (check-worthiness in the US presidential debates 2016) for finding check-worthy claims in context. In particular, we used four transcripts of the 2016 US election: one vice-presidential and three presidential debates. For each debate, we used the publicly-available manual analysis about it from nine reputable fact-checking sources, as shown in Table 1. This could include not just a statement about factuality, but any free text that journalists decided to add, e.g., links to biographies or behavioral analysis of the opponents and moderators. We converted this to binary annotation about whether a particular sentence was annotated for factuality by a given source. Whenever one or more annotations were about part of a sentence, we selected the entire sentence, and when an annotation spanned over multiple sentences, we selected each of them.

Ultimately, we ended up with a corpus of four debates, with a total of 5,415 sentences. The agreement between the sources was low as Table 2 shows: only one sentence was selected by all nine sources, 57 sentences by at least five, 197 by at least three, 388 by at least two, and 880 by at least one. The reason for this is that the different media aimed at annotating sentences according to their own editorial line, rather than trying to be exhaustive in any way. This suggests that the task of predicting which sentence would contain worth-checking claims will be challenging. Thus, below we focus on a ranking task rather than on absolute predictions. Moreover, we predict which sentence would be selected (*i*) by at least one of the media, or (*ii*) by a specific medium.

Note that the investigative journalists did not select the check-worthy claims in isolation. Our analysis shows that these include claims that were highly disputed during the debate, that were relevant to the topic introduced by the moderator, etc. We will make use of these contextual dependencies below, which is something that was not previously tried in related work.

4 Modeling Check-Worthiness

We developed a rich input representation in order to model and to learn the *check-worthiness* concept. The feature types we implemented operate at the sentence- (S) and at the context-level (C), in either case targeting *segments* by the same speaker.[3] The context features are novel and a contribution of this study. We also implemented a set of core features to compare to the state of the art. All of them are described below.

4.1 Sentence-Level Features

ClaimBuster-based (*1,045 S features*; core): First, in order to be able to compare our model and features directly to the previous state of the art, we re-implemented, to the best of our ability, the sentence-level features of *ClaimBuster* as described in (Hassan et al., 2015), namely TF-IDF-weighted bag of words (998 features), part-of-speech tags (25 features), name entities as recognized by *Alchemy API*[4] (20 features), sentiment score from Alchemy API (1 feature), and number of tokens in the target sentence (1 feature).

---

[3]We define a *segment* as a maximal set of consecutive sentences by the same speaker without intervention by another speaker or by the moderator.

[4]http://www.ibm.com/watson/
alchemy-api.html

Apart from providing means of comparison to the state of the art, these features also make a solid contribution to the final system we build for claim-worthiness estimation. However, note that we did not have access to the training data of Claim-Buster, which is not publicly available, and we thus train on our own dataset.

Sentiment (*2 S features*): Some sentences are highly negative, which can signal the presence of an interesting claim to check, as the two example sentences below show (from the 1st and the 2nd presidential debates):

Trump:	Murders are up.
Clinton:	Bullying is up.

We used the NRC sentiment lexicon (Mohammad and Turney, 2013) as a source of words and n-grams with positive/negative sentiment, and we counted the number of positive and of negative words in the target sentence. These features are different from those in the *CB features* above, where these lexicons were not used.

Named entities (NE) (*1 S feature*): Sentences that contain named entity mentions are more likely to contain a claim that is worth fact-checking as they discuss particular people, organizations, and locations. Thus, we have a feature that counts the number of named entities in the target sentence; we use the *NLTK toolkit* for named entity recognition (Loper and Bird, 2002). Unlike the *CB features* above, here we only have one feature; we also use a different toolkit for named entity recognition.

Linguistic features (*9 S features*): We count the number of words in each sentence that belong to each of the following lexicons: Language Bias lexicon (Recasens et al., 2013), Opinion Negative and Positive Words (Liu et al., 2005), Factives and Assertive Predicates (Hooper, 1974), Hedges (Hyland, 1998), Implicatives (Karttunen, 1971), and Strong and Weak subjective words. Some examples are shown in Table 3.

Feature Name	Examples
Bias	capture, create, demand, follow
Negatives	abnormal, bankrupt, cheat, conflicts
Positives	accurate, achievements, affirm
Factives	realize, know, discover, learn
Assertives	think, believe, imagine, guarantee
Hedges	approximately, estimate, essentially
Implicatives	cause, manage, hesitate, neglect
Strong-subj	admire, afraid, agreeably, apologist
Weak-subj	abandon, adaptive, champ, consume

Table 3: Linguistic features and examples.

Tense (*1 S feature*): Most of the check-worthy claims mention past events. In order to detect when the speaker is making a reference to the past or s/he is talking about his/her future vision and plans, we include a feature with three values—indicating whether the text is in past, present of future tense. The feature is extracted from the verbal expressions, using POS tags and a list of auxiliary verbs and phrases such as *will*, *have to*, etc.

Length (*1 S feature*): Shorter sentences are generally less likely to contain a worth-checking claim.[5] Thus, we have a feature for the length of the sentence in terms of characters. Note that this feature was not part of the *CB features*, as there length was modeled in terms of tokens, but here we do so using characters.

4.2 Contextual Features

Position (*3 C features*): A sentence on the boundaries of a speaker's segment could contain a reaction to another statement or could provoke a reaction, which in turn could signal a worth-checking claim. Thus, we added information about the position of the target sentence in its segment: whether it is first/last, as well as its reciprocal rank in the list of sentences in that segment.

Segment sizes (*3 C features*): The size of the segment belonging to one speaker might indicate whether the target sentence is part of a long speech, makes a short comment or is in the middle of a discussion with lots of interruptions. The size of the previous and of the next segments is also important in modeling the dialogue flow. Thus, we include three features with the sizes of the previous, the current and the next segments.

Metadata (*8 C features*): Worth-checking claims often contain accusations about the opponents, as the example below shows (from the 2nd presidential debate):

Trump:	**Hillary Clinton** attacked those same women and attacked them viciously.
Clinton:	They're doing it to try to influence the election for **Donald Trump**.

Thus, we use a feature that indicates whether the target sentence mentions the name of the opponent, whether the speaker is the moderator, and also who is speaking (3 features). We further use three binary features, indicating whether the target sentence is followed by a system message: *applause*, *laugh*, or *cross-talk*.

---

[5] One notable exception are short sentences with negations, e.g., *Wrong.*, *Nonsense.*, etc.

4.3 Mixed Features

The feature groups in this subsection contain a mixture of sentence- and of contextual-level features. For example, if we use a discourse parser to parse the target sentence only, any features we extract from the parse would be sentence-level. However, if we parse an entire segment, we would also have contextual features.

Topics (*300+3 S+C features*): Some topics are more likely to be associated with worth-checking claims, and thus we have features modeling the topics in the target sentence as well as in the surrounding context. We trained a Latent Dirichlet Allocation (LDA) topic model (Blei et al., 2003) on all political speeches and debates in *The American Presidency Project*[6] using all US presidential debates in the 2007–2016 period[7]. We had 300 topics, and we used the distribution over the topics as a representation for the target sentence. We further modeled the context using cosines with such representations for the previous, the current, and the next segment.

Embeddings (*300+3 S+C features*): We further modeled semantics using word embeddings. We used the pre-trained 300-dimensional Google News word embeddings by Mikolov et al. (2013) to compute an average embedding vector for the target sentence, and we used the 300 coordinates of that vector. We also modeled the context as the cosine between that vector and the vectors for three segments: the previous, the current, and the following one.

Discourse (*2+18 S+C features*): We saw above that contradiction can signal the presence of worth-checking claims, and contradiction can be expressed by a discourse relation such as CON-TRAST. As other discourse relations such as BACKGROUND, CAUSE, and ELABORATION can also be useful, we used a discourse parser (Joty et al., 2015) to parse the entire segment, and we focused on the relationship between the target sentence and the other sentences in its segment; this gave rise to 18 contextual indicator features. We further analyzed the internal structure of the target sentence —how many nuclei and how many satellites it contains—, which gave rise to two sentence-level features.

Contradictions (*1+4 S+C features*): Many claims selected for fact-checking contain contradictions to what has been said earlier, as in the example below (from the 3rd presidential debate):

> Clinton: [...] about a potential nuclear competition in Asia, you said, you know, go ahead, enjoy yourselves, folks.
>
> Trump: **I didn't say** nuclear.

We model this by counting the negations in the target sentence as found in a dictionary of negation cues such as *not*, *didn't*, and *never*. We further model the context as the number of such cues in the two neighboring sentences from the same segment and the two neighboring segments.

kNN (*2+1 S+C features*): We used three more features inspired by k-nearest neighbor (kNN) classification. The first one (sentence-level) uses the maximum over the training sentences of the number of matching words between the testing and the training sentence, which is further multiplied by -1 if the latter was not worth-checking. We also used another version of the feature, where we multiplied it by 0 if the speakers were different (contextual). A third version took as a training set all claims checked by *PolitiFact* (excluding the target sentence).

5 Experiments and Evaluation

5.1 Experimental Setting

We experimented with two learning algorithms. The first one is an SVM classifier with an RBF kernel.[8] The second one is a deep feed-forward neural network (FNN) with two hidden layers (with 200 and 50 neurons, respectively) and a softmax output unit for the binary classification. We used ReLU (Glorot et al., 2011) as the activation function and we trained the network with Stochastic Gradient Descent (LeCun et al., 1998).

The models were trained to classify sentences as positive if *one or more media* had fact-checked a claim inside the target sentence, and negative otherwise. We then used the classifier scores to rank the sentences with respect to *check-worthiness*.[9] We tuned the parameters and we evaluated the performance using 4-fold cross-validation, using each of the four debates in turn for testing while training on the remaining three ones.

---

[6] http://www.presidency.ucsb.edu/debates.php

[7] https://github.com/paigecm/2016-campaign

[8] The RBF kernel was clearly superior to a linear kernel in our initial experiments.

[9] We also tried using ordinal regression, and SVM-perf, an instantiation of SVM-struct, to directly optimize precision, but none of them yielded improvements.

For evaluation, we used ranking measures such as *Precision at k* ($P@k$) and *Mean Average Precision* (MAP). As Table 1 shows, most media rarely check more than 50 claims per debate. *NPR* and *PolitiFact* are notable exceptions, the former going up to 99; yet, on average there are two claims per sentence, which means that there is no need to fact-check more than 50 sentences even for them. Thus, we report $P@k$ for $k \in \{5, 10, 20, 50\}$.[10]

MAP is the mean of the Average Precision across the four debates. The average precision for a debate is computed as follows:

$$\text{AvPrec} = \frac{\sum_{k=1}^{n}(P(k) \times rel(k))}{\text{number of relevant utterances}} \quad (1)$$

where n is the number of sentences to rank in the debate, $P(k)$ is the precision at k and $rel(k) = 1$ if the utterance at position k is worth-checking, and it is 0 otherwise.

We also measure the recall at the R-th position of returned sentences for each debate. R is the number of relevant documents for that debate and the metric is known as R-Precision (R-Pr).

5.2   Results

Table 4 shows the performance of our models when using all features described in Section 4: see the SVM$_{All}$ and the FNN$_{All}$ rows.

In order to put the numbers in perspective, we also show the results for five increasingly competitive baselines. The first one is a random baseline. It is then followed by an SVM classifier based on a bag-of-words representation with TF-IDF weights learned on the training data. Then come three versions of the *ClaimBuster* system: CB-Platform refers to the performance of *ClaimBuster* using the scores obtained from their online demo,[11] which we accessed on December 20, 2016, and SVM$_{CBfeat}$ and FNN$_{CBfeat}$ are our reimplementations of *ClaimBuster* using their features, which we then use in our SVM or FNN classifiers trained on our dataset.

We can see that, as expected, all systems perform well above the random baseline. The three versions of ClaimBuster also outperform the TD-IDF baseline on most measures.

Moreover, our reimplementations of *ClaimBuster* are better than the online platform in terms of MAP. This is expected as their system is trained on a different dataset and it may suffer from testing on slightly out-of-domain data. At the same time, this is reassuring for our implementation of the features, and allows for a more realistic comparison to the *ClaimBuster* system.

More importantly, we can see that both the SVM and the FNN versions of our system, when trained with all features, consistently outperform all three versions of *ClaimBuster* on all measures. This means that the extra information coded in our model, mainly more linguistic, structural, and contextual features, has an important contribution to the final performance.

We can further see that the neural network model, FNN$_{All}$, clearly outperforms the SVM model for this task: consistently on all metrics. As an example, with the precision values achieved by FNN$_{All}$, the system would rank on average 4 positive examples in the list of its top-5 choices, and also 14-15 in the top-20 list. Considering the recall at the first R sentences, we will be able to encounter 43% of the total number of check-worthy sentences. This is quite remarkable given the difficulty of the task.

As a next step of the evaluation, we perform error analysis of the decisions made by the Neural Network that uses all available features. We present examples of False Positives (FP) and False Negatives (FN):

1 FP Clinton: He actually was sued twice by the Justice Department.
2 FP Clinton: Five million people lost their homes.
3 FP Clinton: There's no doubt now that Russia has used cyber attacks against all kinds of organizations in our country, and I am deeply concerned about this.
4 FP Trump: Your husband signed NAFTA, which was one of the worst things that ever happened to the manufacturing industry.
5 FN Trump: This is one of the worst deals ever made by any country in history.
6 FN Trump: Well, nobody was pressing it, nobody was caring much about it.
7 FN Trump: So Ford is leaving.
8 FN Trump: It was taken away from her.

Regarding the false positive examples, we can conclude that they could be also interesting for fact-checking, as they make some questionable statements. The list of false negatives contains sentences which belong to a whole group of annotations and some of them are not check-worthy on their own such as the eighth example. Some of the

---

[10]Note that as far as the difference between the $P@k$ metrics (especially between 5 and 10) is in terms of a few sentences, the deviation between them can seem large, while caused by a few correctly/wrongly predicted sentences.

[11]`http://idir-server2.uta.edu/claimbuster/demo`

System	MAP	R-Pr	P@5	P@10	P@20	P@50
Baselines						
Random	.164	.007	.200	.125	.138	.160
TF-IDF	.314	.333	.550	.475	.413	.360
CB Platform	.317	.349	.500	.550	.488	.405
SVM_{CBfeat}	.360	.393	.400	.425	.525	.495
FNN_{CBfeat}	.357	.379	.500	.550	.550	.510
Systems (using all features)						
SVM_{All}	.395	.406	.650	.725	.588	.565
FNN_{All}	**.427**	**.432**	**.800**	**.725**	**.713**	**.600**

Table 4: Evaluation results: our full systems (SVM and FNN) vs. a number of baselines:random and a TF-IDF baselines, also *ClaimBuster* from the platform, and our two reimplementations thereof.

S or C	Feat. Group	MAP	R-Pr	P@5	P@10	P@20	P@50
S+C	Embeddings	.357	.380	.450	.525	.488	.495
S+C	kNN	.313	.322	.800	.725	.612	.445
S	Linguistic	.308	.333	.450	.450	.463	.430
S	Sentiment	.260	.277	.550	.400	.288	.315
C	Metadata	.256	.268	.350	.300	.388	.370
S	Length	.254	.350	.350	.375	.400	.340
S	NEs	.236	.251	.250	.275	.313	.280
S+C	Contradiction	.222	.222	.400	.275	.288	.260
C	Segment size	.217	.231	.100	.150	.150	.245
C	Position	.212	.230	.100	.075	.175	.230
S+C	Discourse	.205	.206	.200	.300	.325	.255
S+C	Topics	.180	.178	.000	.000	.013	.085

Table 5: Performance of each feature group in isolation, using the FNN system. Results sorted by decreasing MAP score.

false negatives, though, need to be fact-checked and our model missed them such as sixth and seventh examples. An interesting observation is that we have two sentences, making the same statements using different wording - fourth and fifth sentences. On the one hand, the annotators should have labeled both of the sentences in the same manner, and on th other hand, our model should have also labeled them equally.

Finally, we can conclude that the false positives of our ranking system also make good candidates for credibility verification and demonstrate that the system has successfully extracted common patterns for check-worthiness. This way, the top-n list will contain mostly sentences which need to be further checked. Given the discrepancies and the disagreement between the annotations, a further cleaning of the corpus might be needed to prevent missing important check-worthy statements.

6 Discussion

In this section, we present some in-depth analysis and further discussion.

6.1 Individual Feature Types

Table 5 shows the performance of the individual feature types described in Section 4, when training using our FNN model, and ordered by their decreasing MAP score. We can see that *embeddings* perform best (MAP=.357, P@50=.495), which shows that modeling semantics and the similarity of a sentence against its context is quite important. Then comes *kNN* with MAP of .313 and P@50 of .455. The high performance of this feature reveals the frequent usage of statements which resemble already fact-checked ones. In the case of

false claims, this can be considered as a testimony for the existence of a post-truth era (Davies, 2016).

Then follow two sentence-level features, *linguistic features* and *sentiment*, with MAP of .308 and .260, and P@50 of .430 and .315. This is on par with previous work, which has focused primarily on similar sentence-level features. Then follow a contextual feature: *Metadata* (MAP=.256, P@50=.370). And two sentence features: *length* and *named entities*, with MAP of .254 and .236, and P@50 of .340 and .280.

At the bottom of the table we find *position*, a general contextual feature with MAP of .212 and P@50 of .230, followed by *discourse* and *topics*.

6.2 Effect of Context Modeling

Next, we study the impact of the contextual features.

Table 6 shows the results when using all features vs. excluding the contextual features vs. using the contextual features only. We can see that the contextual features have a major impact on performance: excluding them yields major drop for all measures, e.g., MAP drops from .427 to .385, and P@5 drops from .800 to .550. The last two rows in the table show that using contextual features only performs about the same as *CB Platform* (which uses no contextual features at all).

System	MAP	R-Pr	P@5	P@10	P@20	P@50
All	.427	.432	.800	.725	.713	.600
All, no contextual	.385	.390	.550	.500	.550	.540
Only contextual	.317	.404	.725	.563	.465	.465
CB Platform	*.317*	*.349*	*.500*	*.550*	*.488*	*.405*

Table 6: Impact of the contextual features on the overall performance (FNN system).

System	MAP	R-Pr	P@5	P@10	P@20	P@50
PolitiFact (PF)						
CB Platform	.154	.213	.200	.300	.238	.210
NN (train on PF)	.218	.274	.450	.325	.300	.270
NN (train on all)	.213	.246	.400	.350	.375	.290
NPR						
CB Platform	.144	.186	.200	.225	.225	.180
NN (train on NPR)	.193	.216	.550	.475	.350	.255
NN (train on all)	.208	.250	.500	.450	.375	.255
The New York Times (NYT)						
CB Platform	.103	.250	.250	.163	.135	
NN (train on NYT)	.136	.178	.250	.225	.188	.135
NN (train on all)	.136	.169	.150	.200	.163	.160
The Guardian (TG)						
CB Platform	.084	.128	.100	.100	.125	.140
NN (train on TG)	.121	.156	.250	.225	.200	.155
NN (train on all)	.128	.185	.100	.150	.188	.165
FactCheck (FC)						
CB Platform	.081	.213	.150	.125	.100	.115
NN (train on FC)	.081	.098	.050	.125	.088	.085
NN (train on all)	.115	.149	.100	.125	.125	.140
CNN						
CB Platform	.082	.096	.150	.125	.088	.085
NN (train on CNN)	.079	.076	.100	.100	.100	.090
NN (train on all)	.095	.087	.000	.075	.088	.100
Chicago Tribune (CT)						
CB Platform	.053	.032	.050	.050	.038	.065
NN (train on CT)	.087	.118	.150	.150	.175	.105
NN (train on all)	.092	.098	.150	.075	.100	.090
ABC						
CB Platform	.065	.066	.150	.125	.088	.080
NN (train on ABC)	.059	.068	.050	.050	.100	.060
NN (train on all)	.088	.090	.150	.150	.113	.100
Washington Post (WP)						
CB Platform	.048	.056	.050	.075	.050	.045
NN (train on WP)	.102	.098	.200	.175	.113	.080
NN (train on all)	.076	.751	.200	.100	.075	.080

Table 7: Training on the target medium vs. training on all media when testing with respect to a particular medium (FNN system).

6.3 Mimicking each Particular Source

In the experiments above, we have been trying to predict whether a sentence is check-worthy in general, i.e., with respect to at least one source; this is how we trained and this is how we evaluated our models. Here, we want to evaluate how well our models perform at finding sentences that contain claims that would be judged as worthy for fact-checking with respect to each of the individual sources. The purpose is to see to what extent we can make our system potentially useful for a particular medium.

Another interesting question is whether we should use our generic system or we should retrain with respect to the target medium. Table 7 shows the results for such a comparison, and it further compares to *CB Platform*. We can see that for all nine media, our model outperforms *CB Platform* in terms of MAP and P@50; this is also true for the other measures in most cases.

Moreover, we can see that training on all data is generally preferable to training on the target medium only, which shows that despite the sizable disagreement between the different media, they do follow some common principles for selecting what is check-worthy; this means that a general system could serve journalists in all these nine, and possibly other, media. One exception is Washington Post, where our system performs better when trained only on the single source, which is an indicator of the difference between Washington Post and the rest sources. Overall, our model works best on PolitiFact, which is a reputable source with fact checking as their primary expertise. We also do well on NPR, NYT, Guardian, and FactCheck; this is quite encouraging.

7 Conclusions and Future Work

We have developed a novel approach for automatically finding worth-checking claims in political debates, which is an understudied problem, despite its importance. Unlike previous work, which has looked primarily at sentences in isolation, here we have focused on the context: relationship between the target statement and the larger context of the debate, interaction between the opponents, and reaction by the moderator and by the public.

Our models have achieved state-of-the-art results, outperforming a strong rivaling system by a margin, while also confirming the importance of the contextual information. We further compiled, and we are making freely available, a new corpus of manually-annotated claims, extracted from the 2016 US presidential and vice-presidential debates, which we gathered from nine reputable sources including FactCheck, PolitiFact, CNN, NYT, WP, and NPR.

In future work, we plan to extend our corpus with additional debates, e.g., from other elections, but also with interviews and general discussions. We would also like to experiment with distant supervision, which would allow us to gather more training data, thus enabling deep learning. We further plan to extend our system with finding claims at the sub-sentence level, as well as with automatic fact-checking of the identified claims.

References

Mouhamadou Lamine Ba, Laure Berti-Equille, Kushal Shah, and Hossam M Hammady. 2016. VERA: A platform for veracity estimation over web data. In *Proceedings of the 25th International Conference Companion on World Wide Web*. International World Wide Web Conferences Steering Committee, Republic and Canton of Geneva, Switzerland, WWW '16 Companion, pages 159–162.

David M Blei, Andrew Y Ng, and Michael I Jordan. 2003. Latent dirichlet allocation. *Journal of machine Learning research* 3(Jan):993–1022.

Carlos Castillo, Marcelo Mendoza, and Barbara Poblete. 2011. Information credibility on Twitter. In *Proceedings of the 20th international conference on World wide web*. ACM, New York, NY, USA, WWW '11, pages 675–684.

Giovanni Luca Ciampaglia, Prashant Shiralkar, Luis M. Rocha, Johan Bollen, Filippo Menczer, and Alessandro Flammini. 2015. Computational fact checking from knowledge networks. *PLOS ONE* 10(6):1–13.

Ido Dagan, Bill Dolan, Bernardo Magnini, and Dan Roth. 2009. Recognizing textual entailment: Rational, evaluation and approaches. *Natural Language Engineering* 15(4):i–xvii.

William Davies. 2016. The age of post-truth politics. *New York Times* 24.

Rob Ennals, Dan Byler, John Mark Agosta, and Barbara Rosario. 2010a. What is disputed on the web? In *Proceedings of the 4th workshop on Information credibility*. ACM, New York, NY, USA, WICOW '10, pages 67–74.

Rob Ennals, Beth Trushkowsky, and John Mark Agosta. 2010b. Highlighting disputed claims on the web. In *Proceedings of the 19th international conference on World wide web*. ACM, pages 341–350.

Xavier Glorot, Antoine Bordes, and Yoshua Bengio. 2011. Deep sparse rectifier neural networks. In Geoffrey Gordon, David Dunson, and Miroslav Dudk, editors, *Proceedings of the Fourteenth International Conference on Artificial Intelligence and Statistics*. Fort Lauderdale, FL, USA, volume 15 of *Proceedings of Machine Learning Research*, pages 315–323.

Momchil Hardalov, Ivan Koychev, and Preslav Nakov. 2016. In search of credible news. In *Proceedings of the 17th International Conference on Artificial Intelligence: Methodology, Systems, and Applications*. Varna, Bulgaria, AIMSA '16, pages 172–180.

Naeemul Hassan, Chengkai Li, and Mark Tremayne. 2015. Detecting check-worthy factual claims in presidential debates. In *Proceedings of the 24th ACM International Conference on Information and Knowledge Management*. CIKM '15, pages 1835–1838.

Naeemul Hassan, Mark Tremayne, Fatma Arslan, and Chengkai Li. 2016. Comparing automated factual claim detection against judgments of journalism organizations. In *Computation + Journalism Symposium*. Stanford, California, USA.

Joan B. Hooper. 1974. *On Assertive Predicates*. Indiana University Linguistics Club. Indiana University Linguistics Club.

Ken Hyland. 1998. *Hedging in scientific research articles*, volume 54. John Benjamins Publishing.

Shafiq Joty, Giuseppe Carenini, and Raymond T. Ng. 2015. CODRA: A novel discriminative framework for rhetorical analysis. *Comput. Linguist.* 41(3):385–435.

Georgi Karadzhov, Pepa Gencheva, Preslav Nakov, and Ivan Koychev. 2017a. We built a fake news & clickbait filter: What happened next will blow your mind! In *Proceedings of the 2017 International Conference on Recent Advances in Natural Language Processing*. Varna, Bulgaria, RANLP '17.

Georgi Karadzhov, Preslav Nakov, Lluís Màrquez, Alberto Barrón-Cede no, and Ivan Koychev. 2017b. Fully automated fact checking using external sources. In *Proceedings of the 2017 International Conference on Recent Advances in Natural Language Processing*. Varna, Bulgaria, RANLP '17.

Lauri Karttunen. 1971. Implicative verbs. *Language* pages 340–358.

Dieu-Thu Le, Ngoc Thang Vu, and Andre Blessing. 2016. Towards a text analysis system for political debates. *LaTeCH 2016* page 134.

Yann LeCun, Lon Bottou, Yoshua Bengio, and Patrick Haffner. 1998. Gradient-based learning applied to document recognition. In *Proceedings of the IEEE*. Anchorage, Alaska, USA, volume 86 of *1998 IEEE*, pages 2278–2324.

Bing Liu, Minqing Hu, and Junsheng Cheng. 2005. Opinion observer: Analyzing and comparing opinions on the web. In *Proceedings of the 14th International Conference on World Wide Web*. New York, NY, USA, WWW '05, pages 342–351.

Edward Loper and Steven Bird. 2002. NLTK: The natural language toolkit. In *Proceedings of the ACL-02 Workshop on Effective Tools and Methodologies for Teaching Natural Language Processing and Computational Linguistics - Volume 1*. Philadelphia, Pennsylvania, ETMTNLP '02, pages 63–70.

Jing Ma, Wei Gao, Prasenjit Mitra, Sejeong Kwon, Bernard J. Jansen, Kam-Fai Wong, and Meeyoung Cha. 2016. Detecting rumors from microblogs with recurrent neural networks. In *Proceedings of the Twenty-Fifth International Joint Conference on Artificial Intelligence*. New York, New York, USA, IJCAI'16, pages 3818–3824.

Tomas Mikolov, Quoc V. Le, and Ilya Sutskever. 2013. Exploiting similarities among languages for machine translation. *CoRR* abs/1309.4168.

Saif M. Mohammad and Peter D. Turney. 2013. Crowdsourcing a word-emotion association lexicon 29(3):436–465.

Preslav Nakov, Tsvetomila Mihaylova, Lluís Màrquez, Yashkumar Shiroya, and Ivan Koychev. 2017. Do not trust the trolls: Predicting credibility in community question answering forums. In *Proceedings of the 2017 International Conference on Recent Advances in Natural Language Processing*. Varna, Bulgaria, RANLP '17.

Marta Recasens, Cristian Danescu-Niculescu-Mizil, and Dan Jurafsky. 2013. Linguistic models for analyzing and detecting biased language. In *ACL 2013 - 51st Annual Meeting of the Association for Computational Linguistics, Proceedings of the Conference*. Sofia, Bulgaria, volume 1 of *ACL '13*, pages 1650–1659.

Arkaitz Zubiaga, Maria Liakata, Rob Procter, Geraldine Wong Sak Hoi, and Peter Tolmie. 2016. Analysing how people orient to and spread rumours in social media by looking at conversational threads. *PloS one* 11(3):e0150989.

Hashtag Processing for Enhanced Clustering of Tweets

Dagmar Gromann
Artificial Intelligence
Research Institute (IIIA-CSIC)
Campus de la UAB,
E-08193 Bellaterra, Spain
dgromann@iiia.csic.es

Thierry Declerck
DFKI GmbH
Stuhlsatzenhausweg 3
D-66123 Saarbrücken, Germany
declerck@dfki.de

Abstract

Rich data provided by tweets have been analyzed, clustered, and explored in a variety of studies. Typically those studies focus on named entity recognition, entity linking, and entity disambiguation or clustering. Tweets and hashtags are generally analyzed on sentential or word level but not on a compositional level of concatenated words. We propose an approach for a closer analysis of compounds in hashtags, and in the long run also of other types of text sequences in tweets, in order to enhance the clustering of such text documents. Hashtags have been used before as primary topic indicators to cluster tweets, however, their segmentation and its effect on clustering results have not been investigated to the best of our knowledge. Our results with a standard dataset from the Text REtrieval Conference (TREC) show that segmented and harmonized hashtags positively impact effective clustering.

1 Introduction

Social media and microblogging platforms continuously produce a wealth of information. The microblogs on Twitter, i.e., tweets, have been mined for nearly everything ranging from the detection of adverse drug reactions (O'Connor et al., 2014) to emergency response (Toriumi and Baba, 2016). One interesting problem in tweet mining is the automated detection of the tweet's topic. Hashtags have been found to be approximate indicators of a tweet's topic(s) (Rosa et al., 2011; Bansal et al., 2015; Zubiaga et al., 2011; Declerck and Lendvai, 2015) as they serve the purpose to point to a previously specified or emerging content. Based on the character limit of the platform, they are heavily used, which is, however, also the reason

why they are frequently composed to save space. Different hashtags are combined to create a new topic reference, such as "#California#Drought", or words within hashtags are concatenated to reference a specific event, e.g. "#PoliticsandCurrentEventsCarolineKennedyMichelleObama".

Complex hashtags are marked by heavy concatenation (see example above) and terminological variation (e.g. "#IranDeal" and "#IranNuclearDeal"). Our research is based on the assumption that preprocessing those concatenations can improve topic identification results of tweets. To evaluate this assumption, this paper presents a method to segment concatenated hashtags and then uses them in a spectral clustering process to group tweets by their topic. We compare the results thereof with clustering results without preprocessing hashtags. We investigate if such a hashtag processing can improve categorizing tweets by topic by comparing the results of both clustering processes. Analysing the internal semantic structure of hashtags holds the promise to predict hashtags for tweets that do not use any hashtags based on the terms in the tweet and a given inventory of potential hashtags used within the same time period. It also facilitates the identification of terminological variation in tweets, which can be useful in scenarios relying on terms, such as emergency response or event detection.

2 Related Work

Hashtags have been previously used as approximate topic indicators in tweets (Rosa et al., 2011; Kapanipathi et al., 2014; Bansal et al., 2015). Rosa et al. (2011) apply supervised and unsupervised clustering algorithms to group tweets by topic based on a gold standard created from assigning a set of hashtags to specific topics. It has been shown before that clustering algorithms using hashtags as features produce good results (Rosa et al., 2011). However, hashtags have been

Proceedings of Recent Advances in Natural Language Processing, pages 277–283,
Varna, Bulgaria, Sep 4–6 2017.

treated as coherent units and their internal structure has not been considered in the clustering process. In this paper we first segment concatenated hashtags to facilitate the detection of similarity between hashtags, e.g. "#IranDeal" and "#IranNuclearDeal".

Hashtags also contain named entities. Their segmentation and linking to entities in knowledge bases has been studied before (Bansal et al., 2015; Kapanipathi et al., 2014). Kapanipathi et al. (2014) semantically enrich tweets with knowledge base content in order to represent user interests hierarchically. This is achieved by classifying named entities extracted from tweets into Wikipedia categories and representing them as a Hierarchical Interest Graph. In contrast to Kapanipathi et al. (2014) and Bansal et al. (2015), we do not limit our approach to entities and instead are interested in any type of term, within or outside of hashtags, while concentrating on the latter in this study with a focus on concatenated hashtags.

3 Dataset

To compare the clustering of tweets with preprocessed and non-preprocessed hashtags, we required a dataset with high-quality topic classifications for each tweet as a ground truth label for our method. Thus, we opted for a gold standard resource where each tweet is thematically classified. A Text REtrieval Conference (TREC-2015) shared task on identifying interest profiles of micro-blogging users (Lin et al., 2015) provides a set of twitter IDs, user-names, and dates for participants to stream the tweets in real-time during the task. When we streamed the tweets based on that list at a later moment in time, not all of them were available. In total, 6,187 tweets from the original dataset were annotated by 6 raters with one of 51 topics ranging from general topics, such as "self-driving cars" or "polar icecap melting", to more time-specific events, such as "Special Olympics 2015" or "Iran nuclear agreement" that was underway and reached in 2015. From those annotated tweets, 5,141 were still available when we streamed the data. Since our main interest in this publication is on hashtags, we limit the dataset to tweets containing hashtags which results in 2,053 tweets.

4 Method

To classify tweets by their topic, the proposed method relies on spectral clustering. Based on the assumption that the segmentation of concatenated hashtags improves this tweet classification, we compare clustering results with and without preprocessing (complex) hashtags. In the long run, we aim at a method for assigning topic labels to the resulting clusters by mining their contents for all types of concatenated sequences and aligning them to knowledge bases.

4.1 Data Preprocessing

To reduce the noise and allow for a separate handling of hashtags, a number of preprocessing steps are performed as described in this section.

URL handling: Instead of URL removal, they are replaced by identifiers and stored in a URL repository, e.g. "https://t.co/UrIygTXM0O" is replaced by "url30075" in all its occurrences. Thus, semantically rich URLs can be utilized as features in the clustering process. Furthermore, other punctuation can be processed without changing any punctuation in URLs.

Marked phrases: Similar to the URLs, hashtags (marked with '#') and replies (marked with '@') have a distinct semantic role and meaning in a tweet and are stored in a separate repository without their marking signs '#' and '@'. We remove those signs since in the segmentation process they would only be attached to the first word.

Stop word removal: The overall frequency of certain stop words, such as articles, is relatively high, while their level of informativeness is very low. For this reason we remove stop words from the microbologging contents in our dataset. Punctuation other than '#', '@', '_', and '-' are considered stop words and are removed from the corpus following Rosa et al. (2011) and for the same reason that stop words are removed. For the purpose of this study we also remove emoticons, which includes hashtags containing only emoticons.

4.2 Hashtag Harmonization

Concatenated hashtags represent an issue for similarity measures since a higher similarity is presumed if a phrase is represented without whitespace than with (Antenucci et al., 2011). But, very often, concatenated hashtags do not follow a consistent way of being built. In our corpus, we have for example "#CaliforniaDrought", "#CADrought", "#cadrought" and more variants of the same concept expressed by using a hashtag. There are more complex examples of this type of term variants, such as "#IranTalksVienna", "#IranTalks", "#IranNuclearDeal", "#Irandeal", "#dealwithiran", "#DisasterIranDeal", "#NoNuclearIran", "#NoIranDeal", "#StopIranDeal", "#stopirandeal", "#StopIranRally", "#badirandeal", etc. Frequently, hashtags are not just attached to the end of a tweet but incorporated into its sentential structure, such as "#IranDeal lifts sanctions". All of those variants relate to one topic, namely the Iran nuclear agreement between Iran and a group of world powers, but some also express opinions about this topic. There is thus a need to segment and normalize hashtags in order to improve measures of similarity, as has also been suggested by other approaches to using Twitter data (Declerck and Lendvai, 2016; Rosa et al., 2011; Kapanipathi et al., 2014).

4.2.1 Orthography

The simplest harmonization step consists in adjusting different typographical versions of a hashtag. A straightforward approach is the lowercasing of the text included in a simple (i.e. not concatenated) hashtag. So for example, in our corpus, the hashtag "#Iran" occurs 236 times, the hashtag "#iran" 28 times and the hashtag "#IRAN" 3 times. After this transformation step, the harmonized hashtag "#iran" will thus occur 267 times. As a result from this simple harmonization process, the "#iran" hashtag can be consistently used as a potential semantic label for (a group of) tweets.

We include in the transformation process the elimination of certain punctuation signs that are attached to the hashtag, like for example "#Iran," or "#Iran:". The lowercasing step is limited in a first phase to simple hashtags, since we need the hashtags using the CamelCase notation as an initial data for the segmentation step. Lowercasing can subsequently be applied to the results of the segmentation process.

4.2.2 Segmentation

In the examples shown in the introduction to this section, we can observe the possibly very large number of concatenated hashtag variants expressing one topic. We aim at providing a segmenta-

tion and harmonization of the components of such hashtags in order to reduce the number of their variants. We apply for this a rather conservative approach in order to avoid the segmentation of hashtags like "#KnockKnockLive" into three "new" hashtags "#Knock", "#Knock" and "#Live" ("Knock Knock Live" is the name of a television series, and should therefore not be segmented into three hashtags.).

A first candidate for segmentation are hashtags that are expressed using a CamelCase notation, such as "#IranDeal" (or even "#KnockKnockLive", which at the end should not be segmented). It is straightforward to segment such hashtags, the segments being defined as the sequences starting with a capital letter. As a preliminary filter for avoiding unwanted segmentations, we request that at least one of the resulting segments occurs as a standalone hashtag (for example "#Iran" in the case of "#IranDeal" or "#NoNuclearIran") in the corpus, and that all the resulting segments are listed in the Unix dictionary `words` file[1]. This way, the segmentation of "#KnockKnockLive" in three components is avoided, as none of the potential segments occurs as a standalone hashtag in the corpus. The algorithm will have to be refined for dealing with other and larger corpora.

This approach offers a basis for the correct segmentation for a set of concatenated hashtags that contain only lowercase letters, for example "#irandeal", as those are typographical variants of the hashtags in CamelCase notation. To give an example on how a concatenated hashtag is segmented, here with the hashtag "#irandeal", which after processing is internally represented as a feature structure:

```
'irandeal':
   {'freq': 9, 0: 'iran', 1: 'deal'}
```

The reader can see that we encode also the order of the components of the segmented hashtag.

As a result of this segmentation process, we can augment the number of times the strings "Iran", "iran" or "IRAN" have been detected within an hashtag from 267 to 468, thus significantly increasing the evidence that the corpus has "iran" as a main topic[2].

---

[1]See for more detailshttps://en.wikipedia. org/wiki/Words_(Unix).

[2]For the sake of the description we have been keeping the # sign in many examples. But for the clustering step, described on 4.3, we remove this marker in order not to have

Current work is dedicated to improving the grouping of terms extracted from the segmented concatenated hashtags, so that for example "#deal-withiran" can be properly associated with "#Iran-NuclearDeal" and similar hashtags. This will be based on structuring 'sub-topics' associated with the 'main' topic, such as "iran". We expect from this step an additionally improved clustering performance. We will also study the possibilities to extend the coverage of "save" and meaningful hashtag segmentations.

4.3 Clustering

To make natural language data useful in an automated fashion they need to be grouped and categorized. The state-of-the-art method to address this task of semantic categorization is unsupervised clustering (Baroni et al., 2014). We perform clustering based on the normalized spectral clustering algorithm proposed by Ng et al. (2001) that has been effectively applied to various lexical acquisition and classification tasks (e.g. Xu and Ke, 2016; Shutova et al., 2016). Spectral clustering is particularly attractive since it is reasonably fast and treats data clustering as a graph partitioning problem. Calculating the distance based on a graph rather than a pair-wise comparison of distances between points is particularly well suited for smaller numbers of clusters, such as the 51 preset clusters in our case based on our dataset.

Even though supervised clustering methods tend to perform better (Shutova et al., 2016), we believe and want to show that simple string harmonization and term variant detection methods can improve both unsupervised and supervised methods. In this paper we start with the improvement of the results of unsupervised methods, while the evidence for supervised methods is yet to come.

The input data are strings consisting of words and urls as well as specially marked words, such as hashtags, replies, and retweets. Some normalization steps are performed to the overall clustering processes as described in Section 4.1. The terms to be clustered are the tweet IDs and their preprocessed contents represent the feature vector with their raw frequencies, e.g. tweet ID "626157993101512704" has the feature vector {when: 37, drought: 489, California: 350, ...} representing the tweets content words and their relative raw frequency. The raw frequency is then

it considered in the frequency count of the resulting feature vectors.

turned into a distance measure in the process of creating a similarity matrix.

Computing a similarity matrix depends on the choice of semantic distance measure that is best for the given data. The most commonly used ones are Term Frequency-Inverse Document Frequency (TF-IDF), Positive Pointwise Mutual Information (PPMI), Kullback-Leibler divergence, string edit distances such as the Jaccard distance, cosine distance, and as of late APSyn (Santus et al., 2016). The Kullback-Leibler divergence is a useful feature to measure mutual information, that is, the concordance among sub-units of phrases (Lin et al., 2015). Thus, it has less bias towards rare-occurring phrases and is particularly adequate for the comparison of compounds. A symmetric and smoothed version of the Kullback-Leibler is the Jensen-Shannon divergence (JSD). Since the similarity matrix represents a weighted but undirected graph, the JSD is more adequate than Kullback-Leibler and for the two feature vectors v_i and v_j is defined as:

$$JSD(v_i||v_j) = \frac{1}{2}D(v_i||M) + \frac{1}{2}D(v_j||M) \quad (1)$$

where D represents the Kullback-Leibler divergence and M is defined as the average of v_i and v_j. We adopt the successful creation of a similarity matrix by Shutova et al. (2016) and define the similarity w_{ij} as

$$w_{ij} = e^{-JSD(v_i,v_j)} \quad (2)$$

We tested with the well-known TF-IDF and PPMI as well as with JSD, but only explain JSD here in detail because it is less well-known than the other two. The similarity matrix build on the respective semantic distance measure and the predefined number of resulting clusters represent the input to the spectral clustering algorithm presented as Algorithm 1.

Based on the input matrix a degree matrix is formed as detailed in Algorithm 1. We followed von Luxburg (2007) and tested the ϵ-neighborhood, k-nearest neighbor (knn), and a fully connected graph building method on our dataset. The difference between the degree and the weighted adjacency matrix form the graph Laplacian L. The normalized matrix of eigenvectors of the normalized L is then used as input to the k-means algorithm. The algorithm provides the

Algorithm 1 Spectral Clustering

1: **Input:** Similarity matrix $S \in \mathbb{R}^{nxn}$, number of k clusters
2: Construct a degree matrix D where $d_i = \sum_{j=1}^{n} w_{ij}$ and $d_{ij} = 0$ if i $\neq$ j
3: Construct a similarity graph and its weighted adjacency matrix W
4: Construct a graph Laplacian $L = D - W$
5: Compute the normalized Laplacian $L_{sym} := D^{-1/2} L D^{-1/2}$
6: Compute the first k eigenvectors $v_1,...v_K$ of L_{sym} and write them as columns into the matrix $U \in \mathbb{R}^{nxk}$
7: Compute the matrix $T \in \mathbb{R}^{nxk}$ from U by normalizing that is set $t_{ij} = u_{ij}/(\sum_k u_{ik}^2)^{1/2}$
8: Let y_i be the vector corresponding to the ith row of T
9: Cluster the points $(y_i)_{i=1,...,n}$ with the k-means algorithm into clusters $C_1,...,C_k$
10: **Output:** Clusters $C_1,...,C_k$ with $C_i = \{j|y_j \in C_i\}$

number of clusters that was initially provided as input. To optimize this variable, we experimented with different sizes of k to be detailed in Section 5. The result of each cluster is the tweet IDs they contain as well as all the preprocessed words that each tweet ID represents. The preprocessing described in Section 4.1 is applied to all tweets and all clustering runs. The decomposition and harmonization of hashtags is only performed for the second clustering run as described below to compare the effect this processing has on the clustering.

5   Results

Before we detail the comparison of the cluster results, we provide some basic statistics on the harmonization of hashtags.

5.1   Hashtag Harmonization Results

In the corpus we had a total of 3.893 hashtags, out of which 2.697 contained at least one capital letter and 1.196 were exclusively in lowercase. In total the number of segmented hashtags in Camel-Case notation amounts to 1.024 and to 91 for hashtags containing only lowercase notation. Lowercase refers to hashtags in which the concatenation is not clearly marked by capitalization, such as "#horseracing". In contrast, in case of Camel-Case notation, the capitalization within a sequence

of characters indicates potential word boundaries, such as "#HorseRacing". Both hashtags refer to the event "horse racing" but different techniques need to be applied for their segmentation, as described in Section 4.2.2.

At first sight the results for the segmentation of lowercase hashtags are accurate, while we need to improve the accuracy of the segmentation process for the hashtags in CamelCase notation. We expect then another improvement of the results presented in Section 5.2

5.2   Clustering Results

Given the ground truth labels of the TREC gold standard dataset and the prediction labels of our clustering algorithm, mutual information can be used to measure the agreement of their assignment. Adjusted Mutual Information (AMI) has been proposed (Vinh et al., 2009) as a measure from information theory that can be used to compare clustering overlaps. It is normalized against chance and particularly adequate for unbalanced reference clustering with varying cluster sizes (Romano et al., 2016).

In Table 1 an AMI-based comparison of the three graph building methods *knn*, ϵ, and *fully connected* with the three main similarity measures is illustrated. The best result is achieved by the combination of a *knn* graph with TF-IDF as similarity measure with 0.754 as highlighted in Table 1. The other graph building methods, however, perform equivalent to *knn* with TF-IDF. We represent the difference between clustering without and with preprocessed hashtags in the columns *unsegmented* (uns.) respectively *segmented* (seg.). Numbers in the segmented column always slightly exceed results without preprocessed hashtags, which shows that the accuracy of clustering can be improved by a basic and straightforward approach to normalizing and segmenting hashtags, even if only slightly.

	knn		ϵ		fully conn.	
	uns.	seg.	uns.	seg.	uns.	seg.
TFIDF	0.687	**0.754**	0.678	0.750	0.677	0.737
PPMI	0.664	0.707	0.676	0.701	0.658	0.701
JSD	0.486	0.531	0.436	0.468	0.442	0.487

Table 1: AMI Unsegmented and Segmented Clustering Results for Tweets

To explain our results in more detail, we provide two example sentences below with their respective feature vector. Without segmentation, it would have been unlikely that "#drought" in example sentence 1 would have achieved a high similarity measure with the concatenated and camel-cased hashtag "#CaliforniaDrought" in example sentence 2. With the preprocessing, their representation in the feature vector is more similar and both are grouped in the same thematic cluster.

```
Example sentence 1: ''When there is
drought in California, people just #paint
their #lawn https://t.co/I0zuBVAXhn
#lifehack #drought''
Feature vector 1: 626157993101512704:
['When', 'drought', 'California',
'people', 'paint', 'lawn', 'lifehack',
'drought', 'url34452']

Example sentence 2: ''In reality the
apocalypse has already happened, but it
came quietly & slowly, so we didn't
notice. #CaliforniaDrought
http://t.co/UOZbMp4yDA''
Feature vector 2: 623383930763366400:
['In', 'reality', 'apocalypse', 'already',
'happened', 'came', 'quietly', 'slowly',
"didn't", 'notice', 'california',
'drought', 'url4850']
```

We were also interested in whether a similar improvement could be achieved when clustering is exclusively performed based on hashtags. A comparison is presented in Table 2 where we can see that this assumption is true other than in the case of the ϵ graph building method. The comparison is only based on JSD since the other two similarity measures returned results lower than 0.2.

	knn		ϵ		fully conn.	
	uns.	seg.	uns.	seg.	uns.	seg.
JSD	0.270	0.332	0.371	0.357	0.404	**0.437**

Table 2: AMI Unsegmented and Segmented Clustering Results for Hashtags

6 Discussion

While the first results obtained are encouraging, we are aware that our approach to the harmonization of (complex) hashtags needs to be refined. We need for example to avoid the segmentation of #YouTube or #FootBall. While this has been already effectively implemented for the latter example, as the word "football" also occurs in the Unix dictionary `words` file, we will need to address the issue of dealing with named entities like "YouTube", since we cannot only rely on the fact that neither "#You" nor "#Tube" occur as standalone in the corpus under investigation. This is

a place where we need to investigate the reuse of approaches dealing with entity linking in the field of Twitter data.

7 Conclusion and Future Work

The experiments conducted in this study on spectral clustering applied to tweets that have undergone basic steps to the segmentation of concatenated hashtags have supported our expectations that harmonized hashtags can lead to a better topic categorization of Twitter texts. This paper provides statistical evidence that the clustering results improve when using processed hashtags. Comparable improvements can be observed when clustering tweet IDs exclusively based on hashtags, leaving the rest of the tweet text aside, which stresses the central role played by hashtags for the categorization of topics of tweets.

In terms of future works, the current experiments need to be extended to more and larger corpora and also the segmentation algorithm could be refined. For example, we think of a hierarchical structure of topics and sub-topics resulting from the segmentation of compounds into main components and modifying components that can be identified by means of dependency analysis. We plan to deal also with other types of compounds in use in micro-blog texts, but concatenated hashtags have the advantage to explicitly mark the combination of words.

A next step will consist in enhancing our spectral clustering approach with graph-based knowledge for an effective semantic classification of tweets, annotating those automatically with DBpedia resources. By linking the resulting terms in the clusters to such a knowledge base, we can improve the identification of the meaning of the cluster and assign it a more accurate topic label.

Acknowledgments

This research has been partially funded by the European Community's Seventh Framework Programme (FP7/2007-2013) under grant agreement no. 607062 /ESSENCE: Evolution of Shared Semantics in Computational Environments/ for the IIIA-CSIC contributions and for the DFKI contribution by the project /ALL-SIDES: Advanced Large-Scale Language Analysis for Social Intelligence Deliberation Support/ funded by the German Federal Ministry of Education and Research (BMBF).

References

Dolan Antenucci, GREGORY Handy, AKSHAY Modi, and Miller Tinkerhess. 2011. Classification of tweets via clustering of hashtags. *EECS* 545:1–11.

Piyush Bansal, Romil Bansal, and Vasudeva Varma. 2015. Towards deep semantic analysis of hashtags. In *European Conference on Information Retrieval*. Springer, pages 453–464.

Marco Baroni, Georgiana Dinu, and Germán Kruszewski. 2014. Don't count, predict! a systematic comparison of context-counting vs. context-predicting semantic vectors. In *ACL (1)*. pages 238–247.

Thierry Declerck and Piroska Lendvai. 2015. Processing and normalizing hashtags. In *RANLP*. pages 104–109.

Thierry Declerck and Piroska Lendvai. 2016. Towards the harmonization and segmentation of german hashtags. *Bochumer Linguistische Arbeitsberichte* page 10.

Pavan Kapanipathi, Prateek Jain, Chitra Venkataramani, and Amit Sheth. 2014. User interests identification on twitter using a hierarchical knowledge base. In *European Semantic Web Conference*. Springer, pages 99–113.

Jimmy Lin, Miles Efron, Yulu Wang, and Garrick Sherman. 2015. Overview of the trec-2015 microblog track. Technical report, DTIC Document.

Andrew Y Ng, Michael I Jordan, Yair Weiss, et al. 2001. On spectral clustering: Analysis and an algorithm. In *NIPS*. volume 14, pages 849–856.

Karen O'Connor, Pranoti Pimpalkhute, Azadeh Nikfarjam, Rachel Ginn, Karen L Smith, and Graciela Gonzalez. 2014. Pharmacovigilance on twitter? mining tweets for adverse drug reactions. In *AMIA annual symposium proceedings*. American Medical Informatics Association, volume 2014, page 924.

Simone Romano, Nguyen Xuan Vinh, James Bailey, and Karin Verspoor. 2016. Adjusting for chance clustering comparison measures. *Journal of Machine Learning Research* 17(134):1–32.

Kevin Dela Rosa, Rushin Shah, Bo Lin, Anatole Gershman, and Robert Frederking. 2011. Topical clustering of tweets. *Proceedings of the ACM SIGIR: SWSM* .

Enrico Santus, Emmanuele Chersoni, Alessandro Lenci, Chu-Ren Huang, and Philippe Blache. 2016. Testing apsyn against vector cosine on similarity estimation. *arXiv preprint arXiv:1608.07738* .

Ekaterina Shutova, Lin Sun, Elkin Darío Gutiérrez, Patricia Lichtenstein, and Srini Narayanan. 2016. Multilingual metaphor processing: Experiments with semi-supervised and unsupervised learning. *Computational Linguistics* .

Fujio Toriumi and Seigo Baba. 2016. Real-time tweet classification in disaster situation. In *Proceedings of the 25th International Conference Companion on World Wide Web*. International World Wide Web Conferences Steering Committee, pages 117–118.

Nguyen Xuan Vinh, Julien Epps, and James Bailey. 2009. Information theoretic measures for clusterings comparison: is a correction for chance necessary? In *Proceedings of the 26th Annual International Conference on Machine Learning*. ACM, pages 1073–1080.

Ulrike Von Luxburg. 2007. A tutorial on spectral clustering. *Statistics and computing* 17(4):395–416.

Zhiqiang Xu and Yiping Ke. 2016. Effective and efficient spectral clustering on text and link data. In *Proceedings of the 25th ACM International on Conference on Information and Knowledge Management*. ACM, pages 357–366.

Arkaitz Zubiaga, Damiano Spina, Víctor Fresno, and Raquel Martínez. 2011. Classifying trending topics: a typology of conversation triggers on twitter. In *Proceedings of the 20th ACM international conference on Information and knowledge management*. ACM, pages 2461–2464.

Natural Language Processing Technologies for Document Profiling

Antonio Guillén, Yoan Gutiérrez and Rafael Muñoz
Department of Software and Computing Systems
University of Alicante, San Vicente del Raspeig (Alicante), Spain
{aguillen, ygutierrez, rafael}@dlsi.ua.es

Abstract

Nowadays, search for documents on the Internet is becoming increasingly difficult. The reason is the amount of content published by users (articles, comments, blogs, reviews). How to facilitate that the users can find their required documents? What would be necessary to provide useful document meta-data for supporting search engines? In this article, we present a study of some Natural Language Processing (NLP) technologies that can be useful for facilitating the proper identification of documents according to the user needs. For this purpose, it is designed a document profile that will be able to represent semantic meta-data extracted from documents by using NLP technologies. The research is basically focused on the study of different NLP technologies in order to support the creation our novel document profile proposal from semantic perspectives.

1 Introduction

The Internet provides large amounts of information through many types of documents. Users require an easy way to filter these documents to find out the most appropriate documents for their interests, capabilities and needs. These documents also can be needed by other entities for market studies, classify and index documents, detect fake information or illegal activities on the Web. These aspects can be treated by the study of NLP areas, tasks, methods and tools.

In this paper, we present a study on some NLP tasks to determinate which NLP technologies are interesting to extract and obtain relevant information from a document. In this study, we want to address which technologies are available currently, estimate its automation and reliability degree, the problems that can be found on applying them and

the most appropriate document's extension. Also, we describe our novel document profile proposal.

A document can be defined as short or long unity of information, principally obtained from websites (a user post, a press article, a comment, a review, etc.). The aim of this study is to investigate the different features that can be extracted by means NLP technologies able to provide enough information for setting up useful meta-data.

For addressing this study we organized the article into two relevant parts. The first part, Section 2, explains what we want to accomplish describing our novel document profile proposal. The second part, Section 3, addresses a study of selected NLP tasks and technologies which serve for supporting the proposal. Finally, Section 4 exposes the conclusions and future works.

2 Document Profile Proposal

Our proposal mainly consists of designing a document profile able to represent different features extracted once NLP technologies are applied on documents, assisted or not by humans. Figure 1 provides a brief overview. As can be seen, there are many features that can only be extracted automatically from documents by using NLP technologies. This work pretends to unify most of these NLP technologies as a whole able to characterize documents from different points of view.

2.1 Documents and NLP Areas

As a first approach, this work will be focused on English documents from the Internet. This is due to NLP technologies have been mostly developed to cover this language and which makes easier to find out NLP tools. Nevertheless, the overall strategy is still valid for other languages. The principal documents addressed are those mostly available on the Internet[1]. Those are press media, social posts, product/service reviews, blogs or per-

---

[1] http://www.quantcast.com/top-sites

Proceedings of Recent Advances in Natural Language Processing, pages 284–290,
Varna, Bulgaria, Sep 4–6 2017.

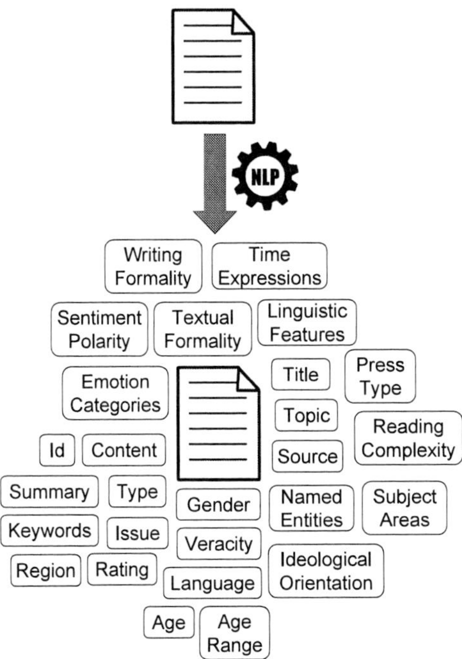

Figure 1: Document profile concept.

sonal websites, academic/science papers, tutorials or instruction manuals, etc. The concrete selection of documents is shown in this schema[2]. Is defined two types of documents (leaf and conceptual), leaf document represents concrete documents that can be obtained the profile, and the conceptual document is defined as group documents that share common features.

For some NLP areas, different NLP tasks require a long or short size document for better results. In our research, a short document is defined as text with 500 words or less, and a long document as texts with 501 words or more. In this research is performed a study of correspondence between short and long documents depending on the NLP task or area. For example, Author Identification tasks give better effectively on long documents, but also some models can give good effectively in short texts (Shrestha et al., 2017) (Green et al., 2013). In the case of Sentiment Analysis, this requires preferably short documents to better focus the different tasks involved, for a long document is necessary to focus on sentence-level or use specific techniques (Basiri et al., 2014). Data Mining requires long text to process in order to reveal common patterns that in single texts are irrelevant.

In general, is highly recommended to process long documents in very similar tasks, like text clustering (Ingaramo et al., 2008). An alternative for getting a brief vision of long documents is generating a summary. At this way, long documents would be represented a minor set of phrases. This idea will be considered by us in such cases where the NLP technology to use requires processing short documents instead of long documents.

2.2 NLP Tasks Selection

In our research, a selection of NLP tasks[3] for designing the profiling meta-data properties is carried out. This list has been taken into consideration to be included in our novel document profile proposal. At this way, it can be obtained a long quantity of meta-data contributing to fill document profiles. As can be seen, we have chosen some of the most active NLP tasks nowadays. So, the main goal at this stage is find out friendly access NLP technologies (i.e. tools, APIs, demos, etc) to test and simulate our proposal in a real scenario. At this way, it would be demonstrated the viability of our proposal, not just providing a document profiling scheme.

2.3 Meta-data Properties

The meta-data properties defined for our proposal can be found in the following link[4]. Notice, that each of these properties indicates the NLP technology acronym from which it is obtained. Is included a brief description of each meta-data property.

2.4 Document Profiling Algorithm

This section presents briefly an algorithm to generate document profiles using the available NLP technologies. Algorithm 1 shows the steps to generate a profile from a Web document. The steps are specified as follows. Firstly, the Web document content is extracted. Then a short version of the document using the summarising technology is generated. It is followed by the detection of the document type. It is generated an initial profile from scratch, only including the meta-data obtained currently (i.e. content, summary and type). Next specific meta-data properties for this document type are obtained as is mentioned in Figure 1. Finally, the results compose the document profile.

---

[2]http://ow.ly/pTaR30dWTj7

[3]http://ow.ly/MPO130e24Jr
[4]http://ow.ly/tQos30dNVcS

Algorithm 1 Document Profiling

Require: *url*, Web document url
1: *cont* ← getContent(*url*)
2: *sum* ← getSummary(*cont*)
3: *type* ← getType(*cont*)
4: *profile* ← newProfile(*cont*, *sum*, *type*)
5: *listProperties* ← getProperties(*type*)
6: **for each** *prop* ∈ *listProperties* **do**
7:    *nlpTech* ← prop.getNlpTech()
8:    *value* ← nlpTech(*cont*, *summ*)
9:    profile.add(*prop*, *value*)

2.5 A Document Profile Example

In order to figure out how would be a document profile, we have prepared an example considering a document taken from the CNN website. The document is a real news article about *Everest's climber George Mallory*. He's the first person who tried climb to summit the Everest. He was disappeared and his body was found 75 years later. Expert people tried to discover if he reached the top of Mount Everest or not. The complete news article it's available in CNN website[5]. The procedure follows as to describe the algorithm 1, based on the technologies presented in Table 1, obtaining the next document profile[6].

A brief description of the features set is commented following: (i) The Id property is auto-generated. (ii) The document type detected is *Press Document*. (iii) *Content*, *Title* and *Issue* meta-data properties can be extracted directly from the article, and the source corresponds to the web URL of article. (iv) The content summary is generated. (v) The topics list represents the most frequently used terms in the text. (vi) The region is obtained analyzing the text, in this case, it talks about the north ridge of Mount Everest located in Tibet (China). About the subject areas detected, we can see *History* because it is a historical news article and *Sports* it talks about climbing. (vii) The language detected is English. (viii) The article does not presents any rating. (ix) Keywords are the more representative words of the whole text. (x) In this article, it is not detected any ideological orientation because it only talks about a historical fact related to sports. (xi) Sentiment polarity determines that it is a positive news for people interested in history, climbing and the Mount

Everest. (xii) It is detected the emotion category *Surprise* because the man's body has been found 75 years later, something unexpected. (xiii) Some time expressions are detected in the text, these expressions have been converted into date format. (xiv) The name entities detected refer persons and locations retrieved in the text. (xv) In this article is not detected any linguistic feature. (xvi) Reading complexity is *Easy* and with *Formal* text and writing. The news article is from a serious press media. The article is feasible to be read by 12 years old people over, since it is a neutral and simplified information. (xvii) The age of author is not predicted due to the high neutrality of the text. However, the gender is predicted as *Female*. (xviii) The press type is classified as *News Article* and its veracity is *Truthful*, taking into account the formality of press media.

3 NLP Technologies Study

This section describes in more detail each NLP task considered in our work and exposes some available technologies: tools, APIs or demos related. In some cases, only methods and algorithms had been found. Mainly works with evaluations and results are presented. In this study, our interests are mainly focused on available technology (Web service/API, programming library) with certain automation degree to be able to be incorporated in future frameworks or prototypes. In the final section, it is exposed a comparison table of some NLP technologies studied in terms of automation and reliability degrees.

Text Classification

Text classification task (TC) consists of identifying the type of document by analyzing its content. The relevance of this task in document profiling is to determinate which type of document is analyzed, depending its type different features would be extracted. For example, Dandelion API[7] categorises plain text on eight categories: business, economy, sports, etc.

Information Extraction

Information Extraction task (IE) as has been addressed by (Vila et al., 2013) is a way to search and obtain text on large volumes of unstructured information to filter relevant information, using regular expressions, rules and patterns. This is use-

---

[5] http://ow.ly/7JtB305V8z6
[6] http://ow.ly/Pnmj30dNVtQ

[7] http://dandelion.eu

ful for document profiling because many complex meta-data can be obtained directly from the document. Since our work is mostly focused on Web documents there are too many tools like DEiXTo[8] that can extract information from the W3C DOM documents. The problem with these tools is the low-automation degree due to they should be reconfigured.

Topic Recognition

Topic Recognition task (TR) consists of identifying topics in the text. This task is interesting to classify a document in multiple categories or topics and know the different aspects that dealt the document. TextRazor[9] is a Web tool that lists topics from a text. Also, another Web demo is Meaning Cloud[10] that offers many NLP services among which topic recognition is included.

Keyword Extraction

Keyword Extraction task (KE) is the automatic extraction of relevant terms from a document. Unlike TR, KE doesn't intend to know the different aspects that dealt the document, KE extracts terms that best describe the subject of the document. Statistical Keyword Extraction Tool (SKET) (Rossi et al., 2013) is a programming library for extracting keywords from the text.

Named Entity Recognition

Named Entity Recognition task (NER) tries to locate and classify named entities according to different categories like names of persons, organizations, etc. Stanford NER (Finkel et al., 2005) is a NLP technology available as a programming library and evaluated in some scenarios, domains and corpora, that offers useful NER services.

Time Expression Recognition

Time Expression Recognition task (TER) consists of obtaining temporal expressions from texts. This information is useful to extract historical facts in texts or documents. Stanford SUTime (Chang and Manning, 2012) is a tested technology and available to be used as a programming library. An alternative is TIPSem (Llorens et al., 2010) which has been tested and available as API.

---

[8] http://dexi.io
[9] http://www.textrazor.com
[10] http://www.meaningcloud.com

Automatic Summarization

Automatic Summarization task (AS) obtains a reduced text from a larger text content. It's interesting to obtain a short version of the same document. (Alcón and Lloret, 2015-07) presents a summarization system for various purposes and domains. This system has been evaluated and is available as API.

Domain Detection

Domain Detection task (DD) is part of Semantic Parsing. This task detects the meaning of sentence using probabilistic semantic models. Our work is focused on ISR-WN (Gutiérrez et al., 2016) which is able to detect domains or categories from different resources obtaining and using relevant semantic trees from a text.

Language Identification

Language Identification task (LI) consists of identifying the language. AlchemyLanguage[11] is a Web demo that offers many NLP services for that purpose.

Polarity Classification

Polarity Classification task (PC) is part of Sentiment Analysis. According to (Mohammad, 2016) this consists of determining whether a text in positive, negative or neutral. Many PC approaches are using machine and deep learning which obtains good results. Among others, we mention two relevant works: (Kiritchenko et al., 2014) which presents an approach using supervised statistical machine learning, and Stanford Sentiment (Socher et al., 2013) that is available as a programming library.

Emotion Detection

Emotion Detection task (ED) is part of Sentiment Analysis. This consists of identifying some emotions expressed in texts. The following set of the basic emotional categories proposed by (Ekman, 2005) are included in this work: Anger, Disgust, Fear, Joy, Sadness and Surprise. One issue of this task is the lack of annotated corpus for evaluation. ToneAnalyzer[12] is a web demo of multiple NLP APIs, including the emotion detection task with 5 Ekman categories: Anger, Disgust, Fear, Joy and Sadness.

---

[11] http://alchemy-language-demo.mybluemix.net
[12] http://tone-analyzer-demo.mybluemix.net

Readability Analysis

Readability Analysis task (RA) according to (Martín Valdivia et al., 2014), the detection of RC consists of determining documents suitable for being read by specific people age ranges. This includes determining reading difficulties or text comprehension. For addressing this task it is necessary to classify documents on the basis of different levels of reading comprehension. Different measures of readability must be selected, we base our work on the study Flesh-Kincaid Grade Level. This study tries to predict the recommended age to understand the text. The tool Readable.io[13] is a web demo for evaluating the readability level of a text using various grade levels, including Flesh-Kincaid Grade Level.

Informality Analysis

Informality Analysis task (IA) tries to detect the degree informality in texts. This task arises due to the necessity of processing in a personalized way non-traditional textual sources existing on the Internet (i.e. blogs, forums, etc.). TENOR (Mosquera and Moreda, 2012) provides functionalities aligned to this task.

Age Estimation

Age Estimation task (AE) is part of the Author Profiling area. According to (Rangel and Rosso, 2016) AE tries to predict some aspects of authors like age or gender. This task will contribute to our research the discovery of various authors types depending on age ranges. Age Analyzer[14] is a web API that provides functionalities aligned to this task.

Gender Detection

Gender Detection task (GD) is strongly related to AE task, but in this case, it tries to detect the gender of text's author. Gender Analyzer[15] is appropriated to this task as has been before mentioned.

Irony Detection

Irony Detection task (ID) tries to detect if a literal message has an opposite meaning, without a negation marker. The difficulty resides the absence of face-to-face contact and vocal intonation. In the automatic detection of irony is used sentiment analysis, information extraction or decision making to obtain textual features for recognizing irony. (Reyes et al., 2013) presents a research for irony detection in Twitter short documents, using the tasks mentioned above.

Ideology Detection

Ideology Detection task (IDD) tries to detect the ideology orientation expressed in a text content based on a set of opinions or beliefs. Usually, this refers to a set of political beliefs or a set of ideas that characterise a particular culture. (Iyyer et al., 2014) presents a research work where political ideology orientation is detected using neural network technologies.

3.1 Automation and Reliability Study

In the present study, the high-reliability degree is defined as technologies that have an evaluation with high scores of performance. Similarly, the high-automation degree is defined as the type of technology easier to implement or use in each case. For example, Web Services, Java or Python libraries, Algorithms, Web application/demo and Desktop tools. Web Services or online APIs present a very-high-automation degree because it is easy to use them in frameworks or meta-tools developments. Java or Python libraries have a high-automation degree, because it is easy to include them in frameworks or meta-tools develops, but sometimes it is needed to proceed with an adaptation stage of the target programming framework. Algorithms present a medium-automation degree because it should be considered the efforts of reproducing them. Web application/demo tools have a low-automation degree because initially it is difficult to automatically include them, however, an alternative is using web crawling. Most experimental approaches that make use of Web application/demo tools apply semi-automatic procedures. Desktop tools have a very-low-automation degree because it is very difficult to include them in frameworks or meta-tools develops, most of the time the procedures are performed by hand. Table 1 shows a detailed comparison at respect. The automation of document profiling procedures, such as this study reveals, is supported by the reliability degree presented in Table 1. The performing scores have been taken from the bibliography before cited, being them the best technologies found in the state of the art. The technologies where is set "Not found", probably it is because they represent developments related to companies or pri-

---

[13]http://readable.io

[14]http://ageanalyzer.com

[15]http://www.genderanalyzer.com

NLP task	Technology	Measure	Score	Type
Text Classification	Dandelion	Not found	Not found	Web demo
Information Extraction	DEiXTo	Not found	Not found	Desktop
Topic Recognition	TextRazor	Not found	Not found	Web demo
	MeaningCloud	Not found	Not found	Web demo
Keyword Extraction	SKET	F1	0.7	Java library
Time Expression	Stanford SUTime	F1	0.92	Java library
	TIPSem	F1	0.85	Web service
Named Entity	Stanford NER	F1	0.8876	Java library
Summarising	Summarise	F1	0.57797	Web service
Domain Detection	ISR-WN	F1	0.52	Web service
Language Identification	Alchemy Language	Not found	Not found	Web demo
Polarity Classification	Kiritchenko et al. (2014)	F1	0.855	Algorithm
	Stanford Sentiment	Accuracy	0.854	Java library
Emotion Detection	Zhang et al. (2017)	F1	0.56	Algorithm
	Tone Analyzer	Not found	Not found	Web demo
Readability Analysis	readable.io	Not found	Not found	Web demo
Informality Analysis	TENOR	Not found	Not found	Algorithm
Age Estimation	Age Analyzer	Not found	Not found	Web service
Gender Detection	Gender Analyzer	Accuracy	0.95	Web service
Irony Detection	Reyes et al. (2013)	F1	0.76	Algorithm
Ideology Detection	Iyyer et al. (2014)	Accuracy	0.702	Algorithm

Table 1: NLP technologies comparisons.

vate research. However, it is interesting to study them for future evaluations. At respect to Web demos, these offer limited NLP services which could be possible resolve through business registration or payment of services. Regarding the type "Algorithm", in some cases, this one is not available in the reference papers. Nevertheless, it is considered because the authors could be contacted in some way.

4 Conclusion and Future Work

In this paper, we presented the study of useful NLP technologies to automate the process of building document's profiles. The study revealed that many NLP technologies are interesting to this aim, however, many of them are difficult to be reused. This depends on the licenses of use, visibility, replicability of their algorithms, etc. Another issue is the lack of annotated corpora to evaluate the technologies involved. Clearly, knowing the difficulties found to reuse the NLP technologies will help us to be more focused on considering those technologies with high-automation degree instead of high-reliability degree.

As result, in this paper we demonstrated that many different NLP technologies can converge all in a unique ecosystem, in our case for profiling documents, to be able to provide advanced sights about documents. Based on this result (a document profile), it can be facilitated searching documents and even be able to recommend documents to users taking into account different perspectives never before considered.

As future work, we plan to create a dataset for further supporting the creation and evaluation of document profile. In addition, the study of the results of evaluating different types of document profiles (i.e. social, press, book, etc.) will be included in our research agenda.

Acknowledgements

This work is funded by the University of Alicante (UAFPU2015-5999 and GRE16-01), Generalitat Valenciana (PROMETEOII/2014/001), the Spanish Government (TIN2015-65100-R, TIN2015-65136-C2-2-R) and Ayudas Fundación BBVA a equipos de investigación científica 2016 (ASAP).

References

Óscar Alcón and Elena Lloret. 2015-07. Estudio de la influencia de incorporar conocimiento léxico-semántico a la técnica de análisis de componentes principales para la generación de resúmenes multilingües.

M E Basiri, A R Naghsh-Nilchi, and N Ghasem-Aghaee. 2014. Sentiment prediction based on dempster-shafer theory of evidence. *Mathematical Problems in Engineering* 2014. https://doi.org/10.1155/2014/361201.

Angel X. Chang and Christopher D. Manning. 2012. Sutime: A library for recognizing and normalizing time expressions. In *In LREC*.

Paul Ekman. 2005. *Basic Emotions*, John Wiley Sons, Ltd.

Jenny Rose Finkel, Trond Grenager, and Christopher Manning. 2005. Incorporating non-local information into information extraction systems by gibbs sampling. In *Proceedings of the 43rd Annual Meeting on Association for Computational Linguistics*. Association for Computational Linguistics, Stroudsburg, PA, USA, ACL '05, pages 363–370. https://doi.org/10.3115/1219840.1219885.

Rachel M Green, John W Sheppard, Jim Cramer, Lauren Young, Josh Brown, and Ben White. 2013. Comparing Frequency- and Style-Based Features for Twitter Author Identification. *Proceedings of the Twenty-Sixth International Florida Artificial Intelligence Research Society Conference* pages 64–69.

Yoan Gutiérrez, Sonia Vázquez, and Andrés Montoyo. 2016. A semantic framework for textual data enrichment. *Expert Systems with Applications* 57:248–269.

Diego Ingaramo, David Pinto, Paolo Rosso, and Marcelo Errecalde. 2008. *Evaluation of Internal Validity Measures in Short-Text Corpora*, Springer Berlin Heidelberg, Berlin, Heidelberg, pages 555–567. https://doi.org/10.1007/978-3-540-78135-6$_4$8.

Mohit Iyyer, Peter Enns, Jordan Boyd-Graber, and Philip Resnik. 2014. Political ideology detection using recursive neural networks. In *Association for Computational Linguistics*.

Svetlana Kiritchenko, Xiaodan Zhu, and Saif M. Mohammad. 2014. Sentiment analysis of short informal texts. *J. Artif. Int. Res.* 50(1):723–762.

Hector Llorens, Estela Saquete, and Borja Navarro. 2010. Temporal expression identification based on semantic roles. In *Proceedings of the 14th International Conference on Applications of Natural Language to Information Systems*. NLDB'09, pages 230–242.

María Teresa Martín Valdivia, Eugenio Martínez Cámara, Eduard Barbu, Luis Alfonso Ureña López,

Paloma Moreda Pozo, Elena Lloret, et al. 2014. Proyecto first (flexible interactive reading support tool): Desarrollo de una herramienta para ayudar a personas con autismo mediante la simplificación de textos .

Saif M. Mohammad. 2016. Sentiment analysis: Detecting valence, emotions, and other affectual states from text. In Herb Meiselman, editor, *Emotion Measurement*, Elsevier.

Alejandro Mosquera and Paloma Moreda. 2012. Tenor: A lexical normalisation tool for spanish web 2.0 texts. In *Text, Speech and Dialogue - 15th International Conference (TSD 2012)*. Springer.

Francisco Rangel and Paolo Rosso. 2016. On the impact of emotions on author profiling. *Information Processing and Management* 52(1):73–92. https://doi.org/10.1016/j.ipm.2015.06.003.

Antonio Reyes, Paolo Rosso, and Tony Veale. 2013. A multidimensional approach for detecting irony in twitter. *Language Resources and Evaluation* 47(1):239–268.

R.G. Rossi, R. M. Marcacini, and S. O. Rezende. 2013. Analysis of statistical keyword extraction methods for incremental clustering.

Prasha Shrestha, Sebastian Sierra, Fabio A González, Paolo Rosso, Manuel Montes-y Gómez, and Thamar Solorio. 2017. Convolutional neural networks for authorship attribution of short texts. *EACL 2017* page 669.

Richard Socher, Alex Perelygin, Jean Wu, Jason Chuang, Christopher D. Manning, Andrew Y. Ng, and Christopher Potts. 2013. Recursive deep models for semantic compositionality over a sentiment treebank. In *Proceedings of the 2013 Conference on Empirical Methods in Natural Language Processing*. Association for Computational Linguistics, Stroudsburg, PA, pages 1631–1642.

Katia Vila, Antonio Fernández, José M. Gómez, Antonio Ferrández, and Josval Díaz. 2013. Noise-tolerance feasibility for restricted-domain Information Retrieval systems. *Data and Knowledge Engineering* 86:276–294. https://doi.org/10.1016/j.datak.2013.02.002.

MappSent: a Textual Mapping Approach for Question-to-Question Similarity

Amir Hazem[1]   **Basma El Amal Boussaha**[1]   **Nicolas Hernandez**[1]

[1] LS2N - UMR CNRS 6004, Université de Nantes, France

{Amir.Hazem,Basma.Boussaha,Nicolas.Hernandez}@univ-nantes.fr

Abstract

Since the advent of word embedding methods, the representation of longer pieces of texts such as sentences and paragraphs is gaining more and more interest, especially for textual similarity tasks. Mikolov et al. (2013a) have demonstrated that words and phrases exhibit linear structures that allow to meaningfully combine words by an element-wise addition of their vector representations. Recently, Arora et al. (2017) have shown that removing the projections of the weighted average sum of word embedding vectors on their first principal components, outperforms sophisticated supervised methods including RNN's and LSTM's. Inspired by Mikolov et al. (2013a); Arora et al. (2017) findings and by a bilingual word mapping technique presented in Artetxe et al. (2016), we introduce MappSent, a novel approach for textual similarity. Based on a linear sentence embedding representation, its principle is to build a matrix that maps sentences in a joint-subspace where similar sets of sentences are pushed closer. We evaluate our approach on the SemEval 2016/2017 question-to-question similarity task and show that overall MappSent achieves competitive results and outperforms in most cases state-of-art methods.

1 Introduction

Since the dawn of the mass access to the Internet fostered by the availability of data, more and more community question answering (CQA) forums such as StackExchange[1] and Qatar Living[2]

have been established and are gaining more and more popularity. It is not unusual to rely on such source of information to find out a correct answer to a given question. However, feeding forums with perpetual questions and answers makes this resource massive and full of duplicate posts and similar question variants. Thus, and to some extent, the search for an answer has become hard to achieve and led to the emergence of an important area of research known as Community Question Answering (CQA).

In the CQA domain, the identification of similar questions is certainly an important preliminary step for providing a correct answer to a posted question. It is necessary to figure out if a question has not already been treated in other posts, essentially for a matter of response effectiveness and to reduce as much as possible duplicate posts. To that end, question-to-question similarity task offers a key challenge while it has to deal not only with similar questions in terms of lexical similarity but also in terms of reformulation, paraphrasing, semantics, etc. It has attracted a great interest as it can be seen in the SemEval shared task where a subtask is dedicated to it since 2015.

In this paper, we propose MappSent, a novel approach for textual similarity that we evaluate on the SemEval question-to-question similarity task. The main idea is to represent questions in a joint sub-space where similar pairs are moved closer thanks to a mapping matrix. Each question is represented by the element-wise addition of its words embedding vectors (Mikolov et al., 2013a; Arora et al., 2017). Then, based on a training set of question pairs equivalence, an optimal linear transformation matrix that minimizes the distance between similar questions is learned. The mapping matrix is built according to Artetxe et al. (2016) approach that was initially introduced for mapping word embeddings of different languages.

---

[1]http://stackoverflow.com/

[2]http://www.qatarliving.com/forum

Proceedings of Recent Advances in Natural Language Processing, pages 291–300,
Varna, Bulgaria, Sep 4–6 2017.

We adapt this approach in a monolingual scenario at the sentence level. Questions are often pieces of texts that contain the context of the question and the question itself. We do not treat separately these two information, on the contrary, we consider both the context and the question as a whole segment that we call by misuse of language: *Sentence*. Our aim is to align two pieces of texts independently of their structures, as long as they exhibit similar characteristics that we try to capture over the proposed mapping matrix. The main contributions of this work are: (i) the introduction of MappSent as a new simple and sound way of representing sentences in an optimized joint sub-space, (ii) an extensive comparison with Arora et al. (2017) approach and, (iii) an empirical study of the impact of removing the first principal components as a preliminary step to questions similarity. We evaluate our approach on the SemEval 2016/2017 question-to-question similarity task (Task3, sub-taskB) and show that overall, MappSent outperforms the state-of-art approaches.

2 Related Work

With the continuous evolution of neural embedding methods, several approaches ranging from a word level embedding representation (Bengio et al., 2003; Collobert and Weston, 2008; Mikolov et al., 2013a; Pennington et al., 2014) to a longer textual level embedding representation such as phrases, sentences, paragraphs or documents (Socher et al., 2011; Mikolov et al., 2013a; Le and Mikolov, 2014; Kalchbrenner et al., 2014; Kiros et al., 2015; Wieting et al., 2016; Arora et al., 2017) have been proposed. Word embedding methods try to capture lexical and semantic word's properties by representing words in a low continuous dimensional space (Bengio et al., 2003; Mikolov et al., 2013a,b). Previous longer textual embedding methods use operations on vectors and matrices like addition or multiplication to represent phrases, sentences or paragraphs (Mitchell and Lapata, 2008, 2010; Mikolov et al., 2013a; Wieting et al., 2016; Arora et al., 2017). Other more sophisticated approaches use recurrent neural networks (RNN) (Socher et al., 2011, 2014; Kiros et al., 2015), long short-term memory (LSTM) to capture long distance dependency (Tai et al., 2015) or convolutional neural networks (CNNs) (Kalchbrenner et al., 2014) to represent sentences. Even if RNNs, LSTMs and CNNs based approaches have shown remarkable improvements in a wide range of applications, their computational cost and the need of large amount of training data, makes these approaches inefficient on small and specific datasets.

While sentence embedding representation is our main focus, it is important to mention Mikolov et al. (2013a) approach where they have shown the possibility to efficiently represent phrases by the sum of their words embedding vectors. In their Skip-Gram model, word vectors are trained to predict surrounding words and thus, to represent the distribution of the context in which a word appears. As word vectors are in a linear relationship, the sum of two word vectors can be seen as the product of the two context distributions. On the phrase analogy task Mikolov et al. (2013a) demonstrated the effectiveness of their model with the hierarchical softmax and subsampling using large amount of data. Recently, using the paraphrase pairs dataset (PPDB), Wieting et al. (2016) have shown that a simple but supervised word averaging model of sentence embeddings leads to better performance on textual similarity tasks. However, the performance of their approach is closely related to the supervision from the paraphrase dateset, while without supervision, their approach did not perform well on textual similarity tasks. More recently, Arora et al. (2017) proposed a new sentence embedding method. Its principle is to first compute a weighted average sum of the word embedding vectors of sentences, and then, to remove the projections of the average vectors on their first principal components. Like Mikolov et al. (2013a) and Wieting et al. (2016), their approach is based on word embedding sum, but the difference is remarkable on the weighted schema and on the use of principal component analysis (PCA) method to remove the correlation of sentence vectors dimensions. They significantly achieved better performance than the unweighted average on a variety of textual similarity tasks. Also, their approach outperformed sophisticated supervised methods such as RNN's and LSTM's.

SemEval question-to-question similarity task offers an appropriate environment to evaluate our approach and validate our intuition. A wide range of approaches have been proposed since the beginning of SemEval. The winners of the 2016 edition (*UH-PRHLT*) for instance (Franco-Salvador et al., 2016), combine lexical and semantic features and representations to measure similarity between pieces of texts. Their approach take advantage of distributed representations of words, graph knowledge constructed from BabelNet and frames extracted from FrameNet. The second best system (*ConvKN*) (Barrón-Cedeño et al., 2016) used convolutional neural networks to represent sentences. They used an SVM operating on three kernels and combined convolutional tree kernels with convolutional neural networks and additional manually extracted features including text similarity and thread specific features. The third best system (*KeLP*) (Filice et al., 2016), used SVM classifier based on a linear combination of kernel functions. Different features were used such as linguistic similarities, shallow syntactic trees encoding lexical and morpho-syntactic information, feature vectors capturing task specific information, etc. Several other systems have been proposed. Wu and Lan (2016) for instance used different ranking methods such as supervised models using traditional features as well as convolutional neural network and long-short term memory. They also proposed two novel methods to improve semantic similarity estimation by integrating ranking information of question-comment pairs. Wang and Poupart (2016) explored a two-layer feedforward neural network with the average of word embedding vectors to predict the semantic similarity score of two questions. While Wu and Zhang (2016) proposed a translation based method that combines a translation model with a cosine similarity based-method to deal with question similarity. Mihaylova et al. (2016) presented a feature rich system based on various types of features: semantic, lexical, metadata and user-related. Their best results were achieved thanks to metadata features. Even if user information conveyed by metadata can be very useful, we make the choice not to exploit it, while our main focus is on text analysis only.

With the success of the 2016 edition and the boom of neural networks, it has been noticed a jump in 2017 on the number of deep learning methods (Nakov et al., 2017). SimBow system, which did not participate in the previous year, is the winner of the 2017 edition on the question-to-question similarity task. The authors proposed a logistic regression on a combination of different unsupervised textual similarities. They introduced a variant of cosine similarity that uses se-

mantic similarity between words to compute cosine between two bag-of-word vectors. The semantic relations were extracted using Word2Vec. LearningToQuestion system achieved the second best result using SVM and logistic regression as integrators of rich features representations (word embeddings, bidirectional LSTMs, gated recurrent unit (GRU), etc.). Kelp system which was ranked 3rd on last year edition, reached also the third place this year but with its contrastive[3] version could reach the first place. Talla system which was ranked at the fourth position, used a random forest classifier based on an ensemble of syntactic, semantic and IR-based features such as semantic word alignment, term frequency Kullback-Leibler divergence, and tree kernels (Nakov et al., 2017). A detailed description of SemEval 2016 and 2017 editions and their participants can be found in Nakov et al. (2016) and Nakov et al. (2017). Overall, the major part of SemEval state-of-art proposed approaches uses sophisticated and complex methods to deal with question-to-question similarity. One advantage of our approach is its simplicity while compared to SemEval systems.

3 MappSent Approach

In order to efficiently align similar sentences[4] and by analogy to word embedding representations, we build a sentence embedding space where sentences are represented by the sum of their word embedding vectors. Similar sentences are moved closer thanks to a mapping matrix (Artetxe et al., 2016) learned from a training dataset containing annotated similar sentences. Basically, a set of similar sentence pairs is used as seed information to build the mapping matrix. The optimal mapping is computed by minimizing the distance between the seed sentence pairs.

MappSent approach consists of the following steps:

1. We train a Skip-Gram [5] model using Gensim (Řehůřek and Sojka, 2010)[6] on a lemma-

---

[3] A contrastive approach refers to the non primary system. It is considered by the authors to be their second or third run.

[4] Or similar pieces of texts.

[5] CBOW model had also been experienced but it turned out to give lower results while compared to the SkipGram model.

[6] To ensure the comparability of our experiments, we fixed the python hash function that is used to generate random initialization. By doing so, we are sure to obtain the same embeddings for a given configuration.

tized training dataset. We use all the questions and answers provided by the *Qatar Living* forum (described in section 4) as training data. We consider all users interactions as a good source of information for context representation.

2. Each training and test sentence is pre-processed. We remove stopwords and only keep nouns, verbs and adjectives while computing sentence embedding vectors and the mapping matrix. This step is not applied when learning word embeddings (cf.Step 1).

3. For each given pre-processed sentence, we build its embedding vector which is the element-wise addition of its words embedding vectors (Mikolov et al., 2013a). Unlike Arora et al. (2017) we do not use any weighting procedure while computing vectors embedding sum[7].

4. We build a mapping matrix where test sentences can be projected. We adapted Artetxe et al. (2016) approach in a monolingual scenario as follows:

   - To build the mapping matrix we need a mapping dictionary which contains similar sentence pairs. To construct this dictionary, we consider pairs of sentences that are labeled as *PerfectMatch* and *Relevant* in the Qatar Living training dataset (cf section 4).
   - The mapping matrix is built by learning a linear transformation which minimizes the sum of squared Euclidean distances for the dictionary entries and using an orthogonality constraint to preserve the length normalization.
   - While in the bilingual scenario, source words are projected in the target space by using the bilingual mapping matrix, in our case, original and related questions are both projected in a similar subspace using the monolingual sentence mapping matrix. This consists of our adaptation of the bilingual mapping.

5. Test sentences are projected in the new subspace thanks to the mapping matrix.

---

[7]We explored this direction without success.

6. The cosine similarity is then used to measure the similarity between the projected test sentences.

As it has been shown in Arora et al. (2017) that removing the projections of the average vectors on their first principal components improves the performance on textual similarity tasks, we apply this technique to our approach. We first compute PCA on the training dataset and then we remove the n first principal components before computing the cosine similarity between two test questions.

4 Data and Resources

In community question answering, the question-to-question similarity task (Task3, SubtaskB in SemEval) consists of reranking the related questions according to their similarity with respect to the original question. Each original question, has 10 candidates to rerank. These candidates are labeled as *PerfectMatch*, *Relevant* or *Irrelevant*. No distinction is made between *PerfectMatch* and *Relevant* labels, both are concidered as good candidates in SemEval task. The training and development datasets consist of 317 original questions and 3,169 related questions[8]. The test sets of 2016 and 2017 respectively consist of 70 original/700 related questions and 88 original/880 related questions. The official evaluation measure towards which all systems are evaluated is the mean average precision (MAP) using the 10 ranked related questions.

For building our Skip-Gram model, we used the training, development and test sets of 2015 (which is a dataset of question-comment pairs, it corresponds to the SubTask A of SemEval), in addition to the training and development sets of 2016 which contain for each original question, its related question and 10 related comments to each related question. It is to note that the training set of 2016 is the same as 2017. The size of the lemmatized training dataset is about 2 million words.

5 Experiments and Results

In this section we first present the results of *Arora*, *MappSent* and the 3 best systems on the SemEval editions 2016 and 2017. Then, we compare MappSent and Arora approaches on the same datasets while varying different embedding

---

[8]http://alt.qcri.org/semeval2016/
task3/index.php?id=data-and-tools

parameters (window size, vectors dimension size, etc.) and the use or not of principal components analysis approach. Finally, we vary the number of principal components to find out the optimal configurations of PCA-based approaches. We note by $Arora$ and $Arora_{pca}$, the approaches presented in Arora et al. (2017). $Arora_{pca}$ is based on PCA removal while $Arora$ does not use PCA and is just a weighted sum of word embedding vectors of a sentence. We also propose four MappSent approaches. We note by $MappSent^-$ and $MappSent^-_{pca}$ our proposed approach that does not use the mapping matrix. It is merely the unweighted sum of word embeddings of a sentence ($MappSent^-$) and its PCA-based variant ($MappSent^-_{pca}$). We also note by $MappSent$ and $MappSent_{pca}$ our proposed approach that uses the mapping matrix ($MappSent$) and its PCA-based variant ($MappSent_{pca}$).

Tables 1 and 2 show the results of SemEval (2016/2017) of our proposed approaches (noted $MappSent^-$, $MappSent^-_{pca}$, $MappSent$ and $MappSent_{pca}$), Arora approaches (noted $Arora$ and $Arora_{pca}$) and the three best systems of the SemEval shared-task that are: $UH\text{-}PRHLT$, $ConvKN$ and $KeLP$ for the 2016 edition and *SimBow*, *LearningToQuestion* and *KeLP* for the 2017 edition. From the two Tables we see that $MappSent$ outperforms the three best systems as well as Arora approaches on both SemEval editions. The best MAP scores obtained by $MappSent$ are 79.18% (2016 edition) and 47.50% (2017 edition). We also notice that MappSent PCA-based approach ($MappSent_{pca}$) obtains the best results on 2017 with a MAP score of 49.29% while it is slightly under $MappSent$ with 79.09% of MAP score for 2016. Concerning $Arora$, $MappSent^-$ as well as their PCA-based variants ($Arora_{pca}$, $MappSent^-_{pca}$), we observe that all of them obtain competitive and sometimes better results while compared to the three best SemEval systems. This is the case for instance on 2016 where the four systems outperform the ranked first system $UH\text{-}PRHLT$. The results are more contrasted concerning the impact of PCA on the performance of $Arora$ and $MappSent$. While we observe a gain using PCA for $Arora_{pca}$ with a jump from 77.87% to 78.81% of MAP score, $MappSent^-_{pca}$ shows a non significant gain (a very little improvement from 78.56% to 78.66%). On the contrary, $MappSent_{pca}$ shows slightly

lower results as it can be seen in Table 1. The results of Table 2 indicate opposite observations. This time $MappSent_{pca}$ shows significant improvements while $MappSent^-_{pca}$ and $Arora_{pca}$ don't. It is necessary to go deeper in parameters analysis to figure out their impact. This is the purpose of the next paragraphs.

Method	MAP(%)
$UH\text{-}PRHLT$	76.70
$ConvKN$	76.02
$KeLP$	75.83
$Arora$	77.87
$Arora_{pca}$	78.81
$MappSent^-$	78.56
$MappSent^-_{pca}$	78.66
$MappSent$	**79.18**
$MappSent_{pca}$	79.09

Table 1: Results on SemEval-2016 Task3 Subtask B

Method	MAP(%)
$Simbow$	47.22
$LearningToQuestion$	46.93
$KeLP$	46.66
$Arora$	46.93
$Arora_{pca}$	46.66
$MappSent^-$	46.90
$MappSent^-_{pca}$	46.53
$MappSent$	47.50
$MappSent_{pca}$	**49.29**

Table 2: Results on SemEval-2017 Task3 Subtask B

5.1 Window and Dimension Size Comparison

Table 3 presents a comparison of MappSent and Arora approaches using different parameters. For embeddings training, we used as settings a window size of 5,10 and 20, negative sampling of 5, sampling of 1e-3 and training over 15 iterations. We applied the Skip-gram model to create vectors of 100, 300, 500 and 800 dimensions. We used hierarchical SoftMax for training the Skip-gram model. Other settings were assessed but on average the chosen ones tend to give the best results on the development data. Concerning the number of principal components, on average the best results were obtained by removing 1 or 2 principal components.

| Approach | SemEval 2016 | | | | SemEval 2017 | | | | Window size |
| | Dimension size | | | | | | | | |
	100	300	500	800	100	300	500	800	
$Arora$	75.86	75.48	75.52	76.41	44.67	44.44	44.36	44.22	
$Arora_{pca}$	77.47	76.98	75.45	77.07	45.07	44.85	45.55	45.26	
$MappSent^-$	76.16	77.01	76.44	76.62	45.39	45.43	45.41	45.15	
$MappSent^-_{pca}$	77.43	76.73	76.47	77.01	45.64	46.01	45.76	45.78	5
$MappSent$	78.47	78.14	77.39	78.03	46.62	46.44	47.38	47.30	
$MappSent_{pca}$	77.13	77.91	76.99	77.91	47.56	48.24	48.66	48.15	
$Arora$	75.71	76.49	76.28	77.16	45.08	45.81	44.90	43.82	
$Arora_{pca}$	76.21	77.02	77.02	77.03	44.81	46.39	**46.66**	45.33	
$MappSent^-$	75.94	76.47	77.37	77.86	45.54	45.60	45.83	45.48	
$MappSent^-_{pca}$	76.26	78.07	78.41	77.36	46.39	45.22	**46.53**	45.33	10
$MappSent$	76.95	78.09	78.74	78.70	47.36	45.92	46.99	46.83	
$MappSent_{pca}$	77.12	77.19	76.55	76.33	48.57	47.22	47.89	48.15	
$Arora$	76.18	76.47	77.45	**77.87**	**46.93**	44.24	44.41	44.36	
$Arora_{pca}$	78.03	**78.81**	78.05	78.11	45.40	44.66	44.50	44.86	
$MappSent^-$	76.39	77.45	77.51	**78.56**	**46.90**	44.66	45.36	45.72	
$MappSent^-_{pca}$	77.72	**78.66**	78.24	78.32	45.74	44.27	46.03	46.28	20
$MappSent$	78.52	**79.18**	79.00	78.83	**47.50**	46.88	46.88	47.44	
$MappSent_{pca}$	78.43	78.39	**79.09**	79.02	47.80	48.03	48.00	**48.72**	

Table 3: Comparison of $Arora$ and $MappSent$ using different window and dimension size (results in bold represent the best score of each approach), the number of PCA components was fixed to 1 or 2 (MAP %)

Our first comparison concerns $Arora$ and $MappSent^-$ which are similar approaches in the idea of computing the sum of word embedding vectors of sentences. The difference mainly resides in the fact that $Arora$ uses a smoothed inverse frequency to weight word vectors while $MappSent^-$ is an unweighted approach[9]. We see that for both editions and in the majority of cases, $MappSent^-$ outperforms $Arora$. The best $Arora$ MAP scores are: 77.87% for 2016 (w=20 and dim=800) and 46.93% for 2017 with the same window size and 100 dimensions. $MappSent^-$ obtained better results on 2016 with a MAP score of 78.56% (w=20 and dim=800) and a slightly lower result on 2017 with a MAP score of 46.90% (w=20 and dim=100). It is to note that both approaches were evaluated under the same conditions that are: lemmatization, stopwords and POS-TAG filtering as well as word embeddings trained on the same corpus. Arora approach under the

original conditions presented in Arora et al. (2017) was tested but the results were much lower using Wikipedia embeddings and no POS-TAG filtering.

The second comparison concerns the use of PCA in $Arora$ and $MappSent^-$. We measure the contribution of removing the first principal components (1 or 2) while varying window and dimension size of word embeddings. The results are obtained using $MappSent^-_{pca}$ and $Arora_{pca}$. We see that the use of PCA almost always improve the performance of $Arora$ approach and except few cases, it also always improve the results of $MappSent^-$. The best $Arora_{pca}$ MAP scores are: 78.81% for 2016 (w=20 and dim=300) and 46.66% for 2017 (w=10 and dim=500). $MappSent^-_{pca}$ obtained higher results on 2016 with a MAP score of 78.66% (w=20 and dim=300) and a slightly lower result on 2017 with a MAP score of 46.53% (w=10 and dim=500).

For the third comparison, we are interested in the performance of the main proposed approach which is $MappSent$ regarding $Arora$

---

[9]It is to note that different weighting schema have been tried, surprisingly they all degraded the results of $MappSent$.

and $Arora_{PCA}$. We notice that $MappSent$ always outperform the latter approaches (except very few cases). The best $MappSent$ MAP scores are: 79.18% for 2016 (w=20 and dim=300) and 47.50% for 2017 (w=20 and dim=100).

Interestingly, the use of PCA improves $MappSent$ performance in most cases on 2017 test set while it degrades its performance in most cases on 2016 test set. The best $MappSent_{PCA}$ MAP scores are: 79.09% for 2016 (w=20 and dim=500) and 48.78% for 2017 (w=20 and dim=800). The number of principal components was fixed to one or two depending on the approach. However it is necessary to conduct an empirical study on the impact of the number of PCA components on PCA-based approaches. This is the purpose of the next Section.

5.2 Principal Components Impact

In this section we compare $Arora$ and $MappSent$ PCA-based approaches regarding the number of principal components that were removed before the computation of sentence similarity. We vary the number of components from 0 to 10 and give an arbitrary upper bound of 20 components.

# PCA	$Arora$	$MappSent^-$	$MappSent$
0	76.47	77.45	**79.18**
1	**78.81**	78.66	78.39
2	77.46	77.80	77.66
3	77.20	78.35	77.63
4	77.91	**78.82**	78.02
5	78.20	78.01	77.13
6	78.59	78.14	77.34
7	78.33	78.09	77.60
8	77.64	77.69	77.51
9	77.64	77.72	78.13
10	77.16	77.14	78.19
20	76.51	75.86	77.08

Table 4: Comparison of $Arora$ and $MappSent$ on SemEval 2016 while removing different numbers of principal components (w=20 and dim= 300)

According to Tables 4 we clearly notice the positive impact of using PCA in $Arora$ and $MappSent^-$. The best results are obtained with one component for $Arora$ and four components for $MappSent^-$. Concerning $MappSent$,

# PCA	$Arora$	$MappSent^-$	$MappSent$
0	44.90	45.83	47.36
1	46.66	46.53	46.77
2	**47.40**	46.81	48.57
3	46.86	46.52	49.07
4	46.50	46.70	**49.29**
5	45.60	46.79	48.69
6	45.72	46.52	47.55
7	47.19	**47.21**	47.77
8	46.97	46.53	47.24
9	45.51	46.48	47.41
10	45.35	46.15	46.84
20	46.53	47.07	46.70

Table 5: Comparison of $Arora$ and $MappSent$ on SemEval 2017 while removing different numbers of principal components (w=10 and dim=500)

the use of PCA degrades its performance which is somehow surprising regarding $MappSent^-$. From Table 5, all the approaches benefit from PCA components removal. The best results are obtained with two components for $Arora$, seven for $MappSent^-$ and four components for $MappSent$. If we can observe the influence of PCA on the experiments, it is however difficult to efficiently fix the the most appropriate number of principle components to use. In addition, it is clear that a high number of principal components is in most cases inefficient.

6 Discussion

The multiple experiments and results have clearly demonstrated the effectiveness of our approach since MappSent and its PCA variant outperformed the best SemEval systems of 2016 and 2017 editions. Hence, the idea of mapping sentences in the same sub-space suggests a better sentence representation. Two key points must however be discussed. First, sentence representation by its words embeddings sum and second, the way of building the mapping matrix and the sentence projection procedure. For sentence representation, it is unclear why a simple words embedding vectors sum performs in most cases better than a weighted sum (as in $Arora$ for instance). That said, this can be partially explained by the fact that we remove stopwords and some POS-TAGs from each sentence. Keeping nouns, verbs and adjectives only, makes sentences smaller and this probably reduce the impact of a weighting schema. The mapping matrix has been built and optimized on a small training dataset using orthogonal constraint, unit normalization and mean centering reduction. The set of training similar sentence pairs was small (about 2000 question pairs). A question remains on how our approach could perform if the mapping matrix was trained on a large sentence database such as the paraphrasing database (PPTB) for instance? We let this question for future work. In addition, one important adaptation of Artetxe et al. (2016) approach is the projection phase. While in a bilingual scenario source words are mapped into the target language, in our monolingual case, we map both source questions (the original questions) and target questions (the related questions). It wouldn't make sense to only map the source questions as we need to represent both pairs in the same sub-space.

In most cases, $MappSent$ and $Arora$ perform better on higher window size (10 or 20). For vector dimensions the results are more contrasted (300, 500 or 800). While it is difficult to clearly pinpoint the reasons of such observation, it is well established that smaller windows capture syntactic/semantic dependencies, while larger windows capture topical structures (Mikolov et al., 2013b). As our datasets treat different topics of the Qatar daily life, one can suppose that topical information maybe more discriminant than the one provided by syntactic information, at least in these experiments.

An important phase is certainly embedding models. Word embedding vectors have been trained using the Skip-Gram model[10]. Here also, and as it has been already shown (Mikolov et al., 2013a,b), the Skip-Gram model performs better than CBOW model on small datasets. Another interesting information is the fact that training word embeddings on a specific dataset (here Qatar living) performs better than using pretrained embeddings such as wikipedia or other bigger size corpora. This can also be explained by the general representation of such embeddings which maybe inappropriate when dealing with specific domains. One interesting direction which we also let for fu-

ture work is to contrast different domains corpora and also use data selection before training our embedding models.

Finally, we could notice the positive impact of PCA in most cases except for $MappSent$[11] on the 2016 test set. Removing principal components from a sum of word embeddings is useful while the resulting sentence embedding vectors are uncorrelated. Hence, similar information is removed which makes sentence comparison more efficient. However, one drawback of PCA among other mathematical transforms is its sensitivity to the original data. One possible reason that can explain PCA performance is probably the correlation between the training and the test datasets. Another PCA drawback is the empirical way to fix the number of principal components. It would be interesting to explore other discriminant mathematical transformations such as canonical correlation analysis (CCA) or independent component analysis (ICA).

7 Conclusion

In this paper we have proposed MappSent, a novel approach for textual similarity. Our approach allows to map sentences in a joint more representative sub-space. Thanks to questions mapping matrix, similar questions are pushed closer suggesting that the new sub-space is more discriminant. The experimental results confirm our intuition while MappSent and its PCA-based variant obtain the best results on SemEval (2016/2017) question-to-question similarity task over state-of-art approaches. One remarkable advantage of MappSent is its simplicity while neither intensive computation nor external resources or metadata are needed. In addition, MappSent can be applied to pieces of text of any length as long as a training set of similar texts is available. That said, no attention has been given to linguistic information and questions were treated as bags-of-words. For future work, we intend to explore linguistic features as well as exploiting the context of a question and the question itself differently. Another exciting challenge is to apply our approach to questions and answers. The use of metadata is also another interesting direction that we leave for the future.

---

[10]It is to note that some experiments using the CBOW model have been conducted but the performance were much lower than using the Skip-Gram model.

[11]Normalization and mean centering embedding vectors as well as a weak correlation between training and test data may explain this behaviour.

Acknowledgments

The current work was both supported by the Unique Interministerial Fund (FUI) No. 17 as part of the ODISAE[12] project and the ANR 2016 PAS-TEL[13].

References

Sanjeev Arora, Liang Yingyu, and Ma Tengyu. 2017. A simple but tough to beat baseline for sentence embeddings. In *Proceedings of the 17th International Conference on Learning Representations (ICLR'17)*. pages 1–11.

Mikel Artetxe, Gorka Labaka, and Eneko Agirre. 2016. Learning principled bilingual mappings of word embeddings while preserving monolingual invariance. In *Proceedings of the 2016 Conference on Empirical Methods in Natural Language Processing (EMNLP'16)*. Austin, TX, USA, pages 2289–2294. https://aclweb.org/anthology/D16-1250.

Alberto Barrón-Cedeño, Giovanni Da San Martino, Shafiq Joty, Alessandro Moschitti, Fahad Al-Obaidli, Salvatore Romeo, Kateryna Tymoshenko, and Antonio Uva. 2016. Convkn at semeval-2016 task 3: Answer and question selection for question answering on arabic and english fora. In *Proceedings of the 10th International Workshop on Semantic Evaluation (SemEval-2016)*. Association for Computational Linguistics, San Diego, California, pages 896–903. http://www.aclweb.org/anthology/S16-1138.

Yoshua Bengio, Rjean Ducharme, Pascal Vincent, and Christian Jauvin. 2003. A neural probabilistic language model. *JOURNAL OF MACHINE LEARNING RESEARCH* 3:1137–1155.

R. Collobert and J. Weston. 2008. A unified architecture for natural language processing: Deep neural networks with multitask learning. In *International Conference on Machine Learning, ICML*.

Simone Filice, Danilo Croce, Alessandro Moschitti, and Roberto Basili. 2016. Kelp at semeval-2016 task 3: Learning semantic relations between questions and answers. In *Proceedings of the 10th International Workshop on Semantic Evaluation (SemEval-2016)*. Association for Computational Linguistics, San Diego, California, pages 1116–1123. http://www.aclweb.org/anthology/S16-1172.

Marc Franco-Salvador, Sudipta Kar, Thamar Solorio, and Paolo Rosso. 2016. UH-PRHLT at semeval-2016 task 3: Combining lexical and semantic-based features for community question answering. In *Proceedings of the 10th International Workshop on Semantic Evaluation, SemEval@NAACL-HLT 2016, San Diego, CA, USA, June 16-17, 2016*. pages 814–821.

Nal Kalchbrenner, Edward Grefenstette, and Phil Blunsom. 2014. A convolutional neural network for modelling sentences. *CoRR* abs/1404.2188.

Ryan Kiros, Yukun Zhu, Ruslan R Salakhutdinov, Richard Zemel, Raquel Urtasun, Antonio Torralba, and Sanja Fidler. 2015. Skip-thought vectors. In C. Cortes, N. D. Lawrence, D. D. Lee, M. Sugiyama, and R. Garnett, editors, *Advances in Neural Information Processing Systems 28*, Curran Associates, Inc., pages 3294–3302.

Quoc V. Le and Tomas Mikolov. 2014. Distributed representations of sentences and documents. *CoRR* abs/1405.4053.

Tsvetomila Mihaylova, Pepa Gencheva, Martin Boyanov, Ivana Yovcheva, Todor Mihaylov, Momchil Hardalov, Yasen Kiprov, Daniel Balchev, Ivan Koychev, Preslav Nakov, Ivelina Nikolova, and Galia Angelova. 2016. Super team at semeval-2016 task 3: Building a feature-rich system for community question answering. In *Proceedings of the 10th International Workshop on Semantic Evaluation, SemEval@NAACL-HLT 2016, San Diego, CA, USA, June 16-17, 2016*. pages 836–843.

Tomas Mikolov, Ilya Sutskever, Kai Chen, Greg S Corrado, and Jeff Dean. 2013a. Distributed representations of words and phrases and their compositionality. In C. J. C. Burges, L. Bottou, M. Welling, Z. Ghahramani, and K. Q. Weinberger, editors, *Advances in Neural Information Processing Systems 26*, Curran Associates, Inc., pages 3111–3119. http://papers.nips.cc/paper/5021-distributed-representations-of-words-and-phrases-and-their-compositionality.pdf.

Tomas Mikolov, Scott Wen-tau Yih, and Geoffrey Zweig. 2013b. Linguistic regularities in continuous space word representations. In *Proceedings of the 2013 Conference of the North American Chapter of the Association for Computational Linguistics: Human Language Technologies (NAACL-HLT 2013)*. Association for Computational Linguistics.

Jeff Mitchell and Mirella Lapata. 2008. Vector-based models of semantic composition. In *Proceedings of ACL-08: HLT*. Columbus, Ohio, pages 236–244.

Jeff Mitchell and Mirella Lapata. 2010. Composition in distributional models of semantics. *Cognitive Science* 34(8):1388–1439.

Preslav Nakov, Doris Hoogeveen, Lluís Màrquez, Alessandro Moschitti, Hamdy Mubarak, Timothy Baldwin, and Karin Verspoor. 2017. SemEval-2017 task 3: Community question answering. In *Proceedings of the 11th International Workshop on Semantic*

---

[12]http://www.odisae.com
[13]http://www.agence-nationale-recherche.fr/?Projet=ANR-16-CE33-0007

Evaluation. Association for Computational Linguistics, Vancouver, Canada, SemEval '17.

Preslav Nakov, Lluís Màrquez, Alessandro Moschitti, Walid Magdy, Hamdy Mubarak, Abed Alhakim Freihat, Jim Glass, and Bilal Randeree. 2016. SemEval-2016 task 3: Community question answering. In *Proceedings of the 10th International Workshop on Semantic Evaluation*. Association for Computational Linguistics, San Diego, California, SemEval '16.

Jeffrey Pennington, Richard Socher, and Christopher D Manning. 2014. Glove: Global vectors for word representation. In *Empirical Methods in Natural Language Processing (EMNLP)*. pages 1532–1543. http://www.aclweb.org/anthology/D14-1162.

Radim Řehůřek and Petr Sojka. 2010. Software Framework for Topic Modelling with Large Corpora. In *Proceedings of the LREC 2010 Workshop on New Challenges for NLP Frameworks*. ELRA, Valletta, Malta, pages 45–50. `http://is.muni.cz/publication/884893/en`.

Richard Socher, Eric H. Huang, Jeffrey Pennington, Andrew Y. Ng, and Christopher D. Manning. 2011. Dynamic Pooling and Unfolding Recursive Autoencoders for Paraphrase Detection. In *Advances in Neural Information Processing Systems 24*.

Richard Socher, Andrej Karpathy, Quoc V. Le, Christopher D. Manning, and Andrew Y. Ng. 2014. Grounded compositional semantics for finding and describing images with sentences. *TACL* 2:207–218.

Kai Sheng Tai, Richard Socher, and Christopher D. Manning. 2015. Improved semantic representations from tree-structured long short-term memory networks. *CoRR* abs/1503.00075.

Hujie Wang and Pascal Poupart. 2016. Overfitting at semeval-2016 task 3: Detecting semantically similar questions in community question answering forums with word embeddings. In *Proceedings of the 10th International Workshop on Semantic Evaluation, SemEval@NAACL-HLT 2016, San Diego, CA, USA, June 16-17, 2016*. pages 861–865.

John Wieting, Mohit Bansal, Kevin Gimpel, and Karen Livescu. 2016. Towards universal paraphrastic sentence embeddings. *Internationa Conference on Learning Representations, CoRR* abs/1511.08198.

GuoShun Wu and Man Lan. 2016. ECNU at semeval-2016 task 3: Exploring traditional method and deep learning method for question retrieval and answer ranking in community question answering. In *Proceedings of the 10th International Workshop on Semantic Evaluation, SemEval@NAACL-HLT 2016, San Diego, CA, USA, June 16-17, 2016*. pages 872–878.

Yunfang Wu and Minghua Zhang. 2016. ICL00 at semeval-2016 task 3: Translation-based method for CQA system. In *Proceedings of the 10th International Workshop on Semantic Evaluation, SemEval@NAACL-HLT 2016, San Diego, CA, USA, June 16-17, 2016*. pages 857–860.

The Impact of Figurative Language on Sentiment Analysis

Tomáš Hercig[†‡]

‡ NTIS – New Technologies
for the Information Society,
Faculty of Applied Sciences,
University of West Bohemia,
Technická 8, 306 14 Plzeň
Czech Republic
`tigi@kiv.zcu.cz`

Ladislav Lenc[†‡]

† Department of Computer
Science and Engineering,
Faculty of Applied Sciences
University of West Bohemia,
Univerzitní 8, 306 14 Plzeň
Czech Republic
`llenc@kiv.zcu.cz`

Abstract

Figurative language such as irony, sarcasm, and metaphor is considered a significant challenge in sentiment analysis. These figurative devices can sculpt the affect of an utterance and test the limits of sentiment analysis of supposedly literal texts. We explore the effect of figurative language on sentiment analysis. We incorporate the figurative language indicators into the sentiment analysis process and compare the results with and without the additional information about them. We evaluate on the SemEval-2015 Task 11 data and outperform the first team with our convolutional neural network model and additional training data in terms of mean squared error and we follow closely behind the first place in terms of cosine similarity.

1 Introduction

Recently there have been several experiments with sarcasm detection e.g. (Ptáček et al., 2014; Ghosh and Veale, 2016; Zhang et al., 2016; Poria et al., 2016). Although these works succeeded in their goal to detect variations of sarcasm, one final step is still missing – the evaluation of sentiment analysis with and without additional sarcasm indicators. There have been attempts at investigating the impact of sarcasm on sentiment analysis (Maynard and Greenwood, 2014) or thorough analysis of hashtags indicating sarcastic tweets (Sulis et al., 2016). However, the impact of figurative language (including sarcasm) on sentiment analysis has not yet been studied in depth.

Our goal is to explore the effect of figurative language (e.g. sarcasm) on sentiment analysis. We incorporate the figurative language indicators into the sentiment analysis process and compare the results with and without the additional information about them. We use additional dataset to examine the results achieved with extra training data.

2 Related Work

2.1 Sarcasm Detection

Maynard and Greenwood (2014) performed experiments with a rule based approach to sarcasm detection and sentiment analysis. They manually annotated 266 sentences from 134 collected tweets. Their corpus contains 68 opinionated sentences (62 negative, 6 positive), out of these 61 were deemed to be sarcastic. Their regular sentiment polarity analyser achieved 0.27 accuracy while the sentiment polarity analyser considering sarcasm achieved 0.77 accuracy using handcrafted rules and lexicons. However this dataset is imbalanced and very small to draw any conclusions.

Second experiment measured the accuracy of sarcasm and polarity detection. The corpus consists of 400 tweets (91 sarcastic sentences). Regrettably, the previous regular vs. sarcasm analyser comparison exploring the impact of sarcasm on polarity detection is not included. They only measured the performance of the sarcastic analyser.

The detection of sarcasm in Czech and English was done by Ptáček et al. (2014). They created large Czech Twitter corpus consisting of 7k manually-labeled tweets and provide it to the community along with the automatically-labeled English balanced (50k sarcastic, 50k normal tweets) and imbalanced corpora (25k sarcastic, 75k normal tweets). They evaluated two classifiers with various combinations of features on each dataset achieving F1 score of 0.947 and 0.924 on the balanced and imbalanced datasets, respectively and

Proceedings of Recent Advances in Natural Language Processing, pages 301–308,
Varna, Bulgaria, Sep 4–6 2017.

F1 score 0.582 on the Czech imbalanced dataset.

2.2 SemEval Workshop

SemEval-2015 Task 10B (Rosenthal et al., 2015) Sentiment analysis in Twitter is a re-run of previous years (SemEval-2013 Task 2 and SemEval-2014 Task 9). The goal of this task is to classify Twitter messages (tweets) into positive, negative, or neutral sentiment classes. Teams evaluate their results on five datasets from previous years and on two new datasets.

Astudillo et al. (2015) treat sentiment analysis as a regression problem which allows more fine-grained sentiment assessment. They model tweets using word2vec (Mikolov et al., 2013) or GloVe (Pennington et al., 2014) embeddings that are averaged or summed over the given tweet. A regression model is than trained on the resulting representations. This model achieved the fourth place.

The goal of **SemEval-2015 Task 11** was to perform fine-grained sentiment analysis over texts containing figurative language. Ghosh et al. (2015) have created a dataset of figurative tweets using Twitter4j API and a set of hashtag queries (*#sarcasm*, *#sarcastic*, *#irony* and words such as *figuratively*). The dataset has been annotated for sentiment analysis on a fine-grained 11-point scale (-5 to 5, including 0). Evaluation measures for this task were mean squared error (MSE) and cosine similarity, both with penalization for not giving scores for all tweets.

CLaC (Özdemir and Bergler, 2015b) presented the best result for SemEval-2015 Task 11 using decision tree regression M5P (Wang and Witten, 1997). They combined various lexicons with negation and modality scopes. They also participated in SemEval-2015 Task 10B achieving ninth place. Özdemir and Bergler (2015a) performed a comprehensive ablation study of features.

CPH (McGillion et al., 2015)[1] and PRHLT (Gupta and Gómez, 2015)[2] teams did not use lexicons and therefore provide comparable baselines to our models, which also do not use lexicons.

Sulis et al. (2016) analyse the corpus from Semeval-2015 Task 11 in terms of hashtags (*#irony*, *#sarcasm*, and *#not*) and confirm that messages using figurative language mostly express a negative sentiment. They experimented with

binary classification (separation) of tweets with these hashtags.

2.3 Neural Networks

A Convolutional Neural Network (CNN) architecture for sentence classification is proposed in (Kim, 2014). The network uses several convolutional kernel sizes simultaneously. It utilizes pre-trained word2vec embeddings. The approach was tested on several tasks including sentiment analysis. It proved state-of-the-art results on the Stanford sentiment treebank (Socher et al., 2013) both for binary and five-level sentiment classification. Best results are obtained using pre-trained embeddings for initialization of the embedding layer.

A neural network model for sarcasm detection is proposed in (Ghosh and Veale, 2016). The model is composed from a CNN followed by a long short term memory (LSTM) network. First a CNN is applied to the input. LSTM is then applied directly on the output of the convolutional layer. Output of the LSTM is fed to a fully connected layer and a softmax layer determines the class. F-score of 0.92 is achieved on their dataset containing 39k tweets.

Another approach is presented in (Zhang et al., 2016). A deep neural network is used for tweet sarcasm detection. The network has two components for local and contextual (history) tweets. The local one is a bi-directional gated recurrent unit that extracts dense real-valued output. The other component applies a pooling layer directly to the word embeddings for words in the contextual tweets and maps it to a fixed length vector. A hidden layer then combines these two components and is followed by a softmax layer. Embeddings are initialized using GloVe. Results are compared with manually created features.

CNNs are utilized for feature extraction in (Poria et al., 2016). Sentiment, emotion, and personality features are utilized for sarcasm detection. CNN models are separately trained on datasets corresponding to the three types of features. The three CNNs are then merged. The final classification is done either using a support vector machines classifier or another CNN which uses the merged features as a static channel and connects it to the penultimate layer before the softmax layer.

---

[1] They used ensemble methods and ridge regression.

[2] They used ensembles of extremely random trees with character n-grams.

Type	Train		Test		Trial	
	Mean Polarity	# Tweets	Mean Polarity	# Tweets	Mean Polarity	# Tweets
Sarcasm	-2.25	5000	-2.02	1200	-1.94	746
Irony	-1.70	1000	-1.87	800	-1.35	81
Metaphor	-1.49	2000	-0.77	800	-0.34	198
Other	–	–	-0.26	1200	–	–
Overall	-1.99	8000	-1.21	4000	-1.89	1025

Table 1: The tweet distributions and mean polarity in SemEval-2015 Task 11 datasets.

Type	Train		Test		Trial	
	Mean Polarity	# Tweets	Mean Polarity	# Tweets	Mean Polarity	# Tweets
Sarcasm	-2.25	4895	-2.05	1107	-2.00	612
Irony	-1.70	1424	-1.85	763	-1.98	23
Metaphor	-1.49	1681	-0.85	878	-0.67	91
Other	–	–	-0.33	1252	–	–
Overall	-1.99	8000	-1.21	4000	-1.83	726

Table 2: The tweet distributions and mean polarity in SemEval-2015 Task 11 datasets by hashtags.

3 Datasets

We use the dataset from SemEval-2015 Task 11 (Ghosh et al., 2015) for training and evaluation. Table 1 shows the mean polarity and the original estimated tweet distributions[3]. The category type labels refer to the authors' expectations of tweet category types in each segment of the dataset. To ensure the validity of the task, the authors added the category *other* to the test dataset.

Table 2 contains the same statistics for our collected datasets[4]. We separated data into the category types by using the harvesting criteria for the datasets' collection (e.g. the *#irony* hashtag)[5]. Table 3 shows the detailed sentiment polarity distributions. The training data were provided with rounded integer values and floating point values. However when we rounded the real-valued scores we got different counts for individual polarity values. This issue corresponds to the *Train* data columns *int* and *rounded*. In our experiments we use *rounded* values wherever it is possible.

To compensate for the missing *other* category in the training data of SemEval-2015 Task 11, we use the dataset from SemEval-2015 Task 10B (Rosenthal et al., 2015) as additional training data. We

were able to download approximately 75.7% of the training data and 78.6% of the test data (see Table 4).

For the SemEval-2015 Task 10B we evaluate on the test data and the sarcasm dataset[6] from the same task in SemEval-2014.

4 Convolutional Neural Network

The architecture of the proposed CNN is depicted in Figure 1. We use similar architecture to the one proposed by Lenc and Král (2017). The input layer of the network receives a sequence of word indices from a dictionary. The input vector must be of a fixed length. We solve this issue by padding the input sequence to the maximum tweet length denoted M. A special "PADDING" token is used for this purpose. The embedding layer maps the word indices to the real-valued embedding vectors of length L. The convolutional layer consists of N_C kernels containing $k \times 1$ units and uses rectified linear unit (ReLU) activation function. The convolutioanl layer is followed by a max-pooling layer and dropout for regularization. The max-pooling layer takes maxima from patches with dimensions $(M - k + 1) \times 1$. The output of the max-pooling layer is fed into a fully-connected layer. The fully connected layer is optionally concatenated with the additional `category-type-binary-input`

---

[3] In the original publication there were some typos, we show the recalculated statistics.

[4] Note that we were unable to download the whole Trial dataset due to perishability of tweets.

[5] Separating tweets into category types is a rule based approach.

[6] We were not able to download sufficient amount of tweets for the sarcasm dataset from SemEval-2015 Task 10B.

Value	Test	Train (int)	Train (rounded)	Trial orig.	Trial downl.
-5	4	0	6	6	4
-4	100	361	364	90	56
-3	737	2954	2971	403	282
-2	1541	2911	2934	255	180
-1	680	909	861	87	67
0	298	347	345	50	40
1	169	164	165	51	39
2	155	197	197	41	29
3	201	106	106	32	23
4	111	49	49	9	6
5	4	2	2	1	0
SUM	4000	8000	8000	1025	726

Table 3: The tweet sentiment polarity distributions in SemEval-2015 Task 11.

Corpus	Positive	Negative	Neutral	Total	Downloaded
Twitter2015-train	3,640	1,458	4,586	9,684	7,326 (76%)
Twitter2015-test	1,038	365	987	2,390	1,878 (79%)
Twitter2014-sarcasm	33	40	13	86	86 (100%)

Table 4: The tweet polarity distributions in SemEval-2015 Task 10B.

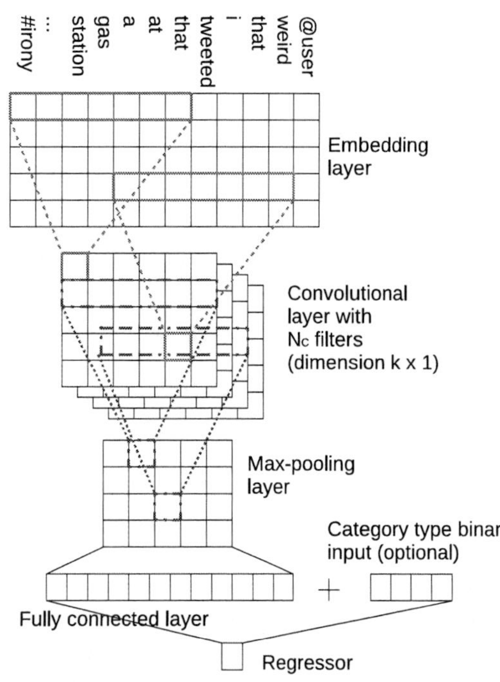

Figure 1: Neural network architecture.

layer that adds the information about hashtags used in the tweet. The output layer is connected to this layer and has just one neuron serving as a regressor.

In our experimental setup we use the embedding dimension $L = 300$ and $N_C = 40$ convolutional kernels with 5×1 units. The penultimate fully-connected layer contains 256 neurons connected with the optional `category-type-binary input` with 4 neurons. We train the network using adaptive moment estimation optimization algorithm (Kingma and Ba, 2014). Mean square error is used as loss function.

5 Experiments

We perform regression experiments on the 11-point scale (-5, .., 0, .., 5) for the SemEval-2015 task 11 and classification into positive, negative, and neutral classes for SemEval-2015 task 10B.

5.1 Preprocessing

The same preprocessing has been done for all datasets. We use UDPipe (Straka et al., 2016) with English Universal Dependencies 1.2 models for POS tagging and lemmatization. Tokenization has been done by TweetNLP tokenizer (Owoputi et al., 2013). Preliminary experiments have shown that lower-casing the data achieves slightly better results, thus all the experiments are performed with lower-cased data. We further replace all user mentions with the token "@USER" and all links with the token "$LINK".

5.2 Regression

Regression has been done using CNN (Section 4) and Weka 3.6.6 (Hall et al., 2009) with the M5P decision tree regression. We use the SemEval-2015 task 11 scorer to evaluate our results. Used features are unigrams with more than two occurrences. We map the additional training data from SemEval-2015 task 10B (-1 negative, 0 neutral, 1 positive) to the 11-point scale by using multiplier 4 (-4 negative, 0 neutral, 4 positive). This corresponds to our intuition that the positive and negative class should contain strong polarity values.

We incorporate the figurative language indicators into the sentiment analysis process and compare the results with and without the additional information about them. We use additional dataset to examine the results achieved with extra training data and to compensate for the missing *other* category in the training data.

First we use the preprocessed dataset. Then we remove the category types harvesting criteria (e.g. the #irony hashtag) from the entire dataset. Finally we add binary features indicating category types to the second experiment.

Table 5 shows the regression results, where system description "-nohash" indicates removing the category types and "-nohash + #" signifies the same plus binary features indicating category types.[7]

Removing the category type indicators deteriorates the results for most cases, except for the category *Metaphor* without additional training data, where the results are actually better. We believe this is due to the removal of words that results in less uncertainty for the model. A similar case is the CNN model for *Irony* without additional training data.

Restoration of the category types using binary features again improves the results in most cases, with the exception of the category *Metaphor*. This suggests that figurative language does matter and information about the given figurative language helps improve sentiment analysis.

Metaphor seems to be very hard to correctly as-

sign sentiment polarity. We believe this is caused by the datasets' composition, because the training dataset does not contain the category *Other*, thus the tweets that do not belong into the *Irony* or *Sarcasm* categories must belong to the *Metaphor* category. This claim presumes that the *Other* category is not present in the training dataset. We believe this is the reason why the *Metaphor* category is suffering in the "-nohash + #" setting. Moreover, tweets from training data in this category such as "@USER we're the proverbial frog getting slowly boiled in the pot of water." may not contain words that can be removed as figurative language indicators.

Additional training data directly improves results for *Metaphor* and *Other*, however the results for *Sarcasm* and *Irony* are worse. This effect is diminished in the "-nohash + #" setting. The results for the "-nohash" setting are consistently worse for all category types.

The best results are achieved with additional training data and basic setting with best results for the category types *Metaphor* and *Other*, which confirms the claim by Ghosh et al. (2015) i.e. there is a strong correlation between the overall performance and performance on the category *Metaphor* and *Other*.

Regardless of the categories, the *Overall* column in Table 5 is directly comparable to the SemEval-2015 Task 11 results. We can see that removing the figurative language indicators always deteriorates the results and their restoration by the binary figurative language features again improves the results for all cases. This supports our hypothesis that figurative language affects sentiment analysis.

5.3 Classification

The classification experiment in Table 6 was performed using the maximum entropy classifier (MaxEnt) from Brainy (Konkol, 2014). This experiment shows that even small in-domain (sarcasm) training data can help improve results. Used features are unigrams and bigrams with more than five occurrences. We train the maximum entropy classifier on the SemEval-2015 Task 10B training data (Twitter2013-train cleansed) and test on Twitter2015-test data and the Twitter2014-sarcasm data.

The F1 score for test data changes just slightly with additional training data (tweets containing

---

[7]Note that the category results are not directly comparable to the SemEval-2015 task 11 results.

Train Data	System Description	Sarcasm		Irony		Metaphor		Other		Overall	
		Cosine	MSE	Cosine	MSE	Cosine	MSE	Cosine	MSE	Cosine	MSE
T11	Best	**0.904**	**0.934**	**0.918**	**0.673**	**0.655**	**3.155**	**0.612**	**3.411**	**0.758**	**2.117**
T11	CLaC	0.892	1.023	0.904	0.779	**0.655**	**3.155**	0.584	**3.411**	**0.758**	**2.117**
T11	CPH	0.897	0.971	0.886	0.774	0.325	5.014	0.218	5.429	0.625	3.078
T11	PRHLT	0.891	1.028	0.901	0.784	0.167	5.446	0.218	4.888	0.623	3.023
T11	CNN	**0.908**	**0.893**	0.863	1.049	0.402	4.641	0.361	4.408	0.652	2.846
T11	-nohash	0.901	0.942	**0.886**	**0.897**	0.420	4.554	0.236	5.822	0.606	3.254
T11	-nohash + #	0.899	0.995	0.879	0.928	0.277	5.134	0.291	4.772	0.620	3.073
T10+T11	CNN	0.900	0.957	0.880	0.924	**0.620**	**3.401**	**0.633**	**2.966**	**0.755**	**2.116**
T10+T11	-nohash	0.851	1.523	0.860	1.163	0.547	3.876	0.518	3.786	0.691	2.679
T10+T11	-nohash + #	0.880	1.269	0.876	0.976	0.573	3.759	0.591	3.219	0.724	2.370
T11	M5P	0.908	0.888	**0.903**	**0.802**	0.291	5.040	0.277	4.588	0.636	2.941
T11	-nohash	0.910	0.874	0.876	0.962	0.378	4.921	0.190	4.917	0.625	3.045
T11	-nohash + #	0.909	0.893	0.891	0.845	0.357	4.825	0.274	4.599	0.640	2.907
T10+T11	M5P	0.834	1.720	0.863	1.140	**0.525**	**3.986**	**0.410**	**4.121**	**0.658**	**2.858**
T10+T11	-nohash	0.816	1.678	0.832	1.295	0.468	4.341	0.388	4.469	0.623	3.063
T10+T11	-nohash + #	**0.912**	**0.858**	0.877	0.958	0.397	4.639	0.381	4.549	0.654	2.862

Table 5: Results on the SemEval-2015 Task 11. Training data T11 and T10 denote the respective tasks' datasets used for training. System description "-nohash" indicates removing the category types harvesting criteria (e.g. the #irony hashtag), "-nohash + #" signifies the same plus binary features indicating category types.

sarcasm from SemEval-2015 Task 11 trial data[8]). The additional training data cause slight improvement on the test data and greatly improve the results on the sarcasm dataset. We would have achieved the seventh place out of 40 participants on the sarcasm dataset. Our simple solution is competitive on the sarcasm dataset with the best results achieved with lexicons, classifier ensembles, and various dictionaries.

Description	Test F1	Sarcasm F1
Best Result	0.648	0.591
CLaC	0.620	0.514
MaxEnt	0.527	0.457
MaxEnt + trial	0.533	0.547

Table 6: Results on the SemEval-2015 Task 10B.

6 Conclusion

In this article we have shown that figurative language can affect sentiment analysis. In our regression experiments removing the figurative language indicators deteriorates the results and their restoration by the binary figurative language features again improves the results on the whole dataset. The classification experiment shows that even small in-domain (sarcasm) training data can help improve results.

Our approach is simple without fine-tuned features and lexicons. We only use extra training data, which was allowed for this task. In the SemEval-2015 Task 11 we would have ranked first with CNN and additional training data in terms of MSE and second in terms of Cosine similarity. Our CNN model without additional training data would have achieved the fourth place in terms of MSE and the seventh place in terms of Cosine similarity.

In the future, we plan to create a dataset with explicitly marked categories for figurative language in both training and test data. Then we will repeat all experiments on this new dataset and compare the results.

Acknowledgments

This work was supported by the project LO1506 of the Czech Ministry of Education, Youth and Sports and by Grant No. SGS-2016-018 Data and Software Engineering for Advanced Applications.

---

[8]We mark tweets as positive for polarity ≥ 1 and negative for polarity ≤ -1.

References

Ramón Astudillo, Silvio Amir, Wang Ling, Bruno Martins, Mario J. Silva, and Isabel Trancoso. 2015. INESC-ID: Sentiment Analysis without Hand-Coded Features or Linguistic Resources using Embedding Subspaces. In *Proceedings of the 9th International Workshop on Semantic Evaluation (SemEval 2015)*. Association for Computational Linguistics, Denver, Colorado, pages 652–656. http://www.aclweb.org/anthology/S15-2109.

Aniruddha Ghosh, Guofu Li, Tony Veale, Paolo Rosso, Ekaterina Shutova, John Barnden, and Antonio Reyes. 2015. SemEval-2015 Task 11: Sentiment Analysis of Figurative Language in Twitter. In *Proceedings of the 9th International Workshop on Semantic Evaluation (SemEval 2015)*. Association for Computational Linguistics, Denver, Colorado, pages 470–478. http://www.aclweb.org/anthology/S15-2080.

Aniruddha Ghosh and Dr. Tony Veale. 2016. Fracking sarcasm using neural network. In *Proceedings of the 7th Workshop on Computational Approaches to Subjectivity, Sentiment and Social Media Analysis*. Association for Computational Linguistics, San Diego, California, pages 161–169. http://www.aclweb.org/anthology/W16-0425.

Parth Gupta and Jon Ander Gómez. 2015. PRHLT: Combination of Deep Autoencoders with Classification and Regression Techniques for SemEval-2015 Task 11. In *Proceedings of the 9th International Workshop on Semantic Evaluation (SemEval 2015)*. Association for Computational Linguistics, Denver, Colorado, pages 689–693. http://www.aclweb.org/anthology/S15-2116.

Mark Hall, Eibe Frank, Geoffrey Holmes, Bernhard Pfahringer, Peter Reutemann, and Ian H. Witten. 2009. The WEKA data mining software: An update. *SIGKDD Explorations* 11(1):10–18. http://www.sigkdd.org/explorations/issues/11-1-2009-07/p2V11n1.pdf.

Yoon Kim. 2014. Convolutional neural networks for sentence classification. In *Proceedings of the 2014 Conference on Empirical Methods in Natural Language Processing (EMNLP)*. Association for Computational Linguistics, Doha, Qatar, pages 1746–1751. http://www.aclweb.org/anthology/D14-1181.

Diederik Kingma and Jimmy Ba. 2014. Adam: A method for stochastic optimization. *arXiv preprint arXiv:1412.6980* .

Michal Konkol. 2014. Brainy: A machine learning library. In Leszek Rutkowski, Marcin Korytkowski, Rafal Scherer, Ryszard Tadeusiewicz, Lotfi Zadeh, and Jacek Zurada, editors, *Artificial Intelligence and Soft Computing*, Springer International Publishing, volume 8468 of *Lecture Notes in Computer Science*, pages 490–499.

Ladislav Lenc and Pavel Král. 2017. Deep neural networks for czech multi-label document classification. *CoRR* abs/1701.03849. http://arxiv.org/abs/1701.03849.

Diana Maynard and Mark Greenwood. 2014. Who cares about sarcastic tweets? investigating the impact of sarcasm on sentiment analysis. In Nicoletta Calzolari (Conference Chair), Khalid Choukri, Thierry Declerck, Hrafn Loftsson, Bente Maegaard, Joseph Mariani, Asuncion Moreno, Jan Odijk, and Stelios Piperidis, editors, *Proceedings of the Ninth International Conference on Language Resources and Evaluation (LREC'14)*. European Language Resources Association (ELRA), Reykjavik, Iceland.

Sarah McGillion, Héctor Martínez Alonso, and Barbara Plank. 2015. CPH: Sentiment analysis of Figurative Language on Twitter #easypeasy #not. In *Proceedings of the 9th International Workshop on Semantic Evaluation (SemEval 2015)*. Association for Computational Linguistics, Denver, Colorado, pages 699–703. http://www.aclweb.org/anthology/S15-2118.

Tomas Mikolov, Kai Chen, Greg Corrado, and Jeffrey Dean. 2013. Efficient estimation of word representations in vector space. *CoRR* abs/1301.3781. http://arxiv.org/abs/1301.3781.

Olutobi Owoputi, Brendan O'Connor, Chris Dyer, Kevin Gimpel, Nathan Schneider, and Noah A. Smith. 2013. Improved part-of-speech tagging for online conversational text with word clusters. In *Proceedings of the 2013 Conference of the North American Chapter of the Association for Computational Linguistics: Human Language Technologies*. Association for Computational Linguistics, Atlanta, Georgia, pages 380–390. http://www.aclweb.org/anthology/N13-1039.

Canberk Özdemir and Sabine Bergler. 2015a. A Comparative Study of Different Sentiment Lexica for Sentiment Analysis of Tweets. In *Proceedings of the International Conference Recent Advances in Natural Language Processing*. INCOMA Ltd. Shoumen, BULGARIA, Hissar, Bulgaria, pages 488–496. http://www.aclweb.org/anthology/R15-1064.

Canberk Özdemir and Sabine Bergler. 2015b. CLaC-SentiPipe: SemEval2015 Subtasks 10 B,E, and Task 11. In *Proceedings of the 9th International Workshop on Semantic Evaluation (SemEval 2015)*. Association for Computational Linguistics, Denver, Colorado, pages 479–485. http://www.aclweb.org/anthology/S15-2081.

Jeffrey Pennington, Richard Socher, and Christopher Manning. 2014. Glove: Global vectors for word representation. In *Proceedings of the 2014 Conference on Empirical Methods in Natural Language Processing (EMNLP)*. Association for Computational Linguistics, Doha, Qatar, pages 1532–1543.

Soujanya Poria, Erik Cambria, Devamanyu Hazarika, and Prateek Vij. 2016. A deeper look into sarcastic tweets using deep convolutional neural networks. In *Proceedings of COLING 2016, the 26th International Conference on Computational Linguistics: Technical Papers*. The COLING 2016 Organizing Committee, Osaka, Japan, pages 1601–1612. http://aclweb.org/anthology/C16-1151.

Tomáš Ptáček, Ivan Habernal, and Jun Hong. 2014. Sarcasm Detection on Czech and English Twitter. In *Proceedings of COLING 2014, the 25th International Conference on Computational Linguistics: Technical Papers*. Dublin City University and Association for Computational Linguistics, Dublin, Ireland, pages 213–223. http://www.aclweb.org/anthology/C14-1022.

Sara Rosenthal, Preslav Nakov, Svetlana Kiritchenko, Saif Mohammad, Alan Ritter, and Veselin Stoyanov. 2015. SemEval-2015 Task 10: Sentiment Analysis in Twitter. In *Proceedings of the 9th International Workshop on Semantic Evaluation (SemEval 2015)*. Association for Computational Linguistics, Denver, Colorado, pages 451–463. http://www.aclweb.org/anthology/S15-2078.

Richard Socher, Alex Perelygin, Jean Wu, Jason Chuang, D. Christopher Manning, Andrew Ng, and Christopher Potts. 2013. Recursive deep models for semantic compositionality over a sentiment treebank. In *Proceedings of the 2013 Conference on Empirical Methods in Natural Language Processing*. Association for Computational Linguistics, pages 1631–1642. http://aclweb.org/anthology/D13-1170.

Milan Straka, Jan Hajič, and Jana Straková. 2016. UDPipe: trainable pipeline for processing CoNLL-U files performing tokenization, morphological analysis, pos tagging and parsing. In *Proceedings of the Tenth International Conference on Language Resources and Evaluation (LREC'16)*. European Language Resources Association (ELRA), Paris, France.

Emilio Sulis, Delia Iraz Hernndez Faras, Paolo Rosso, Viviana Patti, and Giancarlo Ruffo. 2016. Figurative messages and affect in Twitter: Differences between #irony, #sarcasm and #not . *Knowledge-Based Systems* 108:132 – 143. New Avenues in Knowledge Bases for Natural Language Processing. https://doi.org/10.1016/j.knosys.2016.05.035.

Yong Wang and Ian H. Witten. 1997. Induction of model trees for predicting continuous classes. In *Poster papers of the 9th European Conference on Machine Learning*. Springer.

Meishan Zhang, Yue Zhang, and Guohong Fu. 2016. Tweet sarcasm detection using deep neural network. In *Proceedings of COLING 2016, the 26th International Conference on Computational Linguistics: Technical Papers*. The COLING 2016 Organizing Committee, Osaka, Japan, pages 2449–2460. http://aclweb.org/anthology/C16-1231.

Argument Labeling of Explicit Discourse Relations using LSTM Neural Networks

Sohail Hooda　　**Leila Kosseim**

Depart. of Computer Science and Software Engineering
Concordia University
1515 Ste-Catherine Street West
Montréal, Québec, Canada H3G 2W1
`{s_hooda, kosseim}@encs.concordia.ca`

Abstract

Argument labeling of explicit discourse relations is a challenging task. The state of the art systems achieve slightly above 55% F-measure but require hand-crafted features. In this paper, we propose a Long Short Term Memory (LSTM) based model for argument labeling. We experimented with multiple configurations of our model. Using the PDTB dataset, our best model achieved an F1 measure of 23.05% without any feature engineering. This is significantly higher than the 20.52% achieved by the state of the art RNN approach, but significantly lower than the feature based state of the art systems. On the other hand, because our approach learns only from the raw dataset, it is more widely applicable to multiple textual genres and languages.

1 Introduction

In well written texts, discourse relations are used to provide additional meaning to the underlying content by connecting two textual segments logically. This in turn facilitates the reader's understanding of the text. For example, in:

(1) *We would stop index arbitrage* <u>when</u> **the market is under stress**. [1]

two discourse segments, or arguments (`Arg1` in italics and `Arg2` in bold), are explicitly connected via the <u>connective</u> underlined and related by the discourse relation of CONDITION. Discourse relations can be made explicit through the use of discourse connectives such as *although*, *but*, *since*, *because*, etc. or can be left implicit, when no explicit cue phrase is used to signal the relation.

---

[1] This example is taken from the Penn Discourse Treebank (Prasad et al., 2007).

Discourse parsing involves two main tasks: (1) argument labeling, or identifying the boundaries and labeling `Arg1` and `Arg2`, and (2) relation labeling, or identifying the discourse relation that holds between the arguments. Because discourse parsing allows a deeper understanding of the communicative goal of text segments, it has been used in a variety of downstream NLP applications such as text summarization (Barzilay and Lee, 2004; Yoshida et al., 2014) and question-answering (Chai and Jin, 2004; Verberne et al., 2007).

As witnessed in the recent CoNLL shared tasks (Xue et al., 2015, 2016), full end-to-end discourse parsing is still a challenge. In particular, argument labeling is difficult as the exact boundaries of both `Arg1` and `Arg2` must be identified. The state-of-the-art system (Wang and Lan, 2016) achieves an F-measure of only 55.11% and thus leaves much room for improvement. Most work in this domain make use of a variety of hand-crafted features that do not handle long-distance dependencies well. However, the great majority of discourse arguments are not adjacent to one another and long distance features are important for this task.

In this paper, we investigate the use of recurrent neural networks for discourse labeling. Specifically, we investigate the use of Long Short Term Memory (LSTMs) to better handle long term dependencies and automatically extract and embed the features without prior input. We show that a widely applicable model can be produced by learning from the input data alone, and learning the features directly. This allows more generalized applications of our model across multiple text genres as well as languages. We also show that the approach does not suffer from long distance dependencies and achieves stable results regardless of the distance between `Arg1` and `Arg2`. To our knowledge, this is the first attempt at argument

Proceedings of Recent Advances in Natural Language Processing, pages 309–315,
Varna, Bulgaria, Sep 4–6 2017.

labelling using Deep Learning architectures that uses no hand-crafted features and achieves good results in contrast to the existing systems which rely on hand-crafted features during the learning process of the model.

2 Related Work

Due to the CoNLL 2015 and 2016 shared tasks (Xue et al., 2015, 2016), much recent work has addressed the problem of discourse parsing. However, much work is still needed in order to reach the human performance of 82.8% reported by (Miltsakaki et al., 2004). Discourse parsing consists of both: (1) argument labeling and (2) relation labeling (e.g. (Lin et al., 2014; Laali et al., 2015; Kong et al., 2014; Xue et al., 2015, 2016)). The approaches used for argument labeling at CoNLL 2015 (e.g. (Laali et al., 2015; Son et al., 2015; Zhou, 2015) largely consisted of standard supervised machine learning techniques such as Support Vector Machines (SVMs), Conditional Random Fields, Naive Bayes and Maximum Entropy (MaxEnt) and viewed the problem as a sequence labeling task. These models used syntactic positional and lexical features (such as the first word after the discourse connective) to learn to identify discourse arguments. These traditional methods achieved F-scores in the order of 45-55%. In 2016, several Convolutional Neural Networks (CNNs) and Recurrent Neural Networks (RNNs) were introduced for relation labeling (Qin et al., 2016). However, for argument labeling, only (Wang et al., 2015) used RNNs with word embeddings as input which were learned specifically from the training corpus and combined these with hand engineered features based on part of speech tags as well as other linguistic information. The group also used a classifier to determine whether a discourse relation spanned over more than one sentence and based on its output used separate classifiers for same-sentence and multiple-sentence relations. However their F1 score of 20.52% was still significantly below the F1 scores of traditional methods. While applying hand engineered features in a machine learning model does provide good results, it however, forces the model to be specific to the dataset that it is applied to. As a result, the model is unable to perform well with other datasets where either the content of the dataset differs or the language (Prasad et al., 2011). In contrast, if a ma-

chine learning model is configured to learn features solely on the training dataset, it would be able to generalize over larger datasets of different domain with relative ease.

3 Motivation

A major problem in argument labeling is that arguments may be dependent on long distance features. For example, in:

(2) *These are all market excesses* (putting aside the artificial boosts that the tax code gives to debt over equity), <u>and</u> **what we've seen is the market reining them in**.

`Arg1` and `Arg2` are separated by 14 words[2]. These words, known as *attribution*, are a challenge for standard features. For example, features from (Wang et al., 2015) such as "1st Previous Word of Connective", "2nd Previous Word of Connective", "1st Previous POS of Connective " or "2nd Previous POS of Connective", do not handle non-adjacent arguments well. Table 1 shows the number of instances in the PDTB dataset (Prasad et al., 2007) used at CoNLL 2015 and 2016 that do not have consecutive arguments. As Table 1 shows, 78% of `Arg1` and `Arg2` are not located consecutively and 24% are separated by at least 5 words. Standard machine learning techniques have much difficulty to account for these and a standard RNN approach (as used by (Wang et al., 2015)) also suffers from long distance dependencies between `Arg1` and `Arg2` due to the problem of vanishing/exploding gradients (Hochreiter et al., 2001). When attempting to incorporate information between words in arguments that are non-consecutive, as the distance between argument increases, the information collected either converges to zero or to infinity resulting in over- or under-estimating the learning of the neural network. On the other hand, LSTMs can control this behaviour and have been shown to model long distance dependencies much better (Hochreiter and Schmidhuber, 1997). For this reason, we experimented with such an approach.

4 Experiment

4.1 Corpus

To train and validate our LSTM approach, we used the Penn Discourse Treebank Corpus (PDTB) (Prasad et al., 2007). The PDTB has become

---

[2]The connective acts as a marker for the start of `Arg2`, and therefore it is not included in this calculation.

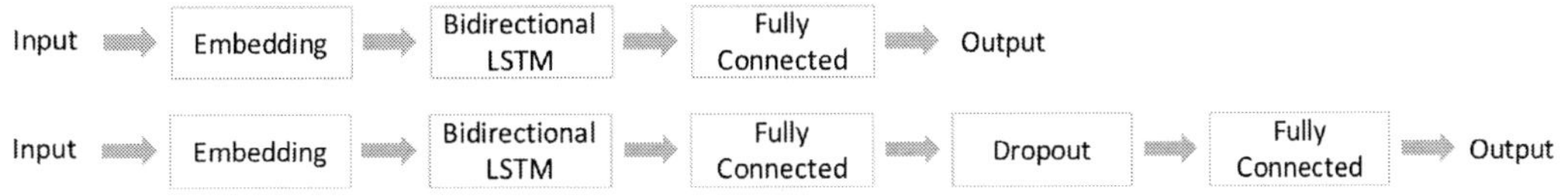

Figure 1: Architecture of model m1 (top) and model m2 (bottom)

Table 1: Statistics on the distance (in number of word tokens) between Arg1 and Arg2 in the explicit relations in the training and test set of the PDTB Dataset (Prasad et al., 2008)

Distance	Number of instances	Percentage
0	3,554	22.29%
1	8,582	53.82%
2-10	1,743	10.93%
>10	2,066	12.96%
Total	**15,945**	**100.00%**

Table 2: Number of instances in the PDTB Dataset

Dataset	Explicit	Non-Explicit	Total
Training	15,246	17,289	32,535
Testing	699	737	1,436
Total	**15,945**	**18,026**	**33,971**

the standard dataset in discourse parsing, thanks, in part, to the CoNLL shared tasks (Xue et al., 2015, 2016). Using this corpus allowed us to compare our work with the state of the art systems. The PDTB contains both explicit relations (marked with discourse connectives such as *because* or *but*) as well as non-explicit relations. Table 2 shows statistics of the dataset.

Since we focused on explicit relations only, the dataset was first cleaned by removing all non-explicit relations. As is standard in the field, we used sections 2-21 of the PDTB for training and section 22 was used for testing. Thus, about 15,246 instances such as example (1) in Section 1 were used for the training process and 699 were used for testing.

4.2 Network Architecture

For our experiments, we used a neural network composed of Long Short-Term Memory (LSTM) cells (Hochreiter and Schmidhuber, 1997). An LSTM is a specialized form of a Recurrent Neural Network (RNN) where a neuron is replaced with a memory cell. The memory cell is able to

learn and hold information to take into account long term dependencies, thus allowing to overcome the problem of vanishing and exploding gradients with RNNs (Hochreiter et al., 2001).

In order to learn the position of Arg1 and Arg2 and the length of these segments from the data only, we experimented with two main architectures. The first architecture shown in Figure 1 (top) is composed of an embedding layer that feeds directly into a Bidirectional LSTM layer. The Bidirectional LSTM layer is composed of 100 LSTM cells (for each direction) and the initialization is performed via the Glorot Uniform technique (Glorot and Bengio, 2010). The Bidirectional LSTM outputs are then fed into a fully connected layer which outputs the probability of 4 possible labels: Arg1, Arg2, connective or none for each input word. In the second architecture, shown in Figure 1 (bottom), we added a dropout layer as well as a fully connected layer at the end of the first model. This is shown in Figure 1. We tested our architectures with different dimensions of word embeddings and decided to use a value of 300 as it resulted in a higher accuracy with the training set (see Section 4.3). Thus, this created the 2 models below:

1. m1: Bidirectional LSTM layer + vectors of 300 words

2. m2: Bidirectional LSTM layers + Dense + Dropout + Dense + vectors of 300 words

Using both models, we also experimented with randomly generated embeddings as well as precomputed word embeddings from (Pennington et al., 2014) (see Section 4.3). All models were learned over 50 epochs. The cost function was minimized via the Adam Optimizer (Kingma and Ba, 2015), a memory efficient stochastic optimizer that relies on first order differentials only and calculates updates via the first and second order moments of the gradients thereby resulting in a linear update process. The cost was minimized over the

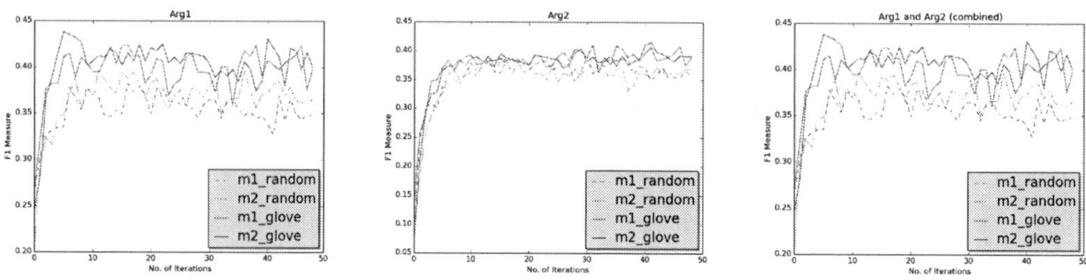

Figure 2: F1 score on the test set as a function of the number of iterations on the training set for `Arg1` (top), `Arg2` (middle) and `Arg1+Arg2` (bottom)

We would have to wait <u>until</u> **we have collected on those assets**
[1,   2,   3,   4, 5,   6,   1, 7,   8,   9, 10,   11,   0, 0,..., 0]

Figure 3: Example with words in a training instance labelled with the corresponding numeric value

mean of the labels for an entire mini batch provided in a single iteration.

4.3 Data Preparation

To provide as input to the neural networks, the training instances were converted into a numeric matrix structure. Since word embeddings are updated dynamically, we used pre-computed `GloVe` embeddings (Global Vectors for Word Representation) (Pennington et al., 2014) in one set of experiments and random values in another set. This was done by creating a dictionary of words and assigning each word to a random numeric value. As shown in Figure 3, a "zero word" was added to the vocabulary as a placeholder to pad sentences to an equal length. This length was set to 1,170 words, which is the size of the longest discourse segment containing both `Arg1` and `Arg2` segments in the PDTB training dataset. Thus the input data was a 2 dimensional matrix of a fixed size of 300 by 1,170. The use of fixed size vectors was not a necessary requirement for the network, but it was mechanically easier to have consistency within the dataset. The label vectors were also correspondingly padded with the `none` class. This allowed the network to learn the end of the `Arg1+Arg2` sequence.

5 Results and Analysis

To evaluate our approach, we used the official CoNLL scoring module[3] and modified it to calculate the performance for explicit relations only. Specifically, the scoring module provides the scores for the exact match for `Arg1` only, `Arg2` only and `Arg1+Arg2`, for every instance in the test set.

For both models, the performance was evaluated at every epoch for a total of 50 evaluation points. Figure 2 shows the F1 scores of the models for `Arg1` only, `Arg2` only and `Arg1+Arg2`. As the graphs show, after about 10 epochs all models seem to stabilize and learn at a much slower rate hence reaching a saturation point.

Table 3 shows the performance of our approaches compared to the state of the art systems. As the table shows, hand-engineered approaches still out perform our LSTM methods with F-measures between 55% to 46% for both `Arg1+Arg2`. However, compared to (Wang et al., 2015), both `m1` and `m2` outperform their RNN approach which did incorporate some hand-engineered features. It is also worthwhile to note that pre-computed embeddings result in slightly higher F1 measures for `Arg1+Arg2` than the random embeddings (25.75% versus 23.75% for `m2` and 24.89% versus 22.75% for `m2`) . This is most likely because of the sparsity of the words used

---

[3] available at https://github.com/attapol/conll16st

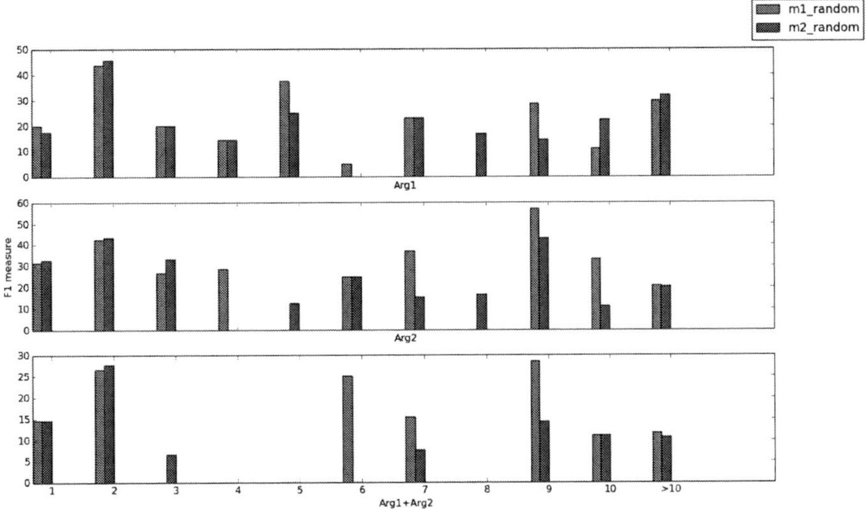

Figure 4: Plot of the distance-based F1 scores for Arg1 (top), Arg2 (middle) and Arg1+Arg2 (bottom)

in the dataset. Since not all words are equally weighted, the system is unable to learn the relationship of those words in a given argument directly from the dataset. Therefore, having precomputed embeddings assist in optimizing the learning process for those words.

Because `Arg2` is structurally bound to the connective, in the case of explicit relations, identifying the connective gives strong evidence to locate `Arg2`. On the other hand, `Arg1` is much harder to identify as it can be located in various positions relative to `Arg2`. In the case of our LSTM based approach, it is interesting to note that while the F1 scores of `Arg1` and `Arg2` independently are quite lower than the state of the art, this difference diminishes drastically for the combined `Arg1+Arg2` F1 scores. This is because the neural network optimizes over an entire instance and hence tries to maximize the score for both arguments combined as opposed to independently optimizing `Arg1` and `Arg2` labeling.

To verify how our LSTM based approach handled long term dependencies, we separated the test dataset by distance and computed a distance-based F1 score. Recall from Section 2 that the distance is measured by the number of words between the closest words of `Arg1` and `Arg2` excluding the connective. Thus we count from the end of `Arg1` to the start of `Arg2` or the connective whichever comes first when `Arg1` precedes `Arg2` and from the end of `Arg2` or the connective whichever

comes last to the start of `Arg1` when `Arg2` precedes `Arg1`. Figure 4 shows the F1 scores for both the models learned with randomly initialized embeddings, calculated at their last epoch, as a function of the distance between `Arg1` and `Arg2`. It is interesting to note that while model `m1_random` seems to perform better on the longer distance based relations (greater than 9), model `m2_random` still gets a better `Arg1+Arg2` accuracy score. Moreover, both models do not show any correlation in their F1 measure as the distance increases. This indicates that both models are unaffected by long and short distances between the arguments of a discourse relation.

6 Conclusion and Future Work

This paper has presented a novel approach for argument labeling based on LSTMs. To our knowledge, this is the first attempt at using Deep Learning for this task that achieves good results without any features in comparison to the existing systems which rely entirely or partially on hand-crafted features. The approach adds value to this domain by decoupling the feature specificity of the PDTB dataset with the problem at hand. Thus, by using LSTM networks, it is possible to generalize the accuracy over different dataset. However, further research is required to prove this hypothesis ¿¿. We experimented with two configurations of our model and showed that using the PDTB training set, our best model achieved 23.05% F1 mea-

Table 3: F1 scores of our LSTM models for explicit relations compared to the best (hand-crafted) approaches and to (Wang et al., 2015)

Model	Arg1+Arg2	Arg1	Arg2	Method
(Wang and Lan, 2016)	55.11%	62.01%	81.26%	Linear classification
(Schenk et al., 2016)	54.41%	61.97%	78.87%	CRF
(Qin et al., 2016)	53.44%	60.99%	79.94%	SVM
(Oepen et al., 2016)	51.37%	60.72%	75.83%	SVM
(Kong et al., 2016)	46.37%	52.89%	74.81%	MaxEnt
m2_GloVe	25.75%	42.06%	41.49%	Bidirectional LSTM
m1_GloVe	24.89%	42.35%	39.48%	Bidirectional LSTM
m2_random	23.75%	39.63%	37.34%	Bidirectional LSTM
m1_random	22.75%	36.62%	38.63%	Bidirectional LSTM
(Wang et al., 2015)	20.52%	28.55%	41.78%	RNN

sure without feature engineering. We have shown that our LSTM-based models deal well with the long term dependencies of explicit discourse relations, an important problem with standard machine learning techniques.

A number of improvements can be suggested over this approach. As shown in Table 3, at this point feature-engineered approaches still provide a better performance than our LSTM-based method especially for labeling Arg2. To address this, it would be interesting to explore the use of a cascading network where a first network identifies the relative location of Arg1 with respect to Arg2 then forwards the discourse to a specialized network capable of learning only that specific type of location. In order to see how much weight is assigned to the discourse connective by the model, one could also test this approach on the implicit relations of the PDTB dataset. Finally, applying this approach on the Chinese Discourse Tree Dataset (Zhou and Xue, 2015) would also be helpful in providing stronger evidence that the features that are learned are independent of the context and language.

References

Regina Barzilay and Lillian Lee. 2004. Catching the drift: Probabilistic content models, with applications to generation and summarization. *Human Language Technology Conference of the North American Chapter of the Association for Computational Linguistics* pages 113–120.

Joyce Y Chai and Rong Jin. 2004. Discourse structure for context question answering. In *Proceedings of the Workshop on Pragmatics of Question Answering at HLT-NAACL.* pages 23–30.

Xavier Glorot and Yoshua Bengio. 2010. Understanding the difficulty of training deep feedforward neural networks. In *Proceedings of the Thirteenth International Conference on Artificial Intelligence and Statistics.* pages 249–256.

Sepp Hochreiter, Yoshua Bengio, Paolo Frasconi, and Jürgen Schmidhuber. 2001. Gradient flow in recurrent nets: the difficulty of learning long-term dependencies. *A field guide to dynamical recurrent neural networks* pages 237–244.

Sepp Hochreiter and Jürgen Schmidhuber. 1997. Long short-term memory. *Neural Computation* 9(8):1735–1780.

Diederik Kingma and Jimmy Ba. 2015. Adam: A method for stochastic optimization. In *Proceedings of ICLR-2015*. San Diego, CA, USA.

Fang Kong, Sheng Li, Junhui Li, Muhua Zhu, and Guodong Zhou. 2016. SoNLP-DP System for ConLL-2016 English Shallow Discourse Parsing. In (Xue et al., 2016), pages 65–69.

Fang Kong, Hwee Tou Ng, and Guodong Zhou. 2014. A Constituent-Based Approach to Argument Labeling with Joint Inference in Discourse Parsing. In *Proceedings of EMNLP-2014*. Doha, Qatar, pages 68–77.

Majid Laali, Elnaz Davoodi, and Leila Kosseim. 2015. The CLaC Discourse Parser at CoNLL-2015. In (Xue et al., 2015), pages 56–60.

Ziheng Lin, Hwee Tou Ng, and Min-Yen Kan. 2014. A PDTB-styled end-to-end discourse parser. *Natural Language Engineering* 20(02):151–184.

Eleni Miltsakaki, Rashmi Prasad, Aravind Joshi, and Bonnie Webber. 2004. Annotating discourse connectives and their arguments. In *Proceedings of the HLT/NAACL Workshop on Frontiers in Corpus Annotation*. Boston, MA, USA, pages 9–16.

Stephan Oepen, Jonathon Read, Tatjana Scheffler, Uladzimir Sidarenka, Manfed Stede, Erik Velldal, and Lilja Øvrelid. 2016. OPT: OsloPotsdamTeesside Pipelining Rules, Rankers, and Classifier Ensembles for Shallow Discourse Parsing. In (Xue et al., 2016), pages 20–26.

Jeffrey Pennington, Richard Socher, and Christopher D Manning. 2014. Glove: Global vectors for word representation. In *EMNLP*. volume 14, pages 1532–1543.

Rashmi Prasad, Nikhil Dinesh, Alan Lee, Eleni Miltsakaki, Livio Robaldo, Aravind Joshi, and Bonnie Webber. 2008. The Penn Discourse TreeBank 2.0. In *Proceedings of LREC-2008*. Marrakech, Morocco.

Rashmi Prasad, Susan McRoy, Nadya Frid, Aravind Joshi, and Hong Yu. 2011. The biomedical discourse relation bank. *BMC bioinformatics* 12(1):188.

Rashmi Prasad, Eleni Miltsakaki, Nikhil Dinesh, Alan Lee, Aravind Joshi, Livio Robaldo, and Bonnie L Webber. 2007. The Penn Discourse Treebank 2.0 Annotation manual. https://www.seas.upenn.edu/ pdtb/PDTBAPI/pdtb-annotation-manual.pdf.

Lianhui Qin, Zhisong Zhang, and Hai Zhao. 2016. Shallow discourse parsing using convolutional neural network. In (Xue et al., 2016), pages 70–77.

Niko Schenk, Christian Chiarcos, Kathrin Donandt, Samuel Rönnqvist, Evgeny A Stepanov, and Giuseppe Riccardi. 2016. Do We Really Need All Those Rich Linguistic Features? A Neural Network-Based Approach to Implicit Sense Labeling. In (Xue et al., 2016), pages 41–49.

Nguyen Truong Son, Ho Bao Quoc, and Nguyen Le Minh. 2015. Jaist: A two-phase machine learning approach for identifying discourse relations in newswire texts. In (Xue et al., 2015), pages 66–70.

Suzan Verberne, Lou Boves, Nelleke Oostdijk, and Peter-Arno Coppen. 2007. Evaluating discourse-based answer extraction for why-question answering. In *Proceedings of the ACM SIGIR*. Amsterdam, Netherlands, pages 735–736.

Jianxiang Wang and Man Lan. 2016. Two End-to-End Shallow Discourse Parsers for English and Chinese in CoNLL-2016 Shared Task. In (Xue et al., 2016), pages 33–40.

Longyue Wang, Chris Hokamp, Tsuyoshi Okita, Xiaojun Zhang, and Qun Liu. 2015. The DCU discourse parser for connective, argument identification and explicit sense classification. In (Xue et al., 2015), pages 89–94.

Nianwen Xue, Hwee Tou Ng, Sameer Pradhan, Rashmi Prasad, Christopher Bryant, and Attapol Rutherford, editors. 2015. *The CoNLL-2015 shared task on shallow discourse parsing*. Beijing, China.

Nianwen Xue, Hwee Tou Ng, Sameer Pradhan, Attapol Rutherford, Bonnie Webber, Chuan Wang, and Hongmin Wang, editors. 2016. *The CoNLL-2016 Shared Task on Shallow Discourse Parsing*. Berlin, Germany.

Yasuhisa Yoshida, Jun Suzuki, Tsutomu Hirao, and Masaaki Nagata. 2014. Dependency-based discourse parser for single-document summarization. In *EMNLP*. Doha, Qatar, pages 1834–1839.

Fang Kong Sheng Li Guodong Zhou. 2015. The SoNLP-DP system in the CoNLL-2015 shared task. In (Xue et al., 2015), pages 32–36.

Yuping Zhou and Nianwen Xue. 2015. The Chinese Discourse TreeBank: A Chinese corpus annotated with discourse relations. *Language Resources and Evaluation* 49(2):397–431.

Non-Deterministic Segmentation for Chinese Lattice Parsing

Hai Hu
Indiana University
huhai@indiana.edu

Daniel Dakota
Indiana University
ddakota@indiana.edu

Sandra Kübler
Indiana University
skuebler@indiana.edu

Abstract

Parsing Chinese critically depends on correct word segmentation for the parser since incorrect segmentation inevitably causes incorrect parses. We investigate a pipeline approach to segmentation and parsing using word lattices as parser input. We compare CRF-based and lexicon-based approaches to word segmentation. Our results show that the lattice parser is capable of selecting the correction segmentation from thousands of options, thus drastically reducing the number of unparsed sentence. Lexicon-based parsing models have a better coverage than the CRF-based approach, but the many options are more difficult to handle. We reach our best result by using a lexicon from the n-best CRF analyses, combined with highly probable words.

1 Introduction

Many Asian languages, such as Chinese, Korean, and Burmese, do not mark word boundaries with spaces, in contrast to Indo-European languages such as English. Traditionally, parsing is preceded by word segmentation in a pipeline model. That is, the segmenter provides the most likely segmentation, which is subsequently passed to the parser, resulting in a propagation of errors from any initial incorrect segmentation. Previous work has demonstrated that performing segmentation and POS tagging jointly improves results (Ng and Low, 2004; Zhang and Clark, 2008; Forst and Fang, 2009), but results in a standard pipeline approach to segmentation and POS tagging have been mixed at best (Jiang et al., 2009).

The interaction between segmentation and unlexicalized constituent parsing for Chinese has not been fully explored. Whereas segmentation is performed on a character level, unlexicalized parsing is based on POS tags. Consequently, there can be a disconnect between the most likely character segmentation and the optimal POS sequence to fit the grammar. If the parser is given multiple segmentations from which to select, it is unclear how consistently and accurately it is able to select the correct segmentation combined with the correct POS sequence. One inherent difficulty is that the most probable segmentation may not actually be the optimal segmentation for the parser, particularly for an unlexicalized parser, since segmentation is done on the character level. Different segmentations may result in completely different sequences of POS tags, resulting in an alteration of the syntactic structure of the sentence that the parser must fit within its grammar.

We investigate a pipeline model where the segmenter provides n-best solutions, and the constituent parser decides on the best segmentation for POS tagging and parsing. I.e., we approach Chinese parsing as similar to morphologically rich languages (MRLs) of Hebrew and Arabic, in which lattice inputs have been used to provide the parser with options from which it chooses the best possible segmentation and morphological analysis. All experiments are based on the Penn Chinese Treebank CTB5 (Xue et al., 2005).

The paper is structured as follows: We present an overview of related work in sec. 2 and a description of the non-deterministic segmenters in sec. 3. We discuss the experimental setup and results plus error analysis in sec. 4 and 5.

2 Related Work

2.1 Word Segmentation

Various approaches to word segmentation have been developed, often during the ACL-SIGHAN

Proceedings of Recent Advances in Natural Language Processing, pages 316–324,
Varna, Bulgaria, Sep 4–6 2017.

segmentation bake-offs (e.g. Sproat and Emerson, 2003; Emerson, 2005)[1]. In the bake-offs, variants of the maximum-length matching algorithm have traditionally been used to establish a baseline for segmentation (Levow, 2006), but more recent approaches have implemented various machine learning algorithms, treating word segmentation as a character sequence labeling task, where each character is given a tag that indicates the position of the character in a word (Xue, 2003; Tseng et al., 2005; Zhao and Kit, 2008, among others). Xue (2003) first employed a Maximum Entropy model to perform character labeling, with character unigrams and bigrams and previous labels as features. Later models also used other machine learning tools, most commonly Conditional Random Field (CRF) (e.g. Zhao et al., 2010; Qian and Liu, 2012). Common features include character types (Zhao et al., 2010), morphological information (Tseng et al., 2005), etc. Word-based F-measures for segmentation of state of the art systems are very high, ranging from 95% to 98%.

2.2 Chinese Parsing

Statistical parsing of Chinese has been approached in many different ways, yielding numerous systems, some Chinese specific. The highest achieved results, to our knowledge, on the Chinese treebank using standard PARSEVAL metrics is 86.6_F achieved by (Wang and Xue, 2014) using a joint POS tagging transition-based constituency parser that incorporates non-local and semi-supervised features using gold segmentation.

Qian and Liu (2012) use a joint system that is an extension of the CYK algorithm achieving 84.13_F using gold segmentation of words, 81.76_F in a pipeline, and 82.85_F for their joint system that includes: segmentation, POS tagging, and parsing. Brackets were only counted as correct if boundaries, label, and segmentation were correct, but this is not directly comparable to standard PARSEVAL metrics, but akin to CParseval (Harper and Huang, 2011).

Successful parsing in a pipeline hinges on the accuracy of the predicted segmentation. Unless the segmentation accuracy is almost 100% (99.9% as suggested by Sun (1999)), passing several segmentations to a downstream application may help resolve ambiguities. Forst and Fang (2009) showed that by applying non-deterministic

segmentation and POS tagging, sentence level segmentation accuracy increases from 47.15% to 65.06%, and passing multiple analyses to an LFG parser increased the accuracy of parseable sentences.

Although Chinese lacks substantial morphology, the problem of identifying words is similar to the need to segment words into syntactic units in morphologically rich languages, which has improved parser performance (Tsarfaty, 2006). Lattice parsing (Chappelier et al., 1999) has been utilized in PCFG parsing; it allows the parser to determine the optimal path through all possible analyses to produce a tree (Goldberg and Tsarfaty, 2008). This technique has been applied to both Hebrew (Cohen and Smith, 2007) and Arabic (Green and Manning, 2010) with significant improvements noted for Hebrew, as well as to recover empty categories for both English and Chinese (Cai et al., 2011).

Directly related work by Wang et al. (2013) used the `blatt` parser, a modified PCFG-LA parser that allows a lattice input, in a pipeline approach. They concluded that non-weighted lattices are not effective for parsing Chinese. They developed a completely lattice-based system that uses a lattice to pass information between analyses (e.g. segmentation to POS tagging), improving results over standard pipeline approaches in all steps.

3 Non-Deterministic Segmentation

3.1 CRF Segmentation

We train a CRF model (crf++[2]) due to its ability to provide the n-best segmentations. We use a standard feature template (see Table 1). Character types are numbers, time (year, month, day, etc.), English letters, punctuation, and other Chinese characters. We use the 6-tag IOB scheme that performed best in a comparison by Zhao et al. (2010): S denotes a single-character word, B and E denote characters at the beginning and end of a multi-character word respectively. B2, B3 and M denote characters in the middle of a multi-character word. For example, the characters in 进出口|总值|达|一千零九十八点二亿|美元 (Eng.: The value of import and export reaches 109.82 billion USD.) are assigned the labels 'B B1 E|B E|S|B B1 B2 M M M M M E'.

[1] http://sighan.cs.uchicago.edu/

[2] http://taku910.github.io/crfpp/

	Features		
Unigram	C_{-1}	C_0	C_{+1}
Bigram	$C_{-1}\,C_0$	$C_0\,C_{+1}$	$C_{-1}\,C_{+1}$
Char. type	type(C_{-1})	type(C_0)	type(C_{+1})

Table 1: CRF Features (C_{-1}: previous character, C_0: current character, C_{+1}: next character).

3.2 Lexicon-Based Segmentation

The second approach to segmentation is lexicon-based, using a Chinese word lexicon. Segmentation is approached as a search that finds all character sequences that occur in the dictionary, returning an unweighted lattice of all possible segmentations. We experiment with different types of input for the parser:

Upper bound: In order to investigate the feasibility of having the parser choose the correct segmentation from the lattice, we first use the lexicon extracted from the *test set*. This ensures full coverage with a minimal lexicon size, but is unrealistic.

Upper bound+Train: In this setting, we add the words from the training set.

Train$n$: In a more realistic setting, we extract the lexicon from the training set. Thus, the lexicon is incomplete with regard to the test set. We use heuristics to handle unknown words: For every unknown segment in a test sentence, we add the segment and a larger sequence of n (1–6) characters to the left and right to the lexicon. The maximal length of the context corresponds to the longest word in the training data. For example, if the sentence is 知识信息网络通讯技术和脱氧核糖核酸生物技术(Eng.: information and web technology and DNA biological technology) and the character 氧 is not present in the lexicon, we add 氧, 脱氧, 氧核, 和脱氧, 脱氧核 and 氧核糖 to the lexicon when $n = 3$. Here the unknown word 脱氧核糖核酸 (DNA) is of length 6, thus we cover this unknown word only when $n = 6$.

Train$n$+Names: Here, we add all person and geographic names, as well as number and time related words from the test data, as gazetteers are fairly easy to gather (c.f. e.g. Yu et al., 2008).

CRFn: Here we create a unique lexicon for each sentence by extracting all words from the n-best CRF analyses for that sentence ($1 < n < 5$).

We also experiment with extracting a lexicon from the CRF analyses for *all* test sentences:

CRF$n$lex: We extract these lexicons from the n-best analyses of the CRF segmenter ($1 < n < 5$).

CRF$n$lex+Train: We add all the words from the training data to CRF$n$lex to increase coverage.

CRF1lex+HiProb: We take advantage of the probability for any segmentation given by the CRF segmenter. Recall that the CRF segmenter provides the sentence probability for each of the n-best options. If the probability of a segmentation is greater than a threshold, we add all the words in that segmentation to the lexicon. By doing so, we add a range of word hypotheses that the CRF segmenter considers probable even though they may not appear in the best segmentation. Non-exhaustive experiments show that the probability threshold 0.30 yields a balance between adding new words to gain coverage and the parser's ability to select the correct segmentation. This setting results in 1901 words in the lexicon, and a reduction of unknown words.

CRF1lex+HiProb+Names+Single: We add names, numbers, times, and all single characters to the lexicon since some single-character words are not captured by the above lexicon. For long sentences (>50 segments) whose best segmentation has a probability <0.35, we extract words from all 5 segmentations. Note that we create individual lexicons for such low probability analyses, by adding a few words that are relevant for this specific sentence to the standard lexicon.

CRF1lex+HiProb+Names+Single+PKU:
Since we still have unknown words, we additionally use the Peking University data (PKU) from the 2nd International Bakeoff in Chinese Word Segmentation (Emerson, 2005), which covers a broader lexicon and thus may increase coverage, but also increases the size of the lexicon, thus making the parser's task more difficult.

We add all words that only appear in the PKU data. Since the segmentation decisions differ between the PKU data and the CTB5, we use a simple filtering method to include only the words for which there is no annotation conflict. For example, the sequence 事实上(事实=fact, 上=grammatical particle, Eng.: in fact) occurs in the CRF analyses only as 事实|上, but in the test data, the only occurrence is segmented as one word, thus adding it from the PKU data reduces the number of unknown words.

System	F
Jiang et al. (2009)	97.58
Jiang et al. (2009) w/ adaptation	98.23
Qian and Liu (2012)	97.85
Zhang and Clark (2011)	97.78
Our CRF model	97.70

Table 2: CRF segmentation results for the 1-best setting.

n-best	# correct sent.	Coverage
1-best	258	74.14%
2-best	296	85.06%
3-best	306	87.93%
4-best	311	89.37%
5-best	318	91.38%

Table 3: Coverage of the CRF n-best analyses.

4 Experimental Setup

We extract the dictionaries and train the CRF model on the Penn Chinese Treebank (CTB5) (Xue et al., 2005), following the split of Qian and Liu (2012): sections 001–270 and 400–1151 for training, and sections 271-300 for testing. We evaluate segmentation using the official evaluation script from the 2nd International Bakeoff (Emerson, 2005). We report coverage and F-score. Coverage is defined as the percentage of sentences with the correct segmentation among the n-best solutions.

For parsing, CTB5 is preprocessed using standard procedures (Harper and Huang, 2011): Function labels are deleted, unary nodes are collapsed, and empty nodes are removed using the Berkeley Parser Analyser (Kummerfeld et al., 2013). We use the blatt parser (Goldberg and Elhadad, 2011), which is a reimplementation of the Berkeley parser (Petrov et al., 2006; Petrov and Klein, 2007), modified to allow lattice input. The parser uses a PCFG-LA (Matsuzaki et al., 2005; Petrov et al., 2006) iterative algorithm that splits each non-terminal category and determines if the split is beneficial. Splits deemed non-beneficial are then merged back together, and smoothing is performed over the non-terminals towards a common ancestor, calculating the EM after each sequence. We train four grammars using four different seeds (1–4) and report averages (unless otherwise noted), using the scorer from the 2013 SPMRL shared task (Seddah et al., 2013), a reimplementation of EVALB (Sekine and Collins, 1997) that allows for the penalization of unparsed sentences by scoring them as completely wrong.

5 Results

5.1 Segmentation Results

5.1.1 CRF Results

The results of our CRF segmenter are compared to other systems in table 2. Our results are similar to state-of-the-art systems, i.e., a CRF segmenter with simple features already works very well. However, table 3 shows that given an F-score of >97%, less than 75% of the test sentences are segmented completely correctly. As the CRF segmenter produces more segmentations, coverage increases to 91.38% given the 5-best analyses.

5.1.2 Dictionary Segmentation Results

Table 4 gives an overview of the coverage and lexicon size of the individual methods. The number of unknown words is the number of words from the gold segmentation of the test set that do not occur in the lexicon. Lexicon size refers to the number of words in the lexicon that occur in the test set. Both numbers give a more general view of the coverage of a lexicon. The training set based methods create much larger lexicons in comparison to the upper bound, but still have a low coverage of 67.53% even with the longest context (6). We reach 76.15% if we include names, etc. The CRF approach, which reaches a segmentation accuracy close to the state of the art (see Table 2), has a similarly low coverage of 74.14%. This shows that a high performance in segmentation does not directly translate into good parsing results. Interestingly, the lexicon extracted from the same 1-best CRF model performs better and reaches a coverage of 79.02%. If we use all 5 segmentations from the CRF to extract a lexicon, we reach a high coverage of 93.07%, at a lexicon size that is similar to the one extracted form the training data.

Combining the CRFn lexicons with the words from the training set gives a good coverage between 85.92% and 91.38%, but also increases the size of the lexicon considerably. Adding highly probable words from the CRF graph to CRF1lex improves coverage by about 8 points, but it does not reach the coverage of CRF5. Adding names and single segments to the lexicon increases coverage by >5.5% absolute. We reach the highest coverage of 94.83% by adding the PKU lexicon. Note that this lexicon only adds 200 words on average,

Lexicon	% coverage	# unk. words	Lex. size
Upper bound	100.00	0	1829
Upper bound+Train	100.00	0	2888
Train1	56.03	263	2755
Train2	58.62	242	2888
Train6	67.53	185	4142
Train1+Names	72.99	162	2785
Train2+Names	75.29	147	2825
Train6+Names	76.15	140	3216
CRF1	74.14	102	1872
CRF2	85.06	50	2164
CRF5	91.38	27	2872
CRF1lex	79.02	102	1872
CRF2lex	89.66	50	2164
CRF5lex	93.97	27	2872
CRF1lex+Train	85.92	57	2926
CRF2lex+Train	91.38	36	3094
CRF5lex+Train	94.83	22	3595
CRF1lex+HiProb	81.90	89	1901
CRF1lex+HiProb+Names+Single	87.64	50	2878
CRF1lex+HiProb+Names+Single+PKU	94.83	19	3028+

Table 4: Coverage of different segmentation methods.

	Wr. seg.	F	Rec.	Prec.
No Penalty				
Gold seg.	0	83.38	82.73	84.04
Upper bound	6.00	83.52	82.87	84.18
Upper+Train	41.25	84.81	84.23	85.39
With Penalty				
Upper bound	6.00	82.07	80.07	84.18
Upper+Train	41.25	75.02	66.90	85.39

Table 5: Initial parsing results

but decreases the number of unknown words by more than half.

5.2 Parsing Results

5.2.1 Initial Results

We establish an upper bound by using the gold segmentation of the *test sentences*, i.e., a deterministic input for the parser. We compare this to a setting using gold standard information, where we use the upper bound lexicon (based on gold segmentations of the test sentences), and a more realistic setting that extracts the lexicon from the combined training and test set. The results are shown in table 5. Note that the standard EVALB metric ignores sentences that have no parse or where the words in the parser output do not match the words in the gold standard. In our case, the latter translates into sentence where the parser did not

choose the correct segmentation. We also present an analysis where both unparsed sentences and incorrectly segmented sentences are counted as completely incorrect, which is overly harsh. We address this issue in section 5.2.2.

The correct segmentation results in an F-score of 83.38. If we present the parser with the upper bound lexicon, the F-score increases minimally to 83.52. This means that the parser is capable of selecting the correct segmentation from the lattice in most cases. The increase in F is due to six incorrectly segmented sentences per grammar/seed, which are consequently ignored in the parser evaluation. Penalizing the parser (lower half of the table) for incorrectly segmented sentences results in a lower F-score of 82.07. When we use a lexicon based the upper bound+train, we achieve results of 84.81 and 75.02 respectively. Note that neither score is very informative. However, we do note that the number of incorrectly segmented sentences increases dramatically when we use a more realistic lexicon. We can conclude that the creation of the lexicon has a considerable influence on parsing quality: We need to provide good coverage without overwhelming the parser with too many segmentation possibilities.

5.2.2 Corrected Evaluation

Here, we have a closer look at how evaluation results are affected by either ignoring incorrectly

	F	Rec.	Prec.
Upper bound	85.14	84.68	85.60
Upper+penalty	76.23	68.71	85.60
Corrected	83.89	83.36	84.42

Table 6: Corrected results (seed 4).

segmented sentences or counting them as completely incorrect. We manually "correct" incorrectly segmented sentences by replacing the wrong tokens by the correct ones and deleting all nodes that cover these tokens in the parses. Thus, we keep the tree that is not affected by the incorrect segmentation but remove the affected part of the tree. As a consequence, recall should suffer from the wrong segmentations while precision should not be affected. This correction gives us a better picture of how incorrect segmentation affects results. Since it requires manual corrections, the analysis is based on a seed of 4, which results in four incorrectly segmented sentences.

Table 6 shows results for individual experiments and settings. Penalizing the parser for an incorrect segment is overly harsh given that the F-Score drops roughly 9% absolute for only four incorrect sentences. The results on the corrected set show higher results overall, i.e., the syntactic analyses for those sentences are mostly correct.

5.2.3 Parsing based on Realistic Segmentation

We have shown that the parser is able to select the correct segmentation with a high level of accuracy if it is present. Given that the gold lexicon is not representative of realistic data, we determine experimentally whether the parser can still perform at a consistently high accuracy with lexicons created from more realistic data. Results are shown in table 7. In the first setting, where we extract the lexicon directly from the training data and use a heuristic to cover unknown words, the parser has difficulties determining the correct segmentation, as evidenced by the high number of incorrectly segmented sentences. Thus, while the parsing results on correctly segmented sentences (no penalty) are high, theF-scores with the penalty are below 50. Adding names and time expressions reduces the number of wrong segmentations and increases the penalty F-scores by about 10 points. Longer contexts do not seem to be useful.

The CRF results show lower numbers of wrong segmentations and higher F-scores under penalty

if we keep the number of lattices low. Creating a lexicon from the best CRF segmentation decreases the number of incorrectly segmented sentence to 82 and increases the F-score slightly. Using the n-best CRF analyses in any form is not useful. These analyses increase the number of wrong segmentations (to 191.75 for CRF5, to 205.25 for CRF5lex and CRF1lex+Train).

When we add the words from the training set to the CRF1 lexicon, we slightly increase the number of incorrectly segmented sentences, which decreased F-scores. Adding the highly probable words decreases the number of incorrectly segmented sentences to 74.50. Also adding names, times, and single characters to the lexicon decreases the number to 65.25, and adding the PKU lexicon reaches the lowest number of 55.25, along with the highest F-score with penalty: 70.69.

These results show clearly that simply increasing the coverage of our lexicon, and thus the input lattice of the parser, does not give us good segmentation and parsing performance. Using the 5-best CRF analyses, the lexicon based on those 5 analyses, and the combination with training words all result in good coverage, but provide unreliable information that does not allow the parser to choose the correct segmentation in many cases. However, adding words from highly likely analyses, and less reliable hypotheses only when necessary, gives the parser a good basis to make correct segmentation decisions. Adding the 200 words from the PKU lexicon helps in another 10 sentences. Thus, we can conclude that the parser is able to select correct segmentations if we have a lexicon that balances quality and good coverage.

5.2.4 Error Analysis

We performed an error analysis for the best setting (CRF1lex+HiProb+Names+Single+PKU), both on the segmentation and the syntax level, using the grammar based on seed 4.

Segmentation. There are 54 incorrectly segmented sentences. For 35 out of these, the correct segmentation is available in the lattice, but the parser did not select it. When analyzing these sentences, we found that in 32 cases, the parser selects a segmentation that has fewer words than the gold segmentation. I.e., the parser prefers analyses with fewer words. In some cases, the wrong segmentation makes sense linguistically, e.g., (NN 全文) (Eng.: full text) instead of the gold segmenta-

Setting	No penalty				With penalty		
	Wrong seg.	F	Rec.	Prec.	F	Rec.	Prec.
Train1	172.25	88.41	87.80	89.04	47.23	32.14	89.04
Train2	163.25	88.17	87.65	88.70	49.30	34.14	88.70
Train6	168.50	88.58	88.01	89.17	48.02	32.87	89.17
Train1+Name	117.25	87.87	87.56	88.18	57.68	42.87	88.18
Train2+Name	109.25	87.63	87.34	87.91	59.21	44.63	87.91
Train6+Name	116.25	87.90	87.61	88.19	57.91	43.12	88.19
CRF1	90.00	85.56	85.32	85.79	63.05	49.83	85.79
CRF2	108.25	85.74	85.05	86.44	61.02	47.16	86.44
CRF5	191.75	85.93	85.32	86.53	41.48	27.28	86.53
CRF1lex	82.00	85.95	85.69	86.21	65.21	52.44	86.21
CRF2lex	110.00	85.64	84.90	86.40	60.59	46.66	86.40
CRF5lex	205.25	86.38	85.75	87.01	35.56	22.34	87.01
CRF1lex+Train	86.50	86.25	85.87	86.63	64.63	51.54	86.63
CRF2lex+Train	117.25	85.66	84.91	86.42	58.73	44.48	86.42
CRF5lex+Train	205.25	86.38	85.75	87.01	35.56	22.34	87.01
CRF1lex+HiProb	74.50	85.84	85.55	86.13	66.51	54.17	86.13
CRF1lex+HiProb+Names+Single	65.25	85.63	85.36	85.91	68.58	57.07	85.91
CRF1lex+HiProb+Names+Single+PKU	55.25	85.73	85.24	86.23	70.69	59.90	86.23

Table 7: Parsing results for the different input lattices.

Error type	Count
NP → NP	20
non-NP → NP	20
non-NP → non-NP	10
NP → non-NP	15

Table 8: Top phrase errors in the best performing setting (CRF1lex+HiProb+Names+Single+PKU).

tion (DP (DT 全))(NP (NN 文)), or (NP (NN 交流会)) (Eng.: a meeting to exchange ideas) instead of (NN 交流) (NN 会).

Syntax. An analysis of the parses based on the upper bound lexicon shows that the most common mistakes made on the 344 correctly segmented sentences consists of frequently over-generated nouns (NN), leading to NP-rich analyses. The same pattern can be found in the correctly segmented sentences from the best setting (CRF1lex+HiProb+Names+Single+PKU). The distribution of parsing errors is shown in table 8. The analysis shows that we have 20 errors of non-NP phrases becoming NPs. For example, a VV retagged as NN causes a VP to become an NP. We also find 20 cases where the parsed NP has the wrong structure.

6 Conclusion & Future Work

We have shown that a pipeline approach to Chinese parsing is feasible and beneficial, but it requires a carefully selected lexicon to guide the parser to make reliable segmentation choices. While lattices from a CRF segmenter with state-of-the-art performance do not allow the parser to select good segmentations, using a lexicon carefully extracted from the n-best CRF analyses gives the parser a good basis. The parser successfully selects the correct segmentation when given the option. The best performing lexicon consists of the 1-best CRF analyses, along with highly probable other analyses, names, dates, and words from the PKU corpus. A lexicon extracted from the CRF analyses has a higher coverage than using the corresponding analyses directly, but analyses beyond the best analysis have a detrimental effect on parsing, as the parser is biased towards its internal POS tag preferences, which may not correspond to the most probable segmentation.

We plan to extend our approach of creating individual lexicons per long sentence into a more general approach where the lexicon for each sentence is determined on an individual basis. We will also investigate the interaction of segmentation and parsing when grammatical functions are present. Preliminary experiments show that they can help resolve segmentation and POS tagging ambiguities, thus also increasing parsing accuracy.

Acknowledgments

H. Hu is funded by the China Scholarship Council.

References

Shu Cai, David Chiang, and Yoav Goldberg. 2011. Language-independent parsing with empty elements. In *Proceedings of the 49th Annual Meeting of the Association for Computational Linguistics: Human Language Technologies*. Portland, Oregon, pages 212–216.

Jean-Cédric Chappelier, Martin Rajman, Ramon Aragües, and Antoine Rozenknop. 1999. Lattice parsing for speech recognition. In *Sixth Conference sur le Traitement Automatique du Langage Naturel (TANL'99)*. Cargèse, France, pages 95–104.

Shay Cohen and Noah Smith. 2007. Joint morphological and syntactic disambiguation. In *Proceedings of the 2007 Joint Conference on Empirical Methods in Natural Language Processing and Computational Natural Language Learning*. Prague, Czech Republic, pages 208–217.

Thomas Emerson. 2005. The second international Chinese word segmentation bakeoff. In *Proceedings of the Fourth SIGHAN Workshop on Chinese Language Processing*. pages 123–133.

Martin Forst and Ji Fang. 2009. TBL-improved non-deterministic segmentation and POS tagging for a Chinese parser. In *Proceedings of the 12th Conference of the European Chapter of the Association for Computational Linguistics*. pages 264–272.

Yoav Goldberg and Michael Elhadad. 2011. Joint Hebrew segmentation and parsing using a PCFG-LA lattice parser. In *Proceedings of the 49th Annual Meeting of the Association for Computational Linguistics: Human Language Technologies*. Portland, Oregon, pages 704–709.

Yoav Goldberg and Reut Tsarfaty. 2008. A single generative model for joint morphological segmentation and syntactic parsing. In *46th Annual Meeting of the Association for Computational Linguistics: Human Language Technologies*. Columbus, Ohio, pages 371–379.

Spence Green and Christopher Manning. 2010. Better Arabic parsing: Baselines, evaluations, and analysis. In *Proceedings of the 23rd International Conference on Computational Linguistics*. Beijing, China, pages 394–402.

Mary Harper and Zhongqiang Huang. 2011. Chinese statistical parsing. In Joseph Olive, Caitlin Christianson, and John McCary, editors, *Handbook of Natural Language Processing and Machine Translation*, Springer Publishing Company.

Wenbin Jiang, Liang Huang, and Qun Liu. 2009. Automatic adaptation of annotation standards: Chinese word segmentation and POS tagging: A case study. In *Proceedings of the Joint Conference of the 47th Annual Meeting of the ACL and the 4th International Joint Conference on Natural Language Processing of the AFNLP*. Singapore, pages 522–530.

Jonathan K. Kummerfeld, Daniel Tse, James R. Curran, and Dan Klein. 2013. An empirical examination of challenges in Chinese parsing. In *Proceedings of the 51st Annual Meeting of the Association for Computational Linguistics*. Sofia, Bulgaria, pages 98–103.

Gina-Anne Levow. 2006. The third international Chinese language processing bakeoff: Word segmentation and named entity recognition. In *Proceedings of the Fifth SIGHAN Workshop on Chinese Language Processing*. Sydney, Australia, pages 108–117.

Takuya Matsuzaki, Yusuke Miyao, and Jun'ichi Tsujii. 2005. Probabilistic CFG with latent annotations. In *Proceedings of the 43rd Annual Meeting on Association for Computational Linguistics*. Ann Arbor, Michigan, pages 75–82.

Hwee Tou Ng and Jin Kiat Low. 2004. Chinese part-of-speech tagging: One-at-a-time or all-at-once? Word-based or character-based? In *Proceedings of the Conference on Empirical Methods in Natural Language Processing*. Barcelona, Spain, pages 277–284.

Slav Petrov, Leon Barrett, Romain Thibaux, and Dan Klein. 2006. Learning accurate, compact, and interpretable tree annotation. In *Proceedings of the 21st International Conference on Computational Linguistics and the 44th Annual Meeting of the Association for Computational Linguistics*. Sydney, Australia, pages 433–440.

Slav Petrov and Dan Klein. 2007. Learning and inference for hierarchically split PCFGs. In *Proceedings of the National Conference on Artificial Intelligence*. Vancouver, Canada, pages 1663–1666.

Xian Qian and Yang Liu. 2012. Joint Chinese word segmentation, POS tagging and parsing. In *Proceedings of the 2012 Joint Conference on Empirical Methods in Natural Language Processing and Computational Natural Language Learning*. Jeju Island, Korea, pages 501–511.

Djamé Seddah, Reut Tsarfaty, Sandra Kübler, Marie Candito, Jinho D. Choi, Richárd Farkas, Jennifer Foster, Iakes Goenaga, Koldo Gojenola Galletebeitia, Yoav Goldberg, Spence Green, Nizar Habash, Marco Kuhlmann, Wolfgang Maier, Joakim Nivre, Adam Przepiórkowski, Ryan Roth, Wolfgang Seeker, Yannick Versley, Veronika Vincze, Marcin Woliński, Alina Wróblewska, and Eric Villemonte de la Clergerie. 2013. Overview of the SPMRL 2013 shared task: A cross-framework evaluation of parsing morphologically rich languages. In *Proceedings of the Fourth Workshop on Statistical Parsing of Morphologically-Rich Languages*. Seattle, Washington, pages 146–182.

Satoshi Sekine and Michael Collins. 1997. Evalb bracket scoring program. http://nlp.cs.nyu.edu/evalb/.

Richard Sproat and Thomas Emerson. 2003. The first international Chinese word segmentation bakeoff. In *Proceedings of the Second SIGHAN Workshop on Chinese Language Processing*. Sapporo, Japan, pages 133–143.

Bin Sun. 1999. Methods for handling segmentation ambiguities. `http://ccl.pku.edu.cn/doubtfire/NLP/Lexical_Analysis/Word_Segmentation_Tagging/Chinese_Word_Seg_Tag/seg_tag_BSWEN.htm`. In Chinese.

Reut Tsarfaty. 2006. Integrated morphological an syntactic disambiguation for Modern Hebrew. In *Proceedings of the COLING/ACL 2006 Student Research Workshop*. Sydney, Australia, pages 49–54.

Huihsin Tseng, Pichuan Chang, Galen Andrew, Daniel Jurafsky, and Christopher Manning. 2005. A conditional random field word segmenter for SIGHAN bakeoff 2005. In *Proceedings of the Fourth SIGHAN Workshop on Chinese Language Processing*. Jeju Island, Korea, pages 32–39.

Zhiguo Wang and Nianwen Xue. 2014. Joint POS tagging and transition-based constituent parsing in Chinese with non-local features. In *Proceedings of the 52nd Annual Meeting of the Association for Computational Linguistics*. Baltimore, Maryland, pages 733–742.

Zhiguo Wang, Chengqing Zong, and Nianwen Xue. 2013. A lattice-based framework for joint Chinese word segmentation, POS tagging and parsing. In *Proceedings of the 51st Annual Meeting of the Association for Computational Linguistics*. Sofia, Bulgaria, pages 623–627.

Naiwen Xue, Fei Xia, Fu-dong Chiou, and Marta Palmer. 2005. The Penn Chinese TreeBank: Phrase structure annotation of a large corpus. *Natural Language Engineering* 11(2):207–238.

Nianwen Xue. 2003. Chinese word segmentation as character tagging. *Computational Linguistics and Chinese Language Processing* 8(1):29–48.

Xiaofeng Yu, Wai Lam, Shing-Kit Chan, Yiu Kei Wu, and Bo Chen. 2008. Chinese NER using CRFs and logic for the fourth SIGHAN bakeoff. In *Proceedings of the Sixth SIGHAN Workshop on Chinese Language Processing*. Hyderabad, India, pages 102–105.

Yue Zhang and Stephen Clark. 2008. Joint word segmentation and POS tagging using a single perceptron. In *46th Annual Meeting of the Association for Computational Linguistics: Human Language Technologies*. Columbus, Ohio, pages 888–896.

Yue Zhang and Stephen Clark. 2011. Syntactic processing using the generalized perceptron and beam search. *Computational Linguistics* 37(1):105–151.

Hai Zhao, Chang-Ning Huang, Mu Li, and Bao-Liang Lu. 2010. A unified character-based tagging framework for Chinese word segmentation. *ACM Transactions on Asian Language Information Processing (TALIP)* 9(2):5.

Hai Zhao and Chunyu Kit. 2008. Unsupervised segmentation helps supervised learning of character tagging for word segmentation and named entity recognition. In *Proceedings of the Third International Joint Conference on Natural Language Processing*. Hyderabad, India, pages 106–111.

Good News vs. Bad News: What are they talking about?

Olga Kanishcheva

Intelligent Computer Systems Department, National Technical University "KhPI"

kanichshevaolga@gmail.com

Victoria Bobichev

Department of Informatics and Systems Engineering

Technical University of Moldova

victoria.bobicev@ia.utm.md

Abstract

Today's massive news streams demand the automate analysis which is provided by various online news explorers. However, most of them do not provide sentiment analysis. The main problem of sentiment analysis of news is the differences between the writers and readers attitudes to the news text. News can be good or bad but have to be delivered in neutral words as pure facts. Although there are applications for sentiment analysis of news, the task of news analysis is still a very actual problem because the latest news impacts people's lives daily.

In this paper, we explored the problem of sentiment analysis for Ukrainian and Russian news, developed a corpus of Ukrainian and Russian news and annotated each text using one of three categories: positive, negative and neutral. Each text was marked by at least three independent annotators via the web interface, the inter-annotator agreement was analyzed and the final label for each text was computed. These texts were used in the machine learning experiments. Further, we investigated what kinds of named entities such as Locations, Organizations, Persons are perceived as good or bad by the readers and which of them were the cause for text annotation ambiguity.

1 Introduction

In news, sentiments are conveyed in a subtle manner without the use of explicit sentiment bearing words, and their detection requires contextual knowledge.
Most research conducted in the field of sentiment analysis has been done for the English language (Zhang and S. Skiena (2010), Liu B. and Zhang L.

(2012)), some more for European Union languages whereas far less research has been completed for East European languages including Ukrainian and Russian.

Sentiment analysis of user generated content has been the focus of many researches; however, mass media news articles deserve the attention of these researches as well. Sentiment analysis of the news helps make their image more transparent, as possible biases in different news sources can be uncovered. The lack of research in this field was the motivation for the current work.

In comparison with the other domains, like product reviews, sentiment polarized words are used less frequently and sentiments are conveyed by complex structures and contextual knowledge as a way for journalists to seem more objective than they actually are. Many newspapers at least want to give an impression of objectivity and journalists desist from using obviously positive or negative vocabulary. This causes the sentiment classification task to become very challenging as we need to find domain-specific methods to handle this complexity.

The paper is organized as follows: in the next Section we describe related work. In Section 3 we described the corpus, its annotation and inter-rater agreement. In Section 4 we present the sentiment analysis experiments. Section 5 interprets the results; this part contains conclusions and future work.

2 Related Work

In recent years, sentiment analysis has been developing faster; it is connected with the growth of online texts and social networks. Some surveys about this area were presented in works Zhang and Skiena (2010), Liu and Zhang (2012).

Proceedings of Recent Advances in Natural Language Processing, pages 325–333,
Varna, Bulgaria, Sep 4–6 2017.

In (Shriniwas Doddi, Haribhakta, Kulkarni, 2014) the authors proposed a platform for serving good news and create a positive environment. They used SVM for sentiment analysis of news in English.

Zhai et al. (2009) developed Java data processing code and used the Stanford Classifier to quickly analyze financial news articles from The New York Times and predict sentiment in the articles. They used Naïve Bayes classifier.

In (Godbole, 2007) the author proposed a system that assigns scores indicating positive or negative opinion to each distinct entity in the text corpus. Their system consists of a sentiment identification part, which associates expressed opinions with each relevant entity, a sentiment aggregation and scoring phase, which scores each entity relative to others in the same class.

Azar (2009) analyzed the numerical information found in financial markets and the verbal information reported in the financial news to classify the news in two classes: positive and negative. The author showed that the performance of Support Vector Machines was comparable to human performance.

In (Kalyani, Bharathi and Jyothi, 2016) the authors compared results obtained using Random Forest: the resulting accuracy varied from 88% to 92%. SVM accuracy was around 86%. Naive Bayes algorithm performance was around 83%.

Recently, deep learning has become a popular method for the sentiment analysis. Lina Maria Rojas-Barahona (2016) and Duyu Tang, Bing Qin, Ting Liu (2015) provide an overview of deep learning for sentiment analysis in order to place these approaches in context.

In the work authors (Cicero Nogueira dos Santos and Maira Gatti, 2014) use deep learning for the Stanford Sentiment Treebank with the accuracy of 86.4%.

In (Koltsova, Alexeeva and Kolcov, 2016) the authors described the development of a system for Russian language sentiment analysis. This system included: a publicly available sentiment lexicon, a publicly available test collection with sentiment markup and a crowdsourcing website for such markup. The sentiment lexicon was aimed at detecting sentiment in user-generated content (blogs, social media) related to social and political issues.

Loukachevitch and Levchik (2016) in their paper presented the Russian sentiment lexicon – RuSentiLex. The current size of the lexicon is more than ten thousand words and phrases. The lexicon entries were classified according to four sentiment categories (positive, negative, neutral, or positive/negative) and three sources of sentiment (opinion, emotion, or fact).

The news sentiment analysis is different from that of other text types. (Balahur, et al., 2013) emphasized that there are several specific problems related to this type of texts; one of them being the problem of positive or negative opinion from good or bad news separation. This problem becomes more evident in the process of news manual annotation (Balahur, Steinberger, 2009). Annotators tend to misinterpret the author intention and mark their interpretation as the true sentiment of the text. In (Balahur, et al., 2009) the annotation experiments of news quotations annotator agreement even for these short pieces of text was relatively low, below 50%. Only for two steps of re-annotation of the same quotations they managed to reach 80% agreement creating detailed annotation guidelines with multiple examples and explanations.

(Bakken et al., 2016) adapted the (Balahur, et al., 2009) methodology in their annotation experiment and annotation made by the first two authors of the paper reached an agreement of 76%.

(Ellis et al., 2014) also stated that in news video transcripts or news articles, the sentiment attached to a statement can be much less obvious. An example presented in the paper demonstrated this: "take the statement that has been relevant in the news in the past year, 'Russian troops have entered into Crimea'. This statement by itself is not polarizing as positive or negative and is in fact quite neutral. However, if it was stated by a U.S. politician it would probably have very negative connotations and if stated by a Russian politician it could have a very positive sentiment associated with it." The annotation was made using Amazon Mechanical Turk and each annotation unit obtained three independent annotations. The paper did not report annotation agreement although they mentioned that around 6% of examples were discarded due to the disagreement of annotators.

In the papers which describe various types of manual annotation (Balahur, et al., 2009, Navarro et al., 2005, Melzi et al., 2014) several reasons of the poor inter-annotator agreement were listed. The ambiguity of the annotation units and subjectivity of the annotators were one of the main problems encountered in this process. A really high inter-annotation agreement can be reached only after several turns of annotations by the same annotators and iteratively improved annotation instructions.

In (Mihalcea, Strapparava, 2010) each news headline in the corpus was annotated by six annotators which had not received any additional instructions, hence, annotated their own sentiments triggered by the text. Then they calculated average annotation of the headlines.

In (Melzi et al., 2014) master students annotated health forum messages with six basic emotions and the calculated Fleiss Kappa (Artstein and Poesio, 2008) was relatively low: 0.26. They explained such disagreement by the variability between people and specifics of the corpus texts. Nevertheless, they continued with automating sentiment classification experiments which give reasonably good results (best F-measure = 0.65).

3 Experiments

3.1 The Data for Annotation

We used two data sets of Ukrainian (https://tsn.ua/) and Russian (http://censor.net.ua/) news. The Ukrainian corpus contains 5,817 news texts and the Russian corpus contains 10,194 news texts. Some statistics are shown in Table I.

The initial set of files was quite large but the great part of these files was neutral. As there was news, not user's comments they were delivered in comparatively neutral texts. Even if the author's attitude was present in a text, it was expressed implicitly, mostly without sentiment bearing words.

TABLE I.   STATISTICS ABOUT DATA SETS

Topic	Number of Ukrainian texts	Number of Russian texts
Society	1,171	2,100
Politics	1,235	2,502
Incidents	1,156	1,393
Sport	1,153	2,100
Economics	1,102	2,099
Total	*5,817*	*10,194*

However, we decided to use sentiment lexicons in order to select the most interesting files. The used sentiment lexicons for Russian (Bobicev et al., 2010) and Ukrainian (Kanishcheva, 2017) were created on the base of WordNetAffect (Strapparava and Valitutti, 2004). WordNet-Affect in its turn was created starting from WordNet DOMAINS (Magnini, B., Cavaglia, 2002). WordNet-Affect produces an additional hierarchy of the effective domain labels, independent from the domain hierarchy for the synsets that represent affective concepts. Only a part of WordNet-Affect synsets provided as a resource for the SemEval-2007 "Affective Text" by Strapparava and Mihalcea (2008) was used for Russian and Ukrainian lexicon creation. There were terms grouped in six subsets in accordance with six basic emotions (Ekman, 1992): anger, joy, surprise, sadness, disgust, fear. Below is presented an example of synset:

a#01943022 awed awestruck awestricken in_awe_of

The created lexicons are comparatively small; the total number of translated synsets is 248 and the number of Russian and Ukrainian words is around 2,000. Sentiment words from the lexicons were compared with the words from the texts. For most text, no one word matched lexicon's terms; these texts were discarded as neutral. If there were some words in texts which matched lexicon terms we left them for the annotation as possible sentiment bearing.

After the filtering described above, 2,018 Russian and 2,133 Ukrainian news texts were left for the manual annotation. For annotation was presented only texts without any additional meta-information such as date, author etc.

3.2 The Annotation and Inter-Annotator Agreement

The annotation was performed by Kharkiv Polytechnic Institute students via the online interface[1]. Around 40 students participated in annotation of each part, Russian and Ukrainian yielding in 7,248 annotations for Russian texts and 6,733 annotations for Ukrainian. Starting the annotation students selected the topic they were willing to work with and the interface randomly selected texts from the folder and offered students. The question they answered was: What sentiments does this text evoke? They also could add some comments if they considered necessary. Finally, each text was annotated by 2 to 5 students using three labels: positive, negative, neutral. The average number of annotators per text was 3.59 for Russian and 3.2 for Ukrainian texts. Inter-annotator agreement calculated on these texts was extremely low: Fleiss Kappa = 0.14 for Ukrainian texts and Fleiss Kappa = 0.24 for Russian.

---

[1] http://lilu.fcim.utm.md/annot_ru/annot_ru.html
http://lilu.fcim.utm.md/annot_ukr/annot_ukr.html

In the case of Ukrainian text, two annotators selected one label and one annotator selected another label for 2/3 of them. Even if in this case we may use the label selected by two annotators as the right one, such distribution of votes is actually identical to the distribution "by chance" and Fleiss Kappa for such annotation is equal to 0.

Nevertheless, we selected the final label by majority voting. This means that for all texts we selected the label which was attached by majority annotators. In the cases, when the text was annotated with three labels and one label was selected by two annotators this label was selected as the final one.

The statistics of documents selected for the annotation are presented in the TABLE II. and TABLE III.

TABLE II.   STATISTICS ON THE RUSSIAN NEWS FILES SELECTED FOR ANNOTATION AND SELECTED FOR THE EXPERIMENTS

Category	Number of files		Emotion category		
	for anno-tation	for expe-ri-ments	Pos-itive	Neu-tral	Nega-tive
Economics	298	202	35	87	80
Incidents	251	209	14	93	102
Politics	526	445	84	259	102
Society	434	322	56	153	113
Sport	509	321	80	134	107
Total	*2,018*	*1,499*	*269*	*726*	*504*

Figures 1 and 2 show the final statistics about the agreement of our data sets. The number of news texts is presented for each emotion category (positive, negative and neutral).

TABLE III.   STATISTICS ON THE FILES UKRAINIAN NEWS SELECTED FOR ANNOTATION AND SELECTED FOR THE EXPERIMENTS

Category	Number of files		Emotion category		
	for an-notation	for ex-peri-ments	Pos-itive	Neu-tral	Neg ative
Economics	254	150	60	65	25
Incidents	493	428	30	137	261
Politics	496	383	82	183	118
Society	449	373	52	189	132
Sport	441	368	153	147	68
Total	*2,133*	*1,702*	*377*	*721*	*604*

3.3 Ambiguous Texts

In this section, we try to analyze reasons of such ambiguous estimation of the news. We explored the news which received three different labels (negative, neutral, positive) from all three annotators. The statistics on these texts are shown in Table IV.

For each category Society, Politics, Incidents, Sport, Economics we extracted named entities (Location, Person, Organization) as we hypothesized that these elements influence the user opinion about the texts. News should be neutral and not impose any opinion. However, the person reading the news has her/his own subjective opinion on this or that object/event/person and this opinion is influence the news evaluation. This is the reason why some of the news have been marked quite ambiguously (TABLE IV.).

TABLE IV.   STATISTICS ABOUT AMBIGUOUS DATA SETS

Category	Number of Ukrainian texts Ambiguous/ un-ambiguous	Number of Russian texts Ambiguous/ un-ambiguous
Society	63/373	62/322
Politics	103/383	65/445
Incidents	58/428	30/209
Sport	58/368	92/321
Economics	68/150	43/202
Total	*350/1,499*	*292/1,702*

In TABLE V. we present entities from completely ambiguous texts and compare with the entities from the unambiguous news. The extracted entities can be divided into several groups. The first group of named entities such as *USA Congress, the US Senate, The German Foreign Ministry* etc. have been met only with the ambiguous news.

The second group, such as *The Verkhovna Rada, Arseniy Yatsenyuk* etc. have been met in two categories: positive and negative. Possibly that's why these entities appeared also in the ambiguous texts.

The third group of entities (*The International Monetary Fund (IMF), Ukraine*) has been met quite often in all categories because these entities are very popular for *Economics* category and for Ukraine in general

Next, we analyzed the frequency of term *IMF* and we can see that it has been met more frequently in the negative context of news. Also, such entity as *Arseniy Yatsenyuk* appeared in positive and negative categories because this politician was at the politic arena of Ukraine in 2016 (our data set was created during the 2016 year) and people who analyzed the news had already their own apparently controversial opinion about him.

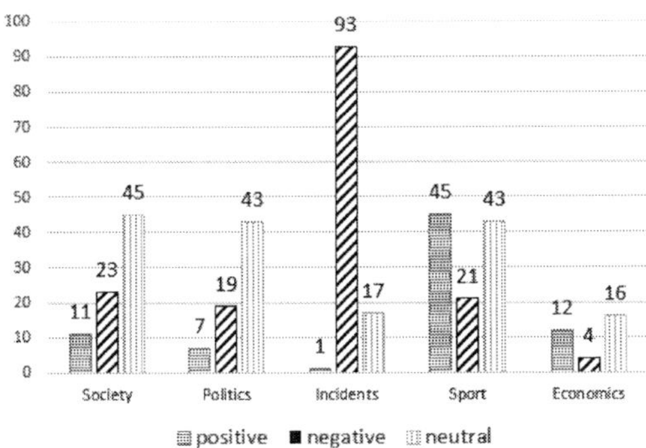

Figure 1: The number of texts with total agreement by emotion categories (Ukrainian news).

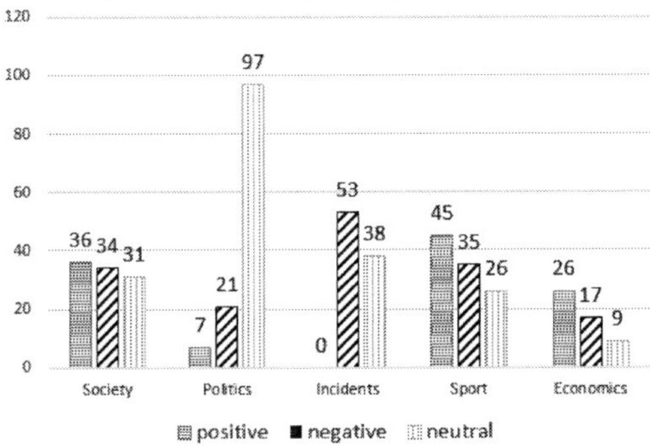

Figure 2: The number of texts with total agreement by emotion categories (Russian news).

TABLE VI. shows that *the Security Service of Ukraine (SSU)* had been met in negative contexts of news but the persons *Arsen Avakov* and *Hatiya Dekanoidze* appeared in the positive context. This positive context may be explained by the people's positive attitude to the reforms they have been carrying out last two years.

The term *Antiterrorist operation (ATO)* had been met in all categories of text but more often in the negative news. It's connected with the war in the East of Ukraine and the annotators used negative labels for texts related to *ATO*.

We observed an interesting fact about the entity *Petro Poroshenko*. This person was mentioned relatively often in positive and in negative categories. This indicates that the president of Ukraine does not have unequivocal support in Ukrainians. This result match with the results of the official surveys[2].

For our texts, we think that the main cause of news ambiguity was the politics. For example, for

<hr>

[2] http://ukraine-elections.com.ua/socopros/parlamentskie_vybory
https://ru.slovoidilo.ua/2017/02/01/infografika/politika/kak-menyalis-elektoralnye-simpatii-ukraincev-v-2016-m

the Economy and Society categories, we detected the following named entities (TABLE V. and TABLE VI.).

Name of Entity (Russian/English)	Tonality		
Organization	Positive	Neutral	Negative
Верховная Рада/ The Verkhovna Rada	+	-	+
Кабинет Министров/ Cabinet of Ministers	+	-	-
Международный валютный фонд (МВФ)/ The International Monetary Fund (IMF)	+	+	+ (many times)
Конгресс США/ USA Congress	-	-	-
Сенат США/ The US Senate	-	-	-
МИД Германии/ The German Foreign Ministry	-	-	-
Евросоюз/ European Union	-	-	-
Антимонопольный комитет/ Antimonopoly Committee	-	-	-
Национальный банк/ National Bank	-	-	-
Кремль/ Kremlin	-	-	-
Location			
Российская Федерация/ Russian Federation	-	-	-
Украина/ Ukraine	+	-	+ (often)
Person			
Президент/ Prezident	-	+	+
Айвараса Абромавичуса/ Aivaras Abromaviichus	-	-	-
Кристин Лагард/ Christine Lagarde	-	+	-
Оксана Сыроид/ Oksana Syroid	-	-	-
Арсений Яценюк/ Arseniy Yatsenyuk	+	-	+
Владимир Гройсман/ Vladimir Groisman	-	-	-
Валерия Гонтарева/ Valeria Gontareva	-	-	+
Павел Жебривский/ Pavel Zhebrivsky	-	-	-
Дмитрий Песков/ Dmitry Peskov	-	-	-
Александр Лукашенко/ Alexander Lukashenko	-	-	-

The same situation is for the news in Ukrainian. Extracted entities show how the society ambiguously perceives the same news especially when it comes to politics. Many categories even non-political ones contain entities that are related to politics and thereby the user's opinion overlaps the evaluation of the news as a whole.

TABLE VI. THE MOST FREQUENT ENTITIES FROM RUSSIAN NEWS (CATEGORY – SOCIETY)

Name of Entity (Russian/English)	Tonality		
Organization	Positive	Neutral	Negative
Минсоцполитики/ Ministry of Social Policy	-	+	-
СБУ/ SSU	-	+	+
Генпрокуратуру/ Prosecutor General's Office	-	-	-
Кабинет Украины/ Cabinet of Ukraine	-	-	-
Верховная Рада/ The Verkhovna Rada	+	+	+
Госпогранслужба Украины/ State Border Service of Ukraine	-	-	-
Луганская Народная Республика/ Luhansk People's Republic	-	-	-
Парламент Канады/ Parliament of Canada	-	-	-
Location			
Майдан/ Maidan	-	-	-
АТО/ ATO	+	+	+ (often)
Евросоюз/ European Union	-	-	-
Дебальцево/ Debaltsevo	-	-	-
Мариуполь/ Mariupol	-	-	+
Чернобыльской АЭС/ Chernobyl nuclear power plant	-	-	-
Person			
Путин/ Putin	-	-	-
Арсен Аваков/ Arsen Avakov	+	+	-
Петр Порошенко/ Petro Poroshenko	+ (often)		+ (often)
Михеил Саакашвили/ Mikheil Saakashvili	-	-	+
Хатия Деканоидзе/ Hatiya Dekanoidze	+	-	-
Вера Савченко/ Vera Savchenko	-	-	+

4 Automated Classification Experiments

In order to evaluate the annotation, we performed Machine Learning experiments using several algorithms: Bayesian classifiers (Naive Bayes Multinomial) and SVM (Support Vector Machine).

The feature set was obtained using bag of word approach and the selection of the best set of attributes by two selection methods: Information Gain feature evaluation which evaluates the worth of a feature by measuring its information gain and Correlation-based Feature Subset Selection (Hall, 1998). We also experimented with lexicon based features[3] but bag of words features gave better results and we are reporting only them. We performed 10-fold cross-validation for each dataset. The best obtained F-measures, the feature sets and the methods of their selection and the machine learning algorithms used to obtain this result on all our categories of texts are presented in the TABLE VII.

We obtained comparatively good results for our texts. The best F-measure 0.776 was obtained for *Sport* category of Russian texts. The third column of the table presents information about the feature set used to obtain this result. In the case of *Sport* category of Russian texts, 91 features selected from the bag of words initial feature set using Correlation-based Feature Subset Selection were used by Naïve Bayes Multinomial algorithm to obtain F=0.779. It is interesting that the worst result F=0.676 was obtained also for the category sport, Ukrainian news. It may be explained by the fact that comparatively neutral reports about scores of sports matches evoke quite different sentiments from competing sport team fans and there was no text element, which indicates these sentiments.

TABLE VII. THE BEST RESULTS OBTAINED FOR EACH CATEGORY

Category	The best F-measure	Feature set for this result	Classification algorithm
Russian news			
Economics	0.728	73 Info Gain	NB Multinomial
Incidents	0.741	71 Info Gain	SVM algorithm
Politics	0.729	160 Info Gain	NB Multinomial
Society	0.695	57 Best subset	NB Multinomial
Sport	0.776	91 Best subset	NB Multinomial
Ukrainian news			
Economics	0.720	29 Info Gain	Naive Bayes
Incidents	0.762	72 Best subset	SVM algorithm
Politics	0.746	77 Info Gain	NB Multinomial
Society	0.763	163 Info Gain	NB Multinomial
Sport	0.676	79 Best subset	SVM algorithm

TABLE VII. TABLE VIII. and 0show the number of features for all our data set which we used for our experiments.

The obtained results are not as good as in (Bobicev et al., 2017) on the similar data set although our corpora are larger. It could be explained

---

[3] https://sites.google.com/site/datascienceslab/projects/multilingualsentiment

by the annotation vagueness. We decided on text polarity by simple majority voting. If a text was labeled by three annotators once with the positive label and two with negative we considered this text negative. However, in such cases, there was not enough evidence that the text was really negative. The possible solutions may be additional annotations of these texts but we already have a number of texts annotated by 4, 5, 6 and even 7 annotators and still, they are ambiguous obtaining for example, 3 positive votes and 2 negative from 5 annotators or 3 positive, 2 negative and 2 neutral from 7 annotators. The possible solutions, in this case, may be (1) creation of an additional category: ambiguous texts or (2) removal of these texts from the training corpus.

TABLE VIII.   THE NUMBER OF FEATURES FOR RUSSIAN NEWS

Category	BOW	Best Subset	Info Gain
Economics	3,483	42	73
Incidents	3,564	40	71
Politics	6,431	78	160
Society	6,107	57	128
Sport	3,482	91	130

TABLE IX.   THE NUMBER OF FEATURES FOR UKRAINIAN NEWS

Category	BOW	Best Subset	Info Gain
Economics	2,878	25	29
Incidents	6,110	72	112
Politics	5,868	68	77
Society	6,088	92	163
Sport	4,531	79	166

5   Conclusion and Future Work

In the paper, we have presented the work on sentiment analysis for news in Ukrainian and Russian news. The news was annotated into three categories (positive, negative and neutral) by three annotators. The inter-annotator agreement was calculated and the final label was attached to each annotated text. The texts that remained ambiguous were not used in the experiments. We have performed experiments with the created annotated corpus of news using Bayesian (Naive Bayes Multinomial) and SVM (Support Vector Machine) classifiers. Bag of word approach with feature selection gave the best results which demonstrated that even the simple learning methods as for example, Naïve Bayes, are able to achieve high results (average F1-score of 0.73) with right features.

We explored what kind of Named Entities have been met in the positive and negative contexts of the news and examined the possibility to use the standard approach of sentiment analysis for prognoses of politician's rating and for some events, such as sports matches, festivals, TV shows etc.

There are several open issues in our study. First, the quality of the annotation needs to be improved. In order to solve this problem we plan to undertake the following steps: (1) to carry more detailed analysis of the most ambiguous texts to detect the common cause of their ambiguity; (2) to introduce one more annotation category: 'ambiguous' for the texts the annotators are not certain about; (3) to experiment with various modifications of the instructions for the annotators.

Second, we plan to search for the better sentiment lexicons for Russian and Ukrainian in order to use them in automate sentiment recognition which currently still need considerable improvement.

Third, the final aim of our work is aspect based sentiment analysis: mining and summarizing opinions from a text about specific entities and their aspects; thus we plan to continue the direction of automating named entities recognition with a close connection to sentiment analysis.

Acknowledgments

We gratefully acknowledge feedback and comments of the anonymous RANLP reviewers, which considerably helped to improve the paper. We would like to thank students from National Technical University "KhPI" for creation and annotation of news collection.

References

Ron Artstein and Massimo Poesio. 2008. Inter-coder agreement for computational linguistics. Journal of the Computational Linguistics, 34(4):555-596. http://dx.doi.org/10.1162/coli.07-034-R2

Pablo Daniel Azar. 2009. Sentiment Analysis in Financial News, Ph.D. thesis, Harvard University.

Patrik F. Bakken, Terje A. Bratlie, Cristina Marco and Jon Atle Gulla. 2016. Political News Sentiment Analysis for Under-resourced Languages. In Proceedings of COLING 2016, the 26th International Conference on Computational Linguistics: Technical Papers, pages 2989–2996.

Alexandra Balahur and Steinberger R. 2009. Rethinking Opinion Mining in News: from Theory to Practice and Back. In Proceedings of the 1st Workshop on Opinion Mining and Sentiment Analysis, Satellite to CAEPIA 2009.

http://publications.jrc.ec.europa.eu/repository/handle/JRC55018

Alexandra Balahur, Ralf Steinberger, Erik van der Goot, Bruno Pouliquen, and Mijail Kabadjov. 2009. Opinion Mining on Newspaper Quotations. In Proceedings of the workshop 'Intelligent Analysis and Processing of Web News Content' (IAPWNC).
http://dx.doi.org/10.1109/WI-IAT.2009.340

Alexandra Balahur, Ralf Steinberger, Mijail A. Kabadjov, Vanni Zavarella, Erik Van der Goot, Matina Halkia, Bruno Pouliquen, and Jenya Belyaeva. 2013. Sentiment Analysis in the News. In the Proceedings of the 7th International Conference on Language Resources and Evaluation (LREC'2010), pages 2216-2220.

Victoria Bobichev, Olga Kanichsheva, and Olga Cherednichenko. 2017. Sentiment Analysis in the Ukrainian and Russian News. In Proceedings of the First Ukraine Conference on Electrical and Computer Engineering (UKRCON 2017), pages 1050-1055.

Victoria Bobicev, Victoria Maxim, Tatiana Prodan, Natalia Burciu and Victoria Angheluş. 2010. Emotions in words: developing a multilingual WordNet-Affect. In Proceedings of the International Conference on Intelligent Text Processing and Computational Linguistics (CICLing 2010), pages 375-384.
http://dx.doi.org/10.1007/978-3-642-12116-6_31

Paul Ekman. 1992. An argument for basic emotions. Cognition and Emotion, vol. 6(3/4), pages 169–200.

Joseph G. Ellis, Brendan Jou, and Shih Fu Chang. 2014. Why We Watch the News: A Dataset for Exploring Sentiment in Broadcast Video News. In the Proceedings of the 16th International Conference on Multimodal Interaction (ICMI 2014), pages 104-111.
http://dx.doi.org/10.1145/2663204.2663237

Mark A. Hall. 1999. Correlation-based Feature Selection for Machine Learning, Ph.D. thesis, University of Waikato.

Namrata Godbole, Manja Srinivasaiah and Steven Skiena. 2007. LargeScale Sentiment Analysis for News and Blogs. In the Proceedings of the International Conference on Weblogs and Social Media.

Joshi Kalyani, Bharathi H. N., and Jyothi Rao. 2016. Stock trend prediction using news sentiment analysis, International Journal of Computer Science & Information Technology (IJCSIT), 8(3), pages 67-76.

Olga Kanishcheva, Catharine Klymenkova, and Catharine Yurieva. 2017. Development of WordNet-

Affect dictionary for the Ukrainian language. In the Proceedings of the 3rd International Academic Conference "Human. Computer. Communication".

Olessia Koltsova, Svetlana Alexeeva, and Sergei Koltcov. 2016. An Opinion Word Lexicon and a Training Dataset for Russian Sentiment Analysis of Social Media. In the Proceedings of the International Conference "Dialogue 2016", pages 277-287.

Bing Liu and Lei Zhang. 2012. A survey of opinion mining and sentiment analysis. Mining Text Data, pages 415-463.

Natalia Loukachevitch and Anatoly Levchik. 2016. Creating a General Russian Sentiment Lexicon. In the Proceedings of the 10th International Conference on Language Resources and Evaluation (LREC 2016), pages 1171-1176.

Bernardo Magnini and Gabriela Cavaglia. 2002. Integrating subject field codes into WordNet. In the Proceedings of the Second International Conference on Language Resources and Evaluation (LREC 2002), pages 1413-1418.

Soumia Melzi, Amine Abdaoui, Jerome Azé, Sandra Bringay, Pascal Poncelet, and Florence Galtier. 2014. Patient's rationale: Patient Knowledge retrieval from health forums. In the Proceedings of the Sixth International Conference on eHealth, Telemedicine, and Social Medicine, pages 140-145.

Borja Navarro, Raquel Marcos, and Patricia Abad. 2005. Semantic Annotation and Inter-Annotators Agreement in Cast3LB Corpus. In the Proceedings of the Fourth Workshop on Treebanks and Linguistic Theories.

Cıcero Nogueira dos Santos and Maıra Gatti. 2014. Deep Convolutional Neural Networks for Sentiment Analysis of Short Texts. In the Proceedings of COLING 2014, the 25th International Conference on Computational Linguistics: Technical Papers, pages 69–78.

Lina Maria Rojas-Barahona. 2016. Deep learning for sentiment analysis. Language and Linguistics Compass, 10(12), pages 701–719.
http://dx.doi.org/10.1111/lnc3.12228

Kiran Shriniwas Doddi, Y. V. Haribhakta, and Parag Kulkarni. 2014. Sentiment Classification of News Articles, International Journal of Computer Science and Information Technologies, 5 (3), pages 4621-4623.

Carlo Strapparava and Rada Mihalcea. 2010. Annotating and Identifying Emotions in Text. Intelligent Information Access, "Studies in Computational Intelligence", pages 21-38.

Carlo Strapparava and Rada Mihalcea. 2008. Learning to identify emotions in text. In the Proceedings

of the 2008 ACM symposium on Applied computing, pp 1556-1560.
http://dx.doi.org/10.1145/1363686.1364052

Carlo Strapparava and Alessandro Valitutti. 2004. WordNet-affect: an affective extension of WordNet. In Proceedings of the 4th International Conference on Language Resources and Evaluation, pages 1083-1086.

Duyu Tang, Bing Qin, Ting Liu. 2015. Deep learning for sentiment analysis: successful approaches and future challenges. Wiley Interdisciplinary Reviews: Data Mining and Knowledge Discovery, 5(6), pages 292-303.
http://dx.doi.org/10.1002/widm.1171

Jinjian Zhai, Nicholas Cohen, and Anand Treya. 2009. CS224N Final Project: Sentiment analysis of news articles for financial signal prediction.

Wenbin Zhang and Steven Skiena. 2010. Trading Strategies to Exploit Blog and News Sentiment. In the Proceedings of the Fourth International AAAI Conference on Weblogs and Social Media, pages 375-378.

We Built a Fake News & Click-bait Filter:
What Happened Next Will Blow Your Mind!

Georgi Karadzhov[1], Pepa Gencheva[1], Preslav Nakov[2], and Ivan Koychev[1]

[1]Sofia University "St. Kliment Ohridski", Bulgaria
[2]Qatar Computing Research Institute, HBKU, Qatar
{georgi.m.karadjov, pepa.k.gencheva}@gmail.com,
pnakov@hbku.edu.qa, koychev@uni-sofia.bg

Abstract

It is completely amazing! Fake news and click-baits have totally invaded the cyber space. Let us face it: everybody hates them for three simple reasons. Reason #2 will absolutely amaze you. What these can achieve at the time of election will completely blow your mind! Now, we all agree, this cannot go on, you know, somebody has to stop it. So, we did this research on fake news/click-bait detection and trust us, it is totally great research, it really is! Make no mistake. This is the best research ever! Seriously, come have a look, we have it all: neural networks, attention mechanism, sentiment lexicons, author profiling, you name it. Lexical features, semantic features, we absolutely have it all. And we have totally tested it, trust us! We have results, and numbers, really big numbers. The best numbers ever! Oh, and analysis, absolutely top notch analysis. Interested? Come read the shocking truth about fake news and click-bait in the Bulgarian cyber space. You won't believe what we have found!

1 Introduction

Fake news are written and published with the intent to mislead in order to gain financially or politically, often targeting specific user groups. Another type of harmful content on the Internet are the so-called *click-baits*, which are distinguished by their sensational, exaggerated, or deliberately false headlines that grab attention and deceive the user into clicking an article with questionable content.

While the motives behind these two types of fake news are different, they constitute a growing problem as they constitute a sizable fraction of the online news that users encounter on a daily basis. With the recent boom of Internet, mobile, and social networks, the spread of fake news increases exponentially. Using on-line methods for spreading harmful content makes the task of keeping the Internet clean significantly harder as it is very easy to publish an article and there is no easy way to verify its veracity. Currently, domains that consistently spread misinformation are being banned from various platforms, but this is a rather inefficient way to deal with fake news as websites that specialize in spreading misinformation are reappearing with different domain names. That is why our method is based purely on text analysis,[1] without taking into account the domain name or website's reliability as a source of information. Our work is focused on exploring various stylistic and lexical features in order to detect misleading content, and on experiments with neural network architectures in order to evaluate how deep learning can be used for detecting fake news. Moreover, we created various language-specific resources that could be used in future work on fake news and clickbait detection for Bulgarian, including task-specific word embeddings and various lexicons and dictionaries extracted from the training data.[2]

---

[1]An earlier version of the system participated in the *Hack the fake news* hackathon, where it was ranked best in terms of classification accuracy and robustness. See the official results here: `https://gitlab.com/datasciencesociety/case_fake_news/blob/master/Teams_Final_Score.xlsx`

[2]The implementation of the final system that we present in this paper is available at `https://github.com/lachezarbozhkov/hack_the_fake_news`

334

Proceedings of Recent Advances in Natural Language Processing, pages 334–343,
Varna, Bulgaria, Sep 4–6 2017.

2 Related Work

Trustworthiness and veracity analytics of online statements is an emerging research direction (Rowe and Butters, 2009). This includes predicting credibility of information shared in social media (Mitra et al., 2017), stance classification (Zubiaga et al., 2016a) and contradiction detection in rumours (Lendvai and Reichel, 2016). For example, Castillo et al. (2011) studied the problem of finding false information about a newsworthy event. They compiled their own dataset, focusing on tweets using a variety of features including user reputation, author writing style, and various time-based features. Canini et al. (2011) analysed the interaction of content and social network structure, and Morris et al. (2012) studied how Twitter users judge truthfulness. They found that this is hard to do based on content alone, and instead users are influenced by heuristics such as user name.

Rumour detection in social media represents yet another angle of information credibility. Zubiaga et al. (2015) studied how people handle rumours in social media. They found that users with higher reputation are more trusted, and thus can spread rumours among other users without raising suspicions about the credibility of the news or of its source. Lukasik et al. (2015) and Ma et al. (2015) used temporal patterns to detect rumours and to predict their frequency, Zubiaga et al. (2016b) focused on conversational threads, and Karadzhov et al. (2017) used deep learning to verify claims using the Web as a corpus.

Veracity of information has been also studied in the context of online personal blogs (Johnson et al., 2007), community question answering forums (Nakov et al., 2017), and political debates (Gencheva et al., 2017).

Astroturfing and misinformation detection represent another relevant research direction. Their importance is motivated by the strong interest from political science, and research methods are driven by the presence of massive streams of micro-blogging data, e.g., on Twitter (Ratkiewicz et al., 2011). While astroturfing has been primarily studied in microblogs such as Twitter, here we focus on on-line news and click-baits instead.

Identification of malicious accounts in social networks is another related research direction. This includes detecting *spam accounts* (Almaatouq et al., 2016; Mccord and Chuah, 2011), *fake accounts* (Fire et al., 2014; Cresci et al., 2015), *compromised accounts* and *phishing accounts* (Adewole et al., 2017). *Fake profile detection* has also been studied in the context of cyber-bullying (Galán-García et al., 2014). A related problem is that of *Web spam detection*, which was addressed as a text classification problem (Sebastiani, 2002), e.g., using spam keyword spotting (Dave et al., 2003), lexical affinity of arbitrary words to spam content (Hu and Liu, 2004), frequency of punctuation and word co-occurrence (Li et al., 2006).

Fake news detection is most closely related to the present work. While social media have been seen for years as the main vehicle for spreading information of questionable veracity, recently there has been a proliferation of fake news, often spread on social media, but also published in specialized websites. This has attracted research attention recently. For example, there has been work on studying credibility, trust, and expertise in news communities (Mukherjee and Weikum, 2015). The credibility of the information published in on-line news portals has been questioned by a number of researchers (Brill, 2001; Ketterer, 1998; Finberg et al., 2002). As timing is crucial when it comes to publishing breaking news, it is simply not possible to double-check the facts and the sources, as is usually standard in respectable printed newspapers and magazines. This is one of the biggest concerns about on-line news media that journalists have (Cassidy, 2007). Finally, Conroy et al. (2015) review various methods for detecting fake news, e.g., using linguistic analysis, discourse, linked data, and social network features.

All the above work was for English. The only work on fact checking for Bulgarian is that of (Hardalov et al., 2016), but they focused on distinguishing serious news from humorous ones. In contrast, here we are interested in finding news that are not designed to sound funny, but to make the reader believe they are real. Unlike them, we use a deep learning approach.

3   Fake News & Click-bait Dataset

We use a corpus of Bulgarian news over a fixed period of time, whose factuality had been questioned. The news come from 377 different sources from various domains, including politics, interesting facts and tips&tricks. The dataset was prepared for the *Hack the Fake News* hackathon. It was provided by the Bulgarian Association of PR Agencies[3] and is available in Gitlab[4]. The corpus was automatically collected, and then annotated by students of journalism. Each entry in the dataset consists of the following elements: URL of the original article, date of publication, article heading, article content, a label indicating whether the article is fake or not, and another label indicating whether it is a click-bait.

The training dataset contains 2,815 examples, where 1,940 (i.e., 69%) are fake news and 1,968 (i.e., 70%) are click-baits; we further have 761 testing examples. However, there is 98% correlation between fake news and click-baits, i.e., a model trained on fake news would do well on click-baits and vice versa. Thus, below we focus on fake news detection only.

One important aspect about the training dataset is that it contains many repetitions. This should not be surprising as it attempts to represent a natural distribution of factual vs. fake news on-line over a period of time. As publishers of fake news often have a group of websites that feature the same deceiving content, we should expect some repetition.

In particular, the training dataset contains 434 unique articles with duplicates. These articles have three reposts each on average, with the most reposted article appearing 45 times. If we take into account the labels of the reposted articles, we can see that if an article is reposted, it is more likely to be fake news. The number of fake news that have a duplicate in the training dataset are 1018 whereas, the number of articles with genuine content that have a duplicate article in the training set is 322. We detect the duplicates based on their titles as far as they are distinctive enough and the content is sometimes slightly modified when reposted.

This supports the hypothesis that fake news websites are likely to repost their content. This is also in line with previous research (Ma et al., 2015), which has found it beneficial to find a pattern of how a rumour is reposted over time.

4   Method

We propose a general framework for finding fake news focusing on the text only. We first create some resources, e.g., dictionaries of words strongly correlated with fake news, which are needed for feature extraction. Then, we design features that model a number of interesting aspects about an article, e.g., style, intent, etc. Moreover, we use a deep neural network to learn task-specific representations of the articles, which includes an attention mechanism that can focus on the most discriminative sentences and words.

4.1   Language Resources

As our work is the first attempt at predicting click-baits in Bulgarian, it is organized around building new language-specific resources[5] and analyzing the task.

Word embeddings: We train 300-dimensional domain-specific word embeddings using word2vec (Mikolov et al., 2013) on 100,000 Bulgarian news articles from the same sources as the main dataset. The labelled dataset we use in our system is a subset of these articles. Finally, we end up with 207,270 unique words that occur in five or more documents. We use these embeddings for text representation, and as an input to our attention-based nevural network.

Latent Dirichlet allocation (LDA): We use LDA (Blei et al., 2003) in order to build domain-specific topic models, which could be useful for inducing classes of words that signal fake/factual news. The LDA model is trained on the same 100,000 Bulgarian news articles as for training the word embeddings. In our experiments, these LDA classes proved helpful by themselves, but they did not have much to offer on top of the word embeddings. Thus, we ended up not using them in our final system, but we chose to still release them as other researchers might find them useful in the future.

---

[3] http://www.bapra.bg/
[4] https://gitlab.com/datasciencesociety/case_fake_news/tree/master/data

Fact-checking lexicon: Using lexicons of sentiment words has been shown to be very successful for the task of sentiment analysis (Mohammad and Turney, 2013), and we applied the same idea to extract a *fact-checking lexicon*. In particular, we use point-wise mutual information (PMI) to find terms (words, word bi-grams, and named entities) that are highly correlated with the fake/factual news class.

We calculated the PMI scores for uni-grams, bi-grams and on extracted named entities. Table 1 shows some of the most significant words for the fake news class. We can see in the table some words that grab people attention, but are not very informative by themselves, such as *mysterious* or *phenomenon*. These words are largely context-independent and are likely to remain stable in their usage across different domains and even over an extended period of time. Thus, they should be useful beyond this task and this dataset.

Other lexicons: Finally, we create four lexicons that can help to model the difference in language use between fake and factual news articles. In particular, we explored and merged/cleansed a number of on-line resources in order to put together the following lexicons: (*i*) common typos in Bulgarian written text, (*ii*) Bulgarian slang words, (*iii*) commonly used foreign words, and (*iv*) English words with Bulgarian equivalents. We separate the latter two, because of the frequent usage of English words in common language. We make these lexicons freely available for future research.

4.2 Features

4.2.1 Stylometric Features

Fake news are written with the intent to deceive, and their authors often use a different style of writing compared to authors that create genuine content. This could be either deliberately, e.g., if the author wants to adapt the text to a specific target group or wants to provoke some particular emotional reaction in the reader, or unintentionally, e.g., because the authors of fake news have different writing style and personality compared to journalists in mainstream media. Disregarding the actual reason, we use features from author profiling and style detection (Rangel et al., 2013).

Original word	Translation	PMI
chemtrails	chemtrails	0.92
феноменните	the phenomenal	0.94
следете в	follow in	0.97
тайнствена	mysterious	0.95
скрит	hidden	0.84

Table 1: Words most strongly associated with the fake news class.

Use of specific words that have strong correlation with one of the classes (48 features). We used the above-described PMI-based fact-checking lexicons to extract features based on the presence of lexicon words in the target article. We end up with the following features: 16 for uni-grams + 16 for bi-grams + 16 for named entities, where we have a feature for the sum and also for the average of the word scores for each of the target classes (click-bait, non-click-bait, fake, non-fake), and we had these features separately for the title and for the body of the article.

Readability index (4 features): We calculate standard readability metrics including the type-token ratio, average word length, Flesch–Kincaid readability test (Kincaid et al., 1975) and Gunning-Fog index (Gunning, 1952). The last two metrics give scores to the text corresponding to the school grade the reader of the target article should have in order to be able to read and understand it easily. These metrics use statistics about the number of syllables, the number of words, and their length.

Orthographic features (12 features): The orthographic features used in our system include: the number of words in the title and in the content; the number of characters in the title and in the content; the number of specific symbols in the title and in the content, counting the following as symbols \$.!;#?:-+%&(), ; the number of capital letters in the title and in the content; the fraction of capital letters to all letters in the title and in the content; the number of URLs in the content; the overlap between the words from the title and the words of the content, relying on the fact that click-baits tend to have content that does not quite match their title. These features can be very effective for modelling the author's style.

Use of irregular vocabulary (4 features):
During the initial analysis of our training
dataset, we noticed the presence of a high
number of foreign words. As it is not common in Bulgarian news articles to use words in
another language, we thought that their presence could be a valuable feature to use. One of
the reasons for their occurrence might be that
they were translated from a foreign resource,
or that they were borrowed. We further found
that many articles that were labelled as fake
news contained a high number of slang words,
and we added this as a feature as well. Finally,
we have a feature that counts the typos in the
text.

4.2.2 Lexical Features

General lexical features are often used in natural language processing as they are somewhat
task-independent and reasonably effective in
terms of classification accuracy. In our experiments, we used TF.IDF-based features over
the title and over the content of the article we
wanted to classify. We had these features twice
– once for the title and once for the the content
of the article, as we wanted to have two different representations of the same article. Thus,
we used a total of 1,100 TF.IDF-weighted features (800 content + 300 title), limiting the
vocabulary to the top 800 and 300 words, respectively (which occurred in more than five
articles). We should note that TF.IDF features should be used with caution as they may
not remain relevant over time or in different
contexts without retraining.

4.2.3 Grammatical Features

The last type of hand-crafted features that
we used are the grammatical features. First,
we evaluate how often stop words are used
in the content of the article. Extensive usage of stop words may indicate irregularities in
the text, which would be missed by the above
features. Additionally, we extract ten coarse-
grained part-of-speech tags from the content
of the article and we use part-of-speech occurrence ratios as features. This makes a total of
twenty features, as we have separate features
for the title and for the contents.

4.2.4 Semantic Features

All the above features are hand-crafted, evaluating a specific text metric or checking
whether specific words highly correlate with
one of the classes. However, we lack features
that target the semantic representation of the
text itself. Thus, we further use two types of
word representations.

Word embeddings (601 features). As we said
above, we trained domain-specific word embeddings. In order to incorporate them as features, we calculate the average vector for the
title and separately for the content of the news
article. We end up with two 300-dimensional
embedding representations of the semantics of
the articles, which we use as 300+300=600 features. We also compute the cosine similarity
between the average vector of the title and the
average vector of the content, because we believe that this is a highly indicative measure
for at least click-bait articles, whose content
differs from what their title says.

Task-specific embeddings. As a more advanced representation, we feed the text into
an attention-based deep neural network, which
we train to produce a task-specific embedding
of the news articles. The network is designed
to recognize words and sentences that contribute to the click-bait class attribution. The
architecture is described in details in Section
4.4.1

4.3 Some Features that we Ignored

As we mentioned above, our method is purely
text-based. Thus, we ignored the publishing
date of the article. In future work, it could
be explored as a useful piece of information
about the credibility of the article, as there is
interesting research in this direction (Ma et al.,
2015). We also disregarded the article source
(the URL) because websites that specialize in
producing and distributing fake content are often banned and then later reappear under another name. We recognize that the credibility of a specific website could be a very informative feature, but, for the sake of creating
a robust method for fake news detection, our
system relies only on the text when predicting
whether the target article is likely to be fake.
We describe our features in more detail below.

4.4 Model

Our framework for fake news detection is comprised of two components, which are used one after the other. First, we have an attention-based deep neural network model, which focuses on the segments of the text that are most indicative of the target class identification, and as a side effect learns task-specific representations of the news articles. We extract these representations from the last hidden layer in the network, and we feed it to the SVM classifier together with the hand-crafted features.

4.4.1 Attention Mechanism

The attention network (Hermann et al., 2015), (Yang et al., 2016) is a powerful mechanism, inspired by the human ability to spot important sections in images or text. We adopt the approach used in (Rocktäschel et al., 2015) and employ an attention neural networks to build attention over the text of a piece of news with respect to the title it has. As far as it is in the nature of click-baits to have titles that are different from the text of the news, the attentional layers of the neural network should spot when the two texts talk about the same thing and when they are not corresponding or accurate. We implemented the attention mechanism using Keras (Chollet et al., 2015) with the Tensorflow back-end (Abadi et al., 2015).

The architecture of the network with attention layers is shown in Figure 1. Our neural model is based on Gated Recurrent Units (GRUs). GRUs are gating mechanism in RNNs which provide the ability to learn long-term dependencies and were first introduced in (Cho et al., 2014). Given the document embedding, the GRUs build representations using input and forget gates, which help storing the valuable information through time. They build embeddings of the title and the text of the news, where at each step the unit has information only about the output from the previous step. This can be considered as a drawback, as far as we would considerably benefit if each step could construct its decision based not only on the previous step's output, but on all of the words that were processed so far. To improve this, the attention layer, for each step in the text sequence, uses the output of the steps in the title sequence. Thus, the layer

learns weights, designating the strength of the relatedness between each word in the title and each word in the content.

For the neural network, we take the first 50 symbols of the title and the content of the news, which we choose after experiments. We train the neural network for 20 epochs and the final classification is derived with sigmoid activation. The optimizer used for the training is Adam optimizer. We feed the neural network with the embedding of the words we built earlier with word2vec.

As we will see below, the neural network is inferior in terms of performance to a feature-rich SVM (even though it performs well above the baseline). This is because it only has access to word embeddings, and does not use the manually-crafted features. Yet, its hidden layer represents a 128-dimensional task-specific embedding of the input article, and it turns out that using it as a list of 128 features in the SVM classifier yields even further great improvement, as we will see below. In this way, we combine a deep neural network with an attention mechanism with kernel-based SVM.

Features	P	R	F1	Acc
Lexical	75.53	74.59	75.02	79.89
Stylometric	74.35	65.99	67.68	77.52
Grammatical	73.23	50.60	42.99	71.48
Embeddings	61.48	53.95	51.67	71.22

Table 2: Performance of the individual groups of hand-crafted features.

4.4.2 SVM

We feed the above-described hand-crafted features together with the task-specific embeddings learned by the deep neural neural network (a total of 1,892 attributes combined) into a Support Vector Machines (SVM) classifier (Cortes and Vapnik, 1995). SVMs have proven to perform well in different classification settings, including in the case of small and noisy datasets.

5 Experiments and Evaluation

We trained on the 2,815 training examples, and we tested on the 761 testing ones. The test dataset was provided apart from the training one, thus we didn't have to partition the

Figure 1: The architecture of our hierarchical attention deep neural network for click-bait news detection.

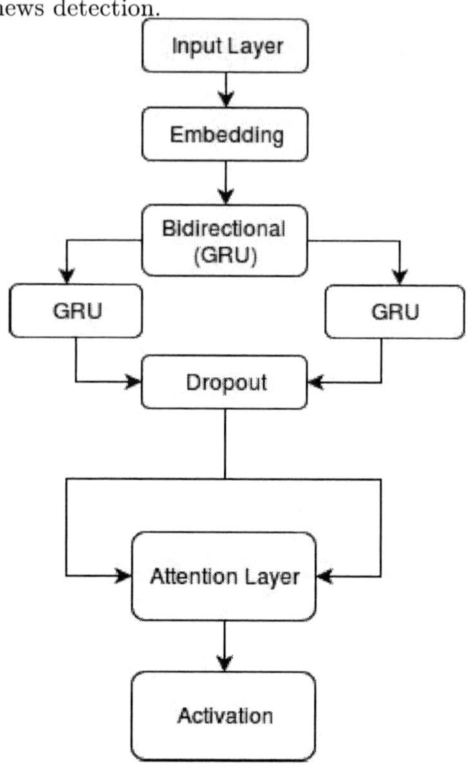

original dataset to receive a testing one. The validation of the models was performed on a randomly chosen subset of sentences - one fifth of the original set. We scaled each feature individually by its maximum absolute value to end up with each feature having values in the [0;1] interval. We used an RBF kernel for the SVM, and we tuned the values of C and γ using cross-validation. We trained the neural network using RMSProp (Tieleman and Hinton, 2012) with a learning rate of 0.001 and mini-batches of size 32, chosen by performing experiments with cross-validation . We evaluated the model after each epoch and we kept the one that performed best on the development dataset.

Table 2 shows the performance of the features in groups as described in Section 4.2. We can see that, among the hand-crafted features, the lexical features yield the best results, i.e., words are the most indicative features. The good results of the stylometric features indicate that the intricacies of language use are highly discriminative. The next group is the one with the grammatical features, which shows good performance in terms of Precision. The last one are the embedding features, which although having low individual performance, contribute to the overall performance of the system as shown in next paragraph.

Evaluating the final model, we set as a baseline the prediction of the majority class, i.e., the fake news class. This baseline has an F1 of 41.59% and accuracy of 71.22%. The performance of the built models can be seen in Table 3. Another stable baseline, apart from just taking the majority class, is the TF.IDF bag-of-words approach, which sets a high bar for the general model score. We then observe how much the attention mechanism embeddings improve the score (AtNN). Finally, we add the hand-crafted features (Feats), which further improve the performance. From the results, we can conclude that both the attention-based task-specific embeddings and the manual features are important for the task of finding fake news.

6   Conclusion and Future Work

We have presented the first attempt to solve the fake news problem for Bulgarian. Our method is purely text-based, and ignores the publication date and the source of the article. It combines task-specific embeddings, produced by a two-level attention-based deep neural network model, with manually crafted features (stylometric, lexical, grammatical, and semantic), into a kernel-based SVM classifier. We further produced and shared a number of relevant language resources for Bulgarian, which we created for solving the task.

The evaluation results are encouraging and suggest the potential applicability of our approach in a real-world scenario. They further show the potential of combining attention-based task-specific embeddings with manually crafted features. An important advantage of the attention-based neural networks is that the produced representations can be easily visualized and potentially interpreted as shown in (Hermann et al., 2015). We consider the implementation of such visualization as an important future work on the task.

Feature Group	P	R	F1	Acc
Baseline	35.61	50.00	41.59	71.22
TF.IDF	75.53	74.59	75.02	79.89
AttNN	78.52	78.74	78.63	81.99
TF.IDF &AttNN	79,89	79.40	79.63	83.44
TF.IDF &Feats &AttNN	80.07	79.49	79.77	83.57

Table 3: Performance of different models: AttNN – Attention Neural Network, Feats – hand-crafted features.

Acknowledgements

We would like to thank Lachezar Bozhkov, who was part of our team in the *Hack the Fake News* hackathon, for his insight. This work is supported by the NSF of Bulgaria under Grant No. DN-02/11/2016 - ITDGate.

References

Martín Abadi, Ashish Agarwal, Paul Barham, and et. al. 2015. TensorFlow: Large-scale machine learning on heterogeneous systems. Software available from tensorflow.org. http://tensorflow.org/.

Kayode Sakariyah Adewole, Nor Badrul Anuar, Amirrudin Kamsin, Kasturi Dewi Varathan, and Syed Abdul Razak. 2017. Malicious accounts: Dark of the social networks. *Journal of Network and Computer Applications* 79:41–67.

Abdullah Almaatouq, Erez Shmueli, Mariam Nouh, Ahmad Alabdulkareem, Vivek K Singh, Mansour Alsaleh, Abdulrahman Alarifi, Anas Alfaris, et al. 2016. If it looks like a spammer and behaves like a spammer, it must be a spammer: analysis and detection of microblogging spam accounts. *International Journal of Information Security* 15(5):475–491.

David M Blei, Andrew Y Ng, and Michael I Jordan. 2003. Latent dirichlet allocation. *Journal of machine Learning research* 3(Jan):993–1022.

Ann M Brill. 2001. Online journalists embrace new marketing function. *Newspaper Research Journal* 22(2):28.

K. R. Canini, B. Suh, and P. L. Pirolli. 2011. Finding credible information sources in social networks based on content and social structure. In *Privacy, Security, Risk and Trust (PASSAT) and 2011 IEEE Third Inernational Conference on Social Computing (SocialCom), 2011 IEEE Third International Conference on.* pages 1–8.

William P Cassidy. 2007. Online news credibility: An examination of the perceptions of newspaper journalists. *Journal of Computer-Mediated Communication* 12(2):478–498.

Carlos Castillo, Marcelo Mendoza, and Barbara Poblete. 2011. Information credibility on twitter. In *Proceedings of the 20th International Conference on World Wide Web.* Hyderabad, India, WWW '11, pages 675–684.

Kyunghyun Cho, Bart Van Merriënboer, Dzmitry Bahdanau, and Yoshua Bengio. 2014. On the properties of neural machine translation: Encoder-decoder approaches. *arXiv preprint arXiv:1409.1259* .

François Chollet et al. 2015. Keras. https://github.com/fchollet/keras.

Niall J Conroy, Victoria L Rubin, and Yimin Chen. 2015. Automatic deception detection: Methods for finding fake .

Corinna Cortes and Vladimir Vapnik. 1995. Support-vector networks. *Machine Learning* 20(3):273–297. https://doi.org/10.1023/A:1022627411411.

Stefano Cresci, Roberto Di Pietro, Marinella Petrocchi, Angelo Spognardi, and Maurizio Tesconi. 2015. Fame for sale: efficient detection of fake twitter followers. *Decision Support Systems* 80:56–71.

Kushal Dave, Steve Lawrence, and David M Pennock. 2003. Mining the peanut gallery: Opinion extraction and semantic classification of product reviews. In *Proceedings of the 12th International World Wide Web conference.* Budapest, Hungary, WWW '03, pages 519–528.

Howard Finberg, Martha L Stone, and Diane Lynch. 2002. Digital journalism credibility study. *Online News Association. Retrieved November* 3:2003.

Michael Fire, Dima Kagan, Aviad Elyashar, and Yuval Elovici. 2014. Friend or foe? fake profile identification in online social networks. *Social Network Analysis and Mining* 4(1):1–23.

Patxi Galán-García, José Gaviria de la Puerta, Carlos Laorden Gómez, Igor Santos, and Pablo García Bringas. 2014. Supervised machine learning for the detection of troll profiles in Twitter social network: Application to a real case of cyberbullying. In *Proceedings of* the International Joint Conference SOCO'13-CISIS'13-ICEUTE'13, Springer International Publishing, Advances in Intelligent Systems and Computing, pages 419–428.

Pepa Gencheva, Preslav Nakov, Lluís Màrquez, Alberto Barrón-Cede no, and Ivan Koychev. 2017. A context-aware approach for detecting worth-checking claims in political debates. In *Proceedings of the 2017 International Conference on Recent Advances in Natural Language Processing*. Varna, Bulgaria, RANLP '17.

Robert Gunning. 1952. The technique of clear writing .

Momchil Hardalov, Ivan Koychev, and Preslav Nakov. 2016. In search of credible news. In *Proceedings of the 17th International Conference on Artificial Intelligence: Methodology, Systems, and Applications*. Varna, Bulgaria, AIMSA '16, pages 172–180.

Karl Moritz Hermann, Tomás Kociský, Edward Grefenstette, Lasse Espeholt, Will Kay, Mustafa Suleyman, and Phil Blunsom. 2015. Teaching machines to read and comprehend. *CoRR* abs/1506.03340. http://arxiv.org/abs/1506.03340.

Minqing Hu and Bing Liu. 2004. Mining and summarizing customer reviews. In *Proceedings of the 10th ACM SIGKDD International Conference on Knowledge Discovery and Data Mining*. Seattle, Washington, USA, KDD '04, pages 168–177.

Thomas J Johnson, Barbara K Kaye, Shannon L Bichard, and W Joann Wong. 2007. Every blog has its day: Politically-interested internet users' perceptions of blog credibility. *Journal of Computer-Mediated Communication* 13(1):100–122.

Georgi Karadzhov, Preslav Nakov, Lluís Màrquez, Alberto Barrón-Cede no, and Ivan Koychev. 2017. Fully automated fact checking using external sources. In *Proceedings of the 2017 International Conference on Recent Advances in Natural Language Processing*. Varna, Bulgaria, RANLP '17.

Stan Ketterer. 1998. Teaching students how to evaluate and use online resources. *Journalism & Mass Communication Educator* 52(4):4.

J Peter Kincaid, Robert P Fishburne Jr, Richard L Rogers, and Brad S Chissom. 1975. Derivation of new readability formulas (automated readability index, fog count and flesch reading ease formula) for navy enlisted personnel. Technical report, Naval Technical Training Command Millington TN Research Branch.

Piroska Lendvai and Uwe D Reichel. 2016. Contradiction detection for rumorous claims. *arXiv preprint arXiv:1611.02588* .

Wenbin Li, Ning Zhong, and Chunnian Liu. 2006. Combining multiple email filters based on multivariate statistical analysis. In *Foundations of Intelligent Systems*, Springer, pages 729–738.

Michal Lukasik, Trevor Cohn, and Kalina Bontcheva. 2015. Point process modelling of rumour dynamics in social media. In *Proceedings of the 53rd Annual Meeting of the Association for Computational Linguistics and the 7th International Joint Conference on Natural Language Processing (Volume 2: Short Papers)*. Association for Computational Linguistics, Beijing, China, pages 518–523.

Jing Ma, Wei Gao, Zhongyu Wei, Yueming Lu, and Kam-Fai Wong. 2015. Detect rumors using time series of social context information on microblogging websites. In *Proceedings of the 24th ACM International on Conference on Information and Knowledge Management*. Melbourne, Australia, CIKM '15, pages 1751–1754.

Michael Mccord and M Chuah. 2011. Spam detection on twitter using traditional classifiers. In *International Conference on Autonomic and Trusted Computing*. Springer, pages 175–186.

Tomas Mikolov, Ilya Sutskever, Kai Chen, Greg S Corrado, and Jeff Dean. 2013. Distributed representations of words and phrases and their compositionality. In *Advances in neural information processing systems*. pages 3111–3119.

Tanushree Mitra, G Wright, and Eric Gilbert. 2017. A parsimonious language model of social media credibility across disparate events. In *Proc. CSCW*.

Saif M. Mohammad and Peter D. Turney. 2013. Crowdsourcing a word-emotion association lexicon. *Computational Intelligence* 29(3):436–465.

Meredith Ringel Morris, Scott Counts, Asta Roseway, Aaron Hoff, and Julia Schwarz. 2012. Tweeting is believing?: Understanding microblog credibility perceptions. In *Proceedings of the ACM 2012 Conference on Computer Supported Cooperative Work*. ACM, New York, NY, USA, CSCW '12, pages 441–450.

Subhabrata Mukherjee and Gerhard Weikum. 2015. Leveraging joint interactions for credibility analysis in news communities. In *Proceedings of the 24th ACM International on Conference on Information and Knowledge Management*. ACM, pages 353–362.

Preslav Nakov, Tsvetomila Mihaylova, Lluís Màrquez, Yashkumar Shiroya, and Ivan Koychev. 2017. Do not trust the trolls: Predicting credibility in community question answering forums. In *Proceedings of the 2017 International Conference on Recent Advances in Natural Language Processing*. Varna, Bulgaria, RANLP '17.

Francisco Rangel, Paolo Rosso, Moshe Moshe Koppel, Efstathios Stamatatos, and Giacomo Inches. 2013. Overview of the author profiling task at pan 2013. In *CLEF Conference on Multilingual and Multimodal Information Access Evaluation*. CELCT, pages 352–365.

Jacob Ratkiewicz, Michael Conover, Mark Meiss, Bruno Gonçalves, Snehal Patil, Alessandro Flammini, and Filippo Menczer. 2011. Truthy: Mapping the spread of astroturf in microblog streams. In *Proceedings of the 20th International Conference Companion on World Wide Web*. Hyderabad, India, WWW '11, pages 249–252.

Tim Rocktäschel, Edward Grefenstette, Karl Moritz Hermann, Tomáš Kočiský, and Phil Blunsom. 2015. Reasoning about entailment with neural attention. *arXiv preprint arXiv:1509.06664* .

Matthew Rowe and Jonathan Butters. 2009. Assessing Trust: Contextual Accountability. In *Proceedings of the First Workshop on Trust and Privacy on the Social and Semantic Web*. Heraklion, Greece, SPOT '09.

Fabrizio Sebastiani. 2002. Machine learning in automated text categorization. *ACM computing surveys (CSUR)* 34(1):1–47.

Tijmen Tieleman and Geoffrey Hinton. 2012. Lecture 6.5-rmsprop: Divide the gradient by a running average of its recent magnitude. *COURSERA: Neural networks for machine learning* 4(2):26–31.

Zichao Yang, Diyi Yang, Chris Dyer, Xiaodong He, Alex Smola, and Eduard Hovy. 2016. Hierarchical attention networks for document classification. In *Proceedings of NAACL-HLT*. pages 1480–1489.

Arkaitz Zubiaga, Geraldine Wong Sak Hoi, Maria Liakata, Rob Procter, and Peter Tolmie. 2015. Analysing how people orient to and spread rumours in social media by looking at conversational threads. *arXiv preprint arXiv:1511.07487* .

Arkaitz Zubiaga, Elena Kochkina, Maria Liakata, Rob Procter, and Michal Lukasik. 2016a. Stance classification in rumours as a sequential task exploiting the tree structure of social media conversations. *arXiv preprint arXiv:1609.09028* .

Arkaitz Zubiaga, Maria Liakata, Rob Procter, Geraldine Wong Sak Hoi, and Peter Tolmie. 2016b. Analysing how people orient to and spread rumours in social media by looking at conversational threads. *PLoS ONE* 11(3):1–29.

Fully Automated Fact Checking Using External Sources

Georgi Karadzhov[1], Preslav Nakov[2], Lluís Màrquez[2], Alberto Barrón-Cedeño[2], and Ivan Koychev[1]

[1]Sofia University "St. Kliment Ohridski", Bulgaria
[2]Qatar Computing Research Institute, HBKU, Qatar
georgi.m.karadjov@gmail.com, {pnakov, lmarquez, albarron}@hbku.edu.qa
koychev@fmi.uni-sofia.bg

Abstract

Given the constantly growing proliferation of false claims online in recent years, there has been also a growing research interest in automatically distinguishing false rumors from factually true claims. Here, we propose a general-purpose framework for fully-automatic fact checking using external sources, tapping the potential of the entire Web as a knowledge source to confirm or reject a claim. Our framework uses a deep neural network with LSTM text encoding to combine semantic kernels with task-specific embeddings that encode a claim together with pieces of potentially-relevant text fragments from the Web, taking the source reliability into account. The evaluation results show good performance on two different tasks and datasets: (*i*) rumor detection and (*ii*) fact checking of the answers to a question in community question answering forums.

1 Introduction

Recent years have seen the proliferation of deceptive information online. With the increasing necessity to validate the information from the Internet, *automatic fact checking* has emerged as an important research topic. It is at the core of multiple applications, e.g., discovery of fake news, rumor detection in social media, information verification in question answering systems, detection of information manipulation agents, and assistive technologies for investigative journalism. At the same time, it touches many aspects, such as credibility of users and sources, information veracity, information verification, and linguistic aspects of deceptive language.

In this paper, we present an approach to fact-checking with the following design principles: (*i*) generality, (*ii*) robustness, (*iii*) simplicity, (*iv*) reusability, and (*v*) strong machine learning modeling. Indeed, the system makes very few assumptions about the task, and looks for supportive information directly on the Web. Our system works fully automatically. It does not use any heavy feature engineering and can be easily used in combination with task-specific approaches as well, as a core subsystem. Finally, it combines the representational strength of recurrent neural networks with kernel-based classification.

The system starts with a claim to verify. First, we automatically convert the claim into a query, which we execute against a search engine in order to obtain a list of potentially relevant documents. Then, we take both the snippets and the most relevant sentences in the full text of these Web documents, and we compare them to the claim. The features we use are dense representations of the claim, of the snippets and of related sentences from the Web pages, which we automatically train for the task using Long Short-Term Memory networks (LSTMs). We also use the final hidden layer of the neural network as a task-specific embedding of the claim, together with the Web evidence. We feed all these representations as features, together with pairwise similarities, into a Support Vector Machine (SVM) classifier using an RBF kernel to classify the claim as True or False.

Figure 1 presents a real example from one of the datasets we experiment with. The left-hand side of the figure contains a True example, while the right-hand side shows a False one. We show the original claims from `snopes.com`, the query generated by our system, and the information retrieved from the Web (most relevant snippet and text selection from the web page). The veracity of the claim can be inferred from the textual information.

Proceedings of Recent Advances in Natural Language Processing, pages 344–353,
Varna, Bulgaria, Sep 4–6 2017.

Example 1   **Example 2**

original claim

Texas, teenager Ahmed Mohamed was arrested and accused of creating a "hoax bomb" after bringing a home-assembled clock to school. snopes.com[a]

Is the popular casual dining chain Chipotle closing all their locations soon? snopes.com[c]

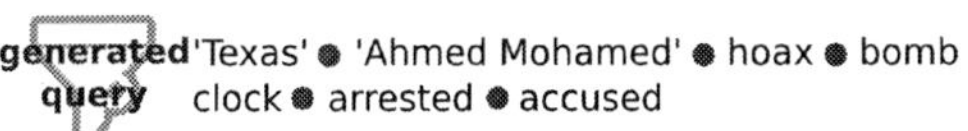

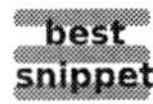

generated query

'Texas' ● 'Ahmed Mohamed' ● hoax ● bomb ● clock ● arrested ● accused

'Chipotle' ● dining ● locations ● popular ● closed

best snippet

knew I'd have a blast playing with [...] Ahmed wasn't accused of making a bomb he was accused of making a look-alike, a hoax [...] it was a bomb, the kid who invented his own digital clock

Chipotle Mexican Grill, Inc is an American chain of fast casual restaurants in the United States, [...] Ellis membership. The restaurant had three locations that operated in 2011 before closing

best webpage sentences

A 14-year-old Texas student was arrested at school for building a clock. ● A ninth grader was arrested on Sept. 14 just outside Dallas, when he brought a homemade clock to school that teachers and authorities said looked like a bomb Business Insider[b]

Chipotle says it plans to open burger restaurant Tribune news services Chipotle, still struggling to win back customers after a series of food scares, plans to open its first burger restaurant this year. ● The chain known for burritos said Thursday it will open a Tasty Made location this fall in Lancaster, Ohio, which is southeast of Columbus. ● The menu will be limited. Chicago Tribune[d]

label

Factually TRUE

Factually FALSE

[a] http://www.snopes.com/2015/09/16/ahmed-mohamed/
[b] http://www.businessinsider.com/ahmed-mohamed-arrested-irving-texas-clock-bomb-2015-9
[c] http://www.snopes.com/chipotle-closing/
[d] http://www.chicagotribune.com/business/ct-chipotle-burger-restaurant-20160728-story.html

Figure 1: Example claims and the information we use to predict whether they are factually true or false.

Our contributions can be summarized as follows:

- We propose a general-purpose light-weight framework for fully-automatic fact checking using evidence derived from the Web.

- We propose a deep neural network with LSTM encoding to combine semantic kernels with task-specific embeddings that encode a claim together with pieces of potentially-relevant text fragments from the Web, taking the source reliability into account.

- We further study factuality in community Question Answering (cQA), and we create a new high-quality dataset, which we release to the research community. To the best of our knowledge, we are the first to study factuality of answers in cQA forums, and our dataset is the first dataset specifically targeting factuality in a cQA setting.

- We achieve strong results on two different tasks and datasets —rumor detection and fact checking of the answers to a question in community question answering forums—, thus demonstrating the generality of the approach and its potential applicability to different fact-checking problem formulations.

The remainder of this paper is organized as follows. Section 2 introduces our method for fact checking claims using external sources. Section 3 presents our experiments and discusses the results. Section 4 describes an application of our approach to a different dataset and a slightly different task: fact checking in community question answering forums. Section 5 presents related work. Finally, Section 6 concludes and suggests some possible directions for future work.

2 The Fact-Checking System

Given a claim, our system searches for support information on the Web in order to verify whether the claim is likely to be true. The three steps in this process are (*i*) external support retrieval, (*ii*) text representation, and (*iii*) veracity prediction.

2.1 External Support Retrieval

This step consists of generating a query out of the claim and querying a search engine (here, we experiment with Google and Bing) in order to retrieve supporting documents. Rather than querying the search engine with the full claim (as on average, a claim is two sentences long), we generate a shorter query following the lessons highlighted in (Potthast et al., 2013).

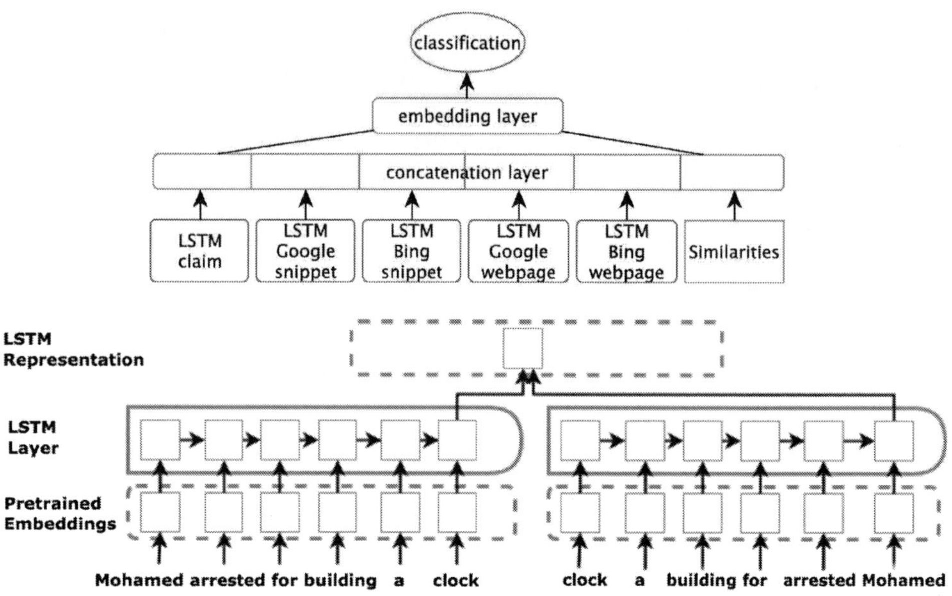

Figure 2: Our general neural network architecture (top) and detailed LSTM representation (bottom). Each blue box in the top consists of the bi-LSTM structure in the bottom.

As we aim to develop a general-purpose fact checking system, we use an approach for query generation that does not incorporate any features that are specific to claim verification (e.g., no temporal indicators).

We rank the words by means of *tf-idf*. We compute the *idf* values on a 2015 Wikipedia dump and the English Gigaword.[1] Potthast et al. (2013) suggested that a good way to perform high-quality search is to only consider the verbs, the nouns and the adjectives in the claim; thus, we exclude all words in the claim that belong to other parts of speech. Moreover, claims often contain named entities (e.g., names of persons, locations, and organizations); hence, we augment the initial query with all the named entities from the claim's text. We use IBM's AlchemyAPI[2] to identify named entities. Ultimately, we generate queries of 5–10 tokens, which we execute against a search engine. We then collect the snippets and the URLs in the results, skipping any result that points to a domain that is considered unreliable.[3] Finally, if our query has returned no results, we iteratively relax it by dropping the final tokens one at a time.

2.2 Text Representation

Next, we build the representation of a claim and the corresponding snippets and Web pages. First, we calculate three similarities (a) between the claim and a snippet, or (b) between the claim and a Web page: (*i*) cosine with *tf-idf*, (*ii*) cosine over embeddings, and (*iii*) containment (Lyon et al., 2001). We calculate the embedding of a text as the average of the embeddings of its words; for this, we use pre-trained embeddings from GloVe (Pennington et al., 2014). Moreover, as a Web page can be long, we first split it into a set of rolling sentence triplets, then we calculate the similarities between the claim and each triplet, and we take the highest scoring triplet. Finally, as we have up to ten hits from the search engine, we take the maximum and also the average of the three similarities over the snippets and over the Web pages.

We further use as features the embeddings of the claim, of the best-scoring snippet, and of the best-scoring sentence triplet from a Web page. We calculate these embeddings (*i*) as the average of the embeddings of the words in the text, and also (*ii*) using LSTM encodings, which we train for the task as part of a deep neural network (NN). We also use a task-specific embedding of the claim together with all the above evidence about it, which comes from the last hidden layer of the NN.

---

[1] catalog.ldc.upenn.edu/ldc2011t07

[2] www.ibm.com/watson/alchemy-api.html

[3] We created such a list by manually checking the 100 most frequent domains in the results, which we accummulated across many queries and experiments.

2.3 Veracity Prediction

Next, we build classifiers: neural network (NN), support vector machines (SVM), and a combination thereof (SVM+NN).

NN. The architecture of our NN is shown on top of Figure 2. We have five LSTM sub-networks, one for each of the text sources from two search engines: *Claim*, *Google Web page*, *Google snippet*, *Bing Web page*, and *Bing snippet*. The claim is fed into the neural network as-is. As we can have multiple snippets, we only use the best-matching one as described above. Similarly, we only use a single best-matching triple of consecutive sentences from a Web page. We further feed the network with the similarity features described above. All these vectors are concatenated and fully connected to a much more compact hidden layer that captures the task-specific embeddings. This layer is connected to a softmax output unit to classify the claim as true or false. The bottom of Figure 2 represents the generic architecture of each of the LSTM components. The input text is transformed into a sequence of word embeddings, which is then passed to the bidirectional LSTM layer to obtain a representation for the full sequence.

SVM. Our second classifier is an SVM with an RBF kernel. The input is the same as for the NN: word embeddings and similarities. However, the word embeddings this time are calculated by averaging rather than using a bi-LSTM.

SVM + NN. Finally, we combine the SVM with the NN by augmenting the input to the SVM with the values of the units in the hidden layer. This represents a task-specific embedding of the input example, and in our experiments it turned out to be quite helpful. Unlike in the SVM only model, this time we use the bi-LSTM embeddings as an input to the SVM. Ultimately, this yields a combination of deep learning and task-specific embeddings with RBF kernels.

3 Experiments and Evaluation

3.1 Dataset

We used part of the rumor detection dataset created by Ma et al. (2016). While they analyzed a claim based on a set of potentially related tweets, we focus on the claim itself and on the use of supporting information from the Web.

The dataset consists of 992 sets of tweets, 778 of which are generated starting from a claim on `snopes.com`, which Ma et al. (2016) converted into a query. Another 214 sets of tweets are tweet clusters created by other researchers (Castillo et al., 2011; Kwon et al., 2013) with no claim behind them. Ma et al. (2016) ignored the claim and did not release it as part of their dataset. We managed to find the original claim for 761 out of the 778 `snopes.com`-based clusters.

Our final dataset consists of 761 claims from `snopes.com`, which span various domains including politics, local news, and fun facts. Each of the claims is labeled as factually *true* (34%) or as a *false* rumor (66%). We further split the data into 509 for training, 132 for development, and 120 for testing. As the original split for the dataset was not publicly available, and as we only used a subset of their data, we had to make a new training and testing split. Note that we ignored the tweets, as we wanted to focus on a complementary source of information: the Web. Moreover, Ma et al. (2016) used manual queries, while we use a fully automatic method. Finally, we augmented the dataset with Web-retrieved snippets, Web pages, and sentence triplets from Web pages.[4]

3.2 Experimental Setup

We tuned the architecture (i.e., the number of layers and their size) and the hyper-parameters of the neural network on the development dataset. The best configuration uses a bidirectional LSTM with 25 units. It further uses a RMSprop optimizer with 0.001 initial learning rate, L2 regularization with λ=0.1, and 0.5 dropout after the LSTM layers. The size of the hidden layer is 60 with *tanh* activations. We use a batch of 32 and we train for 400 epochs.

For the SVM model, we merged the development and the training dataset, and we then ran a 5-fold cross-validation with grid-search, looking for the best kernel and its parameters. We ended up selecting an RBF kernel with $c = 16$ and $\gamma = 0.01$.

3.3 Evaluation Metrics

The evaluation metrics we use are P (precision), R (recall), and F_1, which we calculate with respect to the false and to the true claims. We further report AvgR (macro-average recall), $AvgF_1$ (macro-average F_1), and Acc (accuracy).

---

[4] All the data, including the splits, is available at `github.com/gkaradzhov/FactcheckingRANLP`

	False Claims			**True Claims**			**Overall**		
Model	**P**	**R**	**F1**	**P**	**R**	**F1**	**AvgR**	**AvgF$_1$**	**Acc**
SVM + NN	84.1	86.3	85.2	71.1	67.5	69.2	**76.9**	**77.2**	**80.0**
NN	79.6	92.5	85.5	77.8	52.5	62.7	**72.5**	**74.1**	**79.2**
SVM	75.0	86.3	80.2	60.7	42.5	50.0	**64.4**	**65.1**	**71.7**
all *false*	66.7	100.0	80.0	–	0.0	0.0	50.0	40.0	66.7
all *true*	–	0.0	0.0	33.3	100.0	50.0	50.0	25.0	33.3

Table 1: Results on the *rumor detection dataset* using Web pages returned by the search engines.

3.4 Results

Table 1 shows the results on the test dataset. We can see that both the NN and the SVM models improve over the majority class baseline (all false rumors) by a sizable margin. Moreover, the NN consistently outperforms the SVM by a margin on all measures. Yet, adding the task-specific embeddings from the NN as features of the SVM yields overall improvements over both the SVM and the NN in terms of avgR, avgF$_1$, and accuracy. We can see that both the SVM and the NN overpredict the majority class (false claims); however, the combined SVM+NN model is quite balanced between the two classes.

Table 2 compares the performance of the SVM with and without task-specific embeddings from the NN, when training on Web pages vs. snippets, returned by Google vs. Bing vs. both. The NN embeddings consistently help the SVM in all cases. Moreover, while the baseline SVM using snippets is slightly better than when using Web pages, there is almost no difference between snippets vs. Web pages when NN embeddings are added to the basic SVM. Finally, gathering external support from either Google or Bing makes practically no difference, and using the results from both together does not yield much further improvement. Thus, (*i*) the search engines already do a good job at generating relevant snippets, and one does not need to go and download the full Web pages, and (*ii*) the choice of a given search engine is not an important factor. These are good news for the practicality of our approach.

Unfortunately, direct comparison with respect to (Ma et al., 2016) is not possible. First, we only use a subset of their examples: 761 out of 993 (see Section 3.1), and we also have a different class distribution. More importantly, they have a very different formulation of the task: for them, the claim is not available as input (in fact, there has never been a claim for 21% of their examples); rather an example consists of a set of tweets retrieved using *manually* written queries.

Model	External support	AvgR	AvgF$_1$	Acc
SVM + NN	Bing+Google; pages	76.9	77.2	**80.0**
SVM	Bing+Google; pages	64.4	65.1	**71.7**
SVM + NN	Bing+Google; snippets	75.6	75.6	**78.3**
SVM	Bing+Google; snippets	68.1	69.0	**74.2**
SVM + NN	Bing; pages	77.5	77.0	**79.2**
SVM	Bing; pages	66.9	67.5	**72.5**
SVM + NN	Bing; snippets	76.3	76.4	**79.2**
SVM	Bing; snippets	68.8	69.7	**75.0**
SVM + NN	Google; pages	73.1	74.2	**78.3**
SVM	Google; pages	63.1	63.8	**71.7**
SVM + NN	Google; snippets	73.1	74.2	**78.3**
SVM	Google; snippets	65.6	66.6	**73.3**
baseline (all false claims)		50.0	40.0	**66.7**

Table 2: Results using an SVM with and without task-specific embeddings from the NN on the *Rumor detection dataset*. Training on Web pages vs. snippets vs. both.

In contrast, our system is fully automatic and does not use tweets at all. Furthermore, their most important information source is the change in tweets volume over time, which we cannot use. Still, our results are competitive to theirs when they do not use temporal features.

To put the results in perspective, we can further try to make an indirect comparison to the very recent paper by Popat et al. (2017). They also present a model to classify true vs. false claims extracted from snopes.com, by using information extracted from the Web. Their formulation of the task is the same as ours, but our corpora and label distributions are not the same, which makes a direct comparison impossible. Still, we can see that regarding overall classification accuracy they improve a baseline from 73.7% to 84.02% with their best model, i.e., a 39.2% relative error reduction. In our case, we go from 66.7% to 80.0%, i.e., an almost identical 39.9% error reduction. These results are very encouraging, especially given the fact that our model is much simpler than theirs regarding the sources of information used (they model the stance of the text, the reliability of the sources, the language style of the articles, and the temporal footprint).

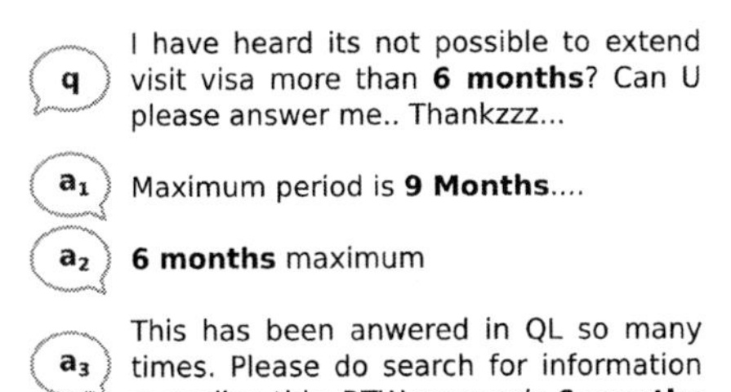

Figure 3: Example from the cQA forum dataset.

	Label	Answers
+	FACTUAL - TRUE	128
−	FACTUAL - PARTIALLY TRUE	38
−	FACTUAL - CONDITIONALLY TRUE	16
−	FACTUAL - FALSE	22
−	FACTUAL - RESPONDER UNSURE	26
−	NONFACTUAL	19
	TOTAL	**249**
	+ POSITIVE	**128**
	− NEGATIVE	**121**

Table 3: Distribution of the answer labels.

4 Application to cQA

Next, we tested the generality of our approach by applying it to a different setup: fact-checking the answers in community question answering (cQA) forums. As this is a new problem, for which no dataset exists, we created one. We augmented with factuality annotations the cQA dataset from SemEval-2016 Task 3 (CQA-QA-2016) (Nakov et al., 2016). Overall, we annotated 249 question–answer, or q-a, pairs (from 71 threads): 128 factually true and 121 factually false answers.

Each question in CQA-QA-2016 has a subject, a body, and meta information: ID, category (e.g., *Education*, and *Moving to Qatar*), date and time of posting, user name and ID. We selected only the factual questions such as *"What is Ooredoo customer service number?"*, thus filtering out all (*i*) socializing, e.g., *"What was your first car?"*, (*ii*) requests for opinion/advice/guidance, e.g., *"Which is the best bank around??"*, and (*iii*) questions containing multiple sub-questions, e.g., *"Is there a land route from Doha to Abudhabi. If yes; how is the road and how long is the journey?"*

Next, we annotated for veracity the answers to the retained questions. Note that in CQA-QA-2016, each answer has a subject, a body, meta information (answer ID, user name and ID), and a judgment about how well it addresses the question of its thread: GOOD vs. POTENTIALLY USEFUL vs. BAD. We only annotated the GOOD answers.[5] We further discarded answers whose factuality was very time-sensitive (e.g., *"It is Friday tomorrow."*, *"It was raining last week."*)[6], or for which the annotators were unsure.

---

[5] See (Nakov et al., 2017a) for an overview of recent approaches to finding GOOD answers for cQA.

[6] Arguably, many answers are somewhat time-sensitive, e.g., *"There is an IKEA in Doha."* is true only after IKEA opened, but not before that. In such cases, we just used the present situation as a point of reference.

We targeted very high quality, and thus we did not use crowdsourcing for the annotation, as pilot annotations showed that the task was very difficult and that it was not possible to guarantee that *Turkers* would do all the necessary verification, e.g., gathering evidence from trusted sources. Instead, all examples were first annotated independently by four annotators, and then *each example* was discussed in detail to come up with a final label. We ended up with 249 GOOD answers to 71 different questions, which we annotated for factuality: 128 POSITIVE and 121 NEGATIVE examples. See Table 3 for details.

We further split our dataset into 185 q–a pairs for training, 31 for development, and 32 for testing, preserving the general positive:negative ratio, and making sure that the questions for the q–a pairs did not overlap between the splits.

Figure 3 presents an excerpt of an example from the dataset, with one question and three answers selected from a longer thread. Answer a_1 contains false information, while a_2 and a_3 are true, as can be checked on an official governmental website.[7]

We had to fit our system for this problem, as here we do not have claims, but a question and an answer. So, we constructed the query from the concatenation of q and a. Moreover, as Google and Bing performed similarly, we only report results using Google. We limited our run to snippets only, as we have found them rich enough above (see Section 3). Also, we had a list of reputed and Qatar-related sources for the domain, and we limited our results to these sources only. This time, we had more options to calculate similarities compared to the rumors dataset: we can compare against q, a, and q–a; we chose to go with the latter. For the LSTM representations, we use both the question and the answer.

---

[7] https://www.moi.gov.qa/site/english/departments/PassportDept/news/2011/01/03/23385.html

Model	False Claims			True Claims			Overall		
	P	R	F1	P	R	F1	AvgR	AvgF1	Acc
SVM + NN	72.2	76.5	74.3	73.3	68.8	71.0	**72.7**	**72.7**	**72.7**
SVM	70.6	70.6	70.6	68.8	68.8	68.8	**69.7**	**69.7**	**69.7**
NN	61.1	64.7	62.9	60.0	56.3	58.1	**60.5**	**60.5**	**60.6**
all *false*	51.5	100.0	68.0	–	0	0	**50.0**	**34.0**	**51.5**
all *true*	–	0.0	0.0	48.5	100.0	65.3	**50.0**	**32.7**	**48.5**

Table 4: Results on the cQA answer fact-checking problem.

Table 4 shows the results on the cQA dataset. Once again, our models outperformed all baselines by a margin. This time, the predictions of all models are balanced between the two classes, which is probably due to the dataset being well balanced in general. The SVM model performs better than the NN by itself. This is due to the fact that the cQA dataset is significantly smaller than the *rumor detection* one. Thus, the neural network could not be trained effectively by itself. Nevertheless, the task-specific representations were useful and combining them with the SVM model yielded consistent improvements on all the measures once again.

5 Related Work

Journalists, online users, and researchers are well aware of the proliferation of false information on the Web, and topics such as information credibility and fact checking are becoming increasingly important as research directions. For example, there was a recent 2016 special issue of the ACM Transactions on Information Systems journal on Trust and Veracity of Information in Social Media (Papadopoulos et al., 2016), there was a SemEval-2017 shared task on Rumor Detection (Derczynski et al., 2017), and there is an upcoming lab at CLEF-2018 on Automatic Identification and Verification of Claims in Political Debates (Gencheva et al., 2017).

The credibility of contents on the Web has been questioned by researches for a long time. While in the early days the main research focus was on online news portals (Brill, 2001; Finberg et al., 2002; Hardalov et al., 2016), the interest has eventually shifted towards social media (Castillo et al., 2011; Zubiaga et al., 2016; Popat et al., 2017; Karadzhov et al., 2017), which are abundant in sophisticated malicious users such as opinion manipulation *trolls*, paid (Mihaylov et al., 2015b) or just perceived (Mihaylov et al., 2015a; Mihaylov and Nakov, 2016), *sockpuppets* (Maity et al., 2017), *Internet water army* (Chen et al., 2013), and *seminar users* (Darwish et al., 2017).

For instance, Canini et al. (2011) studied the credibility of Twitter accounts (as opposed to tweet posts), and found that both the topical content of information sources and social network structure affect source credibility. Other work, closer to ours, aims at addressing credibility assessment of rumors on Twitter as a problem of finding false information about a newsworthy event (Castillo et al., 2011). This model considers user reputation, writing style, and various time-based features, among others.

Other efforts have focused on news communities. For example, several truth discovery algorithms are combined in an ensemble method for veracity estimation in the VERA system (Ba et al., 2016). They proposed a platform for end-to-end truth discovery from the Web: extracting unstructured information from multiple sources, combining information about single claims, running an ensemble of algorithms, and visualizing and explaining the results. They also explore two different real-world application scenarios for their system: fact checking for crisis situations and evaluation of trustworthiness of a rumor. However, the input to their model is structured data, while here we are interested in unstructured text as input.

Similarly, the task defined by Mukherjee and Weikum (2015) combines three objectives: assessing the credibility of a set of posted articles, estimating the trustworthiness of sources, and predicting user's expertise. They considered a manifold of features characterizing language, topics and Web-specific statistics (e.g., review ratings) on top of a continuous conditional random fields model. In follow-up work, Popat et al. (2016) proposed a model to support or refute claims from snopes.com and Wikipedia by considering supporting information gathered from the Web. They used the same task formulation for claims as we do, but different datasets. In yet another follow-up work, Popat et al. (2017) proposed a complex model that considers stance, source reliability, language style, and temporal information.

Our approach to fact checking is related: we verify facts on the Web. However, we use a much simpler and feature-light system, and a different machine learning model. Yet, our model performs very similarly to this latter work (even though a direct comparison is not possible as the datasets differ), which is a remarkable achievement given the fact that we consider less knowledge sources, we have a conceptually simpler model, and we have six times less training data than Popat et al. (2017).

Another important research direction is on using tweets and temporal information for checking the factuality of rumors. For example, Ma et al. (2015) used temporal patterns of rumor dynamics to detect false rumors and to predict their frequency. Ma et al. (2015) focused on detecting false rumors in Twitter using time series. They used the change of social context features over a rumor's life cycle in order to detect rumors at an early stage after they were broadcast.

A more general approach for detecting rumors is explored by Ma et al. (2016), who used recurrent neural networks to learn hidden representations that capture the variation of contextual information of relevant posts over time. Unlike this work, we do not use microblogs, but we query the Web directly in search for evidence. Again, while direct comparison to the work of Ma et al. (2016) is not possible, due to differences in dataset and task formulation, we can say that our framework is competitive when temporal information is not used. More importantly, our approach is orthogonal to theirs in terms of information sources used, and thus, we believe there is potential in combining the two approaches.

In the context of question answering, there has been work on assessing the credibility of an answer, e.g., based on intrinsic information (Banerjee and Han, 2009), i.e., without any external resources. In this case, the reliability of an answer is measured by computing the divergence between language models of the question and of the answer. The spawn of community-based question answering Websites also allowed for the use of other kinds of information. Click counts, link analysis (e.g., PageRank), and user votes have been used to assess the quality of a posted answer (Agichtein et al., 2008; Jeon et al., 2006; Jurczyk and Agichtein, 2007). Nevertheless, these studies address the answers' credibility level just marginally.

Efforts to determine the credibility of an answer in order to assess its overall quality required the inclusion of content-based information (Su et al., 2010), e.g., verbs and adjectives such as *suppose* and *probably*, which cast doubt on the answer. Similarly, Lita et al. (2005) used source credibility (e.g., does the document come from a government Website?), sentiment analysis, and answer contradiction compared to other related answers.

Overall, *credibility* assessment for question answering has been mostly modeled at the feature level, with the goal of assessing the quality of the answers. A notable exception is the work of (Nakov et al., 2017b), where credibility is treated as a task of its own right. Yet, note that *credibility* is different from *factuality* (our focus here) as the former is a subjective perception about whether a statement is credible, rather than verifying it as true or false as a matter of fact; still, these notions are often wrongly mixed in the literature. To the best of our knowledge, no previous work has targeted fact-checking of answers in the context of community Question Answering by gathering external support.

6   Conclusions and Future Work

We have presented and evaluated a general-purpose method for fact checking that relies on retrieving supporting information from the Web and comparing it to the claim using machine learning. Our method is lightweight in terms of features and can be very efficient because it shows good performance by only using the snippets provided by the search engines. The combination of the representational power of neural networks with the classification of kernel-based methods has proven to be crucial for making balanced predictions and obtaining good results. Overall, the strong performance of our model across two different fact-checking tasks confirms its generality and potential applicability for different domains and for different fact-checking task formulations.

In future work, we plan to test the generality of our approach by applying it to these and other datasets in combination with complementary methods, e.g., those focusing on microblogs and temporal information in Twitter to make predictions about rumors (Ma et al., 2015, 2016). We also want to explore the possibility of providing justifications for our predictions, and we plan to integrate our method into a real-world application.

Acknowledgments

This research was performed by the Arabic Language Technologies group at Qatar Computing Research Institute, HBKU, within the Interactive sYstems for Answer Search project (IYAS).

References

Eugene Agichtein, Carlos Castillo, Debora Donato, Aristides Gionis, and Gilad Mishne. 2008. Finding high-quality content in social media. In *Proceedings of the International Conference on Web Search and Data Mining*. Palo Alto, California, USA, WSDM '08, pages 183–194.

Mouhamadou Lamine Ba, Laure Berti-Equille, Kushal Shah, and Hossam M. Hammady. 2016. VERA: A platform for veracity estimation over web data. In *Proceedings of the 25th International Conference Companion on World Wide Web*. Montréal, Québec, Canada, WWW '16, pages 159–162.

Protima Banerjee and Hyoil Han. 2009. Answer credibility: A language modeling approach to answer validation. In *Proceedings of the Annual Conference of the North American Chapter of the Association for Computational Linguistics: Human Language Technologies*. Boulder, Colorado, USA, NAACL-HLT '09, pages 157–160.

Ann M Brill. 2001. Online journalists embrace new marketing function. *Newspaper Research Journal* 22(2):28.

Kevin R. Canini, Bongwon Suh, and Peter L. Pirolli. 2011. Finding credible information sources in social networks based on content and social structure. In *Proceedings of the IEEE International Conference on Privacy, Security, Risk, and Trust, and the IEEE International Conference on Social Computing*. Boston, Massachusetts, USA, Social-Com/PASSAT '11, pages 1–8.

Carlos Castillo, Marcelo Mendoza, and Barbara Poblete. 2011. Information credibility on Twitter. In *Proceedings of the 20th International Conference on World Wide Web*. Hyderabad, India, WWW '11, pages 675–684.

Cheng Chen, Kui Wu, Venkatesh Srinivasan, and Xudong Zhang. 2013. Battling the Internet Water Army: detection of hidden paid posters. In *Proceedings of the 2013 IEEE/ACM International Conference on Advances in Social Networks Analysis and Mining*. Niagara, Ontario, Canada, ASONAM '13, pages 116–120.

Kareem Darwish, Dimitar Alexandrov, Preslav Nakov, and Yelena Mejova. 2017. Seminar users in the Arabic Twitter sphere. In *Proceedings of the 9th International Conference on Social Informatics*. Oxford, UK, SocInfo '17, pages 91–108.

Leon Derczynski, Kalina Bontcheva, Maria Liakata, Rob Procter, Geraldine Wong Sak Hoi, and Arkaitz Zubiaga. 2017. SemEval-2017 Task 8: RumourEval: Determining rumour veracity and support for rumours. In *Proceedings of the 11th International Workshop on Semantic Evaluation*. Vancouver, Canada, SemEval '17, pages 60–67.

Howard Finberg, Martha L Stone, and Diane Lynch. 2002. Digital journalism credibility study. *Online News Association. Retrieved November* 3:2003.

Pepa Gencheva, Preslav Nakov, Lluís Màrquez, Alberto Barrón-Cedeño, and Ivan Koychev. 2017. A context-aware approach for detecting worth-checking claims in political debates. In *Proceedings of the International Conference on Recent Advances in Natural Language Processing*. Varna, Bulgaria, RANLP '17.

Momchil Hardalov, Ivan Koychev, and Preslav Nakov. 2016. In search of credible news. In *Proceedings of the 17th International Conference on Artificial Intelligence: Methodology, Systems, and Applications*. Varna, Bulgaria, AIMSA '16, pages 172–180.

Jiwoon Jeon, W. Bruce Croft, Joon Ho Lee, and Soyeon Park. 2006. A framework to predict the quality of answers with non-textual features. In *Proceedings of the 29th Annual International ACM SIGIR Conference on Research and Development in Information Retrieval*. Seattle, Washington, USA, SIGIR '06, pages 228–235.

Pawel Jurczyk and Eugene Agichtein. 2007. Discovering authorities in question answer communities by using link analysis. In *Proceedings of the 16th ACM Conference on Conference on Information and Knowledge Management*. Lisbon, Portugal, CIKM '07, pages 919–922.

Georgi Karadzhov, Pepa Gencheva, Preslav Nakov, and Ivan Koychev. 2017. We built a fake news & clickbait filter: What happened next will blow your mind! In *Proceedings of the International Conference on Recent Advances in Natural Language Processing*. Varna, Bulgaria, RANLP '17.

Sejeong Kwon, Meeyoung Cha, Kyomin Jung, Wei Chen, and Yajun Wang. 2013. Prominent features of rumor propagation in online social media. In *Proceedings of the 13th IEEE International Conference on Data Mining*. Dallas, Texas, USA, ICDM '13, pages 1103–1108.

Lucian Vlad Lita, Andrew Hazen Schlaikjer, WeiChang Hong, and Eric Nyberg. 2005. Qualitative dimensions in question answering: Extending the definitional QA task. In *Proceedings of the 20th National Conference on Artificial Intelligence*. Pittsburgh, Pennsylvania, USA, AAAI '05, pages 1616–1617.

Caroline Lyon, James Malcolm, and Bob Dickerson. 2001. Detecting short passages of similar text in large document collections. In *Proceedings of the Conference on Empirical Methods in Natural Language Processing*. Pittsburgh, Pennsylvania, USA, EMNLP '01, pages 118–125.

Jing Ma, Wei Gao, Prasenjit Mitra, Sejeong Kwon, Bernard J. Jansen, Kam-Fai Wong, and Meeyoung Cha. 2016. Detecting rumors from microblogs with recurrent neural networks. In *Proceedings of the 25th International Joint Conference on Artificial Intelligence*. New York, New York, USA, IJCAI '16, pages 3818–3824.

Jing Ma, Wei Gao, Zhongyu Wei, Yueming Lu, and Kam-Fai Wong. 2015. Detect rumors using time series of social context information on microblogging websites. In *Proceedings of the 24th ACM International on Conference on Information and Knowledge Management*. Melbourne, Australia, CIKM '15, pages 1751–1754.

Suman Kalyan Maity, Aishik Chakraborty, Pawan Goyal, and Animesh Mukherjee. 2017. Detection of sockpuppets in social media. In *Proceedings of the ACM Conference on Computer Supported Cooperative Work and Social Computing*. Portland, Oregon, USA, CSCW '17, pages 243–246.

Todor Mihaylov, Georgi Georgiev, and Preslav Nakov. 2015a. Finding opinion manipulation trolls in news community forums. In *Proceedings of the Nineteenth Conference on Computational Natural Language Learning*. Beijing, China, CoNLL '15, pages 310–314.

Todor Mihaylov, Ivan Koychev, Georgi Georgiev, and Preslav Nakov. 2015b. Exposing paid opinion manipulation trolls. In *Proceedings of the International Conference Recent Advances in Natural Language Processing*. Hissar, Bulgaria, RANLP '15, pages 443–450.

Todor Mihaylov and Preslav Nakov. 2016. Hunting for troll comments in news community forums. In *Proceedings of the 54th Annual Meeting of the Association for Computational Linguistics*. Berlin, Germany, ACL '16, pages 399–405.

Subhabrata Mukherjee and Gerhard Weikum. 2015. Leveraging joint interactions for credibility analysis in news communities. In *Proceedings of the 24th ACM International on Conference on Information and Knowledge Management*. Melbourne, Australia, CIKM '15, pages 353–362.

Preslav Nakov, Doris Hoogeveen, Lluís Màrquez, Alessandro Moschitti, Hamdy Mubarak, Timothy Baldwin, and Karin Verspoor. 2017a. SemEval-2017 task 3: Community question answering. In *Proceedings of the 11th International Workshop on Semantic Evaluation*. Vancouver, Canada, SemEval '17, pages 27–48.

Preslav Nakov, Lluís Màrquez, Alessandro Moschitti, Walid Magdy, Hamdy Mubarak, abed Alhakim Freihat, Jim Glass, and Bilal Randeree. 2016. SemEval-2016 task 3: Community question answering. In *Proceedings of the 10th International Workshop on Semantic Evaluation*. San Diego, California, USA, SemEval '16, pages 525–545.

Preslav Nakov, Tsvetomila Mihaylova, Lluís Màrquez, Yashkumar Shiroya, and Ivan Koychev. 2017b. Do not trust the trolls: Predicting credibility in community question answering forums. In *Proceedings of the International Conference on Recent Advances in Natural Language Processing*. Varna, Bulgaria, RANLP '17.

Symeon Papadopoulos, Kalina Bontcheva, Eva Jaho, Mihai Lupu, and Carlos Castillo. 2016. Overview of the special issue on trust and veracity of information in social media. *ACM Trans. Inf. Syst.* 34(3):14:1–14:5.

Jeffrey Pennington, Richard Socher, and Christopher Manning. 2014. GloVe: Global vectors for word representation. In *Proceedings of the Conference on Empirical Methods in Natural Language Processing*. Doha, Qatar, EMNLP '14, pages 1532–1543.

Kashyap Popat, Subhabrata Mukherjee, Jannik Strötgen, and Gerhard Weikum. 2016. Credibility assessment of textual claims on the web. In *Proceedings of the 25th ACM International on Conference on Information and Knowledge Management*. Indianapolis, Indiana, USA, CIKM '16, pages 2173–2178.

Kashyap Popat, Subhabrata Mukherjee, Jannik Strötgen, and Gerhard Weikum. 2017. Where the truth lies: Explaining the credibility of emerging claims on the web and social media. In *Proceedings of the 26th International Conference on World Wide Web Companion*. Perth, Australia, WWW '17, pages 1003–1012.

Martin Potthast, Matthias Hagen, Tim Gollub, Martin Tippmann, Johannes Kiesel, Paolo Rosso, Efstathios Stamatatos, and Benno Stein. 2013. Overview of the 5th international competition on plagiarism detection. In *Proceedings of the Conference on Multilingual and Multimodal Information Access Evaluation*. Valencia, Spain, CLEF '13, pages 301–331.

Qi Su, Helen Kai-Yun Chen, and Chu-Ren Huang. 2010. Incorporate credibility into context for the best social media answers. In *Proceedings of the 24th Pacific Asia Conference on Language, Information and Computation*. Sendai, Japan, PACLIC '10, pages 535–541.

Arkaitz Zubiaga, Maria Liakata, Rob Procter, Geraldine Wong Sak Hoi, and Peter Tolmie. 2016. Analysing how people orient to and spread rumours in social media by looking at conversational threads. *PLoS ONE* 11(3):1–29.

Making Travel Smarter: Extracting Travel Information From E-Mail Itineraries Using Named Entity Recognition

Divyansh Kaushik[*], Shashank Gupta[+], Chakradhar Raju[+], Reuben Dias[+], and Sanjib Ghosh[+]

[*]Language Technologies Institute, Carnegie Mellon University
dkaushik@cmu.edu
[+]Amadeus IT Group
{shashank.gupta, mchakradharraju, reuben.dias, sanjib.ghosh}@amadeus.com

Abstract

The purpose of this research is to address the problem of extracting information from travel itineraries and discuss the challenges faced in the process. Business-to-customer emails like booking confirmations and e-tickets are usually machine generated by filling slots in pre-defined templates which improve the presentation of such emails but also make the emails more complex in structure. Extracting the relevant information from these emails would let users track their journeys and important updates on applications installed on their devices to give them a consolidated over view of their itineraries and also save valuable time. We investigate the use of an HMM-based named entity recognizer on such emails which we will use to label and extract relevant entities. NER in such emails is challenging as these itineraries offer less useful contextual information. We also propose a rich set of features which are integrated into the model and are specific to our domain. The result from our model is a list of lists containing the relevant information extracted from ones itinerary.

1 Introduction

We are progressing towards a fully digital and paperless world wherein electronic documents and emails are increasingly becoming more secure and trusted mode of communication. Email has become one of the most popular modes of communication also because of the high adoption of smart and mobile devices that allow email access virtually from anywhere. As a result, an increasing number of businesses are adopting emails as their preferred Business to Consumer (B2C) communication channel to share personalized and sensitive information with their customers. These emails are usually machine generated and composed by filling information from databases into slots in predefined templates and often include personalized greetings and other information. Though these kind of templates enhance presentation of the email, the user is primarily interested in the data relevant to the business.

One such document is the Travel Itinerary sent across by a travel agency or an airline confirming the travel. Travel itineraries vary a lot from simple itineraries in plain text format to tabular itineraries in raw text as well as rich text formats and might contain more than one table or nested tables as well. Extraction of the relevant content from these itineraries and presenting it in a simple structural format would be of great convenience, especially for business travelers who travel very often and have a busy daily routine. In the past, extraction of information has been tried on similar kind of data by the use of wrappers or parsers (Hall et al., 2011; Crescenzi et al., 2001). Since these emails potentially contain personal information, passenger record locater(s) etc. it is essential to maintain the privacy of the traveler while trying to accurately extract the correct information. This problem has been tackled by organizations in the industry by creating parsers for each kind of template used by the travel providers. With more than 1000 registered commercial airlines, varying formats and frequent personalization done by airlines or third party aggregators like Skyscanner or Expedia, it becomes hard to maintain this ever growing number of templates as it demands a significant amount of resources, time and manual effort. This kind of approach is not scalable and a slight change in one template would cause the parser to fail.

First two authors had equal contribution. Work was done when all authors were at Amadeus IT Group.

Proceedings of Recent Advances in Natural Language Processing, pages 354–362,
Varna, Bulgaria, Sep 4–6 2017.

Itinerary

Carrier	Flight #	Departing	Arriving
American Tom Cruise	2379 Seat 22E	MIAMI INTERNTNL SAT 22OCT 5:55 PM Economy	ST THOMAS 8:39 PM FF#: AA123456
American Tom Cruise	1350 Seat 26E	ST THOMAS SAT 29OCT 8:30 AM Economy	MIAMI INTERNTNL 11:27 AM FF#: AA123456

Figure 1: Snapshot of a plain text travel itinerary that looks like a tabular itinerary.

Figure 2: Structured information presentation in applications making use of regular expressions. Flight number, carrier information, boarding and off point, terminal information along with date and time has been extracted. These applications provide real time update to user′s journey.

In this paper, we discuss an approach based on Named Entity Recognition to "parse" such itineraries. For the purpose of this paper, we have considered our scope to be limited to emails that contain flight segments and are in English language. Since we have defined our domain very specifically and we know what we need to extract while also knowing to some extent what kind of data we should expect in an email, a supervised learning approach seems fit. Use of semi-supervised or unsupervised approaches is not feasible at the time given the small amount of data that we have. We investigate the application of Named Entity Recognition (NER) technique towards extracting information from B2C emails in the domain of air travel. The challenge in front of us was not only to extend the application of these NLP techniques to an entirely new domain but also to gather the data and work on it while still following all the laws applied to maintaining one′s privacy. Here, NER is used to label and extract entities like airport, person′s name, location, flight, carrier etc. This will be followed by validating the extracted entities with the open travel data (Arnaud, 2017). The contribution of this paper is twofold: investigate application of named entity recognition on the domain of air travel itineraries and use it to extract information, and present domain specific features to improve the performance of the NER. The end result from our model contains information about various journey legs as extracted from the email after the process of tagging and validation. This concept of NER on restricted domains has been previously used in domains like molecular biology, bioinformatics, and security etc. but extending it to B2C emails is a challenging task. B2C emails especially travel itineraries offer little contextual evidence for the interpretation of the terms that appear in the text. State of the art approaches for named entity extraction from well-edited text rely heavily on orthographic features such as capitalization and part of speech (POS) tagging which are unreliable in case of travel itineraries thereby waning the usefulness of such features for NER in this domain and posing further challenges towards robust entity extraction.

We make use of a Hidden Markov Models which are already verified to be mature and trustworthy on refined text (Zhou and Su, 2002; Minkov et al., 2006b; Ekbal and Bandyopadhyay, 2007; Zhao, 2004) to develop our NER. Our HMM model which when combined with our custom features gives us an F1 value of 70.2% upon experimentation.

2 Related Work

Information extraction from emails is a very complex task. It shares, however, a lot in common with information extraction from the web. Both contain some amount of HTML content which is the very basic similarity. Much work has been done to exploit the HTML structure to extract information from web pages. Buttler et al.(2001) presented rules based on the tree representation of web documents and extracting content from web pages. Crescenzi et al.(2001) presented an approach to extract data from HTML sites based on comparison of HTML pages and then generating wrappers based on their similarities or differences. Their model did not have any predefined knowledge of the organization of web pages which was not the case with either WIEN or STALKER which generated their wrappers by examining a number of labeled examples. Banko et al.(2007) presented the Open IE paradigm which did not require any human input and worked towards extracting relation tuples over a single data driven pass over the corpora, however, it does not build any coherent sets of category or relation instances as constructed by Dalvi et al.(2012) in which concept-instance pairs were extracted from HTML corpus. Their method relied on clustering terms found in HTML tables which was followed by assignment of concept names based on Hearst patterns. A Named Entity Recognition system was also presented for complex named entities in web text which made use of a lexical statistics based approach (Downey et al., 2007). Paşca et al.(2006) applied the NER technique to very large web corpora and demonstrated promising results from a very small seed of example facts. Similarly, Zhang et al.(2015) made use of a semi-supervised approach by making a combination of a weak learner(EM) with plain CRFs. Due to the privacy concerns, work on emails has been limited due to public availability of a few corpora. Klimt and Yang(2004) presented the Enron email corpus for email classification research. Minkov et al.(2005) worked on this dataset towards extraction of personal names from emails. They compared results from a Voted Perceptron HMM and a CRF model. Minkov et al.(2006b) worked towards adjusting the recall-precision tradeoff in NER systems as per user performance criteria. They presented their work on the Enron dataset (Klimt and Yang, 2004) along with other datasets. Major work on emails has been on binary classification of emails as spam or not spam (Koprinska et al., 2007; Youn and McLeod, 2007), and also towards using classification (Klimt and Yang, 2004; Bekkerman et al., 2004; Dredze et al., 2006) and clustering methods (Huang et al., 2004; Huang and Mitchell, 2006; Li et al., 2006) for categorizing emails into folders. Carvalho and Cohen(2004) worked towards learning to extract signatures and reply lines from plain text emails while Minkov et al.(2006a) also worked towards disambiguating names in emails by making use of graph-walk similarity measures. Besides the works on content mining in emails, there have been some works towards event extraction (Nelson et al., 2014) and prioritizing emails for improved user experiences (Eugene and Caswell, 2015; Laclavik and Maynard, 2009). Our

data varies a lot from all these datasets because of the numerous formats in which travel itineraries can come. Also, we cannot make use of features like POS tags or capitalization information as these emails have minimal useful contextual information and are many-a-times present in all caps. This makes our problem statement different from the works that have been done before.

3 Data, Privacy and Characteristics

It is important for businesses to maintain user privacy while sending emails, not just because of the privacy laws - which are very strict and hold businesses to very high principles - but also because of the policies of privacy and ethics such organizations set. Such policies are to ensure that users personal information will not fall into the hands of any third party. This makes it difficult to generate an annotated training set which fares well on the fronts of diversity and complexity as one would encounter in the real world. To counter this, we created a dataset of 2,000 training emails and 600 test emails, none of which correspond to any individual. These were synthetically designed by Amadeus IT Group for testing the regression suites on their email parsing products. These emails have been chosen at random to ensure diversity and complexity. The only difference between emails in our dataset and real world emails is that the data in our emails does not correspond to any real individual. Doing so, we were able to protect one′ privacy. One might wonder what differences are found between our data and well edited data like the newswire corpus on which the performance of NER techniques have been well established. For this purpose we have outlined key characteristics of named entities in our domain along with the emails they are present in to get an understanding of the domain before describing our solution:

- Most emails occur in all caps and have very less usable contextual information making it hard to extract POS features.

- Named entities may have different representations. *John F. Kennedy International Airport, JFK International and JFK Intl. Airp.* refer to the same entity. Similarly *British Airways Flight 9* is same as *BA9* or *BA 9*.

- Sometimes due to character space restraints, an entity may not appear in its complete form.

Entity	Description	Examples
Name	Passenger Name	Tom Cruise, CRUISE/TOM
PNR (Passenger Name Record)	6 character record locater	CC1ORJ, ABC123
Booking Reference	Non 6 char. record locater	S23VG, C7GH1YV
Date	Departure/Arrival date	21-08-2017, 21AUG17
Time	Departure/Arrival time	06:55PM, 1855 hours, 18:55
Airport	Airport Name	Logan International Airport
Location	City of the said airport	Boston
Airport Code	IATA code of the airport	BOS
Carrier	Name of airline	Alitalia, American Airlines
Flight	Carrier name/code follo-wed by flight number	American Airlines 5526, LH400, BA 9

Table 1: Entity classes for the travel itineraries targeted for the probabilistic HMM based NER.

We may see *O Hare Interna* in place of *O Hare International* due to these restraints.

- Entities may appear in a cascaded form like *McCarran Las Vegas International Airport* where *McCarran International Airport* is the airport of *Las Vegas* which is a city. More efforts and validation processes need to be made to identify and extract such entities.

- Two entities might be similar in resemblance. *Indira Gandhi* may be a person traveling from *Indira Gandhi International Airport*. Also, *VS2491* is a *Virgin Atlantic* flight from *New York* to *Pittsburgh* but it might be a PNR as well. It is hard to resolves such ambiguities.

- One named entity may share two or more head nouns for eg: *Envoy Air as American Eagle, Flight 3530 from Buffalo to Chicago*. Here *Envoy Air* and *American Eagle* are two head nouns for flight number *3530*.

Further, the emails may appear in a tabular format without any headers in which case there is usually minimal contextual information for the NER to learn. Such cases make NER difficult on such kind of data. Due to this reason we explore various features that could help us identify such named entities in the text.

4 Methods and Features

4.1 Hidden Markov Model

Emails are processed such that each word in an email is passed as a separate token to an HMM to find and extract the tokens which are part of the entities of interest. In the task of Named Entity Recognition, the hidden state can be thought of as the sequence of tokens while the output sequence is the statistically optimal sequence of labels corresponding to the input word sequence.

Our HMM is inspired from Zhou and Su(2002). The mathematics of their model could be described as follows: Let a sequence of tokens be:

$$S_1^n = S_1 S_2 S_3 S_4 .... S_{n-1} S_n \qquad (1)$$

the objective of the NER is to find the statistically optimum tag sequence

$$T_1^n = T_1 T_2 T_3 T_4 .... T_{n-1} T_n \qquad (2)$$

by trying to maximize the probability $P(T_1^n | S_1^n)$. Each s_i is defined as $\langle f_i, w_i \rangle$ where w_i is the ith word in the sequence and f_i is the set of features attributed to w_i. We follow the BIO notation for labeling and each of our t_i is structurally composed of two parts: the entity class and the feature set. The entity class can be one of the defined classes while labeling the training set along with the OTHER class. The feature set is added in order to represent more accurate and precise models based on the limited number of label boundary categories and entity classes.

From their model, $P(T_1^n | S_1^n)$ can be represented as:

$$log P(T_1^n | S_1^n) = log P(T_1^n) + log \frac{P(T_1^n, S_1^n)}{P(T_1^n) P(S_1^n)} \qquad (3)$$

Assuming mutual independence in the second term, we have:

$$log \frac{P(T_1^n, S_1^n)}{P(T_1^n) P(S_1^n)} = \sum_1^n log \frac{P(t_i, S_1^n)}{P(t_i) P(S_i^n)} \qquad (4)$$

Hence we have,

$$logP(T_1^n|S_1^n) = logP(T_1^n) - \sum_1^n logP(t_i)$$
$$+ \sum_1^n logP(t_i|S_1^n) \qquad (5)$$

by substituting equation 4 in equation 3. Now, we can calculate the first term on the RHS of equation 5 by using the chain rule of probability which allows us to compute joint probabilities by making use of only the conditional probabilities. Each term in our case is assumed to be dependent on the previous two terms (trigram modeling). The second term is the log probability of all label occurrences. We apply the Viterbi algorithm (Forney, 1973; Viterbi, 1967) which makes use of a dynamic programming approach to find the most likely tag sequence for our given sequence of tokens based on the state transition probabilities of the tags and emission probability of s_i given t_i. The emission probability has been smoothened using Lidstone's Law which can be thought of as

$$e_k(s_j) = \frac{N_k(s_j) + \lambda}{\sum_p N_k(s_p) + |NV|}$$

where $N_k(s_j)$ is the number of times a token s_j is emitted in the state k in the training set. λ is a constant whose value lies between 0 and 1 and can be used to vary the degree of discounting offered in smoothing and $|NV|$ is the number of distinct word types in the training set. Similarly smoothing with λ is also applied to the transition probabilities.

4.2 Features

The features defined for this model are domain specific and effort has been put in to craft features that are useful in identifying particular classes. This not only boosts the results of our baseline model but also provides an insight into how specific features effect a particular class. Our features can be classified into three major categories:

1. *Orthographic Features:* In this kind, we have devised special features which are designed to capture the word formation. For eg:- a 6 digit alpha-numeric value which appears in an email in all caps is most likely a passenger record locator. Similarly, an all alphabet token with / in between is most

Feature Name	Example
Common word (StopWord)	from, in
Abbreviation with dot	J.F.K., Jr.
All alphabets	John
Alphabets and Slash - (slash not at extreme)	Paul/John
One Digit	9
Number with length ≤ 6	12
Digit dot digit	1.259
2 char. alphanumeric - slash 6 char. alphanumeric	LX/UV231Y
Digit slash digit	23/10/2016
Digit hyphen digit	23-10-2016
6 character alphanumeric	AB23C5

Table 2: Orthographic Features.

Dictionary Features	Example
Word is in airline name	Lufthansa
Word is in airport name	Port Bouet Airport
Abbreviation is - airline IATA code	LH
Abbreviation is - airline ICAO code	DLH
Abbreviation is - airport code	ABJ
Word is in airport loc.	Abidjan
Word is in alternate - airport name dictionary	Houphouet-Boigny International Airport
Word is in alternate - airline name dictionary	Deutsche Lufthansa
Flight no. in routes dict.	LH404

Table 3: Dictionary Features. All these features are used in the vector creation process as well as the validation process.

likely to be a name in the format of *<last name>/<first name>/MR* as it appears on your boarding pass. Similarly, any token which is an a single alphabet followed by a dot(.) is most likely to be part of an entity name - person's name, airport name, country name etc. A list of such features has been given in Table 2.

2. *Contextual Features:* Features which are based on the previous word or words can be designed on the fly by our model while learning the training set. These features are identified using specially crafted bigrams and tri-

grams which are of the form <*pr. word, current word tag*> and <*pr. pr. word, pr. word, current word tag*>. These are used to identify most likely patterns that could be found for instances such as names, PNRs etc. We identify such patterns and assign a confidence value to such patterns based on the formula:

$$C = \frac{N(correct) - N(incorrect)}{N} \quad (6)$$

where N(Correct) is the total occurences of the pattern when it forms the context of a word having the label of interest and N(incorrect) is the total occurences of such patterns when followed by the label which is not of interest. We generate such patterns on the go for identifying entities such as *Name(s), PNR(s)* and *Booking Reference(s)*. This equation is based on the assumption that such word patterns are useful. After generating all such patterns we make use of a threshold of 60% to shortlist the features of use. Patterns common for a particular entity type are clubbed together as a feature to avoid the problem of data sparseness.

3. *Dictionary features:* We make use of several dictionaries as features. These include airline dictionary, airport dictionary and a dictionary of routes, which not only reflect on the airport/airline names but also allow us access to other information, helping us validate our tags and improve precision. Our dictionary of airports and airlines was obtained from the open travel data repository (Arnaud, 2017). The airport dictionary constructed from this data consists of airport names along with their codes, alternative names, location etc. Similarly our airline dictionary includes airline name, alternative names, IATA and ICAO codes. These help us when there are multiple names for the same airport or the airline and also in deciding whether an abbreviation is an airline code, airport code or none. The routes dictionary consists of information of all the flights operating in the year 2016-17. Not just are these used in feature vector creation but are also used in our later validation stage where we match our airports, flight numbers etc. from the routes data to validate the tags given by the HMM tagger. A few features are listed in Table 3. In validation stage,

while matching *Airport* and *Carrier* entities with dictionary entries we make use of regular expression search (to match partial names as well) using tail recursion for good performance.

5 Experimental Results

Our system was trained on a training set of 2,000 randomly chosen emails which were manually tagged using the BIO tag notation. The tests were performed on a set of 600 randomly chosen e-mails. We evaluate our NER tagger on the metrics of Precision, Recall and F1 Measure. We report the entity-wise results as well as the overall results. Note that the entity-wise results are important for our validation stage which use the same dictionaries mentioned earlier. Table 4 shows our results on various feature sets (the base model remains the same in all cases). The highest score in each category of Precision, Recall and F1 Measure has been written in bold face. entity-wise results are important because of various reasons:

- For entities such as *Name, PNR* and *Booking Reference* which do not have any dictionaries to be validated against, we need high precision. A high recall would be ideal but many times these entities occur multiple times in the same email but have the same value. It would be ideal if the NER tags all the occurrences of a *PNR* as *PNR* but tagging one occurrence of that particular value as PNR is sufficient for our extraction process.

- For entities such as *Airport, Location* and *Carrier*, a validation process is present where use of dictionaries is made. Because of this, a high recall is required. We rule out the incorrectly tagged airports, locations etc. by matching them in the validation dictionaries.

- For entities like *Flight Number* and *Airport Code*, we can validate the journey legs on their basis. We require a high precision as well as recall on these entities to verify and validate the journey legs of an individual.

It can be seen that our baseline features and combination of those features have been able to improve the results of our system. As a general trend, entities involving names (*Name, Airport*) have a low F1 measure of being labeled. One reason for this is that these entities are usually longer than any

Model	Overall	Name	PNR	BRef	Date	Time	ACode	Airp	Loc	Carr	Flt
BASE	0.60	0.31	0.59	0.70	0.72	0.75	0.67	0.45	0.54	0.65	0.31
ORTH	0.66	0.39	0.70	0.83	**0.83**	0.76	0.78	0.46	0.58	0.65	0.55
CTXT	0.63	0.59	0.87	0.73	0.72	0.70	0.73	0.44	0.56	0.65	0.21
DICT	0.62	0.32	0.60	0.70	0.74	0.77	0.93	0.32	0.28	0.80	0.80
O+C	0.69	**0.63**	0.88	0.84	0.80	0.76	0.77	**0.59**	**0.62**	0.65	0.31
O+C+D	**0.70**	0.62	**0.91**	**0.89**	0.82	**0.78**	**0.95**	0.41	0.38	**0.87**	**0.95**

Table 4: F-measure results on the test dataset. The highest values in each column are written in bold. ORTH(O):Orthographic, CTXT(C): Contextual, DICT(D): Dictionary features.

Model	Precision	Recall	F Measure
Base	0.67	0.54	0.60
O+C	**0.72**	0.66	0.69
O+C+D	0.70	**0.70**	**0.70**

Table 5: Overall results on various models.

Entity	Precision	Recall
Name	0.65	0.60
PNR	0.91	0.90
Booking Reference	**0.96**	0.83
Date	0.83	0.81
Time	0.81	0.76
Airport Code	**0.96**	**0.95**
Airport (Name)	0.34	0.53
Location	0.66	0.27
Carrier	0.87	0.86
Flight	**0.96**	0.94

Table 6: Entity-wise Precision and Recall values on final system (O+C+D).

other entity type and not all tokens get the correct labels. The F measure of *Airport Codes, Booking References, PNR* and *Flight* has improved exceptionally with the introduction of features. Also, we can see that *Booking Reference, Flight* and *Airport Code* have the highest precision while *Airport Code, Flight, PNR* and *Carrier* have the highest recall. We haven't used a *Name* dictionary yet because even though our emails are in English, the passenger might be from a region for which such data is not available. We have also analyzed that since the airport names are longer than other entity types, they are have a lesser likelihood to match the dictionary entries for instance: *MIAMI INTERNTNL* as shown in Figure 1 will not match with the dictionary entry of *Miami International Airport*. Similarly *O Hare Intl Airp* will not match with the entire dictionary entry of *O'Hare International Airport* and the maximum subsequence

match will only match *Hare*. This diminishes the value of the *Airport* dictionary and we will discuss this limitation as part of future work. For airlines, since the names are smaller, they match very well with the *Carrier* dictionary entries. Correctly extracting the *Airport Codes* helps us mitigate the poor results shown by the *Airport* entity type. Figures[1] also show extracted journey legs from various itineraries.

6 Conclusion and Future Work

In this paper, we have shown how a probabilistic NER can be applied to B2C emails with focus on travel itineraries and extract relevant data from the same. The emails were chosen randomly to ensure the unpredictability of the format of data representation. We trained our system on the small number of emails that were donated to us for this research and proposed various domain specific features while not using features like POS tagging, capitalization etc. The resulting system was able to extract desired information from test emails with high accuracy and efficiency.

Upon analyzing our results, we have found that the dictionaries are too rigid and we need to find a way to make sure that various representations of the same entity and its aliases are taken care of while matching test data with dictionary entities, especially in the case of *Airport* dictionary. We also plan to improve *Name* extraction by making use of various features as presented by Minkov et al.(2005). With this, we also believe that there is a need to explore CRF and RNN based NER models and compare how each model works. Since our dataset is relatively small, it is also of wondering what impact will increasing the training set have on our system's performance. We intend to gather more training data and evaluate our system's performance as the data increases

---

[1] https://goo.gl/LtvuCb

References

Denis Arnaud. 2017. Open travel data. Amadeus IT Group. https://github.com/opentraveldata/opentraveldata.

Michele Banko, Michael J. Cafarella, Stephen Soderland, Matt Broadhead, and Oren Etzioni. 2007. Open information extraction from the web. In *Proceedings of the 20th International Joint Conference on Artifical Intelligence*. Morgan Kaufmann Publishers Inc., San Francisco, CA, USA, IJCAI'07, pages 2670–2676. http://dl.acm.org/citation.cfm?id=1625275.1625705.

R. Bekkerman, A. McCallum, and G. Huang. 2004. Automatic categorization of email into folders: Benchmark experiments on enron and sri corpora. *Center for Intelligent Information Retrieval, Technical Report IR* 418.

D. Buttler, Ling Liu, and C. Pu. 2001. A fully automated object extraction system for the world wide web. In *Proceedings 21st International Conference on Distributed Computing Systems*. pages 361–370. https://doi.org/10.1109/ICDSC.2001.918966.

Vitor R. Carvalho and William W. Cohen. 2004. Learning to extract signature and reply lines from email. In *In Proceedings of the Conference on Email and Anti-Spam*.

Valter Crescenzi, Giansalvatore Mecca, and Paolo Merialdo. 2001. Roadrunner: Towards automatic data extraction from large web sites. In *Proceedings of the 27th International Conference on Very Large Data Bases*. Morgan Kaufmann Publishers Inc., San Francisco, CA, USA, VLDB '01, pages 109–118. http://dl.acm.org/citation.cfm?id=645927.672370.

Bhavana Bharat Dalvi, William W. Cohen, and Jamie Callan. 2012. Websets: Extracting sets of entities from the web using unsupervised information extraction. In *Proceedings of the Fifth ACM International Conference on Web Search and Data Mining*. ACM, New York, NY, USA, WSDM '12, pages 243–252. https://doi.org/10.1145/2124295.2124327.

Doug Downey, Matthew Broadhead, and Oren Etzioni. 2007. Locating complex named entities in web text. In *Proceedings of the 20th International Joint Conference on Artifical Intelligence*. Morgan Kaufmann Publishers Inc., San Francisco, CA, USA, IJCAI'07, pages 2733–2739. http://dl.acm.org/citation.cfm?id=1625275.1625715.

Mark Dredze, Tessa Lau, and Nicholas Kushmerick. 2006. Automatically classifying emails into activities. In *Proceedings of the 11th International Conference on Intelligent User Interfaces*. ACM, New York, NY, USA, IUI '06, pages 70–77. https://doi.org/10.1145/1111449.1111471.

Asif Ekbal and Sivaji Bandyopadhyay. 2007. A hidden markov model based named entity recognition system: Bengali and hindi as case studies. In *Proceedings of the 2Nd International Conference on Pattern Recognition and Machine Intelligence*. Springer-Verlag, Berlin, Heidelberg, PReMI'07, pages 545–552. http://dl.acm.org/citation.cfm?id=1781034.1781108.

Louis Eugene and Isaac Caswell. 2015. Making a manageable email experience with deep learning.

G. D. Forney. 1973. The viterbi algorithm. *Proceedings of the IEEE* 61(3):268–278. https://doi.org/10.1109/PROC.1973.9030.

Keith B. Hall, Ryan T. McDonald, Jason Katz-Brown, and Michael Ringgaard. 2011. Training dependency parsers by jointly optimizing multiple objectives. In *EMNLP*. ACL, pages 1489–1499. http://www.aclweb.org/anthology/D11-1138.

Yifen Huang, Dinesh Govindaraju, Tom M Mitchell, Vitor Rocha de Carvalho, and William W Cohen. 2004. Inferring ongoing activities of workstation users by clustering email. In *CEAS*.

Yifen Huang and Tom M. Mitchell. 2006. Text clustering with extended user feedback. In *Proceedings of the 29th Annual International ACM SIGIR Conference on Research and Development in Information Retrieval*. ACM, New York, NY, USA, SIGIR '06, pages 413–420. https://doi.org/10.1145/1148170.1148242.

Bryan Klimt and Yiming Yang. 2004. The enron corpus: A new dataset for email classification research. In *Proceedings of the 15th European Conference on Machine Learning*. pages 217–226.

Irena Koprinska, Josiah Poon, James Clark, and Jason Chan. 2007. Learning to classify e-mail. *Inf. Sci.* 177(10):2167–2187. https://doi.org/10.1016/j.ins.2006.12.005.

Michal Laclavik and Diana Maynard. 2009. Motivating intelligent e-mail in business: An investigation into current trends for e-mail processing and communication research. *2009 IEEE Conference on Commerce and Enterprise Computing* pages 476–482.

H. Li, D. Shen, B. Zhang, Z. Chen, and Q. Yang. 2006. Adding semantics to email clustering. In *Sixth International Conference on Data Mining (ICDM'06)*. pages 938–942. https://doi.org/10.1109/ICDM.2006.16.

Einat Minkov, William W. Cohen, and Andrew Y. Ng. 2006a. Contextual search and name disambiguation in email using graphs. In *Proceedings of the 29th Annual International ACM SIGIR Conference on Research and Development in Information Retrieval*. ACM, New York, NY, USA, SIGIR '06, pages 27–34. https://doi.org/10.1145/1148170.1148179.

Einat Minkov, Richard C. Wang, and William W. Cohen. 2005. Extracting personal names from email: Applying named entity recognition to informal text. In *Proceedings of the Conference on Human Language Technology and Empirical Methods in Natural Language Processing*. Association for Computational Linguistics, Stroudsburg, PA, USA, HLT '05, pages 443–450. https://doi.org/10.3115/1220575.1220631.

Einat Minkov, Richard C. Wang, Anthony Tomasic, and William W. Cohen. 2006b. Ner systems that suit user's preferences: Adjusting the recall-precision trade-off for entity extraction. In *Proceedings of the Human Language Technology Conference of the NAACL, Companion Volume: Short Papers*. Association for Computational Linguistics, Stroudsburg, PA, USA, NAACL-Short '06, pages 93–96. http://dl.acm.org/citation.cfm?id=1614049.1614073.

M.F. Nelson, L. Tannenbaum, D. Bhowal, and M. Sharma. 2014. System and method for extracting calendar events from free-form email. US Patent 8,832,205. http://www.google.com/patents/US8832205.

Marius Paşca, Dekang Lin, Jeffrey Bigham, Andrei Lifchits, and Alpa Jain. 2006. Names and similarities on the web: Fact extraction in the fast lane. In *Proceedings of the 21st International Conference on Computational Linguistics and the 44th Annual Meeting of the Association for Computational Linguistics*. Association for Computational Linguistics, Stroudsburg, PA, USA, ACL-44, pages 809–816. https://doi.org/10.3115/1220175.1220277.

A. Viterbi. 1967. Error bounds for convolutional codes and an asymptotically optimum decoding algorithm. *IEEE Transactions on Information Theory* 13(2):260–269. https://doi.org/10.1109/TIT.1967.1054010.

Seongwook Youn and Dennis McLeod. 2007. *A Comparative Study for Email Classification*, Springer Netherlands, Dordrecht, pages 387–391.

Weinan Zhang, Amr Ahmed, Jie Yang, Vanja Josifovski, and Alex J. Smola. 2015. Annotating needles in the haystack without looking: Product information extraction from emails. In *Proceedings of the 21th ACM SIGKDD International Conference on Knowledge Discovery and Data Mining*. ACM, New York, NY, USA, KDD '15, pages 2257–2266. https://doi.org/10.1145/2783258.2788580.

Shaojun Zhao. 2004. Named entity recognition in biomedical texts using an hmm model. In *Proceedings of the International Joint Workshop on Natural Language Processing in Biomedicine and Its Applications*. Association for Computational Linguistics, Stroudsburg, PA, USA, JNLPBA '04, pages 84–87. http://dl.acm.org/citation.cfm?id=1567594.1567613.

GuoDong Zhou and Jian Su. 2002. Named entity recognition using an hmm-based chunk tagger. In *Proceedings of the 40th Annual Meeting on Association for Computational Linguistics*. Association for Computational Linguistics, Stroudsburg, PA, USA, ACL '02, pages 473–480. https://doi.org/10.3115/1073083.1073163.

Graph-Based Approach to Recognizing CST Relations in Polish Texts

Paweł Kędzia
Wrocław University
of Science and Technology

Maciej Piasecki
Wrocław University
of Science and Technology

Arkadiusz Janz
Wrocław University
of Science and Technology

`{pawel.kedzia,maciej.piasecki,arkadiusz.janz}@pwr.edu.pl`

Abstract

This paper presents a supervised approach to the recognition of Cross-document Structure Theory (CST) relations in Polish texts. In the proposed, graph-based representation is constructed for sentences. Graphs are built on the basis of lexicalised syntactic-semantic relations extracted from text. Similarity between sentences is calculated on their graphs, and the values are used as features to train the classifiers. Several different configurations of graphs, as well as graph similarity methods were analysed for this task. The approach was evaluated on a large open corpus annotated manually with 17 types of selected CST relations. The configuration of experiments was similar to those known from SEMEVAL and we obtained very promising results.

1 Introduction

Among large volumes of data available one can find a lot of redundant information, eg. supplementing, overlapping etc. Manual aggregating and synthesizing valuable information from a massive input is laborious. The aim of multi-document discourse parsing is to discover the relations or dependencies linking text passages. The relation we are aiming for are not limited only to the relations between event descriptions. Recognition of discourse relationships linking texts can be useful in many information retrieval applications, and may help in information management.

The Cross-document Structure Theory (CST) (Radev, 2000) introduces an organized structure of semantic links connecting topically related texts. CST relations recognised correctly for text fragments provide a map of the document(s) seman-

tic structure and, e.g., can support multi-document summarization (Kumar et al., 2014). However, due to the large number of relations and often subtle differences between them, CST relation recognition is known to be much harder than Textual Entailment (TE) recognition.

Our goal is to build a tool for the recognition of CST relations in Polish texts. Firstly, we limited the problem to recognition of relations between sentence pairs, that is even a harder task because of the limited text material. to be processed. For training we used a part of the KPWr Corpus (Broda et al., 2012) based on Polish Wikinews[1]. In the work presented here, we focus on the 17 relations with the largest coverage in the corpus.

2 Related Works

In (Zhang et al., 2003) CST relations were recognized by a supervised approach with boosting on the basis of simple, lexical, syntactic and semantic features, extracted from sentence pairs. The evaluation was performed in two steps: binary classification for relationship detection, and multi-class classification for relationship recognition. This idea was expanded Zhang and Radev (2005) by leveraging both labeled and unlabeled data. The exploitation of unlabeled instances improved the performance. Boosting technique was used in combination with the same set of features to classify the data in CSTBank (Radev et al., 2004). Relation detection was significantly improved to F-score = 0.8839. However, recognition of the relation type was still unsatisfactory.

Aleixo and Pardo (2008) is one of a few works that address recognition CST relations for languages other than English. They utilised CST in search for topically related Portuguese documents. They applied a supervised approach based on sim-

---

[1] `https://pl.wikinews.org`

Proceedings of Recent Advances in Natural Language Processing, pages 363–371,
Varna, Bulgaria, Sep 4–6 2017.

ilarity measures calculated for sentence pairs from different documents: cosine similarity and a variant of the Jaccard index. Cut-off thresholds for the similarity were studied in combination with the performance of classifiers.

Zahri and Fukumoto (2011) applied the supervised learning to identify a limited set of CST relations: *Identity, Paraphrase, Subsumption, Elaboration* and *Partial Overlap*. They were used in the multi-document summarization task. SVM algorithm was used and examples from CSTBank. The features of (Aleixo and Pardo, 2008) were expanded with: (i) cosine similarity of word vectors, (ii) intersection of common words measured with the Jaccard Index, (iii) an indicator of longer sentence and (iv) one-sided word coverage ratio.

Kumar et al. (2012a) restricted the set of relations further down to four: *Identity, Subsumption, Overlap* and *Elaboration*. Four features were used: (i) tf-idf based cosine sentence similarity, (ii) words coverage ratio, (iii) sentence length difference and (iv) the indicator of longer sentence. The best performance of SVM in relation recognition was: for *Identity* $F = 0.91$, *Subsumption* 0.59, *Elaboration* 0.54, and 0.62 for *Overlap*. For the same relations Kumar et al. (2012b) presented results obtained with SVM, a Feed-Forward neural network and CBR. The features of (Zahri and Fukumoto, 2011) were extended with the Jaccard based similarity of noun phrases and verb phrases. CBR based on the cosine similarity measure expressed improved results than in (Kumar et al., 2012a): *Identity* 0.966, *Subsumption* 0.803, *Description* 0.786, and 0.722 for *Overlap*.

(Maziero et al., 2014) proposed several refinements to CST in order to reduce the ambiguity. They improved definitions by several additional constraints on the co-occurrence of different relations in texts. The CST taxonomy was amended by introducing a division based on the form and information content of relations. The improved model was used in evaluation of supervised CST relation recognition in three different settings: binary, multi-class and hierarchical (facilitating the proposed taxonomy of relations). The applied features included: sentence length difference, ratio of shared words, sentence position in text, differences of word numbers across PoSs, and the number of shared synonyms between sentences. SVM, Naive Bayes and J48 decision tree were used for classification with the best score of J48. The aver-age F-measure for multi-class scheme was 0.403, while for the binary scheme: 0.673. (without the final decision) and for the hierarchical: 0.724.

3 Dataset

We utilised a dataset of sentence pairs annotated with CST relations from the KPWr Corpus. The corpus consists of complete documents that were grouped by their similarity into groups of 3 news each. The groups include the most similar, potentially topically related documents. The imposed similarity structure facilitated searching for sentence pairs linked by a CST relation. A corpus, with similar distribution of discourse relations linking multiple documents, was also introduced in (Cardoso et al., 2011). It was built from texts from journals in Brazilian Portuguese.

Selected sentences from our corpus were manually annotated with CST relations at least by 3 annotators (linguists) each. Each annotator was exploring the corpus independently, in order to find and annotate inter-document relations inside document groups linking text fragments. The annotators followed the guidelines of CSTBank (Radev et al., 2004) slightly adapted to Polish.

4 Features in Classification

4.1 Baseline Features

As a starting point we used the set features proposed in (Maziero et al., 2014). Our set includes commonly-used, lexical, syntactic and semantic features that were applied for the detection and recognition of CST relationships in supervised approaches. They focus on the grammatical forms in and properties of the linked sentences:

- Shared lemmas – the number of lemmas shared by two sentences,

- Shared PNs – the number of Proper Names shared by two sentences,

- Longest Common Substring – the length of the longest common continuous sub-string of word forms from the two sentences,

- Longest Common Subsequence – the length of the longest common sub-sequence, but the sequences can be discontinuous (i.e. sequence elements can be separated),

- Cosine similarity – the cosine similarity of vectors of the frequency of lemmas,

- Is Longer – equals 1 if the first sentence is longer, 0 for equal, -1 if the second is longer,

- Shared synsets – the number of synsets shared by the two sentences which is normalized by the number of all synsets in the shorter sentence (to make the feature insensitive to sentence length differences),

- PoS similarity – cosine measure of vectors of the frequencies of different Part of Speech in both sentences (4 basic PoS were used),

- SVO Index – the Jaccard Index calculated for vectors of frequencies of triples: subject, verb, object for both texts.

These features were used as a baseline model for the description of text pairs, and compared later with the graph-based representation proposed in the following subsections. Several language tools were used to enrich texts for feature extraction: *Morfeusz* (Woliński, 2006) – a morphological analysis, *WCRFT* (Radziszewski, 2013) – tagger, *Liner2* (Marcińczuk et al., 2013) – recognition of Proper Names, *Maltparser* (Nivre et al., 2007) adapted to Polish (Wróblewska, 2014), *WCCL* (Radziszewski et al., 2011) – recognition of multi-word expressions from plWord-Net (Maziarz et al., 2016; Piasecki et al., 2009), *WoSeDon* (Kędzia et al., 2015; Piasecki et al., 2016) – Word Sense Disambiguation, *IOBBER* (Radziszewski and Pawlaczek, 2013) – a syntactic chunker, *Fextor* (Broda et al., 2013) – tool for feature extraction.

4.2 Graph-based Features

The baseline features do not take into account the linguistic structure of the compared sentences. As the parser for Polish has limited accuracy, instead of depending only on the dependency structure produced by the parser we propose a graph-based representation of a sentence (or text) which is flexible and can accommodate results of processing by different language tools.

4.2.1 Graph-based Sentence Representation

Each sentence S_i is represented as a directed graph G_i. Thus, a relation $R(S_1, S_2)$ between sentences S_1 and S_2 is represented as a relation R between graphs G_1 and G_2: $R(G_1, G_2)$. For them we will calculate a similarity value $v_{sim} = SIM(G_i, G_j)$ where SIM means one of the similarity measures discussed in Sec. 4.2.2. Formally, a directed graph

$G = (V, E)$ where V is a set of vertices and E is set of directed and ordered edges e A directed edge $e = (n_s, n_t)$ where n_s is the source node and n_t is the target node, the direction is from n_s to n_t. The graphs are built in three steps: creation of nodes and edges on the basis of a sentence and merging the graph with subgraphs extracted from external knowledge sources, i.e. plWordNet and SUMO Ontology (Pease, 2011).

In **the first step** an example sentence pair (S_i and S_j) for a relation R is converted into two separate null graphs, respectively: G_i and G_j. Their nodes are of a selected type T (the same for both graphs), represent the words from the sentences and are not connected to each other. If we select more than one node type, we would obtain several null graphs for each sentence. Depending on the chosen type T_i of node, one or more words from S_i could be represented by the same node:

- *Lemma lower* – this is the simplest node type, a node $n_i \in G_j$ represents a lemma from S_j, which is converted to lowercase. All words from a sentence with the same lemma (irrespectively of PoS) are represented by the same node, e.g., for *Z ogrodu zoologicznego we Wrocławiu uciekł wąż Boa Dusiciel i przemieszcza się w stronę Ostrowa Tumskiego.*
we obtain the following null graph:
```
{{w1:z},{w2:ogród},{w3:uciec},
{w4:zoologiczny},{w5:wąż},...}
```

- *Lemma PoS lower* – in a similar way to *Lemma lower*, nodes represent lowercased lemmas, but PoS label is concatenated, e.g. *cat:n* or the Polish word *piec* can be morphologically disambiguated as a verb or noun *Kasia piecze:v ciasto w piecu:n*. Using *Lemma lower* type, the words *piecze* and *piecu* will be represented by a single node labelled as *piec*, while in *Lemma PoS lower* type there will be two different nodes: *piec.n* and *piec.v*. For S_{sample} the node of the type *Lemma PoS lower* are:
```
{{w1:z-prep},{w2:ogród-subst},
{w3:uciec-praet},{w4:wąż-subst},...}
```

- *Synset* – nodes represent plWordNet synsets assigned to the words in a sentence as their lexical meanings by WoSeDon, For S_{sample} and the *Synset* node type, the generated null graph consists of :

```
{{w1:ogród-4772},{w2:uciec-3573},
{w3:zoologiczny-8748},...}
```

- *Concept* – nodes are concepts from SUMO Ontology. The concepts are assigned to words in a sentence on the basis of synsets recognised by WoSeDon and the mapping between plWordNet and SUMO (Kędzia and Piasecki, 2014). The null graph of *Concept* type for S_{Sample} is:

```
{{w1:subsumed-CultivatedLandArea},{w2:
subsumed-Attribute},{w3:subsumed-Reptile}
{w4:equivalent-Snake},...}
```

In **the second step** the null graph constructed in the first step is expanded by adding edges between nodes. If we have multiple null graphs with different node types, we need to expand every null graph from the first step with new edges. The edge types are derived from automatically recognised lexical and semantic relations in a sentence. The e_{type} direction depends on the kind of the relation represented:

- w2w – edges represent the word order in a sentence (*word to word*). If a word w_1 occurs in a sentence before word w_2, then there is a directed edge from w_1 to w_2: e_{w2w} : (w_1, w_2).

- h2h – *head to head* represents the relative order of the heads of *agreement phrases* in a sentence. Each sentence is divided into chunks of three types: Verb Phrase *VP*, Noun Phrase *NP* and Adjective Phrase *AdjP*, that are next subdivided into smaller, *Agreement Phrases* (*AgP*). The relation *h2h* represents the order of *AgPs* heads. If a AgP head w_{hi} occurs in a sentence before the AgP head w_{hj} then the edge is directed from w_{hi} to w_{hj}: e_{h2h} : (w_{hi}, w_{hj}).

- ne2ne – an edge type similar to *w2w* and *h2h*, but in which edges represent the order of the named entities *NE* in a sentence. If named entity w_{nei} occurs before w_{nej} in sentence S, then a directed edge: e_{ne2ne} : (w_{nei}, w_{nej}), is added to the graph.

- malt – edges of this type represent the dependency relations. Each dependency relation between two words w_i and w_j, is modelled in the graph as a directed edge with the same direction. If there is a dependency relation $dep_{rel}(w_i, w_j)$, then it is added into the graph as a directed edge with the same direction dep_{rel}: $e_{dep_{rel}}(w_i, w_j)$.

- defender – the type similar to the *malt*, but relations come from *Defender* parser which is based on IOBBER chunker (Kedzia and Maziarz, 2013). Provides deeper relation structures for NPs. We used *malt* and *defender* relations, because in some situations the relations proposed by Malt are incorrect. If there is a dependency for two words w_i and w_j from *Defender*, then it is added as a directed edge to graph: $e_{def}(w_i, w_j)$.

- semantic roles – edges marked as *srole* represent semantic roles from *NPSemrel*, a Polish shallow semantic parser (Kedzia and Maziarz, 2013). The dependencies proposed by *Defender* are named with semantic roles e.g. *agent*, *theme*. If semantic role is assigned to a pair of words: w_i and w_j, a directed edge is added between the nodes representing w_i and w_j: e_{srole} : (w_i, w_j). The edge is labeled with the semantic role.

All types of edges and nodes were used in our experiments. A single graph G_i represents sentence S_i and contains the edges $E_i \in \{w2w, h2h, ne2ne, malt, def, srole\}$. A graph for sentence $S_{example}$, with *Concept* nodes and full set of possible edge types is shown in Fig. 1. In **the third step** the constructed graphs are merged with a subgraph extracted from an *External Knowledge Graph* (henceforth *EKG*). Our idea is to add to the graphs built from sentences, more semantic information, extracted from *EKG*. Let G will be a graph with node type t built for sentence S during *second step*, $G = (V_t, E \in \{w2w, h2h, ne2ne, malt, def, srole\})$. EKG_{plwn} is a graph built from plWordNet, where the nodes in $EKG(plwn)$ are the synsets from plWordNet, the edges in $EKG(plwn)$ are the relations from plWordNet. $EKG_{S(plwn)}$ is a subgraph of EKG_{plwn}. EKG_{sumo} is the graph built from SUMO Ontology, where nodes represent concepts from SUMO. The edges in EKG_{sumo} correspond to SUMO relations, and $EKG_{S(sumo)}$ is a subgraph of EKG_{sumo}. A subgraph of EKG is extracted from the source in the following way: for each word w in sentence S we identify the corresponding node n_{EKG} in EKG and build a set PN_{EKG} of possible nodes. For each pair of nodes $(n_{EKG,i}, n_{EKG,j})$ in PN_{EKG} we find the shortest path sp_i from $n_{EKG,i}$ to $n_{EKG,j}$, if exists, and

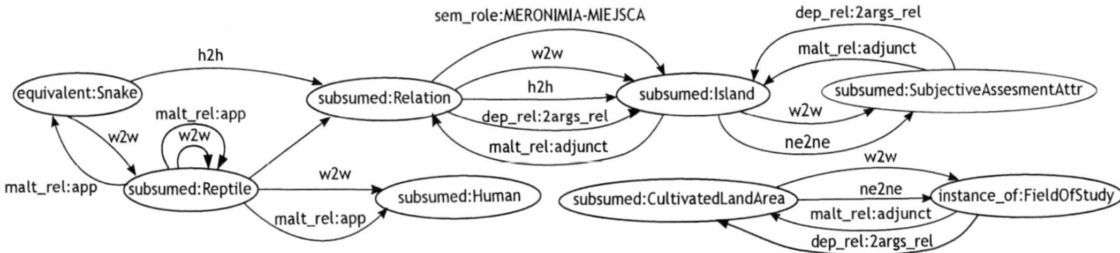

Figure 1: Graph built for sentence $S_{example}$ with *Concept* node type and full set of edges types.

add sp_i to temporary graph $G_{T(S(EKG))}$. After this process $G_{S(EKG)} = G_{T(S(EKG))}$. Using this procedure we can be built three merged graphs.

With plWordNet, $G_{merged} = G \cup EKG_{S(plwn)}$ includes nodes of the type synset (from the first step) edges built in *second step* and edges – relations from plWordNet subgraph.

With SUMO, $G_{merged} = G \cup EKG_{S(sumo)}$ includes concept nodes from the sentence and from the subgraph of SUMO Ontology. The edges are the relations from sentence and relations from the SUMO subgraph.

With plWordNet and SUMO, $G_{merged} = G \cup EKG_{S(plwn)} \cup EKG_{S(sumo)}$ contains full set of nodes: built in *first step*, from plWordNet and SUMO subgraphs, i.e. edges of all types.

There are 12 possible graph types in total, i.e. 4 types of nodes and 3 types of merge with both EKG, namely: *Lemma lower* graph merged with $EKG_{S(SUMO)}$, *Lemma PoS lower* merged with $EKG_{S(plwn)}$, *Concept* merged with $EKG_{S(sumo)}$ or *Synset* graph merged with $EKG_{S(plwn)} \cup EKG_{S(sumo)}$.

4.2.2 Similarity-based Features

For each instance of relation $R_i(S1, S2)$, a sentence pair, from the annotated corpus, see Sec. 3 16 graphs were built for both sentences $S1$ and $S2$: 4 graphs with different node types in the *second step* and 12 graphs with combinations of every node type with both EKG. Thus, each instance of relation R_i is assigned 16 graph-based representations of sentences $R_i(S1, S2) \Rightarrow R_{ik}(G1_k, G2_k), k \in < 1, \ldots 16 >$. Next, we calculate 8 different similarity measures between the graphs for R_i, including 7 similarity measures from the literature and one proposed by us. The measures are explained further on in this section. A single instance of relation R_i from the corpus is converted into a training vector v_i of the size 128 (16 graphs $\times$ 8 measures). The first mea-

sure is well known **Graph Edit Distance** (Fernández and Valiente, 2001) (GED), whose value is the minimal sum of the costs c (labelled as $\gamma(M)$) of atomic operations transforming G_1 to G_2:

$$GED(G_1, G_2) = min(\gamma(M)) \qquad (1)$$

MCS (Bunke and Shearer, 1998) is the ratio of the size of *maximum common subgraph* (mcs) of G_1 and G_2 to the size of bigger graph of ($G1$ or $G2$):

$$MCS(G_1, G_2) = \frac{|mcs(G_1, G_2)|}{max\{|G_1|, |G_2|\}} \qquad (2)$$

Measure **WGU** (Wallis et al., 2001) depends on calculating the ratio of the size of *mcs* G_1 and G_2 to the sum of sizes of both graphs minus *mcs* size:

$$WGU(G_1, G_2) = \frac{|mcs(G_1, G_2)|}{|G_1| + |G_2| - |mcs(G_1, G_2)|} \qquad (3)$$

UGU (Bunke, 1997) is a simple measure, whose value is the difference between the sizes of G_1 and G_2 and the double size of of *mcs* G_1 and G_2:

$$UGU(G_1, G_2) = |G_1| + |G_2| - 2 \cdot |mcs(G_1, G_2)| \qquad (4)$$

Next measure called **MMCS** was proposed by Fernández and Valiente (2001). The *MMCS* value expresses the dissimilarity of graphs G_1 and G_2:

$$MMCS(G_1, G_2) = |MCS(G_1, G_2)| - |mcs(G_1, G_2)| \qquad (5)$$

Measure **MMCSN** (Fernández and Valiente, 2001) depends on calculating ratio of *mcs* and *MCS* for graphs G_1 and G_2.

$$MMCSN(G_1, G_2) = \frac{|mcs(G_1, G_2)|}{|MCS(G_1, G_2)|} \qquad (6)$$

The last measure from literature is **Jaccard** similarity (Jaccard, 1912):

$$J(G_1, G_2) = \frac{|G_1 \cap G_2|}{|G_1 \cup G_2|} \qquad (7)$$

We propose a simple extension of *Jaccard* measure, called **Contextual BOW**, Eq. (8). In it, the context (neighborhood) of the node n_i from G_1 is compared with the context of node n_i in G_2. The neighborhood of node n in graph G is defined as input nodes $G(n)_{in}$ and output nodes $G(n)_{out}$.

$$N(G_1(n)) = \{G_1(n)_{in} \cup G_1(n)_{out}\}$$
$$N(G_2(n)) = \{G_2(n)_{in} \cup G_2(n)_{out}\}$$
$$S(N(G_1(n), G_2(n))) = \frac{|N(G_1(n)) \cap N(G_2(n))|}{|N(G_1(n)) \cup N(G_2(n))|}$$
$$G_{min} = G_1 \iff |G_1| \le |G_2|$$
$$G_{min} = G_2 \iff |G_2| < |G_1|$$

Where $N(G_1(n))$ is the neighborhood of node n in G_1, and $N(G_2(n))$ of node n in G_2. The value of *CTXBowSim* is calculated as:

$$Sim(G_1, G_2) = CTXBowSim(G_1, G_2)$$
$$= \frac{\sum_{n \in G_{min}}^{n} S(N(G_1(n), G_2(n)))}{|G_{min}|} \quad (8)$$

The similarity values are used as features during supervised learning to build a classifier. By changing the way of constructing the graphs and computing their similarity we tune the classification process into different aspects of the sentences being compared. The number of features generated for classification is dependent on the number of different graphs types, used to compare sentences, and the number of applied measures for calculating their similarity. Thus, it is a combination of all node representations, all EKG sources and the applied similarity measures.

5 Results and Evaluation

The corpus contains 3469 examples annotated with one of the possible CST relations. For classification we used SVM (*Suport Vectors Machine* (Steinwart and Christmann, 2008)) and LMT (*Logistic Model Tree* (Landwehr et al., 2005)). The classifiers were evaluated according to 10-fold cross-validation scheme (Kohavi, 1995).

First, the baseline set of features was tested, see Sec. 4.1. The classifiers were tested on relation types, which implies that the training set for the classification was highly unbalanced with respect to different relations. Table 1 shows the results for SVM and LMT and the baseline feature set. Zero values occurred for very specific relations with a small number of instances, e.g. 3 instances of Citation. Moreover, baseline features express only weak discrimination power.

In a multiclass setting, the average F-score value for SVM was 0.334 and 0.309 for LMT.

	SVM			LMT		
Rel.	P	R	F	P	R	F
Cita.	0.000	0.000	0.000	0.000	0.000	0.000
Foll.	0.583	0.023	0.044	0.000	0.000	0.000
Over.	0.454	0.985	0.622	0.465	0.967	0.628
Moda.	0.000	0.000	0.000	0.000	0.000	0.000
IS	0.000	0.000	0.000	0.000	0.000	0.000
Desc.	0.250	0.008	0.016	0.000	0.000	0.000
Equi.	0.000	0.000	0.000	0.000	0.000	0.000
Fulf.	0.000	0.000	0.000	0.000	0.000	0.000
Cont.	0.000	0.000	0.000	0.000	0.000	0.000
Sum.	0.000	0.000	0.000	0.000	0.000	0.000
HB	0.000	0.000	0.000	0.000	0.000	0.000
Iden.	0.900	0.150	0.257	0.430	0.767	0.551
Elab.	0.000	0.000	0.000	0.000	0.000	0.000
Subs.	0.429	0.031	0.058	0.492	0.160	0.241
Chan.	0.000	0.000	0.000	0.000	0.000	0.000
Sour.	0.000	0.000	0.000	0.000	0.000	0.000
NR	0.521	0.246	0.334	0.230	0.116	0.154
Avg.	0.349	0.457	0.307	0.254	0.457	0.309

Table 1: Results for the classifiers trained on the baseline feature set (lexical, syntactic, semantic).

Many CST relations were not recognized at all. Classifiers showed poor precision and recall in the relations detection task (*No relation* result), which means they could not decide whether a pair of sentences represents a CST link or not. The performance at recognition of relations was unsatisfactory, even for the most frequent relations including *Overlap*, *Follow-up*, *Subsumption* or *Description*.

For the graph-based approach, SVM and LMT were used again. Table 2 contains summarized results of classifiers trained with graph-based features. The performance achieved using graph-based features was better than in the previous approach. A significant improvement could be observed for both SVM and LMT. Only for the less frequent relations the classifiers were not able to correctly recognize the type. The average F-score value was 0.442 for SVM and 0.772 for LMT. We can note that LMT outperforms SVM in the classification on almost every class.

Table 3 shows the achieved results on a combined set of the baseline and graph-based features. A combination of these features had a positive impact on the performance of selected classifiers. The average F-score value was increased to 0.749 for SVM and 0.817 for LMT. Our method recognized even more complex relations like *Historical Background*, *Follow-up* or *Elaboration*, with good precision and slightly lower recall. Some of the relations that occur quite rarely in our dataset were also recognized, although performance for them was still low. The corpus used for evaluation has an irregular distribution of CST relations, nega-

	SVM			LMT		
Rel.	P	R	F	P	R	F
Cita.	0.000	0.000	0.000	1.000	0.333	0.500
Foll.	0.965	0.180	0.303	0.772	0.853	0.811
Over.	0.510	0.999	0.675	0.969	0.993	0.981
Moda.	0.000	0.000	0.000	0.000	0.000	0.000
IS	0.750	0.462	0.571	0.000	0.000	0.000
Desc.	0.578	0.070	0.125	0.556	0.739	0.634
Equi.	0.667	0.083	0.148	0.286	0.167	0.211
Fulf.	0.667	0.063	0.114	0.531	0.269	0.357
Cont.	0.000	0.000	0.000	0.000	0.000	0.000
Sum.	0.174	0.073	0.103	0.222	0.073	0.110
HB	0.727	0.103	0.180	0.643	0.756	0.695
Iden.	0.898	0.733	0.807	0.902	0.917	0.909
Elab.	0.378	0.114	0.175	0.707	0.431	0.535
Subs.	0.641	0.129	0.215	0.489	0.474	0.482
Chan.	0.000	0.000	0.000	0.000	0.000	0.000
Sour.	1.000	0.820	0.901	0.813	0.520	0.634
NR	0.956	0.437	0.600	0.776	0.749	0.762
Avg.	0.620	0.544	0.448	0.771	0.786	0.772

Table 2: The results for a graph-based approach.

tively affecting the results of classification. We can notice that for less frequent relations like *Citation*, *Modality*, *Indirect Speech* or *Contradiction*, the classifiers were not able to properly recognize types of the CST links.

	SVM			LMT		
Rel.	P	R	F	P	R	F
Cita.	0.000	0.000	0.000	0.000	0.000	0.000
Foll.	0.800	0.967	0.876	0.964	0.961	0.962
Over.	0.947	1.000	0.973	0.980	0.986	0.983
Moda.	0.000	0.000	0.000	0.000	0.000	0.000
IS	0.000	0.000	0.000	0.393	0.423	0.407
Desc.	0.551	0.728	0.627	0.613	0.707	0.657
Equi.	0.333	0.042	0.074	0.295	0.271	0.283
Fulf.	0.710	0.138	0.230	0.561	0.431	0.488
Cont.	0.000	0.000	0.000	0.167	0.150	0.158
Sum.	0.000	0.000	0.000	0.243	0.167	0.198
HB	0.565	0.724	0.635	0.695	0.753	0.723
Iden.	0.887	0.917	0.902	0.948	0.917	0.932
Elab.	0.933	0.341	0.500	0.607	0.577	0.592
Subs.	0.500	0.629	0.557	0.580	0.526	0.551
Chan.	0.000	0.000	0.000	0.000	0.000	0.000
Sour.	0.800	0.160	0.267	0.818	0.720	0.766
NR	0.777	0.723	0.749	0.873	0.868	0.871
Avg.	0.769	0.786	0.755	0.816	0.820	0.817

Table 3: The results for a combined approach - basis features extended with graph-based features.

As it was noted earlier, a similar distribution of the relations can be observed in the CSTNews corpus (Cardoso et al., 2011). The authors of CSTNews built it from news documents, i.e. the sources were very similar to those utilised in the corpus applied in this work. In (Maziero et al., 2014) CSTNews was used to evaluate recognition methods for the refined CST model. The authors stated that their classifier outperforms other CST parsers. Tab. 4 presents the results of our eval-

uation in comparison to the results reported in (Maziero et al., 2014). The comparison was indirect due to the different languages and data sets, but as both corpora have similar content and structure, this comparison can be informative.

	(Maziero et al., 2014)			Our LMT		
Rel.	P	R	F	P	R	F
Cita.	—	—	—	0.000	0.000	0.000
Foll.	0.282	0.273	0.277	0.964	0.961	0.962
Over.	0.441	0.478	0.458	0.980	0.986	0.983
Moda.	—	—	—	0.000	0.000	0.000
IS	0.529	0.632	0.576	0.393	0.423	0.407
Desc.	—	—	—	0.613	0.707	0.657
Equi.	0.378	0.359	0.368	0.295	0.271	0.283
Fulf.	—	—	—	0.561	0.431	0.488
Cont.	0.273	0.177	0.214	0.167	0.150	0.158
Sum.	—	—	—	0.243	0.167	0.198
HB	0.299	0.260	0.278	0.695	0.753	0.723
Iden.	1.000	1.000	1.000	0.948	0.917	0.932
Elab.	0.405	0.385	0.395	0.607	0.577	0.592
Subs.	0.449	0.447	0.448	0.580	0.526	0.551
Chan.	—	—	—	0.000	0.000	0.000
Sour.	—	—	—	0.818	0.720	0.766
NR	0.773	0.527	0.627	0.873	0.868	0.871
Tran.	0.500	0.500	0.500	—	—	—
Avg.	0.484	0.458	0.467	0.816	0.820	0.817

Table 4: Comparison of the results.

6 Conclusions

In our approach a sentence S is represented by different graphs referring to many types of the word-level representations. It is possible to express the same sentence S on the morphological level (*Lemma PoS Node type*) and/or semantic level (*Synset Node type*). By merging the graphs built from S with some external knowledge graph, we can expand the information stored in the graph of S and calculate similarity between graphs more accurately. The proposed approach to build graphs is language independent and is not depended on the existence of deeper parsers.

Relations extracted from sentence structures, i.e. *semantic roles* or *syntactic dependencies*, and lexical semantic representation assigned to words, i.e. *disambiguated senses* and *SUMO concepts*, were helpful in discriminating CST relation types. In our work we proposed a method for the recognition of the full set of 17 CST relations, in contrast to the limited of subsets used in literature, e.g. in (Kumar et al., 2012a). Our method outperforms also the state of the art algorithm when compared on a corpus of the similar origin and content.

References

Priscila Aleixo and Thiago Alexandre Salgueiro Pardo. 2008. Finding Related Sentences in Multiple Documents for Multidocument Discourse Parsing of Brazilian Portuguese Texts. In *Companion Proceedings of the XIV Brazilian Symposium on Multimedia and the Web*. ACM, New York, NY, USA, WebMedia '08, pages 298–303.

Bartosz Broda, Paweł Kędzia, Michał Marcińczuk, Adam Radziszewski, Radosław Ramocki, and Adam Wardyński. 2013. *Fextor: A Feature Extraction Framework for Natural Language Processing: A Case Study in Word Sense Disambiguation, Relation Recognition and Anaphora Resolution*, Springer Berlin Heidelberg, Berlin, Heidelberg, pages 41–62.

Bartosz Broda, Michał Marcińczuk, Marek Maziarz, Adam Radziszewski, and Adam Wardyński. 2012. KPWr: Towards a Free Corpus of Polish. In Nicoletta Calzolari (Conference Chair), Khalid Choukri, Thierry Declerck, Mehmet Uğur Doğan, Bente Maegaard, Joseph Mariani, Asuncion Moreno, Jan Odijk, and Stelios Piperidis, editors, *Proceedings of the Eight International Conference on Language Resources and Evaluation (LREC'12)*. European Language Resources Association (ELRA), Istanbul, Turkey.

H. Bunke. 1997. On a Relation Between Graph Edit Distance and Maximum Common Subgraph. *Pattern Recogn. Lett.* 18(9):689–694.

Horst Bunke and Kim Shearer. 1998. A Graph Distance Metric Based on the Maximal Common Subgraph. *Pattern Recogn. Lett.* 19(3-4):255–259.

Paula C.F. Cardoso, Erick G. Maziero, María Lucía Castro Jorge, Eloize R.M. Seno, Ariani Di Felippo, Lucia Helena Machado Rino, Maria das Gracas Volpe Nunes, and Thiago Alexandre Salgueiro Pardo. 2011. CSTNews - A discourse-annotated corpus for single and multi-document summarization of news texts in Brazilian Portuguese. In *Proceedings of the 3rd RST Brazilian Meeting*. Cuiabá, Brazil, pages 88–105.

Mirtha-Lina Fernández and Gabriel Valiente. 2001. A Graph Distance Metric Combining Maximum Common Subgraph and Minimum Common Supergraph. *Pattern Recogn. Lett.* 22(6-7):753–758.

Paul Jaccard. 1912. The Distribution of the Flora in the Alpine Zone . *New Phytologist* 11(2):37–50.

Pawel Kedzia and Marek Maziarz. 2013. Recognizing semantic relations within Polish noun phrase: A rule-based approach. In *RANLP*.

Ron Kohavi. 1995. A Study of Cross-validation and Bootstrap for Accuracy Estimation and Model Selection. In *Proceedings of the 14th International Joint Conference on Artificial Intelligence - Volume 2*. Morgan Kaufmann Publishers Inc., San Francisco, CA, USA, IJCAI'95, pages 1137–1143.

Yogan Jaya Kumar, Naomie Salim, Albaraa Abuobieda, and Ameer Tawfik Albaham. 2014. Multi document summarization based on news components using fuzzy cross-document relations. *Applied Soft Computing* 21:265–279.

Yogan Jaya Kumar, Naomie Salim, Ahmed Hamza, and Albarraa Abuobieda. 2012a. *Automatic identification of cross-document structural relationships*, pages 26–29.

Yogan Jaya Kumar, Naomie Salim, and Basit Raza. 2012b. Cross-document Structural Relationship Identification Using Supervised Machine Learning. *Appl. Soft Comput.* 12(10):3124–3131.

Paweł Kędzia and Maciej Piasecki. 2014. Ruled-based, Interlingual Motivated Mapping of plWordNet onto SUMO Ontology. In Nicoletta Calzolari, Khalid Choukri, Thierry Declerck, Hrafn Loftsson, Bente Maegaard, Joseph Mariani, Asunción Moreno, Jan Odijk, and Stelios Piperidis, editors, *Proceedings of the Ninth International Conference on Language Resources and Evaluation (LREC-2014), Reykjavik, Iceland, May 26-31, 2014.*. pages 4351–4358.

Paweł Kędzia, Maciej Piasecki, and Marlena Orlińska. 2015. Word sense disambiguation based on large scale Polish CLARIN heterogeneous lexical resources. *Cognitive Studies / Études cognitives* (15):269–292. https://ispan.waw.pl/journals/index.php/cs-ec/article/download/cs.2015.019/1765.

Niels Landwehr, Mark Hall, and Eibe Frank. 2005. Logistic model trees. *Machine Learning* 59(1):161–205.

Michał Marcińczuk, Jan Kocoń, and Maciej Janicki. 2013. Liner2 – a customizable framework for proper names recognition for Polish. In Robert Bembenik, Lukasz Skonieczny, Henryk Rybinski, Marzena Kryszkiewicz, and Marek Niezgodka, editors, *Intelligent Tools for Building a Scientific Information Platform*, pages 231–253.

Marek Maziarz, Maciej Piasecki, Ewa Rudnicka, Stan Szpakowicz, and Pawel Kedzia. 2016. plWordNet 3.0 - a Comprehensive Lexical-Semantic Resource. In *COLING 2016, 26th International Conference on Computational Linguistics, Proceedings of the Conference: Technical Papers, December 11-16, 2016, Osaka, Japan*. pages 2259–2268.

Erick Galani Maziero, Maria Lucía Del Rosário Castro Jorge, and Thiago Alexandre Salgueiro Pardo. 2014. Revisiting Cross-document Structure Theory for Multi-document Discourse Parsing. *Inf. Process. Manage.* 50(2):297–314.

Joakim Nivre, Johan Hall, Jens Nilsson, Atanas Chanev, Gülsen Eryigit, Sandra Kübler, Svetoslav Marinov, and Erwin Marsi. 2007. MaltParser: A language-independent system for data-driven dependency parsing. *Natural Language Engineering* 13(02):95–135.

Adam Pease. 2011. *Ontology: A Practical Guide*. Articulate Software Press, Angwin, CA.

Maciej Piasecki, Pawel Kędzia, and Marlena Orlińska. 2016. plWordNet in Word Sense Disambiguation task. In *GWC 2016, Proceedings of the 8th Global Wordnet Conference, Bucharest, 27-30 January 2016 Osaka, Japan.* pages 280–290.

Maciej Piasecki, Stanisław Szpakowicz, and Bartosz Broda. 2009. *A Wordnet from the Ground Up*. Oficyna Wydawnicza Politechniki Wroclawskiej, Wrocław.

Dragomir R. Radev. 2000. A Common Theory of Information Fusion from Multiple Text Sources Step One: Cross-document Structure. In *Proceedings of the 1st SIGdial Workshop on Discourse and Dialogue - Volume 10*. Association for Computational Linguistics, Stroudsburg, PA, USA, SIGDIAL '00, pages 74–83.

Dragomir R. Radev, Jahna Otterbacher, and Zhu Zhang. 2004. Cst bank: A corpus for the study of cross-document structural relationships. In *LREC*. European Language Resources Association.

Adam Radziszewski. 2013. A tiered CRF tagger for Polish. In H. Rybiński M. Kryszkiewicz M. Niezgódka R. Bembenik, Ł. Skonieczny, editor, *Intelligent Tools for Building a Scientific Information Platform: Advanced Architectures and Solutions*, Springer Verlag, page to appear.

Adam Radziszewski and Adam Pawlaczek. 2013. *Language Processing and Intelligent Information Systems: 20th International Conference, IIS 2013, Warsaw, Poland, June 17-18, 2013. Proceedings*, Springer Berlin Heidelberg, Berlin, Heidelberg, chapter Incorporating Head Recognition into a CRF Chunker, pages 22–27.

Adam Radziszewski, Adam Wardyński, and Tomasz Śniatowski. 2011. WCCL: A morpho-syntactic feature toolkit. In *Proceedings of the Balto-Slavonic Natural Language Processing Workshop (BSNLP 2011)*. Springer.

Ingo Steinwart and Andreas Christmann. 2008. *Support Vector Machines*. Springer Publishing Company, Incorporated, 1st edition.

W. D. Wallis, P. Shoubridge, M. Kraetz, and D. Ray. 2001. Graph Distances Using Graph Union. *Pattern Recogn. Lett.* 22(6-7):701–704.

Marcin Woliński. 2006. Morfeusz — a practical tool for the morphological analysis of Polish. In Mieczysław A. Kłopotek, Sławomir T. Wierzchoń, and Krzysztof Trojanowski, editors, *Intelligent Information Processing and Web Mining*, Springer-Verlag, Berlin, Advances in Soft Computing, pages 503–512.

Alina Wróblewska. 2014. *Polish Dependency Parser Trained on an Automatically Induced Dependency Bank*. Ph.D. dissertation, Institute of Computer Science, Polish Academy of Sciences, Warsaw.

Nik Adilah Hanin Binti Zahri and Fumiyo Fukumoto. 2011. *Multi-document Summarization Using Link Analysis Based on Rhetorical Relations between Sentences*, Springer Berlin Heidelberg, Berlin, Heidelberg, pages 328–338.

Zhu Zhang, Jahna Otterbacher, and Dragomir Radev. 2003. Learning Cross-document Structural Relationships Using Boosting. In *Proceedings of the Twelfth International Conference on Information and Knowledge Management*. ACM, New York, NY, USA, CIKM '03, pages 124–130.

Zhu Zhang and Dragomir Radev. 2005. Combining Labeled and Unlabeled Data for Learning Cross-document Structural Relationships. In *Proceedings of the First International Joint Conference on Natural Language Processing*. Springer-Verlag, Berlin, Heidelberg, IJCNLP'04, pages 32–41.

Domain Control for Neural Machine Translation

Catherine Kobus and **Josep Crego** and **Jean Senellart**

`firstname.lastname@systrangroup.com`

SYSTRAN International / 5 rue Feydeau, 75002 Paris, France

Abstract

Machine translation systems are very sensitive to the domains they were trained on. Several domain adaptation techniques have already been deeply studied. We propose a new technique for neural machine translation (NMT) that we call domain control which is performed at runtime using a unique neural network covering multiple domains. The presented approach shows quality improvements when compared to dedicated domains translating on any of the covered domains and even on out-of-domain data. In addition, model parameters do not need to be re-estimated for each domain, making this effective to real use cases. Evaluation is carried out on English-to-French translation for two different testing scenarios. We first consider the case where an end-user performs translations on a known domain. Secondly, we consider the scenario where the domain is not known and predicted at the sentence level before translating. Results show consistent accuracy improvements for both conditions.

1 Introduction

Machine translation systems are very sensitive to the domain(s) they were trained on because each domain has its own style, sentence structure and terminology. There is often a mismatch between the domain for which training data are available and the target domain of a machine translation system. If there is a strong deviation between training and testing data, translation quality will be dramatically deteriorated. Word ambiguities are often an issue for machine translation systems. For instance, the English word *"administer"* has to be translated differently if it appears in medical or political contexts. Our work is motivated by the idea that neural models could benefit from having domain information to choose the most appropriate terminology and sentence structure while using the information from *all* the domains to improve the base translation quality. Recently, (Sennrich et al., 2016) report on the neural network ability to control politeness through side constraints. We extend this idea to domain control. Our goal is to allow a model built from a diverse set of training data to produce in-domain translations. This is, to extend the coverage of generic NMT models to specific domains, with their specialized terminology and style, without lowering translation quality on more generic data. We present two frameworks to feed domain meta-information on the NMT encoder side.

The paper is structured as follows: Section 2 overviews related work. Details of our neural MT engine are given in Section 3. Section 4 describes the proposed approach. Experiments and results are detailed in Section 5. Finally, conclusions and further work are drawn in Section 6.

2 Related Work

A lot of work has already been done for domain adaptation in Statistical Machine Translation. The approaches vary from in-domain data selection based methods (Hildebrand et al., 2005) (Moore and Lewis, 2010) (Sethy et al., 2006) to in-domain models mixture-based methods (Foster and Kuhn, 2007) (Koehn and Schroeder, 2007) (Schwenk and Koehn, 2008).

Recent works have especially dealt with domain adaptation for NMT by providing meta-information to the Neural Network. Our work is in line with this kind of approach. (Chen et al., 2016) feeds Neural Network with topic information on

Proceedings of Recent Advances in Natural Language Processing, pages 372–378,
Varna, Bulgaria, Sep 4–6 2017.
"

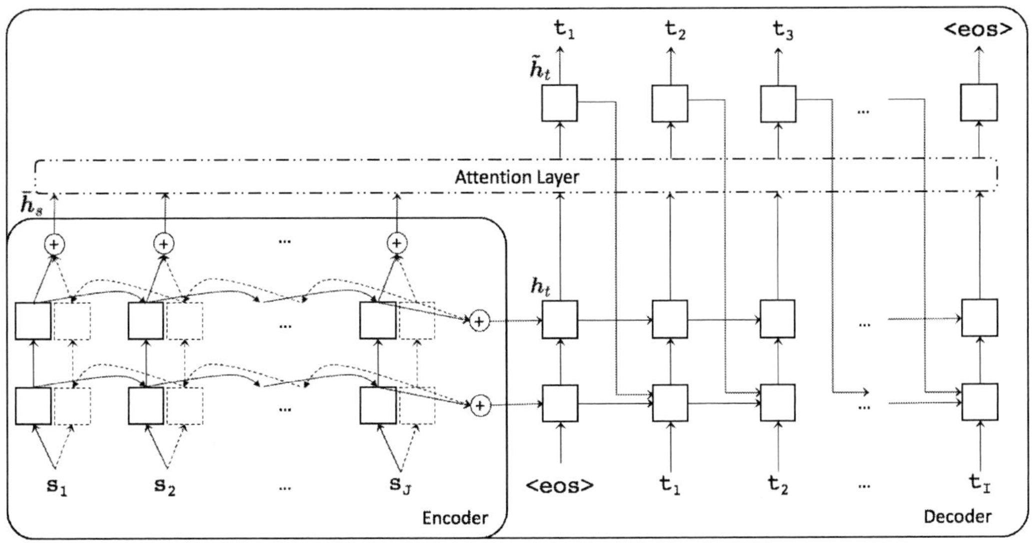

Figure 1: Schematic view of our NMT system.

the decoder side; topics are numerous and consist in human-labeled product categories. (Zhang et al., 2016) includes topic modeling on both encoder and decoder sides. A given number of topics are automatically inferred from the training data using Latent Dirichlet Allocation; each word in a sentence is assigned its own vector of topics. In our work, we also provide meta-information about domain to the network. However, we introduce domain information at the sentence level. (Luong and Manning, 2015) adapt a generic NMT network (trained on out-of-domain data) by running additional training iterations over an in-domain data set. The authors claim to obtain a domain adapted model in a very limited training time. However, it differs from our work since we aim at performing domain-adapted translations using a unique network that covers multiple domains.

3 Neural MT

Our NMT system follows the architecture presented in (Bahdanau et al., 2014). It is implemented as an encoder-decoder network with multiple layers of a RNN with Long Short-Term Memory hidden units (Zaremba et al., 2014). Figure 1 illustrates an schematic view of the MT network.

Source words are first mapped to word vectors and then fed into a bidirectional recurrent neural network (RNN) that reads an input sequence $s = (s_1, ..., s_J)$. Upon seeing the <eos> symbol, the final time step initialises a target RNN.

The decoder is a RNN that predicts a target sequence $t = (t_1, ..., t_I)$, being J and I respectively the source and target sentence lengths. Translation is finished when the decoder predicts the <eos> symbol.

The left-hand side of the figure illustrates the bidirectional encoder, which actually consists of two independent LSTM encoders: one encoding the normal sequence (solid lines) that calculates a forward sequence of hidden states $(\overrightarrow{h}_1, ..., \overrightarrow{h}_J)$, the second encoder reads the input sequence in reversed order (dotted lines) and calculates the backward sequence $(\overleftarrow{h}_1, ..., \overleftarrow{h}_J)$. The final encoder outputs $(\overline{h}_1, ..., \overline{h}_J)$ consist of the sum of both encoders final outputs. The right-hand side of the figure illustrates the RNN decoder. Each word t_i is predicted based on a recurrent hidden state h_i and a context vector c_i that aims at capturing relevant source-side information.

Figure 2 illustrates the attention layer; it implements the "general" attentional architecture from (Luong et al., 2015). The idea of a global attentional model is to consider all the hidden states of the encoder when deriving the context vector c_t. Hence, global alignment weights a_t are derived by comparing the current target hidden state h_t with each source hidden state $\overline{h}_s$:

$$a_t(s) = \frac{exp(score(h_t, \overline{h}_s))}{\sum_{s'} exp(score(h_t, \overline{h}_{s'}))}$$

with the content-based score function:

$$score(h_t, \overline{h}_s) = h_t^T W_a \overline{h}_s$$

Given the alignment vector as weights, the context vector c_t is computed as the weighted average over all the source hidden states.

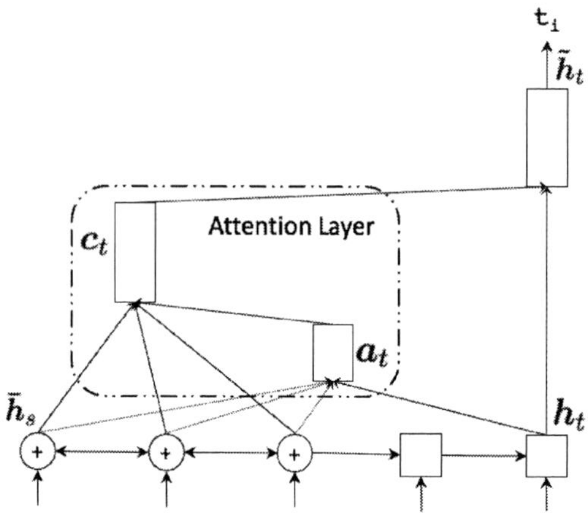

Figure 2: Attention layer of the NMT system.

The framework is available on the open-source project `seq2seq-attn`[1]. More details about our system can be found in (Crego et al., 2016).

4 Domain control

Two different techniques are implemented to integrate domain control: additional token and domain feature.

4.1 Additional Token

The additional token method, inspired by the politeness control technique detailed in (Sennrich et al., 2016) consists in adding an artificial token at the end of each source sentence in order to let the network pay attention to the domain of each sentence pair. For instance, consider the next English-French translation:

Src: `Headache may be experienced`
Tgt: `Des céphalées peuvent survenir`

The network reads off the sentence pair with the appropriate *Medical* domain tag **@MED@**:

Src: `Headache may be experienced `**`@MED@`**
Tgt: `Des céphalées peuvent survenir`

[1]`http://nlp.seas.harvard.edu`

Domain tags are appropriately selected in order to avoid overlaps with words present in the source language vocabulary. This method, though simple, has already proven to be effective to control the politeness level of a translation (Sennrich et al., 2016), or to support multi-lingual NMT models (Johnson et al., 2016).

4.2 Word Feature

We present a second technique to introduce domain control in our neural translation model. We use word-level features as described in (Crego et al., 2016). The first layer of the network is the word embedding layer. We adapt this layer to extend each word embedding with an arbitrary number of cells, designed to encode domain information. Notice that using additional features does not increase the vocabulary of source words; there are separate vocabularies for words and domain tags. Figure 3 illustrates a word embedding layer extended with domain information.

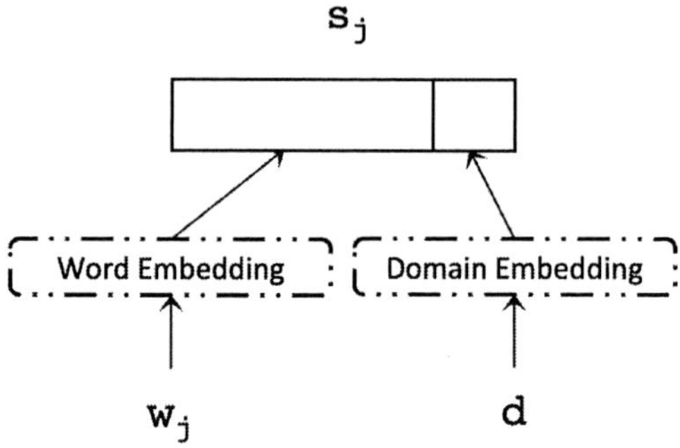

Figure 3: Word embedding layer for word w_j extended with domain label d, which constitutes a new input s_j for the encoder

Following with the example of Section 4.1, the sentence pair is given to the network with the appropriate *Medical* domain tag on each source word as follows:

Src: `Headache    may    be    experienced`
             `MED         MED   MED  MED`
Tgt: `Des céphalées peuvent survenir`

Note that under this feature framework, the sentence-level domain information is added on a word-by-word basis to all the words in a sentence.

Domain	Lines	Src words	Tgt words	Lines	Src words	Tgt words
	Train			Test		
IT	399k	6.0M	7.3M	2k	36,8k	45,1k
Literature	35k	881k	943k	2k	50.1k	54.0k
Medical	923k	10.5M	12.3M	2k	35.6k	43.0k
News	194k	5.4M	6.7M	2k	53.5k	66.4k
Parliamentary	1.6M	37.6M	43.8M	2k	40.7k	49.4k
Tourism	1.1M	23.3M	27.5M	2k	39.1k	45.5k
Total	**4,3M**	**83,7M**	**98.5M**			

Table 1: Statistics for training and test sets of each domain corpus. Note that k stand for thousands and M for millions.

We reuse an existing framework that was originally implemented to include linguistic features at the word level (Crego et al., 2016).

5 Experiments

We evaluate the presented approach on English-to-French translation. Section 5.1 describes the data used for the experiments and details training configurations. Finally, Section 5.2 reports on translation accuracy results.

5.1 Training Details

We used training corpora covering six different domains: *IT*, *Literature*, *Medical*, *News*, *Parliamentary* and *Tourism*. *Medical*, *News*, *Parliamentary* data come from public corpora (respectively EMEA, News Commentary and Europarl), available from the OPUS repository (Tiedemann, 2012). *IT*, *Literature* and *Tourism* are proprietary data. Statistics of the corpora used are given in Table 1.

All experiments employ the NMT system detailed in Section 3 and are performed on NVidia GeForce GTX 1080. We use BPE[2] with a total of $32,000$ source and target tokens as vocabulary, computed over the entire training corpora. Word embedding size is 500 cells. During training, we use stochastic gradient descent, a minibatch size of 64 with dropout probability set to 0.3 and bidirectional RNN. We train our models for 18 epochs. Learning rate is set to 1 and starts decaying after epoch 10 by 0.5. It takes about 10 days to train models on the complete training data set ($4,3$M sentence pairs).

Four different training configurations are considered. The first includes six in-domain NMT models. Each model is trained using its corresponding domain data set (henceforth *Single* models). The *Join* network configuration is built using all the training data after concatenation. Note that this model does not include any information about domain. A *Token* network is also trained using all the available training data. It includes domain information through the additional token approach detailed in Section 4.1. Finally, *Feature* network is also trained on all available training data, it introduces domain information in the model by means of the feature framework detailed in Section 4.2.

5.2 Results

Table 2 shows translation accuracy results for the different training configurations. Accuracies are measured using BLEU[3]. As expected, the *Join* model outperforms all *Single* models on their corresponding test sets, showing that NMT engines benefit from additional training data. Differences in accuracy are lower for domains with a higher representation in the *Join* model, like Parliamentary and Tourism. No domain information is used on these first configurations (*none*).

Results for models incorporating domain information are detailed in columns *Token* and *Feature*. *Oracle* experiments indicate that the test set domains are known in advance, thus allowing to use the correct side-constraint. The additional token approach gives mixed results; it improves translation quality on some tasks and degrades on some others compared to the *Join* model. On the contrary, incorporating domain information through the *Feature* approach consistently improves translation quality on all the tasks. Adding domain information on all the source words seems to be a good technique to convey domain side-constraint

[2]`https://github.com/rsennrich/subword-nmt`

[3]`multi-bleu.perl`

Domain	Single	Join	Token	Feature	Feature	
Constraint	None			Oracle	RNN	Acc (%)
IT	52.73	53.81	53.76	**54.56** (+0.75)	54.42	97.8
Literature	20.25	29.81	29.96	**30.73** (+0.92)	30.71	93.1
Medical	33.97	41.83	42.02	**42.51** (+0.68)	42.34	89.4
News	29.70	33.83	34.47	**34.61** (+0.78)	34.49	88.3
Parliamentary	37.34	37.53	37.13	**37.79** (+0.26)	37.77	82.7
Tourism	37.05	37.46	37.72	**38.30** (+0.84)	38.01	90.6
Dialogs		19.25			19.55	

Table 2: BLEU scores for the different systems and RNN-based domain classifier accuracy.

Src:	Your doctor's instructions should be **carefully observed** .
Ref:	Vous devrez **respecter scrupuleusement** les instructions de votre médecin .
Join:	Les instructions de votre médecin doivent être **soigneusement surveillées** .
Feature:	Les instructions de votre médecin doivent être **suivies attentivement** .
Src:	All injections of Macugen will be **administered** by your doctor.
Ref:	Toutes les injections de Macugen doivent être **réalisées** par votre médecin.
Join:	Toutes les injections de Macugen seront **à l'ordre du jour** de votre médecin.
Feature:	Toutes les injections de Macugen seront **effectuées** par votre médecin.

Table 3: Translation examples of in-domain medical sentences with and without domain feature

and to improve NMT target words choice consistency. Differences between the *Feature* and *Join* configurations are shown in parentheses. Note that an average improvement of 0.80 is observed on all test sets with the exception of Parliamentary translations, for which accuracy was only improved by 0.26. This can be explained by the fact that Parliamentary is the best represented domain in *Join* training set.

Translation examples are shown in Table 3 in a medical context. They show the impact on domain adaptation introduced by the *Feature* approach. The first example shows the preference of the *Feature* model for the French translation *suivies attentivement* of the English *carefully observed*. It seems more suitable than the hypothesis *soigneusement surveillées* output by the *Join*

model. A similar effect is shown on the second example where the French *effectuées* is clearly more adapted as translation of *administered* than *à l'ordre du jour*.

Finally, we also evaluate the ability of our presented approach (*Feature*) to face test sets for which the domain is not known in advance. Hence, before translation, the domain tag is automatically detected using an in-house domain classification module based on Recurrent Neural Networks (RNN) to disambiguate between the six different domains. The tool predicts the domain on a sentence-by-sentence basis, then translation is carried out using the predicted domain value in *Feature* model. Last column of Table 2 shows the accuracy of the domain classification tool for sentences on each of the predefined domains.

Test	Domain feature					
	IT	Literature	Medical	News	Parl.	Tourism
IT	**54.56**	-12.76	-10.25	-12.43	-13.83	-14.18
Literature	-5.96	**30.73**	-5.13	-2.89	-3.50	-3.03
Medical	-4.82	-6.23	**42.51**	-5.06	-5.39	-4.74
News	-3.36	-1.58	-3.04	**34.61**	-0.81	-2.48
Parliamentary	-4.14	-1.92	-3.09	-0.39	**37.79**	-3.01
Tourism	-6.72	-3.2	-4.16	-4.26	-4.35	**38.30**

Table 4: BLEU score decreases using different predefined domain tags

Results for this last condition are shown in column *RNN*. Event though domain is wrongly predicted in some cases, translation accuracy is still improved when compared to the *Join* model. Notice that domain classification at sentence level is a challenging task as short context is considered. We also confront our approach with a final test set from a brand new domain, *Dialogs*, that is not present in our training data. Sentences are selected from TED Talks corpora. The *RNN* toolkit is able to assign each test sentence to one of the source domains, leading to outperform the *Join* model.

In order to better understand the influence of the predicted domain, we conduct a final set of experiments. Using the *Feature* model, we run each test set using all domain values. Results are detailed in Table 4 showing that translation quality can significantly be degraded when translating sentences with the wrong domain tag. It is especially the case for *IT* domain, where translating with the wrong domain tag dramatically reduces accuracy. Results also reveal proximities between different domains like, for example, *News* and *Parliamentary*. Translating the *News* test set with the *Parliamentary* domain tag (and vice versa) does not seem to hurt translation quality compared to other domain tag mismatches.

6 Conclusions and Further Work

We have presented a method that incorporates domain information into a neural network. It allows to perform domain-adapted translations using a unique network that covers multiple domains. The presented method does not need to re-estimate model parameters when performing translations on any of the available domains.

We plan to further improve the feature technique detailed in this work. Rather than providing the network with a hard decision about domain, we want to introduce a vector of distance values of the given source sentence to each domain, thus allowing to smooth the proximity of each sentence to each domain.

Additionally, Table 4 shows indirectly that the neural network has learnt the ability to classify domains at the sentence level. We also plan to implement a joint approach for domain classification and translation, avoiding dependency with the RNN classifier.

Finally, since domain classification is a document level task, it would be interesting to extend the current study to document level translation.

References

Dzmitry Bahdanau, Kyunghyun Cho, and Yoshua Bengio. 2014. Neural machine translation by jointly learning to align and translate. *CoRR* abs/1409.0473. Demoed at NIPS 2014: http://lisa.iro.umontreal.ca/mt-demo/.

Wenhu Chen, Evgeny Matusov, Shahram Khadivi, and Jan-Thorsten Peter. 2016. Guided alignment training for topic-aware neural machine translation. *CoRR* abs/1607.01628v1.

Josep Crego, Jungi Kim, Guillaume Klein, Anabel Rebollo, Kathy Yang, Jean Senellart, Egor Akhanov, Patrice Brunelle, Aurelien Coquard, Yongchao Deng, Satoshi Enoue, Chiyo Geiss, Joshua Johanson, Ardas Khalsa, Raoum Khiari, Byeongil Ko, Catherine Kobus, Jean Lorieux, Leidiana Martins, Dang-Chuan Nguyen, Alexandra Priori, Thomas Riccardi, Natalia Segal, Christophe Servan, Cyril Tiquet, Bo Wang, Jin Yang, Dakun Zhang, Jing Zhou, and Peter Zoldan. 2016. Systran's pure neural machine translation systems. *CoRR* abs/1610.05540.

George Foster and Roland Kuhn. 2007. Mixture-model adaptation for SMT. In *Proceedings of the Second Workshop on Statistical Machine Translation*. Association for Computational Linguistics, Prague, Czech Republic, pages 128–135.

Almut Silja Hildebrand, Matthias Eck, Stephan Vogel, and Alex Waibel. 2005. Adaptation of the translation model for statistical machine translation based on information retrieval. In *Proceedings of the 10th Conference of the European Association for Machine Translation (EAMT)*. Budapest.

Melvin Johnson, Mike Schuster, Quoc V.Le, Maxim Krikun, Yonghui Wu, Zhifeng Chen, and Nikkik Thorat. 2016. Google's multilingual neural machine translation system: Enabling zero-shot translation arXiv:1611.04558v.

Philipp Koehn and Josh Schroeder. 2007. Experiments in domain adaptation for statistical machine translation. In *Proceedings of the Second Workshop on Statistical Machine Translation*. Association for Computational Linguistics, Prague, Czech Republic, pages 224–227.

Thang Luong and Christopher D. Manning. 2015. Stanford neural machine translation systems for spoken language domains. In *IWSLT2015*. Da Nang, Vietnam.

Thang Luong, Hieu Pham, and Christopher D. Manning. 2015. Effective approaches to attention-based neural machine translation. In *Proceedings of the 2015 Conference on Empirical Methods in Natural Language Processing*. Association for Computational Linguistics, Lisbon, Portugal, pages 1412–1421.

Robert C. Moore and William Lewis. 2010. Intelligent selection of language model training data. In *Proceedings of the ACL 2010 Conference Short Papers*. Association for Computational Linguistics, Uppsala, Sweden, pages 220–224.

Holger Schwenk and Philipp Koehn. 2008. Large and diverse language models for statistical machine translation. In *Proceedings of the 3rd International Joint Conference on Natural Language Processing (IJCNLP)*.

Rico Sennrich, Barry Haddow, and Alexandra Birch. 2016. Controlling politeness in neural machine translation via side constraints. In *Proceedings of the 15th Annual Conference of the North American Chapter of the Association for Computational Linguistics: Human Language Technologies*. Association for Computational Linguistics, San Diego, California, USA, pages 35–40.

Abhinav Sethy, Panayiotis Georgiou, and Shrikanth Narayanan. 2006. Selecting relevant text subsets from web-data for building topic specific language models. In *Proceedings of the Human Language Technology Conference of the NAACL, Companion Volume: Short Papers*. Association for Computational Linguistics, New York City, USA, pages 145–148.

Jörg Tiedemann. 2012. Parallel data, tools and interfaces in opus. In *LREC*. pages 2214–2218.

Wojciech Zaremba, Ilya Sutskever, and Oriol Vinyals. 2014. Recurrent neural network regularization. *CoRR* abs/1409.2329.

Jian Zhang, Liangyou Li, Andy Way, and Qun Liu. 2016. Topic-informed neural machine translation. In *COLING*.

Curriculum Learning and Minibatch Bucketing
in Neural Machine Translation

Tom Kocmi and **Ondřej Bojar**
Charles University,
Faculty of Mathematics and Physics
Institute of Formal and Applied Linguistics
surname@ufal.mff.cuni.cz

Abstract

We examine the effects of particular orderings of sentence pairs on the on-line training of neural machine translation (NMT). We focus on two types of such orderings: (1) ensuring that each minibatch contains sentences similar in some aspect and (2) gradual inclusion of some sentence types as the training progresses (so called "curriculum learning"). In our English-to-Czech experiments, the internal homogeneity of minibatches has no effect on the training but some of our "curricula" achieve a small improvement over the baseline.

1 Introduction

Machine translation (MT) has recently seen another major change of paradigms. MT started with rule based approaches which worked successfully for small domains. Generic MT was first reached with statistical methods, the early word-based and the late phrase-based dominant approaches, that build upon large training data. The current change is due to the first successful application of deep-learning methods (neural networks) to the task, giving rise to neural MT (NMT; Collobert et al., 2011; Sutskever et al., 2014). The data-driven methods have always been resource-heavy (e.g. word alignment needing a day or two for large parallel corpora) and NMT pushed this to new extremes: to reach the state-of-the-art performance, the model often needs a few weeks on the highly parallel graphics processing units (GPUs), equipped with large memory (8–12 GB) on a large training corpus.

The complexity of the training is a direct consequence of the complexity of the neural MT model: we need to find optimal setting of dozens millions of real-valued NMT model parameters that, according to the hard-coded model structure, define the calculation that converts the sequence of source words to the sequence of target words. The core of NMT training is thus numerical optimization, gradient descent, towards the least error as defined by the objective function. The common practice is to evaluate cross entropy against the reference translation.

The gradient of the objective function, in which the algorithm progresses, can be established on the whole dataset (called "batch training"), on individual examples ("online training") or a small set of examples ("minibatch training"). The full batch training has a clear advantage of reliable gradient estimates, while online training can easily suffer from instability. As documented by Wilson and Martinez (2003) on 27 learning tasks, online training reaches the same level of optima as the full batch training while having much lower memory demands and faster computation in general.

Minibatches typically contain 50 to 200 examples, calculate and average the error for all of them and propagate the error back through the network to update the weights. They have the advantages of both: the gradient is more stable and we decide how much of the training data it is convenient to handle at each training step. A further benefit comes from parallelizability on GPUs: the error of all the examples in the batch can be calculated simultaneously with the exact same formulas.

The training sets in NMT are simply too large, so full batch training is out of question and everybody uses minibatches.[1] The benefit of parallelization in minibatches can be somewhat diluted if minibatches contain sentences of varying length. In common frameworks for parallel computation, all the items in the minibatch must usually have

---

[1] In fact, the terms "batch" or batch size in NMT refer to minibatches; the whole corpus is then called an "epoch".

Proceedings of Recent Advances in Natural Language Processing, pages 379–386,
Varna, Bulgaria, Sep 4–6 2017.

the same length, and shorter sentences are therefore padded with dummy symbols. Calculations over the padded areas are wasted.

Khomenko et al. (2016) and Doetsch et al. (2017) report improvements in training speed by organizing (bucketing) training sentences so that sentences of identical or similar length arrive in the same minibatches. A related idea is called "curriculum learning" (Bengio et al., 2009) where the network is first trained with easier examples, making the task more complex only gradually.

In this work, we attempt to improve the final translation quality and/or reduce the training time of an NMT system by organizing minibatches in two particular ways. In Section 2, minibatches are created to contain sentences similar not only in length but in other (linguistic) phenomena, hoping for a better quality. In Section 3, similar criteria are used to organize the whole corpus, increasing the complexity of examples as training progresses, aiming at a better quality in shorter time. Section 4 evaluates our ideas in thems of translation quality and discusses the results. Related work is summarized in Section 5 and we conclude in Section 6.

2   Minibatch Bucketing

Minibatches stabilize the online training from fluctuations (Murata and Amari, 1999) and help to avoid a problem with overshooting local optima.

As mentioned, better performance of parallel processing has been achieved by bucketing training examples to contain sentences of similar length. The benefit of this approach however comes purely from the technical reason: avoiding wasted computation on paddings.

Each minibatch leads to one update of the model parameters and each example in the minibatch contributes to the average error. We assume that if all the examples in the minibatch are similar in some *linguistic sense*, they could jointly highlight the fitness of the current model in this particular aspect. Each minibatch would be thus focused on some particular language phenomenon and the gradient derived from this minibatch could improve the behavior of the model in this respect, allowing the network an easier identification of shared features of the examples.

We experiment with several features, by which we bucket the data. Those features are: sentence length, number of coordinating conjunctions, number of nouns, number of proper nouns

and the number of verbs in the training data pairs. In our experiments we do not mix features together, but such mixed-focus minibatches are surely also possible.

The exact procedure of training corpus composition is the following: First, we divide all data based on their features into separate buckets (e.g. one bucket of sentences with at most one verb, another bucket of sentences with two or three verbs etc.). We then shuffle all examples in each bucket and break them down to groups of size same as the minibatch size. Finally, all these groups are shuffled and concatenated. The corpus is then read sequentially but our shuffling procedure ensured that all minibatches contain data having the same feature but among minibatches, the features are shuffled.

3   Curriculum Learning

When humans are trained, they start with easier tasks and gradually, as they gain experience and abstraction, they are able to learn to handle more and more complex situations. It has been shown by Bengio et al. (2009) that even neural networks can improve their performance when they are presented with the easier examples first.

For neural networks, it is important to keep on training also on the easy examples, because the networks are generally prone to very quick overfitting as we discuss in Section 4.5. If the network was presented only with the more difficult examples, its performance on the easy ones would drop. Some mixing strategy is thus needed.

Bengio et al. (2009) propose a relatively simple strategy. They organize all training data into bins of similar complexity. The training then starts with all the examples in the easiest bin (step-by-step in minibatches). With the easiest bin covered, the first and second easiest bins are allowed. In the final stage, examples from all the bins are used in the training.

The disadvantage of this approach is that examples in easier batches are processed several times. This boosts their importance for the training and also prevents us from directly comparing this strategy with the baseline of simply shuffled corpus.

We improve this strategy to use each example only once during an epoch. For our method to work, we require that the number of examples in the bin only decreases as we move to the bin of the higher complexity. This is usually easy to reach as there are generally more easier sentence pairs than complex sentence pairs in parallel corpora. The bin thresholds can be also adjusted to fulfill this condition.

The strategy for selecting examples from the bins is the following. First, we draw examples from the easiest bin only until there remain the same number of examples as in the second most easy bin. We then continue to draw uniformly from the first two easiest bins until in each of them, there remain the same number of examples as in the third one, etc. When taking the examples, we always accumulate one minibatch and feed it to the training. If the number of bins is smaller than the size of the minibatch, the minibatches in the late stages will contain examples from all complexity bins. If there are more bins than the minibatch size, each minibatch will be highly varied in complexity and the training will gradually proceed over examples of all complexities.

3.1 Selected Features

It is not entirely clear which examples are easy and which are hard for NMT (in various stages of the training). We experiment with several linguistically-motivated features.

The first feature is the length of the target sentence. (Source sentences usually have a corresponding length.) Our bins are for sentences of up to 8 tokens, up to 12 tokens, 16, 20, up to 40 tokens and for longer sentences. The thresholds were chosen to satisfy the requirement of more examples in easier bins.

The second binning is based on the number of coordinating conjunctions in the target sentence as one possible (rough) estimate of the number of clauses in the sentence. Conjuctions are also used in lists of items, so a higher number of them suggests that the sentence structure is cluttered with lists. Such examples may be easy to translate but do not correspond well to the generally hierarchical structure of sentences that we want to expose to the network. We use the same thresholds as for sentence length.

Learners of foreign languages often read books written with a simplified vocabulary. To replicate this learning strategy, we sort words by their decreasing frequency and define ranks on this list. For example, the first rank contains the 5000 most frequent words. Sentences are then organized into bins based on the least frequent word in them: the first bin contains sentences with all the words appearing the first rank.

We define the ranks separately for source and for target language and experiment with binning based on one of them or both at the same time.

4 Experiments

This section describes our experiments and results with minibatch bucketing and curriculum learning.

4.1 Model Details

We use Neural Monkey (Helcl and Libovický, 2017), an open-source neural machine translation and general sequence-to-sequence learning system built using the TensorFlow machine learning library.

Neural Monkey is quite flexible in model configuration but we restrict our experiments to the standard encoder-decoder architecture with attention as proposed by Bahdanau et al. (2015). We use the same model parameters as defined for the WMT 2017 NMT Training Task (Bojar et al., 2017). The task defines models of two sizes, one that fits a 4GB GPU and one that fits an 8GB GPU. We use the former one where the encoder uses embeddings of size 300 and the hidden state of 350. Dropout is turned off and maximum input sentence length is set to 50 tokens. The decoder uses attention mechanism and conditional GRU cells, with the hidden state of 350. Output embedding has the size of 300, dropout is turned off as well and the maximum output length is again 50 tokens. The Adam (Kingma and Ba, 2014) optimizer is used as the gradient descend algorithm.

To reduce vocabulary size, we use byte pair encoding (Sennrich et al., 2016) which breaks all words into subword units defined in the vocabulary. The vocabulary is initialized with all letters and larger units are added on the basis of corpus statistics. Frequent words make it to the vocabulary, less frequent words are (deterministically) broken into smaller units from the vocabulary.

As defined for the NMT Training Task, we set the vocabulary of size to 30,000 subword units. The vocabulary is constructed jointly for the source and target side of the corpus.

During the inference, we use simple greedy algorithm which generates the most frequent word depending on the previously generated words, the state of the decoder and attention. We did not employ any better decoding algorithm such as beam

Feature	Performance score
None (baseline)	14.25 ± 0.18 BLEU
Number of conjuctions	14.71 ± 0.24 BLEU
Number of proper nouns	14.58 ± 0.22 BLEU
Number of nouns	14.57 ± 0.24 BLEU
Sentence length	14.43 ± 0.23 BLEU
Number of verbs	14.43 ± 0.21 BLEU

Table 1: Minibatch bucketing after one epoch.

Feature	Performance score
None (baseline)	14.25 ± 0.18 BLEU
Source sentence length	15.41 ± 0.18 BLEU
Target sentence length	15.24 ± 0.27 BLEU
English word ranks	15.07 ± 0.28 BLEU
Czech word ranks	15.06 ± 0.29 BLEU
Number of conjuctions	15.04 ± 0.24 BLEU
Combined word ranks	14.77 ± 0.16 BLEU
Max word ranks	14.73 ± 0.22 BLEU

Table 2: Curriculum learning after one epoch.

search (Sigtia et al., 2015; Graves, 2012) mainly due to technical difficulties. Although this decision leads to a poorer performance, it should not have any influence on the results of our work.

All experiments are based on one epoch of training over whole training dataset. The training takes roughly one week on NVIDIA GeForce GTX 1080. We should note that our model used only 4 GB of memory, instead of 8 GB available in the GPUs.

For the plots and presentation of the results, we compute test score (BLEU, Papineni et al., 2002) after every 100k training examples. To compensate for fluctuations during the training, we report the mean and standard deviation of the last 10 test errors of the training. This simple smoothing method is a substitute for proper significance testing (Clark et al., 2011), since we cannot run all experiments multiple times due to the lack of computing resources.

4.2 Training Data

We use the dataset provided for the WMT 2017 NMT Training Task. The dataset comes from the CzEng 1.6 corpus (Bojar et al., 2016) and it was cleaned by the organizers of the NMT Training Task. The resulting corpus is 48.6 million sentence pairs for English-to-Czech translation.

We use the test set from the WMT 2016 News Translation Task as our only heldout set. We do not need any separate development or validation set, because we are not doing any hyperparameter search or run experiments several times to find the best-performing setup.

4.3 Minibatch Bucketing

Table 1 shows the results of our experiments with minibatch bucketing. The bucketed runs are slightly better than the baseline but they usually fall in the standard deviation range so we cannot claim any significant improvement.

4.4 Curriculum Learning

This sections describes our experiments with curriculum learning. We organized the training data based on the following features: the length of the sentences, the number of coordinating conjunctions, the highest rank of a word in the Czech or the English part and two combinations of the word ranks: "max word rank" which puts sentences into bins based on the maximum rank of their English and Czech words and "combined rank" is based on word ranks derived from concatenated source and target corpora.

As documented in Table 2, several of the curriculum setups improve over the baseline. The most beneficial is to organize the bins by the (source-side) sentence length, reaching a gain of 1.16 BLEU point.

Figure 1 plots learning curves for the baseline, one minibatch bucketing run (Section 2) and some curricula setups. Bucketing closely follows the baseline while curricula start much worse and make up later, as the complexity of training examples matches the fixed complexity of the test set.

The difference between source- and target-length curriculum is particularly interesting. Binning by target length ensures strict target-sentence limits and the decoder indeed follows the restriction never producing longer sentences regardless the source length. This results in serious penalization, see the sharp jumps in "Curriculum by target length". Source-side binning makes target lengths slightly more varied. Assuming some model of sentence length in the decoder (Shi et al., 2016), training it on strictly capped sentences seems to damage its learning while the more varied data better allow to learn to predict output length based on the input length.

4.5 Quick Adaptation or Overfitting

Neural networks are known to quickly adapt to new types of data as they arrive in the training.

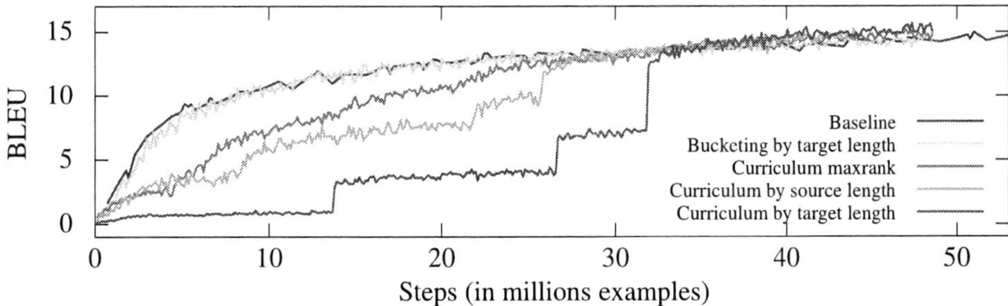

Figure 1: Selected learning curves for minibatch bucketing and curriculum.

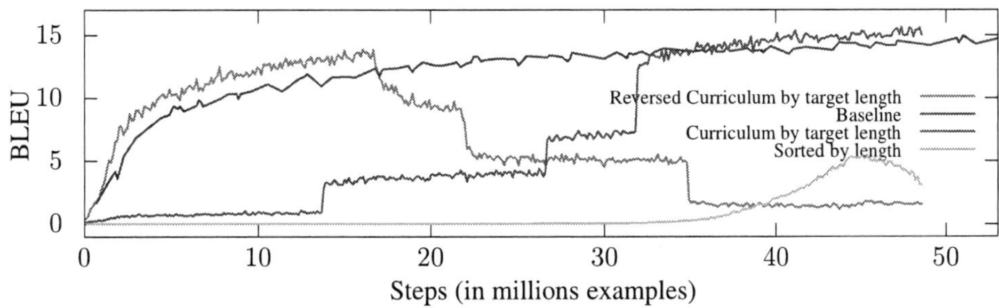

Figure 2: Learning curves of selected curriculum learning runs and other contrastive runs.

This effect is used e.g. in domain adaptation for NMT (Freitag and Al-Onaizan, 2016; Luong and Manning, 2015) but there is a big risk of overfitting to some specialized data.

As shown in Figure 2, our curriculum runs are heavily affected by this quick adaptation. "Baseline" shows the standard behaviour: starting quickly and then more or less flattening towards the end of the epoch.

Our best performing curriculum setup starts with short sentences and the model thus first learns to produce only short sentences. The curve "Curriculum by target length" shows very bad scores for more than a half of the training data, and the particularly striking are the quick transitions whenever a new bin of longer sentences is added. The model adapts and starts producing longer sentences, getting a huge boost in BLEU on the fixed test set. Towards the end of the epoch, "Curriculum by target length" demonstrates its improved generalization power and surpasses the baseline.

If we did not use our strategy of revisiting shorter sentences and simply sorted the corpus by sentence length, the training would fail spectacularly, see the curve "Sorted by length". The model

never reaches any reasonable performance.

The curve "Reversed Curriculum by target length" is very interesting. We simply took the best corpus organization ("Curriculum by target length") and reversed it. The training performs better in the early stages (i.e. minibatches evenly covering all length bins) but very quickly drops as the long-sentence bins get prohibited. Put differently, the model quickly adapts (overfits) to the new "domain" of short sentences and fails to produces normal-length translations of the test set.

4.6 Continuing the Curriculum

It should be noted that all results presented so far are observed after one epoch of curriculum training. It is questionable what would be the best way of subsequent training.

We considered two options, see Figure 3. Starting over from the easiest examples harms the performance terribly early in the epoch but succeeds in improving the performance of the first epoch all the time, see the "Second epoch of curriculum by target length" in Figure 3.

Another option is to continue the training after the first epoch with the training dataset shuffled.

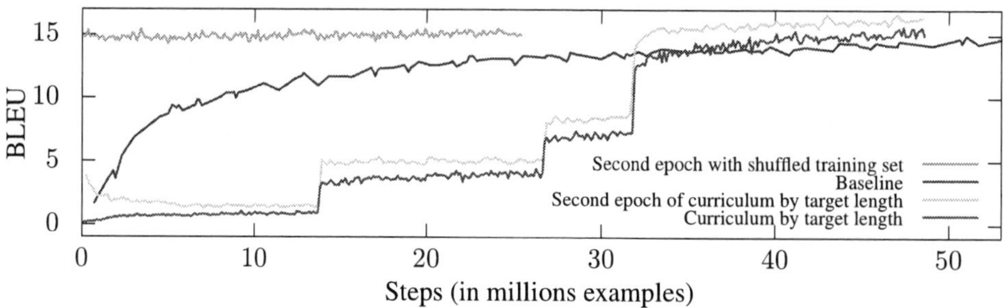

Figure 3: The best run ("Curriculum by target length") and its continuations.

5 Related Work

As the corresponding curve in Figure 3 however shows, the model is probably already quite fixed in the current optimum and we do not see any further improvement on the test set.

Khomenko et al. (2016) used a bucketing technique to accelerate the speed of the training. They prepared minibatches of training data with similar length and got a speedup in the training time of factor up to 4. The buckets are drawn randomly from the training set. A similar approach is also used in Nematus (Sennrich et al., 2017), one of the state-of-the-art open-source toolkits for NMT.

Doetsch et al. (2017) used bucketing and experimented with ordering of the bucketed batches. Their proposed method orders buckets in an alternating way: first in increasing order by length, then decreasing order, then again increasing order etc. This way the buckets of different length are periodically revisited. With this approach, the authors got a speedup in the training time and also obtained better performance results.

Bengio et al. (2009) use curriculum learning for a neural language model, not a full NMT system. They trained the network by iteratively increasing the vocabulary size, starting with the vocabulary of 5000 and increasing by 5000 each epoch. Each epoch used only sentences with words available in the current restricted vocabulary. The last epoch thus used all examples. This curriculum lead to a statistically significant improvement in the performance of the model.

Graves et al. (2017) automatically select examples during multitask learning. The method evaluates training signals from the neural network and uses them to focus on specific subtasks to accelerate the training process of the main task. The authors noted that uniformly sampling from the training data is a strong baseline.

6 Conclusion

We examined the effects of two ways of orderings of training examples for neural machine translation from English to Czech.

Trying to use sentences with similar linguistic properties in each minibatch of the online training (dubbed "minibatch bucketing") did not bring any difference from the baseline of randomly composed minibatches.

Organizing minibatches to gradually include more complex sentences (in terms of length or vocabulary size) helps to reach better translation quality of up to 1 BLEU point.

The actual process of learning is however very interesting, displaying clear jumps in the performance as longer sentences are added to the training data. The strategy cannot be thus used to shorten the training time: unless the gradually-organized epoch is finished, the model performs well below the baseline.

Our experiments also confirm the quick adaptability of deep learning methods, with a high risk of overfitting to particular properties of the very recent training examples.

Acknowledgement

This study was partly supported by the grants SVV 260 453, GAUK 8502/2016, H2020-ICT-2014-1-645442 (QT21) and Charles University Research Programme "Progres" Q18 – Social Sciences: From Multidisciplinarity to Interdisciplinarity. It has been using language resources and tools from LINDAT/CLARIN project of the Ministry of Education, Youth and Sports of the Czech Republic (project LM2015071).

References

Dzmitry Bahdanau, Kyunghyun Cho, and Yoshua Bengio. 2015. Neural Machine Translation by Jointly Learning to Align and Translate. In *Proceedings of the Third International Conference on Learning Representations (ICLR 2015)*. http://arxiv.org/abs/1409.0473.

Yoshua Bengio, Jérôme Louradour, Ronan Collobert, and Jason Weston. 2009. Curriculum learning. In *Proceedings of the 26th annual international conference on machine learning*. ACM, pages 41–48.

Ondřej Bojar, Ondřej Dušek, Tom Kocmi, Jindřich Libovický, Michal Novák, Martin Popel, Roman Sudarikov, and Dušan Variš. 2016. Czeng 1.6: enlarged czech-english parallel corpus with processing tools dockered. In *International Conference on Text, Speech, and Dialogue*. Springer, pages 231–238.

Ondej Bojar, Jindich Helcl, Tom Kocmi, Jindich Libovick, and Tom Musil. 2017. Results of the wmt17 neural mt training task. In *Proceedings of the 2nd Conference on Machine Translation (WMT)*. Copenhagen, Denmark.

Jonathan H. Clark, Chris Dyer, Alon Lavie, and Noah A. Smith. 2011. Better hypothesis testing for statistical machine translation: Controlling for optimizer instability. In *Proceedings of the 49th Annual Meeting of the Association for Computational Linguistics: Human Language Technologies*. Association for Computational Linguistics, Portland, Oregon, USA, pages 176–181. http://www.aclweb.org/anthology/P11-2031.

Ronan Collobert, Jason Weston, Léon Bottou, Michael Karlen, Koray Kavukcuoglu, and Pavel Kuksa. 2011. Natural language processing (almost) from scratch. *Journal of Machine Learning Research* 12(Aug):2493–2537.

Patrick Doetsch, Pavel Golik, and Hermann Ney. 2017. A comprehensive study of batch construction strategies for recurrent neural networks in mxnet. *arXiv preprint arXiv:1705.02414* .

Markus Freitag and Yaser Al-Onaizan. 2016. Fast domain adaptation for neural machine translation. *arXiv preprint arXiv:1612.06897* .

Alex Graves. 2012. Sequence transduction with recurrent neural networks. *Proceedings of the 29th International Conference on Machine Learning (ICML 2012)* .

Alex Graves, Marc G Bellemare, Jacob Menick, Remi Munos, and Koray Kavukcuoglu. 2017. Automated curriculum learning for neural networks. *arXiv preprint arXiv:1704.03003* .

Jindřich Helcl and Jindřich Libovický. 2017. Neural monkey: An open-source tool for sequence learning. *The Prague Bulletin of Mathematical Linguistics* (107):5–17. https://doi.org/10.1515/pralin-2017-0001.

Viacheslav Khomenko, Oleg Shyshkov, Olga Radyvonenko, and Kostiantyn Bokhan. 2016. Accelerating recurrent neural network training using sequence bucketing and multi-gpu data parallelization. In *Data Stream Mining & Processing (DSMP), IEEE First International Conference on*. IEEE, pages 100–103.

Diederik P. Kingma and Jimmy Ba. 2014. Adam: A method for stochastic optimization. *CoRR* abs/1412.6980. http://arxiv.org/abs/1412.6980.

Minh-Thang Luong and Christopher D Manning. 2015. Stanford neural machine translation systems for spoken language domains. In *Proceedings of the International Workshop on Spoken Language Translation*.

Noboru Murata and Shun-ichi Amari. 1999. Statistical analysis of learning dynamics. *Signal Processing* 74(1):3–28.

Kishore Papineni, Salim Roukos, Todd Ward, and Wei-Jing Zhu. 2002. BLEU: a Method for Automatic Evaluation of Machine Translation. In *ACL 2002, Proceedings of the 40th Annual Meeting of the Association for Computational Linguistics*. Philadelphia, Pennsylvania, pages 311–318.

Rico Sennrich, Orhan Firat, Kyunghyun Cho, Alexandra Birch, Barry Haddow, Julian Hitschler, Marcin Junczys-Dowmunt, Samuel Läubli, Antonio Valerio Miceli Barone, Jozef Mokry, and Maria Nadejde. 2017. Nematus: a toolkit for neural machine translation. In *Proceedings of the Software Demonstrations of the 15th Conference of the European Chapter of the Association for Computational Linguistics*. Association for Computational Linguistics, Valencia, Spain, pages 65–68. http://aclweb.org/anthology/E17-3017.

Rico Sennrich, Barry Haddow, and Alexandra Birch. 2016. Neural machine translation of rare words with subword units. In *Proceedings of the 54th Annual Meeting of the Association for Computational Linguistics (Volume 1: Long Papers)*. Association for Computational Linguistics, Berlin, Germany, pages 1715–1725. http://www.aclweb.org/anthology/P16-1162.

Xing Shi, Kevin Knight, and Deniz Yuret. 2016. Why Neural Translations are the Right Length. In *Proceedings of the 2016 Conference on Empirical Methods in Natural Language Processing*. Association for Computational Linguistics, Austin, Texas, pages 2278–2282. https://aclweb.org/anthology/D16-1248.

Siddharth Sigtia, Nicolas Boulanger-Lewandowski, and Simon Dixon. 2015. Audio chord recognition with a hybrid recurrent neural network. In *Proceedings of the 16th International Society for Music Information Retrieval Conference, ISMIR 2015, Málaga, Spain, October 26-30, 2015*. pages 127–133. http://ismir2015.uma.es/articles/227_Paper.pdf.

Ilya Sutskever, Oriol Vinyals, and Quoc V Le. 2014. Sequence to sequence learning with neural networks. In *Advances in neural information processing systems*. pages 3104–3112.

D Randall Wilson and Tony R Martinez. 2003. The general inefficiency of batch training for gradient descent learning. *Neural Networks* 16(10):1429–1451.

Improved Recognition and Normalisation
of Polish Temporal Expressions

Jan Kocoń
Wrocław University
of Science and Technology
Wrocław, Poland
jan.kocon@pwr.edu.pl

Michał Marcińczuk
Wrocław University
of Science and Technology
Wrocław, Poland
michal.marcinczuk@pwr.edu.pl

Abstract

In this article we present the result of the recent research in the recognition and normalisation of Polish temporal expressions. The temporal information extracted from the text plays major role in many information extraction systems, like question answering, event recognition or discourse analysis. We proposed a new method for the temporal expressions normalisation, called Cascade of Partial Rules. Here we describe results achieved by updated version of Liner2 machine learning system.

1 Introduction

Temporal expressions tell us *when* something happens, *how long* something lasts or *how often* something occurs. Recognition of temporal expressions is a sequence labelling task and *normalisation* of temporal expressions is a process of their interpretation. It is often used in many natural language processing tasks, *e.g.*, question answering (Pustejovsky et al., 2005b), text summarisation (Daniel et al., 2003) or event recognition (Andersen et al., 1992; Llorens et al., 2010).

One of the most important thing is the ability to share the temporal information across many languages and systems. A serious problem would be to combine the information from different information extraction systems, *e.g.*, to analyse data from multi-lingual newspapers, where the expected result is the unification of metadata.

A widely used markup language for temporal and event expressions is TimeML (Saurí et al., 2006). At the beginning it was prepared for English, in the context of TERQAS[1] workshop, as

a part of the ARDA-funded program AQUAINT[2] in order to improve the performance of question answering systems (Pustejovsky et al., 2005a). One of the most widely used rule-based system *HeidelTime*[3] (Strötgen and Gertz, 2013; Strötgen et al., 2013) which uses the TIMEX3 annotation standard, currently supports 13 languages: English, German, Dutch, Vietnamese, Arabic, Spanish, Italian, French, Chinese, Russian, Croatian, Estonian and Portuguese.

PLIMEX (Kocoń and Marcińczuk, 2015) is the adaptation of TIMEX3 specification with annotation guidelines presenting how to describe temporal expressions in Polish text documents. It is based on TIDES Instruction Manual for the Annotation of Temporal Expressions (Ferro, 2001), which describes TIMEX2 annotation format. The TIDES manual is also the core of the TIMEX3 annotation format, used in the TimeML specification (Saurí et al., 2006). Both documents present how to use the special Standard Generalized Markup Language tags to annotate temporal expressions, by inserting them directly into the text. We adapted types of temporal expressions from TIMEX3: DATE, TIME, DURATION and SET.

In this work we would like to propose a new method for the temporal expressions normalisation, called Cascade of Partial Rules, which significantly improved the quality of the normalisation system.

2 Related Works

Previous works in this area concerned preparation of a broad description of Polish temporal expressions with annotation guidelines, based in the state-of-the-art solution for English, mainly TimeML specification. The final product, called

---

[1] Time and Event Recognition for Question Answering Systems. An Advanced Research and Development Activity Workshop on Advanced Question Answering Technology

[2] http://www.informedia.cs.cmu.edu/aquaint/index.html

[3] https://code.google.com/p/heideltime/

Proceedings of Recent Advances in Natural Language Processing, pages 387–393,
Varna, Bulgaria, Sep 4–6 2017.

PLIMEX (Kocoń et al., 2015), was extended with the solution to capture the local semantics of temporal expressions, by adapting LTIMEX (Mazur, 2012) specification to Polish. Temporal description also supports further event identification and extends event description model, focusing at anchoring events in time, ordering events and reasoning about the persistence of events. PLIMEX was designed to address these issues. All documents in Polish Corpus of Wroclaw University of Technology (KPWr) were annotated using PLIMEX annotation guidelines with adapted types of temporal expressions (timexes) from TIMEX3: *Date, Time, Duration* and *Set*. In the following examples of timexes, the extent of the annotation in text (if needed) is marked with square brackets. All English translations of Polish examples are given in parentheses. These examples are presented in (Kocoń and Marcińczuk, 2017), and a broad description of each timex type is presented in (Kocoń et al., 2015).

2.1 Types of Temporal Expressions

Date is a type of *timex* which denotes a point on a timeline, i.e., a unit of time greater than or equal to the day. The key question is *when*:

(1) *[poniedziałek, 16 marca 1985 roku] (on [Monday, 16th March 1985])*

Time describes *timexes* which refer to the time of day. The key question is also *when*. For example *Smith wrócił (Smith returned)*:

(2) *[dwadzieścia po dwunastej] (at [twenty past twelve])*

Duration, in contrast to *Date*, has two points on a timeline associated with it – a start and an end point. A different name used in literature is *period* (Saquete et al., 2003). The key question is *how long*. For example *Smith był tutaj (Smith stayed there)*:

(3) *[dwa miesiące] (for [two months])*

Set is relating to more than one instance of a time unit – either a point or a period. The key question is *how often*. Examples – *Jan wraca pijany (John comes back drunk)*:

(4) *co dwa dni (every two days)*

2.2 Global Semantics

In order to describe *timexes* we adopted normalisation format from TimeML. The attribute VAL (Value) attached to the temporal expression is important in the normalisation context. It is a textual representation of a *timex*, which is assigned using guidelines described in the ISO-8601 standard. In order to describe it, the first letters of the English names that specify time are used (e.g. **Y**ear, **M**onth, **D**ay, **h**our, **m**inute, **BC** – before Christ, **AD** – Anno Domini, **T**ime, **MO**rning, **H**alf, **Q**uarter, **SU**mmer, **P**eriod). Each *timex* can be determined with respect to the proper type, using the coding proposed in the ISO-8601 standard, e.g. calendar date (YYYY-MM-DD), week of the year (YYYY-Wxx), hour (hh:mm:ss), date & hour (YYYY-MM-DDThh:mm:ss), duration (PxW).

Table 1 shows example values of the VAL attribute and the semantic meaning (Kocoń and Marcińczuk, 2017).

VAL	Meaning (EN)	Meaning (PL)
1992	year 1992	rok 1992
1992-SU	summer of 1992	lato 1992 roku
BC0346	year 346 BC	346 rok p.n.e.
P2Y	2 years	2 lata
P3W	3 weeks	3 tygodnie
PT8H2M	8 hours and 2 min.	8 godz. i 2 min.
P2DE	2 decades	dwie dekady

Table 1: Examples of VAL attributes and the semantic meaning of *timexes*. VAL values can be assigned manually during annotation or by automatic system.

Normalisation in the TimeML standard involves the determination of the global semantics for a *timex*. There is no indirect form of notation of the local semantics. The introduction of the intermediate stage of determining the global semantics is reasonable from the normalisation point of view. It can be seen in systems that recognise *timexes* in the English language (e.g. HeidelTime [4], (Strötgen and Gertz, 2013)), which often use their own intermediate standard of normalisation. For that purpose LTIMEX standard was adapted (Kocoń and Marcińczuk, 2017). It can be used to determine the local semantics of *timexes*.

---

[4] https://code.google.com/p/heideltime/

2.3 Local Semantics

LTIMEX standard was designed to be compatible with existing annotation schemes, especially TIMEX2 (and TIMEX3). It is beneficial for both design and evaluation to recognise the semantics of the expression with no context involved, what is called *local semantics*, representing the partial and underspecified context-free meaning of temporal expressions (Mazur, 2012). The compatibility with the existing schemes has two purposes:

- It is human-readable and requires minimum effort to use for annotators familiar with TIMEX3.

- It provides a relatively easy means of conversion from local semantics to global semantics.

If the temporal expression is explicit, there is no difference between LVAL and VAL representation. The specification is fully described in work (Kocoń and Marcińczuk, 2017). Table 2 shows the example values of the LVAL attribute and the semantic meaning.

LVAL	Meaning (EN)	Meaning (PL)
xxxx-01-03	January 3rd	3 stycznia
xxxx-xx-19	nineteenth	dziewiętnasty
xxxx-SU	summer	lato
-0000-00-01	yesterday	wczoraj
-0000-02	two months ago	dwa miesiące temu
<M06	last June	ostatni czerwiec
2D4	second Thursday	drugi wtorek
$1M03	last February	ostatni luty

Table 2: Examples of LVAL attributes and the semantic meaning of *timexes*. LVAL values can be assigned manually during annotation or by automatic system.

3 Normalisation Improvement

The previous rule-based normalisation system is presented in work (Kocoń and Marcińczuk, 2017) and contains 224 rules for local normalisation, for 3 classes of temporal expressions: *Date, Time, Duration*. Global normalisation is made as a Java code and contains 16 rules for two classes: *date, time* (for *duration* local and global interpretation is the same). Rules were both created and tuned using *train* data set.

We evaluated rules on *test* set. The evaluation was fully described in the article (UzZaman et al., 2013). We performed the evaluation on a full pipeline for the best model to recognise boundaries of entities and their types (trained on *train+tune* data set). We focus on the end-to-end comparison with other systems presented in the article (UzZaman et al., 2013).

3.1 Metrics

To evaluate temporal expressions we need to check *how many entites* are correctly identified, if *the extents for the entities* are correctly identified and *how many attributes* are correctly identified. We use classical precision, recall and F-measure for the recognition (UzZaman et al., 2013).

3.2 Previous Approach

We prepared module for Liner2 tool (Kocoń and Marcińczuk, 2017) to perform the normalisation process in order to get the local and global meaning of temporal expressions. We created the normalisation process as a two-step rule-based approach. The first step is to get the local meaning of the temporal expression, and the second (created on the basis of the local interpretation) is to get the global meaning. Rules were created by domain experts. For each class of temporal expression we defined several files with rules, patterns and normalisation dictionaries. The whole number of manually prepared resources is presented in Table 3.

Table 3: Previous normalisation resources for determining local value (LVAL) of temporal expressions, prepared using *train* data set. Table presents number of **Rules**, **Patt**erns and **Norm**alisations for each timex **Type**.

Type	Rules	Patt.	Norm.
date	110	75	21
time	93	52	13
duration	21	20	11
SUM	224	147	45

This approach is very similar to method presented in HeidelTime, except the extraction part, which in Liner2 is performed using Conditional Random Fields. In case of HeidelTime, it is necessary to manually specify the extraction rules and corresponding normalisation rules. Because in our solution we have already recognised chunks, we proposed a rule-based method for partial normalisation of timex chunk constituents.

3.3 Cascade of Partial Rules

We observed that in previous approach the further
increase of quality (above 75% of LVAL F1) became very expensive, because only very specific
timex examples not covered by rules left and there
was no option to cover more than 2-3 of these examples with a single rule. Furthermore we saw
that many rules for *time* are simple extensions of
rules for *date* timexes. Because in Liner2 there
is machine learning solution to chunk and classify
timexes, we decided to prepare partial rules, which
can match specific parts of timexes, which, *e.g.*,
always denote *year* part in each timex containing
that part, no matter if its type is *date* or *time*.

Because *durations* strongly differ from timexes
describing points in a timeline, we prepared 2 sets
of rules, the first for *dates* and *times*, the second
for *durations*. Each set contains 3 subsets: *keys*,
maps and *rules*. Examples:

```
{"keys": {
  "digitM_written": ["zero", "jeden",
   "dwa", "trzy", "cztery", ...],
  //zero, one, two, three, four
  "timeM_written": [
   "wieczór", "wieczor", "po północ",
   //evening, evening, after midnight
   "o północ", "północ", "rano", ...],
   //midnight, midnight, morning
  "tomorrowM_written": ["jutro",
  //                      tomorrow
   "następny dzień", "nazajutrz",
   //next day,          morrow
   "dzień następny", "jutrzejszy"]},
   //day after           tomorrow
"maps": {
  "time_written": {
   "wieczór": "EV", "wieczor": "EV",
   //evening           evening
   "po północ": "NI", "rano": "MO",
   //after midnight    morning
   "północ": "24:00", ...]},
   //midnight
  "digit_written": {
   "zero": "0", "jeden": "1",
   //zero         one
   "dwa": "2", "trzy": "3",
   "cztery": "4", "pięć": "5",...}},
"rules": [
{"desc": "[1] jutro",
 "keys": ["tomorrowM_written"],
 "groups": [],
 "match": "($tomorrowM_written)",
 "map": {},
 "value": {"year": "+0000",
  "month": "00", "day": "01"}},
{"desc": "[2] rano",
 "keys": ["timeM_written"],
 "groups": ["hour"],
 "match": "(?<hour>$timeM_written)",
 "map": {"hour": "time_written"},
 "value": {"hour": "$hour",
          "separator": "$hour"}},
{"desc": "[3] godzina 16 . 00",
```

```
 //       hour
 "keys": [],
 "groups": ["hour","minute"],
 "match": "godzina (?<hour>%d%d?)"+
          "%. (?<minute>%d%d?)",
 "map": {}, "value": {
  "hour": "$hour",
  "minute": "$minute"}}]}
```

Keys are `key:value` pairs, where `value` is
a list of words. *Maps* are also `key:value`
pairs, but each value is a `key:value` pair of
`word:word`. *Rules* is a list of items. Each item
consists of the following elements:

- **desc**ription – name of the rule,

- **keys** – a list of keys used in the rule,

- **groups** – a list of group names used in *match*
  regular expression,

- **match** – regular expression for partial
  matching, may contain `groups` in format:
  `(?<group_name>group_regex)`.
  May also contain `$key_name` elements
  which are replaced by `keys[key_name]`
  joined with regexp alternative character, *e.g.*, `$digitM_written` would be
  `zero|jeden|dwa|trzy|...`.

- **map** – a dictionary, where key is a group
  name used in `match`, and value is a map key,

- **value** – a dictionary, where key is a name
  of the final partial normalisation element and
  value is the final form of the timex part.

Consider the following example of *time*:

Pol.: jutro   rano   o godzinie 9:30
Eng.: tomorrow morning at   9:30

This example is covered by the whole
cascade of the given example rules. Rule
[1] is simple: if there is any of words from
`keys["tomorrowM_written"]` (in our ex-
ample it is *jutro*) then set the final partial normal-
isations: `year="+0000"`, `month="00"`,
`"day"="01"`. The order of rules is important,
as the final values set by previous rules may be
overwritten by next rules.

Rule [2] covers *rano* part and the match is:
`(?<hour>$timeM_written)`. All textual
words from temporal expressions are lemma-
tised and *match* looks at the chain of lemmas.
There is one named group in this match: `hour`.
In this case `groups["hour"]="rano"`.

There is also map defined as: `"map": {"hour": "time_written"}`. It means that the group from text has to be transformed like: `groups["hour"]= =maps["time_written"]["rano"]` and after the transformation: `groups["hour"]= "MO"`. Final values to set are: `{"hour": "$hour", "separator": "$hour"}`, so it looks like: `hour="MO", separator="MO"`.

Rule `[3]` covers *godzinie 9:30* part and the match is: `godzina (?<hour>%d%d?) %. (?<minute>%d%d?)`. There are two named groups: `hour` and `minute`, but there is no `map` defined in this rule, so values captured by groups remain unchanged: `hour="9", minute="30"`. Note that rule `[2]` sets the final value of `hour="MO"`, but rule `[3]` overwrites this as `hour="9"`.

After the whole cascade of rules, the final values are: `year="+0000", month="00", "day"="01", hour="9", minute="30", separator="MO"`. These values are combined together to obtain the proper LVAL value, which is: `+0000-00-01T9:30`. Note, that `separator` is important in this case, because without the information about the exact time of a day *rano* (Eng. *morning*), it could be 9AM or 9PM and the final LVAL value would be: `+0000-00-00t9:30` (small letter `t` instead of T, saying that the *hour* part of the local normalisation value is still ambiguous).

There are some other elements, which are not presented in examples, *e.g.,* it is possible to specify the *limit* parameter to apply rule only to a defined subset of temporal types, for example this rule runs only on **Time** expressions:

```
{
  "desc": "3 .",
  "keys": [],
  "groups": ["minute"],
  "match": "^(?<minute>%d+)( %.| %')$",
  "map": {},
  "limit": ["t3_time"],
  "value": {
    "year": "+0000", "month": "00",
    "day": "00", "hour": "+00",
    "minute": "$minute"
  }
}
```

The number of items prepared in this approach is presented in Table 4.

Table 4: Current normalisation resources for determining local value (LVAL) of temporal expressions, prepared using *train* data set. Table presents number of **Rules**, **Pat**terns and **Norm**alisations for each timex **Type**.

Type	Rules	Keys	Maps
date & time	122	24	13
duration	45	4	3
SUM	167	28	16

4 Experiments and Results

Results in Table 5 show, that our system achieves similar quality as the best systems in case of extraction of temporal expressions. It is not easy to compare the quality for different languages, but the result shows, that the complexity of that task for Polish is more close to English in case of normalisation. A strict F-measure of Liner2 tool for the extraction task is very high (88.76%) and outperforms all other systems. In case of global normalisation there is probably still a room for improvement, mainly from the perspective of validating the training data. Still guidelines are not precise enough in case of determining the global value and it requires further work to prepare the exact procedure of determining *VAL* value for temporal expressions. Obtained results for VAL F1 are very close to these achived by best system for English (HeidelTime) and the proposed method (Liner2-new) is almost 11 p.p. better than the previous one (Liner2-old).

5 Conclusions

The comparison of the recognition results (see: Section 3.1) for previous (Liner2-old) and current approach (Liner2-new) is presented in Table 5. We analysed the statistical significance of differences, using paired-differences Student's t-test with a significance level $\alpha = 0.05$ (Dietterich, 1998). The improvement of the recognition quality is statistically significant.

The proposed Cascade of Partial Rules method, applied for determining the LVAL attribute for temporal expressions, outperformed the previous solution by almost 11 p.p. with using only 167 rules instead of 224. We believe, that the further improvement is still possible at the level of de-

System	Extr.	Lang.	Rel.F1	Rel.P	Rel.R	Str.F1	VAL F1	LVAL F1
HeidelTime	RB	SP	90.10	96.00	84.90	85.30	87.50	
TIPSem	DD	SP	87.40	93.70	81.90	82.60	82.00	
HeidelTime	RB	EN	90.30	93.08	87.68	81.34	77.61	
NavyTime	RB	EN	90.32	89.36	91.30	79.57	70.97	
ManTime	DD	EN	89.66	95.12	84.78	74.33	68.97	
SUTime	RB	EN	90.32	89.36	91.30	79.57	67.38	
ATT	DD	EN	85.25	98.11	75.36	78.69	65.57	
TIPSem	DD	EN	84.90	97.20	75.36	81.63	65.31	
ClearTK	DD	EN	90.23	93.75	86.96	82.71	64.66	
JU-CSE	DD	EN	86.38	93.28	80.43	75.49	63.81	
KUL	H	EN	83.67	92.92	76.09	69.32	62.95	
FSS-TimEx	RB	SP	65.20	86.60	52.30	49.50	62.70	
FSS-TimEx	RB	EN	85.06	90.24	80.43	49.04	58.24	
Liner2-old	DD	PL	88.50	90.25	86.81	85.06	66.71	75.14
Liner2-new	DD	PL	92.83	94.56	91.15	88.76	77.23	89.23

Table 5: Evaluation of the end-to-end **System**s for recognition and normalisation of temporal expressions – a comparison of *old* and *new* version of *Liner2* tool with other systems presented during SemEval 2013 (only the best results regarding VAL F1 measure for each tool). **Extr**action methods of temporal entities in these systems are: **RB** – rule-based, **DD** – data-driven, **H** – hybrid. **Lang**uages: **SP**anish, **EN**glish, **PL** – Polish. We used **Str**ict and **Rel**axed variants of evaluation measures presented in Section 3.1, also with measures for **VAL** and **LVAL**.

termining the VAL attribute for temporal expressions.

Acknowledgments

Work financed as part of the investment in the CLARIN-PL research infrastructure funded by the Polish Ministry of Science and Higher Education.

References

Peggy M. Andersen, Philip J. Hayes, Alison K. Huettner, Linda M. Schmandt, Irene B. Nirenburg, and Steven P. Weinstein. 1992. Automatic extraction of facts from press releases to generate news stories. In *In: Processing of the Third Conference on Applied Natural Language Processing*. pages 170–177.

Naomi Daniel, Dragomir Radev, and Timothy Allison. 2003. Sub-event based multi-document summarization. In *Proceedings of the HLT-NAACL 03 on Text Summarization Workshop - Volume 5*. Association for Computational Linguistics, Stroudsburg, PA, USA, HLT-NAACL-DUC '03, pages 9–16. https://doi.org/10.3115/1119467.1119469.

Thomas G. Dietterich. 1998. Approximate statistical tests for comparing supervised classification learning algorithms. *Neural Computation* 10:1895–1923.

Lisa Ferro. 2001. Instruction manual for the annotation of temporal expressions.

Jan Kocoń and Michał Marcińczuk. 2015. Recognition of Polish temporal expressions. *Proceedings of the Recent Advances in Natural Language Processing* pages 282–290. Recent Advances in Natural Language Processing (RANLP 2015).

Jan Kocoń and Michał Marcińczuk. 2017. Supervised approach to recognise Polish temporal expressions and rule-based interpretation of timexes. *Natural Language Engineering* 23(3):385–418. https://doi.org/10.1017/S1351324916000255.

Jan Kocoń, Michał Marcińczuk, Marcin Oleksy, Tomasz Bernaś, and Michał Wolski. 2015. Temporal Expressions in Polish Corpus KPWr. *Cognitive Studies — Etudes Cognitives* 15.

Hector Llorens, Estela Saquete, and Borja Navarro-Colorado. 2010. TimeML events recognition and classification: Learning CRF models with semantic roles. In *Proceedings of the 23rd International Conference on Computational Linguistics*. Association for Computational Linguistics, Stroudsburg, PA, USA, COLING '10, pages 725–733.

Paweł Mazur. 2012. *Broad-Coverage Rule-Based Processing of Temporal Expressions*. Phd thesis, Wrocław University of Science and Technology.

James Pustejovsky, Bob Ingria, Roser Sauri, Jose Castano, Jessica Littman, Rob Gaizauskas, Andrea Setzer, Graham Katz, and Inderjeet Mani. 2005a. The specification language timeml. *The language of time: A reader* pages 545–557.

James Pustejovsky, Robert Knippen, Jessica Littman, and Roser Saurí. 2005b. Temporal and event information in natural language text. *Language Resources and Evaluation* 39(2-3):123–164. https://doi.org/10.1007/s10579-005-7882-7.

Estela Saquete, Rafael Muñoz, and Patricio Martínez-Barco. 2003. Terseo: Temporal expression resolution system applied to event ordering. In Václav Matoušek and Pavel Mautner, editors, *Text, Speech and Dialogue*, Springer Berlin Heidelberg, volume 2807 of *Lecture Notes in Computer Science*, pages 220–228. https://doi.org/10.1007/978-3-540-39398-6_31.

Roser Saurí, Jessica Littman, Robert Gaizauskas, Andrea Setzer, and James Pustejovsky. 2006. TimeML annotation guidelines, version 1.2.1.

Jannik Strötgen and Michael Gertz. 2013. Multilingual and cross-domain temporal tagging. *Language Resources and Evaluation* 47(2):269–298. https://doi.org/10.1007/s10579-012-9179-y.

Jannik Strötgen, Julian Zell, and Michael Gertz. 2013. Heideltime: Tuning english and developing spanish resources for tempeval-3. In *Second Joint Conference on Lexical and Computational Semantics (*SEM), Volume 2: Proceedings of the Seventh International Workshop on Semantic Evaluation (SemEval 2013)*. Association for Computational Linguistics, Atlanta, Georgia, USA, pages 15–19. http://www.aclweb.org/anthology/S13-2003.

Naushad UzZaman, Hector Llorens, Leon Derczynski, Marc Verhagen, James Allen, and James Pustejovsky. 2013. Semeval-2013 Task 1: Tempeval-3: Evaluating time expressions, events, and temporal relations. *Atlanta, Georgia, USA* page 1.

Joint Unsupervised Learning of Semantic Representation of Words and Roles in Dependency Trees

Michal Konkol

NTIS – New Technologies for the Information Society,
Faculty of Applied Sciences, University of West Bohemia,
Technicka 8, 306 14 Plzen, Czech Republic
`konkol@kiv.zcu.cz`

Abstract

In this paper, we introduce WoRel, a model that jointly learns word embeddings and a semantic representation of word relations. The model learns from plain text sentences and their dependency parse trees. The word embeddings produced by WoRel outperform Skip-Gram and GloVe in word similarity and syntactical word analogy tasks and have comparable results on word relatedness and semantic word analogy tasks. We show that the semantic representation of relations enables us to express the meaning of phrases and is a promising research direction for semantics at the sentence level.

1 Introduction

Over the last few years, word level semantics was used with great success in many natural language processing tasks, e.g. named entity recognition (Lample et al., 2016), question answering (Yih et al., 2013), or sentiment analysis (Maas et al., 2011).

Skip-Gram (Mikolov et al., 2013a) and GloVe (Pennington et al., 2014) are among the most successful methods for word level semantics. Both methods are based on the Distributional Hypothesis (Harris, 1954), which says that words appearing in similar contexts have similar meaning. They represent semantics by dense high-dimensional vectors and words with similar vectors are supposed to have similar meaning. Levy et al. (2015) shows that Skip-Gram, GloVe, and some other methods can achieve similar results.

The semantics of higher level text units is currently one of the main research directions of natural language processing. A wide variety of algorithms was proposed, e.g. distributional tree kernels (Ferrone and Zanzotto, 2014), weighted combinations of word embeddings (Brychcín and Svoboda, 2016), neural networks (Socher et al., 2011; He et al., 2015), or extensions to word level semantics methods (Le and Mikolov, 2014).

A few authors extended Skip-Gram with dependency trees. Levy and Goldberg (2014a) redefine the context window to adjacent nodes in the dependency tree. Very similar approach to Levy and Goldberg (2014a) was used by Bansal et al. (2014) and Qiu et al. (2015). Bansal (2015) enhanced the context representation by adding new syntax-related features.

We propose a new method, called WoRel (Word Relations), that uses architecture similar to Skip-Gram, but learns not only word embeddings but also a representation of word relations that can be used to combine words into phrases. WoRel does not use the dependency trees to define syntax-based context as in the previous works, but tries to predict the context based on two words connected by an edge in the dependency tree.

2 Skip-Gram Model

Skip-Gram is a neural network model for word level semantics. It was introduced by Mikolov et al. (2013a). Later, Mikolov et al. (2013b) proposed a more efficient training procedure called negative sampling.

Skip-Gram represents each word by two d-dimensional vectors. We define a *middle word* as the word at the current position in the corpus and a *context word* as any word in a context window (a small neighborhood of the current position). The middle words are represented by vectors $\mathbf{m}_w \in \mathbf{R}$, where w is a word from the vocabulary $\mathbf{V}$. Context words are represented by vectors $\mathbf{c}_w \in \mathbf{R}^d$. We denote w_j the word at position j in the corpus. We maximize the negative sampling objective

Proceedings of Recent Advances in Natural Language Processing, pages 394–400,
Varna, Bulgaria, Sep 4–6 2017.

function

$$\sum_{\substack{k=j-l \\ k \neq j}}^{j+l} \log \sigma(\mathbf{m}_{w_j} \cdot \mathbf{c}_{w_k}) + \sum_{n \in \mathbf{N}} \log \sigma(-\mathbf{m}_{w_j} \cdot \mathbf{c}_n) \tag{1}$$

at each position j in the corpus. The size of the context l is selected randomly from 1 to L. $\mathbf{N}$ is a set of words (random samples) taken from a noise distribution, $\mathbf{N} = \{w \sim P_n(\mathbf{V})\}$.

3 WoRel Model

Skip-Gram uses a middle word (e.g. *food*) from a corpus to guess the words in the context window. If we know that another word (e.g. *rotten*) is related to the middle word, then we can use this information to improve our guess of the context (e.g. *excellent* becomes less probable).

WoRel does not use the middle word in the same way as Skip-Gram, but instead we have a pair of related words, called *phrase* from now on, represented by a vector $\mathbf{p}_j \in \mathbf{R}^d$, where j is the position in the corpus. We define related words as words that are connected by an edge in a dependency tree. A phrase at the position j consists of a word at the position j and its parent (head) in a dependency tree at the position $h(j)$ in the corpus. At position j in the corpus we maximize

$$\sum_{\substack{k=h(j)-l \\ k \notin \{j,h(j)\}}}^{h(j)+l} \log \sigma(\mathbf{p}_j \cdot \mathbf{c}_{w_k}) + \sum_{n \in \mathbf{N}} \log \sigma(-\mathbf{p}_j \cdot \mathbf{c}_n). \tag{2}$$

The phrase vector $\mathbf{p}_j$ is a function of the words w_j, $w_{h(j)}$, and their relation r_j in the dependency tree (e.g. subject or modifier):

$$\mathbf{p}_j = f(\mathbf{m}_{w_j}, \mathbf{m}_{w_{h(j)}}, r_j). \tag{3}$$

There are plenty of functions that can model the meaning of a phrase. We considered three options for the function – matrix multiplication, element-wise linear combination, and linear combination. On one hand, the model is trained on billions of tokens so the function cannot be too complex. On the other hand, too simple function may not be able to express the meaning of the phrase. We ended up with the element-wise linear combination (4) that seems to be a good trade-off between the speed and complexity.

$$f(\mathbf{m}_{w_j}, \mathbf{m}_{w_{h(j)}}, r_j)$$
$$= \boldsymbol{\lambda}_{r_j} \odot \mathbf{m}_{w_{h(j)}} + (1 - \boldsymbol{\lambda}_{r_j}) \odot \mathbf{m}_{w_j} \tag{4}$$

The vector $\boldsymbol{\lambda}_r \in [0, 1]^d$ is a parameter vector for role r and acts as a filter for both words. The symbol $\odot$ denotes an element-wise multiplication.

The parameters of the model (vectors $\mathbf{c}_w$, $\mathbf{m}_w$, $\boldsymbol{\lambda}_r$ for all words w in the vocabulary and roles r) can be found using standard optimization methods, e.g. gradient descent.

4 Word Embeddings Experiments

4.1 Training Setup

We use a combination of the Gigaword corpus and the Wikipedia 2013 dump as the training data (approximately 2.5 billion words). The dependency trees are produced by Stanford neural network parser (Chen and Manning, 2014). The parser was chosen primarily for its speed. We chose universal dependencies parse trees (Nivre et al., 2016) because they can be used across languages and they place the semantically more important words closer to the root[1].

The model has several hyperparameters. They were set according to recommended values for Skip-Gram (Mikolov et al., 2013b; Levy and Goldberg, 2014a). We use maximum context size $L = 10$, number of negative samples $|\mathbf{N}| = 10$, learning rate $\alpha = 0.025$, dimension of semantic vectors $d = 300$, vocabulary size $|\mathbf{V}| = 300\,000$, unigram word distribution raised to 0.75 as the negative sample distribution $P_n(\mathbf{V})$. We do not use subsampling in WoRel and do not remove rare words (it would corrupt the parse trees).

4.2 Evaluation

We evaluate WoRel on two standard tasks: word similarity and word analogy. In evaluation we represent each word with vector $\mathbf{v}_w = \mathbf{m}_w + \mathbf{c}_w$ the same way as in GloVe.

Word similarity. The word similarity and relatedness corpora consists of word pairs and their similarity scores assigned by human annotators. The goal of the algorithm is to assign scores that maximize Spearman correlation

---

[1]See examples of preposition and conjunction roles at `http://universaldependencies.org`

	RG	WordSim			Google Word Analogy		
		all	rel	sim	all	syn	sem
Skip-Gram – recommended [†]	–	–	.623	.773	.599	–	–
Skip-Gram – tuned [†]	–	–	.700	.794	.694	–	–
GloVe – tuned [†]	–	–	**.746**	.643	.702	–	–
Skip-Gram – LS [†]	–	–	.681	.766	**.739**	–	–
GloVe – LS [†]	–	–	.624	.678	.732	–	–
Skip-Gram [‡]	.628	.697	–	–	.691	.660	.730
GloVe [‡]	.778	.658	–	–	.717	.670	**.774**
Skip-Gram – BoW 5 [§]	.776	.686	.607	.751	.613	.615	.610
Skip-Gram – BoW 2 [§]	.727	.657	.567	.737	.539	.627	.532
Skip-Gram – dependency [§]	.771	.626	.492	.754	.361	.526	.162
WoRel	**.817**	**.733**	.685	**.803**	.731	**.727**	.735

Table 1: Results of WoRel compared with other methods on the word similarity datasets WordSim-353 and RG-65 and the Google Word Analogy dataset. [†] Results from (Levy et al., 2015). [‡] Results from (Pennington et al., 2014). [§] Embeddings provided by Levy and Goldberg (2014a).

with the annotated scores. We use Rubenstein-Goodenough corpus (Rubenstein and Goodenough, 1965), WordSim-353 corpus (Finkelstein et al., 2001), and WordSim-353 partitioned to similarity and relatedness corpora (Agirre et al., 2009).

Word analogy. In the word analogy task the model answers questions in the form "What word (d) is related to c in the same way as b is related to a?" E.g. if a is France, b is Paris, and c is Germany we would expect d to be Berlin. The quality of the model is measured by accuracy. We use the Google Word Analogy corpus and its semantic and syntactic partitions. We do not remove questions with out-of-vocabulary words as in (Levy and Goldberg, 2014a) because it favors smaller vocabularies. In our experiments we use the original equation (5) to choose word d, where $\cos \operatorname{sim}(x, y)$ denotes the cosine similarity between x and y. Even though the 3CosMul approach (Levy and Goldberg, 2014b) has better results we use the older approach for a fair comparison with previous works.

$$d = \underset{w \in \mathbf{V} \backslash \{a,b,c\}}{\arg \max} \cos \operatorname{sim}(\mathbf{v}_b - \mathbf{v}_a + \mathbf{v}_c, \mathbf{v}_w) \quad (5)$$

4.3 Results and Discussion

The results for word similarity and analogy tasks are in Table 1 together with previously published results of Skip-Gram and GloVe. We present several results from (Levy et al., 2015). We start with Skip-Gram with the *recommended* hyperparameters. This configuration is used in most cases. The models denoted by *tuned* use hyperparameters that

were found using cross-validation. This approach is not usable in most cases as it requires supervision and it would be too demanding to set all hyperparameters for all tasks to optimal values. But it gives us an upper limit to expected results. The models denoted *LS* use much bigger data than the previous models (10.5 billion words, previous models 1.5 billion tokens) and the hyperparameters are also tuned using cross-validation, but less combinations were tested due to longer training times.

We also compare our results with (Pennington et al., 2014). They provide results for Skip-Gram and GloVe trained on a corpus with 6 billion tokens.

The last comparison is with Skip-Gram with dependency (and also bag-of-word) contexts provided by Levy and Goldberg (2014a). We see that the dependency Skip-Gram is significantly worse than WoRel or even other models. Levy and Goldberg (2014a) showed that their model is very good for different purposes (e.g. classification between relatedness and similarity).

The results show the strengths of WoRel. It significantly outperforms Skip-Gram and GloVe on the syntactical word analogies (5-6% in absolute values). If we consider that we use dependency trees during the training, it may not be so surprising. More surprising are Worel's excellent results on tasks that focus on word similarity (in contrast to relatedness) – RG-65 and WordSim-353 similarity partition. We believe that this is because the similarity is connected to syntax much more than relatedness and WoRel is better at modeling syntax.

Target Phrase	Skip-Gram BoW 5	Skip-Gram Dependency	WoRel
police officer	officers	policeman	policeman
	lapd	officers	sergeant
	inspector	patrolman	constable
	sergeant	síochána	officers
	plainclothes	gardaí	inspector
army officer	corps	artilleryman	sergeant
	commander	brigadeführer	commander
	commandant	nco	soldier
	quartermaster	signaller	colonel
	commanding	militiaman	lieutenant
life partner	mentor	archnemesis	partners
	friend	protegee	girlfriend
	colleague	coworker	friend
	roommate	step-sister	colleague
	partners	love-interest	collaborator
business partner	partners	buisness	partners
	firm	distributorship	firm
	stockbroking	stockholder	shareholder
	partnership	sub-contractor	investor
	import-export	syndicator	supplier
scientific publication	scholarly	bibliographical	periodical
	periodical	musicological	journal
	publications	newpaper	publishing
	journals	journalistic	publications
	triannual	ezine	periodicals
snow falls	rain	snows	snowfall
	sleet	sleet	rain
	snows	thaws	snows
	lake-effect	snowdrifts	snowfalls
	helmcken	rain	rains
make decision	decisions	"to	decide
	overrule	withdrawl	bring
	overturn	kowtow	overturn
	making	forbear	impose
	second-guess	ceteris	give
provide proof	providing	theorise	demonstrate
	substantiation	impute	prove
	verification	proove	give
	provides	substantiation	make
	demonstrate	adduce	satisfy

Table 2: Five best replacements for a target phrase provided by WoRel and Skip-Gram with bag-of-word and dependency contexts.

5 Phrase Embeddings Experiments

We believe the representation of word relations is the most innovative and promising part of WoRel. In this section we use them to create phrase embeddings and provide a qualitative and quantitative analysis of these embeddings. We are not aware of any existing corpora that could be easily used for a standard quantitative analysis of word relation representations thus we propose our own evaluation.

Our experiments with word relations are based on (non-idiomatic) phrases that can be expressed by a single word with a similar meaning. WoRel is compared with two baselines: Skip-Gram embeddings with bag-of-word and dependency con-

texts provided by Levy and Goldberg (2014a). The phrase embeddings are obtained using Equation (4) for WoRel and an unweighted linear combination of the words for the Skip-Gram baselines, a common approach for phrase representation with Skip-Gram (Agirre et al., 2016).

In Table 2 we show five most similar words for a few target phrases. We believe that the provided examples show the quality of WoRel phrase embeddings and that WoRel is able to choose better replacements for the target phrases. We believe that the improvement comes from the WoRel cost function which directly requires a phrase embedding in the same space as word embeddings.

We use the same approach in quantitative analysis. Firstly, we selected a set of phrases that have multiple single-word equivalents. The set was filtered to contain only word phrases where the models differ significantly ($\approx$ 20–30%) in order to reduce annotator work. To avoid author bias we filtered the phrases blindly, i.e. the models were listed in random order. The final set contains 20 phrases. For each phrase the models were ranked blindly by four annotators. Ties (e.g. rankings 1-1-3, 1-1-1, 1-2-2) were allowed. The average standard deviation of the assigned rank is 0.4.

The results of this experiment are in Table 3. For each model we show the sum of all the ranks assigned by individual annotators and the overall results. The best achievable result is 20 for individual annotators and 80 overall (the model is the best for all phrases). The worst result is 60 for individual annotators and 240 overall (third place for all phrases). We can see that WoRel (average rank 1.29) significantly outperforms both baselines (average ranks 2.14 and 2.31).

For a better idea of the relation representations we provide a visualization of a few common dependency roles on Figure 1. By observing some patterns (a few of them circled) in the representations we see that the model learns that the role nsubj (subject) is very similar to role nsubjpass (passive subject) and in both roles there is almost equal importance of child (usually noun) and parent (usually verb). The roles det (determiner) and amod ($\approx$ adjective) are in some aspects similar to each other. For these roles the child words have smaller semantic importance than the parent.

Model	Annotator 1	Annotator 2	Annotator 3	Annotator 4	Total	Average rank
Skip-Gram Dependency	44	43	41	43	171	2.14
Skip-Gram BoW 5	45	51	41	41	185	2.31
WoRel	22	26	27	28	103	1.29

Table 3: The sum of ranks assigned by annotators. Lower numbers are better.

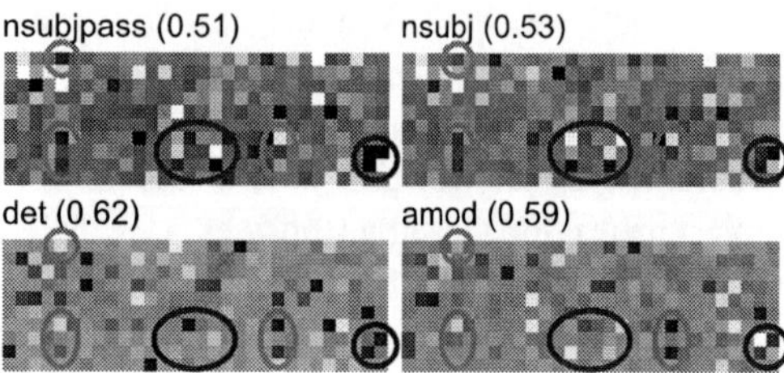

Figure 1: Role representations for selected universal dependency roles. The darker (lighter) the color is, the more information comes from the child (parent). Values in parenthesis show overall importance of the parent (average value of λ_r).

6 Conclusion and Future Work

We proposed WoRel, a new distributional semantics model based on Skip-Gram. The main contribution of WoRel is that it learns not only word embeddings, but also the representations of dependency relations between words.

The word embeddings were tested on word similarity and analogy tasks. WoRel significantly outperformed Skip-Gram and GloVe on syntactical word analogy and word similarity tasks and had similar results to Skip-Gram on semantic word analogy and word relatedness tasks.

Even though the improvement in word embeddings is important, the main innovation lies in the representation of word relations. The relation representations have interesting semantic properties and can be used in a variety of NLP tasks. More importantly, we believe that they can be used to represent semantics at the sentence level.

Our further research will focus on the semantic representation of sentences. WoRel is able to represent meaning of a single edge in a dependency tree (combine a child with its parent), but it is necessary to find a way to properly combine edges with a common parent and ensure transition of the semantic information from leaves of the dependency tree to the root.

Other directions for further research include evaluation on several NLP tasks, finding the op-timal hyperparameters of the model, exploring the effect of data size, proposing other representations of the context (e.g. dependency), or employing more robust and efficient methods for optimization.

The reference implementation and trained word embeddings are publicly available at the authors web pages[2].

Acknowledgments

This publication was supported by the project LO1506 of the Czech Ministry of Education, Youth and Sports under the program NPU I.

References

Eneko Agirre, Enrique Alfonseca, Keith Hall, Jana Kravalova, Marius Paşca, and Aitor Soroa. 2009. A study on similarity and relatedness using distributional and wordnet-based approaches. In *Proceedings of Human Language Technologies: The 2009 Annual Conference of the North American Chapter of the Association for Computational Linguistics*. Association for Computational Linguistics, Stroudsburg, PA, USA, NAACL '09, pages 19–27.

Eneko Agirre, Carmen Banea, Daniel Cer, Mona Diab, Aitor Gonzalez-Agirre, Rada Mihalcea, German Rigau, and Janyce Wiebe. 2016. Semeval-2016 task 1: Semantic textual similarity, monolingual and cross-lingual evaluation. In *Proceedings of the 10th International Workshop on Semantic Evaluation (SemEval-2016)*. Association for Computational Linguistics, San Diego, California, pages 497–511. http://www.aclweb.org/anthology/S16-1081.

Mohit Bansal. 2015. Dependency link embeddings: Continuous representations of syntactic substructures. In *Proceedings of the 1st Workshop on Vector Space Modeling for Natural Language Processing*. Association for Computational Linguistics, Denver, Colorado, pages 102–108.

Mohit Bansal, Kevin Gimpel, and Karen Livescu. 2014. Tailoring continuous word representations for dependency parsing. In *Proceedings of the 52nd*

---

[2]See http://konkol.me/publications/ Konkol-RANLP_2017.html

Annual Meeting of the Association for Computational Linguistics (Volume 2: Short Papers). Association for Computational Linguistics, Baltimore, Maryland, pages 809–815.

Tomáš Brychcín and Lukáš Svoboda. 2016. Uwb at semeval-2016 task 1: Semantic textual similarity using lexical, syntactic, and semantic information. In *Proceedings of the 10th International Workshop on Semantic Evaluation (SemEval-2016)*. Association for Computational Linguistics, San Diego, California, pages 588–594.

Danqi Chen and Christopher D Manning. 2014. A fast and accurate dependency parser using neural networks. In *Empirical Methods in Natural Language Processing (EMNLP)*.

Lorenzo Ferrone and Fabio Massimo Zanzotto. 2014. Towards syntax-aware compositional distributional semantic models. In *Proceedings of COLING 2014, the 25th International Conference on Computational Linguistics: Technical Papers*. Dublin City University and Association for Computational Linguistics, Dublin, Ireland, pages 721–730.

Lev Finkelstein, Evgeniy Gabrilovich, Yossi Matias, Ehud Rivlin, Zach Solan, Gadi Wolfman, and Eytan Ruppin. 2001. Placing search in context: The concept revisited. In *Proceedings of the 10th International Conference on World Wide Web*. ACM, New York, NY, USA, WWW '01, pages 406–414. https://doi.org/10.1145/371920.372094.

Zellig S. Harris. 1954. Distributional structure. *Word* .

Hua He, Kevin Gimpel, and Jimmy Lin. 2015. Multi-perspective sentence similarity modeling with convolutional neural networks. In *Proceedings of the 2015 Conference on Empirical Methods in Natural Language Processing*. Association for Computational Linguistics, Lisbon, Portugal, pages 1576–1586.

Guillaume Lample, Miguel Ballesteros, Sandeep Subramanian, Kazuya Kawakami, and Chris Dyer. 2016. Neural architectures for named entity recognition. In *Proceedings of the 2016 Conference of the North American Chapter of the Association for Computational Linguistics: Human Language Technologies*. Association for Computational Linguistics, San Diego, California, pages 260–270.

Quoc Le and Tomas Mikolov. 2014. Distributed representations of sentences and documents. In Tony Jebara and Eric P. Xing, editors, *Proceedings of the 31st International Conference on Machine Learning (ICML-14)*. JMLR Workshop and Conference Proceedings, pages 1188–1196.

Omer Levy and Yoav Goldberg. 2014a. Dependency-based word embeddings. In *Proceedings of the 52nd Annual Meeting of the Association for Computational Linguistics (Volume 2: Short Papers)*. Association for Computational Linguistics, Baltimore, Maryland, pages 302–308.

Omer Levy and Yoav Goldberg. 2014b. Linguistic regularities in sparse and explicit word representations. In *Proceedings of the Eighteenth Conference on Computational Natural Language Learning*. Association for Computational Linguistics, Ann Arbor, Michigan, pages 171–180. http://www.aclweb.org/anthology/W14-1618.

Omer Levy, Yoav Goldberg, and Ido Dagan. 2015. Improving distributional similarity with lessons learned from word embeddings. *TACL* 3:211–225.

Andrew L. Maas, Raymond E. Daly, Peter T. Pham, Dan Huang, Andrew Y. Ng, and Christopher Potts. 2011. Learning word vectors for sentiment analysis. In *Proceedings of the 49th Annual Meeting of the Association for Computational Linguistics: Human Language Technologies - Volume 1*. Association for Computational Linguistics, Stroudsburg, PA, USA, HLT '11, pages 142–150.

Tomas Mikolov, Kai Chen, Greg Corrado, and Jeffrey Dean. 2013a. Efficient estimation of word representations in vector space. *CoRR* abs/1301.3781.

Tomas Mikolov, Ilya Sutskever, Kai Chen, Gregory S. Corrado, and Jeffrey Dean. 2013b. Distributed representations of words and phrases and their compositionality. In *Advances in Neural Information Processing Systems 26: 27th Annual Conference on Neural Information Processing Systems 2013. Proceedings of a meeting held December 5-8, 2013, Lake Tahoe, Nevada, United States..* pages 3111–3119.

Joakim Nivre, Marie-Catherine de Marneffe, Filip Ginter, Yoav Goldberg, Jan Hajič, Christopher Manning, Ryan McDonald, Slav Petrov, Sampo Pyysalo, Natalia Silveira, Reut Tsarfaty, and Daniel Zeman. 2016. Universal dependencies v1: A multilingual treebank collection. In Nicoletta Calzolari, Khalid Choukri, Thierry Declerck, Marko Grobelnik, Bente Maegaard, Joseph Mariani, Asunción Moreno, Jan Odijk, and Stelios Piperidis, editors, *Proceedings of the 10th International Conference on Language Resources and Evaluation (LREC 2016)*. European Language Resources Association, Paris, France, pages 1659–1666.

Jeffrey Pennington, Richard Socher, and Christopher D. Manning. 2014. Glove: Global vectors for word representation. In *Empirical Methods in Natural Language Processing (EMNLP)*. pages 1532–1543.

Likun Qiu, Yue Zhang, and Yanan Lu. 2015. Syntactic dependencies and distributed word representations for analogy detection and mining. In *Proceedings of the 2015 Conference on Empirical Methods in Natural Language Processing*. Association for Computational Linguistics, Lisbon, Portugal, pages 2441–2450.

Herbert Rubenstein and John B. Goodenough. 1965. Contextual correlates of synonymy. *Commun. ACM* 8(10):627–633. https://doi.org/10.1145/365628.365657.

Richard Socher, Eric H. Huang, Jeffrey Pennin, Christopher D Manning, and Andrew Y. Ng. 2011. Dynamic pooling and unfolding recursive autoencoders for paraphrase detection. In J. Shawe-Taylor, R. S. Zemel, P. L. Bartlett, F. Pereira, and K. Q. Weinberger, editors, *Advances in Neural Information Processing Systems 24*, Curran Associates, Inc., pages 801–809.

Wen-tau Yih, Ming-Wei Chang, Christopher Meek, and Andrzej Pastusiak. 2013. Question answering using enhanced lexical semantic models. In *Proceedings of the 51st Annual Meeting of the Association for Computational Linguistics (Volume 1: Long Papers)*. Association for Computational Linguistics, Sofia, Bulgaria, pages 1744–1753.

Czech Dataset for Semantic Similarity and Relatedness

Miloslav Konopík and **Ondřej Pražák** and **David Steinberger**
NTIS – New Technologies for the Information Society,
Department of Computer Science and Engineering,
Faculty of Applied Sciences, University of West Bohemia, Technická 8, 306 14 Plzeň
Czech Republic
`konopik@kiv.zcu.cz`
`ondfa@ntis.zcu.cz`
`fenic@students.zcu.cz`

Abstract

This paper introduces a Czech dataset for semantic similarity and semantic relatedness. The dataset contains word pairs with hand annotated scores that indicate the semantic similarity and semantic relatedness of the words. The dataset contains 953 word pairs compiled from 9 different sources. It contains words and their contexts taken from real text corpora including extra examples when the words are ambiguous. The dataset is annotated by 5 independent annotators. The average Spearman correlation coefficient of the annotation agreement is $r = 0.81$. We provide reference evaluation experiments with several methods for computing semantic similarity and relatedness.

1 Introduction

Computational methods for automatic assessment of semantic similarity of words significantly changed NLP in recent years.

Evaluation datasets, such as the one introduced in this work, play a crucial role in the development of methods for computing semantic similarity of words. The evaluation datasets consist of word pairs, with associated values of their semantic similarity or relatedness (for example "rooster" and 'hen'" $\rightarrow$ "high"),. The automated methods for computing semantic similarity are then evaluated according to how much the computed output of a method agrees with the human judgment present in the evaluation dataset.

The selection of the words in the dataset is very important. Therefore we introduce four different methods of selecting the word pairs in our dataset. Such diversity of sources ensures that no evaluated method can by a chance or by purpose focus on a

Similar	Related
car – automobile	car – road
rooster – cock	rooster – hen
puck – biscuit	puck – hockey
water – irrigate	irrigate – field

Table 1: Examples of semantically similar and related words.

certain way to prepare the training data to achieve better results in the evaluation.

Semantic relations of words can be perceived as *semantic similarity* or *semantic relatedness*. *Semantic similarity* of words indicates how much of the meaning the words share. The higher similarity of the word, the higher probability is that the words can be replaced one with another in a sentence without changing the meaning of the sentence. On the other hand, *semantic relatedness* describes how much are the words related in meaning. The higher relatedness the higher chance that the words appear in semantically related texts. Some examples are shown in Table 1. Here we can see that similarity implies the same parts of speech for both words whereas relatedness can be high even for words with different parts of speech.

2 Related Work

Several evaluation datasets appeared in the last decade in relation to the increasing interest in the computational models for semantic similarity. The datasets exist primarily for English, however, there are datasets for other languages as well.

The *Rubenstein-Goodenough* (Rubenstein and Goodenough, 1965) dataset was introduced already in 1965. It consists of 65 pairs of regular English words. The similarity is given on scale from 0 to 4. The inter-annotator agreement for the dataset is $r = 0.85$ of Spearman correlation.

Proceedings of Recent Advances in Natural Language Processing, pages 401–406,
Varna, Bulgaria, Sep 4–6 2017.

The *Wordsim* (Finkelstein et al., 2002) dataset was designed with the purpose of enlarging the dataset existing at that time. It contains 353 pairs of nouns. It includes 30 words from the *Rubenstein-Goodenough* dataset and 82 pairs where at least one of the words is not contained in the *Wordnet*. The dataset is divided into similarity and relatedness subsets. The former contains 203 word pairs and the later 252 pairs (102 pairs are shared). 16 annotators participated in creation of the dataset and they evaluated the similarity on a 0–10 discrete scale. The inter-annotator agreement reached $r = 0.72$.

The *MTurk* (Radinsky et al., 2011) dataset consists of 280 word pairs generated from *New York Times* papers. The words must occur in the *DB-Pedia* database (Lehmann et al., 2014). The Amazon's Mechanical Turk service was used to annotate the semantic relatedness scores (1–5 scale).

The *Rare words* (Luong et al., 2013) dataset consists of words that occur rarely in common texts (in this case, Wikipedia articles). The words are divided in 5 groups according to their frequency in Wikipedia. To exclude foreign (non-English) words, all words are checked against the *WordNet* database (Miller, 1995). For generating the pairs, the second words are taken from *Word-Net*. Some relation or relations are selected and the second word is found (e.g. the second word must be a hyponym or a hypernym of the first word). In this way, 2034 word pairs were constructed and consequently annotated via the Amazon's Mechanical Turk service (0–10 scale).

The *MEN* (Bruni et al., 2014) dataset contains words used for tagging images. The dataset is primarily designed to evaluate multi-modal computational models, however, it can be used as well for text data only. The word pairs were generated randomly. In order to avoid majority of pairs with low semantic relatedness, the pairs were scored by the *HAL* semantic model (Lund and Burgess, 1996) and some of the pairs with low scores were discarded. The Amazon's Mechanical Turk service was used to annotate the semantic relatedness scores, however, the annotators were instructed to make binary decisions which of two given word pairs are more related. The relatedness scores for 3000 word pairs were computed from these binary decisions.

There are three evaluation datasets for German. The *Gur65* dataset (Gurevych, 2005) is created

by translating the 65 pairs from the *Rubenstein-Goodenough* English dataset. The scores for semantic similarity were newly annotated by 24 subjects with the inter-annotator agreement of $r = 0.81$. The *Gur350* dataset (Zesch and Gurevych, 2006) consists of 350 word pairs with relatedness scores assigned on a 0-4 scale by 8 annotators (iter-annotator agreement $r = 0.69$). The *ZG222* dataset (Zesch and Gurevych, 2006) contains 222 word pairs annotated by 21 subjects on a 0-4 scale (iter-annotator agreement $r = 0.49$).

A cross-lingual dataset for English, Spanish, Arabic, Romanian languages is described in (Hassan and Mihalcea, 2009). The dataset is created by translation from two English datasets into Spanish, Arabic and Romania. The semantic relatedness scores are taken directly from the English datasets.

The only dataset of semantic similarity scores for Czech is presented in (Krčmář et al., 2011). The dataset consists only of 55 out of 65 word pairs translated from the *Rubenstein-Goodenough* dataset. The 10 pairs were left out due to problems with translation. 55 pairs are insufficient for proper evaluation since the confidence intervals for Spearman correlation coefficient[1] are very wide at these low counts.

3 Dataset Design

3.1 Czech Language

The presented dataset is created in the Czech language. We begin by introducing the very basics of Czech. Czech belongs into the Indo-European, West Slavic language family. Czech is a synthetic language with a high ratio of morphemes per word. The morphology of the Czech language is rich and highly irregular. Czech syntax follows the subject verb object sentence structure, however, the word order is frequently altered to stress out certain words in the sentence.

3.2 Word Pairs Selection

In order to obtain high quality dataset, we use four methods for selecting the words for the word pairs. The first method extracts word pairs used in existing English datasets. The English pairs are translated into Czech and included in the Czech dataset. In the second method, the pairs are extracted from the translation tables for machine translation. The third method of pair generation is based upon the

---

[1]Spearman correlation coefficient is explained in Section 4.1

Method	Source	Count
Translation	RG	46
	Wordsim	205
	MTurk	97
	MEN	121
	Rare Words	85
Translation tables		108
SCIO		118
Own		173
Total		**953**

Table 2: The composition of the new Czech semantic dataset.

bag	brašna	0.039003
bag	batoh	0.013740
bag	balíček	0.005873
bag	balík-1_ˆ(předmět)	0.003546
bag	balení_ˆ(*3it)	0.001995
bag	bago	0.001884
bag	aktovka	0.001662
bag	airbag	0.001662
bag	bags	0.001551
bag	balit_:T	0.000997

Table 3: A snapshot of a translation table. The words are lemmatized.

SCIO language quiz [2]. The rest of the pairs were invented by the annotators. The counts for each method are given in Table 2. We explain the methods in more detail in the following text.

Translating the existing datasets. The annotators translated to Czech randomly selected pairs from the following English datasets: *RG, MTurk, MEN* and *Rare words*. The annotators were instructed to refrain from using any translation service or translation dictionary. Instead, they used their knowledge or an explanatory dictionary. In this way, they were forced to think about the translation in terms of the original pair, not in terms of individual words. The translations were prepared by two annotators for each pair and the different translations were discarded. We also discarded the translations where the original English word can be translated only as a phrase (e.g. "seafood" → "plody moře"). The resulting counts of pairs for each dataset are shown in Table 2. The word pairs in the used English datasets employ different methods of pair selection. Thus, we obtain a multi-source list of pairs just by taking some pairs from each of them.

Extraction from Translation Tables. This method is based upon the bilingual pivoting technique (Bannard and Callison-Burch, 2005). In this technique, bilingual parallel corpora are first aligned on the word level. Next, the pivots are found by looking for foreign words that have different translations. Finally, the different translations are scored according to the alignment probability and frequency in the corpus. The most prob-

able translations for a given pivot are considered as equal in meaning. We simplify the procedure by using the translation tables from a machine translation system. We take a foreign word and look for different translations of the word in the translation tables – see example in Table 3: "brašna" means bag and "bathoh" means backpack whereas "balit_:T" means to pack. To select semantically similar and dissimilar word pairs we always take the first record in the translation table but we randomly select the second record. The similar words tend to be at the top of the translation table, however, at the end the words tend to be somehow related but fairly dissimilar. To generate the translation tables, we use the Moses system (Koehn et al., 2007) and CZENG corpus (Bojar et al., 2011).

SCIO. SCIO tests are used in the Czech Republic for testing the students' general knowledge for university administration exams. The tests include the task to select a most similar, related or antonymous word for a given group of words. We randomly sampled from the groups of words to generate the pairs.

Own Inventions. As the last method, the annotators were asked to invent their own pairs. The annotator were instructed to invent similar, related, antonymous and unrelated pairs.

3.3 Structure of the Dataset

The dataset is structured in records of 8 values:

1. Word 1 – the first word of the pair – e.g. "kohout" (rooster).

2. Word 2 – the second word of the pair – e.g. "slepice" (hen).

---

[2]SCIO tests are used in the Czech Republic for testing the students' general knowledge for university administration exams.

3. Similarity – discrete scale from 0 to 5 – e.g. 3 for "kohout" (rooster) and "slepice" (hen).

4. Relatedness – discrete scale from 0 to 5 – e.g. 5.

5. Context 1 – Context for the word 1 – e.g. "**Kohout** běhal po dvoře" (The **rooster** ran in the yard).

6. Context 2 – Context for the word 2 – e.g. "**Slepice** sedí na vejcích." (A **hen** is sitting on eggs).

7. Ambiguity – An example of ambiguity in case one of the words is ambiguous: "Je otevřen odběrový **kohout**." (The **tap** is open).

8. Common context – A block of text where both words appear together – e.g. "**Slepice** a **kohout** běhali po dvoře" (The **hens** and the **rooster** ran in the yard).

All examples used in the dataset are taken from the SYN corpus (Hnátková et al., 2014). The examples were found via the `Korpus.cz` page.

4   Dataset Annotation

The word pairs in the dataset were annotated by 5 annotators. Two of them were high school teachers of Czech, the others were students. All received oral instructions and a simple annotation manual with examples.

4.1   Inter-annotator Agreement

We use the Spearman correlation coefficient – see Equation 4.1 to compute the inter-annotator agreement of all 5 annotators:

$$r(\mathbf{x}, \mathbf{y}) = 1 - \frac{6 \sum\limits_{i=0}^{n} (r_{x_i} - r_{y_i})^2}{n \times (n^2 - 1)}, \qquad (1)$$

where r_{x_i} a r_{y_i} are two ranks of scores x_i and y_i for the i-th pair and n is the number of word pairs (in our case $n = 953$).

The resulting average Spearman correlation coefficient for all 5 annotators is $r = 0.81$. All of the 5 annotators annotated all the words in the dataset. The correlation is computed for all annotators and it is averaged.

Dataset	Similarity	Relatedness
RG65	90.16	88.56
WS353*	88.70	71.12
MTurk	66.90	70.94
MEN	82.73	87.58
Rare Words	66.25	56.05

Table 4: Spearman correlation coefients for the similarity and relatedness scores between the new Czech corpus and the English corpora. The values are multiplied by 100 for better oriantation. RG65 is the Rubenstein-Goodenough dataset, *WS353* is the Wordsim dataset. * For the WordSim dataset, the similarity corelation is computed on the similarity part of the corpus and the relatedness correlation of the relatedness part.

4.2   Inter-dataset Agreement

Table 4 shows the correlation of similarity and relatedness scores between the new Czech corpus and the English corpora. The Spearman correlation coefficient is computed for the scores of all the translated words and the original scores in the corresponding English corpora. For the WordSim dataset, the similarity correlation is computed on the similarity part of the corpus and the relatedness correlation on the correlation part.

The resulting correlation is high except for the MTurk and the Rare Words datasets. The low correlation for the Rare Words dataset can be explained by the nature of the words in the dataset. The words are rare and difficult to translate. Even when translated using the explanatory dictionaries the translation could not be perfected. The meaning is slighlty different for most of the translated words. It is hard to explain the correlation for the MTurk dataset since no inter-annotator agreement is published for this dataset. For the Rubenstein-Goodenough and the WordSim datasets the obtained correlation coefficients are very close to the published inter-annotator agreements.

4.3   Scores Distribution

Table 5 shows the distribution of similarity and relatedness scores across the dataset. We can observe that trends for similarity and relatedness are reversed. There is a little number of very similar word pairs with score 5 and the counts go up with decreasing similarity (in average). The trend is reversed for semantic relatedness. It is quite expected since when two words are similar then they

Score	Similarity	Relatedness
0	27,60% (263)	1,36% (13)
1	21,20% (202)	8,08% (77)
2	13,33% (127)	11,75% (112)
3	18,36% (175)	14,06% (134)
4	12,91% (123)	35,89% (342)
5	6,61% (63)	28,86% (275)

Table 5: Distribution of scores for similarity and relatedness.

	GloVe	CBOW	S-G	LDA
CZ–sim	50.52	54.69	58.75	40.75
CZ–rel	49.77	50.65	55.55	40.02
RG65	66.20	68.74	71.72	57.63
WS353–sim	57.21	70.85	71.58	56.82
WS353–rel	43.29	52.05	52.50	45.61
MTurk	58.35	66.14	64.83	49.92
RW	24.93	26.02	21.00	16.21
MEN	64.60	71.09	72.06	55.76

Table 6: Reference Evaluation Experiments. *CZ–sim* and *CZ–rel* are results for the new Czech dataset computed for the similarity and relatedness scores. RG65 is the Rubenstein-Goodenough dataset, *WS353–sim* and *WS353–rel* are the similarity and relatedness parts of the Wordsim dataset and *RW* is the Rare words dataset. S-G stands for Skip-gram.

are also related.

5 Reference Evaluation Experiments

Table 6 shows Spearman correlation scores for several popular methods for computing semantic similarity and relatedness. The results are shown for GloVe (Pennington et al., 2014), CBOW and Skip-gram from the Word2Vec toolkit (Mikolov et al., 2013) and for LDA (Blei et al., 2003). Results for several selected English datasets are shown for comparison.

The Czech models were trained on the Wikipedia dump. For English, we have used a subset of Wikipedia articles with comparable size to the Czech corpus.

The results show that the dataset is fairly difficult comparing to its English counterparts. Only the Rare words dataset and the relatedness part of the WordSim dataset provided lower correlations. We believe that the difficulty of the dataset is caused mainly be the properties of the Czech language – see section 4.1. Given the relatively high inter-annotator agreement ($r = 0.81$), there seems to be a sufficient room for further improvements of the methods for computing semantic similarity and relatedness.

6 Conclusion

We introduce not yet another dataset but a dataset different in several areas. It is available for download at: `https://goo.gl/KctX2X`. We introduced a new technique to obtain word pairs for the corpus based upon bilingual pivoting. The obtained inter-annotator agreement of $r = 0.81$ is sufficiently high.

6.1 Distinguishing Properties of the Introduced Dataset

- Semantic similarity and relatedness is provided separately for all words.

- The word pairs are created by four different methods.

- The dataset works with word senses. Each word is considered in its sense that is given by an example.

Acknowledgments

This publication was supported by the project LO1506 of the Czech Ministry of Education, Youth and Sports and by Grant No. SGS-2016-018 Data and Software Engineering for Advanced Applications. Computational resources were provided by the CESNET LM2015042 and the CERIT Scientific Cloud LM2015085, provided under the programme "Projects of Large Research, Development, and Innovations Infrastructures".

References

Colin Bannard and Chris Callison-Burch. 2005. Paraphrasing with bilingual parallel corpora. In *Proceedings of the 43rd Annual Meeting on Association for Computational Linguistics*. Association for Computational Linguistics, Stroudsburg, PA, USA, ACL '05, pages 597–604. https://doi.org/10.3115/1219840.1219914.

David M. Blei, Andrew Y. Ng, and Michael I. Jordan. 2003. Latent dirichlet allocation. *J. Mach. Learn. Res.* 3:993–1022. http://dl.acm.org/citation.cfm?id=944919.944937.

Ondřej Bojar, Zdeněk Žabokrtský, Ondřej Dušek, Petra Galuščáková, Martin Majliš, David Mareček,

Jiří Maršík, Michal Novák, Martin Popel, and Aleš Tamchyna. 2011. Czech-english parallel corpus 1.0 (CzEng 1.0). LINDAT/CLARIN digital library at the Institute of Formal and Applied Linguistics, Charles University. http://hdl.handle.net/11234/1-1458.

Elia Bruni, Nam-Khanh Tran, and Marco Baroni. 2014. Multimodal distributional semantics. *J. Artif. Intell. Res.(JAIR)* 49(1-47).

Lev Finkelstein, Evgeniy Gabrilovich, Yossi Matias, Ehud Rivlin, Zach Solan, Gadi Wolfman, and Eytan Ruppin. 2002. Placing search in context: The concept revisited. *ACM Trans. Inf. Syst.* 20(1):116–131. https://doi.org/10.1145/503104.503110.

Iryna Gurevych. 2005. Using the structure of a conceptual network in computing semantic relatedness. In *Proceedings of the Second International Joint Conference on Natural Language Processing*. Springer-Verlag, Berlin, Heidelberg, IJCNLP'05, pages 767–778. https://doi.org/10.1007/11562214_67.

Samer Hassan and Rada Mihalcea. 2009. Cross-lingual semantic relatedness using encyclopedic knowledge. In *Proceedings of the 2009 Conference on Empirical Methods in Natural Language Processing: Volume 3 - Volume 3*. Association for Computational Linguistics, Stroudsburg, PA, USA, EMNLP '09, pages 1192–1201. http://dl.acm.org/citation.cfm?id=1699648.1699665.

Milena Hnátková, Michal Křen, Pavel Procházka, and Hana Skoumalová. 2014. The syn-series corpora of written czech. In Nicoletta Calzolari (Conference Chair), Khalid Choukri, Thierry Declerck, Hrafn Loftsson, Bente Maegaard, Joseph Mariani, Asuncion Moreno, Jan Odijk, and Stelios Piperidis, editors, *Proceedings of the Ninth International Conference on Language Resources and Evaluation (LREC'14)*. European Language Resources Association (ELRA), Reykjavik, Iceland.

Philipp Koehn, Hieu Hoang, Alexandra Birch, Chris Callison-Burch, Marcello Federico, Nicola Bertoldi, Brooke Cowan, Wade Shen, Christine Moran, Richard Zens, Chris Dyer, Ondřej Bojar, Alexandra Constantin, and Evan Herbst. 2007. Moses: Open source toolkit for statistical machine translation. In *Proceedings of the 45th Annual Meeting of the ACL on Interactive Poster and Demonstration Sessions*. Association for Computational Linguistics, Stroudsburg, PA, USA, ACL '07, pages 177–180. http://dl.acm.org/citation.cfm?id=1557769.1557821.

Lubomír Krčmář, Miloslav Konopík, and Karel Ježek. 2011. Exploration of semantic spaces obtained from czech corpora. In *Proceedings of the Dateso 2011: Annual International Workshop on DAtabases, TExts, Specifications and Objects, Pisek, Czech Republic, April 20, 2011*. pages 97–107. http://ceur-ws.org/Vol-706/paper24.pdf.

Jens Lehmann, Robert Isele, Max Jakob, Anja Jentzsch, Dimitris Kontokostas, Pablo Mendes, Sebastian Hellmann, Mohamed Morsey, Patrick van Kleef, Sören Auer, and Chris Bizer. 2014. DBpedia - a large-scale, multilingual knowledge base extracted from wikipedia. *Semantic Web Journal* .

Kevin Lund and Curt Burgess. 1996. Producing high-dimensional semantic spaces from lexical co-occurrence. *Behavior Research Methods, Instruments, & Computers* 28(2):203–208. https://doi.org/10.3758/BF03204766.

Minh-Thang Luong, Richard Socher, and Christopher D. Manning. 2013. Better word representations with recursive neural networks for morphology. In *CoNLL*. Sofia, Bulgaria.

Tomas Mikolov, Kai Chen, Greg Corrado, and Jeffrey Dean. 2013. Efficient estimation of word representations in vector space. *CoRR* abs/1301.3781. http://arxiv.org/abs/1301.3781.

George A. Miller. 1995. Wordnet: A lexical database for english. *Commun. ACM* 38(11):39–41. https://doi.org/10.1145/219717.219748.

Jeffrey Pennington, Richard Socher, and Christopher Manning. 2014. Glove: Global vectors for word representation. In *Proceedings of the 2014 Conference on Empirical Methods in Natural Language Processing (EMNLP)*. Association for Computational Linguistics, pages 1532–1543. http://aclweb.org/anthology/D14-1162.

Kira Radinsky, Eugene Agichtein, Evgeniy Gabrilovich, and Shaul Markovitch. 2011. A word at a time: Computing word relatedness using temporal semantic analysis. In *Proceedings of the 20th International Conference on World Wide Web*. ACM, New York, NY, USA, WWW '11, pages 337–346. https://doi.org/10.1145/1963405.1963455.

Herbert Rubenstein and John B. Goodenough. 1965. Contextual correlates of synonymy. *Commun. ACM* 8(10):627–633. https://doi.org/10.1145/365628.365657.

Torsten Zesch and Iryna Gurevych. 2006. Automatically creating datasets for measures of semantic relatedness. In *Proceedings of the Workshop on Linguistic Distances*. Association for Computational Linguistics, Stroudsburg, PA, USA, LD '06, pages 16–24. http://dl.acm.org/citation.cfm?id=1641976.1641980.

Improving Discourse Relation Projection to Build Discourse Annotated Corpora

Majid Laali **Leila Kosseim**

Department of Computer Science and Software Engineering
Concordia University, Montreal, Quebec, Canada
`{m_laali, kosseim}@encs.concordia.ca`

Abstract

The naive approach to annotation projection is not effective to project discourse annotations from one language to another because implicit discourse relations are often changed to explicit ones and vice-versa in the translation. In this paper, we propose a novel approach based on the intersection between statistical word-alignment models to identify unsupported discourse annotations. This approach identified 65% of the unsupported annotations in the English-French parallel sentences from Europarl. By filtering out these unsupported annotations, we induced the first PDTB-style discourse annotated corpus for French from Europarl. We then used this corpus to train a classifier to identify the discourse-usage of French discourse connectives and show a 15% improvement of F1-score compared to the classifier trained on the non-filtered annotations.

1 Introduction

The Penn Discourse Treebank (PDTB) (Prasad et al., 2008) is one of the most successful projects aimed at the development of discourse annotated corpora. Following the predicate-argument approach of the D-LTAG framework (Webber et al., 2003), the PDTB associates discourse relations (DRs) to lexical elements, so-called *discourse connectives (DCs)*. More specifically, DRs between two text spans (so-called *discourse arguments*) are triggered by either lexical elements (or *explicit DCs*) such as *however, because* or without any lexical element and are inferred by the reader. If a DR is inferred by the reader, annotators of the PDTB inserted an inferred DC which conveys the

same DR between the text spans (or *implicit DCs*). As a result of this annotation schema, DCs were heavily used to annotate DRs in the PDTB.

Manually constructing PDTB-style discourse annotated corpora is expensive, both in terms of time and expertise. As a result, such corpora are only available for a limited number of languages.

Annotation projection is an effective approach to quickly build initial discourse treebanks using parallel sentences. The main assumption of annotation projection is that because parallel sentences are a translation of each other, semantic annotations can be projected from one side onto the other side of parallel sentences. However, this assumption does not always hold for the projection of discourse annotations because the realization of DRs can change during the translation. More specifically, although parallel sentences may convey the same DR, implicit DRs are often changed to explicit DRs and vice versa (Zufferey and Cartoni, 2012; Meyer and Webber, 2013; Cartoni et al., 2013; Zufferey and Gygax, 2015; Zufferey, 2016). In this paper, we focus on the case when an explicit DR is changed to an implicit one, hence explicit DCs are removed during the translation process. Example (1) shows parallel sentences where the French DC *mais*[1] has been dropped in the English translation.

(1) FR: *Comme tout le monde dans cette Assemblée, j'aspire à cet espace de liberté, de justice et de sécurité, **mais** je ne veux pas qu'il débouche sur une centralisation à outrance, le chaos et la confusion.*
EN: *Like everybody in this House, I want freedom, justice and security. I do not want to see these degenerate into over-centralisation, chaos and confusion.*

According to Meyer and Webber (2013), up to 18% of explicit DRs are changed to implicit ones in the English/French portion of the newstest2010+2012 dataset (Callison-Burch et al.,

---

[1]Free translation: *but*

Proceedings of Recent Advances in Natural Language Processing, pages 407–416,
Varna, Bulgaria, Sep 4–6 2017.

2010, 2012). Because no counterpart translation exists for the new explicit DCs, it is difficult to reliably annotate them and any induced annotation would be unsupported.

To address this problem, we propose a novel method based on the intersection between statistical word-alignment models to identify unsupported annotations. We experimented with English-French parallel texts from Europarl (Koehn, 2005) and projected discourse annotations from English texts onto French texts. Our approach identified 65% of unsupported discourse annotations. Using our approach, we then induced the first PDTB-style discourse annotated corpus for French[2] and used it to train a classifier that identifies the discourse usage of French DCs. Our results show that filtering unsupported annotations improves the relative F1-score of the classifier by 15%.

2 Related Work

Annotation projection has been widely used in the past to build natural language applications and resources. It has been applied for POS tagging (Yarowsky et al., 2001), word sense disambiguation (Bentivogli and Pianta, 2005) and dependency parsing (Tiedemann, 2015) and more recently, for inducing discourse resources (Versley, 2010; Laali and Kosseim, 2014; Hidey and McKeown, 2016). These works implicitly assume that linguistic annotations can be projected from one side onto the other side in parallel sentences; however, this may not always be the case. In this work, we pay special attention to parallel sentences for which this assumption does not hold and therefore, the projected annotations are not supported.

In the context of DR projection, the realization of DRs may be changed from explicit to implicit during the translation, hence explicit DCs are dropped in the translation process (Zufferey and Cartoni, 2012; Meyer and Webber, 2013; Cartoni et al., 2013; Zufferey and Gygax, 2015; Zufferey, 2016). To extract dropped DCs, authors either manually annotate parallel sentences (Zufferey and Cartoni, 2012; Zufferey and Gygax, 2015; Zufferey, 2016) or use a heuristic based approach using a dictionary (Meyer and Webber, 2013; Cartoni et al., 2013) to verify the translation of DCs proposed by statistical word alignment

---

[2]The corpus is available at https://github.com/mjlaali/Europarl-ConcoDisco

models such as IBM models (Brown et al., 1993). In contrast to previous works, our approach automatically identifies dropped DCs by intersecting statistical word-alignments without using any additional resources such as a dictionary.

Note that, because DRs are semantic and rhetorical in nature, even though explicit DCs may be removed during the translation process, we assume that DRs are preserved during the translation process. Therefore, the DRs should, in principle, be transferred from the source language to the target language. Although this assumption is not directly addressed in previous work, it has been implicitly used by many (e.g. (Hidey and McKeown, 2016; Laali and Kosseim, 2014; Cartoni et al., 2013; Popescu-Belis et al., 2012; Meyer, 2011; Versley, 2010; Prasad et al., 2010)).

As a by-product of this work, we also generated a PDTB-style discourse annotated corpus for French. Currently, there exist two publicly available discourse annotated corpora for French: *The French Discourse Treebank (FDTB)* (Danlos et al., 2015) and *ANNODIS* (Afantenos et al., 2012). The FDTB corpus contains more than 10,000 instances of French discourse connectives annotated as *discourse-usage*. However, to date, French discourse connectives have not been annotated with DRs. On the other hand, while *ANNODIS* contains DRs, the relations are not associated to DCs. Moreover, the size of the corpus is small and only contains 3355 relations.

3 Methodology

3.1 Corpus Preparation

For our experiment, we have used the English-French part of the Europarl corpus (Koehn, 2005) which contains around two million parallel sentences and around 50 millions words in each side. To prepare this dataset for our experiment, we used the CLaC discourse parser (Laali et al., 2016) to identify English DCs and the DR that they signal. The CLaC parser has been trained on Section 02-20 of the PDTB and can disambiguate the usage of the 100 English DCs listed in the PDTB with an F1-score of 0.90 and label them with their PDTB relation with an F1-score of 0.76 when tested on the blind test set of the CoNLL 2016 shared task (Xue et al., 2016). This parser was used because its performance is very close to that of the state of the art (Oepen et al., 2016) (i.e. 0.91 and 0.77 respectively), but is more efficient at running time than Oepen et al. (2016). Note that since the CoNLL 2016 blind test set was extracted from Wikipedia and its domain and genre differ significantly from the PDTB, the 0.90 and 0.76 F1-scores of the CLaC parser can be considered as an estimation of its performance on texts with a different domain such as Europarl.

3.2 Discourse Annotation Projection

Once the English side of Europarl was parsed with the CLaC parser, to project these discourse annotations from the English texts onto French texts, we first identified all occurrences of the 371 French DCs listed in LEXCONN (Roze et al., 2012), in the French side of the parallel texts and marked them as French candidate DCs. Then, we looked in the English translation of the French candidate DCs (see Section 3.2.1) and we divided the candidates into two categories with respect to their translation: (1) *supported candidates* (see Section 3.2.2), and (2) *unsupported candidates* (see Section 3.2.3).

3.2.1 Identifying the Translations of Candidate DCs

To automatically identify the translation of French candidate DCs, we used statistical world-alignment models. More specifically, we concatenated all the English words that were aligned with each word of the French candidate DCs and considered this concatenation as their English translation. For example, Figure 1 shows word-alignments for the French DC *d'autre part* where the alignment model found a 1:2 alignment between *d'* and *on the* then three 1:1 alignments. In this case, the English translation of *d'autre part* will be considered to be *on the other hand*.

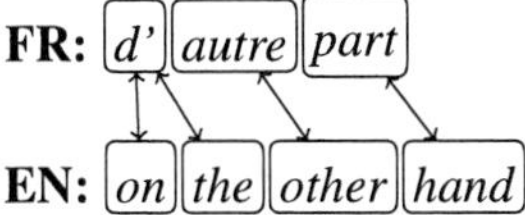

Figure 1: Word-alignment for the French DC *d'autre part*.

To align English and French words, we used the Moses statistical machine translation system (Koehn et al., 2007). As part of its translation model, Moses can use a variety of statistical word-alignment models. While previous works only experimented with the *Grow-diag* model (Versley, 2010; Tiedemann, 2015), in this work we experimented with different models to identify their effect on the annotation projection task. For our experiment, we trained an IBM 4 word-alignment model in both directions and generated two word-alignments:

1. *Direct* word-alignment which includes word-alignments when the source language is set to French and the target language is set to English.

2. *Inverse* word-alignment which is learned in the reverse direction of *Direct* word-alignment (i.e. the source language is English and the target language is French).

In addition to these two word-alignments, we also experimented with:

3. *Intersection* word-alignment which contains alignments that appear in both the *Direct* word-alignment and in the *Inverse* word-alignment. This creates less, but more accurate alignments.

4. *Grow-diag* word-alignment which expands the *Intersection* word-alignment with the alignments that lie in the union of the *Direct* word-alignment and the *Inverse* word-alignment and that satisfy the heuristic proposed by Och and Ney (2003). This heuristic creates more, but less supported alignments.

3.2.2 Supported French Candidate DCs

If a French candidate DC has been translated into English in the parallel sentence and has been aligned to English texts, we consider it as a supported candidate and label it according to the annotation of its English translation identified by the word alignments as follows:

1. *Discourse-Usage (or DU)*: If the English translation was part of a PDTB English DC and was marked by the CLaC discourse parser, then we project the English annotations and assume that the French candidate DC signals the same relation as the English DC.

2. *Non-Discourse-Usage (or NDU)*: If the English translation was not part of a PDTB English DC or was not marked by the CLaC parser, then we project the English NDU label and assume that the French candidate DC is not used in a discourse usage and label it as *NDU*.

#	French	English	Projected Annotation
(2)	*Les États membres ont **aussi** leur part de responsabilité dans ce domaine et ils ne doivent pas l'oublier.*	*The Member States must **also/DU/ CONJUNCTION** bear in mind their responsibility.*	DU/CONJUNCTION ⇒ included in corpus
(3)	*Et quand je parle d'utilisation optimale, j'évoque **aussi** bien le niveau national que le niveau régional.*	*When I speak of optimum utilisation, I am referring **both/NDU** to the national and regional levels.*	NDU ⇒ included in corpus
(4)	*Pour conclure, je dirai que nous devons faire en sorte que les lignes directrices soient larges, indicatives et souples, **afin d'**aider nos gestionnaires de programmes et les utilisateurs des crédits et de valoriser au mieux les potentialités de nos nouveaux domaines de régénération.*	*The conclusion is that we must make the case for guidelines to be broad, indicative and flexible to assist our programme managers and fund-users and to get the maximum potential out of our new fields of regeneration.*	None ⇒ not included in corpus
(5)	*Vous me direz que la croissance ou la pénurie, ce n'est pas **pour** tout le monde.*	*You will tell me that situations of growth or shortage do not affect everyone alike.*	None ⇒ not included in corpus

Table 1: Examples of discourse connective annotation projection in parallel sentences. French candidate DCs and their correct English translation are in bold face[5].

For example, consider Sentences (2) and (3) in Table 1. In Sentence (2), *aussi* is translated to *also* which the CLaC parser tagged as a DC signaling a CONJUNCTION relation. By projecting this annotation, we induce that *aussi* should also be used in discourse usage and signals a CONJUNCTION relation. On the other hand, in Sentence (3), *aussi* is translated to *both* which is not recognized as a DC, therefore, this French candidate DC is assumed to be used in a NDU.

3.2.3 Unsupported French Candidate DCs

If the word-alignment model identified no alignments for a French candidate DC or aligned the candidate to punctuations, then we assume that the candidate has no translation and there is no annotation to be projected. We refer to such French candidate DCs as unsupported candidates and filter them before the annotation projection. Sentences (4) and (5) in Table 1 illustrate two cases of unsupported French candidate DCs. In Sentence (4), the explicit French DC *afin d'*[3] signals a REASON relation, however it has been dropped in the English translation and replaced by the use of *to + infinitive* (*to assist*) to implicitly convey the REASON relation. This example shows how the realization of DRs may be changed from explicit to implicit during the translation process. In Sentence (5), the French candidate DC *pour*[4] does not signal a DR but again, it has no English translation. In both examples, since there is no English translation of the French candidate DCs, they will be filtered because there is no annotation that can be reliably projected onto them.

Our approach is different from previous work as we identify unsupported French candidate DCs before the projection and filter them out. For example, Versley (2010) assumed that French candidate DCs are used in either a DU or a NDU. Anytime there is not enough evidence to label a French candidate DC as a DU (e.g. its translation is not part of an English DC), the candidate is assumed to be a NDU. This means that in Sentences (3), (4) and (5), all French candidate DCs would be tagged as NDU in Versley (2010)'s approach. On the other hand, our approach only labels the French candidate DC in Sentence (3) as NDU and filters out the French candidate DCs in Sentences (4) and (5) as they cannot be reliably annotated.

3.3 Building the ConcoDisco Corpora

Automatically aligning French candidate DCs to their English counterparts allowed us to automatically project discourse annotations from English onto French for each of the four word-alignment models. As a result, we created four different corpora from Europarl where French candidate DCs are labeled with either DU and the DR that they signal or NDU. We called these corpora: the *ConcoDisco corpora*[6]. For comparative purposes, we also extracted a corpus without filtering unsupported candidates, which we refer to as *Naive-Grow-diag*. Table 2 shows statistics of the cor-

---

[3]Free translation: *in order to*

[4]Free translation: *for*

[5]All examples are extracted from the Europarl corpus.

[6]Available at `https://github.com/mjlaali/Europarl-ConcoDisco`.

pora generated from Europarl. As the table shows, all corpora contain about 1 million French candidate DCs that are labelled as true French DC and for which a PDTB DR is assigned, and around 5 million candidates in non-discourse-usage. Compared to the FDTB, these corpora are approximately 100 times larger and French DCs are associated with PDTB relations.

Corpus	# DU	# NDU	Total
ConcoDisco-Intersection	988K	3,926K	4,914K
ConcoDisco-Grow-diag	1,074K	5,191K	6,265K
ConcoDisco-Direct	1,045K	4,279K	5,324K
ConcoDisco-Inverse	1,090K	5,579K	6,668K
Naive-Grow-diag	1,090K	5,191K	6,265K

Table 2: Statistics of the ConcoDisco and Naive-Grow-diag corpora.

As Table 2 shows, the ConcoDisco corpora contain significantly different numbers of NDUs. For example, the *Inverse* word-alignment model generates 1,653 thousands more NDU labels than the *Intersection* word-alignment model (5,579K versus 3,926K). Section 4.1.2 discusses this difference and its relation to unsupported French candidate DCs.

4 Evaluation

To evaluate our approach to filtering unsupported annotations, we proceeded with two methods: 1) an intrinsic evaluation of both DU/NDU labels and the PDTB relations assigned to the French DCs in the ConcoDisco corpora (see Section 4.1) and 2) an extrinsic evaluation of DU/NDU labels using the task of disambiguation of French DC usage (see Section 4.2).

4.1 Intrinsic Evaluation

To intrinsically evaluate the approach, we first built a gold-standard dataset using crowdsourcing (see Section 4.1.1), and then compared the ConcoDisco corpora against the gold-standard dataset (see Section 4.1.2).

4.1.1 Building a Gold-Standard Dataset

To evaluate if French candidate DCs have the same discourse annotations as their translation, we designed a linguistic test, the *Translatable* test, inspired by the *Substitutability Test* of Knott (1996, p. 71). To investigate if two DCs signal the same relation, Knott (1996) compared a set of sentences where the only difference was the DCs used. If

two sentences convey the same meaning then he assumed that the two DCs signal the same relation in that context. For example, the first two sentences in Example (6) (marked with a ✓) convey the same meaning, and therefore we can conclude that *so* and *thereby* signal the same relation in these two sentences. However, the third sentence (marked with a ×) does not convey the same meaning and therefore, it does not support that *in short* can signal the same relation as the other two connectives[7].

(6)   ✓   *She left the country before the year was up; so she lost her right to permanent residence.*

      ✓   *She left the country before the year was up; she thereby lost her right to permanent residence.*

      ×   *She left the country before the year was up; in short she lost her right to permanent residence.*

The *Substitutability Test* has been also used by Roze et al. (2012) as one of their linguistic tests to associate DRs to French DCs.

Inspired by the *Substitutability Test* test, we designed the *Translatable* test. Since parallel sentences are a translation of each other, we can assume that they convey the same meaning and we therefore only need to verify if there is an English expression that is a good substitution for the French DC candidate. If this is the case, then we conclude that the French DC candidate should have the same discourse annotation (discourse usage and relation) as their English substitution. Otherwise, we conclude that the French DC candidate cannot be reliably annotated.

To build a gold-standard dataset, we first randomly selected parallel sentences from a random Europarl file[8] containing French candidate DCs. For each French candidate DC, we selected at most 10 parallel sentences to keep the number of the sentence pairs tractable and to avoid any bias towards frequent French candidate DCs. This approach generated 696 pairs of parallel sentences similar to the examples in Table 1. Then, we used the CrowdFlower platform[9] to run the *Translatable* test on the dataset. To do so, we highlighted the French candidate DCs in each pair of parallel sentences (as shown in the column *French* in Table 1) and asked annotators to identify (i.e. copy and paste) the English expression that is the best translation of the French candidate DC or to indicate if the French candidate DC has

---

[7]All sentences are taken from (Knott, 1996)
[8]ep-00-01-17.txt
[9]https://www.crowdflower.com/

no translation. To ensure more accurate results, we limited the annotators to bilingual English-French speakers. Moreover, we manually aligned 80 test questions using three bilingual English-French speakers with a background in discourse analysis and filtered annotators whose accuracy was below 0.80 against these test questions. Out of 211 initial annotators, only 33 passed our test questions and proceeded with the actual annotation task. We used the webservice[10] provided by Freelon (2010) to calculate the Krippendorff's Alpha agreement (Krippendorff, 2004) between the 33 annotators. The agreement between annotators was 0.787 which shows a strong agreement.

The CrowdFlower annotations allowed us to create a corpus of 696 pairs of sentences which we refer to it as the *CrowdFlower gold-standard* dataset. Table 3 shows statistics of this dataset. According to the crowdsourced annotators, 31.61% of French candidate DCs can be substituted by an English DC which was marked by the CLaC parser and therefore are used in a DU (as in Sentence (2) of Table 1); while 53.74% can be substituted by an English expression which does not signal any DR according to the CLaC parser (as in Sentence (3) of Table 1) and is therefore used in a NDU. Finally, 14.66% of the French candidate DCs have no English translation (as in Sentences (4) or (5) of Table 1), hence they cannot be reliably annotated. Recall that as opposed to previous work such as (Versley, 2010), our approach specifically addresses this significant proportion of explicit relations translated as implicit ones.

French Candidate DCs			
Total	DU	NDU	Dropped
696 (100%)	220 (31.61%)	374 (53.74%)	102 (14.66%)

Table 3: Statistics of the CrowdFlower gold-standard dataset.

4.1.2 Evaluation of the ConcoDisco Corpora

To evaluate the performance of the four word-alignment models in the identification of the English translation of French candidate DCs, we compared the corpora generated by the models against the CrowdFlower gold-standard dataset. Note that this evaluation shows the performance of the word-alignment models for the *Translatable* Test, and therefore can be also considered

as an intrinsic evaluation of the DRs assigned to the French candidate DCs[11]. Table 4 shows precision (P) and recall (R) for both DU and NDU labels, as well as the overall annotations (OA) of the four ConcoDisco corpora. As Table 4 shows, the ConcoDisco-Intersection achieves the highest precision for both DU labels (0.934) and NDU labels (0.902), at the expense of recall. For example, while the ConcoDisco-Intersection achieves a higher overall precision than the Naive-Grow-diag (0.914 versus 0.815), its recall is lower (0.845 versus 0.955).

Because the *Intersection* model suffers from sparsity issues (many words are aligned to null), the *Grow-diag* model is typically used for annotation projection (Tiedemann, 2015; Versley, 2010). However, Table 4 shows that the *Intersection* model is more suitable for discourse annotation projection due to its precision. Because the ConcoDisco corpora are much larger than existing discourse corpora (with around 5 million annotations), a higher precision is preferable in our case.

A further error analysis shows that the main advantage of the *Intersection* model is when French candidate DCs are dropped during the translation (i.e. explicit relations that are changed to implicit ones – see the column *Dropped* in Table 3). For example in Sentence 1, *mais* has been dropped in the English translation. This causes both the *Grow-diag* and the *Inverse* models to incorrectly align *mais* to *and*. Hence, when we project the DR for either of these two models, *mais* will be incorrectly marked as *NDU* because *and* is not an English DC. However, *mais* signals a CONTRAST relation. Therefore, a false-negative instance is generated for *mais*.

Table 5 shows the performance of each alignment model for the identification of dropped French candidate DCs against the CrowdFlower gold-standard dataset. While the *Intersection* model identifies the most dropped DCs (65% out of the 102 dropped candidates), the *Inverse* word alignment is the worst model as it identifies only 6% of the dropped candidates and the naive *Grow-diag* approach clearly identifies none. Note that the alignment models tend to label dropped French candidates DCs as NDU more often than as DU

---

[11]Because we do not have gold discourse annotations for Europarl, we can estimate the quality of the discourse annotations of the English side by evaluating the performance of the CLaC discourse parser on texts with a different domain such as the blind dataset of CoNLL shared task (see Section 3.1).

Corpus	DU		NDU		OA	
	P	R	P	R	P	R
ConcoDisco-Intersection	0.934	0.895	0.902	0.816	0.914	0.845
ConcoDisco-Grow-diag	0.906	0.923	0.814	0.904	0.847	0.911
ConcoDisco-Direct	0.902	0.918	0.883	0.866	0.890	0.886
ConcoDisco-Inverse	0.891	0.927	0.801	0.928	0.832	0.928
Naive-Grow-diag	0.906	0.923	0.771	0.973	0.815	0.955

Table 4: Precision (P) and recall (R) of the four ConcoDisco and the Naive-Grow-diag corpora against the CrowdFlower gold-standard dataset for DU/NDU labels and overall (OA).

when they cannot identify candidates that were dropped during the translation; therefore, dropped French candidate DCs may artificially increase the number of NDU labels. This also explains why the number of NDU labels for the *Intersection* word-alignment is the lowest among the word-alignment models (see Table 2).

Corpus	Identified	Not identified and labeled as	
		DU	NDU
ConcoDisco-Intersection	65%	8%	29%
ConcoDisco-Grow-diag	21%	11%	70%
ConcoDisco-Direct	49%	13%	40%
ConcoDisco-Inverse	6%	17%	79%
Naive-Grow-diag	0%	11%	89%

Table 5: Accuracy of the four ConcoDisco and the Naive-Grow-diag corpora in the identification of dropped candidate DCs (unsupported candidates) against the CrowdFlower gold-standard dataset.

4.2 Extrinsic Evaluation

To extrinsically evaluate the effect of unsupported annotations on the quality of the ConcoDisco corpora models, we used the corpora to train a binary classifier in order to detect the discourse usage of French DCs. Since the classifiers only differ by the training set used, by comparing the results of the classifiers, we indirectly assessed the quality of the corpora.

For our experiment, we used the French Discourse Treebank (FDTB) (Danlos et al., 2015). The FDTB marks French DCs in two syntactically annotated corpora: the Sequoia Treebank (Candito and Seddah, 2012) and the French Treebank (FTB) (Abeillé et al., 2000). We assigned DU labels to the French DCs marked in the FDTB and NDU labels for all other non-discourse occurrences of the French DCs in the FDTB. Table 6 shows statistics of the FDTB.

In our experiments, we used the same classifier

Corpus	# Word	# DU	# NDU
FTB	557,149	10,437	40,669
Sequoia	33,205	544	2,255
Total	579,243	10,735	42,924

Table 6: Statistics of the FDTB.

used in the CLaC discourse parser (Laali et al., 2016) for disambiguating the usage of English DCs and trained it on the ConcoDisco corpora, the Naive-Grow-diag corpus and the FTB section of the FDTB. We reserved the Sequoia section of the FDTB for the evaluation of the trained classifiers. The text of the Sequoia section of the FDTB is extracted from Wikipedia and the ANNODIS corpus (Afantenos et al., 2012). This allowed us to compare the classifiers on datasets of different domains/genres than the training datasets, therefore, introducing no bias toward any of the training datasets.

Table 7 shows the precision, recall and the F1-score of the classifiers. While the precision of classifiers trained on the ConcoDisco corpora is high (0.831~0.857) and actually higher than the one trained on the manually annotated FTB, their recall is much lower (0.309~0.406). We also observed that the classifiers trained on Naive-Grow-diag and on ConcoDisco-Grow-diag have the same performance. This is because the Grow-diag models created many false-negative instances for a set of French DCs. Hence, the classifiers trained on this model labeled all occurrence of these French DCs as NDU. In addition, Naive-Grow-diag also added more false-negative instances to the same set of French DCs so the classifier labeled all those French DCs as NDU.

Among the classifiers trained on the ConcoDisco corpora, the one based on the *Intersection* model again achieves the best performance with an F1-score of 0.546. This confirms that the trade-off between precision and recall achieved by the *In-*

tersection model makes it the most appropriate for discourse annotation projection.

The low recall of the classifiers trained on the ConcoDisco corpora is an indication of a large number of false-negative instances. As discussed in Section 4.1.2, an important source of false-negative instances is due to French candidate DCs that are dropped in the translation. Table 7 shows this by illustrating the same behaviour as in Table 5. As these two tables show, the more accurate a word alignment model is at pruning dropped French candidate DCs, the higher recall the classifier will achieve using the dataset extracted from this word alignment model. In our case, the *Intersection* model is the most accurate model in the identification of dropped candidate DCs with an accuracy of 65% (see Table 5), and the classifier trained on the ConcoDisco-Intersection also achieves the highest recall (i.e. 0.406). This classifier achieves a 15% relative improvement in F1-score compare to the one that was trained on Naive-Grow-diag. This shows the adverse effect of unsupported annotations on the classifiers.

To investigate further the low recall of the classifiers, we manually analyzed the results of three French DCs with a low recall and a high frequency in the CrowdFlower gold-standard dataset: *enfin*, *afin de* and *ainsi*[12]. We observed that while 96% of the French candidate DCs for these English DCs were properly aligned to their translation, 59% of them were incorrectly labeled as NDU because their English translation were not properly annotated. This happened for three main reasons:

1. The English translation is an English DC, but because it is either infrequent in the PDTB (e.g. *finally*) or its NDU usage dominates its DU usage (e.g. *for*), the English DC cannot be reliably annotated.

2. The English translation is an English DC, but it is not listed in the PDTB (e.g. *in order to*).

3. The English translation is not an English DC, but it signals a DRs (e.g. *this would ensure that* or *in this way*). Such expressions are called *AltLex* in the PDTB. We excluded AltLex from our analysis because to our knowledge, no English discourse parser can currently annotate them reliably.

---

¹²Free translation: *enfin = finally, afin de = in order to, ainsi = so.*

Training Corpus	P	R	F1
FTB	0.777	0.756	0.766
ConcoDisco-Intersection	0.831	0.406	0.546
ConcoDisco-Grow-diag	0.837	0.331	0.474
ConcoDisco-Direct	0.834	0.397	0.538
ConcoDisco-Inverse	0.857	0.309	0.454
Naive-Grow-diag	0.837	0.331	0.474

Table 7: Performance of the classifiers trained on different corpora against the Sequoia test set.

5 Conclusion and Future Work

In this paper, we addressed the main assumption of annotation projection and showed that discourse annotations may not always be reliably projected in parallel sentences when DRs are changed from explicit to implicit ones during the translation. We proposed a novel approach based on the intersection between statistical word-alignment models to identify unsupported annotations. This approach was able to identify 65% of the unsupported annotations, hence allowing the automatic induction of more precise corpora. As a by-product of our approach, we automatically induced the ConcoDisco corpora: the first PDTB style discourse corpora for French. We showed that our approach to filtering unsupported annotations improves the F1-score of a classifier that labels the DU and the NDU of French DCs by 15% compared to when the unsupported annotations are not filtered.

There are several ways that this work can be extended. First, our method to induce a classifier to label French DCs with DU/NDU labels lends itself well to a bootstrapping approach. As we used English DCs to label the usage of French DCs, we could also use French DCs to label the usage of English DCs. Second, our approach can be used to automatically identify and annotate implicit DRs within English texts without parsing the English texts by identifying French DCs that are dropped during the translation (see Example (1) or Example (4)). In addition, since our approach only needs the availability of a parallel corpus with English, it can be easy used for other languages. Finally, the results of our work can be used to improve the development of French discourse resources such as LEXCONN and the FDTB.

Acknowledgement

The authors would like to thank the anonymous referees for their insightful comments on an earlier version of the paper. Many thanks also to Andre

Cianflone, Alexis Grondin, Andrés Lou and Félix-Herve Bachand for their help on the CrowdFlower task. This work was financially supported by an NSERC grant.

References

Anne Abeillé, Lionel Clément, and François Toussenel. 2000. Building a treebank for French. In *Proceedings of 2nd International Conference on Language Resources and Evaluation (LREC 2000)*. Athens, Greece, page 165–187.

Stergos D. Afantenos, Nicholas Asher, Farah Benamara, Myriam Bras, Cécile Fabre, Mai Ho-Dac, Anne Le Draoulec, Philippe Muller, Marie-Paule Péry-Woodley, and Laurent Prévot. 2012. An empirical resource for discovering cognitive principles of discourse organisation: The ANNODIS corpus. In *Proceedings of the 8th International Conference on Language Resources and Evaluation (LREC 2012)*. Istanbul, Turkey, page 2727–2734.

Luisa Bentivogli and Emanuele Pianta. 2005. Exploiting parallel texts in the creation of multilingual semantically annotated resources: The MultiSemCor Corpus. *Natural Language Engineering* 11(3):247–261.

Peter F. Brown, Vincent J. Della Pietra, Stephen A. Della Pietra, and Robert L. Mercer. 1993. The mathematics of statistical machine translation: Parameter estimation. *Computational Linguistics* 19(2):263–311.

Chris Callison-Burch, Philipp Koehn, Christof Monz, Kay Peterson, Mark Przybocki, and Omar F. Zaidan. 2010. Findings of the 2010 joint workshop on statistical machine translation and metrics for machine translation. In *Proceedings of the Joint Fifth Workshop on Statistical Machine Translation and MetricsMATR*. Uppsala, Sweden, page 17–53.

Chris Callison-Burch, Philipp Koehn, Christof Monz, Matt Post, Radu Soricut, and Lucia Specia. 2012. Findings of the 2012 Workshop on Statistical Machine Translation. In *Proceedings of the Seventh Workshop on Statistical Machine Translation*. Montréal, Canada, page 10–51.

Marie Candito and Djamé Seddah. 2012. Effectively long-distance dependencies in French: annotation and parsing evaluation. In *The 11th International Workshop on Treebanks and Linguistic Theories (TLT 11)*. Lisbon, Portugal, pages 61–72.

Bruno Cartoni, Sandrine Zufferey, and Thomas Meyer. 2013. Annotating the meaning of discourse connectives by looking at their translation: The translation-spotting technique. *Dialogue & Discourse* 4(2):65–86.

L. Danlos, M. Colinet, and J. Steinlin. 2015. FDTB1: Repérage des connecteurs de discours en corpus. In *Actes de la 22e conférence sur le Traitement Automatique des Langues Naturelles (TALN 2015)*. Caen, France, pages 350–356.

Deen G. Freelon. 2010. ReCal: Intercoder reliability calculation as a web service. *International Journal of Internet Science* 5(1):20–33.

Christopher Hidey and Kathleen McKeown. 2016. Identifying Causal Relations Using Parallel Wikipedia Articles. In *Proceedings of the 54th Annual Meeting of the Association for Computational Linguistics (ACL 2016)*. Berlin, Germany, pages 1424–1433.

Alistair Knott. 1996. *A data-driven methodology for motivating a set of coherence relations*. PhD dissertation, University of Edinburgh, Computer Science Department.

Philipp Koehn. 2005. Europarl: A parallel corpus for statistical machine translation. In *Proceedings of the 10th Machine Translation Summit*. Phuket, Thailand, volume 5, pages 79–86.

Philipp Koehn, Hieu Hoang, Alexandra Birch, Chris Callison-Burch, Marcello Federico, Nicola Bertoldi, Brooke Cowan, Wade Shen, Christine Moran, Richard Zens, Chris Dyer, Ondrej Bojar, Alexandra Constantin, and Evan Herbst. 2007. Moses: Open source toolkit for statistical machine translation. In *Proceedings of the 45th Annual Meeting of the ACL on Interactive Poster and Demonstration Sessions (ACL 2007)*. Prague, pages 177–180.

Klaus Krippendorff. 2004. *Content analysis: An introduction to its methodology*. Sage.

Majid Laali, Andre Cianflone, and Leila Kosseim. 2016. The CLaC Discourse Parser at CoNLL-2016. In *Proceedings of the 20th Conference on Computational Natural Language Learning (CoNLL 2016)*. Berlin, Germany, pages 92–99.

Majid Laali and Leila Kosseim. 2014. Inducing discourse connectives from parallel texts. In *Proceedings of the 25th International Conference on Computational Linguistics: Technical Papers (COLING 2014)*. Dublin, Ireland, pages 610–619.

Thomas Meyer. 2011. Disambiguating Temporal–Contrastive Discourse Connectives for Machine Translation. In *Proceedings of the 49th Annual Meeting of the Association for Computational Linguistics: Human Language Technologies (ACL-HLT 2011)*. Portland, OR, USA, pages 46–51.

Thomas Meyer and Bonnie Webber. 2013. Implicitation of discourse connectives in (machine) translation. In *Proceedings of the 1st DiscoMT Workshop at the 51st Annual Meeting of the Association for Computational Linguistics (ACL 2013)*. Sofia, Bulgaria, pages 19–26.

F.J. Och and H. Ney. 2003. A systematic comparison of various statistical alignment models. *Computational Linguistics* 29(1):19–51.

Stephan Oepen, Jonathon Read, Tatjana Scheffler, Uladzimir Sidarenka, Manfed Stede, Erik Velldal, and Lilja Ovrelid. 2016. OPT: Oslo—Potsdam—Teesside Pipelining Rules, Rankers, and Classifier Ensembles for Shallow Discourse Parsing. In *Proceedings of the 20th Conference on Computational Natural Language Learning (CoNLL 2016)*. Berlin, Germany, pages 20–26.

Andrei Popescu-Belis, Thomas Meyer, Jeevanthi Liyanapathirana, Bruno Cartoni, and Sandrine Zufferey. 2012. Discourse-level Annotation over Europarl for Machine Translation: Connectives and Pronouns. In *Proceedings of the 8th International Conference on Language Resources and Evaluation (LREC 2012)*. Istanbul, Turkey, pages 23–25.

Rashmi Prasad, Nikhil Dinesh, Alan Lee, Eleni Miltsakaki, Livio Robaldo, Aravind K. Joshi, and Bonnie L. Webber. 2008. The Penn Discourse TreeBank 2.0. In *Proceedings of the Sixth International Conference on Language Resources and Evaluation (LREC 2008)*. Marrakech, Morocco, pages 28–30.

Rashmi Prasad, Aravind Joshi, and Bonnie Webber. 2010. Realization of discourse relations by other means: alternative lexicalizations. In *Proceedings of the 23rd International Conference on Computational Linguistics: Posters (COLING 2010)*. Beijing, China, page 1023–1031.

Charlotte Roze, Laurence Danlos, and Philippe Muller. 2012. LEXCONN: A French lexicon of discourse connectives. *Discours [En ligne]* 10. https://doi.org/10.4000/discours.8645.

Jörg Tiedemann. 2015. Improving the Cross-Lingual Projection of Syntactic Dependencies. In *Proceedings of the 20th Nordic Conference of Computational Linguistics (NODALIDA 2015)*. Vilnius, Lithuania, pages 191–199.

Yannick Versley. 2010. Discovery of ambiguous and unambiguous discourse connectives via annotation projection. In *Proceedings of the Workshop on Annotation and Exploitation of Parallel Corpora (AEPC 2010)*. Tartu, Estonia, pages 83–82.

Bonnie Webber, Matthew Stone, Aravind Joshi, and Alistair Knott. 2003. Anaphora and discourse structure. *Computational Linguistics* 29(4):545–587.

Nianwen Xue, Hwee Tou Ng, Attapol Rutherford, Bonnie Webber, Chuan Wang, and Hongmin Wang. 2016. CoNLL 2016 Shared Task on Multilingual Shallow Discourse Parsing. In *Proceedings of the 20th Conference on Computational Natural Language Learning (CoNLL 2016)*. Berlin, Germany, pages 1–19.

David Yarowsky, Grace Ngai, and Richard Wicentowski. 2001. Inducing multilingual text analysis tools via robust projection across aligned corpora. In *Proceedings of the first international conference on human language technology research (HLT 2001)*. San Diego, California, page 1–8.

Sandrine Zufferey. 2016. Discourse connectives across languages: factors influencing their explicit or implicit translation. *Languages in Contrast* 16(2):264–279.

Sandrine Zufferey and Bruno Cartoni. 2012. English and French causal connectives in contrast. *Languages in contrast* 12(2):232–250.

Sandrine Zufferey and Pascal M. Gygax. 2015. The role of perspective shifts for processing and translating discourse relations. *Discourse Processes* 53(7):532–555. https://doi.org/10.1080/0163853X.2015.1062839.

Extracting semantic relations via the combination of inferences, schemas and cooccurrences

Mathieu Lafourcade[1] Nathalie Le Brun[2]
(1) LIRMM, 860 rue de St Priest, 34095 Montpellier cedex 5, France
(2) Imagin@t, 34400 Lunel, France
lafourcade@lirmm.fr, imaginat@imaginat.name

Abstract

Extracting semantic relations from texts is a good way to build and supply a knowledge base, an indispensable resource for text analysis. We propose and evaluate the combination of three ways of producing lexical-semantic relations.

1 Introduction

The semantic relations, whether ontological (*hyperonymous, hyponyms, parts / whole*), lexical (synonyms), or semantic roles (agent, patient, instrument, way, place, etc.) are of a major interest for almost all of the applications of NLP where the system has to "understand" what a text means. That is the case, for instance, in automatic translation, indexing, summary, detection of similar texts, etc. The creation of procedures to produce semantic relations therefore meets multiple needs in the field of NLP.

There are several ways to extract semantic relations. Some methods are manual, as for WorldNet (Miller, 1995), while others are more or less automatic (BabelNet, (Navigli and Ponzetto, 2010)) or contributory (Lafourcade, *et al.*, 2015). Among the many methods of extracting semantic relations from texts, the performances are very unequal. Some are highly accurate, but this precision requires a thorough semantic analysis, which is costly. Moreover, the need to analyze texts with great precision considerably slows down the process of extracting semantic relations. Conversely, some statistical methods include virtually no language processing of the input text.

In this paper, we assess the interest of combining three different strategies to extract semantic relations. This approach is implemented in the context of never ended learning, within the lexical network resulting from the JeuxDeMots project (Lafourcade, 2007). The idea is to implement extraction / exploitation loops in which an automatic extraction system plays the role of contributor within the network. Players / contributors validate or invalidate relations, either through games (GWAPs) or through direct contributions. Thus, we can assess in a holistic way the performance of our SIC (Schema-Inferences-Cooccurrences) system, which feeds the network and uses it to carry out its task.

In the following, we mention, among the previous works in automatic extraction of semantic relations, those whose methodology is similar to ours. Then, we detail three extraction strategies and how we combine them. Finally, we detail and discuss the results.

2 Previous works

Using lexical-semantic schemes to extract synonymy and hyperonymy relations from texts has been proposed by (Hearst, 1992). The schemes may be of "A is a B" type. Herbelot and Copestake (2006) used such diagrams to extract relations in biology from Wikipedia pages with excellent precision (88%) but a fairly low recall (20%). Ruiz-Caasado (2005) and (2007) evoke the automatic learning of such schemas to extract relations from Wikipedia, and insert them into Wordnet. Here again, it is noted that the performances regarding the recall are rather weak. The approach of using automatic learning of schemas from texts has also been exploited by Snow et al., (2004), also to identify hyperonymy or hyponymy relations. In (Girju, *et al.*, 2003), a supervised approach aims to determine the semantic constraints to extract meronymic relations. The constraints are defined by the *part-of* relation of Wordnet and serve as training data. Ramadier and Lafourcade (2016) propose a similar approach, with the difference that they determine the constraints manually and identify many semantic relations.

Proceedings of Recent Advances in Natural Language Processing, pages 417–423,
Varna, Bulgaria, Sep 4–6 2017.

Many authors try to extract relations from Wikipedia by exploiting the structure information of the pages. For example, Sumida and Torisawa, (2008) used this strategy on Wikipedia in Japanese to extract 1.4 million hyponymy relations with an precision of 0.75. In the same way, Ponzetto and Strub (2007) exploit the Wikipedia category links to identify hypernymy relations. Pachenko (2013) presents an in-depth analysis of functions of evaluation of semantic relations between terms. One of the conclusions is that none of the evaluation measures of the semantic relations is better than the others. The proposition of such or such semantic relations, mostly ontological (hypernyms, co-hyponyms, etc.) is conditioned by these different measures of similarity. It should be noted that little work in this field is based on the use of knowledge bases to extract new semantic relations in a continuous loop learning approach. However, such bases are often used for training in automatic learning. Moreover, most approaches are limited to ontological relations, such as hypernymy (*is a*), synonymy (*syn*), and meronymy or holonymy (*has parts / is part of*). Relations like *cause / consequence, characteristics, location, agent, patient* and *instrument* (for verbs) are rarely extracted. In the approach we describe here, we use pure text, exclusively in French, from Wikipedia or otherwise, and we do not exploit the structure of the source document. We also want to extract information from non-encyclopedic texts (such as novels, for example). For each extraction method, we use, at various degrees, the lexical-semantic network JeuxDeMots (JDM).

3 Combining three Relations Extraction Methods

We present three quite simple methods for extracting semantic relations between pairs of terms. We then outline their combination (the first and second ones are new methods).

3.1 Cooccurrences and Relations

At first, we need a cooccurrences network. The method to get it takes into account compound terms and includes a pre-processing on the text, which consists of several steps:

First, a term is replaced by its lemma, but only when the term is a conjugated verb. For example, the segment: *les poules dorment* will become *les poules dormir*. On the other hand, the segment *les poules couvent* remains unchanged since *couvent* can be a conjugate form of the verb *couver* but also the substantive *couvent* (convent).

Secondly, we identify occurrences of compound terms by confronting with the JDM network. The spaces are replaced by underscores, which avoids their segmentation.

The punctuation marks are preserved, but detached from the terms that precede them: *chat, =>chat ,*. Caps are not changed; with the exception of what is mentioned above, neither pos tagging nor parsing is performed.

Compound terms are identified by comparison with those existing in the JDM network. In case of conflict (for example, a segment A B C with two compound words A_B and B_C), a priority is applied to the right (A B_C). Then, segmentation is made using the spaces characters. A *k-word* window is used to establish the co-occurrence relations, with a decreasing weight from *k* (adjacent word) to *1* (word at a distance of *k* terms). We used a window of 10 words, in order to maximize the recall, which is the objective of this method.

We use the JDM knowledge base as a support for the determination of lemmas and morphosyntactic categories, but also for the approximate identification of the types of semantic relations. More precisely, we have rules of this type, which exploit the parts of the speech:

- If X *r_pos* verb & Y *r_pos* adv → X *r_manner* Y
- If X *r_pos* noun & Y *r_pos* adj → X *r_carac* Y
- Default settings : if X is in co-occurrence with Y, → X *r_assoc* Y

The rules are strict and must be understood as: if X is a verb and only a verb and if Y is only an adverb then X will be linked to Y by a *manner* relation. For example, the following sentence: "the cat quickly caught the black rat". The pretreatment phase provides us with the text: "the cat quickly catch the black rat" (we do not indicate weights). The following relations are weighted by the weight of the cooccurrence between the two terms:

cat *r-assoc* catch	rat *r_assoc* black
catch *r_manner* quickly	quicly *r_assoc* rat
catch *r_assoc* rat	cat *r_assoc* rat
catch *r_assoc* black	cat *r_assoc* black
…	quickly *r_assoc* cat

3.2 Lexical-Semantic Schemes with Constraints

Ramadier and Lafourcade (2016) modified the method of Hearst (1992) as well as Herbelot and Copestake (2006), which exploits the semantic schemas, so that the terms satisfy semantic relations coming from the JDM lexical network. For example:

- X of Y with X *r_isa* artefact & Y *r_isa* person → Y *r_own* X (soldier's rifle)
- X of Y with X *r_isa* part of body & Y *r_isa* person → Y *r_part* X (soldier's arm)
- X of Y with X *r_isa* person & Y *r_isa* human place → Y *r_place* X (the girl of the coron)

Of course, some schemas are not associated with constraints, for example:

- X is located in the/my/a/some/ Y → X *r_place* Y
- X is a type of Y → X *r_isa* Y
- X is part of Y → X *r_holo* Y
- X consists of Y → X *r_has_parts* Y

A relation between two terms will be weighted by the number of times it was discovered using different schemes in separate text segments.

3.3 Induction and Abduction within a Lexical-Semantic Network

Zarrouk, *et al.* (2014) and Zarrouk and Lafourcade (2015) proposed an inference-based method to produce new semantic relations. This strictly endogenous approach relies on the JDM network: no text is used. It is based on deduction and various forms of abduction.

3.4 How to Combine these Approaches?

The combination of two methods consists in retaining only the semantic relations found jointly by each of the two methods. Although the co-occurrence method produces non-specific relations (i.e. *associated ideas* relations between terms), which have no equivalences in the other two methods, these neutral relations are used as follows:

X *r_t* Y + X *r_assoc* Y → X *r_t* Y
A neutral relation (type *r_assoc*) validates a typed one (type *r_t*)

We combine approaches in pairs because a combination of the three approaches, while increasing accuracy, would reduce too much the number of retained relations. We will therefore retain the relations produced by at least two of the three methods. The weight of the combination is the geometric mean (square root of product) of the relations.

4 Experimentation and Discussion

The inference approach was tested on the lexical network. For the two others, which require texts, we used a corpus consisting of Wikipedia in French (for schemas and cooccurrences) and the work of Emile Zola (for cooccurrences). This choice of corpus reflects the desire not to limit ourselves to encyclopaedic texts, and to enrich the collection of semantic relations by exploiting the advantages of novelistic literature: to offer (1) a greater diversity of relations between terms, and (2) more common sense information and relating to everyday life.

The extracted relations are: *synonymy* (for verbs, names, adjectives, adverbs), *agent, patient, instrument, manner, take place* (for verbs), *hypernymy, hyponymy, instance, characteristics, is located in, is a place for, parts of, whole, cause, consequence* (for nouns).

The *productivity* is the ability of a method to produce relations. We use this measure in place of the traditional recall, which we are not able to evaluate. Indeed, we do not have linguists / lexicographers to determine the complete set of relations that should be extracted from our corpus. Such a work would be very cumbersome in that it is necessary to go through each text by hand. In addition, the inter-annotator agreement is generally not very high (less than 50% on average). In order to evaluate productivity, we take the inference method as a reference and assign it a productivity value of 1. In practice, this method yielded about 60 million relations (which are potential until they have been validated) between November 1, 2016 and March 30, 2017.

The *precision* is the ratio between relations assessed as fair and all proposed relations. We are of course seeking to maximize this critical criterion, while maintaining good productivity.

Finally, *relevance* is the ratio between the relevant relations and the right relations. Deciding if a relation is relevant remains relatively subjective, but respondents (by crowdsourcing and GWAP) generally agree. Relevance is related to the specificity of a relation; in general, the more a relation is specific to a class of terms, the more it is relevant.

4.1 Methodology

The assessment was carried out jointly by two methods: 1) manual validation of a random sample, and 2) matching of player responses via JeuxDeMots. This evaluation is carried out continuously (the data below are those of the period from November 2016 to March 2017), the results shown below are those at the end of March 2017. For manual validation, the relation to be evaluated is submitted to a player (through the *Askit* game, http://jeuxdemots.org/askit.php), who must decide on its validity and relevance. The matching method involves the classic game of the JeuxDeMots project: a player is offered a game with the first term of the relation to be evaluated, and the type of the relation in question. For example, if the relation *rat r_carac black* has been extracted, then games are proposed with the term *rat* and the instruction to give terms relevant to the relation *r_carac* ; then, the player must give some characteristics of *rat*. If *black* is among its answers, then, the relation *rat r_carac black* is validated. This method is equivalent to questioning people to see if the extracted relation emerges or not. Players can move on if they do not know. We have selected as a priority the relations whose weight corresponds to the 2nd quartile (*i.e.* the 50% with the highest weights).

4.2 General Results

To evaluate the methods independently of each other, we use method I (Inferences) as a reference for the number of relations produced in 5 months, i.e. 60 million. The evaluation of the 3 methods considered individually for the 3 criteria of *productivity, precision* and *relevance* are presented in Table 1.

	Schemas (S)	Infer. (I)	Cooc. (C)
Productivity	0.37 (22 M)	1 (60 M)	3,16 (190 M)
Precision	93 %	65 %	12 %
Relevance	88 %	75 %	47 %

Table 1: Evaluation of the 3 methods individually

The method of extracting through *lexical-semantic schemes* (S) with constraints produces very few false relations but is relatively slow. The 7% error corresponds to the impossibility of applying constraints, when at least one of the two terms of the relation is not sufficiently provided with information. The extracted relations are relevant, which is normal since they are taken directly from the texts.

The *cooccurrence method* (C), as expected, is very productive, fast, and very imprecise (a lot of waste). Correct relations are relevant once in two.

Finally, the *inference method* (I) (which is based only on the JeuxDeMots knowledge base) shows quite good performances. Errors come mainly from the impact of polysemy, which disrupts deductive and abductive inferences. The difference in productivity between S and C is essentially explained by the speed difference of the two methods (S slow and precise, C fast and fuzzy).

The combination of two-by-two methods consists in retaining a relation only if it is proposed by both methods. It is therefore an intersection between the proposals of the two methods.

	S+I	S+C	I+C
Productivity	0.22	0.35	0.78
Precision	96 %	94 %	87 %
Relevance	93 %	84 %	88 %

Table 2: 2-by-2 methods evaluation. The productivity is the highest when *Inference* and *Cooccurrences* are combined. Highest precision is achieved when *Schemas* is combined with *Inferences*.

We find that for each pair productivity decreases with each method taken in isolation, which is an expected result. The S + I combination has very low productivity, indicating that few relations are produced by both S and I methods.

	(S+I) ∪ (S+C) ∪ (I+C)
Productivity	1.28
Precision	99.4 %
Relevance	96 %

Table 3: Evaluation of the approach retaining relations proposed by at least 2 methods (union). Clearly, this method combination tends to maximize the three evaluation criteria.

The approach through combination of the three methods not only produces a 28% increase in productivity compared to method I (taken as a reference), but also increases precision and relevance. If we use method I as a reference, the combination of the approaches allows to reinforce the precision with the method S and the relevance with S and C. Combining S + C allows (again with reference to I) to add relations which could not have been inferred. We recall that C is applied to a corpus of text larger and more general than the method S. This approach tends to increase the common sense relations we are able to capture, without corrupting precision and relevance. Still, relevance seems to be quite difficult to get even though the usage of a large corpus helps focusing on mostly relevant relations.

4.3   Evaluation per Relation Type

We evaluated our approach through relation types.

Relation type	Precision	Relevance
For nouns		
R_isa	98	97
R_carac	99.8	96
R_has-part	98.6	97
R_holo	98.9	98
R_own	97.6	94
R_place_n	99.9	97
R_member_of	98.6	96
R_produce	94.2	98
For verbs		
R_agent	99.5	96
R_patient	99.8	95
R_manner	99.9	97
R_place_v	97.2	98
For both Nouns and Verbs		
R_consequence	97;1	93
R_cause	97.6	93

Table 4: Evaluation detailed by relation type.

There are some variations of precision and relevance amongst the different types of relations. Some relations quite explicit in texts of Wikipedia, for instance the *r_isa, r_carac, r_place* are extracted quite faithfully with a quite high precision and relevance.

The *place* relation (for nouns and verbs) is more difficult to detect for verbs than for nouns. For verbs, some wording about the *manner* may be similar to wording related to the *place*, which can lead to wrong relation type identification.

There is often confusion between *r_holo* and *r_member_of* because these two relations are often expressed in a similar way if not identical. The main distinctive criterion is the use of the singular or plural, or of an entity representing a set.

Le chat fait partie des félins The form *félins* being in the plural, it can be considered as a set, hence leading properly to the *r_member-of* relation. Similarly, for the sentences:

Le soldat fait partie de l'armée. L'abeille fait partie de la ruche

The terms *armée (army)* and *ruche (hive)* have a set aspect, leading also to *the r_member-of* relation. But if we consider:

(a) Les fibres de ce bois sont longues.

(b) Les animaux de ce bois sont craintifs.

It is much more tricky to properly identify the proper relation types between *r_holo* or *r_member* or even *r_place*. Even human validators may hesitate to identify the appropriate relation. For sentence (a), the most appropriate relation is *r_holo* (fibers are part of the wood (matter)). For sentence (b) animals are both part of the woods (forest) (relation *r_member*) and are in the woods (*r_place*). The *cause* and *consequence* relations are much quite difficult to spot, because they are expressed in different ways.

Difficult Cases

We encountered some difficult cases. Consider this definition from Wikipedia:

« La Frégate du Pacifique (Fregata minor) est une espèce d'oiseaux marins appartenant à la famille des Fregatidae. » (Eng : The Frégate du Pacifique (Fregata minor) is a species of sea bird belonging the Fregatidae family.)

The *S* method leads to: *frégate du Pacifique r_isa oiseaux marins*, which stumbles into the problem of the number, as a singular noun (*frégate*) cannot be a plural noun (*oiseaux marins*). We have to deal with some special handling when the lemma of the right part should be considered. In that case, we should obtain: *frégate du Pacifique r_isa oiseau marin*. Note that in this typical case, the cooccurrence and inference mechanisms are very useful. Another relation extracted from this example is *frégate du Pacifique r_member-of Fregatidae*.

Some Typical Failure Examples

Consider the following sentence: *Sa beauté créait bien des tourments (Eng. Her beauty was the origin of many torments.)*

Our approach deduces the following relation: *beauté r_produce tourments*, but in fact the wording is quite metaphorical and misleading, and the proper relation would be *r_consequence*. Such sentences are more frequent in literary texts than in encyclopedic ones (like Wikipedia), nevertheless they are quite common and unless being able to undertake a deep semantic analysis, such relations would remain difficult to identify properly. We also have problem with anaphoric chain, like in this sentence (Wikipedia): *Les chiens de prairie (Cynomys) forment un genre de rongeurs qui comprend cinq espèces.*

Our system identifies wrongly the relation *rongeur r_has part espèces*. In fact, we should have had: *chiens de prairie r_member_of rongeurs*. But such identification is beyond the reach of our methodology, as it requires some reconstruction of the surface expression.

Even if we try to be as precise as possible (at the expense of some recall), there are still some cases in which our approach wrongly identifies the relation types, as some deep understanding seems to be mandatory. Such an automatic understanding could be very costly to obtain in terms of computing on the one hand, and on the other hand requires a quantity of knowledge (at least knowledge of common sense) and … that is precisely what we are trying to capture.

Hence, increasing the size of the corpus can lead to increase the chance to capture a given relation by several different schemas, and thus increasing both precision and relevance. Since common sense relations are the most appropriate for identifying other candidate relations, it would seem that novels are the best source for relation extraction.

4.3 Evaluation with Semantic Class

We evaluated our approach on the basis of the semantic class of the term for which the relations have been discovered (the left-hand side term of discovered relations).

Semantic class	Precision	Relevance
animal	98.3	98
plant	99.7	96
actor/actress	98.3	97
vehicle	98.8	98
disease	98.5	96
medicament	99.2	98
food	99.6	98
movie	97.2	98
city	98.5	97

Table 4: Evaluation detailed by semantic class.

A term belongs to a given semantic class if the word that designates that class is a possible hypernym for it. We should remind that a term could belong at the same time to several semantic classes, as it can be polysemous. For example, the term *frégate* (frigate) is both a bird and a boat/vehicle. The semantic classes listed above account for around 68 % of all terms. The 32% other terms belong to other semantic classes (process, book, geographical place, other types of persons, natural phenomena, etc.). In Table 4, we can see that for the main semantic classes there is not a strong variation amongst precision and relevance values. Perhaps the *movie* semantic class is

an exception for precision, the reason being it is difficult to infer precise relation for a given movie unless analyzing elements of the story. The *disease* semantic class, on the other hand has some good precision but low relevance, the relations found although being correct are quite general.

5 Conclusion

We have presented three methods for the identification of semantic relations between terms. One of them is strictly endogenous and relies on a knowledge base (the JeuxDeMots network), the other two are based on texts, but also use semantic information external to the texts. Overall, these methods are light. Individually, they have defects (productive but imprecise / precise but not very productive). Their union, by offsetting their respective defects, significantly improves productivity, relevance, and precision.

The performance of our method seems not to be very sensible toward the semantic class of the term for which a candidate relation is extracted. We were not able to spot a particular semantic class that would really be underperformed. These results are some good news, as its support the idea that there is no need for some specific treatment for some semantic class of words.

What about extracting automatically some semantic schemes from corpora? We are in the process of undertaking such a task, however there are at least two pitfalls: first, we do extract a very large number of relations that have to be manually validated before being exploited (supervised approach). This is a long and delicate task. Second, it is particularly difficult to automatically determine the semantic constraints to be associated with a semantic scheme. Indeed, on what criteria can we choose in the network the relations that must be verified by the elements of the scheme? To avoid producing schemes with too general constraints, which would lead to erroneous relations, the system tends to select very specific constraints. This has the effect of over-multiplying the schemes (several tens of thousands) and thus considerably increasing the computing time.

Since strictly semantic (and not lexical) relations are independent of languages, a way of further improving the process would be to adapt this approach to the extraction of relations from texts of different languages, using either a translation process, or the multilingual JDM network currently under study.

References

GIRJU, R., BADULESCU, A., and MOLDOVAN, D. (2003) *Learning semantic constraints for the automatic discovery of part-whole relations.* In Proc. Conf. North American Chapter of the Association for Computational Linguistics on Human Language Technology , NAACL '03, pages 1–8. Association for Computational Linguistics, 2003.

HEARST, M. A. (1992) *Automatic acquisition of hyponyms from large text corpora.* In Proc . 14th Conf. on Computational Linguistics, COLING '92, pages 539–545. Association for Computational Linguistics, 1992.

HERBELOT, A. and COPESTAKE, A. (2006) *Acquiring ontological relationships from Wikipedia using RMRS.* In Proc. ISWC 2006 Workshop on Web Content Mining with Human Language Technologies , 2006.

LAFOURCADE, M. (2007) *Making people play for Lexical Acquisition.* In Proc. SNLP 2007, 7th Symposium on Natural Language Processing. Pattaya, Thailande, 13-15 December 2007, 8 p.

LAFOURCADE, M., LE BRUN N., and JOUBERT A. (2015) *Games with a Purpose (GWAPS)*, ISBN: 978-1-84821-803-1 July 2015, Wiley-ISTE, 158 p.

MILLER, G. A. (1995) *Wordnet: A lexical database for English.* Communications of the ACM , 38(11):39–41, November 1995.

NAVIGLI, R.and PONZETTO, S. P. (2010*) Babelnet: Building a very large multilingual semantic network.* In Proc. 48th Annual Meeting of the Association for Computational Linguistics , ACL'10, pages 216–225, 2010.

PANCHENKO, A. (2013) *Similarity Measures for Semantic Relation Extraction.* PhD Dissertation, Université catholique de Louvain & Bauman Moscow State Technical University, 193 p.

RAMADIER, L. ET LAFOURCADE, M. (2016) *Patrons sémantiques pour l'extraction de relations entre termes - Application aux comptes rendus radiologiques.* In 23rd French Conference on Natural Language Processing (JEP-TALN-RECITAL 2016), Paris, France, 4-8 July 2016, 6 p.

RUIZ-CASADO M., ALFONSECA E., AND CASTELLS P. (2005) *Automatic extraction of semantic relationships for Wordnet by means of pattern learning from wikipedia.* In Proc. 10th Int. Conf. Natural Language Processing and Information Systems, NLDB'05, pages 67–79. Springer, 2005

RUIZ-CASADO M., ALFONSECA E., AND CASTELLS P. (2007) *Automatising the Learning of Lexical Patterns: an Application to the Enrichment of Wordnet by Extracting Semantic Relationships from Wikipedia.* In Data & Knowledge Engineering , Issue 3 (June 2007) 25p.

SNOW R., JURAFSKY D., AND ANDREW Y. NG. (2004) *Learning syntactic patterns for automatic hypernym discovery.* In Advances in Neural Information Processing Systems (NIPS), 8 p. 2004.

SUMIDA, A. AND TORISAWA, K. (2008) *Hacking Wikipedia for hyponymy relation acquisition.* In Proc. of IJCNLP 2008 , pages 883–888, 2008.

ZARROUK, M., LAFOURCADE, M., and JOUBERT A. (2014). About Inferences in a Crowdsourced Lexical-Semantic Network, *EACL 2014 (14th Conference of the European Chapter of the Association for Computational Linguistics)*, Gothenburg (Sweden), April 2014

ZARROUK, M. and LAFOURCADE, M. (2014) *Inferring Knowledge with Word Refinements in a Crowdsourced Lexical-Semantic Network.* In proc of the the 25th International Conference on Computational Linguistics (COLING 2014), Dublin, Irlande, 9 p.

If mice were reptiles, then reptiles could be mammals
or
How to detect errors in the JeuxDeMots lexical network?

Mathieu Lafourcade[1] Alain Joubert[1] Nathalie Le Brun[2]
(1) LIRMM, 860 rue de St Priest, 34095 Montpellier cedex 5, France
(2) Imagin@t, 34400 Lunel, France
lafourcade@lirmm.fr, joubert@lirmm.fr, imaginat@imaginat.name

Abstract

Correcting errors in a data set is a critical issue. This task can be either hand-made by experts, or by crowdsourcing methods or automatically done using algorithms. Although even if the rate of errors present in a given lexical network is rather low, it is important to reduce it. We present here automatic methods for detecting potential secondary errors that would result from automatic inference mechanisms when they rely on an initial error manually detected. Encouraging results also invite us to consider strategies that would automatically detect "erroneous" initial relations, which could lead to the automatic detection of the majority of errors in a lexical-semantic network.

1 Introduction

Any collection of data contains errors and, depending on the domain and applications concerned, their quantity is more or less tolerable. Although the anomaly rate is relatively low (well below 1%), the JeuxDeMots (JDM) network is no exception (Lafourcade, 2007). Minimizing this error rate remains a priority and requires effective detection strategies to optimize the correction rate.

The anomalies are various. They may relate either to terms, such as spelling mistakes (eg *théâtre / théatre*) or to the relations between terms (eg, *Milou est_un humain,* or *Dalida,* an *idea_associated* to *Samson,* by confusion between *Dalida* and *Delilah*).

Currently, the detection of anomalies is essentially carried out manually by players / contributors via their activity of enriching the network through the Diko interface[1] (the contributory dictionary of lexical associations of the JDM project). But since errors are discovered by chance, this mode of detection cannot claim to be exhaustive, hence the need to develop a true detection method.

First, we investigate the origin of the anomalies and then present a method that detects and reports a number of relationships as false. It is up to the human validator to decide whether to make corrections or not. Although experimented and exemplified on the JDM data, our approach remains fully generic and can be applied on other lexical-semantic network.

2 Where do the Anomalies in a Lexical-Semantic Network Come from?

The construction method and the characteristics of the JDM network (our test case) as described in (Lafourcade *et al.,* 2015) make it vulnerable to two main types of errors:

"Initial" anomalies introduced by the players and the contributors, voluntarily or not. In our experience, these are essentially unintentional errors, as the interest in voluntarily entering erroneous information is very limited. Indeed,

---

[1] http://www.jeuxdemots.org/diko.php

Proceedings of Recent Advances in Natural Language Processing, pages 424–430,
Varna, Bulgaria, Sep 4–6 2017.

because of the principle of building the JDM network, a relation is created (or reinforced if it already exists) only if both players have proposed it in response to the same instruction. The games being played anonymously and asynchronously, any communication between the players of the same game is not possible, therefore cheating is made very difficult if not impossible. Entering inconsistencies therefore has only an extremely low probability of having consequences on the recorded data. This leads to a significant reduction in risk, but does not completely cancel it.

"Secondary" anomalies are induced by automatic inference mechanisms (deduction, induction, abduction) from initial anomalies. Indeed, the JDM network can be densified automatically by inferences from existing relations (Lafourcade *et al.,* 2014); if some of these "initial" relations are wrong, then the inference mechanisms will generate potentially erroneous relations. When automatically inferred relations are considered doubtful by the system, their validation is subject to a majority vote process and / or expert opinion, which greatly reduces the risk of recording erroneous relations.

Let's take an example: we have the relation *mouse is_a mammal*. Let us suppose that the erroneous "initial" relation has then appeared: *mouse is_a reptile*. The system "knows" that *mammal* and *reptile* are incompatible, just like *mammal* and *fish* or *mammal* and *insect*, for example. It deduces then that *mouse* is polysemous, and thus appear the refinements: *mouse>mammal* and *mouse>reptile*. From this latter refinement, by deduction / induction mechanisms, the system can generate new relations which will probably be erroneous since the refinement *mouse>reptile* is erroneous.

3   How to Detect and Correct Anomalies

Several authors have studied the problem of automatic detection / correction of errors in the domain of NLP. Boudin and Hernandez (2012) propose methods for automatic detection / correction of syntax annotation errors in the French Treebank, based on an approach previously presented by Dikinson and Meurers (2003). Regarding the detection / correction of semantic errors, we find the work of Ben Othmane Zribi *et al.* (2007) for the Arabic language. Bouraoui *et al.* (2009) analyzed the different types of errors encountered in written expression, in order to realize a general typology of errors.

First of all, let us note that in the JDM network, correcting an anomaly does not mean erasing the relation concerned, but more precisely negating it, that is assigning it a negative weight. A relation with a negative weight is deemed to be false.

Indeed, it may be interesting to have (or keep) the information that a relation is not true, rather than having no information about that relation (by deleting it).

For example, if the relation *ostrich* r_agent *fly* is negatively weighted it means that an ostrich cannot fly, while the absence of relation would mean that one does not know whether an ostrich can fly or not.

Moreover, by negating a relation, one ensures that it cannot reappear, which could be the case by suppressing it. Our automatic error detector will prepare this correction process: by contributing by a negative vote on a suspicious relation, it will signal it as such to the human validator, who will decide and negate it (or not ...).

3.1   Initial Anomalies

Initial errors seem difficult to detect by endogenous mechanisms. For example, if two players on the same game proposed the relation *mouse is_a reptile*, the system is not yet able to detect that it is an erroneous relation. It can only deduce from it that *mouse* is polysemous. These relations are currently reported by contributors / players, then they are manually corrected by an expert (again by negating the relations). Exogenous mechanisms, based on knowledge external to the JDM network (Wikipedia, Babelnet ...), could be envisaged, especially with regard to misspelling on terms.

3.2   Secondary Anomalies

When an error is detected (by a contributor), how to find false inferences that the system could make from this error? It turns out that these false relations that the system has inferred have been created either by deduction, or, to a lesser extent, by induction (Lafourcade *et al.*, 2014).

Deduction

The mechanism of deduction is the following (Zarrouk, *et al.*, 2014): let be R an arbitrary semantic relation. If A *is_a* B and B R C, then A R C may be possible (except for exception or polysemy of B). Thus, if A *is_a* B is false, it may be that A R C is also false. It is necessary to indicate as false the outgoing relations from A which come from properties of B, except those which come from hypernyms of A.

Ex: *mouse is_a reptile* => inferences about *mouse* based on *reptile* properties.
(The statement *"mouse is_a reptile* => inferences" is to be read as *"**if** mouse is a reptile **then** some inferences are true")*

How to detect, and thus negate, these false inferences? It is known that *mouse is_a mammal.* In the outgoing relations of *mouse*, it is necessary to point out as potentially false those which come from properties of *reptile* with the exclusion of those that would be in common between *reptile* and *mammal.*

For example, *reptile r_agent to_lay_eggs*, is not a shared relation with *mammal* => thus, the relation *mouse agent to_lay_eggs* (inferred by deduction) is to be reported as false.
A contrario, *reptile has_part vertebrae*, and *mammal has_part vertebrae* => thus, the relation *mouse has_part vertebrae* is to be preserved.

The problem is not limited to the relations concerning the only term for which the anomaly was detected. By deduction process, the system was able to infer new erroneous relations (ex: *mouse agent to_lay_eggs*), and from these erroneous relations, infer new erroneous relations.

The erroneous relation being derived from *mouse*, any specific of *mouse* (like *white mouse* or *laboratory mouse*) would be able to be infected by application of the deduction. It will therefore be necessary to also look for potentially erroneous "secondary" relations deduced from some specifics of *mouse*.

For example, as *white_mouse is_a mouse*, the relation *white_mouse agent to_lay_eggs* could be inferred. How to detect this new erroneous relation? The relation *mouse agent to_lay_eggs* having received a negative vote in the preceding step, the detection system will take this into account and also report this relation as suspicious by assigning it a negative contribution.

Secondary errors may also have spread to the generic chain of the initial term. If A *is_a* B is wrong, in order to search for potentially erroneous "secondary" relations, the human validator must go back in the generic chain of B to check the validity of the different generic relations between A and the terms encountered. As soon as the validator encounters a valid relation, it will no longer be necessary to go back up. For example, *mouse is_a reptile* is wrong. So, do we have :

- *reptile is_a sauropside* => *mouse is_a sauropside* ? answer : erroneous relation, it is put negative and the validator goes on
- *sauropside is_a vertebrate* => *mouse is_a vertebrate* ? answer : valid relation. Thus we can stop the process of searching for potentially erroneous "secondary" relations found by deduction/induction with *mouse is_a sauropside.*

Induction

Induction mechanism (for any R relation type): if A *is_a* B and A R C, then B R C may be possible (except for special cases or polysemy of A). Thus, if A *is_a* B is wrong, it is possible that B R C is also wrong. The outgoing relations of B which originate from the properties of A, with the exception of those derived from the hyponyms of B, must therefore be indicated as false (by affecting them with a negative vote).

Example: let the wrong relation *mouse is_a reptile* => inferences on *reptile* based on the properties of *mouse*

How to detect these false inferences, so as to negate them?

By comparing with the hyponyms of *reptile* that have a lot of information: we know that *tortoise is_a reptile*. Among reptile relations, those derived from *mouse* properties, excluding those from *turtle* properties should be reported as false.

- *mouse has_part hairs*, which is not the case with the *tortoise* => thus, the relation *reptile has_part hairs* (inferred by induction) has to be reported as false.

- on the opposite, *mouse has_part head*, and *tortoise has_part head* => thus, the relation *reptile has_part head* must be retained.

Algorithms

The following two algorithms (Algorithm 1 and 2) reflect the principles developed above. The first algorithm is related to the deduction mechanisms. The second one is related to induction.

The principle of these algorithms is to virtually simulate what could have been specifically deduced (for algorithm 1) or induced (for algorithm 2) and to eliminate what seems to be incompatible.

Note that a relation that is not in the lexical network has a (virtual) weight equal to 0. The hyper function (resp. hypo) returns the list of hypernyms (resp. hyponyms) of the term given as parameter.

For these secondary anomalies, one question remains: do the implemented endogenous mechanisms used detect everything? Or, more precisely, what proportion of anomalies is detected by these mechanisms? Moreover, are these correction mechanisms not likely to introduce errors, indicating as false some relations that are true?

3.3   Actual and Experimental Results

To evaluate the performance of our false relations detection system, we have (on a local copy of the lexical network JeuxDeMots) artificially added false hypernyms to terms.

In fact, we applied our algorithm on the actual JDM data, in order to correct many errors, which was done successfully. But to perform an evaluation in a controlled environment, we made a copy in which we artificially introduced errors.

On the actual data, we were able to halve the number of errors (from 1% to 0.5%). Most of the remaining errors do not fall into the scope of our proposed method, as they were not detectable through hypernym incompatibilities. For those remaining errors, other approaches should be devised.

We verified manually and in depth that the experiments in controlled environment were not biased by the artificial addition of errors. The actual errors and the errors artificially added are of the same nature. We just added much more numerous and various errors in order to assess our method.

We have in JDM a list of pairs of incompatible hypernyms: this means that a given term cannot have the two terms of a pair from this list as generic, unless it is polysemous. For example: *fish - mammal*; *insect - reptile*; *animal - plant*; *plane - ship*; *man - woman*; *car - plane*; *train - boat*, etc. We selected 250 terms having as hypernym one of the generics above but not the second, which we added. We then launched on these 250 terms the mechanisms of inferences. We then applied on this sample of 250 terms our algorithms of detection of false relations to detect the relations to be eliminated.

The inference mechanisms produced 4,500 new relationships that we evaluated through the Askit [2] online application. We retained the 3,600 new relations that were evaluated at least twice. The following board presents the results of the evaluation, globally and for some examples of couples of incompatible generics.

---

[2] http://www.jeuxdemots.org/askit.php

% relations found by both algorithms	global	fish / *mammal	insect / *reptile	animal / *plant	plane / *ship	man / *woman
% correctely found	**97.6**	98.2	95.6	98.4	96.1	99.2
% false positives	**2.4**	1.8	4.4	1.6	3.8	0.8
% false negatives	**0.52**	0.25	0.67	0.35	0.7	0.3

Table 1: Evaluation of found relations with both algorithms according to hypernym terms. The first term is the correct one and the second is the one being invalidated. For the first two lines, the sum of each column is 100% as this refers to the amount of false relations. The last line is the percentage of correct relations that are supposed false by our algorithms.

The terms with a star (*) are the false generics introduced in order to produce erroneous inferences. Overall, our algorithms recover 97.6% of the false relations that have been inferred from an erroneous generic. They "miss" 2.4% of false relationships, and find 0.52% false negatives (i.e. they assume as false some relations that are true). The analysis of false negatives indicates that these are either exceptions or relevant conclusions given the state of completion of the lexical network (important relations may be missing).

Significant differences can be observed depending on the pairs of incompatible generics. Obviously, differences between *man* and *woman* make false inferences more easily detectable than between *insect* and *reptile*. It can be assumed that the network is much more extensively and precisely informed about the human species than about areas of specialty such as zoology; we also notice that in general, performance decreases with the degree of specialization of the field, due to the lesser information in the network.

4 Conclusion

Although the rate of anomalies in the JDM network is low, we can reduce it further by automatic endogenous mechanisms for detecting erroneous relationships. These relatively simple mechanisms make possible to detect a significant proportion of the potentially false "secondary" relations inferred from false "initial" relations. Moreover, since these relations, which are reported as suspicious, are invalidated once an expert has verified that they are erroneous, they can no longer give rise to new false inferences and thus serve as a breeding ground for the birth and spread of new errors; this also favours an overall decrease in the network error rate. On the other hand, "initial" errors are more difficult to detect automatically. However, the use of incompatible generic lists is an interesting lead insofar as it allows the alert to be given when a monosemic term has two incompatible terms as hypernyms.

The method we propose can be applied to any lexico-semantic network whose structure is similar to that of JDM. As our approach relies on quite common relation types (hypernym, hyponym, etc.), it is valid for well known lexical resources like WordNet (Miller, 1995), and HowNet (Dong and Dong, 2006) to cite a few. Moreover, our method is independent of the language because it relies only on relations of a semantic nature.

To conclude, the synergy between manual detection by players/contributors and automatic detection methods helps to maintain a reasonably low error rate in the JDM network. Such methods could be applied with great benefit for other resources.

```
function RelationList erroneousByDeduction (Term A, Term Z)
        // required: A is_a Z is an erroneous relation
        // result: list of the outgoing relations from A, being in the JDM network,
        //              which are potentially erroneous because A is_a Z is erroneous
Begin
        LR = new RelationList()
        LT = hyper (A, Z)                // list of hypernyms of A, but not hypernyms of Z
        For each B ∈ LT
        Do      LR = LR ∪ deduceErroneous (A, B, Z)
                        // list of relations outgoing from A which are potentially erroneous
        EndFor
        Return LR
End


function RelationList deduceErroneous (Term A, B, Z)
        // required: A is_a B > 0 ; A is_a Z is an erroneous relation ; Z is_a B <= 0
        // result: list of outgoing relations from A, being in the JDM network,
        //          which are potentially erroneous because A is_a Z is erroneous.
        /          B is an hypernym of A that the algorithm uses to detect potentially erroneous relations.
Begin
        L = new RelationList()
        For each relation such as ZRY          // we check all the outgoing relations from Z
        Do      If  BRY <= 0                    // BRY does not exist or is negative weighted
                Then    If ARY > 0              // ARY exists (positive weighted)
                        Then L = L ∪ ARY
                        Endif
                EndIf
        EndFor
        Return L
End
```

Algorithm 1: return a list of erroneous relations from a deductive point of view.

```
function RelationList erroneousByInduction (Term A, Term Z)
        // required: A is_a Z is an erroneous relation
        // result: list of the outgoing relations from Z, being in the JDM network,
        //                  which are potentially erroneous because A is_a Z is erroneous
Begin
        LR = new RelationList()
        For each relation such as ARC
                                                // we check all the outgoing relations from A
        Do      If  ZRC > 0                     // if it is outgoing from Z, it may be erroneous
                Then    If erroneousByInduction (A, C, Z)   // is ZRC potentially erroneous?
                        Then LR = LR ∪ ZRC
                        EndIf
                EndIf
        EndFor
        Return LR
End


function boolean isErroneousByInduction (Term A, C, Z)
        // required: ARC > 0 ; A is_a Z is an erroneous relation ; ZRC > 0
        // result: return True if and only if the relation ZRC, being in the JDM network,
        //          is potentially erroneous because A is_a Z is erroneous. C is the target term of an outgoing relation of A
Begin
        LT = hypo (Z,A)                         // list of hyponyms of Z, except A
        Term W = first_term (LT)
        While   W exists and then WRC <= 0      // we check hyponyms of Z
                Do      W = next_term (LT)
        EndWhile
        Return W does not exist
End
```

Algorithm 2: return a list of erroneous relations from an inductive point of view. The *erroneousByInduction* function makes use of the Boolean function *isErroneousByInduction*.

References

BEN OTHMANE ZRIBI C., MEJRI H., AND BEN AHMED M. (2007) Un analyseur hybride pour la détection et la correction des erreurs cachées sémantiques en langue arabe, *TALN 2007*, Toulouse, 5–8 juin 2007

BOUDIN F., AND HERNANDEZ N. (2012) Détection et correction automatique d'erreurs d'annotation morpho-syntaxique du French TreeBank. *TALN 2012*, Juin 2012, Grenoble. pp.281-291.

BOURAOUI J.-L., BOISSIERE P., MOJAHID M., VIGOUROUX N., LAGARRIGUE A., AND VELLA F., NESPOULOUS J.-L. (2009) Problématique d'analyse et de modélisation des erreurs en production écrite. Approche interdisciplinaire. *TALN 2009*, Senlis, 24-26 juin 2009

DICKINSON M., AND MEURERS W.D. (2003) Detecting errors in part-of-speech annotation. *EACL 2003 (10th Conference of the European Chapter of the Association for Computational Linguistics)*, pp.107–114, Budapest, Hungary.

DONG Z. AND DONG Q. (2006) *Hownet and the Computation of Meaning*. World Scientific Publishing Co., Inc., River Edge, NJ, USA.

LAFOURCADE M. (2007) *Making people play for Lexical Acquisition*. In Proc. SNLP 2007, 7th Symposium on Natural Language Processing. Pattaya, Thailande, 13-15 December 2007, 8 p.

LAFOURCADE M., ZARROUK M., AND JOUBERT A. (2014) About Inferences in a Crowdsourced Lexical-Semantic Network, *EACL 2014 (14th Conference of the European Chapter of the Association for Computational Linguistics)*, Gothenburg (Sweden), April 2014

LAFOURCADE M., LE BRUN N., AND JOUBERT A. (2015) *Games with a Purpose (GWAPS)*, ISBN: 978-1-84821-803-1 July 2015, Wiley-ISTE, 158 p.

MILLER G A. (1995) Wordnet: A Lexical Database for English. *Communications of the ACM*. Vol. 38, No. 11: 39-41.

ZARROUK M., LAFOURCADE M., AND JOUBERT A. (2014) About Inferences in a Crowdsourced Lexical-Semantic Network, *EACL 2014 (14th Conference of the European Chapter of the Association for Computational Linguistics)*, Gothenburg (Sweden), April 2014

ZARROUK M. AND LAFOURCADE M. (2014) *Inferring Knowledge with Word Refinements in a Crowdsourced Lexical-Semantic Network.* In proc of the the 25th International Conference on Computational Linguistics (COLING 2014), Dublin, Irlande, 9 p.

Word Embeddings for Multi-label Document Classification

Ladislav Lenc[†‡]
[‡] NTIS – New Technologies
for the Information Society,
University of West Bohemia,
Plzeň, Czech Republic
llenc@kiv.zcu.cz

Pavel Král[†‡]
[†] Department of Computer
Science and Engineering,
University of West Bohemia,
Plzeň, Czech Republic
pkral@kiv.zcu.cz

Abstract

In this paper, we analyze and evaluate word embeddings for representation of longer texts in the multi-label document classification scenario. The embeddings are used in three convolutional neural network topologies. The experiments are realized on the Czech ČTK and English Reuters-21578 standard corpora. We compare the results of word2vec static and trainable embeddings with randomly initialized word vectors. We conclude that initialization does not play an important role for classification. However, learning of word vectors is crucial to obtain good results.

1 Introduction

Text classification (or categorization) is one of the core tasks in natural language processing (NLP) field. The applications of text classification are numerous as for instance sentiment analysis, automatic categorization of e-mails or spam filtering. The main goal of document classification is to assign one or more labels to a given document. The categorization then helps the users to find appropriate documents. Nowadays, computers are heavily utilized for this task and can save a great amount of human labor.

In this paper, we concentrate on multi-label document classification which means that one document can belong to more classes simultaneously. More formally, given a set of documents D and a set of all possible labels C we create a model that assigns a set $C_d \subset C$ to the document $d \in D$.

Multi-label classification is often solved using an ensemble of binary classifiers (Tsoumakas and Katakis, 2006). However, nowadays, neural nets outperform majority of artificial intelligence ap-

proaches including computer vision and natural language processing. Therefore, in this work we use different approaches based on convolutional neural nets (CNNs) which were already presented in Kim (2014) and Lenc and Král (2017).

Usually, the pre-trained word vectors obtained by some semantic model (e.g. word2vec (w2v) (Mikolov et al., 2013a) or glove (Pennington et al., 2014)) are used for initialization of the embedding layer of the particular neural net. These vectors can then be progressively adapted during neural network training. It was shown in many experiments that it is possible to obtain better results using these vectors compared to the randomly initialized vectors. Moreover, it has been proven that even "static" vectors (initialized by pre-trained embeddings and fixed during the network training) usually bring better performance than randomly initialized and trained ones.

However, the experiments were often realized on rather shorter texts and in single-label classification task. In this paper, we would like to analyze and evaluate the use of word embeddings for representation of longer texts in multi-label classification scenario. The embeddings are used in three different convolutional neural network topologies.

The experiments are realized on the Czech ČTK and English Reuters-21578 standard corpora. The Czech language has been chosen as a representative of highly inflectional Slavic language with a free word order. English is used to compare the results of our method with state of the art.

We compare the results with word2vec static and trainable embeddings with randomly initialized word vectors. We conclude that the initialization does not play an important role for classification of these documents. We further analyze and compare the word2vec embeddings with the learned ones from the semantic point of view and discuss the results.

Proceedings of Recent Advances in Natural Language Processing, pages 431–437,
Varna, Bulgaria, Sep 4–6 2017.

The rest of the paper is organized as follows. The following section contains a short review of the usage of neural networks for document classification including word embeddings. Section 3 describes topologies of the convolutional networks. Section 4 deals with experiments realized on the ČTK and Reuters corpora and then analyzes and discusses the obtained results. In the last section, we conclude the experimental results and propose some future research directions.

2 Related Work

Nowadays, neural nets belong to the state-of-the art approaches on many natural language processing tasks as for instance POS tagging, chunking, named entity recognition, semantic role labeling or document classification (Collobert et al., 2011).

First, we mention traditional feed-forward neural nets as shown for instance in (Manevitz and Yousef, 2007). The authors obtain F-measure about 78% on the standard Reuters dataset with a simple multi-layer perceptron with three layers. The standard backpropagation algorithm for multi-label learning of an MLP was improved in (Zhang and Zhou, 2006). The authors use a novel error function which gives better results on functional genomics text categorization.

Nam et al. (2014) propose a novel learning strategy of feed-forward nets for multi-label text classification task. The authors use cross-entropy algorithm for training with rectified linear units activation (Srivastava et al., 2014). The documents are represented by tf-idf and multi-label classification is realized by a simple thresholding of the output layer. The networks are evaluated on several multi-label datasets and obtain results comparable with the state of the art.

Both, standard convolutional networks and recurrent convolutional neural nets are also successfully used for text categorization. The authors (Lai et al., 2015) demonstrated that recurrent CNNs outperform CNNs on four corpora in single-label document classification task.

Another CNN based method with word embeddings as inputs (Kurata et al., 2016) leverages the co-occurrence of labels in the multi-label classification. Some neurons in the output layer capture the patterns of label co-occurrences, which improves the classification accuracy. This method is evaluated on the natural language query classification in a document retrieval system.

An alternative multi-label classification approach is proposed by Yang and Gopal (2012). The conventional representations of texts and categories are transformed into meta-level features. These features are then utilized in a learning-to-rank algorithm. Experiments on six benchmark datasets show good abilities of this approach in comparison with other methods.

Three different types of word embeddings with CNNs are compared in Kim (2014) on 7 NLP tasks including sentiment analysis and question classification. The author proposes a novel CNN topology and shows that word2vec initialization and a subsequent learning plays a crucial role for all sentence-level single-label classification tasks.

3 Network Topologies

In this section we describe the three CNN network topologies used in our experiments. The network inputs are the sequences of word indices into a vocabulary V of the size $|V|$. In order to ensure the fixed length, all documents are padded or shortened to a specified length M. These are then represented as real-valued word vectors of dimension E in the embedding layer. The embedding layer is either initialized randomly or by pre-trained word vectors from word2vec[1]. In the case of word2vec initialization, the layer is either further learned during the training process or is kept static. The input and the embedding layer is similar in all three following network topologies. The concrete values of the main hyper-parameters of the following networks are specified in Section 4.

3.1 Convolutional Network 1

This architecture was proposed in Lenc and Král (2017) for multi-label document classification.

The embedding layer is followed by a convolutional layer, where we use N_C convolution kernels of the size $k \times 1$. It uses rectified linear unit (ReLU) activation function. The following layer performs max pooling over the length $M - k + 1$ resulting in N_C $1 \times E$ vectors. The output of this layer is then flattened and connected with a fully connected layer with d_1 neurons. The output layer uses sigmoid activation function and its size corresponds to the number of categories $|C|$. The final result is obtained by thresholding of the output layer.

---

[1] It is possible to use other semantic model, however based on our previous experiments, we keep word2vec.

This architecture will hereafter be referenced as CNN1.

3.2 Convolutional Network 2

The second architecture is a modified version of a successful net proposed by Kim (2014).

Contrary to the first topology, this network uses two-dimensional convolutional kernels of various widths. The sizes of the kernels are $k \times E$ which means that it takes the whole length of the embedding. The original version is used for single-label classification and therefore it uses softmax activation function in the output layer. In our case, sigmoid is more appropriate due to the multi-label classification task. Similarly as in the previous topology, we also added one fully connected layer before the output. The output layer of the size $|C|$ is also thresholded to determine the set of assigned categories.

This network will be further called CNN2. The architecture is described in detail in Kim (2014). The threshold values for both CNN1 and CNN2 are set on the development corpus.

3.3 Two-level CNN

The first level of this network is the CNN1 topology described above. However, the output is not thresholded as in the former case. This network uses a multi-layer perceptron with one hidden layer to predict the number of labels.

It takes the output of the CNN S and learns a function $l = f(S)$ that maps the vector S to the number of relevant labels l. The output layer has softmax activation. After determining the number of labels the l categories with the highest activations are assigned to the document.

Figure 1 shows the architecture of this network where the CNN and 2nd-level FNN are merged. This topology will be hereafter referenced as 2L-CNN.

4 Experiments

This section describes first the tools and corpora used for evaluation of the approaches. Then we deal with the preprocessing stage and set-up of hyper-parameters of our networks. We describe further our experiments on Czech and English standard corpora and analyze the results.

4.1 Tools and Corpora

For implementation of all neural nets we used Keras tool-kit (Chollet, 2015) which is based on

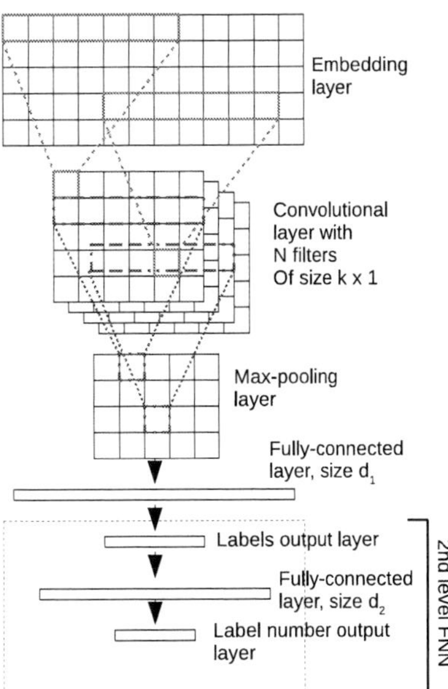

Figure 1: Two-level CNN architecture (2L-CNN).

the Theano deep learning library (Bergstra et al., 2010). It has been chosen mainly because of good performance and our previous experience with this tool. For evaluation of the multi-label document classification results, we use the standard recall, precision and F-measure (*F1*) metrics (Powers, 2011). The values are micro-averaged.

Word2vec vectors for Czech experiments are trained on Czech Wikipedia (Svoboda and Brychcín, 2016). For the English experiments we utilize the standard vectors trained on part of Google News dataset (Mikolov et al., 2013b).

4.1.1 Czech Text Document Corpus v 1.0

This corpus is composed of 11,955 news articles provided by the Czech News Agency (ČTK). The documents are annotated from a set of 60 categories as for instance agriculture, weather, politics or sport out of which we used 37 most frequent ones. The average number of categories per document is 2.55 and the average length of the documents is 277 words. 500 randomly chosen documents are reserved for development set while the remaining part is used for training and testing of our models. Figure 2 shows the distribution of the document lengths (in word tokens). This corpus is freely available for research purposes at `http://home.zcu.cz/~pkral/sw/`. We use the five-fold cross validation procedure for all experiments on this corpus.

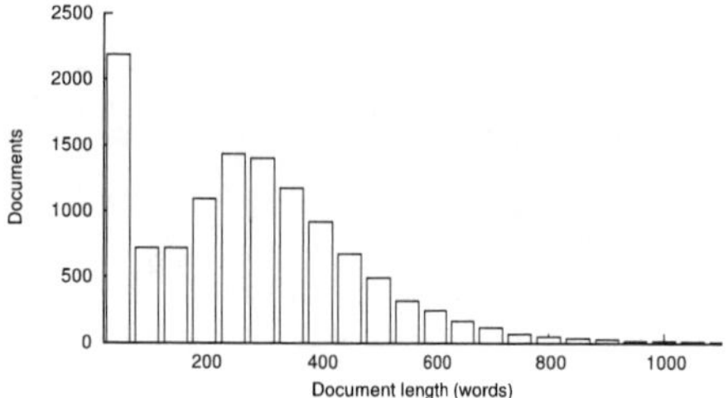

Figure 2: Document lengths in ČTK dataset.

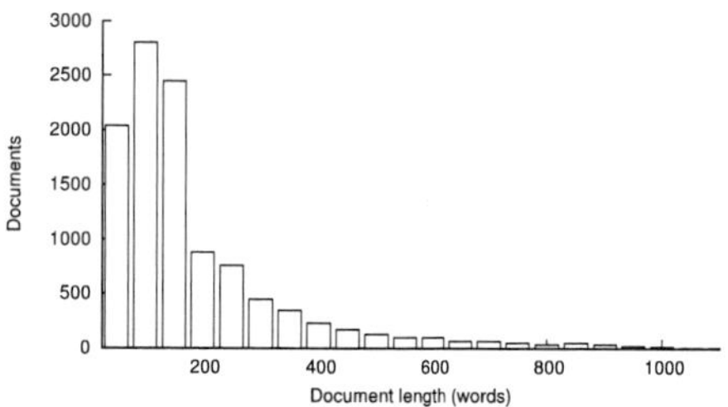

Figure 3: Document lengths in Reuters dataset.

4.1.2 Reuters-21578 English Corpus

The Reuters-21578[2] corpus is a collection of 21,578 documents. However, these documents include examples with no topics and with errors. Therefore, we use the commonly utilized version where the training part is composed of 7769 documents, while 3019 documents are reserved for testing. The number of possible categories is 90 and average label/document number is 1.23. Average document length is 159. This dataset is used in order to compare the performance of our networks with the state of the art. Distribution of document lengths is shown in Figure 3.

4.2 Preprocessing

The same preprocessing was performed for both Czech and English corpora. First we replaced all numbers in the texts by one common token "NUMERIC". The following characters were removed: [.,-_?!#:%()+"] The texts were then lowercased and a simple tokenization according to a space was done. To ensure a fixed length we either shortened the documents to a size of $M = 400$ or padded it by a token "PADDING" to the same length. We used two vocabulary sizes, namely 1000 and 20,000 most frequent words. Words not present in the vocabulary are replaced by an "OOV" (out of vocabulary) token.

---

[2]http://www.daviddlewis.com/resources/testcollections/reuters21578/

4.3 Hyper-parameters Set-up

The embedding vector length is set to 300 in all cases to allow the utilization of the pre-trained vectors and for a straightforward comparison with the learned ones.

The first network (CNN1) uses 40 kernels of length 16 according to (Lenc and Král, 2017). ReLU activation is used in convolutional layer. The following layer contains 256 neurons and the output layer has 37 or 90 neurons according to the used corpus.

The second network (CNN2) utilizes three kernel widths $k \in 3, 4, 5$ as proposed in (Kim, 2014) (100 filters are used for each width). The convolutional layer is followed by a fully-connected layer with 256 neurons and the output layer is the same as in the previous case.

The two-level network (2L-CNN) merges the CNN1 network and an MLP with 100 neurons in the hidden layer and 8 neurons in the output layer indicating the number of assigned labels. The output layer uses softmax activation function.

All networks are trained for 20 epochs using adaptive moment estimation optimization algorithm (Kingma and Ba, 2014). Mean square error loss function is used for the MLP determining the number of labels while binary cross-entropy is used for all CNNs.

4.4 Results on the Czech Corpus

We first present the results of the CNNs on the Czech Corpus (see Table 1). CNN1 and CNN2 are used with thresholding, the thresholds are set experimentally on the development set. Hyper-parameters of the 2L-CNN were also set on this set. The upper part shows the results for vocabulary size 1000 while the lower one uses 20,000 words.

This table shows that the size of the vocabulary plays an important role for document classification. The second interesting observation is that the results of the usage of the embeddings for all networks are consistent. The lowest scores are in all cases obtained with w2v static embeddings while the best classification results are generally achieved with randomly initialized embeddings.

We can thus conclude that initialization of the embeddings with w2v pre-trained vectors does not have any positive impact in this experiment. The best results are obtained using CNN1 and 2L-CNN both with randomly initialized embeddings.

Method	Prec.	Recall	F1[%]
Vocabulary size 1000			
CNN1, w2v static	57.58	70.92	63.56
CNN1, random	71.56	70.84	71.20
CNN1, w2v trainable	72.97	70.02	71.47
CNN2, w2v static	63.86	75.19	69.07
CNN2, random	70.33	71.37	70.84
CNN2, w2v trainable	69.55	71.66	70.59
2L-CNN, w2v static	67.12	62.21	64.57
2L-CNN, random	75.24	68.20	71.55
2L-CNN, w2v trainable	75.76	66.97	71.10
Vocabulary size 20,000			
CNN1, w2v static	64.89	79.88	71.61
CNN1, random	84.84	83.55	84.19
CNN1, w2v trainable	84.62	82.86	83.73
CNN2, w2v static	77.58	80.26	78.90
CNN2, random	80.36	79.59	79.97
CNN2, w2v trainable	79.83	80.96	80.39
2L-CNN, w2v static	76.36	70.20	73.15
2L-CNN, random	87.67	80.95	84.17
2L-CNN, w2v trainable	87.60	79.05	83.10

Table 1: Results of the CNNs on the Czech corpus.

Method	Prec.	Recall	F1[%]
Vocabulary size 1000			
CNN1, w2v static	69.00	62.93	65.82
CNN1, random	75.98	68.10	71.82
CNN1, w2v trainable	78.12	66.46	71.82
CNN2, w2v static	74.13	68.43	71.16
CNN2, random	76.38	67.27	71.54
CNN2, w2v trainable	75.93	67.10	71.24
Vocabulary size 20,000			
CNN1, w2v static	76.06	72.01	73.98
CNN1, random	86.50	82.24	84.32
CNN1, w2v trainable	86.60	81.20	83.81
CNN2, w2v static	82.50	76.45	79.36
CNN2, random	83.16	77.47	80.21
CNN2, w2v trainable	83.75	77.97	80.75

Table 2: Results of CNN1 and CNN2 on the Czech corpus with optimal threshold values.

Another interesting observation is that the role of training of the embeddings in the CNN2 is very small compared to the other two nets. The reason for this behavior can be different size and number of convolutional kernels.

In the second experiment, we show in Table 2 the impact of the optimal thresholds for classification using CNN1 and CNN2 nets. This experiment is done in order to determine the threshold values for English corpus where the development set is missing. Moreover, we also would like to analyze the impact of this optimal value on classification. The thresholds are thus set on the whole corpus. As in the previous case, the upper section of the table uses the vocabulary size 1000 and the lower one 20,000.

We must note that these data cannot be presented as "fair" results for the Czech dataset. However, our goal is to compare the different types of embeddings and this experiment well illustrates the ceiling which can be reached using a particular setting.

This experiment also shows that these results are comparable to the Table 1, therefore we can conclude that the threshold values set on development corpus are appropriate and that the methods are robust to the sub-optimally set thresholds. The second observation is that the behavior of all networks with different kinds of embeddings is similar as in the previous case.

4.5 Results on the English Reuters Dataset

This experiment is realized in order to show the impact of the different embeddings on the standard English corpus. We use the 300-dimensions English word2vec embeddings trained on Google News[3].

This table shows that the role of the embeddings on English language is similar to the previous one, however it slightly differs in the case of the CNN2.

This network gives comparable results for all embedding types. Moreover the best score is obtained with w2v static embeddings, however this difference is not statistically significant.

The behavior of the embeddings in the other two CNNs is similar as in the previous Czech experiments, where word2vec initialization does not play any positive role for classification. A reason for such difference in Czech and English could be caused by the quality of the word2vec embeddings. The best performing network is the 2L-CNN with randomly initialized embeddings. The resulting F-measure is comparable to the value of 87.89% presented in (Nam et al., 2014).

4.6 Embedding Analysis

In this experiment we analyze the semantic similarity of the embedding vectors learned during the network training and compare them with the standard word2vec vectors. We employ the cosine distance to identify 5 most similar words.

We have chosen word "Británie" (Britain) and show the most similar words both for Czech and English embeddings. The results of the Czech experiment are reported in Table 4 while the results

[3]https://code.google.com/archive/p/word2vec

Method	Prec.	Recall	F1[%]
CNN1 w2v static	84.37	73.40	78.50
CNN1 random	87.26	86.14	86.69
CNN1 w2v trainable	90.63	82.18	86.20
CNN2 w2v static	89.42	78.34	83.51
CNN2 random	89.82	76.79	82.79
CNN2 w2v trainable	89.10	78.42	83.42
2L-CNN, w2v static	82.89	74.41	78.42
2L-CNN, random	90.39	84.96	87.59
2L-CNN, w2v trainable	91.03	82.39	86.50

Table 3: Results of the CNNs on the Reuters dataset, vocabulary size is set to 20,000.

Word	Cos.	Word	Cos.
w2v (static)		CNN1, random	
Německo (Germany)	0.65	třetí (third)	0.20
usa	0.63	výroba (production)	0.19
velká (great)	0.60	hlavně (mainly)	0.19
spojené (united)	0.59	Rusko (Russia)	0.18
Rusko (Russia)	0.58	procent (percent)	0.18
CNN2, random		CNN2, w2v trainable	
premiér (p. minister)	0.51	německo (Germany)	0.51
vlády (governments)	0.49	vláda (government)	0.43
vláda (government)	0.48	Londýn (London)	0.40
ústavu (institute)	0.47	tun (tons)	0.39
vládní (governmental)	0.46	prezident (president)	0.38

Table 4: 5 closest words to "Británie (Britain)" in Czech.

Word	Cos.	Word	Cos.
w2v (static)		CNN1, random	
mining	0.41	based	0.24
cents	0.39	tird	0.21
opec	0.38	statistics	0.18
gold	0.34	amount	0.16
quarterly	0.33	october	0.16
CNN2, random		CNN2, w2v trainable	
line	0.19	intervention	0.33
accord	0.19	october	0.33
estimates	0.18	adding	0.31
share	0.18	investment	0.30
same	0.16	ministers	0.29

Table 5: Closest words to "Britain" in English.

on English embeddings shows Table 5. The upper part compares the word2vec (static) embeddings with the vectors learned by CNN1. The lower part then compares the randomly initialized embeddings learned by CNN2 with vectors that were initialized by word2vec and progressively adapted during the training of CNN2.

Table 4 shows that all similarity values except CNN1 values are comparable. The CNN1 vectors differ significantly from the word2vec ones regarding the similarity values. We can observe similar results for both variants learned by CNN2.

From the point of view of the semantic similarity of words, this experiment shows, that the lists of words differ and there is just only few common ones. On the other hand, the majority of words are for all cases really semantically close and related to the word Britain.

Table 5 shows the same experiment carried out with the English word2vec. There is again higher difference between word2vec and CNN1 vectors. However, the variants of CNN2 vectors differ more significantly than in the case of Czech embeddings. This experiment shows, that the lists of words differ as in the previous case and that there is only few common ones.

5 Conclusions and Future Work

This paper analyzed and evaluated word embeddings in convolutional neural networks for representation of longer texts in multi-label classification task. Three different CNNs topologies were used. The experiments were realized on Czech ČTK and English Reuters-21578 corpora.

We compared the results of word2vec static and trainable embeddings with randomly initialized word vectors. We concluded that initialization does not play an important role for multi-label document classification in both languages. However, learning of word vectors is crucial to obtain good classification score. This behavior should be justified by a sufficient amount of the relatively long documents. This fact improves the convergence of our models during training and also decreases the impact of the particular words for the whole classification. We further analyzed both word2vec static and learned embeddings from the semantic point of view and discussed the results. We can conclude that although the semantically closest words differ significantly, they are all close from the semantic point of view.

In future work, we would like to study the impact of document length to the classification results with randomly initialized embeddings and pre-trained word vectors. We could also have used different network topologies to further improve the performance of document classification. A subsequent analysis of the behavior of the embeddings in these nets will be also realized.

Acknowledgments

This work was supported by the project LO1506 of the Czech Ministry of Education, Youth and Sports.

References

James Bergstra, Olivier Breuleux, Frédéric Bastien, Pascal Lamblin, Razvan Pascanu, Guillaume Desjardins, Joseph Turian, David Warde-Farley, and Yoshua Bengio. 2010. Theano: a cpu and gpu math expression compiler. In *Proceedings of the Python for scientific computing conference (SciPy)*. Austin, TX, volume 4, page 3.

Franois Chollet. 2015. keras. `https://github.com/fchollet/keras`.

Ronan Collobert, Jason Weston, Léon Bottou, Michael Karlen, Koray Kavukcuoglu, and Pavel Kuksa. 2011. Natural language processing (almost) from scratch. *The Journal of Machine Learning Research* 12:2493–2537.

Yoon Kim. 2014. Convolutional neural networks for sentence classification. *arXiv preprint arXiv:1408.5882* .

Diederik Kingma and Jimmy Ba. 2014. Adam: A method for stochastic optimization. *arXiv preprint arXiv:1412.6980* .

Gakuto Kurata, Bing Xiang, and Bowen Zhou. 2016. Improved neural network-based multi-label classification with better initialization leveraging label co-occurrence. In *Proceedings of NAACL-HLT*. pages 521–526.

Siwei Lai, Liheng Xu, Kang Liu, and Jun Zhao. 2015. Recurrent convolutional neural networks for text classification .

Ladislav Lenc and Pavel Král. 2017. Deep neural networks for Czech multi-label document classification. *CoRR* abs/1701.03849. http://arxiv.org/abs/1701.03849.

L. Manevitz and M. Yousef. 2007. One-class document classification via neural networks. *Neurocomputing* 70(7-9):1466–1481. https://doi.org/10.1016/j.neucom.2006.05.013.

Tomas Mikolov, Kai Chen, Greg Corrado, and Jeffrey Dean. 2013a. Efficient estimation of word representations in vector space. In *Proceedings of Workshop at ICLR*.

Tomas Mikolov, Ilya Sutskever, Kai Chen, Greg S Corrado, and Jeff Dean. 2013b. Distributed representations of words and phrases and their compositionality. In *Advances in neural information processing systems*. pages 3111–3119.

Jinseok Nam, Jungi Kim, Eneldo Loza Mencía, Iryna Gurevych, and Johannes Fürnkranz. 2014. Large-scale multi-label text classification - revisiting neural networks. In *Joint European Conference on Machine Learning and Knowledge Discovery in Databases*. Springer, pages 437–452.

Jeffrey Pennington, Richard Socher, and Christopher Manning. 2014. Glove: Global vectors for word representation. In *Proceedings of the 2014 Conference on Empirical Methods in Natural Language Processing (EMNLP)*. Association for Computational Linguistics, Doha, Qatar, pages 1532–1543. http://www.aclweb.org/anthology/D14-1162.

DMW Powers. 2011. Evaluation: From precision, recall and f-measure to roc., informedness, markedness & correlation. *Journal of Machine Learning Technologies* 2(1):37–63.

Nitish Srivastava, Geoffrey E Hinton, Alex Krizhevsky, Ilya Sutskever, and Ruslan Salakhutdinov. 2014. Dropout: a simple way to prevent neural networks from overfitting. *Journal of Machine Learning Research* 15(1):1929–1958.

Lukáš Svoboda and Tomávs Brychcín. 2016. New word analogy corpus for exploring embeddings of czech words. *CoRR* abs/1608.00789. http://arxiv.org/abs/1608.00789.

Grigorios Tsoumakas and Ioannis Katakis. 2006. Multi-label classification: An overview. *International Journal of Data Warehousing and Mining* 3(3).

Yiming Yang and Siddharth Gopal. 2012. Multilabel classification with meta-level features in a learning-to-rank framework. *Machine Learning* 88(1-2):47–68.

Min-Ling Zhang and Zhi-Hua Zhou. 2006. Multilabel neural networks with applications to functional genomics and text categorization. *Knowledge and Data Engineering, IEEE Transactions on* 18(10):1338–1351.

Gender Prediction for Chinese Social Media Data

Wen Li
Department of Linguistics
Indiana University
Bloomington, IN, USA
wl9@indiana.edu

Markus Dickinson
Department of Linguistics
Indiana University
Bloomington, IN, USA
md7@indiana.edu

Abstract

Social media provides users a platform to publish messages and socialize with others, and microblogs have gained more users than ever in recent years. With such usage, user profiling is a popular task in computational linguistics and text mining. Different approaches have been used to predict users' gender, age, and other information, but most of this work has been done on English and other Western languages. The goal of this project is to predict the gender of users based on their posts on Weibo, a Chinese micro-blogging platform. Given issues in Chinese word segmentation, we explore character and word n-grams as features for this task, as well as using character and word embeddings for classification. Given how the data is extracted, we approach the task on a per-post basis, and we show the difficulties of the task for both humans and computers. Nonetheless, we present encouraging results and point to future improvements.

1 Introduction and Motivation

Author profiling, the task of determining some demographic property of a language user (gender, age, personality, etc.), has become a significant area within NLP and text mining, with many practical applications (see, e.g., Rangel et al., 2015), and it links to a bevy of related subfields (authorship attribution, native language identification, sentiment analysis, etc.) (cf. Argamon et al., 2009), in that they share in common methods and features (e.g., lexica, n-grams). Despite obtaining promising results in certain tasks with certain data sets (e.g., Schler et al., 2006), the challenges in author profiling increase as the text gets

shorter and noisier, as with social media data, given that there seem to be fewer and less reliable indicators of a demographic trait (e.g., Zhang and Zhang, 2010; Burger et al., 2011), in addition to the fact that many users produce language atypical of their demographic (Bamman et al., 2014; Nguyen et al., 2014). This problem is potentially compounded when examining languages such as Chinese, where: a) the definition of a word is problematic (Sproat et al., 1996); b) the collection of data with links to individual users is challenging, since Weibo (see below) requires users' authorization before data collection; and c) there has been no published work (we are aware of) on this task, most work focusing on English and to some extent other Western languages (Rangel et al., 2015; Nguyen et al., 2013).

We set as our first step that of predicting the gender of users on Weibo[1]—the Twitter analogue in China—based on an individual post. This task reveals two sub-goals. First, we want to identify areas of development in moving to Chinese social media data. Having no work on identifying gender or other author characteristics in Chinese is a pity, as previous work has debated the importance of character-based n-grams vs. word-based n-grams (cf., e.g., Sapkota et al., 2015), and Chinese, with greater difficulty in word segmentation, is an excellent proving ground for such issues. Indeed, although there are many Chinese syntactic issues to deal with (e.g., the nominal classification system), we focus our attention on the impact of different kinds of n-gram models. This is particularly relevant in Chinese as characters in the logographic (meaning-based) Chinese writing system mean something different than characters in alphabetic systems, and with a larger number of characters there will be sparser n-grams. As a side note,

---

[1]http://weibo.com

438

Proceedings of Recent Advances in Natural Language Processing, pages 438–445,
Varna, Bulgaria, Sep 4–6 2017.

there is work utilizing Weibo for word segmentation (e.g., Zhang et al., 2013) and sentiment analysis (e.g., Zhou, 2015); with our work we pave the way for future connections by exploring the impact of data filtering, preprocessing, and n-gram features on system performance.

A second sub-goal is to identify specific difficulties and specific opportunities with a per-post (vs. per-user) method of classification, as this means we have very little data with which to work, as little as a few words (see section 2). Burger et al. (2011) note that their "tweet text classifier's accuracy increases as the number of tweets from the user increases," and Nguyen et al. (2014) point out cases where features associated with one gender are found in tweets of the opposite gender. We assess how accurate such a classifier can be, for humans or machines, and the impact of the choice of features on classification accuracy. Indeed, we find automatic classification accuracy no higher than 63% on this per-post task (section 4.1)—also true for human accuracy (section 4.3)—and our work suggests that per-post classification should focus on the identification of posts which can be reliably classified rather than on improving overall accuracy (sections 4.2 and 4.4).

Given short messages and associated data sparsity, we take the additional step of investigating the role that semantic similarity methods can have in classification. The popularity of word2vec in recent years comes from the weakness of tradiional bag-of-words model: words are represented as isolated indices, and the vectors to represent a document are often sparse (Mikolov et al., 2013). As mentioned in Mikolov et al. (2013), word2vec captures some syntactic regularities and semantic similarities. Some research is starting to use word2vec for text classification of Chinese texts, especially for sentiment analysis (Su et al., 2014; Bai et al., 2014; Zhang et al., 2015), and we would like to explore the use of word2vec techniques in the gender classification task. Because of the attributes of Chinese characters, the "word" vectors could be built based on characters or words. While most approaches train the vectors based on Chinese words, with word segmentation done beforehand, there is also research using character representations (Sun et al., 2014). However, the difference between character and word vectors in Chinese is not clear, and no one has conducted a detailed comparison between them for text classifi-

cation. We would thus like to help fill this gap.

Users are required to specify their gender on Weibo, giving good experimental data (section 2), but making the task less immediately useful.[2] The task is still worth pursuing because the insights are applicable for predicting other demographics (e.g., age) and for (current or future) data beyond Weibo.

2 Data

Weibo (also known as Sina Weibo) is a Chinese microblogging site, with a market penetration similar to the United States' Twitter. According to Wikipedia,[3] as of the third quarter of 2015, Weibo has 222 million subscribers and 100 million daily users. About 100 million messages are posted each day on Weibo.

Weibo implements many features from Twitter. A user may post with a 140-character limit, mention or talk to other people using `@UserName` formatting, add hashtags with `#HashName#` formatting, follow other users to make their posts appear in one's own timeline, re-post with `//@UserName` similar to Twitter's retweet function `RT @UserName`, and select posts for one's favorites list. The users of Weibo include Asian celebrities, movie stars, singers, famous business and media figures, as well as some famous foreign individuals and organizations; like Twitter, Sina Weibo has a verification program for known people and organizations.

URLs are automatically shortened using the domain name `t.cn` like Twitter's `t.co`. Official and third-party applications make users able to access Sina Weibo from other websites or platforms. In January 2016, Sina Weibo decided to remove the 140-character limit for any original posts, and users were thereby allowed to post with up to 2000 characters, while the 140-character limit was still applicable to re-posts and comments.

2.1 Collection

We collected random Weibo users' posts in February and March 2015, using the Weibo developer API.[4] The API allows one to get 200 recent public posts without user authorization. Since short lag times might lead to duplicate documents, we

---

[2]Users may of course falsely report their gender, leaving some noise in the data; an accurate classifier may in the long run help pinpoint such misreporting.

[3]`https://en.wikipedia.org/wiki/Sina_Weibo`

[4]`http://open.weibo.com`

called the API every three minutes. Thus, the collected data are organized by time (i.e., per-post), not by user.

2.2 Filtering

We filter posts from users with more than 500,000 followers, since these accounts are often maintained by organizations or public relations teams (e.g., for celebrities), which produce very different contents than for ordinary users. We also try to filter posts containing headline news, usually starting with " 【".

Some posts on Weibo are written in languages other than Chinese, so we only keep posts with at least 70% Chinese characters in them (punctuation counting as valid Chinese here).

There are some additional challenging posts to filter, namely those automatically generated by third-party applications or ones trying to sell products. Such formulaic posts often result in highly similar contents to each other, overweighting terms, and the notion of user demographics is unclear for them. After some initial examination, we remove these posts using keywords and keyphrases such as "我参加了 (I participated in)" and "请点击 (please click on)". It should be noted, however, that some of the words and phrases used for filtering may occur in posts actually written by users, so we run some risk of overfiltering.

2.3 Summary

After filtering, we use 50,000 posts (2.2 million characters) for classification: 45,000 as training data, 5,000 as test data. 28,901 (57.8%) of the posts are written by female users, 21,099 (42.2%) by males. The average post length is 42 characters. We use 100,000 random posts to train character and word vectors.

3 Methods

3.1 Preprocessing

For preprocessing, we first normalize the data for obtaining more reliable n-grams, by: a) removing all the URLs; and b) replacing Weibo-exclusive emoticons and emojis with a single character that exists nowhere else in the data. In initial experiment, we tried to keep the top 50 most frequent emoticons and emojis, replacing all the others, which resulted in a 0.3% decrease in accuracy.

Secondly, to test different kinds of features, we segment the data into words, using the Stan-

	Char.	Word
Uni.	6,463	81,280
Bi.	333,748	517,639
Tri.	987,781	877,571
Total	1,327,992	1,476,490

Table 1: Number of n-grams in training

ford Chinese Word Segmenter (Tseng et al., 2005). Although developed for well-edited data, hand-examination reveals no major issues for posts; importantly, the segmenter is at least consistent across posts.

3.2 Features

3.2.1 n-gram features

We first focus on features that allow us to explore the impact of segmentation. Starting with **character-based n-grams**, we first extract all unigrams, bigrams, and trigrams in the training data; numbers are in Table 1 for the cleaned data.

We then use information gain (Liu et al., 2014) to select the top 10,000 n-grams, from the set of: a) unigrams ($Uni.$),[5] b) bigrams ($Bi.$), c) trigrams ($Tri.$), d) unigrams and bigrams ($Uni.+Bi.$), or e) all three (All). For condition d (for the cleaned data), among the 10,000 features, there are 1,122 unigrams and 8,878 bigrams; for condition e, there are 842 unigrams, 4,698 bigrams, and 4,460 trigrams.

We then do the same for the **word-based n-grams**; for condition d, we obtain 3,298 unigrams and 6,702 bigrams; for condition e, there are 2,526 unigrams, 4,501 bigrams, and 2,973 trigrams. The features are binary, reflecting n-gram presence/absence.

We currently do not mix character and word-based n-grams, to mitigate the effect of feature overlap in determining utility. Taking an example from English, the character trigram *the* overlaps with word unigrams *the* and *them*, among others. Future work could explore mixing.

3.2.2 Word embeddings

We additionally focus on generalizing beyond simple characters and words by using word vectors; as mentioned in section 2.3, we train the word/character vectors on 100,000 posts. While

---

[5]Since there are fewer than 10,000 character unigrams, we use all 6,643 of them.

training character vectors does not require any pre-processing, word vectors require Chinese word segmentation. To obtain a feature vector for an entire post, we add up the word/character vectors according to the words/characters occurring in a Weibo post and divide the sum by the number of words/characters occurring in the post.

We use Gensim[6] to train our vectors. There are a number of parameters available, and for some of the parameters, there is no intuitive clue of what values would better work for this task. Since we could not try all the combinations exhaustively, in this project we train both continuous bag-of-words (*CBOW*) and skip-gram (*SG*) models; keep the context window size as 5; set the minimum frequency of a word/character as 3; and vary dimensions among *100d*, *200d*, and *500d*. All other parameters are as default settings. For word vectors, there are 40,561 distinct words in the vocabulary; for character vectors, there are 6,581 character types in the vocabulary.

3.3 Classifiers

We use different classifiers implemented by `scikit-learn` (Pedregosa et al., 2011). For classification with n-gram features, we initially employed Multinomial Naive Bayes (MNB), Support Vector Machine (SVM), and Logistic Regression, and found differences that were less than 0.5% in accuracy, with MNB performing the best. We then decide to use MNB for the n-gram experiments, setting α to 0.01.

Since MNB does not work with `word2vec` features—as some values are negative in the feature vector—we use Random Forest for classification with character/word vectors.

4 Evaluation

4.1 Results

4.1.1 Character-based n-grams

Noisy data We first run a MNB classifier with default settings on partly filtered data, namely before using keyword filtering (section 2.2), using character-based unigrams, bigrams, and trigrams. This achieves an overall accuracy of 63.2%; Table 2 shows precision and recall values for the genders. Note that the classifier guesses female 3,085 times and male 1,915.

The results should be taken with a grain of salt, as much of the noisy data has repeated patterns in

[6]https://radimrehurek.com/gensim/index.html

	Acc	Prec	Rec
Female	n/a	66.7	71.6
Male	n/a	57.4	51.7
Avg.	63.2	62.8	63.2

Table 2: Results on noisy data (%), with (10,000) character-based n-grams (*All* model): Test: 2,875 F, 2,125 M.

it; for example, females are more likely to have "我参加了 (I participated in)", but these come from auto-generated messages after participating in, e.g., contests and events that have a change to win some prizes, and males are more likely to have "请点击 (please click on)", but these seem largely to be advertisements.

Cleaned data Results of character n-gram models on cleaned data are given in the left side of Table 3. The best model uses *All* n-gram types, with an overall accuracy of 62.8% and a classifier distribution of 3,289 females and 1,711 males. Individually, unigrams perform better than bigrams or trigrams. Comparing *All* to *Uni.*, some improvement comes from the guessing of males.

4.1.2 Word-based n-grams

The better guessing of females, likely due to more salient features for females (see section 4.4), is repeated with word-based n-grams, as in the right side of Table 3. Overall accuracy of the *All* model is about the same as with character-based n-grams, 62.8%, but with more bias towards females: 3,400 female guesses vs. 1,600 male.

4.1.3 Word embeddings

The accuracy of gender classification using `word2vec` with different settings is shown in the bottom part of Table 3. We can see that in general, word vectors perform better than character vectors, and the *CBOW* model works better than the *SG* model for Chinese data. For the *CBOW* model, increasing the dimension helps accuracy, while the *SG* model performs better with lower dimension vectors.

We plan to explore better `word2vec` training data and different ways of incorporating this information, in addition to a wider range of features. It seems, however, that all of our models are hitting a ceiling, accuracy-wise, leading us to pursue a different approach to the problem.

	Char.					Word				
		Female		Male			Female		Male	
Model	Acc	Prec	Rec	Prec	Rec	Acc	Prec	Rec	Prec	Rec
Uni.	62.0	65.2	74.6	55.6	44.3	61.6	65.3	72.9	54.8	45.9
Bi.	61.7	65.1	74.0	55.0	44.5	61.4	63.8	78.2	55.5	38.0
Tri.	60.7	62.6	81.2	55.0	32.1	60.6	61.5	86.6	56.3	24.3
Uni.+Bi.	62.1	65.9	72.5	55.3	47.5	62.6	65.9	74.1	56.2	46.5
All	**62.8**	66.1	74.5	56.6	46.5	**62.8**	65.6	76.4	57.0	43.7
CBOW_100d	60.9	63.1	78.2	55.2	37.0	62.2	64.1	79.2	57.3	38.7
CBOW_200d	61.0	63.2	78.0	55.3	37.5	62.0	64.1	78.7	56.8	38.9
CBOW_500d	61.2	63.0	80.8	56.1	35.3	**62.9**	64.6	79.9	58.6	39.5
SG_100d	60.8	63.2	77.2	54.9	38.2	62.6	64.4	79.8	58.1	38.8
SG_200d	61.2	63.3	78.7	55.9	37.1	62.5	64.3	79.5	57.8	38.8
SG_500d	60.9	62.8	80.1	55.8	34.6	61.7	63.8	79.1	56.5	37.7

Table 3: Results on cleaned data (%), with n-gram features and `word2vec` features. Training: 45k; Test: 5k.

4.2 More Accurate Cases

Confidence of prediction With very little text, we can use additional information to identify cases for which the classifier is more accurate. Because the classifier assigns a score between 0 (female) and 1 (male), our definition of **confidence** corresponds to the distance from the midpoint (0.5), which ranges from 0.0 to 0.5. A confidence of 0.29, for example, means that the classifier assigned a score of either 0.21 or 0.79.

Post length Within the limit of 140 (Chinese) characters, the Weibo post lengths vary greatly. While a shorter post may not contain enough information for the classifier to make a correct prediction, a longer post is more likely to be a paragraph of famous quotes or a short story, confusing the classifier due to the lack of gender indicators. With regard to character-based and word-based settings, we define the **length of a post** as the number of characters or words, respectively.

Quartiles (Q_1, Q_2, Q_3) of confidence and length for character-based and word-based *All* model are shown in Table 4, with accuracies for the corresponding intervals in Table 5. For example, for character-based confidence, we report an accuracy of 61.2% for confidences between Q_1 (0.29) and Q_2 (0.47), i.e., either in the range (0.03, 0.21) or (0.79, 0.97). By narrowing in on high-confidence cases or posts with sufficient information (i.e., 16–40 words), we can obtain accuracy around 70%. Running the same experiments with `word2vec` features displayed the same trends.

	Confidence		Length	
	Char.	Word	Char.	Word
Q_1	0.2893	0.2357	13.0	9.0
Q_2	0.4726	0.4352	25.0	16.0
Q_3	0.4998	0.4986	62.0	40.0

Table 4: Quartiles for confidence/length of *All* model.

	Confidence		Length	
Interval	Char.	Word	Char.	Word
$\leq Q_1$	57.2	54.3	57.0	60.4
$(Q_1, Q_2]$	61.2	60.5	68.4	63.2
$(Q_2, Q_3]$	63.2	67.8	**68.7**	**70.1**
$> Q_3$	**69.2**	**68.6**	57.3	57.4

Table 5: Accuracy (%) for confidence/length quartiles of *All* model.

4.3 Human Judgment

We asked four people to independently guess the gender of 200 random Weibo posts. The accuracies of two Weibo users are 64.0% (*user_M*) and 59.5% (*user_F*), while the two people who do not use Weibo obtain accuracies of 58.5% (*non_user_F*) and 55.5% (*non_user_M*). For comparison, the character-based, all n-gram classifier achieves an accuracy of 64.5% on the same 200 posts. The detailed results are shown in Table 6.

Not only are the humans no better than automatic classification, but we observe the same tendency of predicting more females than males, with the humans also better at recognizing females than

	Acc	Female		Male	
		Prec	Rec	Prec	Rec
user_M	64.0	65.7	78.3	60.3	44.7
user_F	59.5	63.3	70.4	52.8	44.7
non_user_M	55.0	61.5	58.3	47.3	50.6
non_user_F	58.5	64.0	63.5	51.2	51.8

Table 6: Human judgment results (%) for Weibo (*M/F* = male/female annotator)

males.

4.4 Discussion

We have seen an overall per-post accuracy of approximately 62.8%. Interestingly, this is true regardless of whether it is a model of character-based or word-based n-grams, despite relying on an automatic segmenter. The unigram models perform better individually than either the bigram or trigram models, likely due to fewer issues with sparsity—particularly important for individual posts. Relying on confidence or length can boost accuracy, up to nearly 70%. It is important to note that higher reported performances in previous work deal with per-user classification tasks; more comparably, Burger et al. (2011) report an accuracy of around 64% for per-tweet (per-post) gender classification. Some researchers mentioned using ensemble classifiers to improve the accuracy for text classification tasks (Liu et al., 2016; Li and Zou, 2017), which could be future work for this gender prediction task.

Given that humans also perform with around 60% accuracy, one tentative conclusion is that users only post like their gender about 60% of the time. If true, this may be key for moving from per-post classification to a per-user aggregation.

Additionally, these results support the intuition that it is going to be virtually impossible to correctly classify every post. The quest for identifying posts which can be more accurately classified, as in section 4.2, becomes more important: instead of trying to boost overall accuracy—which various feature settings have failed to do—the important per-post question may be, can one reliably classify some significant portion of the data and identify such a portion automatically? This idea of not attempting to classify every post may thus be useful for a per-user classification, as unreliable posts could distract from an overall trend.

Most important features Classification is better for females than males: as with some previous work (e.g., Burger et al., 2011), this seems attributable to more salient features in female posts. Our MNB classifier does not provide the most important features used in classification, but we use information gain to examine the top 300 features (both character-based and word-based) by hand.

Among the top 40 features, most of them are punctuation marks or repeated characters/emoticons indicating femaleness, such as "！！", "～", "啊啊啊 (ah ah ah)", "嘤嘤嘤 (*sound of sobbing*)", "哈哈哈 (ha ha ha)". Dozens of content words/phrases are in the top 300, such as "开学 (school starts)", "头发 (hair)", "我妈 (my mom)", "姐姐 (sister)", "不开心 (unhappy)", etc. We also observe the names of "鹿晗 (Lu Han)", "王俊凯 (Wang Junkai)", and "TFBOYS" in the list, which indicates the comprehensive popularity of these younger stars on Weibo, especially among female users. Named entity classification may be of future help.

One issue in determining important features from a small set of posts is how to handle multiple instances of the same n-gram within the same file. One may wish to count instances or, alternatively, to normalize repetitive characters or words into single instances. Initial results of incorporating n-gram counts show a slight drop in performance (cf., e.g., Burger et al., 2011).

5 Summary and Outlook

We have set about predicting the gender of users based on their posts on the Chinese micro-blogging platform Weibo. Given issues in Chinese word segmentation, we have explored character and word n-grams as features for this task, as well as using character and word embeddings for classification, and we have shown that all models perform near the same level. With humans performing with the same accuracy on a per-post basis, we have seen a need to explore the identification of high-confidence classification cases. In short, adapting techniques from English to Chinese for identifying gender on social media does not generally seem problematic, as character and word n-gram models seem equally effective. Classifying on a per-post basis, however, requires much more investigation, as well as using the information to move to per-user models.

For short posts, we need to explore ways of linking similar content across lexical variation, such as by incorporating distributional semantic representations (e.g., Ji and Eisenstein, 2013) or paraphrase identification (e.g., Preoțiuc-Pietro et al., 2016). Using aggregate features—post length, presence of sentence-ending particles, emoticon categories, etc.—should also help in this, as well as more data cleaning (e.g., removal of duplicate posts).

References

S. Argamon, M. Koppel, J. Pennebaker, and J. Schler. 2009. Automatically profiling the author of an anonymous text. *Communications of the ACM* 52(2):119–123.

X. Bai, F. Chen, and S. Zhan. 2014. A study on sentiment computing and classification of sina weibo with word2vec. In *2014 IEEE International Congress on Big Data (pp. 358-363). IEEE*.

David Bamman, Jacob Eisenstein, and Tyler Schnoebelen. 2014. Gender identity and lexical variation in social media. *Journal of Sociolinguistics* 18(2):135–160.

John D. Burger, John Henderson, George Kim, and Guido Zarrella. 2011. Discriminating gender on twitter. In *Proceedings of the 2011 Conference on Empirical Methods in Natural Language Processing*. Edinburgh, Scotland, UK., pages 1301–1309.

Yangfeng Ji and Jacob Eisenstein. 2013. Discriminative improvements to distributional sentence similarity. In *Proceedings of Empirical Methods for Natural Language Processing (EMNLP)*. Seattle, WA, pages 891–896.

Wen Li and Liang Zou. 2017. Classifier Stacking for Native Language Identification. In *Proceedings of the 12th Workshop on Building Educational Applications Using NLP*. Association for Computational Linguistics, Copenhagen, Denmark.

Can Liu, Sandra Kübler, and Ning Yu. 2014. Feature feature selection for highly skewed sentiment analysis tasks. In *Proceedings of the Second Workshop on Natural Language Processing for Social Media (SocialNLP), pages 2–11, Dublin, Ireland*.

Can Liu, Wen Li, Bradford Demarest, Yue Chen, Sara Couture, Daniel Dakota, Nikita Haduong, Noah Kaufman, Andrew Lamont, Manan Pancholi, Kenneth Steimel, and Sandra Kübler. 2016. IUCL at SemEval-2016 Task 6: An Ensemble Model for Stance Detection in Twitter. In *Proceedings of SemEval-2016*. San Diego, California, pages 394–400.

Tomas Mikolov, Kai Chen, Greg Corrado, and Jeffrey Dean. 2013. Efficient estimation of word representations in vector space. In *arXiv preprint arXiv:1301.3781*.

Dong Nguyen, Rilana Gravel, Dolf Trieschnigg, and Theo Meder. 2013. "how old do you think i am?"; a study of language and age in twitter. In *Proceedings of the Seventh International AAAI Conference on Weblogs and Social Media*. AAAI Press, Palo Alto, CA.

Dong Nguyen, Dolf Trieschnigg, A. Seza Doğruöz, Rilana Gravel, Mariet Theune, Theo Meder, and Franciska De Jong. 2014. Why gender and age prediction from tweets is hard: Lessons from a crowdsourcing experiment. In *Proceedings of COLING*

2014, the 25th International Conference on Computational Linguistics: Technical Papers. Dublin, Ireland, pages 1950–1961.

F. Pedregosa, G. Varoquaux, A. Gramfort, V. Michel, B. Thirion, O. Grisel, M. Blondel, P. Prettenhofer, R. Weiss, V. Dubourg, J. Vanderplas, A. Passos, D. Cournapeau, M. Brucher, M. Perrot, and E. Duchesnay. 2011. Scikit-learn: Machine learning in Python. *Journal of Machine Learning Research* 12:2825–2830.

Daniel Preoţiuc-Pietro, Wei Xu, and Lyle Ungar. 2016. Discovering user attribute stylistic differences via paraphrasing. In *Proceedings of AAAI 2016*.

Francisco Rangel, Fabio Celli, Paolo Rosso, Martin Pottast, Benno Stein, and Walter Daelemans. 2015. Overview of the 3rd author profiling task at pan 2015. In Linda Cappelato, Nicola Ferro, Gareth Jones, and Eric San Juan, editors, *CLEF 2015 Labs and Workshops, Notebook Papers*. Toulouse, France, CEUR Workshop Proceedings.

Upendra Sapkota, Steven Bethard, Manuel Montes, and Thamar Solorio. 2015. Not all character n-grams are created equal: A study in authorship attribution. In *Proceedings of the 2015 Conference of the North American Chapter of the Association for Computational Linguistics: Human Language Technologies*. Denver, CO, pages 93–102.

J. Schler, Moshe Koppel, S. Argamon, and J. Pennebaker. 2006. Effects of age and gender on blogging. In *Proceedings of the AAAI Spring Symposium on Computational Approaches for Analyzing Weblogs*.

Richard Sproat, William Gale, Chilin Shih, and Nancy Chang. 1996. A stochastic finite-state word-segmentation algorithm for chinese. In *Computational linguistics 22, no. 3 (1996): 377-404*.

Z. Su, H. Xu, D. Zhang, and Y. Xu. 2014. Chinese sentiment classification using a neural network tool — word2vec. In *Multisensor Fusion and Information Integration for Intelligent Systems (MFI), 2014 International Conference on (pp. 1-6). IEEE*.

Y. Sun, L. Lin, N. Yang, Z. Ji, and X. Wang. 2014. Radical-enhanced chinese character embedding. In *International Conference on Neural Information Processing (pp. 279-286). Springer International Publishing*.

Huihsin Tseng, Pichuan Chang, Galen Andrew, Daniel Jurafsky, and Christopher Manning. 2005. A conditional random field word segmenter. In *Fourth SIGHAN Workshop on Chinese Language Processing*.

Cathy Zhang and Pengyu Zhang. 2010. Predicting gender from blog posts. Technical report, University of Massachusetts, Amherst.

D. Zhang, H. Xu, Z. Su, and Y. Xu. 2015. Chinese comments sentiment classification based on word2vec and svm perf. *Expert Systems with Applications* 42(4):1857–1863.

Longkai Zhang, Li Li, Zhengyan He, Houfeng Wang, and Ni Sun. 2013. Improving chinese word segmentation on micro-blog using rich punctuations. In *ACL (2), pp. 177-182*.

Hongzhao Zhou. 2015. Rule-based weibo messages sentiment polarity classification towards given topics. In *ACL-IJCNLP 2015 (2015): 149*.

A Statistical Machine Translation Model with Forest-to-Tree Algorithm for Semantic Parsing

Zhihua Liao
College of Teacher Education
Center for Faculty Development
Hunan Normal University
Changsha, China
cfd@hunnu.edu.cn

Yan Xie
English Department
Foreign Studies College
Hunan Normal University
Changsha, China
xieyanhnnu@163.com

Abstract

In this paper, we propose a novel supervised model for parsing natural language sentences into their formal semantic representations. This model treats sentence-to-λ-logical expression conversion within the framework of the statistical machine translation with forest-to-tree algorithm. To make this work, we transform the λ-logical expression structure into a form suitable for the mechanics of statistical machine translation and useful for modeling. We show that our model is able to yield new state-of-the-art results on both standard datasets with simple features.

1 Introduction

Semantic parsers convert natural language *(NL)* sentences to logical forms *(LFs)* through a meaning representation language *(MRL)*. Recent research has focused on learning such parsers directly from corpora made up of sentences paired with logical meaning representations (Artzi and Zettlemoyer, 2011, 2013; Liao and Zhang, 2013; Liao et al., 2015b,a; Lu et al., 2008; Lu and Ng, 2011; Krishnamurthy, 2016; Kwiatkowski et al., 2010, 2011; Zettlemoyer and Collins, 2005, 2007, 2009). And its goal is to learn a grammar that can map new, unseen sentences onto their corresponding meanings, or logical expressions.

While these algorithms usually work well on specific semantic formalisms, it is not clear how well they could be applied to a different semantic formalism. In this paper, we propose a novel supervised approach to learn semantic parsing task using the framework of the statistical machine translation with forest-to-tree algorithm. This method integrates both lexical acquisition and surface realization in a single framework. In-spired by the probabilistic forest-to-string generation algorithm (Lu and Ng, 2011) and the work of Wong and Mooney (2006; 2007a; 2007b) and Wong (2007) that learn for semantic parsing with statistical machine translation, our semantic parsing framework consists of two main components. Firstly it contains a lexical acquisition component, which is based on phrase alignments between natural language sentences and linearized semantic parses, given by an off-the-shelf phrase alignment model trained on a set of training examples. The extracted transformation rules form a synchronous context free grammar (SCFG), for which a probabilistic model is learned to resolve parse ambiguity. The second component is to estimate the parameters of a probabilistic model. The parametric models are based on maximum-entropy. The probabilistic model is trained on the same set of training examples in an unsupervised manner.

This paper is structured as follows. Section 2 describes how we build the framework of the statistical machine translation with forest-to-tree algorithm to develop a semantic parser, and Section 3 discusses the decoder. Then Section 4 presents our experiments and reports the results. Finally, we make the conclusion in Section 5.

2 The Semantic Parsing Model

Now we present the algorithm for semantic parsing, which translates NL sentences into LFs using a reduction-based λ-SCFG. It is based on an extended version of a reduction-based SCFG (Lu and Ng, 2011). Given a set of training sentences paired with their correct logical forms, the main learning task is to induce a set of reduction-based λ-SCFG rules, which we call a lexicon, a probabilistic model for derivations. A lexicon defines the set of derivations that are possible, so the induction of probabilistic model first requires a lex-

Proceedings of Recent Advances in Natural Language Processing, pages 446–451,
Varna, Bulgaria, Sep 4–6 2017.

icon. Therefore, the learning task can be separated into two sub-tasks:(1) the induction of a lexicon;(2) the induction of a probabilistic model - maximum-entropy model.

2.1 Lexical Acquistion

We introduce the grammar first. Next, we present the generative model for the grammar induction to acquire the grammar rules.

Grammar: We use a weighted λ-SCFG. The grammar is defined as follows: $\tau \rightarrow \langle h_\omega, p_\lambda, \sim \rangle$ where τ is the type associated with the sequence h_ω consisting of natural language words intermixed with types and the λ-production p_λ. The symbol $\sim$ denotes the one-to-one correspondence between nonterminal occurrences in both h_ω and p_λ. Specially, the symbol $\hat{\sim}$ denotes the one-to-one correspondence between terminal occurrence in both $\hat{h}_\omega$ and $\hat{p}_\lambda$, where $\hat{h}_\omega$ is an NL phrase and $\hat{p}_\lambda$ is the LF translation of $\hat{h}_\omega$. Then we allow a maximum of two nonterminal symbols in each synchronous rule (Lu and Ng, 2011). This makes the grammar a binary λ-SCFG.

Grammar Induction: We adopt a generative model for λ-hybrid tree models the mapping from λ-sub-expressions to word sequences with a joint generative process, which Lu and Ng (2011) developed. Figure 1 describes the generative process for a sentence together with its corresponding λ-meaning tree. It results in a λ-hybrid tree[1] (Lu et al., 2008). Figure 2 gives a part of the example λ-hybrid tree. Here, grammar rules are extracted from the λ-hybrid trees. We can use the same grammar for both parsing and generation. Since a SCFG is fully symmetric with respect to both generated strings, the same chart for parsing can be easily adapted for efficient parsing. Now we show how to use the generative model for mapping natural language sentence to λ-expressions. At first, this model finds the Viterbi λ-hybrid trees for all training instances, based on the learned parameters of the generative λ-hybrid tree model. Next, the model extracts grammar rules on the top of these λ-hybrid trees. Specifically, we extract the following tree types of synchronous grammar rules. They are λ-hybrid sequence rules, subtree

---

[1]The internal nodes of the λ-hybrid tree are called λ-productions, which are building blocks of a λ-forest. Each λ-production in turn has at most two child λ-productions. A λ-production has the form $\tau_a : \pi_a \triangleleft \overline{\tau_b}$, where τ_a is the expected type after type evaluation of the terms to its right, π_a is a λ-expression, and $\overline{\tau_b}$ are types of the child λ-productions.

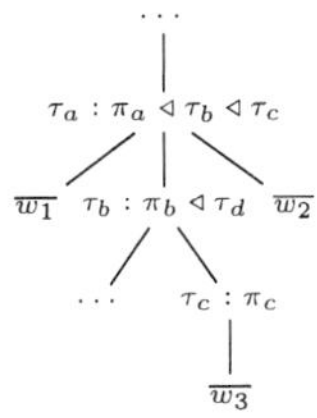

Figure 1: The joint generative process of both λ-meaning tree and its corresponding natural language sentence.

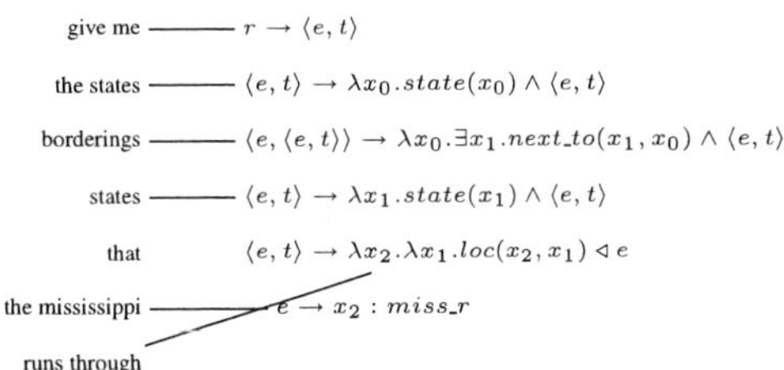

Figure 3: A phrase alignment based on a λ-hybrid tree.

rules and two-level λ-hybrid sequence rules. Here we give an example in Table 1.

1. λ-hybrid sequence rules: these conventional rules are constructed from one λ-production and its corresponding λ-hybrid sequence.

2. Subtree rules: these rules are constructed from a complete substree of the λ-hybrid tree. A mapping between a complete sub-expression and a contiguous sub-sentence can be acquired from each rule.

3. Two-level λ-hybrid sequence rules: these rules are constructed from a tree fragment with one of its grandchild subtrees being abstracted with its type only. These rules are constructed via substitution and reductions. We show how to construct two-level λ-hybrid sequence rules through substitution and reductions. Table 2 gives an example based on a tree fragment of the λ-hybrid tree in Figure 2.

To ground our discussion, we use the phrase alignment in Figure 2 as an example. To represent the logical form in Figure 3, we use its linearized parse — a list of MRL productions that generate the logical form in top-down and left-most order. Since the MRL grammar is unambiguous, every

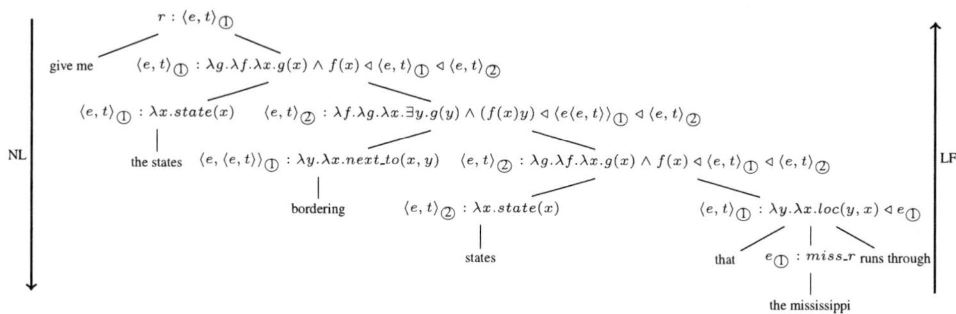

Figure 2: One example λ−hybrid tree for the sentence "give me the states bordering states that the mississippi runs through" together with its logical form "$\lambda x_0.state(x_0) \wedge \exists x_1.[loc(miss\_r, x_1) \wedge state(x_1) \wedge next\_to(x_1, x_0)]$".

type 1:	$\langle e, \langle e, t \rangle \to \langle$ bordering, $\lambda y.\lambda x.next\_to(x, y)\rangle$
	$\langle e, t \rangle \to \langle\langle e, t \rangle_{\textcircled{2}} \langle e, t \rangle_{\textcircled{1}}, \lambda g.\lambda y.\lambda x.g(x) \wedge f(x) \vartriangleleft \langle e, t \rangle_{\textcircled{1}} \vartriangleleft \langle e, t \rangle_{\textcircled{2}}\rangle$
type 2:	$\langle e, t \rangle \to \langle$ states that the mississippi runs through, $\lambda x.loc(miss\_r, x) \wedge state(x)\rangle$
	$\langle e, t \rangle \to \langle$ that the mississippi runs through, $\lambda x.loc(miss\_r, x)\rangle$
type 3:	$\langle e, t \rangle \to \langle$ the states bordering $\langle e, t \rangle_{\textcircled{1}}, \lambda f.\lambda x.state(x) \wedge \exists y.[f(y) \wedge next\_to(y, x)] \vartriangleleft \langle e, t \rangle_{\textcircled{1}}\rangle$
	$\langle e, t \rangle \to \langle$ states that $e_{\textcircled{1}}$ runs through, $\lambda y.\lambda x.loc(y, x) \wedge state(x) \vartriangleleft e_{\textcircled{1}}\rangle$

Table 1: Example synchronous rules that can be extracted from the λ−hybrid tree.

Tree fragment:	$\langle e, t \rangle_{\textcircled{2}} : \lambda g.\lambda f.\lambda x.g(x) \wedge f(x) \vartriangleleft \langle e, t \rangle_{\textcircled{1}} \vartriangleleft \langle e, t \rangle_{\textcircled{2}}$ $\langle e, t \rangle_{\textcircled{2}} : \lambda x.state(x)$ $\langle e, t \rangle_{\textcircled{1}} : \lambda y.\lambda x.loc(y, x) \vartriangleleft e_{\textcircled{1}}$ states that $e_{\textcircled{1}} : \cdots$ runs through
Source: Target:	states that $e_{\square}$ runs through $(\alpha-\text{conversion}) \Rightarrow \lambda y.\lambda x.loc(y, x) \wedge state(x) \vartriangleleft e_{\textcircled{1}}$ $(\beta-\text{conversion}) \Rightarrow \lambda y'.\lambda x.loc(y', x) \wedge state(x) \vartriangleleft e_{\textcircled{1}}$ $(\text{two } \beta-\text{conversion}) \Rightarrow \lambda y'.[\lambda f.\lambda x.loc(y', x) \wedge f(x) \vartriangleleft \lambda x.state(x)] \vartriangleleft e_{\textcircled{1}}$ $(\text{substitution}) \lambda y'.[\lambda y.\lambda f.\lambda x.y(x) \wedge f(x) \vartriangleleft [\lambda y.\lambda x.loc(y, x) \vartriangleleft y'] \vartriangleleft \lambda x.state(x)] \vartriangleleft e_{\textcircled{1}}$
Rule:	$\langle e, t \rangle \to \langle$ states that $e_{\textcircled{1}}$ runs through, $\lambda y.\lambda x.loc(y, x) \wedge state(x) \vartriangleleft e_{\textcircled{1}}\rangle$

Table 2: Construction of a two-level λ−hybrid sequence rule through substitution and reductions from a tree fragment. Note that the subtree rooted by $e_{\square} : miss\_r$ gets "abstracted" by its type e. The auxiliary variable y' of type e is thus introduced to facilitate the construction process.

logical form has a unique linearized parse. We assume the alignment to be n-to-1, where each word is linked to at most one MRL production. Basically, a reduction-based λ-SCFG grammar rule and a phrase alignment (Koehn et al., 2003) can be extracted from an λ-hybrid tree where logical variables are explicitly bound by λ-operators. And these grammar rules are extracted in a bottom-up manner, starting with MRL productions at the leaves of the λ-hybrid tree. Rule extraction continues in this manner until the root of the λ-hybrid tree is reached.

2.2　A Maximum-Entropy Model

Once a lexicon is acquired, the next task is to learn a probabilistic model for the semantic parser. We propose a maximum-entropy model that defines a conditional probability distribution over derivations d given the observed NL string w. Here, the maximum-entropy model is an exponential model:

$$P_\lambda(d|w) = \frac{1}{Z_\lambda(w)} \exp \sum_i \lambda_i f_i(d)$$

where the conditional probability, $P_\lambda(d|w)$, is proportional to the product of weights λ_i assigned to each feature f_i. A feature represents a certain characteristic of a derivation. In this case, the features are the number of times each transformation rule is used in a derivation. The function $Z_\lambda(w)$, called a partition function, is a normalizing factor such that the conditional probabilities sum to *one* over all derivations that yield w. A consequence is that feature weights, λ_i, can be any positive numbers. In a maximum-entropy model, generation of unseen words can be modeled using an extra feature, $f_*(d)$, whose value is the number of all words being skipped. Additional features that correspond to domain-specific word classes can be used for more fine-grained smoothing. The fact that these features may interact with each other is not a concern.

3　Decoding

Decoding of a maximum-entropy model can be done as following:

$$m^* = m(\arg \max_{d \in D(G|w)} P_\lambda(d|w))$$
$$= m(\arg \max_{d \in D(G|w)} \exp \sum_i \lambda_i f_i(d))$$
$$= m(\arg \max_{d \in D(G|w)} \sum_i \lambda_i f_i(d))$$

It can be done in the cubic time with respect to sentence length using the *Viterbi* algorithm. An Earley chart is used for keeping track of all derivations that are consistent with the input. The maximum conditional likelihood criterion is used for estimating a maximum-entropy model parameters λ_i. This means that the conditional likelihood of f_i given w is maximized. This criterion is chosen because it is much easier to work with, and it allows for a form of discriminative learning that focuses on separating good parses from bad ones. A Gaussian prior ($\sigma^2 = 1$) is used for regularizing the model. Since the gold-standard derivations are not available in the training data, correct derivations must be treated as hidden variables. Here, to find a set of parameters λ^* that locally maximize the conditional likelihood, we use a version of improved iterative scaling (IIS) coupled with EM which has been used for estimating probabilistic unification-based grammars. Unlike the fully-supervised case, the conditional likelihood is not concave with respect to λ, so the estimation algorithm is sensitive to initial parameters. To assume as little as possible, λ is initialized to zero. The estimation algorithm requires for a statistics that depend on all possible derivations for a sentence or a sentence-MR pair. While it is not feasible to enumerate all derivations, a variant of the Inside-Outside algorithm can be used for efficiently collecting the required statistics. Only rules that are used in the best parses for the training set are retained in the final lexicon, and all other rules are discarded　(Wong and Mooney, 2006, 2007b,a; Wong, 2007). This heuristic, commonly known as *Viterbi approximation*, is used to improve accuracy, when we assume that rules used in the best parses are the most accurate.

4　Experimental Setup

This section describes our experimental setup and comparisons of the result. We follow the setup of Zettlemoyer and Collins (2007) and Kwiatkowski et al. (2010; 2011), including datasets, and initialization as well as systems, as reviewed below. Finally, we report the experimental results.

Datasets: We evaluate on two benchmark closed-domain datasets. GeoQuery is made up of natural language queries to a database of geographical information, while ATIS contains natural language queries to a flight booking system (Zettlemoyer and Collins, 2007). The Geo880 dataset has been

(a) The Geo250 test set

system	Rec.	Pre.	F1
λ-WASP	75.6	91.8	82.9
UBL	81.8	83.5	82.6
FUBL	83.7	83.7	83.7
SMTFOREST2STRING	85.0	88.5	86.8

(b) The Geo880 test set

system	Rec.	Pre.	F1
ZC07	86.1	91.6	88.8
UBL	87.9	88.5	88.2
FUBL	88.6	88.6	88.6
SMTFOREST2STRING	89.6	91.8	90.7

Table 3: Performance of Exact Match between the different GeoQuery test sets.

system	Rec.	Pre.	F1
ZC07	74.4	87.3	80.4
UBL	65.6	67.1	66.3
FUBL	81.9	82.1	82.0
SMTFOREST2STRING	84.2	90.3	87.3

Table 4: Performance of Exact Match on the ATIS development set.

(a) Exact Match

system	Rec.	Pre.	F1
ZC07	84.6	85.8	85.2
UBL	71.4	72.1	71.7
FUBL	82.8	82.8	82.8
SMTFOREST2STRING	84.2	88.0	86.1

(b) Partial Match

system	Rec.	Pre.	F1
ZC07	96.7	95.1	95.9
UBL	78.2	98.2	87.1
FUBL	95.2	93.6	94.6
SMTFOREST2STRING	96.0	96.8	96.4

Table 5: Performance of Exact and Partial Matches on the ATIS test set.

split into a training set of 600 pairs and a test set of 280 ones. The Geo250 dataset is a subset of the Geo880, and is used 10-fold cross validation experiments with the same splits of this subset. The ATIS dataset is split into a 5000 example development set and a 450 example test set.

Initialization: For our algorithm learning, we use Och and Ney's (2003; 2004) GIZA++ implementation of IBM Model 5 for training word alignment models. IBM Models 1-4 are used for initializing the model parameters during training.

Systems: We compare this performance to those recently-published and directly-comparable results. For GeoQuery, they include the ZC07 (Zettlemoyer and Collins, 2007), λ-WASP (Wong and Mooney, 2007b; Wong, 2007), UBL (Kwiatkowski et al., 2010) and FUBL (Kwiatkowski et al., 2011). For ATIS, we report results from ZC07, UBL and FUBL.

Results: Tables 3-5 present all the results on the GeoQuery and ATIS domains. In all cases, our system achieves at state-of-the-art recall and precision when compared to directly comparable systems and it significantly outperforms ZC07, λ-WASP, UBL and FUBL. The major advantage of our algorithm over other three systems is that it does not require any prior knowledge of the NL syntax. Hence it is straightforward to apply this algorithm to other NL sentences for which training data is available.

5   Conclusion

This paper presents a novel supervised method for semantic parsing which adopts the framework of the statistical machine translation with forest-to-tree algorithm. The experiments on both benchmark datasets (i.e., GeoQuery and ATIS) show that our method achieves suitable performances.

Acknowledgments

We are grateful to the anonymous reviewers for their valuable feedback on an earlier version of this paper. This research was supported in part by the Foreign Language Teaching Research Project of National Universities (grant no.2015HN0009B) and the Social Science Foundation of Hunan Province for Youth Program (grant no.14YBA260).

References

Yoav Artzi and Luke Zettlemoyer. 2011. Bootstrapping semantic parsers from conversations. In *the Conference on Empirical Methods in Natural Language Processing (EMNLP)*.

Yoav Artzi and Luke Zettlemoyer. 2013. Weakly supervised learning of semantic parsers for mapping instructions to actions. *Transactions of the Association for Computational Linguistics (TACL)* .

Philipp Koehn, Franz Josef Och, and Daniel Marcu. 2003. Statistical phrase-based translation. In *the Conference of the North American Chapter of the Association for Computational Linguistics (NAACL-HLT)*.

Jayant Krishnamurthy. 2016. Probabilistic models for learning a semantic parser lexicon. In *the Conference of the North American Chapter of the Association for Computational Linguistics (NAACL-HLT)*.

Tom Kwiatkowski, Luke Zettlemoyer, Sharon Goldwater, and Mark Steedman. 2010. Inducing probabilistic ccg grammars from logical form with higher-order unification. In *the Conference on Empirical Methods in Natural Language Processing (EMNLP)*. Cambridge, MA.

Tom Kwiatkowski, Luke Zettlemoyer, Sharon Goldwater, and Mark Steedman. 2011. Lexical generalization in ccg grammar induction for semantic parsing. In *the Conference on Empirical Methods in Natural Language Processing (EMNLP)*. Edinburgh, UK.

Zhihua Liao, Qixian Zeng, and Qiyun Wang. 2015a. Semantic parsing via ℓ_0-norm-based alignment. In *Recent Advances in Natural Language Processing(RANLP)*. pages 355–361.

Zhihua Liao, Qixian Zeng, and Qiyun Wang. 2015b. A supervised semantic parsing with lexical extension and syntactic constraint. In *Recent Advances in Natural Language Processing(RANLP)*. pages 362–370.

Zhihua Liao and Zili Zhang. 2013. Learning to map chinese sentences to logical forms. In *the 7th International Conference on Knowledge Science, Engineering and Management (KSEM)*. pages 463–472.

Wei Lu and Hwee Tou Ng. 2011. A probabilistic forest-to-string model for language generation from typed lambda calculus expressions. In *the Conference on Empirical Methods in Natural Language Processing(EMNLP)*.

Wei Lu, Hwee Tou Ng, Wee Sun Lee, and Luke S. Zettlemoyer. 2008. A generative model for parsing natural language to meaning representations. In *the Conference on Empirical Methods in Natural Language Processing(EMNLP)*.

Franz Joseph Och and Hermann Ney. 2003. A systematic comparison of various statistical alignment models. *Computational Linguistics* 29(1):19–51.

Franz Joseph Och and Hermann Ney. 2004. The alignment template approach to statistical machine translation. *Computational Linguistics* 30:417–449.

Yuk Wah Wong. 2007. *Learning for Semantic Parsing and Natural Language Generation Using Statistical Machine Translation Techniques*. Ph.D. thesis, Department of Computer Sciences, University of Texas at Austin, Austin, TX.

Yuk Wah Wong and Raymond J. Mooney. 2006. Learning for semantic parsing with statistical machine translation. In *the Human Language Technology Conference of the North American Association for Computational Linguistics (NAACL)*.

Yuk Wah Wong and Raymond J. Mooney. 2007a. Generation by inverting a semantic parser that uses statistical machine translation. In *the Conference of the North American Chapter of the Association for Computational Linguistics (NAACL-HLT-07)*.

Yuk Wah Wong and Raymond J. Mooney. 2007b. Learning synchronous grammars for semantic parsing with lambda calculus. In *the Conference of the Association for Computational Linguistics (ACL)*.

Luke S. Zettlemoyer and Michael Collins. 2005. Learning to map sentences to logical form: Structured classification with probabilistic categorial grammars. In *the 21st Conference on Uncertainty in Artificial Intelligence (UAI)*. pages 658–666.

Luke S. Zettlemoyer and Michael Collins. 2007. Online learning of relaxed ccg grammars for parsing to logical form. In *the Conference on Empirical Methods in Natural Language Processing and the Conference on Computational Natural Language Learning (EMNLP-CoNLL)*. pages 678–687.

Luke S. Zettlemoyer and Michael Collins. 2009. Learning context-dependent mappings from sentences to logical form. In *Joint conference of the 47th Annual Meeting of the Association for Computational Linguistics and the 4th International Joint Conference on Natural Language Processing of the Asian Federation of Natural Language Processing (ACL-IJCNLP)*. pages 976–984.

Summarizing World Speak: A Preliminary Graph Based Approach

Nikhil Londhe
University at Buffalo
nikhillo@buffalo.edu

Rohini K. Srihari
University at Buffalo
rohini@buffalo.edu

Abstract

Social media platforms play a crucial role in piecing together global news stories via their corresponding online discussions. Thus, in this work, we introduce the problem of automatically summarizing massively multilingual microblog text streams. We discuss the challenges involved in both generating summaries as well as evaluating them. We introduce a simple word graph based approach that utilizes node neighborhoods to identify keyphrases and thus in turn, pick summary candidates. We also demonstrate the effectiveness of our method in generating precise summaries as compared to other popular techniques.

1 Introduction & Background

The popularization of social media has fundamentally transformed how news stories are reported and shared (Kwak et al., 2010; Hermida, 2010). As the news stories like the disappearance of flight MH370 (#MH370), or the British referendum to exit EU (#Brexit), or the release of a mobile game based on the popular Pokemon cartoon series (#PokemonGO) – capture global attention, Twitter conversations about them swell in volumes yet vary widely in opinion as well as language, as illustrated in Table 1.

Thus, this begs the question as to how does one begin to *understand* such hashtags in their entirety? Can *true* summaries be generated for such multilingual datasets? Further, how would such summaries circumvent the inherent challenges of language bias, subjectivity of posts and potential Spam (Stafford and Yu, 2013)? Thus, in this work, we explore two primary questions with regards to such multilingual text streams : (a) what consti-

tutes an *ideal* summary? and (b) how can such summaries be evaluated?

1.1 Microblog Summarization

Typically multi-document summarization takes one of two approaches : *abstraction* or *extraction*. Abstractive methods generate a summary by incorporating key information (Kim et al., 2011), whereas extractive methods on the other hand simply aim to choose the most representative sentences (Radev et al., 2002). Typically, longer documents like news stories and blogs have lend themselves better to abstractive summaries whilst shorter documents like social media posts tend to do better with extractive summaries.

As such microblog summarization has received sustained interest in the past few years (Inouye and Kalita, 2011). Overall, two simple techniques based on term frequencies, namely SumBasic (Nenkova and Vanderwende, 2005) and HybridTfIdf (Sharifi et al., 2013) seem to be unanimous choices in most circumstances (Mackie et al., 2014). Thus, for the example hashtags introduced above, we examine the generated summaries for these methods in Table 2. Overall, the problems with the extracted summaries can be enumerated as:

- **Language bias:** Most summaries contained disproportionate number of English posts despite the dataset being more language balanced.[1]

- **Objective vs Subjective posts:** Although in a sense, a representative summary should stay close to the underlying split between subjective and objective posts – for our use case, we would prefer more objective posts, that present an information of some sort beyond just a simple opinion

---

[1]See section 1.2

Proceedings of Recent Advances in Natural Language Processing, pages 452–458,
Varna, Bulgaria, Sep 4–6 2017.

Hashtag	Tweets	Notes
MH370	RT @HuffPostQuebec: #MH370: l'Australie n'a rien détecté près de ses côtes	- Multiple languages : redundancy across languages - Spam and irrelevant data - Mixture of subjective and objective posts
	The Pilots Flight Simulator files were deleted in February. Fishy? #MH370	
	RT @BlackIrishI: St. Jude Pray For Us #MH370 #Flight370	
PokemonGO	RT @BaronVonGamez: Caught my first pokemon...in the gulag #PokemonGO	
	rt gyms pokemongo	
	#PokemonGo - yet another virtual drug for the phone-face generation.	
Brexit	El meme más viral ahora mismo #Brexit	
	British submarine docks in Gibraltar as Spain try to claim sovereignty after Brexit vote	
	#Followback Brexit + uncertainty = market chaos: #TeamFollowBack	

Table 1: Sample tweets for three global hashtags

Hashtag	Algo	Summary
MH370	S	• mh370 • rt mh370 • flight mh370
	H	• rt prayers for the families of missing flight mh370 • rt on the pilots crew and passengers of mh370 • rt what was the cargo of flight mh370
Brexit	S	• brexit • rt brexit • fascinated to see if facebook
	H	• rt on the lessons of brexit for academics • rt in the midst of all brexit fiasco • rt brexit why the british said no to
PokemonGO	S	• pokemongo • rt pokemongo • rt this is the best pokemongo gif so far
	H	• rt pokemongo is out now in the uk • rt caught my first pokemon in the gulag pokemongo • rt this is the magic of pokemongo

Table 2: Initial summarization experiments using SumBasic (S) and HybridTfIdf (H)

Statistic	Min	Max	Avg
Number of tweets	2,153	18,488	7,353
Average Length	6.85	12.46	10.00
Number of tokens	2,445	23,734	10,476
Stopword % (en)	17.91	44.45	30.21
Non english %	24.39	58.10	38.64
Number of languages	38	60	50

Table 3: A summary of the collected tweets

Thus, in essence we seek a summarization algorithm that can be language agnostic whilst preferring objective posts over subjective ones whilst minimizing redundancy within and across languages in the selected posts.

1.2 Evaluating Summaries

Unfortunately, no standard datasets exist for evaluating microblog summarization, largely due to Twitter's data redistribution policies. Although some interest in real-time microblog summarization has been seen in the recent past (Lin et al., 2016), such tasks largely involve stream filtering than summarization. Most researchers in the past have relied on using a variety of trending hashtags to crawl a large number of tweets over an extended period of time. We thus, follow a similar approach and present a summary of the collected datasets between June and July 2016 in Table 3. Note that the crawling process involved using the streaming API for a fixed interval of time. Thus, the number of posts varied between datasets based on the popularity of the hashtag at the time of collection and an additional drop due to deduplication.

Further, there is no consensus on the number of tweets to be considered for a summary. Typically this number has varied from as little as one (Sharifi et al., 2010) to as many as 70 (Chakrabarti and Punera, 2011) and is usually dependent on the method of evaluation. For example, when human summaries are available and recall oriented metrics like ROUGE (Lin, 2004) are used, the target summary size tends to be conservative. However, when precision based metrics are utilized that merely judge the generated outputs, a larger summary size is evaluated.

Given that it is intractable to produce human generated summaries for our use case, we propose an alternate two-pronged approach that seeks to evaluate both precision and recall. First, to evaluate recall, we employ automatic evaluation techniques as proposed by Louis and Nenkova (2009). The basic principle of such evaluation is treating both the input dataset and the generated summary as word distributions and quantifying the quality of the summary as a function of the divergence between these distributions. Although as argued by Saggion et al. (2010), the method through not always reliable works well for multilingual documents as in our case.

We also manually evaluate the precision of the generated summaries for different target summary sizes. The relevance of a post in an ordered set is measured purely in terms of whether it adds any information to the summary. That is, subjective posts or posts that are redundantly similar to previously presented information are deemed as irrel-

Algorithm 1 Neighborhood Summarization

1: **Input:** Dataset D, target summary length n, length parameter λ and phrases P
2: **Output:** Representative n tweets
3: Let $C \leftarrow \emptyset$ be a cache of tweets, $numToks = 0$, $allToks \leftarrow \emptyset$ be a set of unique tokens
4: **for** Tweet T in D **do**
5:     toks = tokenize(T)
6:     **for** Token t in $toks$ **do**
7:         incrementTf(t)
8:         addEdges(t, $toks \setminus t$)
9:         $numToks + +$, $allToks.add(t)$
10:         **if** $t.tf > \eta \times avgTokenProb$ **then**
11:             $C.add(T)$
12:         **end if**
13:     **end for**
14: **end for**
15: Let $S \leftarrow \emptyset$ be a set of seen tweets, $H \leftarrow \emptyset$ be a heap of size n
16: **for** Tweet T in C **do**
17:     **if** $getMaxOverlap(S, T) < 0.8$ **then**
18:         Compute $\tau(T)$
19:         Let $\omega(T) = \tau(T)$
20:         $p = getPhrase(T, P)$
21:         **if** p is not null **then**
22:             $\omega(T) + = w_2(p)$
23:         **end if**
24:         $\omega(T) / = max(\|T\|, \lambda)$
25:         Add $< T, \omega(T) >$ to H
26:         Add T to S
27:     **end if**
28: **end for**
29: Return H

evant. We contend that this two fold evaluation allows us to measure two equally important properties for the generated summaries – how true they are to the underlying term and topic distribution as well as their utility.

Thus, having presented the preliminaries of both the problem and evaluation techniques, we present our graph based summarization technique in the following section.

2   Word Graphs & Keyphrase Extraction

Before we present our summarization technique, it is pertinent that we present how we arrived at a word graph based solution to begin with. Essentially, we were seeking to solve two problems:

- Reduce the language bias by somehow assigning some notion of language independent *importance* to a token

- Incorporate keyphrase extraction (that has shown to produce better summaries (D'Avanzo and Magnini, 2005; Boudin and Morin, 2013)) in a language agnostic setting

We claim that vertex neighborhoods for such graphs are immensely useful in not only determining *important* words (or keyphrase constituents) but also in supplementing context for rarer languages. Algorithm 1 presents a programmatic summary and as can be seen, it proceeds in two stages – graph construction and summary extraction. We present each in the following subsections.

2.1   Graph Construction

Unlike the other graph based summarization algorithms (Olariu, 2014) that index bigrams and trigrams, we instead index an entire post as a clique. Our graph $G = (V, E)$ indexes tokens as vertices (V) and token co-occurrence establishes an edge (E). That is, for a post P with k distinct words, we add it to the graph as k distinct vertices with an edge connecting every possible pair of vertices (i.e. N_2^k edges total). The primary reason for this choice is to circumvent both the relatively free word order associated with hashtag usage but also present a larger context to every token. Further, while adding to the graph, we perform some rudimentary tokenization like lowercasing all text, dropping usernames, URLs, emojis, symbols as well as removing the # prefix. The primary reason for this is to prune the overall graph size. We found that most of such discourse tokens had a low degree and did not affect the system output.

For every token added to the graph, we maintain its term frequency tf as a vertex property that is updated on each subsequent occurrence of the token. Additionally, we maintain a cache of tweets C as we build the graph. A given tweet is added to the cache if it contains any token that occurs more frequently[2] than average. The average token frequency can simply be computed by keeping track of number of tokens ($numToks$) and the number of unique tokens (size of set $allToks$). The cache allows us to reduce the computation time on the next phase.

---

[2]The parameter η allows to control and reduce the cache size

2.2 Summarization

Having described the first stage, i.e., graph construction, we now turn our attention to summarization. In this stage, we iterate over the cached tweets and re-rank them based on two parameters (a) the average importance of all tokens within the tweet and (b) token overlap with previously seen tweets. For a given vertex v, with the set X_v representing all neighbors of v, we assign the following weights to each vertex:

$$w_1(v) = tf(v)/numToks \qquad (1)$$

$$w_2(v) = \frac{1}{n} \sum_{i=1}^{n} w_1(x_i) \qquad (2)$$

where $numToks$ represents the total number of tokens as before , and $x_i \in X_v$. In essence, this is equivalent to weighing each vertex based upon the average probability of occurrence of its neighbors. Finally, given a tweet T, it can be represented numerically as:

$$\tau(T) = \sum_{t}^{T} w_2(t) \qquad (3)$$

We claim that similar to other tf based formulations (Mackie et al., 2014), we are in turn quantifying each post by the *importance* of its constituent tokens. Finally, we additionally boost a tweet if it contains a keyphrase. In defining a keyphrase, we utilize the MWE extraction methodology as outlined by Londhe et al. (2016). They essentially construct a similar graph and use pairwise evaluation of vertices to determine MWEs that include weak MWEs like Named Entities. Although our current algorithm expects the phrases as an external input, a combined algorithm could be developed that simultaneously keeps track of MWE candidates during the graph construction phase.

Note that although we do not explicitly filter out stopwords, they are implicitly controlled by two things. Firstly, by weighing each tweet and not individual tokens, it prevents dominance by specific tokens. Secondly, by restricting permissible tweet overlap prevents the same set of words from reappearing multiple times. We also argue that the implicit inclusion of importance effectively only boosts keyphrases. That is, the boost on MWEs only impacts the final summary if the MWE is important. We now present our experimental results

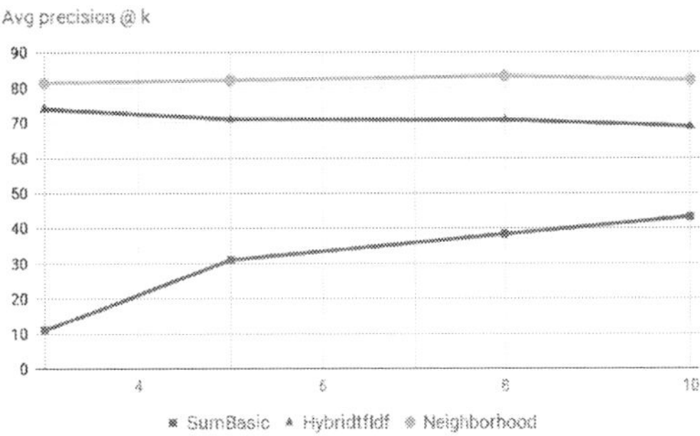

Figure 1: Average Precison @ k

to prove that the said method generates better summaries for our use case as compared to traditional methods.

3 Experiments & Results

3.1 Experiments

As discussed in Section 1.2, we use two fold evaluation for our techniques. Firstly, we compare the divergence statistics and present them in Table 4. The actual divergence values are unbounded, and typically a lower divergence score implies a better summary. However, as described before, a higher divergence score may not imply a bad summary in our case.

Thus, we additionally compare precision at k for a range of values of k and present the results in Figure 1. As described in Section 1.2, precision is manually computed by evaluating information added by a given post. We also list some generated summaries and their assigned relevance labels in Table 5. Note that a grayed out cell indicates a non relevant post.

3.2 Observations

1. The divergence statistics for our method do not vary much from the other techniques, except the KL divergence between the generated summary and the input.

2. However, our method consistently outperforms both on the metrics of precision and compactness.

3. While the precision on HybridTfIdf is comparable to our method, the method is more likely to present posts in the dominant language, i.e English.

Algorithm	JS (Unsmoothened)	JS (Smoothened)	KL (Input to Summary)	KL (Summary to Input)
SumBasic	0.42	0.21	1.60	0.89
HybridTfIdf	0.37	0.18	1.43	0.59
Neighborhood	0.41	0.23	1.69	**1.14**

Table 4: Average Divergence Statistics

Dataset	SumBasic	HybridtfIdf	Neighborhood
PokemonGO	pokemongo	rt pokemongo is out now in the uk	rt icymi pokemongo fiasco ruins the circle of life
	rt pokemongo	rt caught my first pokemon in the gulag pokemongo	pokemons rollen uit de 3dprinter in technobiel pokemongo
	rt this is the best pokemongo gif so far	rt this is the magic of pokemongo	jenkeiss nuoriso saatu liikkeelle paremmin kuin yhdelläkään terveysohjelmalla vau pokemongo lisääliikett
	pokemon pokemongo	rt pokemon go all the time pokemongo	pokemongo oyununda pokemon falan avlamam bur özelliklerime aykır benim ayağıma gelsin
	rt any caamember pokémon trainers find our tiny trucks and get free ride around town to help with your quest pokemongo goo	rt what is the world coming to	all my pokemon stops are churches what you trying to say pokemongo
MH370	mh370	rt prayers for the families of missing flight mh370	rt results of the crowdsourced search for malaysia flight mh370 malaysiaairlines via
	rt mh370	rt on the pilots crew and passengers of mh370	rt the baseless rush to blame pilots of flight 370 via mh370
	flight mh370	rt what was the cargo of flight mh370	rt and this is what the hunt for mh370 has come down to
	malaysia mh370	rt this is who hijacked the malaysian airlines flight mh370	rt prayers for the families of missing flight mh370
	rt breaking news on mh370 plus were ranking your questions right now at 370qs cnn	mh370 where in the world is this plane	rt australia to take charge of southern search for missing flight mh370
Brexit	brexit	rt on the lessons of brexit for academics	rt brexit britain now to suffer the uncertainty that curses switzerland
	rt brexit	rt in the midst of all brexit fiasco	rt how the hokey cokey made me ashamed to be londoner brexit
	fascinated to see if facebook	rt brexit why the british said no to	rt the latest mylbrook vehicle finance news thanks to brexit porsche
	rt watching brexit politics this morning makes me wonder if the snp could field candidates in england and wales sturgeon re	rt brexit poll this is the beginning of end for	rt brexit big fuck to the merchants selling us nwo allwhitesunite
	but were litist for saying brexit is about racism	rt in light of brexit and the ensuing chaos	rt the startling human toll of brexit

Table 5: Summary samples & relevance

4. Although SumBasic seems to perform poorly on precision, its overall performance is comparable for larger values of k. Rather, it seems to produce better summaries for larger values of k.

5. However, we do need a better and ideally a single automatic method of evaluation that could potentially combine these three metrics

4 Related Work

Overall, the work related to hashtag summarization can be divided into two broad categories: (a) Stream clustering (b) Microblog summarization. Stream clustering involves summarizing a live stream of data like the classic CluStream (Aggarwal et al., 2003) method or the more recent Sumblr (Shou et al., 2013) pipeline. However, these methods are suited for large steam processing and require continuous data streaming to create and compare historical summaries. Also, the summaries are query driven implemented as adhoc queries or drill-downs. Thus, we mention them here only for the sake of completeness as they are not directly comparable to our use case.

Microblog summarization, as partially discussed in Section 1.1, has largely evolved from traditional summarization techniques that follow one of the *extraction* or *abstraction* routes. However, although several methods like TextRank (Mihalcea and Tarau, 2004), LexRank (Erkan and Radev, 2004) and MEAD (Radev et al., 2004) have been proposed over the past few years, the two methods compared, viz SumBasic (Nenkova and Vanderwende, 2005) and HybridTfIDF (Sharifi et al., 2013) have been shown to outperfom them (Mackie et al., 2014).

Finally, improvements in parsers and taggers specific to Twitter have also given rise to a new family of Information Extraction based methods for summarization (Xu et al., 2013). However, most such tools are language specific and may not be applied to multilingual datasets without loss of generality and accuracy.

5 Future Work and Conclusions

We believe that the problem warrants much further work. The largest problem would obviously involve finding better ways to evaluate such multilingual summaries without manual intervention. Although considered while designing the algorithm, we did not find a satisfactory way to quantify language divergence as part of the generated summaries. It would also be worthwhile to consider redundancy across languages, especially as applicable for ranking the summary candidates. That is, should a post in the dominant language be preferred against a post in another language that is similar but contains marginally more information?

It would also be worthwhile to incorporate some prior probabilities (like stopword lists) and other semantic equivalences, probably crosslingual dictionaries to improve the generated summaries. It would also be interesting to measure how the summaries evolve for a fixed target summary size as the algorithm sees more posts and use it to measure topic drift and topic divergence. Finally, we would like to explore temporal relationships in a trending topic and possibly generate sub-topical summaries by automatically partitioning the given text stream.

References

Charu C Aggarwal, Jiawei Han, Jianyong Wang, and Philip S Yu. 2003. A framework for clustering evolving data streams. In *Proceedings of the 29th international conference on Very large data bases-Volume 29*. VLDB Endowment, pages 81–92.

Florian Boudin and Emmanuel Morin. 2013. Keyphrase extraction for n-best reranking in multi-sentence compression. In *North American Chapter of the Association for Computational Linguistics (NAACL)*.

Deepayan Chakrabarti and Kunal Punera. 2011. Event summarization using tweets. *ICWSM* 11:66–73.

Ernesto D'Avanzo and Bernado Magnini. 2005. A keyphrase-based approach to summarization: the lake system at duc-2005. In *Proceedings of DUC*.

Günes Erkan and Dragomir R Radev. 2004. Lexrank: Graph-based lexical centrality as salience in text summarization. *Journal of Artificial Intelligence Research* 22:457–479.

Alfred Hermida. 2010. Twittering the news: The emergence of ambient journalism. *Journalism practice* 4(3):297–308.

David Inouye and Jugal K Kalita. 2011. Comparing twitter summarization algorithms for multiple post summaries. In *Privacy, Security, Risk and Trust (PASSAT) and 2011 IEEE Third Inernational Conference on Social Computing (SocialCom), 2011 IEEE Third International Conference on*. IEEE, pages 298–306.

Hyun Duk Kim, Kavita Ganesan, Parikshit Sondhi, and ChengXiang Zhai. 2011. Comprehensive review of opinion summarization. Technical report.

Haewoon Kwak, Changhyun Lee, Hosung Park, and Sue Moon. 2010. What is twitter, a social network or a news media? In *Proceedings of the 19th international conference on World wide web*. ACM, pages 591–600.

Chin-Yew Lin. 2004. Rouge: A package for automatic evaluation of summaries. In *Text summarization branches out: Proceedings of the ACL-04 workshop*. Barcelona, Spain, volume 8.

Jimmy Lin, Adam Roegiest, Luchen Tan, Richard McCreadie, Ellen Voorhees, and Fernando Diaz. 2016. Overview of the trec 2016 real-time summarization track. In *Proceedings of the 25th Text REtrieval Conference, TREC*. volume 16.

Nikhil Londhe, Rohini Srihari, and Vishrawas Gopalakrishnan. 2016. Time-independent and language-independent extraction of multiword expressions from twitter. In *Proceedings of COLING 2016, the 26th International Conference on Computational Linguistics: Technical Papers*. pages 2269–2278.

Annie Louis and Ani Nenkova. 2009. Automatically evaluating content selection in summarization without human models. In *Proceedings of the 2009 Conference on Empirical Methods in Natural Language Processing: Volume 1-Volume 1*. Association for Computational Linguistics, pages 306–314.

Stuart Mackie, Richard McCreadie, Craig Macdonald, and Iadh Ounis. 2014. Comparing algorithms for microblog summarisation. In *International Conference of the Cross-Language Evaluation Forum for European Languages*. Springer, pages 153–159.

Rada Mihalcea and Paul Tarau. 2004. Textrank: Bringing order into texts. Association for Computational Linguistics.

Ani Nenkova and Lucy Vanderwende. 2005. The impact of frequency on summarization. *Microsoft Research, Redmond, Washington, Tech. Rep. MSR-TR-2005* 101.

Andrei Olariu. 2014. Efficient online summarization of microblogging streams. In *EACL*. pages 236–240.

Dragomir R Radev, Timothy Allison, Sasha Blair-Goldensohn, John Blitzer, Arda Celebi, Stanko Dimitrov, Elliott Drabek, Ali Hakim, Wai Lam, Danyu Liu, et al. 2004. Mead-a platform for multidocument multilingual text summarization. In *LREC*.

Dragomir R Radev, Eduard Hovy, and Kathleen McKeown. 2002. Introduction to the special issue on summarization. *Computational linguistics* 28(4):399–408.

Horacio Saggion, Juan-Manuel Torres-Moreno, Iria da Cunha, and Eric SanJuan. 2010. Multilingual summarization evaluation without human models. In *Proceedings of the 23rd International Conference on Computational Linguistics: Posters*. Association for Computational Linguistics, pages 1059–1067.

Beaux Sharifi, Mark-Anthony Hutton, and Jugal K Kalita. 2010. Experiments in microblog summarization. In *Social Computing (SocialCom), 2010 IEEE Second International Conference on*. IEEE, pages 49–56.

Beaux P Sharifi, David I Inouye, and Jugal K Kalita. 2013. Summarization of twitter microblogs. *The Computer Journal* page bxt109.

Lidan Shou, Zhenhua Wang, Ke Chen, and Gang Chen. 2013. Sumblr: continuous summarization of evolving tweet streams. In *Proceedings of the 36th international ACM SIGIR conference on Research and development in information retrieval*. ACM, pages 533–542.

Grant Stafford and Louis Lei Yu. 2013. An evaluation of the effect of spam on twitter trending topics. In *Social Computing (SocialCom), 2013 International Conference on*. IEEE, pages 373–378.

Wei Xu, Ralph Grishman, Adam Meyers, and Alan Ritter. 2013. A preliminary study of tweet summarization using information extraction. *NAACL 2013* page 20.

Human Associations Help to Detect
Conventionalized Multiword Expressions

Natalia Loukachevitch
Lomonosov Moscow State University
Leniskie Gory,1
Moscow, Russia
louk_nat@mail.ru

Anastasia Gerasimova
Lomonosov Moscow State University
Leniskie Gory,1
Moscow, Russia
anastasiagerasimova432@gmail.com

Abstract

In this paper we show that if we want to obtain human evidence about conventionalization of some phrases, we should ask native speakers about associations they have to a given phrase and its component words. We have shown that if component words of a phrase have each other as frequent associations, then this phrase can be considered as conventionalized. Another type of conventionalized phrases can be revealed using two factors: low entropy of phrase associations and low intersection of component word and phrase associations. The association experiments were performed for the Russian language.

1 Introduction

A lot of approaches have been proposed for automatic extraction of idioms, collocations, or multiword terms from texts as potential candidates for inclusion in lexical or terminological resources (Bonial et al., 2014; Gelbukh and Kolesnikova, 2014; Pecina, 2010; Piasecki et al., 2015).

However, developers of computational resources need clear guidelines for the introduction of phrases into their resources. Special instructions on introducing multiword terms exist for constructing information-retrieval thesauri (ANSI/NISO, 2005). Developers of WordNet-like thesauri, a very popular type of resources, discuss the problem of introducing multiword expressions in their resources in several works (Maziarz et al., 2015; Piasecki et al., 2015; Vincze and Almasi, 2014). For example, it is supposed that wordnets have to include only lexicalized concepts as synsets (Miller, 1998). However, Agirre et al., (2006) stress that boundaries of lexicalization are very difficult to draw. Bentivogli and Pianta (2004) argue that there is a necessity to include non-lexicalized phrases into wordnets.

Multiword expressions comprise a broad scope of phrases including idiomatic expressions, noun compounds, technical terms, proper names, verb-particle and light verb constructions, conventionalized phrases, and others (Calzolari et al., 2002; Sag et al., 2002; Baldwin and Kim, 2010). For some of these constructions, such as idioms, it is evident that they should be included in computational lexicons. But for many of other expressions, for example, conventionalized phrases, it is not easy to make a decision about the necessity of their inclusion. To distinguish a multiword expression, it is important to analyze if it has any "idiosincrasies", which can be lexical, syntactical, semantical or statistical.

Conventionalized phrases have statistical idiosyncrasy and usually only one approach is proposed in literature to distinguish such phrases from other compositional phrases. This is so-called substitutionability test, which shows if the phrase components can be easily substituted with their synonyms (Sag et al., 2002; Farahmand et al., 2015; Farahmand and Henderson, 2016; Pearce, 2001; Senaldi et al., 2016).

In this paper, we show that there are at least two more types of statistical idiosyncrasy (and related tests) to distinguish conventionalized expressions:

- association idiosyncrasy when components of a phrase are highly associated with each other, and

- relational idiosyncrasy when a phrase has lexical associations that significantly differ from the associations of its component words; usually it means that the phrase denotes a specific entity or process with a set of its own properties and relations.

Proceedings of Recent Advances in Natural Language Processing, pages 459–466,
Varna, Bulgaria, Sep 4–6 2017.

We provde evidence for these types of phrase idiosyncrasy in association experiments in Russian, in which we asked Russian native speakers what associations they had for phrases and their component words. We have found that the human association experiment is a very efficient tool to detect conventionalized phrases with high accuracy. To the best of our knowledge, this is the first attempt to use human associations for distinguishing conventionalized phrases.

The structure of the paper is as follows. In Section 2 we consider types of phrase idiosyncrasy. Section 3 describes the specificity of RuThes thesaurus, from which we take phrases for the experiments. Section 4 presents the association experiment and its results. In Section 5 we test embedding models on their capability to distinguish conventionalized phrases. Section 6 reviews related work concerning approaches of annotating compositionality/noncompositionality/conventionalization of noun phrases.

2 Types of Idiosyncrasy of Multiword Expressions

Multiword expressions are phrases that have some specificity (idiosyncrasy). Because of this, it is useful to collect them and store in lexicons and thesauri (Calzolari et al., 2002; Sag et al., 2002; Baldwin and Kim, 2010).

The idiosyncrasy can be lexical when a component of a phrase appears only within this phrase (Baldwin and Kim, 2010). It can be syntactical when the syntactic behavior of a phrase differs from usual (for example, fixed word order). Semantical idiosynrasy can be revealed when the meaning of a phrase cannot be inferred from the meanings of its components. If a phrase has one of the above-mentioned types of idiosynrasy it can be called a lexicalized expression (Sag et al., 2002; Baldwin and Kim, 2010).

Statistical idiosyncrasy presupposes that the components of a phrase co-occur more often than expected by chance. Besides, the frequency of phrases with statistical idiosynrasy is much higher than the frequency of the phrase with one component changed to its near-synonym (*weather forecast* vs. *weather prediction*), as the result of the substitutionability test (Sag et al., 2002; Farahmand and Henderson, 2016). Phrases with statistical idiosyncrasy (often called *conventional-*

ized phrases) can be syntactically and semantically compositional.

In many cases conventionalized phrases are difficult to distinguish. For example, one of the often mentioned conventionalized phrase *traffic lights* looks fully compositional. However, if we examine the meaning of this phrase, we can see that the denoted entity can be categorized as a road facility; it has signals; it is usually constructed on road intersections; it is needed for regulating road traffic, etc. This means that the phrase *traffic lights* has thesaurus relations with the correponding words (facilities, road, signals, regulation) that cannot be inferred from the meanings of its component words *traffic* and *lights*.

A lot of similar examples can be found. Compositional *seat belt* has relation to the safety concept. Food courts are usually located in shopping centers, and therefore compositional phrase *food court* has relation with the *shopping center* concept, etc. These relations can be very useful in such NLP applications as textual entailment.

Thus, we can suppose that conventionalized phrases have not only statistical idiosyncrasy, but also *relational idiosyncrasy*, which can be revealed easier than using the substitutionability test. The same idiosynrasy can be found in unclear cases of possible lexicalized expessions.

In (Mel'čuk, 2012) so-called quasi-idioms are discussed. According to Mel'čuk, a phrase *AB* is a quasi-idiom or weak idiom iff its meaning: 1) includes the meaning of both of its lexical components, neither as the semantic pivot, and 2) includes an additional meaning *C* as its semantic pivot. Mel'čuk (2012) gives an example of *barbed wire*, which is an obstacle, but neither *barbed* nor *wire* are obstacles. Thus, it seems than *semantic pivot* in this case is the hypernym relation, that cannot be inferred from the phrase component words. It means that the quasi-idiom is a subtype of relational idiosyncrasy.

In this paper we show that this relational idiosynrasy can be found in association experiments with native speakers. Besides, we can also reveal the association idiosyncrasy of conventionalized phrases in these experiments.

3 RuThes Thesaurus as a Source of Conventionalized Expressions

For the present work, we utilized multiword expressions included in the Russian-language thesaurus RuThes[1] (Loukachevitch and Dobrov, 2014). The RuThes thesaurus is a linguistic ontology for natural language processing, i.e. an ontology, where the majority of concepts are introduced on the basis of actual language expressions.

RuThes has considerable similarities with WordNet: the inclusion of concepts based on senses of real text units, representation of lexical senses, detailed coverage of word senses. At the same time, the differences include attachment of different parts of speech to the same concepts, formulating names of concepts, attention to multiword expressions, the set of conceptual relations, etc.

In particular, the developers of the RuThes thesaurus have special rules for including phrases that appear compositional into the thesaurus. Such phrases are introduced if they have specificity in relations with other single words and/or expressions (Loukachevitch and Lashevich, 2016). The following subtypes of these expressions can be considered:

- A phrase is a synonym to a single word; for example, земельный участок (landing lot) is a synonym to word земля (land), or a phrase has a frequent abbreviation: заработная плата – зарплата (employee wages);

- A phrase has a synonymous phrase and this fact cannot be simply inferred from the components of the phrase: мобильный телефон (mobile phone) – сотовый телефон (cell phone);

- A phrase generalizes several single words. Such phrases as транспортное происшествие (transport accident) or учебное заведение (educational institution) often look compositional but they have a very important function of knowledge representation: they gather together similar concepts;

- A phrase has relations that do not follow from its component words. For example, the compositional phrase дорожное движение (road traffic) has numerous relations with other phrases that cannot be inferred from its components, for example, hyponyms (left-hand traffic, one-way traffic), related concepts (car accident, traffic jam), etc.

Thus, phrases from RuThes without evident non-compositionality were selected for the association experiment in order to understand correlations between choice of phrases made by experts and associations of native speakers.

4 Association Experiment

For the experiment, we took two-word noun phrases (*Adjective + Noun* and *Noun + Noun-in-Genitive*) that have high frequency in Russian newswire text collections.

The multiword expressions were of two main groups. The first group (Thesaurus group) included multiword expressions from the RuThes thesaurus. We chose phrases that either look fully compositional (*increase of prices*) or that have one of components is used in a known (=described in dictionaries) metaphoric sense. This group contained 15 phrases. Another group of phrases comprised fully compositional noun phrases not included in the thesaurus, for example, *end of January, mighty earthquake, result of work*, etc. The non-thesaurus group contained 36 phrases.

We asked respondents (mainly university students) to think of single-word associations to noun phrases. In a separate experiment, we collected associations to the component words of the same phrases. We wanted to understand if the collected associations can serve as a base for distinguishing thesaurus phrases from non-thesaurus phrases (and as a consequence, conventionalized phrases from non-conventionalized). Twenty six native speakers gave their associations for the thesaurus phrases and twenty nine respondents participated in the experiment with non-thesaurus phrases. Forty seven people gave associations for single words.

The study was conducted via Google Forms. The respondents were asked to provide single-word associations. However, some participants could think only of multiword expressions. Such associations were also taken into account. Table 1 contains examples of obtained associations and their frequencies for some thesaurus phrases.

From the associations obtained, we calculated the following characteristics (Tables 2, 3):

- entropy of answers for single words and phrases (currently, only entropy of phrase associations was found useful and included in the tables);

---

[1] http://www.labinform.ru/pub/ruthes/index_eng.htm

- intersection between associations of component words and phrase associations (columns Ph1 and Ph2 in Tables 2, 3); and

- number of times when one component word served as an association of another component word (columns A12 and A21 in Tables 2, 3).

Table 2 contains the results for the thesaurus phrases, and Table 3 shows partial results for the non-thesaurus phrases.

We can see that for thesaurus phrases, the components are associated with each other more often than for non-thesaurus phrases. The average value of such associations for thesaurus phrases is 10 times greater than for non-thesaurus phrases. For some thesaurus phrases, both components are highly connected with another component. Withing non-thesaurus phrases, such frequent mutual associations were not found.

source	associations	freq
w1: земельный (landing)	участок (lot)	**38**
	вопрос (issue)	2
w2: участок (lot)	земля (land)	**11**
	дача (dacha)	**11**
	полицейский (police)	4
	дорога (road)	3
	дом (house)	**2**
phrase: земельный участок (landing lot)	дача (dacha)	**12**
	дом (house)	**2**
	надел (allotment)	2
w1: повышение (increase)	должность (post)	8
	зарплата (wages)	7
	работа (job)	6
w2: цена (price)	ценник (price-tag)	5
	стоимость (cost)	4
	высокая (high)	3
	качество (quality)	2
phrase: повышение цен (increase of prices)	инфляция (inflation)	**12**
	кризис (crisis)	**5**
	нефть (oil)	2

Table 1: Examples of the most frequent associations for thesaurus phrases and its components

Therefore, we think that mutual associations between phrase components are an important sign of phrase **conventionalization**. It seems that such phrases are stored as single units in the human memory. In our case such conventionalized

Phrase	A12	A21	Ph1	Ph2	Entr
транспортное происшествие (transport accident)	0	7	0	6	2.16
учебное заведение (education institute)	1	8	**1**	**1**	**2.52**
программное обеспечение (software program)	**13**	**14**	6	1	2.77
повышение цен (increase in prices)	0	0	**0**	**0**	**2.85**
земельный участок (landing lot)	**38**	**13**	0	14	2.89
квадратный метр (square meter)	**10**	**20**	0	1	3.22
электронная почта (electronic mail)	**6**	**12**	3	4	3.27
дорожное движение (road traffic)	0	2	**0**	**0**	**3.33**
заработная плата (employee wage)	**18**	**10**	8	2	3.42
главный герой (main hero)	5	1	**0**	**3**	**3.56**
медицинская помощь (medical aid)	0	5	**0**	**4**	**3.58**
торговый центр (shopping center)	**26**	0	1	0	3.62
лента новостей (news feed)	**18**	0	1	1	3.79
мобильный телефон (mobile phone)	**26**	**12**	3	7	3.81
температура воздуха (air temperature)	4	0	6	1	3.81
Average	**11**	**6.27**	**1.93**	**2.93**	**3.24**

Table 2: Results of association experiments for the thesaurus phrases

phrases included: программное обеспечение (*software program*), земельный участок (*landing lot*), квадратный метр (*square meter*), электронная почта (*electronic mail*), заработная плата (*employee wages*), мобильный телефон (*mobile phone*), лента новостей (*news feed*), and торговый центр (*shopping center*).

Besides, we found that the average level of entropy (4.07) of phrase associations is much higher for non-thesaurus phrases than for thesaurus phrases (3.24). This means that associations of thesaurus phrases are more concentrated, more motivated by the phrase. But at the same time some clearly compositional non-thesaurus phrases also have fairly low entropy of associations, for example, пресс-служба администрации (*press-service of the administration*).

We can also see that the phrases differ in the number of intersections between the associations obtained for a phrase and for its components. It seems natural that the already found conventionalized phrases have numerous intersections of this kind (Table 2) because the phrase and its components are closely related to each other.

On the contrary, other thesaurus phrases have a relatively small number of such intersections.

Phrase	A12	A21	Ph1	Ph2	Entr
финал лиги (league final)	0	0	2	18	2.16
начало года (beginning of the year)	0	0	1	0	2.66
ежедневный обзор (daily review)	1	0	3	14	2.90
пресс-служба администрации (press-service of administration)	0	0	14	6	2.97
еженедельный обзор (weekly review)	0	0	6	10	3.19
необходимый документ (necessary document)	1	0	0	14	3.64
конец января (end of January)	0	0	2	7	3.81
должность главы (post of the head)	0	0	5	2	3.85
новое поколение (new generation)	0	4	1	8	3.90
член совета (member of council)	5	0	2	5	3.96
повышение эффективности (increase in efficiency)	0	1	6	6	3.98
увеличение объема (growth in volume)	3	0	7	4	4.02
крупный размер (large size)	4	0	6	4	4.07
миллион евро (million of euros)	0	0	5	4	4.11
...					
особое внимание (special attention)	0	2	0	5	4.63
председатель комитета(chairman of committee)	5	0	5	3	4.63
экономический форум (economic forum)	0	2	2	3	4.65
интересный комментарий (interesting comment)	0	0	2	6	4.69
Average	1.22	0.36	2.80	6.36	4.07

Table 3: Results of association experiments for non-thesaurus phrases

It means that the thesaurus phrases evoke their own associations more often. For example, the phrase повышение цен (*increase of prices*) has frequent associations with the words инфляция (*inflation*) (16 of 25) and кризис (*crisis*), which were not mentioned as associations for its component words. On average, intersection between associations of the phrase and its component associations for non-thesaurus phrases is four times less than for thesaurus phrases.

It can also be seen that non-thesaurus phrases with low entropy of associations can have large numbers of intersections between the component associations and the phrase associations. In such cases, low entropy of the phrase associations is mainly detemined by its components, for example, their probable syntactic dependencies. Only one of the non-thesaurus phrases has both low entropy of phrase associations and a few number of intersections of the phrase and component associations at the same time: начало года (begin-

ning of the year). It is highly associated with calendar months: *January* and *September*. For thesaurus phrases, a relatively high number of intersections between the phrase and component associations was revealed for most arguable thesaurus phrases: транспортное происшествие (*transport accident*) and температура воздуха (*air temperature*).

Thus, we can suppose that if a phrase has a low level of entropy of associations together with a small number of the same associations for the phrase and its components then it is also conventionalized.

We can introduce the threshold as 0.8*MaxEntropy of answers. MaxEntropy is the maximal entropy we can obtain if respondents give equiprobable answers. In the current experiment, the threshold is equal to 3.76 for thesaurus phrases and 3.89 for non-thesaurus phrases. In our experiment, such conventionalized phrases include учебное заведение (*educational institute*), повышение цен (*increase in prices*), дорожное движение (*road traffic*), главный герой (*main hero*), медицинская помощь (*medical aid*).

A result, we can say that we have found two signs of phrase conventionalization in the association experiment described:

- component words are frequently associated with each other, and

- associations of a phrase have both low entropy (less than 0.8*MaxEntropy) and a low level of intersection between component and phrase associations (less than 20%).

Using all three factors (association of component words to each other, entropy of phrase associations, and intersection of component word associations and phrase associations), it is possible to differentiate thesaurus phrases and non-thesaurus phrases with greater than 94% accuracy.

It is interesting to compare current results with the smaller amounts of associations. With this aim, we took the first 15 associations obtained for single words and phrases. The same above-mentioned thesaurus phrases have frequent mutual associations between components (that is, have association idiosyncrasy).

Phrases медицинская помощь (*medical aid*) and температура воздуха (*air temperature*) had entropy of associations more than 0.8*MaxEntropy. Only two non-thesaurus phrases had both low entropy (less than 0.8*MaxEntropy) and the low level of intersection between assotiations of the phrase and its components: финал лиги (*league final*) and начало года (*beginning of the year*). As a result, in this smaller experiment, the obtained associations can distinguish thesaurus phrases with accuracy more than 92%.

5 Detecting the Conventionalized Expressions with Distributional Models

We compared the results of the association experiment with the results of distributional models. In previous works, it was supposed that non-compositional phrases can be distinguished with comparison of the phrase distributional vector and distributional vectors of their components: it was supposed that the similarity is less for non-compositional phrases (Cordeiro et al., 2016a; Gharbieh et al., 2016).

We used a Russian news collection (0.45 B tokens) and generated phrase and word embeddings with word2vec tool. For the phrases under consideration, we calculated cosine similarity between the phrase vector $v(w_1 w_2)$ and the sum of normalized vectors of phrase components $v(w_1 + w_2)$ according to formula from (Cordeiro et al., 2016a).

$$v(w_1 + w_2) = \left(\frac{v(w_1)}{|v(w_1)|} + \frac{v(w_2)}{|v(w_2)|} \right)$$

To evaluate different parameter sets, we located all phrases in the ascending order of similarity scores. We wanted to check if the thesaurus phrases with idiosynrasy obtain lesser values of word2vec similarity than non-thesaurus phrases without any specificity. We utilized MAP (mean average precision measure) to evaluate the quality of ordering.

We experimented with different parameters of word2vec and evaluated them with MAP on our data. We found that the best word2vec model (200 dimensions, 3 word window size) achieved quite low value of MAP (**0.391**), which means that it is very difficult for current embedding models to differentiate thesaurus and non-thesaurus phrases in our experiment.

We can also calculate MAP for the same phrase list ordered accoring to the increased entropy of phrase associations. And here we obtain MAP equal to **0.642**. Thus, entropy of human associations without accounting additional factors pre-

dicts thesaurus phrases significantly better than the embedding models.

6 Related Work

The annotation of multiword expressions on compositionality/non-compositionality of noun compounds has been studied in several works (Cordeiro et al., 2016b; Reddy et al., 2011; Ramisch et al., 2016).

Reddy et al. (2011) created the set of 90 noun compounds. The phrases were taken from Word-Net. For each compound, the following types of tasks have been given: a judgement on how literal the phrase is and a judgement on how literal each noun is within the compound. They used 30 turkers to obtain judgements on the compound compositionality in each task.

Ramisch et al. (2016) asked respondents about the degree to which the meaning of an expression follows from its components: separately from each component and from both components in total. The authors of the paper stress that such indirect annotation provides reliable and stable data. However, this approach was confronted with difficulties concerning the inconsistency of the answers in some cases. For example, English speakers agreed on the level of head and head + modifier compositionality for phrase *dirty word*, but disagreed when judging the modifier: it was fully idiomatic for some, but others thought that the phrase just contained an uncommon sense of *dirty*.

Maziarz et al. (2015) try to formulate the procedural definition of multiword lexical units that should be included in the Polish wordnet so that lexicographers could apply these principles consistently. Then they asked linguists to classify phrases using this definition into three categories: *multiword lexical unit, not multiword lexical unit,* and *don't know*. They concluded that a group of 5-7 linguists is able to decide whether multiword lexical units should be introduced in a wordnet with the appropriate agreement. However, this approach was considered too expensive.

In another experiment, Maziarz et al. (2015) directed linguists to answer questions based on non-compositionality criteria of phrases including metaphoric character, hyponymy toward the syntactic head, ability to be paraphrased, nonseparability, fixed word order, terminological register, etc. Then the answers were used to train the decision tree algorithm to predict inclusion or non-inclusion of an expression into the Polish wordnet. However, the obtained decision trees were different for the various phrase sets under analysis.

Farahmand et al. (2015) describe the annotation of non-compositionality and conventionalization of noun compounds. They asked the annotators to make binary decisions about compositionality of phrases. Compositional compounds were further annotated as conventionalized or non-conventionalized. A compound was considered as conventionalized in neither of its constituents can be substituted for their near-synonyms. Sometimes the decision was diffucult because such phrases could really exist (*floor space* vs. *floor area*).

To annotate the compounds, five experts were hired. In such a way, the authors (Farahmand et al., 2015) tried to avoid problems with crowdsourcing, which can lead to flaws in the results (Reddy et al., 2011). The authors stress that identifying conventionalization is not a trivial task and that human agreement on this property can be quite low. The examples of found compositional, but conventionalized phrases included: *cable car, food court, speed limit*, etc. The task of this study to distinguish conventionalized or non-conventionalized phrases among compositional compounds is the closest to our work.

For Russian there are two large resources of human associations. The well-known Russian Association dictionary (Karaulov et al., 1994) is currently obsolete. Another assoicaion-oriented project Sociation.org[2] collected a lot of current Russian associations but it does not have associations for the phrases under analysis.

Practical conclusions from the above-described experiments and related work are as follows:

- In annotating compositionality/non-compositionality of multiword expressions by crowdsourcing as in (Cordeiro et al., 2016b; Reddy et al., 2011; Ramisch et al., 2016), it is also useful to ask respondents about their associations for the phrase and its components to detect relational idiosyncrasy,

- In expert analysis of multiword expressions for inclusion into computational resources as in (Maziarz et al., 2015; Farahmand et al., 2015), it is useful to ask experts about additional lexical or conceptual relations that the phrase have and that do not follow from the phrase components,

- In computational approaches of extracting non-compositional multiword expressions, it is useful to compare contexts of phrase occurrence and contexts of its component word occurrences trying to detect *weirdness* in the phrase context.

7   Conclusion

In this paper, we have shown that if we want to obtain human evidence about conventionalization of some phrases, we can ask native speakers about associations they have for a phrase and its component words.

We have found that there are two forms of manifesting conventionalized phrases. First, we can consider that a phrase is conventionalized if its component words have frequent associations to each other. The second type of conventionalized phrases can be revealed on the basis of two factors: low entropy of phrase associations and a low number of intersections between component word and phrase associations. These three factors allows predicting conventionalized phrases with high accuracy. We have also shown that the existing embedding models distinguish conventionalized phrases from non-conventionalized significantly worse.

In our opinion, developers of thesauri should consider the relational specificity (idiosynrasy) of multiword expressions, which can help them to decide on inclusion of specific phrases into their resources. Weird word co-occurrences with the phrase in comparison with its component contexts can be considered as an additional factor to detect conventionalized expressions in computational approaches.

Acknowledgments.

This study is supported by Russian Scientific Foundationc (project N16-18-02074).

References

Eneko Agirre, Izaskun Aldezabal, and Eli Pociello. 2006. Lexicalization and multiword expressions in the basque wordnet. In *Proceedings of Third International WordNet Conference*. pages 131–138.

ANSI/NISO. 2005. *Z39.19. Guidelines for the Construction, Format and Management of Monolingual Thesauri*. ANSI/NISO.

---

[2] http://sociation.org/

Timothy Baldwin and Su Nam Kim. 2010. Multi-word expressions. In *Handbook of Natural Language Processing, Second Edition,* Chapman and Hall/CRC, pages 267–292.

Luisa Bentivogli and Emanuele Pianta. 2004. Extending wordnet with syntagmatic information. In *Proceedings of second global WordNet conference.* pages 47–53.

Claire Bonial, Meredith Green, Jenette Preciado, and Martha Palmer. 2014. An approach to take multi-word expressions. In *Proc. of the 10th Workshop on Multiword Expressions.* pages 94–98.

Nicoletta Calzolari, Charles J Fillmore, Ralph Grishman, Nancy Ide, Alessandro Lenci, Catherine MacLeod, and Antonio Zampolli. 2002. Towards best practice for multiword expressions in computational lexicons. In *Proceedings of LREC-2002.*

Silvio Cordeiro, Carlos Ramisch, Marco Idiart, and Aline Villavicencio. 2016a. Predicting the compositionality of nominal compounds: Giving word embeddings a hard time. In *Proceedings of the 54th Annual Meeting of the Association for Computational Linguistics (Volume 1: Long Papers).* Association for Computational Linguistics, pages 1986–1997.

Silvio Cordeiro, Carlos Ramisch, and Aline Villavicencio. 2016b. Filtering and measuring the intrinsic quality of human compositionality judgments. In *ACL 2016.* pages 32–37.

Meghdad Farahmand and James Henderson. 2016. Modeling the non-substitutability of multiword expressions with distributional semantics and a log-linear model. In *Proceedings of the 12th Workshop on Multiword Expressions, ACL 2016.* pages 61–66.

Meghdad Farahmand, Aaron Smith, and Joakim Nivre. 2015. A multiword expression data set: Annotating non-compositionality and conventionalization for english noun compounds. In *Proceedings of NAACL-HLT.* Association for Computational Linguistics, pages 29–33.

Alexander Gelbukh and Olga Kolesnikova. 2014. Multiword expressions in nlp: General survey and a special case of verb-noun constructions. *Computational Linguistics: Concepts, Methodologies, Tools, and Applications,* pages 178–197.

Waseem Gharbieh, Virendra C Bhavsar, and Paul Cook. 2016. A word embedding approach to identifying verb–noun idiomatic combinations pages 112–118.

Yuri Karaulov, Yu. Sorokin, E. Tarasov, N. Ufimtseva, and G. Cherkasova. 1994. *Russian Association Dictionary.*

Natalia Loukachevitch and Boris Dobrov. 2014. Ruthes linguistic ontology vs. russian wordnets. In *Proceedings of Global WordNet Conference GWC-2014.* pages 154–162.

Natalia Loukachevitch and German Lashevich. 2016. Multiword expressions in russian thesauri ruthes and ruwordnet. In *Proceedings of the AINL FRUCT 2016.* FRUCT, pages 66–71.

Marek Maziarz, Stan Szpakowicz, and Maciej Piasecki. 2015. A procedural definition of multi-word lexical units. In *Proceedings of Recent Advances in NLP Conference RANLP-2015.* pages 427–435.

Igor Mel'čuk. 2012. Phraseology in the language, in the dictionary, and in the computer. *Yearbook of Phraseology* 3(1):31–56.

George A Miller. 1998. Nouns in wordnet. *WordNet: An electronic lexical database* pages 24–45.

Darren Pearce. 2001. Synonymy in collocation extraction. In *Proceedings of the workshop on WordNet and other lexical resources, second meeting of the north american chapter of the association for computational linguistics.* pages 41–46.

Pavel Pecina. 2010. Lexical association measures and collocation extraction. *Language resources and evaluation* 44(1-2):137–158.

Maciej Piasecki, Michal Wendelberger, and Marek Maziarz. 2015. Extraction of the multi-word lexical units in the perspective of the wordnet expansion. In *RANLP-2015.* pages 512–520.

Carlos Ramisch, Silvio Cordeiro, Leonardo Zilio, Marco Idiart, Aline Villavicencio, and Rodrigo Wilkens. 2016. How naked is the naked truth? a multilingual lexicon of nominal compound compositionality. In *Proceedings of the 54th Annual Meeting of the Association for Computational Linguistics (Volume 2: Short Papers).* Association for Computational Linguistics, pages 114–133.

Siva Reddy, Diana McCarthy, and Suresh Manandhar. 2011. An empirical study on compositionality in compound nouns. In *IJCNLP.* pages 210–218.

Ivan A Sag, Timothy Baldwin, Francis Bond, Ann Copestake, and Dan Flickinger. 2002. Multiword expressions: A pain in the neck for nlp. In *Proceedings of International Conference on Intelligent Text Processing and Computational Linguistics, CICLING-2002.* Springer Berlin Heidelberg, pages 1–15.

Marco SG Senaldi, Gianluca E Lebani, and Alessandro Lenci. 2016. Lexical variability and compositionality: Investigating idiomaticity with distributional semantic models pages 21–31.

Veronika Vincze and Attila Almasi. 2014. Non-lexicalized concepts in wordnets: A case study of english and hungarian. In *Proceedings of Global WordNet, Conference GWC-2014.* Global WordNet Association.

Detecting Hate Speech in Social Media

Shervin Malmasi
Harvard Medical School
Boston, MA, United States
smalmasi@bwh.harvard.edu

Marcos Zampieri
University of Wolverhampton
Wolverhampton, United Kingdom
marcos.zampieri@uni-koeln.de

Abstract

In this paper we examine methods to detect hate speech in social media, while distinguishing this from general profanity. We aim to establish lexical baselines for this task by applying supervised classification methods using a recently released dataset annotated for this purpose. As features, our system uses character n-grams, word n-grams and word skip-grams. We obtain results of 78% accuracy in identifying posts across three classes. Results demonstrate that the main challenge lies in discriminating profanity and hate speech from each other. A number of directions for future work are discussed.

1 Introduction

Research on safety and security in social media has grown substantially in the last decade. A particularly relevant aspect of this work is detecting and preventing the use of various forms of abusive language in blogs, micro-blogs, and social networks. A number of recent studies have been published on this issue such as the work by Xu et al. (2012) on identifying cyber-bullying, the detection of hate speech (Burnap and Williams, 2015) which was the topic of a recent survey (Schmidt and Wiegand, 2017), and the detection of racism (Tulkens et al., 2016) in user generated content.

The growing interest in this topic within the research community is evidenced by several related studies presented in Section 2 and by two recent workshops: Text Analytics for Cybersecurity and Online Safety (TA-COS)[1] held in 2016 at LREC and Abusive Language Workshop (AWL)[2] held in 2017 at ACL.

---

[1] http://www.ta-cos.org/home
[2] https://sites.google.com/site/abusivelanguageworkshop2017/

In this paper we address the problem of hate speech detection using a dataset which contains English tweets annotated with three labels: (1) hate speech (HATE); (2) offensive language but no hate speech (OFFENSIVE); and (3) no offensive content (OK). Most studies on abusive language so far (Burnap and Williams, 2015; Djuric et al., 2015; Nobata et al., 2016) have been modeled as binary classification with only one positive and one negative classes (*e.g.* hate speech vs non-hate speech). As noted by Dinakar et al. (2011), systems trained on such data often rely on the frequency of offensive or non-socially acceptable words to distinguish between the two classes. Dinakar et al. (2011) stress that in some cases "the lack of profanity or negativity [can] mislead the classifier".

Indeed, the presence of profane content does not in itself signify hate speech. General profanity is not necessarily targeted towards an individual and may be used for stylistic purposes or emphasis. On the other hand, hate speech may denigrate or threaten an individual or a group of people without the use of any profanities.

The main aim of this paper is to establish a lexical baseline for discriminating between hate speech and profanity on this standard dataset. The corpus used here provides us with an interesting opportunity to investigate how well a system can detect hate speech from other content that is generally profane. This baseline can be used to determine the difficulty of this task, and help highlight the most challenging aspects which must be addressed in future work.

The rest of this paper is organized as follows. In Section 2 we briefly outline some previous work on abusive language detection. The data is presented in Section 3, along with a description of our computational approach, features, and evaluation methodology. Results are presented in Section 4, followed by a conclusion and future perspectives in Section 5.

Proceedings of Recent Advances in Natural Language Processing, pages 467–472,
Varna, Bulgaria, Sep 4–6 2017.

2   Related Work

There have been several studies on computational methods to detect abusive language published in the last few years. One example is the work by Xu et al. (2012) who apply sentiment analysis to detect bullying in tweets and use Latent Dirichlet Allocation (LDA) topic models (Blei et al., 2003) to identify relevant topics in these texts.

A number of studies have been published on hate speech detection. As previously mentioned, to the best of our knowledge all of them rely on binary classification (*e.g.* hate speech vs non-hate speech). Examples of such studies include the work by Kwok and Wang (2013), Djuric et al. (2015), Burnap and Williams (2015), and by Nobata et al. (2016).

Due to the availability of suitable corpora, the overwhelming majority of studies on abusive language, including ours, have used English data. However, more recently a few studies have investigated abusive language detection in other languages. Mubarak et al. (2017) addresses abusive language detection on Arabic social media and Su et al. (2017) presents a system to detect and rephrase profanity in Chinese. Hate speech and abusive language datasets have been recently annotated for German (Ross et al., 2016) and Slovene (Fišer et al., 2017) opening avenues for future work in languages other than English.

3   Methods

Next we present the Hate Speech Detection dataset used in our experiments. We applied a linear Support Vector Machine (SVM) classifier and used three groups of features extracted for these experiments: surface n-grams, word skip-grams, and Brown clusters. The classifier and features are described in more detail in Section 3.2 and Section 3.3 respectively. Finally, Section 3.4 discusses evaluation methods.

3.1   Data

In these experiments we use the aforementioned Hate Speech Detection dataset[3] distributed via CrowdFlower.[4] The dataset features 14,509 English tweets annotated by a minimum of three annotators.

Individuals in charge of the annotation of this dataset were asked to annotate each tweet and categorize them into one of three classes:

1. (HATE): contains hate speech;

2. (OFFENSIVE): contains offensive language but no hate speech;

3. (OK): no offensive content at all.

Each instance in this dataset contains the text of a tweet[5] along with one of the three aforementioned labels. The distribution of the texts across the three classes is shown in Table 1.

Class	Texts
HATE	2,399
OFFENSIVE	4,836
OK	7,274
Total	14,509

Table 1: The distribution of classes and tweets in the Hate Speech Detection dataset.

All the texts are preprocessed to lowercase all tokens and to remove URLs and emojis.

3.2   Classifier

We use a linear SVM to perform multi-class classification in our experiments. We use the LIBLINEAR[6] package (Fan et al., 2008) which has been shown to be very efficient for similar text classification tasks. For example, the LIBLINEAR SVM implementation has been demonstrated to be a very effective classifier for Native Language Identification (Malmasi and Dras, 2015), temporal text classification (Zampieri et al., 2016a), and language variety identification (Zampieri et al., 2016b).

3.3   Features

We use two groups of surface features in our experiments as follows:

- Surface n-grams: These are our most basic features, consisting of character n-grams (of order 2–8) and word n-grams (of order 1–3). All tokens are lowercased before extraction of n-grams; character n-grams are extracted across word boundaries.

- Word Skip-grams: Similar to the above features, we also extract 1-, 2- and 3-skip word bigrams. These features are were chosen to approximate longer distance dependencies between words, which would be hard to capture using bigrams alone.

---

[5] Each tweet is limited to a maximum of 140 characters.
[6]http://www.csie.ntu.edu.tw/%7Ecjlin/liblinear/

3.4 Evaluation

To evaluate our methods we use 10-fold cross-validation. For creating the folds, we employ stratified cross-validation aiming to ensure that the proportion of classes within each partition is equal (Kohavi, 1995).

We report our results in terms of accuracy. The results obtained by our methods are compared against a majority class baseline and an oracle classifier.

The oracle takes the predictions by all the classifiers in Table 2 into account. It assigns the correct class label for an instance if at least one of the the classifiers produces the correct label for that instance. This approach establishes the *potential* or *theoretical* upper limit performance for a given dataset. Similar analysis using oracle classifiers have been previously applied to estimate the theoretical upper bound of shared tasks datasets in Native Language Identification (Malmasi et al., 2015) and similar language and language variety identification (Goutte et al., 2016).

4 Results

We start by investigating the efficacy of our features for this task. We fist train a single classifier, with each of them using a type of feature. Subsequently we also train a single model combining all of our features into single space. These are compared against the majority class baseline, as well as the oracle. The results of these experiments are listed in Table 2.

Feature	Accuracy (%)
Majority Class Baseline	50.1
Oracle	91.6
Character bigrams	73.6
Character trigrams	77.2
Character 4-grams	**78.0**
Character 5-grams	77.9
Character 6-grams	77.2
Character 7-grams	76.5
Character 8-grams	75.8
Word unigrams	77.5
Word bigrams	73.8
Word trigrams	67.4
1-skip Word bigrams	74.0
2-skip Word bigrams	73.8
3-skip Word bigrams	73.9
All features combined	77.5

Table 2: Classification results under 10-fold cross-validation.

The majority class baseline is quite high due to the class imbalance in the data. The oracle achieves an accuracy of 91.6%, showing that none of our features are able to correctly classify a substantial portion of our samples.

We note that character n-grams perform well here, with 4-grams achieving the best performance of all features. Word unigrams also perform well, while performance degrades with bigrams, trigrams and skip-grams. However, the skip-grams may be capturing longer distance dependencies which provide complementary information to the other feature types. In tasks relying on stylistic information, it has been shown that skip-grams capture information that is very similar to syntactic dependencies (Malmasi and Cahill, 2015, §5).

Finally, the combination of all features does not achieve the performance of a character 4-grams model and causes a large dimensionality increase, with a total of 5.5 million features. It is not clear if this model is able to correctly capture the diverse information provided by the three feature types since we include more character n-gram models than word-based ones.

Next we analyze the rate of learning for these features. A learning curve for the classifier that yielded the best performance overall, character 4-grams, is shown in Figure 1.

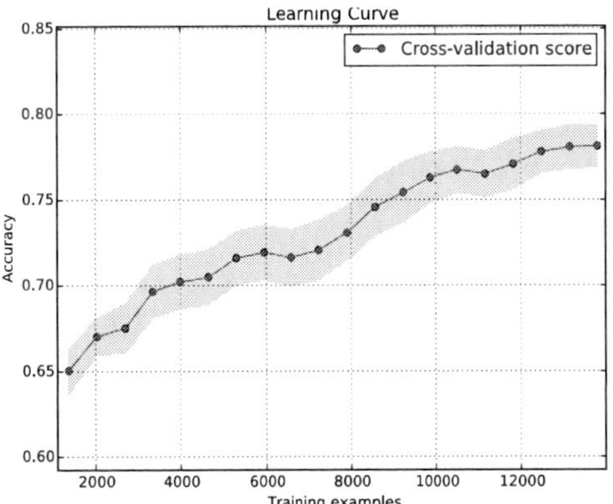

Figure 1: Learning curve for a character 4-gram model, with standard deviation highlighted. Accuracy does not plateau with the maximal data size.

We observe that accuracy increased continuously as the amount of training instances increased, and the standard deviation of the results between the cross-validation folds decreased. This suggests that the use of more training data is likely to provide even higher accuracy. It should be noted, however, that accuracy increases at a much slower rate after $15{,}000$ training instances.

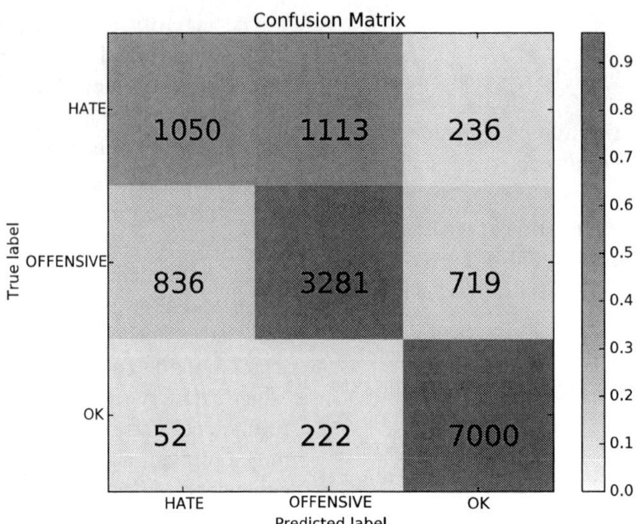

Figure 2: Confusion matrix of the character 4-gram model for our 3 classes. The heatmap represents the proportion of correctly classified examples in each class (this is normalized as the data distribution is imbalanced). The raw numbers are also reported within each cell. We note that the HATE class is the hardest to classify and is highly confused with the OFFENSIVE class.

Finally, we also examine a confusion matrix for the character 4-gram model, as shown in Figure 2. This demonstrates that the greatest degree of confusion lies between hate speech and generally offensive material, with hate speech more frequently being confused for offensive content. A substantial amount of offensive content is also misclassified as being non-offensive. The non-offensive class achieves the best result, with the vast majority of samples being correctly classified.

5 Conclusion

In this paper we applied text classification methods to distinguish between hate speech, profanity, and other texts. We applied standard lexical features and a linear SVM classifier to establish a baseline for this task. The best result was obtained by a character 4-gram model achieving 78% accuracy. The results presented in this paper showed that distinguishing profanity from hate speech is a very challenging task.

This was to the best of our knowledge one of the first experiments to detect hate speech on social media in a scenario including non-hate speech profanity. Previous work so far (e.g. Burnap and Williams (2015) and Djuric et al. (2015)) dealt with the distinction between hate speech and socially acceptable texts in a binary classifi-

cation setting. In binary classification, Dinakar et al. (2011) note that the frequency of offensive words helps classifiers to distinguish between hate speech and socially acceptable texts.

We see a few directions in which this work could be expanded such as the use of more robust ensemble classifiers, a linguistic analysis of the most informative features, and error analysis of the misclassified instances. These aspects are presented in more detail in the next section.

5.1 Future Work

In future work we would like to investigate the performance of classifier ensembles and meta-learning for this task. Previous work has applied these techniques to a number of comparable text classification tasks, achieving success in competitive shared tasks. Examples of recent applications include automatic triage of posts in mental health forums (Malmasi et al., 2016b), detection of lexical complexity (Malmasi et al., 2016a), Native Language Identification (Malmasi and Dras, 2017), and dialect identification (Malmasi and Zampieri, 2017).

Another direction to pursue is the careful analysis of the most informative features for each class in this dataset. Our initial exploitation of the most informative words unigrams and bigrams suggests that coarse and obscene words are very informative for both HATE and OFFENSIVE words which confuses the classifiers. For HATE we observed a prominence of words targeting ethnic and social groups. Finally, an interesting outcome that should be investigated in more detail is that many of the most informative bigrams for the OK feature grammatical words. A more detailed analysis of these features could lead to more robust feature engineering methods.

An error analysis could also help us better understand the challenges in this task. This could be used to provide insights about the classifiers' performance as well as any underlying issues with the annotation of the Hate Speech Detection dataset which, as pointed out by Ross et al. (2016), is far from trivial. Figure 2 confirms that, as expected, most confusion occurs between HATE and OFFENSIVE texts. However, we also note that a substantial amount of offensive content is misclassified as being non-offensive. The aforementioned error analysis can provide insights about this.

Acknowledgments

We would like to thank the anonymous RANLP reviewers who provided us valuable feedback to increase the quality of this paper.

We further thank the developers and the annotators who worked on the Hate Speech Dataset for making this important resource available.

References

David M Blei, Andrew Y Ng, and Michael I Jordan. 2003. Latent Dirichlet Allocation. *Journal of machine Learning research* 3(Jan):993–1022.

Pete Burnap and Matthew L Williams. 2015. Cyber hate speech on twitter: An application of machine classification and statistical modeling for policy and decision making. *Policy & Internet* 7(2):223–242.

Karthik Dinakar, Roi Reichart, and Henry Lieberman. 2011. Modeling the detection of textual cyberbullying. In *The Social Mobile Web*. pages 11–17.

Nemanja Djuric, Jing Zhou, Robin Morris, Mihajlo Grbovic, Vladan Radosavljevic, and Narayan Bhamidipati. 2015. Hate speech detection with comment embeddings. In *Proceedings of the 24th International Conference on World Wide Web Companion*. International World Wide Web Conferences Steering Committee, pages 29–30.

Rong-En Fan, Kai-Wei Chang, Cho-Jui Hsieh, Xiang-Rui Wang, and Chih-Jen Lin. 2008. LIBLINEAR: A Library for Large Linear Classification. *Journal of Machine Learning Research* 9:1871–1874.

Darja Fišer, Tomaž Erjavec, and Nikola Ljubešić. 2017. Legal Framework, Dataset and Annotation Schema for Socially Unacceptable On-line Discourse Practices in Slovene. In *Proceedings of the Workshop Workshop on Abusive Language Online (ALW)*. Vancouver, Canada.

Cyril Goutte, Serge Léger, Shervin Malmasi, and Marcos Zampieri. 2016. Discriminating Similar Languages: Evaluations and Explorations. In *Proceedings of Language Resources and Evaluation (LREC)*. Portoroz, Slovenia.

Ron Kohavi. 1995. A study of cross-validation and bootstrap for accuracy estimation and model selection. In *IJCAI*. volume 14, pages 1137–1145.

Irene Kwok and Yuzhou Wang. 2013. Locate the hate: Detecting tweets against blacks. In *Twenty-Seventh AAAI Conference on Artificial Intelligence*.

Shervin Malmasi and Aoife Cahill. 2015. Measuring Feature Diversity in Native Language Identification. In *Proceedings of the Tenth Workshop on Innovative Use of NLP for Building Educational Applications*. Association for Computational Linguistics, Denver, Colorado.

Shervin Malmasi and Mark Dras. 2015. Large-scale Native Language Identification with Cross-Corpus Evaluation. In *Proceedings of NAACL-HLT 2015*. Association for Computational Linguistics, Denver, Colorado.

Shervin Malmasi and Mark Dras. 2017. Native Language Identification using Stacked Generalization. *arXiv preprint arXiv:1703.06541* .

Shervin Malmasi, Mark Dras, and Marcos Zampieri. 2016a. Ltg at semeval-2016 task 11: Complex word identification with classifier ensembles. In *Proceedings of SemEval*.

Shervin Malmasi, Joel Tetreault, and Mark Dras. 2015. Oracle and Human Baselines for Native Language Identification. In *Proceedings of the Tenth Workshop on Innovative Use of NLP for Building Educational Applications*. Association for Computational Linguistics, Denver, Colorado.

Shervin Malmasi and Marcos Zampieri. 2017. German Dialect Identification in Interview Transcriptions. In *Proceedings of the Workshop on NLP for Similar Languages, Varieties and Dialects (VarDial)*.

Shervin Malmasi, Marcos Zampieri, and Mark Dras. 2016b. Predicting Post Severity in Mental Health Forums. In *Proceedings of the Workshop on Computational Linguistics and Clinical Psychology (CLPsych)*.

Hamdy Mubarak, Darwish Kareem, and Magdy Walid. 2017. Abusive Language Detection on Arabic Social Media. In *Proceedings of the Workshop Workshop on Abusive Language Online (ALW)*. Vancouver, Canada.

Chikashi Nobata, Joel Tetreault, Achint Thomas, Yashar Mehdad, and Yi Chang. 2016. Abusive Language Detection in Online User Content. In *Proceedings of the 25th International Conference on World Wide Web*. International World Wide Web Conferences Steering Committee, pages 145–153.

Björn Ross, Michael Rist, Guillermo Carbonell, Benjamin Cabrera, Nils Kurowsky, and Michael Wojatzki. 2016. Measuring the Reliability of Hate Speech Annotations: The Case of the European Refugee Crisis. In *Proceedings of the Workshop on Natural Language Processing for Computer-Mediated Communication (NLP4CMC)*. Bochum, Germany.

Anna Schmidt and Michael Wiegand. 2017. A Survey on Hate Speech Detection Using Natural Language Processing. In *Proceedings of the Fifth International Workshop on Natural Language Processing for Social Media. Association for Computational Linguistics*. Valencia, Spain, pages 1–10.

Huei-Po Su, Chen-Jie Huang, Hao-Tsung Chang, and Chuan-Jie Lin. 2017. Rephrasing Profanity in Chinese Text. In *Proceedings of the Workshop Workshop on Abusive Language Online (ALW)*. Vancouver, Canada.

Stéphan Tulkens, Lisa Hilte, Elise Lodewyckx, Ben Verhoeven, and Walter Daelemans. 2016. A Dictionary-based Approach to Racism Detection in Dutch Social Media. In *Proceedings of the Workshop Text Analytics for Cybersecurity and Online Safety (TA-COS)*. Portoroz, Slovenia.

Jun-Ming Xu, Kwang-Sung Jun, Xiaojin Zhu, and Amy Bellmore. 2012. Learning from bullying traces in social media. In *Proceedings of the 2012 conference of the North American chapter of the association for computational linguistics: Human language technologies*. Association for Computational Linguistics, pages 656–666.

Marcos Zampieri, Shervin Malmasi, and Mark Dras. 2016a. Modeling language change in historical corpora: the case of Portuguese. In *Proceedings of Language Resources and Evaluation (LREC)*. Portoroz, Slovenia.

Marcos Zampieri, Shervin Malmasi, Octavia-Maria Sulea, and Liviu P Dinu. 2016b. A Computational Approach to the Study of Portuguese Newspapers Published in Macau. In *Proceedings of Workshop on Natural Language Processing Meets Journalism (NLPMJ)*. pages 47–51.

Inforex — a Collaborative System
for Text Corpora Annotation and Analysis

Michał Marcińczuk   **Marcin Oleksy**   **Jan Kocoń**

G4.19 Research Group
Department of Computational Intelligence
Faculty of Computer Science and Management
Wrocław University of Technology, Wrocław, Poland
{michal.marcinczuk,marcin.oleksy,jan.kocon}@pwr.edu.pl

Abstract

We report a first major upgrade of Inforex — a web-based system for qualitative and collaborative text corpora annotation and analysis. Inforex is a part of
Polish CLARIN infrastructure[1]. It is integrated with a digital repository for storing
and publishing language resources[2] and it
allows to visualize, browse and annotate
text corpora stored in the repository. As
a result of a series of workshops for researchers in Humanities and Social Sciences we improved the graphical interface to make the system more friendly and
readable for non-experienced users. We
also implemented a new functionality for
a gold standard annotation which includes
private annotations and annotation agreement by a super-annotator.

1 Introduction

Digital humanities (DH) create new demand and
challenges for development of new or existing
tools and systems for text documents manipulation, processing, analysis and visualization.
CLARIN-PL — the Polish part of CLARIN infrastructure — tries to rise the challenges associated
with DH for Polish language. Among many other
issues, there is a need for an intuitive and easy
to use system for qualitative text corpora management, annotation, analysis and visualization. To
fulfill these needs we develop such a system called
Inforex. In this article we present the current state
of the system development.

The decision to create a system for text corpora annotation was taken in 2009 when there
were no such systems which support collaborative
work. On that time the only existing tools were
desktop applications for individual work such as
GATE (Cunningham et al., 2011) or Manufak-
turzysta Luna (Marciniak et al., 2010). Since
2010 several systems have emerged, like We-
bAnno 3 (Eckart de Castilho et al., 2016) or GATE
Teamware (Bontcheva et al., 2013).

The first version of Inforex system was released in 2010 and its initial role was to construct
corpus-based linguistic resource for various tasks
from the field of natural language processing,
including named entity recognition (Marcińczuk
et al., 2011), shallow parsing (Radziszewski and
Piasecki, 2010), word sense disambiguation (Bas
et al., 2008), recognition of semantic relations
between named entities (Marcińczuk and Ptak,
2012). It was used to develop two major (at that
time) resources for Polish: Corpus of Wrocław
University of Technology called KWPr (Broda
et al., 2012) (within the NEKST[3] project) and
Corpus of Economic News (CEN) (Marcińczuk
et al., 2013) (within the SyNaT project[4]). Later,
in 2013 Inforex was used to construct another major resource, which is Polish Corpus of Suicide
Notes (PCSN)[5] (Marcińczuk et al., 2011) guided
by Monika Zaśko-Zielińska (2013). Until now the
system has been used to access the corpus. The
access is granted on a demand after obtaining a
permission form Wrocław University.

In 2013 Poland joined CLARIN — European
Research Infrastructure for Language Resources
and Technology. The goal of CLARIN is to
make the language technologies more accessible
to researches from humanities and social sciences,
which in most cases do not have the technical
skills to use many of the tools on their own. At that
time we made a decision to make Inforex a part

---

[1] http://clarin-pl.eu
[2] http://clarin-pl.eu/dspace
[3] http://nekst.ipipan.waw.pl/
[4] http://www.synat.pl/
[5] http://pcsn.uni.wroc.pl/

Proceedings of Recent Advances in Natural Language Processing, pages 473–482,
Varna, Bulgaria, Sep 4–6 2017.

of the Polish CLARIN infrastructure. In 2015–2017 we have organized several workshops for researchers in humanities and social sciences. The workshops showed us several user experience issues. System GUI turned out to be not enough intuitive for non-experienced users. Then, first of all, it needed to be simplified. Second problem was connected with the methodology. The researchers use various tools for corpora analysis (including spreadsheets) and Inforex may be treated as some kind of pre-processing tool that allows to prepare corpus for further analysis. Data export was possible but complicated and required an access to a database. Users feedback proved that the easy form of data export is one of the crucial needs. After the set of workshops we gathered more information about other important needs (also in the form of questionnaires) like access to a custom annotation schemas definition or data visualisation. Some of them have been already implemented and the other are under construction.

2 Inforex Features Overview

In the following sections we present the main functionalities and features of the Inforex system.

2.1 Web-based Access

Inforex is a web-based tool which does not require installation. It can be accessed by any web-browser which support JavaScript. Despite Inforex is built on several universal JavaScript libraries and frameworks (jQuery, jQuery extensions and Bootstrap) we suggest using Chrome and Firefox. These two web browsers are used to test the system on daily bases. Users might use other browsers as well, however we are not able to validate all functions in each of the available web browsers, thus some minor issues might occur.

2.2 Authorized and Public Access

Corpora stored in Inforex can be accessed by authorized and unauthorized users. The manager of the corpus (the owner or a user with specific privileges) decides what type of information from the corpora can be publicly available. For instance, only authorized users can have access to documents' content and can modify the corpus annotations while unauthorized users may have access to some statistics or annotation frequency lists.

2.3 Integration with DSpace as a Part of Polish CLARIN Infrastructure

Inforex system is available at `http://inforex.clarin-pl.eu` and it is part of Polish CLARIN infrastructure. This installation is integrated with the official repository for language resources in Polish CLARIN[6]. The repository runs on DSpace system[7]. When a user registers in `https://clarin-pl.eu/dspace/`, he also gains access to Inforex system. At this stage accounts are automatically synchronized. In the future both systems will use unified federation authorization.

2.4 Collaboration

Inforex offers several ways for collaborative work on a single corpus. One of them is the access to the same corpora for different authorized users. The other one is a selective, task-oriented access to the same document. For instance, different groups of users can have access to document's metadata. The last one is the "2+1" annotation, i.e. two or more users annotate the same set of documents independently and the super-annotator creates the final set of annotations based on their input. More about this type of collaboration is presented in Section 3.2.

2.5 Qualitative Document Annotation

Inforex was designed for qualitative document annotation. This means it does not offer a fast and robust search functions over large corpora with millions of documents. Such functionality can be obtained using other existing tools designed for it, for instance Sketch Engine (Kilgarriff et al., 2014) or NoSketch Engine (Rychlý, 2007). Inforex is suited for medium size corpora (containing thousands of small documents) and to manually describe documents in terms of their metadata, annotations (types of phrases organized in a hierarchy), annotation attributes, relations between annotations and annotation frames.

2.6 Language-independent

Inforex is language-independent in the sense that it can handle documents in any natural language. So far it has been used to annotate Polish, English and Hebrew texts (see Section 3.2).

---

[6]`https://clarin-pl.eu/dspace/`
[7]`https://github.com/ufal/clarin-dspace`

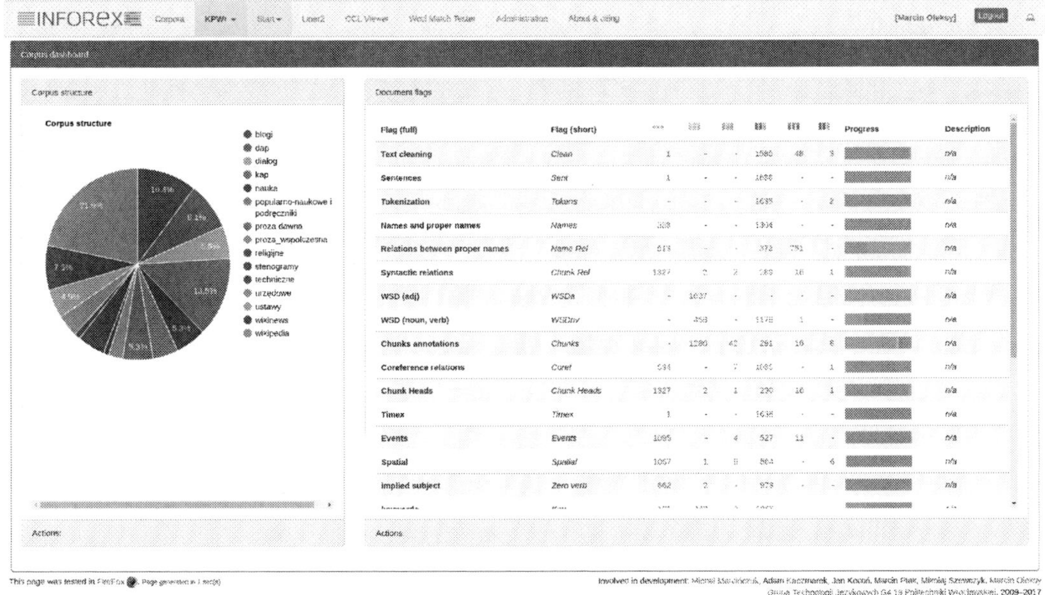

Figure 1: Corpus overview

2.7 Document Visualisation

Inforex can handle documents in two formats: plain text and XML. For XML documents it is possible to display their content in a visually formated way. This allows to highlight the document structure what improves the user experience while browsing and annotating documents. Sample visualizations of different types of documents are presented in Figure 3.

2.8 Document Description

Inforex supports four types of information units which can be used to describe documents content:

1. Metadata — an information unit which is assigned to whole document (author name, document creation time, source, etc.).

2. Annotation — an information unit which is assigned to a sequence of words in the document content. Each annotation is described with a category (categories can be organized in a hierarchy) and a set of attributes. The set of attributes depends on the semantic interpretation of the annotation category. For instance, for named entities it can be a lemma, for temporal expressions it can be a normalized value of the expression and for event mentions it can be an event modality.

3. Relation — an information unit which is assigned to a pair of annotations. It is a directed link between two annotations of some category.

4. Frame — an information unit which is assigned to a set of annotations. Frame consists of a set of annotations with roles assigned to them. This type of structure can be used for event annotations (LCD, 2005).

3 Recent Improvements

In the following sections we present the recent major improvements of Inforex system.

3.1 Modern Layout

A set of workshops carried out from 2015 to 2017 showed that there was the need for an adjustment of user interface to a new group of users — researchers in humanities and social sciences not involved in NLP tools development. New users reported confusion with the large amount of information and the number of available functions. The need of interface simplification appeared while functionalities of the system would remain unchanged. Thus, Inforex layout has been upgraded and modernized. It involved not only a design lifting of the user interface but also changes in navigation panels. The comparision of *old* and *new*

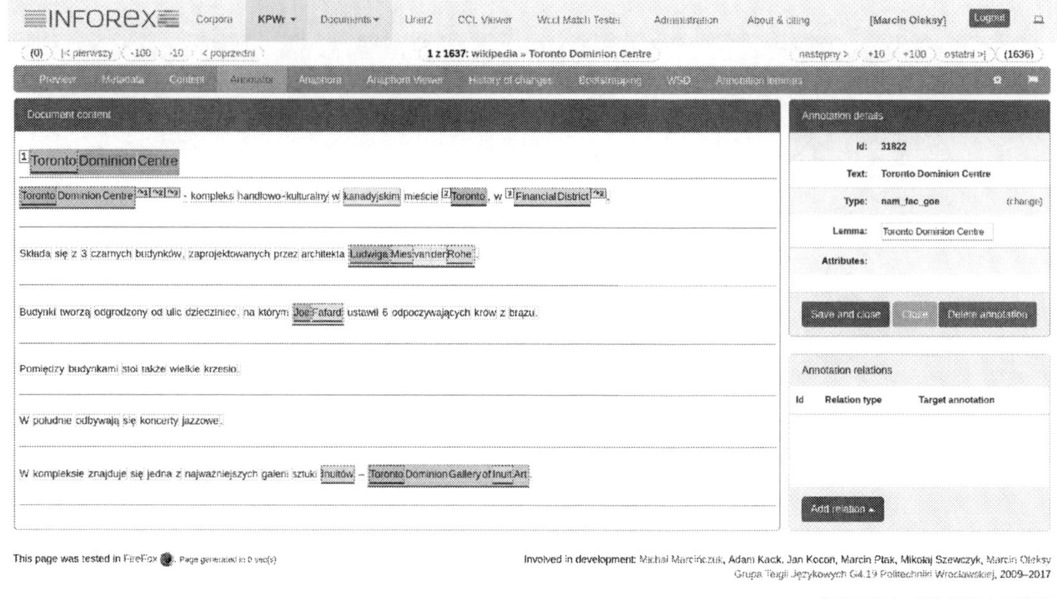

Figure 2: Document annotation view

layout is presented in Figure 4.

3.2 Annotation Agreement

Reliability is a key value in the creation of a good quality corpora for learning and testing of NLP tools. The current version of Inforex enables simultaneous and independent annotation of the same text sample by more than one annotator. Moreover, the annotation process coordinator may keep track of inter-annotator agreement between two raters thanks to the *Agreement module* which uses Positive Specific Agreement (PSA) measure (Hripcsak and Rothschild, 2005) to calculate the reliability (see Figure 5). View configuration gives the opportunity to define annotation layers, subsets or categories, users and set of documents that have to be analysed. The coordinator may also specify a comparison mode: whether the system has to take into consideration the annotation boundaries only or boundaries and categories. It may also include annotation lemmas. Inter-annotator agreement is a very important indicator of the annotation guidelines clearness or cohesion. Keeping track of changes of the inter-annotator agreement between subsequent annotation iterations helps to improve the quality of the annotation guidelines. Agreement module makes that process easier and faster.

Inforex system also supports the curation of the annotation process (see Figure 6). The curator can make choice between two different annotators choices, or even reject consistent but incorrect annotations. Thanks to that module several Gold Standard projects were performed e.g. Polish Coreference Corpus (Ogrodniczuk et al., 2015) for definite descriptions annotation and Polish Spatial Texts corpus for the annotation of dynamic spatial expressions.

4 Applications

In the following sections we present several practical applications of the Inforex system.

4.1 KPWr

KPWr (Polish Corpus of Wrocław University of Technology) (Broda et al., 2012) is a corpus of written and spoken documents available on the Creative Commons license which is intended primarily as a training and testing material for NLP tools being developed at Wrocław University of Science and Technology. It is successively enriched with annotation layers. Inforex recently supported manual text annotation within such layers as temporal expressions and their normalizations, events (and description of event attributes), spatial expressions and semantic roles. In order to prepare temporal expressions annotation (Kocoń et al., 2015) a new annotation scheme based on

(a) Facebook conversation.

(b) Wikipedia article.

(c) Hebrew document.

Figure 3: Sample documents visualizations

TimeML was added. These categories refer to a date, time of a day, duration and frequency of an event. Annotation lemmas perspective was used to provide normalized temporal expressions, revealing that the term 'lemma' in Inforex may function as a broad concept. The Annotator perspective from the system also supports event annotation (Marcińczuk et al., 2015). There are seven coarse-grained categories of events, i.e. action, state, reporting, perception, aspectual, intensional action and intensional state. The categorization was based on the TimeML guidelines with some modifications. It also involved creation of a new annotation scheme. The flexibility in adding new annotation layers (setting the new annotation categories) is one of the most important features. The possibility of establishing relations between annotated fragments is not less relevant. It was crucial e.g. for spatial expressions annotation. Its main goal was to extract different ways of distributing spatial information throughout a sentence by reviewing the lexical and grammatical signals of various relations between objects (Marcińczuk et al., 2016).

4.2 European Legal Texts

As practice shows, although Inforex was primarily developed for Polish language, that it can also be used to work with documents written in other languages. Inforex features and functionalities are useful e.g. in examining current EU official literature related to territorial development and urban planning. Authors of this analysis first uploaded EU Territorial Policy Documents 2007-2016[8] to CLARIN-PL DSpace repository and then imported it to the Inforex system. The corpus was divided into 4 subcorpora and prepared for qualitative and quantitative analysis. The review of the key strands enabled the identification of its 8 core values (or principles) for further statistical and contextual analysis. After ascribing to each category its textual triggers (word forms), a quantitive analysis using words frequency lists generated by Inforex was performed. Manual annotation with a newly defined set of annotations and Annotation Browser with the possibility of exporting data were a great support for qualitative analysis — detailed contextual analysis of the corpus focused on two crucial categories: *Participation* and *Communication*.

---

[8]http://hdl.handle.net/11321/316

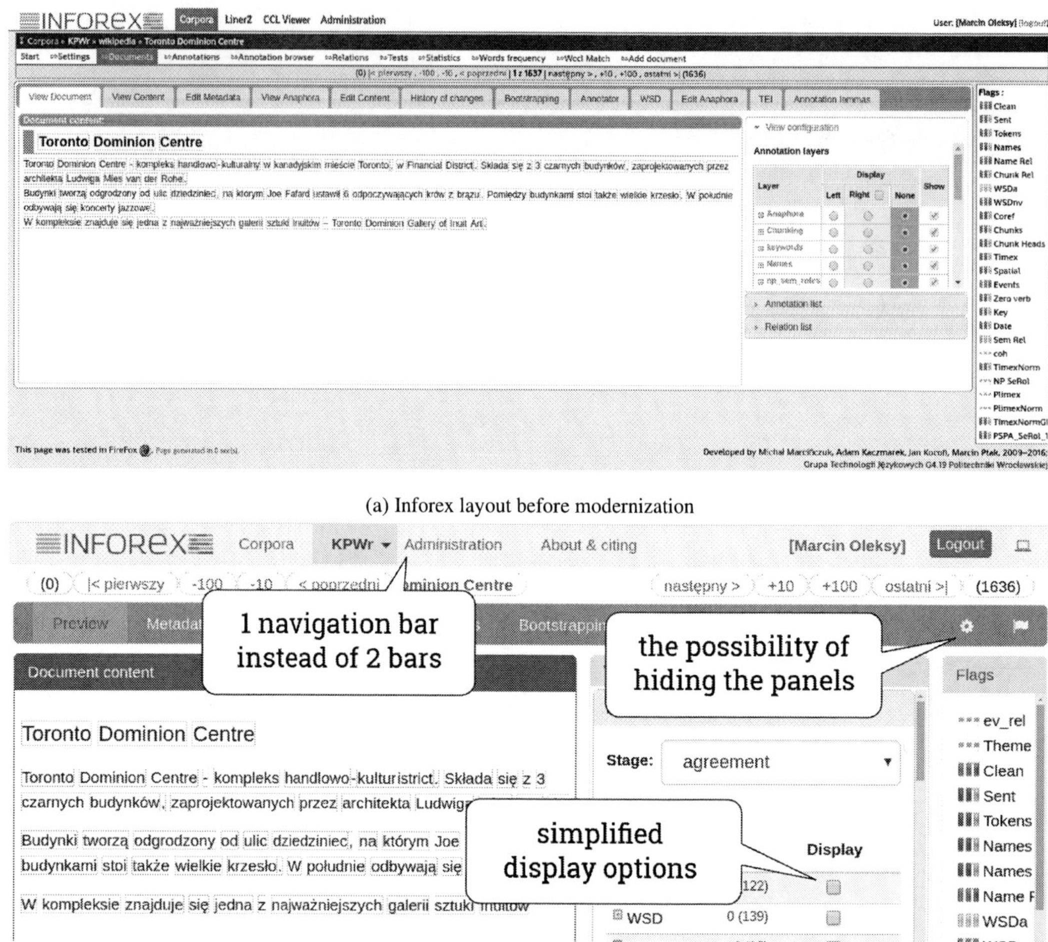

(a) Inforex layout before modernization

(b) Inforex layout after modernization

Figure 4: Inforex layouts comparison

4.3 Hebrew Corpus

Inforex supports manual annotation even if the text is written using non-latin alphabet and a right-to-left notation. One of the system applications was related to a corpus of Hebrew gravestone inscriptions. It also involved the creation of a new annotation schema. Categories referred mainly to the pragmatic level of communication (e.g. initial and final expressions, laudations, death circumstances). The perspective of annotation lemmas was used to enter Polish translations of annotated fragments, which also showed that the lemma attribute may be a broad term especially in the case of practical applications of the system.

4.4 Other Corpora

Inforex was used to prepare the training data during participation in BSNLP 2017 shared task on multilingual named entity recognition aimed at recognizing mentions of named entities in web documents in Slavic languages, their normalization / lemmatization, and cross-language matching (Marcińczuk et al., 2017). The system also supported the annotation of the corpora constructed specially for specific tasks from the field of natural language processing e.g. Polish Coreference Corpus for definite descriptions annotation and Polish Spatial Texts corpus for the annotation of dynamic spatial expressions. It involved creation of dedicated annotation layers but, what is important, in these tasks the new module of the system (Annotation Agreement and "2+1" annotation) was used for the first time, which significantly improved the time of preparation of annotated training and testing corpora.

5   Summary

Inforex system, as a part of CLARIN-PL infrastructure, is gradually developed. Although its initial role was to construct qualitative linguistic resources for various tasks from the field of natural language processing, recently it is also used by scientists for other purposes. We received an important and constructive feedback from users during and after workshops related to CLARIN-PL tools and resources. As users have different needs, we identified the common functionalities and implement them as soon as possible in order to boost their research tasks and provide new possibilities. We also challenged with the fact that many researches from the field of digital humanities are not experienced users of such systems and we made Inforex as easy and intuitive as possible.

Acknowledgments

Work financed as part of the investment in the CLARIN-PL research infrastructure funded by the Polish Ministry of Science and Higher Education.

References

Dominik Bas, Bartosz Broda, and Maciej Piasecki. 2008. Towards Word Sense Disambiguation of Polish. In *Proceedings of the International Multiconference on Computer Science and Information Technology, {IMCSIT} 2008, Wisla, Poland, 20-22 October 2008*. IEEE, pages 73–78. https://doi.org/10.1109/IMCSIT.2008.4747220.

Kalina Bontcheva, Hamish Cunningham, Ian Roberts, Angus Roberts, Valentin Tablan, Niraj Aswani, and Genevieve Gorrell. 2013. Gate teamware: a web-based, collaborative text annotation framework. *Language Resources and Evaluation* 47(4):1007–1029.

Bartosz Broda, Michał Marcińczuk, Marek Maziarz, Adam Radziszewski, and Adam Wardyński. 2012. KPWr: Towards a Free Corpus of Polish. In Nicoletta Calzolari, Khalid Choukri, Thierry Declerck, Mehmet Uğur Doğan, Bente Maegaard, Joseph Mariani, Jan Odijk, and Stelios Piperidis, editors, *Proceedings of LREC'12*. ELRA, Istanbul, Turkey.

Hamish Cunningham, Diana Maynard, Kalina Bontcheva, Valentin Tablan, Niraj Aswani, Ian Roberts, Genevieve Gorrell, Adam Funk, Angus Roberts, Danica Damljanovic, Thomas Heitz, Mark A. Greenwood, Horacio Saggion, Johann Petrak, Yaoyong Li, and Wim Peters. 2011. *Text Processing with GATE (Version 6)*. http://tinyurl.com/gatebook.

Richard Eckart de Castilho, Eva Mujdricza-Maydt, Seid Muhie Yimam, Silvana Hartmann, Iryna Gurevych, Anette Frank, and Chris Biemann. 2016. A web-based tool for the integrated annotation of semantic and syntactic structures. In *Proceedings of the workshop on Language Technology Resources and Tools for Digital Humanities (LT4DH) at COLING 2016*. pages 76–84.

George Hripcsak and Adam S. Rothschild. 2005. Agreement, the f-measure, and reliability in information retrieval. *J. of Am. Medical Informatics Association* 12(3):296–298.

Adam Kilgarriff, Vít Baisa, Jan Bušta, Miloš Jakubíček, Vojtěch Kovář, Jan Michelfeit, Pavel Rychlý, and Vít Suchomel. 2014. The sketch engine: ten years on. *Lexicography* .

Jan Kocoń, Michał Marcińczuk, Marcin Oleksy, Tomasz Bernaś, and Michał Wolski. 2015. Temporal expressions in polish corpus kpwr. *Cognitive Studies— Études cognitives* (15):293–317.

LCD. 2005. ACE (Automatic Content Extraction) English Annotation Guidelines for Events. Technical report, Linguistic Data Consortium.

M. Marcińczuk and M. Ptak. 2012. *Preliminary study on automatic induction of rules for recognition of semantic relations between proper names in Polish texts*, volume 7499 LNAI.

Michał Marcińczuk, Jan Kocoń, and Marcin Oleksy. 2017. Liner2 — a generic framework for named entity recognition. In *Proceedings of the 6th Workshop on Balto-Slavic Natural Language Processing*. Association for Computational Linguistics, Valencia, Spain, pages 86–91. http://www.aclweb.org/anthology/W17-1413.

Michał Marcińczuk, Marcin Oleksy, Tomasz Bernaś, Jan Kocoń, and Michał Wolski. 2015. Towards an event annotated corpus of polish. *Cognitive Studies— Études cognitives* (15):253–267.

Michał Marcińczuk, Michał Stanek, Maciej Piasecki, and Adam Musiał. 2011. Rich Set of Features for Proper Name Recognition in Polish Texts. In *SIIS 2011*. Springer.

Michał Mirosław Marcińczuk, Marcin Oleksy, and Jan Wieczorek. 2016. Towards recognition of spatial relations between entities for polish. *Cognitive Studies— Études cognitives* (16):119–132.

Małgorzata Marciniak, Agnieszka Mykowiecka, and Katarzyna Głowińska. 2010. Anotowany korpus dialogów telefonicznych. In Małgorzata Marciniak, editor, *Anotowany korpus dialogów telefonicznych*, Akademicka Oficyna Wydawnicza EXIT, Warsaw, chapter Anotacja korpusu LUNA–WOZ.PL, pages 217–230.

Michał Marcińczuk, Jan Kocoń, and Maciej Janicki. 2013. Liner2 – a customizable framework for proper names recognition for Polish. In Robert Bembenik, Lukasz Skonieczny, Henryk Rybinski, Marzena Kryszkiewicz, and Marek Niezgodka, editors, *Intelligent Tools for Building a Scientific Information Platform*, pages 231–253.

Michał Marcińczuk, Monika Zaśko-Zielińska, and Maciej Piasecki. 2011. Structure annotation in the polish corpus of suicide notes. In Ivan Habernal and Václav Matoušek, editors, *Text, Speech and Dialogue*, Springer Berlin Heidelberg, volume 6836 of *Lecture Notes in Computer Science*, pages 419–426.

Maciej Ogrodniczuk, Katarzyna Głowińska, Mateusz Kopeć, Agata Savary, and Magdalena Zawisławska. 2015. *Coreference in Polish: Annotation, Resolution and Evaluation*. Walter De Gruyter. http://www.degruyter.com/view/product/428667.

Adam Radziszewski and Maciej Piasecki. 2010. A Preliminary Noun Phrase Chunker for Polish. *Proceedings of the Intelligent Information Systems* pages 169–180.

Pavel Rychlý. 2007. Manatee/bonito - a modular corpus manager. In *1st Workshop on Recent Advances in Slavonic Natural Language Processing*. Masarykova univerzita, Brno, pages 65–70.

M. Zaśko-Zielińska. 2013. *Listy pożegnalne: w poszukiwaniu lingwistycznych wyznaczników autentyczności tekstu*. Quaestio. https://books.google.pl/books?id=QG60ngEACAAJ.

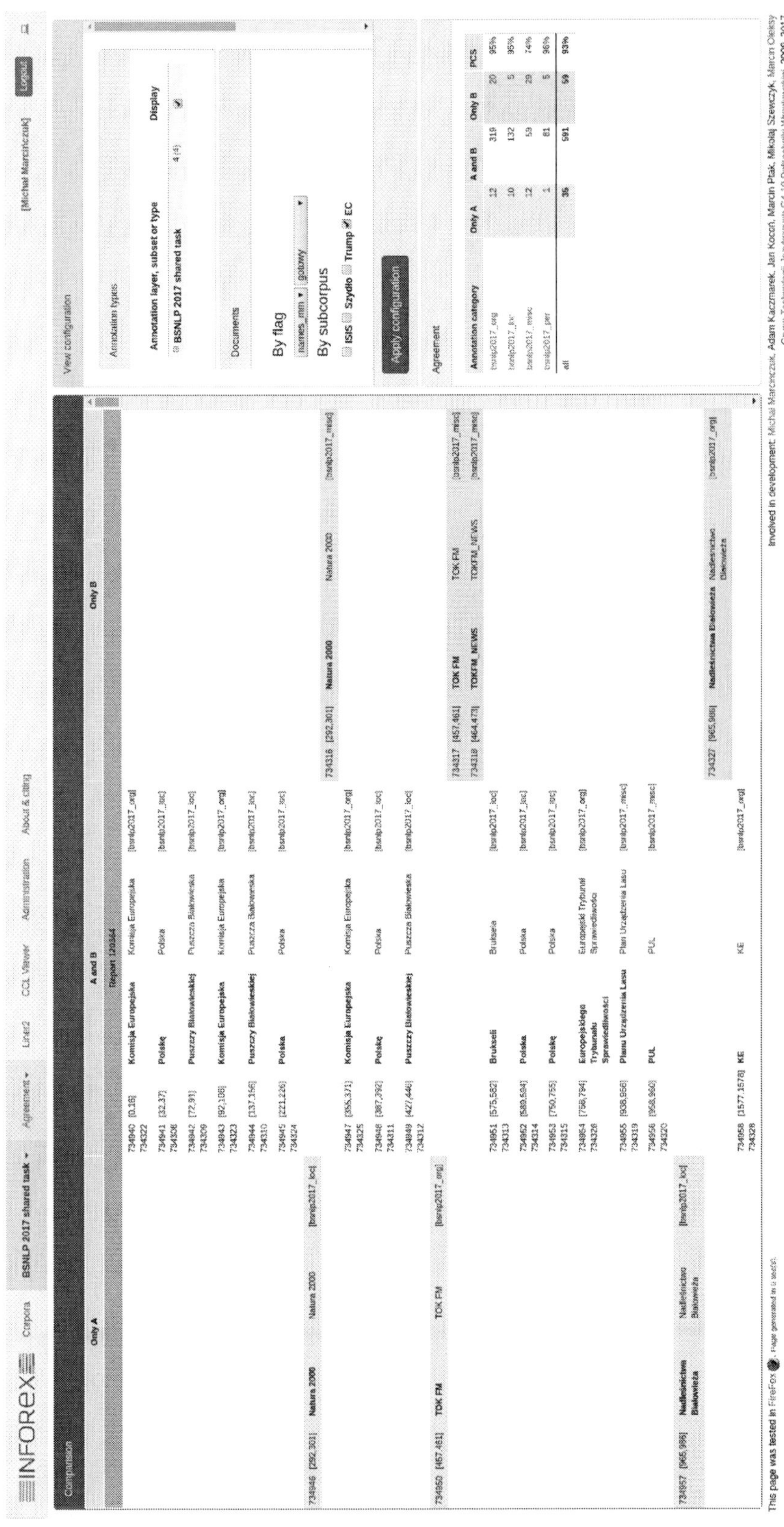

Figure 5: Summary of annotation agreement for a set of document

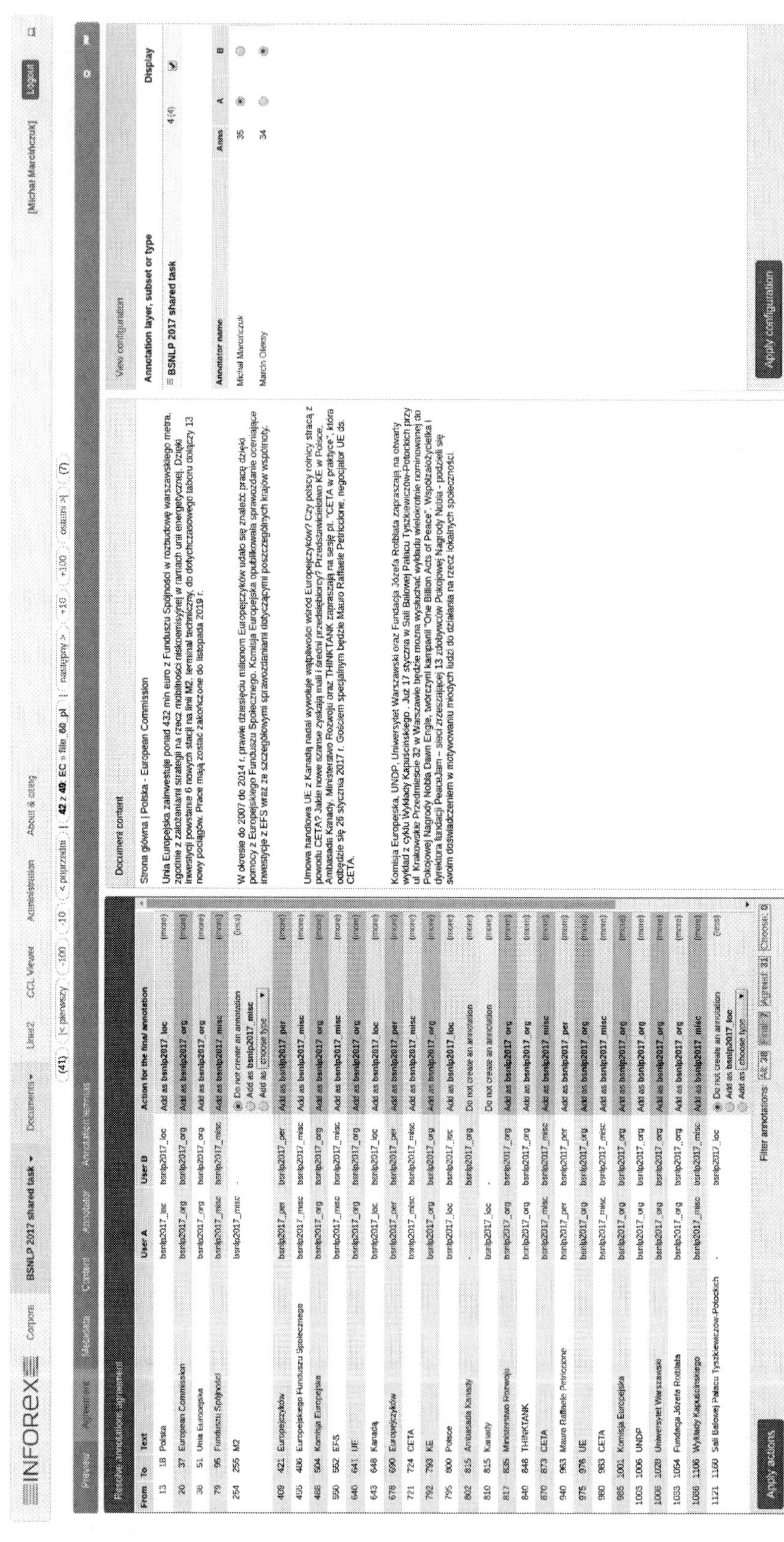

Figure 6: User agreement verification for a single document

Lemmatization of Multi-word Common Noun Phrases and Named Entities in Polish

Michał Marcińczuk
G4.19 Research Group
Department of Computational Intelligence
Faculty of Computer Science and Management
Wrocław University of Technology, Wrocław, Poland
`michal.marcinczuk@pwr.edu.pl`

Abstract

In the paper we present a tool for lemmatization of multi-word common noun phrases and named entities for Polish called PoLem[1]. The tool is based on a set of manually crafted rules and heuristics utilizing a set of dictionaries (including morphological, named entities and inflection patterns). The accuracy of lemmatization obtained by the tool reached 97.99% on a dataset with multi-word common noun phrases and 86.17% for case-sensitive evaluation on a dataset with named entities.

1 Introduction

In the article we cover the problem of multi-word common noun phrase and named entity lemmatization for Polish. The task relies on generating a nominative form of an expression[2]. For example the following named entities — *Janem Nowakiem* (a person name in an instrumental case) and *Jana Nowaka* (a genitive case of the same person name) — should be lemmatized to *Jan Nowak*. Both, lemmatization of multi-word common noun phrases and named entities are challenging because Polish is a highly inflectional language and a single expression can have several inflected forms.

The complexity of multi-word common noun phrase lemmatization is caused by the fact that the expected lemma is not a simple concatenation of base forms for each word in the phrase. In most cases only the head of the phrase is changed to a nominative form and the remaining tokens, which are the modifiers of the head, should remain in

a specific case. For example in the phrase *piwnicy domu* (Eng. *house basement*) only the first word should be changed to their nominative form while the second word should remain in the genitive form, i.e. *piwnica domu*. A simple concatenation of tokens' base forms would produce a phrase *piwnica dom* which is not correct.

In the case of named entities the task is much more complex due to the following reasons:

1. Named entities consist of many words which are not present in the morphological dictionaries. For such words it is impossible to generate the desired form using only a morphological dictionary. A more generic method is required.

2. Some foreign proper names subject to inflection and some not.

3. The desired lemma of a named entity depends on the named entity category. For example *Słowackiego* (a person last name in genitive or accusative) should be lemmatized to *Słowacki* in case of person name and to *Słowackiego* in case of street name.

4. Capitalization do matter. For example a country name *Polska* (Eng. *Poland*) should be lemmatized to *Polska* but not to *polska*.

We took the following assumptions:

Assumption 1 *The lemma should have the same number and gender as the input expression.*

Assumption 2 *The multi-word common noun phrase is neither a proper name nor contains a proper name.*

Assumption 3 *The named entity can consist of any number of tokens, i.e. one or more.*

We also require that:

---

[1] `http://nlp.pwr.wroc.pl/polem`
[2] By *expression* we understand a multi-word common noun phrase or a named entity.

Proceedings of Recent Advances in Natural Language Processing, pages 483–491,
Varna, Bulgaria, Sep 4–6 2017.

Requirement 1 *The expression is described with a disambiguated morphological information.*

Requirement 2 *In case of named entities the semantic category of the named entity is known.*

Our paper is divided into three main parts. In the first part we present the related literature overview, evaluation datasets and baselines. In the second part we present the development of a set of rules for multi-word common noun phrase lemmatization. In the last part we extend the set of rules with some heuristic and new rules in order to increase the coverage and accuracy of named entity lemmatization.

2   Related Works

According to our best knowledge there are several researches on phrase lemmatization for Polish which include both multi-word phrases and named entities. One of them is a rule-base approach in which the lemmatization rules were combined with a grammar for recognition of noun phrases (Degórski, 2012). The lemmatization rules were manually created as an extension to a grammar for Polish (Głowińska, 2008) — the lemmas are generated for the recognized phrases. This method does not produce the final lemmas as it requires a form generator to obtain the desired forms for the generated morphological tags and base forms. The method was evaluated on a set of 336 phrases. 158 of them were correctly recognized and the accuracy for them was 82.9%.

Another approach was presented by Radiszewski (2013b). The method was based on an automatic generation of lemmatization rules using Conditional Random Fields for noun phrases. The authors obtained the accuracy of 80.7% on a set of 564 noun phrases (containing single- and multi-word phrases).

The last approach was also based on an automatic generation of lemmatization rules from a corpus (Małyszko et al., 2015). The method obtained the accuracy of 82.1% on a set of 888 phrases (only 83% of 1063 tested phrases were marked as processable).

3   Evaluation Datasets

The dataset of multi-word common noun phrases was created by extracting occurrences of keywords from the KPWr corpus (Broda et al., 2012)[3]. The corpus contains 1628 documents annotated with keywords. The documents are tagged with the WCRFT tagger (Radziszewski, 2013a). We have extracted 3965 occurrences of keywords from the documents' content. Then we selected those phrases which conform the Assumptions 2 — 1728 in total. Then the set was divided into two random subsets — a train set with 1329 instances and a test set with 399 instances. The train set was used to develop a set of lemmatization rules and the test set was used for the final evaluation. As the keywords were extracted from documents tagged with a morphological tagger the dataset conforms the Requirement 1.

The dataset of named entities was created by extracting named entities from the same corpus. The corpus contains 1349 documents annotated with lemmatized named entities. We have extracted 21 449 occurrences of named entities from the documents' content. The set was also divided into two random subsets — a train set with 14 104 named entities and a test set with 7 345 named entities. The train set was used to extend the basic set of lemmatization rules and the test set was used for the final evaluation.

4   Baseline Results

To establish the baseline we measured the accuracy for three lemmatization methods. For multi-words common noun phrases we used only case-insensitive evaluation. For named entities we used both case-sensitive (CS) and case-insensitive (CI) evaluations. The results are presented in Table 1. The baseline methods are:

1. Concatenation of text forms — the text form is a form which appears in the document content.

2. Concatenation of base forms — base forms were assigned by the morphological tagger for each token.

3. Lemmatization grammar (Degórski, 2012) for the Spejd tool (Przepiórkowski, 2008).

Figure 1 presents a sample phrases with all the mentioned token attributes.

---

[3]`https://clarin-pl.eu/dspace/handle/11321/270`

Lemmatization method	Multi-word phrases		Named entities	
	Train	Test	Train	Test
Number of named entities	*1329*	*388*	*14 104*	*7 345*
Concatenation of text forms CI	41.82%	35.84%	56.62%	57.17%
Concatenation of text forms CS	-	-	56.06%	56.68%
Concatenation of base forms CI	23.80%	22.31%	75.46%	73.08%
Concatenation of base forms CS	-	-	44.02%	43.97%
Spejd (only recognized phrases) CI	79.31%	80.49%	83.42%	82.08%
Spejd (only recognized phrases) CS	-	-	42.83%	42.55%
Spejd (with text forms) CI	69.45%	67.42%	67.37%	67.36%
Spejd (with text forms) CS	-	-	44.01%	44.04%

Table 1: Baseline accuracy of lemmatization for different methods on the train and test sets.

Token	1 (head)	2	3
Text form	organu	pierwszej	instancji
Base form	organ	pierwszy	instancja
Morphological tag	subst:sg:gen:m3	adj:sg:gen:f:pos	subst:sg:gen:f
Expected lemma	organ	pierwszej	instancji
Translation	[3] authority	[1] first	[2] instance

Figure 1: A sample expression with its text form, base form, morphological tags and the expected lemma.

4.1 Baseline for Multi-word Common Noun Phrases

Using the heuristic-based approach we were able to generate lemmas for every phrase in the dataset. However, as expected, the accuracy was very low — 41.82% for the text forms and 23.80% for the base forms on the train set and 35.84% and 22.31% for the test set.

Using the Spejd lemmatization grammar (Degórski, 2012) we were not able to obtain lemmas for every phrase in the dataset. For the train set we were able to generate lemmas for 952 phrases out of 1329 (72% coverage) and for the test set for 287 out of 399 (also 72% coverage). The reason is that the lemmas are generated for specific phrases recognized by the grammar and in some cases our phrases do not overlap with the phrases matched by the grammar. For the recognized phrases the accuracy was 79.31% and 80.49% for the train and the test sets respectively. To overcome the problem of missing lemmas, for the phrases for which Spejd did not generate any lemma we took the text form as a lemma. The final accuracy for the complete dataset was 69.45% and 67.42% for the train and the test sets respectively.

4.2 Baseline for Named Entities

Using text forms as lemmas we obtained accuracy above 56%. The case-sensitive evaluation for the text forms drops the accuracy by less than 1 pp. This indicates that almost all named entities appears in the text in their expected casing, i.e. camel case, all upper, all lower, mix case, etc. In turn, using concatenation of base forms we obtained accuracy near 75%. This means that for 25% of named entities some of the tokens requires a transformation other than the change to their singular masculine nominative form. The case-sensitive evaluation for base form concatenation drops the accuracy to 44% what shows than the token lemmas do not hold the expected capitalization. Even when we apply the casing as for the text forms to the concatenation of base forms we will not increase the accuracy above 75% — by the analogy to the difference between case-insensitive and case-sensitive evaluation for the concatenation of text forms. This shows that in order to handle the remaining 25% of named entities we need a more sophisticated method of lemmatization.

The Spejd lemmatization grammar (Degórski, 2012) obtained the accuracy of 83% but only for near 56% of all named entities. The reason of the low coverage is the same as for multi-word phrases. To handle such cases we combined the Spejd lemmatization grammar with text forms for the named entities which do not match the recognized phrases. The accuracy for case-insensitive evaluation dropped to 67%. For case-sensitive evaluation the accuracy drops even more to 44%.

5 Lemmatization of Multi-word Phrases

5.1 Rule Development

Lemmatization of multi-word common noun phrases mostly relies on finding the correct combination of forms for each word in the phrase. Most of the words and their inflected forms are present in the morphological dictionary. The difficulty is to find the correct form for each token based on the phrase structure. To achieve this goal we developed a set of lemmatization rules.

Each rule consists of two elements — a set of constraints and a set of transformations. When the constrains are satisfied for a given phrase then the transformations are used to obtain the expected word form for each token in the phrase. Sample rules are presented on Figure 2. The constraints test tokens' morphological attributes to check whether they have specific values (text form, base form, case, gender and/or number). The constraints can also check if there is an agreement between specific words in the phrase. To encode the constraints we used the WCCL formalism (Radziszewski et al., 2011). In order to reduce the number of required rules we identified such patterns, where only the first words need some kind of transformation while the remaining words are unchanged. The rules are called the *tail rules*. A sample *tail rule* is presented on Figure 2b.

The transformations (`transformations` tag) are used to generate specific forms of the words matched in the phrase. The transformation can change case or gender of the word. The attribute `index` identifies the word in the phrase and the remaining attributes indicate the expected value of the morphological attributes. For instance, `cas="nom"` means that the word should be in nominative. If the value of a morphological attribute is unchanged then the attribute is omitted.

The initial set of rules did not cover all phrases from the train set because some of them were tagged incorrectly. To overcome the tagger errors we have added some rules with relaxed constraints (for instance we ignored the words agreement). The rules with relaxed constraints are dis-

```
<rule name="SubstAdj_Agr">
    <wccl match="complete">
      and(
        inter(class[1],{adj}),
        inter(class[0],{subst,ger,depr}),
        agrpp(0,1,{nmb,gnd,cas})
      )
    </wccl>
    <transformations>
      <set index="0" cas="nom"/>
      <set index="1" cas="nom"/>
    </transformations>
</rule>
```

(a) A sample standard lemmatization rule.

```
<rule name="AdjSubstTail">
    <wccl match="prefix">
      and(
        inter(class[0],{adj,ppas,pact}),
        inter(class[1],{subst,ger,depr}),
        agr(0,1,{nmb,gnd,cas})
      )
    </wccl>
    <transformations>
      <set index="0" cas="nom"/>
      <set index="1" cas="nom"/>
    </transformations>
</rule>
```

(b) A sample tail lemmatization rule.

```
<rule name="SubstAdvHyphenAdj_FixGndM1">
    <wccl match="complete">
      and(
        inter(class[0],{subst,ger,depr}),
        inter(gnd[0],{m1}),
        inter(class[1],{adv}),
        regex(orth[2],"-"),
        inter(class[3],{adj,ppas,pact}),
      )
    </wccl>
    <transformations>
      <set index="0" cas="nom"/>
      <set index="3" cas="nom" gnd="m1"/>
    </transformations>
</rule>
```

(c) A sample fix lemmatization rule.

Figure 2: Sample lemmatization rules.

tinguished from the remaining set of rules by the *Fix* suffix in their name. The final set of rules consists of 27 rules.

The lemmatization rules are executed in a specific order and the first rule for which the constraints are satisfied for given phrase is used to generate the lemma. At first the set of standard rules is executed. If none of the rules is matched, then the set of *fix rules* is used and, at the end, the set of *tail rules* is used. If the constraints are satisfied, then the transformations for the rule are applied. If a rule does not contain any transformation for a word then the unmodified text form is taken. In other case, the input base form and the morphological tag are taken and the transformation is applied, i.e. the specified attribute values are substituted. Then the modified values are used to generate a new word form using a morphologi-

486

cal analyzer called Morfeusz (Woliński, 2006).

5.2 Evaluation

Table 2 contains the results of evaluation on both sets presented in Section 3. The set of 27 rules was enough to cover all multi-word phrases in the train set and it obtained the accuracy of 99.10%. Also a high accuracy of 97.99% was obtained on the test set which was not used during rule development. In both cases the accuracy was higher than any baseline method presented in Section 4.

Evaluation	Train	Test
Multi-word phrases		
PoLem' CI	99.10%	97.99%
Named Entities		
PoLem' CI	85.56%	84.64%
PoLem' CS	81.96%	80.66%

Table 2: Accuracy of the initial lemmatization rules.

We analyzed the incorrectly generated lemmas for the train set in order to find the sources of errors. We found out that there is no simple solution to handle those cases without any additional resources. We identified the following types of problems:

Tagger errors:

- incorrect number — one of the tokens has incorrect number (singular or plural). Some of the *fix rules* force the correct number for the first or the second token. However, in some cases this leads to an error, because the rule changes the number for the correctly disambiguated word. For such cases the rule should determine for which the disambiguation was incorrect. This is possible for those phrases for which one of the tokens has only plural for singular interpretations. For example for phrase *pytania prawnego* (Eng. *legal question*) the tagger assigned the following interpretations: (1) *subst:pl:nom:n* (2) *adj:sg:gen:m3:pos*, while for the first token it should be *subst:sg:gen:n*. The second token can have only singular interpretation what is a sufficient indicator that the whole phrase should be singular, not plural.

- incorrect part of speech — one of the tokens has incorrect part of speech. For example for

phrase *zmienne środowiskowe* (End. *environmental variables*) the tagger assigned the following part of speeches: *adj adj* for the subsequent words. The first token should be recognized as a noun instead of an adjective. In this case we also should check other possible interpretations to find out the possibly correct tags.

Sense disambiguation — polysemous words might have different schemes of inflection. For example word *pasza* means: (1) fodder or (2) pasha. The word has different plural form for both meanings: *pasz* for (1) and *paszowie* for (2). To handle this problem it might be necessary to check the collocations for those forms. For example, for phrase *pasze lecznicze* (Eng. *healing fodders*) word *healing* will more likely co-occur with *fodder* than *pasha*.

More than one possible form — there are words which have more than one possible form. For example word *koszt* (Eng. *cost*) has two possible plural forms: *koszty* and *koszta*. The first form is more common than the other one. For such cases a frequency list might be helpful to determine the more frequent form.

The initial set of rules also obtained a high accuracy on the dataset of named entities — 85.65% for the train set and 84.64% for the test set. However, for case-sensitive evaluation (marked as CS in the table) the accuracy dropped to 81.96% and 80.66% respectively. The results are also higher than for any presented baseline method. At this stage the dataset of named entities was not used in the development of lemmatization rules. In the next section we present the extension of the initial set of rules based on the analysis of the train set of the dataset of named entities.

6 Lemmatization of Named Entities

In this section we present several extensions of the initial set of lemmatization rules developed for multi-word common noun phrases which improved the accuracy of named entity lemmatization. The following subsections describe in details each of them.

6.1 Generic Lexicons

We used two large lexicons of proper names which are applied before lemmatization rules. The first one was extracted from a morphological dictionary called Morfeusz SGJP (Woliński, 2006). We have selected 39 084 entries marked as geographical names. As the morphological dictionary contains only single words, the lexicon is used to lemmatize single-word named entities.

The second lexicon contains a list of inflected named entities extracted from Polish Wikipedia. The list is a part of NELexicon2[4]. The list of inflected forms was created by extracting internal links from Polish Wikipedia. Each pair consists of a link text and a title of Wikipedia page to which the link directs. The list was filtered by selecting those pairs which have the same number of elements (in the link text and the page title) and the consecutive words have the same base form or have the same prefix of a certain length. The list of pairs was filtered with a list of known proper names. The list consists of 110 178 pairs (single- and multi-word proper names of various categories).

6.2 Category-based Lexicons

For person names we created a separate lexicon which contains solely inflected forms of person names with their lemmas. The lexicon consists of names from NELexicon2 marked as a person name and the lists of first names and last names from Morfeusz SGJP. The lemmatization procedure using this lexicon is based on a rule that for a person name containing only first and last names each part of the name is changed to their respective nominative form. For each person name we divide the name into single words. Then for each word we lookup its' base form in the lexicon. If for every word we can determine the base form then the final lemma is a concatenation of the found base forms. We also defined a list of words which are never inflected, i.e. *św.* (Eng. *Saint*), *von* (and other similar words which appear in foreign last names). If at least one of the words cannot be lemmatized this way we do not generate any lemma.

6.3 Inflection Rules

The dictionaries of person names and geographical names misses many inflected forms of the names. To increase the coverage we have generated a frequency list of suffixes changes based on the morphological dictionary Morfeusz SGJP. Figure 3 presents the most frequent inflection rules

[4]`https://clarin-pl.eu/dspace/handle/11321/247`

for person names. The list consists of lines in the following form: *subst:sg:gen:m1 iego i 1100 0.98*. This means that 98% of names tagged as *subst:sg:gen:m1* which are ended with *iego* have a base form ended with *i*. For instance, the name *Grzybowskiego* tagged as *subst:sg:gen:m1* should be lemmatized to *Grzybowski*. We have created two inflection rule lists, separately for person names and geographical names. In the first run we try to find a set of inflection rules for every single word in the name which leads to a form that is present in the NELexicon2. If we fail to find such a set then we find a set of inflection rules with the highest confidence. On this step we ignore inflections which are less frequent than 50 occurrences. The generated form is treated as a possible lemma.

```
subst:sg:loc:m1   im    i   1112 0.99
subst:sg:inst:m1  im    i   1112 0.99
subst:pl:loc:m1   ich   i   1112 0.99
subst:pl:inst:m1  imi   i   1112 0.99
subst:pl:gen:m1   ich   i   1112 0.99
subst:pl:dat:m1   im    i   1112 0.99
subst:pl:acc:m1   ich   i   1112 0.99
subst:sg:gen:m1   iego  i   1100 0.98
subst:sg:dat:m1   iemu  i   1100 0.98
subst:sg:acc:m1   iego  i   1100 0.98
depr:pl:voc:m2    ie    i   1100 0.93
depr:pl:nom:m2    ie    i   1100 0.93
subst:sg:inst:f   ą     a   1099 1.00
subst:sg:acc:f    ą     a   1061 1.00
subst:sg:loc:m1   kim   ki  1030 0.99
subst:sg:inst:m1  kim   ki  1030 0.99
subst:sg:gen:m1   kiego ki  1030 0.99
subst:sg:dat:m1   kiemu ki  1030 0.99
subst:sg:acc:m1   kiego ki  1030 0.99
subst:pl:loc:m1   kich  ki  1030 0.99
(...)
```

Figure 3: The most common suffix changes for person last names.

6.4 Category-based Rules

The last extension is a set of category-specific lemmatization rules which override the initial set of lemmaitzation rules. The rules reflect the nature of lemmatization of specific proper name categories.

6.4.1 Road Names

The lemma for a road name that is an adjective should be in a genitive case and feminine gender. For instance, *ulicy Białej* (Eng. White street; a locative form) should be lemmatized to *ulica Biała* instead of *biały* which is the base form in the morphological dictionary of the common word.

6.4.2 Voivodeship Names

Similar rule applies for Polish names of voivodeships. The lemmatized form must be in a nominative case and neutral gender instead of masculine which is the default base form in the morphological dictionary. For instance *województwie kieleckim* (Eng. *kieleckie voivodeship*; a locative form) should be lemmatized to *województwo kieleckie* instead of *kielecki*.

6.4.3 Person names

The majority of Polish names consists of a first name and a last name or two first names and a last name, i.e. a sequence of nouns. The generic rule for a sequence of nouns assumes that the first noun is the head of the phrase and the remaining nouns a the head's modifiers. The rule changes the case of the head to the nominative case and keep the case of the modifiers. In case of person names all elements must be changed to their nominative forms. The rule overrides the generic rule by changing all the words to their nominative forms.

6.5 Evaluation

Table 3 contains results for the extended version of PoLem on the dataset of named entities. The final version of PoLem obtained the accuracy of 89.80% for the case-insensitive (CI) evaluation and 87.35% for the case-sensitive (CS) evaluation on the train set. Comparing with the initial set of lemmatization rules we obtained an improvement of near 4–6 pp. Similar improvement was obtained on the test set which was not seen during the development. In the Appendix A we presented the lemmatization accuracy for each named entity category separately. The evaluation shows that there are still some major problems with lemmatization for some categories of named entities.

Evaluation	Train	Test
Named entities		
PoLem" CI	89.80%	88.45%
PoLem" CS	87.35%	86.17%

Table 3: Accuracy of the initial lemmatization rules.

The largest number of incorrect lemmas was obtained for *people names* (`nam_liv_person*`). There are several reasons for this relatively large number of errors. One of them is the gender ambiguity. There are many name forms which can be a male or a female name. For example *Antonia* can be a female name in nominative or a male name in genitive. The dictionaries of person names we used do not contain information about the name gander so we could not utilize the information about the gender assigned by the tagger. On the other hand, the tagger tends to treat most of male names in genitive as female names in nominative. To handle this type of problem some kind of postprocessing with an access to the source document would be required. Similar problem applies to person last names. Different last names have the same inflected form so it is impossible to determine the correct nominative form without considering all variants of the same last name which appeared in the same document.

The second category with a high number of incorrect lemmas was *city name* (`nam_loc_gpe_city`). For this category the majority of errors were caused by the fact that there are many names which are also common words (nouns and adjectives). The names were assigned a nominative form of the common word while the expected lemma has a different form.

7 Summary

In the paper we deal with the problem of multiword phrases and named entity lemmatization for Polish. We presented several baseline methods which do not provide satisfactory results. We showed that a small set of 27 rules was enough to cover all phrases with high accuracy. Latter, the set of initial rules was extended with a set of heuristic utilizing different types of lexicons, inflection rules and several new category-specific lemmatization rules to improve the lemmatization of named entities. The extended version of PoLem improved the accuracy of lemmatization by more than 4 percentage points for the case-insensitive evaluation on the train set and by 6 percentage points for the case-sensitive evaluation. Similar improvement was obtained on the test set which was not used in the development process.

The PoLem tool will be made available in a form of a web-service as a part of the CLARIN-PL infrastructure. The announcement will be published on `http://nlp.pwr.wroc.pl/polem`.

Acknowledgments

Work financed as part of the investment in the CLARIN-PL research infrastructure funded by the Polish Ministry of Science and Higher Education.

A Detailed results for the test set

True	False	Accuracy	Method	Coverage
120	36	76.92%	nam_adj	1.11%
105	18	85.37%	nam_adj_city	0.87%
430	10	97.73%	nam_adj_country	3.12%
10	13	43.48%	nam_adj_person	0.16%
15	22	40.54%	nam_eve	0.26%
141	36	79.66%	nam_eve_human	1.25%
2	1	66.67%	nam_eve_human_aniversary	0.02%
30	1	96.77%	nam_eve_human_cultural	0.22%
20	6	76.92%	nam_eve_human_holiday	0.18%
103	6	94.50%	nam_eve_human_sport	0.77%
1	0	100.00%	nam_eve_natural_phenomenom	0.01%
5	0	100.00%	nam_fac	0.04%
7	4	63.64%	nam_fac_bridge	0.08%
0	2	0.00%	nam_fac_crossroad	0.01%
182	36	83.49%	nam_fac_goe	1.55%
26	13	66.67%	nam_fac_goe_stop	0.28%
8	3	72.73%	nam_fac_park	0.08%
290	35	89.23%	nam_fac_road	2.30%
27	14	65.85%	nam_fac_square	0.29%
15	14	51.72%	nam_fac_system	0.21%
18	1	94.74%	nam_liv_animal	0.13%
8	6	57.14%	nam_liv_character	0.10%
110	26	80.88%	nam_liv_god	0.96%
38	4	90.48%	nam_liv_habitant	0.30%
1945	**314**	86.10%	**nam_liv_person**	16.02%
96	32	75.00%	nam_liv_person_add	0.91%
1366	**122**	91.80%	**nam_liv_person_first**	10.55%
1421	**184**	88.54%	**nam_liv_person_last**	11.38%
7	0	100.00%	nam_liv_plant	0.05%
24	8	75.00%	nam_loc	0.23%
38	10	79.17%	nam_loc_astronomical	0.34%
34	25	57.63%	nam_loc_country_region	0.42%
72	33	68.57%	nam_loc_gpe_admin1	0.74%
21	8	72.41%	nam_loc_gpe_admin2	0.21%
66	4	94.29%	nam_loc_gpe_admin3	0.50%
1121	**140**	88.90%	**nam_loc_gpe_city**	8.94%
11	0	100.00%	nam_loc_gpe_conurbation	0.08%
785	22	97.27%	nam_loc_gpe_country	5.72%
60	10	85.71%	nam_loc_gpe_district	0.50%
42	10	80.77%	nam_loc_gpe_subdivision	0.37%
36	5	87.80%	nam_loc_historical_region	0.29%
1	0	100.00%	nam_loc_hydronym	0.01%
1	0	100.00%	nam_loc_hydronym_bay	0.01%
1	0	100.00%	nam_loc_hydronym_lagoon	0.01%
7	2	77.78%	nam_loc_hydronym_lake	0.06%
3	0	100.00%	nam_loc_hydronym_ocean	0.02%
42	8	84.00%	nam_loc_hydronym_river	0.35%
6	0	100.00%	nam_loc_hydronym_sea	0.04%
4	0	100.00%	nam_loc_land	0.03%
60	0	100.00%	nam_loc_land_continent	0.43%
1	0	100.00%	nam_loc_land_desert	0.01%
23	4	85.19%	nam_loc_land_island	0.19%
48	7	87.27%	nam_loc_land_mountain	0.39%
5	0	100.00%	nam_loc_land_peak	0.04%
7	0	100.00%	nam_loc_land_peninsula	0.05%
4	0	100.00%	nam_loc_land_protected_area	0.03%
19	5	79.17%	nam_loc_land_region	0.17%
1	0	100.00%	nam_num	0.01%
1	0	100.00%	nam_num_flat	0.01%
25	0	100.00%	nam_num_house	0.18%
13	0	100.00%	nam_num_phone	0.09%
2	0	100.00%	nam_num_postal_code	0.01%
6	0	100.00%	nam_org	0.04%
333	43	88.56%	nam_org_company	2.67%
25	23	52.08%	nam_org_group	0.34%
49	10	83.05%	nam_org_group_band	0.42%
227	31	87.98%	nam_org_group_team	1.83%
521	34	93.87%	nam_org_institution	3.93%
17	1	94.44%	nam_org_institution_full	0.13%
153	27	85.00%	nam_org_nation	1.28%
420	30	93.33%	nam_org_organization	3.19%
5	2	71.43%	nam_org_organization_sub	0.05%
141	9	94.00%	nam_org_political_party	1.06%
50	4	92.59%	nam_oth	0.38%
1	0	100.00%	nam_oth_address_street	0.01%
52	18	74.29%	nam_oth_currency	0.50%
7	1	87.50%	nam_oth_data_format	0.06%
1	0	100.00%	nam_oth_ip	0.01%
33	4	89.19%	nam_oth_license	0.26%
1	0	100.00%	nam_oth_mail	0.01%
15	2	88.24%	nam_oth_position	0.12%
118	59	66.67%	nam_oth_tech	1.25%
11	0	100.00%	nam_oth_www	0.08%
2	2	50.00%	nam_pro	0.03%
19	1	95.00%	nam_pro_award	0.14%
135	39	77.59%	nam_pro_brand	1.23%
4	0	100.00%	nam_pro_media	0.03%
194	16	92.38%	nam_pro_media_periodic	1.49%
11	2	84.62%	nam_pro_media_radio	0.09%
31	3	91.18%	nam_pro_media_tv	0.24%
146	48	75.26%	nam_pro_media_web	1.38%
61	33	64.89%	nam_pro_model_car	0.67%
1	0	100.00%	nam_pro_model_phone	0.01%
6	0	100.00%	nam_pro_model_plane	0.04%
57	29	66.28%	nam_pro_software	0.61%
22	1	95.65%	nam_pro_software_game	0.16%
2	2	50.00%	nam_pro_software_os	0.03%
1	0	100.00%	nam_pro_software_version	0.01%
135	19	87.66%	nam_pro_title	1.09%
19	2	90.48%	nam_pro_title_album	0.15%
8	1	88.89%	nam_pro_title_article	0.06%
3	0	100.00%	nam_pro_title_boardgame	0.02%
20	5	80.00%	nam_pro_title_book	0.18%
45	26	63.38%	nam_pro_title_document	0.50%
5	0	100.00%	nam_pro_title_painting	0.04%
2	0	100.00%	nam_pro_title_radio	0.01%
8	3	72.73%	nam_pro_title_song	0.08%
12	2	85.71%	nam_pro_title_treaty	0.10%
28	3	90.32%	nam_pro_title_tv	0.22%
14	2	87.50%	nam_pro_vehicle	0.11%
12307	1797	87.26%	Total	100.00%

References

Bartosz Broda, Michał Marcińczuk, Marek Maziarz, Adam Radziszewski, and Adam Wardyński. 2012. KPWr: Towards a Free Corpus of Polish. In Nicoletta Calzolari, Khalid Choukri, Thierry Declerck, Mehmet Uğur Doğan, Bente Maegaard, Joseph Mariani, Jan Odijk, and Stelios Piperidis, editors, *Proceedings of LREC'12*. ELRA, Istanbul, Turkey.

Łukasz Degórski. 2012. Towards the lemmatisation of Polish nominal syntactic groups using a shallow grammar. *Lecture Notes in Computer Science (including subseries Lecture Notes in Artificial Intelligence and Lecture Notes in Bioinformatics)* 7053 LNCS(250467):370–378.

Katarzyna Głowińska. 2008. Anotacja składniowa NKJP. In (Przepiórkowski, 2008), pages 107–127. https://books.google.pl/books?id=VO76OgAACAAJ.

Jacek Małyszko, Witold Abramowicz, Aagata Filipowska, and Tomasz Wagner. 2015. Lemmatization of Multi-Word Entity Names for Polish Language Using Rules Automatically Generated Based on the Corpus Analysis. *Human Language Technologies as a Challenge for Computer Science and Linguistics* pages 540–544.

Adam Przepiórkowski. 2008. *Powierzchniowe przetwarzanie języka polskiego.* Problemy współczesnej nauki, teoria i zastosowania: Inżynieria lingwistyczna. Akademicka Oficyna Wydawnicza "Exit". https://books.google.pl/books?id=VO76OgAACAAJ.

Adam Radziszewski. 2013a. A tiered CRF tagger for Polish. In R. Bembenik, Ł. Skonieczny, H. Rybiński, M. Kryszkiewicz, and M. Niezgódka, editors, *Intelligent Tools for Building a Scientific Information Platform: Advanced Architectures and Solutions*, Springer Verlag.

Adam Radziszewski. 2013b. Learning to lemmatise Polish noun phrases. In *Proceedings of the 51st Annual Meeting of the Association for Computational Linguistics, {ACL} 2013, 4-9 August 2013, Sofia, Bulgaria, Volume 1: Long Papers*. The Association for Computer Linguistics, pages 701–709. http://aclweb.org/anthology/P/P13/P13-1069.pdf.

Adam Radziszewski, Adam Wardyński, and Tomasz Śniatowski. 2011. WCCL: A Morpho-syntactic Feature Toolkit. In Ivan Habernal and Václav Matousek, editors, *Proceedings of Text, Speech and Dialogue - 14th International Conference, TSD 2011, Pilsen, Czech Republic*. Springer, Pilsen, volume 6836 of *Lecture Notes in Computer Science*, pages 434—-441.

Marcin Woliński. 2006. *Morfeusz — a Practical Tool for the Morphological Analysis of Polish*, Springer Berlin Heidelberg, Berlin, Heidelberg, pages 511–520.

Log-linear Models for Uyghur Segmentation in Spoken Language Translation

Chenggang Mi[1,2], Yating Yang[1,2], Rui Dong[1,2,3], Xi Zhou[1,2],
Lei Wang[1,2], Xiao Li[1,2], and Tonghai Jiang[1,2]
[1]The Xinjiang Technical Institute of Physics & Chemistry of
Chinese Academy of Sciences, Urumqi, China
[2]Key laboratory of speech language information processing of Xinjiang, Urumqi, China
[3]University of Chinese Academy of Sciences, Beijing, China
{micg, yangyt, dongrui, zhouxi, wanglei, xiaoli, jth}@ms.xjb.ac.cn

Abstract

To alleviate data sparsity in spoken Uyghur machine translation, we proposed a log-linear based morphological segmentation approach. Instead of learning model only from monolingual annotated corpus, this approach optimizes Uyghur segmentation for spoken translation based on both bilingual and monolingual corpus. Our approach relies on several features such as traditional conditional random field (CRF) feature, bilingual word alignment feature and monolingual suffix-word co-occurrence feature. Experimental results shown that our proposed segmentation model for Uyghur spoken translation achieved 1.6 BLEU score improvements compared with the state-of-the-art baseline.

1 Introduction

Low resource languages like Uyghur usually suffer from data sparsity in related NLP tasks. Due to need a large scale parallel corpus to train the translation model, this situation becomes even worse in Uyghur - Chinese machine translation. To overcome this problem, morphological segmentation is often used to alleviate the data sparsity.

Most approaches on morphological segmentation such as CRF based model rely on annotated data heavily and do not consider the informal situation like spoken language translation (Table 1). Therefore, using a traditional Uyghur morphological segmentation model to segment the corpus for spoken language translation (SLT) cannot expect to achieve a good performance. In this study, we research on Uyghur morphological segmentation for Uyghur-Chinese spoken language transla-

tion.[1] We proposed a novel method to optimize morphological segmentation for Uyghur SLT. Our approach based on a log-linear model, several features include CRF feature, bilingually-constrained feature and monolingual co-occurrence feature are derived and feed to the model, the model provide an optimized morphological segmentation results for SLT. Experimental results shown that our proposed approach can achieve 1.6+ BLEU improvements, which outperforms other baselines significantly.

The main contributions of this paper can be summarized as following:

- We propose a log-linear based morphological segmentation model for Uyghur-Chinese spoken language translation, several features are integrated into it to optimize the performance of SLT model.

- Our features include CRF feature, bilingual word alignment feature and monolingual suffix-other words (OW, which means words in current Uyghur sentence except current word) co-occurrence feature, which derived from bilingual corpus and monolingual.

- Through exploring the log-linear based model for spoken Uyghur segmentation, we show that these features: CRF, bilingual word alignment and monolingual suffix-OW co-occurrence are all useful to Uyghur-Chinese spoken language translation.

The rest of this paper is organized as follows: we present the features of Uyghur and morphological segmentation for statistical machine translation (SMT) which are related to our research in section 2; in section 3, we give a detailed introduc-

---

[1]In this paper, we write Uyghur with the Latin alphabet and Chinese with Pinyin.

Proceedings of Recent Advances in Natural Language Processing, pages 492–500,
Varna, Bulgaria, Sep 4–6 2017.

Uyghur (source)	Chinese (target)
almighanmu ?	hai mei you na ma ? (Have you ever taken it ?)
shu Otkendimu .	you mei you kao shang ne ? (Have you got it ?)
bishim qalaymiqan .	wo nao zi yi pian hun luan . (My mind goes blank .)

Table 1: Examples of spoken Uyghur-Chinese sentence pairs.

tion of our method; experimental settings and results analysis are described in section 4; we finally review related work in section 5 and conclude in section 6.

2 Background

In this section, we first present some features of Uyghur. Then, we give some introductions about morphological segmentation in SMT. Finally, we describe challenges exist in Uyghur segmentation in SLT.

2.1 Introduction of Uyghur

Uyghur is a Turkic language with 10 to 25 million speakers, which is an official language of the Xinjiang Uyghur Autonomous Region of Western China. Various other countries also have Uyghur-speaking communities.

Uyghur is an agglutinative language with not only a very rich but also a productive derivational and inflectional morphology (Table 2). Also, Uyghur displays vowel harmony, lacks noun classes or grammatical gender, and is a left-branching language with subject-object-verb (SOV) word order.

Uyghur (word)	Uyghur (stem + suffix (es))
aliqanimda	**aliqan**+im+da
etrapidikilerni	**etrap**+i+diki+ler+ni
qurulmasining	**qurulma**+si+ning
qalduridu	**qal**+dur+i+d+u

Table 2: Examples of Uyghur word formation.

2.2 Morphological Segmentation in SMT

Data sparsity is one of the enduring problems in SMT. For low-resourced languages like Uyghur, this situation is even worse in related SMT tasks. As one of the most important parts of SMT, the word alignment model try to capture the probability of $p(e|f)$, where f is a word in source language (Uyghur) and e is the target word (Chinese). When translating between two unrelated languages such as Uyghur (morphologically-rich language) and Chinese (morphologically-poor language), disparate morphological systems can intensifies the problem of data sparsity because the large number of word forms created through morphologically productive processes hinders attempts to find concise mappings between concepts.

To alleviate the data sparsity in SMT, morphological analysis methods are proposed. Morphological analysis identifies functional morphemes to be merged into meaning-bearing stems or to be deleted. In Uyghur, functional morphemes typically belong to suffixes.

2.3 Challenges of Uyghur Segmentation in SLT

Unlike the formal news corpus, which is typically written with a clear intention, and moreover has been editorially controlled according to standards of language use; the informal conversation (dialogues) corpus has different intentions and languages use. Therefore, we may face several challenges in morphological segmentation for Uyghur-Chinese spoken translation:

First, the conversion sentence usually very short compared with news corpus; therefore, limited context can be used in translation model learning.

bilina qala . (ke yi kan chu lai ya .)

uxla tExi ? (hai mei shui jiao ba ?)

Second, a large scale of one-to-many and align to NULL alignments (Figure 1) exist in Uyghur-Chinese spoken corpus due to ellipsis in spoken language, which is very harmful to the translation performance.

Third, most of exist approaches on morphological segmentation are trained on formal corpus such as news, law et al., and these models do not perform well on Uyghur spoken corpus (Table 3).

3 Our Method

To overcome these difficulties, we proposed a novel method to optimize morphological segmentation for SLT. Our approach based on a log-linear model, several features include bilingually-constrained feature, monolingual co-occurrence

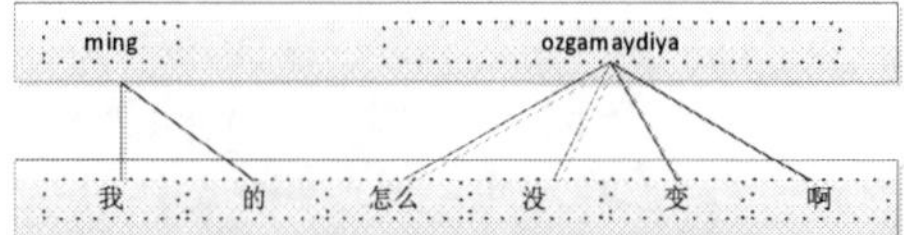

Figure 1: 1-to-many Word Alignments in Spoken Uyghur SMT.

Uyghur (source)	Chinese (translation results)	Chinese (reference)
nim e bol di aka	ge ge de di shen me a	zen me le, da ge.
he shu	jiu shi, shuo shi .	en, jiu shi de.
bol di xudayimgha shvkri	udayimgha shvkri	hao le, xie tian xie di.
chishlimiseng	chishlimiseng	ni bie yao.
he, mubarek bol sun	o, mu ba la ke de shui	en, gong xi ni.

Table 3: Examples of Uyghur sentences, translation results (by previous methods) and reference sentences.

feature are derived and feed to the model, the model provide an optimized morphological segmentation results for SLT.

3.1 Log-linear Model

Log-linear models are widely used in natural language processing (NLP) applications. One of the most important advantages of log-linear models is that they allow a very rich set of features to be used in a model, arguably much richer representations than the other simple estimation techniques (Liu et al., 2005).

We have a set of possible inputs $\mathbf{X}$ (morphemes), and a set of possible labels $\mathbf{Y}$ (R/D). The goal of our task is to model the conditional probability $p(y|x)$. Where for a (morpheme, label) pair $< x, y >$, $x \in \mathbf{X}$ and $y \in \mathbf{Y}$.

In our morphological segmentation task, we have some set $\mathbf{M}$ of possible morphemes, and a set $\mathbf{T}$ of possible tags. The set $\mathbf{Y}$ is simply equal to $\mathbf{T}$, and $\mathbf{X}$ is the set of $\mathbf{M}$ is the set of contexts of the form $< m_1 m_2 m_3 ... m_n, t_1 t_2 t_3 ... t_{i-1} >$. Where n is the length of the input sentence, $m_j \in \mathbf{M}, (j \in \{1..n\})$, $i \in \{1...(n-1)\}$, and $t_j \in \mathbf{T}$ for $j \in \{1...(i-1)\}$.

Accordingly, log-linear model used in our study can be abstractly described as follows. For $m \in \mathbf{M}, t \in \mathbf{T}$

$$p(t|m;v) = \frac{exp(v \cdot f(m,t))}{\sum_{t' \in t} exp(v \cdot f(m,t'))} \quad (1)$$

Here, $\mathbf{M}$ is a set of input morphemes $\mathbf{T}$ is a set of possible labels; f is a feature function, which maps (m,t) pair to a feature vector $f(m,t)$, and

$\mathbf{v}$ is a parameter vector. Note that the number of features and parameters should be the same in log-linear model.

3.2 Feature Functions

In this paper, we use the CRF as the basic feature in our log-linear model. Moreover, we also use additional information like bilingual word alignment and monolingual suffix-OW co-occurrence as two more features.

3.2.1 CRF Feature

We use a CRF based model to train a Uyghur morphological analyzer. Following (Ruokolainen et al., 2013)'s work, we treat the morphological segmentation as a sequence labeling problem.The CRF based morphological segmentation model can be described as

$$p(y|x;w) \propto \prod_{t=2}^{T} exp(w^T f(y_{t-1}, y_t, x, t)) \quad (2)$$

where x are characters in a word, y means corresponding class to each character. t indexes the characters, T is the length of word, $\mathbf{w}$ is the parameter vector, and f the vector-valued feature extracting function.

In this paper, we apply the tagging results of CRF model as the basic feature of our proposed approach. To adapt the spoken Uyghur segmentation situation, we extract the tagging probability of stem in each word in our Uyghur spoken corpus. Therefore, the feature function of CRF feature can be described as

$$h(m, t, fT) = \prod_{i=1}^{l} p_{stem}(t_{stem}|m_i, fT) \quad (3)$$

Where m_i is the ith morpheme, l denotes the number of morphemes. p_stem means the probability of tagging the m_i as "stem" given m_i and a morphological segmentation model **fT**. Which can be calculate as

$$p_{stem}(t_{stem}|m_t) = \frac{N(t_{stem}, m_i)}{N(m_i)} \quad (4)$$

Here, $N(t_{stem}, m_i)$ is the number of times m_i tagging as "stem" and $N(m_i)$ denotes the number of times m_i appeared in training data.

3.2.2 Bilingual Word Alignment Feature

Word alignment is one of the most important topics in SMT, which derive correspondences between words in parallel data as an attempt to explain how translation comes about. Traditional approaches on morphological segmentation for Uyghur SLT suffers from data sparsity seriously. To overcome this problem, we present a bilingual word alignment feature and integrate it into the log-linear model.

Due to the lack of training data and insufficient contextual information in Uyghur-Chinese SLT, we often cannot obtain the correct correspondences of words between Uyghur and Chinese. In word alignment of Uyghur-Chinese spoken corpus, we find that some NULL alignment Chinese words can be aligned to some suffixes of Uyghur words. However, we cannot obtain correspondences between suffixes of Uyghur words and NULL alignment Chinese words directly. In this paper, we first obtain the word alignment results from a large scale Uyghur-Chinese parallel corpus on news domain; one-to-many alignments are extracted and the suffix-word alignment can be obtained accordingly

$$p_{1-to-many}(u) = \frac{N(u, cs)}{N(u)} \quad (5)$$

$N(u, cs)$ is number of times the Uyghur word u correspondding to $n(n > 1)$ Chinese words (1-to-many) in word alignment. $N(u)$ is the number of times Uyghur word u appeared in parallel corpus on news domain.

Accordingly, we define the bilingual word

alignment feature function as

$$h(m, t, u, c, a) = \sum_{i=1}^{l_u} \sum_{j=1}^{n_i} \frac{p_{1-to-many}(u_i)}{n_{ij}} \quad (6)$$

Where l_u is the length of current Uyghur sentence, n_i is the number of suffixes of Uyghur word u_i.

3.2.3 Monolingual Stem-Suffixes Co-occurrence Feature

Uyghur is an agglutinative language. Nouns are inflected for number and case. Verbs are conjugated for tense, voice, aspect and mood. In Uyghur, we find that suffixes of a Uyghur word often appeared with other words (OW), and some of these words are omitted in informal corpus (such as conversion). Accordingly, OW word can express the same meaning with suffixes. Inspired by this, we can reserve certain suffix (es) as a single word if the OWs are not available. We can achieve this by counting the co-occurrence of stem-OW from a monolingual corpus in news domain.

Compare with bilingual parallel corpora, monolingual corpora are easy to build. We first segment a large scale of Uyghur monolingual corpus by a pre-trained morphological analyzer. Then, we obtain the stem-OW co-occurrence probability by counting the relative frequency:

$$p_{sow}(s|ow) = \frac{N_{co}(s, ow)}{N(ow)} \quad (7)$$

Here, $N_{co}(s, ow)$ is the frequency that a suffix is appeared with an OW in Uyghur monolingual corpus, $N(ow)$ is the frequency of one OW appeared.

Therefore, the feature function of stem-OW co-occurrence can be defined as

$$h(m, t, Mono) = \sum_{i=1}^{l} co\_occur(m_{ow(i)}|m_{s(i)}) \quad (8)$$

Where

$$co\_occur(m_{ow(i)}|m_{s(i)}, Mono) = p_{sow}(s|ow) \quad (9)$$

3.3 Model Training

In this study, we train the log-linear model with maximum-likelihood estimation (MLE), which is commonly used in machine learning. We assume that we have a training set, examples (m_i, t_i) are included in it, where m_i belongs to **M**, and t_i belongs to **T**.

For any example, we can calculate the log conditional probability as

$$L(v) = \sum_{i=1}^{n} \log p(t^{(i)}|m^{(j)}; v) \qquad (10)$$

To prevent the log-linear model from overfitting the training data, we follow the common solution that modifies the objective function to include a regularization term. Regularization will prevent overfitting when we have a lot of features. Therefore, the function of the parameters $\mathbf{v}$ can be defined as

$$L'(v) = \sum_{i=1}^{n} \log p(t^{(i)}|m^{(j)}; v) - \frac{\lambda}{2} \sum_{k} v_k^2 \qquad (11)$$

3.4 Decoding

By using the MLE training criteria, the optimal model parameters $\mathbf{v}$ can be estimated. Given the optimized parameters $\mathbf{v}$ and an input $\mathbf{M}$, decoding with the log-linear model defined in section 3.1 can be described as follows:

$$T' = \arg\max_{T} p(T|M, v) \qquad (12)$$

Where $\mathbf{M}$ is a sequence of morphemes, and $\mathbf{T}$ means a sequence of labels tagged by our model. $\mathbf{v}$ is a feature vector which is optimized during model training.

4 Experiments

In this section, we measure the effect of morphological segmentation on Uyghur-Chinese spoken language translation performance.

4.1 Data and settings

For spoken machine translation experiments, we train our model by Moses[2] on a Uyghur-Chinese parallel corpus of approximately 30K sentences, which consists mainly of documents in daily life from QQ, Weixin, etc. Develop set and test set are all collected from the same resources, which include 1K and 1.5K sentences, respectively (Table 4). We train a 5-gram language model on the Sougou corpus using the SRILM[3] with modified Kneser-Ney Smooth algorithm. We use the minimum error rate training (MERT) to optimize the feature weights on the develop set. We evaluate the performance of our model with BLEU.

In morphological segmentation experiments,

[2]http://www.statmt.org/moses/
[3]http://www.speech.sri.com/projects/srilm/

corpus	size of corpus (sentence pairs)		
	training set	dev set	test set
Spoken	30K	1K	1.5K
News	40K	/	/

Table 4: Statistics of data in SMT

we train a traditional model based on CRF with 12K annotated corpus. We extract the bilingually-constrained features on a Uyghur-Chinese parallel corpus on news domain of about 40K sentences, and monolingual co-occurrence features from the Uyghur parts of the same corpus (Table 5). We use a log-linear model to integrate these features together, which is the framework of our proposed method.

4.2 Results and Discussion

Table 6 gives performance of spoken Uyghur morphological segmentation for machine translation using different models. It should be noted that morphological segmentation mentioned in this paper is different from the traditional way. In our approach, we assumed that we already have the segmentation results according to a morphological analyzer; our task is to make a decision that whether to reserve or delete the suffixes of a certain Uyghur word to make a better translation performance. Log-linear model with only the CRF feature do not yield satisfactory results, while our proposed model (log-linear model with CRF, bilingual word alignment and monolingual stem-suffix co-occurrence features) perform significantly better at predicting tags of suffixes on the spoken Uyghur corpus. A single CRF, bilingual word alignment or monolingual stem-suffix co-occurrence feature cannot fully capture bilingual relationship and contexts of current Uyghur word; therefore, performance of these models (LL+XXs) is much lower that our proposed approach.

Table 7& 8 present results on spoken Uyghur-Chinese machine translation with different translation models (Table 7) and segmentation models integrated with different features (Table 8).

From Table 7, we observe that compare with word based model, models based on morphological segmentation achieved better results. That is because segmentation can alleviate data sparsity in model training, especially for low-resource and morphologically rich languages. Although factored translation model can use more linguistic in-

496

corpus	size of corpus (sentences/tokens)		
	training set	dev set	test set
morphseg0	12K/1.2M	/	/
morphseg1	5K/0.5M, 5K/0.6M	0.5K/5K, 0.5K/6K	0.8K/8K, 0.8K/8K
bilingualWA	40K/1M, 40K/1.2M	/	/
monoCO	40K/1M	/	/

Table 5: Statistics of data used in morphological segmentation

models	performance (%)		
	recall	precision	f1
LL+CRF	76.24	78.51	77.36
LL+bilingualWA	75.69	78.20	76.92
LL+monoCO	74.32	77.94	76.09
LL+bilingualWA+monoCO	78.56	78.62	78.59
LL+CRF+bilingualWA	78.70	79.02	78.86
LL+CRF+monoCO	78.93	80.59	79.75
LL+CRF+bilingualWA+monoCO	**82.40**	**85.37**	**83.86**

Table 6: Performance of morphological segmentation for spoken Uyghur translation using different models

models	BLEU	
	test set	dev set
Word based model	15.05	16.81
Factored model	17.18	18.59
Stem based model	18.30	17.52
Stem based model (Ours)	**19.92(+1.62)**	**18.70(+0.11)**

Table 7: Test set and Dev set performance for Uyghur-Chinese spoken machine translation results by models using different translation units.

features	BLEU	
	test set	dev set
CRF	18.30	17.52
bilingualWA	17.28	17.03
monoCoOccur	17.14	16.50
bilingualWA+monoCoOccur	18.29	18.50
CRF+bilingualWA	17.80	17.42
CRF+monoCoOccur	17.68	17.01
CRF+bilingualWA+monoCoOccur(Ours)	**19.92(+1.62)**	**18.70(+0.20)**

Table 8: Test set and Dev set performance for Uyghur-Chinese spoken machine translation (BLEU) results by using our segmentation model with different features.

formation, it can't alleviate the data sparsity effectively in spoken Uyghur-Chinese machine translation. Therefore, stem-based models both outperform factored based translation model in test set. Our proposed approach integrated both bilingual information and monolingual information into the morphological segmentation model, that's why it achieves best translation results in both test and dev sets among four translation models. We also found that the performance of dev set of factored model outperforms stem based model, a possible reason is that stem based model lost some information when Uyghur words segment incorrectly.

In Table 8, we list translation results using different features in log-linear model. The CRF model is just the same as the stem based model. A single bilingualWA or monoCoOccur model has a relative lower performance compared with CRF model that is because CRF model learned from annotated corpus, both bilingualWA and monoCoOccur models learn features unsurpervisedly. With CRF features, the performance of bilingualWA and monoCoOccur both improved. Our proposed log-linear based morphological segmentation model achieved best translation results among seven models, one possible reason is that our method integrates manually annotated information, bilingual word alignment information and monolingual suffix-word co-occurrence information; therefore, it can optimize the morphological segmentation of Uyghur in spoken translation situation.

5 Related Work

Many researchers have focused on morphological segmentation in past few years. These methods can be classified into three categories: unsupervised approaches (Goldsmith, 2001) (Creutz and Lagus, 2002) (Creutz et al., 2007) (Poon et al., 2009) (Abudukelimu et al., 2017), supervised approaches (Sirts and Goldwater, 2013) (Ruokolainen et al., 2013) and semi-supervised approaches (Kohonen et al., 2010) (Ruokolainen et al., 2014) (Tursun et al., 2016). Other people also put their efforts on morphological segmentation for SMT, such as (Lee, 2004) (Grönroos et al., 2016) (Mermer and Saraclar, 2011) (Sereewattana, 2003) (Clifton, 2010) (Bisazza and Federico, 2009) (Al-Haj and Lavie, 2012) (Rasooli et al., 2013) (Mi et al., 2015).

Our proposed approach is different from previous works. One of the most important reasons is that most of above studies are focused on formal corpora, such as news, government documents et al., and our study mainly put efforts on spoken language. Moreover, our method integrates supervised feature (CRF feature) and unsupervised features (bilingual word alignment feature and monolingual suffix-word co-occurrence feature) into the log-linear model.

6 Conclusion

In this paper, we present a bilingually - constrained based Uyghur segmentation method to optimize the performance of Uyghur-Chinese spoken translation. Our approach aims to maintain some useful suffixes of Uyghur words to overcome the information loss and data sparsity exist in spoken translation. The proposed method consists of four parts: 1) Uyghur segmentation based on a CRFs model; 2) bilingual alignment features collection from the GIZA++; 3) monolingual co-occurrence features extract from a large Uyghur corpus; and 4) training a log-linear based Uyghur segmentation model, under the bilingual alignment features and monolingual co-occurrence features. The experimental results show that the proposed model can achieve significant BLEU (+1.6) improvements over several baselines in Uyghur-Chinese spoken translation.

In our future work, we plan to integrate linguistic information such as part-of-speech, syntax into our proposed segmentation approach.

Acknowledgments

We sincerely thank the anonymous reviewers for their thorough reviewing and valuable suggestions. This work is supported by the West Light Foundation of The Chinese Academy of Sciences under Grant No.2015-XBQN-B-10, the Xinjiang Key Laboratory Fund under Grant No. 2015KL031, the Xinjiang Science and Technology Major Project under Grant No.2016A03007-3 and the Natural Science Foundation of Xinjiang under Grant No.2015211B034.

References

Halidanmu Abudukelimu, Yong Cheng, Yang Liu, and Maosong Sun. 2017. Uyghur morphological segmentation with bidirectional gru neural networks. *Journal of Tsinghua*

University(Science and Technology) 57(1):1. https://doi.org/10.16511/j.cnki.qhdxxb.2017.21.001.

Hassan Al-Haj and Alon Lavie. 2012. The impact of arabic morphological segmentation on broad-coverage english-to-arabic statistical machine translation. *Machine Translation* 26(1):3–24.

Arianna Bisazza and Marcello Federico. 2009. Morphological pre-processing for turkish to english statistical machine translation. In *Proceedings of IWSLT 2009*. Tokyo, Japan, IWSLT 2009, pages 129–145.

Ann Clifton. 2010. *Unsupervised morphological segmentation for statistical machine translation*. Simon Fraser University.

Mathias Creutz, Teemu Hirsimäki, Mikko Kurimo, Antti Puurula, Janne Pylkkönen, Vesa Siivola, Matti Varjokallio, Ebru Arisoy, Murat Saraçlar, and Andreas Stolcke. 2007. Morph-based speech recognition and modeling of out-of-vocabulary words across languages. *ACM Trans. Speech Lang. Process.* 5(1):3:1–3:29. https://doi.org/10.1145/1322391.1322394.

Mathias Creutz and Krista Lagus. 2002. Unsupervised discovery of morphemes. In *Proceedings of the ACL-02 Workshop on Morphological and Phonological Learning - Volume 6*. Association for Computational Linguistics, MPL '02, pages 21–30. https://doi.org/10.3115/1118647.1118650.

John Goldsmith. 2001. Unsupervised learning of the morphology of a natural language. *Computational Linguistics* 27(2):153–198. https://doi.org/10.1162/089120101750300490.

Stig-Arne Grönroos, Sami Virpioja, and Mikko Kurimo. 2016. *Proceedings of the First Conference on Machine Translation: Volume 2, Shared Task Papers*, Association for Computational Linguistics, Berlin, Germany, chapter Hybrid Morphological Segmentation for Phrase-Based Machine Translation, pages 289–295. https://doi.org/10.18653/v1/W16-2312.

Oskar Kohonen, Sami Virpioja, and Krista Lagus. 2010. Semi-supervised learning of concatenative morphology. In *Proceedings of the 11th Meeting of the ACL Special Interest Group on Computational Morphology and Phonology*. Association for Computational Linguistics, Uppsala, Sweden, SIGMORPHON '10, pages 78–86. http://dl.acm.org/citation.cfm?id=1870478.1870488.

Young-Suk Lee. 2004. Morphological analysis for statistical machine translation. In *Proceedings of HLT-NAACL 2004: Short Papers*. Association for Computational Linguistics, Boston, Massachusetts, HLT-NAACL-Short '04, pages 57–60. http://dl.acm.org/citation.cfm?id=1613984.1613999.

Yang Liu, Qun Liu, and Shouxun Lin. 2005. Log-linear models for word alignment. In *Proceedings of the 43rd Annual Meeting on Association for Computational Linguistics*. Association for Computational Linguistics, Ann Arbor, Michigan, ACL '05, pages 459–466. https://doi.org/10.3115/1219840.1219897.

Coskun Mermer and Murat Saraclar. 2011. Unsupervised turkish morphological segmentation for statistical machine translation. In *Workshop of MT and Morphologically-rich Languages.*.

Chenggang Mi, Yating Yang, Rui Dong, Xi Zhou, Lei Wang, Xiao Li, Tonghai Jiang, and Turghun Osman. 2015. Optimized uyghur segmentation for statistical machine translation. In *Proceedings of the 20th International Conference on Applications of Natural Language to Information Systems, NLDB 2015*. Springer International Publishing, Passau, Germany, pages 395–398.

Hoifung Poon, Colin Cherry, and Kristina Toutanova. 2009. Unsupervised morphological segmentation with log-linear models. In *Proceedings of Human Language Technologies: The 2009 Annual Conference of the North American Chapter of the Association for Computational Linguistics*. Association for Computational Linguistics, Boulder, Colorado, NAACL '09, pages 209–217. http://dl.acm.org/citation.cfm?id=1620754.1620785.

Sadegh Mohammad Rasooli, Ahmed El Kholy, and Nizar Habash. 2013. Orthographic and morphological processing for persian-to-english statistical machine translation. In *Proceedings of the Sixth International Joint Conference on Natural Language Processing*. Asian Federation of Natural Language Processing, Nagoya, Japan, pages 1047–1051. http://aclweb.org/anthology/I13-1144.

Teemu Ruokolainen, Oskar Kohonen, Sami Virpioja, and Mikko Kurimo. 2013. *Proceedings of the Seventeenth Conference on Computational Natural Language Learning*, Association for Computational Linguistics, Sofia, Bulgaria, chapter Supervised Morphological Segmentation in a Low-Resource Learning Setting using Conditional Random Fields, pages 29–37. http://aclweb.org/anthology/W13-3504.

Teemu Ruokolainen, Oskar Kohonen, Sami Virpioja, and mikko kurimo. 2014. Painless semi-supervised morphological segmentation using conditional random fields. In *Proceedings of the 14th Conference of the European Chapter of the Association for Computational Linguistics, volume 2: Short Papers*. Association for Computational Linguistics, Gothenburg, Sweden, pages 84–89. https://doi.org/10.3115/v1/E14-4017.

Siriwan Sereewattana. 2003. *Unsupervised segmentation for statistical machine translation*. University of Edinburgh.

Kairit Sirts and Sharon Goldwater. 2013. Minimally-supervised morphological segmentation using adaptor grammars. *Transactions of the Association of Computational Linguistics* 1:255–266. http://aclweb.org/anthology/Q13-1021.

Eziz Tursun, Debasis Ganguly, Turghun Osman, Ya-Ting Yang, Ghalip Abdukerim, Jun-Lin Zhou, and Qun Liu. 2016. A semisupervised tag-transition-based markovian model for uyghur morphology analysis. *ACM Trans. Asian Low-Resour. Lang. Inf. Process.* 16(2):8:1–8:23. https://doi.org/10.1145/2968410.

Bootstrapping a Romanian Corpus for Medical Named Entity Recognition

Maria Mitrofan
Research Institute for Artificial Intelli-
gence "Mihai Drăgănescu"
Romanian Academy
Calea 13 Septembrie, nr. 13,
Bucharest, România
maria@racai.ro

Abstract

Named Entity Recognition (NER) is an important component of natural language processing (NLP), with applicability in the biomedical domain, enabling knowledge discovery from medical texts. Due to the fact that for the Romanian language there are only a few linguistic resources specific to the biomedical domain, we have created a sub-corpus specific to this domain. In this paper we present a newly developed Romanian sub-corpus for medical domain NER, which is a valuable asset for the field of biomedical text processing. We provide a description of the sub-corpus, statistics about data-composition and we evaluate an automatic NER tool on the newly created resource.

1 Introduction

There is an increasing need for exploiting and managing the available biomedical texts due to the fact that each day huge amounts of medical data become available (Patel et al., 2009).

MEDLINE, the largest biomedical database resource, currently contains more than 26.9 million abstracts of the world's biomedical journal literature and each month 60,000 new abstracts are added, according to MEDLINE Database Summary Sheet (DBSS). The increasing rate of published biomedical literature has generated a pressing need for computation techniques to be used for information extraction from the available data (Coleman et al., 2009; Gabbay and Le May, 2010).

In general, most of the available data is noisy and/or unstructured as for instance in clinical reports. Consequently, NLP tools are required and used to turn this data into knowledge.

In the NLP domain NER is the task dedicated to the identification and classification of textual units, be they single words or multiple words (such as locations, names of persons, organizations, places).

NER systems are a prerequisite for many text processing applications such as relation extraction (Tasneem and Archana, 2016), question answering (Athenikos and Han, 2009), information extraction (Piskorski and Yangarber, 2012), etc. In fact, NER is a basic step in ordering and structuring all the existing domain information.

In particular, biomedical named entity recognition (BioNER) tools aim to detect biomedical terms such as human anatomical parts (Xu et al., 2014), drug names (Liu et al., 2015), gene and protein mentions (Tanabe and Wilbur, 2002), chemical compounds (Eltyeb and Salim, 2014), diseases (Jimeno et al., 2008) and to assign them the correct categories.

Although the NLP community has invested a lot of efforts in BioNER, the task is complex, because biomedical corpora contain specialized terminology, which is not easy to identify. Nevertheless, it is argued that the vocabulary in biomedical corpora is easier to deal with than the vocabulary in general corpora, due to the closure properties of sublanguages (Temnikova et al., 2013; Temnikova and Cohen, 2013).

Moreover NER systems trained and tested on news articles corpora achieve on average an accuracy of 90% (Passos et al., 2014), but similar techniques do not work well when applied to biomedical corpora, the accuracy obtained being about 10% less (Abacha and Zweigenbaum, 2011).

In this paper, we explore NLP techniques to identify biomedical named entities in text and also we present up-to-date statistics about a newly created Romanian medical sub-corpus.

Proceedings of Recent Advances in Natural Language Processing, pages 501–509,
Varna, Bulgaria, Sep 4–6 2017.

2 Challenges in BioNER

To minimize the gap mentioned before between performances of biomedical NER and other types of NER several techniques and algorithms have been proposed taking into consideration the peculiarities of biomedical texts.

Due to the fact that in biomedical literature there is not a unique naming convention, the spelling variations of the biomedical terms cause recognition ambiguity. For example, the same "diabetes mellitus type 2" entity may be referred to in Romanian in different spelling forms: "T2DM" borrowed abbreviation from English, "DZ tip 2"(En. DM type 2) Romanian abbreviation, "diabet zaharat tip 2"(En. type 2 diabetes mellitus) the full Romanian form. Synonymy is a frequent linguistic feature of the biomedical subcorpus. For exmpample, the terms "natriu" (En. sodium) and "sodiu" (En. sodium) have the same meaning.

The phenomenon of polysemy is also present in Romanian biomedical text, for example for the Romanian abbreviation "PA" there are two possible meanings: "presiune arterială" (En. blood presure) and "forfatază alcalină" (En. alkaline phosphatase).

And also there are no rules for the formation of biomedical terms and words may contain digits (T1DM, T2DM), Greek letters "celula β" (En. β- cell), "celule β-pancreatice" (En. pancreatic β- cells), hyphens "19-nortestosteron" (En. "19-nortestosterone").

Another frequent problem is that biomedical literature is very rich in abbreviations. Many abbreviations are difficult to correctly classify because of their multiple forms. For example "electrocardiogramă" (En. electrocardiogram) has two abbreviation forms "ECG" and "EKG" or "fibrilație atrială" (En. atrial fibrillation) can be abbreviated as "FA" or "FiA".

Chang et al. (2002) have shown that in every 5-10 MEDLINE abstracts there is one new abbreviation and Liu et al. (2002) showed that 81.2% of abbreviations found in MEDLINE abstracts are ambiguous. Moreover, new substances are discovered daily and this causes difficulties in recognizing them, especially for rule based systems.

Furthermore, another BioNER challenge is generated by the fact that one head noun may be shared by two or more biomedical named entities. For example, the following structure with coordination "micro- și macroangiopatiei" (En. micro- and

macroangiopathy) consists of two entityes "microangiopatiei" (En. microangiophaty) and "macroangiopatiei" (En. macroangiopathy), the same case with "ateroscleroza aortei și a vaselor periferice" (En. atherosclerosis of the aorta and peripheral vessels), which should be read as "ateroscleroza aortei și ateroscleroza vaselor periferice" (En. atherosclerosis of the aorta and atherosclerosis of the peripheral vessels).

As a particular type of coordination disjunctions also allow omission for the head noun in the second conjunct: "celule beta pancreatice sau hepatice" (En. pancreatic beta or hepatic cells) should be interpreted as "celule beta pancreatice sau celule hepatice" (En. pancreatic beta cells or hepatic cells).

Cascaded constructions represent another major challenge that can be encountered in BioNER, because one entity may be incorporated in another entity name. In GENIA V3.0 corpus almost 16.57% (Zhou and Su, 2004) of all biomedical entity names have cascaded construction (Sondhi, 2008). For example, for the Romanian language we may find cascaded constructions such as "Anevrismele/B-DISO pot fi fusiforme/I-DISO (aspect cilindric al vasului/B-ANAT sangvin/I-ANAT) sau sacciforme/I-DISO." (En. Aneurysms/B-DISO may be fusiforms/I-DISO (cylindrical appearance of the blood/B-ANAT vessel/I-ANAT) or sacciforms/I-DISO.) (see subsection 5.2).

Even though nowadays there are language independent BioNER systems, most of them rely on linguistic resources, which are not available for all languages and domains (Nadeau and Sekine, 2007), thus when language adaptation is needed the performance of BioNER systems is affected.

Consequently BioNER is much more complex than general named entity recognition applied in newswire domain (Sondhi, 2008).

3 Related Work

3.1 Biomedical Corpora

For English, there are multiple biomedical corpora that can be used for different NLP tasks. Since the release of the GENIA corpus (Kim et al., 2003) and thanks to the availability of annotated biomedical corpora (GENETAG corpus (Tanabe et al., 2005), SCAI IUPAC corpus (Kolarik et al., 2008), AnEM corpus (Ohta et al., 2012), and CellFinder corpus (Neves et al., 2012)), various systems have been developed for information extraction from biomedical documents. Nowadays such systems can find diseases, drug names, clinical problems and gene names with performance (F score) better than 90% (Abacha and Zweigenbaum, 2011; Wang and Patrick, 2009; Boytcheva et al., 2010).

On the other hand, research on medical languages other than English is more scarce.

For the French language, the "Unified Medical Lexicon for French" (UMLF) (Zweigenbaum et al., 2005) has been created and aims at being a reference resource for NLP in the medical domain. Nevertheless, (Cartoni and Zweigenbaum, 2010) showed that even in large collections of terms there is a lack of specialized lexicons and they conducted an experiment to feed a French medical lexicon, in which the dimension of the specialized lexicon increased its coverage of the initial vocabulary from 14.1% to 25.7%.

For Swedish an annotated gold standard corpus of medical records was developed (Velupillai, 2012) and also scientific medical corpus was created for linguistic exploration and terminology management. Mowery et al. (2012) proposed a clinical uncertainty and negation taxonomy and mapped an English annotation schema to a Swedish schema. Recently a corpus for BioNER recognition in Spanish have been created (Moreno et al., 2017).

For Bulgarian language important efforts have been made in collecting biomedical literature usable for NLP tasks. For example (Boytcheva et al., 2009) described a Bulgarian medical corpus formed by 6400 words, with 2000 of them belonging to Bulgarian medical terminology. Nikolova et al. (2016) used free textual data of diabetic patience to determine their smoking status.

3.2 BioNER Approaches

To tackle the challenges posed by BioNER, researchers use different NER approaches including: dictionary-based methods, rule-based methods and machine learning methods.

Terminology-driven BioNER methods such as dictionary and rule-based approaches, use regular expressions to match the information from terminological resources with text phrases. Fukuda et al. (1998) proposed a rule-based system for protein names identification and obtained a precision of 91.90% and a recall of 93.32%, when the system was evaluated on 30 annotated MEDLINE abstracts. Gaizauskas et al. (2000) used used terminology lexicons, standard biomedical suffixes and hand-designed grammar rules for terminology classes and achieved 86% precision and 68% recall. Nevertheless NER systems based on rules perform poorly for large scale tasks because of the spelling variations and different naming conventions of biomedical terms (Gaizauskas et al., 2000; Fukuda et al., 1998; Tuason et al., 2004).

Machine learning (ML) based systems are focused on the recognition of specific named entities using various statistical models. In machine learning area there are taken two main approaches. The former one is based on supervised learning techniques, where based on a learning algorithm a mapping from a known input to a desired output is performed.

The latter broad machine learning approach used for BioNER is unsupervised learning and the aim of this method is to find regularities in the data, based only on input data. The methods of unsupervised learning are mostly built upon clustering techniques, similarity based functions and statistics. Recently, there has been an increasing interest in using word embeddings from unlabeled biomedical corpora (Li et al., 2016).

4 Corpora Description and Annotation Tools

Even though at the international level the challenges of biomedical information processing have changed from where to collect resources to how to make use of them (Shaodian and Elhadad, 2013), at the national level linguistic resources specific to certain domains (biomedical area among them) are difficult to obtain. However, a relevant sub-corpus for biomedical domain has been collected in the context of the CoRoLa project (The reference corpus of the contemporary Romanian language created by the Romanian Academy Research Institute for Artificial Intelligence "Mihai Drăgănescu" and Institute for Computer Science in Iași) (Tufiș et al., 2016).

The Romanian biomedical sub-corpus is composed of about 7 million tokens (including punctuation), about 300,000 sentences extracted from different biomedical sub-domains such as: diabetes, cardiology, endocrinology, neurology, oncology, etc. (Mitrofan and Tufiș, 2016) (Table 1).

# tokens	7,173,396
# words	6,287,246
# unique lemmas	136,330
# sentences	309,948
average tokens per sentence	23.14
average words per sentence	20.28
average punctuation per sentence	2.8

Table 1: Statistics over the Romanian medical sub-corpus.

4.1 Pre-processing Steps

NLP solutions are usually decomposed into subtasks that form processing pipelines that ensure specific functionalities such as: sentence splitting, tokenization, lemmatization and chunking, part-of-speech (POS) tagging, parsing.

In order to process the Romanian medical sub-corpus we used the TTL platform (Ion, 2007), which is a language-independent text processing module (Todirașcu et al., 2011). Another processing tool for Romanian is the Modular Language Processing for Lightweight Applications (ML-PLA) (Dumitrescu et al., 2017), which is a freely available[1] and language-independent processing tool that supports more than 50 languages.

The TTL tool is able to automatically perform specific functionalities (Tufiș et al., 2010) such as: sentence splitting (to identify the end of a sentence it uses regular expressions), tokenization, part-of-speech tagging (with an accuracy of more than 98%, when trained on newswire domain), lemmatization (it recovers for each word the corresponding lemma based on a human-validated Romanian word-form lexicon, the lemma guesser model has an accuracy of 83%), chunking (based on a set of regular expressions for each tagged and lemmatized lexical unit is assigned a syntactic phrase.

After running TTL on the biomedical sub-corpus, about 7 million tokens were assigned a corresponding lemma and a POS tag. Table 6 shows the results after the POS-tagging step. We want to emphasize that most of the B-ANAT, B-DISO, B-PROC, B-CHEM named entity classes tagged as adjectives are in fact POS-tagging errors. This also happens for the category "Others" where nouns can be found tagged as verbs, adverbs, etc.

The TTL tagger marks the unknown words for which the tags and lemmas were predicted on the basis of the language model. This makes it easier to spot wrong predictions (tag, lemma or both) and correct them manually by a linguist. The bootstrapping method we adopted takes advantage of these corrections. It was shown that lexical features, especially part-of-speech tags, are important for BioNER as they may help to identify entity boundaries (Sondhi, 2008). Zhou and Su (2004) reported an increase in performance when part-of-speech features were integrated.

5 The Annotation Process

The first step, in order to apply NER techniques to the medical sub-corpus, was to manually annotate almost 40,000 tokens with BioNER tags and have all these labels checked by a medical expert, who was accustomed to the IOB standard.

Secondly to rapidly grow our sub-corpus used for BioNER we followed a typical bootstrapping procedure, in which, once a sub-portion of the sub-corpus is available, a ML technique is used to learn how to automatically detect and label NEs in the unprocessed sections of the data. This way the manual annotation procedure is enhanced for the remainder corpora, because automatically inferred labels offer good guidelines and greatly speed-up the process. Therefore after the bootstrapping procedure other 60.000 tokens were automatically labeled with BioNER tags and then each one of them was corrected by hand.

5.1 Entity Classes

For the Romanian biomedical sub-corpus four top level entity classes were chosen Anatomy (anatomical structure, body part, organ, organ component,tissue, cell, cell component), Chemicals and Drugs (amino acid, peptide, protein, antibiotic, biologically active substance, chemical, clinical drug, enzyme, hormone, pharmacological substance, receptor), Disorders (anatomical abnormality, acquired abnormality, congenital abnormality, disease or syndrome, injury, mental dysfunction), Procedures (laboratory procedure, therapeutic or preventive procedure), defined by choosing the corresponding UMLS (Unified Medical Language System) semantic groups[2] :

- Anatomy (ANAT): "valvă aortică" (En. aortic valve), "stomac" (En. stomach), "țesut

---

504

epitelial" (En. epithelial tissue), "mitocondrie" (En. mitochondria);

- Chemicals and Drugs (CHEM): "penicilină" (En. penicillin), "acetilcolină" (En. acetylcholine), "lipază" (En. lipase);

- Disorders (DISO): "depresie" (En. depression), "delir" (En. delirium), "accident vascular cerebral" (En. stroke), "diabet zaharat" (En. mellitus diabetes);

- Procedures (PROC): "ecocardiografie transesofagiană" (En. transesophageal echocardiography), "radiografie" (En. radiography).

5.2 IOB Format Tagging

In order to apply language processing algorithms to BioNER, we converted the sub-corpus into IOB2 format (Sang and Veenstra, 1999), where "B" denotes the beginning chunk (a span of tokens) and "I" represents an inside chunk. "O" labels indicate tokens that do not belong to a chunk. Table 2 shows an example of a tagged sentence: "Examenul obiectiv al cordului identifică adesea tulburări de ritm, cele mai frecvente fiind fibrilația atrială și aritmia extrasistolică." (En. The objective examination of the heart often identifies rhythm perturbations, the most common being the atrial fibrillation and the extrasystolic arrhythmia.).

6 Corpus and Automatic Biomedical NER Evaluation

At the time we are writing this paper, the annotation of the sub-corpus is on-going in parallel with enlarging its size. However, we consider that the available data has reached maturity, in the sense that it can already find its use in the field of research. In what follows we provide relevant statistical information about our corpora composition such as: (a) the distributions of the named entities based on their type; (b) the average length and standard deviation of named entities (also based on their types); (c) distribution of underlying part-of-speech type for each NE type and (d) the results obtained by our pretrained NE models.

For clarity, all information regarding the corpus is rendered in subsection 6.1, while subsection 6.2 deals with the process of training and testing our automatic NE technique based on the newly created sub-corpus.

Token	Tag
Examenul (The examination)	O
obiectiv (objective)	O
al (of)	O
cordului (heart)	B-ANAT
identifică (identifies)	O
adesea (often)	O
tulburări (perturbations)	B-DISO
de (of)	I-DISO
ritm (rhythm)	I-DISO
,	O
cele (the)	O
mai (most)	O
frecvente (frequent)	O
fiind (being)	O
fibrilația (the fibrillation)	B-DISO
atrială (atrial)	I-DISO
și (and)	O
aritmia (the arrhythmia)	B-DISO
extrasistolică (extrasistolic)	I-DISO
.	O

Table 2: Example of a tagged sentence

This section is oriented toward providing preliminary information about the sub-corpus and before we proceed with, we will motivate the statistics we extracted.

6.1 Corpus Statistics

- **NE type distribution**: this information is very helpful for establishing if the sub-corpus is well-balanced and what the expected results will be if one trains an automatic NE identification tool on the available data (Table 3).

Tag	Number of tags
B-DISO	3992
I-DISO	2942
B-ANAT	1387
I-ANAT	996
B-PROC	947
I-PROC	714
B-CHEM	2525
I-CHEM	816

Table 3: NE type distribution.

- **Average size (in tokens) of NEs:** knowing what is the average span of a NE is important in the feature-selection process. As such, compact NEs (short and without interleaved non-NE tokens) make it possible to use small context windows in the feature extraction process, while long-range NEs (with interleaved non-NE tokens) require other approaches (in practice modified SHIFT-REDUCE schemes can achieve good results) (Table 5). Table 4 shows that most of the medical NEs are compound of more than one token, as can be seen also in table 5. "CHEM" is the entity class that contains the shortest NEs, 75% of NEs are compound of only one token, and the NEs with length greater than three tokens appear seldom, as can be seen from both tables 5 and 4.

NE	NE length				
	1	2	3	4	5
B-DISO	48%	35%	12%	3%	2%
B-ANAT	43%	42%	12%	2%	1%
B-PROC	40%	47%	10%	2%	1%
B-CHEM	75%	20%	4%	1%	0%

Table 4: NE type length.

Tag	Average	Stdev.
DISO	1.747	0.951
ANAT	1.723	0.743
PROC	1.762	0.177
CHEM	1.329	0.656
Overall	1.626	0.846

Table 5: Average size of NEs.

- **POS statistics:** provide good clues whether one should or should not use the POS information as features for training a automatic NE tool. In our case, it would be expected that most tokens would be nouns, adjectives and abbreviations (Table 6).

6.2 Automatic NE for Biomedical Sub-corpus

As can easily be seen our NEs are mostly compact with a POS distribution that motivates using the grammatical category as a feature. This, combined with the average length of our NEs has driven us to go for a straight-forward NE identification procedure: we trained a classifier to label each token inside a sentence with a IOB tag, based on features extracted from the context windows.

In our approach, the context-window size is 3 (centered on the current token) and the features are composed of the word-form and POS information for each context-word. A particularity is that, instead of using standard approaches (CRF, SVM, Decision Tree etc.) we employed a Partitioned Convolutional Neural Network for classification and we used automatically extracted word-embeddings (Mikolov et al., 2013), computed using Word2Vec[3] from a corpus composed of the Romanian section of Wikipedia, concatenated with our own medical sub-corpus. The architecture of the network is composed of two partitions followed by two fully connected layers and a softmax output layer. Each partition is trained independently on its own feature category:

- The wordform partition works directly over the word embeddings inside the receptive field (window size of 3) and is based on 128 convolutional filters (size 1x64 - a word embeddings size of 64);

- The POS partition is trained on automatically inferred feature embeddings, that feed into 16 convolutional filters. The automatic feature-embeddings process is inspired by (Danqi and Christopher, 2014) and is implemented as a set of deconvolutional filters (one filter for each possible POS label).

In order to evaluate our approach we used 80% of the data for training, 10% for development, and 10% for testing. Table 7 summarizes the results obtained on the test-set: column 2 (ident.) refers to the number of correctly identified instances of the corresponding label and column 3 (act.) represents the actual number of instances in the test-set.

7 The Availability of the Data

The biomedical subcorpus will be available in the context of the CoRoLa project copyright agreement signed with the editorial offices representatives and with the publishing houses. All the data from the CoRoLa will be available for the public through KorAP platform (Bingel et al., 2013). This platform allows various linguistic types of searches in the data, but the corpus will not be downloadable. However, all the results of the interrogation of the corpus outside the scope of the copyright restrictions will be downloadable.

---

[3]https://github.com/dav/word2vec - accessed 2017-05-03

Tag	Nouns	Adjectives	Abbreviations	Others
B-DISO	3634	19	285	54
I-DISO	418	2263	10	251
B-ANAT	1352	19	16	0
I-ANAT	150	788	19	39
B-PROC	907	10	20	10
I-PROC	160	491	15	48
B-CHEM	2195	125	179	26
I-CHEM	248	410	49	109

Table 6: POS-statistics.

Tag	Ident.	Act.	Precision	Recall	F-score
Dev-set					
B-ANAT	63	178	0.67	0.35	0.46
I-ANAT	56	171	0.74	0.32	0.45
B-DISO	208	409	0.64	0.50	0.56
I-DISO	150	341	0.68	0.43	0.53
B-PROC	4	166	0.80	0.02	0.04
I-PROC	13	156	0.81	0.08	0.15
B-CHEM	46	107	0.29	0.42	0.34
I-CHEM	5	26	0.18	0.19	0.18
Test-set					
B-ANAT	52	136	0.75	0.38	0.50
I-ANAT	31	104	0.77	0.29	0.43
B-DISO	162	387	0.61	0.41	0.49
I-DISO	137	297	0.68	0.46	0.55
B-PROC	23	53	0.51	0.43	0.46
I-PROC	17	34	0.47	0.50	0.48
B-CHEM	81	189	0.42	0.42	0.42
I-CHEM	13	74	0.48	0.17	0.25

Table 7: Evaluation results on the development and test sets.

8 Conclusions and Future Work

In this paper we introduced a newly created text sub-corpus aimed at proving support for NLP on biomedical text. We provided relevant information about the sub-corpus itself (at token/NE level), we described our annotation process (both automatic: tokenization, lemmatization and part-of-speech tagging – and manual: the NE labeling procedure).

Additionally, we assessed the validity and maturity of our data by introducing a custom-designed ML method for identifying NEs in the biomedical domain.

Currently our corpus is still under development, but we consider that the available data and the pre-trained tool can already be used on Romanian biomedical text.

The annotated section of the corpus is freely available for download[4] and non-commercial use. Special use-cases require license permissions from the author.

Acknowledgements

We want to thank to my colleague Tiberiu Boroș for helping us with technical issues whenever they have arisen and for the comments that greatly improved the quality of the paper. Moreover we wish to acknowledge the help provided by the PhD student Grigorina Mitrofan. Also Verginica Barbu Mititelu and Elena Irimia, thank you for giving us valuable comments on the draft version of this paper.

---

[4]http://slp.racai.ro/index.php/resources/

References

A. Abacha and P. Zweigenbaum. 2011. Medical entity recognition: a comparison of semantic and statistical methods. In *Proceedings of BioNLP 2011 workshop*. pages 56–64.

Sofia J. Athenikos and Hyoil Han. 2009. Biomedical question answering: A survey.

P. Banskiand J. Bingel, N.Diewald, E. Frick, M. Hanl, M. Kupietz, P. Pezik, C. Schnober, and A. Witt. 2013. The new corpus analysis platform at ids mannheim.

S. Boytcheva, I. Nikolova, E. Paskaleva, G. Angelova, D. Tcharaktchiev, and N. Dimitrova. 2009. Extraction and exploration of correlations in patient status data. in proceedings of the workshop on biomedical information extraction. In *Proceedings of the Workshop on Biomedical Information Extraction*. pages 1–7.

S. Boytcheva, I. Nikolova, E. Paskaleva, G.Angelova, D. Tcharaktchiev, and N. Dimitrova. 2010. Obtaining status descriptions via automatic analysis of hospital patient records.

B. Cartoni and P. Zweigenbaum. 2010. Semi-automated extension of a specialized medical lexicon for french. In *Proceedings of LREC*.

J. Chang, H. Schutze, and R. Altman. 2002. Creating an online dictionary of abbreviations from medline.

K. Coleman, BT. Austin, and C. Brach andEH. Wagner. 2009. *Evidence on the chronic care model in new millenium.*. Millrood.

Chen Danqi and D. Manning Christopher. 2014. A fast and accurate dependency parser using neural networks. In *EMNLP*. pages 740–750.

Stefan Daniel Dumitrescu, Tiberiu Boroş, and Dan Tufiş. 2017. Racai's natural language processing pipeline for universal dependencies. In *Proceedings of the CoNLL 2017 Shared Task: Multilingual Parsing from Raw Text to Universal Dependencies*. Association for Computational Linguistics, Vancouver, Canada, pages 174–181. http://www.aclweb.org/anthology/K/K17/K17-3018.pdf.

Safaa Eltyeb and Naomie Salim. 2014. Chemical named entities recognition: a review on approaches and applications.

K. Fukuda, T. Tsunoda, A. Tamura, and T. Takagi. 1998. Toward information extraction: identifying protein names from biological papers. In *Proceedings of the Pacific Symposium on Biocomputing.*. pages 707–718.

John Gabbay and Andrée Le May. 2010. *Practice-based evidence for healthcare: clinical mindlines*. Routledge.

R. Gaizauskas, G. Demetriou, and K. Humphreys. 2000. Term recognition and classification in biological science journal articles. In *Proceedings of Workshop on Computational Terminology for Medical and Biological Applications.*. pages 37–44.

Radu Ion. 2007. *Word Sense Disambiguation Methods Applied to English and Romanian (in Romanian).*

Antonio Jimeno, Ernesto Jimenez-Ruiz, Vivian Lee, Sylvain Gaudan, Rafael Berlanga, and Dietrich Rebholz-Schuhmann. 2008. Assessment of disease named entity recognition on a corpus of annotated sentences.

J.D. Kim, T. Ohta, Y. Tateisi, and J. I. Tsujii. 2003. Genia corpus—a semantically annotated corpus for bio-textmining.

Corinna Kolarik, Roman Klinger, Christoph M Friedrich, Martin Hofmann-Apitius, and Juliane Fluck. 2008. Chemical names: terminological resources and corpora annotation. In *Workshop on Building and evaluating resources for biomedical text mining (6th edition of the Language Resources and Evaluation Conference)*.

L. Li, L. Jin, Y. Jiang, and D.Huang. 2016. Recognizing biomedical named entities based on the sentence vector/twin word embeddings conditioned bidirectional lstm.

H. Liu, A. Aronson, and C. Friedman. 2002. A study of abbreviations in medline abstracts. In *Proceedings of the American Medical Informatics Association Symposium 2002*. page 327–332.

Shengyu Liu, Buzhou Tang, Qingcai Chen, Xiaolong Wang, and Xiaoming Fan. 2015. Feature engineering for drug name recognition in biomedical texts: Feature conjunction and feature selection.

Tomas Mikolov, Ilya Sutskever, Kai Chen, Greg S Corrado, and Jeff Dean. 2013. Distributed representations of words and phrases and their compositionality. In *Advances in neural information processing systems*. pages 3111–3119.

Maria Mitrofan and Dan Tufiş. 2016. Building and evaluating the romanian medical corpus. In *Proceedings ofthe 12 th International Conference "Linguistic Resources and tools for processing the Romanian language"*. pages 29–36.

I. Moreno, E. Boldrini, P. Moreda, and M. T. Roma-Ferri. 2017. Drugsemantics: a corpus for named entity recognition in spanish summaries of product characteristics.

D. L. Mowery, S. Velupillai, and W. W. Chapman. 2012. Medical diagnosis lost in translation: analysis of uncertainty and negation expressions in english and swedish clinical texts. In *Proceedings of the 2012 Workshop on Biomedical Natural Language Processing. Association for Computational Linguistics*.

D. Nadeau and S. Sekine. 2007. A survey of named entity recognition and classification.

Mariana Neves, Alexander Damaschun, Andreas Kurtz, and Ulf Leser. 2012. Annotating and evaluating text for stem cell research. In *Proceedings of the Third Workshop on Building and Evaluation Resources for Biomedical Text Mining (BioTxtM 2012)*.

I. Nikolova, S. Boytcheva, G. Angelova, and Z. Angelov. 2016. Combining structured and free textual data of diabetic patients' smoking status. in international conference on artificial intelligence: Methodology, systems, and applications. In *Proceedings of the International Conference on Artificial Intelligence: Methodology, Systems, and Applications*. Springer, pages 57–67.

Tomoko Ohta, Sampo Pyysalo, Jun'ichi Tsujii, and Sophia Ananiadou. 2012. Open-domain anatomical entity mention detection. In *Proceedings of ACL 2012 Workshop on Detecting Structure in Scholarly Discourse (DSSD)*. pages 27–36.

Alexandre Passos, Vineet Kumar, and Andrew McCallum. 2014. Lexicon infused phrase embeddings for named entity resolution. In *Proceedings of CoNLL.*.

V.L. Patel, E.H. Shortliffe, M. Stefanelli, P. Szolovits, M.R. Berthold, and R. Bellazzi. 2009. The coming of age of artificial intelligence in medicine.

Jakub Piskorski and Roman Yangarber. 2012. Information extraction: Past, present and future.

E. F. Sang and Jorn Veenstra. 1999. Representing text chunks. In *Proceedings of the ninth conference on European chapter of the Association for Computational Linguistics.*.

Zhang Shaodian and Noémie Elhadad. 2013. Unsupervised biomedical named entity recognition: Experiments with clinical and biological texts.

Parikshit Sondhi. 2008. A survey on named entity extraction in the biomedical domain.

Lorraine Tanabe and John Wilbur. 2002. Tagging gene and protein names in biomedical text.

Lorraine Tanabe, N. Xie, LH. Thom, W. Matten, and WJ. Wilbur. 2005. A tagged corpus for gene/protein named entity recognition.

Almas Tasneem and B. Archana. 2016. A survey on biomedical named entity extraction.

I. P. Temnikova and K. B. Cohen. 2013. Recognizing sublanguages in scientific journal articles through closure properties. In *Proceedings of BioNLP*. pages 72–79.

I. P. Temnikova, I. Nikolova, W.A. Baumgartner Jr, G. Angelova, and K. B. Cohen. 2013. Closure properties of bulgarian clinical text. In *Proceedings of RANLP 2013*.

Amalia Todirașcu, Radu Ion, Mirabela Navlea, and Laurence Longo. 2011. French text preprocessing with ttl. In *PROCEEDINGS OF THE ROMANIAN ACADEMY*. page 151–158.

O. Tuason, L. Chen, H. Liu, J.A. Blake, and C. Friedman. 2004. Biological nomenclature: A source of lexical knowledge and ambiguity. In *Proceedings of Pac Symp Biocomput.*. pages 238–249.

D. Tufis, V. B. Mititelu, E. Irimia, S. D. Dumitrescu, and T. Boros. 2016. The ipr-cleared corpus of contemporary written and spoken romanian language. In *Proceedings of the International Conference on Language Resources and Evaluation - LREC*.

Dan Tufiș, Radu Ion, Alexandru Ceaușu, and Dan Ștefănescu. 2010. Reifying the alignments. accurat-project.eu.

S. Velupillai. 2012. *Shades of certainty: annotation and classification of swedish medical records.*.

Y. Wang and J. Patrick. 2009. Cascading classifiers for named entity recognition in clinical notes. In *Proceedings of the workshop on biomedical information extraction.*. pages 42–49.

Yan Xu, Ji Hua, Zhaoheng Ni, Qinlang Chen, Yubo Fan, Sophia Ananiadou, Eric I-Chao Chang, and Junichi Tsujii. 2014. Anatomical entity recognition with a hierarchical framework augmented by external resources.

G. Zhou and J. Su. 2004. Exploring deep knowledge resources in biomedical name recognition. In *Proceedings of the joint workshop on natural language processing in biomedicine and its applications*. pages 96–99.

P. Zweigenbaum, R. Baud, A. Burgun, F. Namer, É Jarrousse, N. Grabar, and S. Darmoni. 2005. Umlf: a unified medical lexicon for french.

A Domain and Language Independent Named Entity Classification Approach Based on Profiles and Local Information

Isabel Moreno
Department of Software and
Computing Systems,
University of Alicante,
Alicante, Spain
imoreno@dlsi.ua.es

María Teresa Romá-Ferri
Department of Nursing,
University of Alicante,
Alicante, Spain
mtr.ferri@ua.es

Paloma Moreda
Department of Software and
Computing Systems,
University of Alicante,
Alicante, Spain
moreda@dlsi.ua.es

Abstract

This paper presents a Named Entity Classification system, which employs machine learning. Our methodology employs local entity information and profiles as feature set. All features are generated in an unsupervised manner. It is tested on two different data sets: (i) DrugSemantics Spanish corpus (Overall F1 = 74.92), whose results are in-line with the state of the art without employing external domain-specific resources. And, (ii) English CoNLL2003 dataset (Overall F1 = 81.40), although our results are slightly lower than previous work, these are reached without external knowledge or complex linguistic analysis. Last, using the same configuration for the two corpora, the difference of overall F1 is only 6.48 points (DrugSemantics = 74.92 versus CoNLL2003 = 81.40). Thus, this result supports our hypothesis that our approach is language and domain independent and does not require any external knowledge or complex linguistic analysis.

1 Introduction

The goal of Named Entity Recognition and Classification (NERC) is to recognize the occurrences of names in text, which is known as the recognition phase (NER), and assign them a category, which is referred as the classification phase (NEC). Both steps can be performed jointly or separately (Feldman and Sanger, 2007)[pp. 96–97].

NERC systems are fundamental to many text-processing applications. NERC not only is a prerequisite for many tasks, such as general language generation (Vicente and Lloret, 2016) or question answering (Marrero et al., 2013), but also a positive effect in performance has been reported when a NERC is included, as in the case of automatic text summarization (Alcón and Lloret, 2015).

Despite its proven usefulness, their usage is not always direct. Most NERC systems are typically focused on a specific domain, which has diverse requirements and, thus, different types of entities. As a result, these systems are designed ad hoc for a reduced set of predefined categories. If a NERC tool needs to be adapted to a new domain, with different constraints and a new set of entities, considerable effort is required (Marrero et al., 2013).

Furthermore, NERC not only is often domain conditioned, but also language dependent. Most systems are built for a specific corpus and, consequently, there is a dependence on such corpus. The adaptation of a NERC system to a new language is not always possible mainly due to three reasons. First, these systems often rely on linguistic analysis tools, which are not always available for all languages (Indurkhya, 2014). Second, these tools usually need resources which vary between languages (Marrero et al., 2013), if they exists. Lastly, each language poses distinct challenges that may affect the performance of NERC (Tjong Kim Sang, 2002; Sang and De Meulder, 2003).

Towards the advance of such issues, our final objective is to develop a general-purpose NERC system that consists of two separate modules for NER and NEC. To that end, this paper will focus on the development of our NEC module, assuming the output of a "perfect NER" so as to avoid any bias. The implemented NEC module is based on context information using profiles (Lopes and Vieira, 2015) and local information. This NEC approach can be used for different languages and domains.

Aiming to confirm such independence, this work is evaluated on two different corpora: a general-purpose English corpus, CoNLL2003 (Sang and De Meulder, 2003),

Proceedings of Recent Advances in Natural Language Processing, pages 510–518,
Varna, Bulgaria, Sep 4–6 2017.

and a pharmacotherapeutic Spanish corpus, DrugSemantics (Moreno et al., 2017a,b). The former represents general information needs, whereas the latter is related to specific information needs during pharmacotherapeutic day-to-day care. Both corpora are highly representative in terms of linguistic features as well as available NEs. Hence, these datasets allows us to define a language and domain independent evaluation scenario.

The rest of the paper is structured as follows. Section 2 reviews previous NERCs. Then, Section 3 defines our approach. Latter, the experiments set-up is described in Section 4. The evaluation is provided in Section 5, and Section 6 discusses our results. Last, Section 7 concludes the paper and outlines future work.

2 Background

For more than 20 years, several Natural Language Processing forums have promoted shared tasks to evaluate NERC systems. In these cases, research is focalized either in one domain and several languages (Tjong Kim Sang, 2002; Sang and De Meulder, 2003) or on one language and a narrow domain (Segura-Bedmar et al., 2013).

Concerning an example of the former, CoNLL conference hold two shared tasks (Tjong Kim Sang, 2002; Sang and De Meulder, 2003) to deal with NERC in news stories and several languages, namely English, Deutsch, Spanish and German. In both editions, systems obtained different results in each language, thus these NERCs are arguably fully language independent.

Carreras et al. (2002, 2003) obtained the best results in CoNLL 2002 (Spanish F1=81.39 and Dutch F1=77.05) but was ranked 5th on 2003 (NEglish F1=85 and German F1=69.15). This system performs NER and NEC sequentially with separate modules. Both components use Machine Learning (ML), specifically a binary AdaBoost classifier to ensemble small decision trees. Regarding its NEC module, it considers as features lexical (word forms, lemmas, their position and NE length) and orthographic (e.g. capitalization or affixes) information from context and the NE being classified, linguistic tags (such as POS and syntactic chunks) and external gazetteers.

The first place on CoNLL 2003 edition was for Florian et al. (2003) (English F1=88.76 and German F1=72.41). In this case, NER and NEC are addressed as one single task by means of a voting scheme. Specifically, diverse ML algorithms were combined: robust linear classifier, maximum entropy, transformation-based learning, and hidden Markov models. These algorithms take advantage of features of different nature: lexical information (word form in a window), orthographic information (such as affixes), together with linguistic features (e.g. POS tags or lemmas) and gazetteers.

More recently, Konkol et al. (2015) proposed a NERC in one step based on Conditional Random Fields (CRF) algorithm which employs unsupervised features from clusters of semantic spaces (COALS - Correlated Occurrence Analogue to Lexical Semantic - and HAL - Hyperspace Analogue to Language) as well as Latent Dirichlet allocation. This system obtained different results for each language (English F1=89.18, Spanish F1=82.74, Dutch F1=83.01 and Czech F1=74.08). Later, Agerri and Rigau (2016) built ixa-pipes, which tackles NER and NEC jointly, using CoNLL corpora. This tool learns Perceptron models from OpenNLP ML framework[1]. Their inferred model is based on local information (e.g. token, shape, n-grams, prefix and suffix), clusters (i.e. brown, word2vec and clark) and external knowledge (gazetteers). These systems also achieved different results for each language (Spanish F1=84.16, Dutch F1=85.04, English F1=91.36 and German F1=76.42).

Regarding an example of community challenge centered on one narrow domain and one language, the SemEval Workshop organized the DDIExtraction 2013 challenge (Segura-Bedmar et al., 2013). One of its main goals was NERC of drug names from English BioMedical Texts from two textual genres (DrugBank and MedLine abstracts). Most participants employed ML algorithms, specifically three proposals obtained the best results. One of them was the approach of Rocktäschel et al. (2013) who chose CRF algorithm. This strategy not only considers domain independent features (e.g. affixes, capitalization or tokens in a window), but also domain dependent ones such as domain-specific knowledge bases (ChEBI) or tools (ChempSpot). This system achieved the best results. However, the same configuration yield to different results in each genre (F1 STRICT, whole dataset=71.5; MedLine=58.1; DrugBank=87.8).

---

[1] `https://opennlp.apache.org/` (last accessed: May 16th, 2017)

Other proposal was made by Grego and Couto (2013), who used five CRF models that had a domain independent feature set (stem, affixes and whether the token is a number or not). But this system also requires a domain-specific knowledge base (ChEBI) to perform lexical similarity, as well a set of post-processing rules, to obtained good but different results across genres (F1 STRICT, whole dataset=65.6; MedLine=56.7; DrugBank=77.1). Last, the proposal of Björne et al. (2013) selected TEES, which is based on Support Vector Machines (SVM) algorithm. Their features incorporated domain independent information (e.g. affixes), complex linguistic analysis (e.g. dependency chains) as well as information from a domain-specific resource (DrugBank) and a domain-specific tool (MetaMap) to reach adequate results which varied over genres (F1 STRICT, whole dataset=64.8; MedLine=52.2; DrugBank=78.1).

Outside that shared task, on the contrary, few NERC studies are specifically designed to be applied in several domains. Tkachenko and Simanovsky (2012) experimented on different textual genres from OntoNotes corpus and employed the CRF algorithm. CRF was feed with different features: lexical (e.g. tokens and bigrams), orthographic (e.g. hyphenation, shape or affixes), linguistic features (i.e. PoS tags), word clusters (i.e. Brown, Clark, Phrasal) and gazetteers from external sources. In the best case, this method achieved a F1 greater than 70%; while at worst, F1 is less than 50%. DINERS was proposed by Kitoogo and Baryamureeba (2008), who chose two corpora from journalism (CoNLL2003) and law domains. A Maximum entropy classifier was optimized via a genetic algorithm making use of: (i) gazetteers from external resources but also from the training data; (ii) orthographic information (e.g. prefixes, capitalization, presence of hyphens or digits or dollar sign); (iii) lexical information (word form, unigrams, bigrams); and (iv) linguistic information (PoS tags). Their proposal obtained a difference in terms of F1 of more than 20 points between overall law results (F1 = 92.04%) and global journalism performance (F1=70.27%).

In summary, all NERC systems presented here employed different levels of linguistic analysis (ranging from lexical to syntactical). Besides, all of them include certain semantic features to recognise and classify an entity. Such information is gathered from gazetteers, which are derived from external sources (Tkachenko and Simanovsky, 2012; Carreras et al., 2002, 2003; Florian et al., 2003; Kitoogo and Baryamureeba, 2008) or from training data (Kitoogo and Baryamureeba, 2008), from word clusters (Tkachenko and Simanovsky, 2012; Agerri and Rigau, 2016) or from distributional semantics methods (Konkol et al., 2015) or from domain-specific resources and tools (Rocktäschel et al., 2013; Grego and Couto, 2013; Björne et al., 2013). As a consequence of the usage of gazetteers, complex linguistic analysis and domain-specific resources, all these systems have shown that there is a performance gap between different languages and domains or textual genres. Furthermore, none of them analyzed the behavior of their systems changing simultaneously both language and domain or genre. Therefore, our hypothesis is that profile-based entity classification is effective using minimal linguistic information (lemmatizer and PoStagger) and out of external knowledge resources in any domain and language. To this end, our proposed approach is evaluated on two domains (general and pharmacotherapeutic) in different languages (Spanish and English).

3   Method: Named Entity Classification through Profiles

This NEC methodology is based on previous work (Lopes and Vieira, 2015), in which profiles where generated in an unsupervised manner for authorship detection. In addition to the purpose of the profiles usage, there are two main differences between their work and ours. On the one hand, Lopes and Vieira (2015) obtain profiles from a concept extractor system, while ours are derived from lemmas from nouns, verbs, adjectives and adverbs. On the other hand, categorization of Lopes and Vieira (2015) is performed by ranking possible entities using their own similarity measure, but ours calculates similarity between profiles and entities through a ML algorithm. This method consists of two main stages:

1. **Profile generation** process, whose main goal is to train a ML system to perform NEC, is an offline process that works as follows:

   (a) *Linguistic annotation*: a corpus previously annotated with NEs is tokenized, sentence-splitted, morphologically analysed and PoS-tagged. In our case, Freeling (Padró and Stanilovsky, 2012) is used for Spanish whereas Treetagger (Schmid, 1994, 1995) is chosen for English.

(b) *Descriptors extraction*: For each entity instance, we extract descriptors[2] in a window and their frequency as the number of occurrences. The size of the window can be parametrized, but a window of a fixed length is used. In this work, length of the window was set to 10 lemmas (5 descriptors before and 5 after). Then, occurrences (*occ*) of each descriptor (d) are aggregated by entity type (*type*): $occ(d, type)$.

(c) *Split the training corpus*: For each NE type (e), the original training corpus is divided in two sets called target ($\mathcal{T}_e$) and contrasting ($\mathcal{G}_e$). The former set ($\mathcal{T}_e$) represents a fragment of the corpus capable to characterize that a given NE belongs to a certain class (i.e. positive examples of this NE type). While the latter ($\mathcal{G}_e$) is composed by a set of negative examples (i.e. examples of the remaining NE categories) aggregated by entity type.

(d) *Descriptors division*: For each NE type, the extracted descriptors are splitted in two list named unique (U_e) and common (C_e) descriptors list. The former (U_e) contains descriptors only present in the target set ($\mathcal{T}_e$), whereas the latter (C_e) includes common descriptors in both target ($\mathcal{T}_e$) and contrasting sets ($\mathcal{G}_e$) for a given entity type (e).

(e) *Relevance computation*: For both unique and common descriptors lists of each NE type, a relevance index is assigned to weight them and determine their importance for a given NE category. The *Term Frequency, disjoint corpora frequency* (TFDCF) index (Lopes and Vieira, 2015), defined in Equation 1, is applied to items from the unique descriptors list (U_e). Whereas the relevance common index, defined in Equation 2, is computed for each item in the common descriptors list (C_e) to penalize descriptors found in the contrasting set ($\mathcal{G}_e$) as well as in the target set ($\mathcal{T}_e$).

$$idx_{unique}(d, \mathcal{T}_e, \mathcal{G}_e) = \\ \log(1 + \frac{occ(d, \mathcal{T}_e)}{\prod_{\forall g \in \mathcal{G}_e} 1 + \log(1 + occ(d, g))}) \quad (1)$$

$$idx_{common}(d, \mathcal{T}_e, \mathcal{G}_e) = \\ \log(1 + occ(d, \mathcal{T}_e) - \\ \frac{occ(d, \mathcal{T}_e)}{\prod_{\forall g \in \mathcal{G}_e} 1 + \log(1 + occ(d, g))}) \quad (2)$$

where d is a descriptor, $\mathcal{T}_e$ is the target set for an entity type e, g is a contrasting set, $\mathcal{G}_e$ contains all contrasting sets from the contrasting entities for an entity type e, and $occ(d, \mathcal{T}_e)$ is the occurrences of a term d in a set $\mathcal{T}_e$ for an entity type e.

This step produces a profile P_e for each entity type e. It would be constituted by its unique U_e and common C_e descriptors lists: $P_e = \{U_e, C_e\}$. In turn, each item from these lists is a pair $\{d, idx(d)\}$, where d represents a descriptor (i.e. term's lemma) and idx defines its relevance index. It is important to remember that relevance indexes are computed according to descriptors' occurrences extracted from both target $\mathcal{T}_e$ and contrasting $\mathcal{G}_e$. These lists only contain the most frequent descriptors. Specifically, this work employs up to 1000 most habitual descriptors in both lists.

(f) *Local features extraction*: Profiles are complemented with local information from NE itself, regardless of the category. Similarly, such data is obtained easily without requiring semantic or syntactic linguistic analysis or external knowledge. Concretely, three types of features are acquired from state-of-the-art NEC systems and extracted from training data: words of the entity[3](denoted as NE); entity length without stop-words (denoted as NElen); and affixes, distinguishing between suffixes and prefixes up to 4 characters from the first and last words (denoted as affix4).

(g) *Model training*: Our proposal creates a ML model for computing profile similarity between all NE classes, local NE features and its gold standard candidates. Thus, in this step, a multi-classification model is generated joining local features and profiles from all NE types. As a result, profiles are represented as follows: for each NE type, all descriptors' lemmas from the top list T_e are a feature, that has as value its relevance index, idx_{unique} (Equation 1). Similarly, all descriptors' lemmas from the common list

---

[2]Descriptors represent lemmas of content bearing terms that is nouns, verbs, adverbs and adjectives

[3]Please bear in mind that any special character is replaced with "_".

C_e of this NE type are a feature that has as value idx_{common} (Equation 2). Random Forest (RF) algorithm (Breiman, 2001) from Weka 3.6.7 (Hall et al., 2009) has been employed owing to the fact that it is able to deal with more than two classes. Moreover, its selection was motivated due to its fast training, its stability regarding data changes and its automatic variable selection. RF algorithm employs the default parameters, but he number of trees was set to 100.

2. **Profile application** process, whose aim is to classify a previously recognized NE in a set of predefined types, takes these steps:

(a) *Linguistic annotation*: text is tokenized, sentence-splitted, morphologically analyzed and PoS-tagged, as in the generation phase.

(b) *Candidate extraction*: these are gathered directly from the gold standard. It should be noted that candidates can be extracted by any NER module, but here the output of a "perfect NER" is used to avoid any bias.

(c) *Descriptors extraction*: For each candidate and each possible entity type, we extract descriptors that appear in a window using the same restrictions as in the generation phase.

(d) *Relevance computation*: The unique relevance index idx_{unique} (Equation 1) is computed for all candidates and all possible NE types.

(e) *Local features extraction*: For each candidate, local information is gathered (NE, NE-len, affix4).

(f) *Similarity computation and classification*: Once an entity candidate has filled its profile and its local information, these data is compared against the ones generated from the training data, to compute their similarity. RF algorithm estimates similarity with a forest of trees that use as features local information as well as descriptors of all possible types of entities ($P = \{T, C\}$).

4 Datasets and Experimental Set-up

4.1 DrugSemantics Corpus and Set-up

DrugSemantics gold standard (Moreno et al., 2017a,b) is a collection of 5 Spanish Summaries of Product Characteristics (SPC) manually annotated, which contains 780 sentences and more than 2000 entities. This work uses the most frequent NEs from this gold standard: disease (724 entities), drug (657 entities) and unit of measurement (557 entities).

Evaluation uses 5-fold cross-validation at document-level (i.e. 4 SPCs to train and one to evaluate). It is a controlled environment that ensures unknown descriptors. In each fold (f, $F = 5$), the model is assessed for each entity (e, $E = 3$) in terms of traditional Precision (Pr), Recall (Re) and F-measure$_{\beta=1}$ (F1). Then, overall results for a fold are computed as the arithmetic-mean of all entities. Finally, the results of all iterations are averaged as the arithmetic-mean, thus obtaining Macro-averaged (M) figures for each entity e and globally. This decision is motivated to avoid any possible bias to the most frequent NE type.

4.2 English CoNLL2003 Corpus and Set-up

CoNLL2003 dataset (Sang and De Meulder, 2003) is a collection of English news stories from Reuters. It contains four entity types (person, organization, location and miscellaneous). However, miscellaneous is discarded because it has no practical application (Marrero et al., 2013). This corpus is divided in 3 sets: training (23499 entities), development (5942 entities) and testing (5648 entities). A ML model is inferred on the training set for all three NEs and this model is assessed on the test set. The development set is not used since no parameter tunning was done. The performance of the model is assessed for each entity e in terms of traditional Precision (Pr), Recall (Re) and F-measure$_{\beta=1}$ (F1). Last, overall *macro-averaged* results are calculated as the arithmetic-mean for all entities ($E = 3$) so as to avert a possible bias to the most frequent NE type.

5 Evaluation

The aim of our experiments is two fold. On one hand, to verify the appropriateness of our proposed method on two different domains and languages. On other hand, to find out the contribution of our local features (i.e. NE, NElen and affix4). For those reasons, first results on DrugSemantics corpus are shown (Section 5.1) and, then, performance on CoNLL English corpus are presented (Section 5.2). In both cases, local information is included gradually.

features		Pr	Re	F1
p	DR	50.60	47.40	48.39
	DI	62.34	76.14	67.41
	UM	56.42	44.86	49.29
	M	56.45	56.13	55.03
p + NElen	DR	57.17	52.04	53.50
	DI	67.61	75.47	70.19
	UM	56.52	56.29	55.07
	M	60.43	61.27	59.59
p + NE	DR	57.51	52.51	54.43
	DI	62.26	74.69	66.86
	UM	56.16	47.31	50.57
	M	58.65	58.17	57.29
p + affix4	DR	75.90	37.99	50.24
	DI	67.12	79.82	71.95
	UM	51.30	69.88	56.01
	M	64.77	62.56	59.40
p + NElen + NE	DR	59.40	52.07	54.94
	DI	65.89	80.81	71.70
	UM	63.02	55.51	58.30
	M	62.77	62.80	61.65
p + NE + affix4	DR	79.01	51.85	61.91
	DI	78.37	82.58	79.86
	UM	62.50	86.44	71.47
	M	73.29	73.63	71.08
p + NElen + affix4	DR	71.37	40.90	51.08
	DI	73.68	81.50	76.10
	UM	54.34	75.89	59.87
	M	66.47	66.09	62.35
p + NElen + NE + affix4	**DR**	81.95	57.90	66.97
	DI	82.28	84.00	82.62
	UM	66.52	89.22	75.17
	M	**76.92**	**77.04**	**74.92**

Note: (i) p: profile; (ii) NE: entity words;
(iii) NElen: entity length without stopwords;
(iv) affix4: entity suffixes and prefixs up to
4 characters; (v) DR: Drug; (vi) DI: Disease;
(vii) UM: Unit of Measurement; and
(viii) M: Overall Macro-average results.

Table 1: DrugSemantics Precision (Pr), Recall (Re) and $F_{\beta=1}$ (F1) results with different features

5.1 DrugSemantics Results

Table 1 collects overall results and results for each entity type. Disease is the entity type that always obtains the higher results for all measures. All types of entities, but especially Drug and UnitOfMeasurement, perform better when all local information is integrated in our pipeline. In fact, overall MF1 results improve 36.14% (19.89 points) if all local features are combined with context profiles.

5.2 CoNLL2003 Results

Table 2 collects overall results and results for each entity type. All classes, but especially Location, perform better when all local information is integrated in our pipeline. But, overall MF1 increases 50.49% (27.31 points) when profiles are combined with all local features.

6 Discussion

In view of the results, our NEC approach has demonstrated to be appropriated when combining profiles and local information. Using the same configuration, pharmacotherapuetic domain overall reaches almost 75% (MF1=74.92%), whereas general domain obtains an overall MF1 of 81.40%. In spite of this, our NEC system proves to be language as well as domain independent since a small difference is achieved in terms of global MF1 for the same configuration (RF 100 trees, profiles and local information), namely it is 6.48 (MF1: DrugSemantics 74.92%-CoNLL2003 81.40%).

A comparison between our system and NERCs presented in Section 2, it is not free of certain limitations. The corpora is different and, consequently, entities, domain and language also differs. Also, performance is assessed in various ways[4]. Besides, these systems do not provide results for NEC task alone. Still, such comparison is made in two steps. On the one hand, the appropriateness of our approach is compared to determine the extent of our contribution with systems trained on DrugDDI corpus, CoNLL datasets, and NERCs declared domain independent. On the other hand, a comparison in terms of absolute overall F1 difference between best and worst reported resultsis provided in order to prove that such difference is in line with them or lower. This data is summarized in Table 3 as follows: (i) for systems trained

---

[4]For example, CoNLL reported micro-averages; while this paper, macro-averages.

features		Pr	Re	F1
	PER	55.91	43.84	49.15
p	LOC	51.99	58.10	54.88
	ORG	55.82	60.92	58.26
	M	54.57	54.29	54.09
	PER	62.61	51.55	56.55
p +	LOC	57.83	63.15	60.37
NElen	ORG	57.62	62.19	59.82
	M	59.36	58.96	58.91
	PER	69.98	44.65	54.52
p +	LOC	61.06	80.55	69.46
NE	ORG	66.88	68.91	67.88
	M	65.97	64.70	63.95
	PER	82.97	65.73	73.35
p +	LOC	80.65	75.57	78.03
affix4	ORG	67.16	85.00	75.03
	M	76.93	75.43	75.47
	PER	76.07	54.35	63.40
p +	LOC	67.33	82.65	74.21
NElen	ORG	66.19	69.39	67.75
+ NE	M	69.86	68.80	68.45
	PER	89.14	66.85	76.40
p +	LOC	81.04	80.17	80.60
NE +	ORG	71.29	89.23	79.26
affix4	M	80.49	78.75	78.75
	PER	84.59	68.59	75.76
p +	LOC	85.15	76.77	80.74
NElen +	ORG	67.37	86.45	75.73
affix4	M	79.04	77.27	77.41
p +	**PER**	91.99	68.53	78.55
NElen +	**LOC**	85.79	86.25	86.02
NE +	**ORG**	71.86	89.29	79.63
affix4	**M**	**83.21**	**81.36**	**81.40**

Note: (i) p: profile; (ii) NE: entity words;
(iii) NElen: entity length without stopwords;
(iv) affix4: entity suffixes and prefixs up
to 4 characters; (v) PER: Person;
(vi) LOC: Location; (vii) ORG: Organization;
and (viii) M: Overall Macro-average results

Table 2: CoNLL2003 Precision (Pr), Recall (Re)
and $F_{\beta=1}$ (F1) results

D	System	F1	Dif
	Björne et al. (2013)	64.8	25.9
P	Grego and Couto (2013)	65.6	20
	Rocktäschel et al. (2013)	71.5	29.7
	Profiles+local	**74.92**	**6.48**
	Profiles+local	**81.40**	**6.48**
	Freeling	85	12.24
G	Florian et al. (2003)	88.76	16.35
	Konkol et al. (2015)	89.19	15.10
	ixa-pipes	91.36	14.94
I	TkaSim	-	> 25
	DINERS	70.27	> 20

Note: (i) Dif: Absolute difference of overall F1 between
best and worst results; (ii) D: Domain; (iii) G: general;
(iv) P: Pharmacotherapeutic; (v) I: domain
independent systems.

Table 3: Comparison with existing NERC in terms
of F1 and difference between corpora. For each
genre, systems are ranked by F1

on DrugDDI, the difference is computed between
genres using STRICT measure, whose results are
higher than the macro-average (MAVG) reported.
And (ii) Whereas for systems trained on some
CoNLL corpora, the difference is calculated from
the best and the worst language from the results
obtained, which are micro-averaged.

Regarding adequateness of our NEC, our system achieved the best results in the pharmacotherapeutic domain without external knowledge or
complex linguistic analysis. On the contrary, it can
be observed that although our results are slightly
lower than the remaining systems trained on the
CoNLL2003 corpus (F1 column in Table 3), it
should be noted that these are obtained without using external knowledge or complex linguistic analysis.

Regarding domain and language independence
(Dif column in Table 3), our profile-based NEC
systems obtains the smaller difference (6.48
points) when compared to any of these systems.
Furthermore, the two systems declared domain independent, TkaSim (Tkachenko and Simanovsky,
2012) and DINERS (Kitoogo and Baryamureeba,
2008), exhibit the greatest difference when domain or textual genre changes.

7 Conclusions and Future Work

This paper presented a Named Entity Classification system based on profiles and local information. This proposal does not require external resources or complex linguistic analysis. It only needs an annotated corpus with the target NEs and a basic linguistic analyzer able to split sentences and tokens, lemmatize and POS tag this new language.

The evaluation has involved the adaptation of our approach to two different corpora: a Spanish pharmacotherapeutic (corpus MF1: 74.92%) and an English corpus from general domain (MF1: 81.40%). The results are in-line with the state of the art for the narrow domain. But, although our results are encouraging, classification needs to be improved to increase the general domain results. Nevertheless, the difference between the two corpora, employing the same configuration, shows a difference of only 6.48 points. This small change between languages and domains supports our hypothesis: profile-based entity classification is effective using minimal linguistic information (lemmatizer and PoStagger) and out of external knowledge resources in any domain and language.

As future work, we plan to enhance profiles with other features derived automatically from training data. We also consider the generation of profiles using only tokens (instead of lemmas) in order to remove the basic linguistic analyzer requirement. Additionally, aiming at reinforcing our hypothesis, our approach will be evaluated on other available corpora in other language-domain pairs, such as an English pharmacotherapeutic corpus.

Acknowledgements

This research work has been partially funded by the Spanish Government, Generalitat Valenciana, University of Alicante and Ayudas Fundación BBVA a equipos de investigación científica 2016 through the projects TIN2015-65100-R, TIN2015-65136-C2-2-R, PROMETEOII/2014/001, GRE16-01: "Plataforma inteligente para recuperación, análisis y representación de la información generada por usuarios en Internet" and "Análisis de Sentimientos Aplicado a la Prevención del Suicidio en las Redes Sociales" (ASAP).

References

Rodrigo Agerri and German Rigau. 2016. Robust multilingual Named Entity Recognition with shallow semi-supervised features. *Artificial Intelligence* 238:63–82. https://doi.org/10.1016/j.artint.2016.05.003.

Óscar Alcón and Elena Lloret. 2015. Estudio de la influencia de incorporar conocimiento léxico-semántico a la técnica de Análisis de Componentes Principales para la generación de resúmenes multilingües [Studying the influence of adding lexical-semantic knowledge to Principal Component Analysis technique for multilingual summarization]. *Linguamática* 7(1):43–53.

Jari Björne, Suwisa Kaewphan, and Tapio Salakoski. 2013. UTurku : Drug Named Entity Recognition and Drug-Drug Interaction Extraction Using SVM Classification and Domain Knowledge. In *Proceedings of the Seventh International Workshop on Semantic Evaluation*. volume 2, pages 651–659.

L. Breiman. 2001. Random Forests. *Machine Learning* 45(1):5–32. https://doi.org/10.1023/A:1010933404324.

X Carreras, L Marquez, and L Padró. 2002. Named entity extraction using adaboost. In *Proceeding of the 6th Conference on Natural Language Learning*. pages 152–155.

Xavier Carreras, Lluís Màrquez, and Lluís Padró. 2003. A simple named entity extractor using AdaBoost. In *Proceedings of the 7th Conference on Natural Language Learning*. pages 152–155.

R. Feldman and J. Sanger. 2007. *The text mining handbook: advanced approaches in analyzing unstructured data*. Cambridge University Press, New York.

Radu Florian, Abe Ittycheriah, Hongyan Jing, and Tong Zhang. 2003. Named Entity Recognition through Classifier Combination. In *Proceedings of the 7th Conference on Natural Language Learning*. pages 168–171.

Tiago Grego and Francisco M Couto. 2013. LASIGE : using Conditional Random Fields and ChEBI ontology. In *Proceedings of the Seventh International Workshop on Semantic Evaluation*. volume 2, pages 660–666.

Mark Hall, Eibe Frank, Geoffrey Holmes, Bernhard Pfahringer, Peter Reutemann, and Ian Witten. 2009. The WEKA data mining software: An update. *SIGKDD Explorations* 11(1):10–18.

Nitin Indurkhya. 2014. Natural Language Processing. In Teofilo Gonzalez, Jorge Díaz-Herrera, and Allen Tucker, editors, *Computing Handbook, Third Edition: Computer Science and Software Engineering*, CRC Press, chapter 40, pages 40:1–17.

FE Kitoogo and Venansius Baryamureeba. 2008. Towards domain independent named entity recognition. In Janet Aisbett, Gibbon Greg, Anthony J. Rodriguez, Joseph Kizza Migga, Ravi Nath, and Gerald R Renardel, editors, *Strengthening the Role of of ICT in Development*, Fountain publishers, volume IV, chapter 5, pages 84 – 95.

Michal Konkol, T. Brychcín, Konopí, and Miloslav K. 2015. Latent semantics in Named Entity Recognition. *Expert Systems with Applications* 42(7):3470–3479. https://doi.org/10.1016/j.eswa.2014.12.015.

Lucelene Lopes and Renata Vieira. 2015. Building and Applying Profiles Through Term Extraction. In *X Brazilian Symposium in Information and Human Language Technology*. Natal, Brazil, pages 91–100.

Mónica Marrero, Julián Urbano, Sonia Sánchez-Cuadrado, Jorge Morato, and Juan Miguel Gómez-Berbís. 2013. Named Entity Recognition: Fallacies, challenges and opportunities. *Computer Standards and Interfaces* 35(5):482–489. https://doi.org/10.1016/j.csi.2012.09.004.

Isabel Moreno, Ester Boldrini, Paloma Moreda, and María Teresa Romá-Ferri. 2017a. DrugSemantics: A corpus for Named Entity Recognition in Spanish Summaries of Product Characteristics. *Journal of Biomedical Informatics* 72:8 – 22. https://doi.org/10.1016/j.jbi.2017.06.013.

Isabel Moreno, Ester Boldrini, Paloma Moreda, and María Teresa Romá-Ferri. 2017b. DrugSemantics Gold Standard. Mendeley Data, v1. https://doi.org/10.17632/fwc7jrc5jr.1.

Lluís Padró and Evgeny Stanilovsky. 2012. FreeLing 3.0: Towards Wider Multilinguality. In *Proceedings of the Language Resources and Evaluation Conference*. ELRA, Istanbul, Turkey.

Tim Rocktäschel, Torsten Huber, Unter Den Linden, and Tim Rockt. 2013. WBI-NER : The impact of domain-specific features on the performance of identifying and classifying mentions of drugs. In *Second Joint Conference on Lexical and Computational Semantics (*SEM), Volume 2: Proceedings of the Seventh International Workshop on Semantic Evaluation (SemEval 2013)*. pages 356–363.

Erik F. Tjong Kim Sang and Fien De Meulder. 2003. Introduction to the CoNLL-2003 Shared Task: Language-Independent Named Entity Recognition. In *Proceedings of the 7th Conference on Natural Language Learning*. pages 142–147.

H Schmid. 1994. Probabilistic part-of-speech tagging using decision trees. In *Proceedings of International Conference on New Methods in Language Processing*. pages 44–49.

Helmut Schmid. 1995. Improvements In Part-of-Speech Tagging With an Application To German. In *Proceedings of the ACL SIGDAT-Workshop*. pages 47—-50.

I Segura-Bedmar, P Martínez, and M Herrero-Zazo. 2013. SemEval-2013 Task 9: Extraction of Drug-Drug Interactions from Biomedical Texts (DDIExtraction 2013). In *Proceedings of the Seventh International Workshop on Semantic Evaluation*. pages 341–350.

Erik F Tjong Kim Sang. 2002. Introduction to the CoNLL-2002 shared task. In *Proceedings of the 6th Conference on Natural Language Learning*. pages 1–4.

M Tkachenko and A Simanovsky. 2012. Selecting Features for Domain-Independent Named Entity Recognition. In *Proceedings of KONVENS 2012*. pages 248–253.

Marta Vicente and Elena Lloret. 2016. Exploring Flexibility in Natural Language Generation throughout Discursive Analysis of New Textual Genres. In *Proceedings of the 2nd International Workshop Future and Emerging Trends in Language Technologies, Machine Learning and Big Data*. Sevilla, Spain.

Similarity Based Genre Identification for POS Tagging & Dependency Parsing Experts

Atreyee Mukherjee
Indiana University
atremukh@indiana.edu

Sandra Kübler
Indiana University
skuebler@indiana.edu

Abstract

POS tagging and dependency parsing achieve good results for homogeneous datasets. However, these tasks are much more difficult on heterogeneous datasets. In (Mukherjee et al., 2016, 2017), we address this issue by creating genre experts for both POS tagging and parsing. We use topic modeling to automatically separate training and test data into genres and to create annotation experts per genre by training separate models for each topic. However, this approach assumes that topic modeling is performed jointly on training and test sentences each time a new test sentence is encountered. We extend this work by assigning new test sentences to their genre expert by using similarity metrics. We investigate three different types of methods: 1) based on words highly associated with a genre by the topic modeler, 2) using a k-nearest neighbor classification approach, and 3) using perplexity to determine the closest topic. The results show that the choice of similarity metric has an effect on results and that we can reach comparable accuracies to the joint topic modeling in POS tagging and dependency parsing, thus providing a viable and efficient approach to POS tagging and parsing a sentence by its genre expert.

1 Introduction

POS tagging and dependency parsing can be performed reliably on homogeneous datasets such as the Penn Treebank. However, both POS taggers and parsers are often used on out-of-domain data, which generally results in considerably lower accuracies. Domain adaptation provides a poten-

tial for improving out-of-domain accuracy if annotations in the target domain are available. In our work, we assume a more flexible approach in which POS tagging and parsing of an individual sentence is performed by the closest genre expert where the genres are identified automatically prior to training.

In (Mukherjee et al., 2016, 2017), we approach this problem by creating genre/domain experts using topic modeling: We use Latent Dirichlet Allocation (LDA) (Blei et al., 2003; Blei, 2012) for an unsupervised clustering of sentences into topics. We assume that these topics correspond to genres; previous experiments (Mukherjee et al., 2016) have shown that the topic modeler models the split into genres in a very similar way to the original split, with error rates around 2%. We then train one expert per topic. I.e., we train the expert on all the training sentences that were assigned to the corresponding topic. During testing, we assign test sentences to topics, which means that they are POS tagged and parsed by the corresponding expert. We tested the approach on an artificial, heterogeneous corpus, consisting of a balanced mix of sentences from the WSJ portion of the Penn Treebank (financial news) (Marcus et al., 1994) and from the GENIA corpus (biomedical abstracts) (Tateisi and Tsujii, 2004). For POS tagging, we show a moderate increase in performance over a competitive baseline of training on the full training set, and a considerable increase for dependency parsing.

However, in our previous approach, assigning test sentences to the relevant training topic experts is handled in the simplest possible way: We perform topic modeling on the combination of training and test data. Since topic modeling clusters the data but does not create a predictive model, we cannot assign sentences to topics after the initial clustering. This means that each time a new test

Proceedings of Recent Advances in Natural Language Processing, pages 519–526,
Varna, Bulgaria, Sep 4–6 2017.

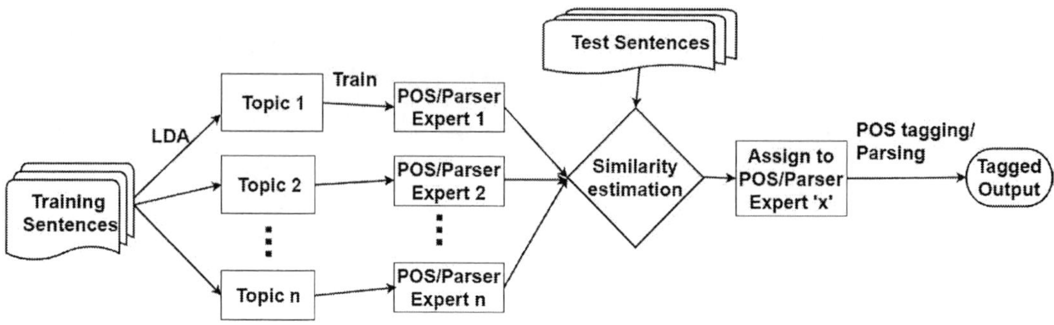

Figure 1: Overview of the architecture of the POS tagging and parsing experts.

sentence is encountered, the topic modeler is re-run to consistently determine the appropriate genres across training and test sentences. In order to avoid retraining, we propose to use similarity estimation techniques to determine which genre the test sentence belongs to. In this setup, we only create the experts once, and then assign new sentences to genres in an asynchronous fashion. For a new test sentence, we evaluate the similarity of the test sentence to the sentences of a genre and then assign it to the expert with the highest similarity score. We investigate a range of different techniques, based on 1) words closely associated with a topic by the LDA, 2) k-nearest neighbors, or 3) perplexity models to estimate the similarity.

Our results indicate that for word based similarity metrics, we reach results very similar to the joint topic modeling approach, thus proving the feasibility of an asynchronous approach. In the case of unigram-based perplexity, parsing accuracy even surpasses the joint modeling approach.

The remainder of the paper is structured as follows: Section 2 outlines our system architecture in greater detail, and section 3 discusses related work. In section 4, we describe the similarity methods, section 5 describes the setup for the experiments, and section 6 shows the results of our experiments. In section 7, we draw conclusions and discuss future steps.

2 Architecture

Following our previous work, we use LDA (Blei et al., 2003; Blei, 2012) to generate genres and train genre experts. But then, instead of having the test sentences clustered along with the training sentences, we assign test sentences to the genres via *similarity metrics*. The test sentences are consequently annotated by the corresponding genre

expert. The complete architecture of our approach is shown in Figure 1.

For the current experiments, we use 2 topics, parallel to the 2 domains, and assign each training sentence via hard clustering to the genre for which LDA showed the highest probability[1]. We then test the different similarity metrics: We compute the similarity of a test sentence to the training sentences of the individual experts and then assign the sentence to the expert for tagging/parsing for which it has the highest similarity. We use the following similarity metrics:

- Topic words from LDA: LDA does not only cluster sentences into genres, it also determines which words are highly correlated with each genre. Thus, we can utilize these words along with their probabilities for a specific genre. We sum over all genre words that we find in the sentence, weighted by their probability, and then assign the sentence to the topic that has the highest score.

- k-nearest neighbors: There exist a wide range of metrics to calculate similarity between two feature vectors. However, since we compare a sentence to a set of genre sentences, we decided to use memory-based classification using the k-nearest neighbors to classify each test sentence into the relevant class (or genre, in our case). This has the advantage over a pure similarity metric that we have a principled way of handling the comparison to a set

---

[1]We have experimented with more topics for POS tagging and shown that we reach good results when using soft clustering rather than hard clustering (Mukherjee et al., 2016). The same holds true for experiments within the Penn Treebank, where we model WSJ internal topics, which are less distinct in their textual characteristics, but the experts still show an improvement over a full training baseline.

of sentences. Additionally, we do not consider the whole search space, as we would if we used a centroid.

- Perplexity: Another obvious choice for determining the similarity of a sentence to a set of sentences is language modeling. We calculate the perplexity of a test sentence with regard to set of sentences of an expert. We then assign a sentence to the expert for which it has the lowest perplexity.

3 Related Work

Our work cannot exactly be called domain adaptation since we automatically determine a range of genres and then train experts per genre while domain adaptation starts from a general model and adapts it to a specific genre. However, the two research questions are closely related and generally face the same problems. Our work is closest to the work by Plank and van Noord (2011) and McClosky et al. (2010). McClosky et al. address the problem of parse adaptation in the case of multiple sources. In their setting, a parser learns the domain differences and various statistics from being trained on datasets from multiple domains. Our approach is comparable to the extent that both approaches profit from a range of domains. Plank and van Noord (2011) adopt an approach where they build a highly specialized training set that is most similar to an out-of-domain document. They create a specialized expert each time the parser encounters a new document. Our approach is more general than Plank and van Noord's in that we do not create an expert for every new document, but rather create experts per genre. In contrast, our approach is more fine grained in that we assign individual sentences to genres rather than complete documents. Plank and van Noord (2011) use the topic distribution from LDA as features for determining the most similar training set. This is comparable to our approach of assigning test sentences to the proper genre (but not to the creation of genres).

Domain adaptation has been studied more extensively in parsing than in POS tagging. For POS tagging, Blitzer et al. (2006) have a similar setup to ours, where they train on WSJ data and test on MEDLINE abstracts. They use structural correspondence learning by identifying "frequently occurring" pivot features which can appropriately represent source as well as target domain. The problem of adapting to a new domain is compounded in cases where no adequate data from the target domain is available. Differences in annotation scheme between the source and target domain can pose additional challenges (Dredze et al., 2007). In our case, GENIA follows a similar annotation scheme as WSJ with a few differences in assigning POS tags to names.

Agreement based approaches and co-training have been employed for domain adaptation of POS tagging. In the agreement-based method adopted by Clark et al. (2003), a Markov model tagger and a maximum entropy tagger are used. For a sentence to be included in the training set, both the taggers have to reach a unanimous decision. Sagae and Tsujii (2007) apply a similar approach but using MaxEnt and SVM to simulate an iteration of co-training. Kübler and Baucom (2011) extended this further by demonstrating that an agreement in terms of word sequences rather than complete sentences is more robust and achieves better results.

In the CoNLL 2007 shared task on domain adaptation for dependency parsing, Attardi et al. (2007) adapt an error correction approach to revise mistakes caused by the base parser in the target domain. Kawahara and Uchimoto (2008) employ a single parser approach using a second order MST parser and combining labeled data from the known domain with unlabeled data of the new domain by simple concatenation and judging the efficacy of the resulting most reliable parses. Finkel and Manning (2009) devise a model for dependency parsing by using a hierarchical Bayesian prior based on the notion that different domains may have different features specific to each domain. Instead of applying a constant prior over all the parameters, a hierarchical Bayesian global is used.

4 Similarity Estimation

There are different ways of determining the similarity of a sentence to the sentences in a genre. We investigate methods based on the topic words from LDA, k-nearest neighbor approaches, and perplexity.

4.1 Topic Words from LDA

LDA provides a list of the words most closely associated with a topic and assigns a weight to each word. Thus, we can use the words that are highly correlated with each topic as good indicators for a sentence belonging to the genre represented by the topic. Additionally, we utilize the probabilities provided by LDA as weights to determine a word's contribution to the similarity. For this experiment, we select the top 50/100/200 words from each topic. I.e., we assume that these words can be considered to be the most representative words in their respective domain. Then, for each sentence, we check how many of those words occur in the current sentence and add up their weights. We then assign the sentence to the topic with the higher value. Since we only look at a small number of words, we have to consider the cases where a sentence does not contain any of the topic words. We resolve these cases by extending beyond the top words and considering all the words in the training set for each genre. If there is a tie in values, we assign the sentence randomly to one of the experts.

4.2 k-Nearest Neighbors

In this method, we perform k-nearest neighbor classification to assign test sentences to topic experts. We create a feature vector by using the top 50/100 words from each genre, as determined by LDA, and assigning the weights as values. We tune the classification parameters on the validation set. For the setting using 50 words, the highest accuracy corresponds to a setting with 7 nearest neighbors, Dice coefficient as the distance metric, and gain ratio for feature weighting. When we increase the number of words per genre to 100, we use Dice coefficient, gain ratio, and 3 nearest neighbors.

4.3 Perplexity-Based Similarity

As the third set of methods, we turn to language modeling and use perplexity as a measure to determine the similarity, i.e., we assign test sentence to the expert which has a lower perplexity. Perplexity is calculated based on unigrams, bigrams, or trigrams.

5 Experimental Setup

5.1 Dataset

We create our corpus manually by combining the Wall Street Journal (WSJ) (Marcus et al., 1994) section of the Penn Treebank and the GENIA corpus (Tateisi and Tsujii, 2004). This gives us an artificial balanced corpus for which we know to which genre a sentence belongs. While WSJ consists of newspaper reports, GENIA consists of biomedical abstracts from Medline.

For the WSJ corpus, we use the POS annotation and syntactic annotations from the treebank. The GENIA Corpus is annotated on different linguistic levels, including POS tags, syntax, coreference, and events, among others. We use GENIA 1.0 trees (Ohta et al., 2002) created in the Penn Treebank format[2]. Both treebanks are converted to dependencies using pennconverter (Johansson and Nugues, 2007).

Following our data split in Mukherjee et al. (2016, 2017), we create a balanced dataset comprising 17 181 sentences from each corpus for the training set and 850 sentences for the test set. Since GENIA is rather small and since there is no standard data split for GENIA, we decided to extract the last 850 sentences for the test set, and the 850 sentences before that for the validation set. The remaining 17 181 sentences are used for training. For WSJ, we chose the same number of sentences for the training, validation, and test set, the training sentences are selected randomly from sections 02-21 and the validation and test sentences from section 22 and 23 respectively.

5.2 Baselines

In Mukherjee et al. (2016, 2017), we have used two baseline cases: The first baseline considers the entire training set and does not employ any topic modeling. Since the topic experts have access to only a fraction of the data, a second and more comparable baseline consists of randomly distributing training and test sentences into sets that correspond in size to the genres. We use these baselines and add a third, which is more relevant to our current setting. In this case, we use the experts trained on the genres but then randomly assign test sentences to the experts. This allows us to gauge how important a correct assignment to the corresponding expert is.

5.3 Topic Modeling

Probabilistic topic modeling is a class of unsupervised algorithms which detects the thematic structure in volumes of documents (Blei, 2012). We use Latent Dirichlet Allocation (LDA), a generative probabilistic model that approximates the underlying hidden topical structure of a collection of texts based on the distribution of words in the documents (Blei et al., 2003).

---

[2]http://nlp.stanford.edu/ mcclosky/biomedical.html

Similarity metric	Setting	Accuracy
joint LDA		98.94
topic words	50	97.59
	100	97.53
	200	97.35
perplexity	unigrams	**99.76**
	bigrams	84.71
	trigrams	81.53
k-NN	50	90.59
	100	91.18

Table 1: Accuracy of genre assignment for different similarity metrics.

We use the topic modeling toolkit MALLET (McCallum, 2002). The topic modeler in MALLET implements Latent Dirichlet Allocation clustering documents into a predefined number of topics.

5.4 POS Tagging and Parsing

For part of speech tagging, we use the Markov model POS tagger TnT (Trigrams'n'Tags) (Brants, 2000). We use TnT mainly because of its speed and because it allows the manual inspection of the trained models (emission and transition frequencies). For the parsing experiments, we use the dependency parser of the MATE Tools[3], a Java implementation of a graph-based parser (Bohnet, 2010). For the parsing experiments, we use gold POS tags.

5.5 Similarity Estimation

For the k-nearest neighbor estimation, we use the Tilburg Memory-Based Learner (TiMBL) (Daelemans et al., 2010). For the perplexity models, we derive n-grams of the training experts using Laplace smoothing, in NLTK (Bird et al., 2009), and compute the perplexity of the training experts to a test sentence.

5.6 Evaluation

We use the script `tnt-diff` that is part of TnT to evaluate the POS tagging results and the CoNLL shared task evaluation script[4] for evaluating the parsing results.

6 Experimental Results

Genre Assignment. We first investigate how well the different similarity metrics can assign the

test sentences to the correct genre. I.e., we calculate accuracy in terms of whether a GENIA sentence is assigned to the GENIA genre, and a WSJ sentence to the WSJ genre. Table 1 shows the results of classification accuracy of using different similarity estimation techniques. The reference here is the joint LDA for training and test data, with an accuracy of 98.94%.

Perplexity based on unigrams reaches the highest accuracy, reaching an accuracy of 99.76%, thus surpassing the joint LDA. Surprisingly, using bi- or trigrams instead decreases accuracy by 15-20 points absolute. We assume that this is due to data sparsity since the language model is trained on a relatively small dataset. The second highest accuracy is reached by the methods based on topic words. Here, the number of words considered does not seem to make a significant difference. The k-NN approach performs at around 91%. These results indicate that using single words without context (i.e., the context in bi- and trigrams) provides the most reliable information. The language model has an additional advantage, potentially because it can smooth over unseen words.

POS Tagging. Table 2 shows the accuracies of the POS tagging experiments for different similarity metrics. We notice that assigning the test sentences randomly to genres has a detrimental effect, and we reach an accuracy of 91.36%, which is more than 5 points absolute lower than the random split baseline. This difference shows how important it is that sentences are assigned to the correct genre.

Perplexity based on unigrams and the method using topic words reach comparable accuracies to the original topic expert results based on the joint LDA clustering. These results follow the same

---

[3]code.google.com/p/mate-tools
[4]http://ilk.uvt.nl/conll/software/eval.pl

Setting	Similarity metric	Accuracy
full training		96.69
random split		96.41
topic experts + random test		91.36
joint LDA		96.95
topic words	50	96.80
	100	96.81
	200	96.81
perplexity	unigrams	**96.92**
	bigrams	95.64
	trigrams	95.22
k-NN	50	96.05
	100	96.09

Table 2: Results for the POS tagging experiments.

Setting	Similarity metric	LAS	UAS
full training		88.67	91.71
random split		87.84	90.86
topic experts + random test		82.17	88.13
joint LDA	-	90.51	92.14
topic words	50	90.30	92.07
	100	90.30	92.07
	200	90.30	92.07
perplexity	unigrams	**90.54**	**92.16**
	bigrams	88.33	91.13
	trigrams	87.50	90.68
k-NN	50	89.45	91.82
	100	89.52	91.84

Table 3: Attachment scores for the dependency parsing experiments.

trends as the genre assignment accuracies, but the differences between the methods are smaller. The perplexity setting using unigrams does not only surpass the joint LDA scores but also all the baselines: by nearly 0.3 percent points for the full training set, by 0.5 percent points for the random split, and by 5 percent points for the random test assignment.

Dependency Parsing. Table 3 shows labeled and unlabeled attachment scores of the dependency parses. These results mirror the trends in the POS tagging experiments: Randomly assigning sentences to genres results in the lowest LAS score of 82.17%, and using perplexity based on unigrams reaches the highest LAS of 90.54%. This LAS is considerably higher than the full training baseline of 88.67%. Note that the differences between the accuracies based on different similarity metrics are considerably more pronounced than in

the POS tagging experiments. This mirrors the trend that we have previously seen for the joint LDA assignment. It is also interesting to see that the results for all the topic word settings are the same. This is due to 5 sentences that did not contain any of the topic words and thus had to be randomly assigned to one genre.

We now have a closer look at the two best settings, i.e., the perplexity experiment using unigrams and 50 topic words: We separate the sentences that were assigned to the wrong genre from the correctly assigned ones and evaluate them separately. For the unigram setting, 4 sentences were assigned to the wrong genre, for the 50 topic words, 41 sentences. The results are shown in Table 4. These results show that the sentences that were assigned to the wrong genre receive POS and dependency analyses with significantly lower accuracies, the difference to the correct ones ranging between 5 points absolute for POS tag-

	setting	Correct genre	Incorrect genre	Overall
POS tagging (acc.)	unigram	96.92	91.84	96.92
	topic words 50	98.23	88.59	96.80
parsing (LAS)	unigram	90.54	85.72	90.54
	topic words 50	90.55	76.19	90.30

Table 4: Results for POS tagging and dependency parsing when we separate incorrectly assigned sentences from correct ones.

ging and 10-14 points for parsing. This corroborates our findings that the correct assignment to a genre is of utmost importance, which also corroborates our conclusion that the genre experts model genre-specific information. If they did not, misassigning sentences would not have any impact.

7 Conclusion

Using topic modeling to create experts can be very beneficial, but this approach is only viable if we can assign new sentences asynchronously to genres without having to retrain the LDA to determine genres that include the new sentences. We have investigated similarity based methods for assigning the new sentences to genres. More specifically, we have investigated the following methods: 1) using topic words that LDA associates with a genre, 2) k-nearest neighbor models, and 3) perplexity in language models. A baseline that assigns test sentences randomly to genres performs poorly, thus showing that the correct assignment to genres is indispensable.

Our results show that the perplexity model based on unigrams surpasses the accuracy of a joint LDA model that assigns the sentences synchronously. For POS tagging, the accuracy of the unigram perplexity model is very close to that of the joint LDA. For parsing, the unigram perplexity model outperforms the joint LDA model. Using the 50 topic words to assign sentences to their genre reaches accuracies close to the best performing model. This shows that word-based methods are more robust in comparison to bigram and trigram methods, which should be able to profit from more context but also face data sparsity issues.

For the future, we plan to investigate models with a more dynamic mix of genres during the POS tagging and parsing process. I.e. rather than creating independent experts, we will investigate methods to create a POS tagger and parser that have access to expert views during each decision about the next POS tag or parsing step. We will also investigate whether we can integrate gold POS tags or dependency information into the topic modeling process, so that the topic modeler has access not only to the specialized lexical information but also to the linguistic information that it is ultimately tasked to distinguish.

References

Giuseppe Attardi, Felice Dell'Orletta, Maria Simi, Atanas Chanev, and Massimiliano Ciaramita. 2007. Multilingual dependency parsing and domain adaptation using DeSR. In *Proceedings of the CoNLL Shared Task Session of EMNLP-CoNLL 2007*. Prague, Czech Republic, pages 1112–1118.

Steven Bird, Ewan Klein, and Edward Loper. 2009. *Natural Language Processing with Python: Analyzing Text with the Natural Language Toolkit*. O'Reilly Media.

David M. Blei. 2012. Probabilistic topic models. *Communications of the ACM* 55(4):77–84. https://doi.org/10.1145/2133806.2133826.

David M. Blei, Andrew Y. Ng, and Michael I. Jordan. 2003. Latent Dirichlet Allocation. *Journal of Machine Learning Research* 3:993–1022.

John Blitzer, Ryan McDonald, and Fernando Pereira. 2006. Domain adaptation with structural correspondence learning. In *Proceedings of the Conference on Empirical Methods in Natural Language Processing (EMNLP)*. Sydney, Australia, pages 120–128.

Bernd Bohnet. 2010. Top accuracy and fast dependency parsing is not a contradiction. In *Proceedings of the 23rd International Conference on Computational Linguistics (COLING)*. Beijing, China, pages 89–97.

Thorsten Brants. 2000. TnT–a statistical part-of-speech tagger. In *Proceedings of the 1st Conference of the North American Chapter of the Association for Computational Linguistics and the 6th Conference on Applied Natural Language Processing (ANLP/NAACL)*. Seattle, WA, pages 224–231.

Stephen Clark, James Curran, and Miles Osborne. 2003. Bootstrapping POS-taggers using unlabelled data. In *Proceedings of the Seventh Conference on Natural Language Learning (CoNLL)*. Edmonton, Canada, pages 49–55.

Walter Daelemans, Jakub Zavrel, Ko van der Sloot, and Antal van den Bosch. 2010. TiMBL: Tilburg memory based learner – version 6.3 – reference guide. Technical Report ILK 10-01, Induction of Linguistic Knowledge, Computational Linguistics, Tilburg University.

Mark Dredze, John Blitzer, Partha Pratim Talukdar, Kuzman Ganchev, João Graca, and Fernando Pereira. 2007. Frustratingly hard domain adaptation for dependency parsing. In *Proceedings of the CoNLL Shared Task Session of EMNLP-CoNLL 2007*. Prague, Czech Republic, pages 1051–1055.

Jenny Rose Finkel and Christopher D. Manning. 2009. Hierarchical Bayesian domain adaptation. In *Proceedings of Human Language Technologies: The 2009 Annual Conference of the North American Chapter of the Association for Computational Linguistics (HLT-NAACL)*. pages 602–610.

Richard Johansson and Pierre Nugues. 2007. Extended constituent-to-dependency conversion for English. In *Proceedings of NODALIDA 2007*. Tartu, Estonia, pages 105–112.

Daisuke Kawahara and Kiyotaka Uchimoto. 2008. Learning reliability of parses for domain adaptation of dependency parsing. In *Proceedings of the Third International Joint Conference on Natural Language Processing (IJCNLP)*. Hyderabad, India.

Sandra Kübler and Eric Baucom. 2011. Fast domain adaptation for part of speech tagging for dialogues. In *Proceedings of the International Conference on Recent Advances in NLP (RANLP)*. Hissar, Bulgaria.

Mitchell Marcus, Grace Kim, Mary Ann Marcinkiewicz, Robert MacIntyre, Ann Bies, Mark Ferguson, Karen Katz, and Britta Schasberger. 1994. The Penn Treebank: Annotating predicate argument structure. In *Proceedings of the ARPA Human Language Technology Workshop, HLT 94*. Plainsboro, NJ, pages 114–119.

Andrew Kachites McCallum. 2002. Mallet: A machine learning for language toolkit. `http://mallet.cs.umass.edu`.

David McClosky, Eugene Charniak, and Mark Johnson. 2010. Automatic domain adaptation for parsing. In *Human Language Technologies: The 2010 Annual Conference of the North American Chapter of the Association for Computational Linguistics*. Los Angeles, CA, pages 28–36.

Atreyee Mukherjee, Sandra Kübler, and Matthias Scheutz. 2016. POS tagging experts via topic modeling. In *Proceedings of the 13th International Conference on Natural Language Processing*. Varanasi, India, pages 120–128.

Atreyee Mukherjee, Sandra Kübler, and Matthias Scheutz. 2017. Creating POS tagging and dependency parsing experts via topic modeling. In *Proceedings of the 15th Conference of the European Chapter of the Association for Computational Linguistics*. pages 347–355.

Tomoko Ohta, Yuka Tateisi, and Jin-Dong Kim. 2002. The GENIA corpus: An annotated research abstract corpus in molecular biology domain. In *Proceedings of the Second International Conference on Human Language Technology Research*. San Francisco, CA, pages 82–86.

Barbara Plank and Gertjan van Noord. 2011. Effective measures of domain similarity for parsing. In *Proceedings of the 49th Annual Meeting of the Association for Computational Linguistics: Human Language Technologies*. Portland, OR, pages 1566–1576.

Kenji Sagae and Jun'ichi Tsujii. 2007. Dependency parsing and domain adaptation with LR models and parser ensembles. In *Proceedings of the CoNLL Shared Task Session of EMNLP-CoNLL 2007*. Prague, Czech Republic, pages 1044–1050.

Yuka Tateisi and Jun'ichi Tsujii. 2004. Part-of-speech annotation of biology research abstracts. In *Proceedings of 4th International Conference on Language Resource and Evaluation (LREC)*. Lisbon, Portugal.

Recognizing Reputation Defence Strategies
in Critical Political Exchanges

Nona Naderi
Department of Computer Science
University of Toronto
Toronto, ON, M5S 3G4, Canada
nona@cs.toronto.edu

Graeme Hirst
Department of Computer Science
University of Toronto
Toronto, ON, M5S 3G4, Canada
gh@cs.toronto.edu

Abstract

We propose a new task of automatically detecting reputation defence strategies in the field of computational argumentation. We cast the problem as relation classification, where given a pair of reputation threat and reputation defence, we determine the reputation defence strategy. We annotate a dataset of parliamentary questions and answers with reputation defence strategies. We then propose a model based on supervised learning to address the detection of these strategies, and report promising experimental results.

1 Introduction

Reputation management and defence is important in personal and professional relations. Every day, individuals, companies, and governments are faced with allegations or threats to their reputation, and they use reputation defence strategies to minimize the damage. One example in recent years was the case of Airbus Helicopters, which faced bribery allegations in a Greek NH-90 helicopter deal. In a statement, it defended its reputation using a denial strategy: *These allegations are groundless and damage the reputation of Airbus Helicopters.*[1] Maintaining good reputation is especially important in political rhetoric, and is considered as one of its primary goals. When faced with criticism, politicians use various strategies to react to it and defend themselves to others—both to their critic and to their audience. These strategies are a component of political argumentation. Recent years have seen a surge of studies that computationally analyze various aspects of arguments, such as identification of arguments (Moens et al., 2007) and analysis of argument structures (Mochales and Moens, 2008; Peldszus and Stede, 2015; Stab and Gurevych, 2014a), and identification of argumentation schemes (Feng and Hirst, 2011). Current approaches, however, have mostly ignored the interaction between the parties involved in the argumentation process, where one party is critical of the other and the other party needs to overcome the doubts.

Consider the question-and-answer sessions in Westminister-style parliamentary debates, where the government of the day is held accountable by the opposition. Opposition members ask confrontational questions, and the government ministers respond. In the face of criticism, they may use various reputation defence strategies to try to maintain a positive image.

In this paper, we propose a novel task of identifying reputation defence strategies in given dialogical argumentation. No annotated data is available for this task, so we examine whether and how reputation defence strategies are used in parliamentary debates to respond to the opposition, and create a new corpus of Canadian parliamentary debates annotated with reputation defence strategies. We focus on the most agreed-upon strategies, namely *denial, excuse, justification,* and *concession* (Benoit, 1995). For example, politicians may deny having caused a bad situation (denial) or try to evade responsibility (excuse), or promise to fix the situation (concession). Table 1(a) presents an example from the Canadian parliament, where the government minister makes an excuse for a situation, and Table 1(b) presents an example of a concession.

We then investigate what features are good predictors of the reputation defence strategies used in each case. The present work is a step towards a

---

[1] *Airbus Helicopters rejects bribery allegations in Greek NH-90 deal*, Reuters, 2015-03-23

527

Proceedings of Recent Advances in Natural Language Processing, pages 527–535,
Varna, Bulgaria, Sep 4–6 2017.

Excuse	Concession
Q. Mr. Speaker, contrary to the Conservatives' claims, we are still short 30,000 jobs to get back to the level we were at before the crisis. For example, the Quebec forestry industry, which has lost 18,000 jobs since 2005, is struggling to get out of this difficult situation. Will the government understand that the crisis is far from over in the forestry industry and that it needs a comprehensive policy to support and modernize the industry, as was the case with the auto industry in Ontario? **A.** Mr. Speaker, all of the forestry experts in the country agree that it is a matter of markets. Unfortunately, the only ones who do not get it are the members opposite. They are playing politics with these people's jobs. The markets are difficult. Our workers are among the best in the world and we will continue to support them. Billions of dollars have been put into improving green practices through the community adjustment fund, and we will continue to support the forestry industry with research and development.	**Q.** Mr. Speaker, on December 9, just a few days from now, the École de médecine vétérinaire de Saint-Hyacinthe will have to report to the American Veterinary Association on the major investments required for its full accreditation to be restored. Does the Prime Minister grasp the urgency of the situation and does he not realize that the Government of Quebec has already put $41 million into the school and that it is now time he and his government did their share? It is urgent, a matter of days. **A.** Mr. Speaker, as has been said many times, this side and the government recognize the importance of the veterinary colleges, not only the one in Quebec but in the other three provinces in this country. We will do all we can to ensure that they maintain and continue their accreditation.

Table 1: Question and answer pairs from Canadian parliamentary proceedings annotated with reputation defence strategies: (a) 2011-02-01, Robert Bouchard (Q) and Denis Lebel (A); (b) 2002-12-03, Lyle Vanclief, (Q) and Yvan Loubier (A).

deeper understanding and evaluation of (political) arguments. Natural arguments are generally enthymematic, which means some of their elements are left implicit. Identifying these implicit argument elements is a very difficult task. Knowing what strategy is used in defence arguments may help in reconstruction of these missing elements. Furthermore, extracting defence strategies can facilitate identifying contradictory and inconsistent arguments.

2 Related Work

While the task of automatically identifying reputation defence strategies has not been addressed previously, some researchers have focused on classifying the relations between argumentative components (Stab and Gurevych, 2014b; Nguyen and Litman, 2016). Others focused on classifying online discussions as agreement and disagreement with respect to a side of the debate on an issue (Abbott et al., 2011; Wang and Cardie, 2014; Rosenthal and McKeown, 2015). They employed various features, such as thread structure features, lexical (e.g., n-grams, number of words), and syntactic features (e.g., POS tags, dependency relations). Mukherjee and Liu (2013) proposed a semi-supervised generative model to extract agreement and disagreement expression types from discussion forums. Cabrio and Villata (2012) used a textual entailment approach to find pro and con arguments in a set of forum debates selected from Debatepedia.

Rosenthal and McKeown (2015) employed a supervised approach to classify forum discussions as agreement and disagreement and found that similar lexical and syntactic structures in a pair of posts were important for the classification task. Biran and Rambow (2011) used discourse markers to classify single sentences as a justification of a claim or not. Peldszus (2014) focused on identifying attack and support relations in microtexts. However, none of these looked at the interactions between arguments of two parties. Here, we aim to analyze these interactions, particularly when one party criticized the other, and the other addresses the criticism.

3 Data

For our analysis, we focus on pairs of questions and answers extracted from Oral Question period from Canadian parliamentary proceedings. The purpose of questions asked in Oral Question period is to hold the government accountable for its actions[2]. While both government backbenchers and opposition members ask questions during this period, the questions asked by opposition members are more confrontational than the questions asked by the backbenchers. The questions asked by government backbenchers tend to be more clarification questions; therefore, we extracted the pairs where the questions were asked by opposition members.

---

[2]http://www.ourcommons.ca/About/Compendium/Questions/c_g_questions-e.htm

Table 2: Conditions for each reputation defence strategy.

Table 3: Disagreement among three annotators, annotated variously as *denial, justification,* and *concession*; 2005-05-30, Lynne Yelich (Q) and Anne McLellan (A).

To study whether reputation defence strategies are used in the parliamentary debates, we first ran a pilot study and asked three expert annotators to annotate 100 random pairs of the extracted questions and answers with one of the reputation strategies or none of the strategies. We prepared detailed guidelines to describe the conditions that need to be satisfied for choosing each reputation defence strategy. Table 2 presents the conditions provided to the annotators (all are adapted from Benoit (1995)).

We further conducted a larger annotation study with 1500 random pairs of the extracted questions and answers on the crowd-sourcing platform (CrowdFlower[3]). Contributors were shown a question and answer pair from the parliamentary debates on various issues, and were asked to choose which strategies (based on the conditions presented in Table 2) had been used by the government in response to criticism. We asked for at least three annotations per pair from the English-speaking countries. To maintain the annotation quality, we allowed only the highest-quality contributors to participate, and also included some test pairs. On each page, each participant was presented with one test pair and three other pairs, and had to maintain 70% accuracy throughout the job. In total, we included 56 test questions for 1500 pairs. Each response was paid $0.04. Only 10% of the question and answer pairs were annotated with *none of the strategies* by the annotators, which shows that these strategies can represent the data reasonably well. Almost 70% of the pairs were agreed upon by two or more annotators, but in order to obtain a more reliable corpus, we accepted the pairs for which at least three annotators agreed on a single answer, and discarded the pairs where fewer than three annotators agreed. For the expert annotations, three annotators achieved full agreement on a single answer for 32 pairs. In total, the

---

[3] https://www.crowdflower.com/

Verb type	Examples
Concealment	conceal
Psych	amuse, admire
Desire	want, long
Judgment	judge, approve
Assessment	estimate
Searching	investigate
Social interaction	correspond, meet
Communication	inquire, advise
Existence	exist, survive
Aspectual	begin, continue
Allow	allow, permit
Admit	admit
Succeed	succeed

Table 4: VerbNet classes that we used.

LIWC category	Examples
Analytic	–
Negations	no, not
Interrogatives	how, what
Affective processes	happy
Positive emotions	nice
Negative emotions	hurt
Cognitive processes	cause
Insight	think
Causation	because
Tentative	perhaps
Certainty	always
Perceptual processes	heard
Achievement	success
Power	superior
Past focus	talked
Present focus	is
Future focus	will
Assent	agree

Table 5: LIWC features that we used.

reliable crowd and expert annotations resulted in a set of 493 pairs, of which 170 were annotated as *denial*, 36 as *excuse*, 173 as *justification*, 95 as *concession*, and 19 as *none of these strategies*. The average number of tokens in each pair is 171, with the longest pair being 356 words. These pairs of questions and answers are on different topics.

We further examined the discarded pairs of questions that were not agreed upon by at least three annotators to investigate the source of disagreements. Disagreements between the annotators were generally due to the use of multiple strategies or vague answers that do not contribute to the goal of the dialogue; they simply look like relevant answers, but they do not really address the questions. Table 3 shows an example of disagreement between three annotators.

Q. Mr. Speaker, contrary to what the Prime Minister says, Canada's actions so far lead us to conclude that it is siding with the United States by supporting, through its silence, comments made by U.S. Secretary of Defense, Donald Rumsfeld, who wants to ignore NATO and the UN if it suits his purposes. Is the Prime Minister aware that his silence is contributing to undermining international institutions and that this complacent attitude breaks with Canada's tradition of respecting major international institutions?

A. Mr. Speaker, I firmly reject the suggestion that the Prime Minister has been silent. Our position is clear. We have always encouraged and supported an approach that goes through the United Nations and through the Security Council. We have gotten here, in some measure, thanks to the efforts of the Prime Minister. He has never been silent, he has been active on the international scene and we are very proud of what he has done.

Table 6: An example *Comparison* relation between two parts of question and answer, specified in bold; 2003-02-12, Francine Lalonde (Q) and Bill Graham (A).

4 Approach

We formulate the task as a classification task. Given a question and answer pair, we identify which of the four reputation defence strategies, *denial*, *justification*, *excuse*, and *concession* is used in the answer. In order to capture the characteristics of each strategy, we explore two classes of features: features that are based solely on the answers, and features that describe the relation between the question and the answer.

4.1 Features from Answers

VerbNet Classes Certain verb classes can indicate defence strategies; for example, *assure* is often used in *justification* or *concession* strategies, e.g., *I want to assure the House that we are taking measures.* To this end, we use the VerbNet lexicon (Schuler, 2005), which groups verbs by their shared semantic meaning and syntactic behavior. Table 4 shows the verb classes that we use. We use the count of verb class occurrences as features.

Positive and Negative Sentiments and Emotions Motivated by the conditions for the *justification* strategy (Table 2), we examined the positive and negative sentiments and emotions expressed in the answers. Emotions are extracted using Linguistic Inquiry and Word Count (Tausczik and Pennebaker, 2010), and sentiments are extracted using OpinionFinder (Wilson et al., 2005).

Features	Acc.(%)	F_1 (%)
Majority Class (justification)	36.50	–
Production rules	49.78	46.31
Unigrams (q + a) (tf-idf)	52.53	49.54
Unigrams (a) (tf-idf)	53.35	51.32
Unigrams (a) (tf-idf) + LIWC	53.57	53.07
Unigrams (a) + VerbNet v class	53.78	51.62
Unigrams (a) + VerbNet v class + Sentiments	56.11	54.02
Unigrams (a) + VerbNet v class + Sentiments + Negation	56.33	55.55
Unigrams (a) + Discourse + Similarity	55.26	53.04
Unigrams (a) + VerbNet v class + Sentiments + Negation + Discourse	56.96	56.33
Unigrams (a) + VerbNet v class + Sentiments + Negation + Discourse + Similarity (best model)	**57.59**	**56.92**

Table 7: The performance of different models for classification of four reputation defence strategies (five-fold cross-validation).

Features	Denial	Excuse	Justification	Concession
Production rules	59.4	0.0	51.8	30.8
Unigrams (q + a) (tf-idf)	62.6	10.0	55.6	28.2
Unigrams (a) (tf-idf)	62.4	13.6	55.6	36.4
Unigrams (a) (tf-idf) + LIWC	64.0	**19.4**	54.2	41.0
Best model	**65.0**	18.0	**59.8**	**48.0**

Table 8: Average F_1 of different models for classification of four reputation defence strategies (five-fold cross-validation).

Past and Future Focus Verb tense can reveal the difference between strategies; for example, in *denial*, the focus is more likely to be on the past, e.g., *as I said in French, I never gave advice about the privatization of the Toronto airport*, whereas in *concession,* the focus tends to be on the future, e.g., *I promise the hon. member and all members of the special forces that I will work with them to ensure they are justly and properly treated.*

Negation *Denials* tend to be expressed using *never, not, no, nobody*, and *none*, e.g., *I never solicited funds.*

Insight and Achievement These categories are mostly associated with *justification* strategies, e.g., *I think when we can help farmers in Canada, it is our duty to do so*, and *We will continue to invest in this fashion. It is a proven success.* To compute these features, we use Linguistic Inquiry and Word Count (LIWC), a tool that counts occurrences of words by their psychological categories. We used 18 LIWC categories, presented in Table 5.

4.2 Features Describing Relations between a Question and Answer Pair

Discourse Relations Discourse relations have been shown to be effective in identifying support and attack relations in persuasive essays (Nguyen and Litman, 2016). While Nguyen and Litman (2016)'s work focused on only the attack and support relations between argumentative components in a paragraph, nonetheless, we believe that discourse relations can be informative features for identifying reputation defence strategies. Here we use shallow discourse relations (*Class level*), including *Comparison*, *Contingency*, and *Expansion* between the question and answer pairs (extracted using End-to-End PDTB-Styled Discourse Parser (Lin et al., 2014)).[4] For example, consider the question and answer pair in Table 6, where the discourse relation (parts in bold) between question and answer is *Comparison* and indicates the *denial* strategy. While fine-grained discourse relations (*type* level) can be informative for identifying reputation strategies, for our analysis, we focused on only major classes of discourse relations because discourse parsers usually yield less reliable results for fine-grained relations.

Syntactic Production Rules Stab and Gurevych (2014b) used production rules to classify support and non-support argument relations in persuasive essays, and found them to be effective features. Their work also focused on

---

[4]*Temporal* relations have not been effective in our classification task, which is also in line with expectations (Biran and Rambow, 2011; Stab and Gurevych, 2014b).

	Features	Denial		Justification		Concession	
		Acc(%)	F_1(%)	Acc(%)	F_1(%)	Acc(%)	F_1(%)
Justification	Best model	**74.35**	**74.74**			70.51	69.14
	BOW + LIWC	72.59	72.49			66.39	64.51
	BOW + VerbNet	70.85	70.79			**70.87**	**69.28**
	BOW + VerbNet + Sent + Neg	72.89	72.72			69.39	68.01
	BOW + Discourse + Similarity	73.18	73.04			67.15	65.48
	Production rules	67.95	67.80			65.32	63.43
	Majority	50.44	–			64.55	–
Concession	Best model	76.23	76.40	70.51	69.14		
	BOW + LIWC	**77.36**	**76.72**	66.39	64.51		
	BOW + VerbNet	75.09	74.52	**70.87**	**69.28**		
	BOW + VerbNet + Sent + Neg	**76.98**	**76.91**	69.39	68.01		
	BOW + Discourse + Similarity	75.85	75.16	67.15	65.48		
	Production rules	76.98	75.90	65.32	63.43		
	Majority	64.15	–	64.55	–		
Excuse	Best model	83.02	81.69	82.31	78.16	66.35	64.74
	BOW + LIWC	84.43	80.28	83.74	79.15	71.68	67.93
	BOW + VerbNet	82.98	78.89	83.28	78.72	68.60	66.15
	BOW + VerbNet + Sent + Neg	81.57	80.25	81.84	77.85	68.60	66.81
	BOW + Discourse + Similarity	84.43	79.91	83.26	78.28	71.71	66.88
	Production rules	82.00	75.01	83.29	76.98	71.71	64.80
	Majority	82.52	–	82.78	–	72.51	–

Table 9: The performance of the models for pairwise classification (five-fold cross-validation). Best model includes discourse relations, cosine similarity, unigrams, verb classes, negations, and positive and negative sentiments in the answers.

the relations in a paragraph. Here, we explore the impact of the production rules in capturing the syntactic characteristics of reputation management strategies. We consider binary features for production rules (e.g., VP → VBZ NP SBAR, VP → VB NP PP) that appear only in the answer, and both in the question and the answer (Lin et al. (2009) and Feng and Hirst (2012) used these features for identifying shallow discourse relations and RST discourse relations, respectively). We used the Stanford parser (Klein and Manning, 2003) to perform the pre-processing.

Similarity Measures Simple lexical similarity methods have been shown to be robust in recognizing textual entailment, which can help capture strategies such as *denial* and *concession*. We compute the average semantic similarity between the question and the answer sentences from the cosine similarity between their vectors. To represent the questions and answers, we sum their word2vec embeddings (Mikolov et al., 2013).

5   Results

The classification is performed using a class-weighted Support Vector Machine model with a linear kernel[5]. The classifiers were trained and

tested with the crowd-sourced data described in section 3 using five-fold cross validation. The baselines that we use are the majority class, where all instances are classified as *justification*, and the bag-of-words representations (weighted using *tf-idf*) of the question and answer pairs and the bag-of-words representations of answers. The bag-of-words representation of answers is the strongest baseline on our dataset and yields an accuracy of 53.35%. To determine the efficacy of the features, we train individual classifiers on the feature classes. The results are reported in terms of accuracy and average F_1-measure.

Multi-class Classification Table 7 reports the results for multi-class classification. The best performance was 57.59% accuracy, which was achieved by using discourse relations and cosine similarity between the question and answer, and verb classes, positive and negative sentiments (extracted using OpinionFinder), negations, and the unigrams from the answers. This model yields a 20-point improvement over the majority baseline and at least a 4-point improvement over bag-of-words baselines. Our ablation studies to measure the contributions of different components show that all features are helpful, with verb classes, sentiments, negations, and unigrams (from answers)

---

[5]LibSVM implementation (Pedregosa et al., 2011).

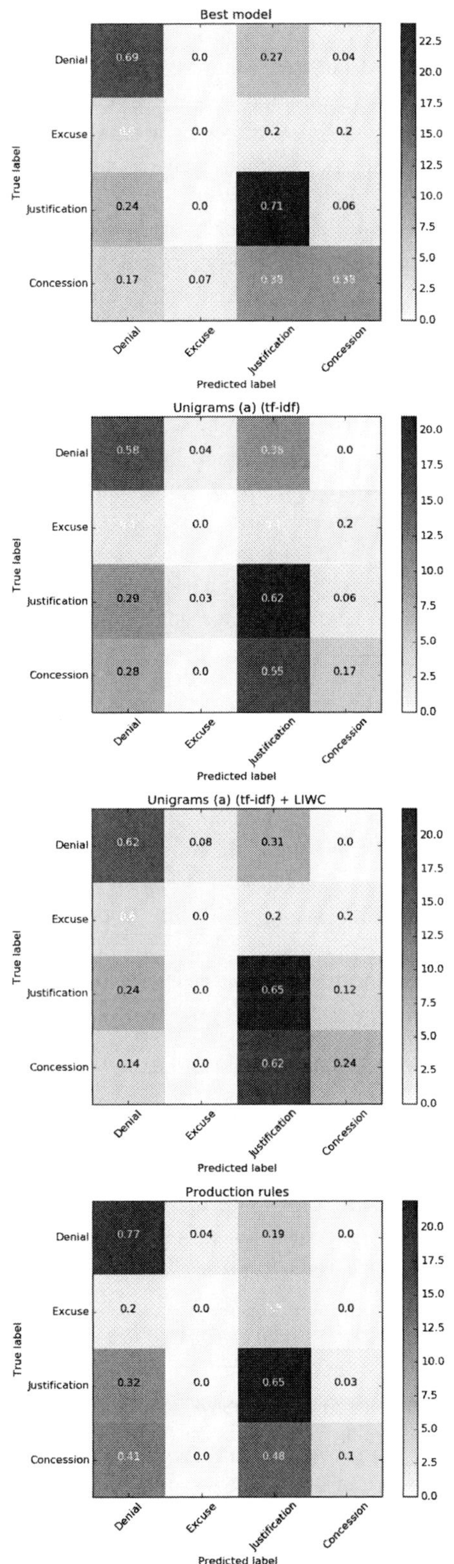

Figure 1: Normalized confusion matrices for reputation defence classification.

being the most helpful for distinguishing between strategies. Using the LIWC features also improves the performance over all the baselines. While production rules are informative features, the performance of this classifier is lower than the bag-of-words baseline.

Table 8 reports the average F_1-measure of five-fold cross validation for each reputation defence strategy in multi-class classification. The best performance for identifying *denial, justification,* and *concession* is achieved by the best model. LIWC features are most informative for identifying *excuse* strategy.

Pairwise Classification We further experimented with *pairwise* classification (one-versus-one) for the six possible pairings of the four strategies to find the most informative features for each strategy (Table 9). For each of the six classifiers, we considered the data for the two strategies against each other. In *pairwise* classification, almost all models improve over the majority baseline, except for *excuse*, for which the training data is very small. In distinguishing between *denial* and *justification*, the combination of verb classes, sentiments, negations, discourse relations, cosine similarity, and unigrams from the answers yields the best performance. The most informative features in distinguishing *concessions* and *justifications* are VerbNet classes. In distinguishing between *denial* and *concession,* the features extracted from the answers contribute the most.

Reputation Defence Errors Figure 1 shows confusion matrices for the best model, the baseline unigram (a) model, LIWC model, and production rule model for the first fold of cross-validation. The most common confusion is misclassifying the *concession* strategy as the *justification* strategy. The best model makes this error less often. Production rules often misclassify the *concession* strategy as the *denial* strategy as well.

6   Discussion

The results show that the features proposed above are successful in distinguishing *denial* and *justification* strategies, but the small training set for *excuse* and *concession* strategies did not allow the model to effectively detect these strategies. While the performance of the model can benefit from more training data, the limited performance could

Q. Mr. Speaker, Canadians are being prevented from obtaining their passports under the guise of increased national security. In the last six months my constituency office has been inundated by hundreds of angry constituents. Some have even been forced to cancel trips, costing them thousands of dollars, due to the incompetence of the government. I have repeatedly raised their concerns with the passport department of foreign affairs to no avail. When the advertised processing time is 45 working days, why are my constituents waiting months for their passports?

A. Mr. Speaker, the hon. member was good enough in the introduction to his question to point out there is a problem in terms of new security measures and there is a great deal of increased flow of demands for passports. The passport office is making a serious and concerted effort to respond to these requests. I regret any inconvenience to the hon. member or to Canadian citizens. I want to assure the House that we are taking measures. We have brought in people this weekend and we will be working around the clock to reduce and eliminate the backlog of requests. We have put in measures to enable people to get their passports more quickly and to deal with it more efficiently. I will be circulating to the hon. member, and all members, statements as to how the department is responding to this.

Table 10: An example of the *justification* strategy used together with the *concession* strategy; 2003-02-12, Andy Burton (Q) and Bill Graham (A).

be also due to the labeling task. By limiting the crowd annotators to choose the most prominent strategy, we attempted to study the characteristics of each strategy in isolation, but the results of the annotation process and classification task show that some defence strategies can be employed in combination with each other. Table 10 shows an example from our corpus that was misclassified by the model as the *concession* strategy, and when we examined the pair[6], we observed that although the main strategy in the defence is *justification* to reduce the offensiveness, corrective actions are further offered (the *concession* strategy).

Moreover, some questions express multiple reputation threats, which may require multiple defence strategies to address the threats. These cases require further analysis of the reputation threats and allegations. We chose parliamentary debates to study reputation defence strategies because reputation threat and defence arguments are more numerous in this data, and the data is easily accessible.

---

[6]Three annotators marked this relation as *justification* and one annotator marked it as *concession*, we considered agreement by three annotators as gold.

7 Conclusion

We have addressed a new task of automatically identifying reputation defence strategies. While reputation defence strategies are used in various social settings and managing reputations against attacks is vital for any individual, in parliamentary settings, they impact decision making as well. Thus, we computationally analyzed reputation defence strategies in parliamentary speeches. We also created a corpus for analysis of reputation strategies. We explored various features for classifying four reputation defence strategies. Our results show that while the models benefit most from the features extracted from the defence, they can be improved using the features that capture the relation between a threat and defence pair. Our promising results suggest a new research direction and allow for a better understanding of political exchanges and large-scale analysis of participant behaviors.

Acknowledgments

This research is financially supported by the Natural Sciences and Engineering Research Council of Canada. We thank Patricia Araujo Thaine and Simon Emond for their contributions to the pilot study of annotations. We thank Gerald Penn, Suzanne Stevenson, and Frank Rudzicz for their valuable feedback, as well as the anonymous reviewers for their suggestions.

References

Rob Abbott, Marilyn Walker, Pranav Anand, Jean E. Fox Tree, Robeson Bowmani, and Joseph King. 2011. How can you say such things?!?: Recognizing disagreement in informal political argument. In *Proceedings of the Workshop on Languages in Social Media*. Association for Computational Linguistics, Stroudsburg, PA, USA, pages 2–11.

William L Benoit. 1995. *Accounts, Excuses, and Apologies: A Theory of Image Restoration Strategies*. State University of New York Press, Albany.

Or Biran and Owen Rambow. 2011. Identifying justifications in written dialogs. In *Proceedings of the 2011 IEEE Fifth International Conference on Semantic Computing*. IEEE Computer Society, Washington, DC, USA, pages 162–168.

Elena Cabrio and Serena Villata. 2012. Natural language arguments: A combined approach. In *Proceedings of 20th European Conference on Artificial Intelligence*. IOS Press, Amsterdam, The Netherlands, pages 205–210.

Vanessa Wei Feng and Graeme Hirst. 2011. Classifying arguments by scheme. In *Proceedings of the 49th Annual Meeting of the Association for Computational Linguistics: Human Language Technologies*. Association for Computational Linguistics, pages 987–996.

Vanessa Wei Feng and Graeme Hirst. 2012. Text-level discourse parsing with rich linguistic features. In *Proceedings of the 50th Annual Meeting of the Association for Computational Linguistics (Volume 1: Long Papers)*. Association for Computational Linguistics, Jeju Island, Korea, pages 60–68.

Dan Klein and Christopher D. Manning. 2003. Accurate unlexicalized parsing. In *Proceedings of the 41st Annual Meeting on Association for Computational Linguistics*. Association for Computational Linguistics, pages 423–430.

Ziheng Lin, Min-Yen Kan, and Hwee Tou Ng. 2009. Recognizing implicit discourse relations in the Penn Discourse Treebank. In *Proceedings of the 2009 Conference on Empirical Methods in Natural Language Processing*. Association for Computational Linguistics, Singapore, pages 343–351.

Ziheng Lin, Hwee Tou Ng, and Min-Yen Kan. 2014. A PDTB-styled end-to-end discourse parser. *Natural Language Engineering* 20(2):151–184.

Tomas Mikolov, Kai Chen, Greg Corrado, and Jeffrey Dean. 2013. Efficient estimation of word representations in vector space. *arXiv preprint arXiv:1301.3781* .

Raquel Mochales and Marie-Francine Moens. 2008. Study on the structure of argumentation in case law. In *Proceedings of the 2008 Conference on Legal Knowledge and Information Systems: JURIX 2008: The Twenty-First Annual Conference*. IOS Press, Amsterdam, The Netherlands, pages 11–20.

Marie-Francine Moens, Erik Boiy, Raquel Mochales Palau, and Chris Reed. 2007. Automatic detection of arguments in legal texts. In *Proceedings of the 11th International Conference on Artificial Intelligence and Law*. ACM, New York, USA, pages 225–230.

Arjun Mukherjee and Bing Liu. 2013. Discovering user interactions in ideological discussions. In *Proceedings of the 51st Annual Meeting of the Association for Computational Linguistics, Sofia, Bulgaria, (Volume 1: Long Papers)*. pages 671–681.

Huy Nguyen and Diane Litman. 2016. Context-aware argumentative relation mining. In *Proceedings of the 54th Annual Meeting of the Association for Computational Linguistics (Volume 1: Long Papers)*. Association for Computational Linguistics, Berlin, Germany, pages 1127–1137.

F. Pedregosa, G. Varoquaux, A. Gramfort, V. Michel, B. Thirion, O. Grisel, M. Blondel, P. Prettenhofer, R. Weiss, V. Dubourg, J. Vanderplas, A. Passos, D. Cournapeau, M. Brucher, M. Perrot, and E. Duchesnay. 2011. Scikit-learn: Machine learning in Python. *Journal of Machine Learning Research* 12:2825–2830.

Andreas Peldszus. 2014. Towards segment-based recognition of argumentation structure in short texts. In *Proceedings of the First Workshop on Argumentation Mining*. Association for Computational Linguistics.

Andreas Peldszus and Manfred Stede. 2015. Joint prediction in MST-style discourse parsing for argumentation mining. In *Proceedings of the 2015 Conference on Empirical Methods in Natural Language Processing*. Association for Computational Linguistics, Lisbon, Portugal, pages 938–948.

Sara Rosenthal and Kathy McKeown. 2015. I couldn't agree more: The role of conversational structure in agreement and disagreement detection in online discussions. In *Proceedings of the 16th Annual Meeting of the Special Interest Group on Discourse and Dialogue*. Association for Computational Linguistics, Prague, Czech Republic, pages 168–177.

Karin Kipper Schuler. 2005. *Verbnet: A Broad-coverage, Comprehensive Verb Lexicon*. Ph.D. thesis, University of Pennsylvania.

Christian Stab and Iryna Gurevych. 2014a. Identifying argumentative discourse structures in persuasive essays. In *Proceedings of the 2014 Conference on Empirical Methods in Natural Language Processing*. Association for Computational Linguistics, Doha, Qatar, pages 46–56.

Christian Stab and Iryna Gurevych. 2014b. Identifying argumentative discourse structures in persuasive essays. In *Proceedings of the 2014 Conference on Empirical Methods in Natural Language Processing*. Association for Computational Linguistics, Doha, Qatar, pages 46–56.

Yla R. Tausczik and James W. Pennebaker. 2010. The psychological meaning of words: LIWC and computerized text analysis methods. *Journal of Language and Social Psychology* 29(1):24–54.

Lu Wang and Claire Cardie. 2014. Improving agreement and disagreement identification in online discussions with a socially-tuned sentiment lexicon. In *Proceedings of the 5th Workshop on Computational Approaches to Subjectivity, Sentiment and Social Media Analysis*. Association for Computational Linguistics, Baltimore, Maryland, pages 97–106.

Theresa Wilson, Janyce Wiebe, and Paul Hoffmann. 2005. Recognizing contextual polarity in phrase-level sentiment analysis. In *Proceedings of the Conference on Human Language Technology and Empirical Methods in Natural Language Processing*. Association for Computational Linguistics, Stroudsburg, PA, USA, pages 347–354.

Classifying Frames at the Sentence Level in News Articles

Nona Naderi
Department of Computer Science
University of Toronto
Toronto, ON, M5S 3G4, Canada
nona@cs.toronto.edu

Graeme Hirst
Department of Computer Science
University of Toronto
Toronto, ON, M5S 3G4, Canada
gh@cs.toronto.edu

Abstract

Previous approaches to generic frame classification analyze frames at the document level. Here, we propose a supervised based approach based on deep neural networks and distributional representations for classifying frames at the sentence level in news articles. We conduct our experiments on the publicly available Media Frames Corpus compiled from the U.S. Newspapers. Using (B)LSTMs and GRU networks to represent the meaning of frames, we demonstrate that our approach yields at least 14-point improvement over several baseline methods.

1 Introduction

Framing is generally conceptualized as a communication process to present an object or an issue. Various typologies are proposed for framing, for example some associate frames with specific issues (Entman (1993); Chong and Druckman (2007)), while others such as Card et al. (2015) believe that framing should be perceived as non-issue-specific, and be analyzed with a fixed set of framing dimensions. We take de Vreese's view that frames can be classified as either generic (issue-independent) or issue-specific (de Vreese (2005)). For example, *economic benefits* can be used as a generic frame for various issues; but the frame *marriage is about more than procreation* is specific to the issue of gay marriage. A single frame may relate to a complete text or only to shorter elements of a text, such as a paragraph or a single clause or sentence. Here, we focus on identifying generic frames at the sentence level in the Media Frames Corpus (Card et al., 2015). We employ both uni- and bi-directional LSTMs and gated recurrent networks, which have

been used effectively to represent long sequences, to automatically learn frame representations.

In Section 2, we summerize the previous work on computational analysis of framing. The problem definition is introduced in Section 3, followed by the data preparation (Section 4). We describe the experimental setup in Section 5. We then report the results in Section 6, and finally conclude in Section 7.

2 Related Work

Researchers have taken different approaches to operationalize the concept of framing. Some work used various kinds of topic models to analyze frames. Tsur et al. (2015) interpreted various contexts of a specific topic as frames, and employed topic models and time series to infer them. In a similar study, Nguyen et al. (2015) modeled issues and frame topics using hierarchical topic models. They used bill texts, votes, and floor speeches of the U.S. Congress for their predictions. Baumer et al. (2015) investigated various lexical and syntactic features to characterize framing language in political news stories. They found that imagery, figurativeness, and other lexical features are important in identifying framing language.

The prior work on the analysis of issue-specific frames mostly focused on a limited list of issues and frames. Boltužić and Šnajder (2014) addressed the task of tagging user postings with a pre-existing set of frames for the two topics of *Pledge of Allegiance* and *gay marriage*. Their supervised classification model made use of entailment and semantic similarity features. To generalize their earlier work for various topics, they subsequently presented an unsupervised model to recognize frames on the topics of *abortion, gay rights, Obama,* and *marijuana* by means of textual similarity (Boltužić and Šnajder, 2015). On

Proceedings of Recent Advances in Natural Language Processing, pages 536–542,
Varna, Bulgaria, Sep 4–6 2017.

the same dataset, Hasan and Ng (2014) employed a probabilistic approach to classify forum posts based on users' stance and reasons. In a similar task, Misra et al. (2015) used a set of lexical and semantic similarity features to classify online forum discussions by "argument facets". Naderi and Hirst (2016) analyzed frames across genres and extracted various frames specific to the *gay-marriage* issue from Canadian parliamentary proceedings. Card et al. (2016) explored the use of persona features to classify entire news articles (on the issue of *immigration*) by their overall frames.

Various frames are used in news articles to persuade the audience by establishing a point of view or supporting one. Frame detection at the sentence level helps in analyzing these persuasive strategies in more detail. Here, we investigate the use of recurrent neural networks for identifying generic frames at the sentence level.

3   Problem Definition

Given a text about a controversial issue, our goal is to classify each sentence that expresses a frame relating to the issue (and not just the entire text with a single frame, as Card et al. (2016) did). We use articles from the Media Frames Corpus (see section 4 below), and our objective in this work is to identify the generic frames expressed in the sentences of these texts.

The following example, an excerpt from an article in the Media Frames Corpus (Card et al., 2015), is annotated with the primary frame *Quality of life* as the overall frame of the article. Individual sentences are annotated with frames (shown in boldface) such as *Fairness and equality* and *Cultural identity*. The annotations do not always cover the entire sentence, for example, only the first part of the third sentence is annotated, and the second part is not. Additionally, in some cases, portions of texts are annotated with multiple frames.

Example 1 *Immigration1.0-171*
*[Overall frame of the article: **Quality of life**]*
Immigrants say bias is 'swift kick' to citizenship
*[**Fairness and equality**]*
*When Eduardo Flores moved to Texas in 1981, he was content straddling two cultures: working in the United States but retaining his Mexican citizenship [**Cultural identity**]. Now, the anti-immigrant sentiment spawned by California's Proposition 187 is making him have second thoughts [**Cultural identity**]: Flores wants a claim*

	Frame	N	N
		I+S	I
1	Economic	7,070	2,597
2	Capacity and resources	1,516	846
3	Morality	1,185	259
4	Fairness and equality	1,368	559
5	Legality, constitutionality and jurisprudence	9,420	4,233
6	Policy prescription and evaluation	6,505	2,716
7	Crime and punishment	6,206	3,857
8	Security and defense	1,730	1,171
9	Health and safety	4,968	1,054
10	Quality of life	3,790	1,674
11	Cultural identity	4,644	2,264
12	Public opinion	2,496	937
13	Political	7,864	4,253
14	External regulation and reputation	888	438
15	Other	623	278
16	*Irrelevant*	1,256	–

Table 1: Frames and number of sentences for each (N), extracted from the Media Frames Corpus. I+S includes frames on immigration and smoking; I includes frames on only immigration

*on the rights available in his adopted land. Legal immigrants like Flores throughout the Southwest have been applying for citizenship at record levels, and many say they want the right to vote to stop the spread of laws like Proposition 187. [**Legality, constitutionality and jurisprudence**]*

4   Data and Pre-processing

The Media Frames Corpus (Card et al., 2015) consists of news articles on three topics of *immigration, smoking,* and *same-sex* marriage.[1] In this corpus, each document is annotated with overall frame (this is what Card et al. (2016) used), and in each sentence, any text that cues a frame is also annotated with that frame, as seen in Example 1 above.

To create our dataset, we first gathered the an-

---

[1]We were able to download 4,315 articles from *smoking,* and 5,686 articles from *immigration* using the scripts provided at https://github.com/dallascard/media_frames_corpus. However, we were not able to obtain any of the *same-sex marriage* articles (according to the authors the inter-annotator agreement on the *same-sex marriage* set was much lower than the other two sets, Krippendorff alpha 0.08 compared to 0.16 for immigration and 0.23 for smoking).

notations that at least two annotators agreed upon; however, that process resulted in a small corpus because a majority of the articles on *smoking* were annotated only once. Therefore, we kept the cases that were annotated only once, and for the more controversial cases, where multiple frame dimensions were assigned, we kept only the annotations that were agreed upon by at least two annotators.

We then pre-processed the articles with a sentence splitter,[2] and gathered all the sentences annotated with the cue words for each frame. This resulted in 61,529 sentences in total. Table 1 shows the statistics of the resulting dataset.

The sentences were further lower-cased and all numeric tokens were converted to $\langle$NUM$\rangle$. Since frames 1, 5, 6, 7, and 13 account for more than 60% of the data, we focused on identifying these five frames; however, we also report the results based on all 15 frames, plus irrelevant category. For all classification tasks, we report 10-fold cross-validation results. For our experiments on immigration and smoking issues, in each fold, we use 30,023 sentences for training, 3,335 for validation, and 3,706 for testing.

As mentioned earlier, the majority of the articles on smoking were annotated only once and the reported inter-annotator agreement on this set is very low, therefore, we further removed the irrelevant category and replicated the experiments on only the immigration set, where at least two annotators agreed upon. Table 1 shows the statistics of the resulting immigration dataset. On this set, in each fold, we use 21,980 sentences for training, 2,442 for validation, and 2,713 for testing.

5   Methods

Here, we present our deep learning–based methods for frame classification. Treating a frame as a sequence of tokens, we explore the use of long short-term memories (Hochreiter and Schmidhuber, 1997) and bi-directional LSTMs (Graves et al., 2013) (BLSTMs), and gated recurrent units (GRU) (Cho et al., 2014) to model the frames. LSTMs and gated recurrent units are types of recurrent neural network that were designed to deal with long-term dependencies, and have been used effectively in the literature to represent long sequences.

To represent the frames, we use word embeddings of the sentences as an input of the model,

followed by a single regular LSTM layer, and a sigmoid output layer for multi-class classification.[3] We decided to use a sigmoid function for the output layer because some sentences in our data are assigned multiple labels. We further replace the sigmoid function with a softmax function in the output layer for comparison. We have two settings for initializing our word representations: (1) publicly available GloVe pre-trained word embeddings[4] (Pennington et al., 2014) (300-dimensional vectors trained on Common Crawl data), and (2) embeddings that are constructed on the fly by the LSTM (without any pre-trained word embeddings; we use dropout of 0.2). [5]

We further explore the use of bi-directional LSTMs to represent frame sentences. A bi-directional LSTM consists of two LSTMs running on the input sequence as well as the reverse of the input sequence, thereby allowing the hidden state to capture past and future information (Graves et al., 2013). The motivation behind using this model is to allow the recurrent neural networks to decide what sentence context is important for the classification. The input layer relies on the word embeddings that we mentioned above. We took two approaches to use the pre-trained embeddings: we allowed the embedding weights to be updated during the training (with dropout of 0.2), and we also prevented the embeddings from being updated. The output of the bi-directional LSTM layer (similar to the experiments with the LSTM model and GRU model) was passed to a dropout layer (Hinton et al., 2012) with a rate of 0.2-0.5 to avoid over-fitting, and then to a sigmoid layer to predict the class label of the input sentence. Similar to the experiment with the LSTM model, we replaced the sigmoid layer with a softmax layer for comparison. We further use gated recurrent units, which have shown to improve the performance of recurrent neural networks. All models (LSTM, BLSTM, and GRU) were trained with categorical cross-entropy with the Adam optimizer (Kingma and Ba, 2014) for 5 epochs. We experiment with 128 units for all models and restrict the vocabulary to 10,000 most frequent words (for the BLSTM model, we also used

---

[2] Using NLTK (Bird et al., 2009).

[3] Using https://keras.io/

[4] http://nlp.stanford.edu/projects/glove/

[5] We further used publicly available word2vec pre-trained word embeddings (Mikolov et al., 2013) (300-dimensional vectors trained on the Google News corpus), but achieved similar results.

Table 2: The performance of different models for classification of 5 frames on both immigration and smoking (10-fold cross-validation).

Model		Accuracy (%)
Majority Class (frame 5)		25.4
Uni-, bi-grams (tf-idf)		54.2
LDA 20-topics		53.3
LDA 50-topics		53.9
LDA 100-topics		53.2
Sum of vectors, pre-trained GloVe		60.2
fastText		62.0
LSTM (128 units) no pre-trained embeddings	10K	64.5
LSTM (128 units) GloVe	10K	66.7
LSTM (128 units) pre-trained GloVe	10K	67.5
BLSTM (128 units) no pre-trained embeddings	10K	64.6
BLSTM (128 units) GloVe	10K	66.8
BLSTM (128 units) pre-trained GloVe	10K	67.8
GRU (128 units) GloVe	10K	68.1
GRU (128 units) pre-trained GloVe	10K	**68.7**

Table 3: The performance of different models for 16-way classification (15 frames plus the irrelevant category) (10-fold cross-validation); B(LSTM) and GRU models use pre-trained GloVe embeddings

Model		Accuracy (%)
Majority Class (frame 5)		15.3
uni-, bi-grams (tf-idf)		38.7
50-topics		36.8
Sum of vectors, word2vec		43.2
Sum of vectors, GloVe		43.2
fastText		48.5
LSTM (128 units)	10K	52.1
BLSTM (128 units)	10K	52.5
GRU (128 units)	10K	**53.7**

Table 4: Confusion matrix for GRU with GloVe (5 classes) specified with frame number

		Predicted				
		1	5	6	7	13
	1	**441**	32	28	31	35
Actual	5	30	**705**	74	159	58
	6	57	149	**268**	55	109
	7	26	78	48	**558**	33
	13	40	40	58	27	**603**

the full vocabulary, but achieved a similar performance).

The baselines that we use are majority class and a random forest classifier[6] with 90 trees trained with bag-of-words representations of the sentences. We use both unigrams and bigrams, weighted using *tf-idf*. We further experiment with 20, 50, 100 topic features derived from the Gibbs-LDA++[7] implementation of Latent Dirichlet Allocation (LDA) (Blei et al., 2003). To represent the sentences with the topics, standard English stopwords were removed, and then tokens were lemmatized to their base form. To estimate the parameters, we used $\alpha = \frac{50}{K}$ (K= number of topics) and $\beta = 0.001$, and ran 1,000 Gibbs sampling itera-

tions and estimated the model at every 100 iterations.

Further, we trained a random forest classifier with sentence vectors obtained by summing the pre-trained word embeddings.

Additionally, we used the fastText (Joulin et al., 2016) classifier based on the skip-gram model, where each word is represented as a bag of character n-grams and the classification is performed through a hierarchical softmax.

6 Results and Discussion

Multi-class Classification All classification results are reported in terms of accuracy. Tables 2 and 3 present the frame detection results for the sets of 5 and 15 frames, plus irrelevant category (sixteen-way classification) respectively on both immigration and smoking issues. The models specified with *"pre-trained"* do not update the embeddings during the training process, whereas the others do update them. All the models reported here used 500 maximum string length with

---

[6]Using scikit-learn (Pedregosa et al., 2011).

[7]http://gibbslda.sourceforge.net/

Table 5: The performance of different models for classification of 5 frames on only immigration (10-fold cross-validation).

Model		Accuracy (%)	F_1(%)
Majority Class (frame 13)		24.1	–
Uni-, bi-grams (tf-idf)		64.8	62.4
LSTM (128 units) GloVe	10K	70.5	69.9
LSTM (128 units) pre-trained GloVe	10K	70.5	70.2
BLSTM (128 units) GloVe	10K	70.0	69.7
BLSTM (128 units) pre-trained GloVe	10K	70.2	69.8
GRU (128 units) GloVe	10K	70.2	69.7
GRU (128 units) pre-trained GloVe	10K	**71.2**	**70.7**

Table 6: The performance of different models for 15-way classification on immigration set (10-fold cross-validation)

Model	Accuracy (%)	F_1 (%)
Majority Class (frame 13)	15.7	–
uni-, bi-grams (tf-idf)	49.7	44.5
LSTM (128 units)	57.7	56.0
BLSTM (128 units)	57.4	56.0
GRU (128 units)	**58.7**	**57.1**

Table 7: The performance of one-against the others classification achieved by GRU model on immigration set (10-fold cross-validation)

Frame	Accuracy	F_1	Majority class
1	**92.5**	**92.2**	85.3
5	**84.3**	**83.8**	76.0
6	84.9	82.6	84.6
7	**89.9**	**89.6**	78.2
13	**89.3**	**89.3**	75.9

mini-batches of 50 (we also experimented with smaller string length and mini-batches; however, the models achieved lower accuracies). On the combined set, the best accuracy (68.7%) was obtained by the GRU model using 300-dimension GloVe word vectors without being updated, 500 maximum string length with mini-batches of 50. This was slightly better than the results of uni-directional LSTM and bi-directional LSTM models, which achieve similar performance. We did not observe any performance improvement for the models when the word embeddings were updated. The models achieved very similar results with sigmoid and softmax functions. None of the models that learned the embeddings on the fly outperformed their counterparts initialized with GloVe embeddings, this shows that the semantics that are captured in word embeddings are useful for representing frames. The LSTM, BLSTM, and GRU models all outperformed the baseline random forest classifier with sentence vectors obtained by summing the pre-trained word-embeddings, this shows that this baseline classifier cannot learn the sentence representation of frames.

Using the full vocabulary (about 30,000) did not impact the performance of the BLSTM model with GloVe embeddings. All LSTM, BLSTM, and GRU models yielded at least a 10-point improvement over the random forest classifier trained with topics. A confusion matrix for the best-performing GRU model is shown in Table 4. The *policy prescription and evaluation* frame is often misclassified as the *legality, constitutionality, and jurisprudence* frame, which can be expected, as these frames are more likely to have overlapping expressions.

Tables 5 and 6 present the frame detection results for the sets of 5 and 15 frames on immigration corpus respectively. LSTM and BLSTM models perform similarly on the immigration set as well. The best performance (71.2%) is achieved again by GRU model, which is about 6-point above the bag-of-words baseline.

One-against-others Classification We wanted to see how different frames were effected by the model, so we performed a one-against-others classification, where each frame is tested against the rest of frames in the corpus. Table 7 presents the results. We only considered the five most frequent frames. The *political* and *crime and punishment* frames are recognized better than the other frames. While the training set for frame *economic* is smaller than the training set for *legality* frame, *economic* frame was detected more accurately. This is probably due to the unambiguous cues and phrases regarding monetary and financial expressions, such as *dollars* and *middle class* that are associated with this frame. The most ambiguous frame is *policy prescription and evaluation*.

7 Conclusion

In this study, we motivated the importance of recognizing generic frames at the sentence level in news articles. In order to represent frames effectively, we employed recurrent neural net models. We showed that our approach achieved better performance compared to classifiers trained with topics and other strong baseline models. There are several potential directions for future work. First, we could study the interaction between the primary frame and the frames at the sentence level found in the article. Another interesting direction is to apply our model to other genre of discourse.

Acknowledgments

We are grateful to Suzanne Stevenson and Frank Rudzicz for helpful comments. This research is financially supported by Natural Sciences and Engineering Research Council of Canada.

References

Eric Baumer, Elisha Elovic, Ying Qin, Francesca Polletta, and Geri Gay. 2015. Testing and comparing computational approaches for identifying the language of framing in political news. In *Proceedings of the 2015 Conference of the North American Chapter of the Association for Computational Linguistics: Human Language Technologies*. Association for Computational Linguistics, Denver, Colorado, pages 1472–1482.

Steven Bird, Ewan Klein, and Edward Loper. 2009. *Natural language processing with Python*. O'Reilly Media, Inc.

David M. Blei, Andrew Y. Ng, and Michael I. Jordan. 2003. Latent dirichlet allocation. *Journal of machine Learning research* 3(Jan):993–1022.

Filip Boltužić and Jan Šnajder. 2014. Back up your stance: Recognizing arguments in online discussions. In *Proceedings of the First Workshop on Argumentation Mining*. pages 49–58.

Filip Boltužić and Jan Šnajder. 2015. Identifying prominent arguments in online debates using semantic textual similarity. In *Proceedings of the 2nd Workshop on Argumentation Mining*. Association for Computational Linguistics, Denver, CO, pages 110–115.

Dallas Card, Amber E. Boydstun, Justin H. Gross, Philip Resnik, and Noah A. Smith. 2015. The Media Frames Corpus: Annotations of frames across issues. In *Proceedings of the 53rd Annual Meeting of the Association for Computational Linguistics and the 7th International Joint Conference on Natural Language Processing*. volume 2, pages 438–444.

Dallas Card, Justin Gross, Amber Boydstun, and Noah A. Smith. 2016. Analyzing framing through the casts of characters in the news. In *Proceedings of the 2016 Conference on Empirical Methods in Natural Language Processing*. Association for Computational Linguistics, Austin, Texas, pages 1410–1420.

KyungHyun Cho, Bart van Merrienboer, Dzmitry Bahdanau, and Yoshua Bengio. 2014. On the properties of neural machine translation: Encoder-decoder approaches. *arXiv preprint arXiv:1409.1259, .*

Dennis Chong and James N. Druckman. 2007. Framing theory. *Annual Review of Political Science* 10.

Claes H. De Vreese. 2005. News framing: Theory and typology. *Information Design Journal + Document Design* 13(1):51–62.

Robert M. Entman. 1993. Framing: Toward clarification of a fractured paradigm. *Journal of Communication* 43(4):51–58.

Alex Graves, Navdeep Jaitly, and Abdel-rahman Mohamed. 2013. Hybrid speech recognition with deep bidirectional LSTM. In *Automatic Speech Recognition and Understanding (ASRU), 2013 IEEE Workshop on*. IEEE, pages 273–278.

Kazi Saidul Hasan and Vincent Ng. 2014. Why are you taking this stance? Identifying and classifying reasons in ideological debates. In *Proceedings of the 2014 Conference on Empirical Methods in Natural Language Processing (EMNLP)*. Association for Computational Linguistics, Doha, Qatar, pages 751–762.

Geoffrey E. Hinton, Nitish Srivastava, Alex Krizhevsky, Ilya Sutskever, and Ruslan R. Salakhutdinov. 2012. Improving neural networks by preventing co-adaptation of feature detectors. *arXiv preprint arXiv:1207.0580 .*

Sepp Hochreiter and Jürgen Schmidhuber. 1997. Long short-term memory. *Neural computation* 9(8):1735–1780.

Armand Joulin, Edouard Grave, Piotr Bojanowski, and Tomas Mikolov. 2016. Bag of tricks for efficient text classification. *arXiv preprint arXiv:1607.01759 .*

Diederik Kingma and Jimmy Ba. 2014. Adam: A method for stochastic optimization. *arXiv preprint arXiv:1412.6980 .*

Tomas Mikolov, Kai Chen, Greg Corrado, and Jeffrey Dean. 2013. Efficient estimation of word representations in vector space. *arXiv preprint arXiv:1301.3781 .*

Amita Misra, Pranav Anand, Jean E. Fox Tree, and
Marilyn A. Walker. 2015. Using summarization to
discover argument facets in online idealogical [sic]
dialog. In *NAACL HLT 2015, The 2015 Conference of the North American Chapter of the Association for Computational Linguistics: Human Language Technologies, Denver, Colorado, USA, May
31 - June 5, 2015*. pages 430–440.

Nona Naderi and Graeme Hirst. 2016. Argumentation mining in parliamentary discourse. In Matteo Baldoni et al., editor, *Principles and Practice
of Multi-Agent Systems*, Springer International Publishing, pages 16–25.

Viet-An Nguyen, Jordan Boyd-Graber, Philip Resnik,
and Kristina Miler. 2015. Tea Party in the house: A
hierarchical ideal point topic model and its application to Republican legislators in the 112th Congress.
In *Proceedings of the 53rd Annual Meeting of the
Association for Computational Linguistics and the
7th International Joint Conference on Natural Language Processing (Volume 1: Long Papers)*. Association for Computational Linguistics, pages 1438–
1448.

F. Pedregosa, G. Varoquaux, A. Gramfort, V. Michel,
B. Thirion, O. Grisel, M. Blondel, P. Prettenhofer, R. Weiss, V. Dubourg, J. Vanderplas, A. Passos, D. Cournapeau, M. Brucher, M. Perrot, and
E. Duchesnay. 2011. Scikit-learn: Machine learning
in Python. *Journal of Machine Learning Research*
12:2825–2830.

Jeffrey Pennington, Richard Socher, and Christopher D. Manning. 2014. GloVe: Global vectors for
word representation. In *Empirical Methods in Natural Language Processing (EMNLP)*. pages 1532–
1543.

Oren Tsur, Dan Calacci, and David Lazer. 2015. A
frame of mind: Using statistical models for detection
of framing and agenda setting campaigns. In *Proceedings of the 53rd Annual Meeting of the Association for Computational Linguistics and the 7th International Joint Conference on Natural Language
Processing (Volume 1: Long Papers)*. Association
for Computational Linguistics, pages 1629–1638.

Robust Tuning Datasets for Statistical Machine Translation

Preslav Nakov and **Stephan Vogel**
ALT Research Group
Qatar Computing Research Institute, HBKU
{pnakov, svogel}@hbku.edu.qa

Abstract

We explore the idea of automatically crafting a tuning dataset for Statistical Machine Translation (SMT) that makes the hyperparameters of the SMT system more robust with respect to some specific deficiencies of the parameter tuning algorithms. This is an under-explored research direction, which can allow better parameter tuning. In this paper, we achieve this goal by selecting a subset of the available sentence pairs, which are more suitable for specific combinations of optimizers, objective functions, and evaluation measures. We demonstrate the potential of the idea with the pairwise ranking optimization (PRO) optimizer, which is known to yield too short translations. We show that the learning problem can be alleviated by tuning on a subset of the development set, selected based on sentence length. In particular, using the longest 50% of the tuning sentences, we achieve two-fold tuning speedup, and improvements in BLEU score that rival those of alternatives, which fix BLEU+1's smoothing instead.

1 Introduction

Modern Statistical Machine Translation (SMT) systems have several, somewhat independent, components that work together to generate a good translation, and are typically combined in a log-linear framework, where the language model, the translation model, the reordering model, etc., contribute to the hypothesis score with different weights. It is now standard to learn these weights discriminatively, from a development dataset, e.g., by optimizing BLEU (Papineni et al., 2002) or some other measure directly.

A tuned system can often yield very significant improvements in terms of translation quality compared to a system that uses standard, untuned default parameters. Thus, a lot of research attention in SMT has been devoted to designing different algorithms for parameter optimization. For years, it was typical to use minimum error rate training, or MERT (Och, 2003), which works quite well when the number of parameters is small. As the number of parameters has grown, rivaling optimizers such as MIRA (Watanabe et al., 2007; Chiang et al., 2008) and PRO (Hopkins and May, 2011) have been developed, as well as various variations thereof (Bazrafshan et al., 2012; Cherry and Foster, 2012; Gimpel and Smith, 2012).

These optimization algorithms have focused on learning from a given fixed dataset, relying on the standard machine learning assumption that the training and the development data come from the same distribution as the test data, e.g., in terms of domain, coverage, genre, length, etc. In practical terms, this is especially important for the development/tuning data, but with standard datasets, there is often no way to guarantee this, and many researchers have determined empirically the most suitable tuning dataset by observing the translation score on the test dataset. Yet, the choice of tuning dataset can considerably affect the results; for example, Zheng et al. (2010) report variation across different standard NIST tuning MTxx datasets of over six BLEU points for Chinese-English SMT when testing on the NIST MT08 test dataset.

Given a *reasonable* tuning set, i.e., one that is really coming from the same distribution as the test dataset, a *good* optimization algorithm should be able to learn to produce optimal weights. Yet, the choice of optimization objective can yield dramatically different translations since different algorithms might need to stress some aspects of the tuning dataset and downplay others.

Proceedings of Recent Advances in Natural Language Processing, pages 543–550,
Varna, Bulgaria, Sep 4–6 2017.

One reason for this is that different optimizers interact differently with different objectives. For example, we have previously shown that sentence-level optimizers yield too short translations when optimizing BLEU+1 (Nakov et al., 2012).

In this paper, we advocate the idea of automatically crafting a tuning dataset that makes tuning parameters *less* susceptible to the deficiencies of the learning algorithms. More specifically, in order to bridge this gap, we propose to customize the tuning dataset by selecting a subset of the available sentence pairs, taking into account the target domain and the peculiarities of the optimization algorithm, objective function, and evaluation measure used. This is important because it brings us a step closer to robust learning, instead of simply overfitting the tuning dataset.

Below, we focus specifically on sentence length as a selection criteria. We chose length because it can have consequences on how translations are scored w.r.t. to metrics like BLEU, and besides, it is a known issue for PRO. Still, to the best of our knowledge, the interaction between the optimizer, the optimization objective, the evaluation measure, and the development dataset has been largely neglected so far. For instance, we show that the problem of short translations when tuning with PRO (Hopkins and May, 2011) is worsened when tuning on short sentence pairs, and alleviated when emphasizing the longer tuning sentences.

Tuning set crafting can be done in various ways, e.g., by removing examples with suboptimal characteristics (e.g., short sentences) or by oversampling the ones with desired characteristics (e.g., longer sentences). Here we focus on selection from a single tuning set because it is applicable to different datasets. We show that significant performance gains are possible with PRO when selecting just a subset of the tuning dataset based on length. Our objective here is to draw the attention of the research community to the possibilities that dataset customization through subset selection can offer for different experimental conditions. We believe that this is a very promising, yet largely underexplored research direction.

Naturally, one could also try to select data from elsewhere and build a completely custom dataset, e.g., by selecting sentences from the training dataset. However, this is not possible in case of multiple references (the training bi-text has only one reference).

One could also try to select/fuse from different available tuning datasets, but it is rare to have multiple tuning datasets.

It has also been observed that having multiple references in the tuning dataset can yield more accurate parameter estimates and thus better test translation scores (Madnani et al., 2008). Thus, adding a few human translations, could significantly boost translation quality. Since this is costly, some researchers have resorted to using automatically generated references, with modest performance gains.

The remainder of the paper is organized as follows: Section 2 introduces related work, Section 3 describes the method, Section 4 presents the experimental setup, Section 5 discusses the evaluation results, and Section 6 provides deeper analysis and further discussion. Finally, Section 7 concludes with possible directions for future work.

2 Related Work

Tuning the parameters of a log-linear model for SMT is an active area of research. The typical way to do this is to use minimum error rate training, or MERT, (Och, 2003), which optimizes the standard dataset-level BLEU directly.

Recently, there has been a surge in new optimization techniques for SMT. Most notably, this includes the margin-infused relaxed algorithm or MIRA (Watanabe et al., 2007; Chiang et al., 2008, 2009), which is an on-line sentence-level perceptron-like passive-aggressive optimizer, and pairwise ranking optimization or PRO (Hopkins and May, 2011), which operates in batch mode and sees tuning as ranking.

A number of improved versions thereof have been proposed including a batch version of MIRA (Cherry and Foster, 2012) and a linear regression version of PRO (Bazrafshan et al., 2012). Another recent optimizer is Rampeon (Gimpel and Smith, 2012). We refer the interested reader to three recent overviews on parameter optimization for SMT: (McAllester and Keshet, 2011; Cherry and Foster, 2012; Gimpel and Smith, 2012).

With the emergence of new optimization techniques, there have been also studies that compare stability between MIRA–MERT (Chiang et al., 2008, 2009; Cherry and Foster, 2012), PRO–MERT (Hopkins and May, 2011), MIRA–PRO–MERT (Cherry and Foster, 2012; Gimpel and Smith, 2012; Nakov et al., 2012).

More relevant to the present work, there has been some interest in analyzing how different optimizers interact with specific metrics. For example, pathological verbosity was reported when tuning MERT on recall-oriented metrics such as METEOR (Lavie and Denkowski, 2009; Denkowski and Lavie, 2011), large variance was observed with MIRA (Simianer et al., 2012), and *monsters* were found when using PRO with too long tuning sentences (Nakov et al., 2013b). In previous work, we also found that MERT learns verbosity, while PRO learns length (Guzmán et al., 2015b).

It has been also observed that having multiple references for the tuning dataset can yield better test-time translation performance (Madnani et al., 2007). Thus, adding a few extra human reference translations could significantly boost translation quality. Since this is costly, some researchers have resorted to using automatically generated references,[1] via paraphrasing (Madnani et al., 2008) and back-translation (Dyer et al., 2011), with modest performance gains.

There has been also work on tuning data selection and/or fusion in the special case when multiple versions of the source sentence are available (Nakov et al., 2013a). This is a fairly rare situation for such approaches to be broadly applicable.

Most relevant to our work, there were efforts to build tuning datasets using information retrieval (Zheng et al., 2010; Tamchyna et al., 2012), text clustering (Li et al., 2010), and sentence-length based features (Guzmán et al., 2012). To avoid data sparseness, most of these approaches require a larger pool of data, which they typically select from the training bi-text, thus reducing the amount of data available for model training. This makes such approaches inapplicable in multi-reference testset contexts since the bi-text only has one translation per source sentence. Moreover, the selection is typically done based on the actual test input, which is not known a priori in a realistic SMT setup, e.g., in online translation.

In contrast, we aim to produce customized datasets that are less susceptible to that, and are suitable for specific combinations of optimizers, objective functions, and evaluation measures. This can yield better parameter estimation, while using less data and more efficient tuning with faster iterations and a smaller computational footprint.

3 Method

Below we present one particular example of tuning dataset customization in order to illustrate the potential of the idea.

In previous work, we have shown that the PRO optimizer yields SMT parameters that yield test-time translations that are shorter than they should be. We have addressed this by changing the objective function, sentence-level BLEU+1, and we have proposed to replace it with one with better smoothing (Nakov et al., 2012). Here we propose an alternative solution, which customizes the tuning dataset by selecting a subset of higher average length.

Observe that, if the reason for PRO yielding too short translations is the add-one smoothing in BLEU+1, this should affect shorter sentences to a greater extent, since the effect of the smoothing is bigger for them. I.e., we should expect that, when tuning with PRO, the translations of short sentences should get relatively shorter translations than those of long sentences. This means that we should expect to get longer translations if we tune on longer sentences, i.e., if we customize the tuning dataset, which can be done, e.g., (*a*) by excluding some of the short sentences or (*b*) by oversampling some of the long sentences. We will explore approach (*a*) below: in particular, we will exclude half of the sentences, keeping the longest 50% only.

4 Experimental Setup

We experimented with Arabic-to-English SMT, training on the Arabic-English data that was made available for the NIST 2012 OpenMT Evaluation.[2] We used all training data except for the UN corpus, we tuned on MT06 (and subsets thereof), and we tested on MT09, which have four English reference translations.

We trained a phrase-based SMT model (Koehn et al., 2003) as implemented in the Moses toolkit (Koehn et al., 2007). We tokenized and truecased the English side of the training/development/testing bitexts, and the monolingual data for language modeling using the standard tokenizer of Moses. We segmented the words on the Arabic side of all bitexts using the MADA ATB segmentation scheme (Roth et al., 2008).

---

[1]Paraphrasing was also applied to the training bi-text (Nakov, 2008; Nakov and Ng, 2009) and to the phrase table (Callison-Burch et al., 2006).

[2]www.nist.gov/itl/iad/mig/openmt12.cfm

	Tuning	BLEU	BP
1	BP-smooth=1, grounded	47.61	0.991
2	BP-smooth=1	47.52	0.984
3	top50	**47.47**	**0.980**
4	mid50	47.44	0.977
5	rand50	47.43	0.978
6	low50	46.38	0.961
7	full	**47.18**	**0.972**

Table 1: Multi-reference PRO experiments: test-set BLEU and BP when tuning on different length-based subsets of the tuning dataset (lines 3-6). For comparison, we also show the results when tuning on the full tuning dataset (line 7), as well as what the PRO-fixes proposed in (Nakov et al., 2012) would achieve when tuning on the full dataset (lines 1-2).

We then built a phrase table using the Moses pipeline with max-phrase-length 7 and Kneser-Ney smoothing, as well as a lexicalized reordering model (Koehn et al., 2005): *msd-bidirectional-fe*. We used a 5-gram language model trained on GigaWord v.5 with Kneser-Ney smoothing using KenLM (Heafield, 2011). On tuning and testing, we dropped the unknown words.

For tuning, we used PRO. In order to avoid instabilities when tuning on long sentences, we used a slightly modified, fixed version of PRO, as we recommended in (Nakov et al., 2013b), where we limited the difference between the positive and the negative example in a training sentence pair to be no more than ten BLEU+1 points. Moreover, in order to ensure convergence, we let PRO run for up to 25 iterations (default: 16); we further used 1000-best lists in each iteration (default: 100).

In our experiments, we performed three reruns of parameter optimization, and we report BLEU averaged over the three reruns, as suggested by Clark et al. (2011) as a way to stabilize MERT. We calculated BLEU using NIST's scoring tool v.13a, in case-sensitive mode.

5 Experiments and Evaluation

In this section, we verify experimentally whether tuning on short sentences can make PRO's length issue worse and whether tuning on longer sentences could help in that respect. We further compare the effect of tuning on long sentences (i.e., of tuning dataset customization) to using better smoothing for BLEU+1 (as we have proposed in our earlier work).

	Tuning	BLEU	BP
1	BP-smooth=1, grounded	29.68	0.979
2	BP-smooth=1	29.43	0.962
3	top50	**29.51**	**0.969**
4	mid50	29.11	0.950
5	rand50	28.96	0.941
6	low50	27.44	0.894
7	full	**28.88**	**0.934**

Table 2: Single-reference PRO experiments: test-set BLEU and BP when tuning on different length-based subsets of the tuning dataset (lines 3-6). We also show the results when tuning on the full tuning dataset (line 7), as well as what the PRO-fixes proposed in (Nakov et al., 2012) would achieve when tuning on the full dataset (lines 1-2).

Lines 3-6 in Table 1 show the results when tuning on the longest (top50), middle (mid50), random (rand50) and shortest (low50) 50% of the tuning sentences. Comparing this to line 7 (tuning on the full MT06), we can see that tuning on the shortest sentences lowers the hypothesis-to-reference ratio (BP), while tuning on top50 improves it,[3] with the BP for mid50 and rand50 in between.

Lines 3-6 further show that better BP corresponds to better BLEU. We can also see that both BP and BLEU for top50 are better than those for the full MT06 tuning dataset. Despite top50 being tuned on less data, its BP and BLEU are comparable to those achieved by the BLEU+1 smoothing approaches shown in lines 1-2 (Nakov et al., 2012), which use the full tuning dataset.

Note that when calculating BP and BLEU, for the 4-reference MT06 dataset, we used the length of the reference sentence that is closest to the length of the hypothesis. This is the *effective reference length* from the original paper on BLEU (Papineni et al., 2002), and it is also the default in NIST scoring tool v13a, which we use.

Using the closest reference yields a very forgiving BP. Yet, few datasets have multiple references. Thus, we also experimented with a single (ref0) reference for both tuning and testing. The results are shown in Table 2. Comparing the corresponding lines of Tables 2 and 1, we see that in this case, the length problem is more severe and affects BLEU more. More importantly, note that the top50 customized tuning dataset is much more effective with a single reference translation.

---

[3] The ideal target value for BP is 1.

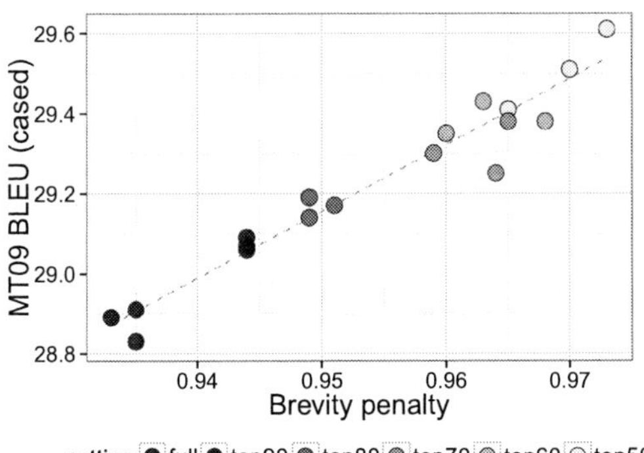

Figure 1: Single-reference PRO experiments. Correlation between cutoff, BP and BLEU score. The x-axis shows the brevity penalty (BP), and the y-axis contains the BLEU score on the testing MT09 dataset. Different colors show the different levels of cutoff. We show the results for three reruns in each setting.

6   Discussion

In this section, we perform further analysis, in order to better understand the improvements when tuning in longer sentences. We consider three aspects: (*i*) amount of training data, (*ii*) genre overlap between tuning and test datasets, and (*iii*) differences in the learned SMT parameters.

6.1   Amount of Tuning Data

In our experiments, we saw that tuning on longer sentences yields better results than tuning on shorter ones. However, one might argue that the subsets with longer sentences have access to more training data in terms of number of word tokens. In order to shed some light on this, we experimented with varying the percentage of longest sentences that we keep in decreasing order: from the full dataset (100%), we gradually removed the shortest sentences in increments of 10% until we ended up with just 50% of the data. The results are shown in Figure 1. We can see that as the cutoff increases, so does BP, which in turn yields better BLEU. This suggests that by varying the length of the tuning sentences, we can effectively control the verbosity that PRO learns. We can further conclude that it is not the amount of tuning data that matters but rather its characteristics.

6.2   Genre Overlap

MT06 is a mixture of three genres: newswire (nw), weblogs (wb) of almost equal sizes, and a much smaller size of broadcast news (bn). MT09 is also a mixture, but of two genres only: it only contains newswire and weblogs. Thus, one could ask the question of whether the observed improvements are due to better overlap between the genres of the tuning and of the testing datasests.

	bn	nw	wb	D_{KL}
MT06				
full	8%	**46%**	**46%**	3.93
low50	7%	25%	64%	7.42
mid50	9%	**46%**	41%	6.41
top50	8%	63%	26%	12.09
MT09				
full		**45%**	**55%**	

Table 3:   Distribution of genres for the different partitions of the tuning data (MT06) and the test data (MT09). While MT06 has newswire (nw), and weblogs(wb) in equal amounts (with a lower proportion of broadcast news (bn)), MT09 has slightly higher proportion of weblog data than newswire. Based on Kullback–Leibler divergence (D_{KL}), the full partition is closest to the test data, followed by the mid50 partition.

Table 3 could help answer this question; it shows the genre distribution for the different partitions of the tuning dataset. We can see that the distribution of genres in the full MT06 dataset is better than for top50, mid50, and low50, having the smallest Kullback–Leibler divergence with the test set; the mid50 partition comes second. In contrast, top50, the best-performing partition among the ones we explored, has the most divergent genre-distribution with respect to the test dataset. From this, we can conclude that the improvements in BLEU for top50 are definitely not due to better genre/domain overlap.

6.3   Better Parameters

The last question we address in this section is the following: Where exactly is the difference in translation quality coming from? I.e., are the improvements in length only the result of decrease in the word penalty or are there other parameters that are being affected? In order to answer this question, we analyzed the optimized weights (averaged over three reruns) for tuning at different cutoffs, from 100% to 50% of the longest sentences in the MT06 development dataset.

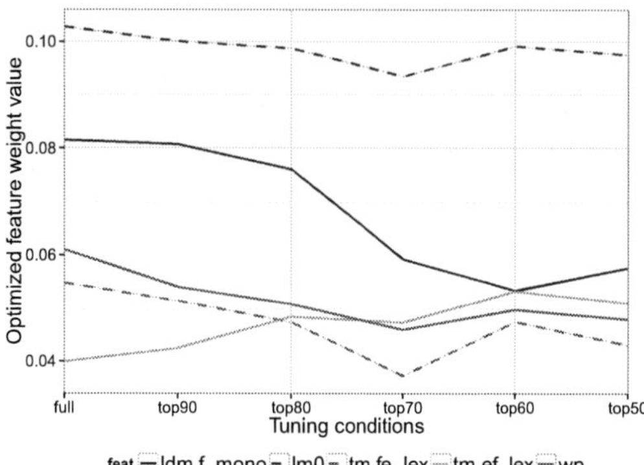

Figure 2: Optimized feature weight values for each of the different tuning settings. Only a subset out of the 14 different tuning weights that are used by the SMT model, and are thus being optimized, are shown in the figure, namely the following: monotone lexicalized reordering (ldm.f_mono), language model (lm0), reverse lexical phrase translation probabilities (tm.fe_lex), direct lexical phrase translation probabilities (tm.ef_lex), and word penalty (wp).

We selected the most important feature weights in terms of their correlation with changes in the brevity penalty (and BLEU). The results are shown in Figure 2. As expected, the average value for the word penalty weight (dark gray solid line) is reduced as we increase the average length of our tuning set. This results in lower costs for longer sentences, explaining why we have higher verbosity.

However, this is not the full picture. The monotone lexicalized reordering model (black solid line) sees significant reduction in its weight, allowing for more reordering. Furthermore, the weight for the direct lexical phrase translation (light gray line) slightly increases as we increase the length of our tuning data. This can be interpreted as increased reliance on word-to-word translations.

Thus, by changing the length of the development set, we not only affect the word penalty, but also allow for changes in other parameters, which jointly yield better translation.[4]

---

[4]To be more precise in this analysis, more careful study needs to be done using the *expected decoding cost*, i.e., multiplying the optimized weights by the mean feature values on a specific set. Nonetheless, there is no clear way to obtain such a mean feature vector without using a specific set of weights for decoding in the first place.

7 Conclusion and Future Work

We have explored the idea of customizing the tuning dataset for Statistical Machine Translation (SMT) that makes the hyper-parameters of the SMT system more robust with respect to some specific deficiencies of the parameter tuning algorithms. This is an under-explored research direction, which can allow better parameter tuning. In this paper, we achieved this goal by selecting a subset of the available sentence pairs, which are more suitable for specific combinations of optimizers, objective functions, and evaluation measures. In particular, we experimented with the pairwise ranking optimization (PRO) optimizer, which is known to yield too short translations. We have shown that the problem can be alleviated by tuning on a subset of the development dataset, selected based on sentence length. In particular, when selecting the longest 50% of the tuning sentences, we achieved two-fold tuning speedup and competitive scores in terms of BLEU, while having a more compact dataset. These results rival those of alternative solutions that we proposed in our previous work, which fix the tuning-time BLEU+1 smoothing instead. Our analysis shows that this is due to improved parameter tuning.

Overall, our goal was not just to show how one can improve PRO, but rather to draw the research attention to the more general idea of customizing a tuning set through subset selection, which can offer a number of opportunities for different experimental conditions, and more efficient training. We believe that this is a very promising research direction, which is worth exploring further.

In the future, we plan to experiment with other language pairs and translation directions, as well as with other optimizers such as MERT and MIRA (instead of PRO), and with other evaluation measures such as TER (Snover et al., 2006), METEOR (Lavie and Denkowski, 2009), and DiscoTK (Joty et al., 2014), including also pairwise measures (Guzmán et al., 2015a) (instead of BLEU). We further want to study the sensitivity of these optimizer and metric combinations with respect to length and other characteristics of the tuning dataset, which would allow us to design targeted dataset customization strategies for them.

Acknowledgements

We would like to thank the anonymous reviewers for their constructive comments.

References

Marzieh Bazrafshan, Tagyoung Chung, and Daniel Gildea. 2012. Tuning as linear regression. In *Proceedings of the 2012 Annual Conference of the North American Chapter of the Association for Computational Linguistics: Human Language Technologies*. Montréal, Canada, NAACL-HLT '12, pages 543–547.

Chris Callison-Burch, Philipp Koehn, and Miles Osborne. 2006. Improved statistical machine translation using paraphrases. In *Proceedings of the Main Conference on Human Language Technology Conference of the North American Chapter of the Association of Computational Linguistics*. New York, NY, USA, HLT-NAACL '06, pages 17–24.

Colin Cherry and George Foster. 2012. Batch tuning strategies for statistical machine translation. In *Proceedings of the 2012 Annual Conference of the North American Chapter of the Association for Computational Linguistics: Human Language Technologies*. Montréal, Canada, NAACL-HLT '12, pages 427–436.

David Chiang, Kevin Knight, and Wei Wang. 2009. 11,001 new features for statistical machine translation. In *Proceedings of the 2009 Annual Conference of the North American Chapter of the Association for Computational Linguistics: Human Language Technologies*. Boulder, Colorado, USA, NAACL-HLT '09, pages 218–226.

David Chiang, Yuval Marton, and Philip Resnik. 2008. Online large-margin training of syntactic and structural translation features. In *Proceedings of the 2008 Conference on Empirical Methods in Natural Language Processing*. Honolulu, Hawaii, USA, EMNLP '08, pages 224–233.

Jonathan H. Clark, Chris Dyer, Alon Lavie, and Noah A. Smith. 2011. Better hypothesis testing for statistical machine translation: Controlling for optimizer instability. In *Proceedings of the 49th Annual Meeting of the Association for Computational Linguistics: Human Language Technologies*. Portland, Oregon, USA, ACL '11, pages 176–181.

Michael Denkowski and Alon Lavie. 2011. Meteor-tuned phrase-based SMT: CMU French-English and Haitian-English systems for WMT 2011. Technical report, CMU-LTI-11-011, Language Technologies Institute, Carnegie Mellon University.

Chris Dyer, Kevin Gimpel, Jonathan H. Clark, and Noah A. Smith. 2011. The CMU-ARK German-English translation system. In *Proceedings of the Sixth Workshop on Statistical Machine Translation*. Edinburgh, Scotland, UK, WMT '11, pages 337–343.

Kevin Gimpel and Noah A. Smith. 2012. Structured ramp loss minimization for machine translation. In *Proceedings of the 2012 Annual Conference of the North American Chapter of the Association for Computational Linguistics: Human Language Technologies*. Montréal, Canada, NAACL-HLT '12, pages 221–231.

Francisco Guzmán, Shafiq Joty, Lluís Màrquez, and Preslav Nakov. 2015a. Pairwise neural machine translation evaluation. In *Proceedings of the 53rd Annual Meeting of the Association for Computational Linguistics and the 7th International Joint Conference on Natural Language Processing*. Beijing, China, ACL-IJCNLP '15, pages 805–814.

Francisco Guzmán, Preslav Nakov, Ahmed Thabet, and Stephan Vogel. 2012. QCRI at WMT12: Experiments in Spanish-English and German-English machine translation of news text. In *Proceedings of the Seventh Workshop on Statistical Machine Translation*. Montréal, Canada, IWSLT '12, pages 298–303.

Francisco Guzmán, Preslav Nakov, and Stephan Vogel. 2015b. Analyzing optimization for statistical machine translation: MERT learns verbosity, PRO learns length. In *Proceedings of the Nineteenth Conference on Computational Natural Language Learning*. Beijing, China, CoNLL '15, pages 62–72.

Kenneth Heafield. 2011. KenLM: Faster and smaller language model queries. In *Proceedings of the Sixth Workshop on Statistical Machine Translation*. Edinburgh, Scotland, UK, WMT '11, pages 187–197.

Mark Hopkins and Jonathan May. 2011. Tuning as ranking. In *Proceedings of the 2011 Conference on Empirical Methods in Natural Language Processing*. Edinburgh, Scotland, UK, EMNLP '11, pages 1352–1362.

Shafiq Joty, Francisco Guzmán, Lluís Màrquez, and Preslav Nakov. 2014. DiscoTK: Using discourse structure for machine translation evaluation. In *Proceedings of the Ninth Workshop on Statistical Machine Translation*. Baltimore, Maryland, USA, WMT '14, pages 402–408.

Philipp Koehn, Amittai Axelrod, Alexandra Birch Mayne, Chris Callison-Burch, Miles Osborne, and David Talbot. 2005. Edinburgh system description for the 2005 IWSLT speech translation evaluation. In *Proceedings of the International Workshop on Spoken Language Translation*. Pittsburgh, Pennsylvania, USA, IWSLT '05, pages 68–75.

Philipp Koehn, Hieu Hoang, Alexandra Birch, Chris Callison-Burch, Marcello Federico, Nicola Bertoldi, Brooke Cowan, Wade Shen, Christine Moran, Richard Zens, Chris Dyer, Ondrej Bojar, Alexandra Constantin, and Evan Herbst. 2007. Moses: Open source toolkit for statistical machine translation. In *Proceedings of the 45th Annual Meeting of the Association for Computational Linguistics*. Prague, Czech Republic, ACL '07, pages 177–180.

Philipp Koehn, Franz Josef Och, and Daniel Marcu. 2003. Statistical phrase-based translation. In *Proceedings of the 2003 Conference of the North American Chapter of the Association for Computational*

Linguistics on Human Language Technology. Edmonton, Canada, HLT-NAACL '03, pages 48–54.

Alon Lavie and Michael J. Denkowski. 2009. The METEOR metric for automatic evaluation of machine translation. *Machine Translation* 23:105–115.

Mu Li, Yinggong Zhao, Dongdong Zhang, and Ming Zhou. 2010. Adaptive development data selection for log-linear model in statistical machine translation. In *Proceedings of the 23rd International Conference on Computational Linguistics*. Beijing, China, COLING '10, pages 662–670.

Nitin Madnani, Necip Fazil Ayan, Philip Resnik, and Bonnie Dorr. 2007. Using paraphrases for parameter tuning in statistical machine translation. In *Proceedings of the Second Workshop on Statistical Machine Translation*. Prague, Czech Republic, pages 120–127.

Nitin Madnani, Philip Resnik, Bonnie J. Dorr, and Richard Schwartz. 2008. Are multiple reference translations necessary? Investigating the value of paraphrased reference translations in parameter optimization. In *Proceedings of the Eighth Conference of the Association for Machine Translation in the Americas*. Waikiki, Hawaii, AMTA '08'.

David McAllester and Joseph Keshet. 2011. Generalization bounds and consistency for latent structural probit and ramp loss. In J. Shawe-Taylor, R.S. Zemel, P. Bartlett, F.C.N. Pereira, and K.Q. Weinberger, editors, *Advances in Neural Information Processing Systems 24*. Granada, Spain, NIPS '11, pages 2205–2212.

Preslav Nakov. 2008. Improved statistical machine translation using monolingual paraphrases. In *Proceedings of the 18th European Conference on Artificial Intelligence*. Amsterdam, The Netherlands, ECAI '08, pages 338–342.

Preslav Nakov, Fahad Al Obaidli, Francisco Guzmán, and Stephan Vogel. 2013a. Parameter optimization for statistical machine translation: It pays to learn from hard examples. In *Proceedings of the International Conference Recent Advances in Natural Language Processing*. Hissar, Bulgaria, RANLP '13, pages 504–510.

Preslav Nakov, Francisco Guzmán, and Stephan Vogel. 2012. Optimizing for sentence-level BLEU+1 yields short translations. In *Proceedings of the 24th International Conference on Computational Linguistics*. Mumbai, India, COLING '12, pages 1979–1994.

Preslav Nakov, Francisco Guzmán, and Stephan Vogel. 2013b. A tale about PRO and monsters. In *Proceedings of the 51st Annual Meeting of the Association for Computational Linguistics*. Sofia, Bulgaria, ACL '13, pages 12–17.

Preslav Nakov and Hwee Tou Ng. 2009. Improved statistical machine translation for resource-poor languages using related resource-rich languages. In *Proceedings of the 2009 Conference on Empirical Methods in Natural Language Processing*. Singapore, EMNLP '09, pages 1358–1367.

Franz Josef Och. 2003. Minimum error rate training in statistical machine translation. In *Proceedings of the 41st Annual Meeting on Association for Computational Linguistics*. Sapporo, Japan, ACL '03, pages 160–167.

Kishore Papineni, Salim Roukos, Todd Ward, and Wei-Jing Zhu. 2002. BLEU: a method for automatic evaluation of machine translation. In *Proceedings of the 40th Annual Meeting of the Association for Computational Linguistics*. Philadelphia, Pennsylvania, USA, ACL '02, pages 311–318.

Ryan Roth, Owen Rambow, Nizar Habash, Mona Diab, and Cynthia Rudin. 2008. Arabic morphological tagging, diacritization, and lemmatization using lexeme models and feature ranking. In *Proceedings of the 46th Annual Meeting of the Association for Computational Linguistics: Human Language Technologies*. Columbus, OH, USA, ACL '08, pages 117–120.

Patrick Simianer, Stefan Riezler, and Chris Dyer. 2012. Joint feature selection in distributed stochastic learning for large-scale discriminative training in SMT. In *Proceedings of the 50th Annual Meeting of the Association for Computational Linguistics*. Jeju Island, Korea, ACL '12, pages 11–21.

Matthew Snover, Bonnie Dorr, Richard Schwartz, Linnea Micciulla, and John Makhoul. 2006. A study of translation edit rate with targeted human annotation. In *Proceedings of the Conference of the Association for Machine Translation in the Americas*. Cambridge, Massachusetts, USA, AMTA '06, pages 223–231.

Aleš Tamchyna, Petra Galuščáková, Amir Kamran, Miloš Stanojević, and Ondej Bojar. 2012. Selecting data for English-to-Czech machine translation. In *Proceedings of the Workshop on Statistical Machine Translation*. Montréal, Canada, WMT '12, pages 374–381.

Taro Watanabe, Jun Suzuki, Hajime Tsukada, and Hideki Isozaki. 2007. Online large-margin training for statistical machine translation. In *Proceedings of the 2007 Joint Conference on Empirical Methods in Natural Language Processing and Computational Natural Language Learning*. Prague, Czech Republic, EMNLP-CoNLL '07, pages 764–773.

Zhongguang Zheng, Zhongjun He, Yao Meng, and Hao Yu. 2010. Domain adaptation for statistical machine translation in development corpus selection. In *Proceedings of the 4th International Universal Communication Symposium*. Beijing, China, IUCS '10, pages 2–7.

Do Not Trust the Trolls:
Predicting Credibility in Community Question Answering Forums

Preslav Nakov[1], Tsvetomila Mihaylova[2], Lluís Màrquez[1], Yashkumar Shiroya[3] and Ivan Koychev[2]

[1]Qatar Computing Research Institute, HBKU, Doha, Qatar
`{pnakov, lmarquez}@qf.org.qa`
[2]Faculty of Mathematics and Informatics, Sofia University "St. Kliment Ohridski", Sofia, Bulgaria
`tsvetomila.mihaylova@gmail.com, koychev@fmi.uni-sofia.bg`
[3]Purdue University, United States
`yshiroya@purdue.edu`

Abstract

We address information credibility in community forums, in a setting in which the credibility of an answer posted in a question thread by a particular user has to be predicted. First, we motivate the problem and we create a publicly available annotated English corpus by crowdsourcing. Second, we propose a large set of features to predict the credibility of the answers. The features model the user, the answer, the question, the thread as a whole, and the interaction between them. Our experiments with ranking SVMs show that the credibility labels can be predicted with high performance according to several standard IR ranking metrics, thus supporting the potential usage of this layer of credibility information in practical applications. The features modeling the profile of the user (in particular *trollness*) turn out to be most important, but embedding features modeling the answer and the similarity between the question and the answer are also very relevant. Overall, half of the gap between the baseline performance and the perfect classifier can be covered using the proposed features.

1 Introduction

Community Question Answering (cQA) forums, such as StackOverflow, Yahoo! Answers and Quora are very popular these days, as they represent effective means for communities of users around particular topics to share information and to collectively solve their information needs. Recent research in natural language processing (NLP) and information retrieval (IR) has focused on automatically finding good answers to newly posed questions using preexisting question-answer threads. This typically requires finding related questions in the forum and ranking the answers according to their goodness for a particular question.

This is precisely the setting of the tasks on Community Question Answering at SemEval 2015 and 2016 (Nakov et al., 2015, 2016). These challenges provide benchmark datasets for the above tasks, with one subtask being specifically about classifying the answers in a question–answer thread as *good* or *bad* answers.

Here, we explore a new dimension in the context of cQA—that of the *credibility* of the answers for a particular question. This aspect is ignored, e.g., in recent cQA tasks at SemEval (Nakov et al., 2015, 2016), where the definition of a *Good* answer is very shallow: an answer is considered *Good* if it tries to answer the question, irrespective of its veracity, accuracy, etc. Figure 1 presents an excerpt of a real example from the Qatar Living forum, with one question and three answers selected from a longer thread. In the above SemEval tasks, all three answers are considered *Good* since they are formally answering the question. However, a_1 contains false information, while a_2 and a_3 are correct. In this case, the credibility of the latter two answers can be inferred from the fact that the "6 months" answer appears many times in the thread.

There are multiple factors explaining the presence of non-credible answers in cQA forums, e.g., misunderstanding of the question, ignorance or maliciousness of the responder, etc. In many cases, the forums are barely moderated and there is no quality control established. The interactions and discussions among the users are usually the means to filter out incorrect or inaccurate answers.

We believe that the *credibility* dimension of an answer is complementary to its *goodness*, i.e., as

Proceedings of Recent Advances in Natural Language Processing, pages 551–560,
Varna, Bulgaria, Sep 4–6 2017.

Q: "I HAVE HEARD ITS NOT POSSIBLE TO EXTEND VISIT VISA MORE THAN 6 MONTHS? CAN U PLEASE ANSWER ME.. THANKZZZ..."

a_1: "Maximum period is 9 Months...."

a_2: "6 months maximum"

a_3: "This has been anwered in QL so many times. Please do search for information regarding this. BTW answer is 6 months." ·

Figure 1: Example from the Qatar Living forum.

a_1 above shows, an answer can be formally *Good*, but it could contain false information. Combining automatic detection of credibility and goodness would offer better experience to the users of cQA systems, e.g., a possible application scenario would be that in which the user is presented with a ranking of all good answers accompanied by credibility scores, where low scores would warn the user not to completely trust the answer or to double-check it.

Below we start by defining the credibility problem in cQA, and by creating an annotated corpus with data from the Qatar Living forum, extending the current annotation from SemEval-2016 Task 3. We specialize the former *Good* label into *Good-Credible* and *Good-NonCredible*, keeping the *Bad* answers unchanged.[1] We then develop a large variety of features to identify non-credible answers. Finally, we train ranking SVMs and we show that they can learn to rank the non-credible answers with performance that is significantly higher than the baselines and quite close to the theoretical upper bound, on a variety of standard IR measures.

Overall, the main contributions of this paper are threefold: (*i*) First, we look at credibility in cQA as a problem on its own right, and we create a new dataset that we release to the research community. To the best of our knowledge, this is the first publicly available dataset specifically targeting credibility in a cQA setting. (*ii*) We experiment with a large variety of features for the problem, some of which have not been compared in

such a configuration before. Our features target the answer, the question, the thread as a whole, and the interaction between them. We show that the most relevant feature types are the user profile (e.g., *trollness* features) text embeddings and the similarity between the answer and the full answer-thread. (*iii*) We show that ranking-based SVMs can learn to rank non-credible answers with good performance. This supports our idea that modeling credibility on its own right can help cQA systems to refine a search that is based on more shallow answer-quality criteria (as the *goodness* from the cQA tasks at SemEval).

2   Related Work

In the context of cQA and general Question Answering (QA), credibility has not been studied on its own right, but rather as a feature to improve good answer identification. Thus, it is typically modeled at the feature level, e.g., Jurczyk and Agichtein (2007) model author authority using link analysis. Similarly, Agichtein et al. (2008) look for high-quality answers in *Yahoo! Answers* by modeling author authority with PageRank and HITS, in addition to other information sources such as intrinsic content quality (e.g., punctuation and typos, syntactic and semantic complexity, and grammaticality), and usage analysis (e.g., number of clicks and dwell time). Su et al. (2010) use verbs and adjectives that cast doubt on an answer, e.g., *doubt, possibly*. Lita et al. (2005) study three qualitative dimensions for answers: source credibility (e.g., does the document come from a government website), sentiment analysis, and potential contradiction compared to other answers. Banerjee and Han (2009) use language modeling for answer validation for QA, which quantifies the reliability of a source document that contains a candidate answer. Jeon et al. (2006) use non-textual features such as click counts, answers activity level, and copy counts. Finally, Pelleg et al. (2016) present a large-scale user study of automatically curating social media content in real time using a combination of syntactic, semantic, and social signals. Unlike this line of research, here we (*i*) study credibility as a task in its own right, (*ii*) using a specialized dataset, and (*iii*) a much richer feature set. As mentioned above, we assume a setting in which credibility is a complementary aspect to answer quality, which can be useful for users in practical application scenarios.

---

[1] *Bad* answers should be ranked lower than *Good* ones in any reasonable scenario; they probably should not be presented to the user at all. Thus, it does not make sense to further try to distinguish between credible and non-credible *Bad* answers.

Information credibility has been also studied in the area of social computing. For instance, Castillo et al. (2011) formulate it as a problem of finding false information about a newsworthy event. They compiled their own dataset, focusing on tweets using variety of features including user reputation, author writing style, and various time-based features. We use some of the features they have proposed; yet, their work is not about QA or cQA. Canini et al. (2011) perform a similar study of the interaction of content and social network structure, and Morris et al. (2012) look into how Twitter users judge truthfulness.

Rumor detection in social media represents yet another angle of information credibility. Zubiaga et al. (2015) studied how people handle rumors in social media, and found that users with higher reputation are more trusted, and thus can spread rumors easily. Zubiaga et al. (2016) also studied the spread of rumors in social media but with focus on conversational threads. Lukasik et al. (2015) and Ma et al. (2015) use temporal patterns of rumor dynamics to detect rumors and to predict their frequency. The interested reader can also see (Zaharia et al., 2010) for a review of methods to detect fake news, including linguistic analysis, discourse, linked data, and social network features.

Finally, there is a recent survey on the assessment and ranking methodologies for user-generated content on the Web, which covers credibility and related topics (Momeni et al., 2015). Several truth discovery algorithms are studied and combined in an ensemble method for veracity estimation in the VERA system (Ba et al., 2016).

3 A New Credibility Corpus

We annotated with credibility judgments data from the Qatar Living forum,[2] using questions from the raw unlabeled data that the organizers of SemEval-2016 Task 3 made available,[3] while preserving the original format with all available metadata. This data is organized into question-answer threads, where each question has a subject, a body, and meta information: ID, category (e.g., *Computers and Internet*, *Education*, and *Moving to Qatar*), date and time of posting, and user name and ID.

Following the setup of SemEval-2016 Task 3, we selected new questions with at least ten answers. Each answer has a subject, a body, and meta information: answer ID, user ID, and user name. We annotated the first ten answers in a thread with two labels: (*i*) goodness (*Good* vs. *Bad*), i.e., whether this answer tries to answer the question, and (*ii*) credibility (*Credible* vs. *Non-Credible*), i.e., whether the answer is credible.

For the *goodness* labels we stick to the definition from SemEval-2016 Task 3, which is agnostic with respect to answer's credibility or veracity: an answer is considered *Good* if "the answer or a portion of it directly answers at least one subquestion of the target question".[4] Regarding *credibility*, we define an answer *Credible* if "the information in the question's thread and/or world knowledge and/or our common sense tells us that the answer is (somewhat) credible". Otherwise, we consider it *NonCredible*.

We used CrowdFlower[5] to obtain five annotations per example. In order to stress the difference between *goodness* and *credibility*, we adopted a three-label annotation schema: *Good-Credible*, *Good-NonCredible*, and *Bad*. In this way, we made sure that the annotators did not confuse credibility and goodness. We annotated a total of 476 questions and 4,760 answers; we further used 24 questions and 240 answers as hidden tests to ensure quality[6]. The inter-annotator agreement in terms of Fleiss' Kappa (Fleiss, 1971) was 0.6245, which corresponds to substantial agreement (Landis and Koch, 1977)

Finally, we converted the 3-way annotations into (*i*) goodness and (*ii*) credibility labels. For goodness, if there were three or more out of five votes for *Bad*, we assigned *Bad*; otherwise, we assigned *Good*. For those examples that were labeled *Good*, we further assigned a credibility label as follows: we set the value to *NonCredible* if at least two annotators assigned *Good-NonCredible*; otherwise, we assigned *Credible*. The rationale here is that since in our application scenario we do not envision to use the credibility information to filter out non-credible answers but to provide extra information to the user, we are interested in characterizing any answer that has a reasonable

---

[2] http://www.qatarliving.com/forum

[3] http://alt.qcri.org/semeval2016/task3/

[4] Questions in the Qatar Living forums can present long stories with multiple embedded subquestions.

[5] CrowdFlower offers a service which allows users to access an online workforce to clean, label and enrich data: https://www.crowdflower.com/

[6] CrowdFlower allows importing of gold-label examples in order to verify that the crowd-annotated labels are of good quality

	Ques-	Good Answers		Bad
	tions	*Credible*	*NonCredible*	**answ.**
TRAIN	376	1,733	73	1,954
DEV	50	137	15	348
TEST	50	213	19	268

Table 1: Statistics about our credibility datasets.

Q: "I need to renew my passport very soon but the Qatari visa stamped on it will expire in 2008. I wonder, what happens to the visa when I get a new passport? Do they need to duplicate it on the new passport or can I just carry old and new passport together when traveling? Does anyone know?"

a_1: "It did happen to me.. but I honestly dont remeber what I did... well I'm not sure I think you keep your old passport with you, for the time being. thats it.. u still need to check on this. You could pop this question to the embassy.. I'm sure the'll help." *NonCredible*

a_2: "They will ussually clip the old and new passport together, that haapened to me when i have to get a new passport coz my old one is full, so everytime i travel my old and new passport are cliped together..." *Credible*

a_3: "You will have to get a new visa stamped on teh new passport. You cannot use your old passport." *Credible*

Figure 2: Example for answers annotated as *Credible* and *NonCredible* from the Qatar Living forum.

chance to be non-credible.[7] We selected randomly 50 questions for dev and for test and used their answers as examples for the classification. The answers of the remaining questions are used for training. Table 1 shows some statistics about the resulting credibility datasets [8] and Figure3 shows an example of credible and non-credible answers.

4 Features

Below we describe the types of features we use.

4.1 Answer Features

CREDIBILITY. (*31 features*) We have features that model the contents of the answer, most of which have been previously used for credibility detection (Castillo et al., 2011): number of URLs/images/emails/phone numbers; number of tokens/sentences; average number of tokens; number of nouns/verbs/adjectives/adverbs/pronouns; number of 1st/2nd/3rd person pronouns; number of positive/negative smileys; number of single/double/triple exclamation/ interrogation symbols; number of interrogative sentences (based on syntactic analysis); number of words that are not in word2vec's Google News vocabulary (this can signal slang, foreign language, etc.)

SENTIMENT (*36 features*) We extract features modeling the sentiment polarity of the answer, which has been previously proposed as a useful feature for credibility (Castillo et al., 2011). We use two sentiment polarity lexicons (Mohammad et al., 2013): the *NRC Hashtag Sentiment Lexicon*, which contains 54,129 words and 316,531 bigrams, and the *Sentiment140 Lexicon*, with 62,468 words and 677,698 bigrams. In these lexicons, for each term there is a real number representing the strength of association of the term with positive/negative sentiment. We use as features the number of positive/negative terms in the answer, both as absolute numbers and normalized by the total number of sentiment-bearing terms in the answer. We also have as features the sum of the scores for the positive/negative/all sentiment-bearing terms. Finally, we have the maximum absolute value for a positive/negative term. We have four copies of these nine features: for words vs. bigrams, and for each of the two lexicons.

GOODNESS (*9 features*) Similarly, we build goodness polarity lexicons that contain 41,633 words, each associated with a real number representing its strength of association with *Good* or *Bad* answers. Following (Balchev et al., 2016), we build this lexicon using pointwise mutual information, starting with the training data from SemEval-2016 task 3, and then extending this to words from the Qatar Living dump. We use the same nine features as for sentiment, but this time we only have one lexicon and we only use words (no bigrams).

GOOGLE_VEC (*300 features*) We use the pretrained, 300-dimensional embedding vectors that Tomas Mikolov trained on 100 billion words from Google News (Mikolov et al., 2013). We compute a vector representation for an answer by simply averaging the embeddings of the words it contains.

QL_VEC (*100 features*) We train 100-dimensional in-domain word embeddings using WORD2VEC on all the available Qatar Living data, which we then use to produce embeddings for the

---

[7] Note that the annotations from all annotators are included in the corpus as complementary information. Thus, other more strict mappings can be considered from the users' annotations to the credibility labels depending on the final application objective.

[8] The full corpus can be found at the following address: https://bitbucket.org/cqa-credibility/cqa-credibility-corpus

answers by averaging the embedding vectors of the answer's words.

SYNTAX_VEC (*25 features*) We parse the answer using the Stanford neural parser (Socher et al., 2013), and we use the final 25-dimensional syntactic embedding vector that is produced internally as a by-product of parsing as a representation for the answer.

4.2 Question-Answer Features

These features measure the similarity between the question and the answer.

MTFEATS (*6 features*) We use the following six machine translation evaluation features: (*i*) BLEU: This is the most commonly used measure for machine translation evaluation, which is based on n-gram overlap and length ratios (Papineni et al., 2002). (*ii*) NIST: This measure is similar to BLEU, and is used at evaluation campaigns run by NIST (Doddington, 2002). (*iii*) TER: Translation error rate; it is based on the edit distance between a translation hypothesis and the reference (Snover et al., 2006). (*v*) Unigram PRECISION and RECALL, which originally come from information retrieval.

BLEUCOMP (*17 features*) We further use as features various components that are involved in the computation of BLEU: n-gram precisions, n-gram matches, total number of n-grams (n=1,2,3,4), lengths of the hypotheses and of the reference, length ratio between them, and BLEU's brevity penalty.

VEC_COSINES (*3 features*) We calculate pairwise similarity features between an answer and the corresponding question using their GOOGLE_VEC, QL_VEC, and SYNTAX_VEC vectors.

4.3 Thread-Answer Features

RANK (*4 features*) We have thread-level features related to the rank of the answer in the thread: (*i*) reciprocal rank of the answer in the thread; (*ii*) percentile of the answer in the thread, calculated as follows: the first answer gets the score of 1.0, the second one gets 0.9, the next one gets 0.8, and so on. We calculate these two features twice: once for the full list of answers, and once for the list of *Good* answers only.

VEC_COS_THREAD (*3 features*) We further use embeddings at the thread-level, which we calculate over the concatenation of all *Good* answers in the thread. The idea is that if a *Good* answer is similar to other *Good* answers, it is likely to be credible; conversely, if it is dissimilar, it is likely to be an outlier, and thus less credible. We use as features the cosines between an answer- and a thread-vector using GOOGLE_VEC, QL_VEC, and SYNTAX_VEC vectors.

4.4 User Profile Features

We further have some features characterizing the user who has posted an answer.

CATEGORIES (*396 features*) We build a vector of the number of answers a user has posted in each of the 197 categories. We have each feature twice: once as a raw feature and once normalized by the total number of answers the user has posted. We further add as features the total number of answers and the number of distinct categories the user has posted in.

QUALITY (*13 features*) We model the quality of the posts by the authors. We first use the SemEval-2016 Task 3 data (Nakov et al., 2016) to train a classifier that predicts whether a given answer is a *Good* answer to the question heading its thread or not. We then run this classifier (which has 80+% accuracy) on the entire Qatar Living dataset dump, and we aggregate its predictions to estimate whether a given user tends to give *Good* answers or not. We have the following features for each user: number of *Good/Bad* answers, total number of answers, percentage of *Good/Bad* answers, sum of the classifier probabilities for *Good/Bad* answers, total sum of the classifier probabilities over all answers, average score for the probability of *Good/Bad* answer, and highest absolute score for the probability of *Good/Bad* answer.

TROLLNESS (*27 features*) These features model the likelihood that the author of the answer is a troll. They are inspired by the trollness definition proposed by Mihaylov et al. (2015), namely that a person who is called a troll by other users is likely to be one. In particular, we have the following features: number of answers that are exactly k (k=1,2,...,10) answers before a troll mention, i.e., an answer that contains words like *troll, trolls, trolling*, and the number of answers that come within $[0;n]$ answers before a troll mention ($n = 3, 5$). These 12 features have two versions each: once as absolute numbers and once normalized by the total number N of answers the user has posted in a thread and they were followed later by a troll mention. This total number is also a feature. Another feature is the average distance of the user's post to a troll mention that comes somewhere below in the thread. Finally, we have a feature that measures the average distance not in terms of number of answers but in terms of average time (days). For users who have never posted answers in a trollness context, the values of these features are zero.

ACTIVITY (*19 features*) These features describe the overall activity of the user (regardless of the quality of the answers and without the requirement for them to appear in a troll context). We use features such as number of answers posted, number of distinct questions to which an answer was posted, number of questions asked, number of posts in the *Jobs*, and in the *Classifieds* sections, number of days since registering in the forum, and number of active days. We also have features modeling the number of answers posted in different hourly periods (note that these intervals overlap): during working hours (7:00-17:00h), after work, at night, early in the morning, and before noon. We further model the day of posting: during a working day vs. during the weekend. Finally, we track the number of answers posted among the first k in a question-answer thread, for $k \in \{1, 3, 5, 10, 20\}$.

5 Experiments

General setup. We experimented with each feature type individually, where the different feature types as well as the features inside larger groups are ordered by their relative MAP (Mean Average Precision) scores. We further combined the best k feature types. The results are shown in Table 2.

Scoring. As we imagine a ranking application scenario, we are interested in ranking evaluation metrics, such as Mean Average Precision (MAP), Mean Reciprocal Rank (MRR) and Average Recall (AvgRec), which were used at SemEval-2016 Task 3. Note that we use the minority class, i.e., *NonCredible*, as the positive class.

Baselines. The last rows of Table 2 show the performance of two baselines. The first one is the chronological ranking, where the answers are ordered by their time of posting; the rationale here is

that later answers might be more credible as over time people tend to gradually converge towards consensus answers. The second baseline classifies all answers as *NonCredible*.

Upper bound. Coming back to ranking, we can see that the scores for MAP and MRR seem quite low, both for the baselines and for the systems trained using various features. The reason for that is shown in the *Oracle* row of the table: we can see that an oracle system (i.e., one that assigns the correct *Credible/NonCredible* label and also assigns such scores that rank all *NonCredible* answers above all *Credible* ones) only achieves a MAP of 0.2273 and an MRR of 22.73. These numbers are an upper bound of what we could possibly achieve. The reason for MAP and MRR being so low is that they are zero by definition when a thread has no *NonCredible* answers, and in our test dataset 34 of the 50 questions have no *Non-Credible* answers (moreover, six of the questions have only *Bad* answers), which pushes the scores down.

Learning algorithm. We used an SVM-rank (Joachims, 2002). We scaled the feature weights, and we experimented with linear and RBF kernels, using grid search to find the best values for the SVM hyper-parameters C and γ.

6 Results and Discussion

Overall, the most important category of features are those modeling the user profile. In particular, this category contains the TROLLNESS feature, which achieves the best results in terms of MAP, AvgRec, and MRR. This shows that users that are seen as trolls by other users in one context, tend to give generally noncredible answers. The success of this feature is somewhat surprising. First, there is no guarantee that a mere mention of words such as *troll*, *trolls*, or *trolling* means that one user accuses some of the previous users who posted in the same thread to be trolls; the word might refer to users in some other thread. Yet, a quick manual analysis of threads containing a troll word shows that most mentions are indeed troll accusations. The problem is that not all users who posted before such an accusation are its target; there are many innocents.[9] Apparently, this is not a big problem,

---

[9]For an illustration, see an example of a thread discussing trolls in Qatar Living here:
```
http://www.qatarliving.com/forum/
qatar-living-lounge/posts/beware-trolls
```

Features	MAP	AvgRec	MRR	P	R	F1	Acc
USER PROFILE FEATURES							
TROLLNESS	**0.1739**	**0.9119**	<u>19.5076</u>	**0.3333**	0.1579	**0.2143**	0.9052
QUALITY	**0.1598**	**0.9024**	17.0455	<u>**0.5000**</u>	0.0526	0.0952	**0.9181**
ACTIVITY	**0.1391**	0.8331	14.3939	0	0	0	**0.9181**
CATEGORIES	0.1230	0.8168	12.0265	**0.1250**	0.1053	0.1143	0.8664
ANSWER FEATURES							
SYNTAX_VEC	**0.1657**	**0.8814**	17.4242	**0.2400**	0.3158	**0.2727**	0.8621
CREDIBILITY	**0.1538**	**0.8829**	15.5682	0.0938	0.1579	0.1176	0.8060
SENTIMENT	**0.1447**	0.8373	16.0227	**0.1176**	0.2105	0.1509	0.8060
GOODNESS	**0.1337**	0.8068	**13.4280**	**0.2000**	0.0526	0.0833	0.9052
GOOGLE_VEC	**0.1331**	**0.8436**	**13.7121**	0.0714	0.1053	0.0851	0.8147
QL_VEC	0.1234	0.7895	**13.5417**	0.0606	0.1053	0.0769	0.7931
QUESTION-ANSWER FEATURES							
VEC_COSINES	**0.1631**	**0.8478**	16.5404	0	0	0	**0.9181**
BLEUCOMP	**0.1426**	**0.8436**	14.5833	0	0	0	**0.9181**
MTFEATS	**0.1341**	0.8162	15.7197	0	0	0	**0.9181**
ANSWER-THREAD FEATURES							
RANK	**0.1512**	**0.8484**	15.6061	0	0	0	**0.9181**
VEC_COSINES_THREAD	**0.1433**	0.8173	**14.2424**	0	0	0	0.9138
THREAD FEATURES							
GOOGLE_VEC_THREAD	**0.1307**	**0.8384**	13.1439	**0.1875**	0.3158	**0.2353**	0.8319
SYNTAX_VEC_THREAD	**0.1307**	**0.8384**	13.1439	**0.1163**	0.2632	**0.1613**	0.7759
QL_VEC_THREAD	**0.1307**	**0.8384**	13.1439	**0.0909**	0.2105	0.1270	0.7629
COMBINATIONS							
TOP-2	**0.1857**	**0.9230**	**18.5606**	**0.1912**	0.6842	**0.2989**	0.7371
TOP-4	**0.1698**	**0.9024**	**17.8030**	**0.2571**	0.4737	<u>**0.3333**</u>	0.8448
TOP-6	<u>**0.1888**</u>	<u>**0.9345**</u>	**19.3182**	0	0	0	**0.9181**
UPPER BOUND							
Oracle	0.2273	1.0000	22.7273	1.0000	1.0000	1.0000	1.0000
BASELINES							
Chronological	<u>0.1307</u>	<u>0.8384</u>	13.1400	—	—	—	—
Random	0.1263	0.8111	<u>13.2386</u>	0.0726	0.4737	0.1259	0.4612
All-Credible	—	—	—	0	0	0	**0.9181**
All-NonCredible	—	—	—	<u>0.0819</u>	**1.0000**	<u>0.1514</u>	0.0819

Table 2: **Evaluation results.** We show the performance for each group of features in isolation, and for the combination of the top-k features groups, as well as for four baselines and an oracle upper bound. For each evaluation measure, we underline the best baseline score, and we mark in bold all system results that are higher than or equal to that score. We further underline the best overall result for each column.

as we model trollness using a number of features, and these only get high values if a user appears many times in a troll-accusation context. Another problem is that we have less than 3,000 users who appeared before a trollness accusation, while there are close to 70,000 users in QatarLiving. Yet, many of those for which we have trollness features, are also those that are among the most active users and thus are likely to be the authors of our test-time answers. Overall, the TROLLNESS feature group has the second-highest precision of 0.3333 among all feature groups we experimented with.

The highest overall precision is achieved by another user profile feature group: QUALITY. The goal here is again to find unreliable users, but the way this is achieved is more indirect: it is hypoth-esized that users who gave mostly bad answers in the past (bad in the sense that they did not try to answer the question, e.g., because they instead engaged in conversation with users, changed topic, started asking new questions, etc.), should not be believed when they actually give seemingly good answers to some question later. This feature has very low recall though.

The second most important feature category is that of answer features. Interestingly, we see at the top SYNTAX_VEC, which is second-best overall on MAP and MRR, but also notably the best in F_1. This suggests that the syntactic structure of an answer is important for human judges when suggesting that a answer is not credible. Indeed, previous work on finding high-quality content in social media has made use of grammaticality as a feature (Agichtein et al., 2008). However, there it was modeled using part-of-speech n-grams, while here we use syntactic answer embeddings.

Naturally, among the top-performing features in this category we find the CREDIBILITY group, which contains some features that have been previously proposed for credibility, but in social media (Castillo et al., 2011). Another strong feature group from this category is SENTIMENT, which has been shown to be useful for credibility.

The third most important feature category in terms of performance is that of the question-answer features. This is to be expected as answers are posted with respect to a question and thus their credibility should take the question into account. The best feature group here is VEC_COSINES; this should not be surprising given the strong performance of SYNTAX_VEC, which is used for one of the three cosines. BLEUCOMP is also relatively strong, which is an indicator of the importance of modeling n-gram overlaps between the question and the answer directly (modeling similarity indirectly as in MTFEATS performs somewhat worse). Finally note that, even though relatively good at ranking, the feature groups in this category never predict NonCredible as a label.

Next in terms of importance comes the answer-thread feature category. We can see that modeling RANK is somewhat important, e.g., maybe because early answers are more likely to be credible as they are more likely to be on topic. Another indication of the importance of the relative ranking of a answer in the thread is the fact that the chronological baselines is a bit better than the random one. The cosines between the vector of a answer and of the corresponding thread, or VEC_COSINES_THREAD, performs relatively well, as it models whether the answer is similar to the set of the other good answers in the thread. The idea is that if several answers say similar things, they should reinforce each other's credibility. Finally, this feature category also cannot predict NonCredible as a label.

The last group of features is that of thread-level feature vectors. Obviously, they are not strong enough in isolation, and perform roughly at the baseline level in terms of ranking measures; yet, they are above the baseline in terms of precision and F_1.

Finally, as we mentioned above, we further combined the prediction scores for the best k features in a meta classifier. This yielded additional improvements, e.g., MAP improved from 0.1739 to 0.1888, AvgRec from 0.9119 to 0.9345, and F_1 from 0.2727 to 0.3333.

7 Conclusion and Future Work

In this paper, we have addressed *information credibility in community Question Answering* as a problem on its own right. To the best of our knowledge, this is done for a first time. We have motivated the problem in the context of answer-quality ranking, and we have created a publicly available corpus, again for the first time for this task. We have also proposed a large set of relatively cheap features, which we used to train ranking SVM classifiers to predict the credibility of an answer with respect to a question in the context of a question-answer thread. The features model the user, the answer, the question, the thread as a whole, and the interaction between them. Our experimental evaluation demonstrate sizable improvements over the baselines across several standard IR ranking-based metrics, which shows that the credibility annotation is indeed learnable. The results further show that features modeling the profile of the user (in particular *trollness*) are the most important for detecting answer credibility. The feature groups based on *semantic similarity of the answer to its associated question as well as to the entire thread* also proved to be relevant. Overall, more than 70% of the gap between the baseline performance and the perfect Oracle classifier (in terms of MAP scores) could be covered by a combination of the most productive feature types. This results support the idea of using the credibility prediction layer in a real-world cQA scenario.

In future work, we plan to enlarge the training and the testing datasets in order to avoid overfitting and to get more reliable conclusions about the utility of our large set of features. In doing so, we also plan to use more complex feature selection algorithms. From machine learning perspective, we are also interested in exploring other approaches, such as deep convolutional neural networks or long short-term memory (LSTM), in order to obtain better embedded representations and to model the structure of the data more adequately, and semi-supervised learning, e.g., exploiting self-training from the entire Qatar Living forum, as a way to partially avoid the need for costly supervision.

References

Eugene Agichtein, Carlos Castillo, Debora Donato, Aristides Gionis, and Gilad Mishne. 2008. Finding high-quality content in social media. In *Proceedings of the 2008 International Conference on Web Search and Data Mining*. Palo Alto, California, USA, WSDM '08, pages 183–194.

Mouhamadou Lamine Ba, Laure Berti-Equille, Kushal Shah, and Hossam M. Hammady. 2016. VERA: A platform for veracity estimation over web data. In *Proceedings of the 25th International Conference Companion on World Wide Web*. Montréal, Québec, Canada, WWW '16 Companion, pages 159–162.

Daniel Balchev, Yasen Kiprov, Ivan Koychev, and Preslav Nakov. 2016. PMI-cool at SemEval-2016 task 3: Experiments with PMI and goodness polarity lexicons for community question answering. In *Proceedings of the 10th International Workshop on Semantic Evaluation*. San Diego, California, SemEval '2016, pages 844–850.

Protima Banerjee and Hyoil Han. 2009. Answer credibility: A language modeling approach to answer validation. In *Proceedings of Human Language Technologies: The 2009 Annual Conference of the North American Chapter of the Association for Computational Linguistics, Companion Volume: Short Papers*. Association for Computational Linguistics, Boulder, Colorado, pages 157–160.

K. R. Canini, B. Suh, and P. L. Pirolli. 2011. Finding credible information sources in social networks based on content and social structure. In *Privacy, Security, Risk and Trust (PASSAT) and 2011 IEEE Third Inernational Conference on Social Computing (SocialCom), 2011 IEEE Third International Conference on*. pages 1–8.

Carlos Castillo, Marcelo Mendoza, and Barbara Poblete. 2011. Information credibility on twitter. In *Proceedings of the 20th International Conference on World Wide Web*. Hyderabad, India, WWW '11, pages 675–684.

George Doddington. 2002. Automatic evaluation of machine translation quality using n-gram co-occurrence statistics. In *Proceedings of the Second International Conference on Human Language Technology Research*. Morgan Kaufmann Publishers Inc., San Francisco, CA, USA, HLT '02, pages 138–145.

Joseph L. Fleiss. 1971. Measuring nominal scale agreement among many raters. *Psychological Bulletin* 76(5):378–382.

Jiwoon Jeon, W. Bruce Croft, Joon Ho Lee, and Soyeon Park. 2006. A framework to predict the quality of answers with non-textual features. In *Proceedings of the 29th Annual International ACM SIGIR Conference on Research and Development in Information Retrieval*. ACM, New York, NY, USA, SIGIR '06, pages 228–235.

Thorsten Joachims. 2002. Optimizing search engines using clickthrough data. In *Proceedings of the Eighth ACM SIGKDD International Conference on Knowledge Discovery and Data Mining*. Edmonton, Alberta, Canada, KDD '02, pages 133–142.

Pawel Jurczyk and Eugene Agichtein. 2007. Discovering authorities in question answer communities by using link analysis. In *Proceedings of the Sixteenth ACM Conference on Conference on Information and Knowledge Management*. ACM, New York, NY, USA, CIKM '07, pages 919–922.

J. Richard Landis and Gary G. Koch. 1977. The measurement of observer agreement for categorical data. *Biometrics* 33(1):159–174.

Lucian Vlad Lita, Andrew Hazen Schlaikjer, WeiChang Hong, and Eric Nyberg. 2005. Qualitative dimensions in question answering: Extending the definitional QA task. In *PROCEEDINGS OF THE NATIONAL CONFERENCE ON ARTIFICIAL INTELLIGENCE*. Menlo Park, CA; Cambridge, MA; London; AAAI Press; MIT Press; 1999, volume 20, page 1616.

Michal Lukasik, Trevor Cohn, and Kalina Bontcheva. 2015. Point process modelling of rumour dynamics in social media. In *Proceedings of the 53rd Annual Meeting of the Association for Computational Linguistics and the 7th International Joint Conference on Natural Language Processing (Volume 2: Short Papers)*. Association for Computational Linguistics, Beijing, China, pages 518–523.

Jing Ma, Wei Gao, Zhongyu Wei, Yueming Lu, and Kam-Fai Wong. 2015. Detect rumors using time series of social context information on microblogging websites. In *Proceedings of the 24th ACM International on Conference on Information and Knowledge Management*. Melbourne, Australia, CIKM '15, pages 1751–1754.

Todor Mihaylov, Georgi D Georgiev, AD Ontotext, and Preslav Nakov. 2015. Finding opinion manipulation trolls in news community forums. In *Proceedings of the Nineteenth Conference on Computational Natural Language Learning, CoNLL*. volume 15, pages 310–314.

Tomas Mikolov, Wen-tau Yih, and Geoffrey Zweig. 2013. Linguistic regularities in continuous space word representations. In *Proceedings of the 2013 Conference of the North American Chapter of the Association for Computational Linguistics: Human Language Technologies*. Atlanta, Georgia, USA, NAACL-HLT '13, pages 746–751.

Saif Mohammad, Svetlana Kiritchenko, and Xiaodan Zhu. 2013. NRC-Canada: Building the state-of-the-art in sentiment analysis of tweets. In *Second Joint Conference on Lexical and Computational Semantics (*SEM), Volume 2: Proceedings of the Seventh International Workshop on Semantic Evaluation*. Atlanta, Georgia, USA, SemEval '2013, pages 321–327.

Elaheh Momeni, Claire Cardie, and Nicholas Diakopoulos. 2015. A survey on assessment and ranking methodologies for user-generated content on the web. *ACM Comput. Surv.* 48(3):41:1–41:49.

Meredith Ringel Morris, Scott Counts, Asta Roseway, Aaron Hoff, and Julia Schwarz. 2012. Tweeting is believing?: Understanding microblog credibility perceptions. In *Proceedings of the ACM 2012 Conference on Computer Supported Cooperative Work*. ACM, New York, NY, USA, CSCW '12, pages 441–450.

Preslav Nakov, Lluís Màrquez, Walid Magdy, Alessandro Moschitti, Jim Glass, and Bilal Randeree. 2015. Semeval-2015 task 3: Answer selection in community question answering. In *Proceedings of the 9th International Workshop on Semantic Evaluation (SemEval 2015)*. Association for Computational Linguistics, Denver, Colorado, pages 269–281.

Preslav Nakov, Lluís Màrquez, Alessandro Moschitti, Walid Magdy, Hamdy Mubarak, Abed Alhakim Freihat, Jim Glass, and Bilal Randeree. 2016. SemEval-2016 Task 3: Community Question Answering. In *Proceedings of SemEval-2016*. Association for Computational Linguistics, San Diego, California, SemEval '16.

Kishore Papineni, Salim Roukos, Todd Ward, and Wei-Jing Zhu. 2002. BLEU: a method for automatic evaluation of machine translation. In *Proceedings of 40th Annual Meting of the Association for Computational Linguistics*. Philadelphia, Pennsylvania, USA, ACL '02, pages 311–318.

Dan Pelleg, Oleg Rokhlenko, Idan Szpektor, Eugene Agichtein, and Ido Guy. 2016. When the crowd is not enough: Improving user experience with social media through automatic quality analysis. In *Proceedings of the 19th ACM Conference on Computer-Supported Cooperative Work & Social Computing*. ACM, New York, NY, USA, CSCW '16, pages 1080–1090.

Matthew Snover, Bonnie Dorr, Richard Schwartz, Linnea Micciulla, and John Makhoul. 2006. A study of translation edit rate with targeted human annotation. In *Proceedings of the 7th Biennial Conference of the Association for Machine Translation in the Americas*. Cambridge, Massachusetts, USA, AMTA '06.

Richard Socher, John Bauer, Christopher D. Manning, and Ng Andrew Y. 2013. Parsing with compositional vector grammars. In *Proceedings of the 51st Annual Meeting of the Association for Computational Linguistics (Volume 1: Long Papers)*. Sofia, Bulgaria, pages 455–465.

Qi Su, Helen Kai yun Chen, and Chu-Ren Huang. 2010. Incorporate credibility into context for the best social media answers. In *Proceedings of the 24th Pacific Asia Conference on Language, Information and Computation*. Institute of Digital Enhancement of Cognitive Processing, Waseda University, Tohoku University, Sendai, Japan, pages 535–541.

Matei Zaharia, Mosharaf Chowdhury, Michael J. Franklin, Scott Shenker, and Ion Stoica. 2010. Spark: Cluster computing with working sets. In *Proceedings of the 2nd USENIX Conference on Hot Topics in Cloud Computing*. Boston, MA, HotCloud '10, pages 10–10.

Arkaitz Zubiaga, Geraldine Wong Sak Hoi, Maria Liakata, Rob Procter, and Peter Tolmie. 2015. Analysing how people orient to and spread rumours in social media by looking at conversational threads. *arXiv preprint arXiv:1511.07487* .

Arkaitz Zubiaga, Maria Liakata, Rob Procter, Geraldine Wong Sak Hoi, and Peter Tolmie. 2016. Analysing how people orient to and spread rumours in social media by looking at conversational threads. *PLoS ONE* 11(3):1–29.

Bulgarian-English and English-Bulgarian Machine Translation: System Design and Evaluation

Petya Osenova
Linguistic Modeling Department
IICT-BAS
petya@bultreebank.org

Kiril Simov
Linguistic Modeling Department
IICT-BAS
kivs@bultreebank.org

Abstract

The paper presents a deep factored machine translation (MT) system between English and Bulgarian languages in both directions. The MT system is hybrid. It consists of three main steps: (1) the source-language text is linguistically annotated, (2) it is translated to the target language with the Moses system, and (3) translation is post-processed with the help of the transferred linguistic annotation from the source text. Besides automatic evaluation we performed manual evaluation over a domain test suite of sentences demonstrating certain phenomena like imperatives, questions, etc.

1 Introduction

The paper describes a Deep Factored Moses system for Bulgarian-English MT in both directions, which includes transfer of linguistic knowledge from the source to the target language in the post-processing phase.

BG↔EN MT architecture presents a hybrid machine translation system that consists of three main steps. The source-language text is linguistically annotated, then translated with the Moses system to the target language and post-processed using the linguistic annotation projected from the source text. In the experiments we use four sets of parallel data — QTLeap corpus: Batch1 to Batch4 (Otegi et al., 2016) — and two versions of the translation systems: **BLMT** — baseline systems trained on pure parallel texts and **DFMT** — deep factored Bulgarian-English MT systems. In DFMT systems during the translation with the Moses system the word alignments are

stored in order to be used for the projection of the linguistic analysis from the source text into the target one.

The structure of the paper is as follows: Section 2 presents the system architecture. Section 3 elaborates on the post-processing procedures. Section 4 presents the manual evaluation results. Section 5 outlines related work. Section 6 concludes the paper.

2 A Hybrid MT Architecture for DFMT

The hybrid architecture for DFMT for both language directions BG↔EN incorporates transfer of linguistic information from the source to the target language. It is depicted in Figure 1. The linguistic analysis for the source language (Analysis — column 1) is projected to a tokenized source text (Analysis — column 2). Then the Moses models (Moses) are applied to produce a target language translation. The translation alignment (Projection — column 1) is used for transferring the information to the corresponding tokens in the target language (Projection — column 2). The projected linguistic information interacts with the linguistic features of the tokens in the target text (for example the morphosyntactic features). The resulting annotation of the target text is used in the post-processing stage.

Note that the number of the tokens in the source and the target language might differ. The alignments can include many-to-many correspondences, not just one-to-one. Nevertheless, in practice about 80 % of the alignments are one-to-one or two-to-two tokens.

Here is an example of aligned texts annotated with morphosyntactic information of the

Proceedings of Recent Advances in Natural Language Processing, pages 561–568,
Varna, Bulgaria, Sep 4–6 2017.

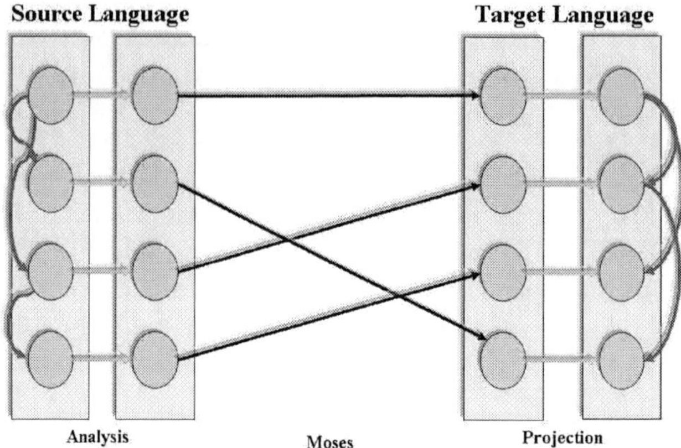

Figure 1: A hybrid architecture for transferring linguistic information from the source to the target text.

English[1] sentence "Place them in the midst of a pile of dirty, soccer kit." and its translation into Bulgarian[2]:

```
(place/VB them/PRP in/IN)
    =
  (postavyaneto/Ncnsd
   im/Ppetdp3;Ppetsp3;Pszt--3 v/R)
(the/DT midst/NN of/IN)
    = (razgar/Ncmsi na/R)
(a/DT pile/NN of/IN)
    = (kup/Ncmsi)
(dirty/JJ)    = (izmyrsyavam/Vpitf-r1s)
(,/,)         = (,/Punct)
(soccer/NN)   = (futbolni/A-pi)
(kit/NN)      = (komplekt/Ncmsi)
(./.)         = (./Punct)
```

From the alignment and rules for mappings between the two tagsets we could establish the following alignments on token level:

```
(them/PRP) = (im/Ppetdp3;Ppetsp3;Pszt--3)
(in/IN)    = (v/R)
(midst/NN) = (razgar/Ncmsi)
(of/IN)    = (na/R)
(pile/NN)  = (kup/Ncmsi)
(,/,)      = (,/Punct)
(soccer/NN)= (futbolni/A-pi)
(kit/NN)   = (komplekt/Ncmsi)
(./.)      = (./Punct)
```

Additionally, the alignment (place/VB) = (postavyaneto/Ncnsd) would be possible because the noun (postavyaneto/Ncnsd) is a deverbal noun, derived from a verb (postavyam/Vpitf-r1s), to place. To establish such an alignment we would need

a derivational lexicon which however is not available to us. Thus, we do not consider this type of alignment. Likewise, the alignment between the English adjective (dirty/JJ) and the Bulgarian verb (izmyrsyavam/Vpitf-r1s), to make dirty would be also possible as much as "something to be dirty" could be a result from the action denoted by the verb. We consider such rules unreliable. Thus we do not use them. Using the alignments, we are able to transfer additional information like dependency links, word senses, etc. It is clear from the example that the transfer is only partial. The alignment (soccer/NN) = (futbolni/A-pi) is allowed when the English noun is a part of a compound. After the transfer of additional information, a set of rules for post processing is applied. For example, here a rule for agreement between the adjective futbolni and the noun komplekt has been applied.

For the EN→BG translation we extended the above architecture by adding an intermediate layer. Thus, the translation consists of two steps — see the modified architecture in Fig. 2. In the first step the English text is annotated with senses from the English WordNet. Then using the mapping between English WordNet and the Bulgarian Wordnet BTB-WN we substitute the English words with Bulgarian lemmas from the corresponding Bulgarian synsets. For each Bulgarian synset a representative lemma is preselected on the basis of a frequency list of Bulgarian lemmas that was

---

[1] For English, the tagset of Penn treebank is used: https://www.ling.upenn.edu/courses/Fall_2003/ling001/penn_treebank_pos.html.

[2] For Bulgarian, the tagset of BulTreeBank was used: http://www.bultreebank.org/TechRep/BTB-TR03.pdf.

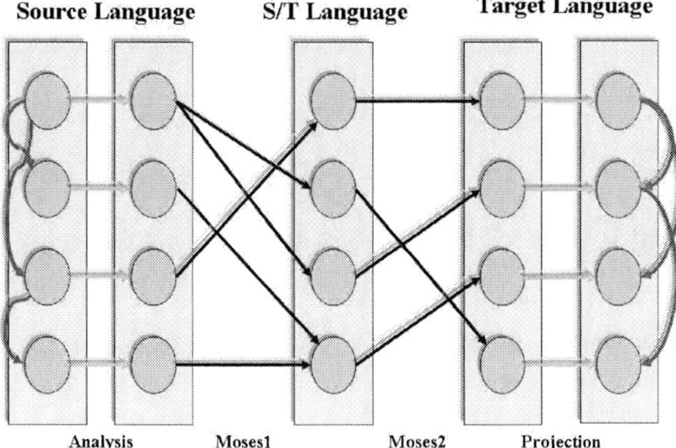

Figure 2: A hybrid architecture of EN→BG for transferring linguistic information from the source to the target language.

constructed over a corpus of 70 million words. The motivation for using the representative lemma in Bulgarian is our expectation for unification of the various synset ids with the similar translations in the target language. For example, the two concepts referred by *donor*: wn30-10025730-n ("person who makes a gift of property") and wn30-10026058-n ("a medical term denoting someone who gives blood or tissue or an organ to be used in another person") are very close to each other. They have the same translation in Bulgarian in both corresponding synsets: донор[3]. Here is an example of the performed processing:

English sentence:
This is real progress .

English sentence with factors:
this|this|dt is|be|vbz realen|real|jj napredyk|progress|nn .|.|.

Bulgarian sentence with factors (S/T Language Layer):
tova|tova|pd e|sym|vx realen|realen|a napredyk|napredyk|nc .|.|pu

Bulgarian sentence:
Tova e realen napredyk.

The intermediate layer is called **S/T Language** text. In addition we use the BLMT system and the alignment produced by the Moses

System (Moses1) in order to substitute some of the functional words in source language with words in the target language. We selected this translation model for EN→BG because in our earlier experiments it performed slightly better than the phrase-based model. The architecture for EN→BG is depicted on Figure 2. Here the source language is analyzed linguistically, then the tokenized text is processed in two ways in order to produce the text for the Source/Target text (in the example above it corresponds to **English sentence with factors**). First, the replacements with the Bulgarian lemmas were performed on the basis of Word Sense annotation of the source text. Additionally, we translated the source text with the phrase-based Moses model (Moses1).

The linguistic analysis for the source language is projected to a tokenized source text; then Moses models (Moses1 and Moses2) are applied for producing a target language translation. The translation alignment is used for transferring the information to the corresponding tokens in the target language. Finally, the target linguistic annotation is used in the post-processing phase. It is important to keep in mind that the number of tokens in the S/T text is the same as in the source text. Thus, the analysis produced for the source text is easy to transfer to the S/T text. Then the actual translation was performed with factor-based Moses model (Moses2) where the alignment is used for the projection of the linguistic analysis over the source text.

---

[3]The corresponding Bulgarian synsets could contain other lemmas and thus for different domains and source language different representative lemmas will be more appropriate.

Our work on the projection of linguistic analysis from the source to the target text is similar to (Ramasamy et al., 2014) and (Mareček et al., 2011).

2.1 Analysis

For both directions the source-language linguistic annotation consists of tokenization, POS tagging, lemmatization, dependency parsing, shallow Minimal Recursion Semantics (MRS) annotation (elementary predicates and arguments) and word sense disambiguation. The analysis of English (tokenization, lemmatization, POS tagging and dependency parsing) was done with the CoreNLP tools.[4] The word sense disambiguation was done by the UKB tool.[5] For the analysis of Bulgarian, we trained Mate tools[6] on the Bulgarian treebank. The MRS structure rules were implemented in our own system.

2.2 Transfer

In the EN→BG system, we used a two-step translation strategy. **The first step**: (Moses1) was done using a phrase-based Moses model. We used the following parallel data: SETimes parallel corpus, LibreOffice parallel corpus, Bulgarian–English Dictionary aligned on wordform level, Microsoft product descriptions and Microsoft Terms. The texts were tokenized with available tokenizers for the corresponding languages. **The second step**: (Moses2) includes a factor-based Moses model which starts from a partially translated source language (S/T language). The training was performed on the same parallel data but processed as in the example given above on page 3. Both the source (**English sentence with factors**) and the target (**Bulgarian sentence with factors**) texts were processed with the corresponding language pipelines.

For the BG→EN system, we used the same parallel corpora and options as for the phrase-based model for EN→BG, but the whole transfer has been done in one step.

For the language model creation we relied on the SETimes corpus, LibreOffice corpus, domain articles from Wikipedia, Microsoft data, and Europarl corpus. The tuning was done on Batch1 of the QTLeap corpus.

3 Post-processing

In the post processing step, a rule-based system was applied, based on linguistically-enhanced information. This information is projected from the source side with the help of the word alignments produced by Moses1 and Moses2. The projected information is the linguistic knowledge in the form of MRS-based elementary predicates, labeled dependencies, word senses (synset ids from WordNet) and POS tags in the source language.

system	metric	BG→EN	EN→BG
BLMT	BLEU	18.54	20.30
DFMT	BLEU	**24.93**	**23.91**

Table 1: BLEU scores of BLMT and DFMT on translations of Batch4 part of the QTLeap Corpus.

It should be noted that the alignment between the source language to the S/T language and from the S/T language to the target language is not one-to-one. It generally maps sets of tokens from the source language to sets of tokens in the target language. Thus, as it was presented above in the example, the transfer of the linguistic information from the analysis of the source language to the target one is not straightforward. Here we apply heuristic rules. Thus, the transferred linguistic information is only partial. For the rules definition we also exploited the language resources and tools for the target language — a morphological lexicon, a lemmatizer, and a morphological generator.

Once the linguistic annotation is projected via the alignment, the post-processing can be applied. It includes various types of rules: morphological, syntactic and semantic. An example of a syntactic rule is the transformation of the English noun compounds into the appropriate syntactic structures in Bulgarian. The direct transfer is rare, since the NN compounds are not so frequent in Bulgarian. The combination in which the first noun is a Named Entity is the most frequent one in the domain data. In the case of a phrase with an adjective and a noun in Bulgarian, a morpho-

---

[4]http://stanfordnlp.github.io/CoreNLP/

[5]http://ixa2.si.ehu.es/ukb/

[6]http://www.ims.uni-stuttgart.de/forschung/ ressourcen/werkzeuge/matetools.en.html

(A)

Source:	Go to the Contacts menu $\geq$ Advanced $\geq$ Back up contacts to file	*2 inst.*
BLMT:	Преход към контактите меню $\geq$ разширени $\geq$ подкрепи контакти до файл	*2 inst.*
DFMT:	Отидете на contacts меню $>$ $>$ разширени назад с контакти за file	*0 inst.*
Reference:	Отидете в менюто Contacts $\geq$ Advanced $\geq$ Back up contacts to file	

logical rule for agreement is applied.

Table 1 shows the results comparing BLMT and DFMT systems. It can be observed that considerable improvements have been achieved in both directions.

4 Manual Evaluation

Here we employ the methodology developed by (Avramidis et al., 2016) to measure the performance of our systems on certain domain specific phenomena like imperatives, questions, terminology, etc. The graphic on Figure 3 as well as the associated Table 2 show the following overall situation: DFMT cannot outperform the baseline BLMT on the mentioned phenomena. It, however, achieves some similar figures on separators, then on imperatives, verbs and terminology. The results drop mostly in the cases of compoundings and quotation marks. As it can be seen, although we have considerable improvements with respect to the automatic metrics, reported above in Table 1, the performance on selected language phenomena might indicate worse results. Thus, the objective evaluation is actually not a trivial task at all.

	#	BLMT	DFMT
imperatives	97	74%	68%
compounds	100	44%	35%
">" separators	60	100%	98%
quotation marks	200	90%	69%
verbs	221	78%	73%
terminology	153	67%	60%
sum	831		
average		76%	56%

Table 2: Translation accuracy on manually evaluated sentences in Bulgarian focusing on particular phenomena. Test sets consist of hand-picked source sentences that include the respective phenomenon.

We present here some examples of the manual evaluation questionnaire in order to show how the evaluation was performed.

Example A depicts the analysis of the menu item. The source contains two instances of the separator. The BLMT system treats all separators correctly. DFMT system places the separators next to each other, so there is no correct instance.

Example B illustrates the translation of imperative forms. There are two correct instances in the source sentence in B. BFMT translates the second verb form from example B (select) correctly, but the first one (press) is translated in the form of a present tense.

Example C illustrates the translation of verbs. The results in this area are satisfactory. DFMT obtains the lower average value. The verb 'duplicate' is translated wrongly by the baseline system. DFMT does not translate it and also there is an English verb form in the Bulgarian sentence.

Example D illustrates the translation of terms. There is only one term in the example. It is translated in BLMT (although not grammatically correctly), but the verb in the sentence is translated like a noun. DFMT does not translate the term at all, but at the same time it translates the verb correctly.

5 Related Work

Our work is closely connected to the transfer-based MT models. Ideally, given the availability of two deep grammars for some language pair, we would be able to translate through the transfer of the deep representations. The transfer in this setting is usually implemented in the form of rewriting rules. For instance, in the Norwegian LO-GON project (Oepen et al., 2004), the transfer rules were hand-written (Bond et al., 2005; Oepen et al., 2007), which involved a large amount of manual work. Graham and van Genabith (2008) and Graham et al. (2009) explored the automatic rule induction approach

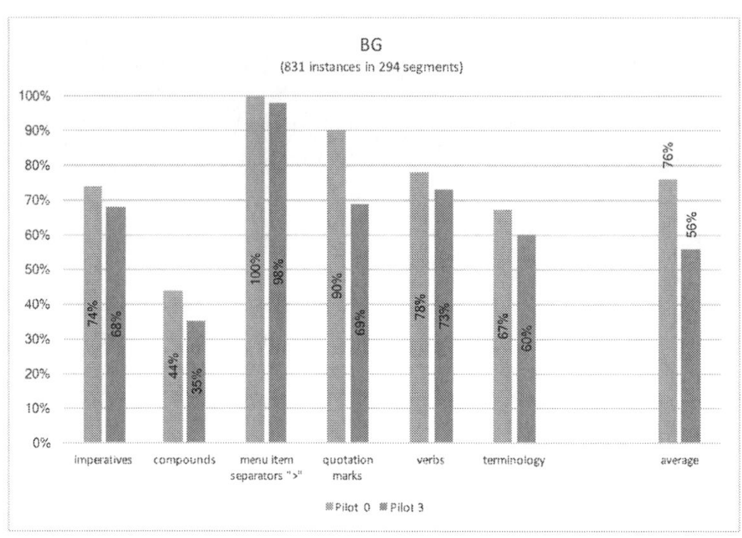

Figure 3: Manual evaluation results for Bulgarian

(B)

Source: If you have WinRAR installed, <u>press</u> the right mouse button on   *2 inst.*
            the file and then <u>select</u> Extract here ...
BLMT: Ако сте winrar инсталирани натискате десния бутон на мишката   *1 inst.*
            върху файла и <u>отметнете</u> добива тук ...
DFMT: Ако имате winrar installed, <u>натиснете</u> десния бутон на мишката   *2 inst.*
            върху файла и след това <u>изберете</u> extract тук ...
Reference: Ако имате инсталиран <u>WinRAR</u>, <u>натиснете</u> десния бутон на
            мишката върху файла и след това <u>изберете</u> Extract here ...

in a transfer-based MT setting two Lexical Functional Grammars (LFGs), which was still restricted by the performance of both – the parser and the generator. Lack of robustness for target side generation is one of the main issues, when various ill-formed or fragmented structures come out after transfer. Oepen et al. (2007) use their generator to generate text fragments instead of full sentences, in order to increase the robustness.

However, since a real large-scale grammar for Bulgarian is still not available, we take an SMT system as our 'backbone' which robustly delivers some translation for any given input. Then, we incrementally augment SMT with deep linguistic knowledge. What we are doing is still along the lines of previous work utilizing deep grammars, but we build a transfer model over dependency parses.

Another stream of research is related to the TectoMT approach (Žabokrtský et al., 2008).

The Prague Dependency Treebank (PDT)[7] is a Czech treebank, annotated in accordance to the linguistic theory of Functional Generative Description (P. Sgall and Panevova, 1986). The tectogrammatical layer[8] is the third layer of the PDT. It represents the syntactic-semantic interface, adding the functional dimension and collapsing the structural information, thus aiming at a more language-independent level of abstraction. The other two layers are the morphological and analytical ones. The morphological layer covers POS tags and lemmas. The analytical layer reflects the surface sentence structure. The tectogrammatical annotation builds on the analytical level. It presents the deep semantic structure of the sentence. The tectogrammatical level representation contains all the in-

---

[7] https://ufal.mff.cuni.cz/pdt2.0/
[8] https://ufal.mff.cuni.cz/pdt2.0/doc/manuals/en/t-layer/html/ch01.html

(C)

| Source: | Press and hold the Alt key and then click the color you want to duplicate. | *5 inst.* |

Source: Press and hold the Alt key and then click the color you want _5 inst._
to duplicate.
BLMT: Натиснете и задръжте върху Alt и щракнете върху цвета, който _4 inst._
желаете да дублира.
DFMT: Натиснете и задръжте клавиша Алт ключ и после щракнете върху _4 inst._
цвят искате да duplicate.
Reference: Натиснете и задръжте клавиша Alt и след това кликнете върху
цвета, който искате да използвате.

(D)

Source: In the terminal, type "netstat-a". _1 inst._
BLMT: В терминал, тип "netstat-a". _1 inst._
DFMT: В terminal, въведете "netstat-a ". _0 inst._
Reference: В терминала напишете „netstat-a".

formation necessary for translating the tectogrammatical representation into the lower levels, as well as for its interpretation in the sense of intentional semantics.

In contrast to the analytical level, the tectogrammatical level highlights the functional dimension (such as the semantic roles *Actor, Patient, Addressee*, etc.). It abstracts away from the synsemantic (functional) parts-of-speech (prepositions, conjunctions, etc.) in the dependency trees, thus focusing on the autosemantic words (nouns, verbs, etc.). The structural information is not lost, but just "collapsed" into the content words representations. In this way, a more abstract level of language representation is achieved, which then is used for the transfer step within the MT systems. Our approach generally follows the ideas behind the tectogrammatical approach in the sense that we also abstract over the sentence structures, focusing on the content words. However, we use MRS as a logical form for sentence representations (elementary predicates, combination rules, etc.).

We also build on the previous language model translation experience described in (Wang et al., 2012a) and (Wang et al., 2012b), enhancing the factored architecture with a more elaborated transfer step and with a more linguistically-aware post-processing step. However, while in the above-mentioned publications only BG→EN translation was explored, in this paper also the EN→BG direction is presented.

6 Conclusions

The presented MT system contains several improvements over the baseline variants of the BG↔EN systems, developed by us. These include: improved knowledge graphs for WSD; extension of the parallel data with aligned terminology and multi-word expressions; rules for generation of shallow MRS structures, rules for transfer of linguistic information from source to target text and post-processing rules that were implemented manually.

The manual evaluation performed on selected language and domain phenomena shows, that even though the automatic evaluation might show improvements, the performance over the selected domain language phenomena might not be good or might even drop.

Our goal in the future is to develop a bigger test suite of phenomena for the language pair of Bulgarian and English. Another improvement we envisage is to add to the test suite a procedure that would allow automatic checking when the translations do not reflect the selected phenomena. Even if done only partially, it would save the manual work during this type of evaluation.

Acknowledgements

This research has received partial funding from the EC's FP7 under grant agreement number 610516: "QTLeap: Quality Translation by Deep Language Engineering Approaches". We are grateful to the anonymous reviewers for their remarks, comments, and suggestions.

References

Eleftherios Avramidis, Aljoscha Burchardt, Vivien Macketanz, and Ankit Srivastava. 2016. DFKI's system for wmt16 it-domain task, including analysis of systematic errors. In *Proceedings of the First Conference on Machine Translation*. Association for Computational Linguistics, Berlin, Germany, pages 415–422.

Francis Bond, Stephan Oepen, Melanie Siegel, Ann Copestake, and Dan Flickinger. 2005. Open source machine translation with DELPH-IN. In *Proceedings of the Open-Source Machine Translation Workshop at the 10th Machine Translation Summit*. pages 15–22.

Yvette Graham, Anton Bryl, and Josef van Genabith. 2009. F-structure transfer-based statistical machine translation. In *Proceedings of the Lexical Functional Grammar Conference*. CSLI Publications, Stanford University, USA, Cambridge, UK., pages 317–328.

Yvette Graham and Josef van Genabith. 2008. Packed rules for automatic transfer-rule induction. In *Proceedings of the European Association of Machine Translation Conference (EAMT 2008)*. Hamburg, Germany, pages 57–65.

David Mareček, Rudolf Rosa, Petra Galuščáková, and Ondřej Bojar. 2011. Two-step translation with grammatical post-processing. In Chris Callison-Burch, Philipp Koehn, Christof Monz, and Omar Zaidan, editors, *Proceedings of the Sixth WMT*. University of Edinburgh, ACL, Edinburgh, UK, pages 426–432.

Stephan Oepen, Helge Dyvik, Jan Tore Lønning, Erik Velldal, Dorothee Beermann, John Carroll, Dan Flickinger, Lars Hellan, Janne Bondi Johannessen, Paul Meurer, Torbjørn Nordgård, , and Victoria Rosén. 2004. Som å kapp-ete med trollet? towards MRS-based norwegian to english machine translation. In *Proceedings of the 10th International Conference on Theoretical and Methodological Issues in Machine Translation*. Baltimore, MD.

Stephan Oepen, Erik Velldal, Jan Tore Lønning, Paul Meurer, Victoria Rosén, and Dan Flickinger. 2007. Towards hybrid quality-oriented machine translation — on linguistics and probabilities in MT. In *Proceedings of the 11th Conference on Theoretical and Methodological Issues in Machine Translation (TMI-07)*. Skovde, Sweden.

Arantxa Otegi, Nora Aranberri, António Branco, Jan Hajic, Martin Popel, Kiril Simov, Eneko Agirre, Petya Osenova, Rita Pereira, João Silva, and Steven Neale. 2016. Qtleap wsd/ned corpora: Semantic annotation of parallel corpora in six languages. In Nicoletta Calzolari (Conference Chair), Khalid Choukri, Thierry Declerck, Sara Goggi, Marko Grobelnik, Bente Maegaard, Joseph Mariani, Helene Mazo, Asuncion Moreno, Jan Odijk, and Stelios Piperidis, editors, *Proceedings of the Tenth International Conference on Language Resources and Evaluation (LREC 2016)*. European Language Resources Association (ELRA), Paris, France.

E. Hajicova P. Sgall and J. Panevova. 1986. *The Meaning of the Sentence in its Semantic and Pragmatic Aspects.*. Dordrecht: Reidel Publishing Company and Prague: Academia.

Loganathan Ramasamy, David Mareček, and Zdeněk Žabokrtský. 2014. Multilingual dependency parsing: Using machine translated texts instead of parallel corpora. *The Prague Bulletin of Mathematical Linguistics* 102:93–104.

Zdeněk Žabokrtský, Jan Ptáček, and Petr Pajas. 2008. TectoMT: Highly Modular MT System with Tectogrammatics Used as Transfer Layer. In *Proceedings of the Third Workshop on Statistical Machine Translation*. Association for Computational Linguistics, Stroudsburg, PA, USA, StatMT '08, pages 167–170.

Rui Wang, Petya Osenova, and Kiril Simov. 2012a. Linguistically-augmented bulgarian-to- english statistical machine translation model. In *Proceedings of the Joint Workshop on Exploiting Synergies Between Information Retrieval and Machine Translation (ESIRMT) and Hybrid Approaches to Machine Translation (HyTra), EACL 2012*. pages 119—128.

Rui Wang, Petya Osenova, and Kiril Simov. 2012b. Linguistically-enriched models for bulgarian-to-english machine translation. In *Proceedings of the Sixth Workshop on Syntax, Semantics and Structure in Statistical Translation, SSST-6, 2012*. pages 10—19.

Identification of Character Adjectives from *Mahabharata*

Apurba Paul
JIS College of Engineering
Kalyani
West Bengal, India
apurba.saitech@gmail.com

Dipankar Das
Jadavpur University
188, Raja S.C. Mullick Road, Kolkata
West Bengal, India
dipankar.dipnil2005@gmail.com

Abstract

The present paper describes the identification of prominent characters and their adjectives from Indian mythological epic, *Mahabharata*, written in English texts. However, in contrast to the traditional approaches of named entity identification, the present system extracts hidden attributes associated with each of the characters (e.g., character adjectives). We observed distinct phrase level linguistic patterns that hint the presence of characters in different text spans. Such six patterns were used in order to extract the characters. On the other hand, a distinguishing set of novel features (e.g., multi-word expression, nodes and paths of parse tree, immediate ancestors etc.) was employed. Further, the correlation of the features is also measured in order to identify the important features. Finally, we applied various machine learning algorithms (e.g., Naive Bayes, KNN, Logistic Regression, Decision Tree, Random Forest etc.) along with deep learning to classify the patterns as characters or non-characters in order to achieve decent accuracy. Evaluation shows that phrase level linguistic patterns as well as the adopted features are highly active in capturing characters and their adjectives.

1 Introduction

The identification of characters from story texts has received a great significance in recent trends. Character (sometimes known as a fictional character) is a person or which may be other beings in a narrative work of art. In literature, characters guide readers through their stories, helping them to understand plots and ponder themes(Freeman,2016). According to Iosif (2014), characters in the stories can either be human or non-human entities, i.e., animals and non-living objects, exhibiting anthropomorphic traits. The interactions among characters can either be human-to-human or human-to-non-human interactions. Sometimes, it also shows the fact that a character may not be necessarily a speaker in context of stories. A character may appear in the story but may not have any quote associated with him/her. It means that it may not have any dialogue or monologue and hence, is not a speaker. Characters play the pivotal roles in order to comprehend the context and help the reader to understand the story in-depth. Thus, for identifying syntactic and semantic level narrative information from any story text, automatic character identification has always been of great significance. In general, we may find two types of characters such as protagonist or antagonist. A protagonist is the main character in any story and it can affect the decisions of main characters and propel the story forward(Duncan,2006). Similarly an antagonist also influences the story.

In a similar context, *The Mahabharata* is an ancient Indian epic where the main story revolves around two branches of a family, Pandavas and Kauravas, battles for the throne of Hastinapura. Interwoven into this, narrative and several smaller stories about people dead or living, and philosophical discourses are discussed in the epic. It is not that merely the names are the characters, often it is found that a noun phrase also refers to a character in an epic such as *The Mahabharata*. Thus, the extraction, identification and analysis of phrases related to a character is required in order to select important attributes with respect to that character.

So, the presence of adjectives and sometimes adverbs in the noun phrase are considered as the crucial attributes that help us to understand the character and its hidden qualities. For example, "*Yudhisthira*" is a character, and "*The Kuru King Yushisthira*" is also considered as a character containing its adjective, "*The Kuru King*" as shown in Example 1.

Proceedings of Recent Advances in Natural Language Processing, pages 569–576,
Varna, Bulgaria, Sep 4–6 2017.

Here, we understand that Yudhisthira is a character who is the king of Kuru dynasty.

Example 1: <*The Kuru King$_{adj}$ Yudhisthira$_{character}$*>

Similarly, in Example 2, "*Krishna*" is a character and "*the highly intelligent and high-souled Krishna*" should obviously be considered as a character. Here, Krishna has a quality of being "*highly intelligent and high-souled*" in the epic *The Mahabharata*.

Example 2: <*the highly intelligent$_{adj}$ and$_{cc}$ high-souled $_{adj}$ Krishna $_{character}$*>

Our goal of this research work is not only to identify characters from text but also to find out its attributive qualities, which we consider as character adjectives.

In this paper, we have formulated some rules which have been employed to extract a word, phrase or a group of words from the parsed sentences which is supposed to be a character. Then, the quality of these rules has been measured. A set of linguistic and statistical features was taken into consideration to identify different properties of the extracted word, phrase or group of words. Such textual units have been manually annotated as *Character* and *Not _a_Character* to prepare a complete tagged data set. Next, different classifiers have been applied on this data set to find out the precision, recall and f-measure; this has been followed by results and error analysis and observations.

In the rest of the paper, we have discussed related work and descriptions of the problem of character identification in *The Mahabharata*. Then, we have explained the data preparation steps followed by experiments, result and error analysis, and conclusion.

2   Related Work

A lot of works has been done on retrieving information from holy book Bible (English language), and Al-Quran (Arabic language). Mamade and Chaleira (2004) developed a system (DID) which was applied to children stories starts by classifying the utterances. The utterances belong to the narrator (indirect discourse) as well as belong to the characters taking part in the story (direct discourse). Afterwards, this DID system tries to associate each direct discourse utterance with the character(s) in the story. Goyal et al. (2010) proposed a system that exploits a variety of existing resources to identify affect states and applies "projection rules" to map the affect states onto the characters in a story. Calix et al. (2013) developed a methodology to detect sentient actors in the spoken stories. Valls-Vargas et al. (2013) proposed a method for automatically assigning narrative roles to characters in stories. Valls-Vargas et al. (2014) proposed a case-based approach to character identification in natural language text in the context of their Voz system. Valls-Vargas et al. (2015) also proposed a feedback-loop-based approach to identify the characters and their narrative roles where the output of later modules of the pipeline is fed back to earlier ones. In the context of keyword extraction, statistical approaches are often built for extracting general terms (Nees et al. 2010); the most basic measure is frequency. C/NC-value (Katerina et al. 2000), another statistical method is well known in the literature and combines statistical and linguistic information for the extraction of multi-word and nested terms.

3   Data Preparation

The English translation of the *Mahabharata* by *Kisari Mohan Ganguli* is the only complete one we can find in the public domain[1]. A total of 18 different chapters are present in the epic. The chapters are marked as *parva* (episode) e.g., *adi, sabha, vana, virata, udyog, bhishma, drona, karna, shalya, sauptika, stri, santi, anusasana, aswamedha, asramvasika, mausala, mahaprasthanika* and *svargarohanika*. It is observed that among the chapters, the 12th chapter, named as *santi parva* has the maximum number of sentences. This chapter contains 14929 uni-grams in a total of 23748 sentences. In contrast, the chapter 17 named as *mahaprasthanika parva* contains the minimum number of sentences and 888 uni-grams in a total of 188 sentences. As a whole, there are 120469 different sentences present in *Mahabharata*.

However, the average length of sentences in these chapters is significantly long (varies from 16 to 22 words). It was also found that *bhishma parva* (chapter 9) has 22 maximum number of average length sentences. Moreover, the characters occupy different floating slots within various text spans and the average number of character entities per sentence is 1.14 . Thus, the challenges lie in two spaces, one is to deal with sentences of varying length as well as to spot

---

[1] http://www.sacred-texts.com/hin/maha/index.htm

multiple characters appeared in different spans of a text. We have used Stanford CoreNLP[2] suite to tokenize the sentences and annotate them with Part-of-Speech (POS) tagger, syntactic parse tree etc. By analyzing the parsed sentences initially, it is observed that the NP which has VP as a right sibling is more tend to be the character in the text. Similar instances are observed when a NNP immediately follows a NP. In this regard, we have formulated a set of rules to extract the subtrees from the parsed sentence where NP holds the above mentioned properties and are considered as the entities. For an example,

R1: {NP<NNP $++ VP, NP<<-NNP}

where, {X<Y} means X immediately dominates Y in parse tree,

{X $++ Y} means X is a left sister of Y in parse tree, and {X<<-Y} means Y is the rightmost descendent of A in parse tree of a sentence.

Entity (e₁) = (NP (DT the) (ADJP (RB highly) (JJ intelligent) (CC and) (JJ high-souled)) (NNP Krishna))

= [the highly intelligent and high-souled Krishna]

Entity (e₂) = (NP (NNP Krishna)) = [Krishna]

The average Support (S_{Avg}) and Confidence (C_{Avg}) of each rule has been given in Table 1.

Rule #	Rules	S_{Avg}	C_{Avg}
R1	NP<NNP	55.45	64.34
R2	NP<NNP $++ (VP<VBD)	7.67	89.35
R3	NP<NNP $++ (VP<VBG)	1.00	83.11
R4	NP<NNP $++ (VP<VBN)	1.16	79.20
R5	NP<NNP $++ (VP<VBP)	0.48	64.10
R6	NP<NNP $++ (VP<VBZ)	0.99	75.21

Table 1: Average Support and Confidence of rules

A rule R can be assessed by its coverage and accuracy. Given a tuple X from a class labelled data set D , let N_{covers} be the total number of tuples covered by R; $N_{correct}$ be the total number of tuples correctly identified by R; and | D | be the total number of tuples in D . We can define the *Coverage* and *Accuracy* of R as follows.

$$\text{Coverage(R)} = \frac{N_{covers}}{|D|} \qquad \text{Accuracy(R)} = \frac{N_{correct}}{N_{cover}} \qquad (1)$$

That is, a rule's coverage is the percentage of tuples that are covered by the rule. For rule's accuracy, we look at the tuples that it covers and see what percentage of them the rule can correctly identify . The observations of coverage and accuracy for each of the rules are described in Table 2. Here |D|=228810.

Rules #	N_{covers}	$N_{correct}$	Coverage %	Accuracy %
R1	**200522**	114053	**87.63**	56.87
R2	17471	15467	7.63	**88.52**
R3	2759	2230	1.20	80.82
R4	3205	2478	1.40	77.31
R5	2012	1137	0.87	56.51
R6	2841	2022	1.24	71.17

Table 2: Coverage and Accuracy of Rules

3.1 Quality Measures of Rules

Sometimes, we find that accuracy, on its own, is not a reliable estimate of judging quality of a rule. Even for a given class, we could have a rule that covers many tuples, but most of which belong to other classes. So, we need other measures for evaluating quality, which may integrate aspects of accuracy and coverage (Han and Kamber, 2009). Here, we look at three measures e.g., Entropy (R), FOIL_Gain and Likelihood Ratio statistics. The quality measures of each rule are given in Table 3.

Rule #	Entropy	FOIL_GAIN	Likelihood
R1	**0.29**	-2683.20	362.24
R2	-3.71	**2608.00**	**3043.77**
R3	-50.29	287.85	238.36
R4	-41.42	272.09	186.71
R5	-75.16	-29.94	2.66
R6	-48.40	149.30	66.4

Table 3: Quality Measures of Each Rule

In addition to such important rules, we have tried to extract more features for employing them in a ML framework.

In this paper, we have extracted two types of features, viz., linguistic features and statistical features for each of the entities. To the best of our knowledge, these features have not been yet explored in literature for character identification.

---

[2] https://stanfordnlp.github.io/CoreNLP

3.2 Linguistic Features

To extract the linguistic features for each of the rules (R_e), we have extracted the set of attributes explained below:

Current head node of extracted entity(C_h), The preterminal nodelist of C_h (P_l), the desired character adjective entity (C_{adj}), List of siblings of C_h (S_l), list of preterminal yields of all siblings of C_h (SP_l), path from C_h to two level up parent node ($Path_{2up}$), immediate ancestor node of C_h (AN_n), list of head nodes of siblings of immediate ancestor node from C_h (AN_l), list of preterminal yield nodes of siblings of immediate ancestor node from C_h (ANP_l).

Consider the rule R_e is *NP<NNP $++ (VP<VBD)* and a sentence S_1="*O ye ascetics, **the great Vyasa** hath composed one hundred and eighty-six sections in this Parva.*"

The corresponding parsed tree of the sentence S_1 is

S_{1p}=" (ROOT (S (NP-TMP (NP (NN O)) (NP (PRP ye) (NNS ascetics))) (, ,) **(NP (DT the) (JJ great) (NNP Vyasa))** (VP (VBP hath) (VP (VBN composed) (NP (NP (CD one) (CD hundred) (CC and) (CD eighty-six) (NNS sections)) (PP (IN in) (NP (DT this) (NN Parva)))))) (. .)))".

The linguistic features (C_h, P_l, C_{adj}, S_l, SP_l, $Path_{2up}$, AN_n) extracted from S_{1p} are shown in Figure 1 .

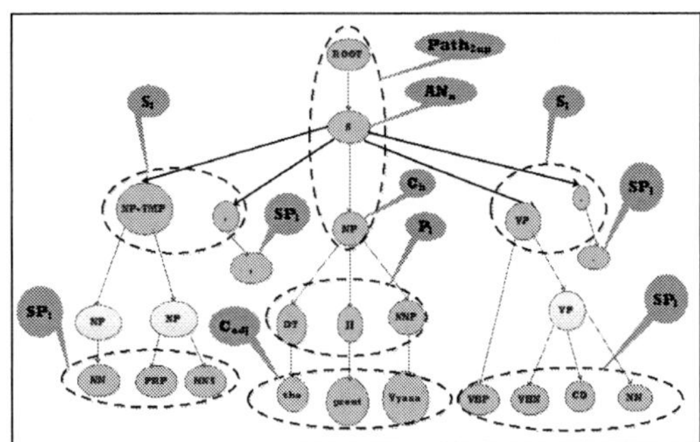

Figure 1: Example of Linguistic features

Again, consider another sentence S_2="***The mighty Jayatsena** the son of Jarasandha, the prince of the Magadhas, O king, hath been slain in battle by the high-souled son of Subhadra.*" and its corresponding parsed tree S_{2p} is:

S_{2p}="(ROOT (S (NP (NP **(NP (DT The) (JJ mighty) (NNP Jayatsena))** (NP (NP (DT the) (NN son)) (PP (IN of) (NP (NNP Jarasandha))))) (, ,) (NP (NP (DT the) (NN prince)) (PP (IN of) (NP (NP (DT the) (NNPS Magadhas)) (, ,) (NP (NNP O) (NN king)))))) (, ,)) (VP (VBP hath) (VP (VBN been) (VP (VBN slain) (PP (IN in) (NP (NN battle))) (PP (IN by) (NP (NP (DT the) (JJ high-souled) (NN son)) (PP (IN of) (NP (NNP Subhadra)))))))) (. .)))"

The linguistic features (AN_l, ANP_l) extracted from S_{2p} are shown in Figure 2 below.

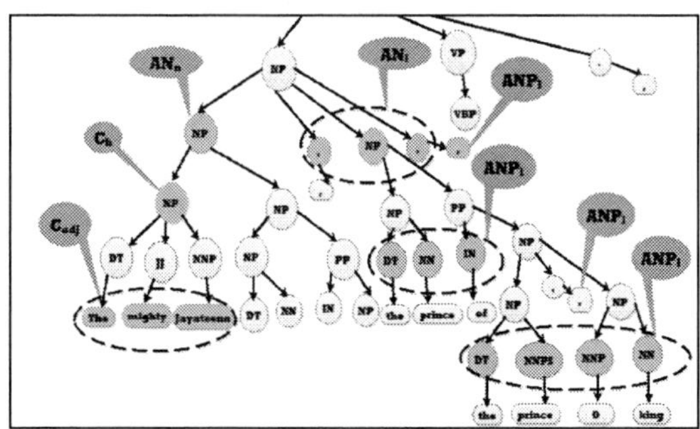

Figure2: Example of Linguistic features

Now, we have applied Stanford Universal Dependency parser[3] to each character adjectives entity (C_{adj}). The parser gives us the relation, governor and dependency of the words present in each NP entity as another set of features. They are relation name of C_{adj} (STR_n), Governor value of C_{adj} (STG_v), Governor tag of C_{adj} (STG_t), dependent value of C_{adj} (STD_v), dependent tag of C_{adj} (STD_t). In S_{2p} , we have C_{adj} ="***The mighty Jayatsena***". Its dependency relation, governor are explained below.

det(mighty/JJ , The/DT) ,
appos(mighty/JJ, Jayatsena/NNP)

There are two relation names of desired character adjective entity found, STR_n , are *det and appos* .The governor value of the desired character adjective entity, STG_v , is *mighty*. The Governor tag of desired character adjective entity, STG_t, is *JJ*. Then the Dependent value of desired character adjective entity, STD_v, are *The and Jayatsena* . After that the Dependent tag of desired character adjective, STD_t, are *DT and NNP*.

3.3 Statistical Features

To extract the statistical features, we have calculated the term frequency (TF) and term frequency-inverse document frequency (TF-IDF) of each character adjectives entity (C_{adj}) found in the dif-

[3] https://nlp.stanford.edu/software/stanford-dependencies.shtml

ferent chapters of *Mahabharata* corpus, considering each chapter as a separate document. The variance and standard deviation of TF-IDF are 0.01779 and 0.13341 respectively. In addition to that, we have calculated C-value and NC-value of each character adjectives entity (C_{adj}). In the list of entities, we have seen that there are single word entities as well as multiword term entities. The degree to which a linguistic unit is related to domain specific concepts is called *Termhood* (Katerina 2000). To find the *Termhood* of each entity, we have applied modified C-value function to all of them. C-value is a domain independent method which aims to improve the extraction of nested terms. The C-value assigns a *Termhood* to an entity, ranking it in the output list of each candidate character adjectives (C_{adj}).

$$C\_value(a) = \begin{cases} \log_2 |a|.f(a) \text{ if } a \text{ is not nested,} \\ \log_2 |a|(f(a) - \dfrac{1}{P(T_a)} \Sigma_{b \in T_a} f(b)) \text{ otherwise} \end{cases} \quad (2)$$

Where,
a = candidate character adjectives entity (C_{adj}), b = longer entity, $|a|$ = length of the entity (number of words), f(a) = frequency of a in the corpus, T_a = set of extracted candidate terms that contain a, $P(T_a)$ = number of candidate terms in T_a, f(b) = frequency of longer entity b in the corpus. After that, we have used NC-value method which incorporates context information into the C-value method. This method re-ranks the C-value list of each candidate character adjectives entity (C_{adj}). The NC-value measure is formally described as

$$NC\_value = 0.8C\_value(a) + 0.2 \sum_{b \in C_a} f_a(b)w(b) \quad (3)$$

where, a = candidate character adjectives entity (C_{adj}), C_a = the set of distinct context words of a, f_a (b) = the frequency of b as a term context words of a, w(b) = weight of b as a term context word. As an example, if we consider C_{adj} = *"the Kuru king Yudhishthira"* then its C-value is 36.00 and NC-value is 46.56. The range of C-value varies from 0 to 7124.92 and the range of NC-value varies from 0.000022 to 193472.6998. In this way, we have collected all the linguistic and statistical features and arranged them in a set named as $Attr_{Total}$ for all the candidate character adjectives (C_{adj}).

$Attr_{Total}$ = { {R_e} ,{C_h, P_l , C_{adj}, S_l , SP_l, $Path_{2up}$, AN_n, AN_l , ANP_l},{STR_n, STG_v , STG_t, STD_v , STD_t}, {TF, TF-IDF}, {C-value, NC-value}}

From the above data preprocessing steps, we have manually tagged all the entities as *Character* and *Not_a_Character*. A total of 228810 objects extracted by the algorithm were manually annotated and for reference, two different independent domain experts were given the task of annotation to determine the *characters* and *non characters* in the dataset D according to their logic and perception. Secondly, they have identified the characters with their attributive qualities named as character adjectives. This identification task was done on the basis of few policies to identify a phrase as a character or character adjectives. Some of the important policies are as follows:

a)Every Name of a person followed by a verb is a Character.

e.g., <*"Yudhisthira"*>

b) Each name of a person with its qualities which is often mentioned before or after the name is a Character.

e.g., < *"the wonderful warrior Drona "*>, <*"Arjuna the foremost "*>

c) Living, non living and celestial things which/who has done some action ,such as: speak, talk, walk or feel etc. and which has an active participation in the script is a *character*.

e.g., <*"the celestial Sakti"*>,<*"the celestial Ganges"*>

d) Each word which is related to some profession of a person (like: *sage, brahmana*) is a *character*.

e.g., *"The Asura architect"*

e) An animal which actively participates in the text is a *character*.

eg:<*"the celestial steed Uchchaihsrava"*>

f) Any special weapon which is very powerful in case of destruction is termed as a Character because it has a particular identity, such as <*"the Sudarshana Chakra (the celestial disc)"*>

eg: <*"the terrible weapon Narayana"*>

To be very precise, every object of dataset D which has anthropomorphic trait is considered to be a character. The confusion matrices for identification of *character* and *Not_a_character* given by annotator-1 and annotator-2 are given in Table 4 and Table 5:

The **kappa measure** of agreement for identification of *Character* is **0.769** and for identification of *Not_a_Character* is **0.753**.

Character Identified in dataset D=137389		Annotator 1	
		Yes	No
Annotator 2	**Yes**	135604	360
	No	304	**1121**

Table 4: Confusion matrix of Characters/Character Adjectives by Annotator 1 and 2

Not_a_Character Identified in dataset D=91421		Annotator 1	
		Yes	No
Annotator 2	**Yes**	88364	632
	No	552	**1873**

Table 5: Confusion matrix of Not_a_Character by Annotator 1 and 2

4 Experiments

We have conducted our experiments on the data set, D that contains 15 linguistic features and 4 statistical features with 228810 entities. The data set seems to a two class problem, where each entity is manually tagged as *Character* or *Not_a_Character*. In order to satisfy the requirements of different classifiers, data preprocessing was conducted to convert textual information into numeric values. We have conducted feature ablation studies in two stages, one at the individual feature level using different attribute selection measures and another at subset level using *Forward Selection* and *Backward Elimination* schemes. Finally, we have applied different classification algorithms available under RapidMiner Studio tool[4] on our data set along with important attributes.

4.1 Attribute Selection Measure

Here, we have applied some popular attribute selection measures like information gain (I_g), gain ratio (G_r), gini index (G_i), Chi Squared Statistic (Chi) to our data set. The results are given below in Table 6. The attribute with highest **Information gain (I_g)** is chosen and the top three attributes with highest Information gain are $\{C_{adj}, P_l, SP_l\}$. The attribute with the maximum **Gain Ratio (G_r)** is selected as the splitting attribute. The top three attributes with highest Gain Ratio are {**NC-value, TF-IDF, C-value**}. On the other hand, **Gini Index (G_i)** is a measure of impurity of any data set. The higher the weight of an attribute, it is considered to be more relevant. The top three relevant attributes can be found from our data set are $\{C_{adj}, P_l, STD_v\}$. The **Chi-Square** statistic is a nonparametric statistical technique used to determine if a distribution of observed frequencies differs from the theoretical expected frequencies. The higher the Chi-Square value of an attribute, the more relevant it is considered . From our data set, the top three attributes selected using Chi-Square are $\{ANP_l, C_{adj}, SP_l\}$.

Attribute	I_g	G_r	G_i	Chi
R_e	0.028	0.038	0.016	7804.304
C_h	0	0	0	0
P_l	0.623	0.126	0.339	161885.5
C_{adj}	**0.924**	0.082	**0.461**	303530.6
S_l	0.261	0.045	0.152	73003.12
SP_l	0.575	0.058	0.297	269168.3
$Path_{2up}$	0.332	0.039	0.183	114295.3
AN_n	0.063	0.035	0.04	18843.35
AN_l	0.18	0.03	0.107	51561.98
ANP_l	0.435	0.05	0.226	**337090.9**
STR_n	0.425	0.142	0.25	119360
STG_v	0.503	0.071	0.278	209395.5
STG_t	0.208	0.116	0.128	61067.99
STD_v	0.541	0.097	0.304	145828.3
STD_t	0.407	0.146	0.24	114517.4
TF	0.121	0.287	0.072	33953.84
TF-IDF	0.189	0.335	0.115	40422.39
C-value	0.149	0.312	0.082	34288
NC-value	0.198	**0.348**	0.119	34571.75

Table 6: Attribute Selection measures

4.2 Feature Subset Selection

We have used two different schemes, e.g. *Forward Selection* and *Backward Elimination* available in Rapid Miner to find out different groups of relevant attributes or features,. Using the *Forward Selection* scheme, we have obtained a new set of attributes FS_F which is a subset of $Attr_{Total}$.

$FS_F = \{ R_e, P_l, C_{adj}, STG_t\ STD_v, STD_t, TF, TF\text{-}IDF \}$;where $FS_F \subset Attr_{Total}$

Next, using the Backward Elimination scheme, we have acquired a new set of attributes BE_F which is also a subset of $Attr_{Total}$.

$BE_F = \{ R_e, C_h, P_l, C_{adj}, S_l, SP_l, Path_{2up}, AN_n, AN_l, ANP_l, STG_t, STD_v, STD_t, TF, TF\text{-}IDF \}$

where $BE_F \subset Attr_{Total}$

---

[4] https://rapidminer.com/products/studio/

In both the schemes, we received a list of attributes as an end product. Then, we have prepared two different data sets D_{FS} and D_{BE} with the relevant attributes.

4.3 Classification Task

First, we have converted our data sets (D, D_{FS}, D_{BE}) into their compatible formats that are acceptable to the classifiers under Rapid Miner tool (e.g. *Deep Learning Classifier, KNN Classifier, Logistic Regression Classifier, NaiveBayes', Decision Tree and Random Forest Classifier*). We have divided the datasets in 7:3 ratio for training and testing. Then, we have applied these classifiers on our data sets to find the accuracy along with different statistical measures.

5 Result Analysis

The detail observation of Precision , Recall and F-Measure for each classifier applied on the data set D, D_{FS} and D_{BE} are given in the Figure 3 and Table 7.

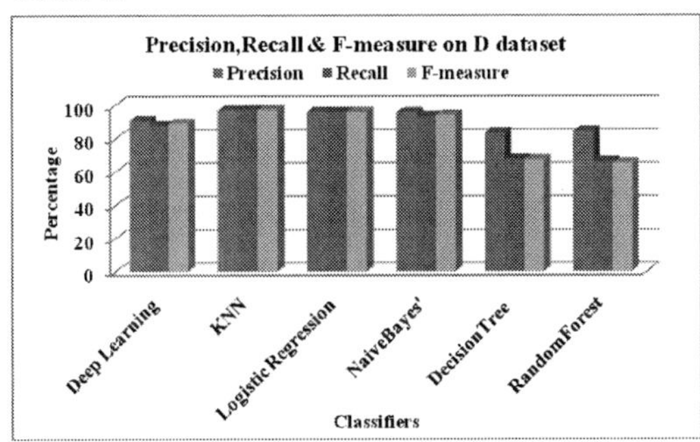

Figure 3: Precision, Recall and F-measure of classifiers on D dataset

It has been observed that KNN classifier obtained the highest Precision, Recall and F-measure on D dataset, whereas RandomForest has the worst Recall and F-measure on D dataset.

	D_{FS} dataset			D_{BE} dataset		
	P	R	F	P	R	F
Deep Learning	88.07	87.03	87.54	89.21	87.23	88.20
KNN	**92.19**	**92.2**	**92.19**	**95.66**	**95.66**	**95.66**
Logistic Regression	85.49	84.43	84.95	85.43	84.43	84.92
NaiveBayes'	**83**	75.81	79.24	81.59	74.1	77.66
DecisionTree	91.94	90.58	91.25	91.95	90.59	91.26
RandomForest	90.29	88.05	89.15	90.99	89.17	90.07
P=Precision; R=Recall; F=F-measure						

Table 7: Precision, Recall and F-measure on D_{FS} and D_{BE} datasets

Similarly, we have observed the Precision, Recall and F-Measure on D_{FS} and D_{BE} datsets as shown in Table7. Here, we found that KNN classifier achieved the best results among the other classifers for both the datasets. But, NaiveBayes' has the worst results for both the datasets. The confusion matrices for each classifier applied on the same data set D, D_{FS} and D_{BE} are observed. Here, N and C are *Not_a_Character* and *Character* respectively.

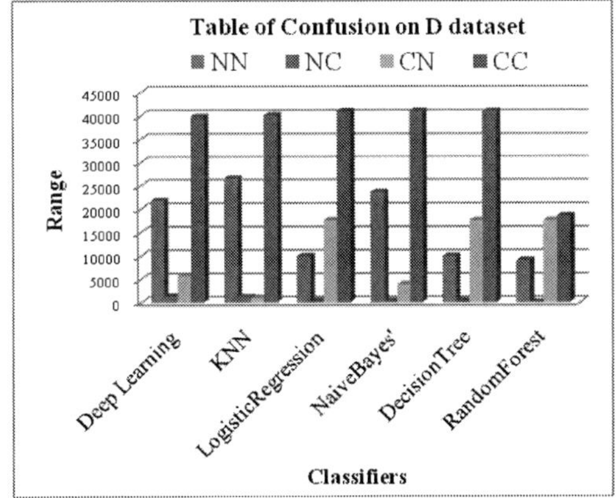

Figure 4: Confusion Table on dataset D

We observed from Figure 4 that NaiveBayes' classifier has maximum number of CC (*Character, Character*) and KNN classifier has maximum number of NN (*Not_a_Character, Not_a_Character*) confusions on dataset D.

	D_{FS} dataset				D_{BE} dataset			
	NN	NC	CN	CC	NN	NC	CN	CC
Deep Learning	7418	200	2283	9759	7687	515	2014	9444
KNN	**9298**	450	403	9509	8985	819	716	**9140**
Logistic Regression	7417	757	2284	9202	7393	732	2308	9227
NaiveBayes'	4856	185	4845	9774	5121	117	4580	9842
DecisionTree	7963	91	1738	9868	7964	93	1737	9866
Random Forest	7677	79	2024	**9880**	7444	63	2257	**9896**
N=Not_a_Character; C=Character								

Table 8: Confusion Table on D_{FS} and D_{BE} datasets

From the Table 8 we can observe that KNN classifier has maximum number of NN (*Not_a_Character, Not_a_Character*) and RandomForest classifier has maximum number of CC (*Character, Character*) in both the datasets D_{FS} and D_{BE} respectively.

6 Error Analysis and Observations

	Classification error(%)		
	D dataset	D_{FS} dataset	D_{BE} dataset
Deep Learning	10.29	12.63	12.86
KNN	**2.67**	4.34	7.81
Logistic Regression	3.83	15.47	15.46
NaiveBayes'	5.35	**25.58**	**23.89**
DecisionTree	25.94	9.3	9.31
RandomForest	27.08	10.7	11.8

Table 9: Error Rate of D, D_{FS} and D_{BE} datasets

It is observed from Table 9 that KNN classifier has the lowest error rate on all the datasets and it implies that KNN has the best performance over other five classifiers. On the other hand, we observed that random classifiers have the worst performances on dataset D and NaiveBayes' has the highest error rate on dataset D_{FS} and D_{BE}.

7 Conclusion

In this paper, we have presented a novel approach to identify *Characters* and *Character Adjectives* from unannotated Indian mythological epic called *Mahabharata* depending on some phrase level rules. Then, we have applied a couple of machine learning algorithms to classify whether an extracted object using the predefined rule is a character/character adjective or not.The experimental results showed that our approach delivers the best results when we have applied KNN classifier followed by Logistic Regresion, NaiveBayes and Deep Learning classifiers. We have also shown that a set of features are very important in classification using feature subset selection schemes. As part of the future work, we have planned to create a larger set of phrase level rules for better evaluation of charcaters and character adjectives.

Acknowledgement

The present work is supported by "Young Faculty Research Fellows of the Visvesvaraya PhD Scheme" of MeitY, Govt. of India.

References

Amit Goyal, Ellen Riloff; and Hal D III.2010. *Automatically producing plot unit representations for narrative text.* In Proceedings of the 2010 Conference on Empirical Methods in Natural Language Processing, pp.77–86. Association for Computational Linguistics.

Ellias Iosif, Taniya Mishra, *From Speaker Identification to Affective Analysis: A Multi-Step System for Analyzing Children Stories.*2014. Proceedings of the 3rd Workshop on Computational Linguistics for Literature(CLfL)@EACL 2014, pp. 40-49.

Jiwaei Han and Micheline Kamber.2009.*Data Mining Concepts and Techniques.*

Josep Valls-Vargas J, Santiago Ontanon ,and Jichen Zhu . 2013.*Toward character role assignment for natural language stories.* Proceedings of the Ninth Artificial Intelligence and Interactive Digital Entertainment Conference.

Josep Valls-Vargas J, Santiago Ontanon and Jichen Zhu . 2014. *Toward automatic character identification in unannotated narrative text.* In Proceedings of the Seventh Workshop in Intelligent Narrative Technologies.

Josep Valls-Vargas, Jichen Zhu, Santiago Ontanon. 2015.*Narrative hermeneutic circle: Improving character role identification from natural language text via feedback loops.* Proceedings of the 24th International Conference on Artificial Intelligence. AAAI Press.

Katerina Frantzi, Sophia Ananiadou and Hideki Mima. 2000. *Automatic Recognition of Multi-Word Terms: the C-value/NC-value Method.* International Journal of Digital Libraries, 3(2), pp.117-132

Matthew Freeman. 2016. *Historicising Transmedia Storytelling: Early Twentieth-Century Transmedia Story Worlds.* Routledge. ISBN 1315439506.

Nees J V Eck , Ludo Waltman L, Ed C M Noyons Ed, and Reindert K Buter. 2010. *Automatic term identification for bibliometric mapping.* SpringerLink, Scientometrics,Volume 82, Number 3.

Numo Mamede and Pedro Chaleira .2004.*Character identification in children stories.* Advances in natural language processing. Springer Berlin Heidelberg, 2004, pp.82-90.

Ricardo A. Calix, Leili Javadpour, Mehdi Khazaeli, and Gerald M. Knapp. 2013. *Automatic Detection of Nominal Entities in Speech for Enriched Content Search.* The Twenty-Sixth International FLAIRS Conference, pp. 190–195

Stephen V Duncan. 2006. *A Guide to Screenwriting Success: Writing for Film and Television.* Rowman & Littlefield. ISBN 9780742553019

Learning Multimodal Gender Profile using Neural Networks

Carlos Pérez Estruch　　　**Roberto Paredes**　　　**Paolo Rosso**
Pattern Recognition and Human Language Technology (PRHLT) Research Center
Universitat Politècnica de València, València, Spain
{carprees, rparedes, prosso}@prhlt.upv.es

Abstract

Gender identification in social networks is one of the most popular aspects of user profile learning. Traditionally it has been linked to author profiling, a difficult problem to solve because of the little difference in the use of language between genders. This situation has led to the need of taking into account other information apart from textual data, favoring the emergence of multimodal data. The aim of this paper is to apply neural networks to perform data fusion, using an existing multimodal corpus, the NUS-MSS data set, that (not only) contains text data, but also image and location information. We improved previous results in terms of macro accuracy (87.8%) obtaining the state-of-the-art performance of 91.3%.

1　Introduction

Nowadays we are experiencing a, more than remarkable, change and growth of technology. Emergence of online social networks has reinvented the form of communication and has taken it to another level. However, it has not been beneficial only to users, since companies and researchers have obtained access to tons of data (aka big data) generated in social media.

This information could be used in multiple ways. There is a growing interest in the search of "who" created the contents, but not exactly as a complete individual identity, rather as a collection of general user profiles traits (gender, age, personality...) in order to construct user groups.

Being able to infer the profile of a user can be beneficial for tasks such as security and marketing. In marketing, we may take advantage of this information, for example, for personalized products recommendations making the selection easier. With respect to security, it is important to have an idea about who could have written a potential threat.

In this paper we aim to approach how to identify the gender of the users taking into account multimodal data. Therefore, the proposed neural networks use different fusion strategies in order to combine the different modalities.

The paper is organized as follows. Section 2 describes related works on gender identification. In Section 3 we present our neural network architectures. In Section 4 we describe the data set, the used techniques and discuss the results. Finally, in Section 5 we draw some conclusions and discuss future work.

2　Related work

The gender identification task has traditionally been related to author profiling. Pennebaker et al. (2003) made some initial approaches to asses how the variation of linguistic characteristics in a text can help in the finding of gender and age of an author with respect to others. Argamon et al. (2003) explored the difference in writing style between male and female, in a large subset of the British National Corpus. Koppel et al. (2002) inferred in the search of gender in a less formal corpus, using a combination of lexical and syntactic features with 80% of accuracy. More related to our study, Schler et al. (2006) analyzed many blogs also looking for differences in writing style between gender and age groups with results closes to 80% of accuracy. Also, Argamon et al. (2009) worked with anonymous texts from blogs using two types of basic features: content-based and style-based features. From a gender perspective, it is interesting to see that with the content-based features they obtained better results (75.1%), 4%

Proceedings of Recent Advances in Natural Language Processing, pages 577–582,
Varna, Bulgaria, Sep 4–6 2017.

more than with the style features. With the combination of style and content features they gained one point of accuracy.

Burger et al. (2011) is one of the first works about gender identification in Twitter. They used a big data set of 184,000 users of which approximately 18,000 are for test set. They obtained very good results: 91.8% of accuracy. Notice that they used names of people which is a very discriminating information about gender. Using only textual information of tweets they reached 74.5% of accuracy.

Since 2013 tasks on author profiling have been organized at the PAN lab of CLEF (Rangel et al., 2013). The focus is on addressing the problem from a perspective exclusively related to the processing of text. The work of Farseev et al. (2015) is possibly the first preliminary study in author profiling from the multimodal perspective with very interesting results: 87.8% in terms of macro accuracy.

3   Model Description

In this work we developed different neural network topologies that operate under a multimodal approach. One of the first questions that can arise when starting to work with multimodal data is how to fuse the data. We can distinguish between two basic types of fusion strategies: early fusion and late fusion.

The idea of the early fusion approach (Figure 1a) is to concatenate all data sources into a new larger vector and feed it directly to the network without doing any previous single source classification (one learning phase). From the perspective of a basic neural network could be more difficult to make a good representation of the data if the different sources have different scales. This can result in a normalization-dependant model, precisely for reducing the variance of the data, and therefore for processing them in a common representation space.

In contrast with the previous one, the late fusion (Figure 1b) is based on performing the fusion after the single source classification is done, at the decision level. We wanted to avoid the use of complex (and usually overmuch heuristic) fusion operations, and in order to address this problem without this disadvantage we developed from scratch a fusion neural network. This modification of the basic multilayer perceptron consists of as many softmax layers as needed, one for each data source (single source learning) and a last softmax layer that modifies the weights of all the network. As we can see, we concatenated each linear output of each single source sofmax layer. Finally, we added one last hidden layer after the concatenation of the outputs, and before the last output in order to discover the last discriminating information of the concatenation vector.

In this case, we consider that one iteration of the network finishes when the 6 learning phases (forward + backward) have been completed. The order in which the single source learning phases are applied should not influence the final result. In our case the last learning phase was the one that modifies the weights of all the network (in Figure 1b, N: Out[2]).

4   Evaluation

In this section we describe the data set, the data preprocesing and all the techniques used to develop the models. Finally, we present and discuss the results.

4.1   Data Set

The data set used in this work was obtained from Farseev et al. (2015). The NUS-MSS data set contains processed social media data from three different cities (Singapore, London and New York) and from three different social networks (Foursquare, Instagram and Twitter) for users of each city. We have focused our research on Singapore users. Following, we analyze each source separately:

- *Foursquare*[1]: We have an user mobility profile as a count (checkins) of visited places. It follows the Foursquare category hierarchy[2] of Singapore, plus more than 150 extra categories. In total we have vectors with 764 components of mobility for each user.

- *Instagram*[3]: This is a preprocessed corpus constructed from users original uploaded images, mapped to a 1000-dimensional (ImageNet labels (Deng et al., 2009)) vector forming an image concept dictionary per user.

---

[1]https://es.foursquare.com/
[2]https://developer.foursquare.com/categorytree
[3]https://www.instagram.com/

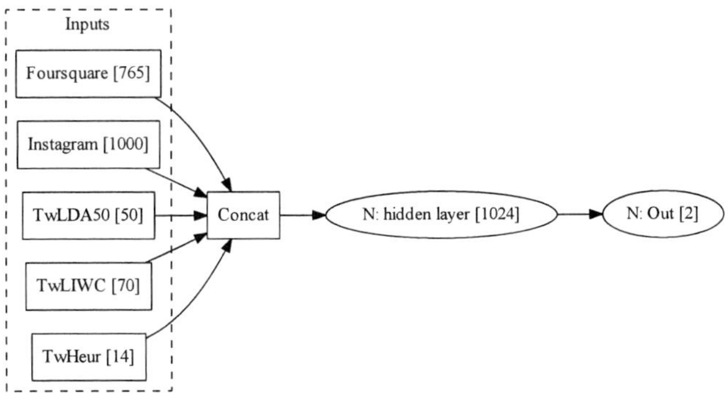

(a) Early fusion architecture

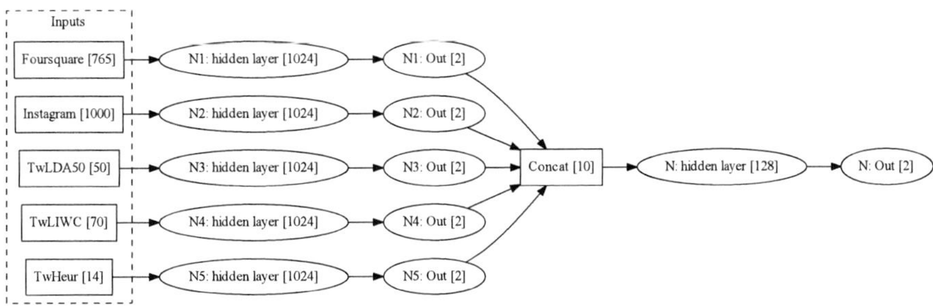

(b) Late fusion architecture

Figure 1: Artificial neural network data fusion strategies. In (a) we can see the basic early fusion topology. In (b) we have the late fusion neural network. Note that the number of hidden layers depends exclusively on the problem to solve.

- *Twitter*[4]: Textual information had been processed in 3 ways: Latent Dirichlet allocation (LDA) 50-dimensional vectors with latent topic space information (Blei et al., 2003); 70-LIWC features vectors (Pennebaker et al., 2001); vectors with 14 manually defined characteristics, "heuristically-inferred features" (Farseev et al., 2015), with for example the number of hashtags, number of emoticons, number of tweets, among others, for each user.

Gender labels were extracted from the Facebook[5] ground truth file provided in the data set.

For the total amount of collected users, we trained our model with the 3172 of which we had data in all three sources. The test set is composed of 222 *other* users.

4.2 Data Preprocessing

There are certain classifiers, such as random forest, that work well regardless of the initial data representation space, but this is not the case of neural networks. Neural network models can learn from non-standardized data, but they will not do it in an optimal way. In this case:

1. Instagram data was modified because the original uploaded data was scaled depending on the number of images for each user. We divided every user's 1000 image concept vector by their number of images to scale them to a more practical range of values.

2. We applied z-score normalization (Eq. 1) for every source (except for Foursquare data)

---

[4]https://twitter.com/

[5]https://www.facebook.com/

in order to accelerate the learning, making stochastic gradient descent convergence faster.

$$z = \frac{x - \mu}{\sigma} \qquad (1)$$

Foursquare vectors were difficult to train in our models because of their sparsity. Some categories, or "visited" places, are 0 for all users. It was not possible to apply z-score normalization to these categories (0 division in the scale operation). Finally, we decided to use this source without pre-processing after testing other types of normalization as for example min-max.

4.3 Training

4.3.1 Activation Function

We used ReLU (Eq. 2 and 3) as activation function for the hidden layers (Nair and Hinton, 2010). At present ReLU is performing better than other activation functions, such as sigmoid, in many scenarios.

$$ReLU(x) = f(x) = max(0, x) \qquad (2)$$

$$f(x) = \begin{cases} x, & \text{if } x > 0 \\ 0, & \text{if } x \leq 0 \end{cases} \qquad (3)$$

He et al. (2015) introduced a modification of ReLU called PReLU (Eq. 4). They proposed to use a small learnable parameter to control the slope of the negative part, in order to avoid zero gradients:

$$f(x) = \begin{cases} x, & \text{if } x > 0 \\ a_i x, & \text{if } x \leq 0 \end{cases} \qquad (4)$$

We tested it, but in comparison with the basic ReLU function we did not see any significant difference in results, although the model converged faster. This can be explained since the trainable parameter acquires a higher value in the first epochs of the training, and therefore the model learns faster because of the highest weights modification.

Finally, we discarded this option because not a big improvement was observed and, on the contrary, it added more training parameters.

4.3.2 Weight Initialization

Weight initialization is linked to the activation functions used in the hidden layers. We used He et al. (2015) initialization for ReLU in all cases. We did not use any pretrained initialization.

4.3.3 Regularization Techniques

We detected overfitting in training, possibly due to the relatively few number of users in the training set. Overfitting is one of the most common problems in neural networks but there are some ways to prevent it.

Dropout (Srivastava et al., 2014) is an extended technique used in these cases. Dropout is based on the idea of leaving disabled a certain number of neurons in each iteration to simulate the train of several networks. The basis is that it is very difficult for the network to see the same data distribution twice and, therefore, the representation should be more distributed.

As we said, data sources were from different social networks, and from different modalities, that means that the vectors were in different representation spaces. Moreover, each source itself has data with a lot of variability. For this reason we decided to apply one interneuron normalization technique known as batch normalization (Ioffe and Szegedy, 2015).

Batch normalization reduces internal covariate shift of data and makes training faster. It can be used jointly with dropout, although there is a better alternative that does the same task as dropout, but with the advantage of data augmentation. We added Gaussian noise with a normal distribution before the scale and shift step (just after the normalization):

$$y_i \leftarrow \gamma(\widehat{x}_i + \widehat{x}_i \mathcal{N}(\mu, \sigma)) + \beta \equiv \text{BN}_{\gamma, \beta}(x_i) \qquad (5)$$

where γ and β are the scale and shift learnable factors respectively, $\mathcal{N}(\mu, \sigma)$ is the random values generator which follows a normal distribution, and $\widehat{x}_i$ is the normalized activation over a mini-batch.

The two learnable parameters (γ and β, eq. 5) learn from different data in each epoch (very low probability that each value appears twice). It is important to know that if we use a too large deviation value, the model is going to learn from random data, and if we use a small parameter the modified values of the data will be too close to their representation without noise. For this reason, the best practice is to generate noise with 0 mean and standard deviation between 0.2 and 0.4. All results presented in this paper were obtained using Batch Normalization with Gaussian noise ($\mu = 0$, $\sigma = 0.3$).

4.3.4 Other Considerations

The learning rate was 0.001 in all cases. It may seem small but according to the data set size we preferred that weight updates were small to control better the training.

We used minibatch stochastic gradient descent (SGD) as optimizer. All parameters were selected applying 10 fold cross-validation, extracting each fold from the training set.

4.4 Results

In Table 1 we show our results together with the previously obtained ones (Farseev et al., 2015). We would like to highlight the improvements we obtained in terms of macro accuracy.

Gender (Macro acc.)	Baseline	Ours
Single source		
Location (Foursquare)	0.649	**0.714•**
LIWC text (Twitter)	0.716	0.737
Heuristic text (Twitter)	0.685	0.712
LDA 50 text (Twitter)	0.788	**0.806**
Img. concepts (Instagram)	0.784	**0.885•**
Multisource combinations (late fusion)		
LDA50 + LIWC	0.784	0.823
LDA50 + heuristic	0.815	0.805
Heuristic + LIWC	0.730	0.755
All text	0.815	0.822
Img. concepts + location	0.802	0.875•
All text + img. concepts	0.824	**0.900•**
All text + location	0.743	0.833•
All sources		
Complete early fusion	0.707	0.910•
Complete late fusion	0.878	**0.913**

Table 1: Macro accuracy results. In the first row we show Farseev et al. (2015) previous results obtained with random forest classifiers. The second row shows the results obtained with our neural network based approach. In bold the best performance on each social media source, the best multisource combination, and all sources. The values with (•) are significantly higher than the baseline (significance level 0.95).

As we can see, there is a high improvement of accuracy on the Instagram set as well as on the other single sources. This is, in part, because random forest classifiers do not have much capacity to discriminate between extensive data vectors that, in contrast, is one of the main advantages of the neural networks. The Instagram source is more related to the liking of a person, and is very helpful from a point of view of gender identification, because males and females (with exceptions) tend to upload very correlated and representative pictures to how they are.

In the case of fusing the LDA-50 characteristics with the heuristic data of the tweets, our result is worse than previous and similar to the LDA-50 single one. In general, the base operation of the late fusion network causes that, if there is contradictory information in the sources, the decision will be related to the most discriminating one.

	Male	Female
Male	97	32
Female	13	80

Table 2: Confusion matrix for single LDA50 model.

	Male	Female
Male	94	35
Female	11	82

Table 3: Confusion matrix for LDA50 + heuristic model.

In this case, the fusion model with the heuristic features contributed to classify better the females but it misclassified some of the males in contrast to single LDA (Tables 2 and 3). These problems do not affect in the same way other classifiers as random forest. A similar behaviour occurs when using only the location information with the image concepts.

Analyzing the results where we used all sources, our approaches worked very well for both fusion techniques. Also, we obtained a very good result employing early fusion, which means that using the right techniques, a neural network has the capacity to classify correctly gender regardless where the fusion takes place.

It is difficult to know which one of the two architectures is better because the macro accuracy difference is not statistically significant (t-test), and both models have a similar number of parameters ($\approx$ 2 million). With relation to its training speed and simplicity, it is clear that the early fusion one can be more efficient, although it worked well in part due to the normalization techniques.

When not using it, the training was more inconsistent than with the late fusion approach, and the accuracy result was worse.

5 Conclusions and Future Work

We developed and tested different neural networks models using multimodal data for a gender identification task with successful results: 91.3% of macro accuracy.

As future work, we will continue working in this direction, searching for the best way to combine and use data. The base fusion neural network models work well and it will be interesting to extend them to add, for example, convolutional neural networks for preprocessing of the raw images and texts, in order to solve these problems using deep learning approaches.

Acknowledgments

This work has been funded by the SomEMBED TIN2015-71147-C2-1-P MINECO research project.

References

Shlomo Argamon, Moshe Koppel, Jonathan Fine, and Anat R. Shimoni. 2003. Gender, genre, and writing style in formal written texts. *TEXT & TALK - An Interdisciplinary Journal of Language, Discourse & Communication Studies* 23:321–346.

Shlomo Argamon, Moshe Koppel, James W. Pennebaker, and Jonathan Schler. 2009. Automatically profiling the author of an anonymous text. *Communications of the ACM* 52(2):119–123.

David M. Blei, Andrew Y. Ng, and Michael I. Jordan. 2003. Latent dirichlet allocation. *The Journal of Machine Learning Research* 3:993–1022.

John D. Burger, John Henderson, George Kim, and Guido Zarrella. 2011. Discriminating gender on twitter. In *Proceedings of the Conference on Empirical Methods in Natural Language Processing*. Association for Computational Linguistics, Stroudsburg, PA, USA, EMNLP '11, pages 1301–1309.

Jia Deng, Wei Dong, Richard Socher, Li-Jia. Li, Kai Li, and Li Fei-Fei. 2009. ImageNet: A Large-Scale Hierarchical Image Database. In *CVPR09*.

Aleksandr Farseev, Liqiang Nie, Mohammad Akbari, and Tat-Seng Chua. 2015. Harvesting multiple sources for user profile learning: A big data study. In *Proceedings of the 5th ACM on International Conference on Multimedia Retrieval*. ACM, New York, NY, USA, ICMR '15, pages 235–242.

Kaiming He, Xiangyu Zhang, Shaoqing Ren, and Jian Sun. 2015. Delving deep into rectifiers: Surpassing human-level performance on imagenet classification. In *Proceedings of the 2015 IEEE International Conference on Computer Vision*. IEEE Computer Society, Washington, DC, USA, ICCV '15, pages 1026–1034.

Sergey Ioffe and Christian Szegedy. 2015. Batch normalization: Accelerating deep network training by reducing internal covariate shift. In *Proceedings of the 32nd International Conference on Machine Learning*. JMLR, Lille, France, volume 37 of *ICML'15*, pages 448–456.

Moshe Koppel, Shlomo Argamon, and Anat R. Shimoni. 2002. Automatically categorizing written texts by author gender. *Literary and Linguistic Computing 17(3), in press.* 17(4):401–412.

Vinod Nair and Geoffrey E. Hinton. 2010. Rectified linear units improve restricted boltzmann machines. In *Proceedings of the 27th International Conference on Machine Learning*. Omnipress, Haifa, Israel, ICML'10, pages 807–814.

James W. Pennebaker, Martha E. Francis, and Roger J. Booth. 2001. *Linguistic Inquiry and Word Count.* Lawerence Erlbaum Associates, Mahwah, NJ.

James W. Pennebaker, Matthias R. Mehl, and Kate G. Niederhoffer. 2003. Psychological aspects of natural language use: Our words, our selves. *Annual review of psychology* 54(1):547–577.

Francisco Rangel, Paolo Rosso, Moshe Koppel, Efstathios Stamatatos, and Giacomo Inches. 2013. Overview of the author profiling task at PAN 2013. In *Working Notes of CLEF 2013 Conference and Labs of the Evaluation forum*. Valencia, Spain.

Jonathan Schler, Moshe Koppel, Shlomo Argamon, and James W. Pennebaker. 2006. Effects of age and gender on blogging. In *AAAI Spring Symposium: Computational Approaches to Analyzing Weblogs*. pages 199–205.

Nitish Srivastava, Geoffrey Hinton, Alex Krizhevsky, Ilya Sutskever, and Ruslan Salakhutdinov. 2014. Dropout: A simple way to prevent neural networks from overfitting. *The Journal of Machine Learning Research* 15(1):1929–1958.

Recognition of Genuine Polish Suicide Notes

Maciej Piasecki
Wrocław University
of Science and Technology
Wrocław, Poland
`maciej.piasecki@`
`pwr.edu.pl`

Ksenia Młynarczyk
Wrocław University
of Science and Technology
Wrocław, Poland
`ksenia.mlynarczyk@`
`gmail.com`

Jan Kocoń
Wrocław University
of Science and Technology
Wrocław, Poland
`jan.kocon@ pwr.edu.pl`

Abstract

In this article we present the result of the research on the recognition of genuine Polish suicide notes (SNs). We provide useful method to distinguish between SNs and other types of discourse, including counterfeited SNs. The method uses a wide range of word-based and semantic features and it was evaluated using Polish Corpus of Suicide Notes, which contains 1244 genuine SNs, expanded with a manually prepared set of 334 counterfeited SNs and 2200 letter-like texts from the Internet. We utilised the algorithm to create the class-related sense dictionaries to improve the result of SNs classification. The obtained results show that there are fundamental differences between genuine SNs and counterfeited SNs. The applied method of the sense dictionary construction appeared to be the best way of improving the model.

1 Introduction

Suicide is a tragedy for the victim and also for their close ones. It is also the third leading cause of violent death among people aged 15 to 44 (Holmes et al., 2007), see also (Gomez, 2014; World Health Organisation, 2014). The reasons for such an act and the mental state of a victim are not open by itself to external observation. However, very often the last language utterances are left in a form of *suicide notes* (henceforth SNs). Such recorded utterances create a unique opportunity to come closer to the way of thinking of someone at risk, and to construct a model of the specific language which is used by people in such a state of mind. The analysis can go in two possible directions: firstly recognition of suicide letters among other types of writing and secondly identification of the features that are characteristic for suicide notes and can provide some insight on the person committing suicide. Both of them are closely correlated and for both development of classification methods to separate SNs from other types of writing is crucial.

Linguistic analysis in (Zaśko-Zielińska, 2013) showed that such differences are mainly of the semantic and pragmatic nature. Moreover, SNs have personal character and varied length but with the dominance of short notes. In addition examples of genuine SNs are available in small data sets. A distinction between genuine SNs and texts intentionally written in such a way that they are meant to resemble SNs may provide crucial evidence for finding out the intrinsic features of SNs, if there are any. Our goal was to develop classification method for the recognition of genuine SNs among other types of texts with a special focus given for sorting out text only resembling SNs, especially counterfeited SNs. The method should analyse a wide range of linguistic features and be a good basis for the automated identification of features that make SNs so specific.

As we can expect that the differences between suicide notes and other types of discourse can be mainly of the semantic and pragmatic natures, we wanted to expand the corpus analysis beyond the simple statistical analysis of word occurrence.

2 Related Works

The study of SNs has a long tradition of qualitative analysis from the point of view of linguistics and clinical psychology (Shneidman and Farberow, 1957). There have also been attempts to perform statistical analysis (Gomez, 2014), e.g. Pennebaker and Chung (2011) used the frequency of verbal elements in a narrative which express a certain mood or sentiment.

Pestian et al. (2008) pioneered automated recognition of differences between genuine SNs

Proceedings of Recent Advances in Natural Language Processing, pages 583–591,
Varna, Bulgaria, Sep 4–6 2017.

and SNs written by volunteers, known as elicited. They worked with a sample of 33 genuine and 33 elicited items. Descriptive features were based on text segmentation and morpho-syntactic tagging only. The trained classifiers achieved performance above the 50% precision baseline. The data set was small and the number of shared words among notes limited, so Pestian et al. (2008) also manually annotated texts with emotion labels from a limited set of categories; that improved the result. Besides the classification itself, they were interested in features which appeared to be significant for the classification. The significant features became a starting point for a linguistic and psychological analysis of the authors of the genuine notes. Pestian et al. (2010) worked with the same 66 SNs. They computed such text characteristics as part of speech, information, readability scores and parse information, and performed manual classification: "trainees accurately classified notes 49% of the time" and "mental health professionals accurately classified notes 63% of the time". The expanded set of features gave a 78% accuracy of automatic classification, but no semantic or emotionally motivated features were considered. The words selected as features seem to be specific only to this particular set of documents. The words arising from feature selection seem to be quite accidental and specific to this particular set of documents, but not specific to SNs.

Matykiewicz et al. (2009) extended that work to a much larger collection of more than 600 genuine SNs. Words frequent enough in SNs were put into overlapping classes with respect to the emotions contained in the Linguistic Inquiry and Word Count tool (LIWC) (Pennebaker et al., 2001). It is worth noting that emotion labels were assigned to words (lemmas), not to word senses (lexical meanings). Matykiewicz et al. (2009) concentrated on document clustering; elicited SNs were not considered. Authors tried to find features which distinguish genuine SNs from other forms of personal communication. As the background, they used posts to different newsgroups, selecting those newsgroups which seemed to be thematically close to the suicide discourse: talk.politics.guns, talk.politics.mideast, talk.politics.misc and talk.religion.misc. There were good clustering results (above 90% of cluster purity), but the background corpus did not include elicited SNs, which seem to be much harder to distinguish from genuine SNs. Spelling errors in SNs have also been left uncorrected; their high frequency is a characteristic feature in Polish SNs (Zaśko-Zielińska, 2013). SNs have been divided by the clustering algorithm into two subgroups (the maximum number of clusters was limited to 4 for the whole corpus). One subgroup showed no emotional content while the other was emotionally charged. Emotions were recognised on the basis of the annotation of words in the LIWC dictionary.

Text analysis of the suicide discourse in literature and poetry has also been attempted. Stirman and Pennebaker (2001) treated word use as an indicator of the mental states of suicidal and non-suicidal poets. Mulholland and Quinn (2013) applied the LIWC tool and dictionary in the analysis of over 70 language dimensions: polarity, affect states, death, sexuality, tense, etc. The dimensions were recognised on the basis of the word annotations in LIWC. The annotation and processing were done for words, not for word senses. Mulholland and Quinn (2013) tried to classify lyricists as suicidal or non-suicidal by their work and their known life stories. The goal of this research was to predict the likelihood of a musician committing suicide. The 70.6% classification rate represents a 12.8% increase over the majority-class baseline in the collected training set.

In (Pestian et al., 2010) a special suicide ontology containing 19 different classes of emotions was prepared and then used to annotate suicide notes. After the feature selection process the final four emotion concepts remained: hopelessness - regret - sorrow - giving things away (that is not strictly speaking an emotion). The final classifier working on the four emotion concepts and also on 42 specific words (among them prepositions, proper names, auxiliary verbs, the words good and love) outperformed mental health professionals in discerning elicited notes from real suicide notes. Following this publication, a special suicide note corpus annotated with 16 emotions was prepared in 2011.

3 Language Data

As the main source for training and testing we used the Polish Corpus of Suicide Notes (PCSN) (Zaśko-Zielińska, 2013). The PCSN is one of very few such resources in the world, e.g. it is significantly larger than the similar collection discussed by (Matykiewicz et al., 2009). It includes 1,244 genuine SNs that have been scanned and manually transcribed. Each SN was manually corrected and linguistically annotated on several levels, including selected semantic and pragmatic phenomena (Zaśko-Zielińska, 2013). The correction was necessary, as the originals include many errors or *ad hoc* abbreviations, that would be very difficult for automated processing. The annotation is stored in a TEI-based format (Marcińczuk et al., 2011) with corrected version in a separate layer. PCSN includes also a subcorpus of 334 counterfeited SNs (elicited). They were created by volunteers who were asked to imitate a real SN for imaginary person whose characteristic had been provided at the beginning of the experiment. The characteristics were randomly generated in a way following the distribution observed among the authors of PCSN genuine notes (the information is stored in the meta-data). Most volunteers were told that the notes written by them would be used 'to deceive' the computer program.

The genuine notes have varied length, but most of them are relatively short (around several sentences). Almost all of them were handwritten, while the counterfeited are all handwritten. The genuine notes include a lot of language errors, while the counterfeited are written in almost correct way. In such a situation, the errors are very clear signal for the genuine notes, that is why we used the corrected version and we used the layer of the corrected versions as the basis for the experiments. Thus the task was much more difficult. It is not clear if the same practice was implemented, e.g. in (Pestian et al., 2008).

As there is imbalance between the numbers of genuine and counterfeited SNs in PCSN, and the counterfeited SNs represent a specific genre, we have collected from Internet for a 2,200 letter-like texts. They represent a wide range of topics, but a have a form of a personal letter. In addition, we have randomly selected 1,000 Wikipedia articles, as examples of non-letters. All these collected texts were treated as negative examples during the experiments.

4   Descriptive Features

In a search for linguistic markers of SNs, we tested a rich set of features of the two main groups: *word-based* and *sense-based*. The first include lemmas (i.e. basic morphological forms), their annotations, derivation types and classes of Proper Names. The second group is based on word senses described in plWordNet (Piasecki et al., 2009) as synsets, their different generalisations, linguistic domains for synsets (Fellbaum, 1998; Piasecki et al., 2009) and the existing mappings of plWordNet onto SUMO ontology (Pease and Fellbaum, 2010; Pease, 2011).

Texts were pre-processed by *WCRFT* – a morpho-syntactic tagger for Polish (Radziszewski, 2013), *Liner2* – a named-entity recogniser (Marcińczuk et al., 2013) and *WoSeDon* – a prototype Word Sense Disambiguation tool (Kędzia et al., 2015) in a version that was based on plWordNet 2.2 (Maziarz et al., 2013). SNs were represented by such features as word lemmas, punctuation, text length, sentence length, grammatical classes of words, proper names and their classes.

4.1   Lexical and syntactic features

The set of word-based features on words and their annotations encompasses the frequencies of:

lemma – basic morphological forms from the tagger,

punctuation – punctuation marks,

big.letter – words started with a big letter,

gram.class – grammatical classes from the tagger,

verb12 – verbs in the 1st or 2nd person,

bigrams – bigrams of grammatical classes,

diminutive – diminutive forms identified on the basis of information from plWordNet,

augmentative – a similar feature to the above one,

PN.class – PN recognised by Liner2 as representing: first and last names, roads, cities and countries.

The feature *verb12* was intended to signal text of personal nature. Diminutives and augmentatives were expected to signal an emotional character, and PNs were assumed to appear more frequently in more concrete texts.

Some experiments replaced lemmas with word senses represented as plWordNet synonym set (synset) identifiers, assigned to words in the SNs by the WSD tool.

4.2 Semantically motivated features

The first group includes several features expressing clear semantic information, but in the case of
the second group we use plWordNet as a basis. To
compute features from the second group, words
are mapped to plWordNet 2.2 synsets by WoSe-
Don. Its accuracy is limited and in practice it
reaches about 75% on running text (the reported is
lower) (Kędzia et al., 2015), but we assumed that
the errors would not significantly influence the result. We used the following semantic features:

synsets – synsets from plWordNet 2.2,

hypernyms5 – all synsets on the hypernymic path
up to five levels from the synset of the given
word,

wn.domains – WordNet Domains (Bentivogli
et al., 2004) assingned to synsets via mapping: plWordNet – Princeton WordNet (Fellbaum, 1998),

sumo – the first SUMO concepts accessible from
the synset of the given word,

synset.hyp – hypernyms that are two levels above
the word synset,

domain – linguistic domains of synsets,

verb.emo – verb lemmas described as expressing emotions in (Zaśko-Zielińska, 2013) on
the basis of the analysis of plWordNet hypernymy structure,

noun.emo – in a similar way to the above one,

adj.emo – as above.

Synsets (as lemmas), can be too specific for particular SNs, and due to the limited number of SNs
in the corpus they can fail in supporting the generalisation of the classifier. That is why we were
looking into different ways of mapping synsets
into classes defined by hypernyms, domains or
SUMO concepts. However, the most sophisticated
way of generalisation is described in the next section.

4.3 Class-related Sense Dictionaries

We aim at generalising particular words to dictionaries of senses that are characteristic for different types of contexts or texts. The underlying hypothesis of this approach is that generalisation of

specific words in a subset of documents from corpus allows to locate synsets in WordNet, for which
we can reconstruct dictionaries, which describe
the observed phenomenon and allows to distinguish between different types of words observed in
the same set of documents. We adapted the algorithm presented in (Kocoń and Marcińczuk, 2016)
for the purpose of selecting a subset of Word-
Net synsets which contain most specific words for
each class of SN to improve classification of SNs.
Algorithm 1 presents the dictionary generation.

On the basis of this method, we have generated dictionaries for three classes of texts: genuine
SNs, counterfeited SNs and other texts. The dictionaries were generated from the held-out (tuning) subset. We calculated the frequency of
synsets from a given dictionary as a feature. The
use of the dictionary occurrence features is marked
as *dictionary* in the description of the experiments.

5 Experiments and Results

The expanded PCSN was randomly divided into
10 parts. One of them was used for feature selection and generation of the class-related sense dictionaries. The rest was used for 10-fold cross validation. After the preliminary pre-experiments, we
decided to use SVM classifier from the LIBSVM
library (Chang and Lin, 2011) and the RBF kernel.
During experiments we used different weighting
methods. Three of them were tested in the final
experiments: Pointwise Mutual Information, its
version called Mutual Information in (Lin, 1998)
and *tf* weighting (i.e. normalisation by the most
frequent lemma/synset). Several other transformations did not bring improvement. All features less
frequent than the threshold $f = 20$ and occurring
in a smaller number of texts than $d = 5$ were filtered out. The feature values were scaled to the
range $[0, 1]$ on the input to the SVM classifier.

We tested a large number of feature combinations, the best are presented in Table 1. They differ
in the number of features selected by the InfoGain
method on the held-out set, weighting method and
the feature set used:

AnnLemmas = *lemmas*, *punctuation*,
gram.class, *verb12*, *PN.class* and *bigrams*,

AnLem+Deriv = **AnnLemmas** plus *big.letter*,
diminutive and *augmentative*,

NonPerLem = **AnLem+Deriv** minus *verb12*,

Algorithm 1 Construction of the class-related sense dictionaries for single class

---

Require:

1: $G = <V, A>$ – WordNet as directed graph, where nodes V are synsets (sets of synonyms) and edges $A \in V \times V$ are hypernym relations;

2: $\vec{d}$ – corpus as vector of words;

3: t – semantic class (e.g. *genuine*);

Ensure:

4: $\mathfrak{P}$ – dictionary of the *greatest positive correlations*;

5: $\mathfrak{M}$ – dictionary of the *lowest negative correlations*;

6: $updateGraph(G)$ — each synset $v \in V$ is extended with its hyponyms' lemmas;

7: $classVector(\vec{d}, t)$ — construction of such a vector $\vec{w}$, where $|\vec{w}| = |\vec{d}|$ and $\vec{w}_n = 1$ if word $\vec{d}_n$ belongs to document classified as t, 0 otherwise;

8: $synsetVector(\vec{d}, V)$ — for each $v \in V$ such a vector $\vec{a}^v$ is constructed, where $|\vec{a}^v| = |\vec{d}|$ and $\vec{a}^v_n = 1$ if $\vec{d}_n \in v$, 0 otherwise;

9: $pearsonCorrelations(\vec{w}, \vec{a}, V)$ — for each $v \in V$ a Pearson correlation value is determined: $P^v = pearson(\vec{w}, \vec{a}^v)$;

10: $bestNodes(V, P, p)$ — creating such synset $v \in V$ collections $\mathcal{P}$ and $\mathcal{M}$, for which P^v was the greatest ($\mathcal{P} \subseteq V$) and the lowest ($\mathcal{M} \subseteq V$) in each *hyponym branch*. Selection of the best nodes is dependent on parameter p, which specifies the minimal absolute value of Pearson correlation P^v to add v to $\mathcal{M}$ or $\mathcal{P}$. In experiments we used $p = 0.001$. for each pair $(v_i, v_j) \in \mathcal{M} \times \mathcal{M} \wedge i \neq j$ there is no path in G between (v_i, v_j), which means, that v_i, v_j cannot be in the same *hyponym branch*. The same applies to $\mathcal{P}$.

11: $bestNodesSubsets(\mathcal{M}, \mathcal{P}, \vec{w})$ — this two-step method joins best nodes and builds two subsets: $\mathfrak{M} \subseteq \mathcal{M}$ and $\mathfrak{P} \subseteq \mathcal{P}$. In the first step a subset $\mathfrak{P}$ is constructed iteratively. In each iteration, the method searches for such element $e \in \mathcal{P}$, for which Pearson correlation $pearson(\vec{\omega}, \vec{w})$ is the greatest after the vector $\vec{\omega}$ is created ($|\vec{\omega}| = |\vec{d}|$ and $\vec{\omega}_n = 1$ if $\vec{d}_n \in \mathfrak{P} \cup \{e\}$, 0 otherwise). Next, $\mathfrak{P} = \mathfrak{P} \cup \{e\}, \mathcal{P} = \mathcal{P} \setminus \{e\}$ and a procedure is repeated until there is no Pearson correlation gain or $\mathcal{P} = \emptyset$. The second step looks similar. In each iteration the method searches for such element $e \in \mathcal{M}$, for which Pearson correlation $pearson(\vec{\omega}, \vec{w})$ is the greatest after the vector $\vec{\omega}$ is created ($|\vec{\omega}| = |\vec{d}|$ and $\vec{\omega}_n = 1$ if $\vec{d}_n \in \mathfrak{P}$ **and** $\vec{d}_n \notin \mathfrak{M} \cup \{e\}$, 0 otherwise). Next, $\mathfrak{M} = \mathfrak{M} \cup \{e\}, \mathcal{M} = \mathcal{M} \setminus \{e\}$ and a procedure is repeated until there is no Pearson correlation gain or $\mathcal{M} = \emptyset$.

Synsets = AnLem+Deriv minus *lemmas* plus *synsets, hypernyms5, wn.domains* and *sumo*,

GenSyn+Dom = AnLem+Deriv minus *lemmas* plus *synset.hyp, domain, verb.emo, noun.emo, adj.emo* and *sumo*,

Dom+SUMO = GenSyn+Dom minus *synset.hyp*,

SenseDict = GenSyn+Dom plus *dictionary*.

The first three vectors, namely **AnnLemmas**, **AnLem+Deriv** and **NonPerLem** do not refer to word senses and do not require pre-processing based on WSD. The basic **AnnLemmas** describe lemmas and punctuation occurring in texts with an intention to identify lemmas characteristic for genuine SNs. In addition bigrams of the grammatical classes provide some hints on syntactic structures, PNs show that text is more concrete and *verbs12* reveals the personal elements and instructions included in the text. **AnLem+Deriv** adds aspects of informal, emotional descriptions (positive and negative). In **NonPerLem** we wanted to find out what is the influence of the *verb12* feature.

Because we expected that words can be quite specific and accidental due to the limited set of documents, in the next group of vectors we tried to map the documents on the semantic space and open possibilities for different kinds of generalisations on the basis of the very large structure of plWordNet and SUMO linked together. The **Synsets** feature vector was the first attempt, in which words were exchanged by synsets and we traced paths across all synsets up several levels the hypernymy structure aiming at expanding the

Exp.	Weight.	Feat.	Acc	F	PosP	NegP	R	Spec	CounterP
Word-based									
AnnLemmas	–	500	88.34	77.78	79.51	91.39	76.13	92.81	69.67
AnnLemmas	PMI	500	93.28	87.14	89.35	94.62	85.04	85.04	73.44
AnnLemmas	MI	500	93.62	87.54	**91.47**	94.32	83.94	**97.15**	74.92
AnnLemmas	MI	1000	91.81	84.91	89.61	92.57	80.68	96.26	76.08
AnLem+Deriv	tf	604	**94.27**	**89.25**	90.40	95.66	88.13	96.54	**77.78**
NonPerLem	tf	603	93.78	88.46	88.56	**95.70**	**88.36**	95.78	74.36
Sense-based									
Synsets	MI	500	92.59	85.70	86.49	95.30	84.93	94.69	66.41
Synsets	MI	2000	92.13	85.34	86.75	94.06	83.95	95.20	70.00
GenSyn+Dom	tf	2000	93.78	88.46	88.56	95.70	88.36	95.78	70.09
Dom+SUMO	tf	1383	94.15	89.07	89.79	95.73	88.36	96.29	73.05
Domains	tf	653	94.33	89.38	**90.42**	95.74	88.36	**96.54**	**76.92**
GenSyn+Dom	tf	500	93.90	88.63	89.15	95.63	88.13	96.04	73.50
SenseDict	tf	2000	**94.64**	**90.06**	90.16	**96.29**	**89.95**	96.37	74.36

Table 1: Results of the classification of Suicide Notes on the basis of different feature vectors (Feat. – the number of the selected features, $Acc = \frac{TP+TN}{TP+FP+TN+FN}$, $PosP = \frac{TP}{TP+FP}$, $NegP = \frac{TN}{TN+FN}$, $R = \frac{TP}{TP+FN}$ – recall, $Spec = \frac{TN}{TN+FP}$, $CounterP$ – the precision in the subset of counterfeited SNs).

description by more general synsets (i.e. lexical meaning), too. As a means of generalisation of the description. In addition we added the mapping to SUMO concepts (that seemed to work well), as an even further generalisation, and WordNet Domains (that introduced too much noise[1]). In the next group of semantic vectors: **GenSyn+Dom**, **Dom+SUMO** and **SenseDict** synsets have been exchanged with their medium-grained generalisations, i.e. every synset was mapped onto a hypernym two levels up and without adding all synsets from the path as it was done in **Synsets**. Moreover, we also used wordnet linguistic domains that were introduced to support wordnet editors (Fellbaum, 1998), but appeared to be a useful way of grouping senses in at least several applications. **Dom+SUMO** do not include synset-based features, but instead mappings to SUMO, while **SenseDict** extends the synset-based vector with the proposed way of extracting domain-related sense dictionaries.

The results were evaluated according to the 10-fold evaluation scheme performed on the training-test set. The average values of the several standard measures across the folds are given in Table 1. The F measure is calculated from the precision $PosP$ and the recall R, which shows how many genuine SNs were recognised. As the counterfeited SNs should be all filtered out by an ideal classifier, we have introduced a separate precision measure for this subset, namely $CounterP$.

In Table 1 we can see that all proposed models present very good performance in general, that is superior to the results achieved so far in the literature for similar tasks. $CounterP$ is much lower, but still much above 50% baseline and this is the most difficult subtask. Moreover in spite of the fact that the size of the set of counterfeited SNs much smaller than the others set, $CounterP$ is still larger than the results reported in the literature.

The results of the first experiment are slightly lower due to the lack of weighting. Word-based models and synsets-based models express similar performance if some mechanisms for generalisation are introduced to the latter, e.g. the simpler **Synsets** model which uses many more specific synsets produced lower results. In the same time **Domains** model that does not refer to synsets and **SenseDict** that utilises classes of word senses achieved higher performance than word-based model. The difference is on the margin of the statistical significance, e.g. in the case of **SenseDict** the difference is on the 95% level of trust. However, we can conclude that looking for the ways of wordnet-based generalisation of the representation is worth attention. The difference between **NonPerLem** and **AnLem+Deriv** shows that the influence of *verb12*, that was meant to represent personal elements in the note, is not clear. On the one hand **NonPerLem** has the best value of $CounterP$, but on the other hand the feature

---

[1] WordNet Domains were extracted automatically from a large English corpus and next transferred from Princeton WordNet to plWordNet via the manually created interlingual mapping – too many places in which noise could appear.

verb12 was selected as a significant one during feature selection for models in which it was included to.

The good results obtained, especially with the classification based on semantic features suggest that the linguistic content of SNs is a strong factor separating them out from other types of writing including non-personal and personal texts (namely letters). Moreover, the linguistic features of SNs make them also different from the counterfeited SNs that were written by humans with intention to deceive 'a computer program'. So we can expect that subjects did all their best during experiments, but still the language used by them express enough differences to be captured by our classifiers.

The feature vectors that produced the best results give some insights into the character of the linguistic differences between true SNs and the other types of writing. In order to take a closer look we have examined the ranking of features selected for the **SenseDict** vector on the basis of the InfoGain algorithm and the held-out set. The top 45 features are presented in Tab. 2. Most of the labels used to name the features are explained in the caption. However the names of the specific plWordNet synsets were too long to fit them into the tables:

synHyp:Group – synHyp:{*grupa* 4 'a group', *zbiór* 1 'a set'}

synHyp:Property – synHyp:{ *właściwość* 1 'property', *przymiot* 1 'attribute' *cecha* 1 'characteristic feature',{ *własność* 2 'property', *atrybut* 1 'attribute'}

sumo:SbjAssessmentAtr – sumo:subsumed by SubjectiveAssessmentAttribute

synHyp:makingRelMag – synHyp:{ [non lexicalised] *wykonywanie czynności religijnych badz magicznych* 1 'performing religious or magical acts'}

synHyp:going away – synHyp:{ *oddalanie si?* 1 'going away' or 'passing away' }

synHyp:ManSocialRel – synHyp:{ [non-lexicalised] *człowiek ze względu na relacje społeczne* 1 'a man distinguished by its social relationships' }

synHyp:State – synHyp:{ *stan* 1 ' a state'}

synHyp:GerDynVerb – synHyp:{ [non-lexicalised, a top synset for a class of gerund nouns] *GERUNDIUM OD CZASOWNIKA DYNAMICZNEGO NIEZMIENNOSTANOWEGO* 1 'a gerund noun derived from a dynamic verb not imposing a change of state'}

Synset dictionaries constructed for general texts (*tex dict.*), as well as genuine and counterfeited SNs are among the top features in Tab. 2. A very high position of *verbs12* seem to reveal the personal character of SNs. The significance of different punctuation symbols is specific for SNs. The general class of punctuations (*lexClass:interp*) is high on the list, but also many bigrams with punctuations (e.g. bigrams:adj+interp), and individual symbols (e.g. *interp:comma*) are close to the top. According to the linguistic analysis, imperative forms of verbs are frequent in genuine SNs, and this is confirmed by *lexClass:impt* representing this specific grammatical class. In the top of the feature ranking, we can also notice several specific semantic features: top hypernyms for different senses referring to groups of people (*synHyp:Group*) including 'a family', for all kinds of situations (*synsetHyp:GERUNDIUM*) but also specific situations of religious acts (e.g. praying) and passing away (*synHyp:going away*). The synset *synHyp:ManSocialRel* dominates many synsets representing social roles of people and this may be caused by frequent referring by authors of SNs to family members or people related to them by naming social roles of those people. The concept *sumo:SbjAssessmentAtr* subsumes many synsets describing man's character – SNs are full of positive and negative description of people. Finally, the specific grammatical class of *aglt* signals more frequent use of the subjunctive mood.

6 Conclusions

The obtained results show that there are fundamental differences between genuine SNs and counterfeited SNs. The differences are even striking in relation to other types of texts. It is worth emphasising that we compared the transcribed versions of SNs not taking into account different types of errors that occur very often in them, the length of the letters, layout of the letters etc. The analysis was intentionally focused only on linguistic properties and the selected feature vectors re-

No	Feature	No	Feature	No	Feature
1	text dict.	16	counterfeited dict.	31	bigrams:num+subst
2	lexClass:subst	17	bigrams:prep+subst	32	bigrams:interp+subst
3	bigrams:interp+empty	18	lexClass:impt	33	PN:country
4	lexClass:interp	19	bigrams:interp+interp	34	domain:zdarz
5	bigrams:adj+interp	20	lexClass:ger	35	synsetHyp:GERUNDIUM
6	genuine dict.	21	interp:question	36	sumo:SbjAssessmentAtr
7	verb12	22	bigrams:adj+subst	37	synHyp:makingRelMag
8	bigrams:subst+interp	23	interp:hyphen	38	synHyp:going away
9	lexClass:ppron12	24	bigrams:subst+subst	39	interp:dash
10	interp:comma	25	interp:fullstop	40	synHyp:ManSocialRel
11	lexClass:noun	26	bigrams:interp+adj	41	synHyp:State
12	lexClass:prep	27	bigrams:subst+ppas	42	synHyp:GerDynVerb
13	bigrams:subst+adj	28	synHyp:Group	43	bigrams:adj+prep
14	domain:rel	29	synHyp:Property	44	lexClass:aglt
15	lexClass:adj	30	bigrams:ppas+prep	45	bigrams:ppron12+praet

Table 2: Characteristic features selected for classifier based on **SenseDict** vector (where *dict.* – a domain dictionary of synsets, *domain:rel* – the domain of relative adjectives, and *domain:zdarz* – domain of event verbs, *lexClass* – a grammatical class. (with *aglt* – aglutinative participle used, e.g., for subjunctive mood, *ger* – gerund, *impt* – imperative verb form, *interp* – punctuation symbol, *num* – numeral, *ppas* – perfective adjectival participle, *ppron12* – personal pronoun of 1st or 2nd person, *praet* – past verb from, but also used for compound future time, *prep* – preposition, *subst* – noun), *verb12* – verbs in 1st or 2nd person.

vealed many features that are characteristic for SNs. In many cases they corresponded to the features identified manually in (Zaśko-Zielińska, 2013).

The models based on synsets are only slightly better than those on words, but the former seem to offer natural ways of generalising the description. The applied method of the sense dictionary construction appeared to be the best way of improving the model. The applied WSD was of a limited accuracy, but it has still some room for improvement.

References

Luisa Bentivogli, Pamela Forner, Bernardo Magnini, and Emanuele Pianta. 2004. Revising wordnet domains hierarchy: Semantics, coverage, and balancing. In *COLING 2004 Workshop on Multilingual Linguistic Resources Geneva, Switzerland, August 28.* pages 101–108.

Chih-Chung Chang and Chih-Jen Lin. 2011. LIB-SVM: A library for support vector machines. *ACM Transactions on Intelligent Systems and Technology* 2:27:1–27:27. Software available at http://www.csie.ntu.edu.tw/~cjlin/libsvm.

Christiane Fellbaum, editor. 1998. *WordNet – An Electronic Lexical Database.* The MIT Press.

J. M. Gomez. 2014. Language technologies for suicide prevention in social media. In *Proceedings of the Workshop on Natural Language Processing in the 5th Information Systems Research Working Days (JISIC 2014).* pages 21–29.

E.A. Holmes, C. Crane, M. J.V. Fennell, and Williams J.M.G. 2007. Imagery about suicide in depression – "flash-forwards"? *Journal of Behavior Therapy and Experimental Psychiatry* 38:423–434.

Paweł Kędzia, Maciej Piasecki, and Marlena J. Orlińska. 2015. Word sense disambiguation based on large scale Polish clarin heterogeneous lexical resources. *Cognitive Studies* 14(To appear).

Jan Kocoń and Michał Marcińczuk. 2016. Generating of Events Dictionaries from Polish WordNet for the Recognition of Events in Polish Documents. In *Text, Speech and Dialogue, Proceedings of the 19th International Conference TSD 2016.* Springer, Brno, Czech Republic, volume 9924 of *Lecture Notes in Artificial Intelligence.*

Dekang Lin. 1998. Automatic retrieval and clustering of similar words. In *Proceedings of the Joint Conference of the International Committee on Computational Linguistics.* ACL, pages 768–774.

M. Marcińczuk, J. Kocoń, and M. Janicki. 2013. Liner2 – a customizable framework for proper names recognition for Polish. In *Intelligent Tools for Building a Scientific Information Platform*, Springer, volume 467 of *Studies in Computational Intelligence*, pages 231–253.

Michal Marcińczuk, Monika Zaśko-Zielińska, and Maciej Piasecki. 2011. Structure annotation in the Polish corpus of suicide notes. In Ivan Habernal and Václav Matousek, editors, *Text, Speech and Dialogue - 14th International Conference, TSD 2011,*

Pilsen, Czech Republic, September 1-5, 2011. Proceedings. Springer, volume 6836 of *Lecture Notes in Computer Science*, pages 419–426.

P. Matykiewicz, W. Duch, and Pestian. J. 2009. Clustering semantic spaces of suicide notes and newsgroups articles. In *Proceedings of the Workshop on BioNLP.* pages 179–184.

Marek Maziarz, Maciej Piasecki, Ewa Rudnicka, and Stan Szpakowicz. 2013. Beyond the Transfer-and-Merge Wordnet Construction: plWordNet and a Comparison with WordNet. In G. Angelova, K. Bontcheva, and R. Mitkov, editors, *Proceedings of International Conference on Recent Advances in Natural Language Processing.* Incoma Ltd., Hissar, Bulgaria.

M. Mulholland and J. Quinn. 2013. Suicidal tendencies: The automatic classification of suicidal and non- suicidal lyricists using nlp. In *International Joint Conference on Natural Language Processing.* pages 680–684.

Adam Pease. 2011. *Ontology - A Practical Guide.* Articulate Software Press, Angwin, CA.

Adam Pease and Christiane Fellbaum. 2010. Formal ontology as interlingua: the SUMO and Word-Net linking project and Global WordNet. In Chu-Ren Huang, Nicoletta Calzolari, Aldo Gangemi, Alessandro Oltramari, and Laurent Prévot, editors, *Ontology and the Lexicon. A Natural Languge Processing Perspective*, Cambridge University Press, Studies in Natural Languge Processing.

J. W. Pennebaker, M. E. Francis, and R. J. Booth. 2001. *Linguistic Inquiry and Word Count: LIWC.* Lawrence Erlbaum Associates, Mahwah.

J.W. Pennebaker and C. K. Chung. 2011. Expressive writing: Connections to physical and mental health. In H. S. Friedman, editor, *The Oxford Handbook of Health Psychology*, Oxford University Press, pages 417–437.

J. Pestian, H. Nasrallah, P. Matykiewicz, A. Bennett, and A. Leenaars. 2010. Suicide note classification using natural language processing. *Biomed Inform Insights* 3:19–28.

John P. Pestian, Pawel Matykiewicz, and Jacqueline Grupp-Phelan. 2008. Using natural language processing to classify suicide notes. In *BioNLP 2008: Current Trends in Biomedical Natural Language Processing.* pages 96–97.

Maciej Piasecki, Stanisław Szpakowicz, and Bartosz Broda. 2009. *A Wordnet from the Ground Up.* Wrocław University of Technology Press. http://www.eecs.uottawa.ca/~szpak/pub /A_Wordnet_from_the_Ground_Up.zip.

Adam Radziszewski. 2013. A tiered CRF tagger for Polish. In *Intelligent Tools for Building a Scientific Information Platform*, Springer, volume 467 of *Studies in Computational Intelligence*, pages 215–230.

E.S. Shneidman and N.L. Farberow, editors. 1957. *Clues to Suicide.* Blakiston Division, New York.

S. W. Stirman and J.W. Pennebaker. 2001. Word use in the poetry of suicidal and nonsuicidal poets. *Psychosomatic Medicine* 63:517–522.

World Health Organisation. 2014. Preventing suicide: A global imperative. Technical report, World Health Organization.

Monika Zaśko-Zielińska. 2013. *Listy pożegnalne: w poszukiwaniu lingwistycznych wyznaczników autentyczności tekstu.* Wydawnictwo Quaestio, Wrocław.

Cross-Lingual SRL Based upon Universal Dependencies

Ondřej Pražák and **Miloslav Konopík**
NTIS – New Technologies for the Information Society,
Department of Computer Science and Engineering,
Faculty of Applied Sciences, University of West Bohemia, Technická 8, 306 14 Plzeň
Czech Republic
ondfa@ntis.zcu.cz
konopik@kiv.zcu.cz

Abstract

In this paper, we introduce a cross-lingual Semantic Role Labeling (SRL) system with language independent features based upon Universal Dependencies. We propose two methods to convert SRL annotations from monolingual dependency trees into universal dependency trees. Our SRL system is based upon cross-lingual features derived from universal dependency trees and supervised learning that utilizes a maximum entropy classifier. We design experiments to verify whether the Universal Dependencies are suitable for the cross-lingual SRL. The results are very promising and they open new interesting research paths for the future.

1 Introduction

The Semantic Role Labeling (SRL) task (Gildea and Jurafsky, 2002) belongs among shallow semantic parsing techniques. The SRL goal is to identify and categorise semantic relationships or *semantic roles* of given *predicates*. Verbs, such as "believe" or "cook", are natural predicates but certain nouns are accepted as predicates as well (see the third example in Figure 1). The simplified definition of semantic roles is that semantic roles are abstractions of predicate arguments. For example, the semantic roles for "believe" can be *Agent* (a believer) and *Theme* (a statement) and for "cook" *Agent* (a chef), *Patient* (a food), *Instrument* (a device for cooking) – see examples in Figure 1. The theory of predicates and their roles is very well established several linguistic resourcesin such as PropBank (Palmer et al., 2005), NomBank (for nouns) (Meyers et al., 2004) , VerbNet (Kipper et al., 2006) or FrameNet (Baker et al., 1998).

(1) [He]$_{\text{AGENT}|\text{A0}}$ <u>believes</u> [in what he plays] $_{\text{THEME}|\text{A1}}$.

(2) Can [you] $_{\text{AGENT}|\text{A0}}$ <u>cook</u> [the dinner] $_{\text{PATIENT}|\text{A1}}$?

(3) [The nation's]$_{\text{AGENT}|\text{AM-LOC}}$ largest [pension]$_{\text{THEME}|\text{A1}}$ <u>fund</u>,

Figure 1: Three examples of shallow semantic annotations: 1) and 2) are examples of verb predicates (labels are from VerbNet v3.2|SRL) and 3) of a noun predicate (labels NomBank|SRL).

In the SRL task, the semantic roles are considered at a higher abstraction level. E.g. for English, there are several core roles denoted by *A0* (usually Agent), *A1* (usually Patient) and *A2*, modifier arguments (*AM-**), restriction arguments (*R-**) and others.

Cross-lingual SRL shares the same goal with monolingual SRL, however, it attempts to provide semantic annotations for languages that lack for training data. The training data are taken from a source language (usually English) and they are transferred to a target language or a language independent model is trained. Cross-lingual SRL contains added value when compared to the monolingual SRL. In cross-lingual SRL, it is ensured that the tagset and the annotation procedure is coherent for all supported languages because the annotation is transferred from one common source (one language) to other languages. This does not apply to the monolingual scenario where we often deal with incompatible tagsets and different annotation guidelines.

In our paper, Universal Dependencies (UD) (Nivre et al., 2016) are the primary vehicle to enable transferring the learned rules from one language to another. UD annotations successfully describe syntax of a high number of languages, however, their annotation structure is somewhat simplified when compared to specific dependencies

Proceedings of Recent Advances in Natural Language Processing, pages 592–600,
Varna, Bulgaria, Sep 4–6 2017.

$(SD)^1$. In this paper, we attempt to find out to what extent the UD annotations are suitable for cross-lingual SRL task.

2   Related Work

Approaches to SRL on languages that lack proper training data can be divided into three main categories: **1)** *Annotation projection* methods attempt to transfer the annotation from one language to the other one and then train a SRL system on the transferred annotation. **2)** *Model transfer* approaches are designed to use language-independent features to train a universal model that can be applied to languages that support the designed features. **3)** Methods based upon *unsupervised training* require no annotated data, however, the models have difficulties to assign meaningful labels to predicate arguments.

Annotation projection   Padó and Lapata (2009) transfer annotation to a target language via word alignments obtained from parallel corpora. Annesi and Basili (2010) use a similar approach and extend it with an HMM model to increase the transfer accuracy.

Model transfer   Kozhevnikov and Titov (2013) use cross-lingual word mappings and cross-lingual semantic clusters obtained from parallel corpora, and cross-lingual features extracted from unlabelled syntactic dependencies to create a cross-lingual SRL system. In (Kozhevnikov and Titov, 2014), they try to automatically find a mapping between language specific models using parallel data.

Unsupervised SRL   Grenager and Manning (2006) deploy unsupervised learning using the EM algorithm based upon a structured probabilistic model of the domain. Lang and Lapata (2011) discover arguments of verb predicates with high accuracy using a small set of rules. A split-merge clustering is consequently applied to assign (nameless) roles to the discovered arguments. Titov and Klementiev (2012) propose a superior argument clustering by using the Chinese restaurant process.

Our approach   belongs among the model transfer approaches. We introduce a first attempt to use Universal Dependencies as cross-language

features in SRL. Most of the state-of-the-art approaches to SRL rely on lexical features (e.g. word lemmas). In the cross-language scenario, such features require bilingual models (e.g. word mapping via machine translation or bilingual clusters). In this paper, we attempt to create a multi-language model that can be potentially trained on many languages and therefore we omit all bilingual features including the lexical features.

3   Universal Dependencies

The main topic of our paper is to utilize the power of Universal Dependencies to analyse syntax in a cross-lingual manner. The UD annotation scheme evolved as a compilation of three universal annotation principles: universal dependency relations from Stanford (de Marneffe and Manning, 2008), part-of-speech tags from Google (Petrov et al., 2012), and morphological features (Zeman, 2008) from UFAL, Charles University.

The design of UD annotations is in principle similar to SD annotations but it differs in some crucial aspects. From the SRL point of view, the most critical difference is making content words the heads. In SD annotation for many languages, the auxiliary verbs, prepositions and conjunctions are often the heads.

Although the specification is quite new, there are several frameworks that enable end-to-end parsing into UDs: UDpipe (Straka et al., 2016), Stanford CoreNLP (Manning et al., 2014), Malt parser (Nivre and Hall, 2005), and others.

4   Annotation Conversion

4.1   Datasets

In our experiment, we use the CoNLL 2009 datasets (Hajič et al., 2009) for the following languages: Czech (CZ), English (EN), German (DE), Spanish (ES) and Chinese (ZH). Only English and Chinese datasets use compatible[2] tagsets of SRL roles. All other languages use different tagsets.

Next, we use a freely available script from Mikhail Kozhevnikov[3] to convert the Czech-English Dependency Treebank (PCEDT) (Hajič et al., 2012) into SRL annotations. The resulting annotations use the same labels for both languages.

---

[1]SD stands for task-Specific or language-Specific Dependencies, e.g. the "old" Stanford dependencies.

[2]The datasets can be mapped to each other by few simple rules.

[3]`http://www.ml4nlp.de/code-and-data/treex2conll`

The CoNLL data are divided into training and evaluation parts. We use the CoNLL 2009 Czech evaluation part also for the PCEDT dataset since it uses the same tagset.

4.2 Existing SD Annotations

SRL copora defined in Section 4.1 use SD trees as the basis of SRL annotations. The annotations label tree heads as predicate arguments (see Figure 2a). The meaning of such an annotation is that the predicate arguments are composed of all words that belong under heads including the head words. Figure 2b illustrates that the *A1* argument is composed of the phrase "in what he plays".

4.3 Conversion Methods

We need SRL annotations built upon UD trees for our experiments. Therefore, we propose two methods to obtain such annotations by converting the annotations built on SD trees into the annotations build on UD trees. Given the UD tree, we label such tree heads so that the predicate arguments cover the same words as in the SD trees – see Figure 2c. In this example, we label the word "what" as the *A1* argument in the UD tree instead of the word "in" which was annotated in the SD tree.

In the first proposed method, we look for such annotations of heads in the given UD trees so that the word coverage of arguments is as close to the original SD trees as possible. For each predicate argument, we look for the optimal head that covers as many of the original words as possible but at the same time as few extra words as possible. In this method, we annotate only one head for each predicate argument. The same constraint is present in some original SRL annotations where only one head per predicate argument is allowed. To formalize the process, we look for an optimal head obtained by the following formula:

$$N_{UD}^\star = \underset{N_{UD} \in T_{UD}}{\arg\max} \; |\mathrm{c}(N_{UD}) \cap \mathrm{c}(N_{SD})| - |\mathrm{c}(N_{UD}) \setminus \mathrm{c}(N_{SD})| : \forall N_{SD} \in \mathrm{arg}(T_{SD}),$$

where N_{SD} and N_{UD} are nodes of an SD tree T_{SD} and an UD tree T_{UD}, respectively; c is coverage operator which returns all nodes that belong under the specified node including the node itself; arg returns all predicate arguments of a given tree.

In the second method, we abandon the constraint of one head per predicate argument (the same holds true e.g. for the original Czech SRL annotations in CoNLL 2009 (Hajič et al., 2009)). We proceed similarly to the first method and we try to optimize the word coverage of the new argument labels in the UD annotations. However, in this approach, we label as many heads as necessary while ensuring that none of the heads is in a subtree of another one. We start by annotating all words that are located under a head of an argument in the original SD tree. Then we iteratively look for common heads (parents) of all the words in the corresponding UD tree. The algorithm stops, when no more common heads are found. We keep the annotation of the heads and discard the annotation of all dependent words (children of the heads). In this way, the SRL labels may be assigned to more than one head for some predicate arguments. The optimization formula is as follows:

$$\{N_{UD}^\star\} = \underset{\{N_{UD}\} \in T_{UD}}{\arg\max} \; |\mathrm{c}(\{N_{UD}\}) \cap \mathrm{c}(N_{SD})| - |\mathrm{c}(\{N_{UD}\}) \setminus \mathrm{c}(N_{SD})| : \forall N_{SD} \in \mathrm{arg}(T_{SD}),$$

where $\{N_{UD}\}$ is a set from T_{UD} and $\{N_{UD}\} \in T_{UD}$ returns all possible sets of distinct subtrees from T_{UD}.

Figure 3b shows different outcomes of the first and the second conversion methods. The first method is constrained to label only one head per predicate. In this case, the optimal head that covers most of the words is "number". The second method is free to label as many heads as necessary and thus it labels both "plants" and "number" heads. This can be confusing for downstream applications, however, in some cases it is the only way to correctly label all argument words.

4.4 Obtaining the UD Trees

So far, we have dealt with the annotation conversion to UD trees but we have not mentioned how to obtain the UD trees in the first place. We have considered two options: **1)** to convert the SD trees to UD trees and **2)** to use syntactic parsers capable of producing UD trees. The first option looks more attractive at first glance since it would produce trees almost without errors. Indeed, the existing UD treebanks were created mostly by conversion from other treebanks. However, it is almost impossible to put this approach into practice. The conversion is not trivial and the result needs to be corrected by hand. The scripts are not publicly available and moreover they are designed to work with specific types of the syntactic annotations. Since we perform experiments on

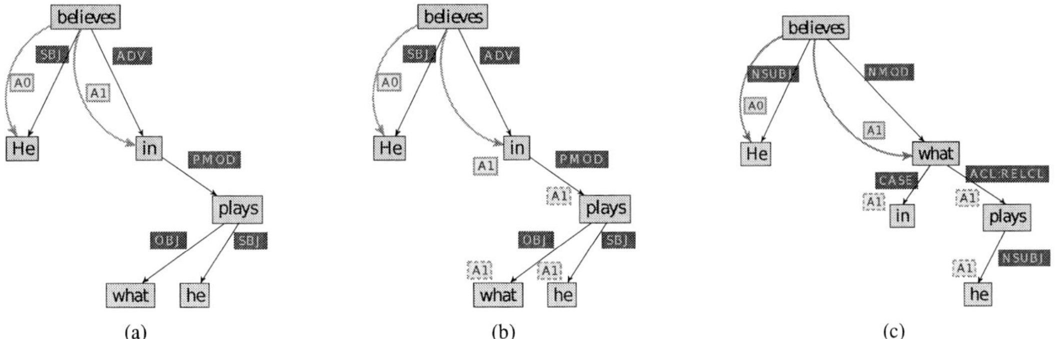

Figure 2: Example of SRL annotations: (a) shows semantic role annotation for an SD tree, (b) shows the coverage of role annotations and (c) shows the result of the conversion to the UD tree. The annotation in sub-figures (a) and (b) are real examples from the Conll 2008 dataset (sentence no. 57 from train.closed.conll08 – all examples in our paper are based upon the CoNLL 2008 and 2009 training data) and sub-figure (c) shows the output of our conversion algorithm.

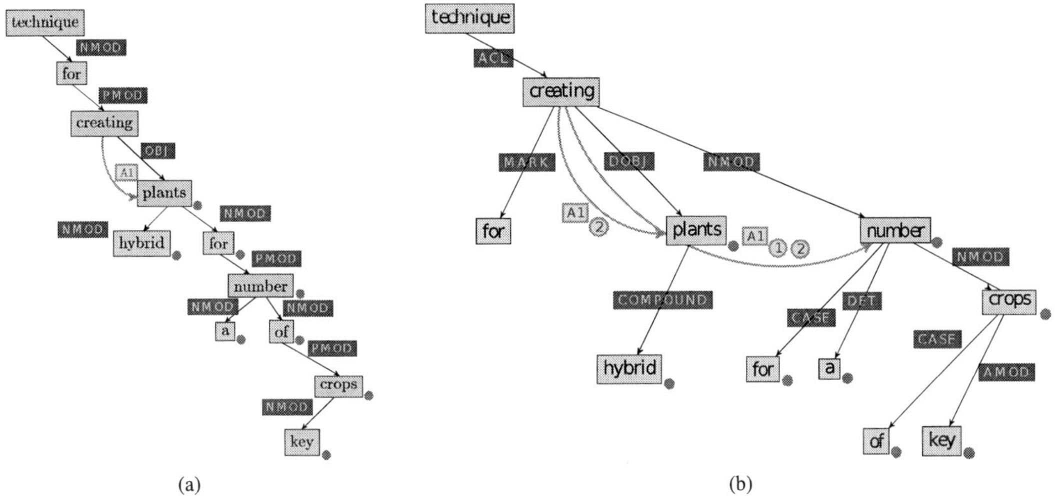

Figure 3: An illustration of a difference of the first and the second conversion method. The dots indicate the coverage of the argument *A1*: (a) is the orginal annotation (sentence no. 117 from train.closed.conll08) and (b) shows the result of the conversion to an UD tree – ① marks the annotation for the first method and ② marks the second method.

five languages, we would have to create or obtain five scripts. These problems lead us to use the second option. We create the UD trees by parsing the sentences in datasets with an UD syntactic parser. This produces trees with errors and complicates the SRL conversion. However, this approach is available for all languages that are supported by an UD parser instantly. In our experiments, we use UDPipe (Straka et al., 2016) for Czech, English, German and Spanish, and Stanford CoreNLP (Manning et al., 2014) for English and Chinese for the cross-lingual experiment (EN-ZH) because UDPipe does not provide a model for

Chinese and Stanford CoreNLP does not provide a model for Czech. We use models provided with parsers based on UD v1.2.

The conversion computed on an UD tree with parsing errors is shown in Figure 4. In the UD tree (Figure 4b), the "1990" node was incorrectly attached to "cars" node instead of the correct node "remain". The results of the SRL annotation conversion are the same for both conversion methods in this case. Both methods labelled the "cars" node with the *AM-MNR* argument because any other annotation would induce a bigger error in the coverage of the argument. The *A3* argument was

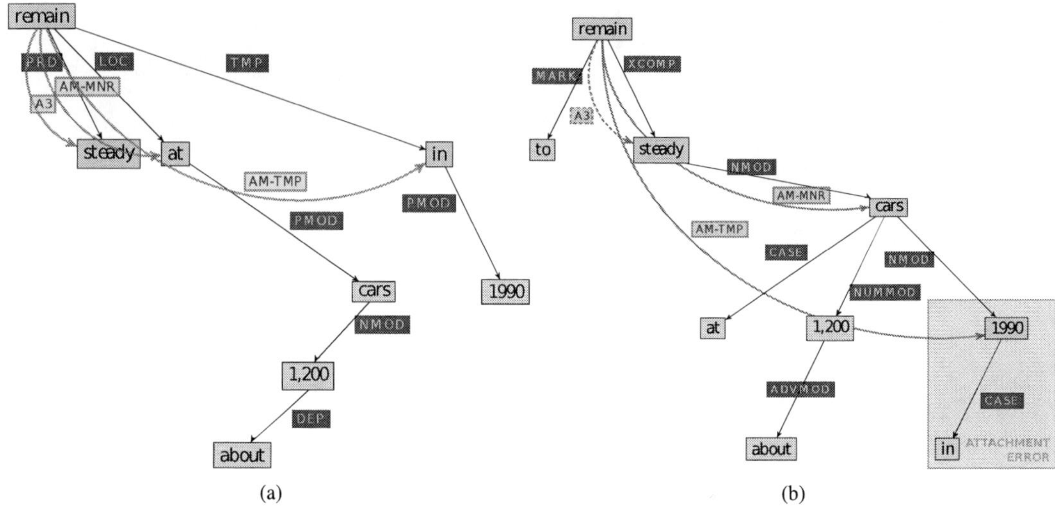

Figure 4: shows the SRL annotation conversion from (a) the SD tree (sentence no. 3 from train.closed.conll08), (b) to an UD tree that contains parsing errors.

discarded completely because labelling any node would cause a bigger error than not labelling any node.

5 Experiments

As in all approaches to SRL, we perform the task in two steps: **1)** *argument identification* and **2)** *argument cassification*.

Argument Identification The goal of the argument identification step is to identify (find) the tree nodes that are the heads of argument phrases. We classify each node into two classes: *argument / not argument*.

Argument Classification The task of the argument classification step is to assign correct labels to the nodes identified as arguments in the previous step. We classify each node identified as an argument into classes that correspond to all possible role labels. We use exactly the same classifiers and features for both steps.

5.1 Evaluation Metrics

For comparison with the state-of-the-art techniques, we compute labelled and unlabelled F1 measure with CoNLL 2009 official evaluation script (marked *us* for unlabelled, *ls* for labelled F1 measures). However, these metrics are computed on heads only which is not suitable for experiments based upon UD trees because the heads of UD trees and SD trees differ significantly. Therefore, we compute F1 score of precision and recall for argument identification (*u*) and accuracy (*l*) for role labelling. Both metrics are evaluated on the whole subtrees. This means that we compute the evaluation score for all words from subtrees, not just for the heads. The labelling accuracy is computed only for correctly identified argument nodes (the same approach is taken in (Kozhevnikov and Titov, 2014)).

The accuracy of argument labelling can be computed only for datasets that use the same labels for arguments. For the cross-lingual experiment, the tagsets of some language pairs differ. In such cases, we compute the F1 score of collocation and purity as defined in (Lang and Lapata, 2010) and denote it F_1^c as in (Kozhevnikov and Titov, 2013).

5.2 Classifier & Features

We train a supervised system based upon the Maximum Entropy classifier using the Brainy tool (Konkol, 2014). We use separate models for verb and non-verb predicates.

All features employed in our system are syntactic:

- *Predicate-argument distance* – distance between locations of a predicate and an argument in a sentence.

- *POS* – part-of-speech of the predicate, the argument and their parent nodes.

- *Dependency relation* – dependency tree relation of the predicate, the argument and their parent nodes.

- *Directed path* – dependency tree path from the predicate to the argument including the indication of dependency directions.

- *Undirected path* – list of relations from the predicate to the argument.

- *Verb voice* – indication of active/passive voice.

- *Other syntactic features* – `feats` column in CoNLL 2009 format with additional information about the words.

- *Bigram features* – predicate-argument bigrams of the part-of-speech and the dependency relations.

The dependency path features are encoded as a probability of a word being a predicate argument (or having a specific role) given the path. These features are more general and the resulting vectors have smaller dimension. Also, the cost function is smoother and thus the model is easier to train.

5.3 Experiment Descriptions

Evaluation of the conversion methods In the first experiment, we evaluate both the conversion methods in order to find out their abilities to transfer the SRL annotations from SD trees to UD trees. We measure the coverage of arguments in the converted annotations and compare it to the original annotations. This experiment should give us a theoretical upper boundary for the experiments based upon UD trees.

Monolingual experiments on SD trees Next, we perform a monolingual SRL experiment on gold SD trees. The experiment uses the same data and conditions as there were at the CoNLL 2009 conference. The results should evaluate the deployed classifier and features in relation to existing monolingual SRL systems. We use the official evaluation metrics as well as our own metric (see Section 5.1) in order to see the relation between the metrics.

Monolingual experiments on UD trees We provide an additional monolingual experiment on converted data in the UD trees. Models for all five languages are trained on the converted data and tested on evaluation parts of the datasets. The test should reveal how well can the features based

upon Universal Dependencies support the model decisions about argument identification and labelling.

Cross-lingual experiments Cross lingual experiments are the most important experiments described in this paper. They show the ability of the proposed method based upon Universal Dependencies to transfer a model learned on one language (English) to other languages Czech (CZ), German (DE), Spanish (ES) and Chinese (ZH).

6 Results

We state the results separately for the verb predicates (V in the tables), non-verb (other) predicates (O) and all predicates (A). When there are no non-verb predicates in the dataset, the corresponding O cell is marked with —.

Annotation Conversion Table 1 shows the performance of our first and second conversion method – see Section 4. In all following experiments we use the second conversion method.

			CZ	EN	DE	ES	ZH
1	u	V	87.10	84.19	81.16	83.79	85.63
		O	85.29	81.52	—	—	-
		A	86.32	83.32	81.16	83.79	85.63
	1	V	98.78	92.75	97.28	96.40	97.81
		O	99.01	89.75	—	—	—
		A	98.88	91.79	97.28	96.40	97.81
2	u	V	89.10	95.06	93.43	91.08	89.87
		O	87.80	89.94	—	—	—
		A	88.55	93.38	93.43	91.08	89.87
	1	V	100.00	100.00	100.00	100.00	100.00
		O	100.00	100.00	—	—	—
		A	100.00	100.00	100.00	100.00	100.00

Table 1: Quality of annotation conversion.

Monolingual Experiments Table 2 gives the results of our system on the SD hand-annotated data (exactly the same task that was at ConLL 2009). The results are measured with the official CoNLL 2009 evaluation script. *ls Zhao* row shows the results of the best system at the CoNLL 2009 shared task. Table 3 shows the results with automatically converted UD annotations.

Cross-lingual Table 4 compares results of the cross-lingual experiments on the UD annotated data. Labelled accuracy (l) is measured only on datasets with the same set of semantic labels (PCEDT for Czech and CoNLL 2009 data for Chinese).

		CZ	EN	DE	ES	ZH
us	A	96.12	91.75	90.42	100.00	92.08
ls	A	87.02	80.52	72.48	75.62	81.73
ls Zhao	A	85.19	85.44	75.99	80.46	78.15
u	V	94.06	95.82	86.52	100.00	87.81
	O	91.41	78.52	—	—	—
	A	92.97	91.07	86.52	100.00	87.81
l	V	74.16	86.02	65.95	69.02	82.99
	O	76.51	79.11	—	—	—
	A	75.11	83.28	65.95	69.02	82.99
F_1^c	V	93.05	93.64	95.09	93.00	92.98
	O	95.38	88.56	—	—	—
	A	94.83	91.10	95.09	93.00	92.99

Table 2: Results on the gold SD trees.

		CZ	EN	DE	ES	ZH
u	V	81.11	83.29	75.19	82.58	67.44
	O	72.12	59.01	—	—	—
	A	77.38	76.51	75.19	82.58	67.44
l	V	63.13	68.70	53.79	53.07	77.71
	O	69.51	64.05	—	—	—
	A	65.60	67.69	53.97	53.07	77.71
F_1^c	V	86.76	83.33	85.75	83.87	89.18
	O	93.22	85.33	—	—	—
	A	91.62	83.72	85.75	83.87	89.18

Table 3: Results with the automatically generated UD trees.

7 Discussion

From the results of the conversion methods (Table 1) we can see that our second conversion method provides better results than the first one. This is a natural outcome since the second method has a higher freedom in selection of the heads. The second method selects only correct heads and therefore the labels can be converted without errors (100% scores in the last section of Table 1). However, some SRL annotations do not permit labelling of more than one head per predicate argument and some SRL systems rely on this constraint. We have designed our systems without the requirement of one head per predicate argument and thus we use the second conversion method in

		EN-CZ	EN-ES	EN-ZH	EN-DE	PCEDT
u	UD	76.28	75.67	64.08	71.66	78.97
	K	—	—	51.70	—	63.90
l	UD	—	—	75.57	—	55.09
	K	—	—	71.70	—	59.00
F_1^c	UD	84.90	81.78	87.94	82.37	83.03
	K	—	—	84.50	—	74.10

Table 4: Cross-lingual results with the UD trees. The *UD* row shows the results of our system based on UD trees and the K row shows the results from (Kozhevnikov and Titov, 2013).

all the following experiments.

The results of the monolingual experiment on the Gold standard trees in Table 2 show that our SRL system performs at a level comparable to the best systems at the CoNLL 2009 shared task (Hajič et al., 2009). Taking into account our reduced feature set (without lexical features), we can safely conclude that the selected features are sufficient for the consequent experiments.

The monolingual experiment performed on the UD trees (Table 3) shows a significant drop of the performance when compared to the Gold standard trees. However, the decrease of the performance is expected since we operate on system generated trees and the annotation conversion introduces additional errors. An additional analysis of the results revealed that most of the errors are caused by incorrect syntactic parses. The CoNLL sentences use a rather complicated structure and the parsing errors are expected. In some cases, the sentences are ambiguous – e.g. see Figure 3a. The node "for" could be easily attached under the node "creating" instead of the node "plant". Such differences directly influence SRL labelling (see the dots in the figure). Taking into account the fact that the obtained SRL annotations are based solely upon syntactic information (we do not use lexical features), we conclude that the UD support the SRL identification and labelling well.

The most interesting results are the outcomes of the cross-lingual experiment in the Table 4. We can see that the predicate argument identification phase (the *u* row, *V* subrow) was very successful except for Chinese. However, we significantly outperformed the results presented in (Kozhevnikov and Titov, 2013) (the *u* row, *K* subrow) for both Czech and Chinese SRL annotations. We believe we can make such a statement even though our results are computed on all argument words and in (Kozhevnikov and Titov, 2013) the results are computed on heads only. From Table 2 we can see that these numbers are highly correlated. The argument classification phase (the *l* row) is similar (diffrence of about 4 points) between our system and the results presented in (Kozhevnikov and Titov, 2013). Both system are able to deal well with the Chinese dataset but the Czech dataset created from PCEDT proved to provide worse scores.

The results of the cross-lingual experiment measured by the unsupervised metrics (Table 4

– F_1^c row) indicate that the transfer of semantic roles from English to all other languages is possible. The high values of F_1^c scores of collocation and purity show that it should be possible to find a mapping of role labels with high agreement between the produced results of the system and the annotations in the evaluation data. Again, the results are better than the ones presented in (Kozhevnikov and Titov, 2013).

8 Future Work

We believe that our system can be improved in several areas. Currently, we work on employing bilingual clusters based upon the Word2Vec model (Mikolov et al., 2013). Next, we plan to train a SRL system on combined annotations from several languages and also to try transferring knowledge from other languages than English. The goal of this experiment would be to evaluate how the differences between languages affect the performance of our approach. Our approach is also capable of training model on more languages and we are currently working on that.

The biggest goal for the future is to propose language-independent semantic roles for the UD trees. Our system introduced in this paper can help significantly in this effort. It can be used for bootstrapping by pre-annotating the UD trees for humans to correct them afterwards.

By studying the UD annotations, we believe that it might be possible to construct language-independent rules for the predicate argument identification. An appropriate consequent clustering phase could be then used to create a language independent unsupervised SRL system.

9 Conclusion

In our paper, we have introduced a model for the cross-lingual SRL based upon the UD annotations. We have outperformed the similar approach presented in (Kozhevnikov and Titov, 2013). However, our primary goal was to evaluate whether the UD trees are suitable for the SRL task. We conclude that UD annotations are a very promising vehicle for creating a SRL system for a broad range of languages. We provide our methods for generating SRL annotations for UD trees freely for download.[4]

---

[4]Available on: goo.gl/rjjhp8.

Acknowledgments

This publication was supported by the project LO1506 of the Czech Ministry of Education, Youth and Sports and by Grant No. SGS-2016-018 Data and Software Engineering for Advanced Applications. Computational resources were provided by the CESNET LM2015042 and the CERIT Scientific Cloud LM2015085, provided under the programme "Projects of Large Research, Development, and Innovations Infrastructures".

References

Paolo Annesi and Roberto Basili. 2010. Cross-lingual alignment of FrameNet annotations through hidden markov models. In *Proceedings of the 11th International Conference on Computational Linguistics and Intelligent Text Processing*. Springer-Verlag, Berlin, Heidelberg, CICLing'10, pages 12–25. https://doi.org/10.1007/978-3-642-12116-6_2.

Collin F. Baker, Charles J. Fillmore, and John B. Lowe. 1998. The Berkeley FrameNet project. In *Proceedings of the 17th International Conference on Computational Linguistics - Volume 1*. Association for Computational Linguistics, Stroudsburg, PA, USA, COLING '98, pages 86–90. https://doi.org/10.3115/980451.980860.

Marie-Catherine de Marneffe and Christopher D. Manning. 2008. The Stanford Typed Dependencies representation. In *Coling 2008: Proceedings of the Workshop on Cross-Framework and Cross-Domain Parser Evaluation*. Association for Computational Linguistics, Stroudsburg, PA, USA, CrossParser '08, pages 1–8. http://dl.acm.org/citation.cfm?id=1608858.1608859.

Daniel Gildea and Daniel Jurafsky. 2002. Automatic labeling of semantic roles. *Computational linguistics* 28(3):245–288.

Trond Grenager and Christopher D. Manning. 2006. Unsupervised discovery of a statistical verb lexicon. In *Proceedings of the 2006 Conference on Empirical Methods in Natural Language Processing*. Association for Computational Linguistics, Stroudsburg, PA, USA, EMNLP '06, pages 1–8. http://dl.acm.org/citation.cfm?id=1610075.1610077.

Jan Hajič, Massimiliano Ciaramita, Richard Johansson, Daisuke Kawahara, Maria Antònia Martí, Lluís Màrquez, Adam Meyers, Joakim Nivre, Sebastian Padó, Jan Štěpánek, et al. 2009. The conll-2009 shared task: Syntactic and semantic dependencies in multiple languages. In *Proceedings of the Thirteenth Conference on Computational Natural Language Learning: Shared Task*. Association for Computational Linguistics, pages 1–18.

Jan Hajič, Eva Hajičová, Jarmila Panevová, Petr Sgall, Silvie Cinková, Eva Fučíková, Marie Mikulová, Petr Pajas, Jan Popelka, Jiří Semecký, Jana Šindlerová, Jan Štěpánek, Josef Toman, Zdeňka Urešová, and Zdeněk Žabokrtský. 2012. Prague czech-english dependency treebank 2.0. LINDAT/CLARIN digital library at the Institute of Formal and Applied Linguistics, Charles University in Prague.

Karin Kipper, Anna Korhonen, Neville Ryant, and Martha Palmer. 2006. A large-scale extension of VerbNet with novel verb classes. In Cristina Onesti Elisa Corino, Carla Marello, editor, *Proceedings of the 12th EURALEX International Congress*. Edizioni dell'Orso, Torino, Italy, pages 173–184.

Michal Konkol. 2014. Brainy: A machine learning library. In Leszek Rutkowski, Marcin Korytkowski, Rafa Scherer, Ryszard Tadeusiewicz, Lotfi A. Zadeh, and Jacek M. Zurada, editors, *Artificial Intelligence and Soft Computing*. Springer International Publishing, volume 8468 of *Lecture Notes in Computer Science*, pages 490–499. https://doi.org/10.1007/978-3-319-07176-3_43.

Mikhail Kozhevnikov and Ivan Titov. 2013. Crosslingual transfer of semantic role labeling models. In *Proceedings of the 51st Annual Meeting of the Association for Computational Linguistics, ACL 2013, 4-9 August 2013, Sofia, Bulgaria, Volume 1: Long Papers*. pages 1190–1200. http://aclweb.org/anthology/P/P13/P13-1117.pdf.

Mikhail Kozhevnikov and Ivan Titov. 2014. Crosslingual model transfer using feature representation projection. In *ACL (2)*. pages 579–585.

Joel Lang and Mirella Lapata. 2010. Unsupervised induction of semantic roles. In *Human Language Technologies: The 2010 Annual Conference of the North American Chapter of the Association for Computational Linguistics*. Association for Computational Linguistics, Stroudsburg, PA, USA, HLT '10, pages 939–947. http://dl.acm.org/citation.cfm?id=1857999.1858135.

Joel Lang and Mirella Lapata. 2011. Unsupervised semantic role induction via split-merge clustering. In *Proceedings of the 49th Annual Meeting of the Association for Computational Linguistics: Human Language Technologies*. Association for Computational Linguistics, Portland, Oregon, USA, pages 1117–1126. http://www.aclweb.org/anthology/P11-1112.

Christopher D. Manning, Mihai Surdeanu, John Bauer, Jenny Finkel, Steven J. Bethard, and David McClosky. 2014. The Stanford CoreNLP natural language processing toolkit. In *Association for Computational Linguistics (ACL) System Demonstrations*. pages 55–60. http://www.aclweb.org/anthology/P/P14/P14-5010.

A. Meyers, R. Reeves, C. Macleod, R. Szekely, V. Zielinska, B. Young, and R. Grishman. 2004. The NomBank project: An interim report. In A. Meyers, editor, *HLT-NAACL 2004 Workshop: Frontiers in Corpus Annotation*. Association for Computational Linguistics, Boston, Massachusetts, USA, pages 24–31.

Tomas Mikolov, Kai Chen, Greg Corrado, and Jeffrey Dean. 2013. Efficient estimation of word representations in vector space. *CoRR* abs/1301.3781. http://arxiv.org/abs/1301.3781.

Joakim Nivre, Marie-Catherine de Marneffe, Filip Ginter, Yoav Goldberg, Jan Hajic, Christopher D Manning, Ryan T McDonald, Slav Petrov, Sampo Pyysalo, Natalia Silveira, et al. 2016. Universal dependencies v1: A multilingual treebank collection. In *LREC*.

Joakim Nivre and Johan Hall. 2005. Maltparser: A language-independent system for data-driven dependency parsing. In *In Proc. of the Fourth Workshop on Treebanks and Linguistic Theories*. pages 13–95.

Sebastian Padó and Mirella Lapata. 2009. Crosslingual annotation projection for semantic roles. *Journal of Artificial Intelligence Research* 36:307–340.

Martha Palmer, Daniel Gildea, and Paul Kingsbury. 2005. The Proposition Bank: An annotated corpus of semantic roles. *Computational Linguistics* 31(1):71–106. https://doi.org/10.1162/0891201053630264.

Slav Petrov, Dipanjan Das, and Ryan McDonald. 2012. A universal part-of-speech tagset. In *Proceedings of the Eight International Conference on Language Resources and Evaluation (LREC'12)*. European Language Resources Association (ELRA), Istanbul, Turkey.

Milan Straka, Jan Hajič, and Jana Straková. 2016. UDPipe: trainable pipeline for processing CoNLL-U files performing tokenization, morphological analysis, pos tagging and parsing. In *Proceedings of the Tenth International Conference on Language Resources and Evaluation (LREC'16)*. European Language Resources Association (ELRA), Paris, France.

Ivan Titov and Alexandre Klementiev. 2012. A bayesian approach to unsupervised semantic role induction. In *Proceedings of the 13th Conference of the European Chapter of the Association for Computational Linguistics*. Association for Computational Linguistics, Stroudsburg, PA, USA, EACL '12, pages 12–22. http://dl.acm.org/citation.cfm?id=2380816.2380821.

Daniel Zeman. 2008. Reusable tagset conversion using tagset drivers. In *Proceedings of the Sixth International Conference on Language Resources and Evaluation (LREC'08)*. European Language Resources Association (ELRA), Marrakech, Morocco. Http://www.lrec-conf.org/proceedings/lrec2008/.

Using Gaze Data to Predict Multiword Expressions

Omid Rohanian, Shiva Taslimipoor, Victoria Yaneva and Le An Ha

Research Group in Computational Linguistics, University of Wolverhampton, UK

{omid.rohanian,shiva.taslimi,v.yaneva,ha.l.a}@wlv.ac.uk

Abstract

In recent years gaze data has been increasingly used to improve and evaluate NLP models due to the fact that it carries information about the cognitive processing of linguistic phenomena. In this paper we conduct a preliminary study towards the automatic identification of multiword expressions based on gaze features from native and non-native speakers of English. We report comparisons between a part-of-speech (POS) and frequency baseline to: i) a prediction model based solely on gaze data and ii) a combined model of gaze data, POS and frequency. In spite of the challenging nature of the task, best performance was achieved by the latter. Furthermore, we explore how the type of gaze data (from native versus non-native speakers) affects the prediction, showing that data from the two groups is discriminative to an equal degree. Finally, we show that late processing measures are more predictive than early ones, which is in line with previous research on idioms and other formulaic structures.

1 Introduction

In order to alleviate the burden that language comprehension poses on the short-term memory, the human brain uses frequently occurring formulaic sequences such as multiword expressions, collocations and idioms, among others, and stores them as units in the long-term memory (Conklin and Schmitt, 2012). As a result of the efficacy of this approach, a large proportion of the spoken and written language is formulaic, with some corpus studies claiming that between 52% and 58% of the language in the analysed corpora falls into this category (Erman and Warren, 2000), and other studies claiming that this figure is around 32% (Foster, 2001). Given the frequency with which this phenomenon occurs, the automatic identification of formulaic language is of paramount importance for a number of Natural Language Processing (NLP) tasks and applications.

Conklin and Schmitt (2012) argue that our brains store and process very frequent and highly fixed combinations as "wholes" as opposed to single words being added together and that this difference in processing is reflected in eye tracking data. A number of eye tracking studies discussed in Section 2 show that there is a processing advantage for formulaic sequences for both native and non-native speakers compared to controlled non-formulaic sequences. Based on this evidence, it could be concluded that the characteristics of formulaic language could be captured through differences in the gaze patterns between formulaic and non-formulaic sequences. In a similar way, gaze data has previously been successfully used in other NLP tasks such as part-of-speech tagging (Barrett et al., 2016a) and evaluation of word embeddings (Søgaard, 2016), and it has been shown that gaze signals transfer across languages (Barrett et al., 2016b). In this sense, automatically identifying formulaic sequences based on gaze features could not only contribute to potentially improving classification accuracy and gaining insight into the cognitive processing of such units, but can also provide a language-independent approach to identification of formulaic phrases. However, it is important to note that almost all studies using gaze data to investigate formulaic language focus solely on idioms and that other types of formulaic units have been significantly understudied.

In the present research we conduct a preliminary study towards the identification of multiword expressions (MWEs) based on gaze features.

Proceedings of Recent Advances in Natural Language Processing, pages 601–609,
Varna, Bulgaria, Sep 4–6 2017.

An MWE is commonly known as a combination of two or more words, not necessarily continuous, that pose difficulties on language processing (Sag et al., 2002) and that typically have syntactic and semantic idiosyncrasies (Fazly and Stevenson, 2006). In particular, we focus on two common types of MWEs, namely, Verb-Particle (e.g. *give up*) and Verb-Noun (e.g. *take place*) constructions.

We use the GECO corpus (Cop et al., 2016), a monolingual and bilingual corpus of the eye-tracking data from participants reading a complete novel. The use of this data allowed comparison between the gaze patterns of native and non-native English speakers, as well as a comparison of the predictive power of data obtained from these two groups. Furthermore, we explore a range of early and late measures of cognitive processing in order to determine which of the two groups of features carries more important linguistic information. In order to account for the fact that MWEs are often processed as unified structures, we used Conditional Random Fields (CRF) classifier to label sequences of words, together with a variety of early and late gaze features.

The contributions of this work are as follows:

- We explore a novel approach to MWE identification based on gaze data. We compare a POS + Frequency baseline to: i) a prediction model based solely on gaze features and ii) a prediction model based on gaze features, POS, and frequency.

- A comparison between the predictive power of gaze data from native and non-native speakers of English in the context of MWE identification.

- A comparison between the predictive power of a number of early and late gaze features in the context of our current task.

The code used in the experiments and the annotation of the MWEs are made freely available[1]. The GECO corpus could be downloaded freely at: `http://expsy.ugent.be/downloads/geco`. For an investigation discussing the cognitive processing of the MWEs in the corpus, refer to (Yaneva et al., 2017).

The rest of this paper is organised as follows. Section 2 presents related work from the fields of

---

[1] `https://github.com/omidrohanian/gaze-mwe-ranlp2017`

eye tracking and MWEs research, while Section 3 describes the data used in this study and Section 4 describes the gaze features. The experimental approach and the actual experiments conducted are presented in Section 5, and are then reported and discussed in Sections 6 and 7, respectively. Finally Section 8 contains the main conclusions and avenues for future work.

2 Related Work

This section presents related work from the fields of eye tracking research and automatic identification of multiword units.

2.1 Eye Tracking and Formulaic Language

Eye tracking is a process where an eye-tracking device measures the point of gaze of an eye (gaze fixation) or the motion of an eye (saccade) relative to the head and a computer screen (Duchowski, 2009). Fixations are eye movements which stabilise the retina over a stationary object of interest, which, in the case of reading research, is the written text and its units (letters, words, phrases, etc). Gaze fixations and revisits (go-back fixations to a previously fixated object) have been widely used as measures of cognitive effort by taking into account their durations and the places in text where longer fixations occur (Duchowski, 2009). Early gaze measures such as first fixation duration give information about the early stages of lexical access and syntactic processing, while late gaze measures such as total dwell time or total number of fixations give information about late stages of processing (e.g. late syntactic processing, textual integration processes, lexical and syntactic/semantic processing and disambiguation in general). A series of studies on eye tracking during reading show that gaze data is sensitive to linguistic phenomena such as word frequency, verb complexity and lexical ambiguity, as well as contextual effects on word perception (Rayner, 1975; Rayner and Duffy, 1986; Rayner, 2009; Rayner et al., 2012).

Gaze data has been previously used to investigate formulaic language with a main focus on idiom research (Underwood et al., 2004; Siyanova-Chanturia et al., 2011; Conklin and Schmitt, 2012; Siyanova-Chanturia, 2013; Cutter et al., 2014; Carrol and Conklin, 2015). For example, Underwood et al. (2004) showed that native speakers read idioms faster and with fewer fixations compared to control non-idiomatic phrases and that the last word of the idiom was read faster than the last word in the control condition. Similarly, non-native readers produced fewer fixations when reading idioms than when reading control phrases but there were no differences in the durations of those fixations (Underwood et al., 2004). Siyanova-Chanturia et al. (2011) corroborated the processing advantages of idioms over novel phrases and showed that idioms required less re-reading and less re-analysis. Interestingly, there were no significant differences in the early gaze measures, suggesting that early eye-tracking measures may not be suitable for investigation of formulaic language (Siyanova-Chanturia et al., 2011). This result may be explained with previous research on predictability of single words showing strong effects in terms of shorter first fixation durations and greater likelihood of skipping (Rayner and Well, 1996). However, Carrol and Conklin (2015) argue that this effect may not scale up to formulaic units in a simple fusion and suggest taking an approach balancing between local, lexical context and global discourse context. Assuming that the case of formulaic language is that "the whole is greater than the sum of the parts", Carrol and Conklin (2015) suggest the use of a *hybrid* approach where formulaic language is analysed both as a whole and at the level of individual words. In order to partly account for this effect we use an algorithm which represents the data as a sequence of words considering their neighbouring word features.

2.2 Identification of MWEs

MWEs have been investigated in computational linguistics based on their many different characteristics such as fixedness (Fazly and Stevenson, 2008), non-compositionality (Baldwin and Kim, 2010), and semi-productivity (Villavicencio, 2003). We have used these properties as the main guidelines for annotating MWEs, specifically following the guidelines provided by the PARSEME project on identifying verbal MWEs.[2] High frequency of MWEs and in particular, the principle that MWEs usually are constructed from high frequency word components have been studied extensively in computational linguistics (Granger and Meunier, 2008; Fazly, 2007).

In the most recent MWE workshop (Savary

---

[2] `https://typo.uni-konstanz.de/ PARSEME/images/shared-task/guidelines/ PARSEME-ST-annotation-guidelines-v6.pdf`

et al., 2017), several language-independent systems have been proposed for identifying or extracting MWEs. When used in conjunction with CRF models (Scholivet and Ramisch, 2017) or structured perceptrons (Schneider et al., 2014), Part-of-Speech (POS) tags have been shown to be useful features (especially when parsing information is not available) to identify MWEs. Schneider et al.'s (2014) statistical sequence model has achieved the best F1-score of 60% in identifying all heterogeneous types of MWEs and truly shows how challenging the task is.

3 Eye Tracking Data

The GECO corpus (Cop et al., 2016) used in this study is, to the best of our knowledge, the most recent eye tracking corpus for English, which: i) contains gaze data from a natural reading task (as opposed to e.g. single sentences), ii) is long enough to contain a sufficient number of MWEs, and iii) contains paired gaze data from native and non-native readers. Eye tracking data was collected for both the English version of the novel and its translation in Dutch; however, in the current study we only focus on the English part of the data.

The text of the corpus is a novel by Agatha Christie entitled "The Mysterious Affair at Styles", the English version of which contains 54,364 tokens and 5,012 unique types. The novel was selected based on the fact that its word frequency distribution had considerable similarity to the one in natural language use, as observed in the Subtlex database (Cop et al., 2016). The novel was read by 14 English monolingual undergraduates from the University of Southampton and 19 Dutch (L1) - English (L2) bilingual students at Ghent University (intermediate and advanced). The two groups were matched on age and education level. The monolingual participants read only the English version of the novel, which amounted to a total of 5,031 sentences. The bilingual participants read chapters 1 - 7 in one language and 8 - 13 in the other in a counterbalanced order, thus reading 2,449 English sentences. The eight bilingual participants who read the first part of the novel in English read 2,852 English sentences.

The sampling rate of the eye tracking device was 1 kHz. Full details about the method and procedure used for the development of the corpus could be found in (Cop et al., 2016).

4   Gaze Features

A number of gaze features were selected for the corpus and are listed in Table 1. All gaze features were averaged over 14 native readers for one set and 19 non-native readers for another set of data. We divided the features into *early* and *late* processing measures. Early measures capture processes such as lexical access and syntactic processing, as well as oculomotor processes and visual properties of the region. An example of such a measure is *first fixation duration* (Demberg and Keller, 2008). Late measures account for late syntactic processing, textual integration processes, lexical and syntactic/semantic processing and disambiguation in general. An example of a late measure is the *total reading time* of a region, which is the sum of all fixations on a region, including refixations of the region after it was left (Demberg and Keller, 2008).

Table 1: Categorised Gaze Features

Early	WORD_FIRST_FIXATION_DURATION WORD_FIRST_RUN_FIXATION_COUNT WORD_FIRST_RUN_FIXATION_% WORD_FIRST_FIXATION_VISITED_WORD_COUNT WORD_FIRST_FIX_PROGRESSIVE WORD_SKIP
Late	WORD_FIXATION_COUNT WORD_FIXATION_% WORD_RUN_COUNT WORD_GO_PAST_TIME WORD_SELECTIVE_GO_PAST_TIME WORD_TOTAL_READING_TIME WORD_TOTAL_READING_TIME_% WORD_SPILLOVER WORD_AVERAGE_FIX_PUPIL_SIZE WORD_SECOND_FIXATION_DURATION WORD_SECOND_RUN_FIXATION_COUNT WORD_SECOND_RUN_FIXATION_% WORD_SECOND_FIXATION_RUN WORD_THIRD_FIXATION_DURATION WORD_THIRD_RUN_FIXATION_COUNT WORD_THIRD_RUN_FIXATION_% WORD_THIRD_FIXATION_RUN WORD_LAST_FIXATION_DURATION WORD_LAST_FIXATION_RUN

5   Experiments

This section presents the annotation procedure, method, and setup used to conduct the experiments, as well as the definition of the baseline.

5.1   Annotation

Two annotators with linguistic background labelled the GECO corpus for Verb + Noun and Verb + Particle constructions. The procedure was as follows. Both annotators read the entire corpus (as opposed to annotating automatically extracted cases) and marked both types of MWEs by considering cases where the components of an MWE can occur with at most three words in between. All Verb + Noun and Verb + Particle expressions (with or without gaps) irregardless of whether they were annotated as MWE or not are considered for evaluating the agreement between the annotators. The kappa inter-annotator agreement is k = 0.7864. Furthermore, we have resolved the annotation differences by employing a third annotator to decide in cases of disagreement.

In order to prepare sequences to be trained by the CRF model, we extract from the corpus all patterns of Verb + Noun and Verb + Prepositions (and Verb + a list of other particles such as *up, down, over, etc*) with at most three words between the components. MWEs are tagged using the IOB format based on the annotations. The (B) tag stands for words appearing at the beginning, (I) for words occurring inside, and (O) for words that are outside of an MWE (Sang, 2002). Verb + Noun and Verb + Particle patterns, with a window of one word before and one word after, are fed into the CRF model as input sequences. In total, there are 381 sequences that contain MWEs and 5,837 which do not. Two examples of annotated sequences are as follows. The first sequence contains an MWE while the second does not.

1) *have   knocked   us   all   down   with   a*
   O   B   O   O   I   O   O

2) *have   been   asked   both   by   my*
   O   O   O   O   O   O

5.2   Method

For our task of sequence labelling with sparse data, we use Conditional Random Fields (CRFs). CRFs are capable of relaxing the strong independence assumptions present in similar models like HMMs, which make them a suitable choice in a structured prediction task where context is of importance (Lafferty et al., 2001).

We use Pycrfsuite[3] which is a freely available Python wrapper around the crfsuite toolkit[4]. For the training algorithm we use Adaptive Regulari-

---

[3]`https://python-crfsuite.readthedocs.io/en/latest/`
[4]`http://www.chokkan.org/software/crfsuite/`

Algorithm 1 Bootstrap aggregating on CRF labels

1: **procedure** BAGGING
2:     $[] \leftarrow result$
3:     $n_{test} \leftarrow \frac{1}{5}\|MW\|$
4:     $n_{train} \leftarrow \frac{4}{5}\|MW\|$
5:     $subIter \leftarrow \frac{\|MW\| - n_{test}}{n_{train}}$
6:     **for** 100 times **do**
7:         $test \leftarrow (sample\,of\,size\,n_{test}\,from\,MW) \cup (sample\,of\,size\,n_{test}\,from\,nonMW)$
8:         **for** i = 1 to subIter **do**
9:             $train \leftarrow (sample\,of\,size\,n_{train}\,from\,(nonMW - test)) \cup (MW - test)$
10:             $C_i \leftarrow CRF(train, test)$
11:         $C^* \leftarrow [\underset{y \in Y}{argmax} \sum_{i:C_i[0]} 1, ..., \underset{y \in Y:C_i[2*n_{test}]}{argmax} \sum 1]$
12:         $result.add(Eval(C^*))$
    return $mean(result), std(result)$

---

sation Of Weight Vector (AROW) that is suitable for handling inherently noisy labels in the training set (Crammer et al., 2009).

In order to extract features for the CRF model, given each sequence:

1. gaze features of each word in the sequence are added;

2. for the verb part of the sequence, we also add the features of the last component of the pattern (Verb + Noun or Verb + Particle);

3. for all other words of the sequence, on the other hand, we add the features of the verb component of the pattern.

The gaze features of the GECO corpus, used in this study are listed in Table 1.

5.3 Setup

In order to tackle the imbalance of data, we employ a bootstrap aggregating strategy (Breiman, 1996). We first randomly select one fifth of the MWEs and the same number from non-MWEs as the test data. Then, we divide the remaining non-MWEs to several different sections with the same size as the remaining MWEs. We train the model on each section of non-MWEs and the whole training set of MWEs. We test the model on the held-out test data by obtaining the majority votes of different training models over the test sample. This process is performed 100 times and the average and standard deviations of the precision, recall and F1-score measures are reported. The formalised approach is presented in Algorithm 1.

5.4 Baseline

We apply the same CRF and aggregating approach only with lexical features as the baseline. POS and word frequency are used as the features. The GECO data is provided with the POS tags for the words, while word frequencies are derived from the BNC corpus (Leech, 1992).

In the case of these lexical features, given each word feature f_w present in the input sequence, contextual features f_{w-1} and f_{w+1} are automatically retrieved and added to the feature set. This informs the model of what is happening in the immediate neighbourhood of each word in the sequence.

6 Results

We report the results of CRF labeling using different sets of features, including POS tags, Frequency (referred to as FREQ), Early and Late gaze measures (Table 2).

Since most of the data are not MWEs and are thus irrelevant to the task, we report the results exclusively for the words at the beginning of the MWEs (B-MWE) and other words occurring within and at the end of the expressions (I-MWE).

In Table 2, we have first shown that augmenting the lexical features (POS and FREQ) with Gaze has slightly improved the performance ($F = 70.05$ for B-MWE and $F = 54.0$ for I-MWE) compared to the baseline ($F = 63.6$ for B-MWE and $F = 48.06$ for I-MWE). Although, based on the reported standard deviation measures, adding Gaze features might not be helpful in some parts of the data, in general, the combination of lexi-

Table 2: The performance (%) and Standard Deviation (std) (%) of CRF labeling models using different sets of features.

Features		Precision (std)	Recall (std)	F1-score (std)
FREQ	B-MWE	46.92 (12.17)	27.59 (13.89)	32.53 (12.03)
	I-MWE	37.00 (14.18)	10.09 (7.06)	14.76 (8.62)
POS	B-MWE	59.14 (4.75)	63.34 (11.92)	60.05 (6.46)
	I-MWE	56.43 (5.44)	39.03 (8.59)	45.44 (6.05)
POS + FREQ	B-MWE	59.95 (3.54)	68.26 (7.96)	63.6 (4.45)
	I-MWE	55.19 (4.78)	43.16 (7.77)	48.06 (5.56)
Gaze features (Early and Late)	B-MWE	51.43 (3.19)	55.55 (9.2)	53.06 (5.22)
	I-MWE	37.43 (5.95)	22.97 (6.07)	27.97 (5.19)
POS + FREQ + Gaze	B-MWE	66.68 (3.36)	74.03 (5.45)	**70.05 (3.48)**
	I-MWE	59.08 (4.8)	50.03 (5.87)	**54.0 (4.41)**
Early features	B-MWE	51.77 (5.14)	55.28 (21.74)	51.02 (12.94)
	I-MWE	37.53 (19.25)	9.73 (10.41)	13.38 (11.7)
Late features	B-MWE	50.16 (3.22)	56.06 (9.41)	52.54 (5.11)
	I-MWE	38.07 (5.0)	21.23 (6.21)	26.8 (5.84)
POS + FREQ + Early features	B-MWE	66.54 (3.68)	74.45 (6.73)	70.11 (3.82)
	I-MWE	60.01 (4.53)	49.16 (5.67)	53.85 (4.1)
POS + FREQ + Late features	B-MWE	65.0 (3.43)	74.12 (5.96)	69.59 (3.69)
	I-MWE	58.85 (4.19)	50.23 (5.77)	53.93 (3.90)

cal features and the gaze information outperforms the baseline model and the model that uses Gaze features alone (Early and Late) ($F = 53.06$ for B-MWE and $F = 27.97$ for I-MWE).

We also compare the performance of Early and Late features in identifying MWEs in the second part of the table. We note that Late features appear to be more discriminative than Early features in identifying MWEs. Although in case of the B-MWE, the improvement over Early features is minimal, the difference is more contrastive for I-MWE. Also the standard deviation for the model using Late features confirms its superior reliability. We see these improvements when using Early or Late features by themselves and not in conjuction with POS+FREQ.

Furthermore, we have conducted an experiment with gaze features extracted from non-native speakers of English. Table 3 presents a comparison between the F1 scores obtained from training on L1 and L2 gaze data. There were no significant differences between the two groups in terms of precision and recall, hence, for the purpose of brevity, we present the comparison only in terms of F1 scores. The better performance when using Late gaze features over Early is well reiterated in the data extracted for non-native speakers in this table.

Table 3: The performance (F1-score%) comparison between data from native (L1) and non-native (L2) speakers.

Features		L1	L2
Gaze	B-MWE	53.06 (5.22)	54.26 (4.8)
	I-MWE	27.97 (5.19)	26.66 (5.11)
POS + FREQ + Gaze	B-MWE	70.05 (3.48)	69.66 (3.07)
	I-MWE	54.0 (4.41)	52.84 (3.89)
Early Gaze	B-MWE	51.02 (12.94)	51.69 (13.3)
	I-MWE	13.38 (11.07)	11.63 (11.66)
Late Gaze	B-MWE	52.54 (5.11)	54.95 (5.04)
	I-MWE	26.8 (5.84)	27.24 (5.78)

7 Discussion

In this section we discuss the results presented above with regards to: i) MWEs identification accuracy, ii) comparison between the predictive power of gaze data of native versus non-native speakers, and iii) the predictive power of Early versus Late gaze features.

In terms of identification accuracy for MWEs, best performance was achieved by the model combining POS + Frequency + Gaze data for both the beginning of the MWE ($F = 70.05$), and the words occurring inside the MWE ($F = 54.0$). Even though gaze features on their own performed significantly worse than the baseline, the combined model of Gaze + Freq + POS outperformed the baseline and achieved a performance comparable to the state-of-the-art in the field (Section 2.2). The lower values for the standard deviations in the combined model for both B-MWE and I-MWE also show that it is more reliable than the baseline in its prediction over 100 iterations. Furthermore, the fact that gaze features improve the classification accuracy means that readers process these structures differently.

We do not observe significant differences in model accuracy when running parallel models on the data from the native speakers and the one from the non-native speakers, which indicates that both data sets are discriminative to an equal extent. It is important to note that the non-native speakers were highly proficient in English and that this result may not be replicated with gaze data from less proficient readers. From a practical perspective this is important with regards to the type of eye-tracking corpora which could be used in similar experiments in the future. Since such resources are scarce and expensive to obtain, it is reassuring to know that data from non-native speakers could be used equally well for the purpose of automatically identifying MWEs. From a psycholinguistic perspective however, this finding is not in line with previous research on the differences in gaze patterns between native and non-native speakers reading formulaic language (Section 2.1). One reason for this could be that previous research using gaze data to explore the processing of formulaic language has focused predominantly on idioms, while we discuss MWEs. Another reason for this could be the different data sets used in these studies and conclusive results can only be drawn if idiom research is performed using the GECO corpus or vice-versa.

Finally, much in line with previous studies (e.g. Siyanova-Chanturia (2013)) we observe that early gaze features are not useful metrics for investigating formulaic language. It is important to note that late features were more discriminative even without using the entire Late feature set; there were no significant differences in performance when removing late features related to the third run and last runs ($F = 0.52$ for B-MWE and $F = 0.23$ for I-MWE). In our experiments the late features were particularly better at identifying the words inside the MWEs and we hypothesise that this effect could be due to the fact that given our pattern of Verb + Noun and Verb + Particle constructions, these were the disambiguation regions of the MWEs. Another possible explanation for the superiority of late features could be that mental processing of MWEs occurs after the fact, meaning, after the word is first encountered in reading. Therefore, early gaze features are not expected to contain much information about whether a particular sequence of tokens are MWE or not.

Some of the limitations of this research are related to averaging of data from multiple participants and the fact that the newly-released GECO corpus (Cop et al., 2016) has not yet been studied in detail and thus it is possible that it contains inaccuracies yet to be spotted. We plan to address the first limitation by conducting a study where separate models are built for each individual participant. This would allow analysis of individual differences and the effects they have on the robustness of the model. We chose to use the GECO corpus since it was the only corpus available which allowed comparison of gaze data from native versus non-native speakers. Nevertheless, it would be interesting to compare our current results on the GECO data to results from more established eye tracking corpora such as the Dundee corpus (Kennedy et al., 2013) in order to further assess the validity of our findings.

8 Conclusions

This paper presents preliminary research towards using gaze data to automatically identify multiword expressions. We show that MWEs are indeed viewed differently and that best classification performance is achieved by a combined model of gaze features, frequency and POS tags, which outperform models based on frequency and POS only and on gaze features only. Furthermore, we show that there is no statistically significant difference between the performance of models using gaze data from native versus highly proficient non-native speakers of English, suggesting that data from both reader groups could be used for similar tasks in the future. Finally, consistent with previous research in the field, we show that late gaze features are better predictors of formulaic language.

Future work includes incorporating different sequence labeling models (including at the level of individual participants) and replicating the experiment with gaze data from different corpora.

References

Timothy Baldwin and Su Nam Kim. 2010. Multiword expressions. In *Handbook of Natural Language Processing, second edition.*, CRC Press, pages 267–292.

Maria Barrett, Joachim Bingel, Frank Keller, and Anders Søgaard. 2016a. Weakly supervised part-of-speech tagging using eye-tracking data. In *Proceedings of the 54th Annual Meeting of the Association for Computational Linguistics.* volume 2, pages 579–584.

Maria Barrett, Frank Keller, and Anders Søgaard. 2016b. Cross-lingual transfer of correlations between parts of speech and gaze features. In *26th International Conference on Computational Linguistics (coling).*

Leo Breiman. 1996. Bagging predictors. *Machine learning* 24(2):123–140.

Gareth Carrol and Kathy Conklin. 2015. Eye-tracking multi-word units: some methodological questions. *Journal of Eye Movement Research* 7(5).

Kathy Conklin and Norbert Schmitt. 2012. The processing of formulaic language. *Annual Review of Applied Linguistics* 32:45–61.

Uschi Cop, Nicolas Dirix, Denis Drieghe, and Wouter Duyck. 2016. Presenting GECO: An eyetracking corpus of monolingual and bilingual sentence reading. *Behavior research methods* pages 1–14.

Koby Crammer, Alex Kulesza, and Mark Dredze. 2009. Adaptive regularization of weight vectors. In *Advances in neural information processing systems.* pages 414–422.

Michael G. Cutter, Denis Drieghe, and Simon Liversedge. 2014. Preview benefit in english spaced compounds. *Experimental Psychology Learning Memory and Cognition* 40(6).

Vera Demberg and Frank Keller. 2008. Data from eye-tracking corpora as evidence for theories of syntactic processing complexity. *Cognition* 109(2):193–210.

Andrew Duchowski. 2009. *Eye Tracking Methodology: Theory and Practice.* Springer, second edition.

Britt Erman and Beatrice Warren. 2000. The idiom principle and the open choice principle. *Text-Interdisciplinary Journal for the Study of Discourse* 20(1):29–62.

Afsaneh Fazly. 2007. *Automatic Acquisition of Lexical Knowledge about Multiword Predicates.* Ph.D. thesis, Department of Computer Science, University of Toronto.

Afsaneh Fazly and Suzanne Stevenson. 2006. Automatically constructing a lexicon of verb phrase idiomatic combinations. In *In Proceedings of EACL-06.* pages 337–344.

Afsaneh Fazly and Suzanne Stevenson. 2008. A distributional account of the semantics of multiword expressions. *Italian Journal of Linguistics* 1(20):157–179.

Pauline Foster. 2001. Rules and routines: A consideration of their role in the task-based language production of native and non-native speakers. *Researching pedagogic tasks: Second language learning, teaching, and testing* pages 75–93.

Sylviane Granger and Fanny Meunier. 2008. *Phraseology: an interdisciplinary perspective.* John Benjamins Publishing Company.

Alan Kennedy, Joël Pynte, Wayne S Murray, and Shirley-Anne Paul. 2013. Frequency and predictability effects in the dundee corpus: An eye movement analysis. *The Quarterly Journal of Experimental Psychology* 66(3):601–618.

John Lafferty, Andrew McCallum, and Fernando Pereira. 2001. Conditional random fields: Probabilistic models for segmenting and labeling sequence data. In *Proceedings of the eighteenth international conference on machine learning, ICML.* volume 1, pages 282–289.

Geoffrey Leech. 1992. 100 million words of english: the british national corpus (bnc). *Language Research* 28(1):1–13.

Keith Rayner. 1975. The perceptual span and peripheral cues in reading. *Cognitive Psychology* 7(1):65–81.

Keith Rayner. 2009. Eye movements and attention in reading, scene perception, and visual search. *The quarterly journal of experimental psychology* 62(8):1457–1506.

Keith Rayner and Susan A Duffy. 1986. Lexical complexity and fixation times in reading: Effects of word frequency, verb complexity, and lexical ambiguity. *Memory & Cognition* 14(3):191–201.

Keith Rayner, Alexander Pollatsek, Jane Ashby, and Charles Clifton Jr. 2012. *Psychology of reading.* Psychology Press.

Keith Rayner and Arnold D Well. 1996. Effects of contextual constraint on eye movements in reading: A further examination. *Psychonomic Bulletin & Review* 3(4):504–509.

Ivan A. Sag, Timothy Baldwin, Francis Bond, Ann A. Copestake, and Dan Flickinger. 2002. Multiword expressions: A pain in the neck for nlp. In *Proceedings of the Third International Conference on Computational Linguistics and Intelligent Text Processing.* Springer-Verlag, London, UK, UK, CICLing '02, pages 1–15.

EF Tjong Kim Sang. 2002. Introduction to the conll-2002 shared task: Language-independent named entity recognition .

Agata Savary, Carlos Ramisch, Silvio Cordeiro, Federico Sangati, Veronika Vincze, Behrang Qasemizadeh, Marie Candito, Fabienne Cap, Voula Giouli, Ivelina Stoyanova, et al. 2017. The parseme shared task on automatic identification of verbal multiword expressions. In *Proceedings of the 13th Workshop on Multiword Expressions (MWE 2017)*. pages 31–47.

Nathan Schneider, Emily Danchik, Chris Dyer, and Noah A. Smith. 2014. Discriminative lexical semantic segmentation with gaps: Running the mwe gamut. *Transactions of the Association for Computational Linguistics* 2:193–206.

Manon Scholivet and Carlos Ramisch. 2017. Identification of ambiguous multiword expressions using sequence models and lexical resources. In *Proceedings of the 13th Workshop on Multiword Expressions (MWE 2017)*. Association for Computational Linguistics, Valencia, Spain, pages 167–175.

Anna Siyanova-Chanturia. 2013. Eye-tracking and erps in multi-word expression research: A state-of-the-art review of the method and findings. *The Mental Lexicon* 8(2):245–268.

Anna Siyanova-Chanturia, Kathy Conklin, and Norbert Schmitt. 2011. Adding more fuel to the fire: An eye-tracking study of idiom processing by native and non-native speakers. *Second Language Research* 27(2):251–272.

Anders Søgaard. 2016. Evaluating word embeddings with fmri and eye-tracking. *ACL 2016* page 116.

Geoffrey Underwood, Norbert Schmitt, and Adam Galpin. 2004. The eyes have it. *Formulaic sequences: Acquisition, processing, and use* 9:153.

Aline Villavicencio. 2003. Verb-particle constructions and lexical resources. In *Proceedings of the ACL 2003 Workshop on Multiword Expressions: Analysis, Acquisition and Treatment - Volume 18*. Association for Computational Linguistics, Stroudsburg, PA, USA, MWE '03, pages 57–64.

Victoria Yaneva, Shiva Taslimipoor, Omid Rohanian, and Le An Ha. 2017. Cognitive processing of multiword expressions in native and non-native speakers of english: Evidence from gaze data. In *Mitkov, R. (Ed.) Computational and Corpus-based Phraseology (to be appeared)*. Springer: Heidelberg, New York, London.

Real-Time News Summarization with Adaptation to Media Attention

Andreas Rücklé[†] and **Iryna Gurevych**[†‡]

[†]Ubiquitous Knowledge Processing Lab (UKP)
Department of Computer Science, Technische Universität Darmstadt
[‡]Ubiquitous Knowledge Processing Lab (UKP-DIPF)
German Institute for Educational Research
`www.ukp.tu-darmstadt.de`

Abstract

Real-time summarization of news events (RTS) allows persons to stay up-to-date on important topics that develop over time. With the occurrence of major sub-events, media attention increases and a large number of news articles are published. We propose a summarization approach that detects such changes and selects a suitable summarization configuration at run-time. In particular, at times with high media attention, our approach exploits the redundancy in content to produce a more precise summary and avoid emitting redundant information. We find that our approach significantly outperforms a strong non-adaptive RTS baseline in terms of the emitted summary updates and achieves the best results on a recent web-scale dataset. It can successfully be applied to a different real-world dataset without requiring additional modifications.

1 Introduction

Important events such as natural disasters, protests, and accidents often trigger an increased information need for many people. These events usually develop over time with the occurrence of multiple sub-events, where publishers on the web create news articles on the topic while the situation is still developing. To stay fully updated, interested persons have to digest a substantial amount of information, which is not feasible in most cases. Some publishers therefore create real-time newsfeeds for selected high-impact events that are regularly updated with short texts to provide a live summary on the recent developments. An excerpt of an example summary is shown in Figure 1. Because the updates are usually created by journalists, the process is laborious and can only be applied to few events.

Figure 1: Three updates for an example summary of the event *Russian Meteor (2013)*.

Automatic approaches to real-time summarization (RTS) on the other hand can generate live summaries for a large number of events without entailing additional editorial cost (Aslam et al., 2014). This summarization process is different to retrospective approaches because all news articles must be processed in a timely fashion as soon as they are available. Thus, real-time in this context refers to the continuous decision-making process over an unbounded stream of news articles where each input document can trigger the emission of new updates.

To deal with this challenge, current approaches to RTS use real-time sentence filtering methods with different heuristics (McCreadie et al., 2014a; Raza et al., 2015) or more complex, real-time capable learning to search methods (Kedzie et al., 2016). They apply the same methods over the full timeframe of an event without explicit adaptation to important changes. However, when major sub-events occur, there is a sudden increase in media attention with a large number of news articles being published on the topic. We hypothesize that the detection of these changes to adapt the summarization process to media attention allows us to create an improved event summary.

In this work, we present an approach to RTS that adapts to changes in news events at run-time

Proceedings of Recent Advances in Natural Language Processing, pages 610–617,
Varna, Bulgaria, Sep 4–6 2017.

by explicitly switching between configurations that determine important parameter choices for summarization. Within our approach, we combine simple yet effective methods for document filtering, single document summarization, and redundancy detection, which is inspired by previous work (McCreadie et al., 2014a). To adjust the parameters of these methods according to important changes in the news events, we continuously predict media attention by measuring moving averages of the number of relevant news articles over time. We switch the summarization configurations according to a ruleset whenever we detect significant changes in our predictions. This allows us to exploit redundancies in content at times with higher media attention to produce more precise updates for the summary of the news event.

Our two main contributions are as follows. First, we show that media attention is an important attribute that can be utilized for improving approaches to RTS. As a result, our approach is able to achieve the best results on a recent web-scale dataset, and can successfully be applied to a different real-world dataset without requiring additional modifications. Second, we demonstrate that simple methods for document filtering, single document summarization, and redundancy detection are very effective for RTS if suitably configured at run-time.

2   Related Work

RTS is strongly related to update summarization, where the goal is to create an update summary with only new and changed information based on a previous summary and a small set of new documents (Dang and Owczarzak, 2008). Early approaches apply standard multi document summarization methods followed by a redundancy removal step (Fisher and Roark, 2008; Copeck et al., 2008), whereas more recent approaches incorporate topic models (Delort and Alfonseca, 2012; Conroy et al., 2011) or specialized sentence re-ranking methods (Du et al., 2010; Li et al., 2013, 2015).

The periodical application of update summarization makes it possible to summarize long-running events that develop over a period of several weeks. McCreadie et al. (2014b), for example, use this approach and select sentences from hourly update summaries according to their prevalence and novelty. A major disadvantage, however, is the inability of being real-time capable. Similar areas are retrospective temporal summarization (Allan et al., 2001) and on-line temporal summarization (Guo et al., 2013).

To accelerate research within summarization of long-running events, the TREC temporal summarization (TREC-TS) tracks were initiated (Aslam et al., 2014). The goal is the emission of updates at arbitrary times based on a large stream of input documents and an event query. Some approaches that use the TREC-TS datasets rely on incremental techniques to create updates over regular time windows. Kedzie et al. (2015), for example, use an incremental salience prediction method and a clustering approach to emit updates in hourly intervals. Other approaches are also real-time capable. McCreadie et al. (2014a) rely on simple filtering and redundancy detection methods and feature-based sentence extraction. Kedzie et al. (2016) use a real-time sequential decision-making process by adapting a learning to search approach. And Raza et al. (2015) rely on cosine-similarity heuristics to emit only the first sentence of relevant news articles.

3   Real-Time News Summarization (RTS)

Problem Definition   Given a stream of input documents (i.e. news articles) $S_{in} \leftarrow d_1, d_2, ..., d_n, ...$ and an event topic in the form of a query q, we want to emit a stream of output sentences $S_{out} \leftarrow u_1, u_2, ..., u_m, ...$ with new and important information related to q. The output sentences are referred to as *updates* whereas the output stream itself is denoted as the *summary*. Each document $d_i \in S_{in}$ is associated with a timestamp t_i where $t_i \leq t_{i+1}$. This reflects a real-life scenario where incoming documents are analyzed in the same order as they are published. Importantly, every document d_i invokes a decision-making process that can lead to the emission of new updates.

Our Approach to RTS   We rely on a multi-step approach with three separate responsibilities: First, we filter S_{in} in regard to q. Second, we process the remaining relevant documents with a single document summarization method and extract the most important sentences. And third, for every extracted sentence, we decide if a new update should be emitted to S_{out}. See Figure 2 for a visualization.

Our approach is similar to the work of McCreadie et al. (2014a) who also rely on a processing pipeline. We however do not bind the individual steps to any particular algorithm. The benefit of this approach is the ability to re-configure all individual responsibilities separately at run-time.

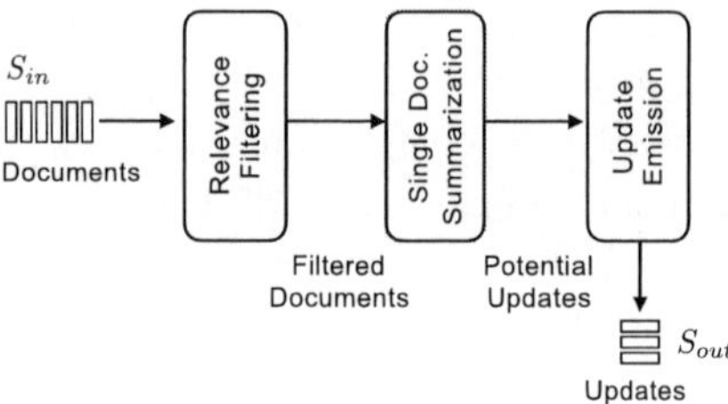

Figure 2: Our multi-step approach to RTS.

4 Adaptation to Media Attention

Measurement of the News Stream To explicitly adapt our approach to media attention at run-time, we continuously measure the stream of news articles in regard to the event query. We calculate moving averages for the number of news articles that pass the document filtering over time windows of 6 ($MA6$) and 24 hours ($MA24$). Moving averages enable us to suppress a certain amount of expected volatility while still being sensitive to important changes. $MA6$ (over $\frac{1}{4}$ day) and $MA24$ (over a full day) thereby allow us to quickly react to increases in media attention ($MA6$) while ignoring common periodical changes, for example day vs. night ($MA24$). A visualization of the moving averages for two events is shown in Figure 4.

With these continuous measurements, we can detect increases in media attention by scanning for sudden increases in $MA6$. We can also detect decreases in media attention by observing decreasing values of both $MA6$ and $MA24$. This enables our approach to select of a suitable configuration for summarization at run-time.

Configuration Selection Our approach can choose from a list of configurations Ψ at run-time, where each configuration $\psi \in \Psi$ determines important parameters for relevance filtering, single document summarization, and update emission. Thus, the two most important properties are Ψ and the behavior to select configurations.

We perform the selection as follows. At the beginning of an event we always select the start configuration $\psi_{current} = \psi_{start}$. During summarization, we obtain important information about media attention of the event through continuous measurements of $MA6$ and $MA24$. Based on this information together with $\psi_{current}$, our approach continuously evaluates a list of transition rules that define conditions for configuration switching. When a rule triggers a switch, the new configuration is im-

mediately selected and all related parameters are changed accordingly.

The transition rules together with the configurations Ψ and the continuous predictions of $MA6$ and $MA24$ enable our approach to explicitly adapt to the event at run-time. In the following, we describe the methods we use in the individual RTS steps and outline all relevant configuration parameters. We present the different configurations and transition rules later in Section 7.

5 Summarization Methods

Document Filtering We use a simple term-based filtering approach to determine the relevance of a news article d in regard to the event query q. If all stemmed words of q appear in the first n sentences of d and at least twice in the full text, we consider d as relevant. Otherwise we discard d. n is an important parameter that is determined by the selected configuration.

This approach to filtering is motivated by the inverted pyramid, which states that news stories usually begin with a story lead that contains the most important information followed by the article body with additional details (Pöttker, 2003).

Single Document Summarization We use the greedy summarization method MMR, which extracts summary sentences by minimizing the summary redundancy and maximizing the query similarity (Carbonell and Goldstein, 1998). The number of extracted sentences m is determined by the selected configuration.

We rely on cosine similarity with *tf·idf* scores to measure the similarity of sentences in MMR. *idf* is approximated by the inverse term count over the static corpus web1t (unigrams).[1] We set the MMR balancing parameter to $\lambda = 0.5$, a common choice to not favor query similarity over redundancy detection. We only consider sentences for extraction that contain between 7 and 30 non-stop words and a named entity. Similar heuristics were applied by McCreadie et al. (2014a).

Update Emission Each individual sentence that was extracted in the prior step invokes a decision-making process for the update emission to determine if a new update u should be emitted to the summary S_{out}. Our approach follows the intuition

---

[1] https://catalog.ldc.upenn.edu/ LDC2006T13

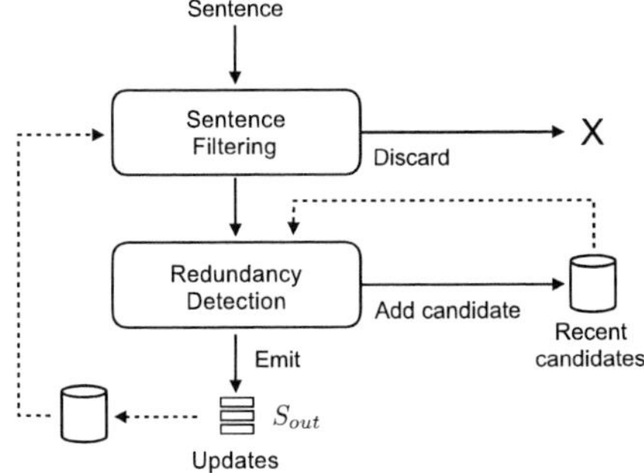

Figure 3: The update emission process.

that in case of important sub-events multiple publishers report about the incident at similar times. We assume that the exploitation of redundancies in content can help us to find important information. Because the amount of available redundant content is proportional to the media attention, run-time adaptation is required.

Our approach is visualized in Figure 3. First, we discard sentences that are redundant to previously emitted updates. We use the same cosine similarity scoring method as described previously and discard sentences if their similarity to a previous update exceeds the threshold t_s. We furthermore employ a Naïve Bayes classifier to discard (obviously) irrelevant sentences,[2] which we trained on manually annotated sentences from the TREC-TS 2013 dataset. We only rely on simple features like term count, frequency of uppercase letters, and frequency of non-alphanumeric letters.

After sentence filtering we apply a real-time capable redundancy detection method. For a sentence s, we check the similarity against a list of recently stored candidate sentences that were not emitted as updates. If we find at least g sentences with similarity greater than a threshold t_c, we emit one sentence from this group as an update. The emitted sentence is the one with the highest similarity to all other sentences of the group. Otherwise, if we cannot find enough similar sentences, we add s itself to the list of candidates.

Parameters that are set by the chosen configuration are t_s, t_c, and g. g is especially important because it determines the required redundancy.

Confidence Scoring In our evaluation, which we describe in Section 6, we rely on manual judge-

ments of the top-n updates for each summary. Thus, it is important to calculate a confidence score that allows us to find these top-n updates.

For an update u, we calculate three different quality indicators that are derived from the group G of redundant sentences that are found in the redundancy detection step of the update emission, and their timestamps T:

$$c_c = \frac{1}{|G \backslash \{u\}|} \sum_{u_{group} \in G \backslash \{u\}} sim(u, u_{group})$$

$$c_t = \frac{max\left(0, \ 24 - max(T) + min(T)\right)}{24}$$

$$c_o = 1 + 0.2 \cdot |G|$$

where c_c is the coherence measured by the average similarity (*sim*) of the redundant sentences, c_t is the timeliness measured by the distance between earliest and latest timestamp (normalized by 24h), and c_o is a value derived from the group size (required redundancy).[3] We calculate the final confidence score as the product of these three indicators.

6 Experimental Setup

Datasets For our experiments we use the TREC-TS corpora of 2014 and 2015. Both are filtered versions of the larger TREC-KBA corpus that contains 1.2 billion web documents (Frank et al., 2012). All documents are timestamped, which allows us to simulate an ordered input stream. We only use news articles and filter out social media content. Besides web documents, the corpora also contain events queries (e.g. *2013 Eastern Australia floods*) and textual *nuggets*, which describe important sub-events (e.g. *Moonie highway flooded*). Nuggets form the gold-standard of information that should be included in a good summary for an event. Dataset statistics are listed in Table 1. Most notable, the 2015 corpus contains significantly fewer news articles per hour and the event duration is 40% shorter on average. We perform experiments on both datasets to compare approaches within different scenarios.

Dataset	News Articles	News Articles per Hour	Avg. Event Duration
2014	6,488,989	2,267	310 [h]
2015	145,266	36	186 [h]

Table 1: Statistics of the employed datasets.

---

[2]E.g. "CBS News CBSNews.com - CBS Evening News - CBS This Morning - 48 Hours"

[3]For each update in the group, we add a 0.2 increase for c_o, which is motivated by a theoretical group size limit of 5.

We split the 2014 corpus into 4 development events[4] and 11 test events. We use all 21 events of the 2015 corpus for testing.

Metrics We adopt the evaluation metrics of TREC-TS 2014, which allows us to score the summary precision, recall, and timeliness. The metrics are heavily dependent on matchings between summary updates and nuggets, where a nugget matches an update whenever the nugget information is contained in the update. For space reasons we refer the reader to (Aslam et al., 2014) for a formal definition of the metrics. We briefly outline them below.

- nEG (Normalized Expected Gain): Measures the expected gain per update ($\sim$ expected relevancy of updates). This is approximated by the number of nuggets a typical update covers. For each nugget, only the first match is considered. This is a *precision* metric.
- C (Comprehensiveness): The ratio of nuggets that have matches (weighted by nugget importance). Measures the amount of relevant content included. This is a *recall* metric.
- EL (Expected Latency): Timeliness of update timestamps compared to nugget timestamps.[5] It measures how fast important information is emitted (larger values = better). This is a *latency* metric.
- $\mathcal{H}$: Harmonic mean of a latency-discounted variant of nEG and C.

Annotations for Evaluation We conducted own annotation studies in accordance to the official TREC-TS track evaluations to obtain matchings between summary updates and event nuggets for all evaluated approaches. We employed three annotators for every event/approach combination who each matched the top-60 updates (determined by confidence score) against the event nuggets. The employed annotators were students with a linguistics and computer science background and prior annotation experience. For the remaining updates (not in top-60) we used exact matches from the pool of past track evaluations. In our results we calculate the mean of the individual scores derived from each annotator.

We measure an inter-annotator agreement of $\kappa = 0.40$ (Cohen's Kappa) on the 2014 dataset and $\kappa =$

0.56 on the 2015 dataset (moderate agreement). Previous work with comparable annotation studies reports similar results (McCreadie et al., 2014b).

Evaluated Approaches We primarily evaluate two different approaches. First, we test our approach with adaptation to media attention (RTS-Adap). The list of configurations and the transition rules are described in Section 7. Second, we evaluate a non-adaptive variant (RTS-Baseline). Compared to RTS-Adap, it relies on the same filtering and single document summarization methods, but employs a reduced update emission step. RTS-Baseline only executes the sentence filtering and skips the redundancy detection. This allows us to choose static configuration parameters, which we determined on the development events. Resulting values are $n = 5$ for the number of sentences that are considered as article lead in the document filtering, $m = 2$ for the number of single document summary sentences, and $t_s = 0.3$ for the similarity threshold to discard updates.

We additionally re-evaluated top-performing systems from the TREC-TS tracks to provide a better overall comparison. We obtained the summary updates from the respective authors.

7 Configurations and Transition Rules

For RTS-Adap, we determined three different configurations ψ_a, ψ_b and ψ_c that are suitable to summarize each of the development events. These configurations were obtained on the development events (using manual annotations for the matchings). The final values for each configuration are shown in Table 2. Whereas ψ_a and ψ_b only differ in the number of required sentences for redundancy detection in the update emission, ψ_c uses a different redundancy threshold and an increased number of sentences that are extracted within single document summarization. Furthermore, the document filtering is less restrictive, where only one token needs to be present in the document text twice (instead of all tokens). This is necessary to handle events with particularly low media attention.

With the individual configurations and the evaluation results on the development events, we determined the list of transition rules. We formulated different constraints that were necessary to obtain a good summary based on the results of the previous parameter search and manually optimized the transition rules to fulfill as many of the constraints as possible. Results are listed in Table 3. A visual-

---

[4]Development events: *Boston Marathon Bombing, Costa Concordia disaster and recovery, 2012 Afghanistan Quran burning protests*, and *2013 Eastern Australia floods*.

[5]The update timestamp is set to the timestamp of the last processed document in S_{in}.

Parameter	ψ_a	ψ_b	ψ_c
n (document filter: article lead)	5	5	20
m (document sum.: extracted sents)	4	4	5
g (emission: redundant candidates)	2	1	1
t_s (emission: update threshold)	0.3	0.3	0.3
t_c (emission: candidate threshold)	0.6	0.6	0.45

Table 2: Parameter values that are determined by the three different configurations.

$\psi_{current}$	Condition	Change to
ψ_c	$MA6 > 6$	ψ_b
ψ_b	$MA6 > 14$	ψ_a
ψ_a	$MA24 < 6$ and $MA6 < 6$	ψ_b
ψ_b	$MA24 < 1$ and $MA6 < 1$	ψ_c
Start configuration: ψ_c		

Table 3: Ruleset for configuration switching.

ization of the adaptive configuration selection with these rules for two events is shown in Figure 4.

8 Experimental Results

2014 Dataset In the first experiment, we study the question of the added value of RTS-Adap compared to RTS-Baseline. We also re-evaluated the best-performing approach of TREC-TS 2014 (CUNLP-AP), which is based on an affinity propagation clustering method (Kedzie et al., 2015).

The results are shown in Table 4. In particular, RTS-Adap outperforms our baseline on all metrics with a significant improvement on $\mathcal{H}$. Most notable, it substantially increases the strong results for the precision-oriented metric nEG. At the same time RTS-Adap also achieves significantly better latency results. These improvements are a result of the effective exploitation of redundancies in content according to media attention, which allows only the most important and timely information to be emitted. Sentences from retrospective reports or opinion texts are usually discarded due to missing redundancies across recent news articles. Information that is already included in the summary is also discarded due to strict filtering in the update emission. Thus, RTS-Adap is highly effective in avoiding emitting irrelevant content.

In comparison to CUNLP-AP, our approach with adaptation to media attention achieves significantly better results on the precision-oriented metric nEG. Even though CUNLP-AP achieves better recall, the summaries of RTS-Adap are more balanced. This is particularly reflected in the combined metric $\mathcal{H}$ where RTS-Adap outperforms CUNLP-AP by a

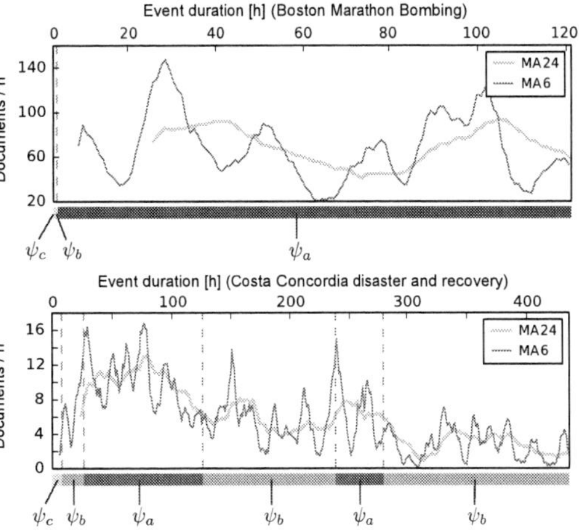

Figure 4: Configuration switches of RTS-Adap.

System	C	nEG	EL	$\mathcal{H}$
(c) CUNLP-AP	**0.32**$_b$	0.07	1.22	0.12
(b) Baseline	0.23	0.11$_c$	1.05	0.12
(a) RTS-Adap	0.26	**0.13**$_c$	**1.23**$_b$	**0.17**$_b$

Table 4: Results on 2014 data. Subscripts indicate statistical significance (Wilcoxon test, $p < 0.05$).

substantial margin. The difference is not statistically significant due to a high variance in the result scores.[6] Additionally, compared to CUNLP-AP, our non-adaptive baseline achieves a similar result on $\mathcal{H}$ because of high precision scores. This particularly demonstrates the effectiveness of the simple three-step approach to RTS.

In our second experiment, we study the performance of RTS-Adap compared to a static variant of the same approach that does not change configurations. To get a better impression of the adaptation itself, we evaluate the static approach for ψ_a, ψ_b, and ψ_c. To keep annotation efforts at a feasible level, we selected five random events from our test set for this evaluation. Table 5 shows the results on $\mathcal{H}$. For only one event RTS-Adap does not select a suitable configuration. On the other hand, in three cases it achieves better results than the best possible individual configuration. This strongly suggests that our method is very effective because it can select the best possible configuration for individual event *segments* to create a better overall summary.

2015 Dataset In the third experiment, we study the question on the influence of a different dataset.

---

[6]Relative std. on $\mathcal{H}$: RTS-Adapt: $\pm47\%$, CUNLP-AP $\pm73\%$. RTS-Adapt produces more consistent results.

Event	ψ_a	ψ_b	ψ_c	RTS-Adap
Egyptian Riots	0.11	0.12	**0.15**	0.14
In Amenas	0.06	0.06	0.07	**0.11**
Russian Prot.	0.14	**0.17**	0.09	0.09
Russia Meteor	0.21	0.24	0.24	**0.29**
Southern Calif.	0.18	0.23	0.23	**0.25**

Table 5: A comparison of RTS-Adap against the same approach with static configurations ($\mathcal{H}$).

System	C	nEG	EL	$\mathcal{H}$
(c) CUNLP-AP	0.27	0.06	1.04	0.07
(s) CUNLP-SD	**0.33**	0.11_c	$\mathbf{1.33}_{cb}$	0.18_c
(b) Baseline	0.32	0.10_c	1.23_c	0.15_c
(a) RTS-Adapt	0.32_{cr}	0.11_c	1.29_c	0.18_{cb}
(r) RTS-Adapt/Re	0.31	$\mathbf{0.11}_{csb}$	1.33_{cb}	$\mathbf{0.19}_{cb}$

Table 6: Results on 2015 data. Subscripts indicate statistical significance (Wilcoxon test, $p < 0.05$).

Besides CUNLP-AP we also re-evaluated CUNLP-SD,[7] a top-performing approach of 2015 that is based on sequential decision-making with a learning to search method (Kedzie et al., 2016). We also created a version of RTS-Adap with conditions that were optimized on results from 2014 (RTS-Re).

Experimental results are listed in Table 6. Most notable, RTS-Adap can successfully be applied to a new real-world dataset without requiring a different ruleset. Compared to RTS-Baseline, our approach, again, achieves a better result on the combined metric $\mathcal{H}$, which is primarily due to better latency scores. On the other hand, the improvements in terms of precision and recall are much smaller. This is an effect of missing high-impact events in the dataset, which results in a small number of relevant news articles per event. This situation strongly favors simple approaches like RTS-Baseline that rely on simple content filtering. RTS-Adap however is still able to achieve better results compared to RTS-Baseline because it correctly selects configurations for low media attention. Our approach performs on the same level as CUNLP-SD and significantly outperforms CUNLP-AP on all measures, which especially shows the effectiveness of adaptation to media attention given its strong performance on the 2014 dataset. Even though RTS-Re achieves the best results in our evaluation, changes are relatively small. This suggests that our approach is robust against changes in the ruleset.

Error Analysis We identified two sources of errors within our approach. First, RTS-Adap some-times selects the wrong configuration when an event is especially long-running with constant low media attention. An example is the event *Russian Protests* in Table 5. Here, our approach chooses the least restrictive configuration ψ_c for the full event timeframe, which results in multiple updates per day. Because the event is active for more than a month, the summary contains too much fine grained updates. As a solution, we could detect especially long-running events with the goal to select better suited configurations.

Second, our simple document filtering approach leads to misclassifications in some cases. As a result, irrelevant news articles are further processed and a small number of irrelevant updates are emitted. We can see this behavior in cases with misleading lexical overlap between the query and an unrelated input document. For example, a news article on Bulgaria protesting against an EU decision passes the filter for the unrelated event query *Bulgarian Protests* (against government). This problem could be solved by using more sophisticated document filtering methods.

9 Conclusion

In this work, we showed that media attention is an important attribute for RTS that can be utilized to improve event summaries. We presented an approach that automatically detects changes within media attention by continuously measuring moving averages for the number of relevant news articles over time. By switching summarization configurations at run-time, we can effectively exploit redundancies in content at times with high media attention and thereby create better, more precise summaries. Our experimental results showed the effectiveness of our approach, which significantly outperforms a strong non-adaptive baseline in terms of the emitted summary updates and achieves the best overall results on a recent web-scale dataset. Strong results on a different real-world dataset furthermore suggest that our approach can also be applied to other scenarios without requiring additional modifications in the employed ruleset. We showed that simple methods are highly effective within RTS if they are suitably configured at run-time.

Acknowledgments

This work has been supported by the German Research Foundation as part of the QA-EduInf project (grant GU 798/18-1 and grant RI 803/12-1).

---

[7]Run id: *3LtoSfltr5*

References

James Allan, Rahul Gupta, and Vikas Khandelwal. 2001. Temporal Summaries of New Topics. In *Proceedings of the 24th Annual International ACM SIGIR Conference on Research and Development in Information Retrieval*. New Orleans, LA, USA, pages 10–18. https://doi.org/10.1145/383952.383954.

Javed Aslam, Fernando Diaz, Matthew Ekstrand-Abueg, Richard Mccreadie, Virgil Pavlu, and Tetsuya Sakai. 2014. TREC 2014 Temporal Summarization Track Overview. *Proceedings of the 23rd Text REtrieval Conference (TREC 2014)* .

Jaime G. Carbonell and Jade Goldstein. 1998. The Use of MMR, Diversity-based Reranking for Reordering Documents and Producing Summaries. In *Proceedings of the 21st Annual International ACM SIGIR Conference on Research and Development in Information Retrieval*. Melbourne, Australia, pages 335–336. https://doi.org/10.1145/290941.291025.

John M. Conroy, Judith D. Schlesinger, Jeff Kubina, Peter A. Rankel, and Dianne P. O'Leary. 2011. CLASSY 2011 at TAC : Guided and Multi-lingual Summaries and Evaluation Metrics. *Proceedings of the Text Analysis Conference* .

Terry Copeck, Anna Kazantseva, Alistair Kennedy, Alex Kunadze, Diana Inkpen, and Stan Szpakowicz. 2008. Update Summary Update. *Proceedings of the Text Analysis Conference* .

Hoa T. Dang and Karolina Owczarzak. 2008. Overview of the TAC 2008 Update Summarization Task. *Proceedings of the Text Analysis Conference* .

Jean-Yves Delort and Enrique Alfonseca. 2012. DualSum: a Topic-Model based approach for update summarization. In *Proceedings of the 13th Conference of the European Chapter of the Association for Computational Linguistics,*. Avignon, France, pages 214–223. http://dl.acm.org/citation.cfm?id=2380845.

Pan Du, Jiafeng Guo, Jin Zhang, and Xueqi Cheng. 2010. Manifold ranking with sink points for update summarization. In *Proceedings of the 19th ACM International Conference on Information and Knowledge Management*. Toronto, ON, Canada, pages 1757–1760. https://doi.org/10.1145/1871437.1871722.

Seeger Fisher and Brian Roark. 2008. Query-focused supervised sentence ranking for update summaries. *Proceedings of the Text Analysis Conference* .

John R. Frank, Max Kleiman-Weiner, Daniel A. Roberts, Feng Niu, Ce Zhang, Christopher Ré, and Ian Soboroff. 2012. Building an entity-centric stream filtering test collection for TREC 2012. Technical report, DTIC Document.

Qi Guo, Fernando Diaz, and Elad Yom-tov. 2013. Updating Users about Time Critical Events. In *Proceedings of the 35th European Conference on Advances in Information Retrieval*. Moscow, Russia, pages 483–494. http://dl.acm.org/citation.cfm?id=2458233.

Chris Kedzie, Fernando Diaz, and Kathleen McKeown. 2016. Real-Time Web Scale Event Summarization Using Sequential Decision Making. In *Proceedings of the International Joint Conference on Artificial Intelligence*. New York, NY, USA, pages 3754–3760. http://www.ijcai.org/Abstract/16/528.

Chris Kedzie, Kathleen McKeown, and Fernando Diaz. 2015. Predicting Salient Updates for Disaster Summarization. In *Proceedings of the 53rd Annual Meeting of the Association for Computational Linguistics and the 7th International Joint Conference on Natural Language Processing*. Beijing, China, pages 1608–1617. http://www.aclweb.org/anthology/P15-1155.

Chen Li, Yang Liu, and Lin Zhao. 2015. Improving Update Summarization via Supervised ILP and Sentence Reranking. In *Human Language Technologies: The 2015 Annual Conference of the North American Chapter of the ACL*. Denver, CO, USA, pages 1317–1322. http://www.aclweb.org/anthology/N15-1145.

Xuan Li, Liang Du, and Yi D. Shen. 2013. Update summarization via graph-based sentence ranking. *IEEE Transactions on Knowledge and Data Engineering* 25(5):1162–1174. https://doi.org/10.1109/TKDE.2012.42.

Richard McCreadie, Romain Deveaud, M-dyaa Albakour, Stuart Mackie, Nut Limsopatham, Craig Macdonald, Iadh Ounis, and Thibaut Thonet. 2014a. University of Glasgow at TREC 2014 : Experiments with Terrier in Contextual Suggestion , Temporal Summarisation and Web Tracks. *Proceedings of the 23rd Text REtrieval Conference (TREC 2014)* .

Richard McCreadie, Craig Macdonald, and Iadh Ounis. 2014b. Incremental Update Summarization: Adaptive Sentence Selection based on Prevalence and Novelty. In *Proceedings of the 23rd ACM International Conference on Conference on Information and Knowledge Management*. Shanghai, China, pages 301–310. https://doi.org/10.1145/2661829.2661951.

Horst Pöttker. 2003. News and its communicative quality: the inverted pyramid – when and why did it appear? *Journalism Studies* 4(4):501–511.

Ahsan Raza, Devin M. Rotondo, and Charles L. A. Clarke. 2015. WaterlooClarke : TREC 2015 Temporal Summarization Track. *Proceedings of the 24th Text REtrieval Conference (TREC 2015)* .

Measuring the Limit of Semantic Divergence for English Tweets

Dwijen Rudrapal
CSE Department
NIT Agartala, India
dwijen.rudrapal@gmail.com

Amitava Das
CSE Department
IIIT Sricity, India
amitava.das@iiits.in

Abstract

In human language, an expression could be conveyed in many ways by different people. Even that the same person may express the same sentence quite differently when addressing different audiences, using different modalities, or using different syntactic variations or may use different set of vocabulary. The possibility of such endless surface form of text while the meaning of the text remains almost same, poses many challenges for Natural Language Processing (NLP) systems like question-answering system, machine translation system and text summarization. This research paper is an endeavor to understand the characteristic of such endless semantic divergence. In this research work we develop a corpus of 1525 semantic divergent sentences generated from 200 English seed tweets.

1 Introduction

A sentence could be expressed in innumerable ways without changing its meaning. Different people may express a sentence in different ways and even that the same person may express a sentence quite differently when addressing different audiences, using different modalities, or tackling different tasks (Dewaele, 1999). Possible number of restatement of the meaning of a sentence in a language is huge (Bell, 1995). These variations may be for different writing styles of different people with diverse background and situations (Karlgren, 1996) (Chambers J.K, 2006), number of polysemous words present in the text, longer/deeper syntactic relations for more than one word or presence of more adjective/ adverb than noun and verb in sentence. For example:

Expression 01: After that game I think Harding deserves another one.

Expression 02: Harding deserves another game after that.

Expression 03: I think Harding should get another chance after that game.

Above expressions are restating the same meaning in different ways. These deviations raise a fundamental question that, *are there any set of rules that govern different factors to determine the degree of semantic divergence of an expression?* To find out the answers i.e. measuring the semantic divergence of English sentence, we prepare a corpus of sentence variants by preserving the meaning of a sentence. In this research work, we concentrate our effort on English social media text specifically on tweets as diverse syntactic variations of texts are more prevalent in informal setting and explore different factors other than situational and personality factors which make presentation variations of a tweet.

The structure of this research paper is as follows. First, we draw the problem definition in section 2, discuss related research work in section 3, followed by corpus development process in section 4. In section 5, we present the explored features behind the semantic variations of an English tweet, explain thematic closeness of variations in section 6. We carry out detail analysis on results in section 7. Finally in section 8, we conclude our work with performance evaluation along with noted limitations and mentioning future scope of work.

2 Problem Description

Semantic diversity nature of natural language is highly influential for a broader range of NLP applications (Madnani and Dorr, 2010). In this regard, we discuss some state-of-the-art NLP sys-

Proceedings of Recent Advances in Natural Language Processing, pages 618–624,
Varna, Bulgaria, Sep 4–6 2017.

tems in this section to draw our research problem.

The performance of one automated NLP system is evaluated by comparing human annotators output against the system generated output. For example, evaluation method for machine translation system, text summarization system, etc. In such evaluations, system outputs are evaluated against reference outputs by measuring the n-gram overlap between them. This measure is completely dependant on exact or partial matching of candidates in both outputs. However, a single reference output may not reflect the best result of matching due to the semantic variation even though both outputs convey the same semantic content. The evaluation process needs to consider all the possible semantically same variants while matching to award better credit. Legitimate variation of a query may retrieve more relevant information. So, the automatic generation of query variants for submission to information retrieval systems should consider all the possible query variants to reach optimal performance.

Our research problem is to explore several important features responsible for arranging information of a tweet into a series of alternatives to reinterpret the tweet in different ways. To address the issue we develop one corpus of semantically same sentences for tweets and present theoretical explanations and evidence in support of the explored features.

3 Related Work

Most of the research work on semantic divergence of expressions focused either on language translation task or to measure formality of document or sub-document units like sentences considering their important applications. But the reinterpretation of a sentence to infer its meaning in different way is also an important research challenge as discussed in section 2. Unfortunately, very few research work have done in this domain. In this section we discuss significant research work on semantic divergence in above two domains.

The work (Hirakawa et al., 1994) proposed an interactive rewriting tool as a part of Japanese-to-English machine translation, where a sentence rewritten based on morphological and syntactical information of the source text. Grammatical transformation of one sentence like syntactic and semantic structure used in the work (Mitamura and Nyberg, 2001) for phrase re-arrangement to rein-

terpret the sentence by preserving its meaning for translation. Proposed model (Galley and Manning, 2008) (Tomoki Fujita and Nakamura, 2013) also used rewriting tool using phrase reordering model to improve machine translation system for Chinese-English and Arabic-English languages. The work (Wang, 2013) proposed a text rewriting decoder, works on the sentence level features like the language model score of the whole sentence. The work (He et al., 2015) introduced grammatically and meaning-preserving syntactic preservation rules such as verb, noun and clause re-ordering on constituent parse trees for Japanese to English machine translation. Query rewriting process in the work (Riezler and Liu, 2010) generated a set of alternative queries which are semantically the same to achieve the best search result from large amounts of user query logs.

Other than machine translation, semantic divergence has a role in formal or informal writing style. The study (Dewaele, 1999) discussed the degree of formality in linguistic expression based on different situational and personality factors. In the work (Lahiri et al., 2011) authors presented an annotated corpus of 600 sentences with variations in formality on a Likert scale (Likert, 1932) of 1-5. Variants of a sentence with the same meaning is possible with re-arranging the grammatical organization of that sentence was discussed in the article (Rafajlovicova, 2002).

In our current research work, we develop a corpus of semantically same sentences for English tweets and made theoretical study to explore possible features which can be utilized in query variants, enlarge sparse human reference data in evaluation and machine translation evaluation system.

4 Corpus Preparation

To develop a corpus of semantic divergent sentences for tweets, initially we take 200 unique English tweets, randomly chosen from SemEval-2015 Task 1 [1] tweet corpus and from Ritter[2] corpus. These tweets are in raw form and include typos, bad grammar, usage of slang, presence of unwanted content like URLs, emoticons, etc. We extract meaningful text content from each tweet by filtering out html entities like <, >, &, emoticons, embedded URLs, usernames, replaced

---

[1] `http://alt.qcri.org/semeval2015/task1/`

[2] `www.github.com/aritter/twitter_nlp`

#hashtag by hashtag, split multiple attached words like *GoldenGlobes* into *Golden Globes*. Apostrophes and punctuation are kept unchanged to retain tweets meaning intact and resourced to help the annotation task for appropriate semantic variations.

We develop one web-page and upload these pre-processed 200 tweets for collecting possible semantic variations for each tweet without altering meaning. Every tweet is hyper-linked to a page where a user can rewrites the tweet and submit. Every submission gets updated instantly and a future user can sees all the previous re-written expressions for that particular tweet. Thus information redundancy is avoided at the time of annotation. While re-writing, when a user see that all the possible variations for that expression are already listed, the user clicks on a check box labeled as *"No more variation possible"* message and submits. This message signifies the limit of the semantic variations of a particular tweet. To be persistent we record *No more variation possible* at least from two different users until we stop showing the particular tweet to other annotators.

Through this web-page, over the course of about 6 weeks, we collect divergent sentences for tweets by human annotators. Human annotators are Post-Graduate students and native English speaker. Total 21 users participated in the annotation task for given 200 tweets. We have collected 1,525 sentences as variants of semantically same sentences for 200 tweets. The highest number of variations for a tweet found was 24 while the lowest number was 4. We also observe that all the tweets reach the message "no more variation possible" two/multiple times ensuring that all the possible variations of a tweet obtained.

5 Measuring of Semantic Divergence

We analyze the developed corpus to determine the important features, responsible for semantic divergence of an English tweet. We observe that there are some grammatical devices like structural, semantic, pragmatic, and textual factors, used for rearranging the information in the message to express it differently. In our work, we select some features such as synonym, passivization, clause re-ordering, idioms and phrase, cleft, negation and use of non-impact words and set up one questionnaire to manually annotate every variation of a tweet by tagging with one of the selected features.

The questionnaire collects responses from two human annotators for two questions. One, does re-written expression represent the same meaning as in original tweet? Two, which feature/features are use to re-written this expression? The response for the first question is yes when the meaning is fully preserved otherwise no. In response to the 2nd question, annotators select one or multiple features from listed features. We calculated inter-annotator agreement statistics (IAAS) on each feature of annotations. Feature wise distribution of the semantic variations for tweets and IAAS is represented in table 1. Observe that there is high agreement on most of the features due to the straight-forward meaning and use of features in variant expressions. The IAAS for the responses of question no.01 is as high as 99.125, reveals that almost all of variants in the corpus preserved the meaning of original tweet while re-written. Theoretical explanations of each feature with an example is discussed in this section to justify the role of the features.

Features	Instance in corpus (%)	IAAS
Activization/ Passivization	5.32	98.67
Synonyms	34.82	98.89
Idioms & phrase	0.4	98.92
Inter-Clause re-ordering	18.29	92.7
Sentence Type Transformation	12.98	100.0
Cleft	1.25	96.7
Addition/deletion of non-impact words	15.4	96.0
Using Multiple features	11.34	100.0

Table 1: Feature wise distribution of semantic variation

5.1 Activization and Passivization:

The representation of a sentence from active to passive or passive to active voice allows structural re-organization of the expression without any alteration of meaning. Active voice describes a sentence where the subject performs the action stated by the verb. Passive voice describes a sentence where the subject is acted upon by the verb. For example:

Original tweet: My phone NEVER sends me Amber Alerts.
Variant: Amber alert is never received by my phone.

In the above variant example, subject (My Phone) is being acted on by the verb (receive) and comes after the action in the sentence. In our developed corpus a total of 81 instances (5.32% of total variants) observe in this category.

5.2 Synonym:

Presence of polysemous words in an expression increases semantic divergent nature. The replacement of a word with its synonym resonate the original sentence meaning without any alteration. A total of 531 variants (34.82% of the corpus) observe for 200 tweets while re-written by preserving meaning. For example:

Original tweet: A walk to remember is so amazing and inspiring.
Variant: A walk to remember is extremely astounding and motivating.

5.3 Idioms and Phrases:

Idiomatic expressions are a type of informal representation that has the same theme as the original expression with restrained meaning. Well-written text utilizes frequent use of idioms and phrases to make expression concise. Only 6 (0.4%) instances were found in the developed corpus where tweets were re-written using idioms and phrases. For example:

Original tweet: I seriously need a screen protector for my ipad
Variant: Need for screen protector for my ipad is dead serious.

5.4 Inter-clause re-orderings:

An expression may be divided into chunks known as information units to make expressions comprehensible. These information units are phonologically realized by the tone units (Rafajlovicova, 2002) (accessed November 7, 2016). Changing the order of tone units in an expression represents it in a different way. Communicatively, the most important positions in a clause/expression are the beginning and the end. Re-ordering of tone units helps to bring a tone unit in initial position or in end position to receive more focus. A total of 279 instances (18.29% of the total corpus) are there in the corpus under this feature. An expression with more number of tone units can be represented proportionally more ways by re-ordering clauses. For example:

Original tweet: a walk to remember is the only movie I like better than the book.
Variant 01: Better than the book I like the movie A Walk To Remember.
Variant 02: The only movie I like better than the book is A walk to remember.

5.5 Sentence Type Transformation:

In different writing style, a sentence may restate in different ways by changing the sentence structure. The work of (Mellon, 1969) (O'Hare, 1973) shows that the change in sentence structure is an effective method for improving content presentation without affecting the meaning of original text. A simple sentence can be transformed into a compound sentence by enlarging phrase or word into a co-ordinate clause or can be transformed into a complex sentence by enlarging a phrase into a subordinate clause such as Noun, Adjective or Adverb. A total of 198 number of instances (12.98%) are there in the corpus, formed by sentence structure transformations. For example:

Original tweet: check out the Yeti on Amazon it 's not too pricey.
Variant: Amazon is offering Yeti at a very cheap price. You can check it there.

5.6 Cleft:

Cleft sentences are used to focus on a particular part of the sentence to emphasize by introducing it with a kind of relative clause. Cleft construction breaks a sentence into two pieces of information in order to provide an extra focus on one piece. There are different types of clefts in English language (Calude, 2008) such as *if-because-cleft, it-cleft, wh-cleft, all-cleft, inferential-cleft and there-cleft*. The cleft structure involves important role in sentence content structure. Speakers/writers seek attention on salient parts of a message (Lambrecht, 2001) by using cleft based on highly linked content structure in the expression. Instances of tweet variants using cleft are less in number (1.25%) than other features in the develop corpus. For example:

Original tweet: I really hate when it rains on cinco de mayo.
*Variant: **When** it rains on cinco de mayo I really hate it.*

5.7 Addition or Deletion of non-impact words:

Natural Language like English becomes less ambiguous and more logical when it takes into account different unstated background assumption (Dewaele, 1999) while writing a sentence. Author / speaker may add or remove a word or more without altering its original meaning depending on the knowledge of context of that expression. This feature helps to resolve semantic ambiguity (Gorfein, 1989) (Grice, 1975) in the expression and makes it more clear, logical and self-possessed. A total of 235 numbers of variations (15.4%) exist in the corpus in this category. For example:

Original tweet: Rocky and john wall in that new quickaintfair Adidas commercial.
Variant: The new quickaintfair Adidas commercial was done by earlier model Rocky and John Wall.

Other than the above feature class, manual annotation process tag 173 number of sentences (11.34%) generated using two or more features (in table 1). For example, inter-clause reordering feature is clubbed with synonyms to restate the tweet here.

Original tweet: The only Nicholas Sparks movie I genuinely like is A Walk To Remember.
Variant: A Walk To Remember by Nicholas Sparks is one of my favorite film.

6 Measuring Thematic Closeness among Variants

We conduct an experiment to measure thematic closeness among the variants and tweets for each feature as in table 1. Our aim of this experiment is to measure the meaning intact status of tweet with its variants. In our experiment, we use three state-of-the-art semantic similarity measuring tools. First, the measure is (M_1) based on the work (Pilehvar et al., 2013). The tool measures similarity between the meanings of the words based on the sense of lexical items in the text by removing the ambiguity of word sense. Second measure (M_2) is based on the work (Pirró and Euzenat, 2010) which measures semantic similarity between ontology concepts of each expression. Equation 1 is used to calculate the similarity between tweet (concept c1) and its variant (concept c2), where msca(c1,c2) is the Most Specific Common Abstraction (msca) (Resnik, 1995) and Extended Information Content (eIC) characterize commonalities and differences.

$$sim_{FaITH}(c_1, c_2) = \frac{eIC(msca(c_1, c_2))}{eIC(c_1) + eIC(c_2) - eIC(msca(c_1, c_2))} \quad (1)$$

Third, the measure (M_3) is based on the method proposed by (Rus et al., 2013a) which uses Latent Semantic Analysis (LSA) model trained on the Wikipedia corpus from early January 2013 and the TASA corpus. The tool outperformed for measuring semantic similarity for paraphrase detection (Rus et al., 2013b).

Details of Average Similarity score of each tool for each feature class is reported in table 2.

Features	M_1	M_2	M_3
Activization/ passivization	0.924	0.946	0.962
Synonyms	0.960	0.907	0.940
Idioms & phrase	0.974	0.968	0.868
Inter-Clause re-ordering	0.913	0.965	0.885
Transforming sentence type	0.967	0.891	0.881
Cleft	0.906	0.899	0.926
Addition/deletion of non-impact words	0.907	0.893	0.969
Combined features	0.947	0.899	0.986

Table 2: Average semantic similarity score of each feature variants

7 Analysis and Discussion

In-depth analysis of semantic divergence of English tweets lead us to the following observations.

First, We observe that shorter length tweets have less variations in comparison to the longer length tweets. This is because longer tweets include more polysemous word as well as more clauses. For example the tweet *"Do not Amber Alert me"* has less semantic variants than the tweet *"I have to watch A Walk to Remember every time it shows"*. Second, thematic closeness of each feature class variants could not reach the maximum level due to two possible reasons. One, wrong spelling of words in tweets, which are corrected during re-writing. For example, the words *I'm* or *I m*, *r*, *NZ* in tweets are written as *I am*, *are*, *New Zealand* respectively in restated sentences. Two, due to the limit of 140 characters, some tweets have incomplete word/clause at the end of tweet. The Rewritten form of that tweets exclude unwanted part. For example the tweet "That AAP Rocky Adidas commerical is hard af" includes incomplete word "af" .

8 Conclusion and Future Work

In this work we generated a corpus of 1525 semantically same sentences for 200 tweets by human annotators. This is the first corpus to represent semantic divergence of tweets. Our work explore the features for reinterpretation of a tweet meaning in different ways. Through human evaluation and experiments we justify meaning preservation in the variants.

We concentrated our current study on tweet corpus where a tweet can have a maximum of 140 characters only. This is an ongoing task. Our next target is to study the characteristics of semantic divergence of social media texts having un-restricted length as well as code-mixed social media texts.

References

A. Bell. 1995. Language style as audience design. In *Language in Society*. volume 13-2, pages 145–204.

Andreea S Calude. 2008. Demonstrative clefts and double cleft constructions in spontaneous spoken english. *Studia Linguistica* 62(1):78–118.

Schiling-Estes N Trudgill P Chambers J.K. 2006. *The handbook of language variation and change*. Blackwell.

Francis Heylighen & Jean-Marc Dewaele. 1999. Formality of language: definition, measurement and behavioral determinants. In *Internal Report, Center "Leo Apostel", Free University of Brussels,*. MIT Press.

Michel Galley and Christopher D. Manning. 2008. A simple and effective hierarchical phrase reordering model. In *Proceedings of the Conference on Empirical Methods in Natural Language Processing*. Association for Computational Linguistics, Stroudsburg, PA, USA, EMNLP '08, pages 848–856.

David S. Gorfein. 1989. *Resolving semantic ambiguity / David S. Gorfein, editor*. Springer-Verlag New York.

H. P. Grice. 1975. Logic and conversation. In Peter Cole and Jerry L. Morgan, editors, *Speech Acts: Syntax and Semantics Volume 3*, Academic Press, New York, pages 41–58.

He He, Alvin Grissom II, John Morgan, Jordan L Boyd-Graber, and Hal Daumé III. 2015. Syntax-based rewriting for simultaneous machine translation. In *EMNLP*. pages 55–64.

Hideki Hirakawa, Kouichi Nomura, and Mariko Nakamura. 1994. An interactive rewriting tool for machine acceptable sentences. In *ANLP*. pages 207–208. http://aclweb.org/anthology-new/A/A94/A94-1043.pdf.

Jussi Karlgren. 1996. Stylistic variation in an information retrieval experiment. *CoRR* cmp-lg/9608003. http://arxiv.org/abs/cmp-lg/9608003.

Shibamouli Lahiri, Prasenjit Mitra, and Xiaofei Lu. 2011. Informality judgment at sentence level and experiments with formality score. *Computational Linguistics and Intelligent Text Processing* pages 446–457.

Knud Lambrecht. 2001. A framework for the analysis of cleft constructions. *Linguistics* 39(3; ISSU 373):463–516.

R.A. Likert. 1932. A technique for the measurement of attitudes. *Archives of Psychology* 22(140):5–55.

Nitin Madnani and Bonnie J Dorr. 2010. Generating phrasal and sentential paraphrases: A survey of data-driven methods. *Computational Linguistics* 36(3):341–387.

John C. Mellon. 1969. *Transformational sentence-combining: a method for enhancing the development of syntactic fluency in English composition [by] John C. Mellon*. National Council of Teachers of English Champaign, Ill.

Teruko Mitamura and Eric Nyberg. 2001. Automatic rewriting for controlled language translation. In *In Proceedings of the NLPRS 2002 Workshop on Automatic Paraphrasing: Theories and Applications*.

Frank. O'Hare. 1973. *Sentence combining; improving student writing without formal grammar instruction*. National Council of Teachers of English Urbana, Ill.

Mohammad Taher Pilehvar, David Jurgens, and Roberto Navigli. 2013. Align, disambiguate and walk: A unified approach for measuring semantic similarity. In *ACL 2013*.

Giuseppe Pirró and Jérôme Euzenat. 2010. A feature and information theoretic framework for semantic similarity and relatedness. In *9th International Semantic Web Conference (ISWC2010)*. Springer, pages 615–630.

R. Rafajlovicova. 2002. Variation of clause patterns - reordering the information in a message. In *http://www.pulib.sk/elpub2/FHPV/Kacmaroval/pdf_doc/05.pdf*.

Philip Resnik. 1995. Using information content to evaluate semantic similarity in a taxonomy. In *In Proceedings of the 14th International Joint Conference on Artificial Intelligence.* pages 448–453.

Stefan Riezler and Yi Liu. 2010. Query rewriting using monolingual statistical machine translation. *Computational Linguistics* 36(3):569–582.

Vasile Rus, Mihai C Lintean, Rajendra Banjade, Nobal B Niraula, and Dan Stefanescu. 2013a. Semilar: The semantic similarity toolkit. In *ACL (Conference System Demonstrations).* pages 163–168.

Vasile Rus, Nobal Niraula, and Rajendra Banjade. 2013b. Similarity measures based on latent dirichlet allocation. In *Computational Linguistics and Intelligent Text Processing*, Springer, pages 459–470.

Graham Neubig Sakriani Sakti Tomoki Toda Tomoki Fujita and Satoshi Nakamura. 2013. Simple, lexicalized choice of translation timing for simultaneous speech translation. In *In Proceedings of Interspeech.*

Pidong Wang. 2013. *A Text Rewriting Decoder with Application to Machine Translation.* Ph.D. thesis, School of Computing, National University of Singapore, Singapore.

Evaluating the Morphological Compositionality of Polarity

Josef Ruppenhofer and Petra Steiner
Institute for German Language
R5, 6-13
D-68161 Mannheim, Germany
`ruppenhofer|steiner@ids-mannheim.de`

Michael Wiegand
Spoken Language Systems
Saarland University
D-66123 Saarbrücken, Germany
`michael.wiegand@lsv.uni-saarland.de`

Abstract

Unknown words are a challenge for any NLP task, including sentiment analysis. Here, we evaluate the extent to which sentiment polarity of complex words can be predicted based on their morphological make-up. We do this on German as it has very productive processes of derivation and compounding and many German hapax words, which are likely to bear sentiment, are morphologically complex. We present results of supervised classification experiments on new datasets with morphological parses and polarity annotations.

1 Introduction

The vast variety of language that speakers use to express evaluations presents a key challenge for sentiment analysis. Any approach to sentiment analysis has to grapple with problems of coverage. Coverage gaps can arise for a number of different reasons, ranging from typos, foreign language material used in code-switching contexts, to rare words. We are interested in the latter sources for coverage gaps. They present a particular problem because, by definition, rare words cannot readily be modeled using a data-driven, corpus-based approach because of the lack of training instances. However, sub-word analysis may give us a significant hook into analyzing such rare words. In this paper, we evaluate the hypothesis that we can model the polarity of German words based on the properties of their morphological make-up, which has parallels to recent work on sentiment composition on the syntactic level (Socher et al., 2013; Haas and Versley, 2015). German has a relatively rich morphology and very productive processes of derivation and compounding. For instance, Baroni et al. (2002) report that 83%

of the compounds in a 28-million word German newswire corpus had a corpus frequency of 5 or less. Since many compounds are hapaxes and since prior work has shown that hapax words are often subjective (Wiebe et al., 2004), it would be particularly desirable to be able to infer the polarity of compounds from their components.

To that end we conduct extensive experiments on a data set with complete morphological parse trees that we compiled from existing resources and which we augmented further.[1] This data set is presented in §2. We lay out the features and the setup of our main experiments in §3. Their results are discussed in §4 where we show the efficacy of psycholinguistic ratings as features and also demonstrate that a shallower analysis at the level of immediate constituents is better than 'going deep' to the leaf level. We present an additional set of experiments in §5 that shed light on the limits of our results from the main experiment when we attempt to generalize to very different data. We discuss related work in section §6 before concluding in §7.

2 Data

Our data mainly consists of lemmas sampled out of the PolArt polarity dictionary (Klenner et al., 2009), a manually curated resource with around 8000 entries, found to be of high precision by (Emerson and Declerck, 2014). Most entries are subjective words but PolArt also includes a few intensifiers (INT)[2], and shifters (SHI). Each subjective entry is labeled as positive (POS), negative (NEG) or neutral (NEU). The polar entries have a discrete score reflecting the degree of their positivity or negativity.

As PolArt has only 55 neutral entries and is

---

[1]Annotations and morphological analyses are available at `https://github.com/josefkr/morphcomp`

[2]PolArt's intensifiers also include downtoners such as *kaum* 'barely'

Proceedings of Recent Advances in Natural Language Processing, pages 625–633,
Varna, Bulgaria, Sep 4–6 2017.

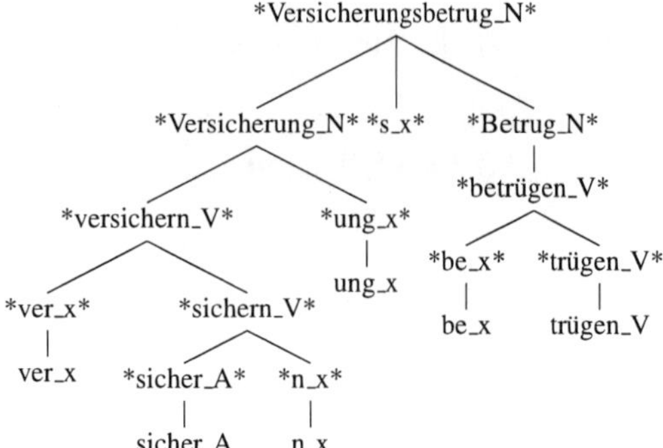

Figure 1: Morphological sample parse for *Versicherungsbetrug* 'insurance fraud'

		Parts of speech					
		N	A	V	R	P	Total
POS	PolArt	886	994	419	0	0	2299
	CELEX	197	57	7	2	0	263
NEG	PolArt	1572	1267	737	0	0	3576
	CELEX	354	78	20	5	1	458
NEU	PolArt	0	53	2	0	0	55
	CELEX	1629	86	6	0	0	1721
SHI	PolArt	0	4	3	0	0	7
	CELEX	0	0	0	0	0	0
INT	PolArt	4	14	2	0	0	20
	CELEX	0	1	0	0	0	1
Total		4642	2554	1196	7	1	8400

Table 1: Distribution of POS and polarity

short on compounds, we added words found in the CELEX database for German (Baayen et al., 1993). CELEX contains information about orthography, phonology, morphology, word class, argument structure as well as word form and lemma frequencies for words in German, Dutch and English. The use of CELEX is motivated by the fact that this resource contains among its morphological information not only segmentations but also complete human-created hierarchical parses, which we use in our experiments. We added polarity annotations for the CELEX entries.

Figure 1 shows the morphological parse for a German compound noun. It contains both components that are themselves words and as such (potentially) have entries in PolArt (e.g. the verb *versichern* 'insure') as well as components that are bound morphemes such as the nominalizing derivational suffix *-ung* or the linking element *s*. We expanded PolArt with entries for 167 affixes, assigning them polarity and intensity values.

Of the total 9300 lemmas, we use 8400 for training and testing in a 10-fold cross-validation setting. While we do not tune parameters for the classifiers, we set aside a development set of 900 lemmas for feature tuning and error analysis.

2.1 Statistics

We use 5937 PolArt entries and 2443 items added from CELEX for training and testing. The CELEX-derived entries are mostly neutral. As shown by Table 1, the distribution of POS (N=noun, A=adjective, V=verb, R=adverb, P=preposition) is dominated by the major lexical classes: nouns, verbs and adjectives.

2.2 Agreement

To test if our polarity annotations are compatible with those of PolArt's creators, we re-labeled a random sample of entries. We also labeled words from our CELEX expansion set to ensure that annotation was consistent on the new data (cf.§2.2.1). As we use novel information on derivational affixes in our experiments, we did a second annotation study (cf.§2.2.2). We sampled 100 derivational morphs. In cases of allomorphy (e.g. the negative prefix *in/im/ir/il-*), we kept only one variant. This cut down our set to 85 instances.

2.2.1 Agreement on Words

A student assistant (A1) and one of the authors (A2) labeled 200 roots for polarity, 100 from PolArt and 100 from CELEX. The kappa scores for all words and the two subsets are given in Table 2. Agreement is high on PolArt as it basically contains only polar words (cf. Table 1). On the added CELEX data, it is high, too, since that set contains many clearly neutral cases such as nouns referring to concrete objects. Agreement is reasonably high, both between the annotators and in comparison to PolArt. Since A2 has higher agreement with PolArt, we use A2's labels when A1 and A2 disagree.

2.2.2 Agreement on Affixes

Observed percent agreement on affixes is 0.85, the Cohen's kappa value is 0.67. The class distribution among affixes is significantly different to roots and words, with neutral affixes accounting for 67% of the affixes types. The disagreements for affixes centered on two distinctions unrelated to the neutral class: SHI vs POS/NEG and INT vs POS/NEG. To illustrate the former, one annotator treated *-frei* 'free of/without' as a shifter, whereas the other treated it as an affix with positive polarity. An example of the latter is *-reich* 'abounding with' which one annotator treated as an intensifier and the other as having positive polarity.

Pair	PolArt	CELEX	All
A1 vs. A2	0.95	0.84	0.90
A1 vs. PolArt	0.72	n/a	n/a
A2 vs. PolArt	0.80	n/a	n/a

Table 2: Kappa measures on all data and subsets

3 Experiments

In our classification experiments we assign a positive, neutral or negative polarity to a composite word based on its morphological make-up. With shifters and intensifiers being so rare (cf. Table 1), we leave them out of consideration.

3.1 Feature Groups

We first discuss the features that we use. They may apply to the composite word, to its immediate constituents (ICs), or to the leaves. In Figure 1, the ICs are *Versicherung*, *s* and *Betrug*.

3.1.1 Structural Features

This group of features considers information about the structure of the word as a whole.

height the height of the morphological parse tree

nt count the number of non-terminal nodes[3]

leaf count the number of leaves on the parse tree

compound is the word a compound formed by its immediate constituents? E.g. *Angsthase* 'scaredy cat' (lit. 'fear bunny/rabbit') is a compound at the level of immediate constituents. The adjective *angsthasenhaft* 'scaredy cat-like' contains this compound but is itself a derived form at the IC level.

category change does the composite word belong to a different POS category than all of its immediate constituents?

3.1.2 POS Features

We use three sets of features representing POS information on three levels. Each set consists of five indicator variables, one for each POS.

comp pos part of speech of the composite word

ic pos POS present among the ICs

leaf pos POS present among the leaves

3.1.3 Psycholinguistic Features

If possible, we extract psycholinguistic ratings for the whole word, its immediate constituents and the leaves. These features have been successfully used in the task of identifying metaphor, which also has a significant expressive function (Turney et al., 2011; Gargett et al., 2014). Psycholinguistic ratings were also explored for the task of polar intensity scoring by Ruppenhofer et al. (2014).

The first dimension places words on a scale from abstract to concrete (**abstconc**). Abstract words denote things we do not perceive directly (*integer*, *politics*, ...) whereas concrete words refer to things we can perceive (*sound*, *scent*, ...). The second feature concerns imageability. A large subset of concrete words have a high imageability (**img**). These words refer to things that we can actually see (*chestnut*, *police jeep*, ...). The third rating dimension is valence (**val**), which measures the pleasantness of a word (*gift* vs. *punishment*). The **arousal** dimension represents the intensity of emotion caused by a stimulus (*alert* vs *calm*).[4]

Our affective ratings derive from the work of Köper and Schulte im Walde (2016). While the creation of this resource involved some automatic translation from two English resources (Brysbaert et al. (2014); MRC database[5]) as well as score harmonization, it holds information for 350k words and is thus far more comprehensive than the affective norm data of Kanske and Kotz (2010) or Lahl et al. (2009). It is also much larger than common polarity lexicons such as PolArt (Klenner et al., 2009) or GermanPolarityClues (Waltinger, 2010).

3.1.4 Polarity Features

We use polarity information for immediate constituents and leaves. We take it from PolArt itself or our own supplemental annotations. We define one set of count features (**ic pol**) for the number of immediate constituents that are (i) positive, (ii) negative, or (iii) neutral, (iv) intensifying or downtoning, or (v) negating. We define a parallel group of features (**leaf pol**) for the leaves. Both feature sets include two more features representing the minimum and maximum polarity values present.

3.1.5 Lexical Features

One group of lexical features captures the presence or absence of individual derivational affixes at the level of immediate constituents (**ic affix**). Another set represents the presence of frequent lexical words or morphemes among the ICs (**ic lex**). An item must occur in at least 5 composite words to qualify as a lexical feature.

3.2 Classifiers

We employ a set of standard classifiers, Naive Bayes (NB), logistic regression, and linear SVM in the implementations of scikit-learn (Pedregosa

---

[3]This feature is highly correlated with height.

[4]Valence and arousal are part of (Osgood et al., 1957)'s well-known theory of emotions.

[5]http://websites.psychology.uwa.edu.au/school/MRCDatabase/uwa_mrc.htm

```
 1: pol="NEU"
 2: if $pos_{ct} > neg_{ct}$ then
 3:     pol="POS"
 4: else if $pos_{ct} < neg_{ct}$ then
 5:     pol="NEG"
 6: else if $pos_{ct} == 0$ and $neg_{ct} == 0$ then
 7:     pass
 8: else if $pos_{ct} > 0$ and $neg_{ct} > 0$ then
 9:     pol="NEG"
10: else
11:     pass
12: end if
13: if $shi_{ct}\%2 == 0$ then
14:     pass
15: else
16:     if $pol == "NEG"$ then
17:         pol="POS"
18:     else if $pol == "POS"$ then
19:         pol="POS"
20:     else
21:         pol="NEG"
22:     end if
23: end if
```

Figure 2: Baseline algorithm

et al., 2011). Our evaluation setup is 10-fold cross-validation. We compare different classifiers using McNemar's test with continuity correction (Japkowicz and Shah, 2011). Its χ^2 statistic depends on the number of cases where the classifiers disagree but one matches gold. We apply the test to the concatenated predictions across all folds.

3.2.1 Rule-based Polarity Baseline

A weak majority-class baseline would have a low accuracy of 48.2% on train/test. We define a much stronger rule-based baseline using simple heuristics about polarity and shifting. The algorithm is portrayed in Figure (2). It consists of two steps. The first condition block (lines 1-11) produces an initial polarity for the whole word based on the quantitative relations between positive, negative and neutral morphemes. The second block (12-20) potentially modifies the initial polarity, if there is an odd number of shifters present (12). A negative bias is built in in two places. When positive and negative items occur in equal non-zero number, we default to negative (8-9). When an odd number of shifters occurs only with neutral items, we still assign negative polarity (19-20).

4 Results

We first report basic three-way classification results for training and testing on all multi-morphemic words with our best setting. The results in Table 3 show that the SVM and logistic regression classifiers can beat the baseline in terms of accuracy, while Naive Bayes cannot. Consider-

ing the F1-score for the individual classes (+ = pos, $\sim$ = neu, $-$ = neg), we see that while there is better performance for the largest class (negative) the classifiers do learn the properties of the less frequent classes quite well, too. The linear SVN and logistic regression classifiers differ little but Naive Bayes is consistently lower-performing. As classifier optimization is not our focus, we henceforth only use the logistic regression classifier.

classifier	data	feats.	Acc.	+ F1	$\sim$ F1	- F1
baseline	all	all	0.74	0.70	0.67	0.81
Naive Bayes	all	all	0.74	0.70	0.76	0.77
SVM	all	all	$0.84^{\diamond}$	0.80	0.84	0.87
logistic	all	all	$0.85^{\star}$	0.81	0.86	0.88

statistical significance testing: McNemar's; $\star$ better than SVM at p< 0.001; $\diamond$ better than Naive Bayes at p< 0.001

Table 3: 3-way classification performance on multi-morphemic words on train/test (10-fold CV)

The results on the dev set (not shown for lack of space) pattern like those for the train/test-data.

4.1 Results per POS

Table 4 shows accuracy per POS on the train/test set, comparing the logistic regression classifier to our negatively-biased baseline. For nouns the improvement over the baseline is smallest, which is no surprise as the baseline is strongest for nouns. The biggest gains are seen for verbs.

	N	V	A	all
baseline	0.79	0.59	0.69	0.74
logistic	0.87	0.83	0.84	0.85

Table 4: 3-way classification accuracy per POS on train/test

4.2 Compounding vs Derivation

Table 5 shows, somewhat surprisingly, that compounds seem to be no harder to handle than derived forms for the logistic regression classifier, which is significantly better than the baseline for both sets. For the baseline, there is more of a gap.

data	classifier	Acc.	+ F1	$\sim$ F1	- F1
compounds	baseline	0.80	0.74	0.85	0.78
compounds	logistic	$0.86^{\flat}$	0.72	0.90	0.85
derived forms	baseline	0.72	0.71	0.53	0.82
derived forms	logistic	$0.85^{\flat}$	0.82	0.79	0.88

statistical significance testing: McNemar's; $\flat$ better than baseline at p< 0.001;

Table 5: Average 3-way classification performance on train/test

4.3 Impact of Feature Groups

Table 6 shows the effect of using only particular feature groups when carrying out 3-way classification in a cross-validation setting on the dev set. The dev set contains 460 negative words, 153 neutral items and 284 positive ones.[6] As expected, overall performance is a bit lower than on the much larger train/test set.

Polarity information about leaves (leaf pol) is useful but information on immediate constituents (ic pol) is more so. Combining the two does not improve over IC-level features alone. Afective ratings (psych) are also helpful. Affective ratings for the composite word (comp psych) are very valuable. The valence dimension by itself has the greatest impact while the other dimensions (arousal, abstconc and img) are not very predictive individually. However, the full set of ratings is markedly better than valence alone. Affective ratings below the level of the composite word (leaf psych, ic psych) still carry significant information. The pattern observed for polarity repeats here: information at the IC-level is better than information about leaves. Combining the two gives no significant boost. More generally, relying on the combination of all features at the level of ICs (ic all) is better than using the features at the leaf level (leaf all). This concords with the observation that structural features are not very predictive.

features	Acc.	+ F1	∼ F1	- F1
all	0.83★	0.79	0.81	0.86
structural	0.50	0.00	0.00	0.66
lexical	0.52	0.38	0.31	0.64
leaf pos	0.56	0.09	0.58	0.68
ic pos	0.51	0.00	0.48	0.65
ic & leaf pos	0.55	0.12	0.57	0.68
comp pos	0.50	0.00	0.00	0.66
ic pol	0.74	0.70	0.61	0.84
leaf pol	0.65	0.58	0.46	0.77
ic & leaf pol	0.74	0.69	0.61	0.83
ic psych	0.64	0.55	0.57	0.72
leaf psych	0.60	0.49	0.52	0.68
ic & leaf psych	0.64	0.55	0.58	0.71
comp psych	0.76	0.73	0.59	0.81
comp val	0.68	0.68	0.00	0.79
comp arousal	0.49	0.00	0.26	0.66
comp imageability	0.50	0.00	0.00	0.66
comp abstconc	0.50	0.00	0.05	0.67
ic all	0.80◇	0.76	0.77	0.85
leaf all	0.73	0.67	0.69	0.78
ic & leaf all	0.80	0.75	0.78	0.83

statistical significance testing: McNemar's; ★ better than *all ic & leaf* at p< 0.001; ◇ better than *all leaf* at p< 0.001

Table 6: Average 3-way classification performance on the dev set for multi-morphemic words, omitting some features

---

[6]The set also contains 3 intensifiers but we leave these aside as we perform only a three-way classification.

4.4 Error Analysis

Table 7a shows a confusion matrix for three-way classification, summed across all 10 folds. The confusions between the polar classes (neg for pos, or pos for neg) make up most (51%) of the errors. This picture seems, however, to be due to the derived forms but not the compounds. As Table 7b shows, for compounds the 'fatal' confusions between the two polar classes are much less frequent (17%). Instead, we observe many confusions of what is actually polar as neutral (59%).

	pos	neu	neg	pos	neu	neg
pos	**1741**	143	288	**159**	64	20
neu	117	**1547**	110	21	**889**	37
neg	242	138	**2936**	20	78	**441**

(a) Derivations and compounds (b) Compounds only

Table 7: Confusion matrices for train/test

Inspection of the predicted and gold labels on the dev set suggests the key source of error is that our lemma-based approach cannot deal with polysemy and the effects of idiosyncratic lexicalization. One example of this is the complex noun *Blinddarm* 'appendix' (lit. 'blind intestine'). The first component of this noun is the adjectival root *blind* 'blind' which is listed in PolArt as negative. The negative polarity of the adjective is however irrelevant to the rare meaning of 'lacking an opening' which *blind* has in *Blinddarm*. Similarly, the derived verb *umsorgen* was tagged as negative due to a PolArt entry that reflects a negative sense of 'worry' for *sorgen*, whereas the prefix *um-* is treated as neutral. Within *umsorgen*, however, *sorgen* occurs in its positive meaning of 'care (for)'. A third illustrative example is the derived adjective *lachhaft* 'laughable', which was predicted to be positive since the root *lach-* 'laugh' has positive polarity while the suffix *-haft* is neutral. But like its English gloss, *lachhaft* is negative.

These issues have clear parallels in the syntactic domain with multi-word expressions, which are well known to pose problems of compositionality (Sag et al., 2002). And in fact, most German compounds translate to English compounds which are considered a core part of the typology of multi-word expressions (Schneider et al., 2016). Likewise many German prefix verbs correspond to English particle verbs, which are MWEs in English.

5 Out of Domain Testing for Compounds

We suspect that the conclusions we can draw based on our PolArt and CELEX data may not carry over to other types of vocabulary. Consider that 8226 (88.4%) out of our total 9300 items are also listed in GermaNet (Hamp and Feldweg, 1997), the German counterpart of WordNet, and 93% of the items are contained in dlexdb, a lexical database for psycholinguistic research (Heister et al., 2011). These words are thus rather frequent and common. We now want to look at less common words and at compounds in particular. While the results for compounds on PolArt suggested that they were potentially as easy to handle as derived forms, that result was counter-intuitive: compound interpretation usually poses considerable challenges. The other reason to focus on compounds is that compounds are often hapaxes and that hapaxes in turn often express subjectivity.

We add data from two sources: from the collaborative online lexicon Wiktionary and from Wortwarte[7]. Wortwarte ('word watch') is a project that aims to extract neologisms from web-data, mostly from online newspapers. Words from these sources are less likely to be covered by GermaNet or dlexdb than PolArt entries (cf. Table 8).

	Wiktionary	Wortwarte
sample size	200	100
pos/neu/neg	3/38/159	9/53/38
% in GermaNet	36	1
% in dlexdb	68	1

Table 8: Wiktionary and Wortwarte data

So that the new items are not at a disadvantage relative to the PolArt and CELEX-derived items, we augment our polarity resource with new annotations for any unseen component words and morphemes introduced by the Wiktionary and Wortwarte data and also produce morphological parses as needed. With both data sets, we use the best system configuration found on the train/test data.

5.1 Wiktionary Compounds

The Wiktionary compounds were extracted by looking for lemmas labeled as compounds, with at least one sense marked as positive or negative/pejorative. We selected a random sample of 200 items. We re-annotated polarity as we consider the items as lemmas and a negative or positive word sense may not be salient to an annotator making a lemma-level judgment. The polarity distribution among the items is very biased (cf. Table 8).

On Wiktionary, the polarity baseline achieves an accuracy of 0.40. Unsurprisingly, it does worst on the few positive instances but for the neutral and negative classes the F1-scores are not far apart

(0.38 vs 0.44). The gravest source of error are actual negatives predicted as neutral. This results from the fact that the sample contains many cases such as *Quotenfrau* 'token woman' (lit. quota woman), which lack polar components but have a negative connotation. With an accuracy of 0.49, our system outperforms the baseline. The difference is significant at the α=0.01-level according to a McNemar's test. Like the baseline, our system does worst on the positive class. However, it handles the negative class significantly better than the rule-based baseline. Still, the same overall picture holds: the main source of error are negative instances predicted as neutral (cf. Table 9a).

	pos	neu	neg	pos	neu	neg
pos	**0**	3	0	**7**	1	1
neu	1	**31**	6	20	**18**	15
neg	8	85	**66**	6	7	**25**
	(a) Wiktionary			(b) Wortwarte		

Table 9: Confusion matrices for Wortwarte and Wiktionary compounds

On the Wiktionary data there are hardly any confusions between the polar classes. In this regard, the Wiktionary compounds are like PolArt's compounds and unlike PolArt's derived forms.

5.2 Wortwarte Compounds

Many Wortwarte items are of a domain-specific technical nature (e.g. *Ankertaumine* 'tethered mine') while others are playful (*Egoaufbauprogramm* 'ego-boosting program'). Typically, the items remain low-frequency and do not enter the general lexicon (cf. Table 8). As with Wiktionary, the classification results for Wortwarte are low: we achieve an accuracy of 0.50. The confusion matrix (cf. Table 9b) shows that many actually neutral items are predicted as positive or negative. The low accuracy is not due to missing polarity information: recall that we augmented our lexicon with this information for any unseen items. Two factors seem to be at play. On the one hand, Wortwarte includes words that are more creative and less predictable than the words in PolArt, and on the other hand many more neutral items than are found in the polarity lexicon. Note that the biased rule-based baseline outperforms our system significantly (according to McNemar's test), achieving an accuracy of 0.73, mainly due to much better recognition of neutral cases. Comparing the confusion matrix for Wortwarte to those for Wiktionary and PolArt (Table 7a) suggests that the

Wortwarte data represents its own kind of challenge.

6 Related Work

Moilanen and Pulman (2008) carried out a study on English that explored how well it was possible to classify unknown English words into one of three polarity classes based on morphological analysis that mainly considered affixation and zero conversion. Our work is different in several respects. First, we focus exclusively on morphology, whereas Moilanen and Pulman (2008) also used information about the syllable structure of words. Second, Moilanen and Pulman (2008) evaluated on a combination of infrequent words from the BNC and what they called 'junk' entries from a web-corpus. We did not use entries of the latter sort as we did not want to mix the issue of normalization into our setup. While we did test on low-frequency words, we purposefully also used high-frequency words to investigate the differences in compositionality in between words of different frequency bands. Because we used a polarity lexicon, we only have citation forms, whereas Moilanen and Pulman (2008) used inflected word forms. Finally, because the division of labor between morphology and syntax differs between German and English, our data included many cases that in English would be encountered as multi-word expressions.

Neviarouskaya et al. (2011) use morphological knowledge about derivation and compounding to perform a rule-based expansion of a base polarity lexicon. Newly proposed formations are added only if they are listed in WordNet (Miller, 1995). By comparison, our work is learning-based, unrestricted in terms of the morphological rules by which composite words are built up, and it addresses neutral items in addition to polar ones. Our results are consistent with the work of Neviarouskaya et al. (2011): entries in a human-curated sentiment lexicon are likely to be sufficiently compositional so that an expansion based on derivation and restricted compounding (within the bounds of a general language resource such as WordNet) makes sense.

In other related work, Wiegand et al. (2016) developed an approach to classify the modifiers of German compounds as expressing either the source or target of evaluation, or neither. For compounds whose head words are not always subjective, they use distributional similarity to first classify the compounds as a whole as being either subjective or not. Their setting assumes that the compounds in question are reasonably frequent to make distributional information reliable. In our research, we are interested in the predictive value of word-internal information by itself, especially with an eye towards handling rare words.

7 Conclusion

We presented a learning-based approach to the task of predicting the polarity of German words from their morphological make-up, focusing on derived forms and compounds in a new data set that we compiled and which we will make available. Using knowledge about the polarity of components and information about polarity shifting morphemes, we achieved a maximum performance of 85% accuracy on the train/test-set derived from the PolArt and CELEX lexical resources. Our results showed that psycholinguistic ratings for affective dimensions, even automatically generated ones as those of Köper and Schulte im Walde (2016), can substitute for or be combined with polarity features. The experiments also demonstrate that information at the immediate constituency level is more reliable than those at the level of leaves. As other structural features did not have a large impact, it seems advisable to proceed top down and only as far as is necessary to find known components. The experiments further suggested that derivations and compounds both seemed amenable to morphological analysis for the purposes of polarity prediction.

However, experiments on data from Wiktionary and Wortwarte showed that the knowledge we learned on the augmented PolArt resource does not readily transfer to compounds that are rarer and either more domain-specific, colloquial and/or more playful. Lexicalized compounds such as *Zeitungsente* 'canard' (lit. 'newspaper duck') which contain no polar part do not seem to be well represented in PolArt and they most likely cannot be handled sufficiently well on the basis of morphological knowledge alone. In future work, we therefore want to focus on a) using local context to analyze particular instances of compounds and on b) using corpus-derived information about the polarity of a given sub-word unit across multiple complex words it occurs in. The latter seems a promising addition to using polarity information about the uses where the items occur as free words.

Acknowledgments

The authors were partially supported by the German Research Foundation (DFG) under grants RU 1873/2-1 and WI 4204/2-1.

References

R. Harald Baayen, R. Piepenbrock, and H. van Rijn. 1993. *The CELEX lexical data base on CD-ROM*. Linguistic Data Consortium, Philadelphia, PA.

Marco Baroni, Johannes Matiasek, and Harald Trost. 2002. Predicting the components of German nominal compounds. In *Proceedings of the 15th European Conference on Artificial Intelligence*. IOS Press, pages 470–474.

Marc Brysbaert, Amy Beth Warriner, and Victor Kuperman. 2014. Concreteness ratings for 40 thousand generally known english word lemmas. *Behavior research methods* 46(3):904–911.

Guy Emerson and Thierry Declerck. 2014. SentiMerge: Combining sentiment lexicons in a Bayesian framework. In *Proceedings of the Workshop on Lexical and Grammatical Resources for Language Processing*.

Andrew Gargett, Josef Ruppenhofer, and John Barnden. 2014. Dimensions of metaphorical meaning. In *Proceedings of the 4th Workshop on Cognitive Aspects of the Lexicon (COGALEX)*. pages 166–173.

Michael Haas and Yannick Versley. 2015. Subsentential sentiment on a shoestring: A crosslingual analysis of compositional classification. In *HLT-NAACL*. pages 694–704.

Birgit Hamp and Helmut Feldweg. 1997. GermaNet - a Lexical-Semantic Net for German. In *In Proceedings of ACL workshop Automatic Information Extraction and Building of Lexical Semantic Resources for NLP Applications*. pages 9–15.

Julian Heister, Kay-Michael Würzner, Johannes Bubenzer, Edmund Pohl, Thomas Hanneforth, Alexander Geyken, and Reinhold Kliegl. 2011. dlexDB–eine lexikalische Datenbank für die psychologische und linguistische Forschung. *Psychologische Rundschau* .

Nathalie Japkowicz and Mohak Shah. 2011. *Evaluating learning algorithms: a classification perspective*. Cambridge University Press.

Philipp Kanske and Sonja A Kotz. 2010. Leipzig affective norms for German: A reliability study. *Behavior research methods* 42(4):987–991.

Manfred Klenner, Angela Fahrni, and Stefanos Petrakis. 2009. Polart: A robust tool for sentiment analysis. In *Proceedings of the 17th Nordic Conference on Computational Linguistics (NODALIDA 2009)*. pages 235–238.

Maximilian Köper and Sabine Schulte im Walde. 2016. Automatically generated affective norms of abstractness, arousal, imageability and valence for 350000 german lemmas. In *Proceedings of the 10th International Conference on Language Resources and Evaluation*. pages 2595–2598.

Olaf Lahl, Anja S. Göritz, Reinhard Pietrowsky, and Jessica Rosenberg. 2009. Using the World-Wide Web to obtain large-scale word norms: 190,212 ratings on a set of 2,654 German nouns. *Behavior Research Methods* 41(1):13–19. https://doi.org/10.3758/BRM.41.1.13.

George A Miller. 1995. WordNet: a lexical database for English. *Communications of the ACM* 38(11):39–41.

Karo Moilanen and Stephen Pulman. 2008. The Good, the Bad, and the Unknown: Morphosyllabic Sentiment Tagging of Unseen Words. In *Proceedings of the 46th Annual Meeting of the Association for Computational Linguistics on Human Language Technologies: Short Papers*. Association for Computational Linguistics, Stroudsburg, PA, USA, HLT-Short '08, pages 109–112. http://dl.acm.org/citation.cfm?id=1557690.1557719.

Alena Neviarouskaya, Helmut Prendinger, and Mitsuru Ishizuka. 2011. SentiFul: A lexicon for sentiment analysis. *IEEE Transactions on Affective Computing* 2(1):22–36.

Charles E. Osgood, George J. Suci, and Percy H. Tannenbaum. 1957. The measurement of meaning. *Urbana: University of Illinois Press* .

F. Pedregosa, G. Varoquaux, A. Gramfort, V. Michel, B. Thirion, O. Grisel, M. Blondel, P. Prettenhofer, R. Weiss, V. Dubourg, J. Vanderplas, A. Passos, D. Cournapeau, M. Brucher, M. Perrot, and E. Duchesnay. 2011. Scikit-learn: Machine learning in Python. *Journal of Machine Learning Research* 12:2825–2830.

Josef Ruppenhofer, Michael Wiegand, and Jasper Brandes. 2014. Comparing methods for deriving intensity scores for adjectives. In *Proceedings of the 14th Conference of the European Chapter of the Association for Computational Linguistics, volume 2: Short Papers*. Association for Computational Linguistics, Gothenburg, Sweden, pages 117–122. http://www.aclweb.org/anthology/E14-4023.

Ivan A Sag, Timothy Baldwin, Francis Bond, Ann Copestake, and Dan Flickinger. 2002. Multiword expressions: A pain in the neck for NLP. In *International Conference on Intelligent Text Processing and Computational Linguistics*. Springer, pages 1–15.

Nathan Schneider, Dirk Hovy Anders Johannsen, and Marine Carpuat. 2016. SemEval-2016 Task 10: Detecting Minimal Semantic Units and their Meanings (DiMSUM). *Proceedings of SemEval* pages 546–559.

Richard Socher, Alex Perelygin, Jean Y Wu, Jason Chuang, Christopher D Manning, Andrew Y Ng, Christopher Potts, et al. 2013. Recursive deep models for semantic compositionality over a sentiment treebank. In *Proceedings of the conference on empirical methods in natural language processing (EMNLP)*. Citeseer, volume 1631, page 1642.

Peter D. Turney, Yair Neuman, Dan Assaf, and Yohai Cohen. 2011. Literal and metaphorical sense identification through concrete and abstract context. In *Proceedings of the Conference on Empirical Methods in Natural Language Processing*. Association for Computational Linguistics, Stroudsburg, PA, USA, EMNLP '11, pages 680–690. http://dl.acm.org/citation.cfm?id=2145432.2145511.

Ulli Waltinger. 2010. GermanPolarityClues: A Lexical Resource for German Sentiment Analysis . In Nicoletta Calzolari, Khalid Choukri, Bente Maegaard, Joseph Mariani, Jan Odijk, Stelios Piperidis, Mike Rosner, and Daniel Tapias, editors, *LREC*. European Language Resources Association, pages 1638–1642.

Janyce Wiebe, Theresa Wilson, Rebecca Bruce, Matthew Bell, and Melanie Martin. 2004. Learning subjective language. *Computational linguistics* 30(3):277–308.

Michael Wiegand, Christine Bocionek, and Josef Ruppenhofer. 2016. Opinion Holder and Target Extraction on Opinion Compounds - A Linguistic Approach. In Kevin Knight, Ani Nenkova, and Owen Rambow, editors, *NAACL HLT 2016, The 2016 Conference of the North American Chapter of the Association for Computational Linguistics: Human Language Technologies, San Diego California, USA, June 12-17, 2016*. The Association for Computational Linguistics, pages 800–810. http://aclweb.org/anthology/N/N16/N16-1094.pdf.

Introducing EVALD – Software Applications
for Automatic Evaluation of Discourse in Czech

Kateřina Rysová, Magdaléna Rysová, Jiří Mírovský, Michal Novák
Charles University
Faculty of Mathematics and Physics
Institute of Formal and Applied Linguistics
`{rysova, magdalena.rysova, mirovsky, mnovak}@ufal.mff.cuni.cz`

Abstract

In the paper, we introduce two software applications for automatic evaluation of coherence in Czech texts called EVALD – Evaluator of Discourse. The first one – EVALD 1.0 – evaluates texts written by native speakers of Czech on a five-step scale commonly used at Czech schools (grade 1 is the best, grade 5 is the worst). The second application is EVALD 1.0 for Foreigners assessing texts by non-native speakers of Czech using six-step scale (A1–C2) according to CEFR. Both applications are available online at `https://lindat.mff.cuni.cz/services/evald-foreign/`.

1 Introduction

Students of Czech often have problems with writing a comprehensive and continuous text. The reason is that creating texts is more demanding for them than creating separate sentences. The text is not simply "a cluster of sentences" but its structure has its own rules whose failure can result in the so called incoherent text, i.e. a text that is not fully functional in communication (see e.g. Halliday and Hasan, 1976). The ability of creating text should thus be encouraged already in the teaching process. At the same time, appropriate tools developed to assess such texts may reduce the amount of teachers' manual work.

In this paper, we present the results of our investigation of automatic evaluation of texts in Czech (written by native and non-native speakers), more specifically, possibilities of automatic evaluation of text coherence. We present the linguistic features (concerning mainly discourse phenomena) that may be observed and evaluated automatically. Our experiments in this area resulted in a development of two software applications:

Evaluator of Discourse 1.0 (EVALD 1.0) and Evaluator of Discourse 1.0 for Foreigners (EVALD 1.0 for Foreigners).

The EVALD applications can function as assistant tools for evaluation of essays in Czech[1] and they can be also used by students and learners who can easily verify their level of coherence in Czech.

EVALD applications are available as online services[2] and also as downloadable Docker containers.[3]

1.1 Czech as a Foreign Language – Assessing Criteria

The process of learning a foreign language is long-lasting and continuous. The learner goes through several stages from a beginner to a highly advanced language user. These stages (or phases of learning) are described in the document of the Council of Europe *Common European Framework of Reference for Languages* (CEFR). CEFR distinguishes six categories: A1 (basic language user – lower level), A2 (basic language user – higher level), B1 (independent language user – lower level), B2 (independent language user – higher level), C1 (proficient language user – lower level), C2 (proficient language user – higher level).

---

[1] The EVALD applications were created for assessing the coherence of authentic essays written by native and non-native speakers of Czech. In other words, they are trained to evaluate (prosaic) texts whose content and form (e.g. length) correspond to the common essays created as a comprehensive piece of writing on a given topic, e.g. during the Czech language exam. When evaluating a different type of text (e.g. too short texts, poems etc.), the software cannot work reliably because it is not trained for such text type.
[2] https://lindat.mff.cuni.cz/services/evald/index.php; https://lindat.mff.cuni.cz/services/evald-foreign/
[3] See http://ufal.mff.cuni.cz/evald/documentation for detailed installation instructions.

Proceedings of Recent Advances in Natural Language Processing, pages 634–641,
Varna, Bulgaria, Sep 4–6 2017.

Motivations behind learning foreign languages, including the languages of smaller countries, may be diverse. For example, learning Czech is useful for foreigners who want to study in the Czech Republic (most of the Czech universities require the CEFR level of B2). The knowledge of Czech is also compulsory for foreigners to be granted permanent residence in the Czech Republic (the required CEFR level is A1) or state citizenship (the required CEFR level is B1). Therefore, it is of a great importance to assess these examinations as objectively as possible and according to uniform criteria.

This requirement is rather difficult to meet because the writing samples are evaluated only manually by human assessors (although according to the uniform rating grid) who naturally bring in a subjective human factor to the evaluation.

Therefore, we tried to find several objective criteria (concerning text coherence) for distinguishing the individual CEFR levels automatically. Specifically, we carried out research on text coherence concerning mainly various discourse phenomena (e.g., the use and frequency of discourse connective expressions) and we tested the possibility of their automatic monitoring and evaluation.

1.2 Czech of Native Speakers

Creating a coherent text that is fully functional in communication is not easy and obvious even for native speakers. Native speakers are also gradually learning to write a well-structured and comprehensive text.

At the same time, students' ability to create a coherent text is often examined at schools. For instance, writing an essay has been a compulsory part of the graduation examination at secondary schools in the Czech Republic for decades.

The essays by native speakers are not evaluated according to the CEFR levels, but according to a five-step scale commonly used at Czech schools (grade 1 is the best, grade 5 is the worst). EVALD 1.0 thus distinguishes 5 rating grades.

2 Previous Research

2.1 Text Coherence and Discourse

Text coherence (continuity) is a common property of each text that is fully functional in authentic communication. Linguistically, it is a complex phenomenon realized through various language aspects like semantico-pragmatic relations, coreference and anaphoric relations, lexical relations, substitution or ellipsis (see e.g. Dressler and de Beaugrande, 1972, 1981; Halliday and Hasan, 1976 or Hoey, 1979, 2001). In present-day linguistics, text coherence is thus often studied through language interactions (see e.g. Long and Chong, 2001; Camblin et al., 2007 or Hajičová, 2011).

This paper describes especially the automatically measurable aspects of semantico-pragmatic discourse relations (i.e. relations such as condition, opposition, reason, succession etc.) as one of the most important aspects of coherence. Discourse relations constitute the whole structure of a text and each text thus may be imagined as a net of semantico-pragmatic relations that are arranged hierarchically, i.e. the smallest units are linked to form higher units etc.

The right interpretation of semantico-pragmatic relations (which is a core of discourse analysis, see mainly Harris, 1952) then leads to the right interpretation of the whole text. To make this interpretation easier for the reader to comprehend, each language has its specific expressions that signal these types of relations explicitly – discourse connectives (cf. examples like *proto* "therefore", *avšak* "however", *v důsledku* "in consequence" etc.). Discourse connectives may be divided into two groups: primary and secondary (see Rysová and Rysová, 2014, 2015). In short, primary connectives are mostly grammaticalized expressions often consisting of a single word, e.g *když* "when", *protože* "because", *a* "and", *nebo* "or". On the other hand, secondary connectives are not yet fully grammaticalized, mainly multi-word structures, e.g. *za podmínky, že* "on condition that", *v důsledku* "in consequence", *z tohoto důvodu* "for this reason" etc.

2.2 Studies on Automatic Evaluation of Coherence

Automatic evaluation of various language aspects (grammatical accuracy etc.) is studied in a number of projects (see e.g. Bangalore et al., 2000; Leacock and Chodorow, 2000 or Papineni et al., 2002). On the contrary, assessment of text coherence has been carried out so far rather manually by human assessors. Experiments on automatic evaluation of text coherence are thus relatively new in contemporary research. In this area, there exist only few studies (mainly for English) concerning various aspects of text coherence and co-hesion.

In earlier studies, Foltz et al. (1998) and Wiemer-Hastings and Graesser (2000) have developed systems which examine text coherence in students' essays. Their systems focus on local coherence (i.e. on such aspects of coherence occurring in smaller sequence of sentence, mostly between adjacent sentences or within a single paragraph) and they measure lexical relatedness between text units by using vector-based similarity between adjacent sentences.

Their work relates in terms of similarity scoring to the TextTiling scheme (see Hearst and Plaunt, 1993 or Hearst, 1997) that may be used to recognize the subtopic of a text. Miltsakaki and Kukich (2000) also deal with text coherence in students' writing. They work with Rough Shift element of Centering Theory (Grosz et al., 1995) by examining the similarity of adjacent text units.

Possibilities of automatic evaluation of global coherence is studied by Higgins et al. (2004) focusing on four points: i) relatedness of a text to its topic, ii) relatedness to the thesis, iii) relatedness within a segment (i.e. each sentence in a text segment should be related to at least one other sentence within the segment), iv) grammar accuracy (a text is of a low coherence if it contains grammatical errors, incomplete sentences etc.).

To date, few attempts have been made to develop new methods for automatic evaluation of coherence in non-native (learners') texts, see e.g. Yannakoudakis and Briscoe (2012) investigating learners' coherence by monitoring part-of-speech distribution, number of (primary) discourse connectives (based on a fixed list) or word length.

Up to now, the research on automatic evaluation of students' essays (written by both native and non-native speakers) seems to be a relatively unexplored topic. In this paper, we thus aim to contribute to it by discussing new aspects of coherence that may be evaluated automatically (e.g. apart from primary connectives, we reflect also some types of secondary connectives, see Section 4.4). [4] At the same time, the EVALD applications are the first attempts to measure text coherence automatically on Czech data.

---

⁴ The long-term investigation of discourse resulted in publication of the first discourse annotated corpus for Czech – the Prague Discourse Treebank, see the first version in Poláková et al, 2012 and the second one in Rysová et al., 2016.

3   Language Material

Three corpora served as a source for basic linguistic research on coherence in Czech as well as for training of both software applications. Texts by the non-native speakers were obtained from the MERLIN corpus (Boyd et al., 2014) and CzeSL-SGT (Šebesta et al., 2014). Texts by the native speakers were taken from the corpus Skript2012 / AKCES 1 (Šebesta et al., 2016). EVALD 1.0 for Foreigners was trained on 945 texts in total and EVALD 1.0 on 1,118 texts.

4   Components of EVALD Applications

EVALD applications are based on supervised machine learning. Therefore, coherence must be first assessed on the text from the training corpora manually. Trained EVALD models then try to mimic this manual annotation using a set of linguistically motivated features. Many of the features take advantage of the linguistic information collected automatically on the texts during the pre-processing stage.

4.1   Assessment of the Texts by Linguists

Manual evaluation of texts from the corpora mentioned in Section 3 was performed by two trained evaluators.[5] The texts of non-native speakers were categorized into 6 classes differentiated by CEFR (A1, A2, B1, B2, C1 and C2) according to their coherence. The texts of native speakers were divided into 5 categories in accordance with the ratings used at Czech schools: 1 (excellent), 2 (very good), 3 (good), 4 (satisfactory), 5 (fail/unsatisfactory). The inter-annotator agreement (IAA) was measured on 100 texts of non-native speakers and on 100 texts of native speakers of Czech assessed (simultaneously) by the two evaluators. The exact IAA agreement reached 51% (on texts by non-native speakers) and 64% (on texts by native speakers). With tolerance of one level distance (e.g. evaluator 1: A1, evaluator 2: A2), the IAA agreement is 93% on texts by non-native speakers and 90% on texts by native speakers. Our IAA agreement is comparable to other similar projects, see e.g. Östling et al. (2013) reaching 45.8% of exact agreement among teachers evaluating 1,702 school essays in Swedish.

---

⁵ The evaluation of texts from the MERLIN corpus was taken directly from this corpus, as the texts from MERLIN already contained a reliable coherence evaluation according to CEFR.

4.2 Automatic Pre-processing of the Texts

A highly modular Treex processing system (Žabokrtský, 2011) was used for the automatic analysis of the text from its surface representation to deep syntactic dependency trees. The analysis pipeline for Czech comprises word tokenization, sentence splitting, part-of-speech tagging and lemmatization with MorphoDiTa (Straková et al. 2014), surface dependency parsing with MST parser adapted to Czech (Novák and Žabokrtský, 2007), and rule-based transition to deep syntactic trees. Such trees are then ready to be labeled with discourse-related annotation.

An algorithm designed by Jínová et al. (2012) was used to find intra-sentential discourse relations expressed by the primary connectives (e.g. *a* "and", *ale* "but", *protože* "because"). Inter-sentential discourse relations were addressed by our own method exploiting the list of inter-sentential primary connectives in Czech (compiled from the data of the Prague Discourse Treebank 2.0). Furthermore, an algorithm for automatic annotation of inter-sentential discourse relations expressed by secondary connectives containing pronominal anaphor (e.g. *díky tomu* "thanks to that", *kvůli tomu* "due to that", *kromě toho* "besides that") was created. It takes advantage of an adjusted version of the Treex Coreference Resolver (Bojar et al., 2012) module for demonstrative pronouns. The module does not seek an antecedent. Instead, it determines whether the pronoun refers to an entity, event or is non-anaphoric.

4.3 Feature Extraction Based on Linguistic Research

On the manually assessed texts, we carried out a comparative linguistic research, whose aim was to find language features that are distinctive for each level of text coherence. Our attention was paid to those features that are automatically detectable in the text. Based on this research, we have compiled a list of distinctive features, see Section 4.4.

For illustration, we present some partial results of this research phase on the example of connective expressions in the texts written by learners of Czech. Table 1 shows the distribution of these expressions[6] over A2, B1 and B2 categories in the MERLIN corpus, measured in terms of absolute and relative (per 100 sentences) frequencies.

---

[6] The table captures the occurrence of the most frequent connective expressions, i.e. those that have more than 100 tokens in the MERLIN corpus texts.

The table reveals that B2 learners of Czech use markedly more connective expressions than learners at lower levels (A2 or B1). On the other hand, there is no difference between levels A2 and B1 in this respect.

In addition, Graphs 1, 2 and 3 capture the distribution of the most frequently used connective expressions in the A2, B1 and B2 texts (the graphs are based on the values from Table 1). In all cases, the most common connective is *a* "and". However, the CEFR levels vary in the proportion of the connective *a* "and" among the other frequently used connective expressions. Basic language users (A2) use the connective *a* "and" substantially more often (compared to their use of other common connective expressions) than independent language users (B1, B2). By contrast, language users in categories B1 and B2 do not differ in this respect.

The examples above illustrate that the individual language features do not always distinguish all the coherence categories but they sometimes distinguish only some of them. It is thus interesting that some of the language phenomena are not improving evenly, when moving from A2 to B2. This observation demonstrates that the learning process of the individual language phenomena is not always linear. That is, it does not always follow the process of gradual improvement but some aspects of the second language are acquired rather "in jumps" by the learners. Similarly, we searched for further linguistic criteria according to which it would be possible to distinguish individual coherence categories of texts (written both by native and non-native speakers of Czech). Subsequently, the identified distinctive features (automatically detectable in texts) have been implemented in the EVALD software.

Most frequent connective means	A2		B1		B2	
	Tokens in 102 texts	Tokens per 100 sentences	In 171 texts	Per 100 sent.	In 157 texts	Per 100 sent.
a "and"	369	32	709	23	1,107	45
ale "but"	47	4	231	7	320	13
když "when"	11	1	66	2	230	9
protože "because"	43	4	136	4	104	4
tak "so"	5	0	64	2	133	5
aby "in order to"	2	0	35	1	140	6
také "too"	17	1	52	2	85	3
taky "too"	22	2	56	2	73	3
proto "therefore"	19	2	22	1	74	3
Total	535	47	1,371	44	2,266	91

Table 1: Most frequent connective expressions of A2, B1 and B2 CEFR levels in MERLIN corpus.

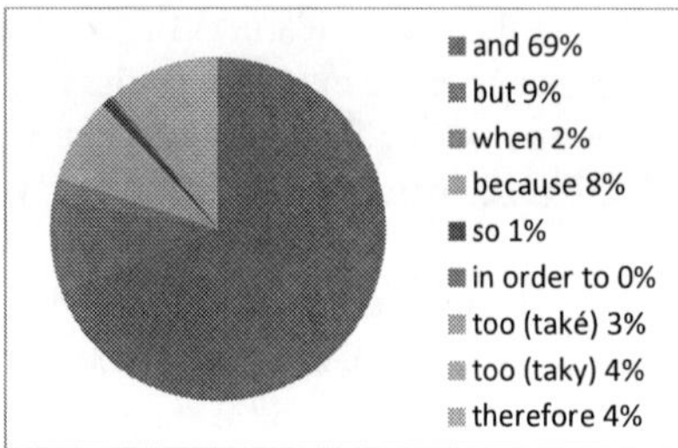

Graph 1: Distribution of most frequent connective expressions in A2 of MERLIN texts.

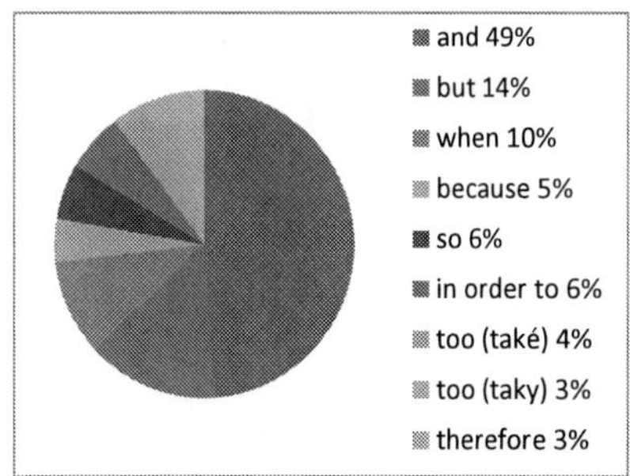

Graph 2: Distribution of most frequent connective expressions in B1 of MERLIN texts.

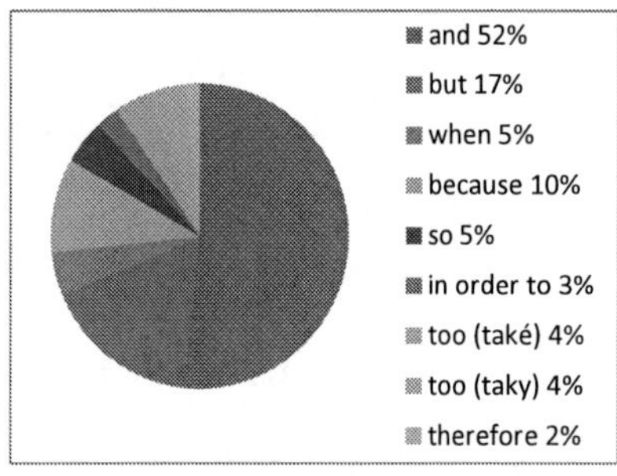

Graph 3: Distribution of most frequent connective expressions in B2 of MERLIN texts.

4.4 Final List of Linguistic Features Evaluated by Both Software Applications

EVALD 1.0 and EVALD 1.0 for Foreigners work with the following language features.

Surface features consist of those using only tokenization and sentence segmentation, i.e. not any advanced part of the text analysis such as syntactic parsing and discourse parsing:

• number of all connective words per 100 sentences; • number of coordinating connective words per 100 sentences (e.g. *a* "and", *ale* "but", *nebo* "or"); • number of subordinating connective words per 100 sentences (e.g. *aby* "in order to", *když* "when", *protože* "because"); • number of tokens (words) per sentence (i.e. sentence length); • richness of the vocabulary (i.e. variety of lemmas).

Advanced features extract information from the automatically parsed tree structures and from automatically annotated discourse relations:

• number of intra-sentential discourse relations per 100 sentences; • number of inter-sentential discourse relations per 100 sentences; • number of all discourse relations per 100 sentences; • number of different connectives in all discourse relations; • ratio of discourse relations with connectives *a* "and", *ale* "but", *protože* "because", *také* "too", *potom* "then", *pak* "then", *když* "when", *nebo* "or", *proto* "therefore", *tak* "so", *aby* "in order to", *totiž* "that is"; • ratio of inter-sentential discourse relations expressed by secondary connectives containing pronominal anaphor; • number of predicate-less sentences per 100 sentences (i.e. constructions without finite verbs like *Lovely!*); • ratio of discourse relations from class of Temporal, Contingency, Contrast and Expansion relations; • ratio of occurrence of the most common connective within all connectives in a text; • ratio of occurrence of the first and second most common connective within all connectives in a text.

4.5 Machine Learning Modelling

For machine learning experiments, the Random Forest algorithm implemented in WEKA toolkit (Hall et al., 2009) was chosen, as it provided the best results in the initial stages of the experiments among many other algorithms available in WE-KA. Details on machine learning experiments and discussion on them can be found in Rysová et al. (2016).

5 Experiments and Evaluation

EVALD applications were trained and evaluated using 10-fold cross validation. In the first experiment, the whole datasets described in Section 3 were used (L1: 1,118 texts, L2: 945 texts) and for the evaluation, the F-score was measured, see Table 4 (the column F-Score).

Since the available data do not reflect the real distribution of the individual assessed classes in population, the data sets were uniformed for the second experiment – the instances in all classes were reduced to achieve a uniform distribution of them across the individual categories (L1: 475 texts, L2: 600 texts; more details are given in Novák et al., 2017). Confusion matrices are presented in Tables 2 and 3. The information for overall accuracy on these uniformed data sets is captured in the second column of Table 4.

EVALD 1.0		Assessed automatically				
		1	2	3	4	5
Assessed manually	1	84	1	1	9	0
	2	82	5	2	6	0
	3	53	9	6	27	0
	4	20	0	3	66	6
	5	2	0	0	35	58

Table 2: EVALD 1.0 – Confusion Matrix for Random Forest.

EVALD 1.0 for Foreigners		Assessed automatically					
		A1	A2	B1	B2	C1	C2
Assessed manually	A1	64	27	5	2	2	0
	A2	30	35	17	14	2	2
	B1	5	14	62	14	4	1
	B2	1	3	0	81	5	10
	C1	11	22	8	37	6	16
	C2	0	0	3	10	2	85

Table 3: EVALD 1.0 for Foreigners – Confusion Matrix for Random Forest.

As we can see in Tables 2 and 3, many of the errors are a result of misclassifying to a neighbouring class. Therefore, we measured not only the exact accuracy of the classifier, but also its accuracy with tolerance of "one-level" error (e.g. a human annotator classifies the text as B1 and EVALD as B2), see the third column of Table 4.

	Accuracy (Random Forest algorithm with 10-fold cross-validation method)		
	F-score on the whole data set	Exact accuracy on balanced data set	Accuracy with tolerance of "one-level" error on balanced data set
EVALD 1.0	44.9	46.1	80.8
EVALD 1.0 for Foreigners	51.3	55.5	82.5

Table 4: Accuracy of EVALD applications.

6 Discussion

The accuracy presented in Table 4 is an encouraging result because it is natural even among human evaluators (teachers) to hold the assessment within one level distance, see Section 4.1.

The EVALD accuracy is also comparable to other automatic systems developed for other languages. However, the comparison is rather difficult because the existing systems focus rather on evaluation of grammatical, lexical and semantic aspects than on text coherence (which is a complex language phenomenon more difficult to monitor than e.g. spelling, grammar errors etc.). At the same time, the other systems often do not evaluate all the existing levels (e.g. A1–C2).

For example, Vajjala and Lõo (2013) reach 79% accuracy in automatic evaluation of A2–C1 CEFR levels in Estonian using especially morphosyntactic and lexical features. Volodina et al. (2016) present 67% accuracy in evaluation of A1–C1 of CEFR levels in Swedish using count-based, lexical, syntactic, morphological, and semantic features. Hancke and Meurers (2013) demonstrate 62.7% accuracy of A1–C1 CEFR levels in German with syntactic, lexical and morphological features. Concerning automatic evaluation of native speakers' essays, Östling et al. (2013) reach 62.2% accuracy in automatic evaluation of high school essays written in Swedish, using especially grammatical and lexical features.

The research on EVALD applications is going to be further deepened by implementing features concerning other language phenomena. Currently, the applications are being enriched by features reflecting coreference and anaphora (see Novák et al., 2017). In the next step, the applications will also be enriched by features concerning sentence information structure.

7 Conclusion

In our paper, we have introduced two software applications that automatically estimate a coherence level of the text created by native or non-native speakers of Czech. Their accuracy achieves around 80% with one-level error tolerance. As far as we know, a similar tool for Czech has not yet been developed. The EVALD applications are unique especially in the way that they evaluate text coherence, which is not yet fully explored topic not only for Czech but also in international context.

Acknowledgement

The authors acknowledge support from the Ministry of Culture of the Czech Republic (project no. DG16P02B016 *Automatic Evaluation of Text Coherence in Czech*).

This work has been using language resources developed, stored and distributed by the LINDAT/CLARIN project of the Ministry of Education, Youth and Sports of the Czech Republic (project LM2015071).

References

Srinivas Bangalore, Owen Rambow, and Steve Whittaker. 2000. Evaluation metrics for generation. In *Proceedings of the INLG*, pages 1–8.

Robert-Alain de Beaugrande and Wolfgang Dressler. 1981. *Introduction to Text Linguistics*. London: Longman.

Ondřej Bojar, Zdeněk Žabokrtský et al. 2012. The Joy of Parallelism with CzEng 1.0. In *Proceedings of the 8th International Conference on Language Resources and Evaluation (LREC 2012)*. European Language Resources Association, İstanbul, Turkey, pages 3921–3928.

Adriane Boyd, Jirka Hana, Lionel Nicolas, Detmar Meurers, Katrin Wisniewski, Andrea Abel, Karin Schöne, Barbora Štindlová, and Chiara Vettori. 2014. The MERLIN corpus: Learner language and the CEFR. In *Proceedings of the 9th International Conference on Language Resources and Evaluation (LREC 2014)*. European Language Resources Association, Reykjavík, Iceland, pages 1281–1288.

Christine C. Camblin, Peter C. Gordon, and Tamara Y Swaab. 2007. The interplay of discourse congruence and lexical association during sentence processing: Evidence from ERPs and eye tracking. *Journal of Memory and Language*, 56(1):103–128.

Common European Framework of Reference for Languages. Language Policy Unit, Strasbourg. http://www.coe.int/t/dg4/linguistic/Source/Framework_EN.pdf. [cite 2017-04-30]

Wolfgang Dressler. 1972. *Einführung in die Textlinguistik*. Tübingen: Niemeyer.

Peter Foltz, Walter Kintsch, and Thomas K. Landauer. 1998. The measurement of textual coherence with Latent Semantic Analysis. *Discourse Processes*, 25(2&3):285–307.

Barbara J. Grosz, Scott Weinstein, and Aravind K. Joshi. 1995. Centering: A framework for modeling the local coherence of discourse. *Computational linguistics* 21(2): 203–225.

Eva Hajičová. 2011. On interplay of information structure, anaphoric links and discourse relations. In *Societas linguistica europaea SLE 2011, 44th Annual Meeting, Book of Abstracts*. Universidad de la Rioja, Center for Research in the Applications of Language, Logrono, Spain, pages 139–140.

Mark Hall. Eibe Frank, Geoffrey Holmes, Bernhard Pfahringer. Peter Reutemann, Ian H. Witten. 2009. The WEKA data mining software: an update. *ACM SIGKDD explorations newsletter* 11(1), pages 10–18.

Julia Hancke and Detmar Meurers. 2013. Exploring CEFR classification for German based on rich linguistic modeling. *Learner Corpus Research*, 54–56.

Marti A. Hearst and Christian Plaunt. 1993. Subtopic structuring for full-length document access. In *Proceedings of ACM SIGIR*, pages 59–68.

Marti A. Hearst. 1997. TextTiling: Segmenting text into multi-paragraph subtopic passages. *Computational Linguistics*, 23(1):33–64.

Derrick Higgins et al. 2004. Evaluating multiple aspects of coherence in student essays. In *Proceedings of the NAACL*, pages 185–192.

Michael Hoey. 1979. *Signalling in discourse*. Birmingham UK: English Language Research Unit, University of East Angllia.

Michael Hoey. 2001. *Textual Interaction: An Introduction to Written Discourse Analysis*. London: Routledge.

Pavlína Jínová, Jiří Mírovský, and Lucie Poláková. 2012. Semi-Automatic Annotation of Intra-Sentential Discourse Relations in PDT. In *Proceedings of the Workshop on Advances in Discourse Analysis and its Computational Aspects (ADACA) at Coling 2012*. Organizing Committee, Mumbai, India, pages 43–58.

Michael Alexander Kirkwood Halliday and Ruqaiya Hasan. 1976. *Cohesion in English*. London: Longman.

Claudia Leacock and Martin Chodorow. 2000. An unsupervised method for detecting grammatical errors. In *Proceedings of the First Meeting of the North American Chapter of the Association for Computational Linguistics (NAACL 2000)*, pages 140–147.

Debra L. Long, D. L and Jennifer L. Chong. 2001. Comprehension skill and global coherence: A paradoxical picture of poor comprehenders abilities. *Journal of Experimental Psychology Learning, Memory and Cognition, 27*(14):24–1429.

MERLIN for CEFR-related language learning, teaching, and testing. 2014. WWW: <http://merlin-platform.eu/index.php>

Eleni Miltsakaki and Karen Kukich. 2000. Automated evaluation of coherence in student essays. In *Proceedings of LREC 2000*, Athens, Greece.

Michal Novák, Kateřina Rysová, Magdaléna Rysová, and Jiří Mírovský. 2017. Incorporating Coreference to Automatic Evaluation of Surface Coherence in Essays. In *Proceedings of the Statistical Language and Speech Processing (SLSP 2017)*.

Václav Novák and Zdeněk Žabokrtský. 2007. Feature Engineering in Maximum Spanning Tree Dependency Parser. *Lecture Notes in Computer Science*, 4629(17):92–98. Springer, Berlin.

Robert Östling, Andre Smolentzov, Björn Tyrefors Hinnerich, and Erik Höglin. 2013. Automated essay scoring for Swedish. In *Proceedings of the Eighth Workshop on Innovative Use of NLP for Building Educational Applications*, pages 42–47, Atlanta, Georgia.

Kishore Papineni et al. 2002. BLUE: a method for automatic evaluation of machine translation. In *Proceedings of the ACL*, pages 311–318.

Lucie Poláková, Pavlína Jínová, Šárka Zikánová, Eva Hajičová, Jiří Mírovský, Anna Nedoluzhko, Magdaléna Rysová, Veronika Pavlíková, Jana Zdeňková, Jiří Pergler, and Radek Ocelák. 2012. *Prague Discourse Treebank 1.0.* Data/software, ÚFAL MFF UK, Prague, Czech Republic, http://ufal.mff.cuni.cz/pdit/.

Kateřina Rysová, Jiří Mírovský, Michal Novák, and Magdalćna Rysová. 2016. *EVALD 1.0.* Data/software, ÚFAL MFF UK, Prague, Czechia, http://hdl.handle.net/11234/1-1820. [https://ufal.mff.cuni.cz/evald].

Kateřina Rysová, Jiří Mírovský, Michal Novák, and Magdaléna Rysová. 2016. *EVALD 1.0 for Foreigners.* Data/software, ÚFAL MFF UK, Prague, Czechia, http://hdl.handle.net/11234/1-1821. [https://ufal.mff.cuni.cz/evald/evald-10-foreigners].

Kateřina Rysová, Magdaléna Rysová, Jiří Mírovský. Automatic evaluation of surface coherence in L2 texts in Czech. 2016. In *Proceedings of the 28th Conference on Computational Linguistics and Speech Processing ROCLING XXVIII.* 2016. Taipei, Taiwan: The Association for Computational Linguistics and Chinese Language Processing (ACLCLP), pages 214–228.

Magdaléna Rysová, Pavlína Synková, Jiří Mírovský, Eva Hajičová, Anna Nedoluzhko, Radek Ocelák, Jiří Pergler, Lucie Poláková, Veronika Pavlíková, Jana Zdeňková, and Šárka Zikánová. 2016. *Prague Discourse Treebank 2.0.* Data/software, ÚFAL MFF UK, Prague, Czech Republic, http://hdl.handle.net/11234/1-1905.

Magdaléna Rysová and Kateřina Rysová. 2015. Secondary Connectives in the Prague Dependency Treebank. In *Proceedings of the Third International Conference on Dependency Linguistics (Depling 2015)*, Uppsala University, Uppsala, Sweden, pages 291–299.

Magdaléna Rysová and Kateřina Rysová. 2014. The Centre and Periphery of Discourse Connectives. In *Proceedings of the 28th Pacific Asia Conference on Language, Information and Computing (PACLIC 28)*. Bangkok, Thailand: Department of Linguistics, Faculty of Arts, Chulalongkorn University, pages 452–459.

Jana Straková, Milan Straka and Jan Hajič. 2014. Open-Source Tools for Morphology, Lemmatization, POS Tagging and Named Entity Recognition. In *Proceedings of 52nd Annual Meeting of the Association for Computational Linguistics: System Demonstrations.* Association for Computational Linguistics, Baltimore, Maryland, pages 13–18.

Karel Šebesta, Zuzanna Bedřichová, Kateřina Šormová et al. 2014. *AKCES 5 (CzeSL-SGT).* LINDAT/CLARIN digital library at the Institute of Formal and Applied Linguistics, Charles University in Prague, http://hdl.handle.net/11858/00-097C-0000-0023-95B1-E.

Karel Šebesta, Hana Goláňová, Jana Letafková et al., 2016. *AKCES 1.* LINDAT/CLARIN digital library at the Institute of Formal and Applied Linguistics, Charles University in Prague, http://hdl.handle.net/11234/1-1741.

Sowmya Vajjala and Kaidi Lõo. 2014. Automatic CEFR level prediction for Estonian learner text. Proceedings of the third workshop on NLP for computer-assisted language learning. NEALT Proceedings Series 22 / Linköping Electronic Conference Proceedings 107, pages 113–127.

Elena Volodina, Ildikó Pilán, and David Alfter. 2016. Classification of Swedish learner essays by CEFR levels. In S. Papadima-Sophocleous, L. Bradley & S. Thouësny (Eds), CALL communities and culture – short papers from EUROCALL 2016, pages 456–461.

Peter Wiemer-Hastings and Arthur Graesser. 2000. Select-a-Kibitzer: A computer tool that gives meaningful feedback on student compositions. *Interactive Learning Environments*, 8(2):149–169.

Helen Yannakoudakis and Ted Briscoe. 2012. Modeling coherence in ESOL learner texts. In *Proceedings of the Seventh Workshop on Building Educational Applications Using NLP.* Association for Computational Linguistics, pages 33–43.

Zdeněk Žabokrtský. 2011. Treex – an open-source framework for natural language processing. In *Information Technologies – Applications and Theory*. Univerzita Pavla Jozefa Šafárika v Košiciach, Košice, Slovakia, pages 7–14.

Idiom Type Identification with Smoothed Lexical Features and a Maximum Margin Classifier

Giancarlo D. Salton and **Robert J. Ross** and **John D. Kelleher**
School of Computing
Dublin Institute of Technology
Ireland
`giancarlo.salton@mydit.ie` `{robert.ross,john.d.kelleher}@dit.ie`

Abstract

In our work we address limitations in the state-of-the-art in idiom type identification. We investigate different approaches for a lexical fixedness metric, a component of the state-of-the-art model. We also show that our Machine Learning based approach to the idiom type identification task achieves an F1-score of 0.85, an improvement of 11 points over the state-of-the-art.

1 Introduction

Idioms are a figurative form of language whose meaning is non-compositional, i.e., their meaning cannot be derived from their individual constituents. Examples of idioms, from English, are *pull one's leg* ("to trick someone by telling something untrue") and *hit the mark* ("be successful in an attempt or accurate in a guess").

Any natural language processing (NLP) system must be able to correctly process and interpret idioms (Villavicencio et al., 2005). A common practice in NLP systems is to use an idiom dictionary as part of the process for handling idioms. However, compiling and maintaining a dictionary by hand is expensive and time consuming. Therefore, reliable ways of automatically identifying idioms are important to keep idiom dictionaries in NLP systems up-to-date (Bannard, 2007).

The automatic construction of idiom dictionaries using idiom type identification (i.e., identifying expressions that have an associated idiom[1]) is an active topic of research. Within this field, researchers have mainly followed two approaches: supervised methods that rely on manually encoded knowledge (e.g., (Copestake et al., 2002)

and (Villavicencio et al., 2004)); and unsupervised methods that rely on knowledge extracted from corpora (e.g, (Lin, 1999), (Bannard, 2007) and (Fazly et al., 2009)). Note that to date the supervised methods are idiom-specific and cannot be generalized to a broader class of expressions.

Our research focuses the task of identifying expressions composed of a verb and a noun occurring in its direct object position that have an idiomatic meaning associated with them (Nunberg et al., 1994). These expressions are referred to as VNICs, short for *verb+noun idiomatic combination*. VNICs are the most frequent class of idioms (Villavicencio et al., 2004) and occur across languages (Baldwin and Kim, 2010). We refer to this task as VNIC type identification.

We consider the state-of-the-art method within the field of VNIC type identification to be the work of Fazly et al. (2009). Fazly et al. devise a set of fixedness metrics based on the observation that VNICs are generally more lexically and syntactically fixed than other verb+noun combinations.

In our current work, we identify a number of problems with Fazly et al.'s model and propose modifications to overcome these difficulties. Also, we show that using the fixedness metrics as input features to a Support Vector Machine (SVM) classifier results in an improved method for VNIC type identification compared to Fazly et al.'s model.

The paper is organized as follows: §2 reviews existing fixedness metrics; §3 describes our new fixedness metrics; §4 outlines related work; §5 presents our evaluation methodology; §6 describes the SVM trained using the new fixedness metrics and our results; and §7 presents our conclusions.

2 Fazly et al.'s Fixedness Model

Fazly et al. (2009) present a set of fixedness metrics designed to identify verb+noun pairs that have

---

[1] As distinct from *idiom token identification* which is the task of distinguishing between idiomatic and literal instances of an expression with an associated idiomatic meaning.

Proceedings of Recent Advances in Natural Language Processing, pages 642–651,
Varna, Bulgaria, Sep 4–6 2017.

an associated VNIC. Fazly et al. base their approach on the evidence that idioms are more syntactically and lexically fixed than literal constructions. In this approach all verb+noun pairs receive an overall fixedness score that is a linear combination of a syntactic fixedness metric and a lexical fixedness metric. In the following subsections we present and analyse the details of this approach.

2.1 Syntactic Fixedness

Fazly et al. (2009) propose a metric to capture the syntactic fixedness of idioms based on the observation of Riehemann (2001) that idiomatic expressions are expected to appear more frequently under their canonical syntactic form than literal combinations. Fazly et al. describes three types of syntactic variations that can be characteristic of idiomatic combinations: "Passivization"; "Determiner type"; and "Pluralization". Merging these three syntactic variations, they obtained a set $\mathcal{P}$ of eleven syntactic patterns, see Table 1

No.	Verb	Determiner	Noun
pt_1	v_{active}	DET:*NULL*	$n_{singular}$
pt_2	v_{active}	DET:*a/an*	$n_{singular}$
pt_3	v_{active}	DET:*the*	$n_{singular}$
pt_4	v_{active}	DET:*DEM*	$n_{singular}$
pt_5	v_{active}	DET:*POSS*	$n_{singular}$
pt_6	v_{active}	DET:*NULL*	n_{plural}
pt_7	v_{active}	DET:*the*	n_{plural}
pt_8	v_{active}	DET:*DEM*	n_{plural}
pt_9	v_{active}	DET:*POSS*	n_{plural}
pt_{10}	v_{active}	DET:*other*	$n_{singular,plural}$
pt_{11}	$v_{passive}$	DET:*any*	$n_{singular,plural}$

Table 1: Syntactic patterns: the verb v can be active (v_{act}) or passive (v_{pass}); the determiner (DET) can be NULL, indefinite (*a/an*), definite (*the*), demonstrative (DEM), or possessive (POSS); the noun n can be in singular (n_{sg}) or plural (n_{pl}).

The goal of Fazly et al.'s syntactic fixedness is to compare the behaviour of a target verb+noun pair to the behaviour of a "typical" verb+noun pair. The syntactic behaviour of a "typical" verb+noun pair is defined as a prior distribution over the set $\mathcal{P}$. The syntactic behaviour of the target verb+noun pair is defined as a posterior distribution over the set $\mathcal{P}$ given the pair's constituents. Thus, its syntactic behaviour is calculated as the

posterior estimate for a pattern $pt \in \mathcal{P}^2$. The difference between the behaviour of the target verb+noun pair and the "typical" verb+noun pair is calculated as the divergence between the posterior and the prior distributions over $\mathcal{P}$ as measured using the Kullback-Leibler divergence. Syntactic fixedness takes values in the range $[0, +\infty]$ where larger values denote higher degrees of syntactic fixedness, i.e., the verb+noun pair is more likely to have a VNIC meaning.

2.2 Lexical Fixedness

Typically, idioms do not have lexical variants and, when they have, they are generally unpredictable (Fazly et al., 2009). Therefore, Fazly et al. assume that a verb+noun pair is lexically fixed (and likely to be a VNIC) to the extent that replacing one of its constituents by a semantically similar word does not generate another valid idiomatic combination. Based on this, Fazly et al. propose a measure to capture the degree to which a given verb+noun pair is lexically fixed with respect to the set of its variants. These variants are generated by replacing either the verb or the noun by a word from a set of semantically similar words and is defined as:

$$S_{sim}(v,n) = \{\langle v_i, n\rangle | 1 \leq i \leq K_v\}$$
$$\cup \{\langle v, n_j\rangle | 1 \leq j \leq K_n\}$$

where $\{\langle v_i, n\rangle | 1 \leq i \leq K_v\}$ is the set of similar combinations generated by replacing the verb by a word from the set of K_v most similar verbs; and $\{\langle v, n_j\rangle | 1 \leq j \leq K_n\}$ is the set of similar combinations generated by replacing the noun by a word from the set of K_n most similar nouns.

To measure the strength of the association between the target verb+noun pair's constituents, Pointwise Mutual Information (PMI) (Church et al., 1991) is applied to the pair and to its set of similar combinations $S_{sim}(v,n)$.

The idea behind lexical fixedness is that the target verb+noun pair $\langle v, n\rangle$ is lexically fixed, and likely to be a VNIC, to the extent its PMI deviates from the mean PMI of the set $S_{sim}(v,n) \cup \langle v, n\rangle$. Following this assumption, lexical fixedness of a verb+noun pair is calculated as a standard z-score:

$$\mathcal{F}_{lex}(v,n) = \frac{PMI(v,n) - \overline{PMI}}{s} \tag{1}$$

---

[2] For more details on the definition of the prior and posterior distributions see (Fazly et al., 2009).

where $PMI(v, n)$ is the PMI of the target pair $\langle v, n \rangle$; $\overline{PMI}$ and s are the mean and standard deviation of PMI applied to the verb+noun pairs listed in $S_{sim}(v, n) \cup \langle v, n \rangle$. Lexical fixedness falls into the range of $[-\infty, +\infty]$, where higher values mean higher degrees of lexical fixedness (i.e., the verb+noun pair is more likely to be a VNIC).

2.3 Overall Fixedness

Fazly et al. (2009) merge the lexical and syntactic metrics using a weighted linear combination to score the overall fixedness of a verb+noun pair. Note, lexical and syntactic fixedness have different ranges so we rescale them to the range $[0, 1]$ before combining them. Overall fixedness is defined as follows:

$$\mathcal{F}_{over}(v, n) = \omega \mathcal{F}_{syn}(v, n) + (1 - \omega)\mathcal{F}_{lex}(v, n) \tag{2}$$

where the weight ω controls the relative contribution of each measure for predicting the VNIC's idiomaticity. Values close to 1 means higher degrees of overall fixedness. Moreover, when a particular pair score higher than a certain threshold it is assumed to have an idiomatic expression associated with it, i.e., the pair is identified as a VNIC. In previous work, Fazly et al. used the median value of the test set as the threshold. We see this as problematic and we discuss it in Section 5.2.

2.4 Analysis of Fazly et al.'s Fixedness Model

Fazly et al. have shown their fixedness model to be useful in VNIC type identification. However, their model does have limitations. The definition of lexical fixedness is based on PMI which is known to be biased towards infrequent events (Turney and Pantel, 2010). This property of PMI may lead to undesired results when computing lexical fixedness using counts obtained from a corpus. Furthermore, it is difficult to interpret PMI for those pairs listed in $S_{sim}(v, n)$ that are not observed in the corpus. All pairs are generated by using synonyms (or at least similar related words) and should be acceptable combinations in language. Therefore, the pairs' components should carry information about each other, even if it is small. Thus, we see that just discarding the pairs[3] would affect the result and reduce the power of the model. Therefore, especially for under-resourced

---

[3]In other words, discarding the pairs is the same as setting PMI = 0, following *Information Theory* conventions.

languages with small corpora (where the chance of many pairs in $S_{sim}(v, n)$ not being observed is high), a more efficient way to measure the pair's association strength is needed.

3 Alternative Lexical Fixedness Metrics

In our work we have investigated four ways to replace PMI by other metrics in order to deal with the limitations faced by a lexical fixedness metric based on PMI. In the following we describe these alternatives, and consider how these alternatives can be most effectively combined.

3.1 Probabilities

As mentioned early, a VNIC is expected to be more likely to occur in language than its semantically similar variants. From a probabilistic perspective, we can assume that a VNIC has a higher probability of occurring in language than its semantically similar variants (e.g., literal variants). Following this intuition, we first propose to replace the PMI of a target verb+noun pair by the pair's probability estimated from the corpus as a base for a lexical fixedness metric. The probability for a verb+noun pair is estimated as:

$$P(v, n) = \frac{f(v, n)}{f(*, *)} \tag{3}$$

where $f(v, n)$ is the frequency of the verb+noun pair in a direct object relation (be it a target verb+noun pair or one of its similar variants), occurring in the corpus; and $f(*, *)$ is the frequency of all verb+noun pairs that occur in a direct object relationship in the corpus.

We assume that a target verb+noun pair $\langle v, n \rangle$ is lexically fixed, and likely to be a VNIC, to the extent its probability of occurring in language deviates positively from the mean probability of the set $S_{sim}(v, n) \cup (v, n)$. Thus, we also calculate lexical fixedness based on probabilities as a z-score:

$$\mathcal{F}_{lex} = \frac{P(v, n) - \overline{P}}{s} \tag{4}$$

where $P(v, n)$ is the probability of the target verb+noun pair; and $\overline{P}$ and s are the mean and standard deviation of Equation 3 applied to elements of $S_{sim}(v, n) \cup (v, n)$.

3.2 Smoothed Probabilities

A lexical fixedness metric using raw probabilities may have some of the same disadvantages as a PMI-based metric when estimated with counts from a corpus. For example, when a verb+noun pair listed in $S_{sim}(v, n)$ does not occur in the corpus we end up with a probability of zero. Just because a particular verb+noun pair does not appear in a corpus this does not mean that this combination cannot occur in language at all.

Inspired by the use of smoothing techniques in language modelling research to overcome the problem of unseen n-grams with zero probabilities, for our second metric we cast a VNIC as a bi-gram composed of a verb+noun pair ignoring the words in between the verb and the noun. This framing allows us to apply *Modified Kneser-Ney smoothing*[4] to the probabilities of our verb+noun pairs thereby ensuring that all verb+noun pairs in our experiments (including unseen variants listed in $S_{sim}(v, n)$) have non-zero probabilities[5].

As with the lexical fixedness metric based on probabilities, we stick with the same assumption regarding how likely a verb+noun pair is to be a VNIC. Thus, the lexical fixedness based on smoothed probabilities is calculated using a z-score as in Equation (4).

3.3 Interpolated Back-off Probabilities

When estimating a language model from corpora, we may suffer with occurrences of outliers or under-representative samples of n-grams (Koehn, 2010). This problem happens if the higher-order n-grams are too sparse and, thus, they may be unreliable. The problem is more common when small corpora are used to estimate the model. As we are now considering the verb+noun pair as a bi-gram we may also have to face this problem. To overcome these difficulties, it is a common practice to rely on lower-order n-grams, which are considered more robust, even if the higher-order n-gram have been observed. To do that, one can simply interpolate the high- and low-order n-grams into a single probability and, thus, bring together the benefits of longer contexts in higher-order n-grams and the robustness of low-order n-grams.

A simple but efficient way to interpolate higher- and lower-order n-grams is to first apply *Modified Kneser-Ney smoothing* and then sum the smoothed probabilities. We propose to interpo-

late the probability for the bi-gram composed by a verb+noun pair using an interpolation weight of 0.5 the higher- and lower-order n-grams (i.e. we give the same weight for bi-grams and one-grams).

We keep the same assumption of lexical fixedness based on probabilities regarding how likely a verb+noun pair is to be a VNIC. Therefore, the lexical fixedness based on interpolated back-off probabilities is calculated as in Equation 4.

3.4 Normalized Google Distance

So far, we base our propositions on probabilistic and language models approaches. Nevertheless, there are other metrics that can be used to measure the association strength between two words. Thus, we also investigate the use of Normalized Google Distance (NGD) (Cilibrasi and Vitányi, 2007).

NGD is a metric that relies on page counts returned by a search engine on the Internet to measure the strength of the association between two words. As we are interested in VNICs type identification in monolingual corpora, we decided to experiment with an NGD version that uses counts directly extracted from a corpus rather then returned from a search engine on the Internet. A property of NGD that makes it of interest for us to apply is its smooth space of values, granted by removing the dependency of multiplications in the formula. Our NGD variant[6] is defined as:

$$NGD(v, n) = \frac{max\left\{\log(f(v)), \log(f(n))\right\} - \log(f(v, n))}{\log(f(*, *)) - min\left\{\log(f(v)), \log(f(n))\right\}} \tag{5}$$

where $f(v)$ is the frequency of the verb v occurring with any noun as its direct object; $f(n)$ is the frequency of the noun n occurring as a direct object of any transitive verb in the corpus; $f(v, n)$ is the frequency of the verb+noun pair occurring in a direct object relation; and $f(*, *)$ is the frequency of all verb+noun pairs in a direct object relation.

Lexical fixedness based on NGD also follows the assumption that if the NGD of the target verb+noun pair $\langle v, n \rangle$ deviates positively from the mean NGD of the set $S_{sim}(v, n) \cup (v, n)$ then the pair is likely to be a VNIC. Thus, lexical fixedness based on NGD is also calculated as a z-score following Equation 4.

---

[4]For details on the *Modified Kneser-Ney* please refer to Chen and Goodman (1999).

[5]There are a number of (simpler) smoothing techniques that we could have used, such as add-1 or Laplace smoothing. However, we chose *Modified Kneser-Ney smoothing* as it is considered the state-of-the-art smoothing technique for n-grams, for more see (Brychcín and Konopík, 2014).

[6]Where we also set $\log 0 = 0$, following *Information Theory* conventions, when any of the frequencies involved in NGD calculation is 0.

3.5 Converting the Fixedness Metrics into Classification Models

In the previous section we presented four new lexical fixedness metrics. Similar to Fazly et al., we can use each of these lexical fixedness metrics to compute an overall fixedness score for a verb+noun pair by combining each of them with Fazly et al.'s syntactic fixedness metric using a weighted linear combination as in Equation 2. In the case of our proposed metrics, we replace the original Fazly et al.'s lexical fixedness with one of our own proposed metrics. Including Fazly et al.'s model described in Section 2, these combinations of syntactic and lexical metrics give us the following five models:

1. **Fazly et al.'s model**: Fazly et al.'s syntactic + Fazly et al.'s lexical
2. **Syntactic+Probabilities**: Fazly et al.'s syntactic + Lexical based on probabilities
3. **Syntactic+Smoothed** Fazly et al.'s syntactic + Lexical based on smoothed probabilities
4. **Syntactic+Interpolated**: Fazly et al.'s syntactic + Lexical based on interpolated back-off probabilities
5. **Syntactic+NGD**: Fazly et al.'s syntactic + Lexical based on NGD

While these models provide a real valued measure of the fixedness of a given verb+noun pair, we need to apply a thresholding function to construct a useful classifier. We do this using the logistic function: The logistic function is defined as:

$$ sigmoid(x) = \frac{1}{1 + \mathrm{e}^{-(x)}} \qquad (6) $$

We applied a different threshold to each of the above models. All the pairs that scored above the threshold for a model were classified as VNICs by that model. The process of setting the threshold for each model is described in Subsection 5.2.

4 Related Work

Although this paper focuses on idiom type identification it is worth noting that there has been a substantial amount of research on idiom token identification. Peng et al. (2014) frame idiom token identification in terms of modeling the global lexical context (essentially using topic models to distinguish idiomatic and literal uses of expressions). Salton et al. (2016) study the use of distributed sentential semantics generated by Sent2Vec (Kiros et al., 2015) to train a general classifier that can take any sentence containing a candidate expression and predict whether the usage of that expression is literal or idiomatic. More recently, Peng and Feldman (2017) presented a model using word embeddings to analyze the context a particular expression is inserted in and predict if its usage is literal or idiomatic.

Turning to the general problem of identifying multiword expressions (MWEs) with associated non-compositional meanings research recent includes Yazdani et al. (2015) model for noun compounds in English and Farahmand and Henderson (2016) work on identifying of collocations. Focusing on the specific task of idiom type identification, Muzny and Zettlemoyer (2013) describes a model that classifies multi-word Wiktionary entries as idiomatic or literal. The model uses a number of lexical and graph based features to calculate the relatedness between the words in the entry and the definition. Muzny and Zettlemoyer (2013) model relies on the Wiktionary structure both in terms of the entry-definition relationship and the definition of the lexical features. Consequently, porting the model for use on an unstructured mono-lingual corpus is non-trivial. Also, although we consider Fazly et al. (2009) the state-of-the-art in VNIC type identification in English, Senaldi et al. (2016) present a model using distributed semantics to identify idiom types in Italian. The authors analysed the differences between idiomatic and literal phrases in embedding spaces, in a similar fashion to lexical fixedness.

Also, previous work has used smoothing and counts obtained from the web for infrequent combinations of words. Keller and Lapata (2003) showed that the web can be used to obtain reliable counts for unseen bigrams but did not evaluate their work on idiom type identification. Ramisch et al. (2010) used the web as a corpus to obtain better counts for n-grams in a language model setting to identify English noun compounds.

5 Evaluating the Classification Models

In order to assess the performance of the classification models we compare them in a classification task over a balanced dataset. We proceed by explaining our data preparation (Subsection 5.1) and describing the methodology to set the thresholds for each model (Subsection 5.2). Finally, we present and discuss the results (Subsection 5.3).

5.1 Data Preparation

We started our data preparation by parsing the written portion of the BNC corpus (Burnard, 2007) using the Stanford Parser (Manning et al., 2014). From the parsed sentences we extracted all verb+noun pairs that occurred in at least one of the syntactic patterns in Table 1. For these extracted verb+noun pairs we recorded the total count of the pair and the total count of the pair in each pattern.

Following the first step, we proceeded by applying Fazly et al.'s syntactic and Fazly et al.'s lexical fixedness metrics and our modified versions of lexical fixedness to all pairs given the recorded counts. To generate the similar combinations required by the lexical fixedness metrics, we used the automatically built thesaurus of Lin (1998). As reported by Fazly et al. (2009), there is little variation on the results for a K number of similar combinations when $20 \leq K \leq 100$, where $K = (K_v + K_n)$. We thus choose $K = 40$ for all lexical models, with $K_v = K_n$[7].

After calculating all fixedness metrics, we kept only those verb+noun combinations which occur at least 10 times in the corpus (note that we did not take into account the determiners introducing the noun). We expect this constraint to balance the distributions of all models tested. Range normalization was then performed on all fixedness metrics before the five overall fixedness scores were determined. To set the weighted linear combination parameter ω, we choose the same value ($\omega = 0.6$) reported by Fazly et al. as the most reasonable choice for all overall models.

Given the five overall scores calculated in the previous step, we selected the top 1,000 verb+noun pairs ranked by each model. Using this methodology, we found only 2,091 different pairs among the 5 lists, i.e., there is an overlap among all metrics. For each of these 2,091 verb+noun pairs, we checked in the Cambridge Idioms[8] and the Collins COBUILD[9] dictionaries whether the verb+noun pair was listed as an idiom[10]. Of the 2,091 pairs, a total of 414 verb+noun pairs were found to be VNICs (and thus, 1,677 were literal combinations). Using this labelled set of 2,091

---

[7]This means we generate 20 similar pairs by changing the verb constituent and 20 similar pairs by changing the noun constituent, with 40 similar combinations in total.

[8]http://dictionary.cambridge.org/

[9]http://www.collinsdictionary.com/

[10]If a verb+noun pair was listed as an idiom in at least one of these two dictionaries we considered it to be a VNIC.

Overall Metric	Threshold
Fazly et al.'s Model	0.63
Syntactic+Probabilities	0.64
Syntactic+Smoothed	0.61
Syntactic+Interpolated	0.62
Syntactic+NGD	0.62

Table 2: Thresholds for each overall metric determined based on the F1-scores on the "Training Set" after applying the logistic function to the scores.

pairs we created a training and test set.

Fazly et al. used a balanced test set for their evaluations. In order to make our evaluation comparable we also created a balanced test set. To generate our test set we selected VNICs and literal pairs from the 2,091 pairs found in the previous step. From the 414 VNICs, we constrained the selection process so that the selected VNICs occurred with similar frequencies in the corpus as the literal pairs (which were extracted from the 1,677 remaining pairs). This process resulted in a test set of 95 VNICs and 95 literal pairs (called "Test-Set"). The remaining 319 VNICs were held as training data in which we added another 319 verb+noun non-idiomatic pairs, also extracted from the remaining literal pairs (once again with similar frequencies), to create a balanced "Training-Set".

5.2 Setting the Thresholds

In order to create a VNIC type classification model from a fixedness metric we need to apply a threshold to the scores. Fazly et al. choose the median value of their test set as their threshold. We see this as problematic as this provides the model with information about the distribution of the test set and thus biases the evaluation. To avoid this problem, we performed a K-fold cross-validation (with $k = 3$) on our "Training-Set" to find the threshold for each model that maximized the F1-score on the set. This step gave us 5 thresholds, one for each model (see Table 2[11]).

Each model was run on the test set and classified verb+noun pairs with scores greater or equal than the threshold as VNICs and, otherwise, as non-idioms. Table 3 presents the Precision, Recall and

---

[11]In fact, Fazly et al. recognized the use of the median value as problematic and suggested that a suitable threshold should be determined based on development data.

Model	Pr.	Rec.	F1
Syntactic+Smoothed	**0.83**	**0.78**	**0.77**
Fazly et al.'s Model	0.83	0.75	0.74
Syntactic+Probabilities	0.82	0.73	0.70
Syntactic+Interpolated	0.79	0.64	0.59
Syntactic+NGD	0.78	0.62	0.56

Table 3: Results in terms of precision (Pr.), recall (Rc.) and F1-score (F1) ordered by their F1-scores compared to Standard Fixedness as baseline.

F1-score of the models, ordered by F1-scores.

5.3 Discussion of the Linear Models

Analysing the results in Table 3, we can observe that the worst performance is from the Syntactic+NGD model. We believe the poor results are due to the fact that we are limiting the NGD formulation to consider the counts obtained in the corpus and thus reducing the power of the model. The second worst result is from the Syntactic+Interpolated model, which is slightly higher than the worst model. The intuition for the low results is that, when we apply the interpolation after smoothing the probabilities, we are actually reducing too much the difference between the probability of our target pair and the mean probability of the pair and its variants. In other words, we are over-smoothing the probability distributions across each target pair and its variants.

The Syntactic+Probabilities model, has notable higher scores than the two worst models but it still performs worse than Fazly et al.'s Model. We believe that the difficulties encountered when the similar verb+noun pairs does not occur in the corpus, framed as one of the limitations of the state-of-the-art, are somewhat accentuated when applying raw probabilities as the basis for the lexical fixedness metric. Fazly et al.'s Model scored the second best result over the fixedness models.

The best fixedness model is the Syntactic+Smoothed model. Analysing this model one can also point that the difference between the probability of the target and the mean probability of its variants should be reduced and thus incurring on the same problem as the Syntactic+Interpolated model. Nevertheless, we believe the higher results for this model are due to the fact that when we only smooth the probabilities and not interpolate them, the deviations captured on the z-score are closer to the true deviation. We credit these good

results to the use of smoothing to save probability mass for the unseen pairs as it enabled the metric to approximate the true degree of deviation in this lexical fixedness metric. In addition, our results were tested for significance by pairing all the models and applying McNemar's test (McNemar, 1947) to those pairs. We found all $p < 0.05$.

6 Support Vector Machines

An analysis of the scores returned by the fixedness metrics revealed a strong non-linearity in the decision boundary between VNIC and non-idiom verb+noun pairs. One limitation of the VNIC type classifiers in §5 is the weighted linear combination used to merge the syntactic and lexical metrics. This linear approach cannot model non-linear decision boundaries. To overcome this limitation, we trained an SVM classifier (Vapnik, 1995) using the fixedness metrics as inputs.

The SVM is a classification tool designed to find the optimal hyperplane that maximizes the distance between two classes (Zaki and Meira Jr., 2014). An SVM projects the input features into a higher-dimensional feature space and attempts to find a linear separating hyperplane in this higher-dimensional space. The intuition is that a linear separating hyperplane may exist in the higher-dimensional feature space even though the classes are not linearly separable in the original input feature space (Kelleher et al., 2015). For the cases where the classes are not perfectly linearly-separable even in the higher-dimensional feature space the SVM introduces "slack variables" for each datapoint which indicates how much that point violates the separable hyperplane. Then, the goal of the SVM training turns into finding the hyperplane with the maximum margin and that also minimizes the slack terms. This new SVM structure is called a "Soft-margin SVM".

The task of training an SVM with a linear kernel is usually framed as a constrained quadratic programming problem in the dual space. However, in its native form, it is an unconstrained empirical loss minimization including a penalty term for the classifier being learned in direct space (Shalev-Shwartz et al., 2007). Framed this way, SVM can be trained by solving this minimization problem applying Stochastic Gradient Descent (SGD) (Bottou, 2010).

6.1 Building SVM Models from Fixedness Metrics

We used Scikit-Learn (Pedregosa et al., 2011) to train a soft-margin SVM with a linear kernel using SGD training and the fixedness metrics as input features. The training algorithm required two hyper-parameters to be set: an α value (a constant that multiplies the regularization term) and the regularization function. To set these we performed a grid search using k-fold cross-validation (with $k = 3$) over the "Training-Set" using all metrics as features. Based on the results, we set $\alpha = 0.0001$ and the regularization function to be the L2-norm. This step gave us a model which we called "SVM-All". We trained it for 20 epochs.

We also performed feature selection using the weights values of a fitted SVM (Guyon et al., 2002). We selected the three features with the highest weights in "SVM-All": Fazly et al.'s syntactic fixedness, Fazly et al.'s lexical fixedness and the lexical fixedness based on probabilities. Another grid search for the best parameters was performed using k-fold cross-validation (with $k = 3$) over the "Training-Set" using only these three features. Based on the results, we set $\alpha = 0.01$ and set the regularization function to be the L1-norm. This step gave us a model which we called "SVM-Select". We trained this for 20 epochs.

As a matter of comparison, we trained a SVM model using only the original Fazly et al.'s metrics as features. Once again, we performed a grid search using k-fold cross validation (with $k = 3$) over the "Training-Set" to set the α parameter and the regularization function. For this model we set $\alpha = 0.0001$ and the regularization function to be the L2-norm. We called this 2-feature SVM model "SVM-Fazly" and we trained it for 20 epochs.

6.2 Discussion of the SVM Models

Table 4 presents the results of the SVM models, Fazly et al.'s model and the Syntactic+Smoothed (our best linear model). Two SVM models outperformed the fixedness models in the classification task. Surprisingly, the results obtained by the SVM-All model are just slightly higher than those obtained by the fixedness models. We believe the high-dimensional space obtained by this 7-feature SVM is too sparse and thus the classification problem become more difficult. The best general result is from the SVM-Select model. In addition to that, we can observe that the SVM model using only

Model	Pr.	Rec.	F1
SVM-Select	**0.87**	**0.85**	**0.85**
SVM-All	0.80	0.78	0.78
Syntactic+Smoothed	0.83	0.78	0.77
Fazly et al.'s Model	0.83	0.75	0.74
SVM-Fazly	0.83	0.73	0.71

Table 4: Precision, Recall and F1-Score results for the 3 SVM models and the 2-best linear models: Fazly et al.'s model Syntactic+Smoothed model.

Fazly et al.'s original set of fixedness features had the worst performance in terms of F1-score.

A final point worth considering is the type of errors each of the models is prone to. Taking the VNIC class as the positive class, most of the errors for the two SVM models and our Syntactic+Smoothed models were false negatives (they classified VNICs as non-VNICS). By comparison, the other models all had higher rates of false positives. In our opinion, for this context, false positives are more problematic than false negatives because a false positive may result in a non-idiom being included in an idiom dictionary. In conclusion, not only do our SVM and Syntactic+Smoothed models outperform the other models in terms of F1 but they are also less prone to false positives. Once again, our results were tested for significance by pairing the models and applying McNemar's test to pairs of models. We found all $p < 0.05$.

7 Conclusions

In this paper we presented four different models to overcome the limitations of the state-of-the-art model for VNIC type identification. We took a probabilistic approach by reinterpreting a previous claim that a VNIC is more likely to appear in language use then its semantically similar variants. In addition, we experimented with a different association measure (Normalized Google Distance) applied to a monolingual corpus.

We have shown that a fixedness model using a lexical metric based on smoothed probabilities out-performs the state-of-the-art model in VNIC type identification. At the same time, we showed that feeding the fixedness metrics to an SVM also improves the F1-score on the same VNIC type identification task by 11 points. We see this work as a significant contribution that will lead to improved models for idiom type identification.

Acknowledgments

This research was partly funded by the ADAPT Centre. The ADAPT Centre is funded under the SFI Research Centres Programme (Grant 13/RC/2106) and is co-funded under the European Regional Development Fund. Giancarlo D. Salton would like to thank CAPES ("Coordenação de Aperfeiçoamento de Pessoal de Nível Superior") for his Science Without Borders scholarship, proc n. 9050-13-2.

References

Timothy Baldwin and Su Nam Kim. 2010. Multiword expressions. In Nitin Indurkhya and Fred J. Damerau, editors, *Handbook of Natural Language Processing, Second Edition*, CRC Press, Taylor and Francis Group, Boca Raton, FL.

Colin Bannard. 2007. A measure of syntactic flexibility for automatically identifying multiword expressions in corpora. In *Proceedings of the Workshop on a Broader Perspective on Multiword Expressions (MWE '07)*. pages 1–8.

Léon Bottou. 2010. Large-scale machine learning with stochastic gradient descent. In *Proceedings of the 19th International Conference on Computational Statistics (COMPSTAT'2010)*. pages 177–187.

Tomáš Brychcín and Miloslav Konopík. 2014. Semantic spaces for improving language modeling. *Comput. Speech Lang.* 28(1):192–209.

Lou Burnard. 2007. Reference guide for the british national corpus (xml edition). Technical report, http://www.natcorp.ox.ac.uk/.

Stanley F. Chen and Joshua Goodman. 1999. An empirical study of smoothing techniques for language modeling. *Computer Speech and Language* (13):359–394.

Kenneth Church, William Gale, Patrick Hanks, and Donald Hindle. 1991. Using statistics in lexical analysis. In *Lexical Acquisition: Exploiting On-Line Resources to Build a Lexicon*. Erlbaum, pages 115–164.

Rudi L. Cilibrasi and Paul M.B. Vitányi. 2007. The google similarity distance. *IEEE Transactions On Knowledge And Data Engineering* 19(3):370–383.

Ann Copestake, Fabre Lambeau, Aline Villavicencio, Francis Bond, Timothy Baldwin, Ivan A. Sag, and Dan Flickinger. 2002. Multiword expressions: linguistic precision and reusability. In *Proceedings of the Third International Conference on Language Resources and Evaluation (LREC-2002)*. pages 1942–1947.

Meghdad Farahmand and James Henderson. 2016. Modeling the non-substitutability of multiword expressions with distributional semantics and a log-linear model. In *Proceedings of the 12th Workshop on Multiword Expressions, MWE@ACL 2016, Berlin, Germany, August 11, 2016.*.

Afsanesh Fazly, Paul Cook, and Suzanne Stevenson. 2009. Unsupervised type and token identification of idiomatic expressions. In *Computational Linguistics*, volume 35, pages 61–103.

Isabelle Guyon, Jason Weston, Stephen Barnhill, and Vladimir Vapnik. 2002. Gene selection for cancer classification using support vector machines. *Machine Learning* 46(1-3):389–422.

John D. Kelleher, Brian Mac Namee, and Aoife D'Arcy. 2015. *Fundamentals of Machine Learning for Predictive Data Analytics: Algorithms, Word Examples and Case Studies*. MIT Press.

Frank Keller and Mirella Lapata. 2003. Using the web to obtain frequencies for unseen bigrams. *Comput. Linguist.* 29(3):459–484. https://doi.org/10.1162/089120103322711604.

Ryan Kiros, Yukun Zhu, Ruslan R Salakhutdinov, Richard Zemel, Raquel Urtasun, Antonio Torralba, and Sanja Fidler. 2015. Skip-thought vectors. In *Advances in Neural Information Processing Systems 28*. pages 3276–3284.

Philipp Koehn. 2010. *Statistical Machine Translation*. Cambridge University Press, New York, NY, USA.

Dekang Lin. 1998. Automatic retrieval and clustering of similar words. In *Proceedings of the 17th International Conference on Computational Linguistics and the 36th Annual Meeting of the Association for Computational Linguistics (COLING-ACL'98)*. pages 768–774.

Dekang Lin. 1999. Automatic identification of non-compositional phrases. In *Proceedings of the 37th Annual Meeting of the Association for Computational Linguistics on Computational Linguistics*. pages 317–324.

Christopher D. Manning, Mihai Surdeanu, John Bauer, Jenny Finkel, Steven J. Bethard, and David McClosky. 2014. The Stanford CoreNLP natural language processing toolkit. In *Proceedings of 52nd Annual Meeting of the Association for Computational Linguistics: System Demonstrations*. pages 55–60. http://www.aclweb.org/anthology/P/P14/P14-5010.

Quinn McNemar. 1947. Note on the sampling error of the difference between correlated proportions or percentages. *Psychometrika* 12(2):153–157. https://doi.org/10.1007/BF02295996.

Grace Muzny and Luke S. Zettlemoyer. 2013. Automatic idiom identification in wiktionary. In *Proceedings of the 2013 Conference on Empirical Methods in Natural Language Processing, EMNLP 2013,*

18-21 October 2013, Grand Hyatt Seattle, Seattle, Washington, USA, A meeting of SIGDAT, a Special Interest Group of the ACL. pages 1417–1421.

Geoffrey Nunberg, Ivan A. Sag, and Thomas Wasow. 1994. Idioms. *Language* 3(70):491–538.

F. Pedregosa, G. Varoquaux, A. Gramfort, V. Michel, B. Thirion, O. Grisel, M. Blondel, P. Prettenhofer, R. Weiss, V. Dubourg, J. Vanderplas, A. Passos, D. Cournapeau, M. Brucher, M. Perrot, and E. Duchesnay. 2011. Scikit-learn: Machine learning in Python. *Journal of Machine Learning Research* 12:2825–2830.

Jing Peng and Anna Feldman. 2017. *Automatic Idiom Recognition with Word Embeddings*, Springer International Publishing, Cham, pages 17–29.

Jing Peng, Anna Feldman, and Ekaterina Vylomova. 2014. Classifying idiomatic and literal expressions using topic models and intensity of emotions. In *Proceedings of the 2014 Conference on Empirical Methods in Natural Language Processing (EMNLP).* pages 2019–2027.

Carlos Ramisch, Aline Villavicencio, and Christian Boitet. 2010. Web-based and combined language models: A case study on noun compound identification. In *Proceedings of the 23rd International Conference on Computational Linguistics: Posters.* Association for Computational Linguistics, Stroudsburg, PA, USA, COLING '10, pages 1041–1049.

Susanne Riehemann. 2001. *A Constructional Approach to Idioms and Word Formation.* Ph.D. thesis, Stanford University.

Giancarlo D. Salton, Robert J. Ross, and John D. Kelleher. 2016. Idiom token classification using sentential distributed semantics. In *Proceedings of the 54th Annual Meeting on Association for Computational Linguistics.*

Marco Silvio Giuseppe Senaldi, Gianluca E. Lebani, and Alessandro Lenci. 2016. Lexical variability and compositionality: Investigating idiomaticity with distributional semantic models. In *Proceedings of the 12th Workshop on Multiword Expressions, MWE@ACL 2016, Berlin, Germany, August 11, 2016..*

Shai Shalev-Shwartz, Yoram Singer, and Nathan Srebro. 2007. Pegasos: Primal estimated sub-gradient solver for svm. In *Proceedings of the 24th International Conference on Machine Learning.* pages 807–814.

Peter D. Turney and Patrick Pantel. 2010. From frequency to meaning: Vector space models of semantics. *Journal of Artificial Intelligence Research* (37):141–188.

Vladimir N. Vapnik. 1995. *The Nature of Statistical Learning Theory.* Springer-Verlag New York, Inc., New York, NY, USA.

Aline Villavicencio, Francis Bond, Anna Korhonen, and Diana McCarthy. 2005. Editorial: Introduction to the special issue on multiword expressions: Having a crack at a hard nut. *Comput. Speech Lang.* 19(4):365–377.

Aline Villavicencio, Ann Copestake, Benjamin Waldron, and fabre Lambeau. 2004. Lexical encoding of mwes. In *Proceedings of the Workshop on Multiword Expressions: Integrating Processing (MWE '04).* pages 80–87.

Majid Yazdani, Meghdad Farahmand, and James Henderson. 2015. Learning semantic composition to detect non-compositionality of multiword expressions. In *Proceedings of the 2015 Conference on Empirical Methods in Natural Language Processing, EMNLP 2015, Lisbon, Portugal, September 17-21, 2015.* pages 1733–1742.

Mohammed J. Zaki and Wagner Meira Jr. 2014. *Data Mining and Analysis: Fundamental Concepts and Algorithms.* Cambridge University Press.

A Calibration Method for the Evaluation of Sentiment Analysis

F. Sharmila Satthar, Roger Evans and Gulden Uchyigit
Computing, Engineering and Mathematics
University of Brighton
Brighton, UK
{F.Satthar,R.P.Evans,G.Uchyigit}@brighton.ac.uk

Abstract

Sentiment analysis is the computational task of extracting sentiment from a text document – for example whether it expresses a positive, negative or neutral opinion. Various approaches have been introduced in recent years, using a range of different techniques to extract sentiment information from a document. Measuring these methods against a gold standard dataset is a useful way to evaluate such systems. However, different sentiment analysis techniques represent sentiment values in different ways, such as discrete categorical classes or continuous numerical sentiment scores. This creates a challenge for evaluating and comparing such systems; in particular assessing numerical scores against datasets that use fixed classes is difficult, because the numerical outputs have to be mapped onto the ordered classes. This paper proposes a novel calibration technique that uses precision vs. recall curves to set class thresholds to optimize a continuous sentiment analyser's performance against a discrete gold standard dataset. In experiments mapping a continuous score onto a three-class classification of movie reviews, we show that calibration results in a substantial increase in f-score when compared to a non-calibrated mapping.

1 Introduction

Sentiment analysis is the computational study of people's opinions, appraisals, emotional attitudes toward entities, events and their attributes. The sentiment analysis task involves classifying texts according to the sentiment content they contain.

Sentiment analysis is a very active research area in natural language processing, with many research projects working on building sentiment classifiers using different techniques and algorithms. Evaluation is an important process when estimating the performance of text/data classification in information retrieval or natural language processing systems. The accuracy of a (binary) classifier is typically measured based on its *precision*, *recall* and *f-score* values when applied to a gold standard dataset. This approach has been adopted for the evaluation of sentiment analysis systems too (Turney, 2002; Pang et al., 2002; Nasukawa and Yi, 2003; Prabowo and Thelwall, 2009), but it is complicated by the fact that sentiment analysis is usually a multi-class classification task.

Many sentiment analysis approaches focus on three classes such as *positive*, *negative* and *neutral*. However Saif et al. (2016) introduced an extra class, in addition to the neutral class, called *mixed-sentiment*, which is a mixture of positive and negative opinions, while Pang and Lee (2005) and Nakov et al. (2016) explored 4 or 5 star scales/classifications. To evaluate these types of multi-class classification tasks, precision, recall and f-score values are calculated for each class separately, and the performance measures for the whole system are then calculated by averaging those values using micro or macro-averaging (Prabowo and Thelwall, 2009).

Most supervised machine learning methods for sentiment analysis produce categorical outputs such as *positive*, *negative* and *neutral*, with no assumptions about the relationship between classes; they simply map texts into classes by associating text features with class labels. But other multi-class systems use rated or scaled methods so that their categorical outputs are implicitly ordered in a natural 'sentiment order' based on sentiment polarity and/or magnitude/intensity, such as the fol-

Proceedings of Recent Advances in Natural Language Processing, pages 652–660,
Varna, Bulgaria, Sep 4–6 2017.

lowing examples:

Positive > Neutral > Negative

Strong-Positive > Positive > Weak-Positive >
Neutral>
Weak-Negative > Negative > Strong-Negative

3 stars > 2 stars > 1 star

In addition, some sentiment analysis applications are based more explicitly on sentiment scores, rather than sentiment classes, and produce numerical values with positive and negative signs as the output for a given text, such as $+0.987$, $-0.786 \ldots$ or $+187$, $-243 \ldots$ etc. Such methods typically use the sign to indicate the polarity of the given text and numerical values to define the sentiment strength (generally over a system-dependent range), with a sentiment value of 0 indicating a neutral text. A simple mapping from such scores to a 3-class sentiment model just uses the sign (+,0,-) to identify sentiment classes (positive, neutral, negative). However, there is no correspondingly simple way to use the magnitude to extend this to more classes (such as *'strong positive'*, *'weak positive'*, *'positive'* ... etc.), and no clear justification for the implicit claim that *neutral* is a single point (0). This paper introduces a method to address these concerns, by calibrating the mapping from a numerical score to a semantic class in a way that optimises the system's performace as a multi-class classifier.

To transform a numeric scale to an ordinal (categorical) scale, boundaries (upper and lower) for each sentiment class needed to be identified from the given numeric scale. These boundary values are 'cut-off values' for the sentiment classes, and are the parameters for a multi-class sentiment classification system based on the numerical scores. This paper proposes new techniques to assign cut-off values for each class using a learning-based evaluation technique. This transformation allows us to both optimise and evaluate a system that gives numeric outputs against a gold standard dataset that contains fixed categorical outputs.

We use evaluation performance measures (precision and recall) on a training subset of the dataset to adjust the parameters to produce an optimal result, by using Precision vs Recall (PR) curve visualisation. The parameters are optimised to give the best performance on the training set, and then evaluated using test set. In addition we can determine how far misclassified texts deviate from actual classes in multi-class ordered classification

tasks, by computing macro-averaged mean absolute error which is the popular approach for ordinal classification (Nakov et al., 2016; Baccianella et al., 2009; Gaudette and Japkowicz, 2009).

We demonstrate our technique for tuning the parameters using the *Galadriel* sentiment analysis system (Satthar, 2015), which we built for sentiment analysis using an inheritance-based lexicon. *Galadriel* is an example of a class of systems which calculate sentiment scores by combining raw lexical scores using a range of arithmetic rules (summming, scaling, averaging etc.). The final output of *Galadriel* for a text is a signed real number which reflects sentiments expressed by the lexical items in quite a complex way, making the intepretation of scores as classes challenging. The calibration method achieves this mapping in an optimal way.

In this paper, section 2 discusses relevant previous research, in particular pre-evaluation processes and some general methods involved in sentiment classification (section 2.1) and use of the PR curve for evaluation (rsection 2.2). In section 3, we present our novel techniques for tuning the parameters. In section 4, we present our experiments with the *Galadriel* system, and the results of optimising cut-off values for sentiment classes. Section 5 compares the evaluation results using the cut-off values which are computed in the previous section with evaluation without calibration. Finally, section 6 provides the conclusion.

2   Related Work

2.1   Approaches to sentiment classification

Sentiment classification is most simply expressed as a two-class (*positive* and *negative*) or three-class (including *neutral*) classification problem. In recent work, sentiment analysis researchers have also been interested in greater than three class classification such as *strong positive* to *strong negative* and *scale-1* to *scale-5* (Aly, 2005; Lee and Grafe, 2010; Pang and Lee, 2005).

For supervised machine learning methods, the classes come directly from the labelled training data, which means that such systems can directly produce *positive* or *negative* labelled outputs without any direct intepretation of what the classes 'mean' (Pang et al., 2002; Hsu et al., 2010). Similarly, unsupervised learning methods directly produce *positive* or *negative* labelled outputs using different techniques and algorithms such as k-

Word	Bing Liu	Harvard GI	Vader	SentiWordNet	SenticNet	Taboada
good	+1	POS	+1.9	0.75 (POS)	+0.883	+3
glad	+1	POS	+2.0	0.5 (POS)	+0.413	+2
incapable	−1	NEG	−1.6	0.625 (NEG)	−0.736	−1
sad	−1	NEG	−2.1	0.25(NEG)	−0.306	−2
bad	−1	NEG	−2.5	0.875(NEG)	−0.367	−3

Table 1: Some lexical entries with their semantic orientation according to different lexicon dictionaries.

means, TF-IDF and PMI-IR algorithms (Turney, 2002; Zagibalov and Carroll, 2008; Unnisa et al., 2016), but again without a clear interpretation of the classes identified. Lexicon-based approaches (as well as some unsupervised learning methods methods such as Turney (2002)) have proceeded by calculating the semantic orientation (a numerical score) and deciding the polarity of the document depending on its sign and the sentiment strength based on its magnitude. Such methods calculate the semantic orientation of a document by the aggregating semantic orientation of words or phrases, using various arithmetic combinations of scores (Taboada et al., 2011; Palanisamy et al., 2013).

The sentiment analysis approaches based on semantic orientation use different semantic dictionaries (lists of sentiment words/lexical items with their semantic orientation or sentiment scores) to determine each individual word's semantic orientation. The range of the sentiment scores assigned to words in these dictionaries varies considerably. For instance, Taboada et al. (2011) used a dictionary with a sentiment score range between −5 and +5 whereas Esuli and Sebastiani (2007) has positive and sentiment words with scores between 0 and 1. Table 1 shows the different semantic scores for some common sentiment words in a number of recent semantic dictionaries[1]. In addition, the aggregation operations involved also vary, and do not always have straightforward semantic interpretations (for example, sentiment negation is achieved in some systems but inverting the score polarity, and in others by shifting the value towards zero). Comparing the outputs of such systems, or evaluating them against a gold standard, is therefore, very challenging.

2.2 The Precision vs. Recall Curve

The use of graphical representations to visualise classifer performance is well-established. The Receiver Operation Characteristic (ROC) curve, originally used in signal detection theory (Egan, 1975), has also been adopted to visualise classifier performances in text classification. The ROC is created by plotting true positive rates (TPR) against false positive rates (FPR) at various thresholds, and the area under the curve has been used as a measure of accuracy in evaluation methods. More recently, researchers have used the Precision-Recall (PR) curve, which plots precision against the true positive rate, and taken the area under this curve as a measure of performance (West et al., 2014; Manning and Schütze, 1999; Raghavan et al., 1989). Both curves can be used to visualise classifier performance; however, PR curves produce a more informative visualisation, particularly for highly imbalanced data sets (Davis and Goadrich, 2006). Moreover, a PR curve is more useful for problems where one class is considered to be more important than other classes. On the other hand, there are issues with PR curves too, for example unlike in ROC space it is complicated to interpolate two points in PR space. Furthermore, the area under a PR curve produces the arithmetic mean, whereas the also commonly used f-score is the harmonic mean of precision and recall[2]. However, these issues do not affect this work as in our calibration method we only use visualisation of the PR curve to set values for boundaries of sentiment classes.

---

[1]Bing Liu's opinion lexicon: `www.cs.uic.edu/~liub/`; Harvard General Inquirer: `www.wjh.harvard.edu/~inquirer/`; Vader Sentiment: `github.com/cjhutto/vaderSentiment/tree/master/vaderSentiment`; SentiWordNet: `www.sentiwordnet.isti.cnr.it/`; SenticNet: `www.sentic.net/downloads/`; Taboada et al. (2011)'s lexicon kindly made available by the authors for this research.

[2]Such issues can be mitigated by plotting a Precision-Recall-Gain curve (Flach and Kull, 2015) and considering its associated area. However this is beyond the scope of this paper.

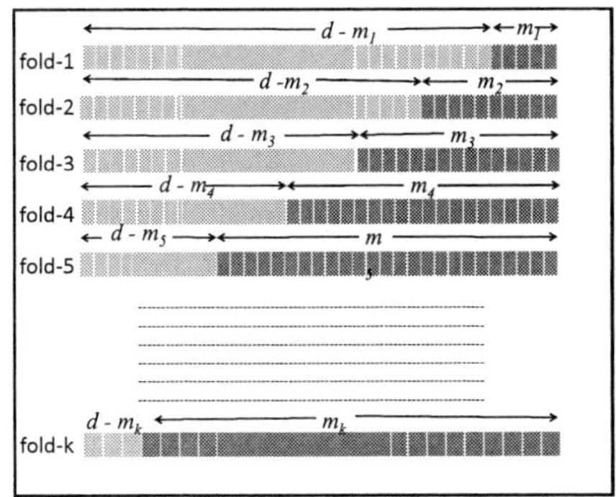
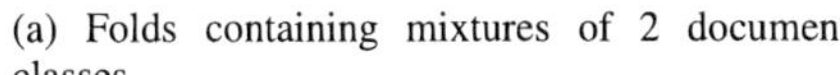
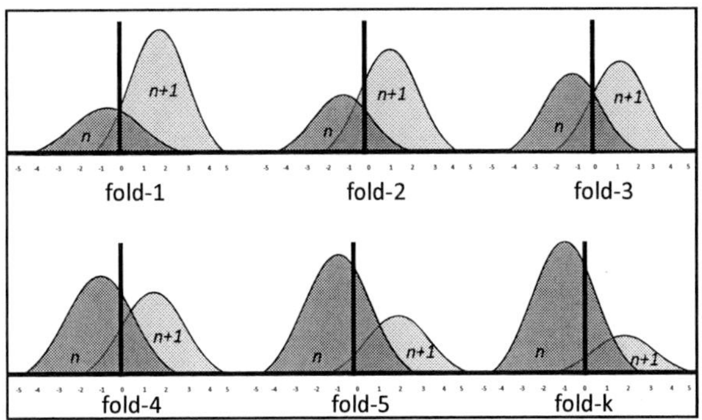

(a) Folds containing mixtures of 2 document classes

(b) Example histograms and cut-off points for different balances between n^{th} and $n+1^{th}$ classes in different folds

Figure 1: k-fold class mixtures, to produce PR curves for each cut-off candidate

3   A Calibration Method for Cut-off Values of Sentiment Classes

In this section, we introduce a calibration method for setting sentiment class cut-off values from numerical sentiment scores using learning-based techniques. We use a training data set to assign boundaries of sentiment classes, where the classes have a natural 'sentiment order'. Our method is inspired by the cross-validation method. We calculate upper and lower boundary values of each sentiment class at a time in sentiment order. For instance, in a three-class classification, we first calculate boundary values for *negative* (1st class), then *neutral* (2nd class) and then *positive* (3rd class). We then determine the optimal *cut-off* value between these two boundaries to delimit the classes.

To compute the cut-off value, first we reduce the problem of multi-classes and convert it into the standard binary class problem. That is, we consider the nth order class and the $(n + 1)^{th}$ order class to compute the cut-off values between those two classes. We select documents belonging to the nth and $(n + 1)^{th}$ classes from the training dataset and run our semantic classifier over these two sets. As a result, we get a set of numerical scores, one for each document in each class. We consider the maximum score for the nth class, Max_n, and the minimum score for the $(n + 1)^{th}$ class, Min_{n+1}. The cut-off value, $C_{n/n+1}$, for those two classes should lie between these two scores[3]. We plot different PR curves for candidate cut-off values between these scores to determine the cut-off value

which gives optimum performance.

For a given candidate cut-off value, the PR curve plots the classifier system's ability to classify using that cut-off as the class boundary, for different mixtures of the two classes. The data set is divided into k subsets (folds) with an equal number (d) of documents. We assume the data set is normally distributed. Each subset contains n^{th} class documents and $(n + 1)^{th}$ class documents in different proportions. For example, the 1st subset contains m_1 number of nth class documents and $(d - m_1)$ number of $(n+1)^{th}$ class documents, the 2nd subset contains m_2 number of nth class documents and $(d - m_2)$ number of $(n + 1)^{th}$ class documents, and the kth subset contains m_k number of nth class documents and $(d - m_k)$ number of $(n + 1)^{th}$ class documents (see figure 1a). Each fold represents a different distribution of sentiment scores for the two classes (see figure 1b) and hence a different precision and recall score for each class for the given cut-off. We then calculate the macro-average precison and recall across the two classes; the PR curve plots these different precision/recall values for a single cut-off value across all the folds.

The best cut-off value produces high and almost equal values of precision and recall. Therefore, the PR curve of the best cut-off value lies to the top right hand corner of the graph as well as close to the diagonal line ($p = r$). We originally hoped that we could choose the best PR curve by visual inspection, but in practice, while this is sufficient to rule out many candidates, the final choice was also supported by additionally plotting average recall and precision for each PR curve.

Once the best cut-off value, $C_{n/n+1}$, has been

---

[3]Note that the classes score ranges may overlap — Max_n may be greater than Min_{n+1}.

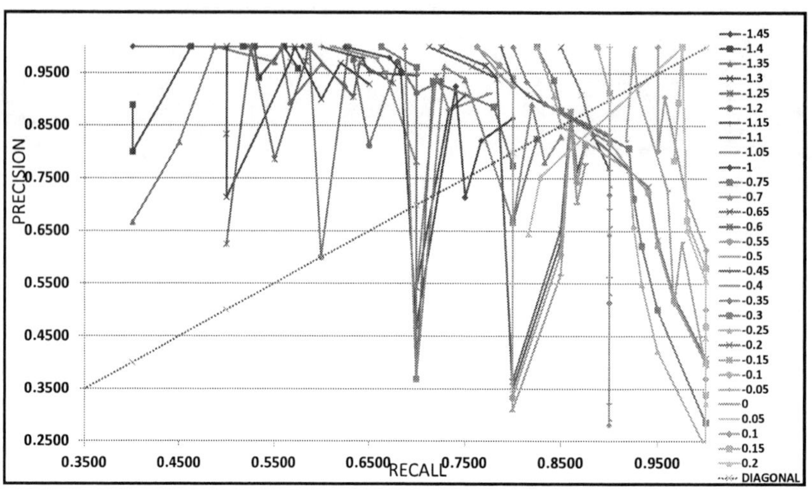

Figure 2: PR curves for all candidate cut-off values

established, we repeat the process for the other class boundaries ($C_{n+1/n+2}$ etc.). These cut-off values can then be used to map the numerical scores to classes in an optimal way. For example, in the three class *negative, neutral, positive* case, with classes 1, 2 and 3, we use $C_{1/2}$ as the boundary between *negative* and *neutral*, and $C_{2/3}$ as the boundary between *neutral* and *positive*, and classify as follows:

$$S_i = \begin{cases} positive, & \text{If } Tot_i > C_{2/3} \\ neutral, & \text{If } C_{1/2} < Tot_i < C_{2/3} \\ negative, & \text{If } Tot_i < C_{1/2} \end{cases} \quad (1)$$

where S_i is the sentiment class of document i and Tot_i is the total sentiment score of the document i.

4 Experiments and Results

To test the above method, we performed an experiment with the *Galadriel* sentiment analysis system (Satthar, 2015) on a scaled dataset[4] used by Pang and Lee (2005). The dataset is a collection of movie reviews labelled with values of $0, 1, 2$. When analysed by the *Galadriel* system, the documents in this dataset return scores ranging between -10 and $+25$. The purpose of this experiment was to show that by assigning optimal cut-off values for *Galadriel* scores according to this scaled dataset, we can map the system's output into this three-class system in a way which maximises its performance as a sentiment classifier.

We selected 300 documents of approximately equal length from the dataset (100 documents for each scale value in an approximately normal distribution). First we divided the dataset into two parts, one for training and other for testing. We used 240 documents (80 documents from each scale) as our training set. First, we computed boundaries for the *scale-0* class, then for the *scale-1* class and finally for the *scale-2* class. Since *scale-0* is the lowest class it is not necessary to compute the lower boundary for *scale-0*. To determine the upper boundary of the *Galadriel* score for *scale-0*, the cut-off value of the *Galadriel* score between *scale-0* and *scale-1* needed to be computed. For this, we used our *scale-0* and *scale-1* training documents (160 documents). We found that the maximum normalised *Galadriel* score for *scale-0* documents was $+0.17$ and minimum *Galadriel* score for *scale-1* documents was -1.41 (rounded up to two decimals). Therefore, we set up candidate cut-off values (C_i) between -1.45 and $+0.2$ in an equal interval of 0.05, i.e., $-1.45, -1.40, -1.35, -1.30, -1.25, -1.20, -1.15, -1.10, -1.05, -1.00, -0.05, 0.00, +0.5, +0.1, +0.15, +0.2$. Then, for each candidate cut-off value, we calculated precision and recall value for 5 sub training data sets, each subset containing a mixture of 35 *scale-0* and *scale-1* documents. For each cut-off values (C_i) precision and recall values were calculated for *scale-0* class and *scale-1* class. Then the precision and recall values were summarised by taking macro average of both classes' values. Finally, we had 5 pairs of precision and recall values for each of our 28 candidate

---

[4]`www.cs.cornell.edu/people/pabo/`
`movie-review-data/`

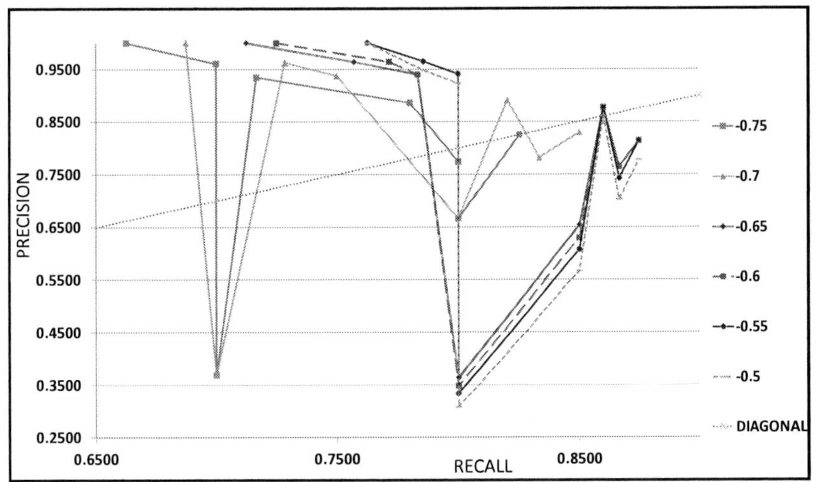

Figure 3: Most appropriate PR curves

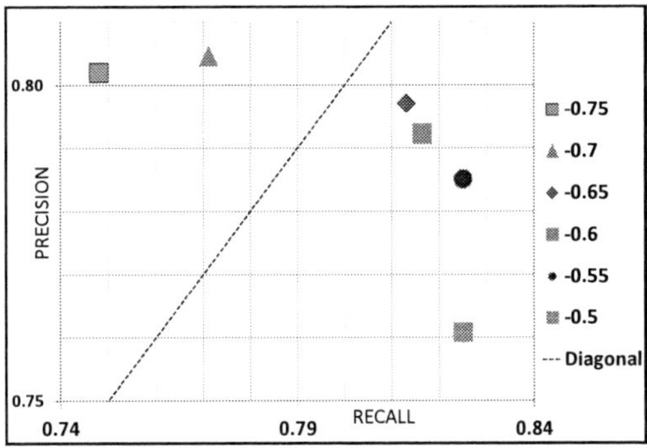

Figure 4: Average of Precision and Recall values

Cut-off values	Recall	Precision	F-score
-0.75	0.7480	0.8020	0.7741
-0.70	0.7712	0.8046	0.7875
-0.65	0.8131	0.7972	0.8050
-0.60	0.8164	0.7922	0.8042
-0.55	0.8250	0.7851	0.8046
-0.50	0.8250	0.7608	0.7916

Table 2: Average Precison, Recall and F-score measures for candidate cut-off values

cut-off values. Figure 2 shows the resulting 28 different PR curves.

The ideal cut-off value will have a PR curve as close to the diagonal, and as far towards the top right corner as possible. As can be seen in figure 2, although the general trend is for all the curves to be in the top right half of the graph, many of them deviate significantly from the diagonal line. We focused on the six curves closest to the diagonal (by visual inspection), shown in figure 3, for further analysis.

The 6 candidate cut-off values remaining after this step are -0.75, -0.70, -0.65, -0.60, -0.55 and -0.50. The PR curves of those values lie closest to the diagonal line, and largely in the upper right corner. Thus we concluded that one of those 6 test values is the optimal cut-off value $C_{0/1}$ for *scale-0* and *scale-1* classes. Looking more closely, we can see that the PR curves for $-0.65, -0.60$, -0.55 and -0.5 lie noticeably closer to the top right-hand corner compared to the PR curves for -0.75 and -0.70. We therefor discard these two, but the remaining curves track each other very closely — too closely for visual discrimination. We therefore calculated the (macro-)average precision and recall values of each cut-off value and plotted these in a scatter plot(figure 4). From this plot, we concluded that the best cut-off value for *scale-0* and *scale-1* classes is -0.65.

To validate this cut-off value, we also compared f-scores for the candidate cut-off values from these macro-averaged recall and precision values. We only considered the candidate values used in figure 3 as the remaining cut-off values had already been rejected. Table 2 also shows these numbers for the different candidate cut-off values. The f-score of the cut-off value -0.65 has the maximum value.

Similarly, the cut-off value $C_{1/2}$ for *scale-1* and *scale-2* classes were computed with an optimal value of $+1.05$.

Document Scales	Calibrated system			Uncalibrated system		
	Precision	Recall	F-Score	Precision	Recall	F-Score
scale-0	0.9375	0.7500	0.8333	0.6522	0.7500	0.6977
scale-1	0.7619	0.8000	0.7805	0.3333	0.0500	0.0870
scale-2	0.7826	0.9000	0.8372	0.5294	0.9000	0.6667
Macro-average	0.8273	0.8167	0.8220	0.5050	0.5667	0.4838

Table 4: Comparing performance measures calculated by the calibrated and uncalibrated versions of *Galadriel*.

Galadriel scores of documents	Scaled documents		
	0	1	2
$-0.65 > \text{Gal}_i$	15	1	0
$-0.65 < \text{Gal}_i < +1.05$	3	16	2
$+1.05 < \text{Gal}_i$	2	3	18

Table 3: Confusion Matrix for the classification

5 Evaluation of the Calibrated System

In order to demonstrate the effect of the calibration process, we evaluated the calibrated *Galadriel* system against Pang and Lee (2005)'s dataset and compared this with evaluation of the uncalibrated version. For this evaluation, we selected 50 random unseen test documents from the dataset and analysed them using *Galadriel*, giving numerical scores for each document as its output. The output scores were classified according to *Galadriel* cut-off values -0.65 ($C_{0/1}$) and $+1.05$ ($C_{1/2}$). Table 3 shows the resulting confusion matrix. It is interesting to note that this optimum score range for the *neutral* class is quite small in comparison to the total score range of the system (1.70 out of 30), and also not balanced around zero.

Table 4 shows precison, recall and f-score results for each class and overall macro-average results, for both the calibrated system and the uncalibrated system, which maps sentiment scores simply on the basis of their sign (negative, zero or positive). The effect of calibrating is to increase the macro-averaged f-score from 0.48 to 0.82. Moreover, the calibrated system gives overall macro-averaged mean absolute error (MAE) of 0.2167 whereas the uncalibrated system shows 0.5166.

6 Conclusion

This paper presented a novel calibration method to transform numerical sentiment scores into fixed ordered classes. This method uses corpus-based evaluation techniques, as widely used in supervised machine learning approaches, calibrating a system using gold standard labelled data. The effect is to optimise a continuous sentiment analysis system for the discrete classification model represented by the gold standard data. The calibrated system can then be evaluated and compared with other systems by using additional unseen gold standard data for the same model, or applied to new data assumed to follow the same model, with the confidence provided by the evaluation results. The availability of a general calibration method also means that the same system can be calibrated independently for different classification tasks as required.

We also presented a comparison between the performance of a calibrated system and the corresponding uncalibrated system, where sentiment scores are mapped into classes based solely on their sign, and showed that calibration can provide a substantial increase in performance. Although the uncalibrated system might be considered a poor baseline for comparison, it is worth bearing in mind that it is a simple model such as this which often guides the assignment of lexical semantic orientation scores such as those given in table 1. The effectiveness of calibration is a measure of the extent to which the document analysis process as a whole deviates from the simple lexical model, in a way that is difficult to capture by other means, and reveals interesting biases in the way the process maps sentiment onto scores.

In future work, we hope to look at automating the process of selecting the best PR curve, so that the entire calibration process is essentially automatic.

References

Mohamed Aly. 2005. Survey on multiclass classification methods. *Neural Networks* 19:1–9.

Stefano Baccianella, Andrea Esuli, and Fabrizio Sebastiani. 2009. Evaluation measures for ordinal regression. In *Intelligent Systems Design and Applications, 2009. ISDA'09. Ninth International Conference on*. IEEE, pages 283–287.

Jesse Davis and Mark Goadrich. 2006. The relationship between precision-recall and roc curves. In *Proceedings of the 23rd International Conference on Machine Learning*. ACM, New York, NY, USA, ICML '06, pages 233–240. https://doi.org/10.1145/1143844.1143874.

James P. Egan. 1975. *Signal detection theory and ROC analysis*. Academic Press, New York.

Andrea Esuli and Fabrizio Sebastiani. 2007. Sentiwordnet: A high-coverage lexical resource for opinion mining. *Evaluation* pages 1–26.

Peter Flach and Meelis Kull. 2015. Precision-recall-gain curves: Pr analysis done right. In C. Cortes, N. D. Lawrence, D. D. Lee, M. Sugiyama, and R. Garnett, editors, *Advances in Neural Information Processing Systems 28*, Curran Associates, Inc., pages 838–846. http://papers.nips.cc/paper/5867-precision-recall-gain-curves-pr-analysis-done-right.pdf.

Lisa Gaudette and Nathalie Japkowicz. 2009. Evaluation methods for ordinal classification. In *Canadian Conference on Artificial Intelligence*. Springer, pages 207–210.

Raymond Hsu, Bozhi See, and Alan Wu. 2010. Machine learning for sentiment analysis on the Experience project. Accessed on July 31, 2017. http://cs229.stanford.edu/proj2010/HsuSeeWu-MachineLearningForSentimentAnalysis.pdf.

Moontae Lee and Patrick Grafe. 2010. Multiclass sentiment analysis with restaurant reviews. Accessed on July 31, 2017. https://nlp.stanford.edu/courses/cs224n/2010/reports/pgrafe-moontae.pdf.

Christopher D. Manning and Hinrich Schütze. 1999. *Foundations of Statistical Natural Language Processing*. MIT Press, Cambridge, MA, USA.

Preslav Nakov, Alan Ritter, Sara Rosenthal, Fabrizio Sebastiani, and Veselin Stoyanov. 2016. Semeval-2016 task 4: Sentiment analysis in twitter. In *Proceedings of the 10th International Workshop on Semantic Evaluation (SemEval-2016)*. Association for Computational Linguistics, San Diego, California, pages 1–18. http://www.aclweb.org/anthology/S16-1001.

Tetsuya Nasukawa and Jeonghee Yi. 2003. Sentiment analysis: Capturing favorability using natural language processing. In *Proceedings of the 2Nd International Conference on Knowledge Capture*. ACM, New York, NY, USA, K-CAP '03, pages 70–77. https://doi.org/10.1145/945645.945658.

Prabu Palanisamy, Vineet Yadav, and Harsha Elchuri. 2013. Serendio: Simple and practical lexicon based approach to sentiment analysis. In *proceedings of Second Joint Conference on Lexical and Computational Semantics*. Citeseer, pages 543–548.

Bo Pang and Lillian Lee. 2005. Seeing stars: Exploiting class relationships for sentiment categorization with respect to rating scales. In *Proceedings of the 43rd Annual Meeting on Association for Computational Linguistics*. Association for Computational Linguistics, Stroudsburg, PA, USA, ACL '05, pages 115–124. https://doi.org/10.3115/1219840.1219855.

Bo Pang, Lillian Lee, and Shivakumar Vaithyanathan. 2002. Thumbs up?: sentiment classification using machine learning techniques. In *Proceedings of the ACL-02 conference on Empirical methods in natural language processing-Volume 10*. Association for Computational Linguistics, pages 79–86.

Rudy Prabowo and Mike Thelwall. 2009. Sentiment analysis: A combined approach. *Journal of Informetrics* 3(2):143–157.

Vijay Raghavan, Peter Bollmann, and Gwang S. Jung. 1989. A critical investigation of recall and precision as measures of retrieval system performance. *ACM Trans. Inf. Syst.* 7(3):205–229. https://doi.org/10.1145/65943.65945.

Hassan Saif, Yulan He, Miriam Fernandez, and Harith Alani. 2016. Contextual semantics for sentiment analysis of twitter. *Information Processing & Management* 52(1):5–19.

F Sharmila Satthar. 2015. Modelling so-cal in an inheritance-based sentiment analysis framework. In *OASIcs-OpenAccess Series in Informatics*. Schloss Dagstuhl-Leibniz-Zentrum fuer Informatik, volume 49.

Maite Taboada, Julian Brooke, Milan Tofiloski, Kimberly Voll, and Manfred Stede. 2011. Lexicon-based methods for sentiment analysis. *Computational linguistics* 37(2):267–307.

Peter D Turney. 2002. Thumbs up or thumbs down?: semantic orientation applied to unsupervised classification of reviews. In *Proceedings of the 40th annual meeting on association for computational linguistics*. ACL, pages 417–424.

Muqtar Unnisa, Ayesha Ameen, and Syed Raziuddin. 2016. Opinion mining on twitter data using unsupervised learning technique. *International Journal of Computer Applications* 148(12).

Robert West, Hristo S Paskov, Jure Leskovec, and Christopher Potts. 2014. Exploiting social network structure for person-to-person sentiment analysis. *arXiv preprint arXiv:1409.2450* .

Taras Zagibalov and John Carroll. 2008. Automatic seed word selection for unsupervised sentiment classification of chinese text. In *Proceedings of the 22nd International Conference on Computational Linguistics-Volume 1*. Association for Computational Linguistics, pages 1073–1080.

Building Multiword Expressions Bilingual Lexicons for Domain Adaptation of an Example-Based Machine Translation System

Nasredine Semmar, Meriama Laib

CEA, LIST, Vision and Content Engineering Laboratory, F-91191, Gif-sur-Yvette, France

`nasredine.semmar@cea.fr, meriama.laib@cea.fr`

Abstract

We describe in this paper a hybrid approach to build automatically bilingual lexicons of Multiword Expressions (MWEs) from parallel corpora. We more specifically investigate the impact of using a domain-specific bilingual lexicon of MWEs on domain adaptation of an Example-Based Machine Translation (EBMT) system. We conducted experiments on the English-French language pair and two kinds of texts: in-domain texts from Europarl (European Parliament proceedings) and out-of-domain texts from Emea (European Medicines Agency documents) and Ecb (European Central Bank corpus). The obtained results indicate that integrating domain-specific bilingual lexicons of MWEs improves translation quality of the EBMT system when texts to translate are related to the specific domain and induces a relatively slight deterioration of translation quality when translating general-purpose texts.

1 Introduction

Multiword Expressions (MWEs) play a major role in several natural language processing applications such as Machine Translation (MT) and Cross-Language Information Retrieval (CLIR) because they often characterize specific-domains vocabularies. The identification and the alignment of MWEs from parallel texts is a complex task (Sag et al., 2002; Hurskainen, 2008; DeNero and Klein, 2008; Bouamor et al., 2012; Ramisch, 2014; Semmar and Laib, 2017). Statistical approaches for word alignment (Brown et al., 1993) are unable to handle many-to-many alignments and as a result they cannot take into account correctly MWEs present in parallel corpora. For instance, the automatic word alignment tool Giza++ (Och and Ney, 2002) which implements IBM models can produce noisy (non perfect) outputs in particular when it aligns MWEs (Fraser and

Marcu, 2007). As Statistical Machine Translation (SMT) systems use the translation table probabilities produced by this word alignment tool, the translation quality of these systems is highly impacted by the performance of Giza++.

In this paper, we discuss the application of domain adaptation to an Example-Based Machine Translation (EBMT) system. In particular, our investigation focuses on the impact of using a domain-specific bilingual lexicon of MWEs on the performance of this system. Two kinds of texts corpora are used in our investigation: in-domain texts from Europarl (European Parliament proceedings) and out-of-domain texts from Emea (European Medicines Agency documents) and Ecb (European Central Bank corpus).

The remainder of the paper is organized as follows. In section 2, we first present a state-of-the-art on domain adaptation for SMT, and then, we survey previous work on the use of multiword expressions in MT. Section 3 describes a hybrid approach to build bilingual lexicons of multiword expressions from parallel corpora. Section 4 presents briefly the EBMT system. In section 5, the experimental results are reported and discussed. Finally, the conclusions and future work are presented in section 6.

2 Related Work

In the last few years, a number of approaches have been explored to deal with domain adaptation in SMT (Hildebrand et al., 2005; Lewis et al., 2010; Banerjee et al., 2010; Bungum and Gambäck, 2011; Axelrod et al., 2011; Pecina et al., 2011; Wang et al., 2012; Mathur et al., 2015; Semmar et al., 2015). These approaches can be classified into three distinct categories: supervised (Daumé III, 2007; Foster and Kuhn, 2007; Koehn and Schroeder, 2007; Civera and Juan, 2007), semi-supervised (Ueffing, 2006; Ueffing et al., 2007; Ueffing et al., 2008) and unsupervised (Wu et al., 2008; Bertoldi and Federico, 2009). The first category (supervised approaches) consists in manipu-

Proceedings of Recent Advances in Natural Language Processing, pages 661–670,
Varna, Bulgaria, Sep 4–6 2017.

lating in-domain and out-of-domain data in order to adapt language and translation models (Eck et al. 2004; Daumé III, 2007; Foster and Kuhn, 2007; Koehn and Schroeder, 2007; Civera and Juan, 2007; Daumé III and Jagarlamudi, 2011). Daumé III (2007) used dictionary mining techniques to find translations for unseen words from comparable corpora and integrated these translations into a statistical phrase-based translation system. Likewise, Civera and Juan (2007) used monolingual corpora to adapt MT systems designed for Parliament domain to work in News domain. The obtained results showed significant gains in performance. On the other hand, Eck et al. (2004) limited adaptation to the target language model. The general-purpose language model is combined with one estimated on documents retrieved from the Web. These documents are obtained by using cross-language information retrieval techniques. The objective of the second category (semi-supervised approaches) is to train an SMT system on a small amount of data and then iteratively improve its performance by translating additional monolingual source language corpora and adding the reliable translations to the training corpus (Ueffing, 2006; Ueffing et al., 2007; Ueffing et al., 2008). Ueffing et al. (2007) explored monolingual texts in the source language to improve the MT system performance. They used an initial version of the translation system to translate texts in the source language. The generated translations and their sources are then used as a new parallel corpus for training an additional translation model. In this way, the translation system is adapted to the new source texts even if no bilingual corpus in this domain is available. The third category includes (unsupervised) approaches where in-domain bilingual corpora do not exist (Langlais, 2002; Wu et al., 2008; Bertoldi and Federico, 2009). Langlais (2002) added the content of a domain-specific lexicon into the training corpus used to generate the translation model of a SMT system. Wu et al. (2008) described a method which first uses out-of-domain corpora to train a baseline system and then uses in-domain translation dictionaries and in-domain monolingual corpora to improve the in-domain performance. Bertoldi and Federico (2009) investigated cross-domain adaptation of the state-of-the-art SMT system Moses (Koehn et al., 2007) by exploiting large monolingual corpora. They generated a synthetic parallel corpus by translating a monolingual

adaptation corpus with an existing machine translation system, and they trained statistical models from the synthetic corpus. They reported that the most important improvement is provided by adapting the language model. The adaptation of the translation model and the reordering model produces small improvement.

As regards exploiting multiword expressions in domain adaptation, several works attempted to integrate these units in machine translation systems (Hurskainen, 2008; Ren et al., 2009; Carpuat and Diab, 2010; Pal et al., 2011; Bouamor et al., 2012; Semmar and Laib, 2017). Hurskainen (2008) described different ways to identify and isolate MWEs, and presented a method to mark MWEs in order to integrate this resource in a rule-based MT system. The author observed that when MWEs have been described in the linguistic analyzer of the MT system, they can be automatically included as part of the bilingual lexicon of the system. Ren et al. (2009) integrated bilingual MWEs into the decoder of the SMT system Moses. They observed a high improvement when they added a feature that identifies whether or not a bilingual phrase contains bilingual MWEs. Carpuat and Diab (2010) generalized this approach by replacing the binary feature by a count feature representing the number of MWEs in the source language phrase. Pal et al. (2011) converted the MWEs present in the parallel training corpus into single tokens in order to improve the phrase alignment quality. They reported that this preprocessing step improved the translation quality of a phrase-based statistical machine translation system. Recently, Semmar and Laib (2017) described, on the one hand, a hybrid approach to identify and find bilingual MWEs correspondences from a parallel corpus, and on the other hand, three strategies to integrate a bilingual lexicon of MWEs into the SMT system Moses.

The approach we implemented to deal with domain adaptation in our Example-Based Machine Translation system is close to the work of (Langlais, 2002) and (Hurskainen, 2008). It consists in adding a domain-specific bilingual lexicon of MWEs to the general-purpose bilingual dictionary of the EBMT system.

3 Building Bilingual Lexicons of Multiword Expressions

There are mainly two strategies to extract bilingual MWEs from parallel corpora. The first strategy consists to acquire translations of phrases from parallel corpora in one step. Phrases are not necessary MWEs, they are contiguous sequences of a few words that encapsulate enough context to be translatable (DeNero and Klein, 2008; Marchand and Semmar, 2011). The second strategy firstly, identifies monolingual MWEs candidates and then applies alignment approaches to find bilingual correspondences (Daille et al., 1994; Blank, 2000; Barbu, 2004). In the second strategy, the MWEs extraction can be processed by using symbolic methods founded on morphosyntactic patterns, or, through statistical approaches, which use automatic measures to rank MWEs candidates. Finally, MWEs extraction can be done by using hybrid approaches, which combine the two first strategies.

Our hybrid approach for MWEs alignment performs terminology extraction and alignment of MWEs from parallel texts in one step (Marchand and Semmar, 2011). The main idea of this approach is to consider the global task of identification and alignment of MWEs as an optimization problem. In order to linearize this optimization problem, we made the hypothesis that a MWE is composed of contiguous units. We use, then, integer linear programming to find an approximated optimal solution (DeNero and Klein, 2008). In this model, a sentence pair consists of two word sequences e and f, e_{ij} is the MWE from between-word positions i to j of e, and f_{kl} is the MWE from between-word positions k to l for f. A link is an aligned pair of MWEs, denoted (e_{ij}, f_{kl}). Each e_{ij} is allowed to be linked with several f_{kl} and each f_{kl} with several e_{ij}. An alignment a of the sentence pair (e, f) is a segmentation of the two sentences in MWEs with the set of links between these MWEs. We use a real-valued function ϕ to score links.

$$\phi : \{e_{ij}\} \times \{f_{kl}\} \to R$$

The score of an alignment a is the product of all the links inside it:

$$\phi(a) = \prod_{(e_{ij}, f_{kl}) \in a} \phi(e_{ij}, f_{kl})$$

In order to find the alignment (segmentation + links) that maximizes this score, we, first, introduce binary variables A_{ijkl} denoting whether a link exists between e_{ij} and f_{kl}. Furthermore, we introduce binary indicators E_{ij} and F_{kl} that denote whether some $(e_{ij}, .)$ and $(., f_{kl})$ appear in a, respectively. Finally, we use $W_{ijkl} = log(\Phi(e_{ij}, f_{kl}))$ to

transform the product into a sum. When optimized, the integer program yields the optimal alignment:

$$\begin{cases} \max \sum_{i,j,k,l} W_{i,j,k,l} A_{i,j,k,l} \\[2mm] \forall\, x : 1 \leq x \leq |e| \qquad \sum_{i,j:i<x\leq j} E_{i,j} = 1 \qquad (1) \\[2mm] \forall\, y : 1 \leq y \leq |f| \qquad \sum_{k,l:k<y\leq l} F_{k,l} = 1 \qquad (2) \\[2mm] \forall\, i,j \qquad \sum_{k,l} A_{i,j,k,l} \geq E_{i,j} \qquad (3) \\[2mm] \forall\, k,l \qquad \sum_{i,j} A_{i,j,k,l} \geq F_{k,l} \qquad (4) \\[2mm] \forall\, i,j,k,l \qquad 2 \cdot A_{i,j,k,l} \leq E_{i,j} + F_{k,l} \qquad (5) \end{cases}$$

Under the following constraints:

$$\begin{cases} 0 \leq i < |e|, \quad 0 < j \leq |e|, \quad i < j \\ 0 \leq k < |f|, \quad 0 < l \leq |f|, \quad k < l \end{cases}$$

Constraints (1) and (2) indicate that a word is inside exactly one phrase. Constraint (3) ensures that each phrase in the selected partition of e appears in at least one link (and likewise constraint (4) for f). Finally, constraint (5) ensures that if a link exists between e_{ij} and f_{kl} ($A_{ijkl} = 1$) then e_{ij} and f_{kl} are in the selected partitions of e and f. This constraint allows a phrase to be aligned with several other phrases. This integer program can work with any real-valued scoring function.

3.1 Scoring Based on Co-occurrence of MWEs

We use a sentence aligned corpus to compute the co-occurrence score. For each MWE, we consider its presence or absence in each sentence, and thus, the score between two MWEs e_{ij} and f_{kl} is computed as follows:

$$\phi_c(e_{ij}, f_{kl}) = \frac{\sum_{s' \in S} N_{s'}(e_{ij}) \times N_{s'}(f_{kl})}{\sum_{s \in S} N_s(e_{ij}) + N_s(f_{kl}) - N_s(e_{ij}) \times N_s(f_{kl})}$$

Where $N_s(e_{ij})$ is 1 if the phrase e_{ij} of the first language is present in the sentence s of the corpus S and 0 otherwise. $N_s(f_{kl})$ is similar for the other language. This score calculates the number of common presence of both MWEs divided by the number of total presence of either MWE. Note that if none of e_{ij} or f_{kl} appears in the whole corpus, the score is set to 0. Indeed, if two MWEs appear exactly in the same bi-sentences, they are probably translation of each other and the score will be 1.

3.2 Filtering MWEs Candidates

After obtaining an ordered list of bilingual MWEs, we filter the results, on the one hand, by removing the longer MWEs if a shorter MWE occurs in these candidates, and on the other hand, by keeping only MWEs which match with a list of morpho-syntactic patterns built manually (Bouamor et al., 2012).

4 Example-Based Machine Translation System

The translation process of the proposed EBMT system consists of several steps (Figure 1): retrieving translation candidates from a monolingual corpus using a cross-language search engine, producing translation hypotheses using a bilingual reformular, and generating the n-best translations from the combination of translation candidates and translation hypotheses (Semmar et al., 2015).

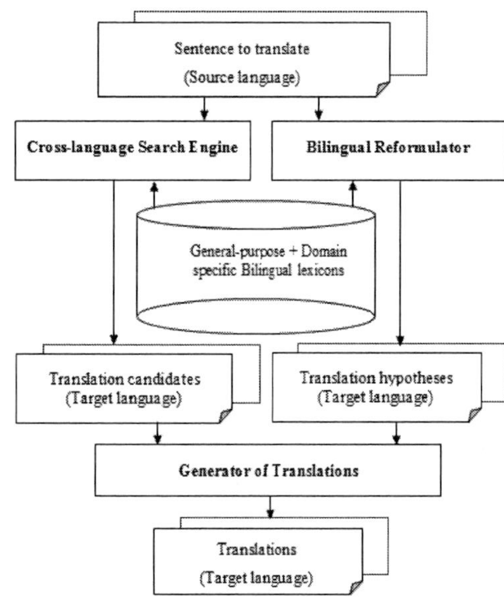

Figure 1: Main components of the Example-Based Machine Translation system.

The Cross-language Search Engine extracts for each sentence to translate (user's query) sentences or sub-sentences from an indexed monolingual corpus in the target language. These sentences or sub-sentences correspond to a total or a partial translation of the sentence to translate. This cross-language search engine is based on a deep linguistic analysis of the query and the monolingual corpus to be indexed, a bilingual lexicon and a weighted vector space model (Besançon et al., 2003). The deep linguistic analysis is achieved by means of the multilingual analyzer LIMA (Besançon et al., 2010) and the English-French lexicon is composed of 243539 entries[1]. The cross-language search engine returns translation candidates represented as graphs of words and encoded with Finite-State Machines (FSMs). Each transition of the automaton corresponds to the lemma and its linguistic information (Part-Of-Speech, gender, number, etc.) which is provided by LIMA.

The role of the Bilingual Reformulator consists, on the one hand, in transforming into the target language the syntactic structure of the sentence to translate, and, on the other hand, in translating its words. The reformulator uses a set of linguistic rules to transform syntactic structures from the source language to the target language (Syntactic transfer) and the bilingual lexicon of the cross-language search engine to translate words of the sentence to translate (Lexical transfer). These rules are built manually and are based on morpho-syntactic patterns (Table 1). Phrases corresponding to each pattern are identified by the syntactic analyzer of LIMA during the step of recognition of verbal and nominal chains. These phrases are extracted from the sentence to translate and are accepted by a FSM transducer whose outputs are instances of these phrases in the target language.

English pattern	French pattern
Adj-Noun	Noun-Adj
Adj-Adj-Noun	Noun-Adj-Adj
Noun-Prep-Noun	Noun-Prep-Noun
Noun-Prep-Adj-Noun	Noun-Prep-Adj-Noun
Noun-Noun	Noun-Noun

Table 1: Some frequent patterns to transform syntactic structures from English to French.

The Generator of Translations produces the n-best translations from a set of word lattices. These word lattices correspond to the combination of the results returned by the cross-language search engine and the bilingual reformulator. The combination process consists in composing FSMs corresponding to the translation candidates with FSMs corresponding to the translation hypotheses. The FSM state where the composition is made is determined by words which link the nominal chains of the translation candidates and the translation hypotheses. In order to find the best translation hypothesis from the set of word lattices, we first

---

[1] http://catalog.elra.info/product_info.php?products_id=666.

use a statistical language model learned on lemmas and Part-Of-Speech tags of the target language corpus, and then, we apply a morphological generator (flexor) associated with linguistic information provided by LIMA to generate the n-best translations with words in their surface (inflected) forms.

5   Experimental Results

In this section, we first describe the corpora and the experimental setup used to train the Example-Based Machine Translation system and our baseline which is the state-of-the-art SMT system Moses[2]. Then, we give some details concerning the integration of the bilingual lexicons extracted from domain-specific corpora in these two systems, and we present the different sets of experiments that we carried out with a brief discussion.

5.1   Data and Experimental Setup

In order to study the impact of using a domain-specific bilingual lexicon on the performance of the EBMT system and Moses, we conducted our experiments on three English-French parallel corpora (Table 2): Europarl (European Parliament proceedings), Emea (European Medicines Agency documents) and Ecb (European Central Bank corpus). These corpora were extracted from the open parallel corpus OPUS (Tiedemann, 2012). We use the factored translation model of Moses. It is an extension of the phrase-based models which are limited to the mappings of phrases without any explicit use of linguistic information. The factored model enables the use of additional markup at the word level. Our model operates on lemmas instead of surface forms because the entries of the general-purpose dictionary and the bilingual lexicon of MWEs are in lemma forms. Therefore, training corpora are lemmatized using the multilingual analyzer LIMA.

Evaluation consists in comparing translation results produced by Moses and the EBMT system on in-domain and out-of-domain texts. The English-French training corpus is used to build Moses's translation and language models. The French sentences of this training corpus are used to create the indexed database of the cross-language search engine integrated in the EBMT system. We conducted six runs and two test experiments for each run: In-Domain and Out-Of-Domain. For this, we

randomly extracted 500 parallel sentences from Europarl as an In-Domain corpus, 500 pairs of sentences from Emea and 500 pairs of sentences from Ecb as Out-Of-Domain corpora.

Run n°.	Training (# sentences)	Tuning (# sentences)
1	150K+10K (Europarl+Emea)	2K+0.5K (Europarl+Emea)
2	150K+20K (Europarl+Emea)	2K+0.5K (Europarl+Emea)
3	150K+30K (Europarl+Emea)	2K+0.5K (Europarl+Emea)
4	500K+10K (Europarl+Ecb)	2K+0.5K (Europarl+Ecb)
5	500K+20K (Europarl+Ecb)	2K+0.5K (Europarl+Ecb)
6	500K+30K (Europarl+Ecb)	2K+0.5K (Europarl+Ecb)

Table 2: Corpora details used to train Moses language and translation models, and to build the database of the EBMT system (K refers to 1000).

The goal of our experiments is to show the impact of the domain vocabulary on the translation results. The domain vocabulary is identified by a bilingual lexicon of MWEs which is extracted automatically from the specialized parallel corpus (Emea or Ecb) using our MWEs alignment approach. In the case of the EBMT system, the specialized bilingual lexicon is added to the general-purpose English-French lexicon which is used jointly by the cross-language search engine and the bilingual reformulator. In the case of Moses, on the one hand, we added the English-French lexicon of the cross-language search engine to the training data (Europarl), and on the other hand, we integrated the domain-specific bilingual lexicon of MWEs using the following three methods (Bouamor et al., 2012):

- $Moses_{CORPUS}$: In this method, we include the extracted MWE pairs of the bilingual lexicon to the training data of Moses.

- $Moses_{TABLE}$: This method consists to insert the extracted MWE pairs in the phrase table which is generated while training Moses.

- $Moses_{FEATURE}$: In this method, we extend $Moses_{TABLE}$ by adding a new feature indicating whether a phrase is a MWE or not.

[2] http://www.statmt.org/moses.

5.2 Results and Discussion

The performance of Moses and the EBMT system is evaluated using the BLEU score (Papineni et al., 2002) on the two test sets for the six runs described in the previous section. Note that we consider one reference per sentence. Table 3 illustrates the performance of the EBMT system for In-Domain and Out-Of-Domain texts. Table 4 and Table 5 report the BLEU scores of the different integration strategies of the specialized bilingual lexicon in Moses respectively for In-Domain and Out-Of-Domain texts.

Run n°.	In-Domain (Europal)	Out-Of-Domain (Emea and Ecb)
1	32.05	29.02
2	31.03	30.26
3	29.92	31.84
4	33.82	32.64
5	33.31	33.71
6	32.93	37.74

Table 3: BLEU scores of the EBMT system for In-Domain and Out-Of-Domain texts.

Run n°.	In-Domain (Europal)		
	$Moses_{CORPUS}$	$Moses_{TABLE}$	$Moses_{FEATURE}$
1	32.79	32.10	32.91
2	34.06	33.51	34.12
3	34.61	34.19	34.68
4	37.58	37.44	37.63
5	37.61	37.52	37.72
6	37.79	37.76	37.84

Table 4: BLEU scores of Moses for In-Domain texts.

Run n°.	Out-Of-Domain (Emea and Ecb)		
	$Moses_{CORPUS}$	$Moses_{TABLE}$	$Moses_{FEATURE}$
1	23.38	23.05	23.59
2	23.95	23.71	24.12
3	25.37	24.87	25.40
4	25.92	25.67	26.15
5	26.85	26.73	27.07
6	31.04	30.94	31.39

Table 5: BLEU scores of Moses for Out-Of-Domain texts.

As shown in Table 3 and Table 4, for In-Domain texts, Moses and the EBMT system achieve a relatively high BLEU score and the score of Moses is better in all the runs. For the Out-Of-Domain test corpora, the EBMT system performs better than Moses. This may be due to the bilingual lexicon of MWEs which is built automatically from the specialized parallel corpus (Emea or Ecb). It seems that it has had a significant impact on the result of the EBMT system, it improved regularly its BLEU score in all the runs. These results also show that adding a specialized lexicon of MWEs to the translation model of Moses improves translation quality of Out-Of-Domain texts without loss of translation quality when translating In-Domain texts, and confirm the results obtained by Ren et al. (2009) and Bouamor et al. (2012). However, in the case of the EBMT system, adding the specialized lexicon to the general-purpose bilingual dictionary of the search engine translation has had a negative impact on the translation quality of In-Domain texts. For example, adding a bilingual lexicon of MWEs built from the Emea specialized parallel corpus composed of 30K sentences to the 150K sentences of Europarl reported a gain of 2.82 BLEU points when translating Out-Of-Domain texts but had led to a loss of 2.13 BLEU points when translating In-Domain texts (Table 3: runs 1 and 3). Likewise, adding a bilingual lexicon of MWEs built from the Ecb specialized parallel corpus composed of 30K sentences to the 150K sentences of Europarl reported a gain of 5.10 BLEU points when translating Out-Of-Domain texts but had led to a loss of 0.89 BLEU points when translating In-Domain texts (Table 3: runs 4 and 6). The other important point to mention here is that the integration method $Moses_{FEATURE}$ provides the best BLEU score in all the runs for In-Domain texts (Table 4) and Out-Of-Domain texts (Table 5).

In order to evaluate and analyze the translation quality of the EBMT system and Moses when translating specific-domain texts, we take an example of translations drawn from the Ecb test corpus (Table 6). For this sentence, the EBMT system and Moses provide close translations and these translations are more or less correct, but translations provided by Moses contain many spelling and grammatical errors. In this example, the English word "shares" was identified by the morpho-syntactic analyzer used by the EBMT system as a noun and is translated as "actions". This translation is the right one despite the fact that the English-French lexicon contains for the word "share" several translations (avoir part à, contingent, diviser, lot, lotir, part, partager, participer, etc.). On the other hand, Moses translates the word "shares" with the word "partage" which is not a correct translation. It seems that Moses has taken this translation from Europal training corpus instead of the Ecb corpus. Likewise, Moses fails to translate correctly the word "investors" (plural of the word "investor") even if it has translated correctly the singular form of this word (investor).

Example Input (Ecb): for example, in France, statistics show that a non resident *investor* holds *shares* on average only for five months (compared to eleven months for resident *investors*).	
Reference	en France, par exemple, les statistiques montrent qu'un *investisseur* non résident ne conserve, en moyenne, ses *actions* que pour une période de cinq mois (contre onze mois pour un *investisseur* résident).
EBMT system: Run 6	par exemple, en France, les statistiques montrent qu'un *investisseur* non résident garde des *actions* en moyenne seulement pour cinq mois (par comparaison avec onze mois pour les *investisseurs* résidents).
Moses_{FEATURE}: Run 6	par exemple, en France, les statistiques montrent qu'un *investisseur* non résidente détient *partage* en moyenne seulement pour cinq mois (par rapport à onze mois pour résidant *investors*).

Table 6: Translations produced by the EBMT system and Moses for a sentence from Ecb corpus.

After analyzing some translations, we observed that the major issues of our EBMT system are related to errors from the source language syntactic analyzer, the non-isomorphism between the syntax of the two languages and the polysemy in the bilingual lexicon. We think that taking into account translation candidates returned by the cross-language search engine even if these translations correspond only to a part of the sentence to translate could reduce the impact of the issues related to syntactic parsing. However, for the presence of the polysemy in the bilingual lexicon, the EBMT system has no specific treatment. On the other hand, we noted that most of Moses's translation errors for Out-Of-Domain sentences are related to vocabulary. In another example of translation, Moses proposes the compound word "capitalisation du marché" as a translation for the expression "market capitalisation" instead of the compound word "capitalisation boursière" which is more precise. In SMT systems such as Moses, phrase tables are the main knowledge source for the machine translation decoder which consults these tables to figure out how to translate an input sentence. These tables are built using Giza++ but, as we mentioned before, this tool could produce errors in particular when it aligns multiword expressions (Fraser and Marcu, 2007). Finally on this point, we can observe that the major issues of Moses concern errors produced by Giza++ when aligning MWEs (translation model), incorrect spelling and poor grammar generated by the decoder (language model). To handle the first issue, we proposed to take into account the specialized bilingual lexicon extracted with the MWEs aligner into Moses's phrase table and we added a new feature indicating whether a word comes from this lexicon or not (Moses_{FEATURE} method). However, for spelling and poor errors, statistical machine translation toolkits like Moses have no specific treatment because they have not been designed with grammatical error correction in mind.

6   Conclusion and Future Work

We have presented in this paper a hybrid approach to build automatically bilingual lexicons of Multiword Expressions (MWEs) from parallel corpora. We have also investigated the impact of using a domain-specific bilingual lexicon of MWEs on domain adaptation for two MT systems: the state-of-the-art SMT system Moses and an Example-Based Machine Translation (EBMT) system. The obtained results have showed that adding a specialized bilingual lexicon of MWEs to the general-purpose dictionary of the EBMT system improves significantly its performance for Out-Of-Domain texts. We have compared the results of the EBMT system with those of Moses, and the results of the EBMT system are always better for Out-Of-Domain texts and almost comparable for In-Domain texts. This study offers several open issues for future work. First, we plan to analyze the obtained translations for both the EBMT and the SMT systems in terms of perplexities in order to improve the modeling of Out-Of-Vocabulary words. The second perspective is to adapt and evaluate the MWEs alignment approach and the EBMT system to new language pairs and new domains. We also expect to explore the use of recurrent neural networks language models for rescoring the n-best translations produced by the EBMT system.

Acknowledgments

This project has received funding from the European Union's Horizon 2020 research and innovation programme under grant agreement No 700381.

References

A. Axelrod, X. He, and J. Gao. 2011. Domain adaptation via pseudo in-domain data selection. In *Proceedings of EMNLP 2011*.

P. Banerjee, J. Du, B. Li, S.K. Naskar, A. Way, and J. van Genabith. 2010. Combining Multi-Domain Statistical Machine Translation Models using Automatic Classifiers. In *Proceedings of AMTA 2010*.

A. M. Barbu. 2004. Simple linguistic methods for improving a word alignment algorithm. In *Proceedings of the 7th International Conference on the Statistical Analysis of Textual Data*.

N. Bertoldi and M. Federico. 2009. Domain adaptation for statistical machine translation with monolingual resources. In *Proceedings of the 4th Workshop on Statistical Machine Translation*.

R. Besançon, G. De Chalendar, O. Ferret, F. Gara, M. Laib, O. Mesnard, and N. Semmar. 2010. LIMA: A multilingual framework for linguistic analysis and linguistic resources development and evaluation. In *Proceedings of LREC 2010*.

R. Besançon, G. De Chalendar, O. Ferret, C. Fluhr, O. Mesnard, and H. Naets. 2003. Concept-Based Searching and Merging for Multilingual Information Retrieval: First Experiments at CLEF 2003. *C. Peters et al. (Ed.): CLEF 2003,* Springer Verlag.

I. Blank. 2000. Terminology extraction from parallel technical texts. *Parallel text processing*, Springer.

D. Bouamor, N. Semmar, and P. Zweigenbaum. 2012. Automatic Construction of a MultiWord Expressions Bilingual Lexicon: A Statistical Machine Translation. In *Proceedings of the 3rd Workshop on Cognitive Aspects of the Lexicon (CogALex-III), COLING 2012*.

P. F. Brown, S. A. Della Pietra, V. J. Della Pietra, and R. L. Mercer. 1993. The mathematics of statistical machine translation: parameter estimation. *Computational Linguistics, 19(2)*.

L. Bungum and B. Gambäck. 2011. A Survey of Domain Adaptation in Machine Translation Towards a refinement of domain space. In *Proceedings of the India-Norway Workshop on Web Concepts and Technologies*.

M. Carpuat and M. Diab. 2010. Task-based Evaluation of Multiword Expressions: a Pilot Study in Statistical Machine Translation. In *Proceedings of Human Language Technology conference and the North American Chapter of the Association for Computational Linguistics conference*.

J. Civera and A. Juan. 2007. Domain adaptation in statistical machine translation with mixture modelling. In *Proceedings of the Second Workshop on Statistical Machine Translation*.

B. Daille, E. Gaussier, and J. M. Langé. 1994. Towards automatic extraction of monolingual and bilingual terminology. In *Proceedings of the 15th conference on Computational linguistics ACL 1994*.

H. Daumé III. 2007. Frustratingly easy domain adaptation. In *Proceedings Conference of the Association for Computational Linguistics. ACL 2007*.

H. Daumé III and J. Jagarlamudi. 2011. Domain Adaptation for Machine Translation by Mining Unseen Words. In *Proceedings of ACL 2011*.

J. DeNero and D. Klein. 2008. The complexity of phrase alignment problems. In *Proceedings of the 46th annual meeting of the association for computational linguistics on human language technologies*.

M. Eck, S. Vogel, and A. Waibel. 2004. Language model adaptation for statistical machine translation based on information retrieval In *Proceedings of the 4th International Conference on language resources and evaluation LREC 2004*.

G. Foster and R. Kuhn. 2007. Mixture-model adaptation for SMT. In *Proceedings of the Second Workshop on Statistical Machine Translation*.

A. Fraser and D. Marcu. 2007. Measuring word alignment quality for statistical machine translation. *Computational Linguistics, 33(3)*.

A. S. Hildebrand, M. Eck, S. Vogel, and W. Alex. 2005. Adaptation of the translation model for statistical machine translation based on information retrieval. In *Proceedings of the EAMT 2005*.

A. Hurskainen. 2008. Multiword Expressions and Machine Translation. In *Technical Report No 1 in Language Technology, Institute for Asian and African Studies*, University of Helsinki, Finland.

P. Koehn and J. Schroeder. 2007. Experiments in domain adaptation for statistical machine translation. In *Proceedings of the second workshop on statistical machine translation*.

P. Koehn, H. Hoang, A. Birch, C. Callison-Burch, M. Federico, N. Bertoldi, B. Cowan, W. Shen, C. Moran, R. Zens, C. Dyer, O. Bojar, A. Constantin, and E. Herbst. 2007. Moses: open source toolkit for statistical machine translation. In *Proceedings of the 45th Annual meeting of the Association for Computational Linguistics ACL 2007*.

P. Langlais. 2002. Improving a general-purpose statistical translation engine by terminological lexicons. In *Proceedings of COLING: Second international workshop on computational terminology.*

W. D. Lewis, C. Wendt, and D. Bullock. 2010. Achieving Domain Specificity in SMT without Overt Siloing. In *Proceedings of LREC 2010.*

M. Marchand and N. Semmar. 2011. A Hybrid Multi-Word Terms Alignment Approach Using Word Co-occurrence with a Bilingual Lexicon. In *Proceedings of the 5th Language & Technology Conference: Human Language Technologies as a Challenge for Computer Science and Linguistics LTC'11.*

P. Mathur, M. Federico, S. Köprü, S. Khadivi, and H. Sawaf. 2015. Topic Adaptation for Machine Translation of E-commerce Content. In *Proceedings of MT Summit XV.*

F. J. Och and H. Ney. 2002. Discriminative training and maximum entropy models for statistical machine translation. In *Proceedings of ACL 2002.*

S. Pal, T. Chakraborty, and S. Bandyo-padhyay. 2011. Handling Multiword Expressions in Phrase-Based Statistical Machine Translation. In *Proceedings of the XIII Machine Translation Summit.*

K. Papineni, S. Roukos, T. Ward, and W. Zhu. 2002. BLEU: a method for automatic evaluation of machine translation. In *Proceedings of ACL 2002.*

P. Pecina, A. Toral, A. Way, V. Papa-vassiliou, P. Prokopidis, and M. Giagkou. 2011. Towards Using Web-Crawled Data for Domain Adaptation in Statistical Machine Translation. In *Proceedings of EAMT 2011.*

C. Ramisch. 2014. Multiword Expressions Acquisition: A Generic and Open Framework. *Theory and Applications of Natural Language Processing Monographs*, Springer.

Z. Ren, Y. Lu, J. Cao, Q. Liu, and Y. Huang. 2009. Improving statistical machine translation using domain bilingual multiword expressions. In *Proceedings of the Workshop on Multiword Expressions, ACL-IJCNLP 2009.*

I. Sag, T. Baldwin, F. Bond, A. Copestake, and D. Flickinger. 2002. Multiword expressions: A pain in the neck for NLP. In *Proceedings of CICLing '02.*

N. Semmar, O. Zennaki and M. Laib. 2015. Evaluating the Impact of Using a Domain-specific Bilingual Lexicon on the Performance of a Hybrid Machine Translation Approach. In *Proceedings of Recent Advances in Natural Language Processing RANLP 2015.*

N. Semmar and M. Laib. 2017. Integrating Specialized Bilingual Lexicons of Multiword Expressions for Domain Adaptation in Statistical Machine Translation. In *Proceedings of PACLING 2017.*

J. Tiedemann. 2012. Parallel Data, Tools and Interfaces in OPUS. In *Proceedings of LREC 2012.*

N. Ueffing. 2006. Using monolingual source-language data to improve MT performance. In *Proceedings of the international workshop on spoken language translation IWSLT 2006.*

N. Ueffing, G. Haffari, and A. Sarkar. 2007. Semi-supervised model adaptation for statistical machine translation. *Machine Translation*, 21(2).

N. Ueffing, G. Haffari, and A. Sarkar. 2008. Semi-supervised learning for machine translation. *Learning machine translation*, NIPS Series, MIT Press.

W. Wang, K. Macherey, W. Macherey, F. Och, and P. Xu. 2012. Improved Domain Adaptation for Statistical Machine Translation. In *Proceedings of AMTA 2012.*

H. Wu, H. Wang, and C. Zong. 2008. Domain adaptation for statistical machine translation with domain dictionary and monolingual corpora. In *Proceedings of the 22nd International Conference on Computational Linguistics COLING'08.*

Identifying the Authors' National Variety
of English in Social Media Texts

Vasiliki Simaki[1,2], Panagiotis Simakis[3], Carita Paradis[1] and Andreas Kerren[2]

[1]Centre for Languages and Literature, Lund University, 221 00 Lund, Sweden

{vasiliki.simaki, carita.paradis}@englund.lu.se

[2]Department of Computer Science, Linnaeus University, 351 95 Växjö, Sweden

andreas.kerren@lnu.se

[3]XPLAIN, 153 42 Athens, Greece

simakis@xplain.com

Abstract

In this paper, we present a study for the identification of authors' national variety of English in texts from social media. In data from Facebook and Twitter, information about the author's social profile is annotated, and the national English variety (US, UK, AUS, CAN, NNS) that each author uses is attributed. We tested four feature types: formal linguistic features, POS features, lexicon-based features related to the different varieties, and data-based features from each English variety. We used various machine learning algorithms for the classification experiments, and we implemented a feature selection process. The classification accuracy achieved, when the 31 highest ranked features were used, was up to 77.32%. The experimental results are evaluated, and the efficacy of the ranked features discussed.

1 Introduction

The spread of social media has been rapid and impressive during the past decade. More and more people use social media on a daily basis and they often choose this channel to express their opinions about various topics such as politics, music, lifestyle, environment, or personal matters. This activity produces a massive number of sound data, images, and text data everyday that needs to be further analysed and grouped according to different criteria that we set in each case. Text data from social media can provide important information about social media users, their preferences, habits and the trends they follow. The identification of authors' sociodemographic and personality information has attracted a great deal of attention in the research community, and numerous studies and methodologies about this task have been proposed.

The identification of sociodemographic information about the social media authors is an interesting task for a number of reasons and contributes to the monitoring of the users' opinions on various topics. This information provides an important input to sociological studies, and at the same time it is indispensable for Market Analysis and e-commerce services. Text Mining and Natural Language Processing are among the scientific fields that benefit from this development. New methods and tools have been proposed, and significant results have been observed in Author Profiling, Language Variety Identification, and other similar tasks. The research activity in these domains is also a result of the significant expansion the past few years of the available resources due to the data and information flow.

The present study can provide useful information to the field of dialectology as well. Studies in this field have observed the different linguistic choices that speakers of different English varieties make at various language levels (morphology, phonology, lexicon, syntax, etc.). The varieties of the English language that we investigate are used by 315 million speakers approximately[1] (225 million speaker in the USA, 55 in the UK, 19.4 in Canada, and 15.6 in Australia). Previous studies in this topic (Schneider, 2007) that have observed different linguistic choices among the various varieties can be evaluated in new data, and new clues about the linguistic attitude of speakers that use different English varieties can be detected.

In this paper, we present a study for the identification of the authors' national variety of the English. The annotation labels used for this study is

---

[1]According to the information provided on wikipedia: https://en.wikipedia.org/wiki/Varieties_of_English

Proceedings of Recent Advances in Natural Language Processing, pages 671–678,
Varna, Bulgaria, Sep 4–6 2017.

US for the American English speakers, *UK* for the British English speakers, *AUS* for the Australian English variety and *CAN* for the Canadian English variety. The non-native speakers of the English are annotated with the *NNS* label. This label is attributed according to the information that the authors provide about themselves on their profile pages on social media or other internet sources (their place of birth, and/or the place they were raised). For this study, we used data from both Facebook and Twitter that are annotated with various information about the authors (gender, age, profession) additionally to the authors' national English variety. We extracted four different feature sets: formal linguistic features, Part-of-speech features, lexicon-based features that are related to the different linguistc variety, and data-based features from each English variety. We performed classification experiments by using a set of various machine learning algorithms, and we implemented a feature selection process. After the experimental results, we achieved classification accuracy of 77.32% with the 31 most infromative features and the NaiveBayesMultinomial classifier. The efficacy of the different features used in this study is an interesting finding, which is evaluated and discussed.

2   Related Work

Identifying information about the author of a text has been the subject of various studies in the fields of Text Mining and Natural Language Processing. Researchers approached the problem of the automatic identification of authors' identity and personality information from different angles.

The first studies in this field were about the Authorship Attribution (Stamatatos, 2009; Koppel et al., 2009; Grieve, 2007; Zheng et al., 2006), where researchers used linguistic features to detect authors' identity in texts from literary works, journalism, and other sources. These studies set the research basis in the identification of a text's author, and motivated the investigation of more refined characteristics. Their methodological approach motivated our work, and many features used in these studies, especially in Zheng et al. (2006) were used in this study.

The detection of gender, age, and other clues of the author's personality and language has also attracted a great deal of attention (Argamon et al., 2007a; Cheng et al., 2011; Schler et al., 2006; Arg-

amon et al., 2007b; Peersman et al., 2011; Rangel and Rosso, 2013; Simaki et al., 2015a,b, 2016, 2017; Sboev et al., 2016; Lins and Gonçalves, 2004). These studies investigate one or more sociodemographic factors, and many of them use data from social media. The profiling of the author (Wright and Chin, 2014; Stamatatos et al., 2015; Rangel et al., 2016) is a recent task, and the findings are important for Forensic Linguistics among other disciplines (van de Loo et al., 2016; Zaeem et al., 2017).

Studies in the field of Native Language Identification (NLI) can be considered as relevant to ours, with Koppel et al. (2005) being the first to infer the native language of an author based on texts written in a second language by using various NLP and Second Language Acquisition features. The studies in this topic that followed implemented different methods and characteristics for the identification of the author's native language by using various feature types like syntactic clues and grammars (Wong and Dras, 2011; Wong et al., 2012) or different resources and evaluation techniques (Tetreault et al., 2012). In his doctoral thesis, Malmasi (2016) offers an extensive presentation of the field's literature, and describes his numerous studies, application and evaluative tasks.

Our task is part of the *Language Variety Identification* research topic. Studies in this field aim at labeling texts in a native language with their specific variation. This topic has become quite popular within the NLP community and numerous events have been organized to this end, with the 5th Author Profiling Task at PAN 2017 as the most recent one (Rangel et al., 2017b). In some of the investigations with different languages, the problem of identifying between pairs of similar languages and language variants on sentences from newspaper corpora is adressed (Zampieri et al., 2014; Tan et al., 2014). Lui and Cook (2013) evaluate various approaches to classify documents into Australian, British and Canadian English, including a corpus of tweets. For Spanish, there are various studies in this task, and researchers achieve good results in terms of classification accuracy mostly by using character and word n-gram models as well as POS and morphological information (Maier and Gómez-Rodrıguez, 2014; Franco-Salvador et al., 2015; Rangel et al., 2017a). Other languages, as for instance the Portuguese (Zampieri and Gebre, 2012) and the Arabic (Sadat et al., 2014), have also been investigated in term of their different varieties.

Most of the studies in the above domains share common methodologies and similar features, and tackle the search task mainly as a classification problem, which usually involves machine learning algorithms and classification experiments.

3 Data Description and Methodology

3.1 Data description

For this study, we used a data set of 712,033 posts (13,424,523 words and 89,347,103 characters in total). The posts were extracted from the official Facebook and Twitter profiles of public figures like actors, authors, singers, athletes, politicians, and they were annotated with the author's sociodemographic clues. To extract the data, we used the *Facepager* software (Keyling and Jünger, 2013). The average size of the corpus posts is 125 characters per post, and the topics discussed vary from personal branding, opinions about social and political matters, nature, etc. The corpus was compiled from September to December 2015, and data from 838 different users (535 male and 302 female users) were manually annotated with information about the author's gender, age, professional activity, national variety of the English and any other additional information available such as his/her educational background or professional details. Concerning the author's national English variety, 584 different users are native speakers of the American English (US), 117 of the British English (UK), 21 of the Australian English (AUS), 31 of the Canadian English (CAN), and 84 of the authors are not native speakers of the English language (NNS). The annotation labels were given according to the information that the users provide about themselves in their social media accounts, and in some cases according to the information that Wikipedia[2] entries or other internet sources provide (as most authors are well-known personalities).

3.2 Methodology

In this study, a text classification methodology was followed for the identification of the authors' national variety of English in our data set. For the experiments four feature sets were extracted:

Formal Features
Frequency of all symbols
Frequency of all punctuation
Frequency of spaces
Frequency of upper case characters
Frequency of alphabetical characters
Frequency of digit characters
Frequency of short words (less than 3 characters)
Total number of word characters
Average word length
Average sentence length/word
Average sentence length /characters
Number of different words
Hapax legomena
Hapax dislegomena
Frequency of each symbol (˜ , @, /, \$, %, ˆ , &, *, -, =, +, >, <, _)
Frequency of each punctuation ((,), [,]. —, ,, ;, ?, ., !, :, ', ", ")

Table 1: The formal features extracted in the data set.

- *formal features*, which are general linguistic characteristics used in a wide set of studies in Text Mining and Author Profiling. This feature set contains basic counts of character frequencies,word and sentence metrics, as Table 1 presents. The formal features are 41 in total.

- *Part-of-Speech (POS) features*, which count the following basic grammatical categories (according to NLTK' POS tags) in the data set: nouns, prepositions, pronouns, adjectives, determinants, verbs, adverbs, conjunctions, interjections and particles. The number of the POS features is 10.

- *lexicon-based features* from slang and national varieties lexicons for the English language (4 features in total). We extracted idiomatic terms from slang and geographical lexicons[3] that had at least one hit in the data set. Some examples are presented in Table 2.

- *data-based features* based in the different forms used by each national variety of English, which are frequent in the data set (5

[2] https://en.wikipedia.org/wiki/Main_Page

[3] http://www.manythings.org/slang/
https://www.anglotopia.net/
http://aussie-slang.com/
https://www.fluentland.com/

US	UK	AUS	CAN
cool	taking	mate	click
call	brilliant	legit	rad
eat	fit	togs	flat
kick	throw	grit	hoodie
clip	pants	footy	hosed
cut	wicked	barbie	pissed
con	bloody	arvo	frog
dope	chips	dag	grit
vibes	ace	slab	tad
chicken	sorted	prawn	emo
grand	uni	goon	hammered
jam	chap	wuss	puck
joint	bangers	hydro	randy
cop	gutted	aboriginal	beaver

Table 2: Some of the lexicon-based features extracted in the data set.

features in total). We kept only the forms that were frequent and unique in each national group by eliminating the frequent forms that appeared in more than one national class. We show some examples in Table 3. We observe in Table 3 that many of these characteristics are related to the trends and popular subjects of each national group during the data collection period, which means that these features are corpus-sentitive characteristics, and have to be re-extracted when different resources are used.

To extract these features, we used the NLTK[4] toolkit. For the classification stage, we used a number of different machine learning algorithms, which are well studied and have been used extensively in several text classification tasks. All classifiers are implemented using the WEKA[5] toolkit (Witten et al., 2016). For all algorithms, the free parameters that are not reported were kept in their default values.

4 National Variety Classification Experiments

4.1 Experimental Setup

For the classification experiments of our study, we tested the performance of various machine learning techniques. In particular, we used the following algorithms:

[4]http://www.nltk.org/
[5]http://www.cs.waikato.ac.nz/ml/weka/

- a multilayer perceptron neural network (MLP),

- a bayesian classifier (NaiveBayesMultinomial),

- a bagging algorithm using decision trees (Bagging),

- a simple decision table majority classifier (DecisionTable),

- a fast decision tree learner (RepTree),

- a tree algorithm that considers K randomly chosen attributes at each node (RandomTree),

- a classifier for building linear logistic regression models(SimpleLogistic),

- various support vector machine classifiers (SVM, SMO, SVM with radial kernel).

The classifiers are implemented using WEKA, and a 10-fold cross validation protocol for each algorithm was followed. The classification accuracy was evaluated in terms of percentages of correctly classified posts. The classification results when all features were used achieved an accuracy up to 73.86% with the Bagging algorithm, as Table 4 shows.

In Table 4, the results of the classification process are presented. The results are tabulated in descending order, from the highest accuracy percentage to the lowest one. We observe that four classifiers achieved classification accuracy above 70%.

4.2 Feature Selection

The large number of the features used in our preliminary experiments, as well as the promising results in terms of classification accuracy, led us to the investigation of the feature informativity.

We performed a feature selection process in order to highlight the most efficient features and/or feature types for the identification of the national variety of English. We used a Relief feature selection algorithm (Kira and Rendell, 1992), which is heuristics-independent, noise-tolerant, robust to feature interactions and it runs in low-order polynomial time. In our case, we used the updated ReliefF algorithm proposed by Koronenko (1994), which improves the reliability of the probability

US	UK	AUS	CAN	NNS
trump	jamieol	ambrose	nelly	gric
msnbc	easytolove	trashed	celine	bieniek
pbs	maxipriest	rpmotorsports	btmontreal	jamaica
slumerican	paulmccartney	bala	furtado	fiberboard
fam	recipeoftheday	aussiecycling	celinedion	ineedyourlove
mypinkfriday	ziggy	cyclingaus	avril	nonfiction2015
bitly	gandy	stanleyracing	makeovers	usain
yall	stardust	aussie	abuse	charlize
cmt	whosay	athletics	gaza	reggae
xzibit	amg	keithurban	palestinian	protocol
jukebox	mercedes	canberra	getinspired	iriesocial
gat	wuss	itsstephrice	beerscontemporary	lama
postmodern	itv	tires	sarahstyle	un
hillary	labour	dymocks	adespatie	por

Table 3: The most salient data-based features extracted in the data set.

Classifier	Accuracy
Bagging	**73.86%**
DecisionTable	73.07%
MLP	73.05%
RepTree	72.93%
RandomTree	59.44%
NaiveBayes	30.65%

Table 4: The classification results when all features are tested.

approximation, it is robust to incomplete data, and generalized to multi-class problems. Our dataset was processed by the ReliefF algorithm, implemented using the WEKA machine learning toolkit, and feature ranking scores were estimated. The 31 highest ranked features are presented in Table 5.

In Table 5, the 31 highest ranked features are presented. We observe that all data-based features and three lexicon-based features (only the US lexicon-based feature is not among the most informative ones) are among them. The POS features appear to be particularly important (nine from a set of ten features). From the set of formal features, the characteristics that are related to word and sentence length, punctuation use, and other lexical clues (e.g., hapax and dis legomena, number of different words, number of short words, etc.) that authors of a different English national variety use, appear to be very informative. This list highlights that the main differences among speakers of a different national variety of English are primarily found at lexical and syntactic levels. In

a future study, a more descriptive and qualitative analysis of these findings can be an interesting task.

The results of the feature selection process are evaluated and presented in the Subsection below.

4.3 Second Round of Classification Experiments

We performed a second round of classification experiments where only the most informative features were used. The best results achieved are presented in Table 6.

We observed that the best results were achieved when the Bayesian (NaiveBayesMultinomial) algorithm was used. The Bagging algorithm, which achieved the highest classification accuracy when all features were used, is not that effective and achieved a low accuracy (32.74%). The results which show that the feature selection process improved the performance of the classification algorithms are promising. One interesting finding is that the best results with the reduced feature set are achieved with a Bayesian classifier (the same classifier that performed the worst in the first round of experiments). This confirms the fact that Bayesian models suffer from the curse of dimensionality, and that dimensionality reduction helps improving their performance.

5 Conclusion

In this paper, our study of the identification of the author's national variety of English from social media texts is presented. In our data set, which

Ranking	ReliefF Score	Feature
1	0.00231732	NNS data-based
2	0.00230444	AUS data-based
3	0.00229047	upper case char.
4	0.0021488	spaces
5	0.00174613	symbol char.
6	0.00163237	word length
7	0.00127163	alphabetical char.
8	0.00115416	short words
9	0.00113051	punctuation char.
10	0.00106681	CAN data-based
11	0.00106118	UK data-based
12	0.00096111	char. in words
13	0.00083135	digit char.
14	0.00075679	sent. length/char.
15	0.00070453	nouns
16	0.00052172	prepositions
17	0.00047358	pronouns
18	0.00040154	AUS lexicon-based
18	0.00034311	adjectives
20	0.00034107	determinants
21	0.00033963	verbs
22	0.00022508	hapax legomena
23	0.00020172	adverbs
24	0.00019028	different words
25	0.00013848	US data-based
26	0.00012652	conjunctions
27	0.00010855	hapax dislegomena
28	0.00003396	interjections
29	0.00001187	sent. length/words
30	0.00000442	UK lexicon-based
31	0.00000197	CAN lexicon-based

Table 5: The 31 highest ranked features.

Classifier	Accuracy
NaiveBayesMultinomial	**77.32%**
SVM(radial kernel)	76.02%
SMO	73.45%
MLP	54.92%
SimpleLogistic	41.43%
Bagging	32.74%

Table 6: The classification results for our data set, when the highest ranked features are tested.

proaches the identification of the author's national variety of English from a NLP perspective. Our results confirm the theoretical work in dialectology, stating that basic differences among English national varieties (in written discourse) can be detected at the level of lexical choices and syntactic patterns. This study can be further expanded, more resources from different sources can be tested, and new methods can be implemented. Also, the feature selection findings can be analysed and used for further qualitative studies. Additionally, the thematic patterns and the trending subjects found in the data of each variety can be analysed for sociological and cultural purposes.

Acknowledgments

This research is funded by the StaViCTA project[6], supported by the Swedish Research Council (framework grant the Digitized Society Past, Present, and Future, No. 2012-5659).

is annotated with various sociodemographic variables, we searched for the national variety of English of each author based on the labels US, UK, AUS, CAN, NNS that were attributed to each author/post. For this task, we tested various linguistic, lexicon- and data-based features and we performed a number of classification experiments by implementing various algorithms. We also tested the informativity of the features and we showed that the lexicon- and data-based features, as well as lexical and syntactic-related features can improve the classification accuracy of our experiments. For the 31 most informative features we achieved 77.32% accuracy.

This preliminary work is among the recent studies in Language Variety Identification field that ap-

References

Shlomo Argamon, Moshe Koppel, James W Pennebaker, and Jonathan Schler. 2007a. Mining the blogosphere: Age, gender and the varieties of self-expression. *First Monday* 12(9).

Shlomo Argamon, Casey Whitelaw, Paul Chase, Sobhan Raj Hota, Navendu Garg, and Shlomo Levitan. 2007b. Stylistic text classification using functional lexical features. *Journal of the Association for Information Science and Technology* 58(6):802–822.

Na Cheng, Rajarathnam Chandramouli, and KP Subbalakshmi. 2011. Author gender identification from text. *Digital Investigation* 8(1):78–88.

Marc Franco-Salvador, Francisco Rangel, Paolo Rosso, Mariona Taulé, and M Antònia Martít. 2015. Language variety identification using distributed representations of words and documents. In *International*

---

[6]`http://cs.lnu.se/stavicta/`

Conference of the Cross-Language Evaluation Forum for European Languages. Springer, pages 28–40.

Jack Grieve. 2007. Quantitative authorship attribution: An evaluation of techniques. *Literary and linguistic computing* 22(3):251–270.

R Keyling and Jakob Jünger. 2013. Facepager (version, fe 3.3). *An application for generic data retrieval through APIs* .

Kenji Kira and Larry A Rendell. 1992. A practical approach to feature selection. In *Proceedings of the ninth international workshop on Machine learning.* pages 249–256.

Igor Kononenko. 1994. Estimating attributes: analysis and extensions of relief. In *European conference on machine learning.* Springer, pages 171–182.

Moshe Koppel, Jonathan Schler, and Shlomo Argamon. 2009. Computational methods in authorship attribution. *Journal of the Association for Information Science and Technology* 60(1):9–26.

Moshe Koppel, Jonathan Schler, and Kfir Zigdon. 2005. Automatically determining an anonymous authors native language. *Intelligence and Security Informatics* pages 41–76.

Rafael Dueire Lins and Paulo Gonçalves. 2004. Automatic language identification of written texts. In *Proceedings of the 2004 ACM symposium on Applied computing.* ACM, pages 1128–1133.

Marco Lui and Paul Cook. 2013. Classifying english documents by national dialect. In *Proceedings of the Australasian Language Technology Association Workshop.* pages 5–15.

Wolfgang Maier and Carlos Gómez-Rodrıguez. 2014. Language variety identification in spanish tweets. In *Proceedings of the EMNLP2014 Workshop: Language Technology for Closely Related Languages and Language Variants (LT4CloseLang 2014).* pages 25–35.

Shervin Malmasi et al. 2016. Native language identification: explorations and applications .

Claudia Peersman, Walter Daelemans, and Leona Van Vaerenbergh. 2011. Predicting age and gender in online social networks. In *Proceedings of the 3rd international workshop on Search and mining user-generated contents.* ACM, pages 37–44.

Francisco Rangel, Marc Franco-Salvador, and Paolo Rosso. 2017a. A low dimensionality representation for language variety identification. *arXiv preprint arXiv:1705.10754* .

Francisco Rangel and Paolo Rosso. 2013. Use of language and author profiling: Identification of gender and age. *Natural Language Processing and Cognitive Science* 177.

Francisco Rangel, Paolo Rosso, Martin Potthast, and Benno Stein. 2017b. Overview of the 5th author profiling task at pan 2017: Gender and language variety identification in twitter. *Working Notes Papers of the CLEF* .

Francisco Rangel, Paolo Rosso, Ben Verhoeven, Walter Daelemans, Martin Potthast, and Benno Stein. 2016. Overview of the 4th author profiling task at pan 2016: cross-genre evaluations. *Working Notes Papers of the CLEF* .

Fatiha Sadat, Farnazeh Kazemi, and Atefeh Farzindar. 2014. Automatic identification of arabic language varieties and dialects in social media. *Proceedings of SocialNLP* page 22.

Aleksandr Sboev, Tatiana Litvinova, Dmitry Gudovskikh, Roman Rybka, and Ivan Moloshnikov. 2016. Machine learning models of text categorization by author gender using topic-independent features. *Procedia Computer Science* 101:135–142.

Jonathan Schler, Moshe Koppel, Shlomo Argamon, and James W Pennebaker. 2006. Effects of age and gender on blogging. In *AAAI spring symposium: Computational approaches to analyzing weblogs.* volume 6, pages 199–205.

Edgar W Schneider. 2007. *Postcolonial English: Varieties around the world.* Cambridge University Press.

Vasiliki Simaki, Christina Aravantinou, Iosif Mporas, Marianna Kondyli, and Vasileios Megalooikonomou. 2017. Sociolinguistic features for author gender identification: From qualitative evidence to quantitative analysis. *Journal of Quantitative Linguistics* 24(1):65–84.

Vasiliki Simaki, Christina Aravantinou, Iosif Mporas, and Vasileios Megalooikonomou. 2015a. Automatic estimation of web bloggers age using regression models. In *International Conference on Speech and Computer.* Springer, pages 113–120.

Vasiliki Simaki, Christina Aravantinou, Iosif Mporas, and Vasileios Megalooikonomou. 2015b. Using sociolinguistic inspired features for gender classification of web authors. In *International Conference on Text, Speech, and Dialogue.* Springer, pages 587–594.

Vasiliki Simaki, Iosif Mporas, and Vasileios Megalooikonomou. 2016. Age identification of twitter users: Classification methods and sociolinguistic analysis. In *17th International Conference on Intelligent Text Processing and Computational Linguistics.* Springer Verlag.

Efstathios Stamatatos. 2009. A survey of modern authorship attribution methods. *Journal of the Association for Information Science and Technology* 60(3):538–556.

Efstathios Stamatatos, Martin Potthast, Francisco Rangel, Paolo Rosso, and Benno Stein. 2015. Overview of the pan/clef 2015 evaluation lab. In *International Conference of the Cross-Language Evaluation Forum for European Languages*. Springer, pages 518–538.

Liling Tan, Marcos Zampieri, Nikola Ljubešic, and Jörg Tiedemann. 2014. Merging comparable data sources for the discrimination of similar languages: The dsl corpus collection. In *Proceedings of the 7th Workshop on Building and Using Comparable Corpora (BUCC)*. pages 11–15.

Joel R Tetreault, Daniel Blanchard, Aoife Cahill, and Martin Chodorow. 2012. Native tongues, lost and found: Resources and empirical evaluations in native language identification. In *COLING*. pages 2585–2602.

Janneke van de Loo, Guy De Pauw, and Walter Daelemans. 2016. Text-based age and gender prediction for online safety monitoring. *International Journal of Cyber-Security and Digital Forensics (IJCSDF)* 5(1):46–60.

Ian H Witten, Eibe Frank, Mark A Hall, and Christopher J Pal. 2016. *Data Mining: Practical machine learning tools and techniques*. Morgan Kaufmann.

Sze-Meng Jojo Wong and Mark Dras. 2011. Exploiting parse structures for native language identification. In *Proceedings of the Conference on Empirical Methods in Natural Language Processing*. Association for Computational Linguistics, pages 1600–1610.

Sze-Meng Jojo Wong, Mark Dras, and Mark Johnson. 2012. Exploring adaptor grammars for native language identification. In *Proceedings of the 2012 Joint Conference on Empirical Methods in Natural Language Processing and Computational Natural Language Learning*. Association for Computational Linguistics, pages 699–709.

William R Wright and David N Chin. 2014. Personality profiling from text: introducing part-of-speech n-grams. In *International Conference on User Modeling, Adaptation, and Personalization*. Springer, pages 243–253.

Razieh Nokhbeh Zaeem, Monisha Manoharan, Yongpeng Yang, and K Suzanne Barber. 2017. Modeling and analysis of identity threat behaviors through text mining of identity theft stories. *Computers & Security* 65:50–63.

Marcos Zampieri and Binyam Gebrekidan Gebre. 2012. Automatic identification of language varieties: The case of portuguese. In *KONVENS2012-The 11th Conference on Natural Language Processing*. Österreichischen Gesellschaft für Artificial Intelligende (ÖGAI), pages 233–237.

Marcos Zampieri, Liling Tan, Nikola Ljubešic, Jörg Tiedemann, and Nikola Ljube. 2014. A report on the dsl shared task 2014. In *Proceedings of the First Workshop on Applying NLP Tools to Similar Languages, Varieties and Dialects (VarDial)*. pages 58–67.

Rong Zheng, Jiexun Li, Hsinchun Chen, and Zan Huang. 2006. A framework for authorship identification of online messages: Writing-style features and classification techniques. *Journal of the Association for Information Science and Technology* 57(3):378–393.

Towards Lexical Chains for Knowledge-Graph-based Word Embeddings

Kiril Simov   **Svetla Boytcheva**   **Petya Osenova**

Linguistic Modeling and Knowledge Processing Department
Institute of Information and Communication Technology
Bulgarian Academy of Sciences
`kivs@bultreebank.org, svetla.boytcheva@gmail.com,`
`petya@bultreebank.org`

Abstract

Word vectors with varying dimensionalities and produced by different algorithms have been extensively used in NLP. The corpora that the algorithms are trained on can contain either natural language text (e.g. Wikipedia or newswire articles) or artificially-generated pseudo corpora due to natural data sparseness.

We exploit Lexical Chain based templates over Knowledge Graph for generating pseudo-corpora with controlled linguistic value. These corpora are then used for learning word embeddings. A number of experiments have been conducted over the following test sets: WordSim353 Similarity, WordSim353 Relatedness and SimLex-999.

The results show that, on the one hand, the incorporation of many-relation lexical chains improves results, but on the other hand, unrestricted-length chains remain difficult to handle with respect to their huge quantity.

1 Introduction

Recent research in NLP has focused on distributional semantic models that incorporate linguistic information from various resources. Such models are trained with different algorithms, among which: Network Language Model (NNLM), Latent Semantic Analysis (LSA), etc. Word embeddings have become lately a popular distributed representation. Word vectors with varying dimensionalities and produced by different algorithms have been extensively put forward in the literature. The corpora that the algorithms are trained on can contain either natural language text (e.g.

Wikipedia or newswire articles) or artificially-generated pseudo corpora, such as the output of the Random Walk on Graphs algorithm, when run to select sequences of nodes from a knowledge graph (KG) — see (Goikoetxea et al., 2015) and (Ristoski and Paulheim, 2016). We denote the pseudo corpus generated via Random Walk on Graphs algorithm as *Pseudo Corpus RWG*.

In this paper we present the results from our initial experiments of training word embeddings on the basis of generated pseudo corpora over a knowledge graph via lexical chain patterns. We name the pseudo corpus generated via lexical chain patterns *Pseudo Corpus LC*. The main knowledge graph in the experiments is the English WordNet (WN) (Fellbaum, 1998). It is represented as nodes corresponding to synsets in WN and arcs corresponding to relations encoded in WN, such as hypernymy, meronymy, entailment, etc. We have extended the graph with new relations between synsets (i.e. additional arcs in the graph). These new relations come from sources outside WordNet, such as relations extracted from semantically annotated corpora or explication of implicit knowledge in WordNet on the basis of inference procedures (e.g. transitive closure over the relations). In our previous work we showed that enriching the knowledge graph with more relations can lead to accuracy improvement in the Word Sense Disambiguation (WSD) task — (Simov et al., 2016b), (Simov et al., 2016a).

However, the relevant evaluation of such distributed semantic models still faces some issues. Here a few of the typical problems in this line of work are listed: a) the evaluation datasets merge similarity and association relations, while the models typically favor one subset and suppress the role of the other; b) uneven frequency of the words in the corpus; c) the impossibility to cover all words with all their meanings in all

Proceedings of Recent Advances in Natural Language Processing, pages 679–685,
Varna, Bulgaria, Sep 4–6 2017.

possible contexts. In this paper we aim to evaluate the obtained word embeddings for the similarity and association (relatedness) tasks. We report our initial experiments on training word embeddings over pseudo corpora generated with the help of lexical chain templates as measured on the following datasets: WordSim353 Similarity, WordSim353 Relatedness (see (Finkelstein et al., 2001) for introducing WordSim353) and SimLex-999 (Hill et al., 2015). We compare these results to the results over a pseudo corpora generated over the same knowledge graph with the help of Random Walk over Graphs as presented within (Goikoetxea et al., 2015). Our currently generated *Pseudo Corpora LC* do not lead to better word embeddings (with respect to the above mentioned evaluation) in comparison to the *Pseudo Corpora RWG*. However, they provide valuable additional knowledge which improves the performance of joint corpora.

The structure of the paper is as follows: the next section discusses related work; Section 3 describes the experimental setups including the used knowledge graphs, tools and evaluation datasets; Section 4 presents the results from the experiments; Section 5 concludes the paper.

2 Related Work

The content as well as the relation distribution within the knowledge graph play an important role in the successful performance of the various NLP tasks. One of the most approached tasks is Knowledge-based Word Sense Disambiguation (KWSD) — see (Agirre et al., 2014). Our own experiments showed that the manipulation of the knowledge graph with respect to adding new relations, combining various lexical relations or combining syntagmatic (corpus-based) and paradigmatic (lexicon-based) relations can improve the results in this task. For example, in (Simov et al., 2016b) we experimented with lexical relations from WN, glosses from eXtended WN as well as semantic relations, extracted from the syntactic annotation of SemCor (Miller et al., 1993). We reuse the sets of relations developed in these works to generate our *Pseudo Corpora LC*.

Goikoetxea et al. 2015 (Goikoetxea et al., 2015) describe an architecture in which a run of the Random Walk algorithm (Agirre et al., 2014) produces an artificial corpus from WordNet. The graph that is fed to the algorithm is composed of WordNet synsets (the graph nodes) and of different types of relations between them (the graph arcs; some relation types are antonymy, hypernymy, derivation, etc.). This corpus is then fed into a shallow neural net which creates distributed word representations. The authors use the Continuous Bag of Words (CBOW) and Skip-gram algorithms as introduced in (Mikolov et al., 2013). They show that training on the artificial corpus gives improvements over text-trained models on some datasets (WordSim353 Similarity, WordSim353 Relatedness and SimLex-999). They also conclude that all explored methods are complementary to each other. In Goikoetxea et al. 2016 (Goikoetxea et al., 2016), the idea described above is further developed with the inclusion of a text corpus in addition to the corpus generated from WordNet. Learning is first performed on each of the two resources, and then various combination methods are introduced. The combined system outperforms the other systems on similarity, equals in relatedness, showing the advantages of simple combinations (like concatenation of independently learned embeddings) to the more complex ones.[1]

In addition to the usage of Random Walks algorithm, we promote the idea of using the lexical chains for handling graph contexts. In (Hirst and St-Onge, 1996) this idea was exploited for detecting and correcting malapropisms. Lexical chains introduce light context in a meaningful, i.e. not random way. WordNet was used as source for word similarity in order to form various types of lexical chains. Three types of relations have been constituted: extra-strong (literal word repetition), strong (between words in the same synsets, direct horizontal links[2] - similarity, antonymy, etc.) and medium-strong (defined by allowable paths in the knowledge graph, like between an apple and a carrot). The authors investigate only noun chains. The procedure is monotonic. First, an extra-strong relation is sought for a word. If found, it is added to the corresponding chain. If not, a strong relation is sought with search scope limitation. Similarly, medium-strong relation is sought with even stricter context window. If nothing is found, a new chain is started. The lexical chainer has been tested intrinsically (omissions and misplacements in chains) as well as extrinsically (in a spelling correction task).

---

[1] Due to space limitations we do not present an extensive overview of the literature on word embeddings.

[2] For the directions of the relations see next section.

3   Experimental Setup

Our experimental setup adopts the idea of the lexical chains as a mechanism for generation of *Pseudo Corpora LC*. There are some important differences from (Hirst and St-Onge, 1996). First, we use relations not only between nouns, but also among other parts-of-speech (POS)— noun (N), verb (V), adjective (A), and adverb (R). Second, we construct lexical chains over a knowledge graph, instead of constructing lexical chains over texts. Our experience in Word Sense Disambiguation task showed that usually two types of context play important role for the task (Mihalcea et al., 2004): (1) **Local context** — where the semantic measures are used for disambiguating words additionally connected by syntactic relations; and (2) **Global context** — where the semantic measures are employed to derive lexical chains, which are viewed as threads of meaning throughout an entire text. In usual text-based word embeddings only the local context is mainly considered. The creation of pseudo corpora on the basis of knowledge graphs additionally provides information about words that are usually distributed in the global context.

In order to simulate lexical chains in a *Pseudo Corpus LC* we exploited the formula of (Hirst and St-Onge, 1996) for calculation of the word similarity within the medium-strong relations:

$$weight = C - pathLen - k * numberChDir$$

$pathLen$ is the length of the path in the graph, $numberChDir$ is the number of the changes in the relation path directions, C and k are parameters. In our first experiment, reported here, we consider as pseudo sentences in the *Pseudo Corpus LC* the paths starting from a given synset in WordNet and having weight above some threshold. We called such a path *lexical chain path*. Unfortunately, the number of paths starting at a given synset with appropriate weights has become exponentially huge. This prevented the practical usage of this set of paths. Thus, reduction of the number of paths generated for each synset was needed.

First, we define the number of occurrences of each relation in the lexical chain path. In such a way, the allowable paths are selected that provide bigger diversity of relations in the pseudo sentences. Even with these restrictions the number of the generated paths remained huge. Thus, we had to impose additional restrictions on the basis of the relation types. Two types of relations were

considered: *paradigmatic* and *syntagmatic*. We alternated the relations according to their types. For example, after up to three paradigmatic relations we allowed up to three syntagmatic ones.

3.1   Knowledge Graph Relations

The WordNet-based KG (WN) has been constructed out of the relations in the Princeton WordNet (PWN3.0) and additional relations added by us from different sources. PWN3.0 groups together words in synsets, which in the knowledge graph are represented as nodes. The relation types that are possible between the different synsets are 16 original relations from PWN3.0 and 7 additional relations (Table 1[3]). We also consider their reverse relations which allows us to have more freedom for navigating over the knowledge graph.

The relation `defby` is taken from set of relations **WNG**[4]. It contains relations extracted from WN3.0 glosses, as the glosses are annotated with synset ids in eXtended WordNet (XWN) — (Mihalcea and Moldovan, 2001). The relations in **WNG** are constructed as co-occurrences of a synset and the synsets for open class words in its gloss. For example, from the gloss: "a set of data arranged in rows and columns" for the synset {table, tabular array} the following relations are extracted: {table, tabular array} `defby` {set ...}; {table, tabular array} `defby` {data ...}; {table, tabular array} `defby` {arrange ...}; etc.

The relations `coinc`, `moda`, `modn`, `modv`, `hpart`, and `condto` are extracted from two sources: logical representation of glosses in XWN and dependency analyses of sentences in SemCor corpus. For example, the synset {disyllable, dissyllable} is defined by "a word having two syllables." The logical form for this gloss in XWN is the following

```
disyllable:NN(x1) ->
    word:NN(x1) have:VB(e1, x1, x2)
    two:JJ(x2) syllable:NN(x2)
```

In our opinion, each predicate that originates from a verbal, adjectival, adverbial, or prepositional lemma expresses an event. In the example, `have:VB(e1, x1, x2)` denote the event of "holding" of object denoted by `x2` by the object denoted by `x1`. Both of these objects are participants of the event of "holding" `e1`. From this

---

[3]Each relation is represented by its acronym, name, number of instances, POS combination (X-X denote all combinations of POS.), type (**S**yntagmatic and **P**aradigmatic) and direction (⇑ (UP), ⇓ (Down), and ⇔ (Horizontal)).

[4]This set of relations is downloaded from the web page of UKB System: http://ixa2.si.ehu.es/ukb/

Acronym	Name	Number	POS	Type	Direction
		WordNet Original Relations			
hyp	*hypernymy*	**89 089**	N-N, V-V	P	⇑
ant	*antonymy*	**8 689**	A-A, N-N, R-R, V-V	P	⇔
at	*attribute relation*	**886**	N-A, A-N	S	⇔
cls	*a member of a class*	**9 420**	A-N, N-N, R-N, V-N	S	⇑
cs	*cause*	**192**	V-V	S	⇓
der	*derivational morphology*	**74 644**	A-N, N-A, N-N, N-V	S	⇔
ent	*entailment*	**408**	V-V	S	⇓
ins	*instance*	**8 576**	N-N	P	⇑
mm	*member meronym*	**12 293**	N-N	P	⇑
mp	*part meronym*	**9 097**	N-N	P	⇑
ms	*substance meronym*	**797**	N-N	P	⇑
per	*pertains*	**8 505**	A-N, R-A	S	⇔
ppl	*participle*	**79**	A-V	S	⇔
sa	*additional information*	**3 269**	A-A, V-V	P	⇔
sim	*similar in meaning*	**21 386**	A-A	P	⇔
vgp	*similar in meaning verb*	**1 725**	V-V	S	⇔
		Additional Relations			
defby	*defined by*	**419 387**	X-X	P	⇑
coinc	*cooccurrences*	**93 221**	A-A, N-N, V-V, R-R	S	⇔
moda	*adverb modifier*	**1 970**	R-A, R-V	S	⇓
modn	*adjective modifier*	**69 857**	A-N, V-N	S	⇓
modv	*adverb modifying verb*	**10 653**	R-V	S	⇓
hpart	*has participant*	**128 444**	V-N	S	⇓
condto	*condition to*	**2 494**	V-V	S	⇑

Table 1: Relations in Knowledge Graph.

we extract the following relations: {have} hpart {word} — "word" is a participant in the event denoted by "have"; {have} hpart {syllable} — "syllable" is a participant in the event denoted by "have"; {word} coinc {syllable} — co-participants in the same event; and {two} moda {syllable} — "two" modifies "syllable".

Similarly from {ice-cream cone} defined by "ice cream in a crisp conical wafer" the following logical form is presented:

```
ice-cream_cone:NN(x1) ->
    ice_cream:NN(x1) in:IN(x1, x2)
    crisp:JJ(x2) conical:JJ(x2)
    wafer:NN(x2)
```

From it we extracted the following relation: {crisp} coinc {conical} in the appropriate senses, because they modified the same noun.

The reverse relations have the same characteristics as the original ones, except for the direction which is changed to the opposite one. For some relations the reverse ones are not added because they are symmetric like ant relation. The knowledge graph used in the experiments is defined as a set of nodes formed by the synsets of WN, and the arcs corresponds to all above relations. This knowledge graph is called **WNUnion**.

3.2 Pseudo-corpus Generation

For the pseudo corpus generation on the basis of the knowledge graph **WNUnion** we used a cascade vertical approach (fig. 1). We started with the generation of relation templates — combinations of relations without concrete synset ids. Here is an example of a path consisting of three relations: ○–modn–○–mp–○–hpart-1–○[5]. This determines a set of lexical chains that contain an adjective modifying a noun (local context), then part-of relation between two nouns (global context), and then connection between a noun and a verb where the noun refers to a participant predicated by the verb (local context). For each template we used a mapping to the knowledge graph and identified all possible

---

[5]In this case "-1" in hpart-1 denotes the reverse relation from a noun to a verb.

paths — the empty nodes (⃝) in templates were filled by synset identifiers in KG. For the template above we generated 8 866 possible combinations of synset ids. Here is one example: {02176178-a}–modn–{03614007-n}–mp–{03928116-n}–hpart-1–{00599992-v}. Finally we applied lemma substitution to each path and generated pseudo sentences. From the above example we generated the following pseudo sentence: `complex keyboard piano learn`. Keep in mind that the relation `hpart` (and thus `hpart-1`) does not distinguish between the syntactic roles of the event participants. Thus, in the example `piano` could be a direct object in a real sentence.

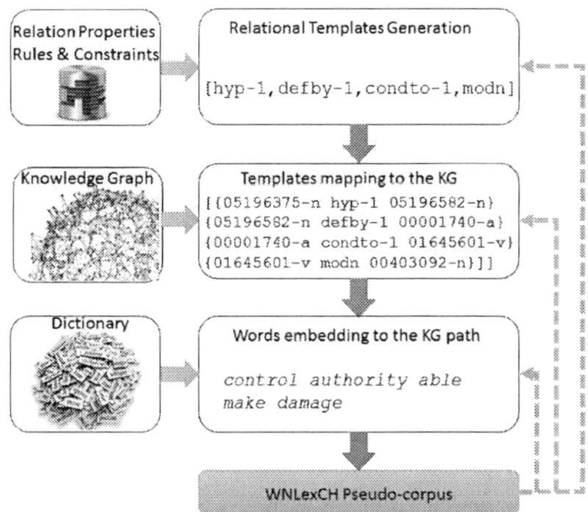

Figure 1: WNLexCH pseudo-corpus generation

The method was applied several times iterating the length of the generated templates from 2 up to the desired maximal pseudo sentence length. At each step the method reused the generated templates, paths and pseudo-sentences by joining them into a longer one. The combination of relations in the templates reflects their properties like direction, transitivity, allowed maximal number of repetitions, scope, relation type - paradigmatic and syntagmatic. In addition, some constraints for templates generation were used, like penalties for each direction change; consecutive relation and its opposite were allowed only for transitive relations etc. Note that in these experiments we used only pseudo-sentences generated on the first 3 steps because of the exploding size of the pseudo corpus. In the experiments we used subcorpora of **WNLexCH**, depending on the length of the paths involved in the corresponding subcorpora: **WN-LexCH 2R** — paths of length 2 (466 285 957 pseudo sentences); **WNLexCH 3R** — paths of length 3 (733 998 728 pseudo sentences); **WNLexCH 4R** — paths of length 4 (143 416 212 pseudo sentences); and the whole corpus **WN-LexCH**.

4 Experiment Results

The generated corpora have been fed into the Word2Vec tool[6] in order for the models to be trained. Initially, we performed experiments with different settings of the system parameters: context window size varying from 1 to 19 words, with the best results in most cases being for context window of 5 and context window of 15 words (reported below); iterations from 1 to 9, with best results for 7 iterations; negative examples set to 5; and frequency cut sampling was set to 7.

The evaluation of the word embeddings was done over the following datasets: *Word-Sim353 Similarity*, *WordSim353 Relatedness*[7], and *SimLex-999*[8]. Each of the datasets consists of pair of words and numeric value of their similarity (*WordSim353 Similarity* and *SimLex-999*) or their relatedness (*WordSim353 Relatedness*). The numerical values were established on the basis of consultation with a number of human subjects. The evaluation was done in the following manner: first, the distance between the words in each pair was calculated on the basis of the corresponding word embedding; then, Spearman's rank correlation between the predicted distances and the gold standard values was calculated.

We have performed a number of experiments through the different subcorpora as described above. As baselines, we evaluated two text-corpus-based word embeddings that are freely available on the web, as well as the best result of Goikoetxea et al. (Goikoetxea et al., 2015), available from the UKB web page[9]. Thus, the pseudo-corpus-based embeddings have been compared with text-based embeddings. We have selected two text-based sets of word vectors[10]: Google News trained over 100 billion running words — named **GoogleNews**; and Wikipedia dependency trained over context extracted from a dependency analysis of Wikipedia articles — named **Depen-**

---

[6]https://code.google.com/archive/p/word2vec/
[7]http://alfonseca.org/eng/research/wordsim353.html.
[8]https://www.cl.cam.ac.uk/fh295/simlex.html
[9]http://ixa2.si.ehu.es/ukb/
[10]https://github.com/3Top/word2vec-api

Embedding	WordSim353 Similarity	WordSim353 Relatedness	SimLex-999
GoogleNews	0.77145	**0.61988**	0.44196
Dependency	0.76699	0.46764	0.44730
WN+WNG$_{best}$	**0.78670**	**0.61316**	**0.52479**
WNLexCH 2R	0.45172	0.29896	0.33593
WNLexCH 3R	0.66728	0.55904	0.48925
WNLexCH 4R	0.59042	0.41102	0.47418
WNLexCH	0.70038	0.52050	0.47907
WNUnion Random	0.74378	0.59988	0.51650
WNUnion Random + WNLexCH 3R	0.74998	**0.63375**	*0.52302*
WNUnion Random + WNLexCH	*0.75916*	0.62848	0.52125

Table 2: Results from experiments with different extensions of the WordNet knowledge graph. All our embeddings were trained with the same options for word2vec.

dency. The results for these baselines are presented in the first three rows of Table 2.

The experiments were divided into two groups: (1) experiments by our algorithm with corpora generated with different numbers of relations; and (2) experiments by the UKB system with a pseudo corpus generated over the same knowledge graph, and its combinations with the corpora generated by our algorithm. In Table 2 we present some results for each type of the experiments.

The results from the experiments show that increasing the length of the lexical chain path improves the results of the word embeddings with respect to both similarity and relatedness measures. In order to compare our approach to the *Pseudo Corpus RWG* we have generated a pseudo corpus over the same knowledge graph **WNUnion**. The result shows that the *Pseudo Corpus RWG* is better in comparison to the *Pseudo Corpus LC* with its length of the paths up to four. But on the other hand, the combination of the *Pseudo Corpus RWG* and the *Pseudo Corpus LC* produces better results than each of them separately — the last two rows in Table 2.

5 Conclusion

The paper presents an approach to the generation of pseudo corpora on the basis of lexical chain templates over knowledge graphs. We showed that the knowledge within the closer neighborhood of the synsets plays an important role for the similarity and relatedness evaluation. In some cases they outperformed the embeddings trained on text corpora. The improvement over Pseudo Corpora RWG, generated on the same KG, shows also that

longer lexical chain paths are necessary. In our view the main reason for the current results is the fact that the pseudo corpus **WNLexCH** reflects all the relations in the local context of the synsets in the KG. In our work (Simov et al., 2017) we demonstrated that different combinations of relations in the KG generally improved performance of similarity and relatedness. Our hope is that knowledge learned by the embeddings over *Pseudo Corpus LC* is more homogeneous comparing to embeddings over text corpora where the problem is with the infrequent words. In these cases the embeddings learned less features than the ones for the frequent ones. The problem with the embeddings over *Pseudo Corpus RWG* is that there is no way to control the coverage.

Our research is in-line with the current tendency of building artificial corpora for various NLP tasks due to sparseness and bias of the available data. In future, we envisage to do experiments with selections of longer lexical chain paths. Also we will perform extrinsic evaluation incorporating the various embeddings in Neural Network systems for different NLP tasks. On the basis of the results we plan to do experiments with different lexical chain templates in order to determine the most appropriate models for each target NLP task.

Acknowledgements

This research has received partial support by the grant 02/12 — *Deep Models of Semantic Knowledge (DemoSem)*, funded by the Bulgarian National Science Fund in 2017–2019 . We are grateful to the anonymous reviewers for their remarks, comments, and suggestions.

References

Eneko Agirre, Oier López de Lacalle, and Aitor Soroa. 2014. Random walks for knowledge-based word sense disambiguation. *Comput. Linguist.* 40(1):57–84.

Christiane Fellbaum, editor. 1998. *WordNet An Electronic Lexical Database.* The MIT Press, Cambridge, MA ; London.

Lev Finkelstein, Evgeniy Gabrilovich, Yossi Matias, Ehud Rivlin, Zach Solan, Gadi Wolfman, and Eytan Ruppin. 2001. Placing search in context: The concept revisited. In *Proceedings of the 10th International Conference on World Wide Web.* ACM, New York, NY, USA, WWW '01, pages 406–414.

Josu Goikoetxea, Eneko Agirre, and Aitor Soroa. 2016. Single or multiple? combining word representations independently learned from text and wordnet. In *AAAI.* AAAI Press, pages 2608–2614.

Josu Goikoetxea, Aitor Soroa, and Eneko Agirre. 2015. Random walks and neural network language models on knowledge bases. In *HLT-NAACL.* The Association for Computational Linguistics, pages 1434–1439.

Felix Hill, Roi Reichart, and Anna Korhonen. 2015. Simlex-999: Evaluating semantic models with (genuine) similarity estimation. *Computational Linguistics* .

Graeme Hirst and David St-Onge. 1996. *Lexical chains as representations of context for the detection and correction of malapropisms,* The MIT Press.

Rada Mihalcea and Dan I. Moldovan. 2001. extended wordnet: progress report. In *in Proceedings of NAACL Workshop on WordNet and Other Lexical Resources.* pages 95–100.

Rada Mihalcea, Paul Tarau, and Elizabeth Figa. 2004. Pagerank on semantic networks, with application to word sense disambiguation. In *Proceedings of Coling 2004.* COLING, Geneva, Switzerland, pages 1126–1132.

Tomas Mikolov, Kai Chen, Greg Corrado, and Jeffrey Dean. 2013. Efficient estimation of word representations in vector space. *CoRR* abs/1301.3781.

George A. Miller, Claudia Leacock, Randee Tengi, and Ross T. Bunker. 1993. A semantic concordance. In *Proc. of HLT '93.* pages 303–308.

Petar Ristoski and Heiko Paulheim. 2016. Rdf2vec: Rdf graph embeddings for data mining. In *International Semantic Web Conference.* Springer, pages 498–514.

Kiril Simov, Petya Osenova, and Alexander Popov. 2016a. Using context information for knowledge-based word sense disambiguation. In Christo Dichev and Gennady Agre, editors, *Proceedings of Artificial Intelligence: Methodology, Systems, and Applications (AIMSA 2016).* Springer International Publishing, Cham, pages 130–139.

Kiril Simov, Petya Osenova, and Alexander Popov. 2017. Comparison of word embeddings from different knowledge graphs. In *Proceedings of Language, Data, and Knowledge Conference.* Springer International Publishing, pages 213–221.

Kiril Simov, Alexander Popov, and Petya Osenova. 2016b. The role of the wordnet relations in the knowledge-based word sense disambiguation task. In *Proceedings of Eighth Global WordNet Conference..* pages 391–398.

Word Embeddings as Features for Supervised Coreference Resolution

Iliana Simova
Saarland University
Saarbrücken, Germany
ilianas@coli.uni-saarland.de

Hans Uszkoreit
Language Technology Lab, DFKI
Alt-Moabit 91c, Berlin, Germany
uszkoreit@dfki.de

Abstract

A common reason for errors in coreference resolution is the lack of semantic
information to help determine the compatibility between mentions referring to
the same entity. Distributed representations, which have been shown successful
in encoding relatedness between words,
could potentially be a good source of such
knowledge. Moreover, being obtained
in an unsupervised manner, they could
help address data sparsity issues in labeled
training data at a small cost. In this work
we investigate whether and to what extend
features derived from word embeddings
can be successfully used for supervised
coreference resolution. We experiment
with several word embedding models,
and several different types of embedding-
based features, including embedding cluster and cosine similarity-based features.
Our evaluations show improvements in the
performance of a supervised state-of-the-
art coreference system.

1 Introduction

Coreference resolution is the task of automatically
identifying expressions in a text which refer to the
same real-world entity. It is an important intermediate step for a number of Natural Language Processing (NLP) applications which depend on text
understanding, such as machine translation, relation extraction, and question answering, to name a
few.

There is a wide range of approaches for solving coreference resolution. Some successful systems rely on rules and heuristics (Lee et al., 2011),
others employ a variety of machine learning models (Martschat et al., 2015; Björkelund and Kuhn,

2014). One aspect they have in common is the
recognition that the process could benefit from
some form of lexical and encyclopedic knowledge.
For instance, lexical relations such as synonymy
and hyperonymy (e.g., *a capital* is *a city*), world
knowledge (e.g., *France* is *a country*), and even
attributive knowledge (e.g., *countries* have *areas*
and *population*) could all prove helpful for the
task.

Durrett and Klein (2013) have shown that to
achieve state-of-the-art performance in coreference resolution, one does not need complicated
heuristic-driven features. However, they identify
the task of including semantics into the process as
an "uphill battle". Many works explore sources of
semantic knowledge for the task. Some include
mining unannotated data (Bean and Riloff, 2004;
Mohit Bansal, 2012), structured lexical databases
(Daumé III and Marcu, 2005), and knowledge
bases (Rahman and Ng, 2011). In this work we
explore a different source of semantic knowledge,
namely distributed word representations.

Word embeddings are representations of word
meaning taking the perspective that the sense of
a word is defined by the company it keeps, or its
context words. In some models, these representations are learned as a prediction task using neural
networks (Mikolov et al., 2013), other approaches
use dimensionality reduction on a co-occurrence
matrix (Pennington et al., 2014). The resulting
representations have been shown to encode word
relatedness and similarity. Depending on the context selected to represent a word's sense, this similarity can take different forms (Levy and Goldberg, 2014). Such representations are typically
learned from large collections of text in an unsupervised manner. If we employ them to a supervised task, they could also prove useful in addressing some data sparsity issues in the training data.
Therefore they are an attractive source of semantic

Proceedings of Recent Advances in Natural Language Processing, pages 686–693,
Varna, Bulgaria, Sep 4–6 2017.

knowledge, which can be obtained at a small cost and be beneficial in multiple ways.

In this work we explore the usefulness of features derived from word embeddings for the task of coreference resolution. We experiment with several general purpose word embedding models, and several different types of features derived from word embeddings, including embedding cluster and cosine similarity-based features.

2 Related Work

Word embeddings generally serve as input to deep learning architectures. Several works have applied such techniques successfully to the task of coreference resolution (Wiseman et al., 2016; Clark and Manning, 2016). While such systems reach state-of-the-art performance without the need for elaborate handcrafted features, complexity is added in terms of the model. In this work we investigate whether word embeddings could also be beneficial when used in another simpler way and a standard setting - in the form of features for supervised learning. To the best of our knowledge this is the first work to apply such features to supervised coreference resolution.

Several works have explored the application of word embedding features to supervised learning systems for other NLP tasks.

Turian et al. (2010) compare several unsupervised word representation models for Named Entity Recognition (NER) and chunking. The authors find that each of them improves on state-of-the-art supervised baselines. Yu et al. (2013) further explore other ways of encoding word embedding information at a lower computational cost by performing prior clustering of the embeddings and inducing a cluster label feature.

In (Guo et al., 2014), word embedding-based features are studied in relation to the task of NER. The work further explores several different ways of deriving features from word embeddings - 1) by creating a binarized version of the embedding to consider features with strong opinions on each dimension, 2) by clustering of the embedding via k-means and including the cluster label as a feature, and 3) as a distributional prototype feature. In the latter, a few examples are automatically selected to represent each type of named entity, and then cosine similarity is calculated between the embeddings of the word in question and these prototypes. All word embedding-based features brought improvements to the baseline, and over the direct use of the embedding. Moreover, a combination of the features led to a greater improvement in performance, indicating that the knowledge represented by them is not overlapping completely.

Similarly to Guo et al. (2014), in this work we experiment with several different word embedding-based features. We employ prior clustering of the word embeddings and include the obtained cluster label as a feature, with the expectation that it would encourage semantic compatibility between candidate coreferring expressions. One difference here lies in choice of clustering algorithm - spherical k-means was selected due to its use of cosine similarity as a distance metric as opposed to Euclidean distance which is employed in standard k-means. We consider this metric more suitable when comparing word embeddings, and expect that its use would result in more meaningful clusters. In addition to also directly using the original word embedding as a feature, we experiment with reduced version of it. While a prototype-based feature could also prove useful for this task, we plan to investigate it in future work.

3 Experimental Setup

This section offers more details on the way in which we use word embeddings as features for supervised learning, as well as on the word embedding models selected for the current experiments. We further present the baseline coreference system.

3.1 Word Embedding Models

There is a fairly big selection of available pre-trained general purpose word embedding models. As a first step towards designing word embedding-based features, we have selected three of them with varying properties. These include: the word2vec embedding (Mikolov et al., 2013) trained on part of the Google News dataset, with a vocabulary of 3 million words and phrases (e.g., New_York), a GloVe embedding (Pennington et al., 2014) trained on Wikipedia and Gigaword 5 with a vocabulary of 400 thousand words, and the dependency-based word embedding (Levy and Goldberg, 2014) model trained on part of Wikipedia, with a vocabulary size of about 180 thousand words. All of the selected embeddings are of dimension 300. For simplicity we refer to them as *w2v*, *glove* and *deps*, respectively.

Our aim is not to provide a fair comparison of these models, but rather to see if some of them with their specific characteristics would prove particularly useful for our task. For instance, the first two embedding models have different types of training data. The word2vec model is trained on news data, which coincides with the majority of the data in the OntoNotes corpus, and has the largest vocabulary of the three. The GloVe model, in addition to news data present in Gigaword, also incorporates the encyclopedic knowledge of Wikipedia. The dependency embedding, on the other hand, takes a different perspective on which words in the context of a word are important for determining it's sense, and make use of dependency analysis in order to select meaningful contexts. The resulting embeddings have been shown to exhibit more functional similarity (Levy and Goldberg, 2014).

3.2 Features Derived from Word Embeddings

3.2.1 Embedding Cluster

We perform a clustering of word embeddings and assign a cluster label to the head words of each mention pair under consideration. The motivation behind this is that this clustering would provide us with a form of a semantic tag which could either ensure semantic compatibility between the mentions directly when two mentions fall into the same cluster, or be used by the supervised system to learn compatible anaphor-antecedent combinations from the training data. During clustering, each word embedding vector is treated as a single instance, and the resulting clusters consist of the words with the most similar embeddings according to a distance metric.

The selection of clustering algorithm is guided by the choice of suitable distance metric. As cosine similarity is popularly used to compare embeddings of words, our clustering algorithm of choice is spherical k-means[1].

We experiment with several different values for number of clusters in order to determine what granularity is most suitable for the task. The values include 50, 100, 500 for less fine-grained clusters, and 1k to 10k in steps of 2.5k for more fine-grained ones.

3.2.2 Dense Embedding Features

Another way to deliver word embedding information to the coreference system is by including the embedding vector directly. In this setting each dimension of the vector of a mention's head word is a separate numeric feature. This is justified by the fact that different dimensions of each embedding can be considered as latent features encoding different properties of a word (Turian et al., 2010).

One consideration here is that by including the whole vector we increase the amount of features substantially. Therefore we also experimented with reduced versions of the original vectors by Principal Component Analysis (PCA)[2]. PCA examines the correlation between different dimensions in the word embedding vector, and identifies a smaller number of variables that best explain the original vector. The vectors were reduced to retain different amounts of variability present in the original data, which addresses over-fitting, and effectively reduces the amount of features to be added. We experiment with variance levels of 10% to 100% in steps of 10%.

3.2.3 Cosine Similarity Features

The third set of word embedding features is based on cosine similarity. Cosine similarity computes the cosine of the angle between two vectors, and in the case of word embeddings, provides a measure of relatedness between words. We estimate the similarity between the head words of each anaphor and antecedent (ANA, ANTE) in a candidate pair, as well as between their governing words (GOV_{ana}, GOV_{ante}) in the dependency tree, and the combinations ANA-GOV_{ante} and ANTE-GOV_{ana}.

This feature could prove useful in cases of pronoun resolution, where the context of the pronoun referring expression is a deciding factor. Consider the example from (Jespersen, 1949), "If the *baby* does not thrive on *raw milk*, boil *it*.", where the pronoun *it* has two candidate antecedents. The cosine similarity between the governing word of the anaphor, *boil*, and the second antecedent candidate, *milk*, is very high, as opposed to between the alternative pairing which leads to an undesirable interpretation. As GOV_{ana} and GOV_{ante} are often verbs, this feature could also prove useful when coreferring mentions carry out related actions ("During an interview he *said* [..] He further *reported* that [..]").

---

[1] https://github.com/clara-labs/spherecluster

[2] package sklearn.decomposition.PCA

Feature set	F1
baseline	59.19
$+\text{EC}_{w2v,2.5k}$	59.56
$+\text{CS}_{glove,pca\text{-}20}$	59.49
$+\text{WE}_{glove,pca\text{-}50}$	59.67
$+\text{EC}_{glove,2.5k}$ $+\text{CS}_{glove,pca\text{-}20}$	59.68
$+\text{CS}_{deps,pca\text{-}60}$ $+\text{WE}_{glove,pca\text{-}50}$	59.66
$+\text{EC}_{glove,2.5k}$ $+\text{WE}_{glove,pca\text{-}50}$	59.66
$+\text{EC}_{glove,5k}$ $+\text{CS}_{deps,pca\text{-}90}$ $+\text{WE}_{glove}$	**59.72**

Table 1: Summary of the performance of the coreference system (CoNLL F1) with different sets of features. Individual features include: embedding cluster (EC) label, cosine similarity (CS) features, and word embedding (WE) features, as described in subsection 3.2.

When calculating the cosine similarity between two words, we use the vectors of the original word embeddings, as well as PCA-reduced versions of them.

3.3 Coreference Resolution System

The coreference resolution toolkit *cort* (Martschat et al., 2015; Martschat and Strube, 2015) was used to obtain the baseline, and extended in our further experiments. The system offers several implementations of popular coreference resolution approaches, as well as ways of visualizing and comparing the outputs of different models. In this work we employ a *mention-pair* model with *best-first* clustering. This model breaks down the task of coreference resolution into pairwise coreference decisions. The construction of coreference chains is then enabled via clustering.

The baseline employs a standard set of features, including: number, gender, various string matching and distance features, semantic class ("person", "object", "numeric"), fine type (name, definite/indefinite noun phrase, etc.), and others [3].

4 Results

4.1 Evaluation

Table 1 contains the best results achieved by the coreference resolution tool per feature and feature combination. All of the models were trained and tested on the CoNLL-2012 training and test data sets with automatic preprocessing. The evaluation

metric is CoNLL-F1 score (average of MUC, B^3, and CEAF_e). Due to space limitations we do not provide a detailed list of results, but a discussion of the most important ones is included below.

When considering the embedding cluster feature in isolation, we observed that the best performing setting is that with the *w2v* embedding and 2.5K number of clusters. For the other two embedding models, the same amount of clusters was also most successful. We observed a drop in performance for high number of clusters (over 7.5K) with all three models. In 12% of the experiments we obtained a small drop in performance below the baseline score.

For the cosine similarity set of features, the best performance was achieved by *glove* with explained variance of 20%. Using the whole word embedding vectors to compute this feature lead to worse results for all embedding models, and the performance of the feature across different reductions was unstable, often dropping slightly below the baseline level (results were in the range 58.97-59.49, with 36% worse than the baseline).

The best result with the word embedding feature was achieved with *glove* and variance of 50%. Here we also observed that when the original embeddings were used, the performance was worse compared to the reduced versions. The models' performance ranged from 59.06 to 59.67, with 25% of them performing worse than the baseline.

The second part of Table 1 shows the best pairwise combinations of features. We experimented with combinations of some of the best performing individual features. Our goal is to determine if the knowledge they encode is complementary to each other. The most complementary feature combination is embedding cluster and cosine similarity. For the rest of the combinations we did not observe any gains in performance over the use of the best individual feature.

With a combination of three of the feature types we obtained the highest scoring model of 59.72 F1 score.

4.2 Error Analysis

As the automatic evaluation doesn't offer a very good insight on where the word embedding feature models differ with respect to the baseline model and each other, we include a more detailed recall and precision error analysis.

We use the methodology proposed in

---

[3] see https://github.com/smartschat/cort for a complete list

Precision Error Analysis					
Error Category	Feature Set				
ANA → ANTE	baseline	$+EC_{w2v,2.5k}$	$+CS_{glove,pca\text{-}20}$	$+WE_{glove,pca\text{-}50}$	$+EC+CS+WE_{best}$
Pron → Pron	33%	33%	34% △	35% △	33%
Pron → Name	5%	5%	5%	5%	5%
Pron → Noun	7%	7%	7%	**6%**	7%
Name → Pron	1%	2% △	2% △	1%	1%
Name → Name	21%	21%	21%	22% △	22% △
Name → Noun	1%	2% △	1%	1%	1%
Noun → Pron	1%	1%	1%	1%	1%
Noun → Name	2%	**1%**	2%	2%	2%
Noun → Noun	27%	**26%**	**25%**	**26%**	**26%**
total num. errors	4758	**4712**	**4638**	**4500**	**4565**

Table 2: Precision error analysis of some of the best models per type of anaphor and antecedent. A decrease in the amount of errors is marked in **bold**, and an increase: with the symbol △.

(Martschat and Strube, 2014). In this study, coreference chains are viewed as complete one directional graphs, following the order in which mentions occur in the text. Error analysis is then viewed as comparing graphs in terms of edges. A system's output is transformed into a maximum spanning tree using a notion from accessibility theory to select the most likely missing links needed to reach the reference graph. If an edge in the resulting graph is missing from the reference entity, this is considered a recall error. To extract precision errors, the anaphor and antecedent decisions made by a system are used in a similar manner. This representation allows for the recall and precision errors to be categorized in terms of type of anaphor and antecedent.

4.2.1 Precision Error Analysis

The results of our precision error analysis are provided in Table 2. In bold we mark all cases where a reduction of the amount of errors is visible as compared to the baseline system, while an increase in the amount of errors is marked with the symbol △. The percentages denote the proportion of errors per error type from the total number of errors a system made. For instance, in the baseline system, resolving a link between a pronoun anaphor and a pronoun antecedent ("Pron → Pron") was responsible for 33% of the total number of errors, 4758.

All of the systems manage to achieve a reduction in the total number of precision errors compared to the baseline system (see "total number of errors"). The word embedding model comes first with 258 fewer errors, followed by the best combination model with 193 fewer errors.

We observe interesting results for the category "Noun → Noun", where both the anaphor and antecedent are noun phrases. All of the systems manage to improve over the baseline, showing the influence of the semantic knowledge introduced by the word embedding features. Here surprisingly the most improvement is achieved by the cosine similarity model (25% or 105 fewer errors in raw counts).

Our initial hypothesis that the cosine similarity model would be especially useful for pronoun resolution was not supported by the evaluation results. For the category "Pron → Pron", it even lead to more precision errors.

The word embedding model is the one which stands out in terms of overall performance, but it leads to more errors in two of the categories: "Pron → Pron" and "Name → Name". For the first one, it is perhaps to be expected, as the word embedding of a pronoun is not particularly informative, given no additional context information. The latter result was surprising, as we anticipated that the model would be able to detect more aliases and name variations.

The combination model does not seem to inherit some of the negative properties of the other models, as it does not have worse performance than the baseline for most of the categories which were

<table>
<tr><td colspan="6" align="center">Recall Error Analysis</td></tr>
<tr><td>Error Category</td><td colspan="5" align="center">Feature Set</td></tr>
<tr><td>ANA → ANTE</td><td>baseline</td><td>+EC$_{w2v,2.5k}$</td><td>+CS$_{glove,pca\text{-}20}$</td><td>+WE$_{glove,pca\text{-}50}$</td><td>+EC+CS+WE$_{best}$</td></tr>
<tr><td>Pron → Pron</td><td>7%</td><td>7%</td><td>7%</td><td>7%</td><td>7%</td></tr>
<tr><td>Pron → Name</td><td>10%</td><td>10%</td><td>10%</td><td>10%</td><td>10%</td></tr>
<tr><td>Pron → Noun</td><td>17%</td><td>17%</td><td>17%</td><td>17%</td><td>17%</td></tr>
<tr><td>Name → Pron</td><td>1%</td><td>1%</td><td>1%</td><td>1%</td><td>1%</td></tr>
<tr><td>Name → Name</td><td>18%</td><td>18%</td><td>18%</td><td>18%</td><td>18%</td></tr>
<tr><td>Name → Noun</td><td>3%</td><td>3%</td><td>3%</td><td>4% △</td><td>4% △</td></tr>
<tr><td>Noun → Pron</td><td>1%</td><td>1%</td><td>1%</td><td>1%</td><td>1%</td></tr>
<tr><td>Noun → Name</td><td>9%</td><td>9%</td><td>9%</td><td>9%</td><td>9%</td></tr>
<tr><td>Noun → Noun</td><td>21%</td><td>21%</td><td>21%</td><td>21%</td><td>21%</td></tr>
<tr><td>total num. errors</td><td>4844</td><td>4800</td><td>4853 △</td><td>4861 △</td><td>4835</td></tr>
</table>

Table 3: Recall Error Analysis of some of the best models per type of anaphor and antecedent. A decrease in the amount of errors is marked in **bold**, and an increase: with the symbol △.

problematic for the individual feature models.

4.2.2 Recall Error Analysis

The error analysis in terms of recall presented in Table 3 was not as informative as the precision one. Most of the systems perform similarly, with small variations in raw counts per error category.

Only two of the models manage to obtain lower total number of recall errors compared to the baseline: the embedding cluster with 44 fewer errors, and the combination model with 9. The overall good performance of the word embedding model in terms of precision is a result of a Precision-Recall trade-off.

5 Discussion

On the topic of selecting a word embedding model, we made several observations. In the automatic evaluation and error analysis for most of our experiments, including ones not reported here, the *glove* word embedding proved to be most useful. The *deps* model stood out in conjunction with the cosine similarity feature. Given that it has the smallest vocabulary of the three, it would be interesting so see how this type of embedding performs for the task when trained on a bigger data set. This would also allow us to fairly compare the former model, encoding more topical similarity, and the latter with more functional similarity. We believe that both types of knowledge are of importance with respect to coreference resolution.

The error analysis presented in subsection 4.2 suggests the need for a task-specific word embedding with a special handling of pronouns and names. While all tested feature configurations were beneficial for resolving coreferences involving common nouns, for several other categories involving the aforementioned types of expressions, they did not improve and sometimes even lead to a degradation in precision. The exploration of suitable task-specific models which address these issues is left to future work.

We observed a trade-off between performance in terms of F1 measure and computational cost. Our results partially support the findings of Yu et al. (2013) - the embedding cluster feature was the most cost-effective way to provide word embedding information to the coreference tool. However, it did not lead to better coreference resolution performance over the direct use of the word embedding. The word embedding feature did lead to longer training and testing, but using the PCA reduction technique improved on both running time and F1 measure.

Additional complexity is added to the coreference model when attempting to combine several of the word embedding features. Moreover, it is not trivial to find a good combination - selecting the features configurations which perform best in isolation did not necessarily lead to a more successful combination, as can be seen in Table 1.

We performed an additional study of the effect of the newly introduced word embedding features when some of the original features had been re-

Feature set	F1	ΔF1
baseline	59.19	
+EC$_{w2v,2.5k}$	59.56	+0.37
+WE$_{glove,pca\text{-}50}$	59.67	+0.48
-gender	59.10	-0.09
-gender, +EC$_{w2v,2.5k}$	59.18	-0.01
-gender, +WE$_{glove,pca\text{-}50}$	59.34	+0.15
-number	59.39	+0.20
-number, +EC$_{w2v,2.5k}$	59.33	+0.14
-number, +WE$_{glove,pca\text{-}50}$	59.43	+0.24
-head	59.19	+0.00
-head, +EC$_{w2v,2.5k}$	59.28	+0.09
-head, +WE$_{glove,pca\text{-}50}$	59.29	+0.10
-head_NE	59.14	-0.05
-head_NE, +EC$_{w2v,2.5k}$	59.34	+0.15
-head_NE, +WE$_{glove,pca\text{-}50}$	59.34	+0.15
-semclass	59.23	+0.04
-semclass, +EC$_{w2v,2.5k}$	59.44	+0.25
-semclass, +WE$_{glove,pca\text{-}50}$	59.46	+0.27
-finetype	55.50	-3.69
-finetype, +EC$_{w2v,2.5k}$	55.98	-3.21
-finetype, +WE$_{glove,pca\text{-}50}$	55.74	-3.45

Table 4: Interaction of some of the original and newly introduced features. ΔF1 denotes the difference in the performance of a model compared to the baseline.

moved. The goal of this experiment was to determine to what extend the knowledge encoded by these features overlaps with some of the semantic information already present in the original ones, and whether they might be better alternatives to them. These include: gender and number information, head word and Named Entity (NE) tag of the head word, and semantic class and fine type of the mention. Table 4 presents a summary of the results.

None of the new features seem to completely cover the information encoded by the original ones. Rather, they work best in the setting where they interact with each other. The dense word embedding feature includes more of the *number* and *gender* information, compared to the embedding cluster feature. An explanation for this could be that the different dimensions of an embedding of a word encode some of these properties. Thus the

word embedding feature is a better way of providing them to the coreference system, as each dimension is kept as a separate numeric feature. This information is partially lost when performing clustering. For head word, its NE tag, and semantic class, we do not observe a big difference between the performance of the two new features. Both of them seem to successfully encode information on the semantic class of a word. For the fine type feature, the embedding cluster outperforms the word embedding feature, but neither manage to cover much of this information.

6 Conclusion

This work offers some insights on how word embeddings can be applied to the task of coreference resolution. We present three different features derived from word embeddings, and show that they influence the coreference resolution process in different ways. These include a setting in which each dimension of the embedding is a separate numeric feature, an embedding cluster which approximates a semantic class, and a set of cosine similarity features, which incorporate some contextual information.

Our evaluation results and error analysis show that each of these features helps to improve over the baseline coreference system's performance. We observed a reduction in the total number of precision errors. Moreover, all features lead to a reduction in the amount of precision errors in resolving references between common nouns. These results indicate that they successfully incorporate some lexical semantic and world knowledge into the process.

One of the ways in which we would like to extend the current experiments in future work is by creating a task-specific word embedding. Our error analysis shows that the current approach degraded the precision for the resolution of pronouns and names. For the former, word embeddings do not contribute much without the availability of more contextual information. We will investigate some specific examples to determine the reason for the latter.

We would further like to study the influence of models encoding more topical in comparison to ones with more functional similarity to the coreference resolution task.

References

David L. Bean and Ellen Riloff. 2004. Unsupervised learning of contextual role knowledge for coreference resolution. In *HLT-NAACL*. The Association for Computational Linguistics, pages 297–304.

Anders Björkelund and Jonas Kuhn. 2014. Learning structured perceptrons for coreference resolution with latent antecedents and non-local features. In *Proceedings of the 52nd Annual Meeting of the Association for Computational Linguistics (Volume 1: Long Papers)*. Association for Computational Linguistics.

Kevin Clark and Christopher D. Manning. 2016. Improving coreference resolution by learning entity-level distributed representations. *CoRR* .

Hal Daumé III and Daniel Marcu. 2005. A large-scale exploration of effective global features for a joint entity detection and tracking model. In *Proceedings of the Conference on Human Language Technology and Empirical Methods in Natural Language Processing*. Association for Computational Linguistics, Stroudsburg, PA, USA, HLT '05.

Greg Durrett and Dan Klein. 2013. Easy victories and uphill battles in coreference resolution. In *Proceedings of the 2013 Conference on Empirical Methods in Natural Language Processing*.

Jiang Guo, Wanxiang Che, Haifeng Wang, and Ting Liu. 2014. Revisiting embedding features for simple semi-supervised learning. In *Proceedings of the 2014 Conference on Empirical Methods in Natural Language Processing (EMNLP)*. Association for Computational Linguistics, Doha, Qatar, pages 110–120.

Otto Jespersen. 1949. *A Modern Grammar On Historical Principles. Part 7 Syntax*. Taylor and Francis Ltd, London, UK.

Heeyoung Lee, Yves Peirsman, Angel Chang, Nathanael Chambers, Mihai Surdeanu, and Dan Jurafsky. 2011. Stanford's multi-pass sieve coreference resolution system at the conll-2011 shared task. In *Proceedings of the Fifteenth Conference on Computational Natural Language Learning: Shared Task*. pages 28–34.

Omer Levy and Yoav Goldberg. 2014. Dependency-based word embeddings. In *Proceedings of the 52nd Annual Meeting of the Association for Computational Linguistics*.

Sebastian Martschat, Patrick Claus, and Michael Strube. 2015. Plug latent structures and play coreference resolution. In *ACL*.

Sebastian Martschat and Michael Strube. 2014. Recall error analysis for coreference resolution. In *In proceedings of the 2014 Conference on Empirical Methods in Natural Language Processing*.

Sebastian Martschat and Michael Strube. 2015. Latent structures for coreference resolution. In *ACL*.

Tomas Mikolov, Ilya Sutskever, Kai Chen, Greg Corrado, and Jeffrey Dean. 2013. Distributed representations of words and phrases and their compositionality. In *Proceedings of the 26th International Conference on Neural Information Processing Systems*. Curran Associates Inc., NIPS'13.

Dan Klein Mohit Bansal. 2012. Coreference semantics from web features. The Association for Computational Linguistics.

Jeffrey Pennington, Richard Socher, and Christopher D. Manning. 2014. Glove: Global vectors for word representation. In *Empirical Methods in Natural Language Processing (EMNLP)*. pages 1532–1543.

Altaf Rahman and Vincent Ng. 2011. Coreference resolution with world knowledge. In *Proceedings of the 49th Annual Meeting of the Association for Computational Linguistics: Human Language Technologies - Volume 1*. Association for Computational Linguistics, HLT '11, pages 814–824.

Joseph Turian, Lev Ratinov, and Yoshua Bengio. 2010. Word representations: A simple and general method for semi-supervised learning. In *Proceedings of the 48th Annual Meeting of the Association for Computational Linguistics*. Association for Computational Linguistics, Stroudsburg, PA, USA, ACL '10, pages 384–394.

Sam Wiseman, Alexander M. Rush, and Stuart M. Shieber. 2016. Learning global features for coreference resolution. *CoRR* .

Mo Yu, Tiejun Zhao, Daxiang Dong, Hao Tian, and Dianhai Yu. 2013. Compound embedding features for semi-supervised learning. In *HLT-NAACL*.

Cross-lingual Flames Detection in News Discussions

Josef Steinberger[1,2] , **Tomáš Brychcín**[1,2] , **Tomáš Hercig**[1,2] , and **Peter Krejzl**[2]

[1]NTIS – New Technologies for the Information Society,
Faculty of Applied Sciences, University of West Bohemia, Czech Republic
[2]Department of Computer Science and Engineering,
Faculty of Applied Sciences, University of West Bohemia, Czech Republic
`{jstein,brychcin,tigi,krejzl}@kiv.zcu.cz`
`http://mediagist.kiv.zcu.cz/flames`

Abstract

We introduce Flames Detector, an online system for measuring flames, i.e. strong negative feelings or emotions, insults or other verbal offences, in news commentaries across five languages. It is designed to assist journalists, public institutions or discussion moderators to detect news topics which evoke flames. We propose a machine learning approach to flames detection and calculate an aggregated score for a set of comment threads. The demo application shows the most flaming topics of the current period in several language variants. The search functionality gives a possibility to measure flames in any topic specified by a query. The evaluation shows that the flame detection in discussions is a difficult task, however, the application can already reveal interesting information about the actual news discussions.

1 Introduction

News portals are highly busy online places where people express their opinions. Journalists write about controversial topics because these attract the readers. The large number of commentaries is a sign that the topic was read by a lot of readers and it could be viewed as a sign of success of the article. Besides journalists who need to identify such topics, political institutions have to know the current trends of the society to react accordingly. International institutions (e.g. European Commission) find useful cross-lingually organized news and commentaries, as they can quickly find and understand different views on controversial topics in different countries.

There are many news aggregators and analy-

sers. Google News[1] aggregates headlines and displays the stories according to each reader's interests. IBM Watson News Explorer[2] gives a more analytical way to read news through linked data visualizations. Europe Media Monitor (EMM)[3] produces a summary of news stories clustered near real-time in various languages and compares how the same events have been reported in the media written in different languages. MediaGist[4] exploits together with news articles another source of information: the commentaries. Including comments opens many above-mentioned use cases.

Natural language processing (NLP) technology can help to make sense out of this data, in particular, the field of argumentation mining (Habernal and Gurevych, 2017). Sentiment analysis, in its basic definition, reveals the polarity of the texts (positive, negative, neutral). Habernal et al. (2014) state that posts in social media often contain sarcasm and irony, they later experiment with sarcasm detection in (Ptáček et al., 2014).

Stance detection (Mohammad et al., 2016) is a related field which tries to infer whether the author of the comment is in favor or against a predefined topic. The migration crisis in Europe raised attention to the *hate speech*, which is defined as "abusive speech targeting specific group characteristics, such as ethnic origin, religion, gender, or sexual orientation" (Djuric et al., 2015). Detecting offensive language was studied by Razavi et al. (2010) or Chen et al. (2012), who analyzed the use case of protecting adolescent online safety by detecting offensive language in social media.

Here, we study *flames*, which were defined as

---

[1]`https://news.google.com/`

[2]`http://news-explorer.mybluemix.net/`

[3]Europe Media Monitor is developed at Joint Research Centre, European Commission: `http://emm.newsbrief.eu` (Atkinson and van der Goot, 2009).

[4]`http://mediagist.eu` (Steinberger, 2016).

Proceedings of Recent Advances in Natural Language Processing, pages 694–700,
Varna, Bulgaria, Sep 4–6 2017.

non constructive, aggressive posts, which do not contribute to the discussion, where users attack each other at a personal level instead of contrasting the discussion partner for his/her approach, ideas, contribution or argumentation (Pazienza and Tudorache, 2011). We consider *flaming* those comments which carry strong negative feelings or emotions, insults or other verbal offences regardless of agreement or disagreement with the given topic. Flames detection can help discussion moderators to manage and filter the discussion.

We propose a machine learning approach to detect flames in news discussions, and an aggregation metric. Another contribution is the corpus we developed. It contains flames annotations in news discussions for 5 languages (English, Czech, German, French and Italian). The developed application, running at `http://mediagist.kiv.zcu.cz/flames`, is unique as near real-time flames detection in online discussions has not been realized yet. It displays the most flaming topic of the current week and the search functionality provides a way to measure flaming of the topic defined by the query. Because the topics are linked across languages, the topic can be easily studied and compared across the languages. The trend figures provide a historical view on the flaming of the query topic.

In the next Section we introduce the functionality of the web application for detecting flames in news discussions. Section 3 reveals how a flaming dialogue interaction can be recognized. It is followed by a definition of the aggregation measure which calculates the intensity of a set of comment threads (Section 4). In Section 5, we describe the corpus we developed in order to train and test the flame classifier. In the rest, we discuss the performance and future extensions.

2 Proposed System

The proposed system uses data feed from MediaGist (Steinberger, 2016) and brings flame detection. MediaGist processing starts with a crawler. It gathers articles and their comments from predefined news sites[5]. It creates an RSS file for each article, which goes through the NLP pipeline. The pipeline first recognizes entities, in both the article and its comments, and assigns a cross-lingual id to each mention. The named entity recognizer is based on JRC-Names[6], which is a highly multilingual named entity resource for person and organization names (Steinberger et al., 2011c). The coreference resolver (Steinberger et al., 2011a) then enriches the list of entity mentions by name part references and definite descriptions. Sentiment analyzer (Steinberger et al., 2011b) assigns to each article, comment and entity mention a sentiment score. Here comes the place to assign a flame label (FLAME/NO-FLAME) to each interaction (i.e. to every response). Except the posts which start a new thread, each comment receives a flame annotation.

Article comments are then summarized according to (Kabadjov et al., 2013). These fully annotated article RSS files enter the clustering phase. Every four hours, for each language, the clustering takes the articles published during the current week and creates monolingual clusters. After this step, RSS files contain information about all articles in the cluster. The cross-lingual linker then connects the most similar clusters across languages. Cross-lingual linking uses two kinds of features: entities and descriptors from EuroVoc[7]. Using Eurovoc features ensures that the linked clusters share the same topic. If at the same time the clusters share the same entities[8], it is very likely that the clusters are about the same story (Steinberger, 2013). The last step is creating a summary of clustered articles and a summary of cluster's comments. The RSS now contains all information needed by the presentation layer, the MediaGist website.

The clustered data are then indexed in ElasticSearch[9]. During displaying the front page, Elasticsearch runs a query which returns the cluster, which has the largest sum of flame scores (defined in Section 4) across languages. The cross-lingual links are used to calculate flame scores of the other language variants of the cluster. As the sum is used, highly cross-lingual topics have more chances to be selected.

The core of the flames detector is the search functionality. The language of the query is currently set to English. After submitting a query ElasticSearch finds relevant English news clusters

---

[5]Currently, it gathers data from 8 sources in 5 languages: English (theguardian.com), Czech (idnes.cz, ihned.cz, novinky.cz), Italian (corriere.it, repubblica.it), French (lemonde.fr) and German (spiegel.de).

[6]`https://ec.europa.eu/jrc/en/language-technologies/jrc-names`
[7]`http://eurovoc.europa.eu`
[8]The entity ids are unified across languages.
[9]`https://www.elastic.co/`.

in the last 10 weeks. The fields used for searching are: article titles, descriptions (initial sentence/paragraph), the summary of articles and the summary of comments. The cross-lingual links are then used to receive the relevant clusters in other languages. It can thus find, e.g., French topics relevant to the English query. For every language (a set of clusters), it measures the flame score and its confidence interval. It uses all comment threads in all retrieved clusters for the calculation. It also detects the most flaming cluster, the most flaming article and also the post which triggered the most flaming discussion. In the case of the post, the ratio of flame replies and all replies is taken as a score. For all the flame extremes (cluster, article, post) it requires a minimum number of replies (set to 10) unless there is no post having such an amount of replies. A search result can be seen at Figure 1. Each row shows information about a language. On the left, statistic about the whole retrieved set of clusters, the most flaming cluster, article and flame trigger post can be found. On the right, a historical trend is drawn. The trend is based on weekly flame scores because week is the clustering unit.

The extracted clusters are linked with MediaGist, which can be further used to analyze the results. The articles are linked to the source site from both ends (Flames detector and MediaGist).

3 Flames Detector

Distinguishing between flaming/not-flaming utterances is in fact a binary classification task. We employ Maximum Entropy (ME) classifier (Berger et al., 1996) implemented in the Brainy machine learning library (Konkol, 2014). The following feature functions were used:

- **GloVe**: We express the meaning of an utterance as the real-valued vector. Each value in the vector is then used as a separate feature. We use semantic composition approach. It is based on *Frege's principle of compositionality* (Pelletier, 1994), which states that the meaning of a complex expression is determined as a composition of its parts, i.e. words. We use linear combination of word vectors, where the weights are represented by the inverse-document-frequency (IDF) values of words. We use Global Vectors (GloVe) (Pennington et al., 2014) for word vector representation. We trained the word vectors

on data from MediaGist gathered during the last 17 month (approximately 1M comments for each language). Brychcín and Svoboda (2016) showed that this approach leads to very good sentence representation.

- **BoW**: We use bag-of-words (BoW) representation of an utterance, i.e. separate binary feature representing the occurrence of a word in the utterance.

- **DisSize**: The number of utterances in the discourse. The larger discourses are assumed to be about the more controversial topic or at least the topic which worth discussing.

- **Level**: The number expressing how many preceding utterances occur in the sequence of replies. The larger number means the people are paying attention to the discussed topic.

- **CharNgrams**: Separate binary feature for each character n-gram in the utterance text. We do it separately for different orders $n \in \{1, 2, 3\}$.

- **WordShape**: We tried to improve pattern features by using word-shape classes for words. We assign words into one of 24 classes[10] similar to the function specified in (Bikel et al., 1997). Each class is separate binary feature.

GloVe and *BoW* features use preprocessed text. We lowercase the text, remove stop-words, and apply stemming for remaining words. We use HPS unsupervised stemmer (Brychcín and Konopík, 2015). We trained HPS on the same data as GloVe word vectors. The surface features (*CharNgrams* and *WordShape*) work with the text in the form it was originally written. When the current comment starts with a repetition of a part of the previous comment, we remove the repetition.

4 Flaming Intensity Metric

A not nested post (i.e. a post on the top level of the discussion) with its replies (and replies on replies, etc.), which evolve the discussion, make a tree of utterances. The tree is in the following text denoted simply as discourse. Assume we have a set of n discourses and we want to determine the

---

[10]We use edu.stanford.nlp.process.WordShapeClassifier with the WORDSHAPECHRIS1 setting available in Standford CoreNLP library (Manning et al., 2014).

Figure 1: The search results for query "israel, palestine".

flaming intensity. For i-th discourse we firstly calculate the ratio of flaming utterances and the discourse size. We denote this ratio as w_i. The flaming intensity is then simply a mean, $\bar{w}$. In addition, we calculate t-statistics confidence interval for the mean $\bar{w}$. In our system we use 90% confidence level. Flaming intensities across less and highly discussed topics can be then better compared.

5 Proposed Dataset

We created a corpus for five languages (Czech, English, French, Italian, and German), in which we annotated flames. The data comes from noisy user-generated news article discussions. The statistics of the corpus are shown in Table 1.

Language	Size	Flame ratio
CS	1812	702 (38.7%)
DE	1122	149 (13.3%)
EN	1007	250 (24.8%)
FR	487	144 (29.6%)
IT	649	249 (38.4%)

Table 1: Data statistics.

For every language, we used the same annotation scheme and we included topics from multiple domains. The annotators were given instructions to label a comment as flame when it contained strong negative feelings, negative emotions, insults or other verbal offenses regardless of agreement or disagreement with the given topic. See the examples of flame comments bellow:

- `You mean like Bullsh!t?`
- `Rubbish.`
- `Thats a lovely collection of random thought bubbles.`
- `you really think you speak for everyone eh? Says a lot about you.`
- `When do you leave school, Tim?`
- `Cool story, bro. But you still seem to be suffering from the view that walking and chewing gum is impossible. Try it.`

Czech and English data were annotated by three experts. The annotators each labeled approximately a third of the data and a small sample was annotated by all to assess their agreement. The majority voting scheme was applied on the gold label selection. Table 2 shows the inter-annotator agreement metrics for the Czech corpus (100 comments) and the English corpus (76 comments). Only one annotator labeled French, Italian and German data.

Metric	EN	CS
AVG Accuracy	79.83%	86.67%
Fleiss' κ	0.590	0.578
AVG Cohen's κ	0.591	0.580
Krippendorff's α	0.592	0.579

Table 2: Inter-annotator agreement.

The corpus will be available for research purposes at `http://nlp.kiv.zcu.cz/projects/flame`.

6   Results and Discussion

We used the same settings and features for experiments in all languages. The proposed datasets for different languages have different ratios of flaming/not flaming posts. Due to the small size, the datasets are not assumed to cover all discussion topics. We apply Maximum Entropy principle to achieve the best estimate for previously unknown topic, i.e. we balance the training data to contain the same number of flaming/not flaming posts.

Model	CS	DE	EN	FR	IT
ME BoW	53.5%	62.4%	53.2%	51.7%	55.6%
ME GloVe	56.4%	64.4%	68.0%	54.2%	54.0%
ME all	62.8%	67.8%	72.2%	60.1%	60.2%

Table 3:   Accuracy of flame detection across all five languages.

The results reported in Table 3 are achieved by 20-fold cross-validation on balanced datasets. The difficulty of flames detection is similar to polarity or stance detection (accuracy 60%–70% in the case of commentary data). The best accuracy was for English (72.2%), the worst for French (60.1%). The size of the training data (Table 1) clearly affects the classification accuracy. Note the best contributing feature was *GloVe*. Also *DisSize* and *Level* were proved to be very useful.

To illustrate the search functionality we show results of query "climate change" in Table 4. We can observe that the supplied query actually defines the topic. As the cross-lingual linking is based on topical words and entities it gives the answer wider than just climate change. The top entities mentioned in the clusters relevant to climate change were: *Donald Trump, Barrack Obama, United Nations*, and *European Commission*. These play an important role in cross-lingual linking and thus the topics related to them are retrieved for the other languages.

7   Conclusion and Future Work

This is the first study for detecting flames in news commentaries across languages. The flame classification performance very much depends on the size of training data. An extension of the corpus will directly lead to an improved performance.

The application measures the flames in discussions in near real-time and extracts the flaming topics which can be further analyzed in the news aggregator (MediaGist) or at the source news site itself. Future plans include increasing the data volume on both vertical (sources) and horizontal (historical data) axes. This will allow us to study the evolution of flames on a larger scale.

The system currently consumes raw commentaries. Measuring the flames among real Internet users will require to fight trolls and filter the conversations (Mihaylov et al., 2015). On the other hand, without fighting the trolls, the system can identify those discussions in which trolls are active because such comments many times raise negative emotions and thus help to identify the trolls.

Flame ratio depends very much on the source. We will search for a way how to remove the source bias. This will make the flaming more comparable across languages.

Acknowledgements

This publication was supported by the project LO1506 of the Czech Ministry of Education, Youth and Sports under the program NPU I., by Grant No.   SGS-2016-018 Data and Software Engineering for Advanced Applications and by project MediaGist, EUs FP7 People Programme (Marie Curie Actions), no. 630786.

References

Martin Atkinson and Erik van der Goot. 2009.   Near real time information mining in multilingual news. In *Proceedings of the 18th International World Wide Web Conference (WWW 2009)*. Madrid, Spain, pages 1153–1154.

Adam L. Berger, Vincent J. D. Pietra, and Stephen A. D. Pietra. 1996.   A maximum entropy approach to natural language processing. *Computational Linguistics* 22:39–71.

Daniel M. Bikel, Scott Miller, Richard Schwartz, and Ralph Weischedel. 1997.   Nymble: a high-performance learning name-finder. In *Proceedings of the fifth conference on Applied natural language processing*. Association for Computational Linguistics, pages 194–201.

Tomáš Brychcín and Miloslav Konopík. 2015.   Hps: High precision stemmer. *Information Processing & Management* 51(1):68–91.

Tomáš Brychcín and Lukáš Svoboda. 2016.   UWB at SemEval-2016 Task 1: Semantic Textual Similarity using Lexical, Syntactic, and Semantic Information. In *Proceedings of the 10th International Workshop on Semantic Evaluation (SemEval-2016)*. Association for Computational Linguistics, San Diego, California, pages 588–594.

Language	Clusters	Articles	Comments	Flame score	Threads	Flame cluster
CS	7	30	4556	0.307	691	Lidé mohou domů. Přehrada Oroville je podle šerifa na bouři připravena
DE	7	23	265	0.552	153	Rede zur Amtseinführung Das hat Donald Trump versprochen
EN	110	388	186,640	0.461	30,301	Trump can save his presidency with a great deal to save the climate
FR	8	23	237	0.492	44	Téhéran teste la détermination de Washington
IT	9	34	947	0.479	39	Brexit, governo sconfitto a Camera Lord su emendamento che protegge diritti cittadini Ue

Table 4: An example of queries and their results.

Ying Chen, Yilu Zhou, Sencun Zhu, and Heng Xu. 2012. Detecting offensive language in social media to protect adolescent online safety. In *Proceedings of the 2012 ASE/IEEE International Conference on Social Computing and 2012 ASE/IEEE International Conference on Privacy, Security, Risk and Trust*. IEEE Computer Society, Washington, DC, USA, SOCIALCOM-PASSAT '12, pages 71–80.

Nemanja Djuric, Jing Zhou, Robin Morris, Mihajlo Grbovic, Vladan Radosavljevic, and Narayan Bhamidipati. 2015. Hate speech detection with comment embeddings. In *Proceedings of the 24th International Conference on World Wide Web*. ACM, New York, NY, USA, WWW '15 Companion, pages 29–30.

Ivan Habernal and Iryna Gurevych. 2017. Argumentation mining in user-generated web discourse. *Computational Linguistics* 43(1):(in press).

Ivan Habernal, Tomáš Ptáček, and Josef Steinberger. 2014. Supervised sentiment analysis in czech social media. *Information Processing & Management* 50(5):693–707.

Mijail Kabadjov, Josef Steinberger, and Ralf Steinberger. 2013. Multilingual statistical news summarization. In *Multilingual Information Extraction and Summarization*, Springer, volume 2013 of *Theory and Applications of Natural Language Processing*, pages 229–252.

Michal Konkol. 2014. Brainy: A machine learning library. In Leszek Rutkowski, Marcin Korytkowski, Rafa Scherer, Ryszard Tadeusiewicz, Lotfi A. Zadeh, and Jacek M. Zurada, editors, *Artificial Intelligence and Soft Computing*, Springer-Verlag, Berlin, volume 8468 of *Lecture Notes in Computer Science*.

Christopher D. Manning, Mihai Surdeanu, John Bauer, Jenny Finkel, Steven J. Bethard, and David McClosky. 2014. The Stanford CoreNLP natural language processing toolkit. In *Association for Computational Linguistics (ACL) System Demonstrations*. pages 55–60.

Todor Mihaylov, Georgi Georgiev, and Preslav Nakov. 2015. Finding opinion manipulation trolls in news community forums. In *Proceedings of the 19th CoNLL*. ACL, pages 310–314.

Saif Mohammad, Svetlana Kiritchenko, Parinaz Sobhani, Xiaodan Zhu, and Colin Cherry. 2016. Semeval-2016 task 6: Detecting stance in tweets. In *Proceedings of SemEval-2016*. Association for Computational Linguistics, San Diego, California, pages 31–41.

Maria Teresa Pazienza and Alexandra Gabriela Tudorache. 2011. Interdisciplinary contributions to flame modeling. In *Congress of the Italian Association for Artificial Intelligence*. Springer, pages 213–224.

Francis Jeffry Pelletier. 1994. The principle of semantic compositionality. *Topoi* 13(1):11–24.

Jeffrey Pennington, Richard Socher, and Christopher Manning. 2014. Glove: Global vectors for word representation. In *Proceedings of the 2014 Conference on Empirical Methods in Natural Language Processing (EMNLP)*. Association for Computational Linguistics, Doha, Qatar, pages 1532–1543.

Tomáš Ptáček, Ivan Habernal, and Jun Hong. 2014. Sarcasm detection on czech and english twitter. In *Proceedings of COLING 2014*. Dublin City University and Association for Computational Linguistics, Dublin, Ireland, pages 213–223.

Amir H. Razavi, Diana Inkpen, Sasha Uritsky, and Stan Matwin. 2010. Offensive language detection using multi-level classification. In Atefeh Farzindar and Vlado Kešelj, editors, *Advances in Artificial Intelligence: 23rd Canadian Conference on Artificial Intelligence*. Springer Berlin Heidelberg, Berlin, Heidelberg, pages 16–27.

Josef Steinberger. 2016. Mediagist: A cross-lingual analyser of aggregated news and commentaries. In *Proceedings of ACL-2016 System Demonstrations*. Association for Computational Linguistics, Berlin, Germany, pages 145–150.

Josef Steinberger, Jenya Belyaeva, Jonathan Crawley, Leonida Della-Rocca, Mohamed Ebrahim, Maud Ehrmann, Mijail Kabadjov, Ralf Steinberger, and Erik Van der Goot. 2011a. Highly multilingual coreference resolution exploiting a mature entity repository. In *Proceedings of the 8th RANLP Conference*. Incoma Ltd., pages 254–260.

Josef Steinberger, Polina Lenkova, Mijail Kabadjov, Ralf Steinberger, and Erik Van der Goot.

2011b. Multilingual entity-centered sentiment analysis evaluated by parallel corpora. In *Proceedings of the 8th RANLP Conference*. pages 770–775.

Ralf Steinberger. 2013. Multilingual and cross-lingual news analysis in the europe media monitor (emm). In *Multidisciplinary Information Retrieval*, Springer, volume 8201 of *LNCS*, pages 1–4.

Ralf Steinberger, Bruno Pouliquen, Mijail Kabadjov, Jenya Belyaeva, and Erik Van der Goot. 2011c. Jrc-names: A freely available, highly multilingual named entity resource. In *Proceedings of the International RANLP Conference*. Incoma Ltd.

Pyramid-based Summary Evaluation
Using Abstract Meaning Representation

Josef Steinberger[1,2] , **Peter Krejzl**[2] , and **Tomáš Brychcín**[1,2]

[1]NTIS – New Technologies for the Information Society,
Faculty of Applied Sciences, University of West Bohemia, Czech Republic
[2]Department of Computer Science and Engineering,
Faculty of Applied Sciences, University of West Bohemia, Czech Republic
{jstein,krejzl,brychcin}@kiv.zcu.cz

Abstract

We propose a novel metric for evaluating summary content coverage. The evaluation framework follows the Pyramid approach to measure how many summarization content units, considered important by human annotators, are contained in an automatic summary. Our approach automatizes the evaluation process, which does not need any manual intervention on the evaluated summary side. Our approach compares abstract meaning representations of each content unit mention and each summary sentence. We found that the proposed metric complements well the widely-used ROUGE metrics.

1 Introduction

Evaluating the quality of automatic summaries is a known problem, which has attracted many computational linguists. Summary quality has different aspects, mainly the readability and the content coverage. Readability scores the summary by its grammaticality, non-redundancy, referential clarity, focus, structure or coherence. For many use cases (e.g. skimming through a summary of related news articles), content coverage decides whether the summary is useful or not.

The Pyramid method (Nenkova et al., 2007) is a well-designed framework for measuring content coverage. It computes how many summarization content units (SCUs) are shared between model summaries and the target system summary. The matching cannot be done on the lexical level, because the same information is often expressed in different words. In the past DUC/TAC[1] challenges the matching was done by humans. Although the participants received a precise feedback on their summaries, it was not possible to evaluate a new set of summaries after the evaluation exercise.

There has been many approaches to perform a fully automatic evaluation, including the most widely used ROUGE (Lin, 2004). Although they can rank the systems well enough on the whole corpus, their correlation with human judgements on the summary level is limited.

Abstract meaning representation (AMR) was introduced by Banarescu et al. (2013). AMR is intended to abstract meaning away from syntax. Sentences, which are similar in meaning should be assigned the same AMR, even if they are not identically written. The abstractive ability makes it very suitable for summarization, already shown by Liu et al. (2015). And as the pyramid matching requires dealing with paraphrases, it led us to the idea to use AMR for automatic pyramid evaluation.

Next, we discuss the past summarization shared tasks and evaluation metrics. An overview of the AMR format, a state-of-the-art parser, and an AMR graph similarity metric are described in Section 3. In Section 4, we define a novel metric, denoted as APE[2]. We evaluate the metric and compare/combine it with other metrics in Section 5.

2 Related Work

The most widely used automatic content evaluation metric is ROUGE (Lin and Hovy, 2003; Lin, 2004). It measures the word n-gram overlap between evaluated summary (*peer*) and the reference summaries (*models*, ideally written by humans). DUC/TAC evaluations showed that ROUGE correlates well with human judgements when scores of each peer are averaged over all topics of a corpus (Pearson's r is greater than .9).On the other hand, when as-

---

[1]Document Understanding Conference (DUC), followed by Text Analysis Conference (TAC), was a series of summarization shared tasks initiated by NIST (Over et al., 2007).

[2]APE denotes using **A**MR for **P**yramid-based **E**valuation.

Proceedings of Recent Advances in Natural Language Processing, pages 701–706,
Varna, Bulgaria, Sep 4–6 2017.

sessing individual summaries, correlation drops to
$\sim .6$).ROUGE-2 (bigrams) and ROUGE-SU4 (bigrams with skip distance up to 4 words) correlated best on most of the corpora. Basic Elements (Hovy et al., 2005; Tratz and Hovy, 2008) were designed to address the problem of variable-size of semantic units by scoring syntactically coherent units. Head-modifier (BE-HM) pairs performed the best.

In the first DUC conferences, only a manual scale-based evaluation method was used. Later, it was complemented by the Pyramid method. The pyramid approach involves two tasks. First, human annotators identify SCUs, sets of text fragments that express the same basic content, in model summaries and create a pyramid (SCUs are weighted according to the number of models, in which they appear). Second, they evaluate a new summary against the pyramid. The *pyramid score* is computed by the total weight of all SCUs present in the candidate divided by the total SCU weight possible for an average-length summary (Nenkova et al., 2007). Although, creating a pyramid automatically would be useful for creating a new evaluation corpora, having an automated scoring of a new summary against a human-produced pyramid would make the method far more useful for developers. They would use a standard corpus and evaluate different versions of summarizers.

Several approaches for automating the pyramid scoring has been proposed. Harnly et al. (2005) tested several similarity metrics for matching SCUs against summaries and achieved the best results with unigram overlaps and single-linkage clustering. Passonneau et al. (2013) added two semantic similarities: a string comparison and a distributional semantics method, which performed better.

Emulating the pyramid method was one of the goals of the past TAC AESOP tasks in 2009 (Dang and Owczarzak, 2009), 2010 (Owczarzak and Dang, 2010), and 2011 (Owczarzak and Dang, 2011; Owczarzak et al., 2012). In 2009, several submissions achieved high correlations on the summarizer level. In 2010, ROUGE metrics were ranked very high, again based on summarizer-level correlations. In 2011, summary-level correlations revealed a room for improvement as the best Pearson correlation was .752 (Giannakopoulos and Karkaletsis, 2011), followed by ROUGE-SU4 (.736). Many models have been already proposed for the pyramid matching (Harnly et al., 2005; Passonneau et al., 2013), but the use of semantic relations between the sentence units has not been discussed yet.

3 Abstract Meaning Representation

Graph-structured semantic representations enable a direct semantic analysis of sentences. Banarescu et al. (2013) started annotating the logical meaning of sentences into AMR. In a nutshell, AMR graph is a rooted, labeled, directed acyclic graph, comprising a sentence. It is intended to abstract away from syntax and incorporates semantic roles, coreference, questions, modality, negation, and further linguistic phenomena[3].

Formally, we define a set of all possible triples:

$$T = \left\{ (r, n_1, n_2) \,\middle|\, \begin{array}{l} r = \text{relation type} \\ n_1 = \text{variable} \\ n_2 = \text{variable or concept} \end{array} \right\} \quad (1)$$

AMR is then a subset of T: $A \subseteq T$.

An example sentence, logical triples and corresponding AMR graph is illustrated in Figure 1 (left part). AMR introduces variables (graph nodes) for entities, events, properties, and states. Each node in the graph represents a semantic concept. These concepts can either be English words (*boy*), PropBank framesets (*want-01*) (Palmer et al., 2005), or special keywords. The *instance* relation assigns to each concept a variable which can be reused in other triples. Edge labels denote the relations that hold between entities (e.g. *ARG-0* relation between *want-01* and *boy*). The AMR triples take one of these forms: *relation(variable, concept)* or *relation(variable₁, variable₂)*.

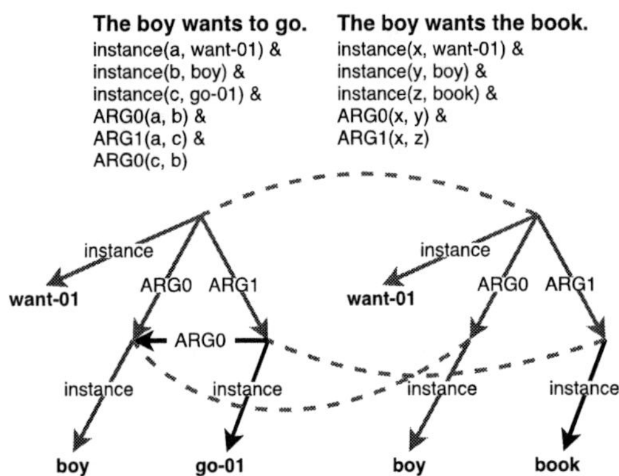

Figure 1: AMR trees and semantic matching.

Flanigan et al. (2014) introduced the first approach to parse sentences into AMR, which re-

---

[3]The AMR language is described in more detail in the AMR annotation guidelines: http://amr.isi.edu/language.html.

quires algorithms for alignment, structured prediction, and statistical learning (JAMR[4]). In order to automatically parse English into AMR, JAMR employs a two-part algorithm. First, it identifies the key concepts using a semi-Markov model. Second, it identifies the relations between the concepts by searching for the maximum spanning, connected subgraph, a similar approach to maximum spanning tree described in McDonald et al. (2005).

Cai and Knight (2013) introduced semantic match (Smatch), a metric that calculates the degree of overlap between two semantic feature structures. It first computes the maximum number of matching triples among all possible variable mappings. To obtain the best variable mapping, Smatch executes a brief search which uses integer linear programming and a hill climbing method (described by Cai and Knight (2013)). We define a function (*mmt*) which takes two AMRs, finds the optimal variable mapping, and returns the maximum number of matching triples:

$$\text{mmt} : \boldsymbol{T} \times \boldsymbol{T} \to \mathbb{Z}^+ \qquad (2)$$

Given the maximum number of matching triples, we can compute precision, recall, and F1 score, which is the Smatch score.

For our example (Figure 1), the highest scoring variable alignment is if $a = x$, $b = y$ and $c = z$. The blue-arrow relations are matched (4), the black-arrow relations are not matched (2 left, 1 right). Thus recall is $4/6$, precision is $4/5$. and the resulting Smatch score is .73.

4 APE – AMR-based Pyramid Evaluation

The aim is to measure how many SCUs identified by humans in a set of model summaries are contained in the target (evaluated) peer summary. Assume we have a sequence of C SCUs $\boldsymbol{c} = \{\boldsymbol{c}_i\}_{i=1}^C$. Their weights ($\lambda_i$) are based on the number of models, in which they were mentioned. Each SCU is described by a sequence of its mentions $\boldsymbol{c}_i = \{d_j\}_{j=1}^{D_i}$, where D_i is the number of models, in which SCU $\boldsymbol{c}_i$ is mentioned. Model summaries contain a sequence of M sentences $\boldsymbol{m} = \{m_i\}_{i=1}^M$, and the peer summary is a sequence of P sentences $\boldsymbol{p} = \{p_i\}_{i=1}^P$.

Every sentence from all models and from the peer is parsed by an AMR parser, resulting in a sequence of AMR trees. $\boldsymbol{A}_{m_i} \subseteq \boldsymbol{T}$ is the set of AMR triples of sentence m_i, similarly $\boldsymbol{A}_{p_i} \subseteq \boldsymbol{T}$ is the set of AMR triples of sentence p_i. As each SCU mention d_j is a part of a model sentence m_i, $\boldsymbol{A}_{d_j}$ contains only those triples of $\boldsymbol{A}_{m_i}$ whose constituents are contained in the SCU mention: $\boldsymbol{A}_{d_j} \subseteq \boldsymbol{A}_{m_i}$. These represent the "gold triples", which are searched in the peer summary sentences.

For each sentence in the peer summary, we get the corresponding AMR tree and match its triples against the gold ones. The Smatch variable mapping is used for getting a common set of triples (function mmt, see Equation 2). If there is a sentence that contains a larger percentage of gold triples than a threshold (τ), the SCU is considered covered by the peer summary. Note that compared to the Smatch score, which calculates the F1 score, APE is a recall measure. The pyramid score is then computed the same way as discussed in Section 2: the total weight of all SCUs present in the candidate (w_p) divided by the total SCU weight possible for an average-length summary (w_{ideal}) (Nenkova and Passonneau, 2004). The APE algorithm[5] follows:

Algorithm 1 APE: computes the pyramid score for a given peer summary ($\boldsymbol{p}$) and SCUs ($\boldsymbol{c}$). w_{ideal} acts as a normalization factor.

> **function** APE($\boldsymbol{p}$, $\boldsymbol{c}$)
> $w_p \leftarrow 0$
>   **for all** $1 \leq i \leq C$ **do**
>   *matched* $\leftarrow$ false
> $\boldsymbol{d} \leftarrow \boldsymbol{c}_i$
>   **for all** $1 \leq j \leq D_i$ **do**
>   **for all** $1 \leq k \leq P$ **do**
>   **if** $\text{mmt}(\boldsymbol{A}_{d_j}, \boldsymbol{A}_{p_k}) / |\boldsymbol{A}_{d_j}| > \tau$ **then**
> $w_p \leftarrow w_p + \lambda_i$
>   *matched* $\leftarrow$ true
>   break
>   **if** *matched* **then** break
>   **return** w_p / w_{ideal}

---

5 Results and Discussion

We selected TAC'09 corpus for evaluation, because 2009 was the last time DUC/TAC contained a general summarization task[6]. The corpus contains 44 topics. For each topic, there are 4 model summaries and the manually created pyramid. 55 participating systems were ranked according to the manual Pyramid scores, producing a gold ranking of the systems for each topic. Overall, there are

---

[4]Available at http://github.com/jflanigan/jamr.

[5]Altough the complexity of the algorithm is quite large, the runtime was not an issue in our experiments.

[6] In 2010 and 2011, TAC shifted towards aspect-based summarization. We also consider only initial summaries. Evaluating update summaries would need some changes similarly to the ROUGE adaptation in (Conroy et al., 2011).

$44 \times 55 = 2420$ evaluation scores. An automatic evaluation metric runs 2420 evaluations as well, and we can study its correlation with the manual pyramid score (the *per-summary* scenario). The other option is to calculate an average score for each system and look at the correlation of the averages (55 scores): the *per-system* scenario. The TAC'09 AESOP task concluded that on the system level, the correlation is sufficient (the best Pearson's r was .978, ROUGE-SU4: .921), but the metrics are much worse on the summary level.

ROUGE-SU4[7] and BE-HM were taken as baselines. We report three types of correlations. Pearson's tests the strength of a linear dependency between the two sequences. Spearman rank correlation is preferable for ordinal comparisons, absolute values are less relevant. Kendall's tau is less sensitive to outliers. Results are in Table 1.

We can observe that ROUGE-SU4 correlates better than BE-HM and about the same as APE (.66 Pearson, .62 Spearman, .45 Kendall). These numbers do not show whether the information added by APE's relations improves the summary evaluation. However, if we combine APE and ROUGE-SU4 by a linear combination ($\alpha \times$ APE $+ (1 - \alpha) \times$ ROUGE-SU4), we see a significant improvement. In the case of a "blind combination" (i.e. without looking at the test data, $\alpha = .5$), we notice an absolute improvement of 3.7% in Pearson, 4.0% in Spearman, and 3.2% in Kendall. In the case of the optimal $\alpha = .2$, a lower weight of the AMR relations, we see an improvement of 5.1% in Pearson, 6.4% in Spearman, and 5.5% in Kendall. The improvement is much larger than if BE-HM is combined with ROUGE-SU4. Combining all the three metrics yields only a marginal improvement. Figure 2 shows how the correlation depends on α.

We also noticed a large correlation between the gold number of SCUs (annotated in peers) and APE's number of SCUs: Pearson's r was .769. This further shows the positive effect of AMR relations.

The optimal setting for τ was .75, we tested all levels of τ with step .05. This means that 3/4 of the triples has to match between an SCU mention and a peer sentence to consider the SCU captured.

We further studied how different relation types affect the metric. The JAMR parser found 57 relation types. 51 relation types affected the correlation positively. These included verb arguments,

---

[7]ROUGE-SU4 was selected to represent the ROUGE family because it correlated best in the TAC AESOP experiments.

Metric	α	Pearson	Spearman	Kendall
ROUGE-SU4		.662	.624	.453
BE-HM		.612	.579	.413
APE		.661	.623	.456
APE + ROUGE-SU4	.2	**.713**	**.688**	**.508**
APE + ROUGE-SU4	.5	.695	.664	.485
BE-HM + ROUGE-SU4	.2	.666	.633	.460
BE-HM + ROUGE-SU4	.5	.661	.634	.461

Table 1: Correlations of the evaluation metrics with the manual pyramid score. Except for ROUGE-SU4 vs. APE, all differences are statistically significant with p-value=.01 measured by t-test and Fisher's transformation.

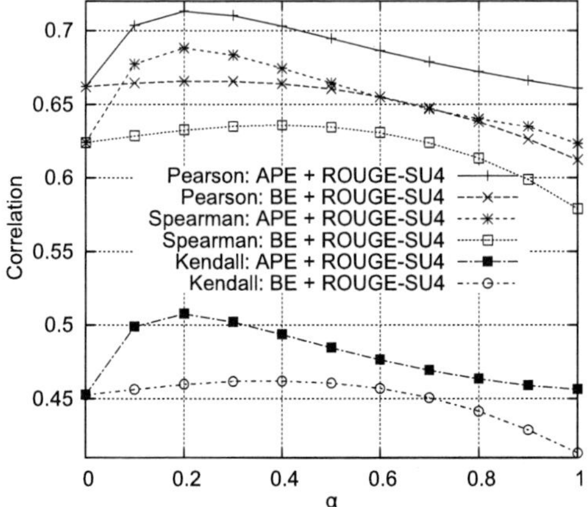

Figure 2: Linear combination of the metrics compared with human scores.

operands[8] (relations linking entity name parts), number-based relations (e.g. *unit*), time-based (e.g. date parts), prepositions, and most of the semantic relations, including the *polarity*. Six relation types had a negative effect. The *name* relation probably boosted the weight of the named entities too much. Syntactically oriented relations (e.g. *mod*) do not seem to be useful.

6 Conclusion

We showed that semantic relations among sentence items can improve the current summarization evaluation metrics. The approach is very sensitive to the quality of the AMR parser. It is expected to improve when AMR parsing advances. Our future work includes experiments with the latest findings in AMR parsing, e.g. Wang et al. (2015); Damonte et al. (2016). There has been made much progress on the Semantic Textual Similarity (STS) shared task in recent years (Agirre et al., 2016). We plan

---

[8]The opX relations were merged into a common "op" type.

to incorporate the metrics to further boost the evaluation performance. We found optimal settings of the parameters (τ and α), however, we need to investigate whether it generalizes across all summarization domains. As SCUs need to be manually created before performing summary evaluation, our final future work includes finding a way to use AMR to extract SCUs from model summaries and create the pyramid.

Acknowledgements

This publication was supported by the project LO1506 of the Czech Ministry of Education, Youth and Sports under the program NPU I., by Grant No. SGS-2016-018 Data and Software Engineering for Advanced Applications and by project MediaGist, EUs FP7 People Programme (Marie Curie Actions), no. 630786.

References

Eneko Agirre, Carmen Banea, Daniel Cer, Mona Diab, Aitor Gonzalez-Agirre, Rada Mihalcea, German Rigau, and Janyce Wiebe. 2016. Semeval-2016 task 1: Semantic textual similarity, monolingual and cross-lingual evaluation. In *Proceedings of the 10th International Workshop on Semantic Evaluation (SemEval-2016)*. Association for Computational Linguistics, San Diego, California, pages 497–511. http://www.aclweb.org/anthology/S16-1081.

Laura Banarescu, Claire Bonial, Shu Cai, Madalina Georgescu, Kira Griffitt, Ulf Hermjakob, Kevin Knight, Philipp Koehn, Martha Palmer, and Nathan Schneider. 2013. Abstract meaning representation for sembanking. In *Proceedings of the 7th Linguistic Annotation Workshop and Interoperability with Discourse*. Association for Computational Linguistics, Sofia, Bulgaria, pages 178–186. http://www.aclweb.org/anthology/W13-2322.

Shu Cai and Kevin Knight. 2013. Smatch: an evaluation metric for semantic feature structures. In *Proceedings of the 51st Annual Meeting of the Association for Computational Linguistics (Volume 2: Short Papers)*. Association for Computational Linguistics, Sofia, Bulgaria, pages 748–752. http://www.aclweb.org/anthology/P13-2131.

John M. Conroy, Judith D. Schlesinger, and Dianne P. O'Leary. 2011. Nouveau-rouge: A novelty metric for update summarization. *Computational Linguistics* 37:1–8.

Marco Damonte, Shay B. Cohen, and Giorgio Satta. 2016. An incremental parser for abstract meaning representation. *arXiv preprint at arXiv:1608.06111*.

Hoa T. Dang and Karolina Owczarzak. 2009. Overview of the tac 2009 summarization track. In National Institute of Standards and Technology, editors, *Proceedings of Text Analysis Conference (TAC-09)*. Gaithersburg, MD.

Jeffrey Flanigan, Sam Thomson, Jaime Carbonell, Chris Dyer, and Noah A. Smith. 2014. A discriminative graph-based parser for the abstract meaning representation. In *Proceedings of the 52nd Annual Meeting of the Association for Computational Linguistics (Volume 1: Long Papers)*. Association for Computational Linguistics, Baltimore, Maryland, pages 1426–1436. http://www.aclweb.org/anthology/P14-1134.

George Giannakopoulos and Vangelis Karkaletsis. 2011. Autosummeng and memog in evaluating guided summaries. In National Institute of Standards and Technology, editors, *Proceedings of Text Analysis Conference (TAC-11)*. Gaithersburg, MD.

Aaron Harnly, , Ani Nenkova, Rebecca Passonneau, and Owen Rambow. 2005. Automation of summary evaluation by the pyramid method. In *Proceedings of the International Conference on Recent Advances in Natural Language Processing (RANLP 2005)*. Borovets, Bulgaria.

Eduard Hovy, Chin-Yew Lin, and Liang Zhou. 2005. Evaluating duc 2005 using basic elements. In *Proceedings of the Fifth Document Understanding Conference (DUC)*. Vancouver, Canada.

Chin-Yew Lin. 2004. ROUGE: a package for automatic evaluation of summaries. In *Proceedings of the Workshop on Text Summarization Branches Out*. Barcelona, Spain.

Chin-Yew Lin and Eduard Hovy. 2003. Automatic evaluation of summaries using n-gram co-occurrence statistics. In *Proceedings of HLT-NAACL*. Edmonton, Canada.

Fei Liu, Jeffrey Flanigan, Sam Thomson, Norman Sadeh, and Noah A. Smith. 2015. Abstract meaning representation for sembanking. In *Proceedings of the 2015 Annual Conference of the North American Chapter of the ACL*. Association for Computational Linguistics, Denver, Colorado, page 10771086.

Ryan McDonald, Fernando Pereira, Kiril Ribarov, and Jan Hajic. 2005. Non-projective dependency parsing using spanning tree algorithms. In *Proceedings of Human Language Technology Conference and Conference on Empirical Methods in Natural Language Processing*. Association for Computational Linguistics, Vancouver, British Columbia, Canada, pages 523–530. http://www.aclweb.org/anthology/H/H05/H05-1066.

Ani Nenkova and Rebecca Passonneau. 2004. Evaluating content selection in summarization: The pyramid method. In *Proceedings of the Meeting of the*

North American Chapter of the Association for Computational Linguistics (NAACL).

Ani Nenkova, Rebecca Passonneau, and Kathleen McKeown. 2007. The pyramid method: incorporating human content selection variation in summarization evaluation. *ACM Transactions on Speech and Language Processing* 4(2).

Paul Over, Hoa Dang, and Donna Harman. 2007. DUC in context. *Information Processing and Management* 43(6):1506–1520. Special Issue on Text Summarisation (Donna Harman, ed.).

Karolina Owczarzak, John M. Conroy, Hoa Trang Dang, and Ani Nenkova. 2012. An assessment of the accuracy of automatic evaluation in summarization. In *Proceedings of Workshop on Evaluation Metrics and System Comparison for Automatic Summarization*. Association for Computational Linguistics, Montréal, Canada, pages 1–9. http://www.aclweb.org/anthology/W12-2601.

Karolina Owczarzak and Hoa T. Dang. 2010. Overview of the tac 2010 summarization track. In National Institute of Standards and Technology, editors, *Proceedings of Text Analysis Conference (TAC-10)*. Gaithersburg, MD.

Karolina Owczarzak and Hoa T. Dang. 2011. Overview of the tac 2011 summarization track: Guided task and aesop task. In National Institute of Standards and Technology, editors, *Proceedings of the Text Analysis Conference (TAC-11)*. Gaithersburg, MD.

Martha Palmer, Paul Kingsbury, and Daniel Gildea. 2005. The proposition bank: An annotated corpus of semantic roles. *Computational Linguistics* 31(1):71–106.

Rebecca J. Passonneau, Emily Chen, Weiwei Guo, and Dolores Perin. 2013. Automated pyramid scoring of summaries using distributional semantics. In *Proceedings of the 51st Annual Meeting of the Association for Computational Linguistics*. Association for Computational Linguistics, Sofia, Bulgaria, page 143147.

Stephen Tratz and Eduard Hovy. 2008. Summarization evaluation using transformed basic elements. In National Institute of Standards and Technology, editors, *Proceedings of Text Analysis Conference (TAC-08)*. Gaithersburg, MD.

Chuan Wang, Nianwen Xue, and Sameer Pradhan. 2015. Boosting transition-based amr parsing with refined actions and auxiliary analyzers. In *Proceedings of the 53rd Annual Meeting of the Association for Computational Linguistics and the 7th International Joint Conference on Natural Language Processing (Volume 2: Short Papers)*. Association for Computational Linguistics, Beijing, China, pages 857–862. http://www.aclweb.org/anthology/P15-2141.

Large-scale news entity sentiment analysis

Ralf Steinberger, Stefanie Hegele, Hristo Tanev & Leonida Della Rocca

European Commission – Joint Research Centre (JRC), Via E. Fermi 2749, 21027 Ispra, Italy
Ralf.Steinberger@ec.europa.eu

Abstract

We work on detecting positive or negative
sentiment towards named entities in very
large volumes of news articles. The aim is to
monitor changes over time, as well as to
work towards media bias detection by comparing differences across news sources and
countries. With view to applying the same
method to dozens of languages, we use linguistically light-weight methods: searching
for positive and negative terms in bags of
words around entity mentions (also considering negation). Evaluation results are good
and better than a third-party baseline system,
but precision is not sufficiently high to display the results publicly in our multilingual
news analysis system *Europe Media Monitor*
(EMM). In this paper, we focus on describing
our effort to improve the English language
results by avoiding the biggest sources of errors. We also present new work on using a
syntactic parser to identify safe opinion
recognition rules, such as predicative structures in which sentiment words directly refer
to an entity. The precision of this method is
good, but recall is very low.

1   Introduction

This work is being carried out in the context of our
large-scale multilingual media monitoring effort
EMM (*Europe Media Monitor*, Steinberger et al.
2017, 2009). EMM processes a daily average of
300,000 news articles in about 70 languages. EMM
groups related articles, tracks them over time, categorises them, extracts information such as entities
and reported speech by and about people, translates
eleven languages into English and produces various types of statistics. The intention is to add
graphs showing how positive or negative certain
persons or organisations are being talked about,
how this differs between news sources and countries, and how this changes over time. Due to the
high number of languages covered, EMM works
mostly with knowledge-poor methods, using language-agnostic rules. EMM therefore does not rely
on part-of-speech tagging, syntactic parsers or
large-scale dictionaries (Steinberger 2012). EMM
uses machine learning for other purposes, but there
is not sufficient suitable data to train our multilingual sentiment analysis components.

The practical requirement in the context of
EMM is to achieve reasonable *precision in positive
and negative mentions*. The strongly dominant
class of neutral mentions in the news domain is less
relevant and would at best serve to measure the
overall heat around an entity (subjectivity level).
Due to the large number of partially redundant
news articles, *recall* is secondary. As a future goal,
it would be good to also recognise sentiment separately for different aspects (Kumar & Sebastian
2012), such as types of policy of a politician. **Table 1** lists snippets that show readers the types of
phenomena we encounter in our work.

The term *sentiment analysis* is often used as the
generic term to mean the computational treatment
of opinion, sentiment and subjectivity in text (Pang
& Lee 2008), but the terms are not identical: It is
possible to state an opinion without expressing a
sentiment (Soo-Min & Hovy 2004). We aim to detect *polar* (positive or negative) judgements or appraisals towards entities (our *opinion target*), independently of the *opinion holder*. We are mostly interested in cases where the *journalists* (representing the news source) express a biased judgement.
However, as quoting other persons who make an
evaluative statement is the journalist's wilful
choice, we currently make the simplifying approximation to equate the opinion holder with the author. By searching for polar words in the news text,
we mostly aim to detect the newspaper's *framing
bias*; We do not currently consider *epistemological
bias* (focusing on the believability of a proposition;
Recasens et al. 2013). We have no means to detect
content bias (not giving equal treatment to both
sides in a political conflict; Entman 2007), such as
the selection of stories a newspaper chooses to
cover (tackled by Fortuna et al. 2009).

Proceedings of Recent Advances in Natural Language Processing, pages 707–715,
Varna, Bulgaria, Sep 4–6 2017.

N°	Sentence with <u>Entity</u> (opinion target) and possible **sentiment word**
1	Statement by the HR/VP <u>Federica Mogherini</u> on cessation of **hostilities** in Syria:
2	… and as **humiliated** leaders like <u>Deng Xiaoping</u> came back from their internal exiles …
3	…began in the 1960s, **inspired** by Chinese revolutionary leader <u>Mao Zedong</u>, and has cost thousands of lives.
4	… published a post that poked **fun** at the Microsoft web browser <u>Internet Explorer</u>.
5	<u>Donald Trump</u> **supports** the so-called "First Amendment Defense Act," (FADA), a bill to enable Kim Davis-style **discrimination** against LGBTQ people nationwide.
6	Chief Minister <u>Shivraj Singh Chouhan</u> has **good** intentions but there's little one man can do.
7	<u>Facebook</u> ended up hiring one of its **best** bug hunters, Reginaldo Silva …
8	The suit, filed in July 2012, alleged that <u>JPMorgan Chase</u> issued **false** and **misleading** statements regarding its trading activity …
9	<u>Margaret Thatcher</u>'s former PR guru **shocked** listeners when he told a **poor-taste** 'joke' …
10	There's a simple reason why <u>Lewis Hamilton</u> is the **favorite** for this year's Monaco Grand Prix,
11	It has taken out billboards in New York's Times Square praising Charles Schumer […] for opposing the deal and **chastising** Senator <u>Kirsten Gillibrand</u> for backing it.
12	General Hassan Firouzabadi highlighted rifts between <u>Rouhani</u> and **critics** who say negotiations don't serve Iran's national interest …
13	In Ohio <u>Obama</u> was **not supported** by various groups of people.
14	The claims made by the three US carriers that <u>Etihad Airways</u> and other Gulf carriers are **damaging** their business …
15	Oliver Letwin, the Prime Minister's **troubleshooter**, had advised <u>Cameron</u> to stay for the stability of the country.

Table 1. Real-life news sentences. The task is to identify sentiment towards the entity.

Sentiment analysis can be performed at different levels: It can be document, sentence, word and feature-based (Liu 2012). We only look at a window of up to six words around the entity in order to limit the potential impact of good or bad *news* (as opposed to *sentiment*) on the resulting sentiment value (see Section 3).

In the following sections, we first give an overview of related work (Section 2) and explain our method to perform sentiment analysis (3). We will present the evaluation results, including a detailed error analysis and the steps undertaken to reduce the error rate (4). Section 5 summarises additional experiments in which we learned and used syntactic patterns for sentiment analysis. In Section 6, we summarise and conclude.

2   Related work

Here, we want to mention some relevant work in the field of sentiment analysis, including annotation efforts and competitive events, especially in the news domain.

Sentiment analysis is usually based on lexical knowledge encoded explicitly as dictionaries and taxonomies or indirectly, as machine learning models. *SentiWordNet* (Esuli & Sebastiani 2006; Baccinella et al. 2010) is a lexical resource specific to sentiment analysis that assigns to each WordNet synset – sets of synonyms for groups of English words – three sentiment scores: positivity, negativity, or objectivity. Other approaches for sentiment lexicon building make use of bootstrapping (e.g. Banea et al. 2008). J Steinberger et al. (2012) used triangulation to generate polar dictionaries in fifteen languages.

Most researchers look at sentiment analysis as a text classification task (Pang & Lee 2008; Kiritchenko et al. 2014; Grimmer & Stewart 2013). Features used typically are word classes and word types such as adjectives, verbs and sentiment shifters. Other researchers like Vilares et.al. (2015) demonstrate the usefulness of using syntactic representations for carrying out sentiment analysis. Socher et al. (2013) present the so-called Recursive Neural Tensor Network, which – trained on annotated treebanks and considering sentiment compositionality – assigns polarity to whole sentences.

The dominant part of current academic sentiment analysis work applies supervised or semi-supervised classification techniques trained on manually annotated data such as movie or product reviews while there is relatively little work on the news genre. Li et al. (2008) annotated 108 German political news documents involving German politicians following the annotation scheme developed in Wiebe et al. (2005). The Interest Group on German Sentiment Analysis provides 605 annotated sentences from a parliamentary corpus as training data for their 2016 IGGSA Shared Task (Ruppenhofer et al. 2016). Deng & Wiebe's (2015b) English language MPQA 3 corpus contains some 70 annotated texts, including news. The sentiment slot filling track at the NIST *Text Analysis Conference* (TAC) also contains a news part (Mitchell 2013). Unfortunately, resources are altogether relatively small. No annotated resources exist for the many languages we need to cover, and each annotated corpus is annotated with different objectives and definitions in mind. For instance, Li et al. (2008) use the words *polarity, opinions* and *tones of voice*, without defining what is deemed to be positive or negative. They list the word *Krieg* (war) as being negative and *Erfolg* (success) as positive. The word 'success' could indeed be seen as a positive judgement of the writer towards the entity, but in our view, the word 'war' usually refers to a factual event that has nothing to do with sentiment or judgement. See Section 3 for more detail on our viewpoint that good/bad sentiment should be separated from good/bad news content.

While a lot of sentiment-related work does not well define what positive or negative means, we feel that work around Soo-Min and Hovy (2004) and Wiebe et al. (2005) is more mature. Soo-Min and Hovy (2004) use a more conceptually motivated model. They describe an opinion as a "quadruple [Topic, Holder, Claim, Sentiment], in which the Holder believes a Claim about the Topic, and in many cases associates a Sentiment, such as *good* or *bad*, with the belief". Sentiments always involve the Holder's emotions or desires, and may be present explicitly (lexically) or only implicitly. Soo-Min & Hovy only try to identify those cases where the opinion holder is mentioned in the text while we are particularly interested in those cases where the author (the journalist) holds a biased or judgemental view. Wiebe et al. (2005, pp. 4ff) aim to describe linguistic expressions of so-called *private states*, a term coined by Randolph Quirk that includes internal states that cannot be directly observed by others, such as *opinions, emotions, sentiments, speculations* and *evaluations*. They distinguish (a) explicit mentions of private states (e.g. *the US fears a spill-over*), (b) speech events expressing private states (*Person A said "The report is full of absurdities"*) and (c) expressive subjective elements. The latter are "used by people to express their frustration, anger, wonder, positive sentiment, mirth, etc., without explicitly stating that they are frustrated, angry, etc.". Sarcasm and irony often involve expressive subjective elements. In their terms, *experiencers* hold *attitudes* toward *targets* (e.g. in *John hates Mary*). SenticNet (Cambria & Hussain 2015; Cambria et al. 2012) and WordNet-Affect (Strapparava & Valitutti 2004) provide more fine-grained information covering various aspects of emotion and sentiment. We can expect better multilingual resources for more informed sentiment analysis systems in the future, but producing such linguistic resources is much more time-consuming than producing lists of polar words.

Starting in 2013, there have been sentiment slot filling tracks as part of the NIST *Text Analysis Conference* (TAC) series. The 2013 task (Mitchell 2013) was to identify sentiment polarity together with opinion holder and opinion target in English language open domain texts, using news, forum texts and the general web. While this task differs from our own in that it focuses on cases where the opinion holder is explicitly mentioned in the text, it is interesting to see that the best system reached a precision of 10% and the best F-Score reached (by another system) was 13.15%. Performance was best in fora texts. In 2016, the track's objective was to identify beliefs or sentiments (private states) and the track was extended to include also smaller portions of Spanish and Chinese language texts. Due to the inclusion of beliefs, the task is even harder to compare to our own.

Deng & Wiebe (2015a) worked on an entity/event-level sentiment analysis system recognising and inferring both explicit and implicit sentiments. In addition to recognising polarity and opinion target, they also aim at recognising the opinion holder. They evaluate their system on the annotated English language MPQE 3.0 corpus (Deng & Wiebe 2015b). The best experimental results for this complex task yielded a precision of almost 38% for positive, and almost 36% for negative pairs. The best F-measure achieved was 24% and 33%, respectively.

3 Approach to news sentiment analysis

In a nutshell, our base sentiment analysis method searches for words from four different sentiment classes in a bag-of-words window around the entities (For details, see J Steinberger et al. 2011). Subjectivity is assumed if a sentiment word is present in this window (see the discussion in Section 6). The added positive and negative sentiment values in that word window help identify the polarity regarding the mentioned entity. We distinguish the four classes *positive/negative* and *highly positive/negative*. Altogether, there are about 2,300 sentiment dictionary entries. These were created by combining in-house and various publicly available resources, by learning more terms using distributional semantics, and by then manually curating the resulting list. The best-performing combination of several existing sentiment dictionaries were empirically identified by using a training set (Balahur et al. 2010). Sentiment value calculation is compositional in our system as it also considers lists of about 125 intensifiers, diminishers and negators. The optimal window size (six words on both sides of the entity, but not passing sentence borders) was also empirically identified using a training set (Balahur et al. 2010). The cumulative sentiment values are normalised for the varying window size (in case of sentence borders). Due to a lack of large enough training data, we did not have the opportunity to further optimise the sentiment value assignment algorithm automatically nor the final lists of sentiment words or their relative weights. Some of the sentiment words contain wildcards in order to capture possible variants (e.g. *intelligen%*).

An important issue for us was that *good/bad news* should not have an impact on the sentiment values for the entities that may be randomly associated with the event, e.g. when a politician visits an area affected by a natural disaster. We therefore kept factual words that may be perceived negatively such as *war, death* or *injured* out of the sentiment word lists and our algorithm ignores potential sentiment words that are part of the defining vocabulary of the article's news category. For instance. When a news item was categorised into the news category NATURAL DISASTER, we ignore the category-defining words *natural* and *disaster*.

In order to evaluate the system performance, we produced a manually annotated news corpus consisting of 1274 sentences mentioning entities. Two annotators were asked to annotate the entity mentions as being positive (POS), negative (NEG) or neutral (NEUT), following the guidelines described in Balahur & Steinberger (2009). The annotators reached an agreement of 80%, resulting in

Prec/Rec	IAA	Original	Improved	Base/SSA
ALL	0.80	.737 / .737	.742 / .742	.260 / .260
NEUT	0.86	.788 / .900	.788 / .910	.718 / .133
POS	**0.78**	**.436 / .323**	**.431 / .294**	**.219 / .323**
NEG	**0.87**	**.578 / .312**	**.592 / .310**	**.181 / .820**
POS/NEG	**0.83**	**.500 / .317**	**.507 / .303**	**.189 / .587**
Base/ALL NEUT		.72	.72	.72

Table 2. Inter-annotator agreement (IAA, column 2), Precision/Recall for English language entity sentiment analysis before (Column 3) and after the improvement rules (Column 4, see Section 4), as well as by the Stanford tool (Base, Column 5). 2nd. baseline results: ALL NEUT, i.e. assigning only the neutral class.

a fair kappa agreement of 0.65 (see **Table 2**, second column, *IAA*). In comparison, the inter-annotator agreement for Portuguese news entity sentiment in Domingos de Arruda et al. (2015) is reported as 40% (kappa = 0.28). Our first annotator assigned POS to 16% of cases, NEG to 17% and NEUT to 67%. The second annotator assigned non-neutral polarity more often: 26% POS, 24% NEG and 50% NEUT. In order to reach a gold standard annotation, a third annotator decided in those cases where the first two disagreed. In the resulting gold-standard set of 1274 sentences, 167 entity mentions were deemed to be positive (13%), 189 negative (15%) and 918 neutral (72%). This neutral majority class serves as a tough performance baseline (ALL NEUT).

The third column of **Table 2** (*Original* system) shows the system performance. The overall accuracy achieved was 74%. However, the precision for only the positive and the negative classes (POS/NEG) in the three-way classification was 50%, which is useless for practical purposes. The comparison in J Steinberger et al. (2011) showed very similar results for all seven languages tested. Column 5 (Base/SSA) shows a second baseline: the results of the *Stanford Sentiment Annotator* (SSA; Socher et al. 2013). SSA assigns polarity at the sentence level, using semantic compositionality, a sentence parser and the Recursive Neural Tensor Network, trained on a movie review sentiment treebank. The results in Column 5 were calculated by assigning the sentence polarity to the entities they contain. While the authors report 81% accuracy for movie reviews, SSA as we used it yielded 26% on our news corpus, and 19% for the polar cases POS/NEG. We observe that SSA classified an overwhelming 67% of sentences as being negative.

Word	Freq.	Perc.
support	310446	2.68%
won	183227	1.58%
win	178328	1.54%
well	165016	1.42%
help	124610	1.07%
best	101223	0.87%
supporters	100810	0.87%
accused	97665	0.84%
victory	91059	0.78%
agreed	87384	0.75%
crisis	87295	0.75%
warned	84082	0.72%
good	82835	0.71%
clear	75171	0.65%
emergency	72486	0.62%
better	70896	0.61%
called for	67307	0.58%
pressure	63878	0.55%
lost	61996	0.53%
cooperation	59970	0.52%
allies	59439	0.51%
aid	57188	0.49%
militants	57001	0.49%
criticism	52584	0.45%
winning	50878	0.44%
wins	49233	0.42%
failed	47805	0.41%
criticized	46628	0.40%
ally	45362	0.39%
supporting	44996	0.39%

Table 3. Sentiment words and their occurrence frequency and percentage (out of all sentiment words) in 12 months of English language news analysis.

The difficulty of our task lies in the fact that only two out of nine possible combinations can be considered correct and that the neutral class (which is the only one we are *not* interested in) is by far the largest (72% of cases). Random assignment would yield 9.3% for only the polar cases POS and NEG. Considering the difficulty of the task and the odds at play, a precision of 50% is a good achievement, but it is not sufficient for practical purposes.

4 Error analysis and rules to improve the output

The entity opinion mining system described in Section 3 was run for more than one year (May 2015-April 2016), on altogether about 20 million English language news articles. The sentiment word forms most frequently found next to an entity are shown in **Table 3.** There are minor variations from one month to the next. The cumulated frequency for all 11,303 sentiment word forms is 11.76 million. The top ten most frequent sentiment word forms account for 12.3% of all sentiment terms found and the top one hundred for 42% of all sentiment word occurrences. As improving the sentiment value assignment accuracy of the most frequent terms should thus have a high impact on the overall performance of the system, we focused our effort on the ten most frequent sentiment words by first analysing the system output errors and then writing rules to avoid them. For this purpose, we used the SketchEngine (Kilgarriff et al. 2014) and HTML-based in-house tools to analyse the usage of each polar word.

4.1 Sentiment assignment errors and solutions implemented

We found the following major sources of errors:

1. **Wild cards capture wrong strings:** Our sentiment dictionaries contain a few words with wild cards to capture variants. To avoid words such as *supporting-actor* (support%) or *intelligence-gathering* (intelligen%), the wild cards in our sentiment dictionaries were refined and some wrong matches were included in a stop word list of terms that should not be used.

2. **Multi-word expressions and non-sentiment uses:** Some sentiment words also occur as multi-word expressions that do not have sentiment meaning, e.g. *well* in *as well as*. We used SketchEngine and the TenTen web corpus (included with the Sketch Engine service) to produce the most frequent word n-grams containing our top frequent sentiment words and selected those manually where we did not perceive the intended sentiment meaning of the word. We identified 52 such multi-word expressions (e.g. *best known, with respect to, super PAC, artificial intelligence, well-known*, etc.) and added them to a stop word list.

3. **Sentiment words in uppercase:** Uppercase words are usually part of entity names and should be ignored, e.g. *crisis* in the organisation name *Judicial Crisis Network* and *super* in *Super Tuesday*. To test the hypothesis, three evaluators not part of the team judged 40 sentences, of which 20 contained uppercase and 20 lowercase sentiment words. Their agreement with the system more than doubled when filtering out the uppercase words: Agreement rates with the system went from 20, 40 and 20% to 40, 75 and 55%, respectively. This confirmed our hypothesis.

4. **Reported speech:** Sentiment words found inside direct or indirect speech must not be linked to the entity who is the author of the quotations because the entity is the opinion *holder* and not the opinion *target*. Markers of direct and indirect speech should thus act like sentence borders. Patterns to recognise indirect speech were added, consisting of reporting verbs combined with the conjunction *that*. This rule eliminates 1% of all entity mentions followed by a sentiment word. To test our hypothesis, three evaluators not part of the team judged 100 sentences containing sentiment words, of which 50 contained indirect speech. When filtering out the indirect speech sentences, their agreement with the system rose significantly, i.e. from 31, 40 and 67% to 54, 72 and 78%, respectively. This confirmed our hypothesis.

5. **Scope of sentiment words and passive constructions:** Some sentiment verbs have a scope that only extends in one direction. For instance, only the object (patient) of the verb *support* is positively affected by the action verb while the subject (agent) could be considered the 'opinion holder'. In passive sentences, the roles are inverted (*A was supported by B*). We thus formulated filters ensuring that the system does not recognise a positive sentiment towards the agent. To test this hypothesis, three evaluators judged 95 sentences containing the verb 'support', of which 53 were then filtered out to avoid that the sentiment word was associated with the agent of the sentence. The agreement of the evaluators with the system output went up from 52, 44 and 51% to 57, 52 and 60%, respectively. Considering the success of this rule, we then used distributional semantics to identify lists of further verbs behaving like 'support'. We checked the results manually and added them to the filtering rules (e.g. *criticise, accuse, praise, reject, blame*).

These were the main cases where the system regularly went wrong. However, there are numerous cases where polar words do not refer to the nearby entity and where we were not able to find a regularity that could be exploited in a filtering rule.

4.2 Sentiment analysis results after incorporating these insights – Results

After implementing the filters and improvements described in Subsection 4.1, we carried out a new evaluation to see whether the overall results have improved (See the fourth column in **Table 2** - *Improved*). In the test set of 1274 sentences with entity mentions, there were 52 occurrences of the top ten sentiment words (the ones we focused our improvement efforts on), of which 19 were filtered out by the filtering rules 3 to 5 mentioned in Section 4.1. This filter improved the accuracy, but not significantly: precision for negative mentions improved by 1.35% to 59.2% and it diminished by 0.3% for positive mentions (43.1%).

Due to the large neutral portion of the test sentences, the sample of subjective sentences is too small. We therefore compiled an additional test set consisting of 200 potentially subjective sentences, i.e. sentences containing an entity name and at least one polar word in its word window. The system assigned 89 positive and 111 negative sentiment values to this set. Four evaluators annotated this collection. Two of them were part of the team and they had ample opportunities to come to a common understanding of the task, while the other two simply followed the annotation instructions. The agreement overlap between the six pairs of human annotators ranged from 67.5% to 81.5%, which is rather good even though the kappa scores only ranged from 0.13 to 0.40 because the neutral class was so dominant. However, the annotators agreed very little with the system output, namely in between 7% and 31% of cases. The in-house annotators, who had a clearer understanding of the task, agreed less with the system (7 and 13%) than the two outsiders (18 and 31%). Annotators agreed slightly more with our baseline, the Stanford Sentiment Annotator, i.e. 36, 36.5, 37 and 43.5%, but still clearly below the 50% threshold.

These results are extremely disappointing. They are worse than those of the previous evaluation carried out. It looks like the majority of entity mentions in the news sentence test set are neutral/objective even when they are mentioned in close vicinity to words from our sentiment dictionaries: Our four annotators marked only between 18% and 39% as either positive or negative in spite of the presence of sentiment words in the immediate vicinity of entities.

5 Syntactic rules for news entity sentiment analysis

The flaw of our system seems to be the recognition of subjective mentions. We furthermore observed that polar words close to the entity mentions do not necessarily refer to the entity itself, i.e. the bag-of-words approach is too coarse-grained. We therefore worked on identifying safe rules capturing syntactic constructions in which there is a clear relationship between the polar word and the entity. We developed patterns for two predicative constructions (Rules 1 and 2) and two more generic syntactic paths (Rules 3 and 4), as shown in the following pattern list:

1. NAME is (who is, to be, was, may be....) SENTIMENT
   ENTITY is impressive.
2. SENTIMENT<-adjective- NAME
   Impressive ENTITY.
3. SENTIMENT word and the Entity have a common verbal or nominal ancestor in the syntactic tree, e.g.
   ENTITY delivered an impressive speech (here 'delivered' is the common verbal ancestor of 'impressed' and ENTITY)

   The impressive speech of ENTITY (with 'speech' as a common nominal ancestor).
4. Sentiment word under the name in the syntactic dependency tree, e.g.
   intelligent politician ENTITY.

We analysed the test set of 200 sentences to evaluate our heuristics, using the Stanford dependency parser (Manning et al. 2014). We took as ground truth the two evaluators with the highest agreement. These were the two EMM team members, who had classified most sentences as neutral. They disagreed in only one of the sentences captured by the four rules, which they discussed and for which they then came to an agreement.

Altogether, the four rules matched 25 of the 200 sentences (12.5%). The precision was 44% and the recall 32%. Rules 1 and 2, which are the safest and most obvious, matched three times and all three analyses were correct (precision 100%) while Rules 3 and 4 matched 22 times, of which eight were correct (precision is 36%). The imposed relationship between the sentiment word and the entity in Rules 3 and 4 is thus too vague to be useful. This shows that if the sentiment word does not directly syntactically refer to the entity, things can go wrong. Jiang et al (2011) seem to have come to the same conclusion for Twitter sentiment analysis. More information would be needed to determine the correct sentiment judgement in such cases. This becomes obvious with the constructed example *the intelligent/impressive liar ENTITY* (matching Rule 4), where the generally positive words contribute to a negative judgement due to the negative noun *liar*.

6 Discussion and Conclusion

The EMM news entity sentiment annotation module was developed using linguistically shallow methods so that it could be applied to dozens of languages. The tool has an accuracy of 74%, which goes much beyond a baseline system trained for movie reviews (the *Stanford Sentiment Annotator SSA*, Socher et al. 2013). However, its precision is only 50% for positive and negative entity mentions (SSA: 19%; Random: 9.3%). In this paper, we presented a large-scale error analysis and hand-crafted rules to improve the results by avoiding the major errors. This did not significantly improve precision. Major challenges are the dominant number of neutral entity mentions (72%) and the fact that polar words often do not refer to the nearby entity. A separate subjectivity filter should be applied rather than assuming polarity in all cases where a sentiment word is present. We should also review our list of polar words to ensure that they have a polar sentiment value, rather than pointing to positive or negative news content (e.g. *win, victory, support*).

In separate experiments, we applied a syntactic parser and rules imposing a scope relationship between the polar word and the entity. While predicative structures (*X is NEG*, or *the NEG X*) yielded 100% precision, their recall is unacceptably small.

In view of sentiment analysis work trained on social media data such as movie reviews (Socher et al. 2013) reaching over 80% of accuracy, the results presented in this paper may look sub-standard. However, it does make a difference whether large numbers of manually classified reviews on a specific product are available to train the system or whether wide-coverage news is being analysed. Our comparative results reported in **Table 2** (performance drop of the SSA tool from 80% on the training data to 26% on our data) show that tools cannot simply be ported to another domain.

Secondly, even our system achieves 74% accuracy when including the neutral class, but if the aim is to achieve a *precision* that goes significantly above 50% for the minority classes POS and NEG, the task is harder. The precision for various subtasks at evaluations and shared tasks (of course partially on more complex tasks) often does not go much above the 50% threshold either (Mitchell 2013; Ruppenhofer et al. 2016). The reported results furthermore typically include the neutral class. It looks like generic systems like ours are not yet ready to be deployed automatically for uncontrolled public display.

References

Baccinella Stefano, Andrea Esuli & Fabrizio Sebastiani. 2010. SentiWordNet 3.0: An enhanced lexical resource for sentiment analysis and opinion mining. LREC'2010, pp. 2200-2204.

Balahur Alexandra & Ralf Steinberger. 2009. Rethinking Sentiment Analysis in the News: from Theory to Practice and back. Proceeding of WOMSA.

Balahur Alexandra, Ralf Steinberger, Mijail Kabadjov, Vanni Zavarella, Erik Van Der Goot, Matina Halkia, Bruno Pouliquen, Jenya Belyaeva. 2010. Sentiment analysis in the news. Proceedings of the 7th Intern. Conf. on Language Resources and Evaluation (LREC'2010), pp. 2216-2220. Valletta, Malta, 19-21 May

Banea Carmen, Rada Mihalcea & Janyce Wiebe. 2008. A bootstrapping method for building subjectivity lexicons for languages with scarce resources. Proceedings of LREC'2008. .

Cambria Erik & Amir Hussain. 2015. SenticNet. In: Sentic computing. A common-sense-based framework for concept-level sentiment analysis, pp. 23-71. Springer

Cambria Erik, Andrew Livingstone & Amir Hussain. 2012. The hourglass of emotions. In: A. Esposito et al. (eds.) Cognitive Behavioural Systems. Springer LNCS 7403, pp. 144-157.

Deng Lingjia & Janyce Wiebe. 2015a. Joint Prediction for Entity/Event-Level Sentiment Analysis using Probabilistic Soft logic Models. Proceedings of EMNLP, pp. 179-189.

Deng Lingjia & Janyce Wiebe. 2015b. MPQA 3.0: An entity/event-level sentiment corpus. Proceedings of NAACL, pp. 1323-1328.

Domingos de Arruda Gabriel, Norton Trevisan Roman, Ana Maria Monteiro. 2015. An Annotated Corpus for Sentiment Analysis in Political News. Proceedings of Symposium in Information and Human Language Technology. Natal, RN, Brazil, pp. 101-110.

Entman Robert. 2007. Framing Bias: Media in the Distribution of Power. Journal of Communication 57 (2007) pp. 163-173.

Esuli A & Fabrizio Sebastiani. 2006. SentiWordNet: a high-coverage lexical resource for opinion mining. Technical Report. Institute of Information Science and Technologies of the Italian National Research Council.

Fortuna Blaž, Carolina Galleguillos & Nello Cristianini. 2009. Detection of bias in media outlets with statistical learning methods. In Ashok Srivastava & Mehram Sahami (eds.): Text Mining. Classification, Clustering, and Applications. Chapman and Hall, pp. 27-50.

Grimmer Justin & Brandon Stewart. 2013. Text as data: The promise and pitfalls of automatic content analysis methods for political texts. Political Analysis 21(3), pp 267-297.

Jiang Long, Mo Yu, Ming Zhou, Xiaohua Liu & Tiejun Zhao. 2011. Target-dependent Twitter sentiment classification. Proceedings of ACL'2011, pp. 151-160.

Kilgarriff Adam, Vít Baisa, Jan Bušta, Miloš Jakubíček, Vojtěch Kovář, Jan Michelfeit, Pavel Rychlý, Vít Suchomel. 2014. The Sketch Engine: ten years on. Lexicography, Volume 1, Issue 1, pp 7–36.

Kiritchenko Svetlana, Xiaodan Zhu & Saif Mohammed. 2014. Sentiment analysis of short informal texts. Journal of Artificial Intelligence Research (JAIR) 50 (2014, pp. 723-762.

Kumar A. & T. M. Sebastian. 2012. Sentiment analysis: A perspective on its past, present and future. International Journal of Intelligent Systems and Applications, 4(10):1-14.

Liu B. 2012. Sentiment analysis and opinion mining. Morgan and Claypool Publishers: Synthesis Lectures on Human Language Technologies.

Manning Christopher, Mihai Surdeanu, John Bauer, Jenny Finkel, Steven Bethard & David McClosky. 2014. The Stanford CoreNLP natural language processing toolkit. Proceedings of 52nd Annual Meeting of the Association for Computational Linguistics: System Demonstrations, pp. 55-60.

Mitchell Margaret. 2013. Overview of the TAC2013 Knowledge Base Population Evaluation: Sentiment Slot Filling. https://tac.nist.gov/publications/2013/.

Pang L. & L. Lee. 2008. Opinion mining and sentiment analysis. Foundations and trends in information retrieval 2 (1-2), 1-135.

Recasens Marta, Cristian Danescu-Niculescu-Mizil & Dan Jurafsky. 2013. Linguistic models for analyzing and detecting biased language. Proceedings of the ACL conference, pp. 1650-1659.

Socher Richard, Alex Perelygin, Jean Wu, Jason Chuang, Christopher Manning, Andrew Ng & Christopher Potts. 2013. Recursive deep models for semantic compositionality over a sentiment treebank. Proceedings of EMNLP 2013, pp. 1631-1642. Seattle, Washington.

Soo-Min Kim & Eduard Hovy. 2004. Determining the sentiment of opinions. CoLing Conference, Geneva.

Steinberger Josef, Mohamed Ebrahim, Maud Ehrmann, Ali Hürriyetoglu, Mijail Kabadjov, Polina Lenkova, Ralf Steinberger, Hristo Tanev, Silvia Vázquez, Vanni Zavarella. 2012. Creating sentiment dictionaries via triangulation. Decision Support Systems 53(4), pp. 689-694

Steinberger Josef, Polina Lenkova, Mijail Kabadjov,
Ralf Steinberger & Erik van der Goot. 2011. Multilingual entity-centered sentiment analysis evaluated
by parallel corpora. Proceedings of the RANLP
Conference, pp. 770-775.

Steinberger Ralf, Bruno Pouliquen & Erik van der
Goot. 2009. An Introduction to the Europe Media
Monitor Family of Applications. In: Fredric Gey,
Noriko Kando & Jussi Karlgren (eds.): Information
Access in a Multilingual World - Proceedings of the
SIGIR 2009 Workshop (SIGIR-CLIR'2009), pp. 1-
8. Boston, USA.

Steinberger Ralf. 2012. A survey of methods to ease the
development of highly multilingual text mining applications. Language Resources and Evaluation,
Vol. 46 (2), pp. 155-176, Springer.

Steinberger Ralf, Martin Atkinson, Teófilo Garcia,
Erik van der Goot, Jens Linge, Charles Macmillan,
Hristo Tanev, Marco Verile & Gerhard Wagner.
2017. EMM: Supporting the analyst by turning multilingual text into structured data. In: Deggendorfer
Forum zur digitalen Datenanalyse e.V. Verantwor-
tung in der digitalen Datenanalyse, pp. 85-108. Berlin, Erich Schmidt Verlag.

Strapparava Carlo & Alessandro Valitutti. 2004. Word-
Net Affect: an affective extension of WordNet.
LREC, vol. 4, pp. 1083-1086.

Vilares David, Miguel Alonso & Carlos Gómez-Rodrí-
guez. 2015. On the usefulness of lexical and syntactic processing in polarity classification of Twitter
messages. Journal of the Association for Information Science and Technology, 66: pp. 1799-1816.

Predicting the Law Area and Decisions of French Supreme Court Cases

Octavia-Maria Şulea[1], Marcos Zampieri[2], Mihaela Vela[3], Josef van Genabith[3,4]
[1]University of Bucharest, Romania
[2]University of Wolverhampton, United Kingdom
[3]Saarland University, Germany
[4]German Research Center for Artificial Intelligence (DFKI), Germany
`mary.octavia@gmail.com, marcos.zampieri@uni-koeln.de`
`m.vela@mx.uni-saarland.de, josef.vangenabith@uni-saarland.de`

Abstract

In this paper, we investigate the application of text classification methods to predict the law area and the decision of cases judged by the French Supreme Court. We also investigate the influence of the time period in which a ruling was made over the textual form of the case description and the extent to which it is necessary to mask the judge's motivation for a ruling to emulate a real-world test scenario. We report results of 96% f1 score in predicting a case ruling, 90% f1 score in predicting the law area of a case, and 75.9% f1 score in estimating the time span when a ruling has been issued using a linear Support Vector Machine (SVM) classifier trained on lexical features.

1 Introduction

Text classification methods have been used in a wide range of NLP tasks. This includes predicting information about authors of texts, such as age (Nguyen et al., 2013), gender (Ciobanu et al., 2017), personality traits (Sulea and Dichiu, 2015), and native language (Gebre et al., 2013), estimating the period in which a text was published (Niculae et al., 2014), the amount of subjectivity or sentiment expressed in texts (Balahur et al., 2014), and detecting pastiche (Dinu et al., 2012), plagiarism (Barrón-Cedeño et al., 2013), and influences from other authors (Ganascia et al., 2014). Classic machine learning algorithms such as Multinomial Naive Bayes and SVMs proved to be very reliable for these tasks, achieving high performance.

In this paper, we apply text classification methods to legal documents. We explore the use of bag of words (BOW) and linear SVM classifiers in predicting a case's ruling, law area, and the date in which a ruling was issued. We apply these methods to a large corpus of court rulings issued by the French Supreme Court with over 126,000 documents, spanning from the 1800s until the present day.

To the best of our knowledge, several NLP tasks have been carried out on legal texts, most notably text summarization (Farzindar and Lapalme, 2004; Galgani et al., 2012), however, as evidenced in Section 2, the use of text classification to predict court rulings is an under-explored area. The recent study by Aletras et al. (2016) on predicting decisions of the European Court of Human Rights (ECHR) is among the few examples of such attempts.

2 Related Work

In the legal domain, text classification has been more important to forensics (De Vel et al., 2001; Sumner et al., 2012; Pérez-Rosas and Mihalcea, 2015) than to predict information in legal texts such as case descriptions, rulings, and court decisions. General NLP methods, on the other hand, have played an important role in the intersection between artificial intelligence and law, a vibrant sub-area of research with international associations (e.g. IAAIL[1]) and a number of specialized scientific conferences and workshops.

Palau and Moens (2009) investigate the extent to which one can automatically identify argumentative propositions in legal text, along with their argumentative function and structure. They use a corpus containing legal texts extracted from the European Court of Human Rights (ECHR) and classify argumentative vs. non-argumentative sentences with an accuracy of 80%.

Boella et al. (2011) present a classification approach to identify the relevant domain to which a

---

[1]`http://www.iaail.org/`

Proceedings of Recent Advances in Natural Language Processing, pages 716–722,
Varna, Bulgaria, Sep 4–6 2017.

specific legal text belongs. Using TF-IDF weighting and Information Gain for feature selection and SVM for classification, reporting an f1-measure of 76% for the identification of the domains related to a legal text and 97.5% for the correct classification of a text into a specific domain.

The studies by Farzindar and Lapalme (2004) and by Galgani et al. (2012) apply computational methods for the automatic summarization of legal texts. Such applications are developed to help law professionals in speeding up their work by providing shorter summaries of very long documents which are abundant in legal processes.

Studies applying text classification to legal documents include Hachey and Grover (2006), which proposed a system of classifying sentences for automatic court rulings summarization, and Gonçalves and Quaresma (2005), which used BOW, POS tags, and TF-IDF to classify legal text in 3,000 categories, based on a taxonomy of legal concepts. Authors of this study reported performance of 64% and 79% f1 score.

A few papers have been published on court ruling prediction. This includes the work by Katz et al. (2014), using extremely randomized trees, reporting 70% accuracy in predicting the US Supreme Court's behavior and, more recently, Aletras et al. (2016) proposed a computational method to predict decisions of the ECHR and reported 78% accuracy as their highest score.

To the best of our knowledge, so far most work on predicting court rulings has been carried out on English data. No work has yet been carried out on French, such as the Supreme Court decisions we analyze in this paper. Moreover, to the best of our knowledge, previous work on court rule prediction did not take a temporal dimension into account and our work fills this gap.

Finally, another innovative aspect of our work is the masking step described in 3.2. French High Court rulings contain (near) explicit mentions of our targeted predictions in the running text of the ruling (e.g. law area, court ruling, and time issued). In order to simulate a realistic application scenario where a text classification-based system is supposed to make a prediction on "draft" case description data that do not mention the predicted variables, we present a method of automatically masking such data based on feature ranking on the full data. All our experiments reported in this paper are carried out with masked data sets.

3 Data

We use a diachronic collection of rulings from the French supreme court (*Court de Cassation*).[2] The complete collection[3] contains 131,830 documents, each consisting of a unique ruling and metadata formatted in XML. Common metadata available in most documents includes: law area, time stamp, case ruling (e.g. *cassation, rejet, non-lieu*, etc.), case description, and cited laws. In our supervised learning approach we use the metadata provided as 'natural' labels to be predicted by the machine learning system. In order to simulate realistic test scenarios, we identify and mask all mentions from the training and test data that refer to our target prediction classes. In a pre-processing step we remove all surface forms of the words within the labels from the text data used to derive the predictive features.

All duplicate and incomplete entries in the dataset were excluded resulting in a corpus comprising 126,865 unique court rulings, each containing a case description and four different types of labels: a law area, the date of ruling, the case ruling itself, and a list of articles and laws cited within the description.

3.1 Tasks and Labels

In this section we present the process of defining labels in the dataset for the three tasks presented in this paper. The tasks and the respective section of the paper containing the results are summarized as follows:

1. Predicting the law area of a case (Section 5.1).

2. Predicting the court ruling based on the respective case description (Section 5.2).

3. Estimating when a case description and a ruling were issued (Section 5.3).

To reduce the feature and label space, we first removed accents and punctuation and lowercased all words in the description and ruling. Further pre-processing was needed to reduce the label space for each task. For task 1, we kept in the corpus all entries corresponding to the labels that had over 200 examples. This left us with 8 law area classes. Table 1 shows their distribution.

[2]https://www.courdecassation.fr/about_
the_court_9256.html
[3]https://www.legifrance.gouv.fr

Law Area	# of cases
CHAMBRE_SOCIALE	33,139
CHAMBRE_CIVILE_1	20,838
CHAMBRE_CIVILE_2	19,772
CHAMBRE_CRIMINELLE	18,476
CHAMBRE_COMMERCIALE	18,339
CHAMBRE_CIVILE_3	15,095
ASSEMBLEE_PLENIERE	544
CHAMBRE_MIXTE	222

Table 1: Distribution of Law Area labels over the Case Descriptions

In establishing the ruling label set for predicting the case ruling (task 2), we were faced with a bigger challenge since, after the initial preprocessing, we were left with a list of 475 unique labels (from the initial 635). Looking at this list, we noticed that there were some entries which contained the same keyword repeated several times without having an overt interpretation for the repetition (e.g. *cassation partielle rejet rejet cassation* appeared 145 times in the dataset) as opposed to other multi-word labels which could be easily interpreted (e.g *cassation partielle sans renvoi* which appeared 1,015 times).

An initial step, for better visualization of the ruling label space, was to do hierarchical clustering on the BOW occurrence vector representation for each label. We achieved this using Python's SciPy hierarchical functions with Ward distance. (Figure 1). The results show good evidence for a high level clustering of labels into 6-8 groups. We then investigate what might be the basis of this clustering and determined that keeping only the labels which had at least 200 examples was a good way to obtain this grouping.

On court ruling prediction, we carried out two sets of experiments. In the first one we considered only the first word within each label and only those labels which had over 200 entries in the corpus (first word setup). This lead to an initial set of 6 unique labels: *cassation, annulation, irrecevabilite, rejet, non-lieu,* and *qpc (question prioritaire de constitutionnalit)*. The motivation behind using the first word, rather than using a more complex approach for the identification of the "correct" label, was based on the fact that in French the adjective follows the noun and that the labels consisted only of nouns, adjectives, and stop words.

In the second set of experiments, we consid-

ered all labels which had over 200 dataset entries and this time we did not reduce them to their first word. Table 2 shows the distribution of the ruling labels with over 200 examples each. Italics were used here to emphasize those labels which do not have an overt semantic interpretation. An important observation here is that, in the full, multi-word label extraction setup, *non-lieu* and *qpc*, which are known to be valid decisions of the French Supreme Court, are not selected as final labels, unlike in the first-word setup. This happens because they appear at the beginning of several rare labels (e.g. non-lieu a statuer, non-lieu a recevoir, qpc seule irrecevabilite, etc.). Therefore, there are not enough instances in the dataset with these labels for these labels to be selected. A similar phenomenon occurs with the rest of the labels when comparing the first-word to the multi-word setup.

First-word ruling	# of cases
rejet	68,516
cassation	53,813
irrecevabilite	2,737
qpc	409
annulation	377
non-lieu	246

Full ruling	# of cases
cassation	37,659
cassation sans renvoi	2,078
cassation partielle	9,543
cassation partielle sans renvoi	1,015
cassation partielle cassation	1,162
cassation partielle rejet cassation	906
rejet	67,981
irrecevabilite	2,376

Table 2: Distribution of Case Ruling labels over the Case Descriptions

Finally, for the temporal text classification (task 3), we initially considered the decade of the ruling and the case description. The distribution is shown on Table 3, with the 1970 being the most prolific in cases.

As discussed in Zampieri et al. (2016) the definition of time spans for supervised temporal text classification is often arbitrary. Given that most cases were dated after 1960 and previous decades had only a few cases each, we divided the dataset into 7 classes by grouping all cases before 1960 under one label. Secondly, we considered fine-grained intervals by dividing the dataset into 14

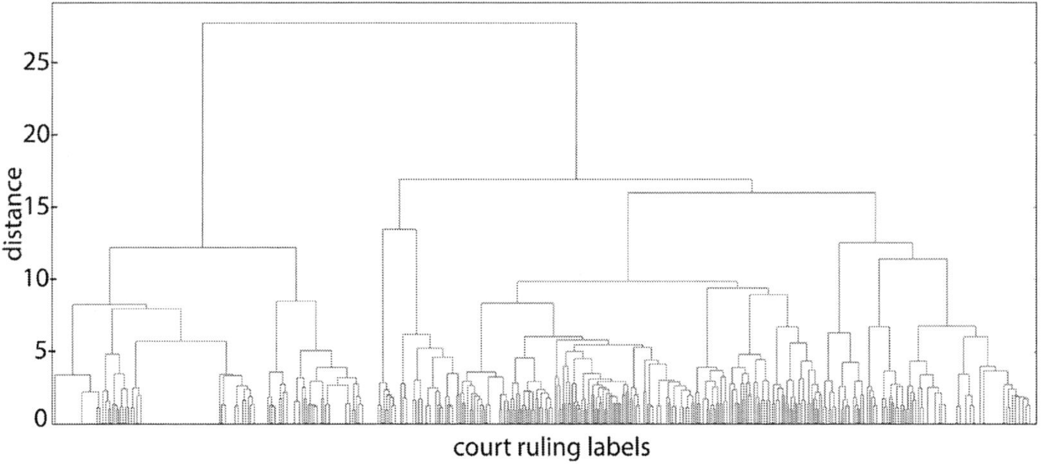

Figure 1: Dendrogram showing hierarchical clustering of ruling labels

classes merging classes before 1920 as follows: 1830-1840, 1850-1860, 1870-1880, 1890-1910.

Period	# of CR	Period	# of CR
1880s	1	1870s	8
1810s	2	1880s	10
1820s	2	1890s	8
1830s	1	1910s	2
1840s	4	1920s	17
1850s	9	1930s	29
1860s	9	1940s	15
1950s	84	1960s	4,797
1970s	23,964	1980s	18,233
1990s	16,693	2000s	12,577
2010s	4,541		

Table 3: Distribution of Ruling Date labels over the Case Descriptions

3.2 Masking and Feature Selection

To emulate a real-world scenario in which a system would operate on a "draft" case description which does not indicate the desired target features to be predicted, we had to eliminate the occurrence of each word of the labels to predict from the text of the corresponding case description.

For task 1, law area prediction, we eliminated all words contained in the respective label. For task 2, predicting the ruling, we initially eliminated from the case description all occurrences of the ruling word itself. We run ANOVA testing on the feature set used for classification (bag of words) and looked at the top 20 features to make sure that none of them could be construed as being directly linked to the label we were attempting to predict, so that a complete masking of the ruling was done within the case description text. In doing so, we realized the label was present both in its nominal form (e.g. *cassation, irrecevabilite*) and in its verbal forms (e.g. *casse, casser*). We eliminated these forms too.

We finally investigated whether this technique of picking the top k classification features was good for identifying facts in the case description, aspects by which one would expect a lawyer to predict the judge's ruling. We did this by looking at the highest-ranking 20 word bigrams and trigrams from the feature set. What we found instead were nouns with their articles (e.g. *la cause, le pourvoi*), prepositions with verbs and nouns (e.g. *pour etre, sur interpretation*), for bi-grams, and infinitival constructions (e.g. *et pour etre, occasion de faire*), for trigrams.

Finally, for task 3, estimating the data of the case, we eliminate all digits from the case description. This has the disadvantage of removing digits that may refer to cited laws thus making the task even more challenging.

4 Computational Approach

We approach the tasks using a text classification system based on the scikit-learn implementation (Pedregosa et al., 2011) of the LIBLINEAR SVM classifier (Fan et al., 2008). As features, we investigate word unigrams (bag of words) and bigrams (bag of bigrams) frequencies to capture the appropriate differences between case descriptions. We extract these features using scikit-learn's CountVectorizer.

Since these features rendered lower performance in temporal classification than in the first two tasks, we also look at other features as proposed in Niculae et al. (2014) to improve the performance. Specifically, we couple BOW with the type-token ratio of each case description computed in the following way:

$$word\_type\_token = \frac{\#unique\_words}{\#total\_words}$$

As the dataset is imbalanced, we employ stratified 10-fold cross-validation for all experiments, since this validation method maintains the initial distribution over each fold. We compare our scores against a random baseline classifier implemented in scikit-learn as the DummyClassifier which takes into consideration the dataset's initial distribution. We report average precision, recall, and f1 scores over all labels. The C hyperparameter for the linear SVM was set to 0.1 in all experiments employing SVMs.

5 Results

In this section we report the results obtained for the three tasks all under the masking regimes described in Section 3.2: (1) predicting the law area of a case, (2) predicting the ruling of a case based on a case description, and (3) estimating the date of a case.

5.1 Law Area

In the first experiment, we apply the SVM classifier to predict the law area of a case. Table 4 shows the results of this classifier applied to 8 classes containing at least 200 instances each presented in Table 2.

Model	P	R	F1	Acc.
SVM	90.9%	90.2%	90.3%	90.2%
baseline	17.7%	17.7%	17.7%	17.%

Table 4: Classification results for the law area prediction task using Linear SVM on 8 classes

The results show that on average our system is able to predict the law area of a case and court ruling with high precision, recall, and f1 score, well above those of the random baseline.

5.2 Court Ruling

In this section we present the results obtained in the second task, ruling prediction based on a case description. The results are presented in Table 5. We report the scores of the experiments when run on the first-word (6 classes) as well as multi-word setups (8 classes) for label extraction discussed in Section 3.1.

We observe an apparent 6 percentage points decrease in average scores when the classifier is trained on the dataset with more classes. This is in tune with the characteristic of classifiers such as SVM which suffer from imbalanced data and is to a certain extent expected since the class imbalance is significant. However, it is important to note that the drop is only apparent, since the increase in number of classes leads to a decrease in the random baseline performance and thus the difference between the baseline scores and our method actually grows by 4 percentage points from the first-word setup.

Model	P	R	F1	Acc.
6 cls SVM	97.1%	96.9%	97.0%	96.9%
6 cls baseline	47.7%	47.7%	47.7%	47.7%
8 cls SVM	93.2%	92.8%	92.7%	92.8%
8 cls baseline	40.6%	40.6%	40.6%	40.6%

Table 5: Classification results for the ruling prediction task using Linear SVM

In terms of previous work, unfortunately a systematic and thorough comparison with Katz et al. (2014) and Wongchaisuwat et al. (2016) is not possible since we are not using the same corpus nor working on the same language as these two papers. Even so, our method appears to surpass both, in terms of f1 score, in predicting the ruling of a court, based on previous examples. One main difference might be the judicial system which is known to be more predictable (offering the judges less interpretation freedom) in the case of the French Supreme Court.

5.3 Temporal Text Classification

For the third task, estimating the date of case and ruling, we use the same approach as previous experiments, a linear SVM classifier trained on bag of unigrams and bag of bigrams as features. Results in two settings, one containing 7 classes and the other containing 14 classes, are reported in Table 6

Subtask	Model	Precision	Recall	F1	Accuracy
7-class	SVM 1-gram	69.9%	68.3%	68.2%	68.3%
7-class	SVM 2-gram	**75.9%**	**74.3%**	**73.2%**	**74.3%**
7-class	baseline	19.2%	19.2%	19.2%	19.2%
14-class	SVM 1-gram	69.1%	68.6%	68.5%	68.6%
14-class	SVM 2-gram	**75.6%**	**74.2%**	**73.9%**	**74.2%**
14-class	baseline	19.1%	19.1%	19.1%	19.1%

Table 6: Classification results for temporal prediction using Linear SVM

The general tendency of traditional supervised classification algorithms is to increase their performance as the number of classes or imbalance between classes decreases. Our experiments show that we manage to preserve the difference between the baseline performance and that of our system on different tasks (ruling prediction and temporal classification), with varying number of classes and initial distributions, which suggests that these techniques are robust for our purpose. However, from a user perspective, where error rate needs to be low, we expect this observation to not be useful and we therefore also run the SVM experiments with type-token ratios as features. On their own, they were able to reach a little above the random baseline (43% f1 score vs. 19% for the random). Interestingly, type-token ratio did not increase the performance of the classifier when combined with BOW.

6   Conclusions and Future Work

In this paper we investigated the application of text classification methods to legal texts from the French Supreme Court. To the best of our knowledge, this is the first work to: (1) apply text classification to predict the rulings on a French dataset, (2) carry out temporal text classification experiments on legal texts. The paper also reports high performance in the task of predicting court rulings.

We showed that a linear SVM classifier trained on BOW can obtain high f1 scores in predicting the law area and the ruling of a case, given the case description. Estimating the date of cases turned out to be more difficult to learn using bag of words and lexical richness features (type-token ratio), but this may be due to the highly imbalanced dataset (i.e. too few examples from the minority classes) or to the possible fact that the language used by judges of the French Supreme Court over the years has not changed much. This final observation is worth further investigation.

We also looked at ways of masking the case description to convey as little information as possible regarding the ruling itself making the task more challenging. This method showed that the word bigrams and trigrams deemed to be the most salient in predicting the ruling are not actually tied to any factual information particular to one case, but more related to formulaic expressions typical for a particular ruling. In future work, we would like to extend this investigation to the sentence level and see if the sentences that are considered most effective in predicting the ruling are of factual nature.

Our work is proof of concept that text classification techniques can be used to provide valuable assistive technology for law professionals in obtaining guidance and orientation from large corpora of previous court rulings. In the future we would like to investigate more sophisticated methods of masking features in the original text data that explicitly list and "give away" the desired target prediction to simulate realistic application scenarios, where text classification predicts the target features from "draft" case descriptions that do not yet contain the target predictions.

Finally, we would like to improve the performance of our system by exploring the combination of other features and the use of ensembles and meta-classifiers which proved to achieve high performance in other text classification tasks (Malmasi et al., 2016).

Acknowledgements

This work was carried out while the first and the second author, Octavia-Maria Şulea and Marcos Zampieri, were at the German Research Center for Artificial Intelligence (DFKI).

References

Nikolaos Aletras, Dimitrios Tsarapatsanis, Daniel Preoţiuc-Pietro, and Vasileios Lampos. 2016. Predicting Judicial Decisions of the European Court of Human Rights: A Natural Language Processing Perspective. *PeerJ Computer Science* 2:e93.

Alexandra Balahur, Rada Mihalcea, and Andrés Montoyo. 2014. Computational Approaches to Subjectivity and Sentiment Analysis: Present and Envisaged Methods and Applications. *Computer Speech & Language* 28(1):1–6.

Alberto Barrón-Cedeño, Marta Vila, M Antònia Martí, and Paolo Rosso. 2013. Plagiarism Meets Paraphrasing: Insights for the Next Generation in Automatic Plagiarism Detection. *Computational Linguistics* 39(4):917–947.

Guido Boella, Luigi Di Caro, , and Llio Humphreys. 2011. Using Classification to Support Legal Knowledge Engineers in the Eunomos Legal Document Management System. In *Proceedings of JURISIN*.

Alina Maria Ciobanu, Marcos Zampieri, Shervin Malmasi, and Liviu P Dinu. 2017. Including Dialects and Language Varieties in Author Profiling. In *Proceedings of CLEF*.

Olivier De Vel, Alison Anderson, Malcolm Corney, and George Mohay. 2001. Mining E-mail Content for Author Identification Forensics. *ACM Sigmod Record* 30(4):55–64.

Liviu P Dinu, Vlad Niculae, and Octavia-Maria Şulea. 2012. Pastiche Detection Based on Stopword Rankings: Exposing Impersonators of a Romanian Writer. In *Proceedings of the Workshop on Computational Approaches to Deception Detection*.

Rong-En Fan, Kai-Wei Chang, Cho-Jui Hsieh, Xiang-Rui Wang, and Chih-Jen Lin. 2008. LIBLINEAR: A Library for Large Linear Classification. *Journal of Machine Learning Research* 9:1871–1874.

Atefeh Farzindar and Guy Lapalme. 2004. Legal Text Summarization by Exploration of the Thematic Structures and Argumentative Roles. *Proceedings of the Text Summarization Branches Out Workshop* .

Filippo Galgani, Paul Compton, and Achim Hoffmann. 2012. Combining Different Summarization Techniques for Legal Text. In *Proceedings of the Hybrid Workshop*.

Jean-Gabriel Ganascia, Pierre Glaudes, and Andrea Del Lungo. 2014. Automatic detection of reuses and citations in literary texts. *Digital Scholarship in the Humanities* 29(3).

Binyam Gebrekidan Gebre, Marcos Zampieri, Peter Wittenburg, and Tom Heskes. 2013. Improving Native Language Identification with TF-IDF Weighting. In *Proceedings of the BEA Workshop*.

Teresa Gonçalves and Paulo Quaresma. 2005. Evaluating Preprocessing Techniques in a Text Classification Problem. In *Proceedings of the Conference of the Brazilian Computer Society*.

Ben Hachey and Claire Grover. 2006. Extractive Summarisation of Legal Texts. *Artificial Intelligence and Law* 14(4):305–345.

Daniel Martin Katz, Michael J. Bommarito II, and Josh Blackman. 2014. Predicting the Behavior of the Supreme Court of the United States: A General Approach. *CoRR* abs/1407.6333.

Shervin Malmasi, Marcos Zampieri, and Mark Dras. 2016. Predicting Post Severity in Mental Health Forums. In *Proceedings of the CLPsych Workshop*.

Dong-Phuong Nguyen, Rilana Gravel, RB Trieschnigg, and Theo Meder. 2013. "How old do you think I am?" A Study of Language and Age in Twitter. In *Proceedings of ICWSM*.

Vlad Niculae, Marcos Zampieri, Liviu P Dinu, and Alina Maria Ciobanu. 2014. Temporal Text Ranking and Automatic Dating of Texts. *Proceedings of EACL* .

Raquel Mochales Palau and Marie-Francine Moens. 2009. Argumentation Mining: The Detection, Classification and Structure of Arguments in Text. In *Proceedings of the ICAIL*.

F. Pedregosa, G. Varoquaux, A. Gramfort, V. Michel, B. Thirion, O. Grisel, M. Blondel, P. Prettenhofer, R. Weiss, V. Dubourg, J. Vanderplas, A. Passos, D. Cournapeau, M. Brucher, M. Perrot, and E. Duchesnay. 2011. Scikit-learn: Machine learning in Python. *Journal of Machine Learning Research* 12:2825–2830.

Verónica Pérez-Rosas and Rada Mihalcea. 2015. Experiments in Open Domain Deception Detection. In *Proceedings of EMNLP*.

Octavia-Maria Sulea and Daniel Dichiu. 2015. Automatic Profiling of Twitter Users Based on Their Tweets: Notebook for PAN at CLEF 2015. In *Proceedings of CLEF*.

Chris Sumner, Alison Byers, Rachel Boochever, and Gregory J. Park. 2012. Predicting Dark Triad Personality Traits from Twitter Usage and a Linguistic Analysis of Tweets. In *Proceedings of ICMLA*.

Papis Wongchaisuwat, Diego Klabjan, and John O McGinnis. 2016. Predicting Litigation Likelihood and Time to Litigation for Patents. *arXiv preprint arXiv:1603.07394* .

Marcos Zampieri, Shervin Malmasi, and Mark Dras. 2016. Modeling Language Change in Historical Corpora: The Case of Portuguese. In *Proceedings of LREC*.

Unsupervised Learning of Morphology with Graph Sampling

Maciej Sumalvico
University of Leipzig
NLP Group, Department of Computer Science
Augustusplatz 10, 04109 Leipzig
sumalvico@informatik.uni-leipzig.de

Abstract

We introduce a language-independent, graph-based probabilistic model of morphology, which uses transformation rules operating on whole words instead of the traditional morphological segmentation. The morphological analysis of a set of words is expressed through a graph having words as vertices and structural relationships between words as edges. We define a probability distribution over such graphs and develop a sampler based on the Metropolis-Hastings algorithm. The sampling is applied in order to determine the strength of morphological relationships between words, filter out accidental similarities and reduce the set of rules necessary to explain the data. The model is evaluated on the task of finding pairs of morphologically similar words, as well as generating new words. The results are compared to a state-of-the-art segmentation-based approach.

1 Introduction

The aim of unsupervised learning of morphology is to explain structural similarities between words of a language and discover mechanisms allowing one to predict or analyze unseen words using only a plain wordlist or an unannotated corpus as input. A vast majority of approaches to this problem concentrates on *morphological segmentation*, i.e. segmentation of words into minimal structural units, called *morphs* (Hammarström and Borin, 2011), usually employing statistical or machine learning methods.

While the segmentation approach has proven successful in some applications (especially compound splitting), it is known to suffer from seri-

ous limitations, like e.g. its intrinsic difficulty of handling non-concatenative morphology. Furthermore, phenomena like morphophonological rules (reflected by the orthography), allomorphs, or interactions between morphemes, are especially difficult to discover in an unsupervised setting, which is why most approaches limit themselves to rudimentary marking of postulated morpheme boundaries in the word's surface form. Because of the lack of morphotactical information, there is also no straightforward way to utilize such methods for generating new words: considering arbitrary morpheme sequences overgenerates massively and additional filtering approaches are needed, like the ones presented by (Rasooli et al., 2014). Finally, the notion of morpheme itself, although widely accepted in linguistics, has also been subject to criticism (e.g. Aronoff, 1976, 2007; Anderson, 1992).

An alternative linguistic theory, called Whole Word Morphology (Ford et al., 1997; Singh et al., 2003) (henceforth WWM), seems in our opinion particularly useful from the point of view of unsupervised learning. In WWM, the structural regularities between words are expressed as patterns operating simultaneously on multiple levels of lexical representation (phonological, syntactic, semantic). For example, the structural relationship between *cat* and *cats* would be captured by the following rule:[1]

$$
\begin{bmatrix} \text{PHON:} & \text{/X/} \\ \text{SYNT:} & \text{N, SG} \\ \text{SEM:} & \spadesuit \end{bmatrix} \leftrightarrow \begin{bmatrix} \text{PHON:} & \text{/Xs/} \\ \text{SYNT:} & \text{N, PL} \\ \text{SEM:} & \text{many } \spadesuit \end{bmatrix} \quad (1)
$$

The bidirectional arrow postulates, that if there is a word matching the pattern on one side of the rule, a counterpart matching the other side should also be a valid word. There is no notion of 'internal word structure' and neither of the words is

---

[1] For the sake of simplicity, we discard the allophony in the phonological representation and present the semantic layer in an extremely schematic way.

Proceedings of Recent Advances in Natural Language Processing, pages 723–732,
Varna, Bulgaria, Sep 4–6 2017.

said to be morphologically 'more complex' than the other. The variable X stands for an arbitrary sequence of phonemes, which is retained on both sides of the rule. While the particular representations are further decomposable, for instance the phonological one in syllables and phonemes, the smallest unit of the language that combines all three layers is the word, and not the morpheme.

In this way, the morphological structure of a lexicon can be expressed as a graph, in which words constitute vertices and pairs of words following a regular structural pattern are connected with an edge, labeled with the corresponding rule. For the task of unsupervised learning, we see it as an advantage to learn a relation operating directly on observable objects (i.e. words), rather than some vaguely defined and theory-dependent underlying representation, like morpheme segmentation.

In the remainder of this paper, we briefly review previous unsupervised approaches to morphology (Sec. 2), present a generative probabilistic model for graphs of word derivations (Sec. 3), along with inference algorithms suited for unsupervised learning (Sec. 4). Our method is evaluated in Sec. 5.

2 Related Work

The approaches focusing on segmentation of words into smaller meaningful units have a long history, ranging from heuristic methods (Harris, 1955; Goldsmith, 2006) to the more recent approaches employing complete probabilistic models. A particularly successful example of the latter is Morfessor (Creutz and Lagus, 2005; Virpioja et al., 2013). Further probabilistic models include probabilistic hierarchical clustering (Can, 2011) and log-linear models (Poon et al., 2009). The yearly competition MorphoChallenge (Kurimo et al., 2010), which took place from 2005 until 2010, provides a good overview on the state of the art in morphological segmentation.

Another line of research concentrates on finding pairs of morphologically related words and using them to discover more general patterns. Various similarity measures are often used to identify such pairs, including orthographic and context similarity, or a combination of both (Yarowsky and Wicentowski, 2000; Baroni et al., 2002; Kirschenbaum, 2013). The first approach explicitly mentioning Whole Word Morphology as lin-

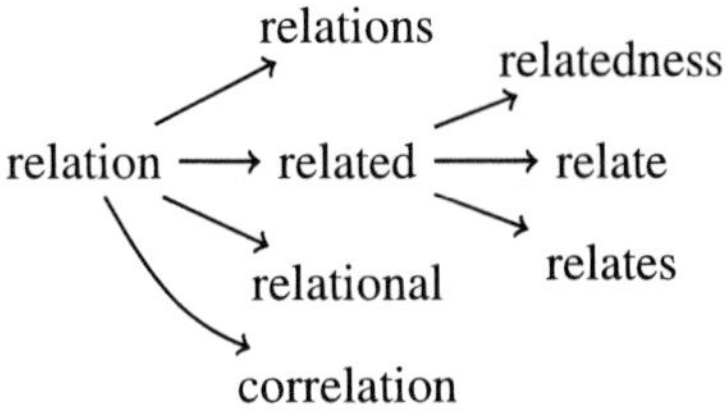

Figure 1: An example tree of word derivations. Edge labels are omitted for better readability.

guistic foundation has been presented by (Neuvel and Fulop, 2002), followed by a graph clustering method (Janicki, 2013) and a graph-based probabilistic model (Janicki, 2015). Recently, also word embeddings have been used to induce word-based transformation rules (Soricut and Och, 2015; Narasimhan et al., 2015). The latter method also produces graph-based representations of morphology, but is eventually evaluated on the segmentation task.

While, to our best knowledge, sampling from a probability distribution over graph structures has not yet been applied in the task of learning morphology, it has been successfully applied in other NLP tasks, notably unsupervised dependency parsing (Mareček, 2012; Teichmann, 2014) and machine translation (Peng and Gildea, 2014).

3 The Probabilistic Model

The model described here is a slight modification of the one introduced by (Janicki, 2015). Our goal is a probability distribution $Pr(V, E|R)$ over graphs (consisting of a set of vertices V and a set of labeled edges E), given a set of transformation rules R. A single graph represents a hypothesis about the origin of words: the root nodes constitute the idiosyncratic part of the lexicon, i.e. they correspond to words, that are not derived from any other and must be memorized. Once some words are introduced, further ones can be derived using the transformation rules. Such derivations correspond to edges leading to new nodes. We restrict the allowed structure of the graphs to directed forests: they must not contain cycles and every node has at most one ingoing edge, i.e. every word has a unique analysis. Accordingly, we consider directed transformation rules.

An example of such graph is shown in Fig. 1. In this case, *relation* is the base for the whole word family: it is used to derive, among others, *related*, which in turn serves as a base for further words. Note that the tree shown in Fig. 1 does not constitute a linguistically correct analysis, nor does it have to. A unique 'correct' tree usually does not exist, e.g. the decision of whether the correct analysis of *correlation* should be *correlation* ← *correlate* ← *relate* or *correlation* ← *relation* ← *relate*, or yet another, is from our point of view completely arbitrary. This is the reason why we are not going to focus on single graphs, but rather on large samples, in which such multiple possibilities are accounted for.

Moving on to the probabilistic formulation of the model outlined above, let ρ be a probability distribution over strings, which should be nonzero at least for all well-formed words of the language. The root nodes of the graph are drawn from ρ. Then, we iteratively try to apply every rule on every word, resulting in a (possibly empty) set of candidate derivations. Each derivation is an independent[2] Bernoulli trial with probability θ_r: if it succeeds, the new word is introduced into the graph, along with the edge deriving it. We thus arrive at the following distribution:[3]

$$Pr(V, E|R, \Theta_R) \propto \prod_{v \in V_0} \rho(v)$$

$$\times \prod_{v \in V} \prod_{r \in R} \prod_{v' \in r(v)} \begin{cases} \theta_r & \text{if } \langle v, v', r \rangle \in E, \\ 1 - \theta_r & \text{if } \langle v, v', r \rangle \notin E \end{cases}$$

$$(2)$$

V_0 denotes the set of root nodes in the graph $\langle V, E \rangle$. Θ_R is the parameter vector, which contains θ_r values for each rule r. $r(v)$ is the set of words derived from v by applying r. Note that $r(v)$ might be empty if v does not match the left-hand side of r. As to the distribution ρ, we learn it from the observed vocabulary V using the ALERGIA algorithm (de la Higuera and Thollard, 2000;

de la Higuera, 2010), which learns distributions over strings from samples. Once learnt, it is considered fixed and not changed by our inference procedure.

Furthermore, let n_r denote the number of edges in the graph $\langle V, E \rangle$ labeled with r and m_r denote the total number of words, that can be derived with r from words from V. More formally:

$$n_r := |\{\langle v, v', r' \rangle \in E : r' = r\}| \quad (3)$$

$$m_r := \sum_{v \in V} |r(v)| \quad (4)$$

Then (2) can be rewritten as:

$$Pr(V, E|R, \Theta_R) \propto \prod_{v \in V_0} \rho(v) \prod_{r \in R} \theta_r^{n_r} (1 - \theta_r)^{m_r - n_r}$$

$$(5)$$

From (5), we can easily see, that the number of edges derived by a rule follows a Binomial distribution. Following the Bayesian approach, we use Beta distribution as conjugate prior for θ_r:

$$\theta_r \sim Be(\alpha, \beta) \quad (6)$$

In practice, α and β are always set to 1.1 (an almost uniform prior, but with exclusion of extreme values). The parameters can be integrated out:

$$Pr(V, E|R) = \int_{(0,1)^{|R|}} Pr(V, E|R, \Theta_R)$$

$$\times Pr(\Theta_R|R) d\Theta_R$$

$$\propto \prod_{v \in V_0} \rho(v) \prod_{r \in R} \frac{B(n_r + \alpha, m_r - n_r + \beta)}{B(\alpha, \beta)}$$

$$(7)$$

Finally, we introduce a probability distribution for the rule set. For this purpose, we represent the rules as sequences of edit operations. For example, the rule $/X\text{ation}/ \rightarrow /X\text{ate}/$ deriving *relate* from *relation* is represented as the following sequence:

$$\star \quad \text{a:a} \quad \text{t:t} \quad \text{i:e} \quad \text{o:0} \quad \text{n:0} \quad \# \quad (8)$$

The item denoted by $\star$ means leaving an arbitrary sequence of characters unchanged and # is a special item terminating the sequence. The probability $\pi(r)$ of a rule is simply a product of the probabilities of individual sequence items (i.e. edit operations), which are treated as symbols of an alphabet. The item probabilities are learnt from the initial set of candidate rules and considered fixed, just like the ρ distribution for root words. The

---

[2]The well-formedness conditions of the graphs do not introduce any dependency between the edges. Note that each rule application derives a new word, so each edge leads to a new node. If multiple rules derived the same word, it should correspond to multiple graph nodes with the same label. However, our set of vertices V (which is considered given and fixed) contains one node per word, so such graphs are ruled out.

[3]The proportionality sign is due to the first term: the probability of a random set of independently chosen elements is proportional, but not equal, to the product of the probabilities of the elements. However, with the right choice of set size distribution (Poisson with mean 1), we can obtain a fixed and simple normalizing constant e^{-1}. The choice of Poisson distribution is motivated only by mathematical convenience. See (Janicki, 2015) for a more detailed explanation.

probability of the rule set is then proportional to the product of probabilities of individual rules:

$$Pr(R) \propto \prod_{r \in R} \pi(r) \qquad (9)$$

The distribution $Pr(R)$ penalizes complex models: it attributes lower probabilities to large rule sets and specific, sophisticated rules.

4 Inference

While (Janicki, 2015) used an optimization approach to find the single best graph, our goal is to base the inference on large samples from the distribution over graphs using a Markov Chain Monte Carlo sampler. In particular, we are going to be interested in expected values of certain functions of the graph with respect to the edge structure, which is a latent variable. Thus, for a given function h (e.g. measuring the frequency of a rule or the likelihood of the graph), we want to be able to approximate the expectations of the following form:

$$\mathbb{E}_{E|V,R} h(V, E) = \sum_E h(V, E) Pr(E|V, R) \quad (10)$$

4.1 Finding Candidate Rules

We begin by extracting all pairs of words that might be morphologically related from the given vocabulary. We follow the approach of (Janicki, 2015): we apply a modified FastSS algorithm (Bocek et al., 2007) to find all pairs of words, that differ with at most 5 characters at the beginning and at the end and with at most 3 characters within a single slot inside the word. Those numbers are configurable parameters, but we have found the above values to be sufficient to capture most morphological rules in many languages.

Each pair of words is used to extract a number of transformation rules of the form (cf. (1)):

$$/a_1 X_1 a_2 X_2 a_3/ \rightarrow /b_1 X_1 b_2 X_2 b_3/ \qquad (11)$$

where X_1, X_2 are variable elements, a_1, a_3, b_1, b_3 are constants of at most 5 characters, and a_2, b_2 are constants of at most 3 characters.[4] There are usually many rules that can be derived from a single pair of words, depending on whether we assign common substrings of both words to the variable elements X_1, X_2, resulting in more general rules, or to the constants, resulting in more specific rules.

For example, three of many rules that can be extracted from the pair $\langle relate, correlate \rangle$ are given below:

$$
\begin{aligned}
/X/ &\rightarrow /\mathrm{cor}X/ \\
/\mathrm{r}X/ &\rightarrow /\mathrm{corr}X/ \\
/\mathrm{r}X\mathrm{ate}/ &\rightarrow /\mathrm{corr}X\mathrm{ate}/ \qquad (12)
\end{aligned}
$$

In order to reduce the number of candidate rules and edges to tractable sizes, we apply the following filtering criteria:

max. number of rules: only $N_{\max}$ most frequent rules are kept;

max. number of edges per word pair: only k most general rules are extracted from each word pair;

min. rule frequency: only rules occurring in at least $n_{\min}$ word pairs are kept.

In all our experiments, we used fixed values of $N_{\max} = 10000$, $k = 5$, $n_{\min} = 3$, which led to good results for training data of various sizes. Those values can thus be safely used as default setting, without the need of parameter tuning.

4.2 The Sampler

Having a set of rules R and a vocabulary V, we are ready to draw samples of edge sets from the distribution $Pr(E|V, R)$, which is proportional to $Pr(V, E|R)$ up to a normalizing constant. In the following, we will define a sampler based on the Metropolis-Hastings algorithm, which belongs to a larger family of Markov Chain Monte Carlo methods.

The key idea of Markov Chain Monte Carlo methods is, given a probability distribution f, to construct a Markov chain, for which f is the limiting distribution (Robert and Casella, 2005). The Metropolis-Hastings algorithm (Metropolis et al., 1953; Hastings, 1970) provides a relatively simple recipe for such chain. It involves an instrumental distribution $q(y|x)$ used to propose the next item y of the sample given the current item x. Then, the next item of the sample is taken to be either y or x, depending on whether the proposal is accepted or rejected. The probability of acceptance is:

$$\alpha(x, y) = \min \left\{ \frac{f(y)}{f(x)} \frac{q(x|y)}{q(y|x)}, 1 \right\} \qquad (13)$$

Note that the distributions f and q only have to be known up to a multiplicative constant, since the

---

[4] In case a_2 and b_2 are both empty, X_1 and X_2 are merged into a single variable X.

computation only involves quotients of their values. Also, q does not have to bear any relationship to f. It is sufficient that every point of the sample space, for which f is nonzero, can be reached from any other in a finite number of steps using q. Then (13) implies that the resulting Markov chain has f as its limiting distribution. Although the sample obtained from such chain is not independent, it can be used for approximating expectations like (10).

The preprocessing step described in the previous section provides us with a set of all candidate edges $\mathcal{E}$, which can be created by the rules from R. The idea for a proposal distribution $q(\cdot|E)$, given the current set of edges E, is the following: we choose an edge e uniformly from $\mathcal{E}$. If it is already present in E, we delete it, if not, we add it. In this way, we obtain a proposal for the next set of edges E'. Note that in this way we can reach any graph from any other in a finite number of steps by first deleting all the edges of the first graph and then adding all the edges of the second graph one by one.

There is however one problem with this approach: while deleting an edge is always possible, adding one could result in an ill-formed graph (e.g. create a cycle). If we simply discarded such proposals and proposed staying with the current graph instead, such procedure would still yield a valid instrumental distribution and a valid MCMC sampler. While the resulting chain would still be theoretically correct, its so-called *mixing properties* would be very bad, meaning that it would need an extremely large number of iterations to converge to the limiting distribution. For this reason, we are going to introduce additional moves which make adding of an edge possible in most cases.

Let's consider adding a new edge $v_1 \xrightarrow{r} v_2$. The first problematic case is when the new edge would create a cycle, i.e. v_1 is already a descendent of v_2. Let v_3 denote the parent of v_2, v_5 the immediate child of v_2 which leads to v_1 and v_4 the parent of v_1 (see Fig. 2). We have two possibilities to add an edge between v_1 and v_2 by 'cutting out' either v_1 or v_2 from its place in the tree. Both variants involve adding and deleting two edges. We refer to this kind of operation as 'flip'. The variant to be used is chosen randomly each time a 'flip' move is to be applied. Note that a 'flip' move might be impossible if the other edge to be added ($v_3 \rightarrow v_1$ or $v_3 \rightarrow v_5$, respectively) is not available in $\mathcal{E}$.

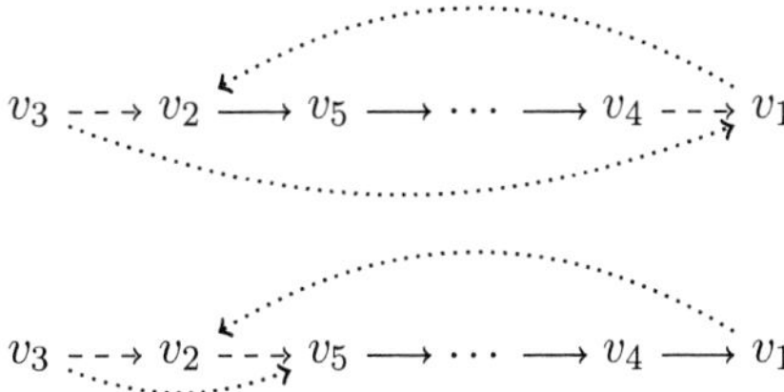

Figure 2: The two variants of the 'flip' operation. The deleted edges are dashed and the newly added edges dotted. The goal of the operation is to make possible adding an edge from v_1 to v_2 without creating a cycle.

In this case, we propose staying with the current graph, which, as already mentioned, does not undermine the validity of the sampler. The absence of other involved edges (e.g. $v_3 \rightarrow v_2$ in case v_2 is a root) or the overlapping of some nodes (e.g. $v_5 = v_1$ and $v_4 = v_2$ if v_1 is a child of v_2 directly) can be simply ignored as the move is still valid.

Another problematic case arises when the newly added edge $v_1 \xrightarrow{r} v_2$ would not create a cycle, but v_2 already has an ingoing edge (possibly even from v_1, but with a different label). In this case, we simply exchange the previous ingoing edge of v_2 for the new one.

It is important to point out, that all moves are reversible and that the resulting proposal distribution is symmetric. The move is uniquely determined by the choice of the edge e to be added or deleted, except for the 'flip' case, where additionally one of the two variants of the move is randomly chosen. In case of adding or removing a single edge without side effects, selecting the same edge again reverses the operation. If the edge to be added is exchanged for another, selecting the previously deleted edge will reverse it. Finally, the first variant of 'flip' on $v_1 \rightarrow v_2$ can be reversed by the second variant on $v_4 \rightarrow v_1$ and the second variant on $v_1 \rightarrow v_2$ can be reversed by the first variant on $v_2 \rightarrow v_5$.

Note, that the complexity of a single sampling iteration is only $O(h)$, with h being the maximum height of a tree, since h operations are needed to determine whether v_1 is a descendant of v_2. In practice, h is usually bounded by a small constant. Also, we do not need to memorize the graphs seen in the sample, we only have to keep track of the current graph and the current values of the expectations we are interested in. The latter can be updated dynamically. A single sampling iteration is thus computationally very cheap, which enables us to draw large samples. In the experiments, we use sample sizes of 50 million graphs.

4.3 Model Selection

The sampler developed in the previous section has multiple applications. One of them is *model selection*, i.e. the task of selecting an optimal set of rules.[5] For the purpose of comparing models, we introduce the following expected log-likelihood function:

$$
\begin{aligned}
\ell(R) = \ & \mathbb{E}_{E|V,R} \ln Pr(V, E|R) + \ln Pr(R) \\
= \ & \mathbb{E}_{E|V,R} \left[\sum_{v \in V_0} \ln \rho(v) \right. \\
& + \sum_{r \in R} \ln B(n_r + \alpha, m_r - n_r + \beta) \\
& \left. - |R| \ln B(\alpha, \beta) \right] + \sum_{r \in R} \ln \pi(r) \quad (14)
\end{aligned}
$$

We use the graph sampler for computing the value of $\ell(R)$ for a single rule set. The model selection task is to maximize ℓ, i.e. to find:

$$
\hat{R} = \arg\max_R \ell(R) \quad (15)
$$

For this optimization task, we use the *simulated annealing* algorithm (Kirkpatrick et al., 1983), which is closely related to MCMC sampling. In this algorithm, we also use an instrumental distribution $q(y|x)$ to propose the next point y given the current point x. Let h denote the function to optimize. Then the acceptance probability of y while being at x is defined as:

$$
\alpha(x, y) = \min \left\{ \frac{q(x|y)}{q(y|x)} e^{\frac{h(y)-h(x)}{t}}, 1 \right\} \quad (16)
$$

The parameter t is called *temperature* and is meant to decrease with each iteration, thus decreasing the algorithm's willingness to move to points with lower h value. As (Besag, 2004) points out, if we consider a distribution $f(x) \propto \exp h(x)$, then simulated annealing corresponds to MCMC sampling from a distribution proportional to $f^{\frac{1}{t}}$. As t goes towards zero, the latter will converge to a uniform distribution over global maxima of h. In this way, the algorithm is able to find a global maximum and escape local maxima.

---

[5] Each set of rules R defines a *model*, parametrized by Θ_R.

We are now going to define the instrumental distribution $q(R'|R)$ used to propose the next rule set. All considered rule sets are going to be subsets of $\mathcal{R}$, which denotes the set of rules obtained after the preprocessing step described in Sec. 4.1. We begin by defining the *score* of a single rule, which is the expected contribution of this rule to the log-likelihood of the graph:

$$
\begin{aligned}
\zeta(r) = \ & \mathbb{E}_{E|V,R} \left[- \sum_{\substack{\langle v,v',r' \rangle \in E \\ r'=r}} \ln \rho(v') \right. \\
& + \ln B(n_r + \alpha, m_r - n_r + \beta) \\
& \left. - \ln B(\alpha, \beta) \right] + \ln \pi(r) \quad (17)
\end{aligned}
$$

The first term corresponds to the log-likelihood, that is gained by deriving words using r, rather than having them as roots. We subsequently apply the logistic function to turn the rule score into a probability:

$$
g(r) = \frac{1}{1 + \exp(-\gamma \cdot \zeta(r))} \quad (18)
$$

where γ is a configurable parameter. $g(r)$ is the probability of r being selected to the next rule set. Note that $g(r)$ is also defined for rules not occurring in the current rule set: the first term and n_r are then simply always zero. Finally, we propose the next rule set R' by randomly determining for each rule from $\mathcal{R}$, whether it is going to be selected or not. Basing the selection probability on $\zeta(r)$ means that the chances of a rule to 'survive' in the next iteration depend on its usefulness in the current iteration. Once a rule is dropped, it can still be re-selected, but the probability of it happening is rather small. Finally, γ is set to be equal to inverse temperature of the annealing algorithm, which means that the importance of rule performance increases over time, allowing less and less changes in later iterations.

In practice, the cost of one iteration of the annealing algorithm is high, since it involves a whole run of the graph sampler. We are thus only going to perform a few annealing iterations (typically 20 or 30) which is obviously not enough to find the global maximum. Thus, we use this algorithm only as a local optimizer: to reduce the set of rules as much as possible within a reasonable runtime. However, it is still a plausible choice because of its flexibility, e.g. being able to move across a parameter space composed of discrete sets (unlike e.g.

	training	testing
English	45,391	15,608
German	76,813	221,190
Dutch	103,190	145,354

Table 1: The size (number of words) of datasets used for the analysis task.

the EM algorithm, which requires a space of real-valued vectors).

4.4 Model Fitting

Once the optimal model is selected, we can determine optimal values for the parameter vector Θ_R. For this purpose, we use the Monte Carlo EM algorithm (Wei and Tanner, 1990), which is a variant of EM using a sampler to approximate the expected values. In the maximization step, we set the θ_r values to their maximum a-posteriori likelihood estimates:

$$\theta_r^{(t+1)} := \frac{\mathbb{E}_{E|V,R,\Theta_R^{(t)}}[n_r] + \alpha - 1}{m_r + \alpha + \beta - 2} \qquad (19)$$

5 Evaluation

We evaluate our approach on the tasks of morphological *analysis* and *generation*.

5.1 Analysis

As we intend to avoid postulating internal word structure, the task of analysis is defined as linking an unknown word to morphologically similar words from a known lexicon. We consider a pair of words to be morphologically similar if one word can be derived from the other using a single morphological operation (e.g. affix insertion, deletion or substitution). Pairs of morphologically similar words can also be extracted from segmentations by computing edit distance on morpheme sequences – words are considerered morphologically similar if such distance is equal to 1 and the difference does not include stems.

Dataset   We use the CELEX lexical database to derive training and evaluation data. CELEX provides data for English, German and Dutch, including morphological segmentation, labeling of inflectional classes and corpus frequency. For training, we use words with nonzero corpus frequency, while the remaining words, i.e. those with zero frequency, constitute the testing dataset. The size of the datasets is shown in Table 1.

	–MS	+MS
English	9,434	3,943
German	8,432	4,888
Dutch	9,026	4,743

Table 2: The model size (number of rules) before and after model selection.

Language	Model	Precision	Recall	F-score
English	Morfessor	74.4 %	41.4 %	53.2 %
	–MS	38.5 %	73.2 %	50.5 %
	+MS	53.8 %	69.3 %	60.6 %
German	Morfessor	75.1 %	38.8 %	51.2 %
	–MS	56.4 %	67.8 %	61.6 %
	+MS	65.1 %	62.8 %	63.9 %
Dutch	Morfessor	73.1 %	39.2 %	51.0 %
	–MS	42.5 %	68.1 %	52.3 %
	+MS	54.1 %	63.1 %	58.3 %

Table 3: Results for the analysis task.

Experiment setup   We report the results for two different setups: with model selection (+MS) and without it (–MS). We also compare our results to Morfessor Categories-MAP (Creutz and Lagus, 2005). In addition to morpheme segmentations, this tool labels each morpheme as prefix, affix or stem, which enables us to convert its output into morphologically similar pairs using the edit distance method.[6] The training dataset also constitutes the known lexicon, i.e. we evaluate pairs of similar words (w_1, w_2) with w_1 coming from the training and w_2 from the testing dataset.

Results   The results are shown in Table 3. The setup with model selection achieves the best performance for all three languages, which demonstrates the usefulness of this step. The difference is especially clear for English, where the setup without model selection performs worse than Morfessor. Our method also manages to capture non-concatenative morphology: pairs like German (*findet*, *fändet*) or Dutch (*televisiekanalen*, *televisiekanaal*), are successfully detected. On the other hand, the method based on Morfessor segmentations suffers from low recall: even small errors in segmentation can result in a failure to discover many similar pairs.

Table 2 shows another benefit of model selection: reducing the number of rules approximately by half, which has a significant impact on the speeed of the analysis.

---

[6]Unfortunately, such conversion is not possible for most other approaches to unsupervised segmentation, which do not provide additional labeling for stems.

Language	Model	1k	5k	10k	50k	100k	200k	500k
English	−MS, −F	72.2 %	52.5 %	48.4 %	37.3 %	26.9 %	20.4 %	11.1 %
	−MS, +F	69.8 %	64.9 %	62.3 %	42.5 %	31.1 %	22.3 %	17.5 %
	+MS, +F	71.9 %	66.4 %	62.7 %	43.4 %	32.7 %	22.9 %	17.0 %
German	−MS, −F	85.6 %	80.0 %	74.3 %	56.0 %	42.3 %	32.2 %	17.5 %
	−MS, +F	86.0 %	82.0 %	83.7 %	68.0 %	51.2 %	35.7 %	21.4 %
	+MS, +F	86.4 %	83.0 %	83.9 %	67.8 %	51.5 %	35.9 %	21.1 %
Dutch	−MS, −F	50.0 %	53.3 %	53.3 %	31.6 %	24.6 %	18.0 %	10.3 %
	−MS, +F	73.9 %	60.1 %	60.5 %	38.7 %	29.4 %	20.6 %	11.2 %
	+MS, +F	73.9 %	62.2 %	62.2 %	38.8 %	29.8 %	21.0 %	11.4 %

Table 4: Results for the generation task. The scores show precision depending on the number of generated words. ('k' means 'thousand').

5.2 Generation

In generation task, we evaluate the capability of the model to derive new, valid words using the learnt morphological rules. As the recall measure for this task is hardly possible to compute (it would involve listing all and only words derivable from the training set), we evaluate the precision against the number of generated words.

Dataset For training, we use the same datasets as in the analysis task (CELEX words with nonzero corpus frequency). The testing wordlists, which are supposed to contain at least all words obtainable from the training words within a single morphological operation, are built by merging the complete CELEX vocabulary with lists of Wiktionary entries for the relevant language.

Experiment setup We conduct the experiment on three different settings, depending on whether the model selection (MS) and the fitting (F) step are carried out or omitted.[7] In case of omitting the fitting step, the rule probabilities (θ_r) are set according to (19), but using maximum rule frequency, i.e. the number of candidate edges in $\mathcal{E}$ labeled with this rule, as n_r. The generated words are ordered by their contribution to the log-likelihood of the data, which is equivalent to sorting according to the probability of the rule used to derived the word.

For this task, we do not include any comparison to a segmentation-based approach. Such approaches usually do not model morphotactics at all, or do it in a very simple way (like Morfessor Categories-MAP). Applying them to generate new words leads to a disastrous overgeneration (e.g. every common morpheme can be repeated many times), which renders a comparison

pointless. Segmentation models are simply not designed for the generation task.

Results The results shown in Table 4 highlight the importance of a proper fitting step, which in most cases improves the results considerably. On the other hand, the impact of the model selection step is rather insignificant. This is understandable: the goal of model selection is to eliminate weak, useless rules, while in the word generation task, the strongest rules are applied first.

6 Conclusion

We have presented a method for unsupervised discovery of pairs of morphologically related words without performing morpheme segmentation. Our method is based on a probabilistic model describing graphs of word derivations. We developed a Markov Chain Monte Carlo sampler for such graphs, which allows us to approximate expectations over the latent edge structure. The evaluation results confirm our intuition, that the discovery of morphologically related words, as well as prediction of unseen words, is easier without the need of morpheme segmentation. While we limited ourselves to unannotated string forms of words, the formalism can be easily extended to include various other word features, like POS-tags or frequency. In the further work, we especially intend to follow the recent trend and include word embeddings as a feature. Furthermore, we are going to examine practical applications of a whole-word morphology model, like e.g. increasing the performance of statistical language models in dealing with unknown words. We believe that morpheme segmentation is neither sufficient nor necessary for learning morphology, especially in the unsupervised setting.

---

[7]The results for the +MS, −F case are omitted, because they are very similar to −MS, −F, and thus do not contribute anything noteworthy to the evaluation.

References

Stephen R. Anderson. 1992. *A-Morphous Morphology*.

Mark Aronoff. 1976. *Word Formation in Generative Grammar*. MIT Press.

Mark Aronoff. 2007. In the Beginning was the Word. *Language* 83(4):803–830.

Marco Baroni, Johannes Matiasek, and Harald Trost. 2002. Unsupervised discovery of morphologically related words based on orthographic and semantic similarity. In *Proceedings of the 6th Workshop of the ACL Special Interest Group on Phonology*. volume 6, pages 48–57.

Julian Besag. 2004. An introduction to Markov chain Monte Carlo methods. In Mark Johnson, Sanjeev P. Khudanpur, Mari Ostendorf, and Roni Rosenfeld, editors, *Mathematical Foundations of Speech and Language Processing*, Springer-Verlag New York, Inc., pages 247–270.

Thomas Bocek, Ela Hunt, and Burkhard Stiller. 2007. Fast Similarity Search in Large Dictionaries. Technical report, University of Zurich.

Burcu Can. 2011. *Statistical Models for Unsupervised Learning of Morphology and POS Tagging*. Ph.D. thesis, University of York.

Mathias Creutz and Krista Lagus. 2005. Inducing the Morphological Lexicon of a Natural Language from Unannotated Text. In *Proceedings of the International and Interdisciplinary Conference on Adaptive Knowledge Representation and Reasoning (AKRR'05)*.

Colin de la Higuera. 2010. *Grammatical Inference: Learning Automata and Grammars*. Cambridge University Press, New York, NY, USA.

Colin de la Higuera and Franck Thollard. 2000. Identification in the Limit with Probability One of Stochastic Deterministic Finite Automata. In *ICGI '00*. pages 141–156.

Alan Ford, Rajendra Singh, and Gita Martohardjono. 1997. *Pace Pāṇini: Towards a word-based theory of morphology*. American University Studies. Series XIII, Linguistics, Vol. 34. Peter Lang Publishing, Incorporated.

John Goldsmith. 2006. An algorithm for the unsupervised learning of morphology. *Natural Language Engineering* 12(1):353.

Harald Hammarström and Lars Borin. 2011. Unsupervised Learning of Morphology. *Computational Linguistics* 37(2):309–350.

Zellig S Harris. 1955. From phoneme to morpheme. *Language* 31(2):190–222.

Wilfred K. Hastings. 1970. Monte Carlo Sampling Methods Using Markov Chains and Their Applications. *Biometrika* 57(1):97–109.

Maciej Janicki. 2013. Unsupervised Learning of A-Morphous Inflection with Graph Clustering. In *Proceedings of the Student Research Workshop associated with RANLP 2013*. pages 93–99.

Maciej Janicki. 2015. A Multi-purpose Bayesian Model for Word-Based Morphology. In Cerstin Mahlow and Michael Piotrowski, editors, *Systems and Frameworks for Computational Morphology – Fourth International Workshop, SFCM 2015*. Springer.

S. Kirkpatrick, C.D. Gelatt, and M. P. Vecchi. 1983. Optimization by Simulated Annealing. *Science* 220(4598):671–680.

Amit Kirschenbaum. 2013. Unsupervised Segmentation for Different Types of Morphological Processes Using Multiple Sequence Alignment. In *1st International Conference on Statistical Language and Speech Processing, SLSP*. Tarragona, Spain, pages 152–163.

Mikko Kurimo, Sami Virpioja, Ville Turunen, and Krista Lagus. 2010. Morpho Challenge 2005-2010: Evaluations and results. In *Proceedings of the 11th Meeting of the ACL-SIGMORPHON, ACL 2010*. pages 87–95.

David Mareček. 2012. *Unsupervised Dependency Parsing*. Ph.D. thesis, Charles University in Prague.

Nicholas Metropolis, Arianna W. Rosenbluth, Marshall N. Rosenbluth, Augusta H. Teller, and Edward Teller. 1953. Equation of state calculations by fast computing machines. *Journal of Chemical Physics* 21(6):1087–1092.

Karthik Narasimhan, Regina Barzilay, and Tommi S. Jaakkola. 2015. An unsupervised method for uncovering morphological chains. *TACL* 3:157–167.

Sylvain Neuvel and Sean A. Fulop. 2002. Unsupervised Learning of Morphology without Morphemes. In *Proceedings of the 6th Workshop of the ACL Special Interest Group in Computational Phonology (SIGPHON)*. pages 31–40.

Xiaochang Peng and Daniel Gildea. 2014. Type-based MCMC for Sampling Tree Fragments from Forests. *Proceedings of the 2014 Conference on Empirical Methods in Natural Language Processing (EMNLP 2014)* pages 1735–1745.

Hoifung Poon, Colin Cherry, and Kristina Toutanova. 2009. Unsupervised morphological segmentation with log-linear models. In *Proceedings of Human Language Technologies The 2009 Annual Conference of the North American Chapter of the Association for Computational Linguistics on NAACL 09*. page 209.

Mohammad Sadegh Rasooli, Thomas Lippincott, Nizar Habash, and Owen Rambow. 2014. Unsupervised Morphology-Based Vocabulary Expansion. In *ACL*. pages 1349–1359.

Christian P. Robert and George Casella. 2005. *Monte Carlo Statistical Methods (Springer Texts in Statistics)*. Springer-Verlag New York, Inc., Secaucus, NJ, USA.

Rajendra Singh, Stanley Starosta, and Sylvain Neuvel. 2003. *Explorations in Seamless Morphology*. SAGE Publications.

Radu Soricut and Franz Josef Och. 2015. Unsupervised Morphology Induction Using Word Embeddings. In *NAACL 2015*. pages 1626–1636.

Christoph Teichmann. 2014. *Markov Chain Monte Carlo Sampling for Dependency Trees*. Ph.D. thesis, University of Leipzig.

Sami Virpioja, Peter Smit, Stig-Arne Grönroos, and Mikko Kurimo. 2013. Morfessor 2.0: Python Implementation and Extensions for Morfessor Baseline. Technical report, Aalto University, Helsinki. http://urn.fi/URN:ISBN:978-952-60-5501-5.

Greg C. G. Wei and Martin A. Tanner. 1990. A Monte Carlo Implementation of the EM Algorithm and the Poor Man's Data Augmentation Algorithms. *Journal of the American Statistical Association* 85(411):699–704.

David Yarowsky and Richard Wicentowski. 2000. Minimally Supervised Morphological Analysis by Multimodal Alignment. In *ACL '00*. pages 207–216.

Multi-entity sentiment analysis using entity-level feature extraction and word embeddings approach

Colm Sweeney
Queen's University,
Belfast
csweeney17@qub.ac.uk

Deepak Padmanabhan
Queen's University,
Belfast
D.Padmanabhan@qub.ac.uk

Abstract

The sentiment analysis task has been traditionally divided into lexicon or machine learning approaches, but recently the use of word embeddings methods have emerged, that provide powerful algorithms to allow semantic understanding without the task of creating large amounts of annotated test data. One problem with this type of binary classification, is that the sentiment output will be in the form of '1' (positive) or '0' (negative) for the string of text in the tweet, regardless if there are one or more entities referred to in the text. This paper plans to enhance the word embeddings approach with the deployment of a sentiment lexicon-based technique to appoint a total score that indicates the polarity of opinion in relation to a particular entity or entities. This type of sentiment classification is a way of associating a given entity with the adjectives, adverbs, and verbs describing it, and extracting the associated sentiment to try and infer if the text is positive or negative in relation to the entity or entities.

1. INTRODUCTION

Sentiment Analysis incorporates the use of natural language processing, statistics and text analysis to identify and extract subjective information in source materials that can refer to a named entity. A Named Entity (NE) is considered: a person, an organization, a location, an expression of time, a quantity and others, referred to by name. Once the entities have been identified using POS tagging or entity extraction processing, they can be used to identify the main subjects of a sentence, and once identified, the descriptive words, for example, adjectives, verbs or adverbs can be used to identify sentiment towards the entity.

The advent of social media has allowed users write large numbers of short text messages to comment about current events, politics and products. As a form of communication, in some situations, it provides information that can be more up-to-date than conventional news sources, and this has encouraged the research community to analyze ways to extract information from this data source. Microblogging sites have established themselves as a main communication tool, for example Twitter has attracted "over 500 million registered users and publish 340 million tweets per day" (Lunden, 2012). These tweets often contain mentions of numerous entities and additional information, like an opinion, that is being viewed more and more, as valuable currency, that can make or break a product in the marketplace.

Some of the problems encountered when processing social media content include: the length of texts (texts are typically very short, for example Twitter's limit is 140 characters); noisy texts (informal text snippets include misspellings and do not contain grammatically correct sentences); and the reliability of information in this type of text messages is uncertain, compared to news media texts. The short message length limits the amount of context available to allow an understanding of the text content (Lim, et al., 2013), but these short snippets of text can be used to provide real-time insights into the aggregated sentiments of people and capture public opinion about product preferences.

While machine learning can identify the expressed sentiment, they ignore any implicit sentiment that relates to one specific entity or another. This paper will attempt to analyze sentiment at the entity level, to designate the sentiment associated with the individual entity and not to the text snippet. For example, the following comment "Applause! Insurelife recognized for best practices unlike Busibank, worst ever", indicates two sentiments for

Proceedings of Recent Advances in Natural Language Processing, pages 733–740,
Varna, Bulgaria, Sep 4–6 2017.

two different financial companies, Insurelife and Busibank. While the sentiment towards Insurelife would be read as positive, the sentiment relating to Busibank is negative. It would be ineffective to label the overall opinion of this post, as it does not solely relate to one entity. With this in mind, the key aim of this project is to investigate how entities and their descriptor words can be used to identify the sentiment of the tweet in relation to the entity or entities, where more than one entity exists.

This can be approached through the use of one of the most popular sentiment lexicons – SentiWordNet 3.0, which evolved from annotating WordNet synonym entries in relation to their polarity scoring (Baccianella, et al., 2010). The scores given for positive, negative and neutral classes range between zero and one, and the summation of all three scores is 1. SentiWordNet has been shown to perform better than other lexicon dictionaries (Taboada, et al., 2011).

2. RELATED WORK

The main objective of Sentiment Analysis is to associate a given entity with a word or phrase describing the entity and extract the associated sentiment identifiers to infer if the text is positive or negative in relation to the main entity. This can also be called opinion mining/extraction and is now a topic of active research interest in many different communities. Until recently, the main body of research in the area of Sentiment Analysis has been conducted on news feeds and in particular types of domain, for example movie review websites, and most of the existing Twitter-specific Sentiment Analysis research seems to be term-based (see (Pak, et al., 2010), (Go, et al., 2009), (Barbosa, et al., 2010)), where certain words are extracted from Twitter posts that contain a certain term, and the sentiments of these terms are analysed from the tweets.

There are two traditional approaches to this type of sentiment classification. The first is the knowledge based approach, where predefined dictionaries of opinion words are used to search the input words to find the appropriate instances. The publicly available corpus SentiWordNet (Baccianella, et al., 2010) is an extension of WordNet where each

synset is annotated with labels indicating how objective, positive, and negative the terms in the synset are. The sentiment is determined by comparing tweets against the pre-defined entry in the dictionary, which makes it easy to determine the polarity of a specific sentence. As the core objective is to identify sentiments with respect to entities (and their attributes) from natural language, following on from the last stage, the attributes (adjectives, adverbs and verbs) that have been identified as being associated with a main entity or topic ((Hatzivassiloglou, et al., 2000) (Taboada, et al., 2011) (Volkova, et al., 2013)) can be checked to see if they have a corresponding sentiment polarity in the sentiment dictionaries to indicate a positive or negative scoring for the overall tweet.

The second (language based) approach involves supervised machine learning, where trained classifiers can be used for sentiment classification. The most common algorithms for machine learning approaches include: Naive Bayes; Support Vector Machines; (SVM) and Maximum Entropy, and different algorithms achieved different results for the different research parties - SVM being preferred by (Pang, et al., 2002) and Naïve Bayes by (Pak, et al., 2010) and (Parikh, et al., 2009) who found that the Naive Bayes classifiers worked much better than the Maximum Entropy model.

As opinions are usually targeted at an entity, an appropriate approach to Sentiment Analysis is the use of Part-Of-Speech (POS) tagging to label the entity types and any other words, or phrases that are relevant to the entity. POS tagging is also useful as noun and verb forms of the same word may have different sentiments. Early work by (Hatzivassiloglou, et al., 2000) found that the presence and type of certain terms like adjectives can be used to indicate whether a sentence is being subjective or objective. Other parts of speech have been found to be useful in Sentiment Analysis, such as adverbs ((Benamara, et al., 2007), (Taboada, et al., 2011)) nouns (Nasukawa, et al., 2003), and verbs (Wiebe, et al., 2004), or all three, ((Volkova, et al., 2013), (Jmal, et al., 2013), (Subrahmanian, et al., 2008)) as these types of words have been found to play an important role in Sentiment Analysis.

While the majority of sentiment analysis relates to text where the opinions are focused on a central topic, this may not always be the case, as opinions can be expressed about a number of entities. According to Liu (Liu, 2012), there can be two types of opinions, regular opinions and comparative opinions (Jindal, et al., 2006). Regular opinions relate to one entity or an aspect of the entity, for example "The iPhone screen is small," which expresses a negative sentiment on the aspect - screen of the iPhone. A comparative opinion, on the other hand compares more than one entity based on any number of shared aspects, for example "The Samsung Galaxy S8 looks better than iPhone 7" compares a Samsung phone and an iPhone based on their appearance (an aspect) and expresses a preference for the Samsung phone.

Most sentiment analysis research considers the whole document or text snippet as having a single polarity, in relation to a movie, for example. But in many cases a segment of text can have opinions on more than one entity with differing polarities. This suggests that the polarity classification should be performed at an entity level. One of the earliest approaches to sentiment analysis for multiple entities was proposed by (Moilanen, et al., 2009) in 2009. Their approach was to use a dependency parser to establish at entity level, the polarity of each entity in the text. A later approach by (Gryc, et al., 2010) applied the same techniques to infer the polarity in the political domain on blog messages.

Recently, word embedding-based approaches ((Mikolov, et al., 2013), (Pennington, et al., 2014)) have become popular, as they are able to capture the semantics and context of words, by using the machine learning approach of Neural Networks (Socher, et al., 2011). The Word2Vec method (Mikolov, et al., 2013) can be a supervised or unsupervised word embedding-based approach that aims to detect the meaning and the relationships between words by learning how the words co-occur in a corpus. It produces a vector space where each unique word in the corpus is allocated a corresponding vector in the space.

These vectorized representations of words, learned through the Word2Vec algorithm, have proven to efficiently manage semantic meanings of those words, where words that have a similar context in the training corpus are located in close proximity in the word vector. This type of model has proven very useful in the field of Natural Language Processing (NLP) applied to Sentiment Analysis.

This research proposes a dual classification approach for the task of polarity analysis. An initial classification of tweets identifies those that relate to a single entity, and the word embedding-based approach will be used to determine the opinion polarity of these tweets. Only the subjective tweets are being used as (Pang, et al., 2002) have found that polarity classification is improved by the removal of objective sentences from the training set. The next step will analyse and classify the emotion relating to multiple entities in the Twitter text by using a sentiment lexicon-based technique that appoints a score to indicate the polarity of opinion in relation to each particular entity in text that contains multiple entities.

3. METHODOLOGIES

The goal is to build a classification system that can decide whether a tweet is positive or negative towards each given entity. The training dataset that is used contains only positive or negative tweets, as they denote subjective opinion.

For those tweets that are identified as containing more than one, different entity, they are removed for processing as described in section 3.2 and 3.3. These tweets are analyzed, where particular descriptor words are extracted as features from the text, and the sentiment of these words are identified using the SentiWordNet lexicon. The remaining tweets are processed using the Word2Vec algorithm, as below. The dataset used for training and testing contains 1,578,627 classified tweets, where each row is marked as 1 for positive sentiment and 0 for negative sentiment. Approximately 1/10 of the corpus was used for testing the algorithm, while the rest was used for training.

3.1. Training

Before training the Word2Vec model, the data was pre-processed, where all uppercase letters and words were changed to lower case letters to ensure uniformity. In addition, the sentences were split into individual tokens by using NLTK's **punkt** tokenizer. Additional pre-processing steps clean the data by removing any HTML markup and punctuation. Stop words which refer to the most common words in a language, such as "a" and "the", are usually removed for NLP tasks. In the case of training the Word2Vec model, stop words are not removed, as the algorithm relies on the broader context of the sentence in order to produce high-quality word vectors. With the pre-processing complete, the Word2Vec model is trained on the given training dataset that was derived from a total of over a million tweets (dataset sourced from Kaggle[1]), with the sentiment tag removed to provide unlabelled training, as Word2Vec does not need labels in order to create meaningful representations (Ye, et al., 2015).

3.2. Word2Vec algorithm

The Word2Vec algorithm uses the genism method in Python to create the word vectors. Word2Vec can employ one of two training algorithms – Continuous bag- of-words (CBOW) or skip-gram. As the skip-gram algorithm approach has proved to be more efficient for big datasets, as is the case of the corpus adopted, it is selected for this work. Word2Vec works in a way that is comparable to deep approaches like deep neural networks, where it allows for a representation of semantically similar words with neighboring points in the same vector space.

3.3. Dependency Parser

The Twitter texts that contain more than one entity will be processed further by taking the descriptor features and using SentiWordNet for an overall score per entity. SentiWordNet has been chosen as the sentiment lexicon for this task, as it has been shown to perform better than other lexicon dictionaries (Taboada, et al., 2011). First the Twitter specific dependency parser, TweeboParser from (Kong, et al., 2014), is used to generate a syntactic structure of each tweet. The tokenized tweet is

created with the associated part-of-speech tags and syntactic dependencies. The parsed file is structured according to the CoNLL format showing different information in different columns.

The generated syntactic structure for the following tweet is presented in Table 1:

"Applause! Insurelife recognized for best practices unlike Busibank, worst ever"

ID	FORM	LEMMA	CPOSTAG	POSTAG	FEATS	HEAD
1	Applause	_	N	N	_	0
2	!	_	,	,	_	_
3	Insurelife	_	^	^	_	4
4	recognized	_	V	V	_	0
5	for	_	P	P	_	4
6	best	_	A	A	_	7
7	practices	_	N	N	_	5
8	unlike	_	P	P	_	4
9	Busibank	_	^	^	_	9
10	,	_	,	,	_	_
11	worst	_	A	A	_	6
12	ever	_	R	R	_	6

Table 1. TweeboParser output

The fields in Table 1 include: ID showing token position; FORM showing the form of the word (or punctuation symbol); CPOSTAG and POSTAG showing the coarse grained and fine grained part-of-speech tags respectively; the HEAD denotes the head of the current token; and DEPREL shows any dependencies and the type of dependency relation (CNNL-2006).

For the example tweet above, two separate entities – Insurelife and Busibank have been identified by the '^' symbol in the POSTAG field. The 2 entities do not match and are therefore different. With the entities identified, any neighboring words showing

---

1   http://thinknook.com/twitter-sentiment-analysis-training-corpus-dataset-2012-09-22/

part-of-speech tags for Adverbs, Adjectives and Verbs will be analysed for sentiment, using entity-level feature extraction.

3.4. Entity-level feature extraction

This involves the identification of the dependent words in relation to the entities, where these words are used to identify the polarity towards a given entity. The tweet level and the entity level polarity (towards a given topic) can be different, when relating to different topics or entities, resulting in contrasting opinions in the one tweet. The entity-level feature extraction is applied using the SentiWordNet lexicon against the parsed text to identify the polarity of the descriptor words, to better identify the sentiment of a tweet towards a given entity or entities.

Continuing on from feature extraction research based on associated token words on either side of the topic (Sweeney, et al., 2017), the dependency of descriptor words on a topic or entity, can be considered more intuitive as an effective method, as neighboring tokens (2 words on either side of the entity) can emphasize the correct sentiment value. With only descriptor words being used as neighboring tokens, this research aims to improve on this by identifying the descriptor words and using them to identify the sentiment directed towards individual entities.

Figure 1 shows the architectural components of the proposed hybrid supervised solution. Tweets are processed using the TweeboParser application. The parsed output is used to differentiate tweets that relate to more than one entities and the remaining, that relate to one entity only.

3.5. Scoring tweets

The descriptor words of the multi-entity tweets are scored using SentiWordNet sentiment lexicon. The overall scoring per entity is printed out as output for the multi-entity tweets. The remaining tweets are classified using a Random Forest classifier that uses feature vectors created by a Word2Vec model that was trained on a large classified Twitter corpus. The output includes the tweet number and the sentiment

scoring per tweet – 1 for a positive sentiment and 0 for a negative sentiment.

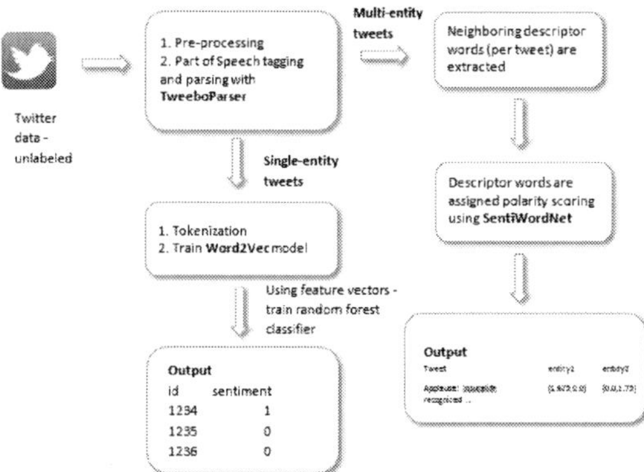

Figure 1. Flowchart of application

4. Results

As a baseline, the texts were parsed with the Tweet specific parser - TweeboParser and by extracting descriptor words (Adverbs, Adjectives and Verbs) only per tweet and using SentiWordNet to score each of the descriptor words, the scoring for this system is providing **69%** accuracy. To improve on this system, the subjective tweets that relate to only one entity are processed by the Word2vec modelling technique integrating a neural network implementation to learn the distributed representations for words to allocate a scoring per tweet. The tweets that relate to more than one entity are processed separately using TweeboParser, and the descriptor words neighboring each entity are used to score sentiment relating to that entity. With all entities in multi-entity tweet being correctly scored, this provided an improvement in accuracy to **71%**. So, by integrating a word embeddings approach for single entity tweets, accompanied by a sentiment lexicon approach on parsed text for multi-entity tweets, this has improved the accuracy of sentiment scoring on Twitter texts.

To evaluate the performance of sentiment classification systems, the following three performance measures are used: Precision; Recall and F1-Measure. Precision and Recall are calculated and combined to produce the averaged F1-measure. Positive or negative reference values were used to calculate the precision, recall, and F-measure of the lexicon-based classification approach (see table 2).

	Precision	Recall	F1-score
Classification using SentiWordNet + POS	0.68	0.68	0.68
Classification using Word2Vec +SentiWordNet + POS	0.72	0.69	0.71

Table 2. Application results

5. CONCLUSIONS AND FUTURE WORK

Most research in the field of sentiment analysis usually integrates either machine learning algorithms or lexicon based approaches. With the increased popularity of word embeddings methods, this research aims to highlight how a hybrid word embeddings and lexicon based approach can be used to tackle the problem of sentiment analysis on multiple entities. Using a Twitter-specific parser to identify the descriptor words that relate to a specific entity for text that contains multiple entities, this research is able to achieve very good results.

Future work could involve other factors that can have a high impact on sentiment for a tweet containing more than one entity, for example identifying negation to improve the accuracy of the lexicon based part of the classification. Further investigation of entity and descriptor word relationship could also be investigated further. For example, if the word is a noun preceded by an adjective, or if the preceding word is an adverb, this could be indicators of a possible descriptor/entity relationship.

REFERENCES

Baccianella S., Esuli A. and Sebastiani F. SentiWordNet 3.0: An Enhanced Lexical Resource for Sentiment Analysis and Opinion Mining [Conference] // Proceedings in Language Resources and Evaluation Conference (LREC-10). - 2010. - pp. 2200-2204.

Baccianella S., Esuli A. and Sebastiani F. SentiWordNet 3.0: An Enhanced Lexical Resource for Sentiment Analysis and Opinion Mining [Conference] // International Conference on Language Resources and Evaluation (LREC - 2010). - 2010.

Barbosa L. and Feng J. Robust sentiment detection on Twitter from biased and noisy data [Conference] // In Proceedings of the 23rd International Conference on Computational Linguistics: Posters, pages . - [s.l.] : Association for Computational Linguistics, 2010.

Benamara F. [et al.] Sentiment analysis: Adjectives and adverbs are better than adjectives alone [Conference] // International Conference on Weblogs and Social Media (ICWSM '07). - 2007.

CNNL-2006 CoNLL-X Shared Task: Multi-lingual Dependency Parsing [Online] // http://ilk.uvt.nl/. - ILK Research Group. - http://ilk.uvt.nl/conll/#dataformat.

Go A. and Bhayani R. Huang, L. Twitter sentiment classication using distant supervision - CS224N Project Report [Report]. - [s.l.] : Stanford, 2009.

Gryc W. and Moilanen K. Leveraging Textual Sentiment Analysis with Social Network Modelling [Conference] // In Proceedings of the "From Text to Political Positions" Workshop. - Amsterdam : [s.n.], 2010.

Hatzivassiloglou V. and Wiebe J.M. Effects of adjective orientation and gradability on sentence subjectivity [Conference] // In Proceedings of the 18th conference on Computational linguistics. - [s.l.] : Association for Computational Linguistics, 2000.

Jindal N. and L. Bing Mining comparative sentences and relations [Conference] // Proceedings in National Conference on Artificial Intelligence (AAAI-2006). - 2006.

Jmal J. and Faiz R. Customer review summarization approach using Twitter and SentiWordNet [Conference] // Proceedings of the 3rd International Conference on Web Intelligence, Mining and Semantics. - [s.l.] : ACM, 2013. - p. 33.

Khan F. H., Bashir S. and Qamar U. TOM: Twitter opinion mining framework using hybrid classification scheme [Journal] // Decision Support Systems. - 2014. - pp. 245-257.

Kiritchenko S., Zhu X. and Mohammad S. M. Sentiment analysis of short informal texts [Journal] // Journal of Artificial Intelligence Research. - 2014. - pp. 723-762.

Kong L. [et al.] A dependency parser for tweets [Conference] // Proceedings of the 2014 Conference on Empirical Methods in Natural Language Processing (EMNLP-14). - [s.l.] : Association for Computational Linguistics, 2014. - pp. 1001–1012.

Kouloumpis E., Wilson T. and Moore J. D. Twitter sentiment analysis: The good the bad and the omg! [Conference] // The International AAAI Conference on Web and Social Media (ICWSM-2011) . - [s.l.] : Association for the Advancement of Artificial Intelligence (AAAI), 2011.

Lim E-P., Chen H, and Chen G. Business Intelligence and Analytics: Research Directions [News Article] // Transactions on Management Information Systems (TMIS). - [s.l.] : ACM, 2013 йил. - 4 : Vol. 3.

Liu B. Sentiment analysis and opinion mining [Journal] // Synthesis lectures on human language technologies. - 2012. - 1 : Vol. 5. - pp. 1-167.

Lunden I. Analyst: Twitter Passed 500M Users In June 2012, 140M Of Them In US; Jakarta 'Biggest Tweeting' City [Online] // http://techcrunch.com. - 2012 йил. - 2014 йил 12-10. - http://techcrunch.com/2012/07/30/analyst-twitter-passed-500m-users-in-june-2012-140m-of-them-in-us-jakarta-biggest-tweeting-city/.

Mikolov T. [et al.] Efficient estimation of word representations in vector space. - [s.l.] : arXiv preprint arXiv:1301.3781, 2013.

Mohammad S. and Turney P.D. Crowdsourcing a Word-Emotion Association Lexicon [Article] // Computational Intelligence. - 2013.

Moilanen K. and Pulman S. Multi-entity Sentiment Scoring [Conference] // Proceedings in RANLP (Recent Advances in Natural Language Processing) 2009. - 2009.

Nasukawa T. and Yi J. Sentiment analysis: capturing favorability using natural language processing [Conference] // Proceedings of the Conference on Knowledge Capture. - 2003.

Owoputi O. [et al.] Improved Part-of-Speech Tagging for Online Conversational Text with Word Clusters [Conference] // Conference of the North American Chapter of the Association for Computational Linguistics: Human Language Technologies. - [s.l.] : Association for Computational Linguistics, 2013.

Pak A. and Paroubek P. Twitter as a corpus for sentiment analysis and opinion mining [Conference] // Proceedings of the International Conference on Language Resources and Evaluation (LREC '10). - 2010.

Pang B., Lee L. and Vaithyanathan S. Thumbs up? Sentiment classification using machine learning techniques [Conference] // In Proceedings of the ACL-02 conference on Empirical methods in natural language processing. - [s.l.] : Association for Computational Linguistics, 2002. - Vol. 10.

Parikh R. and Movassate M. Sentiment Analysis of User-Generated Twitter Updates using Various Classification Techniques - CS224N Final Report [Report]. - 2009.

Pennington J., Socher R. and Manning C.D. GloVe: Global vectors for word representation [Conference] // In Proceedings of the conference on empirical methods on natural language processing (EMNLP '14). - 2014.

Socher R. [et al.] Semi-supervised recursive autoencoders for predicting sentiment distributions [Conference] // In Proceedings of the 2011 conference on empirical methods in natural language processing (EMPLP '11). - 2011.

Subrahmanian V. S. and Reforgiato D. AVA: Adjective-verb-adverb combinations for sentiment analysis [Journal] // IEEE Intelligent Systems. - 2008. - pp. 43-50.

Sweeney C.J., Hong J and Liu W Sentiment Analysis using entity-level feature extraction [Conference] // In Proceeding of Conference on Computational Linguistics and Intelligent Text Processing (CICLing '17). - Budapest : [s.n.], 2017.

Taboada M. [et al.] Lexicon-based methods for sentiment analysis [Journal] // Computational linguistics. - 2011. - pp. 267-307.

Volkova S., Wilson T. and Yarowsky D. Exploring Sentiment in Social Media: Bootstrapping Subjectivity Clues from Multilingual Twitter Streams [Conference] // Proceedings of the 51st Annual Meeting of the Association for Computational Linguistics. - [s.l.] : Association for Computational Linguistics, 2013. - pp. 505-510.

Wiebe J. M. [et al.] Learning subjective language [Journal] // Computational Linguistics. - 2004. - Vol. 30.

Ye K. [et al.] Summarizing Product Aspects from Massive Online Review with Word Representation [Conference] // In International Conference on Knowledge Science, Engineering and Management. - [s.l.] : Springer, Cham, 2015.

Finding Individual Word Sense Changes
and their Delay in Appearance

Nina Tahmasebi
Språkbanken,
University of Gothenburg, Sweden
`nina.tahmasebi@gu.se`

Thomas Risse
University Library J.C. Senckenberg,
Germany
`t.risse@ub.uni-frankfurt.de`

Abstract

We present a method for detecting word
sense changes by utilizing automatically
induced word senses. Our method works
on the level of individual senses and allows a word to have e.g. one stable sense
and then add a novel sense that later experiences change. Senses are grouped
based on polysemy to find linguistic concepts and we can find broadening and narrowing as well as novel (polysemous and
homonymic) senses. We evaluate on a
testset, present recall and estimates of the
time between expected and found change.

1 Introduction

When interpreting the content of historical documents, knowledge of changed word senses play an
important role. Without knowing that the meaning
of a word has changed (*word sense change*) we
might falsely place a more current meaning on the
word and thus interpret the text wrongly.

Recent work on detecting word sense change
utilize word embeddings and have several drawbacks: (i) they look at all senses of a word at once
and thus only track changes in a word's dominant
sense, (ii) they can find *when* a word changes but
not *what* has changed; and (iii) they cannot separate stable senses from changing senses for a word,
e.g. the *stone* sense of *rock* stayed stable while a
music sense was added and later changed.

In this paper, we propose a method that utilizes
automatically extracted word senses by means of
word sense induction, to find sense changes given
a text collection. We test the hypothesis that automatically induced word senses and the temporal
comparison of these has the potential to capture
changes in all senses of a word separately. We apply unsupervised methods and show the potential

of our method on a set of words that have experienced change in the past centuries. We perform
word sense change detection per sense rather than
considering a word and all its senses as one. We
measure the time between an expected change in
word sense and the corresponding found change
to investigate not only *if* but *when* changes can be
found and with which time delay.

We consider continuous data from two centuries, which leads to a high complexity; If all
senses of a word can relate between adjacent time
periods, the relation graph would result in a combinatorial explosion. Therefore, we reduce complexity by first detecting coherent senses over
time and then comparing these. Nonetheless, the
complexity is high with many relations to evaluate. Because we lack automatic evaluation methods and common testsets, we present a proof-of-
concept of our method.

The contributions of this paper are as follows:
- Methodology for tracking word sense
  changes for individual senses.
- Analysis of time delay for detected changes
  with respect to ground truth.
- Testset for word sense change detection, the
  WSC dataset (Tahmasebi and Risse, 2017).

2 State of the Art

The first methods for automatic sense change detection were based on context vectors; they investigated semantic density (Sagi et al., 2009) and utilized mutual information scores (Gulordava and
Baroni, 2011) to identify semantic change. Both
methods detect signals of change but neither aligns
senses over time or determines what changed.

Topic-based models (where topics are interpreted as senses) have been used to detect novel
senses in one collection compared to another by
identifying new topics in the later corpus ((Lau
et al., 2012; Cook et al., 2014)), or to cluster top-

Proceedings of Recent Advances in Natural Language Processing, pages 741–749,
Varna, Bulgaria, Sep 4–6 2017.

Table 1: Comparison of evaluation in previous work.

Reference	words			Time		Change
	# pos.	# neg.	# points	# span	# types	
Lau et al. (2012)	5	5	2	43	1	
Cook et al. (2014)	20	204	2	43/17	1	
Sagi et al. (2009)	4	0	4	560	2	
Gulordava and Baroni (2011)	x	100-x[1]	2	30	1	
Mitra et al. (2014)	69	0	8	488^2	4	
Kulkarni et al. (2015)	20^3	0	21/12/24	105/15/2	1	
Hamilton et al. (2016)	28^4	0	20	200/190	1	
This paper	35	26	222	222	4	

[1] A random subset of 100 words were chosen. pos./neg. ratio unclear.
[2] The first portion of the data consists of 1520-1908 and contains roughly the same amount of data as the last portion spanning 2006-2008.
[3] An additional 20 words/method evaluated, pos./neg. ratio unclear.
[4] Same as [3] but 10 words/method

ics over time (Wijaya and Yeniterzi, 2011). A dynamic topic model that builds topics with respect to information from the previous time point is proposed by Frermann and Lapata (2016) and again sense novelty is evaluated. With the exception of Wijaya et al. that partition topics, no alignment is made between topics to allow following diachronic progression of an individual sense.

Graph-based models (Tahmasebi, 2013; Mitra et al., 2014, 2015) aim at revealing complex relations between a word's senses by (a) modeling senses per se using WSI; and (b) aligning senses over time. The models allow identification of individual senses in different time periods and Tahmasebi also groups senses into related concepts.

The largest body of work is done using word embeddings of different kind in the last years (Kim et al., 2014; Basile et al., 2016; Zhang et al., 2016). Embeddings are trained on different time-sliced corpora and compared over time. Kulkarni et al. (2015) project words onto their frequency, POS and word embeddings and propose a model for detecting statistically significant changes between time periods on those projections. Hamilton et al. (2016) investigate both similarity between a priori known pairs of words, and between a word's own vectors over time to detect change. Kulkarni et al. (2015); Basile et al. (2016); Hamilton et al. (2016) all propose different methods for projecting vectors from different time periods onto the same space to allow comparison.

Word embeddings do not allow us to recover the senses that have changed and therefore, no way of detecting *what* changed. Most methods use similar words to the changing word as a method to illustrate what happens. However, the most similar words will only represent the dominant sense and not reflect changes among the other senses or capture stable parts of a word.

Table 1 shows a summary over the evaluation performed by some of the methods described. We present the number of positive and negative examples of change, the number of time points and the total timespan as well as the number of considered change types. Currently no standard datasets or evaluation metrics are available for comparison across methods or datasets.

3 Modeling Word Sense Change

As a basis for our analysis we consider automatically induced word sense clusters. Each cluster represents a distinct time period and consists of a set of nouns and noun phrases of length two. These clusters are approximations of word senses and to some extent capture also contexts. Throughout the paper we use **word senses** and **clusters** interchangeably and refer to these automatically derived approximations. A **concept** consists of senses that are related (i.e., polysemous) following Cooper (2005). To model word sense change, we should allow each sense to change individually; worst case, this results in a graph where, for a maximum number of senses S in each time period $t \in T$, we have in the order of $S^{|T|}$ edges representing sense similarity. Even for a small number of time periods, this graph becomes infeasible to investigate and evaluate. Therefore, we reduce this complexity by first considering coherent senses over time (units) and then following the units over time. Units that are related are placed in a *path*. A unit can contain an arbitrary number of clusters so in order to get a good representation, we create a *unit representative*.

We define a **unit** $u_i(w) = u_i$ as an ordered sequence of clusters $\{c_1^{t_i}, c_2^{t_j}, \ldots, c_n^{t_k}\}$ such that each cluster contains the word w and comes from a distinct time period t_j where $t_i \leq t_j \leq t_k$. We allow time gaps between the clusters, i.e., $t_k \geq t_j + 1$, in order to capture senses that have lost in popularity or are underrepresented for a period of

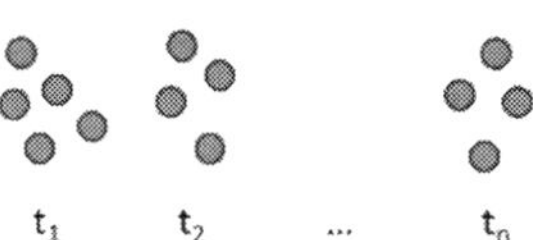

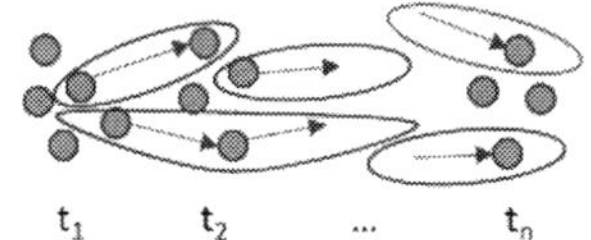

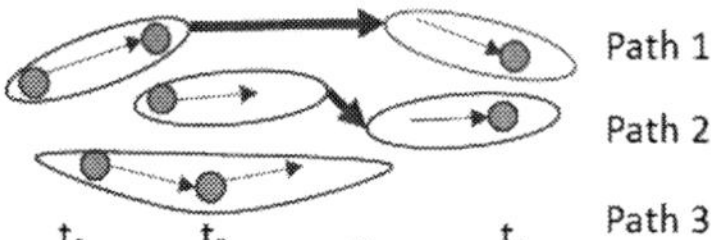

Figure 1: Process for word sense change detection.

time. The unit representative, r_{u_i}, contains a set of words that can be used to represent all participating clusters. A **single unit** is a unit with one cluster where the cluster words are the unit representative. A unit set $U_{t_i}(w)$ consists of all units for w that start at t_i. We measure **similarity between units** as similarity between unit representatives.

A **path** is an ordered sequence of units $\{u_i, u_j, \ldots, u_k\}$ such that units have a similarity above α. A path represents polysemous senses and all their changes for a word. Different paths represent homonymic concepts.

4 Methodology

Our method consists of three steps (Figure 1). We begin with an example and then provide details.

We choose an example with three time points t_1, t_2, t_3 and unit sets $U_{t_1}(w) = \{u_1\}$, $U_{t_2}(w) = \{u_2, u_3\}$ and $U_{t_3}(w) = \{u_4, u_5\}$ for the target word *tape*. Each unit represents a cluster chosen from the word sense change (WSC) dataset.

$u_1 = \{stereo, cassette, tape, radio, record\}$,
$u_2 = \{pin, thread, tape, silk, chair, cotton\}$,
$u_3 = \{tape, radio, record, cassette\}$,
$u_4 = \{tape, sparkplug cable, wire, clip\}$,
$u_5 = \{television, record, tape, video, book, film, magazine, video industry\}$.

In the first step, similarity between pairs (u_1,u_2) and (u_1,u_3) is measured. Pairs are ranked according to similarity and the pair with the highest similarity is merged. In this case, u_1 and u_3 are merged into $u' = \{u_1, u_3\}$ because u_3 is a subset of u_1. The unit representative consists of the words $\{cassette, tape, record\}$. The pair (u_1,u_2) is removed because u_1 is merged with one unit from $U_{t_2}(w)$.

The resulting unit set is $U_{[t_1,t_2]}(w) = \{\{u_1, u_3\} = u', u_2\}$. At time t_3, unit u_4 and u_5 are compared to the two units in $U_{[t_1,t_2]}(w)$. u_5 is merged with u' resulting in $u'' = \{u_1, u_3, u_5\}$. u_4 remains a single unit and is placed in $U_{[t_1,t_3]}(w)$ without being merged. When we merge two units,

we add up all their clusters and build a new representative. When unit u_5 is merged with $u' = \{u_1, u_3\}$ we consider this to be a broadening because the single unit u_5 has a broader sense than the merged unit u'. The resulting unit set consists of $U_{[t_1,t_3]}(w) = \{\{u_1, u_3, u_5\} = u'', u_2, u_4\}$.

As a final step, to create paths, we measure similarity between the pairs (u'',u_2) and (u'',u_4). In this example, no units are related into paths (i.e., they all form their own path) which tells us that there are three different concepts for *tape*, one regarding *sewing tape*, one regarding *scotch tape* and one regarding *musical tape* which later includes also the *video tape*, matching well the main senses of tape but also capturing *sewing tape*, a sense less common today (OED, 2000).

4.1 Deriving Word Sense Clusters

We find word senses using an unsupervised word sense induction algorithm called *curvature clustering* (Dorow et al., 2005). These clusters have been evaluated by Tahmasebi et al. (2013) and were shown to have 85% precision using the Pantel and Lin (2002) evaluation method. To the best of our knowledge, the curvature clustering method is the only induction method that has been evaluated on historical texts and therefore, is used as a starting point for our word sense change detection. However, our method can make use of senses derived by any induction algorithm, or the combination of several, where the output is a set of words.

Measuring Unit Similarity A central part of word sense tracking is to measure similarity between the induced senses (by means of unit similarity). We consider equality between words $w_i \in r_{u_i}$ and $w_j \in r_{u_j}$ in two ways; 1. full match and 2. partial match. If there is no full match, we split all words into their (space separated) parts $w_i = w_1\, w_2$ and a word w_i is accepted as a partial match to w_j only if any w_1 or w_2 is a suffix or prefix in w_j, e.g. *motor car* and *motorcar* as well as *monitor* and *color monitor* but not *rave* and *gravel*.

Our similarity measure, lin (Lin, 1998; Pantel and Lin, 2002), is semantic and based on closeness of WordNet synsets (Miller, 1995). We measure similarity between clusters by considering them as single units and measuring unit similarity.

$$sim(u_i, u_j) = \frac{\sum_{u \in r_{u_i}} \max_{v \in r_{u_j}} lin(u, v)}{\min(|r_{u_i}|, |r_{u_j}|)} \qquad (1)$$

4.2 Creating Units

We use the unit similarity to determine which clusters represent coherent senses and merge these into units. In the merging step, we calculate the similarity between all pairs of units (u, v) such that $u \in U_{[t_1, t_k]}(w)$ and $v \in U_{t_{k+1}}(w)$. In the first step we set $k = 1$ and simply perform merging by looking at clusters (i.e., single units) from t_1 and t_2. In the subsequent steps, we merge single units from time t_{k+1} with all units up to time k.

For each unit v, we normalize similarity s.t. the sum of the similarities between v and all units u amounts to 1 and keep only pairs with similarity above a threshold α. We then merge the pair (v, u) with the highest similarity and remove all pairs $(u, *)$ and $(*, v)$. If the similarity of v and several units u is the same, we assume that there are polysemous concepts. By uniquely assigning and merging v with one unit u we reduce the complexity of the method. It remains future work to investigate how much information is lost by not allowing a more complex graph structure.

Capturing the Core of Units Once we determined which clusters that should form a unit, we need a representation of the participating clusters, i.e., we need to chose the words for the unit representative. For this, we make use of *local clustering coefficient* (*lcc*) (Watts and Strogatz, 1998).We also measure participation rate *part* as the amount of participating clusters where the word is present. To allow a word in the unit representative, the word must be highly central in its cluster (high *lcc*) or participate in many clusters (high *part*). Each time a new cluster is added, we update the unit representative, and thus allow a slow shift of the unit representatives capturing broadening, narrowing and evolved senses (e.g. adding *video* to the *music tape* sense).

4.3 Creating Paths

Once all clusters and units have been merged, the final set $U_{[t_{start}, t_{end}]}(w)$ consists of units that rep-

resent individual senses over time. To find concepts, we seek to group units s.t. the units are related, i.e., have a similarity above α, following an idea by Mei and Zhai (2005). We compare each unit $u \in U_{[t_{start}, t_{end}]}(w)$ to all other units that start at the same or later time point. We allow time gaps between units to capture relations between underrepresented senses. All units that are related are placed in a *path*.

Table 2: Extract of units for *aeroplane*. Units only display some of the internal clusters and words.

Year	Cluster words
	Unit u_1: 1908-1930 (defining the construction)
1908	airship, aeroplane, balloon, aeroplane construction
1930	aeroplane, automobile, airship, engine work, liner
	Unit u_2: 1917-1943 (as a weapon of war)
1917	piping, gun, aeroplane, shafting, tank, infantry
1933	armoured car, aeroplane, tank
1943	tank, aeroplane, ship, gun, ammunition
	Unit u_3: 1914-1941 (as a means of transportation)
1914	plane, aeroplane, motor bicycle, motor lorry, car
1920	train, lorry, car, aeroplane
1930	motorcycle, lorry, motorcar, aeroplane
1941	tank, machineguns, gun, lorry, motorcycle, aeroplane
	Unit u_4: 1916-1974 (unit with all senses)
1916	aeroplane, bird, ship
1930	train, aeroplane, ship
1941	gun, artillery, machineguns, aeroplane, ship, tank
1974	car, train, aeroplane, motor car

Table 2 shows units for *aeroplane*. The three first units represent the individual senses and the last unit contains the changes all in one unit. We find two paths $u_1 \rightarrow u_2 \rightarrow u_4$, and $u_3 \rightarrow u_4$.

5 Experiments

The aim of our experiments is to find the quality and degree (i.e., recall) to which word sense change can be found using our proposed methodology against the main changes according to a set of knowledge sources. We use *The Times Archive*, a large sample of modern English spanning 1785 – 1985 and append the *New York Times Annotated Corpus*, a modern collection spanning 1987 – 2007, giving us a total of 222 years.

5.1 Testset

As a testset, we manually chose a set of 23 words that we know have experienced word sense change during the past centuries. The main changes for each word were found using Wikipedia, dictionary.com and the Oxford English Dictionary, and the automatically found changes were compared against the manually found counterpart. For comparison purposes we also chose a set of 11 words that have experienced minimal change during the period, i.e., **stable words**. The full testset can be found in (Tahmasebi and Risse, 2017).

We categorize changes into several classes:

- **evolved sense** A sense that changes by means of broadening or narrowing. Should be found within one unit, e.g. *mail* as *electronic mail*;

- **novel related sense** (polysemy) A sense that is related to at least one existing sense. Should be found as a new unit in an existing path, e.g. *record* as a *musical record* related to *official record*, to constitute a concept;

- **novel unrelated sense** (homonomy) A sense that is unrelated to any existing senses or corresponds to a new word (neologism). Should be found in a separate path, e.g. *Internet* or *rock as music* different from *rock as stone*;

- **existing sense** A sense that appears before the start of our dataset and is stable during the entire period, e.g. the *stone* sense of *rock*. This class is used for words without any change events (existing – stable) and words that later experience change (existing – evo).

The resulting testset consists of 16 evolved senses, 9 novel related and 10 novel unrelated senses, 15 existing senses for changing and 11 existing senses for stable words. To sum up, we have **35 change events** and **26 non-change events**.

5.2 Setup

We cluster using a minimum clustering coefficient of 0.3. A word w from any participating cluster is placed in the unit representative r_u if; (1) $lcc \geq 0.7$; (2) $part \geq 60\%$; or (3) if $lcc \geq 0.4$ and $part \geq 50\%$ hold. To filter out noise, we remove all single units once the paths are created.

We use the WordNet Similarity for Java implementation (WS4J, 2014) for the lin measure. We set $\alpha = 0.1$ to be as inclusive as possible while keeping the number of possible pairs down.

5.3 Evaluation

For each experiment, we firstly measure **recall** and discuss false positives; and secondly the **average time delay** as the difference in time between the *expected*, according to our ground truth, and the *found* events. Finally, we measure the **average path length** to see if we can differentiate between stable and changing words.

Recall is straightforward and measures the portion of expected change present in our paths, according to our ground truth. The expected time of change is more complex; true time of change is the first time that a word is used in a collection with the correct corresponding sense. We do not know this and therefore we approximate it using two different time points.

The first expected time point is the *time of definition* or *time of invention* of a word w, $t_{DI}(w)$, in a given dictionary or knowledge resource. However, that an invention has been made does not necessarily correspond to newspapers reporting on it frequently. E.g. the *computer* was invented in its modern form in the 1940s, but was not mentioned in newspapers often in the early 40's, most likely due to WWII. Therefore, as a second expected time point, we consider the *first cluster evidence*, $t_{CE}(w)$, indicating the first time the word appears in a cluster. This represents the first possible time point for tracking, given the curvature clustering algorithm for extracting word sense clusters. The true expected time point lies in the interval $[t_{DI}, t_{CE}]$. Finally, we have the time point of the detected change event, $t_{found}(w)$.

The time delay is $T_{DI}(w) = t_{found}(w) - t_{DI}(w)$ and $T_{CE}(w) = t_{found}(w) - t_{CE}(w)$. The average time delay is summed over all words,
$$AT_{DI} = \frac{\sum_{\forall w} T_{DI}(w)}{|w|} \text{ and } AT_{CE} = \frac{\sum_{\forall w} T_{CE}(w)}{|w|}.$$

Experimental setup We split our experiments into two parts; In the first experiment, *best case experiment*, we investigate how much can be detected in the units. We do not make any distinction between different change events and we view this as an upper bound on our recall and a lower bound on avg. time delay. This experiment aims to answer the question; how suitable are the units for capturing the expected word senses and their changes? Implicitly, we capture the potential of the induced word senses as a basis for word sense change detection. Are the senses present among the induced senses and can the change events be found among the units?

The second experiment is to evaluate units and paths for capturing and differentiating between change events. We call this the *all classes experiment* and consider each class (existing, novel unrelated, novel related and evolved) separately. This is the full evaluation of our method and shows how well the classes can be differentiated. Thus we require each change type to appear in the correct

Table 3: Recall and time delay for all words in the testset, where *BC* is the best case and *All* is the all class experiments. The *value* in *bold* represents delay time from first cluster evidence AT_{CE} and the second represents time of definition AT_{DI}.

	Recall		Avg. time delay	
	BC	All	BC	All
Evolved sense	1.00	1.00	**6.2** - 11.0	**16.1** - 20.9
New related sense	0.89	0.11	**5.8** - 27.8	**26.0** - 36.0
New unrelated sense	0.80	0.80	**1.6** - 19.8	**1.9** - 20.0
Existing sense – evo	1.00	1.00	**11.7**- 59.0	**11.7**- 59.0
Existing – stable	1.00	1.00	**2.7** -20.5	**2.7** -20.5
Average excl. stable	0.94	0.80	**7.1** - 30.7	**11.8** - 35.4
Total average	0.95	0.84	**6.3** - 28.7	**9.9** - 32.2

form (see Sec. 5.1).

6 Experimental Results

6.1 Recall

Table 3 shows the recall for the best case (*BC*) and all classes (*All*). For the **evolved sense** class (broadening and narrowing within an existing unit), we have full recall and found all 16 events within units. For **new unrelated senses** (new units in their own path) we correctly found 8 out of 10. The only senses that are not found are the first senses for *Internet* and *computer*, most likely because of few mentions in the dataset. The **existing senses** are all found, regardless of if they are senses attached to a stable word or to a word that will later gain or change meaning.

The **new related sense** (new unit related to an existing path) is the hardest class to find. The units contain evidence for 89% of all changes, however, they cannot be found related to other units. By looking at examples from this class, it is obvious that the linguistic definition is very hard to detect automatically. E.g. the word *memory* in a digital sense is related to *human memory*, but rarely used in similar context and *train* as a *mechanical train* with a locomotive differs largely from a *train of people* (e.g. funeral train). Therefore, we cannot place them in the correct path and they are placed in their own path.

To sum up, our recall is 95% for all changes and stable senses in our units. In the correct form within the paths, we have a recall of 84%, only missing out on new related senses where the linguistic definition does not match the usage.

False positives Providing precision requires a definition of precision in the case of word sense change detection using paths. When do we achieve full precision? In a unit with 70-80 cluster or a path with hundreds of units, evaluation becomes extremely complex. Therefore, instead of precision, we analyze false positives by looking at the average number of change events per word and leave the definition of precision for future work.

On average, there are 3 paths/word and 5.3 units/path for change words and 13.3 for stable words. Among the changing words, we have an average of 2.2 change events and thus we would expect around 2 false positives (5.3 units mean 4 change events on average out of which we expect 2 to be correct). Among the stable words, all change events and thus different units are per definition wrong, that means on average 13.3 false positives. However, there are some words that stand out, *horse*, *bank* and *music* are very common words and have, on average, 47.5, 21.4 and 24.9 units per path when we would expect only one. For these we observe very long spanning units with 206, 197 and 204 years for the longest unit. Excluding these three words, the average number of unit per path drops to 6.6 and represents 5 change events.

Though this is an approximation of the false positive rate, it does tell us that the number of elements to manually filter is limited and thus the results can be of great use for digital archive users and researchers in e.g. the digital humanities.

6.2 Average Time Delay

Table 3 shows the average time delays for our experiments. Bold values are delay times with respect to first cluster evidence, AT_{CE} and the second values time of definition AT_{DI}.

For the **evolved sense** class, the change events are found in our units 6.2 years after first appearing in a cluster and 11 years after being invented or defined in a dictionary. We consider the true time delay to be between 6.2 – 11 years. To appear in the correct form, i.e., inside an existing unit, the average time delay is 16.1 – 20.9 year. For the **new related senses** we have a time delay of 5.8 – 27.8 years for the words to appear in any unit. However, to appear in the correct form, the time delay is much higher (26.0 – 36.0 years) and gives evidence for the fact that this class is very hard to detect using context-based methods.

The **new unrelated senses** have the lowest time delay of all classes and take between 1.6 – 19.8 years to appear in any unit and only marginally more, 1.9 – 20.0, to appear in the correct form.

Existing senses show an interesting behavior; the existing senses for words that later have a change event have significantly longer average time delays compared to existing senses of stable words, 11.7 compared to 2.7. One possible explanation is that words are less likely to change their meanings, if they are commonly used and hence we cannot find them in our dataset.

For all change events, we find an average delay of 7.1 – 30.7 years for any evidence to appear in a unit and 11.8 – 35.4 for our method to find the change in its correct form (see Sec. 5.1). Including existing senses, all delay times decrease slightly. We consider 7.1 years to appear in a unit a reasonable time delay given the 222 year time span. The delay of 4.7 years (between 7.1 to 11.8) for the change to appear in the correct form could be decreased by optimizing thresholds and merging strategies. To find the reason for the upper limit (30.7 and 35.4 years) we need to use linguists and historians with in depth knowledge of the datasets, time period and place of publication.

6.3 Average Path Length

To further investigate if the stable senses can be differentiated from changing ones, we measure the *average length of a path* as the difference between the earliest to last participating cluster. We find that stable words have statistically significantly longer paths (181 years) than words that change their meanings over time (114 years), clearly differentiating the classes with our method.

7 Discussions

Our units capture 94% of all expected changes. As comparison, a natural baseline is concordances; where we would expect an upper bound close to 100%. For certain words, concordances are enough and can e used to deduce a new sense. However, mostly, an induction mechanism is needed which will result in reduced recall. Therefore, we consider our recall good evidence for the choice of methods for creating clusters and units.

Our similarity measure relies on WordNet that suffers from having a low coverage of older texts.We re-ran our experiments using a modified Jaccard similarity and found small differences that were not statistically significant. We find that set similarity measures can therefore offer a viable option for resource poor languages.

Our method goes beyond those using distributional semantics that embed words to vectors and detect changes by comparing the vectors. These methods can find changes in the dominant sense of a word but cannot differentiate between senses or allow some senses to stay stable while others change. We believe that the future lies in a combined approach, using embeddings (possibly multi-sense embeddings (Trask et al., 2015; Li and Jurafsky, 2015; Pelevina et al., 2016)) and sense-differentiated techniques.

8 Conclusions and Future Work

In this paper, we presented a method for word sense change detection that relies on an existing induction algorithm and uses the induced word senses as a basis for finding coherent senses (units) and grouping units into polysemous concepts (paths). By tracking individual sense changes, we can differentiate a word's changing senses from its stable ones.

On average, 94% of the change events and 95% of all events, including stable senses, were found with a time delay of between 6.3 and 7.1 from the first cluster evidence. Our *all classes* experiment shows how well the different change events can be differentiated. For the evolved sense category, we have a 100% recall. The new unrelated (homonymic) senses yield 80% recall. Only the new related (polysemous) category perform badly; a high-level linguistic relation is not captured in the context of a word.

Our method detected change in the correct form 9.9 – 11.8 years after the first cluster evidence and is the first work to report such time analysis. Given the 222 year timespan, we consider this delay to be a good starting point for future work. Moving forth, we will use a combined approach, utilizing the potential of embeddings with sense-differentiated graph-based techniques.

Acknowledgments

This work has been funded in part by a framework grant *Towards a knowledge-based culturomics*; contract 2012-5738), funding to Swedish CLARIN (*Swe-Clarin*; contract 2013-2003), both awarded by the Swedish Research Council, and by the European Research Council under Alexandria (ERC 339233). We would like to thank Times Newspapers Limited for providing the archive of The Times for our research.

References

Pierpaolo Basile, Annalina Caputo, Roberta Luisi, and Giovanni Semeraro. 2016. Diachronic analysis of the italian language exploiting google ngram. In *Proceedings of Third Italian Conference on Computational Linguistics (CLiC-it 2016)*.

Paul Cook, Jey Han Lau, Diana McCarthy, and Timothy Baldwin. 2014. Novel word-sense identification. In *Proceedings of COLING 2014*. Dublin, Ireland, pages 1624–1635. http://www.aclweb.org/anthology/C14-1154.

Martin C. Cooper. 2005. A Mathematical Model of Historical Semantics and the Grouping of Word Meanings into Concepts. *Computational Linguistics* 32(2):227–248. https://doi.org/10.1162/0891201054223995.

Beate Dorow, Jean-pierre Eckmann, and Danilo Sergi. 2005. Using curvature and markov clustering in graphs for lexical acquisition and word sense discrimination. In *Proceedings of the Workshop MEANING-2005*.

Lea Frermann and Mirella Lapata. 2016. A bayesian model of diachronic meaning change. *TACL* 4:31–45.

Kristina Gulordava and Marco Baroni. 2011. A distributional similarity approach to the detection of semantic change in the Google Books Ngram corpus. In *Proceedings of the GEMS 2011 Workshop on GEometrical Models of Natural Language Semantics*. Association for Computational Linguistics, Stroudsburg, PA, USA, GEMS '11, pages 67–71. http://dl.acm.org/citation.cfm?id=2140490.2140498.

William L. Hamilton, Jure Leskovec, and Dan Jurafsky. 2016. Diachronic word embeddings reveal statistical laws of semantic change. *CoRR* abs/1605.09096. http://arxiv.org/abs/1605.09096.

Yoon Kim, Yi-I Chiu, Kentaro Hanaki, Darshan Hegde, and Slav Petrov. 2014. Temporal analysis of language through neural language models. In *Workshop on Language Technologies and Computational Social Science*.

Vivek Kulkarni, Rami Al-Rfou, Bryan Perozzi, and Steven Skiena. 2015. Statistically significant detection of linguistic change. In *Proceedings of the 24th International Conference on World Wide Web*. ACM, pages 625–635.

Jey Han Lau, Paul Cook, Diana McCarthy, David Newman, and Timothy Baldwin. 2012. Word sense induction for novel sense detection. In *EACL 2012, 13th Conference of the European Chapter of the Association for Computational Linguistics*. pages 591–601. http://aclweb.org/anthology-new/E/E12/E12-1060.pdf.

Jiwei Li and Dan Jurafsky. 2015. Do multi-sense embeddings improve natural language understanding? In *Proceedings of the 2015 Conference on Empirical Methods in Natural Language Processing*. ACL, pages 1722–1732.

Dekang Lin. 1998. Automatic retrieval and clustering of similar words. In *Proceedings of the 36th Annual Meeting of the Association for Computational Linguistics and 17th International Conference on Computational Linguistics - Volume 2*. Association for Computational Linguistics, Stroudsburg, PA, USA, ACL '98, pages 768–774. https://doi.org/10.3115/980691.980696.

Qiaozhu Mei and ChengXiang Zhai. 2005. Discovering evolutionary theme patterns from text: an exploration of temporal text mining. In *Proceedings of the eleventh ACM SIGKDD international conference on Knowledge discovery in data mining*. ACM.

George A. Miller. 1995. Wordnet: A lexical database for english. *Commun. ACM* 38(11):39–41. https://doi.org/10.1145/219717.219748.

Sunny Mitra, Ritwik Mitra, Suman Kalyan Maity, Martin Riedl, Chris Biemann, Pawan Goyal, and Animesh Mukherjee. 2015. An automatic approach to identify word sense changes in text media across timescales. *Natural Language Engineering* 21(05):773–798.

Sunny Mitra, Ritwik Mitra, Martin Riedl, Chris Biemann, Animesh Mukherjee, and Pawan Goyal. 2014. That's sick dude!: Automatic identification of word sense change across different timescales. In *Proceedings of the 52nd Annual Meeting of the Association for Computational Linguistics, ACL 2014 USA*. pages 1020–1029. http://aclweb.org/anthology/P/P14/P14-1096.pdf.

OED. 2000. The Oxford English Dictionary 2nd ed. 1989. OED Online. Oxford University Press. 4 Apr. 2000. http://dictionary.oed.com.

Patrick Pantel and Dekang Lin. 2002. Discovering word senses from text. In *Proceedings of the eighth ACM SIGKDD international conference on Knowledge discovery and data mining (KDD'02)*. ACM, Edmonton, Alberta, Canada, pages 613–619. https://doi.org/10.1145/775047.775138.

Maria Pelevina, Nikolay Arefyev, Chris Biemann, and Alexander Panchenko. 2016. Making sense of word embeddings. In *Proceedings of the 1st Workshop on Representation Learning for NLP*. pages 174–183.

Eyal Sagi, Stefan Kaufmann, and Brady Clark. 2009. Semantic density analysis: comparing word meaning across time and phonetic space. In *Proceedings of the Workshop on Geometrical Models of Natural Language Semantics*. Association for Computational Linguistics, Stroudsburg, PA, USA, GEMS '09, pages 104–111. http://dl.acm.org/citation.cfm?id=1705415.1705429.

Nina Tahmasebi, Kai Niklas, Gideon Zenz, and Thomas Risse. 2013. On the applicability of word sense discrimination on 201 years of modern english. *International Journal on Digital Libraries* 13(3-4):135–153. https://doi.org/10.1007/s00799-013-0105-8.

Nina Tahmasebi and Thomas Risse. 2017. Word Sense Change Test Set. https://doi.org/10.5281/zenodo.495572.

Nina N. Tahmasebi. 2013. *Models and Algorithms for Automatic Detection of Language Evolution*. Ph.D. thesis, Gottfried Wilhelm Leibniz Universitt Hannover. http://edok01.tib.uni-hannover.de/edoks/e01dh13/771705034.pdf.

Andrew Trask, Phil Michalak, and John Liu. 2015. sense2vec - A fast and accurate method for word sense disambiguation in neural word embeddings. *CoRR* abs/1511.06388.

Duncan J. Watts and Steven Strogatz. 1998. Collective dynamics of "small-world" networks. *Nature* 393:440–442.

Derry Tanti Wijaya and Reyyan Yeniterzi. 2011. Understanding semantic change of words over centuries. In *Proceedings of the 2011 international workshop on DETecting and Exploiting Cultural diversiTy on the social web*. ACM, New York, NY, USA, DETECT '11, pages 35–40. https://doi.org/10.1145/2064448.2064475.

WS4J. 2014. WordNet Similarity for Java. `https://code.google.com/p/ws4j/`. [Online; accessed 2014-09-23].

Yating Zhang, Adam Jatowt, and Katsumi Tanaka. 2016. Detecting evolution of concepts based on cause-effect relationships in online reviews. In *Proceedings of the 25th International Conference on World Wide Web*. ACM, pages 649–660.

Streaming Text Analytics for Real-Time Event Recognition

**Philippe Thomas, Johannes Kirschnick, Leonhard Hennig, Renlong Ai,
Sven Schmeier, Holmer Hemsen, Feiyu Xu, Hans Uszkoreit**
Deutsches Forschungszentrum für Künstliche Intelligenz, Germany
`firstname.lastname@dfki.de`

Abstract

A huge body of continuously growing
written knowledge is available on the web
in the form of social media posts, RSS
feeds, and news articles. Real-time information extraction from such high velocity, high volume text streams requires
scalable, distributed natural language processing pipelines. We introduce such a
system for fine-grained event recognition
within the big data framework Flink, and
demonstrate its capabilities for extracting
and geo-locating mobility- and industry-
related events from heterogeneous text
sources. Performance analyses conducted
on several large datasets show that our system achieves high throughput and maintains low latency, which is crucial when
events need to be detected and acted upon
in real-time. We also present promising
experimental results for the event extraction component of our system, which recognizes a novel set of event types. The
demo system is available at `http://
dfki.de/sd4m-sta-demo/`.

1 Introduction

In the last few years text analytics has assumed a
very important role in the area of large scale data
processing, in particular, big data analytics of unstructured textual data. Its applications range from
fulfilling very specific information needs to building up knowledge resources serving a variety of
purposes (e.g. social media monitoring, business
intelligence, and knowledge organization). An important task of text analytics is detection and monitoring of events reported in various texts. For example, mobility providers may wish to better serve
their customers by incorporating real-time infor-

mation about short-term disruptions across the
general mobility infrastructure (e.g. accidents, delays, roadblocks), whereas supply chain managers
require timely information about critical supplier
events (e.g. liquidity problems, strikes, disasters).

While general text analytics pipelines for event
detection focus on detecting and tracking "news
topics", such as earthquakes or crisis events (Allan et al., 1998; Osborne et al., 2014), monitoring fine-grained events, such as strikes at a particular facility of a company, or a traffic accident
on a specific road crossing, raises additional challenges. It requires more extensive linguistic analysis of texts, including named entity recognition
(NER) for non-standard entity types such as roads
or facility locations, entity linking (EL) (Dredze
et al., 2010) and relation extraction (RE) (Mintz
et al., 2009). Furthermore, much larger and more
domain-specific knowledge bases for NER and
EL have to be incorporated, as opposed to existing systems (Ji et al., 2014). For real world
applications, it is also necessary to combine information extracted from unstructured texts with
(semi-)structured information provided by domain
databases such as public transport timetables, and
traffic information systems.

The ever-increasing volume and velocity of textual data available on the web raises additional
challenges from an engineering point of view, especially if we aim for real-time processing. Data
must be processed and transformed "on the fly" so
that, when it reaches a persistent data store, it is
immediately available for querying and interpretation (Orenstein et al., 2015). The system also
needs to be able to handle the burstiness of input
data streams, i.e. it must be capable of adapting
to the high variability in input volume and handle
the resulting back-pressure appropriately. Existing
NLP pipeline frameworks, such as UIMA (Ferrucci and Lally, 2004), often only allow for some

Proceedings of Recent Advances in Natural Language Processing, pages 750–757,
Varna, Bulgaria, Sep 4–6 2017.

degree of parallelization, but are not designed to handle big data streams.

In this paper, we introduce a scalable, distributed linguistic analysis pipeline to detect fine-grained events from heterogeneous text sources. The pipeline's main functionalities include entity recognition, entity linking to well established knowledge bases and event recognition. To ensure scalability, robustness, and near real-time distributed processing, our platform is implemented within the big data analytics framework Flink (Alexandrov et al., 2014). Our contributions in this paper are as follows:

- A linguistic analysis pipeline for detecting and localizing events, including NER for fine-grained and non-standard entity types, and a novel entity linking approach for resolving highly ambiguous geo-entities such as street or train station names
- A scalable, distributed architecture for fault-tolerant processing of data streams in (near) real-time and a performance analysis in terms of throughput and scalability
- Experimental results on the event extraction quality of the pipeline, based on a dataset collected over a 3 month period

Moreover, we will discuss some observations on the performance of our NER, EL and RE approaches (see Section 4).

2 NLP Pipeline

We give an overview of the pipeline architecture, which is shown in Figure 1. The current system is designed to deal with various text types such as Twitter messages, RSS feeds, and web pages, and simultaneously handles German- and English-language documents. For each resource type, an example is shown in Figure 2.

2.1 Preprocessing

Preprocessing consists of the following steps: boilerplate detection, language detection, sentence segmentation and tokenization, POS tagging and dependency parsing.

Due to the high heterogeneity of website contents, processing HTML websites is an inherent challenge. Boilerplate detection is used to retain the main content of an HTML document (Kohlschütter et al., 2010), langid.py (Lui and Baldwin, 2012) for language detection –

Type	Size	Resource	Examples
Company	112,347	Internal	BMW, Bayer AG
City	27,075	OSM	Berlin, Hof
Street	104,598	OSM	Hauptstrasse, A1
Station	9,860	Dt. Bahn	S+U Hauptbahnhof
Route	25,907	Dt. Bahn	ICE 557, U2, M47

Table 1: Named entity types and size of the corresponding gazetteers recognized by our pipeline. *Route* refers to public transport identifiers.

which achieves high accuracy for various text types and short documents. In our current implementation, we focus on English and German documents. POS tagging and dependency parsing is performed by the Mate Tools suite (Bohnet, 2010) for German, and with Stanford CoreNLP (Manning et al., 2014) for English.

2.2 Named Entity Recognition

Table 1 represents the main entity types covered by our system, besides standard types such as date and time expressions. NER is realized by a combination of Stanford CoreNLP (Manning et al., 2014) and the general purpose entity recognition toolkit SProUT (Drozdzynski et al., 2004). SProUT is a rule-based framework that unifies analyzed features of each module (e.g. tokenizer, morphology, and gazetteer) as typed feature structures and applies grammar rules based on regular expressions to recognize entities.

Besides some general rules for recognizing organizations and datetime expressions, we implemented particular rules to deal with frequent morphologic variations of names (e.g. German "Strasse" and "Straße" for "street") and abbreviations (e.g. "Pl." for "Platz" ("place")), as well as special time or date formats often used in RSS feeds and news articles. We construct gazetteers for companies, cities, streets, public transport stations, and routes from existing knowledge resources. The gazetteers store information about naming variants, database identifiers, and geospatial shapes[1]. For geographic entities (i.e., cities and streets) we utilize data from Open-StreetMap (OSM). The public transport datasets provided by Deutsche Bahn AG contain information and geo-shapes for public transport stations, timetables, and interconnecting routes within Germany. The company gazetteer is constructed from

---

[1]Shapes consist of a set of geo-coordinates describing a polygon.

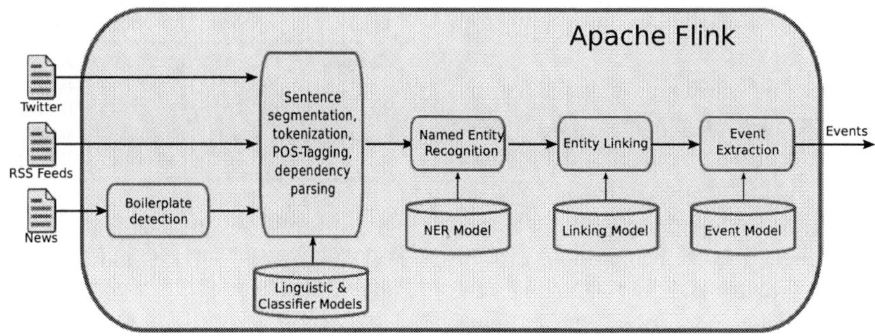

Figure 1: System Architecture

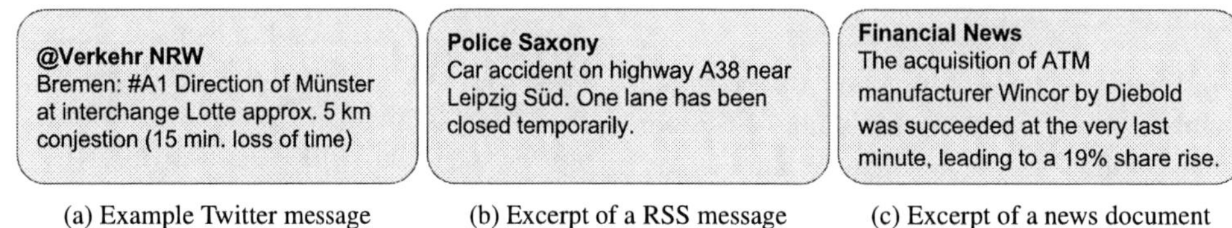

(a) Example Twitter message   (b) Excerpt of a RSS message   (c) Excerpt of a news document

Figure 2: Examples for the three different data sources covered by our pipeline.

a large dataset of enterprises, which includes small and medium-sized enterprises, and thus considerably extends the data available e.g. in Wikipedia or Freebase (Bollacker et al., 2008).

2.3 Entity Linking

An entity linking step is required after NER to disambiguate the recognized candidate entities. Since our system utilizes a large set of company and geo-location entities, entity linking is particularly challenging. For example, many public transport route names are synonymous across German cities (e.g. "S1" for "suburban train line #1" exists in more than 15 metropolitan regions) and street names are also very often re-used in different municipalities (see Table 2).

We implemented a novel geo-location based disambiguation strategy. For ambiguous entities the algorithm chooses the candidate whose coordinates are contained or intersect with the geo-shape of "larger" entities co-occurring in the same text. For example, a street name is typically resolved to the correct database entry by testing if the street's shape is contained in the geo-shape of a city mentioned in the same document. In turn, unambiguous stop or street entities can also sometimes be used to disambiguate other entities, e.g. transit routes, using a similar strategy. In other words, we combine document context and geo-location context to link entity mentions to their

Streetname	# concepts
Hauptstraße	6,889
Schulstraße	5,190
Dorfstraße	5,138
Gartenstraße	4,918
Bahnhofstraße	4,761

Table 2: List of the five most frequently found street names in our dataset of German cities.

correct knowledge base entry.

Additionally, Twitter allows users to tag locations in a message. This can either be a precise location (longitude, latitude) or a general location label (e.g. a city name with geo-shape). In our corpus of more than 3.8 million tweets, we observe 2.7 % to be tagged with a location shape. For tweets with a location label, we prioritize recognized entities within the user tagged region.

We manually identified more than 150 Twitter channels which are frequently used to communicate mobility related information. This includes channels from mobility providers, local radio stations, police departments, and community forums. Overall, approximately 31.21 % of all collected tweets are sent over one of these channels. For each of these channels we manually identified their regions of main interest, usually a list of cities or a county. During linking, we use this information to remove entities located outside of the region of interest.

Name	Arguments
Accident	Street, route, loc, trigger, time
Delay	Street, route, cause, loc, time
Disaster	Type, trigger, casualties, loc, time
Traffic Jam	Street, loc, trigger, direction, time
Rail Replac.	Route, loc, trigger, direction, time
Road Closure	Street, cause, trigger, loc, time
Acquisition	Buyer, acquired, seller, trigger, time
Merger	Old, new, trigger, loc, time
Spin-off	Parent, child, trigger, loc, time
Layoffs	Company, trigger, number, loc, time
Strike	Company, trigger, number, loc, time
Insolvency	Company, trigger, cause, loc, time

Table 3: Event types and their arguments recognized by our pipeline.

2.4 Event Detection

In this work, we define events in the spirit of the definitions of ACE (Automatic Content Extraction) guidelines (Doddington et al., 2004) as n-ary relations with a set of required and optional arguments, including location and time. For example, a *strike* event has a required argument *company*, one or multiple *location* arguments, and an optional argument *time* (see Table 3). We hence use a more fine-grained definition of what constitutes an event than the document-level view typically assumed in topic detection and tracking (Allan et al., 1998).

We detect events by matching dependency parse trees of sentences to relation-specific patterns, as described by Xu et al. (2007). The dependency patterns for each relation are extracted automatically from a set of 2,000 training documents, which have been manually annotated for event type, argument types, and roles. For Twitter, we additionally implement a keyword-based event detection strategy, since dependency parsing is likely to often produce erroneous results given the very informal language of many tweets. We define a set of relation-specific trigger phrases to detect events, which are matched both to hashtags and general tweet text. By carefully selecting the trigger phrase set, we can identify events with high precision. Figure 3 shows a screenshot of our web demo for NER, EL and RE.

3 Stream Processing Architecture

Our system is separated into three distinct functions: document retrieval, processing and annotation, and data storage - which are connected via a distributed message queue system, Kafka[2].

Retrieval is handled by individual data source adapters that fetch a continuous stream of new documents and forward the results into the message bus. This relieves the annotation processor from source specific data handling as well as buffers documents in case of large traffic bursts. A similar, less versatile, message–based architecture, has been presented by Kirschnick and Thomas (2017) for NER in the biomedical domain.

The core processing itself is handled by Apache Flink, a distributed, streaming data flow engine that provides data distribution, communication, and fault tolerant stream computation. We modeled the NLP pipeline within Flink as a series of transformations, that each wrap one NLP aspect. Flink connects to the message bus and forwards each new document through the pipeline. Fault tolerance, using check-pointing, guarantees exactly once processing, avoiding to double process the same document in case of failures. Furthermore, with adaptive back pressure handling, Flink will back off from retrieving new documents when the pipeline itself falls behind in processing, which guarantees the fastest possible processing across all compute nodes.

Together, these frameworks can handle back pressure in case of data stream peaks, and provide high throughput. Our system thus can easily scale to larger and faster data streams than those we currently handle, for example when extending the system to monitor more data streams, other languages, or a wider range of events.

Transformations subsequently enrich an internal document representation whose schema is inspired by the Common Analysis Structure implemented in UIMA. This schema defines major elements, such as sentences, tokens, concepts, relations and generic attributes, including provenance information, consisting of annotator, confidence and license information for traceability. Other annotations are either realized as attributes of these classes, or in a generic fashion using a labeled span scheme. The data schema is extensible and allows us to easily integrate additional annotation components, as well as multiple different annotators for the same annotation type (e.g. when using both Stanford and SProUT for NER). We use Avro[3], a compact binary data format, to efficiently serialize documents between pipeline processing

---

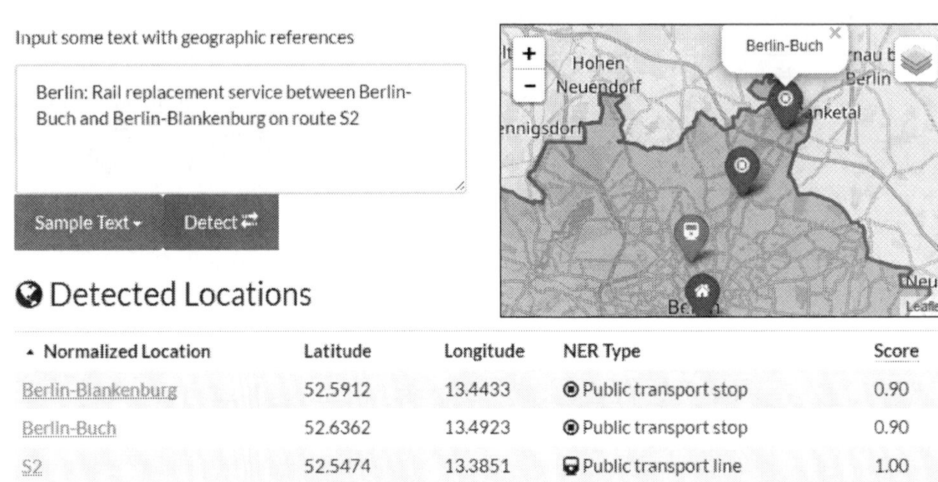

Figure 3: Screenshot of our web based demo system for location detection.

steps.

Finally, annotated documents are pushed back to the message system, where they can be read by multiple consumers. In our implementation we archive all results for offline analysis and index a rolling window of the results for immediate querying through a dashboard. The dashboard can be used to serve alerts and notifications of extracted events in near real-time, as they are happening.

4 Observations and Insights

In this section we share observations made during the development of our linguistic pipeline.

Preprocessing: During preprocessing we observed that boilerplate detection sometimes retains navigational text, which impacts the subsequent linguistic steps. Twitter and RSS feeds are easier to process due to the structured and well-defined format they are provided in (JSON and XML).

Named entity recognition: Our current approach substantially relies on gazetteers and grammatical rules implemented in SProUT. This approach provides some inherent difficulties for NER: First, we are unable to detect specific-type entities not covered by the gazetteers (since Stanford only detects 'larger' locations). To ameliorate this problem, we implemented a fuzzy matching strategy, but lower than desirable recall is still an issue. Second, cross-type ambiguity of e.g. public transport stop names sharing the name with the street or borough they are located in, remains a challenge. For example, "Baumschulenweg" can refer to a public transport train station in Berlin, a street in more than 15 cities,

or a locality in Berlin. Third, we observe a high ambiguity between smaller cities and German nouns, e.g. Regen (rain), Dom (cathedral), or Strom (stream/river, but also electricity). In this work we utilize a blacklist of frequent terms to identify and remove such entities. As an alternative to SProUT, we plan to incorporate conditional random field models (Lafferty et al., 2001), trained for non-standard entity types in the future (Schwarzenberg et al., 2017).

Entity linking: Entity linking is implemented using a geo-location based disambiguation strategy. This strategy works best for documents, mentioning the larger area (e.g. a city) and smaller locations contained within this area in the same sentence. In cases where multiple cities match a named entity, we require a popularity measure to rank target concepts. A simple measure currently implemented is the surface area of a shape. However, this measure can sometimes be misleading in case of relatively large but sparsely populated places (e.g. Frankfurt (Oder) is only 40 % smaller than Frankfurt (Main), but with only 8 % of the inhabitants). A potentially helpful measure is the number of inhabitants in a specific area, which is only provided for approximately 4.6 % of all areas contained in OSM.

Event extraction: Event extraction uses relation-specific dependency patterns for RSS-feeds and news articles. For Twitter we define a set of relation-specific trigger phrases. The latter event detection strategy poses a problem for metaphoric word usage. For instance, *"a landslide victory in Berlin"* would be tagged as nat-

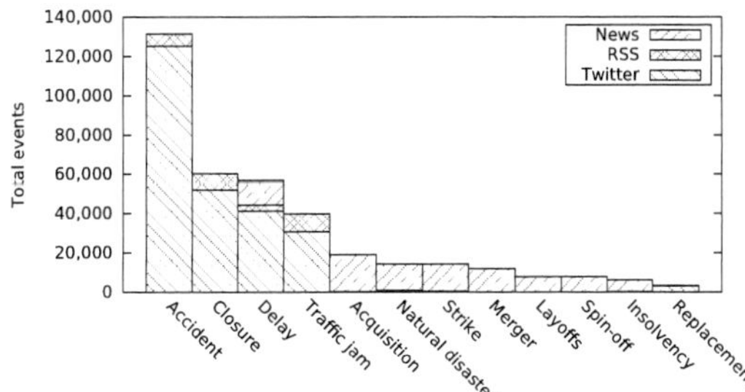

Figure 4: Distribution of extracted events for the three different text sources.

Event type	Twitter	RSS	News	Avg
Traffic jam	0.28	1.0	–	0.64
Strike	0.58	–	0.66	0.62
Delays	0.74	0.94	0.26	0.65
Disaster	0.52	0.94	0.48	0.57
Layoffs	0.66	–	0.76	0.71

Table 4: Precision of event recognition for selected event types. Empty cells indicate that the corresponding event did not occur in the given document type.

ural disaster. Currently, the event extraction module recognizes events and arguments according to the types defined in Table 3. In the next step, we would like to aggregate a detected event into a geospatial representation. For instance, a traffic jam event on the motorway A9 between Munich and Eching should be reduced to this specific section, and not the full length of the highway.

5 Relation Extraction Experiments

We applied our pipeline to a dataset of 3,789,803 tweets, 412,652 RSS feeds, and 860,307 news documents collected in the time period of Jan 1st, 2016 to March 31st, 2016. Figure 4 visualizes the distribution of the 12 different event types across all sources. The largest proportion of events is extracted from Twitter messages, which also constitutes the majority of all processed documents. Company related events are mostly extracted from news documents, while mobility related events are almost exclusively detected in Twitter and RSS feeds.

For each event type, we manually judge the correctness of a random sample of 50 documents per source (if available for a given relation). Documents were considered to *correctly* state an event if their text explicitly reported the event, regard-

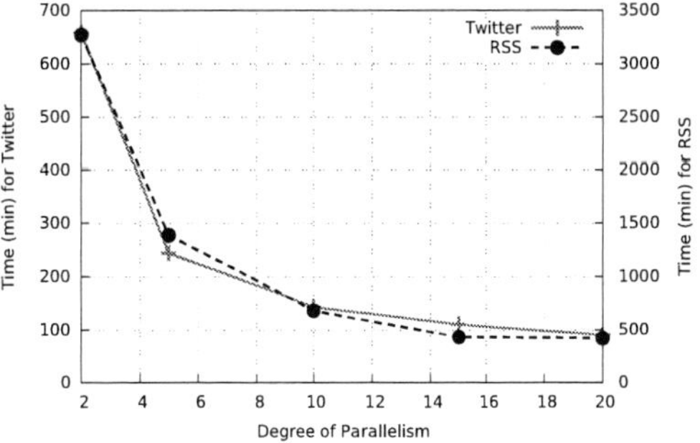

Figure 5: Experiment runtime with varying degrees of parallelism on the testing corpus.

less of whether it was ongoing, took place in the past, or was announced for the future (e.g. in the case of strikes). Events that were only implied were labeled as *incorrect*. Table 4 lists the precision scores of a subset of the events, for all three sources and micro-averaged across sources.

Best results are generally observed for RSS feeds. This is an expected result, as we selectively collect only RSS feeds from traffic information sources. Some event types are more reliably observed in specific sources, e.g. *Strike* and *Layoffs* in news. The overall accuracy of event recognition on Twitter is surprisingly high, with the exception of *Traffic Jam* events. This, however, can be attributed to the fact that the keyphrase pattern approach employed for Twitter used the German word "Stau" ("jam"), which is often used in other, non-traffic contexts to denote slow or halting progress. On average, 64% of the identified events are judged to be correct.

6 Performance and Scalability

To assess the performance of our system we selected 2,875,000 Tweets and 3,093,456 RSS messages, corresponding to a weekly data sample.

We first measured the time that each individual step of the processing pipeline takes, to assess the latency that an ideal streaming pipeline would possess. This determines the delay between message acquisition and availability for querying or inspection of downstream systems. Overall, RSS documents contain more text, and thus incur higher processing costs, compared to the much shorter Twitter messages. On average, our pipeline takes roughly $1s$ to process a RSS document and $250ms$ for a Twitter message.

We are also interested in the scaling properties

of distributing the processing across multiple machines. We observed that the volume of messages is not constant across each source, instead these sources show a bursty behavior. Large events, for example, can generate huge temporary spikes in message volume – but at the same time we would like to retain the ability to process all messages in near real-time by scaling out. The experiment setup consisted of a cluster of 4 machines (32 logical CPUs and 256 GB RAM each), running Ubuntu 14.04 and Flink v1.1.2. We varied the degree of parallelism by specifying the number of task managers that Flink could utilize to distribute the processing and measured the overall runtime to process each dataset sample.

Figure 5 shows the results of the scaling experiment, varying the parallelisms from 2 to 20. For both datasets the processing time drops significantly when more and more tasks managers are added. The performance gains are smaller for larger degrees of parallelism, due to a corresponding increase in communication costs between worker nodes. In the highest setting, we measured a throughput of 530 docs/sec and 123 docs/sec for Twitter and RSS respectively.

The price for the gained throughput is a modest processing overhead introduced by Flink itself as well as the time it takes to transport the documents over the network. With 20 task managers we observed an overall processing overhead of 10%.

7 Related Work

The ReDites real-time event detection and tracking system presented by Osborne et al. (2014) focuses on events from the security domain, and uses Twitter as its sole data source. As our system, it is fully automatic, geo-locates events, and supports multiple languages. Its scope, however, does not encompass deep linguistic analyses of input documents for NER, EL and RE, since it uses a shallow definition of event detection in the spirit of Topic Detection and Tracking (TDT). The system can therefore not be used e.g. for knowledge base population. Other TDT-like systems include Trend Miner (Preoţiuc-Pietro and Cohn, 2013) and the Social Sensor system (Aiello et al., 2013).

Most similar to our system is the approach presented by Tanev et al. (2008). Their system also extracts ACE-style events together with their arguments from news texts. They utilize, in their own words, a 'linguistically poor' approach that relies on simple 1 and 2-slot extraction patterns that are acquired by bootstrapping. The system focuses on security-related events, employs TDT-style clustering techniques, but for efficiency reasons processes only the first sentence of each document. Our system scales to full documents, and can hence detect a much larger set of events from each document. Piskorski and Atkinson (2011) later extend the approach of Tanev et al. to more fine-grained event schemas, and to support event detection in 7 languages.

8 Conclusion

In this work we introduced a system for scalable, realtime event extraction. Our system currently implements both German and English analysis pipelines that include components for NER, EL and RE. It processes different input text data streams, including high-volume, high-velocity sources such as Twitter, but also continuous crawls of web documents and RSS feeds. A performance analysis conducted on several large datasets shows that processing large volumes in near-realtime is possible when running on the distributed stream processing platform Flink – not only achieving high throughput, but also maintaining low latency, crucial when extracted events need to be monitored and acted upon. The demo is available at `http://dfki.de/sd4m-sta-demo/`.

We find that linking fine-grained geo-entities (such as street or route names) is especially challenging, and will require better models. Furthermore, in future work we would like to extend our relation extraction component to handle more relations and event types, and to correctly distinguish between factual and future (or rumored) events, such as for example planned road works, or company acquisition offers.

Acknowledgments

This research was partially supported by the German Federal Ministry of Economics and Energy (BMWi) through the projects SDW (01MD15010A) and SD4M (01MD15007B), and by the German Federal Ministry of Education and Research (BMBF) through the project BBDC (01IS14013E).

References

L. M. Aiello, G. Petkos, C. Martin, D. Corney, S. Papadopoulos, R. Skraba, A. Gker, I. Kompatsiaris, and A. Jaimes. 2013. Sensing Trending Topics in Twitter. *IEEE Transactions on Multimedia* 15(6):1268–1282.

A. Alexandrov, R. Bergmann, S. Ewen, J. Freytag, F. Hueske, A. Heise, O. Kao, M. Leich, U. Leser, V. Markl, F. Naumann, M. Peters, A. Rheinländer, M. Sax, S. Schelter, Ma. Höger, K. Tzoumas, and D. Warneke. 2014. The Stratosphere Platform for Big Data Analytics. *The VLDB Journal* 23(6).

J. Allan, J. Carbonell, G. Doddington, J. Yamron, and Y. Yang. 1998. Topic detection and tracking pilot study: Final report. In *Proc. of DARPA Broadcast News Transcription and Understanding Workshop*.

B. Bohnet. 2010. Top accuracy and fast dependency parsing is not a contradiction. In *Proc. of COLING*. pages 89–97.

K. Bollacker, C. Evans, P. Paritosh, T. Sturge, and J. Taylor. 2008. Freebase: A Collaboratively Created Graph Database for Structuring Human Knowledge. In *Proc. of SIGMOD*. pages 1247–1250.

G. Doddington, A. Mitchell, M. Przybocki, L. Ramshaw, S. Strassel, and R. Weischedel. 2004. The Automatic Content Extraction (ACE) Program - Tasks, Data, and Evaluation. In *Proc. of LREC*.

M. Dredze, P. McNamee, D. Rao, A. Gerber, and T. Finin. 2010. Entity disambiguation for knowledge base population. In *Proc.of COLING 2010*.

W. Drozdzynski, H. Krieger, J. Piskorski, U. Schäfer, and F. Xu. 2004. Shallow processing with unification and typed feature structures — foundations and applications. *Künstliche Intelligenz* 1:17–23.

D. Ferrucci and A. Lally. 2004. UIMA: An architectural approach to unstructured information processing in the corporate research environment. *Nat. Lang. Eng.* 10(3–4):327–348.

H. Ji, J. Nothman, and B. Hachey. 2014. Overview of TAC-KBP2014 Entity Discovery and Linking Tasks. In *Proc. of the Text Analysis Conference*.

J. Kirschnick and P. Thomas. 2017. SIA: Scalable Interoperable Annotation Server. In *Proc. of BeCalm*. pages 138–145.

C. Kohlschütter, P. Fankhauser, W. Nejdl, C. Kohlschütter, P. Fankhauser, and W. Nejdl. 2010. Boilerplate Detection Using Shallow Text Features. In *Proc. of WSDM*. pages 441–450.

J. D. Lafferty, A McCallum, and F .C. N. Pereira. 2001. Conditional Random Fields: Probabilistic Models for Segmenting and Labeling Sequence Data. In *Proc. of ICML*. pages 282–289.

M. Lui and T. Baldwin. 2012. langid.py: An off-the-shelf language identification tool. In *Proc. of ACL: System Demonstrations*. pages 25–30.

C. D. Manning, M. Surdeanu, J. Bauer, J. Finkel, S. J. Bethard, and D. McClosky. 2014. The Stanford CoreNLP Natural Language Processing Toolkit. In *Proc. of ACL: System Demonstrations*. pages 55–60.

M. Mintz, S. Bills, R. Snow, and D. Jurafsky. 2009. Distant Supervision for Relation Extraction Without Labeled Data. In *Proc. of ACL-IJCNLP*. pages 1003–1011.

G. Orenstein, C. Doherty, K. White, and S. Camiña. 2015. *Building Real-Time Data Pipelines*. O'Reilly.

M. Osborne, S. Moran, R. McCreadie, A. Von Lunen, M. Sykora, E. Cano, N. Ireson, C. Macdonald, I. Ounis, Y. He, T. Jackson, F. Ciravegna, and A. O'Brien. 2014. Real-time detection, tracking, and monitoring of automatically discovered events in social media. In *Proc. of ACL: System Demonstrations*.

J. Piskorski and M. Atkinson. 2011. Frontex real-time news event extraction framework. In *Proc. of KDD*. KDD '11, pages 749–752.

D. Preoţiuc-Pietro and T. Cohn. 2013. A temporal model of text periodicities using gaussian processes. In *Proc. of EMNLP*. pages 977–988.

R. Schwarzenberg, L. Hennig, and H. Hemsen. 2017. In-Memory Distributed Training of Linear-Chain Conditional Random Fields, with an Application to Fine-Grained Named Entity Recognition. In *Proc. of GSCL*.

H. Tanev, J. Piskorski, and M. Atkinson. 2008. Real-time news event extraction for global crisis monitoring. In *Proc. of NLDB 2008*. pages 207–218.

F. Xu, H. Uszkoreit, and H. Li. 2007. A Seed-driven Bottom-up Machine Learning Framework for Extracting Relations of Various Complexity. In *Proc. of ACL*. pages 584–591.

An Eye-tracking Study of Named Entity Annotation

Tokunaga, Takenobu[†]   **Nishikawa, Hitoshi**[†]   **Iwakura, Tomoya**[‡]

[†]Tokyo Institute of Technology
{take, hitoshi}@c.titech.ac.jp

[‡]Fujitsu Laboratories LTD.
iwakura.tomoya@jp.fujitsu.com

Abstract

Utilising effective features in machine learning-based natural language processing (NLP) is crucial in achieving good performance for a given NLP task. The paper describes a pilot study on the analysis of eye-tracking data during named entity (NE) annotation, aiming at obtaining insights into effective features for the NE recognition task. The eye gaze data were collected from 10 annotators and analysed regarding working time and fixation distribution. The results of the preliminary qualitative analysis showed that human annotators tend to look at broader contexts around the target NE than recent state-of-the-art automatic NE recognition systems and to use predicate argument relations to identify the NE categories.

1 Introduction

Corpus-based natural language processing (NLP) has been the mainstream of NLP research for the past quarter of a century. In this approach, given a task and manually annotated answers in a corpus, machine learning (ML) techniques are employed to induce a system for the task. The system adopts various kinds of information in the texts for solving the task, which is represented as a set of features for the ML algorithm. These features have often been determined based on heuristics such as adopting words and their POS within a certain size of a window around target words. Features based on human linguistic knowledge have also been employed through referring to manually constructed linguistic resources such as Word-Net (Miller, 1995) and linguistic theories such as Centring Theory (Grosz et al., 1995).

Unlike the past attempts, we explore effective features in human behaviour during their annotation of answers in corpora. Considering an NLP system as a replacement of annotators, the replacement could follow the human annotators on their annotation behaviour as well as their annotation results. The information that human annotators refer to during their annotation process would provide useful clues to find effective features for the ML algorithms.

Recently utilising human behaviour information, particularly eye gaze information in various NLP tasks has begun attracting attention. The target tasks are diverse, including word sense disambiguation (Joshi et al., 2013), named entity recognition (Tomanek et al., 2010), syntactic analysis (Barrett and Søgaard, 2015), coreference resolution (Ross et al., 2016), predicate argument structure analysis (Iida et al., 2013; Mitsuda et al., 2013; Maki et al., 2016), sentiment analysis (Joshi et al., 2014), sentence compression (Klerke et al., 2016) and translation (Mishra et al., 2013; Sajjad et al., 2016).

In the present work, following Tomanek et al. (2010), we adopt the named entity (NE) recognition task. Having been motivated to select difficult training instances for active learning, Tomanek et al. (2010) utilised annotator eye gaze during their annotation of NEs in texts. They tried to define "difficulty" of NE instances regarding a cognitive load for annotating each NE instance. Annotation time and eye gaze were used for explaining the cognitive load. By relating the cognitive load of NE instances to their linguistic characteristics, they extracted features for a regression model estimating the difficulty of NE instances. In their attempt the resolution of eye gaze was very coarse, i.e. four regions around a target NE word (above, left, right and below) in addition to the target word itself, and eye gaze data was not fully quantitatively utilised for estimating the cognitive load.

Proceedings of Recent Advances in Natural Language Processing, pages 758–764,
Varna, Bulgaria, Sep 4–6 2017.

The main advances of our work over Tomanek et al. (2010) are twofold. (1) We collect eye gaze on more precise regions, i.e. phrase chunks instead of the coarse regions around a target word. (2) We try to find effective features for solving the task itself instead of selecting training instances for the task. In what follows, we report a data collection experiment in which annotator eye gaze during their annotation are collected (section 2) and results of a preliminary qualitative analysis of the collected data (section 3).

2 Data Collection

2.1 Materials and Procedure

We conducted an experiment for collecting annotator eye gaze and tool operations during the annotation of NEs in Japanese texts. The material for annotation was selected from the development data of the IREX named entity recognition task[1] consisting of 1,279 Japanese news articles. The named entities in these articles have been manually annotated with one of 8 categories: person, location, organisation, artefact, date, time, money and percent.

All articles were processed by a Japanese syntactic analyser KNP 4.11[2] to automatically annotate the NE categories in the texts. To collect difficult NE instances for the automatic NE recognition system, we compared the human-annotated categories and the KNP's outputs and extracted incorrectly annotated instances for four kinds of categories: person, location, organisation and artefact, which were more difficult than the rest. By selecting a single incorrectly annotated NE for each text, we made a set of texts consisting of 72 texts each of which included only a single NE target. The average length of the texts is 315 characters, which is roughly equivalent to 150 English words. The numbers of each NE category are 11 persons, 15 locations, 29 organisations and 17 artefacts.

We recruited sixteen Japanese native speakers, six males and ten females; ten of them had some experience of text annotation but not necessarily the NE annotation. After having been explained the objective of the experiment and the operation of a custom-made annotation tool, the participants were instructed to assign one of the following categories to a highlighted NE in each text.

---

[1] http://nlp.cs.nyu.edu/irex/Package/IREXfinalB.tar.gz
[2] http://nlp.ist.i.kyoto-u.ac.jp/?KNP

⟨PSN⟩ person or pseudo-person name

⟨LOC⟩ location names, addresses and name of natural things such as rivers and mountains

⟨ORG⟩ organisation names, group names etc.

⟨ART⟩ name of artefacts such as products, service

⟨OTH⟩ none of the above

⟨UKW⟩ unable to decide

The participant gaze during annotation was captured by the Tobii T60 eye tracker at intervals of 1/60 second. The display size was $1,280 \times 1,024$ pixels, and the distance between the display and participant's eyes was maintained at about 50 cm. A text on display was presented with the MS Gothic font at the size of 24×24 pixels in black colour with a white background. The line space was set to 72 pixels, and the top, left and right margins were set to 96 pixels respectively. A target NE was highlighted with a yellow background.

The text set was divided into two annotation sets each of which contains 36 texts. All participants had two sessions for these two sets in the same order. Since we had a small number of participants, we did not consider counterbalancing the text order. We allowed the participants to take a break as much as needed between the sessions. Before starting the actual sessions, the participants annotated five texts for practice which were not included in the annotation sets. The five-point calibration was run before starting each session.

A session starts with showing a marker at the centre of the display for guiding the annotator eye gaze to the display centre. Clicking the marker shows a text with a highlighted target NE to annotate. When the participant decides on its category, they click the target NE and choose its category from a pop-up menu shown at the target. Choosing a category makes the display back to the centred marker screen. This cycle goes on until the 36th text in a session. Three click time points: a click on the marker, a click on the target and a click on a category, were recorded for each text.

This task design is simplified than actual NE annotation in two respects: the task concerns only NE category classification without NE span identification, and a single target NE is specified in a text at a time. This simplification enables us to directly relate the annotator eye gaze and their decision process on the category for the target NE; thus it makes the analysis of the collected data easier.

Table 1: Annotator Accuracy

annotator	01	02	04	08	10	11	12	13	14	15	ave.
accuracy	0.82	0.75	0.88	0.79	0.89	0.92	0.89	0.65	0.82	0.92	0.83

Table 2: Distribution of NEs over their Error Rate

error rate	0.0	0.1	0.2	0.3	0.4	0.5	0.6	0.7	0.8	0.9	1.0
#NEs	32	12	10	9	3	0	2	0	0	2	2

2.2 Results

Recent eye-tracking devices like Tobii have made it drastically easier to capture gaze positions. However, there remain eye-tracking errors in the experiments. Tobii delivers the gaze point regarding the display coordinates of both eyes separately together with the timestamp and the error code denoting the validity of the gaze point. Based on the Tobii's error code of each gaze point, we selected the data from the participants fulfilling the following conditions:

- the total error rate (total number of the erroneous gaze points against the number of overall gaze points in the two sessions) is less than 15%, and

- more than half texts have the text-wise error rate less than 10%.

As a result, we discarded data from six participants, retaining the data from ten. The six participants have annotation experience, and the rest four do not.

3 Data Analysis

3.1 Accuracy of Annotators

Table 1 shows the accuracy of each annotator, i.e. the ratio of the correct annotations by each annotator against the overall 72 NEs. The underlined annotators in Table 1 have some annotation experience but not necessarily the NE annotation. The table shows that past annotation experience does not necessarily work favourably. The average annotator accuracy is 0.83, which looks not so high comparing to the performance of the state-of-the-art automatic NE recognition systems (Iwakura, 2011; Darwish, 2013; Passos et al., 2014). However, considering that we collected NE instances that could not be correctly analysed by the automatic NE tagger, humans perform the NE recognition task far better than computers.

Table 3: Distribution of Working Time on NE

duration (sec)	T1	T1+T2	duration (sec)	T2
(0, 4]	18	2	(0, 1]	0
(4, 8]	27	34	(1, 2]	30
(8, 12]	15	15	(2, 3]	19
(12, 16]	10	12	(3, 4]	15
(16, 20]	1	7	(4, 5]	6
(20, 24]	0	0	(5, 6]	0
(24, 28]	0	1	(6, 7]	1
(28, 32]	0	0	(7, 8]	0
(32, 36]	0	0	(8, 9]	1
(36, 40]	0	0		
(40, 44]	1	1		

Table 4: Average Working Time for each Response Type

response	T1		T2		
	ave.	SD	ave.	SD	N
correct	6.7	7.4	2.2	2.3	599
incorrect	9.0	9.0	4.0	3.5	63
$\langle$OTH$\rangle$	11.5	12.8	6.0	6.1	51
$\langle$UKW$\rangle$	32.5	9.7	2.5	0.5	7

Table 2 shows the number of NEs according to their error rate. The error rate of an NE is defined by the ratio of the correctly responding annotators for the NE against the overall ten annotators. The greater error rate value indicates more difficult NEs. The table indicates that the most NEs are easy for a human to identify their category.

3.2 Working Time

Table 3 shows the distribution of average working time on each NE, in which T1 indicates a duration from clicking a start marker until clicking a target NE, T2 indicates a duration from clicking the NE until selecting its category. Comparing the distribution between T1 and T2, we can find that the distribution of T1 is more diffused than that of T2. Their standard deviations over the NE instances are 7.80 for T1 and 3.20 for T2. Considering this difference, we can assume that decision on the category is mostly made in T1. The Pearson's correlation coefficient between the NE error rate and the average T1 was calculated, resulting in a positive correlation (0.47; $p < 0.00005$), i.e.

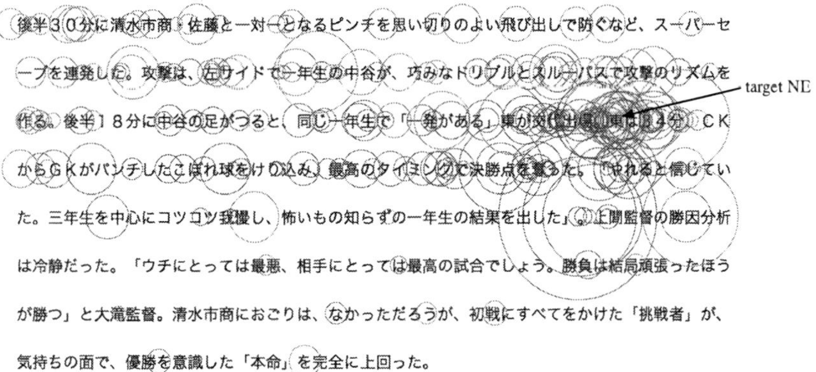

Figure 1: Example of Fixations

the annotators tend to make mistakes for the NEs that require longer T1. There was no significant difference in T1 across the NE categories.

We further investigated the average working time for each type of responses: correct response, incorrect response, response with ⟨OTH⟩ and response with ⟨UKW⟩ as shown in Table 4. The table shows a tendency that annotators need more time when they make mistakes and choose ⟨OTH⟩ and ⟨UKW⟩ categories than when they correctly choose the category. Moreover, short T2 in cases for the correct response and ⟨UKW⟩ selection indicates that they already made a decision during T1, while longer T2 in the incorrect response and ⟨OTH⟩ selection indicates the annotators are still wondering during T2.

3.3 Preprocessing Eye-gaze Data

Eye-gaze data, a sequence of display coordinates with the timestamp, were grouped into gaze fixations based on their spatial and temporal closeness (Richardson et al., 2007). We used the Dispersion-Threshold Identification (I-DT) algorithm (Salvucci and Goldberg, 2000) for clustering eye-gaze data into a sequence of fixations. The I-DT algorithm has two parameters: spatial and temporal; considering the experimental configurations, i.e. (i) the display size and resolution, (ii) the distance between the display and the annotator's eyes, and (iii) the eye-tracker resolution, the spatial parameter was set to 24 pixels, and the temporal parameter was set to 100 msec following Richardson et al. (2007).

The current eye-tracking technology is more error-prone in the vertical direction than in the horizontal direction. Several methods for error correction in fixation coordinates have been proposed (Mishra et al., 2012; Cohen, 2013; Carl, 2013). They employ, however, task specific heuristics and are not necessarily applicable to our current task (Carl et al., 2008). To compensate tracking errors in the vertical direction, we took larger line spaces than usual, i.e. three character heights, and utilised a simple heuristics that a fixation located between lines was forced to aligned to the nearest line. We did not conduct any error correction for the horizontal direction.

Figure 1 shows fixations mapped on a text, where a circle indicates a fixation with its radius representing duration and its centre representing the centre of gravity of all gaze points belonging to the fixation cluster. The circle colour indicates different annotator groups, which are described later. The temporal information, i.e. a chronological sequence of fixations, is not presented in this figure. The target NE is highlighted with a yellow background (the 8th character from the right in the third line). The fixation on a word in texts is widely believed to have some relation with a cognitive process on that word (Just and Carpenter, 1980).

3.4 Distribution of Fixations

It is common to use a local context around the target NE for identifying its category in recent state-of-the-art automatic NE recognition. To be more concrete, surface strings and POS of the target NE and its neighbouring two words have been reported to be effective for NE recognition in many languages, e.g. English (Passos et al., 2014), Arabic (Darwish, 2013), and Japanese (Iwakura, 2011). We investigated to what extent a human also relies on the local context in the NE recog-

Table 5: Fixation Ratio in Local Contexts during T1

window width	± 1 chunk		± 2 chunks	
type/token	type	token	type	token
fixation frequency	0.24	0.34	0.31	0.41
fixation duration	0.24	0.38	0.31	0.44

nition. Since our target texts were in Japanese, we firstly segmented texts into phrasal chunks called *bunsetu* consisting of a sequence of content words followed by function words. We used an off-the-shelf analyser CaboCha[3] for the segmentation. Every fixation was then aligned to a chunk if the fixation centre fell within that chunk's bounding box on display. The average length of the chunks is 4.7 characters in our text set. Since the parafoveal vision in reading Japanese texts is reported to range from five to seven characters (Ikeda and Saida, 1978; Osaka, 1992) and a Japanese *bunsetu* is a basic unit for a grammatical role, it is reasonable to deal *bunsetu* chunks as the fixation target.

Table 5 shows the ratio of fixations locating within one or two chunks in both sides of the target NE during the T1 period, i.e. a duration from clicking the target until selecting its category. Assuming a word consists of two characters, a single chunk roughly corresponds to two words. We can see that only 24% in type and less than 40% in token of fixations are located within one chunk ($\sim$ two words) of both sides. Here the "token" column counts the fixated chunk tokens, while the "type" column counts the fixated chunk types. Even with the doubled context, i.e. two chunks wide, this ratio does not rise significantly. This observation suggests that a human tends to look at broader contexts than the automatic NE recognition, and this difference might suggest clues to improve the performance of the automatic NE recognition.

3.5 Fixations for Correct Annotation

We investigated the difference in fixation distribution between the annotators who correctly identified the NE category and those who did not. As shown in Table 2, the most NEs were correctly annotated by almost all the annotators, i.e. many NEs have small error rate values. To collect the NEs on which the numbers of correct and incorrect annotations are comparable, we chose the 14

NEs the error rate of which ranges from 0.3 to 0.6 for the further analysis. To see the difference of fixations between the correct and incorrect annotator groups, we calculated the number of fixations and the sum of fixation duration on each chunk normalised by the number of annotators in each group. Having investigated the differences of these metrics, we observed the following tendencies.

First, in nine out of the 14 NEs, the correct annotator group tends to look at the predicate that takes the target NE as an argument, and other argument chunks that share the same predicate with the target NE argument more than the incorrect annotator group. This suggests that predicate argument relations involving the target NEs would provide effective information for identifying NE categories. For instance, in Figure 1, the colour of the fixations denotes the corresponding annotator groups: correct one (blue) and incorrect one (red). The target NE is located in the right part of the third line. This example illustrates that the correct group looks at the succeeding context which includes several predicates having the target NE as a nominative argument, while the incorrect group looks at the preceding context where there is no chunk having predicate argument relations with the target NE. This observation is consistent with the result by Sasano and Kurohashi (2008) that empirically showed the effectiveness of dependency relations for named entity recognition.

Second, the range of fixation distribution is not decisive for the correct annotation. The broad look is necessary for the correct annotation in some cases, but concentrated fixations in a local context around the target NE do not necessarily suggest incorrect annotations. There are cases in which the annotators are biased toward an incorrect category because of the local context containing decisive clues for that category, although the correct one can only be found by referring to broader contexts. On the other hand, there are cases that the correct category is impossible to be guessed even having read the whole text. Such cases crucially require annotator's background knowledge for the correct annotation.

4 Concluding Remarks

This paper described a pilot study on the analysis of eye-tracking data during named entity (NE) annotation. The results revealed potential usefulness

---

[3] http://taku910.github.io/cabocha/

of eye gaze data in designing an effective feature set for the NE recognition. Particularly it showed that human annotators tend to use predicate argument relations, and they look at broad contexts around the target NEs. It would be interesting to see to what extent the latter tendency, i.e. considering broader contexts, could be captured by the recent LSTM-based NE methods (Ma and Hovy, 2016; Chiu and Nichols, 2016).

However, this study remains in its pilot phase because of the limitation of the collected data size. To confirm the present preliminary results, analysis with larger data would be indispensable. At the same time, selection of NE instances to be annotated in the data collection should be designed carefully. In the present study, we used the NE instances that were not correctly analysed with one of the state-of-art NE recognition systems. The eye gaze data for the NE instances that can be correctly analysed by the systems should also be collected and analysed. Because of the limited data size, we have not conducted analysis on a chronological sequence of fixations. That kind of analysis is also necessary with large scale data.

Other future research direction includes concretising the feature design and the evaluation of its effectiveness through NE recognition systems. Also, a further analysis of the eye gaze data is necessary for other potential purposes such as improving annotator expertise by comparing the gaze patterns of novice and expert annotators and enhancing the usability of annotation tools.

Acknowledgement

This work was supported by JSPS KAKENHI Grant Number JP16H02865.

References

Maria Barrett and Anders Søgaard. 2015. Using reading behavior to predict grammatical functions. In *Proceedings of the Sixth Workshop on Cognitive Aspects of Computational Language Learning*. pages 1–5.

Michael Carl. 2013. Dynamic programming for remapping noisy fixations in translation tasks. *Journal of Eye Movement Research* 6(5):1–11.

Michael Carl, Arnt Lykke Jakobse, and Oleg Spakov. 2008. Towards an annotation standard for eye tracking data. In *Proceedings of Measuring Behavior*. page 223.

Jason P.C. Chiu and Eric Nichols. 2016. Named entity recognition with bidirectional LSTM-CNNs. *Transactions of the Association for Computational Linguistics* 4:357–370.

Andrew L. Cohen. 2013. Software for the automatic correction of recorded eye fixation locations in reading experiments. *Behavior Research Methods* 45(3):679–683.

Kareem Darwish. 2013. Named entity recognition using cross-lingual resources: Arabic as an example. In *Proceedings of the 51st Annual Meeting of the Association for Computational Linguistics (ACL 2013)*. pages 1558–1567.

Barbara J. Grosz, Aravind K. Joshi, and Scott Weinstein. 1995. Centering: A framework for modeling the local coherence of discourse. *Computational Linguistics* 21(2):203–225.

Ryu Iida, Koh Mitsuda, and Takenobu Tokunaga. 2013. Investigation of annotator's behaviour using eye-tracking data. In *Proceedings of the 7th Linguistic Annotation Workshop and Interoperability with Discourse*. pages 214–222. http://www.aclweb.org/anthology/W13-2326.

Mitsuo Ikeda and Shinya Saida. 1978. Span of recognition in reading. *Vision Research* 18(1):83–88. https://doi.org/10.1016/0042-6989(78)90080-9.

Tomoya Iwakura. 2011. A named entity recognition method using rules acquired from unlabeled data. In *Recent Advances in Natural Language Processing, (RANLP 2011)*. pages 170–177.

Aditya Joshi, Abhijit Mishra, Nivvedan Senthamilselvan, and Pushpak Bhattacharyya. 2014. Measuring sentiment annotation complexity of text. In *Proceedings of the 52nd Annual Meeting of the Association for Computational Linguistics (ACL 2014)*. pages 36–41.

Salil Joshi, Diptesh Kanojia, and Pushpak Bhattacharyya. 2013. More than meets the eye: Study of human cognition in sense annotation. In *Proceedings of the 2013 Conference of the North American Chapter of the Association for Computational Linguistics: Human Language Technologies (NAACL-HLT 2013)*. pages 733–738.

Marcel Adam Just and Patricia A. Carpenter. 1980. A theory of reading: From eye fixations to comprehension. *Psychological Review* 87(4):329–354.

Sigrid Klerke, Yoav Goldberg, and Anders Søgaard. 2016. Improving sentence compression by learning to predict gaze. In *Proceedings of the 2016 Conference of the North American Chapter of the Association for Computational Linguistics: Human Language Technologies*. pages 1528–1533. http://www.aclweb.org/anthology/N16-1179.

Xuezhe Ma and Eduard Hovy. 2016. End-to-end sequence labeling via bi-directional LSTM-CNNs-CRF. In *Proceedings of the 54th Annual Meeting of the Association for Computational Linguistics (ACL 2016)*. pages 1064–1074. http://www.aclweb.org/anthology/P16-1101.

Ryosuke Maki, Hitoshi Nishikawa, and Takenobu Tokunaga. 2016. Parameter estimation of japanese predicate argument structure analysis model using eye gaze information. In *Proceedings of the 26th International Conference on Computational Linguistics (Coling 2016)*. pages 2861–2869.

George A. Miller. 1995. WordNet: a lexical database for English. *Communications of the ACM* 38(11):39–41. https://doi.org/10.1145/219717.219748.

Abhijit Mishra, Pushpak Bhattacharyya, and Michael Carl. 2013. Automatically predicting sentence translation difficulty. In *Proceedings of the 51st Annual Meeting of the Association for Computational Linguistics (ACL 2013)*. pages 346–351.

Abhijit Mishra, Michael Carl, and Pushpak Bhattacharya. 2012. A heuristic-based approach for systematic error correction of gaze data for reading. In *Proceedings of the First Workshop on Eye-tracking and Natural Language Processing*. pages 71–80.

Koh Mitsuda, Ryu Iida, and Takenobu Tokunaga. 2013. Detecting missing annotation disagreement using eye gaze information. In *Proceedings of the 11th Workshop on Asian Language Resources*. pages 19–26.

Naoyuki Osaka. 1992. Size of saccade and fixation duration of eye movements during reading: Psychophysics of japanese text processing. *Journal of Optical Society of America* 9(1):5–13.

Alexandre Passos, Vineet Kumar, and Andrew McCallum. 2014. Lexicon infused phrase embeddings for named entity resolution. In *Proceedings of the 18th Conference on Computational Natural Language Learning (CoNLL 2014)*. pages 78–86.

Daniel C. Richardson, Rick Dale, and Michael J. Spivey. 2007. Eye movements in language and cognition: A brief introduction. In Monica Gonzalez-Marquez, Irene Mittelberg, Seana Coulson, and Michael J. Spivey, editors, *Methods in Cognitive Linguistics*, John Benjamins., pages 323–344.

Joe Cheri Ross, Abhijit Mishra, and Pushpak Bhattacharyya. 2016. Leveraging annotators' gaze behaviour for coreference resolution. In *Proceedings of the 7th Workshop on Cognitive Aspects of Computational Language Learning*. pages 22–26.

Hassan Sajjad, Francisco Guzmán, Nadir Durrani, Ahmed Abdelali, Houda Bouamor, Irina Temnikova, and Stephan Vogel. 2016. Eyes don't lie: Predicting machine translation quality using eye movement. In *Proceedings of the 2016 Conference of the North American Chapter of the Association for Computational Linguistics: Human Language Technologies (NAACL-HLT 2016)*. pages 1082–1088. http://www.aclweb.org/anthology/N16-1125.

Dario D. Salvucci and Joseph H. Goldberg. 2000. Identifying fixations and saccades in eye-tracking protocols. In *Proceedings of the 2000 symposium on Eye tracking research & applications (ETRA '00)*. pages 71–78. https://doi.org/10.1145/355017.355028.

Ryohei Sasano and Sadao Kurohashi. 2008. Japanese named entity recognition using structural natural language processing. In *Proceedings of the Third International Joint Conference on Natural Language Processing (IJCNLP 2008)*. pages 607–612. http://aclweb.org/anthology/I/I08/I08-2080.pdf.

Katrin Tomanek, Udo Hahn, Steffen Lohmann, and Jürgen Ziegler. 2010. A cognitive cost model of annotations based on eye-tracking data. In *Proceedings of the 48th Annual Meeting of the Association for Computational Linguistics (ACL 2010)*. pages 1158–1167. http://www.aclweb.org/anthology/P10-1118.

A Graph-based Text Similarity Measure That Employs Named Entity Information

Leonidas Tsekouras
Institute of Informatics
and Telecommunications,
N.C.S.R. "Demokritos",
Greece,
ltsekouras@iit.demokritos.gr

Iraklis Varlamis
Department of Informatics
and Telematics,
Harokopio University
of Athens, Greece,
varlamis@hua.gr

George Giannakopoulos
Institute of Informatics
and Telecommunications,
N.C.S.R. "Demokritos",
Greece,
ggianna@iit.demokritos.gr

Abstract

Text comparison is an interesting though hard task, with many applications in Natural Language Processing. This work introduces a new text-similarity measure, which employs named-entities' information extracted from the texts and the n-gram graphs' model for representing documents. Using OpenCalais as a named-entity recognition service and the JINSECT toolkit for constructing and managing n-gram graphs, the text similarity measure is embedded in a text clustering algorithm (k-Means). The evaluation of the produced clusters with various clustering validity metrics shows that the extraction of named entities at a first step can be profitable for the time-performance of similarity measures that are based on the n-gram graph representation without affecting the overall performance of the NLP task.

1 Introduction

The development of a text comparison algorithm is a critical step in many Natural Language Processing and Text Mining tasks, such as text clustering, categorization and summarization. However, the easy -for a human- task of understanding whether two texts are talking about the same topic or are somehow related, still remains an open challenge for NLP programs.

The main difficulties behind automatic text comparison are semantic ambiguity of words (Sanderson, 1994), lexical and syntactic differences (Ferreira et al., 2016) between sentences. According to Stavrianou et al. (2007), additional issues that affect text similarity performance and must be considered during text preprocessing are: stopwords and noisy data (e.g. misspelled words)

removal, stemming, part of speech (POS) tagging, multi-word terms (collocations), tokenization and text representation. Text preprocessing in this direction aims at reducing the amount of information used for representing the document, only to the information that is really useful (e.g. by ignoring misspelled words or stopwords), by reducing semantic ambiguity (e.g. by defining the POS of a polysemous word) and the dimensions of the feature space (e.g. by mapping set of words to a multi-word term or by replacing words with stems).

Apart from the popular algebraic text representation model of VSM (Vector space model), where each word is a feature (Unigram or Bag-of-words model) and its multi-word (or multi-character) extensions (n-gram models), there has been significant work in representing texts as graphs. In the former cases, cosine similarity is used to calculate the similarity between two texts, whereas graph comparison methods are used in the latter case.

N-gram graphs (nGG) (Giannakopoulos and Karkaletsis, 2009; Giannakopoulos, 2009) capture the word order in the text, by connecting neighboring n-grams with edges that denote their frequency of co-occurrence within a given window of text and allow the detection of partial similarity in the morphology of text, with some resilience to noise and no need for preprocessing.Although n-gram graphs have shown improved performance in text mining tasks, their complexity significantly grows for large texts. In order to address this, we focus only on the most informative terms thus reducing the graph complexity, without losing significant information. It is typical in text representation models used in text mining or NLP tasks to select the most informative terms (e.g. the terms with the highest tf/idf weights or terms with special meaning, such as named entities). For example, Kumaran and Allan (2004) used Named Entity (NE)

Proceedings of Recent Advances in Natural Language Processing, pages 765–771,
Varna, Bulgaria, Sep 4–6 2017.

terms to improve performance in the "new event detection" task, Nadeau and Sekine (2007) provide an interesting survey on the uses of Named Entities in information extraction tasks, Toda and Kataoka (2005) employ Named Entities for clustering search results, whereas Sinoara et al. (2014) and Montalvo et al. (2015) used NEs as privileged information in text clustering.j

In this work, we combine the informativeness of Named Entities with the ability of the n-gram graph representation to capture word sequence information and define a new graph-based text similarity measure. We evaluate the performance of our approach in a text clustering task, using two different datasets. Results show that term selection can improve the time-performance of n-gram graph similarity and that named entities can be a useful addition to the set of terms selected using a "Term Frequency — Inverse Document Frequency" (TF-IDF) weighting scheme.

2 Related Work

In the past years, there has been significant research on text similarity. Gomaa and Fahmy (2013) provide a survey on text similarity measures, dividing them into three groups: i) string-based measures that operate on character sequences, ii) corpus-based measures that take into account information that comes from corpora, and iii) knowledge-based measures that use semantic networks (or similar knowledge-driven constructs) to determine the similarity between words.

Bos and Markert (2005) used surface string similarity, model building and theorem proving in order to assess text similarity. They extended the set of words in the text with synonyms from WordNet, and employed Google API to measure a weight for each word using the web as a corpus. Mihalcea et al. (2006) also used external information from semantic networks and defined a knowledge-based similarity metric for short texts, which reduced the error rate in a text paraphrasing task by up to 13% compared to other vector-based similarity metrics.

Friburger et al. (2002) found that the combined use of a "named entities" vector and an "all-words" vector with an increased weight to the entities vector had the best overall performance.

Schenker et al. (2005) performed text clustering and classifications tasks using graph representation models and graph-based similarity measures. They also introduced graph edit distance metrics,

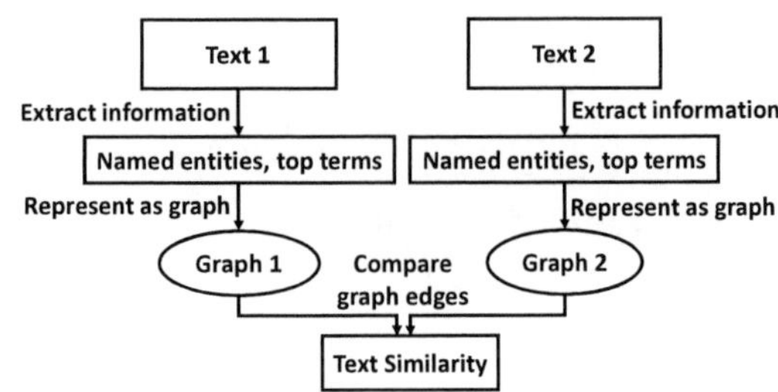

Figure 1: General diagram of how the algorithm works

in order to tackle the complexity (NP-complete) of graph isomorphism problem. Giannakopoulos and Karkaletsis (2009) represented texts as n-gram graphs, using a sliding window of length n and compared their graphs using metrics such as Value Similarity, Normal Value Similarity, Value Ratio and Size Similarity.

The proposed approach builds on the metrics introduced by (Giannakopoulos and Karkaletsis, 2009) using the findings of (Friburger et al., 2002). Instead of taking all terms into account, we distinguish between named entities and top-ranked terms (by TF-IDF), and all other words and weight the n-gram graph accordingly.

3 Proposed Method

The aim of this work is to define a text comparison methodology that takes into account the named entities mentioned in the texts and represents texts as *n-gram graphs*, which are compared using graph comparison operators. For each pair of input texts T_i, T_j, a similarity function f will output a score $s = f(T_i, T_j)$, where $\{s \in \mathbb{R} | 0 \leq s \leq 1\}$ indicating how similar the two texts are. Values of s close to 1, indicate high similarity between the texts, when s is close to 0 the texts are dissimilar. The whole process is depicted in Figure 1.

In the information extraction step, two types of terms are extracted from text: i) named entities, ii) top-ranked terms using TF-IDF. The extraction of named entities has been done using the Open-Calais API[1], although any other entity extraction service or program can be used instead.

Using the named entities and the top terms extracted in the first step, we proceed to the text representation step, where: i) all entities are replaced with a hash value that allows multi-word entities to appear as single words in the word graph repre-

---

[1] http://www.opencalais.com/

sentation model and ii) all the remaining words are replaced with a placeholder word. In the experiments, we chose the word "A" as a placeholder. The use of a single placeholder word causes the word graph to have only one node for all the non-important words, which significantly reduces the size of the n-gram graph and the complexity of comparison operators. Similarly, the mapping of the entity names to hash values minimizes the memory footprint of the graph further since a hash value takes up less memory than the full entity name in most cases.

Using the graph-based representation of the texts, the text similarity function is based on the comparison of the word n-gram graphs, which counts in tandem the value, size, containment and normalized value similarity of the two graphs as detailed in the following paragraphs.

3.1 Creation and Comparison of N-gram Graphs

For the creation of the word n-gram graph the JIN-SECT toolkit[2] has been employed, which supports both character and word n-gram graphs and implements several graph similarity measures. The word n-gram graphs are created using a sliding window of size n over the words, which means that a node is created for each word in the text (i.e. term hashcode or replacement word) and graph edges connect words (nodes) that are in proximity to each other (i.e. within a d words distance; we use $d = n$). The graph is weighted and weights denote the number of times two words were found close to each other (within the sliding window distance). For the comparison of two graphs, let's call them G_i and G_j, four similarity metrics that give a value in $[0, 1]$ have been employed. The metrics — Value Similarity, Size Similarity, Containment Similarity and Normalized Value Similarity — are defined by (Giannakopoulos, 2009) and for the comparison of a graph G_i against another graph G_j can be described as follows:

- *Value Similarity* indicates how many edges of G_i are present in G_j, but also takes into account the weights of these edges. If e is a given common edge of G_i, G_j with a respective weight of w_e^i, w_j^i, the we define $VR(e) =$

$$\frac{min(w_e^i, w_j^i)}{max(w_e^i, w_j^i)}$$

$$VS(G_i, G_j) = \frac{\sum_{e \in G_i \cap G_j} VR(e)}{max(|G_i|, |G_j|)} \quad (1)$$

- *Size Similarity* takes into account only the size of the graphs.

$$SS(G_i, G_j) = \frac{min(|G_i|, |G_j|)}{max(|G_i|, |G_j|)} \quad (2)$$

- *Normalized Value Similarity* is assigned a value of 0, if Size Similarity is zero, otherwise it is the ratio of Value Similarity to Size Similarity. It is a measure of similarity that ignores the relative size of the graphs when comparing them.

$$NVS(G_i, G_j) = \frac{VS(G_i, G_j)}{SS(G_i, G_j)} \quad (3)$$

Below, we provide an example of a text that has been processed for extracting useful terms and has been represented as a word n-gram graph.

> **Original text:** ...Make your reservation early. Our **workshop** coincides with other **Cornell** events...
>
> **Processed text:** ...A A A A A WORK-SHOP A A A -1675268131 A...

In addition, Figure 2 gives a visual representation of the word n-gram graph created by JIN-SECT for the example mentioned above, using a sliding window of size 3. The graph is quite small because all unimportant words are replaced with the same replacement word (i.e. "A") and consequently result to a single node in the graph. The edge going from node "A" to itself has a much bigger weight than other edges, because frequently in the text we have sequences of non-important words. The other nodes represent the named entities (the node with the hashcode value which corresponds to the entity Cornell) and top TF-IDF ranking words of the text (the top-1 word — Workshop — has been used). Both nodes are connected with the "A" node since they neighbor non-important words but not with each other.

The size of the word graph is small, because of the term extraction step. If the full text had been

---

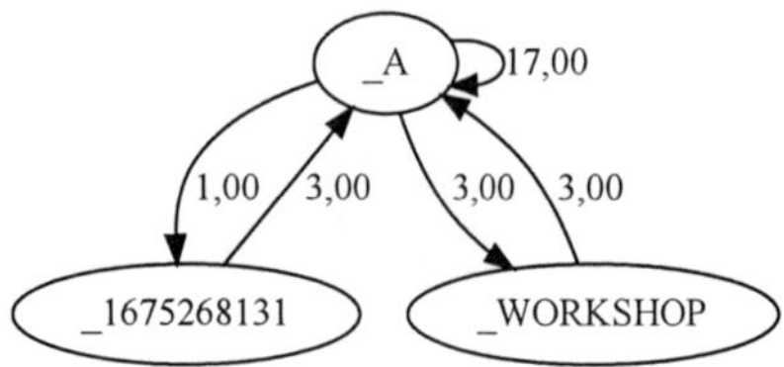

Figure 2: Example word graph with entities & top TF-IDF terms

used, then the graph would be larger and the time needed for graph and consequently text comparison would be larger. In the experiments, both the time complexity and the overall performance of the proposed methodology and of other methods are compared.

4   Experiments

This section describes the experimental evaluation process followed by an evaluation of the proposed text similarity measure performance in text clustering tasks. The datasets employed for the study are first presented (one English and one multilingual corpus), then the measures used for the evaluation of the cluster quality and finally the different steps of the processing pipeline, which have been evaluated for their time performance are explained. The presentation of results follows the same structure, starting with the clustering quality performance by dataset and continuing with the time complexity of the different tasks.

4.1   Datasets and Analysis Process

In the experiments, two datasets have been employed: i) the 20 Newsgroups data set, which consists of around 20,000 news documents, quite evenly distributed into 20 groups and ii) the MultiLing 2015 dataset, which comprises 1350 WikiNews articles in total about 15 events written in 10 different languages.

More specifically, for the 20 Newsgroups, we used the texts in the "test" set of the "bydate" version[3], which comprises documents from 20 different groups. Two texts have been excluded from the experiments, because they were in Swedish and this was not supported by the OpenCalais API and another five texts were excluded because they exceeded the maximum file size and maximum processing timeout set by the OpenCalais API. This resulted to a final set of 7525 texts.

In the case of the MultiLing 2015 dataset[4], which comprises texts derived from the publicly available WikiNews about various events, the dataset contains a number of events (15), each described by several documents (10–15). The documents have been translated across a number of languages. In our experiments, we used the English, Spanish and French versions, resulting in a set of 400 texts that cover the 15 events.

For evaluating the performance of the proposed text similarity measure in a text clustering task, we used a simple, centroid-based, clustering algorithm (i.e. k-Means) with a fixed number of clusters (k) that equals the number of predefined classes (i.e. $k = 20$ for 20 newsgroups, $k = 15$ for the MultiLing dataset). The input for the algorithm was a text similarity matrix, which was computed using i) the proposed similarity measure with entities only (ent_graph) and with top tf-idf terms ($ent\&tfidf\_graph$), ii) word n-gram graph similarity using the whole text to create the graph (all_graph), as defined by (Giannakopoulos and Karkaletsis, 2009), and iii) cosine similarity using the VSM representation and the top TF-IDF terms ($tfidf\_VSM$). Entities are extracted using OpenCalais and TF-IDF weights for words are computed using custom Java code. The n-gram graphs are constructed using the JINSECT library, using the replacement strategy described in section 3. The word n-gram graphs are compared using the JINSECT graph similarity metrics in order to create the document similarity matrix.

Using the text similarity matrix as input to k-Means, we produce a set of clusters. The ELKI software[5] has been employed for clustering the documents and more specifically the k-Means Lloyd implementation.

4.2   Clustering Validity Metrics

For the evaluation of clustering algorithms, the options are either to use external metrics that compare the clustering schema against a "ground truth" clustering or internal validity metrics that comparatively examine the cohesiveness and separation of clusters across different clustering schemata. In the current experiment, the "ground truth" is the actual classification of documents to the 20 newsgroups or the 15 MultiLing topics respectively, so external metrics are preferred. Since

---

[3]http://qwone.com/~jason/20Newsgroups/

[4]http://multiling.iit.demokritos.gr/
pages/view/1516/multiling-2015

[5]https://elki-project.github.io/

all experiments have been done using the same clustering algorithm (k-Means), the only factor that affects the cluster quality is the text similarity measure, so the results are directly comparable.

For measuring the validity of the produced clustering schemes, we implemented a wide range of external clustering quality indexes: Precision, Recall and F_1-measure as described by (Hassanzadeh et al., 2009), Folkes and Mallows ($F\&M$), Jaccard and Rand as described in (Desgraupes, 2013).

Since k-Means' results depend on the selection of the initial k centroid documents, we repeat the clustering many times (100 for the MultiLing dataset and 10 for the much larger 20-newsgroups dataset) and we report the mean values and the 95% confidence intervals in Tables 1 and 2.

4.3 Time Performance

The whole pipeline of information extraction (entities and TF-IDF weights), text representation (as graphs or vectors), text similarity computation and clustering was wrapped in a Java program that employs the JINSECT library, the OpenCalais API and the ELKI clustering algorithms. This allows to measure the time needed for the different steps of the comparison procedure:

TF-IDF weights refers to the time needed for the computation of TF-IDF weights for all the texts in the dataset. In the case of word n-gram graphs created using the whole text, this step is omitted.

Graph creation is the time needed for the creation of all word n-gram graphs (one for each text). The graphs are cached in memory in order to accelerate the steps that follow.

Graph comparison is the time needed to create the similarity matrix, containing the pairwise similarities of all texts in the dataset.

We do not report the time for extracting named entities, since it involves accessing the external OpenCalais API, and time performance depends on factors that cannot be controlled, such as the network latency. In the future, we aim to replace this step with an offline Named Entity Recognition service based on the open source OpenNLP project. We do not also report the time for running the clustering algorithm or for evaluating the clustering results, since it is expected to be equivalent in all cases, given the fixed size of the similarity matrices.

4.4 Results

The quality of the clusters produced by k-Means, using the four different similarity measures (i.e. the baseline cosine similarity that uses TF-IDF — $tfidf\_VSM$, the n-gram graph similarity using all words — all_graph, the proposed n-gram graph similarity measure with entities only — ent_graph, and an extension that combines entities and the top TF-IDF terms — $ent\&tfidf\_graph$) has been evaluated using the validity indexes.

4.4.1 English Texts (20 Newsgroups)

The results for 20 Newsgroups are summarized in Table 1. Results in bold are significantly better (at 95% confidence interval) than that of the baseline $tfidf - VSM$ method, which employs cosine similarity and the TF-IDF weighting scheme. All the approaches demonstrate a rather low performance (at least in Precision and F_1 Measure), which is mainly due to the large number of categories and the sparsity of the unigram (i.e. words) feature space (less than .5% non-zero features). This sparsity is even greater in the case of entities, where only 3% of the document pairs have at least one common entity. This explains the poor performance of the ent_graph method, which still outperforms the original all_graph method and the $tfidf\_VSM$ baseline.

The approach that adds to the entities n-gram graph a few more nodes that correspond to important document words (high TF-IDF values) improves the results significantly (all values have been computed at the 95% confidence interval) against the VSM and the simple n-gram graph model, but also outperforms the graph based similarity that uses only the entities in the graph. In this case, the important document terms increase the overlap between the document graphs.

	$tfidf\_VSM$	all_graph	ent_graph	$ent\&tfidf\_gr.$
$F\&M$	**0.15 ± 0.012**	0.10 ± 0.012	0.14 ± 0.019	0.09 ± 0.005
Jaccard	0.05 ± 0.001	0.04 ± 0.002	0.05 ± 0.001	0.04 ± 0.002
Rand	0.58 ± 0.067	0.81 ± 0.044	0.65 ± 0.099	**0.87 ± 0.016**
Precision	0.06 ± 0.005	0.06 ± 0.009	0.08 ± 0.017	**0.10 ± 0.017**
Recall	**0.61 ± 0.075**	0.32 ± 0.077	0.52 ± 0.122	0.24 ± 0.037
F_1	0.10 ± 0.008	0.10 ± 0.008	0.13 ± 0.020	**0.14 ± 0.012**

Table 1: Clustering performance for the 20 Newsgroups dataset (95% C.I.)

4.4.2 Multilingual Texts (MultiLing)

The results are even more interesting in the case of the multi-lingual dataset of MultiLing and are

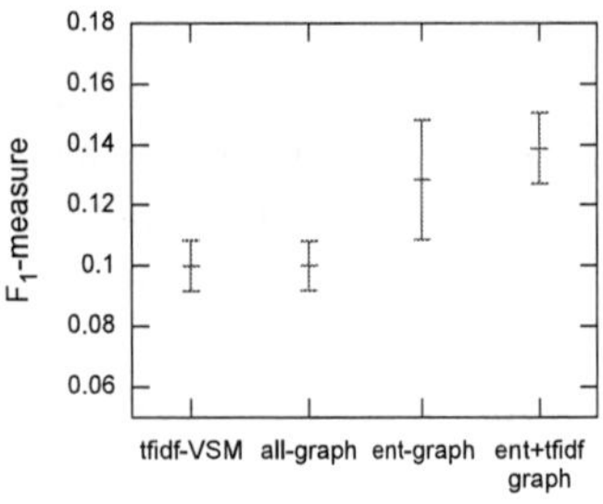

Figure 3: F_1-measure performance of the algorithms for the 20 Newsgroups dataset

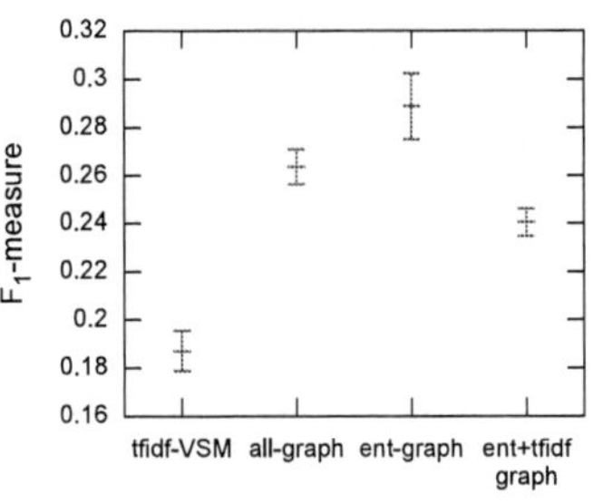

Figure 4: F_1-measure performance of the algorithms for the MultiLing 2015 dataset

summarized in Table 2. In this dataset, the *ent_graph* method significantly outperforms all other methods (in terms of Recall and F_1), and the entities seem to be more useful than all the other words in the texts. These results highlight one of the main advantages of the proposed graph-based similarity measure, which is the ability to process texts in multiple languages. The entity extraction mechanism reduces the feature space only to the named entities, which frequently remain the same between languages, thus reduce sparsity. In this dataset, 38% of the document pairs had at least one common entity.

What is also interesting here is that the performance degrades when important document terms (according to TF-IDF) are added to the graph. This is because such terms are translated across languages are not matched thus reduce the similarity of the corresponding document graphs.

	$tfidf\_VSM$	all_graph	ent_graph	$ent\&tfidf\_gr.$
F&M	0.16 ± 0.001	0.16 ± 0.001	$\mathbf{0.21 \pm 0.003}$	0.15 ± 0.002
Jaccard	0.08 ± 0.001	0.08 ± 0.001	0.08 ± 0.002	0.08 ± 0.001
Rand	0.77 ± 0.006	0.82 ± 0.006	0.62 ± 0.021	$\mathbf{0.85 \pm 0.003}$
Precision	0.13 ± 0.008	0.23 ± 0.010	0.20 ± 0.013	0.21 ± 0.008
Recall	0.35 ± 0.008	0.33 ± 0.005	$\mathbf{0.62 \pm 0.020}$	0.29 ± 0.004
F_1	0.19 ± 0.008	0.26 ± 0.007	$\mathbf{0.29 \pm 0.014}$	0.24 ± 0.006

Table 2: Clustering performance for the MultiLing 2015 dataset (95% C.I.)

4.4.3 Time Complexity

Figure 3 presents the time for the various text comparison steps for the 20 Newsgroups dataset only, since the respective times for the 400 texts of the MultiLing 2015 dataset where very small. The time for graph construction for the 7525 texts almost doubles when all words are used whereas time for text comparison almost triples.

The TF-IDF time for $tfidf\_VSM$ is longer than that of $ent\&tfidf\_graph$'s because we in-

clude the time required to create vectors of the same size for each document, which is required to calculate their cosine similarity but not to just identify a document's top terms.

	all_graph	$ent\&tfidf\_graph$	$tfidf\_VSM$
TF-IDF	0	3.97	26
Graph creation	38.46	17.6	0
Text comparisons	1697.3	509.4	543.2

Table 3: Times for the various text comparison steps (in seconds)

5 Conclusion

This work presented a graph-based text similarity measure that takes advantage of named entities' information and improves the performance of text clustering tasks. The similarity measure employs named entities and the most important document terms (by TF-IDF) for the construction of the n-gram graph and improves the time complexity of the n-gram graph similarity measures that employ all the document information since it results in a smaller and simpler graph. The first results show that the method can be useful in cases where the documents are rich in entities and have an overlap in the entities space, and is not very useful in the absence of entities. The proposed measure is appropriate for multilingual text collections (e.g. for news collected in many different languages), since the named entities seem to be less affected by translation than any other word in the text.

It is on our plans to evaluate the performance of our entity based similarity measure to character n-gram graphs, which are expected to capture better the small variations across languages. Even, when named entities are translated from a language to another, the differences are small and could be possibly captured by a character n-gram graph model.

References

Bos, J. and Markert, K. (2005). Recognising Textual Entailment with Logical Inference. In *Proceedings of the Conference on Human Language Technology and Empirical Methods in Natural Language Processing*, HLT '05, pages 628–635, Stroudsburg, PA, USA. Association for Computational Linguistics.

Desgraupes, B. (2013). Clustering indices. *University of Paris Ouest-Lab ModalX*, 1:34.

Ferreira, R., Lins, R. D., Simske, S. J., Freitas, F., and Riss, M. (2016). Assessing sentence similarity through lexical, syntactic and semantic analysis. *Computer Speech & Language*, 39:1–28.

Friburger, N., Maurel, D., and Giacometti, A. (2002). Textual similarity based on proper names. In *Proc. of the workshop Mathematical/Formal Methods in Information Retrieval*, pages 155–167.

Giannakopoulos, G. (2009). *Automatic Summarization from Multiple Documents*. Ph. D. dissertation, University of the Aegean, Department of Information and Communication Systems Engineering.

Giannakopoulos, G. and Karkaletsis, V. (2009). N-gram graphs: Representing documents and document sets in summary system evaluation. In *Proceedings of Text Analysis Conference TAC2009 (To appear)*.

Gomaa, W. H. and Fahmy, A. A. (2013). A survey of text similarity approaches. *International Journal of Computer Applications*, 68(13).

Hassanzadeh, O., Chiang, F., Lee, H. C., and Miller, R. J. (2009). Framework for evaluating clustering algorithms in duplicate detection. *Proceedings of the VLDB Endowment*, 2(1):1282–1293.

Kumaran, G. and Allan, J. (2004). Text classification and named entities for new event detection. In *Proceedings of the 27th annual international ACM SIGIR conference on Research and development in information retrieval*, pages 297–304. ACM.

Mihalcea, R., Corley, C., and Strapparava, C. (2006). Corpus-based and knowledge-based measures of text semantic similarity. In *AAAI*, volume 6, pages 775–780.

Montalvo, S., Martínez, R., Fresno, V., and Delgado, A. (2015). Exploiting named entities for bilingual news clustering. *Journal of the Association for Information Science and Technology*, 66(2):363–376.

Nadeau, D. and Sekine, S. (2007). A survey of named entity recognition and classification. *Lingvisticae Investigationes*, 30(1):3–26.

Sanderson, M. (1994). Word sense disambiguation and information retrieval. In *Proceedings of the 17th annual international ACM SIGIR conference on Research and development in information retrieval*, pages 142–151. Springer-Verlag New York, Inc.

Schenker, A., Kandel, A., Bunke, H., and Last, M. (2005). *Graph-theoretic techniques for web content mining*, volume 62. World Scientific.

Sinoara, R. A., Sundermann, C. V., Marcacini, R. M., Domingues, M. A., and Rezende, S. O. (2014). Named entities as privileged information for hierarchical text clustering. In *Proceedings of the 18th International Database Engineering & Applications Symposium*, pages 57–66. ACM.

Stavrianou, A., Andritsos, P., and Nicoloyannis, N. (2007). Overview and semantic issues of text mining. *ACM Sigmod Record*, 36(3):23–34.

Toda, H. and Kataoka, R. (2005). A search result clustering method using informatively named entities. In *Proceedings of the 7th annual ACM international workshop on Web information and data management*, pages 81–86. ACM.

Detecting Metaphorical Phrases in the Polish Language

Aleksander Wawer   **Agnieszka Mykowiecka**
Institute of Computer Science, Polish Academy of Sciences
Jana Kazimierza 5
01-248 Warsaw, Poland
$\{axw, agn\}$@ipipan.waw.pl

Abstract

In this paper we describe experiments with automated detection of metaphors in the Polish language. We focus our analysis on noun phrases composed of an adjective and a noun, and distinguish three types of expressions: with literal sense, with metaphorical sense, and expressions both literal and methaphorical (context-dependent). We propose a method of automatically recognizing expression type using word embeddings and neural networks. We evaluate multiple neural network architectures and demonstrate that the method significantly outperforms strong baselines.

1 Introduction

Language expressions can be interpreted literally or metaphorically, e.g. *round table* is just a table which is round, but it can also describe a way of organizing a discussion. The chances of these two interpretations are not equal for all expressions. With some of them, e.g. *zielony długopis* 'green pen' it is hard to imagine when they get figurative meaning – they are strictly compositional – while others, e.g. *biały szum* 'white noise' are used only in figurative meaning. There is also a third group of phrases (to which *round table* belongs) used both literally and metaphorically. Identification of potentially figurative usage may improve the performance of many NLP applications. It is crucial for information extraction task as literal interpretation of metaphors can lead to incorrect results (Patwardhan and Riloff, 2007), machine translation (Shutova, 2011) and textual entailment (Agerri, 2008). In particular, Thibodeau and Boroditsky (2011) even analyze the role of metaphor in reasoning about social policy on crime. Although the

ultimate goal is to decide on every phrase occurrence whether it could be interpreted compositionally (literally) or not, such task requires annotated data which are quite hard to prepare. In this work we concentrate on the initial classification of isolated phrases – we try to categorize Polish phrases build up from a noun and a modifying adjective into these three categories, i.e. phrases which are nearly for sure interpreted literally (L), phrases which have only metaphorical meaning (M) and phrases which occur in both interpretations (B). We test our approach on a set of about 500 phrases selected (mainly) from the top frequent phrases of Polish National Corpus, NKJP, (Przepiórkowski et al., 2012), and manually categorized into these three classes. We tested methods which do not require to build vectors of the analyzed phrases. Our models use only vectors representing phrase constituents.

2 Existing Work

Discrimination of literal and metaphorical (compositional and non-compositional) phrases is not a new idea. First attempts to solve this problem use different type of measures. Lin (1999) compared the mutual-information measures of the constituents with the mutual information of similar expressions obtained by substituting one of the elements with a related word, while Schone and Jurafsky (2001) evaluated a number of co-occurrence based measures. Both approaches did not give satisfactory results. In many later works distributional models were used. Baldwin et al. (2003) showed that LSA-based similarity between the multiword expression and each of its components is indicative for compositionality. Katz and Giesbrecht (2006) compared the actual phrase vector to the estimated compositional meaning vector calculated as a sum of the meaning vectors of the

Proceedings of Recent Advances in Natural Language Processing, pages 772–777,
Varna, Bulgaria, Sep 4–6 2017.

parts. The hypothesis was that the similarity between these two vectors should be larger in case of phrases which are not used non-compositionally. The test set contained 81 potential German multi word (preposition-noun-verb) collocation candidates) from a database described in Krenn (2000). When the threshold of similarity value was set to 0.2, the method achieved F-measure of 0.48. The results of (Baldwin et al., 2003) method on the same set were 0.16 for verbs and 0.51 for nouns. Several other solutions consist in training classifiers: Tsvetkov et al. (2014) used abstractness, imageability (whether or not a word can be easily associated with image), wordnet-like, but specifically defined, supersenses, and word vectors, in random forest classifier to distinguish metaphoric and literal adjective-noun pairs. On the set of 884 metaphoric and 884 literal phrases and 360 features, they obtained results with 0.86 accuracy (in 10-fold cross validation). Hovy et al. (2013) employed the idea of selectional preference violation as the indicator of metaphor and trained an SVM classifier with tree kernels to capture compositional properties of metaphorical language. Their hypothesis is that unusual semantic compositions in the data may be indicative of the use of metaphor. They trained the model on labeled examples of literal and metaphorical uses of 329 words (3872 sentences) using word vectors, part of speech tags and WordNet supersenses introduced into dependency trees as features and obtained F-score=0.75. The detailed comparison of these earlier methods can be found in (Shutova, 2015).

A recent attempt in metaphor analysis using compositional semantic method is presented in Gutierrez et al. (2016). The authors classify 8592 adjective-noun pairs as either metaphoric or literal. They build compositional DS models in which adjectives are treated as linear maps from nouns to AN phrases. For each adjective they split the phrases involving that adjective into two subsets, the literal subset and the metaphorical subset and build three models representing literal, metaphorical and both types of usage of every adjective from the traininig phrases. An unseen phrase involving a known adjective is classified as metaphorical if the vector representing the phrase is more similar to the vector representing the same phrase with the adjective replaced by its metaphoric usage representation than to the vec-

tor obtained for its literal usage. The resulting F-measure and accuracy are 0.79 and 0.81 respectively.

As the state-of-the-art methods of contextual recognition of figurative phrases we can cite Peng and Feldman (2017) who explored the idea that idioms and their non-idiomatic counterparts do not appear in the same contexts and that the words which are representatives of the local context are likely to associate strongly with a literal expression. The association was measured as in terms of projection (inner product) of word vectors onto the vector representing the literal expression. For different data sets they achieved the accuracy of 0.57 to 0.87. However, in their work, phrases are recognized in sentential context and the analyze concerns verb-noun pairs.

3 Training and Test Data

Annotation of phrases with the type of their usage was done specially for this experiment. A list of 437 figurative expressions of the form adjective-noun were composed from two different sources. About 100 phrases were proposed by several project members being native speakers of Polish. This list was then enriched with the examples manually selected from the top of the frequency list of the adjective+noun phrases occurring in NKJP. Next, all phrases were verified by a linguist who classified them into two categories: M – phrases which are only used metaphorically, e.g. *barwna historia* 'colourful story' and B – phrases which can be used both in literal and metaphorical senses, like *biała karta* 'white page' which in Polish can mean that we start from the beginning without any judgments on the previous work or behaviour or just a page which is not covered with text. Only one phrase from this set was eventually classified as used only literally (*linia autobusowa*) 'bus line'. The phrases are also annotated with information on the domain which is described by an adjective, e.g. for *chłodne oko* 'cool eye' the adjective domain is *temperature*, and the type of a noun (abstract or specific). The second list contain adjective-noun phrases which have only literal meaning (at least in not very awkward situations) and they include the same adjectives as phrases on the first list. These phrases were also manually selected from the top of the frequency list of NKJP. Their type was verified by the second annotator and only phrases on which both of them agreed are included in the final list. In total, our data comprises 282 phrases with only metaphorical meaning, 1041 with literal meaning and 154 phases which can have both types of usage.

4 Data Analysis

In order to obtain better understanding of our data set, we analyzed properties of adjectives and nouns included in phrases of all types.

In the case of nouns, we manually annotated whether the noun is concrete or abstract (two possible values). In the case of adjectives, we manually annotated its domain. By *domain* we understand the root of hypernymy tree for an adjective (eg. for "red", the root hypernym is "color"). However, we did not use any existing typology, but the annotators (linguists) proposed semantic groupings into which words with more specific meanings fall, not necessarily based on hyperonymy in the strict sense (eg. "sensual experience" for taste such as "bitter", "dimension" for "high"). The number of the topmost classes in this hierarchy is 47.

In the two sections below we analyse whether adjective and noun types are related to metaphorical use of a phrase (each constituted of a verb and a noun).

4.1 Adjective Types

Adjective type appears to have an influence whether the phrase is metaphorical. To confirm this, we compute $\tilde{\chi}^2$ statistics ($\tilde{\chi}^2$=151 with 96 degrees of freedom and p=0.0002), therefore we conclude that the relationship between adjective domain and metaphorical character of the phrase is significant. Table 1 illustrates frequencies of selected adjective types in literal (L), metaphorical (M) and both metaphorical and literal (B) phrases.

4.2 Noun Types

Turney et al. (2011) prove that metaphorical word usage is correlated with the degree of abstractness of the word's context. As we analyse isolated phrases we cannot use information about the context, but we observe similar relation between the abstractness of the noun and the metaphorical usage of the phrase to which it belongs. Table 2 shows frequencies of phrase types and noun types. As could be expected, the observation to be made is that in metaphorical phrases nouns tend to be abstract, while those used in both metaphorical and

	L	B	M
good/bad	25	5	0
sound	11	3	7
emotions	27	4	5
order	42	6	0
colour	185	22	29
material	77	13	13
state of body/mind	12	0	12
temperature	50	10	22
dimension	137	10	27
physical property	25	14	24
supernatural phenomenon	0	8	3
weather phenomena	1	1	9
sensual experience	21	7	50

Table 1: Selected adjective types and metaphorical phrases

literal and only literal phrases are more often concrete.

	abstract		concrete
M	193	(0.68%)	89
B	41	(0.27%)	112
L	253	(0.24%)	789

Table 2: Noun types and metaphorical phrases

5 Network Architectures

The observations made in previous section allow to hypothesize that certain information influencing the metaphorical character of a phrase, namely adjective type and noun type (such as for instance relation to sensual experiences of an adjective and high abstractness of a noun), can be contained in word embeddings trained on large corpora. For this reason we try to predict metaphorical character of each phrase using word embeddings provided as input to neural network models. In the following sections we describe our experiments with this approach.

We attempt to recognize the type of a phrase (as literal, metaphorical, and both) consisting of an adjective and a noun using several types of neural network structures. As word embeddings we used word2vec vectors trained on a dump of Polish language Wikipedia and NKJP. All word2vec parameters had default values as in (Řehůřek and Sojka, 2010).

5.1 Multiplicative

This model implements Marco Baroni et al. hypothesis that adjectives act as functions on nouns (Baroni et al., 2014). In this view, computing meaning of a noun phrase is based on multiplication of noun embeddings by adjective embeddings (functions). Success of this idea might depend on training adjective and noun embeddings according to different objectives, which obviously is not the case for word2vec embeddings.

We experiment with three set-ups of this idea, each with different sets of weight vectors. Let adj-v denote the embedding of an adjective, noun-v the embedding of a noun, and w, w-1 and w-2 trainable weight layers. In each case, the presented formulas were followed by multiplication by trainable softmax weights layer with bias weights. The size of all weight vectors and softmax weight vector was equal to word embedding size.

The three implementations we tested are as follows:

- M1: adj-v * noun-v

- M2: adj-v * w * noun-v

- M3: adj-v * w-1 * noun-v * w-2

All of these architectures have been implemented in TensorFlow.

5.2 Concatenated

In this type of models, embeddings of an adjective and a noun were concatenated, and this concatenated vector was subsequently passed to neural network layers. By dense we denote a regular layer of weights (called also dense).

Implementations we tested were as follows:

- C1: dense $\rightarrow$ softmax

- C2: dense $\rightarrow$ dense $\rightarrow$ softmax

In the case of these architectures, C1 was implemented in TensorFlow, while C2 in Keras.

6 Results

Because of overwhelming majority of one class (those with literal meaning) we compare our methods to the most frequent class baseline. The accuracy of this baseline can be computed as 0.70. We perform the experiments on all 1457 phrases in our data set, evaluating each combination of parameters in a 10-fold cross-validation.

Table 6 contains results of evaluations of each neural network architecture as average micro precision (P) and recall (R) for each phrase type over 10 folds and three consecutive runs for each parameter combination. Reporting 'micro' values (e.g., precision P, recall R) means giving each observation (phrase) an equal contribution to the overall metric and is often preferred in multilabel settings, as in our case. We experimented with multiple embedding vector sizes. In each case batch size was equal to one.

| | | embedding size | | | | | |
| | | 50 | | 100 | | 200 | |
		P	R	P	R	P	R
M3	Both	0.32	0.16	0.27	0.25	N/A	N/A
	Lit.	0.84	0.91	0.85	0.86	N/A	N/A
	Met.	0.62	0.58	0.58	0.57	N/A	N/A
	All	0.74	0.77	0.74	0.74	N/A	N/A
C2	Both	0.29	0.27	0.29	0.29	0.31	0.31
	Lit.	0.87	0.88	0.87	0.88	0.87	0.91
	Met.	0.63	0.61	0.65	0.61	0.74	0.62
	All	0.76	0.77	0.77	0.77	0.79	0.79

Table 3: Average micro precision (P) and recall (R) in 10-fold cross-validation

In Table 6 we report results only for M3 and C2 architectures, each proven superior within their type.

The M1 architecture could not be successfully trained as the weights did not converge during learning. In the case of M1 and M2, between 10% and 30% of the models also did not converge. The same thing occurred to M3 models with embedding size 200 (marked as N/A in the table). Surprisingly, M3 model with embedding size 50 turned to have better recall than the one with embedding size 100, maintaining the same precision value. Therefore, embedding size appears to be reversely proportional to prediction quality in the case of M-type models.

Concatenative models C2 (with two dense layers) turned to be superior from C1 (one dense layer) by few percentage points in each measure. In the case of M-type models, embedding size appears to be directly proportional to prediction quality.

Generally it must be stated that concatenative models proved quite promising. Their quality increased with embedding size and the best model achieved the overall precision (and recall) of 0.79.

		corr.	ass.
biała gorączka	white fewer	M	B
biały kolor	whilte colour	L	M
ciężka atmosfera	heavy atmosphere	B	+
ciężki bagaż	heavy luggage	L	+
ciężka bitwa	heavy battle	M	B
ciężka doniczka	heavy pot	L	+
ciężka próba	ordeal	B	+
ciężka kłódka	heavy paddlock	L	+
ciężki konar	heavy bough	L	+
ciężka ręka	hard hand	B	+
ciężki wykład	heavy lecture	B	M
wściekły lis	rabid fox	L	L
wściekły upał	furious heat	M	M
zdrowy chłopiec	healthy boy	L	M
zdrowy psiak	healthy dog	L	L
zdrowy rozsądek	common sense	M	B

Table 4: Sample correct (+) and incorrect results.

7 Analysis of the Results

Incorrectly assigned labels were nearly equally frequent B, L and M tags. Mistakes are made in all directions. In Table 7 there are selected examples for test phrases with the adjectives of all test phrases with adjectives *biały* ''white', and *zdrowy* 'healthy' and all test phrases with the adjectives *ciężki* and *wściekły*. The first one means 'heavy' but is frequently used as 'difficult'. The latter is ambiguous and means in Polish both 'furious' and 'rabid'. Phrases with *ciężki* are classified quite well. The only severe error is for *heavy battle*. The other error is smaller as the phrase *heavy lecture* should be probably rather classified as M. The next group of two phrases are both correctly tagged while phrases while 'healthy dog' is labelled correctly and 'healthy boy' is not.

8 Conclusions and Future Work

We performed multiple experiments with automatic recognition of metaphorical expressions, noun phrases composed of a noun and an adjective. We divided those expressions into three types: strictly metaphorical, both metaphorical and literal (where actual meaning is determined by the context of usage), and finally strictly literal (that are not used in non-literal, metaphorical sense). The paper contains an analysis, supported by manual annotation, that demonstrates relationships between phrase type (falling into one of metaphorical classes) and types of involved nouns and adjectives.

We proposed to automatically recognize phrase types using word embeddings to represent word meaning. We described several experiments us-ing selected neural network architectures. We predicted phrase type without using sentence contexts, only based on word embeddings of adjectives and nouns that constitute each phrase. Results significantly outperform strong baseline of the most frequent class.

In future we plan to focus on sentence-level, context-dependent detection of metaphorical phrases. This involves detecting when phrases of B type (contextually metaphorical) take their non-literal meaning. Also we plan on applying our models on large corpora to detect more phrases of B type than in our current data set.

Acknowledgments

The paper is partially supported by the Polish National Science Centre project *Compositional distributional semantic models for identification, discrimination and disambiguation of senses in Polish texts* number 2014/15/B/ST6/05186.

References

Rodrigo Agerri. 2008. Metaphor in textual entailment. In *Coling 2008: Companion volume – Posters and Demonstrations*. pages 3–6.

Timothy Baldwin, Colin Bannard, Takaaki Tanaka, and Dominic Widdows. 2003. An empirical model of multiword expression decomposability. In *Proceedings of the ACL 2003 Workshop on Multiword Expressions: Analysis, Acquisition and Treatment - Volume 18*. Association for Computational Linguistics, Stroudsburg, PA, USA, MWE '03, pages 89–96.

Marco Baroni, Raffaella Bernardi, and Roberto Zamparelli. 2014. Frege in space: A program for compositional distributional semantics. *Linguistic Issues in Language Technology* 9:5–110.

Dario Gutierrez, Ekaterina Shutova, Tyler Marghetis, and Benjamin Bergen. 2016. Literal and metaphorical senses in compositional distributional semantic models. In *Proceedings of ACL 2016 (short papers)*.

Dirk Hovy, Shashank Srivastava, Sujay Kumar Jauhar, Mrinmaya Sachan, Kartik Goyal, Huiying Li, Whitney Sanders, and Eduard Hovy. 2013. Identifying metaphoricalword use with tree kernels. In *Proceedings of the First Workshop on Metaphor in NLP*. Association for Computational Linguistics, pages 52–57.

Graham Katz and Eugenie Giesbrecht. 2006. Automatic identification of non-compositional multiword expressions using latent semantic analysis. In *Proceedings of the ACL/COLING-06 Workshop on Multiword Expressions: Identifying and Exploiting Underlying Properties*. pages 12–19.

Brigitte Krenn. 2000. *The Usual Suspects: Data-Oriented Models for Identification and Representation of Lexical Collocations*. DFKI-LT - Dissertation Series.

Dekang Lin. 1999. Automatic identification of non-compositional phrases. In *Proceedings of the 37th Annual Meeting of the Association for Computational Linguistics on Computational Linguistics*. Association for Computational Linguistics, Stroudsburg, PA, USA, ACL '99, pages 317–324.

Siddharth Patwardhan and Ellen Riloff. 2007. Effective information extraction with semantic affinity patterns and relevant regions. In *Proceedings of the 2007 Joint Conference on Empirical Methods in Natural Language Processing and Computational Natural Language Learning (EMNLP-CoNLL)*. Association for Computational Linguistics, Prague, Czech Republic, pages 717–727. http://www.aclweb.org/anthology/D07-1075.

Jing Peng and Anna Feldman. 2017. Automatic idiom recognition with word embeddings. In Juan Antonio Lossio-Ventura and Hugo Alatrista-Salas, editors, *Information Management and Big Data: Second Annual International Symposium, SIMBig 2015, Cusco, Peru, September 2-4, 2015, and Third Annual International Symposium, SIMBig 2016, Cusco, Peru, September 1-3, 2016, Revised Selected Papers*, Springer International Publishing, Cham, pages 17–29.

Adam Przepiórkowski, Mirosław Bańko, Rafał L. Górski, and Barbara Lewandowska-Tomaszczyk, editors. 2012. *Narodowy Korpus Języka Polskiego*. Wydawnictwo Naukowe PWN, Warsaw.

Radim Řehůřek and Petr Sojka. 2010. Software Framework for Topic Modelling with Large Corpora. In *Proceedings of the LREC 2010 Workshop on New Challenges for NLP Frameworks*. ELRA, Valletta, Malta, pages 45–50.

Patrick Schone and Daniel Jurafsky. 2001. Is knowledge-free induction of multiword unit dictionary headwords a solved problem? In *Proceedings of Empirical Methods in Natural Language Processing*. Pittsburgh, PA.

Ekaterina Shutova. 2011. *Computational Approaches to Figurative Language*. Ph.D. thesis.

Ekaterina Shutova. 2015. Design and evaluation of metaphor processing systems. *Computational Linguistics* 41(4):579–623.

Paul H. Thibodeau and Lera Boroditsky. 2011. Metaphors we think with: The role of metaphor in reasoning. *PLOSone* 6(2). https://doi.org/10.1371/journal.pone.0016782.

Yulia Tsvetkov, Leonid Boytsov, Anatole Gershman, Eric Nyberg, and Chris Dyer. 2014. Metaphor detection with cross-lingual model transfer. In *Proceedings of the 52nd Annual Meeting of the Association for Computational Linguistics*. Association of Computational Linguistics, pages 248–258.

Peter D. Turney, Yair Neuman, Dan Assaf, and Yohai Cohen. 2011. Literal and metaphorical sense identification through concrete and abstract context. In *Proceedings of the 2011 Conference on Empirical Methods in Natural Language Processing*. Association of Computational Linguistics, pages 680–690.

Efficient Encoding of Pathology Reports Using Natural Language Processing

Rebecka Weegar
Dept. of Computer and
Systems Sciences
Stockholm University
rebeckaw@dsv.su.se

Jan F Nygård
The Cancer Registry of Norway
jfn@kreftregisteret.no

Hercules Dalianis
Dept. of Computer and
Systems Sciences
Stockholm University
hercules@dsv.su.se

Abstract

In this article we present a system that extracts information from pathology reports. The reports are written in Norwegian and contain free text describing prostate biopsies. Currently, these reports are manually coded for research and statistical purposes by trained experts at the Cancer Registry of Norway where the coders extract values for a set of predefined fields that are specific for prostate cancer. The presented system is rule based and achieves an average F-score of 0.91 for the fields Gleason grade, Gleason score, the number of biopsies that contain tumor tissue, and the orientation of the biopsies. The system also identifies reports that contain ambiguity or other content that should be reviewed by an expert. The system shows potential to encode the reports considerably faster, with less resources, and similar high quality to the manual encoding.

1 Introduction

A cancer diagnosis is often based on an examination of a biopsy, a small tissue sample taken from a patient with a suspected cancer disease. These samples are visually examined by a pathologist, using a microscope. To document the examination, the pathologist writes a report describing findings and a diagnosis.

Pathology reports are primarily a tool used for communicating findings done by the pathologist to the physician treating the patient, but if the findings in the reports are encoded and registered in a systematic way, they can also be used for research purposes.

In Norway, all pathology reports concerning cancer diseases are reported to The Cancer Reg-

istry of Norway. The contents of each report is read and encoded by a trained coder. This is an area where an efficient information extraction system could prove very useful, since about 180,000 reports are sent yearly to the registry where they are coded by 25 full time coders. The coding of a single report takes between two and ten minutes. (Observe that Norway has a population of 5.2 million inhabitants).

In this study we have focused on pathology reports written in Norwegian describing results from prostate biopsies. The goal of the system presented in this paper is to accurately extract information from the unstructured textual content of pathology reports, so that the extracted information can be stored in a structured data format suitable for a cancer registry.

2 Previous Research

A number of studies have applied information extraction techniques to pathology reports for several types of cancer, including breast cancer, colorectal cancer, lung cancer, and prostate cancer. Scharber (2007) provides an overview of various available tools.

Most of the work in this field has been done for English text, and both rule based and machine learning methods as well as combinations thereof have been applied. For a review of the research area, see Spasić et al. (2014).

Coden et al. (2009) extracted information from pathology reports for colon cancer. A combination of rules and machine learning were used to extract nine different classes from the reports.

Ou and Patrick (2014) extracted 28 different concepts from pathology reports for primary cutaneous melanoma (skin cancer).

Martinez and Li (2011) classified colorectal cancer according to the *TNM (Tumor, Node and*

Proceedings of Recent Advances in Natural Language Processing, pages 778–783,
Varna, Bulgaria, Sep 4–6 2017.

Metastases) scale using Naïve-Bayes and Support Vector Machines.

Nguyen et al. (2011) applied rule based methods to pathology reports for lung cancer.

The mentioned studies present results in the terms of F-score ranging from 0.7 to 0.9.

Currie et al. (2006) used rules to extract concepts in 5,826 breast cancer and 2,838 prostate cancer pathology reports. The extracted around 80 fields and obtained 90-95 percent accuracy. The evaluation was carried out by domain experts.

Two studies have applied rule based methods to Norwegian pathology reports. Dahl et al. (2016) extracted values for nine concepts from 25 pathology reports describing prostate biopsies. They obtained F-scores ranging from 0.24 to 0.94. Weegar and Dalianis (2015) extracted values for ten concepts related to breast cancer with an F-score ranging from 0.67 to 1.0 using 40 reports. Both studies were done on small data sets, but the results show that rule based methods are a promising approach for information extraction from pathology reports written in Norwegian.

3 Materials

Each document in the data set consists of the report written by the pathologist and the corresponding manual encoding of the report. There are no additional annotations of the reports, meaning that the documents contain no information about which parts of the text that an encoded value is based on. The full text of each report is therefore used as input for each encoded value. The reports do not contain names or other identifiers and have been securely stored and remotely accessed to ensure privacy protection.

The data was divided into a development set containing 70 percent of the documents and a test set with the remaining 30 percent. After removing duplicate files, there were 388 documents in the development set and 176 in the test set.

The reports in the development set contain 276 tokens on average, and each report describes between one and 21 biopsies, the average number of biopsies per report is 8.25. An example of a pathology report can be seen in Figure 1.

A specific set of fields is associated with and encoded for each type of cancer. For prostate cancer biopsies, 9 fields are extracted and each of them is encoded as an integer value. The fields are:

- Primary Gleason grade, a numerical value

```
Biopsier fra  venstre prostatalapp.
2:          Prostatakarsinom, Gleason
score  3+4=7(utbredelse 4/13 mm)
4:          Prostatakarsinom, Gleason
score 3+3=6(utbredelse 0,5/12 mm)
1,3:Ikke påvist malignitet

Biopsier fra høyre prostatalapp:
5-7,9:   HPIN og adenokarsinom, Gleason
score 3+3=6(utbredelse 1/13 mm)
8:   Prostatakarsinom, Gleason
score 3+4=7(utbredelse 5/15,4/15 mm)

Perinevral infiltrasjon: ikke påvist
Infiltrasjon i fettvev: ikke påvist
```

Figure 1: A pseudonymized example of text from a pathology report describing prostate biopsies. The text contains descriptions of 9 biopsies, four from the left side and five from the right side.

ranging from 1 to 5.

- Secondary Gleason grade, a numerical value ranging from 1 to 5.

- Gleason score, the sum of the primary and secondary Gleason grade.

- The number of biopsies.

- The number of malign biopsies.

- The number of biopsies with orientation right/left.

- The number of malign biopsies with orientation right/left.

A biopsy is malign if it contains cancerous cells and the Gleason grades and score are a type of cancer staging specific to prostate cancer. Gleason score is calculated as primary grade + secondary grade = score, for example:

```
Gleason score 4+3=7
```

gives that primary grade is 4, secondary grade is 3 and that Gleason score is 7. Primary here means the dominant grade seen in the biopsy. Different grades and score can be observed in different biopsies, and this means that there can be several different values for Gleason grades and score given in the same report. Of these values, the most prominent is selected and encoded.

The biopsies are typically indexed by numbers or letters and grouped together if they have the same characteristics. For example, the sentence

```
A-E, G: Biopsies from left side,
benign samples
```

	gleason	L	prostatacarcinom	L	adenocarcinom	L	venstre	L	høyre	L
1	*gleaoson*	1	*prostatakarsinom*	2	*adenokarsinom*	1	*vesntre*	2	*høye*	1
2	*glelason*	1	*prostatakarinom*	3	*adenocarcnom*	1	vekst	3	*h?yre*	1
3	*glerason*	1	*prostatakarsionom*	4	*adenokarsinom*	2	minste	3	*hlyre*	1
4	*gleaosn*	2	*protatakarsinom*	4	*adneocarcinom*	2	høystre	3	høre	1
5	*gelason*	2	*medprostatakarsinom*	5	*denokarsinom*	3	lengste	3	høyt	2
6	glass	3	*prostatatakarsinom*	6	*adenokarsinomet*	4	meste	3	nøye	2
7	glasa	3	prostatabiopiser	7	carcinom	5	tettere	4	høystre	2
8	glas	3	prostatakjertler	8	karsinom	7	hentet	4	sørre	2
9	glemt	4	adernocarcinom	8	derimot	8	beskr	4	høy	2
10	reaksjon	4	prostatasylindre	8	prostatacarcinom	8	nesten	4	score	3

Table 1: Spelling variants of key concepts *Gleason*, *Prostate carcinoma*, *Adenocarcinoma*, *Left* (venstre), and *Right* (høyre) identified by and ranked using Levenshtein distance (L) . Relevant variants are in boldface.

describes six biopsies (as indicated by the indices A-E, G) without tumor tissue with *left* orientation, and the sentence

```
3: Biopsy with prostate carcinoma,
Gleason grade 3+3=6
```

indicates one biopsy with tumor tissue and a Gleason score of six.

4 Methods

4.1 Value Extraction

A rule based solution has been implemented since the texts in reports are relatively structured. Using rules also has the benefit of transparency, the user always knows why a specific value was given by the system.

The rules included in the system were manually written using regular expressions and string matching and the system is implemented in Java. Firstly, the system reads the texts and the corresponding encoding from the documents. The text is preprocessed and the extraction rules are applied. The results of the extractions are evaluated and finally encoded.

The nine fields that are encoded for the current task can be divided into two groups, Gleason fields and Biopsy fields. The values of the fields in each group are highly dependent on each other and a set of rules have been written for each of the groups.

The Gleason grades and score are in most cases extracted together, as they are typically written as *primary grade + secondary grad = score*, with a number of minor variations. The exception is when only one or a few biopsies are reported, in those cases there is a larger variation in the reports, which requires additional rules.

For the biopsy group, six values are extracted, and the correct extraction of each value is necessary to get correct values for the subsequent fields. As a first step, each biopsy in the reports needs to be correctly identified to get the correct value for the field *Number of biopsies*. Then each identified biopsy is classified as benign or malignant and as having either the orientation left or right. The performance of the the extraction of the number biopsies that are malignant and the orientation each biopsy is limited by the performance of the first step.

4.2 Spelling Variations of Key Concepts

We identified a set of key concepts that are central to the encoding process, these concepts are *Gleason*, *Prostate carcinoma*, *Adenocarcinoma*, *Left* and *Right*. The texts contain a number of spelling variants of the key concepts and it is essential to correctly identify each of them, both standard variants, such as the two spellings of prostate carcinoma: *prostatakarsinom* and *prostatacarcinom*, and misspellings, in order to correctly encode the reports. Using the concept representation reduces the number of rules needed, since individual rules are not needed for each spelling variation.

The alternative spellings of the key concepts were found using Levenshtein distance (Levenshtein, 1966). The Levenshtein distance can be used as a measurement for how similar two strings are, and the distance is calculated by counting the number of substitutions, deletions, and insertions of characters that are required to make two strings equal.

To find the variations, the texts in the reports

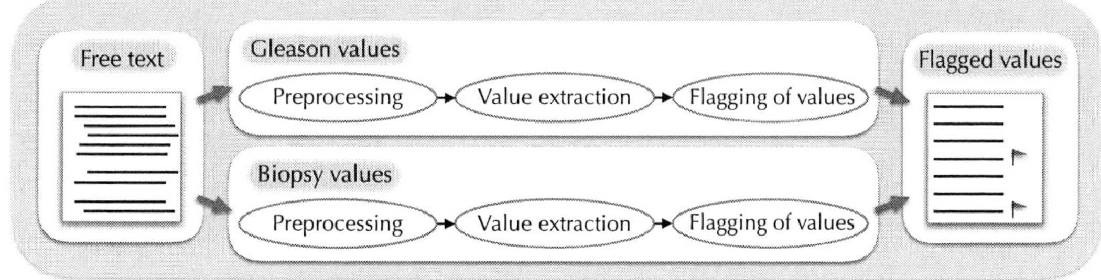

Figure 2: The contents of each report is processed separately for the two groups of fields, Gleason and Biopsy. After the values are extracted any inconsistencies in the values are flagged for manual review.

were tokenized and the Levenshtein distances between the tokens and the concept strings was calculated. Strings that are highly similar receive a low score, and the ten lowest scoring tokens for each concept are shown in Table 1. The relevant variants were manually selected from lowest scoring tokens and these tokens were included in the set of key concepts. For the concepts *Left* and *Right*, a number of abbreviations were also included.

4.3 Identifying Reports for Manual Review

The texts in the reports are relatively structured, but there are exceptions where the system might fail to extract the correct values. It would therefore be beneficial if the system itself could identify the reports that it is incapable of handling correctly. This would increase the precision of the system and allow the difficult cases to be manually reviewed.

To achieve this, a module was added that evaluates the extracted values. If inconsistencies are found, the values are flagged for review, see Figure 2. In total, three indicators for flagging were identified, and for the Gleason group, there is one such flag; a report gets marked for manual review if the concept *Gleason* is mentioned, but none of the extraction rules matches the contents of the text.

For the Biopsy group, the main source of error is that many of the reports lack information on the orientation of biopsies in the text. This information is instead often located in a sketch accompanying the reports. Since the current system is not able to process these images, the first mechanism is to flag any report that mentions neither the concept *left* nor the concept *right*.

The system contains a set of heuristic rules for inferring the orientation of the biopsies when the

orientation is not explicitly stated for each biopsy. For example, if a report only mentions the concept *Left*, all biopsies in that report are considered as having the orientation left. These heuristics improve performance when applied to all files, but in some cases they also introduce errors. These errors are partly due to the fact that the orientation of the malign biopsies is more often mentioned than the orientation of the benign biopsies.

The second mechanism for the Biopsy group therefore flags the files where the sum of the biopsies identified as having orientation left or right does not match the total number of biopsies identified, or when the total sum of malign biopsies does not match the sum of malign biopsies identified as left or right.

5 Results

The system has been evaluated against the test set containing 176 reports, using precision, recall and F-score. The results for are presented in Table 2.

Field	P	R	F
Gleason grade 1	1.0	0.98	0.99
Gleason grad 2	1.0	0.99	0.99
Gleason score	1.0	0.99	0.99
Number of biopsies	0.96	0.98	0.97
Biopsies w. tumor tissue	0.92	1.0	0.96
Biopsies, right	0.69	1.0	0.82
Biopsies, left	0.69	1.0	0.82
With tumor tissue, right	0.68	1.0	0.81
With tumor tissue, left	0.69	1.0	0.82

Table 2: Precision (P), recall (R) and F-score (F) for the nine extracted fields.

The next step was then to separate out the reports which the system determines should be manually reviewed. This procedure was applied at group level, first to the Gleason group and next to the Biopsy Group.

The system identified and flagged three reports in the test set for which the values in the Gleason group should be manually reviewed. When excluding these reports (< 2 percent of the test set), the performance was improved, see Table 3.

Field	P	R	F
Gleason grade 1	1.0	1.0	1.0
Gleason grad 2	1.0	1.0	1.0
Gleason score	1.0	1.0	1.0

Table 3: Precision (P), recall (R) and F-score (F) when excluding the three reports that the system flagged for manual review

The same process was applied to the Biopsy group. The first method for discovering challenging reports was to exclude all reports not mentioning the orientation of the biopsies. This step marked and excluded 67 reports in the test set (43 percent), and the results for remaining reports are shown in Table 4.

Field	P	R	F
Number of biopsies	0.98	0.99	0.99
Biopsies w. tumor tissue	0.95	1.0	0.97
Biopsies, right	0.89	1.0	0.94
Biopsies, left	0.9	1.0	0.95
With tumor tissue, right	0.90	1.0	0.95
With tumor tissue, left	0.91	1.0	0.95

Table 4: Precision (P), recall (R) and F-score (F) for the extracted fields in the Biopsy group, when only including the 110 reports mentioning the concepts right or left.

The second flagging mechanism for the Biopsy group marks 25 additional reports, meaning that the system is confident in correctly determining the values for all the fields in the Biopsy group for 48 percent of the reports in the test data. This step also improves the precision of the system, as shown in Table 5.

6 Error Analysis

The errors produced by the system are either due to the system not being able to handle previously unseen text structure or text content, or due to the data lacking information or containing noise. Lack of information is mostly regarding orientation, and

Field	P	R	F
Number of biopsies	0.99	0.99	0.99
Biopsies w. tumor tissue	0.97	1.0	0.98
Biopsies, right	0.95	1.0	0.98
Biopsies, left	0.97	1.0	0.98
With tumor tissue, right	0.97	1.0	0.98
With tumor tissue, left	0.95	1.0	0.98

Table 5: Precision (P), recall (R) and F-score (F) for the extracted fields in the Biopsy group, when only including the 85 reports mentioning the concepts right or left and reports where the sum of the fields left and right is equal to the total number of biopsies found

noise can for example be typos, such as when two different biopsies are indexed with the same number.

System errors can be corrected by updating the rule set, and errors due to noise or lack of information is most often caught by the flagging mechanisms

The data also contains a small number of cases where there is a mistake in the encoding.

A manual error analysis has been performed on the reports that are not marked by any flagging mechanism but still contain errors. There are no such reports for the Gleason group and eight reports for the Biopsy group.

Two of the reports contain one biopsy each that is erroneously classified as malign by the system. The system fails on correctly identifying the orientation of biopsies for two reports (one because of an unusual file structure and one because of some of the biopsies actually having the orientation "center"). Three reports contain an error in the encoding and one report is correctly encoded by the system based on the actual contents of the text, but where there likely is a typo in the text corrected during the manual encoding.

7 Conclusions and Future Work

We have demonstrated the possibility of automatically extracting and encoding information from free text pathology reports with a high level of accuracy. The developed system is not designed to be implemented as fully automatic, but to reduce the amount of manual work currently needed for the encoding of the reports. The results in this study in terms of precision and recall were high for a majority of the extracted fields, and will enable the Cancer Registry to encode the reports considerably faster, with less resources. A vital part of the system is marking the cases which should be manually reviewed, and notifying the coding experts to be extra vigilant in the coding of the flagged reports. Thus, contributing to a more consistent encoding and further improving the quality of the data.

The results in term of precision, recall and F-score are similar to the ones described in the studies in Section 2, but though the studies all share the domain of free text pathology reports, the actual task depends on the cancer type, the number of extracted fields, availability of annotations, and language, making a fair comparison difficult. The study by Dahl et al. (2016) was developed for a similar, but much smaller, data set and achieved an average F-score of 0.73 for the nine fields, whereas the current system has a significantly higher performance with an average F-score of 0.91.

The fields concerning orientation of the biopsies are the most challenging for the system, and the encoding produced by the system for these fields are somewhat difficult to evaluate. This is largely due to the fact that the values of these fields often are based on sketches not available to the system. Excluding the reports flagged by the system as not containing the concepts *Left* and *Right* improves the results for the orientation fields, but also reduces the number of reports that the system is able to handle automatically. A high precision is prioritised over a high recall in this case since it is necessary to produce data of a high enough quality for the registry.

This study focuses only on prostate cancer, but each cancer type that is encoded by the registry is associated with a specific set of fields. Future work therefore includes to extend the system to other cancer types as well as to investigate methods for automatic rule creation.

Acknowledgments

This work was supported by the Nordic Center of Excellence in Health-Related e-Sciences (NI-ASC); financed by NordForsk (Project number 62721).

References

Anni Coden, Guergana Savova, Igor Sominsky, Michael Tanenblatt, James Masanz, Karin Schuler, James Cooper, Wei Guan, and Piet C De Groen. 2009. Automatically extracting cancer disease characteristics from pathology reports into a Disease Knowledge Representation Model. *Journal of Biomedical Informatics* 42(5):937–949. https://doi.org/10.1016/j.jbi.2008.12.005.

Anne-Marie Currie, Travis Fricke, Agnes Gawne, Ric Johnston, John Liu, and Barbara Stein. 2006. Automated Extraction of Free-Text from Pathology Reports. In *AMIA Annual Symposium Proceedings*.

Anders Dahl, Atilla Özkan, and Hercules Dalianis. 2016. Pathology text mining on norwegian prostate cancer reports. In *Data Engineering Workshops (ICDEW), 2016 IEEE*. IEEE, pages 84–87. https://doi.org/10.1109/ICDEW.2016.7495622.

Vladimir Iosifovich Levenshtein. 1966. Binary codes capable of correcting deletions, insertions, and reversals. *Soviet Physics Doklady* 10(8):707–710.

David Martinez and Yue Li. 2011. Information extraction from pathology reports in a hospital setting. In *Proceedings of the 20th ACM international conference on Information and knowledge management*. ACM, pages 1877–1882. https://doi.org/10.1145/2063576.2063846.

Anthony Nguyen, Michael Lawley, David Hansen, and Shoni Colquist. 2011. Structured pathology reporting for cancer from free text: Lung cancer case study. *Electronic Journal of Health Informatics* 7(1):8.

Ying Ou and Jon Patrick. 2014. Automatic population of structured reports from narrative pathology reports. In *Proceedings of the Seventh Australasian Workshop on Health Informatics and Knowledge Management*. Australian Computer Society, Inc., HIKM '14, pages 41–50. http://dl.acm.org/citation.cfm?id=2667680.2667685.

Wendy Scharber. 2007. Evaluation of Open Source Text Mining Tools for Cancer Surveillance. *CDC* 24:28. https://www.cdc.gov/cancer/npcr/pdf/aerro/text_mining_tools.pdf.

Irena Spasić, Jacqueline Livsey, John A. Keane, and Goran Nenadić. 2014. Text mining of cancer-related information: Review of current status and future directions. *International Journal of Medical Informatics* 83(9):605–623. https://doi.org/10.1016/j.ijmedinf.2014.06.009.

Rebecka Weegar and Hercules Dalianis. 2015. Creating a rule based system for text mining of Norwegian breast cancer pathology reports. In *Sixth International Workshop in Health Text Mining and Information Analysis (LOUHI), in conjunction with EMNLP 2015, Portugal.* pages 73–78. https://doi.org/10.18653/v1/W15-2609.

Neural Reranking for Named Entity Recognition

Jie Yang and **Yue Zhang** and **Fei Dong**
Singapore University of Technology and Design
{jie_yang, fei_dong}@mymail.sutd.edu.sg
yue_zhang@sutd.edu.sg

Abstract

We propose a neural reranking system for named entity recognition (NER), leverages recurrent neural network models to learn sentence-level patterns that involve named entity mentions. In particular, given an output sentence produced by a baseline NER model, we replace all entity mentions, such as *Barack Obama*, into their entity types, such as *PER*. The resulting sentence patterns contain direct output information, yet is less sparse without specific named entities. For example, "PER was born in LOC" can be such a pattern. LSTM and CNN structures are utilised for learning deep representations of such sentences for reranking. Results show that our system can significantly improve the NER accuracies over two different baselines, giving the best reported results on a standard benchmark.

1 Introduction

Shown in Figure 1, named entity recognition aims to detect the entity mentions in a sentence and classify each entity mention into one out of a given set of categories. NER is typically solved as a sequence labeling problem.

Traditional NER systems use Hidden Markov Models (HMM) (Zhou and Su, 2002) and Conditional Random Fields (CRF) (Lafferty et al., 2001) with manually defined discrete features. External resources such as gazetteers and human defined complex global features are also incorporated to improve system performance (Ratinov and Roth, 2009; Che et al., 2013). Recently, deep neural network models have shown the ability of learning more abstract features compared with traditional

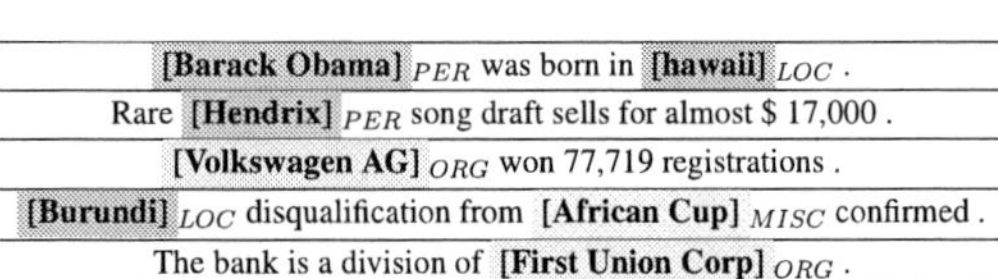

Figure 1: Named Entity Recognition.

statistical models with indicator features for NER (Zhang et al., 2015).

Recurrent Neural Network (RNN), in particular Long Short-Term Memory (LSTM) (Hochreiter and Schmidhuber, 1997), shows the ability to automatically capture history information over input sequences, which makes LSTM a proper automatic feature extractor for sequence labeling tasks. Different methods have been proposed by stacking CRF over LSTM in NER task (Chiu and Nichols, 2016; Huang et al., 2015; Lample et al., 2016; Ma and Hovy, 2016). In addition, it is possible to combine discrete and neural features for enriched information, which helps improve sequence labeling preformance (Zhang et al., 2016).

Reranking is a framework to improve system performance by utilizing more abstract features. A reranking system can take full advantage of global features, which are intractable in baseline sequence labelling systems that use exact decoding. The reranking method has been used in many NLP tasks, such as parsing (Collins and Koo, 2005), QAs (Chen et al., 2006) and machine translation (Wang et al., 2007; Shen et al., 2004).

Some work has adopted the reranking strategy for NER. Collins (2002) tried both a boosting algorithm and a voted perceptron algorithm as reranking models on named-entity boundaries (without classification of entities). Nguyen et al. (2010) applied Support Vector Machine (SVM) with kernels to reranking model, obtaining significant improvements in F-measure on CoNLL 2003 datasets. Yoshida and Tsujii (2007) used a sim-

Proceedings of Recent Advances in Natural Language Processing, pages 784–792,
Varna, Bulgaria, Sep 4–6 2017.

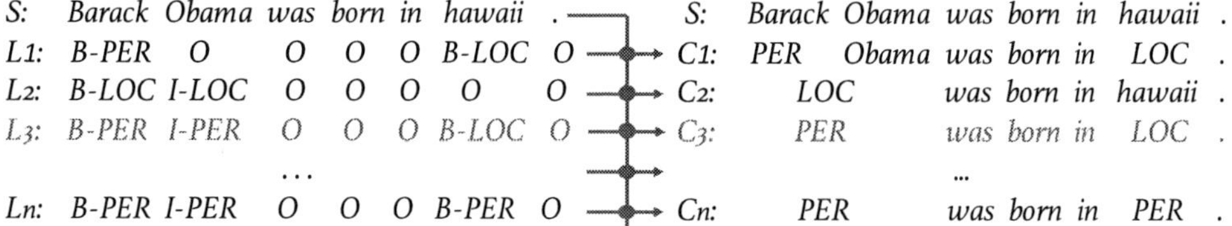

Figure 2: Example of generating collapsed sentence patterns from baseline NER output label sequences.

ple log-linear rerank model on a biomedical NER task, also obtaining slight improvemts. All the above methods use sparse manual features. To the best of our knowledge, there has been no neural reranking model for NER task.

Our work is also in line with neural sentence representation topic. Related tasks such as paraphrase detection (Socher et al., 2011), sentiment classification (HLTCOE, 2013; Le and Mikolov, 2014) are all benifiting from neural models. Le and Mikolov (2014) proposed an unsupervised algorithm to learn the representation of sentences, paragraphs and even documents. Convolution Neural Network (CNN) structure has been used to represent sentences for classification task (Kim, 2014). Palangi et al. (2016) embedded sentences with simple LSTM model but got good results on the web document retrieval task. Zhu et al. (2015b) utilized syntactic information into sentence representation using tree-LSTM.

In this paper, we propose a simple neural reranking model for NER. The model learns sentence patterns that involve output named entities automatically, using neural network. Take the sentence *"Barack Obama was born in hawaii ."* as an example, Figure 2 illustrates several candidate sentence patterns such as *"PER was born in LOC ."* (C_3) and *"LOC was born in hawaii ."* (C_2), where *PER* represents entity type *persons* and *LOC* means *locations*. It is obvious that C_3 is a much more reasonable sentence pattern compared to C_2. To generate the sentence patterns above, we replace predicted entities in candidate sequences with their entity type names. This can effectively reduce the sparsity of candidate sequences, as each entity type contains open vocabulary names (e.g. *PER* can be *Donald Trump*, *Hillary Clinton* etc.), which can bring noise when learning the sentence patterns. In addition, since the learned sentence patterns are global over output structures, it is difficult for baseline sequence

Description	Feature Template
word grams	w_i, w_iw_{i+1}
shape, capital	$Sh(w_i), Ca(w_i)$
capital + word	$Ca(w_i)w_i$
connect word	$Co(w_i)$
capital + connect	$Ca(w_i)Co(w_i)$
cluster grams	$Cl(w_i), Cl(w_iw_{i+1})$
prefix, suffix	$Pr(w_i), Su(w_i)$
POS grams	$P(w_i, w_iw_{i+1}, w_{i-1}w_1w_{i+1})$
POS + word	$P(w_0)w_0$

Table 1: Features of discrete *CRF* for NER, $i \in \{-1, 0\}$.

labeling systems to capture such patterns.

We develop a neural reranking model which captures candidate pattern features using LSTM and auxilliary neural structures, including CNN (Kim, 2014; Kalchbrenner et al., 2014) and character based neural features. The learned global sentence pattern representations are then used as features for scoring by the reranker. Results over a state-of-the-art discrete baseline using CRF and a state-of-the-art neural baseline using LSTM-CRF show significant improvements. On CoNLL 2003 test data, our model achieves the best reported result.

Our main contributions include (a) leveraging global sentence patterns that involve entity type information for NER raranking, (b) exploiting auxilliary neural features to enrich basic LSTM sequence representation and (c) achieving the best F1 result on CoNLL 2003 data. The source codes of this paper are released under GPL at `https://github.com/jiesutd/RerankNER`.

2 Baselines

Formally, given a sentence S with t words: $S = \{w_1, w_2, ..., w_t\}$, the task of NER is to find out all the named entity mentions from S. The dominate approach takes the task as a sequence labelling problem, where the goal is to generate a label sequence $L = \{l_1, l_2, ..., l_t\}$, where $l_i = p_i e_i$. Here p_i is an entity label, $p_i \in \{B, I, O\}$, where B indicates the beginning of an entity mention, I denotes a non-beginning word of a named entity mention and O denotes a non-named-entity word [1]. e_i indicates the entity type. In the CoNLL dataset that we use for our experiments, $e_i \in \{PER, ORG, LOC, MISC\}$, where "$PER$" indicates a *person* name; "LOC", "ORG", "$MISC$" represent *location*, *organization* and *miscellaneous*, respectively.

We choose two baseline systems, one using discrete CRF with handcrafted features and one using neural CRF model with bidirectional LSTM structure, both baselines giving the state-of-the-art accuracies among their respective category of models.

2.1 Discrete CRF

We choose a basic discrete CRF model as our baseline tagger. As shown in Figure 3(a), discrete word features are first extracted as binary vectors (black and white circles) and then fed into a CRF layer. Taking those discrete features as input, the CRF layer can give *n-best* predicted sequences as well as their probabilities. Table 1 shows the discrete features that we used, which follow the definition of (Yang et al., 2016). Here *shape* means whether characters in word are belonging to number, English character or not. *capital* is the indication if word starts with *upper-case* English character, *connect words* include five types: "of", "and", "for", "-" and other. Prefix and suffix include the 4-level prefixes and suffixes of each words.

2.2 Neural CRF

A neural CRF with bidirectional LSTM structure is used as our second baseline, which is shown in Figure 3(b). Word representations are represented with continious vectors (gray circles), which are fed into a bidirectional LSTM layer to extract neural features. A CRF layer with *n-best* output is stacked on top of the LSTM layer to decode the label sequences based on the neural features. We use the neural structure of Ma and Hovy (2016), where the word representation is the concatenation of word embedding and a CNN output on the character sequence of the word.

---

[1] When $p_i = O$, e_i equals to NULL.

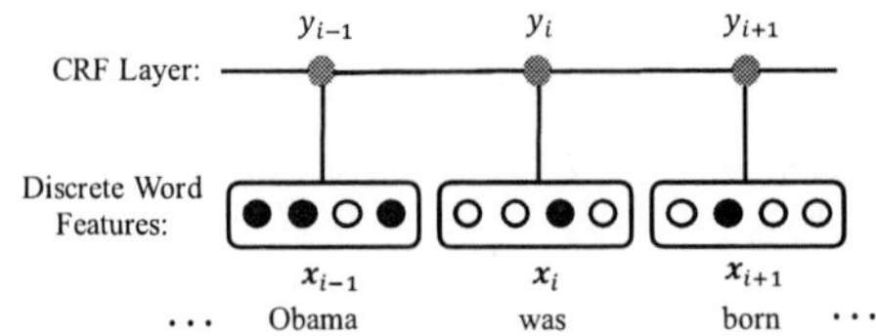

(a) Discrete CRF baseline.

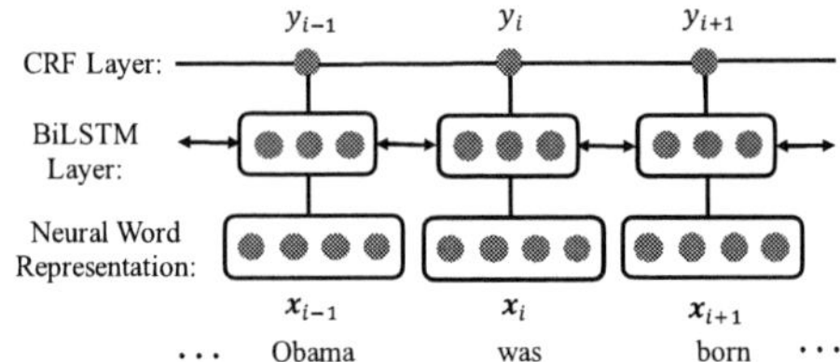

(b) Neural CRF baseline.

Figure 3: Baselines.

3 Reranking Algorithms

3.1 Collapsed Sentence Representation

Given the *n-best* output label sequences of a baseline system $\{L_1, L_2, ..., L_i, ..., L_n\}$, where $L_i = \{l_{i1}, l_{i2}, ..., l_{it}\}$, we learn a reranking score $s(L_i)$ for L_i by firsting converting L_i into a sequence pattern C_i, and then learning a representation $h(C_i)$ as its dense representation. To convert candidate sequence L_i to collapsed sequence C_i. We use the following rules to convert each label sequence L_i into a collapsed sentence pattern C_i.

If the L_i include entity labels (e.g. l_{i1} =B-PER, l_{i2}=I-PER), then the entity labels are replaced with the corresponding entity type name (e.g. $\{l_{i1}, l_{i2}\}$ → PER, $C_{i1} = PER$), else labels are replaced by its corresponding words ($C_{ix} = w_x$). In the example shown in Figure 2, $S = \{Barack\ Obama\ was\ born\ in\ hawaii\ .\}$ and $L_3 = \{B\text{-}PER\ I\text{-}PER\ O\ O\ O\ B\text{-}LOC\ O\}$. The corresponding collapsed sequence is $C_3 = \{PER\ was\ born\ in\ LOC\ .\}$, *Barack Obama* and *hawaii* are regarded as entities and hence are replaced by the entity names, i.e. *PER* and *LOC*, respectively.

3.2 Neural Features

Given a collapsed sentence representation C_i, we use neural network to learn its overall representation vector $h(C_i)$, which is used for the scoring of C_i.

Word Representation: We use *SENNA* (Collobert et al., 2011) embedding to initialize the word embedding of our reranking system. For out of vocabulary words , embeddings are randomly initialized within $(-\sqrt{\frac{3.0}{wordDim}}, \sqrt{\frac{3.0}{wordDim}})$, where $wordDim$ is the word dimension size (Ma and Hovy, 2016).

Character features are proved useful in capturing morphological features, such as word similarity and dealing with the out-of-vocabulary problem (Ling et al., 2015). As shown in Figure 4(a), we follow Ma and Hovy (2016) by utilizing CNN to extract character-level representation [2]. Input character sequences are firstly passed through the embedding layer to lookup the character embeddings. To extract local features, a *convolution layer* with a fixed window-size is applied on top of the embedding layer. Then we use a *max-pooling* layer to map varying length vectors into a fixed size output vector. Finally, word representation is the concatenation of character CNN output vectors and word embeddings.

LSTM features: We choose a word-based LSTM as the main network, using it for capturing global sentence pattern information. For input sequence vectors $\{x_1, x_2, ..., x_t\}$, our LSTM model is implemented as follows:

$$
\begin{aligned}
h_t &= tanh(M_t) \odot o_t \\
i_t &= \sigma(W_1 h_{t-1} + W_2 x_t + \mu_1 \odot M_{t-1} + b_1) \\
f_t &= \sigma(W_3 h_{t-1} + W_4 x_t + \mu_2 \odot M_{t-1} + b_2) \\
\widetilde{M_i} &= tanh(W_5 y_{t-1} + W_6 x_i + b_3) \\
M_t &= i_i \odot \widetilde{M_i} + f_i \odot M_{t-1} \\
o_t &= \sigma(W_7 h_{t-1} + W_8 x_t + b_4),
\end{aligned}
$$

where $\odot$ is the element-wise multiply operator, σ is the sigmoid function, and $\{W, b, \mu\} \in \Theta$ are parameters. i_t, f_t, M_t and o_t are the *input gate, forget gate, memory cell* and *output gate*, respectively. h_t is the hidden vector at step t in the input sentence. As shown in Figure 4(b), word representations are the concatenation of word embeddings and character CNN output (red block). We choose the hidden vector in last word h_{LSTM} as the representation of the input sequence.

CNN features: We introduce CNN to capture local features of the candidate sequences. It consists of a *filter* $W \in R^{h \times k}$ which operates on a context of k words to produce local order features. Max pooling layer is employed over the convolutional layer to extract the most salient features.

---

[2] Characters are padded into a fixed length by using a special token *Pad*.

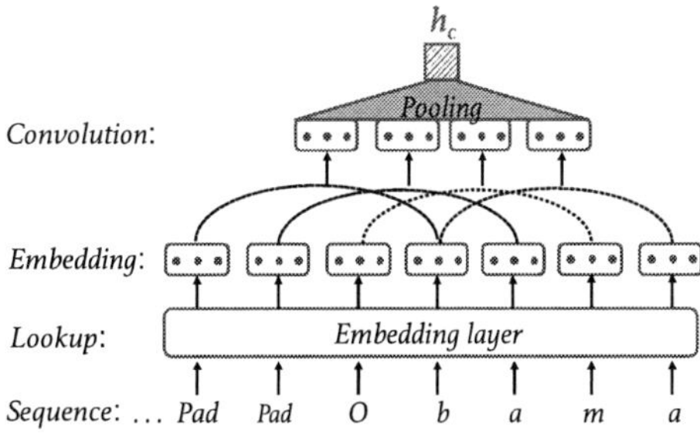

(a) CNN character sequence representation for word.

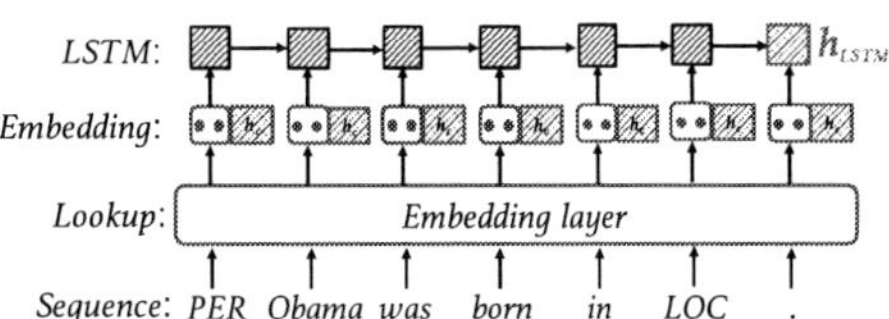

(b) LSTM word sequence representation for sentence.

Figure 4: Representation.

Assume u_j is the concatenation of word representations in Eq. (1) centralized in the embedding z_j in a given sequence $u_1, u_2, ..., u_L$, CNN applies a matrix-vector operation to each window of size k successive window along the sequence in Eq. (2).

$$
\begin{aligned}
u_j &= (z_{j-(k-1)/2}, ..., z_{j+(k-1)/2}) &\quad (1) \\
r_i &= max_{1<j<L}(W u_j + b)_i, i = 1, ..., d, &\quad (2)
\end{aligned}
$$

where z_j is the j-th word embedding in the given sequence, d is the output dimension of the CNN. $h = [r_1, ..., r_i, ..., r_d]$ is the fixed-size feature representation for the sequence after pooling.

The *CNN* representation structure is similar to Figure 4(a) but its input is word representations rather than character embeddings. We define the CNN features of word sequence as h_{CNN}.

3.3 Score Calculation

After the LSTM and CNN features of collapsed sequence C_i are extracted, we concatenate them together and feed the result into a *softmax* layer.

$$
\begin{aligned}
h(C_i) &= h_{LSTM} \oplus h_{CNN} \\
s(C_i) &= \sigma(W h(C_i) + b),
\end{aligned} \quad (3)
$$

where $\oplus$ represents the concatenating operation, $h(C_i)$ is the final representation of collapsed sequence C_i and $s(C_i)$ is the output score of C_i.

Parameter	Value	Parameter	Value
n-best	10	peepholes	no
wordDim	50	charDim	50
LSTM hidden	100	dropout	0.2
charCNN filter	50	batch size	128
wordCNN filter	100	λ	0.001
charCNN length	3	*Adam* β_1	0.1
wordCNN length	3	*Adam* β_2	0.999
learning rate	0.001	*Adam* ϵ	1e-8

Table 2: Hyperparameters of reranker.

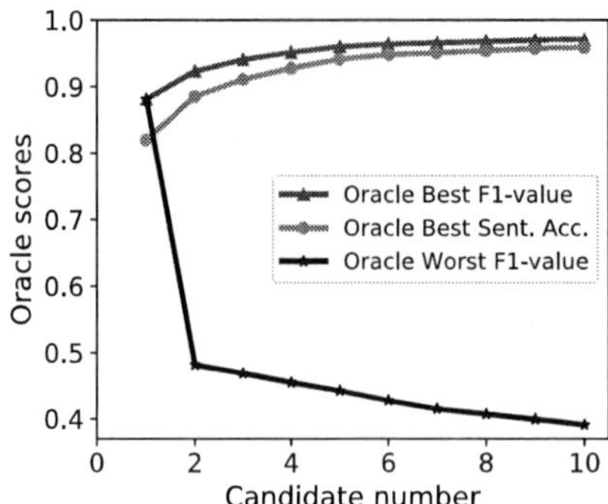

Figure 5: Oracle scores in baseline outputs.

3.4 Decoding

We use a mixture reranking strategy during decoding. Denote the candidate label sequence set on sentence S as $C(S) = \{C_1, C_2, ..., C_n\}$. We take advantage of both the reranker prediction score and the baseline tagger's output probability, using the score

$$\hat{y}_i = \arg \max_{C_i \in C(S)} (\alpha s(C_i) + (1 - \alpha)p(L_i)), \quad (4)$$

where $\alpha \in [0, 1]$ is an interpolation weight, which is a hyperparameter tuned on the development set. $p(L_i)$ is the probability of label sequence L_i in the baseline tagger.

3.5 Training

For each training triplet $\{S, L_i, C_i\}$, given the golden sequence L_{golden}, we calculate the tag accuracy $y_i \in [0, 1]$ of each candidate sequence based on L_i and L_{golden}. The same decoding process is applied to each collapsed sequence (C_i, y_i). We use a logistic regression model with mean square error (MSE) as the loss function, with a l_2-regulation term [3] :

$$J(\Theta) = \frac{1}{|\mathcal{D}|} \sum_{(C_i, y_i) \in \mathcal{D}} (y_i - s(C_i))^2 + \frac{\lambda}{2} ||\Theta||_2^2 \quad (5)$$

where Θ are all the parameters to be trained, $\mathcal{D}$ is the training set and λ is the regulation factor.

Adam (Kingma and Ba, 2015) is used to update model parameters.

4 Experiments

4.1 Settings

We use *CRF++* [4] as our discrete baseline CRF implementation and default parameters are used.

For neural baseline, we follow the same structure and settings of the state-of-the-art system (Ma and Hovy, 2016). When building the neural reranking system, *SENNA* embedding with 50 dimensions is used to initialize word embeddings. Hyperparameters of reranking system are listed in Table 2.

As we use the mixture strategy in Eq. (4) during decoding, we search the ideal interpolation weight α within $[0, 1]$ in a step of *0.005* based on the preformance under the development set.

4.2 Reranking Data

All of our experiments are evaluated on the standard CoNLL 2003 English dataset (Tjong Kim Sang and De Meulder, 2003), which is a collection of Reuters newswire articles. The CoNLL 2003 English dataset includes 14,987 training sentences, 3,466 development sentences and 3,684 test sentences, annotated into 4 entity types, i.e. *persons(PER), locations(LOC), organizations(ORG)* and *miscellaneous(MISC)*.

To construct the reranking training data, we conduct five-fold jackknifing, splitting the training set into 5 equal parts. In each case, the baseline tagger trains the model with 4/5 of the data and decode the remaining 1/5 to generate *n-best* candidate label sequences. For the reranking development and test data, the full training set is used to encode baseline tagger and decode development/test sentences with *n-best* output. All the *n-best* candidate sequences are converted into collapsed sequences following Section 3.1.

4.3 Baseline Oracle Results

The discrete baseline achieves 92.13% of F1-measure in development set and 88.15% in test set. Our neural baseline gives 94.58% and 91.25% on

---

[3] We also tried *max-margin* criterion like (Zhu et al., 2015a), while the results are similar with regression model.

[4] https://taku910.github.io/crfpp/

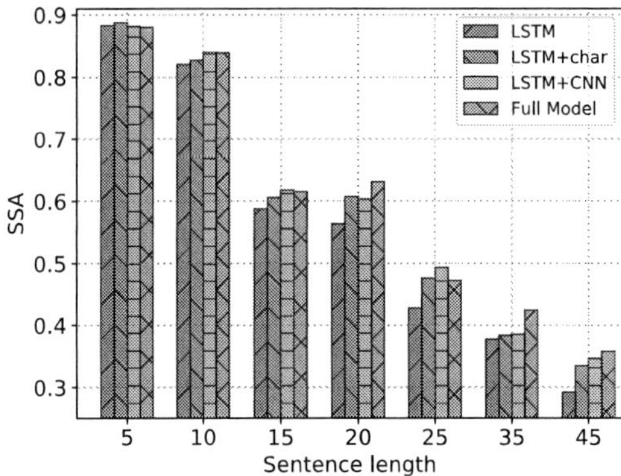

Figure 6: SSA with sentence length.

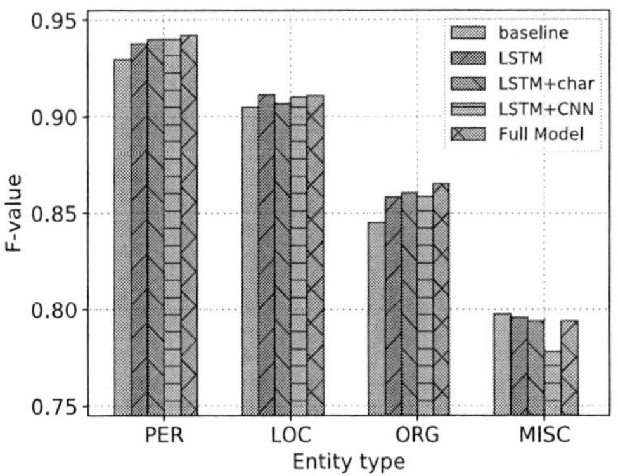

Figure 7: F1-value comparision by entity types.

development and test data, respectively. The discrete baseline for example. Figure 5 shows different oracle scores varying with *n-best* in discrete baseline. The oracle best is obtained by always chooseing the best sequence in the *n-best* candidates, and *vice versa* for the oracle worst. The orcale best sentence accuracy (OBA) [5] represents the accuracy of the sequence choice within the *n-best* candidates under oracle best assumption, and the orcale best F1-value (OBF) is the corresponding F1-value similarly. Orcale worst F1-value (OWF) is the F1-value under the worst choice situation.

As the figure shows, the larger n is, the better is the OBA, which means that a potentially better reranking result is possible. On the other hand, the OWF also drops, which means that the reranking task is more difficult. In our experiments, *n-best* is set as 10, the orcale best F1-value of test set achieves 97.13% (+8.98%) while its orcale worst F1-value drops 49.07% to 39.08%.

4.4 Influence of Sentence Length

We perform development experiments to evaluate model performance on various sentence lengths. Figure 6 shows results by reranking the discrete baseline. Here sentence select accuracy (SSA) is calculated using the corrected number of sentences divided by the total number of sentences. The *x-axis* is the sentence length range (e.g. 10 means sentence length range from 5 to 10), while the *y-axis* corresponds to SSA within 10-best candidates before the mixture strategy (without mixing baseline output probability).

As shown in the Figure 6, the accuracies of all model settings drop as the size of the sentence increases, which demonstrates that longer sentences are more challenging to our neural rerankers as they are to the baseline models. This can be because for longer sentences, candidate collapsed sequences have higher overlapping proportions and hence are more difficult to distinguishing by reranker. Both character information and CNN local features are useful for enhancing the SSA over a LSTM-only baseline. With the integration of character information and CNN features, our full model reranker can improve its performance on all sentence length ranges, especially for long sentences.

4.5 Influence of Entity Type

Figure 7 shows the comparision of models on different entity types. Compared with the baseline, entities with type of *PER* and *ORG* receive the most improvements, showing that sentence patterns are useful for those types. The performance on entities with type of *MISC* decreases slightly, since *MISC* includes various entity types which bring noise on learning sentence patterns. We believe that our model can benifit more from the NER corpus with fine-grained entity type. Table 3 shows the F1-value and SSA (after mixing baseline output probability) of our reranker on test data with different neural features on the discrete baseline. The word based LSTM reranker achieves the F1-value of 88.75%, with 0.6% absolute improvement over the baseline tagger. Cooperating with CNN features on word only does not make much improvement, while character CNN features are more effective (+0.78%). However, the full

---

[5]Notice this is different with accuracy which represents the correct rate of tags, OBA represents the correct rate in sentence level.

Model (%)	F1	ΔF1	SSA	ΔSSA
Baseline	88.15	0	83.31	0
LSTM	88.75	0.60	84.41	1.10
LSTM+CNN	88.79	0.64	84.63	1.32
LSTM+char	88.93	0.78	84.69	1.38
Full model	**89.25**	1.10	**85.12**	1.82

Table 3: F1-value and SSA on test set.

combination of character representation and word CNN features improves the F-value to 89.25% (+1.10%) with the significance level of $p < 0.05$ with *t-test*. The trend of SSA is the same as the F1-value, the accuracy is improved from the baseline 83.31% to 85.12% using the full model reranker, with an absolute improvement of 1.82%.

4.6 Effectiveness of Reranking

Table 4 shows our rerank results on two baselines and the comparison with state-of-the-art systems. Our reranker on discrete baseline compares favourably to the best discrete models, including the use of external corpus (Kazama and Torisawa, 2007; Suzuki and Isozaki, 2008). It also outperforms Nguyen et al. (2010) which builds a discrete reranking model by utilizing SVM with kernels. Ratinov and Roth (2009)* achieves 90.57% in discrete model by combining global features and abundant external lexicons, while its performance drops to 88.55% when removing the global features (Ratinov and Roth, 2009). Luo et al. (2015) gives the best discrete result (91.20%) by jointing NER with disambiguation task together.

Collobert et al. (2011) builds a first neural NER model with comparable performance to discrete models on CoNLL 2003 corpus. Most state-of-the-art neural NER models utilize bidirectional LSTM with a CRF layer (Huang et al., 2015). Lample et al. (2016) and Ma and Hovy (2016) concatenate character representation with word embedding and Chiu and Nichols (2016) even merge lexicon features into word representation. Passos et al. (2014) obtain a 90.90% by combining discrete features and neural word embeddings in a CRF model. Our neural baseline, which takes the same features as Ma and Hovy (2016), achieves 91.25% in F-value. Our reranker on this baseline outperforms all the previous models with the F-value of 91.62%, which is the best reported F-score on CoNLL 2003.

Discrete Model (%)	F1
Kazama and Torisawa (2007)	88.02
Suzuki and Isozaki (2008)	89.92
Nguyen et al. (2010)	88.16
Ratinov and Roth (2009)	88.55
Ratinov and Roth (2009)*	90.57
Luo et al. (2015)	91.20
Discrete baseline	88.13
Our reranker	89.25

Neural Model (%)	F1
Collobert et al. (2011)	89.59
Passos et al. (2014)	90.90
Huang et al. (2015)	90.10
Chiu and Nichols (2016)	90.77
Lample et al. (2016)	90.94
Ma and Hovy (2016)	91.21
Neural baseline	91.25
Our reranker	**91.62**

Table 4: Comparison of state-of-the-art systems.

4.7 Examples

Figure 8 gives some example outputs on the development dataset for which discrete baseline gives incorrect outputs yet the reranker corrects the mistake. Our reranker learns better sentence patterns by correcting both named entity boundary errors and named entity type errors.

In the first case, example 1 shows that *"U.N. Ambassador Albright"* in sentence *"U.N. Ambassador Albright arrives in Chile ."* is incorrectly tagged as a *organization* by the baseline and the entity boundary is incorrect either. By building the collapsed sentences as the input of our reranker, entities such as *"U.N. Ambassador Albright"* are replaced as a single entity name *"ORG"*. Our reranking model learns that *"... PER arrives in LOC ..."* is more possible compared to *"... ORG arrives in LOC ..."*, thereby the candidate with the reasonable entity boundary and type is picked by our reranker.

For the second case, the entity type of *"EL SALVADOR"* in example 3 *"SOCCER - U.S. BEAT EL SALVADOR 3-1 ."* is incorrectly recognized as *organization* by baseline. Our reranker corrects this entity type error by giving higher score to sentence pattern *"... LOC BEAT LOC ..."* rather than pattern *"... LOC BEAT ORG ..."*.

Baseline 1	[U.N. Ambassador Albright] $_{ORG}$ arrives in [Chile] $_{LOC}$.
Reranker 1	[U.N.] $_{ORG}$ Ambassador [Albright] $_{PER}$ arrives in [Chile] $_{LOC}$.
Baseline 2	West [Indian] $_{MISC}$ all-rounder [Phil Simmons] $_{PER}$ took four ...
Reranker 2	[West Indian] $_{MISC}$ all-rounder [Phil Simmons] $_{PER}$ took four ...
Baseline 3	SOCCER - [U.S.] $_{LOC}$ BEAT [EL SALVADOR] $_{ORG}$ 3-1 .
Reranker 3	SOCCER - [U.S.] $_{LOC}$ BEAT [EL SALVADOR] $_{LOC}$ 3-1 .
Baseline 4	... prisoners are held in [Rangoon] $_{LOC}$'s [Insein Prison] $_{PER}$.
Reranker 4	... prisoners are held in [Rangoon] $_{LOC}$'s [Insein Prison] $_{LOC}$.
Baseline 5	[PAKISTAN] $_{LOC}$ WIN TOSS , PUT [ENGLAND] $_{ORG}$ INTO BAT.
Reranker 5	[PAKISTAN] $_{LOC}$ WIN TOSS , PUT [ENGLAND] $_{LOC}$ INTO BAT.

Figure 8: Output examples. The first two examples illustrate the correction of entity boundary errors and the followings show the correction of entity type errors.

5 Conclusion

We proposed a neural reranking architecture for NER by exploiting neural structure to learn sentence patterns. Given the candidate label sequences generated from a baseline tagger, we replace the predicted entity words with the corresponding entity type names to build collapsed sentences, which are used as inputs of a neural reranking model. A mixture reranking strategy is used to combine both the knowledge of the probability from the baseline tagger and the reranker score. Experiments on both discrete and neural baselines show our reranking system improves NER performance significantly, obtaining the best results on CoNLL 2003 English task .

One problem of current method is that all the candidates share the same non-entity words, which lead the neural representations similar, especially for long sentences. In future work, we will develop neural tree structures based on entity position, which can enlarge the difference between candidate sequences. Intuitively, we believe the entities contribute more than non-entity when modeling the sequence vector, *attention* model (Bahdanau et al., 2015) may help collect more information from the intermediate vector of sentences.

Acknowledgments

We thank the anonymous reviewers for their insightful comments and Zhiyang Teng, Zhongqing Wang for their meaningful discussion. Yue Zhang is the corresponding author.

References

Dzmitry Bahdanau, Kyunghyun Cho, and Yoshua Bengio. 2015. Neural machine translation by jointly learning to align and translate. *International Conference on Learning Representations* .

Wanxiang Che, Mengqiu Wang, Christopher D Manning, and Ting Liu. 2013. Named entity recognition with bilingual constraints. In *HLT-NAACL*. pages 52–62.

Yi Chen, Ming Zhou, and Shilong Wang. 2006. Reranking answers for definitional qa using language modeling. In *Proceedings of the 21st International Conference on Computational Linguistics and the 44th annual meeting of the Association for Computational Linguistics*. Association for Computational Linguistics, pages 1081–1088.

Jason Chiu and Eric Nichols. 2016. Named entity recognition with bidirectional lstm-cnns. *Transactions of the Association for Computational Linguistics* 4:357–370. https://transacl.org/ojs/index.php/tacl/article/view/792.

Michael Collins. 2002. Ranking algorithms for named-entity extraction: Boosting and the voted perceptron. In *Proceedings of the 40th Annual Meeting on Association for Computational Linguistics*. Association for Computational Linguistics, pages 489–496.

Michael Collins and Terry Koo. 2005. Discriminative reranking for natural language parsing. *Computational Linguistics* 31(1):25–70.

Ronan Collobert, Jason Weston, Léon Bottou, Michael Karlen, Koray Kavukcuoglu, and Pavel Kuksa. 2011. Natural language processing (almost) from scratch. *Journal of Machine Learning Research* 12(Aug):2493–2537.

JHU HLTCOE. 2013. Semeval-2013 task 2: Sentiment analysis in twitter. *Atlanta, Georgia, USA* 312.

Sepp Hochreiter and Jürgen Schmidhuber. 1997. Long short-term memory. *Neural computation* 9(8):1735–1780.

Zhiheng Huang, Wei Xu, and Kai Yu. 2015. Bidirectional lstm-crf models for sequence tagging. *arXiv preprint arXiv:1508.01991* .

Nal Kalchbrenner, Edward Grefenstette, and Phil Blunsom. 2014. A convolutional neural network for modelling sentences pages 655–665. http://www.aclweb.org/anthology/P14-1062.

Junichi Kazama and Kentaro Torisawa. 2007. Exploiting wikipedia as external knowledge for named entity recognition. In *EMNLP-CoNLL*. pages 698–707.

Yoon Kim. 2014. Convolutional neural networks for sentence classification pages 1746–1751. http://www.aclweb.org/anthology/D14-1181.

Diederik Kingma and Jimmy Ba. 2015. Adam: A method for stochastic optimization. *International Conference for Learning Representations* .

John Lafferty, Andrew McCallum, and Fernando Pereira. 2001. Conditional random fields: Probabilistic models for segmenting and labeling sequence data. In *Proceedings of the eighteenth international conference on machine learning, ICML*. volume 1, pages 282–289.

Guillaume Lample, Miguel Ballesteros, Sandeep Subramanian, Kazuya Kawakami, and Chris Dyer. 2016. Neural architectures for named entity recognition pages 260–270. http://www.aclweb.org/anthology/N16-1030.

Quoc Le and Tomas Mikolov. 2014. Distributed representations of sentences and documents. In *Proceedings of the 31st International Conference on Machine Learning (ICML-14)*. pages 1188–1196.

Wang Ling, Chris Dyer, Alan W Black, Isabel Trancoso, Ramon Fermandez, Silvio Amir, Luis Marujo, and Tiago Luis. 2015. Finding function in form: Compositional character models for open vocabulary word representation pages 1520–1530. http://aclweb.org/anthology/D15-1176.

Gang Luo, Xiaojiang Huang, Chin-Yew Lin, and Zaiqing Nie. 2015. Joint named entity recognition and disambiguation. In *Proc. EMNLP*.

Xuezhe Ma and Eduard Hovy. 2016. End-to-end sequence labeling via bidirectional lstm-cnns-crf pages 1064–1074. http://www.aclweb.org/anthology/P16-1101.

Truc-Vien T Nguyen, Alessandro Moschitti, and Giuseppe Riccardi. 2010. Kernel-based reranking for named-entity extraction. In *Proceedings of the 23rd International Conference on Computational Linguistics: Posters*. Association for Computational Linguistics, pages 901–909.

Hamid Palangi, Li Deng, Yelong Shen, Jianfeng Gao, Xiaodong He, Jianshu Chen, Xinying Song, and Rabab Ward. 2016. Deep sentence embedding using long short-term memory networks: Analysis and application to information retrieval. *IEEE/ACM Transactions on Audio, Speech and Language Processing (TASLP)* 24(4):694–707.

Alexandre Passos, Vineet Kumar, and Andrew McCallum. 2014. Lexicon infused phrase embeddings for named entity resolution pages 78–86. http://www.aclweb.org/anthology/W/W14/W14-1609.

Lev Ratinov and Dan Roth. 2009. Design challenges and misconceptions in named entity recognition. In *Proceedings of the Thirteenth Conference on Computational Natural Language Learning*. Association for Computational Linguistics, pages 147–155.

Libin Shen, Anoop Sarkar, and Franz Josef Och. 2004. Discriminative reranking for machine translation. In *HLT-NAACL*. pages 177–184.

Richard Socher, Eric H Huang, Jeffrey Pennin, Christopher D Manning, and Andrew Y Ng. 2011. Dynamic pooling and unfolding recursive autoencoders for paraphrase detection. In *Advances in Neural Information Processing Systems*. pages 801–809.

Jun Suzuki and Hideki Isozaki. 2008. Semi-supervised sequential labeling and segmentation using gigaword scale unlabeled data. In *ACL*. pages 665–673.

Erik F Tjong Kim Sang and Fien De Meulder. 2003. Introduction to the conll-2003 shared task: Language-independent named entity recognition. In *Proceedings of the seventh conference on Natural language learning at HLT-NAACL 2003-Volume 4*. Association for Computational Linguistics, pages 142–147.

Wen Wang, Andreas Stolcke, and Jing Zheng. 2007. Reranking machine translation hypotheses with structured and web-based language models. In *Automatic Speech Recognition & Understanding, 2007. ASRU. IEEE Workshop on*. IEEE, pages 159–164.

Jie Yang, Zhiyang Teng, Meishan Zhang, and Yue Zhang. 2016. Combining discrete and neural features forsequence labeling. In *International Conference on Intelligent Text Processing and Computational Linguistics*.

Kazuhiro Yoshida and Jun'ichi Tsujii. 2007. Reranking for biomedical named-entity recognition. In *Proceedings of the Workshop on BioNLP 2007: Biological, Translational, and Clinical Language Processing*. Association for Computational Linguistics, pages 209–216.

Meishan Zhang, Jie Yang, Zhiyang Teng, and Yue Zhang. 2016. Libn3l: a lightweight package for neural nlp. In *Proceedings of the Tenth International Conference on Language Resources and Evaluation*.

Meishan Zhang, Yue Zhang, and Duy-Tin Vo. 2015. Neural networks for open domain targeted sentiment. In *Proceedings of the 2015 Conference on EMNLP*. pages 612–621.

GuoDong Zhou and Jian Su. 2002. Named entity recognition using an hmm-based chunk tagger. In *proceedings of the 40th Annual Meeting on Association for Computational Linguistics*. Association for Computational Linguistics, pages 473–480.

Chenxi Zhu, Xipeng Qiu, Xinchi Chen, and Xuanjing Huang. 2015a. A re-ranking model for dependency parser with recursive convolutional neural network pages 1159–1168. http://www.aclweb.org/anthology/P15-1112.

Xiaodan Zhu, Parinaz Sobihani, and Hongyu Guo. 2015b. Long short-term memory over recursive structures. In *International Conference on Machine Learning*. pages 1604–1612.

Online Deception Detection Refueled by Real World Data Collection

Wenlin Yao, Zeyu Dai, Ruihong Huang, James Caverlee
Department of Computer Science and Engineering
Texas A&M University
{wenlinyao, jzdaizeyu, huangrh, caverlee}@tamu.edu

Abstract

The lack of large realistic datasets presents a bottleneck in online deception detection studies. In this paper, we apply a data collection method based on social network analysis to quickly identify high-quality deceptive and truthful online reviews[1] from Amazon. The dataset contains more than 10,000 deceptive reviews and is diverse in product domains and reviewers. Using this dataset, we explore effective general features for online deception detection that perform well across domains. We demonstrate that with generalized features – advertising speak and writing complexity scores – deception detection performance can be further improved by adding additional deceptive reviews from assorted domains in training. Finally, reviewer level evaluation gives an interesting insight into different deceptive reviewers' writing styles.

1 Introduction

Online reviews are increasingly being used by consumers in making purchase decisions. A recent survey by the Nielsen Company shows that 57% of electronic shoppers and 45% of car shoppers were influenced by online reviews. However, due to the widespread growth of crowdsourcing platforms like Mechanical Turk, large-scale organized campaigns can be quickly launched and create massive malicious reviews in order to promote products or to defame competitors. Deceptive product reviews can easily bias and mislead consumers' perception of product quality.

Deceptive opinion spam detection is challenging because deception makers can target various objects and domains (e.g., commercial products or services) and the language is dynamic to adapt to distinct objects. Basically, the goal of deception detection is to recognize varied and generalized linguistic cues that can indicate deceit across domains, which is dramatically different from semantic analysis (e.g. sentiment analysis). So far, understanding of deceptive language in general is still scarce. One major obstacle is that it is difficult to obtain ground truth deceptive and authentic reviews. Ott et al. (2011) revealed that it is impossible for humans to accurately identify and label deception. Therefore, a common method to have ground truth labels for deception detection (Li et al., 2014) is to ask customers or domain experts to write down deceptive reviews following a carefully designed and strictly controlled procedure. Such a data collection approach is slow, costly and hard to scale. Consequently, most of the prior research has used small datasets containing several hundred of reviews that usually take weeks to collect (Ott et al., 2011). Moreover, this data collection method is too strict and cannot reflect real world online review manipulation processes.

Due to the difficulty of deception data collection, most research has been limited to study deception within an individual domain such as hotel or restaurant (Ott et al., 2011; Feng et al., 2012; Ott et al., 2013; Li et al., 2014). Consequently, only several conceptual types of features have been studied for deception detection including genre indicative Part-Of-Speech (POS) features and psychologically motivated Linguistic Inquiry and Word Count (LIWC) (Pennebaker et al., 2015) category features. What is surprising is that among all the studied features, Bag-Of-Word (BOW) features remain the most effective type of features for deception detection. Until very recently, Li et al. (2014) suggested that POS fea-

---

[1]Dataset will also be released

Proceedings of Recent Advances in Natural Language Processing, pages 793–802,
Varna, Bulgaria, Sep 4–6 2017.

tures and LIWC features are better than BOW features in generalizing across domains, solely based on their experiments with several hundred reviews and three domains. Without large scale realistic data, it is difficult to gain a deeper understanding of general rules for online deception detection.

In this paper, we apply an existing online deception data collection method (Fayazi et al., 2015) that recognizes online campaigns of malicious review posting and further employ social network analysis on reviewer-reviewer graphs, which can quickly accumulate the list of deceptive reviewers as well as deceptive reviews. The deceptive reviews collected in this manner are rich in terms of authors and domains. We constructed a dataset containing around 10,000 deceptive reviews written by 1,540 deceptive reviewers, ranging over more than 30 domains including books, electronics, movies, etc. Using such an author and domain diversified dataset, we are able to conduct extensive cross-domain experiments in order to search for general rules on deception detection. Then we demonstrate that with generalized sets of features, increasing amounts of data from arbitrarily different domains can continuously improve the performance of deception detection, which also shows the value of this scalable deception data collection method. In addition, our preliminary experiments on reviewer level deception analysis shows that detection systems trained with data from reviewers of a type might perform poorly in detecting opinion spam written by reviewers of a contrasting type.

This paper has two major contributions. First, we connect two communities – social media analysis and language analysis – that have worked on online deception detection but with a different focus. We apply an existing social network analysis based algorithm for collecting a large and rich dataset from the wild online world. Second, we are the first to conduct linguistically motivated deception detection analysis using such a diverse dataset that is two orders of magnitude larger than the datasets used in previous studies. Most prior studies are based on manually collected unreal and small datasets, and the lack of large and real datasets significantly limits the depth of deception detection research. Our experiments show that general rules for deception detection are likely to be revealed by large-scale cross-domain experiments in modeling writing styles instead of modeling contents as in single-domain experiments.

2   Related Work

Previous studies mainly relied on four types of methods to obtain deceptive reviews. The first method is to ask human annotators to label deceptive reviews (Jindal et al., 2010; Mukherjee et al., 2012). However, studies show that humans are not good at identifying deceptive reviews and the annotation performance is poor (Ott et al., 2011). Therefore, Ott et al. (2011, 2013) introduced the second approach that they asked Amazon Mechanical Turkers to compose 400 deceptive and 400 non-deceptive reviews. Similarly, Li et al. (2014) asked both Mechanical Turkers and domain experts to write deceptive reviews. There are two main drawbacks of this method. First, it is too strict to scale. Second, this strict method does not reflect how deceptive reviews are posted in the real online environment.

The third approach used rule-based heuristics to filter reviews which are likely to be deceptive (Jindal and Liu, 2007, 2008; Hammad, 2013). The rules include labeling reviews that contain certain keywords as deceptive, labeling duplicate or near duplicate reviews as deceptive, labeling product irrelevant reviews as deceptive, etc. Nonetheless, such methods can be easily fooled by careful deceptive review creators. Lastly, the fourth method (Mukherjee et al., 2013) proposed a deceptive review dataset by simply collecting reviews filtered by the Yelp website as ground truth deceptive reviews and collecting reviews not filtered as authentic reviews. However, the filtering mechanism used by Yelp is still a black box and unknown. Therefore, the data collected by such method is not trustworthy.

So far, due to the lack of a large and realistic dataset, language analysis research for online deception detection are restricted. Jindal and Liu (2008) first studied the problem of deceptive opinion spam. They discussed the evolution of opinion mining, which focused on summarizing the opinions from text in order to identify duplicate opinions as spam. Ott et al. (2011) presented three different types of basic features for deceptive spam detection including n-grams, POS tags and LIWC. Feng et al. (2012) found that syntactic stylometry features derived from Context Free Grammar (CFG) parse trees improved deception detection performance over several baselines that use shallow lexico-syntactic features. Li et al. (2014) found that LIWC and POS are more robust than n-grams features when applied to cross-domain adaptation. More recently, a multi-task learning method (Hai et al., 2016) for deception detection is developed to exploit domain relatedness and to use unlabeled data.

3 Dataset Construction

Crowdsourcing platforms have been shown their effectiveness in organizing large amounts of individuals to work on a target task. These platforms also provide an alternative strategy to request deceptive reviews in order to promote their own products. Recently, Fayazi et al. (2015) introduced an approach to understand massive manipulation of online reviews. For our purpose, we employed their approach to collect real world manipulation of online reviews.

Briefly, this deceptive review collection approach has two steps. First, we identified deceptive review request tasks from crowdsourcing platforms. Tracking the Amazon URL in each task which links to a specific product, we collected reviews associated with the product as well as reviewers' information. We next augmented this base set of reviews, reviewers and products via a three hop breadth-first search, and applied social network analysis techniques to a rich product-reviewer-review graph in order to identify additional deceptive review composers and their written deceptive reviews (Figure 1). Details are given in section 3.1 and section 3.2.

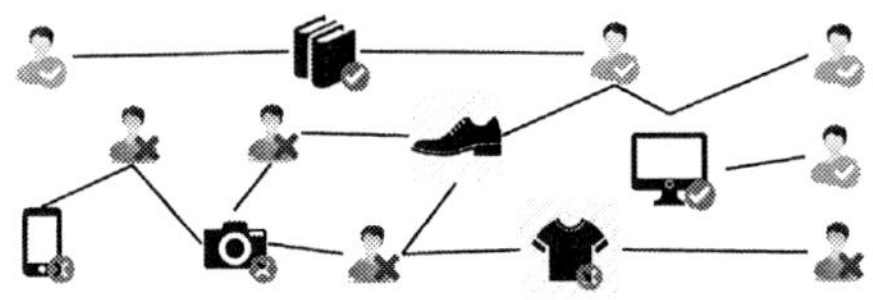

Figure 1: Online Deceptive Review Collection using Social Network Analysis

3.1 Initial Products, Reviewers and Reviews

First, we followed the framework presented by (Fayazi et al., 2015) and crawled deceptive review creation tasks posted on ShortTask.com, Rapid-Workers.com, and Microworkers.com. Starting from this as *root task set*, we collect initial deceptive products, reviews and reviewers. Then we crawled three hops to identify a larger candidate set of potential deceptive reviews, reviewers and products.

3.2 Discovering Additional Deceptive Reviewers

In order to identify additional deceptive reviewers who have contributed deceptive reviews, we applied a reviewer-reviewer graph clustering algorithm using a pairwise Markov Random Field (MRF) that defines individual and pair potentials (Fayazi et al., 2015). Specifically, every node in the random field corresponds to one reviewer. Individual level potential (single reviewer) and pairwise potential (between two reviewers) functions are used to capture two intuitions. (i) Two reviewers who collaborated (responded to the same task) heavily should be assigned to the same cluster. (ii) Two reviewers who behave similarly in posting reviews probably belong to the same cluster (deceptive or authentic). For instance, one reviewer who actually purchased a product and another reviewer who did not purchase the product should be put to different clusters.

Then, we formalized the goal of identifying additional deception making reviewers using a maximizing the likelihood function, which is optimized using an Expectation Maximization (EM) algorithm. EM iterates over two steps to increase the overall likelihood. In specific, E-Step finds the best cluster assignments given current parameters and M-Step updates parameters given the best cluster assignment.

3.3 Ground Truth

The aforementioned social network analysis approach also identifies various deceptive reviewers and deceptive products. To get ground truth labels of reviews, deceptive or authentic, we applied multiple sieves on reviews, based on their reviewers and targeted products. Specifically, we deem a review as deceptive if it satisfies the following two conditions: (i) Its author is marked as a deceptive reviewer; and (ii) The product this review commented on appears in an initial deceptive review request task. Meanwhile, we deem a review as authentic if neither its reviewer nor its commented product has been labeled as deceptive by the data collection system [2].

---

[2] All deceptive and authentic reviews were collected from 3-hop breadth-first search over the social network graph, as described in Section 3.1.

This method of collecting deceptive reviews and authentic reviews is reasonable. First, Fayazi et al. (2015) reported that their social analysis model can achieve high performance - 0.96 AUC (Area Under the ROC Curve) on balanced training and test sets and 0.77 AUC on unbalanced sets[3]. Second, our double filtering (reviewer-level and product-level) further controls the quality in labeling deceptive and authentic reviews.

4 Dataset Overview

The dataset we collected contains more than 10,000 deceptive reviews, which is significantly larger than the datasets examined in previous studies. In addition, the dataset is from the real world manipulation and is diverse in reviewers and products (Table 1 shows dataset statistics).

	deceptive	truthful
reviews	10114	101226
reviewers	1540	16497
products	994	72266

Table 1: Number of Reviews, Reviewers and Products

The deceptive products that were targeted in crowdsourcing websites can be organized into 32 domains based on the product hierarchy on Amazon. Therefore, it is impossible to train a deception detection system for each domain, which motivates our research on deriving general rules for deception detection that can apply across domains. We further see that the domains are highly unbalanced in size, for instance, 4,555 deceptive reviews were identified for "Kindle Edition" books while only 38 deceptive reviews were identified for "Kitchen" related products, which reflects skewed distribution of deceptive reviews in reality to certain degree. In contrast, the datasets used in prior studies are small and roughly balanced.

5 General Linguistic Features

We first discuss linguistic features that have been used in previous studies (section 5.1). Then we introduce our new types of features in order to model advertising language that is commonly used in deceptive reviews (section 5.2) and syntactic complexities (section 5.3).

5.1 Basic Features

N-gram Based Lexical Features: Both unigrams and bigrams (Brown et al., 1992) features have been used for deception detection (Ott et al., 2011). To be consistent with the cross-domain experimental settings in Li et al. (2014), we only consider unigram lexical features (BOWs) in our experiment.

LIWC Features: Features derived using the Linguistic Inquiry and Word Count (LIWC) lexicon (Pennebaker et al., 2015) has been shown effective in both within-domain (Ott et al., 2011; Shojaee et al., 2013; Ott et al., 2013) and cross-domain (Li et al., 2014) deceptive opinion spam detection. We use features derived from the LIWC 2015 lexicon, which consists of 125 psychologically interesting semantic classes.

POS Features: It has been observed that the distribution of words' POS tags in a document is indicative of its genre or certain writing style. Part-Of-Speech features (Biber et al., 1999; Rayson et al., 2001) have been shown useful for deception detection.

Syntactic Production Rule Features: Feng et al. (2012) introduced syntactic production rule features for deception detection that are drawn from Context Free Grammar (CFG) syntactic parse trees of sentences. We used the Stanford coreNLP tool[4] to obtain both POS tags and CFG production rules for product reviews. In addition, we realized that the bottom level syntactic production rules have the form of POS tag $\rightarrow$ WORD and include lexical words, which are dependent on specific domains and their vocabularies overlap with BOWs features. Therefore, we experiment with the extracted syntactic production rule features with or without the bottom level rules in order to understand their generalities in deception detection, and distinguish them as All Production (AP) rules and Unlexicalized Production (UP) rules.

5.2 Features Modeling Advertising Language

Commonly Used Advertising Phrases: The purpose of deceptive review writing is to promote a certain product or to directly persuade customers

[3]In their evaluation, the unbalanced training and test sets each contains half of the original data, so real world deceptive to authentic ratio can be kept. Balanced sets undersample authentic reviews so that each set has equal number of deceptive and authentic reviews.

[4]http://stanfordnlp.github.io/CoreNLP/

to buy the product.[5] Therefore, we hypothesize that deceptive reviews are likely to adopt marketing phrases more frequently than truthful reviews. Specifically, we crawled lists of advertising phrases from online blogs[6] and websites[7] that provide suggestions for writing persuasive product advertisements. The advertising phrases include efficient phrases to persuade people to make purchase, including cause-and-effect phrases (e.g., due to, thus, accordingly), premium adjectives (e.g., exclusive, guaranteed, unique), premium verbs (e.g., try it, discover, love) and phrases that inspire safety (e.g., authentic, certificated, privacy), etc. Finally, all advertising phrases are used as a set of binary features (presence vs. absence). [8]

Ngrams in Product Description Titles: We observed that many faked reviews repeatedly mention entire or partial product name. For some specific models or products, they even mention five or more successive words same as in their descriptions. Reasonably, deceptive review composers have not purchased and used the products, so they more frequently refer back to the product descriptions in order to imagine relevant reviews. In contrast, truthful customers write reviews describing their real experience using the products and rely less on product descriptions. In specific, we count the number of common features shared by a review and corresponding product description in terms of unigram and bigram and put two frequency scores as new features.

5.3 Syntactic Complexity Features Indicating Deceptive Writing Styles

Syntactic complexity scores (Lu, 2010) have been shown useful in measuring text readability and distinguishing authorships. These scores have not been used in deception detection. But intuitively, deceptive reviewers do not want to invest too much time to get paid so they unconsciously tend to use simple sentence syntactic structure to write.[9] Following (Lu, 2010), we use a range of measurement scores to represent sentence syntactic complexity, including sentence length, clause length, average number of clauses or specific syntactic constructions per sentence, etc. Specifically, we use the Tregex (Levy and Andrew, 2006) system to query syntactic parse trees[10] using predefined Tregex patterns.

6 Experimental Results

6.1 Data and Settings

As shown in Table 2, we merge similar product categories and create four broad product domains. All the remaining product domains were put under the catch-all "Other" category, which is a mixture of a variety of product domains. Table 3 shows the number of deceptive reviews in each category.

Large domains	Contain categories
Books	Hardcover Paperback Kindle Edition
Health/Beauty	Health and Beauty Health and Personal Care
Electronics	Electronics Personal Computers Cell Phones
Movies	Movies and TV DVD

Table 2: Four Broad Product Domains

Books	Health	Electronics	Movies	Other
6244	2118	228	292	1232

Table 3: Number of Reviews for Each Domain

In the experiments, we use Maximum Entropy (Berger et al., 1996) classifiers[11]. Specifically, we use the implementation of Maxent models in the LIBLINEAR library (Fan et al., 2008) with default parameter settings. In reality, there are generally many more authentic reviews than deceptive ones. In order to reflect the actual skewed label distribution, we randomly selected truthful reviews three times of deceptive reviews across our experiments. In contrast, the previous studies on deception detection often artificially enforce deceptive and truthful reviews to be balanced.

---

[5]Interestingly, we observed that almost all tasks we crawled from crowdsourcing websites are promoting specific products which might reflect real-life manipulation behavior that promoting is the majority.

[6]https://blog.bufferapp.com/words-and-phrases-that-convert-ultimate-list

[7]http://systemagicmotives.com/Effective%20Ad%20Words.htm

[8]299 advertising phrases are used in total

[9]In our dataset, average sentence length is 17.8 for deceptive reviews versus 20.9 for authentic reviews. Average number of clauses per sentence 1.97 for deceptive reviews versus 2.28 for authentic reviews.

[10]http://nlp.stanford.edu/software/tregex.shtml

[11]We also tried Support Vector Machines and achieved similar results.

6.2 In-domain Evaluation

First, we restrict the experiments within one domain where both the training and test data are from one domain. Specifically, we conduct in-domain experiments for each of the four broad product domains using 5-fold cross validation. We experiment with each of the basic features as described in subsection 5.1, with one type of features each time.

Features	Macro Average
unigram	80.2/88.0/83.9
POS (Biber et al., 1999)	32.9/56.7/41.6
LIWC (Pennebaker et al., 2015)	46.0/63.4/53.3
AP (Feng et al., 2012)	76.0/86.0/80.7
UP (Feng et al., 2012)	56.6/62.6/59.5

Table 4: In-domain Experimental Results Using Different Features, Recall/Precision/F1-score

Table 4 shows the macro average scores across four domains when using each type of features. Consistent with the previous studies (Ott et al., 2012, 2013; Li et al., 2014), the best in-domain performance is achieved using unigrams. In addition, the second best performed type of features is AP features that include the bottom-level syntactic production rules with lexical words. The three other types of features, POS, LIWC and UP features, perform significantly worse on in-domain deception detection.

6.3 Cross-domain Evaluation

To test whether deception detection classifiers implementing general rules perform well across distinct domains, we conduct extensive cross-domain experiments. Specifically, with a set of features we train a classifier using reviews from each of four domains – *Books, Health, Electronics, Movies* – and test the classifier on the rest three domains. In each of the four runs, we train a classifier using one domain and report the macro-average recall/precision/F1-score of the classifier across the rest three test domains with respect to deceptive reviews detection. To measure how the set of features performs overall for deception detection, we further calculate the meta macro-average scores over the four sets of macro-average scores resulted from each run.

Table 5 shows the macro-average scores from each run trained with one domain as well as the meta macro-average scores across the four separate runs. From the first section of Table 5, we can see that in cross-domain experiments with each of the five basic types of features, the classifier using UP features outperforms the classifier using Unigrams or AP features overall. Especially in the runs trained with three smaller domains, *Health, Electronics, Movies*, UP features are promising in deriving generalized deception detection classifiers. Next, we add each of the first three types of basic features on top of UP features. It turns out that POS features slightly improve the overall performance, while both Unigrams and LIWC features hurt the overall performance.

Table 5 (With New Features section) shows the cross-domain experimental results when we increasingly add two new types of linguistic features. We can see that the features modeling advertising language can clearly improve the performance of deception detection across the four classifiers trained on each domain, showing that advertising language is commonly seen across four domains. Furthermore, adding the syntactic complexity features can slightly improve both the macro-average recall and precision in deception detection.

Long Short-Term Memory (LSTMs) (Hochreiter and Schmidhuber, 1997) and Convolutional Neural Networks (CNNs) (LeCun et al., 1998) have been shown effective on deriving compositional meanings of texts and have achieved great success across many NLP tasks (Sutskever et al., 2014; Zaremba et al., 2014; Kim, 2014). For comparison purposes, we also conduct cross-domain experiments using both LSTMs and CNNs trained on top of word2vec 300 dimensions word embeddings (Mikolov et al., 2013). [12] From the second section of Table 5, we can see that the performance of both neural net models are worse than our feature-based classifiers using well selected generalized features. One explanation for the lower performance of neural nets on deception detection is that this task is not about understanding semantic meanings of reviews, rather, deception detection is about understanding and recognizing subtle syntactic or stylistic clues and footprints of deceptive writing. Our strong claim is that general rules for deception detection cannot

---

[12]For LSTMs, we use one hidden-layer of 128 hidden units. For CNNs, we use filter window size 3, 4 and 5, and a hidden-layer of 100 hidden units. For both LSTMs and CNNs, we run Adam optimizer with a learning rate of 0.001, dropout rate of 0.5.

Features	Books	Health	Electronics	Movies	Macro Average
Unigrams	53/73/61	19/73/31	24/67/35	22/79/34	29.3/72.9/41.8
POS (Biber et al., 1999)	36/48/41	16/52/24	22/48/30	28/47/35	25.5/48.7/33.4
LIWC (Pennebaker et al., 2015)	35/53/42	13/51/21	34/46/39	23/50/31	26.0/50.1/34.2
AP (Feng et al., 2012)	56/71/**63**	20/74/31	27/62/38	24/72/36	31.7/69.8/43.6
UP (Feng et al., 2012)	48/55/51	32/55/40	38/48/43	43/48/45	40.2/51.5/45.1
UP + POS	48/55/52	32/56/41	39/50/44	41/48/44	40.0/52.3/45.3
Results from Neural Net Models					
LSTM (Zaremba et al., 2014)	45/67/54	31/65/42	39/57/47	34/66/45	37.5/63.7/47.2
CNN (Kim, 2014)	45/57/50	31/58/40	30/52/38	41/60/48	36.7/57.1/44.7
With New Features					
UP + POS + ad	50/60/55	33/63/**44**	42/54/**47**	43/55/48	42.0/58.0/48.8
UP + POS + ad + comp	51/61/56	32/64/43	42/54/**47**	44/55/**49**	42.3/58.5/**49.1**

Table 5: Cross-domain Experimental Results Using Different Features, Recall/Precision/F1-score

Features	Books	Health	Electronics	Movies	Macro Average
UP + POS	41/62/49	40/58/48	49/53/51	47/55/50	44.3/56.9/49.8
With New Features					
UP + POS + ad	45/71/55	45/66/**54**	63/58/60	59/60/59	52.9/63.6/57.8
UP + POS + ad + comp	45/73/**56**	44/67/53	62/60/**61**	59/62/**60**	52.4/65.4/**58.2**

Table 6: Cross-domain Experimental Results after Adding Training Data from Other Domains

be obtained continuing single-domain studies (in which simple unigram is the best) and we have shown that cross-domain experiments are promising in revealing general rules.

6.3.1 Adding Training Data from Distinct Domains

We have seen that classifiers trained with generalized features perform well across the rest three domains. So far, all the classifiers we have used in cross-domain evaluation were trained with data from a single domain. However, we hypothesize that generalized features should enable deception detection classifiers to further benefit from additional training data, even when the data is from dramatically different domains.

Therefore, we augment each single domain set of reviews with additional reviews from "Other" domains (assorted domains) which contain 1,232 deceptive reviews (Table 3), and rerun the cross-domain experiments. From Table 6, we can see that using the best set of basic features, UP+POS, the detection performance of classifiers were significantly improved after including additional reviews from assorted domains in training. The improvements are 6-7% across domains except *Books*, where adding 1,232 more deceptive reviews to 6,244 deceptive instances on Books may

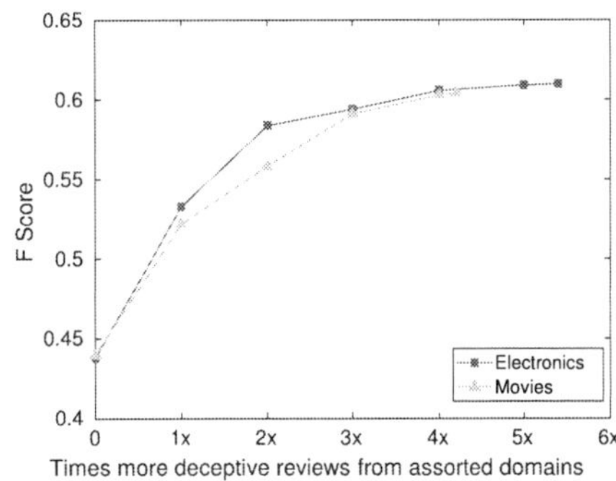

Figure 2: Learning Curves

not notably change its overall review distribution. Especially, with the feature sets enriched with our advertising speak features and syntactic complexity features, the performance of the classifier even further improves using additional mixed-domain training data, by 10-14% across the latter three categories (Health, Electronics and Movies).

Note that for the smallest two domains, *Electronics* and *Movies* have deceptive reviews of 228 and 292, so the newly added deceptive reviews (1,232) are several times of their original deceptive reviews. In order to understand how the performance of the classifier was influenced when increasingly adding times more training reviews from assorted domains, we drew a learning curve (shown in Figure 2) for each classifier that was initially trained with deceptive reviews from one of *Electronics* and *Movies*. We can see that the performance is consistently growing with times more deceptive reviews added in training. We expect to see further improvements if more data were provided.

These improvements confirm that with generalized features, deception detection performance can be remarkably improved using more data, even with data from dramatically different domains. It further emphasizes the value of the new deceptive data collection method that relies on social network analysis to generate amounts of ground truth deceptive reviews across diverse domains.

7 Effects of Reviewers and Personalized Deceptive Writing Styles

Intuitively, reviewers of distinct personalities write differently, which implies that reviewers should be considered in deriving general rules for online deception detection. Our dataset includes deceptive reviews that were written by a diverse set of reviewers and many reviewers contributed dozens of deceptive reviews, which enables us to study the effects of reviewers in deception detection. In the following, we present our initial findings.

Reviewer 1	Reviewer 2	Reviewer 3	Reviewer 4
113	112	78	80

Table 7: Number of Reviews for Each Person

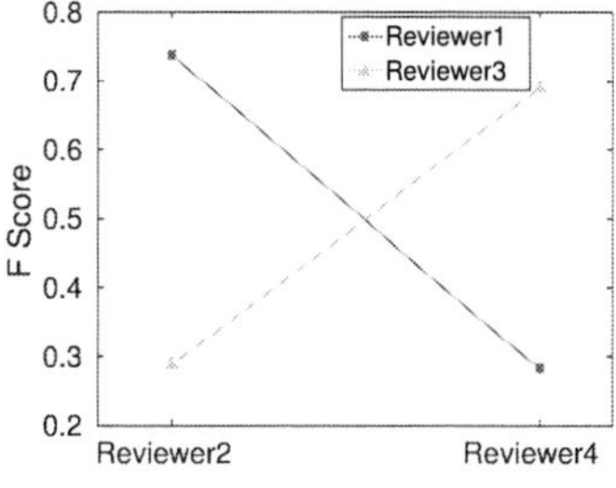

Figure 3: Reviewer level evaluation

We identified four deceptive reviewers that fall into two groups based on their writing styles (Table 7 shows the number of deceptive reviews for each reviewer). Specifically, we observed that reviews by the first group of reviewers use shorter sentences and advertising words more frequently in making comparisons. In contrast, reviews by the second group of reviewers tend to use longer and generally more complex sentences, more numbers and more words related to personal feelings. Figure 3 shows the result when we train the classifier using reviews from one reviewer taken from each category, say reviewer R1 and R3, and apply the classifier to deceptive reviews written by the other two reviewers, R2 and R4, also one from each category. The detection performance can achieve F-scores as high as 70-80% when it is trained and tested on the same type of reviewers. In contrast, detection F-scores can be as low as 30% when it is trained on one type and tested on another type. Deceptive examples from each reviewer is also listed in Table 8.

Reviewer 1: LOVE TO BAKE. I love these type of recipes especially for cupcakes and cakes! I have tried almost them all so far. It's the best book for finding that perfect flavor for that perfect event your planning. Highly recommended!
Reviewer 2: A cute kids book! I was honestly impressed with this childrens book. I read it to my son and it kept his interest, which is no easy task! He liked the front cover picture. This was a hit with my son. Great book!
Reviewer 3: Very Valuable Information. The reason why I bought this book is because I really needed a boost in self confidence, my main luck of confidence was in social situation where I tended to shy away and keep quite, I must say that after reading this book my confidence level went up and I feel much more comfortable when I am out with friends, I now talk more, engage more in the conversations and feel much better when out with friends.
Reviewer 4: Diet is awesome. Well..you know life is hard when you're fat, but if you get this you may succeed in your diet and you will lose some pounds. My grandmother was fat i bought this book for her and she is pretty well now if you want to lose your weight you may seriously want to try this book. I recommend it to anyone congrats to the maker and good luck selling more copies.

Table 8: One Example Deceptive Review per Reviewer

8 Conclusion

We applied a new method for real world deceptive review collection leveraging social network analysis. The newly collected dataset is rich in products and reviews and has two orders of magnitude more deceptive reviews than previously used artificial datasets. We demonstrate that such a large dataset facilitates the development of identifying generalized features for deception detection. We further show that with generalized features, additional deceptive review data from assorted domains can be used to improve both recall and precision of online deception detection.

References

Adam L Berger, Vincent J Della Pietra, and Stephen A Della Pietra. 1996. A maximum entropy approach to natural language processing. *Computational linguistics* 22(1):39–71.

Douglas Biber, Stig Johansson, Geoffrey Leech, Susan Conrad, and Edward Finegan. 1999. Grammar of spoken and written english. *Harlow: Longman* .

Peter F Brown, Peter V Desouza, Robert L Mercer, Vincent J Della Pietra, and Jenifer C Lai. 1992. Class-based n-gram models of natural language. *Computational linguistics* 18(4):467–479.

Rong-En Fan, Kai-Wei Chang, Cho-Jui Hsieh, Xiang-Rui Wang, and Chih-Jen Lin. 2008. Liblinear: A library for large linear classification. *Journal of machine learning research* 9(Aug):1871–1874.

Amir Fayazi, Kyumin Lee, James Caverlee, and Anna Squicciarini. 2015. Uncovering crowdsourced manipulation of online reviews. In *Proceedings of the 38th International ACM SIGIR Conference on Research and Development in Information Retrieval*. ACM, pages 233–242.

Song Feng, Ritwik Banerjee, and Yejin Choi. 2012. Syntactic stylometry for deception detection. In *Proceedings of the 50th Annual Meeting of the Association for Computational Linguistics: Short Papers-Volume 2*. Association for Computational Linguistics, pages 171–175.

Zhen Hai, Peilin Zhao, Peng Cheng, Peng Yang, Xiao-Li Li, and Guangxia Li. 2016. Deceptive review spam detection via exploiting task relatedness and unlabeled data pages 1817–1826.

Ahmad SJ Abu Hammad. 2013. *An approach for detecting spam in arabic opinion reviews*. Ph.D. thesis, Islamic University of Gaza.

Sepp Hochreiter and Jürgen Schmidhuber. 1997. Long short-term memory. *Neural computation* 9(8):1735–1780.

Nitin Jindal and Bing Liu. 2007. Review spam detection. In *Proceedings of the 16th international conference on World Wide Web*. ACM, pages 1189–1190.

Nitin Jindal and Bing Liu. 2008. Opinion spam and analysis. In *Proceedings of the 2008 International Conference on Web Search and Data Mining*. ACM, pages 219–230.

Nitin Jindal, Bing Liu, and Ee-Peng Lim. 2010. Finding unusual review patterns using unexpected rules. In *Proceedings of the 19th ACM international conference on Information and knowledge management*. ACM, pages 1549–1552.

Yoon Kim. 2014. Convolutional neural networks for sentence classification. *arXiv preprint arXiv:1408.5882* .

Yann LeCun, Léon Bottou, Yoshua Bengio, and Patrick Haffner. 1998. Gradient-based learning applied to document recognition. *Proceedings of the IEEE* 86(11):2278–2324.

Roger Levy and Galen Andrew. 2006. Tregex and tsurgeon: tools for querying and manipulating tree data structures. In *Proceedings of the fifth international conference on Language Resources and Evaluation*. Citeseer, pages 2231–2234.

Jiwei Li, Myle Ott, Claire Cardie, and Eduard H Hovy. 2014. Towards a general rule for identifying deceptive opinion spam. In *ACL (1)*. Citeseer, pages 1566–1576.

Xiaofei Lu. 2010. Automatic analysis of syntactic complexity in second language writing. *International Journal of Corpus Linguistics* 15(4):474–496.

Tomas Mikolov, Ilya Sutskever, Kai Chen, Greg S Corrado, and Jeff Dean. 2013. Distributed representations of words and phrases and their compositionality. In *Advances in neural information processing systems*. pages 3111–3119.

Arjun Mukherjee, Bing Liu, and Natalie Glance. 2012. Spotting fake reviewer groups in consumer reviews. In *Proceedings of the 21st international conference on World Wide Web*. ACM, pages 191–200.

Arjun Mukherjee, Vivek Venkataraman, Bing Liu, and Natalie S Glance. 2013. What yelp fake review filter might be doing? In *ICWSM*.

Myle Ott, Claire Cardie, and Jeff Hancock. 2012. Estimating the prevalence of deception in online review communities. In *Proceedings of the 21st international conference on World Wide Web*. ACM, pages 201–210.

Myle Ott, Claire Cardie, and Jeffrey T Hancock. 2013. Negative deceptive opinion spam. In *HLT-NAACL*. pages 497–501.

Myle Ott, Yejin Choi, Claire Cardie, and Jeffrey T Hancock. 2011. Finding deceptive opinion spam by any stretch of the imagination. In *Proceedings of the 49th Annual Meeting of the Association for Computational Linguistics: Human Language Technologies-Volume 1*. Association for Computational Linguistics, pages 309–319.

James W Pennebaker, Ryan L Boyd, Kayla Jordan, and Kate Blackburn. 2015. The development and psychometric properties of liwc2015. Technical report.

Paul Rayson, Andrew Wilson, and Geoffrey Leech. 2001. Grammatical word class variation within the british national corpus sampler. *Language and Computers* 36(1):295–306.

Somayeh Shojaee, Masrah Azrifah Azmi Murad, Azreen Bin Azman, Nurfadhlina Mohd Sharef, and Samaneh Nadali. 2013. Detecting deceptive reviews using lexical and syntactic features. In *Intelligent*

Systems Design and Applications (ISDA), 2013 13th International Conference on. IEEE, pages 53–58.

Ilya Sutskever, Oriol Vinyals, and Quoc V Le. 2014. Sequence to sequence learning with neural networks. In *Advances in neural information processing systems*. pages 3104–3112.

Wojciech Zaremba, Ilya Sutskever, and Oriol Vinyals. 2014. Recurrent neural network regularization. *arXiv preprint arXiv:1409.2329* .

A Weakly Supervised Approach to Train Temporal Relation Classifiers and Acquire Regular Event Pairs Simultaneously

Wenlin Yao, Saipravallika Nettyam, Ruihong Huang
Department of Computer Science and Engineering
Texas A&M University
`{wenlinyao, n1005120, huangrh}@tamu.edu`

Abstract

Capabilities of detecting temporal relations between two events can benefit many applications. Most of existing temporal relation classifiers were trained in a supervised manner. Instead, we explore the observation that regular event pairs show a consistent temporal relation despite of their various contexts, and these rich contexts can be used to train a contextual temporal relation classifier, which can further recognize new temporal relation contexts and identify new regular event pairs. We focus on detecting *after* and *before* temporal relations and design a weakly supervised learning approach that extracts thousands of regular event pairs and learns a contextual temporal relation classifier simultaneously. Evaluation shows that the acquired regular event pairs are of high quality and contain rich commonsense knowledge and domain specific knowledge. In addition, the weakly supervised trained temporal relation classifier achieves comparable performance with the state-of-the-art supervised systems.

1 Introduction

Capabilities to recognize temporal relations between two events can benefit many Natural Language Processing applications, including event timeline generation, script knowledge extraction, text summarization and event prediction.

This is a challenging task because temporal relations can be described in dramatically different contexts depending on domains and pairs of events, signifying different semantic meanings. In order to capture various contexts, large amounts of labeled data are needed to train a high-coverage temporal relation classifier. However, almost all existing datasets that contain event-event temporal relation annotations are limited in size and domains, such as Automatic Context Extraction (ACE) (Strassel et al., 2008) and TimeBank (Pustejovsky et al., 2003), which generally contain several hundred documents. Most of the existing temporal relation classifiers were trained using these small manually annotated datasets, relying on sophisticated lexical, grammatical, linguistic (e.g., tenses and aspects of events), semantic (e.g., semantic roles and lexicon derived features) and discourse (e.g., temporal discourse connectives (Mirza and Tonelli, 2014b)) features.

We observed that event pairs presenting regularities tend to show the same temporal relation despite of various contexts they may occur in. For instance, *arrest* events tend to happen after *attack* events, and the following sentential contexts all indicate the same temporal relation:

Under pressure following suicide <u>attacks</u>, police <u>arrested</u> scores of activists on Monday.

Two men were <u>arrested</u> on suspicion of carrying out the Mumbai <u>attacks</u>.

Carlos was <u>arrested</u> in Sudan in August in connection with two bomb <u>attacks</u> in France in 1982.

Mamdouh Habib was <u>arrested</u> in Pakistan three weeks after the Sept.11 <u>attacks</u>.

Leveraging this key observation, we propose a bootstrapping approach that focuses on recognizing *after* or *before* temporal relations and substantially reduces the reliance on human annotated data. We start by identifying regular event pairs that have occurred enough times with an explicit temporal pattern, i.e., EV_A *after (before)* EV_B. We then populate these seed event pairs in a large unlabeled corpus to quickly collect hundreds of thousands of sentences that contain a regular event pair, which are then used as training instances to

Proceedings of Recent Advances in Natural Language Processing, pages 803–812,
Varna, Bulgaria, Sep 4–6 2017.

obtain an initial contextual temporal relation classifier. Next, the classifier is applied back to the text corpus and label new sentential contexts that indicate a specific *after* or *before* temporal relation between events. Then new regular event pairs can be identified, which are event pairs that have a majority of their sentences labeled as describing a particular temporal relation. The newly identified regular event pairs will be used to augment seed event pairs and identify more temporal relation sentential contexts in the unlabeled corpus. The bootstrapping learning process iterates.

In summary, this paper makes the following contributions: (1) Through this weakly supervised learning method, we obtain both a contextual temporal relation classifier and a list of regular event pairs that usually show a particular "after/before" temporal relation; (2) Our experiments show that the weakly supervised trained contextual temporal relation classifier achieves comparable performance with state-of-the-art supervised models using benchmark evaluation data provided by TempEval-3; (3) We obtained around 4,400 regular event pairs with the overall accuracy of 69%. The learned regular event pairs demonstrate rich common sense knowledge, furthermore, our evaluation shows that about 90% of temporally related regular event pairs are causally related as well.

2   Related Work

Most of existing temporal relation classifiers were learned in a supervised manner and depend on human annotated data. In the TempEval campaigns (Verhagen et al., 2007, 2010; UzZaman et al., 2013), various classification models and linguistic features (Bethard, 2013; Chambers et al., 2014; Llorens et al., 2010; D'Souza and Ng, 2013; Mirza and Tonelli, 2014b) have been applied to identify temporal relations between two events. For example, a recent study by (D'Souza and Ng, 2013) applied sophisticated linguistic, semantic and discourse features to classify temporal relations between events. They also included 437 hand-coded rules in building a hybrid classification model. CAEVO, a CAscading EVent Ordering architecture by Chambers et al. (2014), applied a sieve-based architecture for event temporal ordering. CAEVO is essentially a hybrid model as well. While the first few sieves are rule based and deterministic, the latter ones are machine learned

using human annotated data.

In contrast, we present a weakly supervised approach that requires minimal human supervision (i.e., several patterns), and simultaneously learns a contextual temporal relation classifier and a collection of regular event pairs. In particular, our approach has a co-training (Blum and Mitchell, 1998) flavor, and the contextual temporal relation classifier learning and the regular event pair acquisition process collaborate and dependent on each other.

Pattern based methods have been applied to acquire event pairs in a specific semantic relation. Specifically, VerbOcean (Chklovski and Pantel, 2004) extracted fine-gained semantic relations between verbs including the happens-before relation using lexico-syntactic patterns. It turns out that the temporal relation patterns used in VerbOcean (e.g., "to X and then Y") are too specific and not capable of identifying many event pairs that are rarely seen in one of the specified patterns. Evaluation shows that our approach induces very different event pairs from VerbOcean, by using the weakly supervised trained temporal relation classifier to recognize diverse contexts that describe a particular temporal relation. Our work is also related to previous research on generating narrative event chains (Chambers and Jurafsky, 2008, 2009), however, as indicated by the authors, their focus is not to detect temporal orders between events and the generated event chains are only partially ordered.

Detecting causality between events is challenging and has been addressed by several pilot studies (Girju, 2003; Bethard and Martin, 2008; Riaz and Girju, 2010; Do et al., 2011; Riaz and Girju, 2013). Recently, Mirza and Tonelli (2014a) presented annotation guidelines and annotated explicit causality between events in Timebank. With the resulted corpus, called Causal-TimeBank, they built supervised models to identify causal relations. Then Mirza and Tonelli (2016) proposed a sieve-based method to perform joint temporal and causal relation extraction, exploiting interactions between temporal and causal relations.

3   Event Representations

Our bootstrapping approach relies on identifying regular event pairs that tend to unambiguously show a particular temporal relation. However, an event word can refer to a general type of events or more than one type of events, and therefore has varied meanings depending on contexts. To make individual events expressive and self-contained, we find and attach arguments to each event word and form event phrases. Specifically, we consider both verb event phrases (Section 3.1) and noun event phrases (Section 3.2). We further require that at least one argument is included in an event pair which may be attached to the first or the second event. In other words, we do not consider event pairs in which neither event has an argument.

3.1 Verb Event Phrases

To ensure a good coverage of regular event pairs, we consider all verbs[1] as event words except reporting verbs[2]. The thematic patient of a verb refers to the object being acted upon and is essentially part of an event, therefore, we first include the patient of a verb in forming an event phrase. We use Stanford dependency relations (Manning et al., 2014) to identify the direct object of an active verb or the subject of a passive verb. The agent is also useful to specify a event especially for a intransitive verb event, which does not have a patient. Therefore, we include the agent of a verb event in an event phrase if its patient was not found. Agents are usually the syntactic subject of an active verb or *by* prepositional object of a passive verb.

For instance, in the sentence *"They win the lottery."*, the verb *win* can refer to various *win* events, but with its direct object, *win lottery* refers to a specific type of event. For another instance, *"Water evaporates when it's hot."*, the verb *evaporates* itself is not very meaningful without contexts, but after including its subject, the event *water evaporates* becomes self-contained. If neither a patient nor an agent was found, we include a prepositional direct object of a verb in the event representation to form an event phrase.

3.2 Noun Event Phrases

We include a prepositional object of a noun event in forming an noun event phrase. We first consider an object headed by the preposition *of*, then an object headed by the preposition *by*, lastly an object headed by any other preposition.

Note that many noun words do not refer to an event. In order to compile a list of noun event words, we use two intuitive textual patterns *participate in* EVENT and *involve in* EVENT. By the semantics of these two patterns, their prepositional direct objects refer to events. However, due to language vagueness and dependency analysis errors, non-event words were seen in the EVENT position too. Therefore, we only consider words that have occurred with one of the two patterns at least 20 times as potential noun event words. To further remove noise, we quickly went through the list of nouns and manually removed non-event words. Finally, we obtained 721 noun event words.

3.3 Generalizing Event Arguments Using Named Entity Types

Including arguments into event representations generates specific event phrases though. In order to obtain generalized event phrase forms, we replace specific name arguments with their named entity types (Manning et al., 2014). We also consider replacing pronouns with their types, but concerned with poor quality of full coreference resolution, we only replace personal pronouns with their type PERSON. We observed that this strategy greatly improves generality of event phrases and facilitates the bootstrapping learning process. In section 5.1.2, we compare bootstrapping learning performance using generalized event representations v.s. using non-generalized event representations.

3.4 Regular Event Pair Candidates

Considering that it is not feasible to test all possible pairs of events in Gigaword and often two events that co-occur in a sentence have no temporal relation. In order to narrow down the search space, we identify candidate event pairs which are likely to have temporal relations.

Two strategies are used to identify candidate event pairs. First, by intuition, if two event phrases co-occur (within a sentence) many times, the likelihood of the two events being related and having a temporal relation should be higher compared to event phrases that rarely co-occur. Therefore, we select event phrase pairs that co-occur within a sentence for more than 100 times as candidate event pairs. Second, we use two specific temporal relation patterns, EV_A *after (before)* EV_B, that explicitly indicate two events are in a after (before) relation. We extract an event pair as a candidate

---

[1] We used POS tags to detect verb events.

[2] Reporting verbs, such as "said", "told" and "added", are commonly seen in news articles. We determined that most of event pairs containing a reporting verb are not very interesting and informative and we therefore discarded these event pairs.

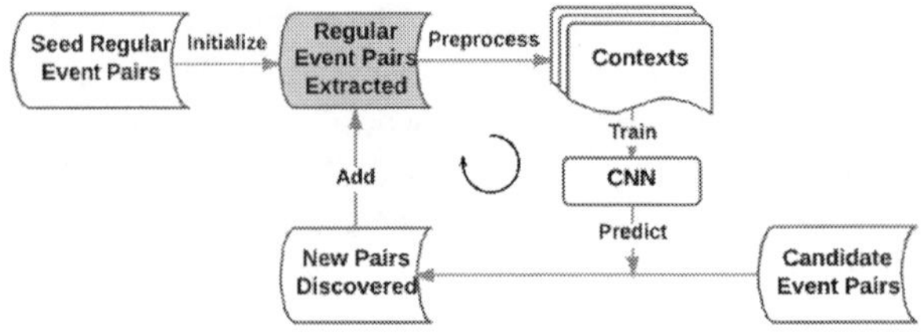

Figure 1: Overview of the Bootstrapping System

regular pair if it occurs three or more times with one of the patterns in the text corpus. The assumption is that if a pair of events shows a particular temporal relation regularly, it is likely to be seen in the above textual patterns as well. Specifically, we extract the governor and dependent word of the dependency relation *prep_after (prep_before)* in the annotated English Gigaword (Napoles et al., 2012) and check whether each word is an event[3]. If yes, we form an event phrase for each event and obtain an event pair. In addition, we expect regular event pairs to occur mostly in a single temporal order, either *before* or *after*, and discard event pairs that have showed mixed temporal orders. Specifically, a regular event pair is required to occur in a particular temporal relation more than 90% of times.

Overall by applying the two strategies, we obtained a candidate event pair pool that consists of 40,278 event pairs.

4 Bootstrapping both Regular Event Pairs and a Temporal Relation Classifier

Figure 1 illustrates how the bootstrapping system works. We first populate seed regular event pairs in the text corpus and identify sentences that contain a regular event pair as training instances. We train a contextual temporal relation classifier, using Convolutional Neural Nets (CNNs), to identify specific contexts describing a temporal *after (before)* relation. We then apply the classifier to the corpus to identify new sentences that describe a particular temporal relation, from which new regular event pairs can be extracted. Note that the classifier is only applied to sentences that contain a candidate regular event pair. The bootstrapping process repeats until the number of newly identified regular event pairs is less than 100.

While we used the whole Gigaword (Napoles

---

[3]Note we consider any verb and a noun that is in our noun event list as an event.

et al., 2012) to identify regular event pairs, we only use the New York Times section of Gigaword for bootstrapping learning.

4.1 Regular Event Pair Seeds

In order to ensure high quality of seed pairs, we only consider event pairs that have occurred in explicit temporal relation patterns, EV_A *after (before)* EV_B, as seed event pairs. Furthermore, we require each seed regular event pair to have occurred in a temporal relation pattern for at least ten times. Specifically, we identified 2,110 seed regular event pairs using the Gigaword corpus[4].

4.2 Contextual Temporal Relation Classification

We use a neural net classifier to capture compositional meanings of sentential contexts and avoid tedious feature engineering. Specifically, we used a Convolutional Neural Net (CNN) as our classifier, inspired by recent successes of CNN models in various NLP tasks and applications, such as sentiment analysis (Kalchbrenner et al., 2014; Kim, 2014), sequence labeling (Collobert et al., 2011) and semantic parsing (Yih et al., 2014). As shown in figure 2, our CNN architecture is a slight variation of the previous models as described in (Kim, 2014; Collobert et al., 2011). It has one convolutional layer with 100 hidden nodes, one pooling layer and one fully connected softmax layer.

The input are word embeddings of an array of sentential context words. A convolution filter is applied to a sliding window of every h words to provide input for each hidden node. We use Rectified Linear Unit (ReLU) as the non-linear activation function. We next apply a max-pooling operation to take the maximum value over a feature map. The final softmax layer output probability

---

[4]By populating seed regular event pairs in the New York Times section of the Gigaword corpus, we extracted 7191 sentences and 11339 sentences that contain an event pair in a "before" and "after" temporal relation respectively.

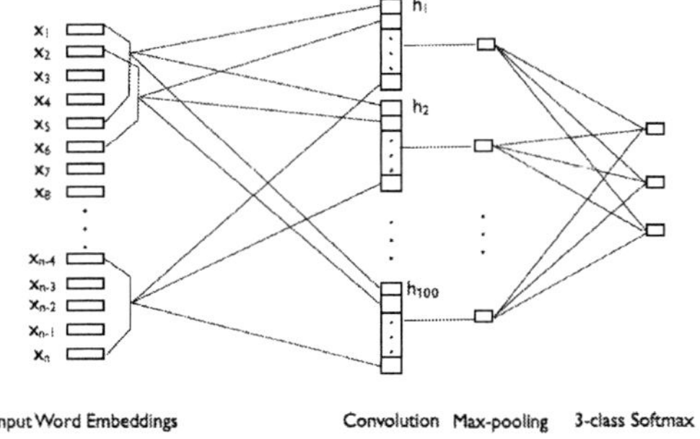

Figure 2: CNN Model Architecture

distributions over three classes (AFTER, BEFORE and OTHER) indicating the temporal relation between a pair of events in a sentence. Specifically, the temporal relations are defined with respect to the textual order the two events are presented in a sentence. If the first event is temporally BEFORE the second event as described in a sentence, this instance will be labeled as BEFORE. Otherwise if the first event is temporally AFTER the second event as described in a sentence, the instance will be labeled as AFTER. The class OTHER is to capture all the rest contexts that may describe a temporal relation other than *after (before)* or do not describe a temporal relation.

In our experiments, we use pre-trained 300-dimention word2vec word embeddings (Mikolov et al., 2013) that are trained on 100 billion words of Google News and we use a filter window size of 5. In training, we used stochastic gradient descent with Adadelta update rule (Zeiler, 2012) and mini-batch size of 100, in addition, we applied dropout (Hinton et al., 2012) with rate $p = 0.5$ to avoid overfitting of the CNN model. We also randomly selected 10% of the training data as the validation set and chose the classifier with the highest validation performance within the first 10 epochs.

4.2.1 Sentential Contexts: Local Windows v.s. Dependency Paths

We explore two types of contexts, local windows v.s. dependency paths, in order to identify contexts that effectively describe temporal relations between two events.

First, the local window based context for an event pair includes five words before the first event, five words after the second event and all the words between the two events. Note that two event phrases can be arbitrarily far from each other and long contexts are extremely challenging for a

classifier to capture. In our experiments, we only consider sentences where two event mentions are at most 10 words away.

Second, we observed that not every word between two events is useful to predict their temporal relation. In order to concentrate on relevant context words, we further construct dependency path[5] based context representation. Specifically, considering a dependency tree as an undirected graph, we use breadth-first-search to extract a sequence of words connecting the first event word to the second event word. In addition, to capture important information in certain syntactic structures such as conjunctions, we extract children nodes for each word in the path. Finally, we sort extracted words according to their textual order in the original sentence and the sorted sequence of words is provided as an input to the CNN classifier.

4.2.2 Negative Training Instances

Reasonably, most sentences in a corpus do not contain an event pair that is in a temporal "before/after" relation. Therefore, we use negative instances that are 10 times of the total number of positive training instances (i.e., sentences that contain an event pair in a *after (before)* relation). Specifically, we require a negative instance to contain an event pair that does not appear in seed pairs nor the candidate event pair set. We randomly sampled negative instances satisfying the condition. Then these deemed negative instances were labeled as the class OTHER, a class that compete with the two temporal relation classes, BEFORE and AFTER.

4.3 New Regular Event Pair Selection Criteria

Recall that regular event pairs are event pairs that tend to show a particular temporal relation despite of their various contexts. Therefore, we identify a candidate event pair as a new regular event pair if majority of its sentential contexts, specifically 60% of contexts, were consistently labeled as a particular temporal relation (*after* or *before*) by the CNN classifier. In addition, we require that at least 15 instances of a regular event pair have been labeled as the majority temporal relation. In order to control semantic drift (McIntosh and Curran, 2009) in bootstrapping learning, we increase the threshold by 5 after each iteration.

---

[5] Stanford CoreNLP (Manning et al., 2014) were used to generate dependency trees.

Systems	0 (Seeds)	1	2	3	4	5	Total
Basic System	1057	213	102	48	–	–	1420
+ Arg Generalization	2110	638	323	81	–	–	3152
+ Dependency Path Contexts (Full System)	2110	1230	555	288	156	62	4401

Table 1: Number of New Regular Event Pairs Generated after Each Bootstrapping Iteration

Furthermore, in order to filter out ambiguous event pairs that can be in either *before* or *after* temporal order depending on concrete contexts, we require the absolute difference between number of instances labeled as AFTER and labeled as BEFORE to be greater than a ratio of the total number of instances, specifically, we set the ratio to be 40%.

5 Evaluation

Our bootstrapping system learned regular event pairs as well as a contextual temporal relation classifier. We evaluate each of the two learning outcomes separately.

5.1 Regular Event Pair Acquisition

5.1.1 System Variations

We compare three variations of our system:

Basic System: in the basic system, we did not apply event argument generalization as described in section 3.3. In addition, we use local window based sentential contexts as input for the classifier.

+ Arg Generalization: on top of the basic system, we apply event argument generalization.

+ Dependency Path Contexts (Full System): in the full system, we apply event argument generalization and use dependency path based sentential contexts as input for the classifier.

Table 1 shows the number of regular new pairs that were generated after each bootstrapping iteration by each of the three systems. First, we can see that event argument generalization is useful in obtaining roughly two times of seed regular event pairs. Second, event argument generalization is useful in recognizing additional regular event pairs in bootstrapping learning as well. Third, dependency path based sentential contexts are effective in capturing relevant sentential contexts for temporal relation classification, which enables the bootstrapping system to maintain a learning momentum and learn more regular event pairs.

5.1.2 Accuracy of Regular Event Pairs

For each of the three system variations, we randomly selected 50 pairs from seed regular event

Systems	Seed Pairs	New Pairs
Basic System	0.73	0.55
+ Arg Generalization	0.71	0.63
+ Dependency Path Contexts		0.67

Table 2: Accuracy of 100 Randomly Selected Event Pairs

pairs and 50 from bootstrapped event pairs[6] and asked two human annotators to judge the correctness of these acquired regular event pairs.

Specifically, for each selected event pair, we ask two annotators to label whether a temporal AFTER or BEFORE relation exists between the two events. In addition to the two temporal relation labels, we provide the third category OTHER as well. We instruct annotators to assign the label OTHER to an event pair if the two events (i) generally have no temporal relation, (ii) have a temporal relation other than AFTER or BEFORE, or (iii) one or both mentions do not refer to an event at all.[7] For each event pair, only one label is allowed. Before the official annotation, we trained the two annotators with system generated event pairs for several iterations. The event pairs we used in training annotators are different from the final event pairs we used for evaluation purposes.

Table 2 shows the accuracy of regular event pairs learned by each system variation. We determine that an event pair is correctly predicted by a system if the system predicted temporal relation is the same as the label that has been assigned by both of the two annotators. The overall kappa inter-agreement between the two annotators is 72%. We can see that with event argument generalization, the quality of acquired seed regular event pairs is roughly equal to that using specific name arguments. Furthermore, because we obtained two times of seed event pairs after using event argument generalization, the second and third bootstrapping systems received more guidance and continued to learn regular event pairs

---

[6]The seed pairs for the second and the third system are the same, so we evaluate the same 50 randomly selected seed pairs for the two systems.

[7]This can happen due to Part-Of-Speech errors or ambiguous event words.

Common Sense	PERSON **worked** ← **graduation** **career** → **announced** retirement **wash** hands → **eating** PERSON **returned** ← **visit**
Politics	government be **formed** ← **elections** **fled** mainland ← **losing** war **imposed** sanctions ← **invasion** of LOCATION LOCATION **split** ← **war**
Business	**reached** agreement ← **negotiations** **hosted** banquet ← **meeting** **trading** → stock **closed**
Health	**cause** of death ← **cancer** PERSON be **hospitalized** ← **suffering** stroke PERSON **died** ← **admitted** to hospital
Sports	**games** → **ended** season PERSON be **sidelined** ← **undergoing** surgery PERSON be **suspended** ← **testing** for cocaine PERSON **returned** ← **recovering** from injury
Crime	**shooting** → PERSON be **arrested** **spending** in jail → PERSON be **released** PERSON be **arrested** ← **bombings** driver **fled** ← **accident**

Table 3: Examples of Learned Regular Event pairs. → represents *before* relation and ← represents *after* relation.

with a high quality. In addition, using dependency path based sentential contexts enables the classifier to further improve the accuracy of bootstrapped regular event pairs.

5.1.3 Examples and Constructed Knowledge Graphs

We have learned around 4,400 regular event pairs that are rich in commonsense knowledge and domain specific knowledge for domains including politics, business, health, sports and crime. Table 3 shows several examples in each category.

In addition, related event pairs form knowledge graphs, figure 3 shows two examples. The first one describes various scenarios that cause deaths while the second one describes contingent relations among events specific in sports.

5.1.4 Causally Related Events

We observed that a large portion of the learned regular event pairs are both temporally and causally related. We adopt the force dynamics theory and determine that two events are causally related if one event causes, enables or prevents the other event to happen. Then we asked two annotators [8] to annotate causal relations for the same set of 100 randomly selected regular event pairs

---

[8] We used the same two annotators that have conducted temporal relation annotations. For this task, the annotator inter-agreement is 0.82 in kappa.

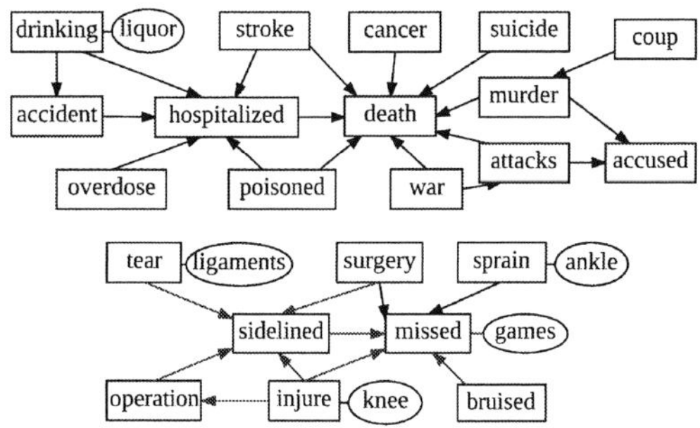

Figure 3: Knowledge Graphs

	0 (Seeds)	1	2	3	4	Total
Full System	112	179	271	95	–	657

Table 4: Bootstrapping Using VerbOcean Patterns

generated by the full bootstrapping system. Surprisingly, out of 69 event pairs that have been assigned with the same temporal relation by both annotators, 61 event pairs were deemed as causally related. This shows that most of our temporally related regular event pairs are causally related as well.

5.1.5 Using VerbOcean Patterns

VerbOcean Chklovski and Pantel (2004) created lexico-syntactic patterns in order to extract event pairs with various semantic relations from the Web. Specifically, for the temporal relation *happens-before*, VerbOcean used ten patterns such as "to X and then Y", "to X and later Y" and acquired 4,205 event pairs with a temporal "before/after" relation from the Web.

Therefore, we replace our two straightforward temporal relation patterns, EV_A *after (before)* EV_B, with the ten patterns proposed by VerbOcean and use these patterns to acquire seed regular event pairs. However, with exactly the same settings and frequency threshold we used in seed identification, we can only identify seven seed regular event pairs using the same complete Gigaword corpus. In order to obtain more seed event pairs, we lowered the frequency threshold of seeing an event pair in patterns from ten to three. In this case as shown in table 4, we obtained 112 seed event pairs, which is still much less than 2110 event pairs that we have acquired. Then with the initial 112 seed regular event pairs, around 500 new event pairs were later learned using exactly the same bootstrapping learning settings we have used. In total, only 657 event pairs were learned by using VerbOcean patterns. Note that the Gigaword corpus we used is much smaller in volume than the Web. Therefore, we hypothesize that VerbOcean patterns are too specific to be productive in identifying regular event pairs from a limited text corpus.

In addition, we compared our learned 4,401 regular event pairs with the 4,205 verb pairs in the *happens-before* relation acquired by VerbOcean[9]. Interestingly, among these two sets, only eight event pairs are the same. This shows that our bootstrapping learning approach recognizes diverse sentential contexts and learns a dramatically different set of temporally related event pairs, compared with VerbOcean which mainly uses specific lexico-syntactic patterns to query the giant Web.

5.2 Weakly Supervised Contextual Temporal Relation Classifier

5.2.1 Accuracy of the Classifier

Recall that the contextual temporal relation classifier was trained on the New York Times section of Gigaword. In order to evaluate the accuracy of the classifier, we applied the weakly supervised learned classifier (the full system) to sentential contexts between pairs of events extracted from the Associated Press Worldstream section of Gigaword. We randomly sampled 100 instances from the ones that were labeled by the classifier as indicating a *after* or *before* relation and with a confidence score greater than 0.8. Then for each instance and its pair of events, we asked our two annotators to judge whether the sentence indeed describes a *after (before)* temporal relation between the two events. According to the annotations[10], the classifier predicted the correct temporal relation 74% of time.

5.2.2 Evaluation Using a Benchmark Dataset

To facilitate direct comparisons, we evaluate both our weakly supervised trained classifier and two supervised trained systems using a benchmark evaluation dataset, the TempEval-3-platinum corpus, which contains 20 news articles annotated with several temporal relations between events. We only evaluate system performance on identifying temporal "before/after" relations.

	Approaches	F1	P	R
1	ClearTK (Bethard, 2013)	0.27	0.36	0.22
2	Mirza and Tonelli (2014b)	0.29	0.24	0.38
3	Our classifier	0.28	0.35	0.24

Table 5: Performance on TempEval-3 Test Data

We compare with two feature-rich supervised trained systems. ClearTK (Bethard, 2013) uses event attributes such as tense, aspect and class, dependency paths and words between two events as features in identifying temporal relations between events. More recently, (Mirza and Tonelli, 2014b) proposes even more sophisticated features including various lexical, grammatical and syntactic features, event durations, temporal signals and temporal discourse connectives etc. In contrast, our neural net based temporal relation classifier is simpler and does not require feature engineering.

Table 5 shows the comparison results between these three systems. Note that we ran the original ClearTK system and we re-implemented the system described in (Mirza and Tonelli, 2014b). In addition, both supervised systems were trained using TimeBank v1.2 (Pustejovsky et al., 2006). The performance across the three systems is overall low, one reason is that the pairs of events that are in a temporal relation were not provided to the classifiers. Therefore, the classifiers had to identify temporally related event pairs as well as classify their temporal relations. We can see that the weakly supervised classifier achieved roughly equal performance as ClearTK, while the other supervised system presents a a different precision-recall tradeoff. Overall, without using any annotated data or sophisticated hand crafted features, our weakly supervised system achieved a F1-score comparable to both supervised trained systems.

6 Conclusion

We presented a weakly supervised bootstrapping approach that learns both regular event pairs and a contextual temporal relation classifier, by exploring the observation that regular event pairs tend to show a consistent temporal relation despite of their diverse contexts. Evaluation shows that the learned regular event pairs are of high quality and rich in commonsense knowledge and domain knowledge. In addition, the weakly supervised trained temporal relation classifier achieves comparable performance with state-of-the-art supervised classifiers.

---

[9]Because event pairs in VerbOcean do not contain arguments, we removed event arguments from our event pairs for direct comparisons.

[10]The two annotators achieved a Kappa inter-agreement score of 0.71.

References

Steven Bethard. 2013. Cleartk-timeml: A minimalist approach to tempeval 2013. In *Second Joint Conference on Lexical and Computational Semantics (* SEM)*. volume 2, pages 10–14.

Steven Bethard and James H Martin. 2008. Learning semantic links from a corpus of parallel temporal and causal relations. In *Proceedings of the 46th Annual Meeting of the Association for Computational Linguistics on Human Language Technologies: Short Papers*. Association for Computational Linguistics, pages 177–180.

Avrim Blum and Tom Mitchell. 1998. Combining labeled and unlabeled data with co-training. In *Proceedings of the eleventh annual conference on Computational learning theory*. ACM, pages 92–100.

Nathanael Chambers, Taylor Cassidy, Bill McDowell, and Steven Bethard. 2014. Dense event ordering with a multi-pass architecture. *Transactions of the Association for Computational Linguistics* 2:273–284.

Nathanael Chambers and Dan Jurafsky. 2009. Unsupervised learning of narrative schemas and their participants. In *Proceedings of the Joint Conference of the 47th Annual Meeting of the ACL and the 4th International Joint Conference on Natural Language Processing of the AFNLP: Volume 2-Volume 2*. Association for Computational Linguistics, pages 602–610.

Nathanael Chambers and Daniel Jurafsky. 2008. Unsupervised learning of narrative event chains. In *ACL*. Citeseer, volume 94305, pages 789–797.

Timothy Chklovski and Patrick Pantel. 2004. Verbocean: Mining the web for fine-grained semantic verb relations. In *Proceedings of Conference on Empirical Methods in Natural Language Processing (EMNLP-04)*.

Ronan Collobert, Jason Weston, Léon Bottou, Michael Karlen, Koray Kavukcuoglu, and Pavel Kuksa. 2011. Natural language processing (almost) from scratch. *Journal of Machine Learning Research* 12(Aug):2493–2537.

Quang Xuan Do, Yee Seng Chan, and Dan Roth. 2011. Minimally supervised event causality identification. In *Proceedings of the Conference on Empirical Methods in Natural Language Processing*. Association for Computational Linguistics, pages 294–303.

Jennifer D'Souza and Vincent Ng. 2013. Classifying temporal relations with rich linguistic knowledge. In *HLT-NAACL*. pages 918–927.

Roxana Girju. 2003. Automatic detection of causal relations for question answering. In *Proceedings of the ACL 2003 workshop on Multilingual summarization and question answering-Volume 12*. Association for Computational Linguistics, pages 76–83.

Geoffrey E Hinton, Nitish Srivastava, Alex Krizhevsky, Ilya Sutskever, and Ruslan R Salakhutdinov. 2012. Improving Neural Networks by Preventing Co-adaptation of Feature Detectors. In *arXiv preprint arXiv:1207.0580*.

Nal Kalchbrenner, Edward Grefenstette, and Phil Blunsom. 2014. A convolutional neural network for modelling sentences. In *Proceedings of the 52nd Annual Meeting of the Association for Computational Linguistics*.

Yoon Kim. 2014. Convolutional neural networks for sentence classification. In *Proceedings of 2014 the Conference on Empirical Methods in Natural Language Processing (EMNLP-2014)*.

Hector Llorens, Estela Saquete, and Borja Navarro. 2010. Tipsem (english and spanish): Evaluating crfs and semantic roles in tempeval-2. In *Proceedings of the 5th International Workshop on Semantic Evaluation*. Association for Computational Linguistics, pages 284–291.

Christopher D. Manning, Mihai Surdeanu, John Bauer, Jenny Finkel, Steven J. Bethard, and David McClosky. 2014. The stanford corenlp natural language processing toolkit. In *Proceedings of the 52nd Annual Meeting of the Association for Computational Linguistics (ACL)*. pages 55–60.

Tara McIntosh and James R Curran. 2009. Reducing semantic drift with bagging and distributional similarity. In *Proceedings of the Joint Conference of the 47th Annual Meeting of the ACL and the 4th International Joint Conference on Natural Language Processing of the AFNLP: Volume 1-Volume 1*. Association for Computational Linguistics, pages 396–404.

Tomas Mikolov, Ilya Sutskever, Kai Chen, Greg S Corrado, and Jeff Dean. 2013. Distributed representations of words and phrases and their compositionality. In *Advances in neural information processing systems*. pages 3111–3119.

Paramita Mirza and Sara Tonelli. 2014a. An analysis of causality between events and its relation to temporal information. In *COLING*. pages 2097–2106.

Paramita Mirza and Sara Tonelli. 2014b. Classifying temporal relations with simple features. In *EACL*. volume 14, pages 308–317.

Paramita Mirza and Sara Tonelli. 2016. Catena: Causal and temporal relation extraction from natural language texts. In *The 26th International Conference on Computational Linguistics*. pages 64–75.

Courtney Napoles, Matthew Gormley, and Benjamin Van Durme. 2012. Annotated gigaword. In *Proceedings of the Joint Workshop on Automatic Knowledge Base Construction and Web-scale Knowledge Extraction*. Association for Computational Linguistics, pages 95–100.

James Pustejovsky, Patrick Hanks, Roser Sauri, Andrew See, Robert Gaizauskas, Andrea Setzer, Dragomir Radev, Beth Sundheim, David Day, Lisa Ferro, et al. 2003. The timebank corpus. In *Corpus linguistics*. volume 2003, page 40.

James Pustejovsky, Marc Verhagen, Roser Saurí, Jessica Littman, Robert Gaizauskas, Graham Katz, Inderjeet Mani, Robert Knippen, and Andrea Setzer. 2006. Timebank 1.2. *Linguistic Data Consortium* 40.

Mehwish Riaz and Roxana Girju. 2010. Another look at causality: Discovering scenario-specific contingency relationships with no supervision. In *Semantic Computing (ICSC), 2010 IEEE Fourth International Conference on*. IEEE, pages 361–368.

Mehwish Riaz and Roxana Girju. 2013. Toward a better understanding of causality between verbal events: Extraction and analysis of the causal power of verb-verb associations. In *Proceedings of the annual SIGdial Meeting on Discourse and Dialogue (SIGDIAL)*. Citeseer.

Stephanie Strassel, Mark A Przybocki, Kay Peterson, Zhiyi Song, and Kazuaki Maeda. 2008. Linguistic Resources and Evaluation Techniques for Evaluation of Cross-Document Automatic Content Extraction. In *Proceedings of the Sixth International Language Resources and Evaluation Conference (LREC-08)*.

Naushad UzZaman, Hector Llorens, James Allen, Leon Derczynski, Marc Verhagen, and James Pustejovsky. 2013. SemEval-2013 task 1: TempEval-3 evaluating time expressions, events, and temporal relations. In *Proceedings of the 7th International Workshop on Semantic Evaluation (SemEval 2013)*.

Marc Verhagen, Robert Gaizauskas, Frank Schilder, Mark Hepple, Graham Katz, and James Pustejovsky. 2007. Semeval-2007 task 15: Tempeval temporal relation identification. In *Proceedings of the 4th International Workshop on Semantic Evaluations*. Association for Computational Linguistics, pages 75–80.

Marc Verhagen, Roser Sauri, Tommaso Caselli, and James Pustejovsky. 2010. Semeval-2010 task 13: Tempeval-2. In *Proceedings of the 5th international workshop on semantic evaluation*. Association for Computational Linguistics, pages 57–62.

Wen-tau Yih, Xiaodong He, and Christopher Meek. 2014. Semantic parsing for single-relation question answering. In *Proceedings of the 52nd Annual Meeting of the Association for Computational Linguistics*.

Multilingual and Cross-Lingual Complex Word Identification

Seid Muhie Yimam[†], Sanja Štajner[‡], Martin Riedl[†], and Chris Biemann[†]

[†]Language Technology Group, Department of Informatics, Universität Hamburg, Germany
[‡]Data and Web Science Group, University of Mannheim, Germany
{yimam, riedl, biemann}@informatik.uni-hamburg.de
sanja@informatik.uni-mannheim.de

Abstract

Complex Word Identification (CWI) is an important task in lexical simplification and text accessibility. Due to the lack of CWI datasets, previous works largely depend on Simple English Wikipedia and edit histories for obtaining 'gold standard' annotations, which are of mixed quality, and limited to English only. We collect complex words/phrases (CP) for English, German and Spanish, annotated by both native and non-native speakers, and propose language independent features that can be used to train multilingual and cross-lingual CWI models. We show that the performance of cross-lingual CWI systems (using a model trained on one language and applying it on the other languages) is comparable to the performance of monolingual CWI systems.

1 Introduction

The goal of lexical simplification (LS) is to replace words and phrases that are infrequent and difficult to understand with their simpler variants, which are easier to understand for various target readers, e.g. language learners (Petersen and Ostendorf, 2007; Aluísio et al., 2008), children (De Belder and Moens, 2010), and people with various cognitive or reading impairments (Feng et al., 2009; Rello et al., 2013; Saggion et al., 2015). Most LS systems have a Complex Word Identification (CWI) module at the beginning of their pipeline, which is then followed by the generation of possible substitution candidates, and the substitution candidates ranking (Paetzold and Specia, 2015, 2016a). Other systems do not have a separate CWI module but rather try to simplify any content word in the text, e.g. (Bott et al., 2012a; Glavaš

and Štajner, 2015). They, however, still compare the complexity of the target word to all its substitution candidates, and in this way, perform the CWI task implicitly. The complexity comparison is usually performed taking into account the words frequency, length, ambiguity, or their combinations (Bott et al., 2012a; Glavaš and Štajner, 2015).

The 'gold standard' CWI datasets should ideally be compiled using human annotation of complex words and phrases in a controlled experiment (differentiating between target groups, e.g. native and non-native speakers). However, this is not always the case, e.g. (Shardlow, 2013; Horn et al., 2014). Currently the only existing 'gold standard' CWI corpus is the Semeval-2016 shared task CWI corpus for English (Paetzold and Specia, 2016b), annotated by non-native English speakers. In spite of the fact that such datasets are necessary for consistent automatic evaluation of LS systems and that CWI systems are known to improve the performance of automated LS systems (Paetzold and Specia, 2015), no similar datasets were built for any other language so far.

We address these needs by:

1) Collecting human annotations of complex words and phrases[1] by both native and non-native speakers in three languages (English, German, and Spanish), and for English, for three different text genres (Sections 3 and 4);

2) Proposing a language-independent set of features to build state-of-the-art automated CWI systems for all three languages (Section 5);

3) Showing that CWI systems using our language-independent feature set can be successfully trained on a dataset in one language and ap-

---

[1]In this paper, we interchangeably use **complex word**, **complex phrase**, or **hard word**, defined as a single word or a multi-word expression that causes difficulties in understanding the sentence or paragraph for a target reader.

Proceedings of Recent Advances in Natural Language Processing, pages 813–822,
Varna, Bulgaria, Sep 4–6 2017.

plied on another language, thus reducing the need for compiling CWI datasets for various languages (Section 6).

2 Related Work

2.1 CWI Datasets

Currently the largest and most widely used CWI dataset, only available for English, is the SemEval-2016 shared task dataset (Paetzold and Specia, 2016b), which consists of 9,200 sentences collected from the older CW dataset created by Shardlow (2013), LexMTurk corpus (Horn et al., 2014), and Simple Wikipedia (Kauchak, 2013). Those previous datasets relied on Simple Wikipedia and edit histories as a 'gold standard' annotation of CWs, despite the fact that the use of Simple Wikipedia as a 'gold standard' for text simplification has been disputed (Štajner et al., 2012; Amancio and Specia, 2014; Xu et al., 2015). The SemEval-2016 CWI dataset, in contrast, is a collection of human annotations of CWs. Another improvement over the previous datasets is that all annotators were non-native English speakers, and therefore the two user groups (native and non-native English speakers) were not mixed as in the previous cases.

In the SemEval-2016 CWI dataset, for each given sentence, annotators were asked to annotate all content words (nouns, verbs, adjectives, and adverbs as tagged by Freeling (Padró and Stanilovsky, 2012)) that they could not understand individually even if they could understand the meaning of the sentence as a whole. Annotators were presented only one target word at the time. In the training dataset (200 sentences), each target word was annotated by 20 people, while in the test set (9,000 sentences), each target word was annotated only by a single annotator. The goal of the shared task was to predict the complexity of a word for a single non-native speaker based on the annotations of a larger group of non-native speakers. This introduced a strong bias and inconsistencies in the test set (test sentences were annotated by only one annotator, but not all of them by the same one, involving a total of 400 different annotators), reflected in very low F-scores obtained across all systems (Paetzold and Specia, 2016b; Wróbel, 2016).

To the best of our knowledge, there are no CWI datasets for any language other than English, neither there are English CWI datasets covering different text genres and both native and non-native English speaker's needs.

2.2 State-of-the-Art CWI Systems

The systems of the SemEval-2016 shared task were ranked based on F-score (the standard F_1-measure) and G-score (a harmonic mean between accuracy and recall) on the *complex* class only.

The best system with respect to the G-score (77.40%), but at the cost of F-score being as low as 24.60%, uses a combination of threshold-based, lexicon-based and machine learning approaches with minimalistic voting techniques (Paetzold and Specia, 2016b). The second best system by the G-score (77.30%) also uses various lexical, morphological, semantic and syntactic features. The highest scoring system with respect to F-Score (35.30%), which obtained a G-score of 60.80%, uses threshold-based document frequencies on Simple Wikipedia (Wróbel, 2016).

The problem of those best performing systems is that their features cannot be obtained for other languages, as the lexicons used and Simple Wikipedia do not exist for other languages than English. Therefore, we propose a language-independent set of features and build fully-automated CWI systems using those features, which perform en par with the best SemEval-2016 shared task systems. Furthermore, we show that our systems, taking advantage of the language-independent set of features, can even be trained on one language and successfully applied on CWI task in a different language.

3 Collection of the New CWI Datasets

We collect the annotations of complex words and phrases (longer sequences of words, up to maximum 50 characters), using the MTurk crowdsourcing platform, from multiple native and non-native English speakers (collecting the information about whether they are native speakers or not) on three different text genres. Similarly, we collect complex phrases for German and Spanish, using the same UI and instructions given in the respective languages.[2]

---

[2]Data available under CC-BY at: `https://www.inf.uni-hamburg.de/en/inst/ab/lt/resources/data/complex-word-identification-dataset.html`.

3.1 Data Selection

The English dataset comprises texts from three different text genres: professionally written news, Wiki news (amateur written news), and Wikipedia articles (amateur written encyclopedic articles). For the NEWS dataset, we used 100 news stories from the EMM NewsBrief[3] compiled by Glavaš and Štajner (2013) for their event-centered simplification task. For the WIKINEWS, we collected 42 news articles from the Wikipedia news articles. To resemble the existing CW resources (Shardlow, 2013; Horn et al., 2014; Paetzold and Specia, 2016b), we also collected 500 sentences from Wikipedia, belonging to different categories (politics, economics, science, etc.) to ensure that we do not introduce a topic bias. For German and Spanish, a total of 978 and 1,387 sentences, respectively, were collected from German and Spanish Wikipedia articles; we take one HIT (Human Intelligence Task) from each article when there are enough sentences for a HIT.

3.2 Procedure

For each language, we follow the same procedure except that the instructions and examples are provided in the same language as the dataset. Every single annotation task is cast into a HIT, which consists of 5–10 sentences forming a paragraph and is completed by 10 workers each. To select a complex phrase, workers can highlight single words or sequences of words using their mouse pointer. In order to control the annotation process, we do not allow users to select simple words such as determiners, numbers and stop words,[4] and very long phrases (more than 50 characters). We also have a compulsory question about whether the annotator is a native speaker or not, with a comment that the answer to this question does not influence the payment. To encourage annotators to carefully read the text and to only highlight complex words, we offer a bonus that doubles the original reward if at least half of their selections match selections from other workers. To discourage arbitrarily larger annotations, we limit the maximum number of selections that annotators can highlight to 10. If an annotator cannot find any complex word, we ask them to provide a comment. Examples 1, 2,

and 3 show some of the CPs examples that were provided to the annotators for English, German and Spanish, respectively.

> **Example 1**: *The Israeli official said the new ambassador to Cairo, Yaakov Amitai, was expected to travel to the Egyptian capital in December to present his* credentials *, but the embassy would not be* staffed *or resume normal activity until acceptable* security arrangements *were in place. Many Egyptians view Israel, which signed a* peace treaty *with Egypt in 1979 after four wars between the two countries, with* hostility *.*
>
> **Example 2**: *Die Falschmeldung hatten die Yes Men (* Kommunikationsguerilla *)* lanciert *um an die Katastrophe in* Bhopal *vor 20 Jahren zu erinnern. Offiziellen Angaben zufolge starben 1.600 Menschen sofort und rund 6.000 weitere an den unmittelbaren Nachwirkungen. Bis heute* summiert *sich die Zahl der Opfer auf mindestens 20.000 Personen. Rund ein Fnftel der 500.000 Menschen die dem Gas ausgesetzt waren, leiden heute unter* chronischen *und unheilbaren Krankheiten , die sich offensichtlich zum Teil weiterverben knnen. Tausende erblindeten.*
>
> **Example 3**: *Se ubica exactamente* en la falda *del cerro Uliachin y* al pie de la *laguna Patarcocha en la regin geogrfica de la* puna *donde est rodeada de montaas y lagunas.* Se encuentra *a pocos kilmetros del* santuario *nacional "Bosque de piedras de Huayllay" famoso por las misteriosas formas que le han dado el viento y el agua a los grandes* macizos rocosos *.*

Our data collection differs from previous works in several regards: 1) we allow annotators to select both single words and sequences of words. We think that such datasets are helpful in upstream tasks such as lexical simplification or paraphrasing. 2) We do not show a single sentence at a time, but rather multiple sentences (5-10), which allows annotators to select complex phrases based on larger contexts.

4 Analysis of Collected Annotations

A total of 181 workers (134 native and 47 non-native) participated in the annotation task and 25,617 complex phrase (CP) annotations have been collected, out of which 6,830 are unique CPs. The distribution of selected CPs across all annotators (*All*), native and non-native annotators separately, and the number of CPs selected by at least one native and one non-native annotator (*Both*) is presented in Table 1. The distribution of selected

[3]Freely available at: `http://takelab.fer.hr/data/evsimplify/`

[4]`https://github.com/6/stopwords-json/`

Dataset	All		Native		Non-native		Both
	Sing.	Mult.	Sing.	Mult.	Sing.	Mult.	
NewsBrief	2,373	10,358	2,032	5,981	1,824	2,923	1,860
WikiNews	1,565	5,687	1,253	4,052	1,091	756	896
Wikipedia	1,170	4,464	1,031	2,792	832	979	773
German	1,525	5,878	1,225	1,727	1,306	3,145	11,66
Spanish	3,983	10,297	3,952	10,080	236	12	172

(a) Annotation statistics (raw counts)

Dataset	All		Native		Non-native		Both
	Sing.	Mult.	Sing.	Mult.	Sing.	Mult.	
NewsBrief	18.64	81.36	25.36	74.64	38.42	61.58	14.61
WikiNews	21.58	78.42	23.62	76.38	59.07	40.93	12.36
Wikipedia	20.77	79.23	26.97	73.03	45.94	54.06	13.72
German	20.60	79.40	41.50	58.50	29.34	70.66	15.75
Spanish	27.89	72.11	28.16	71.84	95.16	4.84	1.21

(b) Annotation statistics in percentages

Table 1: Distributions of selected CPs across all annotators (*All*), native and non-native annotators separately, and the number of CPs selected by at least one native and one non-native annotator (*Both*). The column *Sing.* shows the number/percentage of annotations selected by only one annotator while the column *Mult.* shows the number/percentage of annotations selected by at least two annotators.

dataset	uni-gram	bi-gram	tri-gram+	total
NewsBrief	10,631	1,592	508	12,731
WikiNews	6,242	727	289	7,258
Wikipedia	4,776	661	197	5,634
German	6,832	356	215	7,403
Spanish	11,000	1,975	1,305	14,280

(a) Distribution of collected CW (raw counts)

dataset	uni-gram	bi-gram	tri-gram+
NewsBrief	83.50	12.50	3.99
WikiNews	86.00	10.02	3.98
Wikipedia	84.77	11.73	3.50
German	92.29	4.81	2.90
Spanish	77.03	13.83	9.14

(b) Distribution of collected CW in percentages

Table 2: Distribution of collected CW annotations across different text genres and languages with CP lengths.

dataset	Number of Annotators		Avg. annotators per HIT	
	Native	Non-native	Native	Non-native
NewsBrief	67	29	5.8	4.2
WikiNews	56	12	7.6	2.4
Wikipedia	31	13	6.9	3.1
German	12	11	3.9	6.1
Spanish	48	6	9.8	0.2

Table 3: Distribution of number of annotators (native and non-native) per each language and on average per HIT.

CPs according to their length is presented in Table 2, while the distributions of annotators (native and non-native) per each language and on average per HIT are presented in Table 3.

4.1 Analysis of English CPs

As we can see from Table 1, around 80% of English CPs have been selected by at least two annotators. However, when we separate the selections made by native and non-native speakers, we see that: (1) the percentage of multiply-selected CPs by native speakers stays stable across differ-

ent genres, while this is not the case for the non-native speakers; (2) the percentage of multiply selected CPs by non-native speakers is always significantly lower (54%–62%) than the percentage of multiply selected CPs by native speakers (73%–75%), regardless of the text genre; and (3) the percentage of CPs selected by at least one native and one non-native annotator is very low (12%–15%).

These results indicate a higher heterogeneity of complex phrases among non-native speakers, raising doubts in how well can we predict complex phrases for a non-native speaker based on the annotations of other non-native speakers, and thus offering a possible explanation for the very low F-scores obtained by the best systems on the SemEval-2016 shared task. The low inter-annotator agreement (IAA) between native and non-native speakers (column *Both*) further indicates that the lexical simplification needs are very different for those two target groups. The IAA is calculated based on percentage of exact matches of annotations.

4.2 Analysis of German CPs

For German CWI task, we had fewer annotators (23 in total, 12 native and 11 non-native). They highlighted a total of 7,403 complex phrases (2,952 were selected by native and 4,451 by non-native speakers), out of which 2,711 are unique CPs. In this task, we had more non-native than native annotators per HIT (6.1 non-native and 3.9 native on average per HIT, see Table 3). In contrast to English and Spanish CP annotations, in the German task, more than 92% of the annotations are single words (Table 2). Unlike in the English CWI task, we found a higher IAA among non-native German annotators (70.66%) than native German annotators (58.5%). This might be due to the fact that we have more non-native than native annotators per HIT. The IAA between the native and non-native annotators was also higher for the German task (15.75%) than for the English task (Table 1).

4.3 Analysis of Spanish CPs

For the Spanish CWI task, we had 54 annotators, 48 native speakers and 6 non-native speakers. A total of 14,280 annotations are collected (14,032 from the native and 248 from the non-native speakers) with 6,061 CPs being unique. Given a low number of participating non-native speakers, we excluded the non-native Spanish annotations from further experiments. We found a lower IAA among Spanish native speakers than among English native speakers. This lower IAA for Spanish is mainly due to the fact that annotators highlighted mostly multiple phrases (23% of the annotations, see Table 2).

5 Classification Experiments

We developed a binary classification system for the CWI task with a performance comparable to the state-of-the-art systems of the SemEval-2016 shared task. We base our discussions on the F-scores, but also report on the G-score (both calculated on the *complex* class only, as in the shared task) to compare our systems with the SemEval-2016 best systems. We have normalized and transformed all features to a common and language-independent feature space in order to build a multilingual CWI system. This multilingual CWI sys-

tem design help us to conduct cross-lingual experiments.

5.1 Language-independent Feature Space

We use four different, language-independent sets of features.

Length and frequency features: Lexical substitution systems (Bott et al., 2012b; Glavaš and Štajner, 2015), and most of the CWI systems in the SemEval-2016 shared task use length- and frequency-related features. We use three length features: the number of vowels, the number of syllables, and the number of characters in the word. The number of syllables in the word are computed using the *texhyphj* tool,[5] which is a Java implementation of the Liang (1983) hyphenation algorithm available in multiple languages. We also use three sets of frequency features: frequency of the word in Wikipedia, frequency of the word in the Google Web 1T 5-Grams, and frequency of the word in the HIT/paragraph. In order to build a language independent feature representation, we normalized all the length and frequency features. For the length of vowels and syllables features, we normalize the count by dividing it with the token length. The length of the word (number of characters) was normalized by dividing the observed length with the average length of all words in the specific language of the datasets used to collect CPs. We have found that, for the English dataset, the average length of a word was 5.3 while for German and Spanish, it was 6.5 and 6.2 characters, respectively. Similarly, the frequency of the word in Wikipedia and Web1T corpus was normalized by dividing the frequency of the word by the maximum frequency of the word in the Wikipedia and Web1T corpus of the respective language.

Syntactic features: Based on the work of Davoodi and Kosseim (2016), the part of speech (POS) tag influences the complexity of the word. We used POS tags predicted by the Stanford POS tagger (Toutanova et al., 2003). However, the pre-trained models for the Stanford POS tagger are trained based on various POS tagged data: Penn Treebank[6] for English, the Stuttgart-Tübingen tag set (STTS)[7] for German, and the DEFT Spanish

---

[5] github.com/dtolpin/texhyphj

[6] https://www.ling.upenn.edu/courses/Fall_2003/ling001/penn_treebank_pos.html

[7] http://www.ims.uni-stuttgart.de/forschung/ressourcen/lexika/TagSets/stts-table.html

Treebank tag set[8] for Spanish. We have transformed the tag sets into universal POS tags based on the work of Petrov et al. (2012)[9].

Word embeddings features: The work of Ammar et al. (2016) introduced a single shared embedding space for more than fifty languages. For estimating multilingual embeddings, two methods called *multiCluster* and *multiCCA*, are designed with dictionaries and monolingual data. For our task, we have used the pre-trained embeddings model for the 3 languages.[10] We use the word2vec representations of content words (both complex and simple) as a feature, and also compute cosine similarities between the vector representations of the word and its context paragraph or sentence. The paragraph and sentence representations are computed by averaging the vector representations of the content words.

Topic Features: We use topic-relatedness feature that is extracted based on an LDA (Blei et al., 2003) model, which was trained on English, German and Spanish Wikipedia using 100 topics. We compute the cosine similarity between the word-topic vector and the document (the HIT in this case) vector as a feature. While this requires training a topic model for each language, the feature is still language-independent since we merely use the similarity between complex word candidate and context to gauge its in-topic-ness.

5.2 Classification Algorithms

We have used different machine learning algorithms from the scikit-learn machine leaning framework:[11] KNeighborsClassifier (KNN), NearestCentroid (NC), ExtraTreesClassifier (EXT), RandomForestClassifier (RF), and GradientBoostingClassifier (GB), and Support Vector Machines (SVM), and report only the results of the best classifiers based on NearestCentroid (NC).

On the SemEval-2016 shared task dataset, our system obtains an F-score of 35.44% and a G-score of 75.51%. The best system of the shared task by G-score obtained a 77.40% G-score, but with much lower F-score (24.60%) than ours, and the best shared task system by F-score obtained a 35.50% F-score, but with much lower G-score (60.80%) than ours. Therefore, our best system can be seen as comparable to the state-of-the-art CWI systems, but with the crucial difference of using a language-independent feature set.

5.3 Experimental Setups

We first build nine new datasets (three different genres times two different groups of annotators for English, native and non-native datasets for German and the native dataset for Spanish), by marking a word as *complex* if at least one annotator selected it as complex.

We further perform three sets of experiments:
Set I: Monolingual experiments on nine datasets (for all three languages).
Set II: Cross-language experiments.
Set III: Cross-group experiments.

The first set of experiments can be seen as benchmarking of CWI task on different languages and text genres. The second set of experiments explores the possibility of training a CWI system on one language and applying it on another language, which if possible, would imply that we do not need to collect CWI datasets for all languages. The third set of experiments explores whether the simplification needs of native and non-native speakers can be generalized.

In all three sets of experiments, we use the NC classifier and the same set of features (cf. Section 5.1), and we always use training sets of 200 sentences (to have the same size training dataset as in the SemEval-2016 shared task) and the rest of each dataset for testing (controlling for not having the same sentences in training and test sets in any experiment).

The distributions of the *complex* class in our nine new datasets and the SemEval-2016 shared task dataset are presented in Table 4. As can be noted, the percentages of *complex* instances are similar for both training and test sets in all our datasets, while this is not the case for the SemEval-2016 shared task. The unbalanced percentage of *complex* instances in training and test sets of the SemEval-2016 shared task is the consequence of the training dataset being annotated by 20 annotators and the test set being annotated by only one annotator, which is probably the cause for the very

---

[8]https://web.archive.org/web/20160325024315/http://nlp.lsi.upc.edu/freeling/doc/tagsets/tagset-es.html

[9]https://github.com/slavpetrov/universal-pos-tags

[10][http://128.2.220.95/multilingual/data/

[11]http://scikit-learn.org/stable/supervised_learning.html

Dataset	Native				Non-Native			
	Train		Test		Train		Test	
	Simple	Complex	Simple	Complex	Simple	Complex	Simple	Complex
NewsBrief	970	459	768	360	1,068	361	860	270
Wiki news	898	531	436	250	1,119	310	516	170
Wikipedia	856	573	268	225	985	444	355	133
German	1,117	393	586	187	1,014	497	536	238
Spanish	1,529	647	1,189	435	–	–	–	–
Shared	–	–	–	–	1,531	706	84,090	4,131

(a) Raw counts of *complex* and *simple* instances in our training and test sets

Dataset	Native				Non-Native			
	Train		Test		Train		Test	
	Simple	Complex	Simple	Complex	Simple	Complex	Simple	Complex
NewsBrief	67.88	32.12	68.09	31.91	74.74	25.26	76.11	23.89
Wiki news	62.84	37.16	63.56	36.44	78.31	21.69	75.22	24.78
Wikipedia	59.90	40.10	54.36	45.64	68.93	31.07	72.75	27.25
German	73.97	26.03	75.81	24.19	67.11	32.89	63.73	28.06
Spanish	70.27	29.73	73.21	26.79	–	–	–	–
Shared	–	–	–	–	68.44	31.56	95.32	4.68

(b) Percentages of *complex* and *simple* instances in our training and test sets

Table 4: Distribution of *complex* and *simple* instances in our nine new datasets and the SemEval-2016 shared task dataset.

low F-scores achieved by all systems on the shared task (Section 2). In order to avoid this problem, we used exactly the same annotation procedure for both training and test sets. For Spanish, we only report results for native annotators since we did not collect enough non-native annotations (cf. Section 4.3).

6 Results and Discussion

We present and discuss the results of each set of experiments in a separate subsection. In all experiments, as a baseline system, we use threshold-based document frequency using the English Simple Wikipedia, German Wikipedia and Spanish Wikipedia articles. We present results of all experiments based on the F_1-measure.

6.1 Monolingual Results (Setup I)

Table 5 presents the baseline as well as the results of the CWI systems for the nine datasets using the multilingual features. All of the CWI systems perform better than the baseline system. We can also see that for English, the CWI systems based on the datasets collected from native speakers perform better than CWI systems based on the datasets collected from non-native annotators.

6.2 Cross-Language Results (Setup II)

In the cross-language CWI systems, we train the source model in one language and test on the

Dataset	Native		Non-native	
	Our (NC)	Baseline	Our (NC)	Baseline
NEWS	**69.97**	66.01	**62.35**	60.28
WIKINEWS	**69.25**	66.56	**57.89**	51.50
WIKIPEDIA	**70.79**	67.20	**58.31**	53.53
GERMAN	**54.92**	51.37	**58.50**	56.57
SPANISH	**45.83**	44.04	–	–

Table 5: Results of our CWI system (NC) and the baseline system on our nine datasets using the multilingual features. The baseline is based on document frequency thresholds of Wikipedia corpora in the respective languages, with better system marked in bold. (Setup I)

datasets for other languages (both native and non-native datasets separately). As we can see from Table 6, when we use a CWI model trained on one of the English datasets and test it on the German datasets annotated by native or non-native speakers, we obtain similar results to (and, in some cases, even better than) those of the CWI models trained on German datasets. The same holds when we test the English CWI models on the native Spanish dataset.

When we train the CWI system on the Spanish native dataset and test it on the German datasets, we observe a slight decrease in performance in comparison to monolingual German CWI systems, but still very close.

The CWI systems trained on German datasets and applied on English datasets, however, show a

Training		Testing								
		NEWS		WIKI NEWS		WIKIPEDIA		GERMAN		SPANISH
		Native	Non-Native	Native	Non-native	Native	Non-native	Native	Non-native	Native
NEWS	Native	**69.97**	60.13	**71.45**	**59.76**	67.24	**57.14**	53.89	58.32	45.19
	Non-Native	67.49	**62.35**	69.24	58.53	67.95	55.28	53.02	58.92	44.79
WIKI NEWS	Native	69.25	57.69	70.91	58.84	64.98	54.34	54.54	58.42	44.48
	Non-Native	68.56	57.89	69.49	58.37	66.36	51.67	56.03	58.31	43.26
WIKIPEDIA	Native	69.75	58.54	71.02	58.64	**70.79**	55.61	52.93	58.64	45.29
	Non-Native	68.80	59.95	68.63	57.36	67.12	58.31	51.53	**59.14**	44.39
GERMAN	Native	67.42	57.55	64.12	51.01	61.99	50.48	**54.92**	57.69	42.76
	Non-Native	66.99	58.51	68.33	55.53	67.27	54.09	53.83	58.50	41.52
SPANISH	Native	66.07	58.17	68.69	55.43	62.67	51.89	53.53	56.82	**45.83**

Table 6: Results of the cross-group and cross-language experiments using for the nine datasets, with better system marked in bold.) (Setups II and III)

drop in the performance in comparison to monolingual English CWI systems. The same holds for the CWI systems trained on the Spanish native dataset and applied on the English test sets.

Therefore, we see that the CWI systems trained on one language can be used to identify complex words in another language.

6.3 Cross-Group Results (Setup III)

For the English datasets, training the CWI systems on native datasets and using them to identify complex words for non-native speakers seems to lead to worse performances than training the CWI systems on the non-native English datasets (Table 6). The opposite (training the CWI systems on non-native English datasets and using them to identify complex words for native speakers), however, seems to lead to better results than training the systems on the native English datasets.

For the cross-group German experiments, the results are exactly the opposite from those for English. One possible explanation could be the higher IAA between English native annotators and German non-native annotators (cf. Table 1) and the number of annotators per HIT being higher for English native and German non-native annotators (cf. Table 3).

7 Conclusions

Complex word identification (CWI) task is an important task in text accessibility and text simplification. So far, however, this task has only been addressed on the Wikipedia sentences and taking into account mostly the needs of non-native English speakers. Moreover, languages other than English did not receive any attention with regard to building either the CWI datasets or automated CWI systems.

We have collected a total of nine 'gold-standard' CWI datasets: six datasets for English (three genres times two groups of annotators), two datasets for German (for native and non-native speakers), and one dataset for Spanish native speakers.

Furthermore, we have developed a state-of-the-art automated CWI system with language-independent feature representations, and showed that it performs well regardless of text genre and language.

Most importantly, we demonstrated that it is possible to train CWI systems in one language and use them to identify complex words in a different language, by demonstrating that CWI systems trained with English datasets annotated by native and non-native speakers can be used to reliably identify complex words in German and Spanish with a drop of only 1-2% in performance, whereas CWI systems trained with German training sets annotated by non-native speakers can be used to identify complex words in English with maximal drop of only 2-4% in performance.

These results imply that state-of-the-art CWI systems can be built for many languages without a need for collecting new CWI datasets in those languages: it is safe to use existing CWI datasets for other languages.

The full dataset is available for download via the first author's homepage.

References

Sandra M. Aluísio, Lucia Specia, Thiago A.S. Pardo, Erick G. Maziero, and Renata P.M. Fortes. 2008. Towards Brazilian Portuguese automatic text simplification systems. In *Proceedings of the eighth ACM symposium on Document engineering*. New York, NY, USA, DocEng '08, pages 240–248.

Marcelo Adriano Amancio and Lucia Specia. 2014. An Analysis of Crowdsourced Text Simplifications. In *Proceedings of the 3rd Workshop on Predicting and Improving Text Readability for Target Reader Populations (PITR)*. Gothenburg, Sweden, pages 123–130.

Waleed Ammar, George Mulcaire, Yulia Tsvetkov, Guillaume Lample, Chris Dyer, and Noah A. Smith. 2016. Massively multilingual word embeddings. *CoRR* abs/1602.01925.

David M. Blei, Andrew Y. Ng, and Michael I. Jordan. 2003. Latent dirichlet allocation. *Journal of Machine Learning Research (JMLR)* 3:993–1022.

Stefan Bott, Luz Rello, Biljana Drndarevic, and Horacio Saggion. 2012a. Can Spanish be simpler? LexSiS: Lexical simplification for Spanish. In *Proceedings of COLING 2012*. Mumbai, India, pages 357–374.

Stefan Bott, Luz Rello, Biljana Drndarević, and Horacio Saggion. 2012b. Can Spanish be simpler? LexSiS: Lexical simplification for Spanish. In *Proceedings of COLING 2012*. Mumbai, India, pages 357–374.

Elnaz Davoodi and Leila Kosseim. 2016. CLaC at SemEval-2016 Task 11: Exploring linguistic and psycho-linguistic Features for Complex Word Identification. In *Proceedings of the 10th International Workshop on Semantic Evaluation (SemEval-2016)*. San Diego, California, USA, pages 982–985.

Jan De Belder and Marie-Francine Moens. 2010. Text simplification for children. In *Proceedings of the SIGIR workshop on accessible search systems*. Geneva, Switzerland, pages 19–26.

Lijun Feng, Noémie Elhadad, and Matt Huenerfauth. 2009. Cognitively motivated features for readability assessment. In *Proceedings of the 12th Conference of the European Chapter of the Association for Computational Linguistics*. Athens, Greece, EACL '09, pages 229–237.

Goran Glavaš and Sanja Štajner. 2013. Event-centered simplification of news stories. In *Proceedings of the Student Research Workshop at the International Conference on Recent Advances in Natural Language Processing*. Hissar, Bulgaria,, pages 71–78.

Goran Glavaš and Sanja Štajner. 2015. Simplifying Lexical Simplification: Do We Need Simplified Corpora? In *Proceedings of the 53rd Annual Meeting of the Association for Computational Linguistics and the 7th International Joint Conference on Natural Language Processing (Volume 2: Short Papers)*. Beijing, China, pages 63–68.

Colby Horn, Cathryn Manduca, and David Kauchak. 2014. A Lexical Simplifier Using Wikipedia. In *Proceedings of the 52nd Annual Meeting of the Association for Computational Linguistics (Volume 2: Short Papers)*. Baltimore, Maryland, USA, pages 458–463.

David Kauchak. 2013. Improving Text Simplification Language Modeling Using Unsimplified Text Data. In *Proceedings of the 51st Annual Meeting of the Association for Computational Linguistics (Volume 1: Long Papers)*. Sofia, Bulgaria, pages 1537–1546.

Franklin M. Liang. 1983. *Word hy-phen-a-tion by com-put-er*. Ph.D. thesis, Stanford University, Department of Linguistics, Stanford, CA., USA.

Lluís Padró and Evgeny Stanilovsky. 2012. FreeLing 3.0: Towards Wider Multilinguality. In *Proceedings of the Eight International Conference on Language Resources and Evaluation (LREC'12)*. Istanbul, Turkey, pages 2473–2479.

Gustavo Paetzold and Lucia Specia. 2015. LEXenstein: A Framework for Lexical Simplification. In *Proceedings of ACL-IJCNLP 2015 System Demonstrations*. Beijing, China, pages 85–90.

Gustavo Paetzold and Lucia Specia. 2016a. Benchmarking Lexical Simplification Systems. In *Proceedings of the Tenth International Conference on Language Resources and Evaluation (LREC 2016)*. Portorož, Slovenia, pages 3074–3080.

Gustavo Paetzold and Lucia Specia. 2016b. SemEval 2016 Task 11: Complex Word Identification. In *Proceedings of the 10th International Workshop on Semantic Evaluation (SemEval-2016)*. San Diego, California, USA, pages 560–569.

Sarah E. Petersen and Mari Ostendorf. 2007. Text Simplification for Language Learners: A Corpus Analysis. In *Proceedings of Workshop on Speech and Language Technology for Education*. Farmington, Pennsylvania, USA, pages 69–72.

Slav Petrov, Dipanjan Das, and Ryan McDonald. 2012. A Universal Part-of-Speech Tagset. In *Proceedings of the Eight International Conference on Language Resources and Evaluation (LREC'12)*. Istanbul, Turkey, pages 2089–2096.

Luz Rello, Ricardo Baeza-Yates, Laura Dempere-Marco, and Horacio Saggion. 2013. Frequent words improve readability and short words improve understandability for people with dyslexia. In *Proceedings of the INTERACT 2013: 14th IFIP TC13 Conference on Human-Computer Interaction., 2013*. Cape Town, South Africa, pages 203–219.

Horacio Saggion, Sanja Štajner, Stefan Bott, Simon Mille, Luz Rello, and Biljana Drndarević. 2015. Making It Simplext: Implementation and Evaluation of a Text Simplification System for Spanish. *ACM Transactions on Accessible Computing* 6(4):14:1–14:36.

Matthew Shardlow. 2013. The CW Corpus: A New Resource for Evaluating the Identification of Complex Words. In *Proceedings of the Second Workshop on Predicting and Improving Text Readability for Target Reader Populations*. Sofia, Bulgaria, pages 69–77.

Kristina Toutanova, Dan Klein, Christopher Manning, and Yoram Singer. 2003. Feature-Rich Part-of-Speech Tagging with a Cyclic Dependency Network. In *North American Chapter of the Association for Computational Linguistics - Human Language Technologies (NAACL HLT 2003)*. Edmonton, Canada, pages 982–985.

Sanja Štajner, Richard Evans, Constantin Orasan, and Ruslan Mitkov. 2012. What Can Readability Measures Really Tell Us About Text Complexity? In *Proceedings of the LREC'12 Workshop: Natural Language Processing for Improving Textual Accessibility (NLP4ITA)*. Istanbul, Turkey.

Krzysztof Wróbel. 2016. PLUJAGH at SemEval-2016 Task 11: Simple System for Complex Word Identification. In *Proceedings of the 10th International Workshop on Semantic Evaluation (SemEval-2016)*. San Diego, California, USA, pages 953–957.

Wei Xu, Chris Callison-Burch, and Courtney Napoles. 2015. Problems in current text simplification research: New data can help. *Transactions of the Association for Computational Linguistics* 3:283–297.

Automatic Generation of Situation Models for Plan Recognition Problems

Kristina Y. Yordanova

University of Rostock
18059 Rostock
Germany
`kristina.yordanova@uni-rostock.de`

Abstract

Recent attempts at behaviour understanding through language grounding have shown that it is possible to automatically generate models for planning problems from textual instructions. One drawback of these approaches is that they either do not make use of the semantic structure behind the model elements identified in the text, or they manually incorporate a collection of concepts with semantic relationships between them. We call this collection of knowledge situation model. The situation model introduces additional context information to the model. It could also potentially reduce the complexity of the planning problem compared to models that do not use situation models. To address this problem, we propose an approach that automatically generates the situation model from textual instructions. The approach is able to identify various hierarchical, spatial, directional, and causal relations. We use the situation model to automatically generate planning problems in a PDDL notation and we show that the situation model reduces the complexity of the PDDL model in terms of number of operators and branching factor compared to planning models that do not make use of situation models.

1 Introduction

Libraries of plans combined with observations are often used for behaviour understanding (Ramirez and Geffner, 2011; Krüger et al., 2014; Yordanova and Kirste, 2015). Such approaches rely on PDDL-like notations to generate a library of plans and then reason about the agent's actions, plans, and goals based on observations. Models describing plan recognition problems for behaviour understanding are typically manually developed (Ramírez and Geffner, 2009; Ramirez and Geffner, 2011; Baker et al., 2009). The manual modelling is however time consuming and error prone and often requires domain expertise (Nguyen et al., 2013).

To reduce the need of domain experts and to reduce the time required for building the model, one can substitute them with textual data (Philipose et al., 2004). More precisely, one can utilise the knowledge encoded in textual instructions to learn the model structure. Textual instructions specify tasks for achieving a given goal without explicitly stating all the required steps. On the one hand, this makes them a challenging source for learning a model (Branavan et al., 2010). On the other hand, they are usually written in imperative form, have a simple sentence structure, and are highly organised. Compared to rich texts, this makes them a better source for identifying the sequence of actions needed for reaching the goal (Zhang et al., 2012).

According to (Branavan et al., 2012), to learn a model for planning problems from textual instructions, the system has to: 1. **extract the actions' semantics** from the text, 2. **learn the model semantics** through language grounding, 3. and finally to **translate it into computational model** for planning problems.

In this work we add the **learning of a situation model** as a requirement for learning the model structure. As the name suggests, it provides context information about the situation (Ye et al., 2012). It is a collection of concepts with semantic relations between them. In that sense, the situation model plays the role of the common knowledge base shared between different entities.

In this work, we show that a computational

823
Proceedings of Recent Advances in Natural Language Processing, pages 823–830,
Varna, Bulgaria, Sep 4–6 2017.

model for plan recognition problems can benefit from a situation model, which describes the semantic structure of the model elements, as it (1) introduces additional context to the model and (2) it can be used to reduce the model complexity through action specialisation. We propose a method for learning the situation model from textual instructions that relies on language taxonomies, word dependencies and implicit causal relations to identify the semantic structure of the model. We use the situation model to generate planning operators for a planning problem in a Planning Domain Definition Language (PDDL) notation. We evaluate our approach by generating a model that describes the preparation of brownies. We compare the model complexity with and without the usage of the situation model in terms of number of operators and mean branching factor.

2   Related Work

The goal of grounded language acquisition is to learn linguistic analysis from a situated context (Branavan et al., 2011; Vogel and Jurafsky, 2010). This could be done in different ways: through grammatical patterns that are used to map the sentence to a machine understandable model of the sentence (Li et al., 2010; Zhang et al., 2012; Branavan et al., 2012); through machine learning techniques (Sil and Yates, 2011; Chen and Mooney, 2011; Benotti et al., 2014; Goldwasser and Roth, 2014; Kollar et al., 2014); or through reinforcement learning approaches that learn language by interacting with an external environment (Branavan et al., 2012, 2011, 2010; Vogel and Jurafsky, 2010; Babeş-Vroman et al., 2012; Goldwasser and Roth, 2014; Kollar et al., 2014).

Models learned through language grounding have been used for plan generation (Li et al., 2010; Branavan et al., 2012), for learning the optimal sequence of instruction execution (Branavan et al., 2011, 2010), for learning navigational directions (Vogel and Jurafsky, 2010; Chen and Mooney, 2011), and for interpreting human instructions for robots to follow them (Kollar et al., 2014; Tenorth et al., 2010).

All of the above approaches have two drawbacks. The first problem is the way in which the preconditions and effects for the planning operators are identified. They are learned through explicit causal relations, that are grammatically expressed in the text (Li et al., 2010; Sil and Yates, 2011). The existing approaches, however, either rely on initial manual definition to learn these relations (Branavan et al., 2012), or on grammatical patterns and rich texts with complex sentence structure (Li et al., 2010). Textual instructions however usually have a simple sentence structure where grammatical patterns are rarely discovered (Yordanova, 2015). The existing approaches do not address the problem of discovering causal relations between sentences, but assume that all causal relations are expressed within the sentence (Tenorth et al., 2010). In textual instructions however, the elements representing cause and effect are usually found in different sentences (Yordanova, 2015).

The second problem is that existing approaches either rely on manually defined situation model (Sil and Yates, 2011; Branavan et al., 2012; Goldwasser and Roth, 2014), or do not use one (Li et al., 2010; Branavan et al., 2011, 2010; Zhang et al., 2012; Vogel and Jurafsky, 2010). However, one needs a situation model to deal with model generalisation problems and as a means for expressing the semantic relations between model elements (Yordanova and Kirste, 2016; Yordanova, 2016). What is more, the manual definition is time consuming and often requires domain experts.

To address these two problems, in previous works we outlined an approach for automatic generation of behaviour models from texts (Yordanova and Kirste, 2016; Yordanova, 2016, 2017). In this work, we extend the approach by proposing a method for automatic generation of situation models. The method adapts the idea proposed by (Yordanova, 2015) to use time series analysis to identify the causal relations between text elements. Our approach uses this idea to discover causal relations between actions. It also makes use of existing language taxonomies and word dependencies to identify hierarchical, spatial and directional relations, as well as relations identifying the means through which an action is accomplished. The situation model is then used to generate planning operators that use the situation model's semantic structure in order to specialise the operators and thus to reduce the model complexity. In the following, we describe the approach in details.

3   Approach

The goal of the work is to build a situation model for a given planning problem. In this sense, a situation model is the knowledge base containing all relevant information about a given situation. This information is represented in terms of entities describing the relevant elements for a given situation and the semantic relations between these entities. In the following we first discuss which elements are of interest for us and then we describe our approach for generating the situation model from textual instructions.

3.1 Identifying Elements of Interest

The first step in generating the situation model is to identify the elements of interest in the text. We consider a text to be a sequence of sentences divided by a sentence separator.

Each sentence in the text is then represented by a sequence of words, where each word has a tag describing its part of speech (POS) meaning.

In a text we have different types of words. We are most interested in verbs as they describe the actions that can be executed in the environment. The actions are then verbs in their infinitive form or in present tense, as textual instructions are usually described in imperative form with a missing agent.

We are also interested in those nouns that are the direct (accusative) objects of the verb. These nouns give us the elements of the world with which the agent is interacting (in other words, objects on which the action is executed).

Apart from the direct objects, we are also interested in any indirect objects of the action. Namely, any nouns that are connected to the action through a preposition. These nouns give us spacial, locational or directional information about the action being executed, or the means through which the action is executed (e.g. an action is executed "with" the help of an object). We denote the set of direct and indirect objects with O.

3.2 Building the Initial Situation Model

Given the set of objects O, the goal is to build the initial structure of the situation model from these elements. This structure consists of words, describing the elements of a situation and the relations between these elements. If we think of the words as nodes and the relations as edges, we can then represent the situation model as a graph.

Definition 1 (*Situation model*) *Situation model* $G := (W, R)$ *is a graph consisting of nodes represented through words W and of edges represented through relations R, where for two words $a, b \in W$, there exists a relation $r \in R$ such that $r(a, b)$.*

The initial structure of the situation model is represented by a taxonomy that contains the objects O and their abstracted meaning on different levels of abstraction. To do that, a language taxonomy L containing hyperonymy relations between the words of the language is used (this is the is-a relation between words).

To build the initial situation model, we start with the set O as the leaves of the taxonomy and for each object $o \in O$ we recursively search for its hypernyms. This results in a hierarchy where the bottommost layer consist of the elements in O and the uppermost layer contains the most abstract word, that is the least common parent of all $o \in O$. In that sense, a word at a higher abstraction level is the least common parent of some words on a lower abstraction level.

3.3 Extending the Situation Model

As the initial situation model contains only the abstraction hierarchy of the identified objects, we extend it by first including the list of all actions to the situation model and then adding the relations between actions and indirect objects and actions and direct objects to the graph.

On one hand, this step is performed in order to enrich the semantic structure of the model. On the other hand, it gives the basis for the planning operators, as the list of arguments in an operator is represented by all objects that are related to the action.

3.4 Adding Causal Relations

The last step is extending the situation model with causal relations. The causal relations provide the cause-effect relation between actions in the model. It is important for the planning problem, as the planning operators are defined through preconditions and effects, which in turn build up the causal structure of the planning problem.

To discover causal relations between actions in the text, we consider two cases: (1) relations between two actions in the text; (2) relations between two action-object pairs in the text. We consider the first case as there are actions that are not related to a specific direct or indirect object but that still are causally related to other actions. We consider the second case because applying one action on an object can cause the execution of another action on the same object. We can think of the second case as a special case of the first, where we have filtered out any elements that could cause "noise" when searching for causality.

To discover causal relations between actions, we adapt the algorithm proposed by (Yordanova, 2015), which makes use of time series analysis. We start by representing each unique action (or each action-object tuple) in a text as a time series. Each element in the series is a tuple consisting of the number of the sentence in the text, and the number of occurrences of the action (tuple) in the sentence.

In order to discover causal relations based on the generated time series, we make use of the Granger causality test. It is a statistical test for determining whether one time series is useful for forecasting another. More precisely, Granger testing performs statistical significance test for one time series, "causing" the other time series with different time lags using auto-regression (Granger, 1969).

Generally, for two time series, we perform Granger test, and if the p value of the result is under the significance threshold, we conclude that the first time series causes the second, hence the first word causes the second. For example, we generate time series for the words "take" and "put" and after applying the Granger test, it concludes that the lagged time series for "take" significantly improve the forecast of the "put" time series, thus we conclude that "take" causes "put".

Now that we have identified the causal relations between actions, we add them in the situation model. We do that by adding the set of new relations to the existing set of relations in the situation model. An example of a situation model can be seen in Figure 2.

3.5 Generating Planning Operators

In order to test whether the situation model reduces the complexity of the planning problem, we generate operators based on the situation model. Figure 1 shows an example of an operator in the Planning Domain Definition Language (PDDL). It consists of action name, parameters (or arguments), and preconditions, which tell us what constraints have to be satisfied for an action to be executable, and effects, which define how the action execution changes the world.

```
(:action put
 :parameters (?o - object ?to -
     location)
 :precondition (and
         (not (executed-put ?o ?to)))
 :effect     (and
         (executed-put ?o ?to))
)
```

Figure 1: Example of an action template *put* in the PDDL notation.

To generate an operator, we take the name from the set of actions in the situation model. Then, for each action a, we take the set of arguments from the objects $o \in O$ in the situation model that have object-verb relations to the action.

The set of preconditions of an operator is then generated from the set of causal relations to actions, which cause a given action a to become executable. The set of effects consists of marking the action as executed with the given set of arguments and of negating the execution of another action if they are cyclic. Cyclic actions are actions that negate each other's effects. For example, the execution of "put the apple on the table" negates the effect of the action "take the apple". In that respect, for two operators a and b with cyclic relation, we have to negate the effects of a after executing b and vice versa, otherwise it will not be possible to execute these actions again.

4 Evaluation

To evaluate the approach, we generated a planning model from experiment instructions describing the preparation of brownies. Table 1 shows a small excerpt of the instructions.

```
1  Open the brownie bag.
2  Put the scissors in the drawer.
3  Take the brownie bag and rip the brownie bag.
4  Put the ripped brownie bag in the sink.
5  Close the drawer.
```

Table 1: Excerpt from instruction describing how to prepare brownies.

The instructions consisted of 110 short sentences describing the step by step execution of the experiment. To obtain the part of speech tags and dependencies between words, we used the Stanford NLP parser. We used the taxonomy of English language WordNet (Miller, 1995) to obtain the hyperonyms of the identified objects. As some

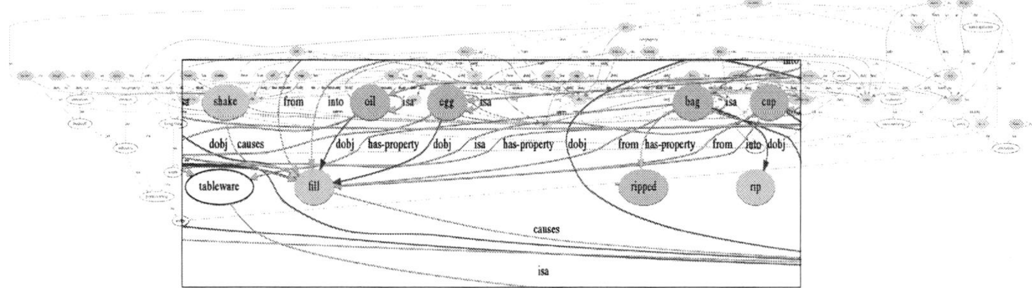

Figure 2: Extract of the situation model for the brownies instruction. Blue circles indicate actions, grey – objects, lila – properties, white taxonomy of objects. Dark blue relations indicate direct object – verb relation, yellow – different types of relations between indirect objects and verbs or nouns, light blue – causal relations, grey – abstraction hirarchy.

words have different meanings, we took the most frequently used meaning for each object. The Granger causality test was implemented in R in order to discover causal relations between the actions. Finally, the automatic generation of the situation model and the PDDL model were implemented in Haskell.

We generated a situation model which consisted of 29 objects and 10 actions identified in the text. Furthermore, 38 unique hyperonyms were identified for the 29 objects as well as 6 hyperonyms based on the relations of the indirect objects to the action. Finally, 12 causal relations were discovered. The resulting situation model contained 138 unique relations between the above identified elements. Figure 2 shows the resulting situation model for the brownies.

To evaluate the situation model, we investigated two hypotheses.

H1 The situation model provides additional context knowledge and semantic structure to the planning problem.

H2 The situation model reduces the planning model complexity compared to models that do not use situation models or only use manually defined situation models.

To investigate H1, we compared the PDDL model that makes use of the situation model ($PDDL_{sm}$) to: 1. a PDDL model containing only actions and no arguments. We call this model $PDDL_1$; 2. a PDDL model containing only the unique actions – arguments pairs discovered in the instructions. We call this model $PDDL_2$.

To investigate H2, we compared $PDDL_{sm}$ to: 1. a PDDL model that does not use a situation model. That is, each action template in the model has the same number of parameters, but they are all of the same type. In other words, any object can be used as argument for this action. We call this model $PDDL_3$; 2. a PDDL model that makes use of the hyperonyms extracted through Word-Net. We assume this model represents a manually built situation model. We call this model $PDDL_4$; 3. a PDDL model that makes use of the hyperonyms extracted through WordNet and of the abstraction achieved through the relations between indirect objects and actions. We call this model $PDDL_5$.

We use the following metrics: number of operators and mean branching factor.

4.1 Results

The results for H1 can be seen in Table 2. They show that $PDDL_{sm}$ has much more operators than $PDDL_1$ and $PDDL_2$. This is apparent, as $PDDL_1$ uses only the action classes and does not have any arguments. $PDDL_2$ has arguments but these are only the concrete action – arguments pairs discovered in each sentence, so the model does not make any other combinations of arguments that might be applicable to the same action. $PDDL_{sm}$, however, generates the operators based on the identified PDDL action templates, making use of the situation model. This allows for various combinations of arguments when grounding the templates. On the one hand, this has the positive effect of actions and plan variability. The model will be able to explain many more varia-

Metrics	$PDDL_{sm}$	$PDDL_1$	$PDDL_2$
N: operators	1426	11	74
mean br. factor	1071	11	74

Table 2: Comparison between $PDDL_{sm}$, $PDDL_1$, and $PDDL_2$.

tions in the behaviour of the agent then $PDDL_1$ and $PDDL_2$. On the other hand, the high number of operators also increases the mean branching factor of the model. In other words, it would be much easier to recognise the correct actions and plan of the agent in the case of 11 (respectively 74) choices than 1136.

The results for H2 show that the situation model generated through our approach reduces the complexity of the model compared to models, which do not make use of situation models or use manually defined situation models (see Table 3). Ta-

Metrics	$PDDL_{sm}$	$PDDL_3$	$PDDL_4$	$PDDL_5$
oper.	1426	3053	1736	1426
br. fac.	1071	3053	1736	1426

Table 3: Comparison between $PDDL_{sm}$, $PDDL_3$, $PDDL_4$, and $PDDL_5$.

ble 3 shows that $PDDL_3$ has the highest number of operators (3053), which is to be expected as each action template can be grounded with any of the available objects. The number of operators in $PDDL_4$ decreases compared to $PDDL_3$ (1736). This is due to the introduced type hierarchy extracted through WordNet. The number of operators decreases further when one takes into account the additional relations identified between indirect objects and actions ($PDDL_5$ with 1426 operators). Adding the causal relations does not decrease the number of operators ($PDDL_{sm}$) compared to $PDDL_5$. It is also to be expected as the causal relations are not part of the type hierarchy.

The causal relations, however, reduce the mean branching factor of the model. It decreases from 1426 in $PDDL_5$ to 1071 in $PDDL_{sm}$. In other words, in the rest of the models each action is always executable as there are no constraints to reduce the number of applicable actions. Adding the causal relations to operators reduces the branching factor allowing for better execution of the correct action. This is also visible in Figure 3. It shows the branching factor over time given a plan the model had to explain. The plan consists of 66 actions and was manually built by watching the video log of the brownies experiment. It can be seen that for the models, which do not make use of

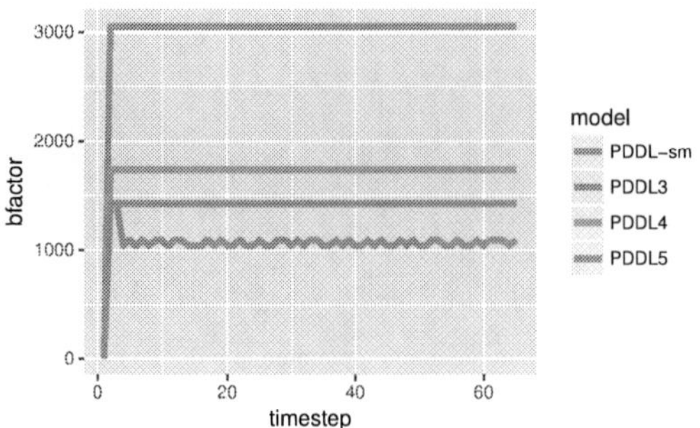

Figure 3: Branching factor for the different models for each time step.

causal relations, the branching factor is constant. For $PDDL_{sm}$, however, we see both fluctuation and reduction of the branching factor, which is due to the preconditions and effects introduced in the model.

5 Discussion and Conclusion

In this work we proposed an approach that generates situation models from textual instructions. It then uses the situation model to generate PDDL operators for planning problems. The results showed that the situation model introduces additional context information and semantic structure to the PDDL model. It also reduces the model complexity compared to models, which do not use situation models or which use manually developed situation models.

The automatically generated situation model provides valuable additional context information about the semantic structure behind the executed behaviour. It can potentially be used as a means to reason beyond the actions and the goal in the executed plan, namely by providing information about the situation in which the agent is acting.

Acknowledgments

This work is funded by the German Research Foundation (DFG) within the context of the project TextToHBM, grant number YO 226/1-1.

References

Monica Babeş-Vroman, James MacGlashan, Ruoyuan Gao, Kevin Winner, Richard Adjogah, Marie desJardins, Michael Littman, and Smaranda Muresan. 2012. Learning to interpret natural language instructions. In *Proceedings of the Second Workshop on Semantic Interpretation in an Actionable Context*. Association for Computational Linguistics, Stroudsburg, PA, USA, SIAC '12, pages 1–6. http://dl.acm.org/citation.cfm?id=2390927.2390928.

Chris L. Baker, Rebecca Saxe, and Joshua B. Tenenbaum. 2009. Action understanding as inverse planning. *Cognition* 113(3):329–349.

Luciana Benotti, Tessa Lau, and Martín Villalba. 2014. Interpreting natural language instructions using language, vision, and behavior. *ACM Trans. Interact. Intell. Syst.* 4(3):13:1–13:22. https://doi.org/10.1145/2629632.

S. R. K. Branavan, Nate Kushman, Tao Lei, and Regina Barzilay. 2012. Learning high-level planning from text. In *Proceedings of the 50th Annual Meeting of the Association for Computational Linguistics: Long Papers - Volume 1*. Association for Computational Linguistics, Stroudsburg, PA, USA, ACL '12, pages 126–135. http://dl.acm.org/citation.cfm?id=2390524.2390543.

S. R. K. Branavan, David Silver, and Regina Barzilay. 2011. Learning to win by reading manuals in a monte-carlo framework. In *Proceedings of the 49th Annual Meeting of the Association for Computational Linguistics: Human Language Technologies - Volume 1*. Association for Computational Linguistics, Stroudsburg, PA, USA, HLT '11, pages 268–277. http://dl.acm.org/citation.cfm?id=2002472.2002507.

S. R. K. Branavan, Luke S. Zettlemoyer, and Regina Barzilay. 2010. Reading between the lines: Learning to map high-level instructions to commands. In *Proceedings of the 48th Annual Meeting of the Association for Computational Linguistics*. Association for Computational Linguistics, Stroudsburg, PA, USA, ACL '10, pages 1268–1277. http://dl.acm.org/citation.cfm?id=1858681.1858810.

David L. Chen and Raymond J. Mooney. 2011. Learning to interpret natural language navigation instructions from observations. In *Proceedings of the 25th AAAI Conference on Artificial Intelligence (AAAI-2011)*. pages 859–865. http://www.cs.utexas.edu/users/ai-lab/?chen:aaai11.

Dan Goldwasser and Dan Roth. 2014. Learning from natural instructions. *Machine Learning* 94(2):205–232. https://doi.org/10.1007/s10994-013-5407-y.

C. W. J. Granger. 1969. Investigating Causal Relations by Econometric Models and Cross-spectral Methods. *Econometrica* 37(3):424–438. https://doi.org/10.2307/1912791.

Thomas Kollar, Stefanie Tellex, Deb Roy, and Nicholas Roy. 2014. Grounding verbs of motion in natural language commands to robots. In Oussama Khatib, Vijay Kumar, and Gaurav Sukhatme, editors, *Experimental Robotics*, Springer Berlin Heidelberg, volume 79 of *Springer Tracts in Advanced Robotics*, pages 31–47. https://doi.org/10.1007/978-3-642-28572-1_3.

Frank Krüger, Martin Nyolt, Kristina Yordanova, Albert Hein, and Thomas Kirste. 2014. Computational state space models for activity and intention recognition. a feasibility study. *PLoS ONE* 9(11):e109381. https://doi.org/10.1371/journal.pone.0109381.

Xiaochen Li, Wenji Mao, Daniel Zeng, and Fei-Yue Wang. 2010. Automatic construction of domain theory for attack planning. In *IEEE International Conference on Intelligence and Security Informatics (ISI), 2010*. pages 65–70. https://doi.org/10.1109/ISI.2010.5484775.

George A. Miller. 1995. Wordnet: A lexical database for english. *Commun. ACM* 38(11):39–41. https://doi.org/10.1145/219717.219748.

Tuan A Nguyen, Subbarao Kambhampati, and Minh Do. 2013. Synthesizing robust plans under incomplete domain models. In C.J.C. Burges, L. Bottou, M. Welling, Z. Ghahramani, and K.Q. Weinberger, editors, *Advances in Neural Information Processing Systems 26*, Curran Associates, Inc., pages 2472–2480. http://papers.nips.cc/paper/5120-synthesizing-robust-plans-under-incomplete-domain-models.pdf.

Matthai Philipose, Kenneth P. Fishkin, Mike Perkowitz, Donald J. Patterson, Dieter Fox, Henry Kautz, and Dirk Hahnel. 2004. Inferring activities from interactions with objects. *IEEE Pervasive Computing* 3(4):50–57. https://doi.org/10.1109/MPRV.2004.7.

Miquel Ramírez and Hector Geffner. 2009. Plan recognition as planning. In *Proceedings of the 21st International Jont Conference on Artifical Intelligence*. Morgan Kaufmann Publishers Inc., San Francisco, CA, USA, IJCAI'09, pages 1778–1783. http://dl.acm.org/citation.cfm?id=1661445.1661731.

Miquel Ramirez and Hector Geffner. 2011. Goal recognition over pomdps: Inferring the intention of a pomdp agent. In *Proceedings of the Twenty-Second International Joint Conference on Artificial Intelligence*. AAAI Press, Barcelona, Spain, volume 3 of *IJCAI'11*, pages 2009–2014. https://doi.org/10.5591/978-1-57735-516-8/IJCAI11-335.

Avirup Sil and Alexander Yates. 2011. Extracting strips representations of actions and events. In *Proceedings of the International Conference Recent Advances in Natural Language Processing 2011*. RANLP 2011 Organising Committee, Hissar, Bulgaria, pages 1–8. http://aclweb.org/anthology/R11-1001.

M. Tenorth, D. Nyga, and M. Beetz. 2010. Understanding and executing instructions for everyday manipulation tasks from the world wide web. In *IEEE International Conference on*

Robotics and Automation (ICRA). pages 1486–1491. https://doi.org/10.1109/ROBOT.2010.5509955.

Adam Vogel and Dan Jurafsky. 2010. Learning to follow navigational directions. In *Proceedings of the 48th Annual Meeting of the Association for Computational Linguistics*. Association for Computational Linguistics, Stroudsburg, PA, USA, ACL '10, pages 806–814. http://dl.acm.org/citation.cfm?id=1858681.1858764.

Juan Ye, Simon Dobson, and Susan McKeever. 2012. Review: Situation identification techniques in pervasive computing: A review. *Pervasive Mob. Comput.* 8(1):36–66. https://doi.org/10.1016/j.pmcj.2011.01.004.

Kristina Yordanova. 2015. Discovering causal relations in textual instructions. In *Recent Advances in Natural Language Processing*. RANLP 2015 Organising Committee, Hissar, Bulgaria, pages 714–720. http://www.aclweb.org/anthology/R15-1091.

Kristina Yordanova. 2016. From textual instructions to sensor-based recognition of user behaviour. In *Companion Publication of the 21st International Conference on Intelligent User Interfaces*. ACM, New York, NY, USA, IUI '16 Companion, pages 67–73. https://doi.org/10.1145/2876456.2879488.

Kristina Yordanova. 2017. TextToHBM: A generalised approach to learning models of human behaviour for activity recognition from textual instructions. In *Proceedings of the AAAI Workshop on Plan, Activity and Intent Recognition (PAIR)*. AAAI, San Francosco, USA, pages 891–898. https://www.aaai.org/ocs/index.php/WS/AAAIW17/paper/view/15110.

Kristina Yordanova and Thomas Kirste. 2015. A process for systematic development of symbolic models for activity recognition. *ACM Transactions on Interactive Intelligent Systems* 5(4):20:1–20:35. https://doi.org/10.1145/2806893.

Kristina Yordanova and Thomas Kirste. 2016. Learning models of human behaviour from textual instructions. In *Proceedings of the 8th International Conference on Agents and Artificial Intelligence (ICAART 2016)*. Rome, Italy, pages 415–422. https://doi.org/10.5220/0005755604150422.

Ziqi Zhang, Philip Webster, Victoria Uren, Andrea Varga, and Fabio Ciravegna. 2012. Automatically extracting procedural knowledge from instructional texts using natural language processing. In Nicoletta Calzolari, Khalid Choukri, Thierry Declerck, Mehmet Uğur Doğan, Bente Maegaard, Joseph Mariani, Jan Odijk, and Stelios Piperidis, editors, *Proceedings of the Eighth International Conference on Language Resources and Evaluation (LREC-2012)*. European Language Resources Association (ELRA), Istanbul, Turkey, pages 520–527. ACL Anthology Identifier: L12-1094. http://www.lrec-conf.org/proceedings/lrec2012/pdf/244_Paper.pdf.

Gap in pagination due to unavailable paper.

**Pages 831-838

Using NLP for Enhancing Second Language Acquisition

Leonardo Zilio   **Rodrigo Wilkens**   **Cédrick Fairon**

CENTAL
Université catholique de Louvain
{leonardo.zilio,rodrigo.wilkens,cedrick.fairon}@uclouvain.be

Abstract

This study presents SMILLE, a system that draws on the Noticing Hypothesis and on input enhancements, addressing the lack of salience of grammatical information in online documents chosen by a given user. By means of input enhancements, the system can draw the user's attention to grammar, which could possibly lead to a higher intake per input ratio for metalinguistic information. The system receives as input an online document and submits it to a combined processing of parser and hand-written rules for detecting its grammatical structures. The input text can be freely chosen by the user, providing a more engaging experience and reflecting the user's interests. The system can enhance a total of 107 fine-grained types of grammatical structures that are based on the CEFR. An evaluation of some of those structures resulted in an overall precision of 87%.

1 Introduction

Research on the field of second language acquisition (SLA) has already shown that the mere presentation of input to a language learner is not enough for ensuring that some linguistic information will be retained (Meurers et al., 2010). This means that the language learner may process the input for its meaning alone, without noticing its linguistic structures, because there is no salient grammatical information. Input is, therefore, understood as "potentially processible language data which are made available, by chance or by design, to the language learner" (Smith, 1993). On the other hand, the intake is the part of the input which is actually internalized by the user and that can

potentially be connected to the long-term memory (Reinders, 2012).

As such, an input in its raw form has lower chances of being converted into intake by the learner, and may thus not provide any new linguistic information. In the early 90's, Schmidt (1990) developed the hypothesis that, in order to convert input into intake, a language learner needs to notice the relevant information in the input. More recently, Schmidt (2012) stated, in a less controversial way, that "people learn about the things that they attend to and do not learn much about the things they do not attend to". There is much discussion regarding the assumptions of the Noticing Hypothesis, and it has some fierce contesters, such as Truscott (1998). Nevertheless, it seems to be of general agreement that noticing is at least a facilitator of the language learning process, even though there is differences in the way that authors view the process of noticing, either as a purely conscious process or as a possibly unconscious process (Cross, 2002).

To solve the lack of salience in raw input, Smith and Truscott (2014) suggested the use of "input enhancements", so as to give prominence to the relevant linguistic information. This focus-on-form strategy (Doughty, 1991) provides a way to assist language learners, and recent studies on SLA have shown that input enhancements represent a positive step in transforming input into intake (Plonsky and Ziegler, 2016; Simard, 2009).

CALL systems that are able to deal with authentic texts and uses NLP for rendering a better presentation of linguistic information are called Authentic Texts Intelligent Computer-Assisted Language Learning (ATICALL) Meurers (2012). In this paper, we present the Smart and Intelligent Language Learning Environment (SMILLE), an ATICALL system that enhances authentic Web pages by using available NLP tools. It extracts the

Proceedings of Recent Advances in Natural Language Processing, pages 839–846,
Varna, Bulgaria, Sep 4–6 2017.

text content of a Web page chosen by the user (i.e., the language learner) and processes it, retrieving linguistic information that can be enhanced according to the user's specific language learning needs. To ensure that the highlighted information is relevant, SMILLE is linked to the users' language level, as described by the Common European Framework of Reference for Languages (CEFR) (Council of Europe, 2011).

SMILLE was developed based on a scenario in which the users are already pursuing a foreign language course and wish to continue the language learning activity by means of reading Web-based material that corresponds to their interests. In this case, SMILLE can help not only with the text-understanding process, for it has built-in access to dictionaries and meaning-related information, but also with improving the users' awareness of the grammatical structures that correspond to their language learning level. As such, the system can be seen as a complementary application to a language course, where the grammatical structures of the user's level will be in focus (by means of text highlighting), with the bonus of having a plethora of new vocabulary available, since it is designed to process any user-chosen, Web-based text.

Some of the grammatical structures that should be highlighted are complex linguistic structures that are not always recognized by parsers and need hand-written rules to cover this lack of parser information. Since these rules are not trivial to implement and require specialized knowledge, in this paper we evaluate the performance of the specialized rules against a gold standard. In specific, we focus on rules precision, because it is a key point of the pedagogical purpose of our system. In addition, we compare our specialized rules performance against parser dependency tagging performance.

This paper is organized as follows: we present information on systems that automatically enhance grammatical structures in Section 2, specially focusing on what type of information and what resources they use for text enhancements; in Section 3, we describe SMILLE, some of its features, and briefly discuss the CEFR and its language learning levels; we then describe the evaluation process of some of SMILLE's features in Section 4; lastly, in Section 5 we present our final remarks.

2 Related Work

CALL systems have recently started to use NLP applications for aiding in reading activities (Azab et al., 2013b), so, in this section, we describe a selection of ATICALL systems that use text enhancements for SLA: SmartReader (Azab et al., 2013a,b), WERTi (Meurers et al., 2010), and FLAIR (Chinkina and Meurers, 2016; Chinkina et al., 2016).

The *SmartReader* provides a reading assistant tool that uses a parser to process texts and highlights information for the user based on the parser analysis. The system presents definitions for content words, grammatical information for function words, and encyclopedic information for named entities. It also displays the syntactic function (such as subject, object) of selected words in the given sentence and generates simple questions about named entities, provided the answers are in the near context.

The *WERTi* system allows for text enhancements of selected linguistic elements of English, Spanish and German. It also presents exercises corresponding to the selected structure, such as clicking on relevant words, filling the gaps with multiple choice questions or writing the correct word in a gap. The user can choose any URL as input, and WERTi will highlight (by means of color coding) the linguistic structure that was selected by the user or modify the text for testing the user's skills based on the selected activity. It uses parsing combined with rules and regular expressions to retrieve text information for seven linguistic structures.

The *FLAIR* system is described as an online information retrieval system "that uses efficient algorithms to retrieve, annotate and rerank Web documents based on the grammatical constructions they contain" (Chinkina et al., 2016). FLAIR searches online documents based on keywords selected by the user, parses the first twenty documents retrieved by the search engine and ranks them according to the settings the user selected as most important. It can also recognize 87 different types of grammatical structures described in the official curriculum for German schools. These structures are annotated in the texts and highlighted for the user.

In addition to these systems, there are also other CALL systems that present information from texts to the user, but do not focus on grammatical highlighting. This is the case, for instance, of the REAP system (Brown and Eskenazi, 2004), which is more focused on text retrieval based on user profile and on vocabulary information, and the CoBRA system (Deville et al., 2013), which has a database of aligned multilingual texts and relies on the teacher to select the relevant information for the language learner. There are also systems that were developed within the field of text simplification or readability, but they usually focus on the text properties themselves and on L1 instead of L2.

3 System Description

SMILLE is being developed for English, but there will be an effort to port it to other languages as well. Following the idea of WERTi (Meurers et al., 2010) and the SmartReader (Azab et al., 2013a,b), SMILLE was designed in a way that the users have independence for choosing online reading materials in the foreign language, so that the freedom of choice should serve as an incentive for further developing the learning process. Using the selected, Web-based text, SMILLE provides a reading assistant module that helps the user to notice linguistic content of the target language by highlighting (i.e., enhancing) language structures in context, while also offering the possibility of looking up meaning and word class.

In the way it presents the text enhancements and the features of the reading assistant module, SMILLE bears some similarities with the systems presented in Section 2. However, it distinguishes itself in how the enhancements are selected. For instance, in WERTi, only a few grammatical structures are highlighted for the user, and, in SmartReader, only information more relevant to the meaning of the lexical units is presented, and only parser information is shown as part of the grammatical training. And, while FLAIR and SMILLE share a bigger scope in terms of enhancements, the types and granularity of grammatical structures are different (for instance, FLAIR does not distinguish between gerund and present participle, but SMILLE does). In addition, SMILLE links the displayed information to the guidelines of the CEFR and to other language learning resources, so that the enhancements are not limited to isolated linguistic structures, but covers the needs for the different language levels. As such, users can read texts that are interesting according

to their own preference, while keeping an eye on important information in terms of linguistic structures that are relevant for their process of acquiring a second language.

For retrieving the relevant content in the chosen Web page, SMILLE crawls over the HTML structure and extracts its text content. This text content is then parsed for part-of-speech (PoS) and syntactic dependencies with the Stanford parser (Manning et al., 2014). The parsed text content is then analyzed with hand-written rules for creating new tags for each relevant grammatical structure. After this process, a new Web page is constructed, showing the same information extracted from the original one, but with new HTML code and different JavaScript and CSS scripts that allow for real-time modifications of the text.

Some of the grammatical information that is detected by SMILLE requires only that the parser correctly analyzes the word or structure in question. Such is the case, for instance, of adverbs, adjectives and simple verb tenses. Other structures require some rules for retrieving more complex word formations, such as compound verb tenses, phrasal verbs and passive voice, but the information is mostly retrieved from the dependency and PoS tags. Still other structures though, such as WH-questions and question tags, are retrieved based on rules specifically written for them. As such, SMILLE combines the analysis done by the parser with hand-written rules to extract text information that would not be easily identified, and would not be salient, in a raw input.

3.1 CEFR Levels

The Common European Framework of Reference (CEFR) for Languages (Council of Europe, 2011) presents a guide in terms of language levels and content. It provides a description for the communication goals of a language learner.

As a general guide, it leaves various gray areas in which the content of the learning process is not so clear. The information at each level also does not cover the different needs for language learners with different native languages. As such, the specific curricula of different language courses do not need to be necessarily the same regarding the six language mastery levels (Alderson, 2007; Little, 2007).SMILLE is being developed in the framework of a partnership between the Université catholique de Louvain and Altissia[1], so, our information regarding the grammatical structures and CEFR levels are linked to the language course structure of our enterprise partner.

While developing the system, we had to make a decision regarding the granularity of grammatical structures and the escalation of knowledge associated to each language levels. The CEFR was designed for language learning, but Web-based documents normally don't have this instructive approach by design. In a language course, different grammatical structures can be learned in progressive steps, so, for instance, today a language learner may study the modal verb "can" and later, during another session, it is possible to learn the modal verb "must". In an online text, the chances are that different modal verbs will appear at the same time, interwoven in the text. To address this fine-grained differentiation, SMILLE would have to encompass specific rules for each case, sometimes for each word in a grammatical category. This would require more processing and an undesired increase in the number of rules. So, although the system respects the escalation related to different language levels (e.g., different grammatical structures in levels B1 and B2 were separated in specific rules), the progression in the same level was overruled and generalized.

3.2 System Resources

SMILLE is responsible for analyzing a text that was chosen by the user and for outputting an enhanced text. For example, if the user is currently studying phrasal verbs, the system can highlight phrasal verbs in the chosen text, so that the user's attention is more easily drawn to the in-context occurrence of this kind of syntactical construct of the English language. The output of SMILLE is a new Web page that can highlight relevant grammatical structures based on the user's language level, but it can also help the user to understand the meaning of different vocabulary that is present on the text.

For the grammatical content of the text, there is a sidebar menu showing all the grammatical information available on the text that corresponds to a given language level. The highlighting is done in real-time, so that the user can change the highlighted structures on the fly. The highlighted text is modified in terms of color coding (font and background colors) and by changing the format

to bold. The option for these three modifications are based on the results of Simard (2009), which have shown that the use of three modifications was among the best ways of enhancing a text structure without saturation.

Our system is designed to be able to show grammatical information corresponding to levels A1 to C1 of the CEFR[2]. Depending on the chosen level, a number of grammatical structures will be displayed on the sidebar menu. These structures can vary from simple part-of-speech information, such as adjectives, adverbs, nouns, proper nouns, etc. in level A1 to more complex structures such as the use of gerund as object in B1 or the use of passive voice and phrasal verbs in B2. Figure 1 exemplifies structures that can be highlighted by SMILLE's reading assistant module.

If the user wants to look up the meaning of a word, SMILLE offers two possibilities: if it is not a content word, there is the possibility to look it up online on the Merriam-Webster[3]; on the other hand, if it is a content word, then both the Merriam-Webster's definitions and the WordNet's (Fellbaum, 1998) glosses can be looked up online[4]. The access to both online resources was implemented by CTRL-clicking on the desired word and selecting the desired resource from a context menu. In addition, by hovering the mouse over a word, the system displays PoS and lemma information. In Figure 2, the word *speculative* was selected and the information from two online resources (Merriam-Webster and WordNet) is displayed; lemma *speculative* and PoS *adjective* of the word are also shown in the form of a tooltip.

The CTRL-click menu has yet another function, and it is related to the grammar information. Any word that is part of a grammatical structure that can be highlighted also has a link to a database of grammatical rules. Since the clicked-on word also belongs to a relative clause, by hovering over the relative clause menu, the gerund sub-menu would collapse and a new sub-menu would be displayed with links to information on relative clauses. This provides for further grammatical training when needed by the user.

---

[1]Site: http://altissia.com/

[2]Level C2 is focused on reviewing the grammatical knowledge acquired in previous levels.

[3]Site: www.merriam-webster.com/

[4]The WordNet was included as a lexical resource because it presents semantic relations between words, such as hypernyms, meronyms, that are usually not present in a regular dictionary.

Figure 1: Example of highlighting of quantifiers in the text

4 System Evaluation

The system was evaluated to verify its performance in retrieving grammatical information with rules. Since SMILLE has language learners as target users, and has a pedagogical function as goal, it is important that the information highlighted on the text really corresponds to the grammatical categories selected by the user. If the system has too low precision, than it may impair the user's capacity of understanding the correct use of the different grammatical structures.

For the evaluation process, a gold standard was manually annotated with the required information. The necessity to create a gold standard is due to the fact that, to our knowledge, there exists no corpus annotated with more complex grammatical structures. There do exist many corpora annotated with PoS and dependency information, but those do not present information such as the ones we are working with here. So, in this section, we first describe our gold standard and the annotation process, and later present and discuss the results of the evaluation.

4.1 Gold Standard

The gold standard comprises online newspaper articles and excerpts from literary texts. The newspaper articles were extracted from the sites of *The New York Times*[5] (20 articles; 31k tokens), *The Guardian*[6] (20 articles; 18k tokens), *The Washington Post*[7] (10 articles; 23k tokens), and the *USA Today*[8] (5 articles; 9k tokens). These were selected for being dedicated to nation wide and international news, and the articles were collected in a time period that starts at the beginning of March 2017 and ends at the beginning of April 2017. Since newspaper articles generally do not present much dialogue and interaction, and some of the grammatical structures (e.g., short answers,

WH-questions, question tags) appear more often in dialogues, we further selected seven literary texts from the Project Gutenberg[9] which contained longer dialogues: *The Yellow Sign* (9k tokens), *Varney, the Vampyre* (chapters II to V; 20k tokens), *The Great God Pan* (chapter V; 11k tokens), and *An Ideal Husband* (First Act; 2k tokens).

The corpus was annotated with the following grammatical structures: (1) phrasal verbs, (2) relative clauses, (3) WH-questions, (4) question tags, (5) short answers, (6) gerunds, (7) present participles, (8) infinitives with "to", and (9) infinitives without the particle "to". Most of these structures were selected because they are not retrievable based only on PoS or dependency information, and, although phrasal verbs are indeed recognized based on dependency information, we decided to include this structure for its importance in the learning of English as second language. Each type of grammatical structure was annotated following specific criteria, which were laid out in an annotation manual. Since some grammatical structures are rarer than others, the annotation was not done equally in all texts. Structures that are not abundant in most texts (i.e., wh-questions, question tags, short answers, and phrasal verbs) were annotated in all documents of the corpus, whenever they appeared. The other ones (i.e., gerunds, present participles, infinitives with and without "to", and relative clauses) were annotated in only a part of the corpus. Since there is this different distribution along the corpus, Table 1 presents the number of documents (newspaper articles and literary texts) that contains the structure and the token and sentence count in the gold standard.

Table 1 shows how many structures were annotated in the gold standard. As can be seen, even though the whole corpus was scrutinized in the search for certain structures, we couldn't find many instances of question tags and short answers.

4.2 Evaluation

The evaluation was made on a sentence basis. Table 2 shows precision, recall and F-measure for each of the nine tested grammatical structures.

The overall precision, recall and f-measure of the rule-based annotation[10] was, respectively, 85.20%, 82,40% and 83.78%. Since the system

---

[5]Site: www.nytimes.com.
[6]Site: www.theguardian.com.
[7]Site: www.washingtonpost.com.
[8]Site: www.usatoday.com.

[9]Site: www.gutenberg.org.
[10]This excludes the evaluation of phrasal verbs, which was just based on parser information.

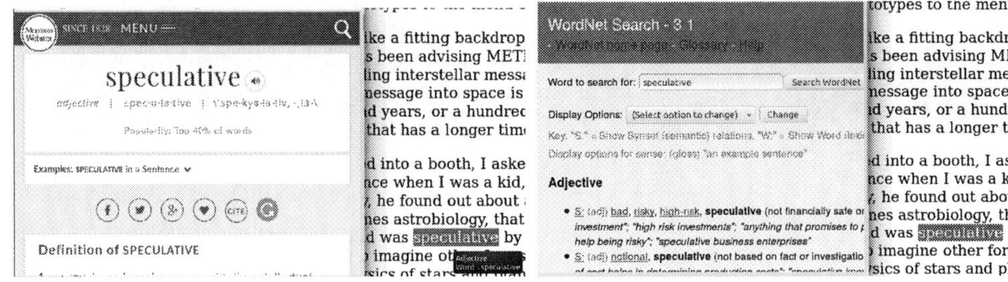

<table>
<tr><td>(a) Merriam-Webster's definitions</td><td>(b) WordNet's glosses</td></tr>
</table>

Figure 2: SMILLE can show dictionary information for a given word.

Table 1: Gold standard description

Grammatical Structure	# Texts	# Sentences	# Tokens	# Structures Annotated
Phrasal Verb	58	6,052	121.1 k	534
Infinitive with "to"	14	1,478	31.9 k	444
Infinitive without "to"	13	1,477	31.8 k	564
Gerund	26	3,920	66.8 k	282
Present Participle	13	2,443	35.0 k	453
Relative Clause	34	2,217	56.7 k	425
WH-Question	20	4,044	66.9 k	176
Question Tag	3	1,992	22.6 k	25
Short Answer	7	3,024	42.3 k	42

Table 2: The SMILLE's Evaluation: Precision, Recall and F-measure

Grammatical Structure	P	R	F
Phrasal Verbs	.951	.673	.878
Gerunds	.879	.697	.778
Present Participles	.891	.799	.843
Infinitives with "to"	.983	.859	.917
Infinitives without "to"	.840	.979	.904
Relative Clauses	.870	.780	.823
WH-Questions	.957	.779	.859
Question Tags	.905	.760	.826
Short Answers	.215	.676	.327

is focused on the learning process, the higher precision score is positive, because showing correct structures is more important than showing a lot of structures that may be incorrect. So, as Meurers et al. (2010) point out, in CALL, the balance tends to be more inclined to the precision side, and less to recall.

The results showed an f-measure that is above the mean ($\alpha = 0.05$) for generating labeled dependency parsing (Cer et al., 2010). We also compared the performance of our rules for relative clauses with the performance of an annotation solely based on the relative clause annotation that the Stanford parser provides, and the annotation based only on the parser had 59.32% of precision, 94.04% of recall and 72.75% of f-measure, which ranks below the annotation with our rules.

In terms of comparison to state-of-the-art systems, the only other work we know of that presents a similar evaluation is FLAIR (Chinkina and Meurers, 2016), which used 9 newspaper articles as corpus to evaluate 87 different rules used in the FLAIR system for retrieving grammatical information from web-based texts. Unfortunately, the rules and the evaluation process were different than the ones presented here. For instance, Chinkina and Meurers (2016) did not separate gerunds and present participles, considering both as "-ing verb forms"; thus, they use a rule that is more broad in scope than ours and do not have the problem of distinguishing between the structures. So, although some of the patterns are probably similar, such as the ones for WH-questions and question tags, the different corpora that were used represent a hindrance for a more detailed comparison.

To better understand the results we got from the

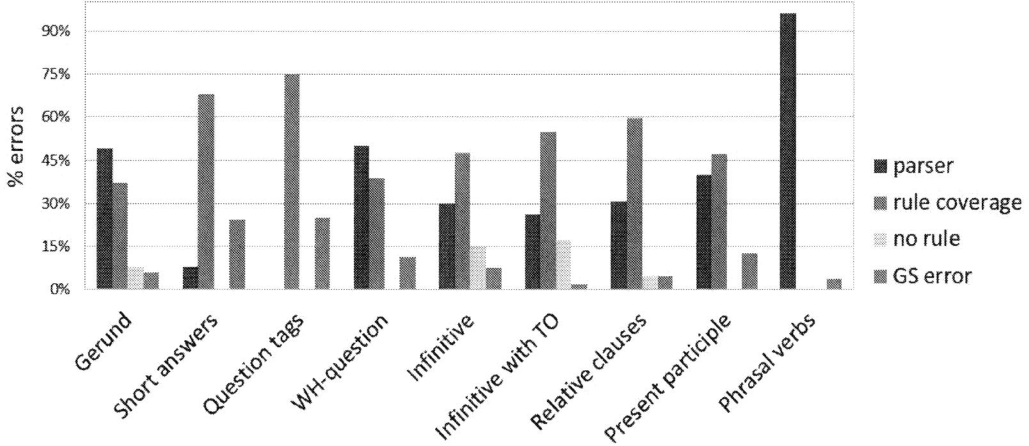

Figure 3: Error analysis

evaluation, we conducted an error analysis. The errors (false positives and false negatives) of the evaluated structures were classified into four categories: parser (parsing error), rule coverage (the rules do not address the specific structure or are too permissive in scope), no rule (there is no rule designed for the structure), GS error (gold standard annotation error), as can be seen in Figure 3. While errors made by the parser annotation (in which some of the rules are based) are responsible for a great part (48%) of the errors, the coverage of our rules (responsible for 38% of the errors) was the main reason for the lack of recall of the system and, especially, for the low precision we got for short answers (in this case, because of a single, too permissive rule). The errors in the gold standard annotation, while not very frequent, prevented, for instance, that our question tag precision reached 100% (which would be the correct precision for this type of structure). This error analysis was a very important step for the future developments of the system, since it allowed us to better pinpoint where there is room for improvement in the rules.

5 Conclusion

This paper presented a system that combines available NLP resources for enhancing language learning. SMILLE extracts raw text from a Web page chosen by the user and enhances its contents by providing the user with tools for a more independent language learning that can take place anywhere with available Internet access. The text is parsed, and a set of rules specific for the different grammatical structures is then applied. By processing texts with NLP tools and rules, the system presents a series of linguistic information, aiding the user to notice in-context grammatical structures and providing access to glosses and definitions for words, while also offering grammatical explanations for specific types of structures.

SMILLE performed above 85% in terms of precision in most of the evaluated grammatical structures, but lacked a bit in terms of recall. The case of short answers can be considered an outlier, since it presented a very low precision, and so will require special attention. Future improvements will take into account the full error analysis that was carried out and that pinpointed how the flaws in the rules can be addressed.

In terms of the system as a whole, further developments have to be implemented to cover other languages, and to create a database for keeping track of user information and user activity concerning language learning (e.g., words that are looked up in dictionaries, grammatical rules consulted, etc.). With these features in place, SMILLE will be able to provide a more customizable user experience.

Acknowledgments

The authors would like to thank the Walloon Region (Projects BEWARE n. 1510637 and 1610378) for support, and Altissia International for research collaboration.

References

J Charles Alderson. 2007. The cefr and the need for more research. *The Modern Language Journal* 91(4):659–663.

Mahmoud Azab, Ahmed Salama, Kemal Oflazer, Hideki Shima, Jun Araki, and Teruko Mitamura. 2013a. An english reading tool as a nlp showcase. In *The Companion Volume of the Proceedings of IJCNLP 2013: System Demonstrations*. Asian Federation of Natural Language Processing, Nagoya, Japan, pages 5–8. http://www.aclweb.org/anthology/I13-2002.

Mahmoud Azab, Ahmed Salama, Kemal Oflazer, Hideki Shima, Jun Araki, and Teruko Mitamura. 2013b. An nlp-based reading tool for aiding non-native english readers. *Recent Advances in Natural Language Processing* page 41.

Jonathan Brown and Maxine Eskenazi. 2004. Retrieval of authentic documents for reader-specific lexical practice. In *InSTIL/ICALL Symposium 2004*.

Daniel M Cer, Marie-Catherine De Marneffe, Daniel Jurafsky, and Christopher D Manning. 2010. Parsing to stanford dependencies: Trade-offs between speed and accuracy. In *LREC*. Floriana, Malta.

Maria Chinkina, Madeeswaran Kannan, and Detmar Meurers. 2016. Online information retrieval for language learning. *ACL 2016* page 7.

Maria Chinkina and Detmar Meurers. 2016. Linguistically aware information retrieval: providing input enrichment for second language learners. In *Proceedings of the 11th Workshop on Innovative Use of NLP for Building Educational Applications, San Diego, CA*.

Council of Europe. 2011. *Common European Framework of Reference for Languages: learning, teaching, assessment*. Cambridge University Press.

Jeremy Cross. 2002. Noticing'in sla: Is it a valid concept. *TESL-EJ* 6(3):1–9.

Guy Deville, Laurence Dumortier, Jean-Roch Meurisse, and Marc Miceli. 2013. Ressources lexicales pour laide a lapprentissage des langues. *Ressources lexicales: contenu, construction, utilisation, évaluation* 30:291–311.

Catherine Doughty. 1991. Second language instruction does make a difference. *Studies in second language acquisition* 13(04):431–469.

Christiane Fellbaum. 1998. *WordNet*. Wiley Online Library.

David Little. 2007. The common european framework of reference for languages: Perspectives on the making of supranational language education policy. *The Modern Language Journal* 91(4):645–655.

Christopher D. Manning, Mihai Surdeanu, John Bauer, Jenny Finkel, Steven J. Bethard, and David McClosky. 2014. The Stanford CoreNLP natural language processing toolkit. In *Association for Computational Linguistics (ACL) System Demonstrations*. pages 55–60. http://www.aclweb.org/anthology/P/P14/P14-5010.

Detmar Meurers. 2012. Natural language processing and language learning. *The Encyclopedia of Applied Linguistics* .

Detmar Meurers, Ramon Ziai, Luiz Amaral, Adriane Boyd, Aleksandar Dimitrov, Vanessa Metcalf, and Niels Ott. 2010. Enhancing authentic web pages for language learners. In *Proceedings of the NAACL HLT 2010 Fifth Workshop on Innovative Use of NLP for Building Educational Applications*. Association for Computational Linguistics, pages 10–18.

Luke Plonsky and Nicole Ziegler. 2016. The call-sla interface: Insights from a second-order synthesis .

Hayo Reinders. 2012. Towards a definition of intake in second language acquisition .

Richard Schmidt. 2012. Attention, awareness, and individual differences in language learning. *Perspectives on individual characteristics and foreign language education* 6:27.

Richard W Schmidt. 1990. The role of consciousness in second language learning1. *Applied linguistics* 11(2):129–158.

Daphnée Simard. 2009. Differential effects of textual enhancement formats on intake. *System* 37(1):124–135.

Michael Sharwood Smith. 1993. Input enhancement in instructed sla. *Studies in second language acquisition* 15(02):165–179.

Mike Sharwood Smith and John Truscott. 2014. Explaining input enhancement: A mogul perspective. *International Review of Applied Linguistics in Language Teaching* 52(3):253–281.

John Truscott. 1998. Noticing in second language acquisition: A critical review. *Second Language Research* 14(2):103–135.

AUTHOR INDEX

AUTHOR INDEX

AUTHOR INDEX